The Good Britain Guide 2004

Edited by Alisdair Aird

Deputy Editor: Fiona Stapley

Associate Editors: Karen Fick, Robert Unsworth

Research Officer: Elizabeth Adlington

Additional Research: Emily Bone

Walks Consultant: Tim Locke

EBURY PRESS
LONDON

Please send reports to:

The Good Britain Guide
FREEPOST TN1569
WADHURST
E. Sussex
TN5 7BR

This edition published in 2003 by
Ebury Press
Random House, 20 Vauxhall Bridge Road
London SW1V 2SA

www.randomhouse.co.uk

10 9 8 7 6 5 4 3 2 1

ISBN 0 09 188894 8

Typeset from author's disks by Textype Typesetters, Cambridge
Printed and bound in Great Britain by Cox and Wyman, Reading, Berks

Contents

INTRODUCTION

WATCH OUT, THAT BEACH IS DISAPPEARING

With warmer summers (its long spells of unbroken dry sunny weather and some record temperatures made 2003 one of the best summers ever), it's good news that bathing water off many of Britain's beaches has become much cleaner in the last few years. The bad news is that some of those beaches are vanishing. In recent years we have noted sand being lost from lots of popular beaches, including Hayling Island (Hampshire), parts of the Kent coast between Folkestone and Hythe, Happisburgh and Winterton-on-Sea (Norfolk), Minehead (Somerset), Filey (Yorkshire) and Rhossili and Oxwich on the Gower (Wales).

This is usually part of the natural evolution of the coastline, changing gradually through the millennia. But sometimes it is because of ill-conceived sea defence schemes elsewhere. And global warming, raising sea levels and making inroads on coasts everywhere, is intensifying the threat to our beaches. Of course coastal change also has many other effects, on farming, wildlife, even housing. So efforts are being made to deal with the threat. Voluntary coastal defence groups have been drawing up shoreline management plans for each stretch of coast, consulting the various interests involved. But there are three big problems with this approach. The first is that as the groups are voluntary and non-statutory, there's no guarantee that every interest including that of the beach-loving public is taken into account properly. The second is that responsibility for drawing up the plans and putting them into effect is split between too many different authorities. And the third is that so far most plans have taken the Canute line, opting to try to hold the line against the sea, with very few planning for the managed retreat that in most places will be necessary as global warming raises sea levels.

We fear that there will not be a happy end to this story. The obvious solution is a national approach, with one single authority taking clear control to ensure that all the management plans mesh into a unified and successful strategy, and having national funds to pay for all the costs involved, including not just sea defence works but compensation for all affected by any managed retreat, and restoration of eroded beaches. But this would be a deeply painful nettle for any government to grasp, stirring up all sorts of local resentments, quite apart from seeing the cost going into national rather than local accounts. So it's probably more realistic for us simply to say: go out and enjoy those beaches while they're still there.

GIVE LOCAL PRODUCE A BREAK

Many of the smaller places to stay in, and the places we recommend for food, are now making huge efforts to track down local suppliers and local ingredients for what they cook and serve. In most parts of the country, regional or more local organisations are springing up to link local producers in the area and get their products on to local shelves. The explosive growth of farmers' markets has added an interesting new factor to many a day out. A growing number of shows, fairs and festivals such as Ludlow's September food and drink festival celebrate the quality and diversity of what is produced in the area.

All this can be a special bonus for visitors. We know from our readers that they really relish the chance of eating good genuinely local foods, and buying things that truly capture and recall the flavour of the places they visit, rather than mass-produced items that they could get on any high street.

What tourist attractions earn from their cafés and shops has become tremendously important to them. In places with free entry, catering and sales are the only sources of income from visitors apart from donations. In places that do charge for admission, for each £1 they get from the entry fee, on average they earn another 72p from what they sell. So the shops and cafés attached to visitor attractions have become very big business indeed. We estimate that this year they will earn a total of around £1,200 million.

This should be an ideal sales channel between an area's local producers and its visitors. But it very rarely is. What you get for your money generally has very little to do with the place you are visiting. It's true that the smallest places do often take the trouble to organise genuinely local supplies. But it's the bigger ones, often run by national organisations, that tot up the great majority of visits. And these generally seem more interested in finding the cheapest suppliers, even overseas, than the local ones which visitors would prefer - even plants for sale are unlikely to have come from their own gardens.

Chatsworth in Derbyshire, with over half a million visitors a year, is a shining example of what can and should be done by even the biggest places. Its farm shop is a first-class local showcase. We believe that the national heritage organisations and local authorities should all now set a target for sourcing a significant proportion of what each of their properties sells - say, 30% - from within 50 miles of the property.

Historic houses and gardens
UNFAIRLY PENALISED

Defeated at the end of a 10-year court battle, Customs & Excise now have to allow exemption from VAT for non-profit cultural organisations run primarily by volunteers. The test cases involved the society which runs the London Zoo and Whipsnade, and the Brontë Society which runs the Parsonage Museum in Haworth. The Brontë Society got back nearly £600,000, representing VAT payments since 1990. Many other similar organisations which get a fair number of visitors (say, over 50,000 a year) and charge more than a pound or two will now benefit from this ruling. Most heritage railways, for example, are run largely by volunteers. Exemption means an organisation can't claim back VAT on its spending, so all that might qualify for this exemption will be doing their sums carefully to see whether or not they'd benefit. But the court ruling will be a great boon to many, with the rebates helping to fund maintenance or even expansion. And it seems to us to point firmly towards another tax change that is now needed.

We believe the owners of historic houses and gardens open to the public are right in their current campaign - backed by the boss of English Heritage - to offset the cost of repairs and maintenance against their own tax bills. It seems to us unfair that these places, which now operate as tourist businesses, can't count repairs and maintenance as a business expense, when virtually all other businesses can. What's more, this stately homes' tax works against the public interest. Because it makes maintenance up to 40% more expensive than it would otherwise be, it means that maintenance is often put off for too long - until disaster looms, and an immense grant is needed instead. Moreover, many smaller buildings and gardens of great interest and beauty which are not at the moment open might well be opened, in return for being allowed maintenance and repairs as a business expense. After all, it was the original exemption from capital transfer tax, offered in the 1970s to houses opening to the public and meeting certain conservation standards, which led almost at once to the opening of so many stately homes. This would be a small dent in Gordon Brown's total tax take, but a big boost to the range of heritage houses and gardens open to the public.

WATCH OUT EDINBURGH, HERE COMES PORTSMOUTH

For decades, even centuries, London has been *the* city to visit, full of interest and an obvious draw for people from all over the world. And since the first edition of this *Guide* we have been pushing the strong claims of Edinburgh, York, Chester and Bath for really enjoyable weekend breaks, while Cambridge, Oxford and (perhaps particularly for visiting Americans) Stratford have always been on overseas visitors' hit lists.

Now, however, there's a new phenomenon. Other cities, industrial or post-industrial places which, rightly, very few people would even have considered weekending in, have been quietly building up an impressive roster of visitor attractions, and at the same time perking up their street scenery and atmosphere. Now, there's suddenly a much wider choice of cities to go on the Must Visit One Day list. Certainly, we'd now add Leeds, Manchester, Liverpool, Portsmouth, Glasgow and Birmingham to that list. And before very long these former ugly ducklings might well be joined by places like Hull, Coventry, Sheffield, Leicester and perhaps Bradford, now all fluffing out their exciting new plumage.

AWARD WINNERS

Bird Centre of the Year is Beale Park at Lower Basildon (Berkshire), a smashing place with broad family appeal though birds are still the stars.

Farm Park of the Year is Dairyland near Newquay (Cornwall), dairy farming with an entertaining twist, lots of fun things to do.

Aquarium of the Year is the National Sea Life Centre in Birmingham, surrounding you with a tropical ocean, and dozens of other intriguing displays as well.

Adventure of the Year is North Wales's Llechwedd Slate Caverns in Blaenau Ffestiniog: an unforgettable hard-hat encounter with the world of the Victorian miners.

Garden of the Year is Trebah in Cornwall: this subtropical ravine is beautiful for a summer's day out, with its private beach down at the bottom.

Zoo of the Year is Bristol Zoo Gardens (Somerset chapter), all sorts of exotic creatures in lovely surroundings.

Oddity of the Year is Real Mary King's Close in or rather under Edinburgh - the city from a startlingly different angle.

Railway of the Year is the Bluebell Line at Sheffield Park Station (Sussex) - it set the steam railway waggon rolling back in the 1950s, and is still first class.

Tour of the Year is Nottingham's Caves - two tours actually, one giving an in-depth look at the past of these intriguing caverns, the other a lively family affair.

Discovery Centre of the Year is Newcastle Discovery (Northumbria): it's not just kids who are captivated by this great place.

Castle of the Year is Edinburgh Castle (Scotland), its battlements towering over the charming city - crossing the cobbles under that portcullis gate takes you into another world.

Theme Park of the Year is Alton Towers (Staffordshire), with dozens of mind-blowing rides, plenty of gentler stuff too - a thrilling day out.

Specialist Museum of the Year is the Royal Armouries Museum in Leeds (Yorkshire), a mind-boggling array of armaments not just in glass cases but in action too - if you don't have an interest in the subject when you go in, you will when you come out.

Living Museum of the Year is the North of England Open-Air Museum in Beamish (Northumbria), drawing you deeply into the life and work of your great grandparents' generation.

Historic House of the Year is Tatton Park on the edge of Knutsford (Cheshire) - magnificent mansion, 1920s farm, delightful grounds, with lots going on.

Gallery of the Year is the Barber Institute of Fine Arts in Birmingham, a comprehensive collection of european art by the great masters, approachably hung in a friendly-sized building.

Museum of the Year is the Horniman Museum in London, fresh out of a £13 million extension, full of extraordinary things - you'll be amazed.

Visitor City of the Year is thriving Leeds in Yorkshire, tempting now for all sorts and ages - plenty to see, nice hotels, restaurants and shops, and a good optimistic feel.

Newcomer of the Year is Living Coasts in Torquay, a fresh new look at the birds, animals and plants of the world's shorelines.

Family Attraction of the Year is the Portsmouth Historic Dockyard (Hampshire), Nelson's *Victory* and the *Mary Rose* of course, but masses more to enjoy - and the all-in ticket means you don't have to crowd it all into just one day.

We have been particularly impressed this year by the friendliness and helpfulness of all the people we dealt with in the West Country (especially Dorset, Cornwall and Devon), and up towards the north-west (Cheshire, Derbyshire and Nottinghamshire). And a word of praise for the thousands of volunteers helping to staff so many of the country's attractions, from little local museums to great historic buildings.

USING THE GUIDE

THE COUNTIES

England has been split alphabetically into county chapters. Scotland and Wales have each been covered in single chapters, and London appears immediately before them at the end of England.

WHERE TO STAY

In each section, hotels, inns and other places to stay such as farmhouses are listed alphabetically by town or village.

The price we show is the total for two people sharing a double or twin-bedded room with its own bathroom, for one night in high season. It includes full english breakfast (unless only continental is available, in which case we say so), VAT and any automatic service charge that we know about. So the price is the total price for a room for two people. We say if dinner is included in this total price. It is commonly included in some of the more remote places, especially in Cumbria and Scotland, and may also be in some other places where the quality of the food is a main attraction; in these cases, the establishment concerned does not normally offer B&B on its own. In some of the places we list, some or occasionally even all the bedrooms share bathrooms; we say if this is the case.

An asterisk beside the price means that the establishment concerned assured us that that price would hold until the end of summer 2004. Many establishments were unable to give us this assurance; it would be prudent to allow for an increase of around 5% by then.

A few hotels will do a bargain break price at weekends even if you're staying for just one night. If so, that's the price we give, and we show this with a **w** beside the price. Many more hotels have very good value short break prices, especially out of season, if you stay a minimum of nights; if you plan to stay in one area rather than tour around, it's well worth asking if there's a special price for short breaks when you book. Many more hotels than previously now offer short-notice bargains which don't appear on their tariffs if they are underbooked on a particular night, so as to fill their rooms even at a discount. So, especially if you are not booking in advance, ask what price they can quote you for that particular night.

If we know that the back rooms are the quietest or the front ones have the best views or the ones in the new extension are more spacious then we say so. If you want a room with a sea view or whatever, you should always ask specifically for this, and check whether it costs extra.

If the hotel closes for any day or part of the year, we say so. But there may be unscheduled closures, and some go out of business altogether. So don't head off into an area where there are no nearby alternatives without checking by telephone first. We always mention a restaurant if we know the inn or hotel has one. Note that we always commend food if we have information supporting a positive recommendation. So a bare mention that food is served shouldn't be taken to imply a recommendation of the food.

WHERE TO EAT

The price in ordinary type is for one person having a typical three-course restaurant meal with half a bottle of wine, including any automatic service charge. So double it to get a meal for two. The second price, in **bold** type after the |, is for a more informal single-dish meal, if that's available.

We list any scheduled closing dates. Many of the restaurants we list are very popular, and without a booking you may find there's no room for you.

If you want a good meal out in any area, look at the places to stay as well as the restaurants, especially in country areas. When we praise a hotel or inn for its food, that means it's well worth consideration as a place for a good meal out. In some parts of the country, it's in these hotel restaurants that you'll find the best food.

Our brief mentions of places to eat in the text of the **To see and do** sections are based on our own inspections or firm recommendations from readers.

CHILDREN AND DOGS

We asked all hotels, restaurants and other places to stay in and eat at which have full entries in the *Guide* whether they allow children. If the entry doesn't mention children, that means the establishment has told us that it welcomes them, with no restrictions. If there are restrictions (either an age limit, or segregated early evening meals for them), we spell these out. We have found that very occasionally establishments turn out in practice to be more restrictive about children than they claim. And of course managements change, and so do their policies. If you are travelling with children, to avoid misunderstandings it's always worth checking ahead. Please let us know if you find any difference from what we say. We have picked out a few places to stay that are really special for families. We've marked these in the text with ☺, our good for families symbol. This year we also asked all places to stay whether they allowed dogs; we say if they do.

LOCATIONS

Generally, we list places to see (and hotels and restaurants) under the name of the nearest village or town. We use **BOLD CAPITALS** to name the locality, and **bold type** like this to name the establishment. If the village is so small that you probably wouldn't find it on a road map, we've listed it under the name of the nearest sizeable village or town instead.

Places well known in their own right - famous castles, great houses, for example - are shown in **BOLD CAPITALS** instead of the locality name. The maps use the same locality name as the text.

We include places in their true geographical locations - so if a village is actually in Buckinghamshire that's where we list it, even if its postal address is in Oxfordshire.

EUROPEAN HERITAGE OPEN DAYS

On European Heritage Open Days, many notable buildings will be open to the public which are normally closed. English National Heritage Open Days were 12-15 Sept in 2003, with places all over England taking part, which provide visitors with a unique opportunity to explore these sometimes hidden, always interesting places in English cities, towns and villages - and completely free of charge. For more information ring (020) 7930 0914 or look at their helpful web site: www.civictrust.org.uk. The Welsh Civic Trust run open establishments through the three last weekends of September, ring (029) 2048 4606 for details. The Scottish equivalent, Doors Open Days, takes in over 700 properties and will run most weekends in September; ring (0141) 221 1466. During London Open House Weekend, 18-19 September, there will be free admission to over 500 buildings; anything from City Hall to private residences. For more details write to London Open House, PO Box 25361, London, NW5 1GY or call (020) 7267 2070.

PRICES AND OTHER FACTUAL DETAILS

Information about opening times and so forth is for 2004. In some cases establishments were uncertain about these when the *Guide* went to press during the late summer of 2003; if so, we say in the text. (And of course there's always the risk of changed plans and unexpected closures.) When we say 'cl Nov-Mar' we mean closed from the beginning of November to the end of March, inclusive; however, when we say 'cl Nov-Easter' we mean that the establishment reopens for Easter.

Where establishments were able to guarantee a price for 2004, we have marked this with an asterisk. In many cases establishments could not rule out an unscheduled price increase, and current experience suggests that about half these places - ie, no asterisk against the price - will put up their prices by 10-15% in around April 2004.

🔟 OUR DISCOUNT VOUCHER

In this edition over 700 places to visit have a 🔟 symbol immediately after their name. These have said they will honour our discount voucher until the end of 2004 (or of course the end of their season, if they close earlier). To get the discount, you must hand one of the vouchers in at the admissions kiosk; there are six vouchers on the tear-out card in the centre of the book. Usually, the discount is that one child will be admitted free for two adults paying the full price. Please also note the general conditions on the voucher itself, and in some instances we have spelt out different conditions in the text for an establishment. Note that the offer is generally not available on bank holidays or special event days.

NATIONAL TRUST

NT after price details means that the property is owned by the National Trust, and that for members of the Trust admission is free. There is a similar arrangement for properties owned by the National Trust for Scotland (NTS); the two Trusts have a reciprocal arrangement, so that members of one may visit the properties of the other free. Membership is therefore well worth while if you are likely to visit more than a very few properties in the year - quite apart from its benefit to the Trusts' valuable work. NT membership is £34 a year (£62 family membership); details from National Trust, PO Box 39, Bromley, Kent BR1 3XL; (020) 8315 1111. NTS membership is £32 (£52 family); details from National Trust for Scotland, 28 Charlotte Sq, Edinburgh EH2 4ET; (0131) 243 9300.

FRIENDS OF HISTORIC HOUSES

The Friends of Historic Houses Association has NT-style membership offering free entry to around 280 historic houses and gardens in private ownership throughout Britain - we recommend a high proportion of these. Membership is £30 a year (£44 for joint membership), so you only have to go to four or five houses and you've got your money back. Details from Historic Houses Association, Heritage House, PO Box 21, Baldock, Herts SG7 5SH; (01462) 896688.

ENGLISH HERITAGE

A similar membership scheme gives free access to those EH properties (about half) which charge admission. It costs £34 (£58 family). Details from English Heritage Membership Dept, PO Box 570, Swindon, SN2 2UR; (0870) 3331182. Cadw (for Wales) (029) 2050 0200: £27, (family £49.50), details from Cadw, Crown Building, Cathays Park, Cardiff, CF10 3NQ, and Historic Scotland (0131) 668 8600: £30 (family £57.50), details from Historic Scotland, Longmore House, Salisbury Place, Edinburgh, EH9 1SH, have similar schemes.

MAP REFERENCES

Most place names are given four-figure map references, looking like this: NT4892. The NT means it's in the square labelled NT on the map for that area. The first figure, 4, tells you to look along the grid at the top and bottom of the NT square for the figure 4. The third figure, 9, tells you to look down the grid at the side of the square to find the figure 9. Imaginary lines drawn down and across the square from these figures should intersect near the locality itself. The second and fourth figures, the 8 and the 2, are for more precise pinpointing, and are really for use with larger-scale maps such as road atlases or the Ordnance Survey 1:50,000 maps, which use exactly the same map reference system. On the relevant Ordnance Survey map, instead of finding the 4 marker on the top grid you'd find the 48 one; instead of the 9 on the side grid you'd look for the 92 marker. This makes it very easy to locate even the smallest village.

DISABLED ACCESS

We always ask establishments if they can deal well with disabled people. We mention disabled access if a cautious view of their answers suggests that this is reasonable, though to be on the safe side anyone with a serious mobility problem would be well advised to ask ahead (many establishments tell us that this helps them to make any special arrangements needed). There may well be at least some access even when we or the establishment concerned have not felt it safe to make a blanket recommendation - again, well worth checking ahead. There are of course many places where we can't easily make this sort of assessment - particularly the less formal attractions such as churches, bird reserves, waterside walks, viewpoints. In such cases (which should be obvious from the context) the absence of any statement about disabled access doesn't mean that a visit is out of the question, it simply means we have no information about that aspect. We're always grateful to hear of readers' own experiences. An important incidental point: many places told us that they would give free admission to a wheelchair user and companion.

CHANGES DURING THE YEAR – PLEASE TELL US

Changes are inevitable during the course of the year. Managements change, and so do their policies. We very much hope that you will find everything just as we say. But if you find anything different, please let us know, using the report card in the middle of the book, the forms at the end of the book, or just a letter. This *Guide* depends very heavily indeed on readers reporting back to it. In that sense it's very much a collaborative venture: and the more people that send us reports, the better the book will be. So please do help us by telling us about places you think should be added to the book, or removed from it, or even just confirming that places still deserve their entry. We try to answer all letters (though there may be a delay - and between the end of May and October we put all letters aside until after the end of the hectic editorial rush). People who help us do get a special offer discount price on the next edition. There's a note on the sort of information we need at the back of the book, with report forms; and a tear-out report card in the middle of the book. For letters posted in Britain you don't need a stamp: the address is The Good Britain Guide, FREEPOST TN1569, WADHURST, E. Sussex TN5 7BR. Alternatively you can use our web site, www.goodguides.co.uk (see below), to send us reports.

Our web site combines material from *The Good Britain Guide* and its sister publication *The Good Pub Guide*. It additionally includes a day-by-day list of thousands of events that will be taking place this year.

SYMBOLS

For simplicity's sake we use just five symbols in the text:

☺ Good places for families to stay   ⇌ Surface rail – former British Rail
⊖ London Underground   🖅 Our special offer discount (see
                                                        details above and tear-out card)

* indicating that a price is for 2004

Additionally, the map uses these two symbols:

🛏 places to stay
✗ places to eat

BEDFORDSHIRE

Some outstanding days out, and great outings for animal lovers

Picturesque Old Warden has enough for a nicely varied day out: a fascinating collection of vintage aeroplanes, a friendly birds of prey centre and an unusual Swiss Garden combine to make this year's Family Attraction.

Bedfordshire is home to two of the best animal attractions in the whole country. With a splendid Safari Park and the more sophisticated glories of county's finest stately home, Woburn Abbey wraps together plenty of interest for all ages; at Whipsnade Wild Animal Park too, there is a tremendous variety of exotic animals, in lovely surroundings (plus a children's farm, big adventure playground and indoor discovery centre). Slip End, Billington and Thurleigh all have good family-friendly farms, and Bedford Butterfly Park at Wilden also has quite a bit to keep children entertained.

At Lower Stondon, you can see one of the largest private collections of vehicles in the country, while at Leighton Buzzard Museum they have trains from all over the world. The Cecil Higgins Art Gallery in Bedford houses its impressive collection in a beautifully furnished Victorian mansion. Guided tours of Moggerhanger Park are a new addition, and this year we've added little military museums in Clapham and Thurleigh. In Luton, the Stockwood Craft Museum and Gardens have enough to fill a contented afternoon (and we've now added the local history museum here too). Gardeners will get a lot out of a visit to Wrest Park, while bird lovers (and strollers) enjoy the Lodge at Sandy, and Harrold Odell Country Park.

Although the county's scenery is generally not memorable, there are some charming villages to wander through, and Dunstable Downs have decent walking and remarkable views. The relative flatness makes cycling a pleasure, and a tourist board leaflet details good circular cycle routes; other good leaflets detail guided walks through some of the prettier villages and countryside.

Where to stay

BLETSOE TL0259 **North End Barns** *Riseley Rd, Bletsoe, Bedford, Bedfordshire MK44 1QT (01234) 781320* **£50**; 8 rms. 16th-c farmhouse with carefully converted barn on a working arable and sheep farm; fine barn beams, cheerful décor, a wide choice of breakfast dishes eaten around a large communal table in the farmhouse, and nearby pubs for evening meals; no smoking; children over 4; disabled access; dogs welcome in bedrooms

FLITWICK TL0234 **Flitwick Manor** *Church Rd, Flitwick, Bedford, Bedfordshire MK45 1AE (01525) 712242* **£204**, plus special breaks; 17 thoughtfully decorated rms. 17th-c country house surrounded by interesting gardens, with log fire in entrance hall, comfortable lounge and library, and smart restaurant with fine french wines and imaginative food using home-grown and local produce; tennis, putting,

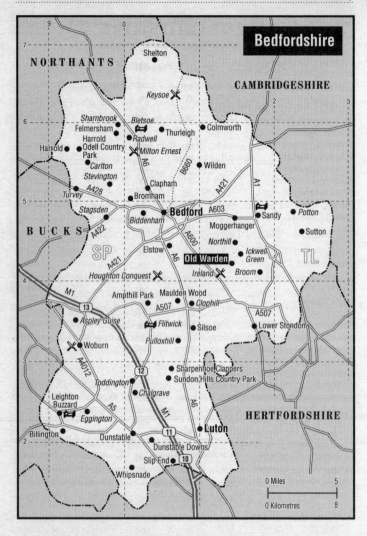

croquet; children over 12 in evening restaurant; dogs welcome in bedrooms

LEIGHTON BUZZARD SP9224 **Swan** *High St, Leighton Buzzard, Bedfordshire LU7 7EA (01525) 372148* **£70***, plus wknd breaks; 38 rms. Handsome Georgian coaching inn with pleasant lounge, relaxed Hunter's Bar, and attractive conservatory restaurant with english cooking

SANDY TL1651 **Highfield Farm** *Tempsford Rd, Sandy, Bedfordshire SG19 2AQ (01767) 682332* **£65**; 8 rms (2 in former stables). Neatly kept whitewashed house (no smoking) set well away from A1 and surrounded by attractive arable farmland with plenty of room; warmly friendly, helpful owner, open fire in comfortable sitting room, and communal breakfasts in pleasant dining room; disabled access; dogs welcome in bedrooms ☺

To see and do

Bedfordshire Family Attraction of the Year

OLD WARDEN TL1544 **Shuttleworth Collection, English School of Falconry and the Swiss Garden** The three excellent attractions spread around the park here are each worth visiting in their own right, but if you've got the time you can combine them into one busily rewarding and very varied day out. Even better, you can get a joint ticket covering admission to them all, which at £12.50 for adults and £4.50 for children is good value considering how much there is to see. You'll get most out of a visit on a dry day. The prices below are the costs of visiting each attraction separately. The one with the most general appeal to children is the very good birds of prey centre opened by the English School of Falconry; splendidly positioned in the grounds of Shuttleworth Mansion, it's one of the best of its type, showing off a collection of over 300 birds such as hawks, owls, eagles, falcons and vultures in a very pleasant woodland setting. Many of the birds are rare or unusual (after much deliberation they recently introduced some african hornbills), and there are up to four well organised flying displays every day (10.30, 12.30 and 2.30, plus 4pm in summer). They also have races between kestrels and even ferrets, there's a walk-through aviary with free-flying owls, and you may be able to have a go at flying a hawk. The staff are particularly helpful. Snacks and pleasant picnic areas by the lake, shop, disabled access; cl 25-26 Dec; 1 Jan; (01767) 627527; £6 adults, £4 children 5-16. A family ticket for two adults and two children is £16, a good saving if this is the only attraction you plan to visit (if you're doing all three, the joint ticket is better). Close by, the outstanding Shuttleworth Collection is a fascinating assemblage of nearly 40 historic aircraft, going right back to the early days of aviation. There's everything from a 1909 Blériot to a 1942 Spitfire, in purpose-built hangars on a classic grass aerodrome. Several exhibits are the only surviving examples of their type, and, uniquely, they're all still in working condition. It's worth going on one of the days when some are flown - usually at least twice a month in summer, but best to phone for exact dates. Even on other days, a visit can last a couple of hours, and as well as the planes there are plenty of old cars and motorbikes. Meals, snacks, shop, disabled access; cl Mon and Tues in Jan and Feb, and all Christmas week; (01767) 627288; £7.50 adults (more on flying days, when the joint ticket isn't valid), children up to 16 free. Finally, next to the Shuttleworth Collection's shop in Old Warden Park, the delightful Swiss Garden is a prime example of the 'Swiss Vogue' popular in the early 19th c. Ten acres of romantic wilderness garden, it's very nice for a wander, with pretty vistas and colourful trees and shrubs. Meals, snacks, shop, disabled access; open afternoons Mar-Sept, all day Sun and bank hols; (01767) 627666; £3 adults, £2 children. Further broadening the appeal for families, the Shuttleworth estate has recently opened an impressive adventure play area in the park, covering around two and a half acres; it's free, though if you're not going in any of the other attractions, you'll need to pay £2 for parking.

AMPTHILL PARK TL0239
Former hunting grounds of Henry VIII, surprisingly heathy but landscaped by Capability Brown, with lovely trees and a water-lily lake. In the little market town the Queens Head has cheap food, and Church St has some handsome buildings. On the outskirts are the ruins of a Jacobean hunting lodge (thought to be House Beautiful in Bunyan's *The Pilgrim's Progress*).
BEDFORD TL0549
Despite its long history, this is a straightforwardly modern town, but there are decent riverside gardens and a few nice buildings. The Corn

Exchange (St Paul's Sq) has a bronze bust of Glenn Miller, who made many of his morale-boosting broadcasts from here. Lincolns (Goldington Green) is an interesting old place for lunch.

Cecil Higgins Art Gallery & Museum (Castle Close) Bedford's outstanding attraction, this rewarding place boasts the kind of paintings most other museums can only dream about, inc great works by Turner, Constable, Rembrandt, Matisse, Picasso and Dali. The Victorian mansion's beautifully furnished rooms make it look as if the family that lived here have just popped out - it's clear that careful thought has gone into the displays, and nothing seems unnatural or out of place. An extension has collections of local lace, most notably by Thomas Lester, and european glass and ceramics; changing exhibitions. Snacks, shop, disabled access; cl Mon (exc pm bank hols), am Sun, 25-26 Dec, 1 Jan, Good Fri; (01234) 211222; £2.10, free on Fridays. Included in the admission price, the traditional **Bedford Museum** is housed in the former Higgins & Sons Brewery (open the same times).

John Bunyan Museum (Bunyan Meeting Free Church, Mill St) In the grounds of the church where John Bunyan was minister; stained-glass windows show scenes from *The Pilgrim's Progress*, and the bronze entrance doors are impressive. Visitors can walk through a series of tableaux of his life, and they've some of his possessions - there's also a trail around Bunyan-related sites in the town. Snacks, shop, disabled access; cl Sun, Mon, Good Fri, and Nov-Feb; (01234) 213722; free.

BILLINGTON SP9422

Mead Open Farm (Stanbridge Rd) Children enjoy themselves at this well arranged place, with trailer rides, indoor and outdoor play areas (inc one for under-3s), and a variety of hands-on activities such as egg collecting and pony grooming; occasional falconry displays. Meals, snacks, shop, disabled access; cl around a wk over Christmas, best to check; (01525) 852954; £4.50.

BROMHAM TL0050

Bromham Mill (Bridge End) Picturesque working 17th-c watermill on River Ouse, and a gallery with local

art and crafts. Snacks and picnic area, shop, disabled access to ground floor only; open Sun pm and bank hols Apr-Oct; (01234) 824330; free. The Swan is a pleasant family dining pub.

CLAPHAM TL0254

Glenn Miller Museum This World War II control tower was the last place Glenn Miller was seen alive before his ill-fated flight to Paris in 1944, and has an exhibition dedicated to him. The top floor has been restored, and there are lots of wartime photographs, a little aviation art gallery and a collection of military vehicles. Snacks, shop, disabled access to ground floor; open wknds and most bank hols; (01234) 350413; £3.

COLMWORTH (BUSHMEAD) TL1160

Bushmead Priory Ruins of late 12th-c Augustinian priory, well preserved, with medieval wall paintings and timber-framed roof. Open a few wknds in summer, ring to check times and prices; (01234) 376614; EH; free.

DUNSTABLE TL0221

Priory Church of St Peter (Church St) This remarkable priory church incorporates part of a 12th-c abbey (where Henry VIII's first marriage was annulled). Disabled access; cl bank hols; free. The Old Sugarloaf (High St) is useful for lunch.

DUNSTABLE DOWNS TL0019 Very popular with kite-fliers and gliders at wknds or in summer; there's a countryside centre (open Apr-Oct, plus wknds Nov-Mar), three car parks, and lots of space to run around. The downs give great views from a spectacular escarpment path, amid ancient grasslands. They can be linked to a circuit incorporating Whipsnade village and the nearby Tree Cathedral - the best walk in Beds. **Five Knolls** is an important Bronze Age burial mound, excavated by Agatha Christie's husband Sir Max Mallowan and Gerald Dunning. The Horse & Jockey (A5183) is a useful family food pub.

ELSTOW TL0546 The county's finest village, with a very attractive core of fine old timbered houses by the green. Bunyan was baptised in the handsome church, which has an unusual detached tower and a Pilgrim's Progress window. The

Three Tuns at Biddenham is the closest good place for lunch.

Moot Hall Outstanding brick-and-timber medieval market house with a collection of John Bunyan's works (he was born nearby) and a reconstruction of his writing room. Shop; cl am, Mon (exc bank hols), Fri and Sat, plus end Sept-Easter; (01234) 266889; £1.

FELMERSHAM SP9957

A lovely church by a medieval tithe barn and attractive old houses, some thatched, with the River Ouse below. Nearby Pavenham is also pretty, with a stroll down to the river. The Bedford Arms in peaceful Souldrop has good interesting food, and a play fort in its garden.

HARROLD SP9556

Pretty riverside village with 13th-c church and pack-bridge, and an early circular 19th-c lock-up on the village green. The Magpie is useful for lunch, and in Odell the Bell is good.

Harrold Odell Country Park (Carlton Rd) One for the bird-watchers; with two lakes and nature reserve, it's especially good for waterfowl, particularly in winter. Bedfordshire CC publish a circular route incorporating three waymarked walks up to 13 miles long. Snacks, disabled access; visitor centre and wildlife hide; (01234) 720016; free.

LEIGHTON BUZZARD SP9224

Leighton Buzzard Railway (Pages Park Station, Billington Rd) Good collection of locomotives from around the world, with a fleet of steam trains to trundle you through gently varied countryside. The Stonehenge Works terminus has industrial heritage displays and crafts shop. Snacks, shop, disabled access; open Sun and bank hol wknds Mar-Sept, wknds in Dec, and other days in school hols; (01525) 373888 for timetable; £5.50 (discount voucher not valid over Christmas). The Globe in Linslade is a nicely set canalside pub, with pleasant nearby walks.

LOWER STONDON TL1535

Stondon Museum (Station Rd) One of the largest private collections of vehicles in Britain, with around 400 exhibits in eight halls, covering motoring from 1890-1990. As well as the usual cars, bikes and military

vehicles, they do guided tours around a replica of Captain Cook's ship the *Endeavour* (12, 2 and 3.30pm). Snacks, shop, disabled access; cl Christmas wk; (01462) 850339; £5.

LUTON TL0822

Luton Museum and Art Gallery (Wardown Park) Local history museum in a Victorian mansion, with an interesting display on hats, also lace collection and military history; hands-on activities, touch-screen computers and special events. Snacks, shop, disabled access; cl Sun, Mon, 25-26 Dec, 1 Jan; 01582 546722; free. The surrounding park has a playground and crazy golf.

Stockwood Craft Museum & Gardens (Stockwood Country Park, Farley Hill) Ideal for a restrained and uncomplicated day out. Besides a museum and several lovely period garden settings (inc a 17th-c knot garden and a Victorian cottage garden), there's a refreshingly witty sculpture garden, and an adjacent children's play area. Also here, the **Mossman Collection** concentrates on the history of horse-drawn transport from Roman times onwards with more than 70 vehicles - the Royal Mail coach is particularly noteworthy. Snacks, shop, disabled access; cl Mon (exc bank hols), wkdys Nov-Mar, 25-26 Dec, 1 Jan; (01582) 738714; free.

MAULDEN WOOD TL0638

Ancient woodland with a picnic site, marked walks and muntjac deer; in the village (Clophill Rd) the pretty thatched Dog & Butcher has good value food.

MOGGERHANGER TL1349

Moggerhanger Park They hope to do guided tours of this recently restored Georgian manor, designed by Sir John Soane, on about 90 days of the year (though the grounds and a little exhibition on the house will be open more often). Meals, snacks, shop, disabled access; due to open late spring, phone for opening times and prices; (01767) 64100. The Anchor overlooking the River Ouse in Great Barford does generous food.

OLD WARDEN TL1343

An attractive village, built deliberately quaintly in the 19th c; the village church has a number of european wood carvings, inc some from the private chapel of Henry VIII's wife Anne of Cleves. The Hare & Hounds has imaginative food, and a play area in its nice garden.

Shuttleworth Collection, English School of Falconry and the Swiss Garden See separate family panel on p.3.

SANDY TL1847

The Lodge (RSPB Nature Reserve) The elegant 19th-c Tudor-style house is the RSPB's HQ, and though it isn't open to the public, it's surrounded by formal gardens, a wildlife garden, and a nature reserve covering 106 acres of heath, lake and woodland, with plenty of birds, animals and numerous trails of varying lengths. Perfect for watching birds undisturbed, but even if bird-spotting's not your thing, this is a relaxing place to explore, especially charming in spring when the woods are carpeted with bluebells. Snacks, good shop, some disabled access and parking; cl 25-26 Dec; (01767) 680541; £3 (free for RSPB members).

SHARPENHOE CLAPPERS TL0629

Steep-sided downland with chalkland flora and butterflies, crowned with a fine beechwood and Iron Age hill fort; the area is owned by the National Trust and is laced with paths. The Chequers at Streatley has good value food (and often jazz in its garden on summer Sun lunchtimes).

SHELTON TL0368

Pretty little cottages, hall and rectory grouped around the quite delightful church, with 13th-c work inside and a 14th-c font on seven legs. The St John Arms at Melchbourne is useful for something to eat, with a nice cottagey garden.

SILSOE TL0935

Wrest Park House & Gardens (off A6) Inspired by french chateaux, the 19th-c house has a few ornately plastered rooms open to visitors, but the enormous formal gardens are the main attraction. They go on for over 90 acres and give a good example of the changes in gardening styles between 1700 and 1850. Perhaps best of all is the Great Garden, designed by the Duke of

Kent between 1706 and 1740 and later modified by Capability Brown, with lovely views down the water to the baroque pavilion. Snacks, shop, disabled access to grounds only (can be tricky in the grassy gardens); open wknds and bank hols Apr-Oct; (01525) 860152; £4; EH. The Star & Garter by the church has a good range of home-made food.

SLIP END TL0818

Woodside Farm & Wildlife Park Good value friendly farm (much of it under cover) where children can collect eggs from the hen house, and have fun seeing and touching some of the 250 different breeds of animals and birds. Their monkey house has particularly friendly lemurs and marmosets - some have been hand-reared. There are good indoor and outdoor play areas, and a crazy golf course. You can buy feed for the animals from their very well stocked farm shop; tractor and pony and trap rides, trampolines and bouncy castles usually available during school holidays. Meals, snacks, indoor and outdoor picnic areas, shops, good disabled access; cl 25-26 Dec, 1 Jan; (01582) 841044; £4.95.

SUNDON HILLS COUNTRY PARK TL0528

Sheep-cropped downland with good views and marked walks (some quite steep). The Fancott Arms at nearby Fancott has food all day, and short children's train rides, at holiday times.

SUTTON TL2247

Notable for its steeply humpbacked packhorse bridge; ironically, cars have to use a more ancient crossing, the shallow ford beside it. A decent pub nearby is named after John o' Gaunt, the village's former owner.

THURLEIGH TL0459

306 Bombardment Group Museum Displays on life at home during World War II, with memorabilia, and various re-creations inc a wartime kitchen and GI bride scene. Open wknds and most bank hols Mar to end Oct; snacks, shop, disabled access; (01234) 708715; £3.

Monster-Events Centre You can have a go at riding or even driving the enormous trucks at this outdoor activity centre; also quad bikes, 4x4s and radio-controlled trucks. Age restrictions for some vehicles; meals, snacks, disabled access; phone to book (01234) 771904. Rides from £3.50 (the price we quote is a minimum; you can pay up to £100 for some rides.

Thurleigh Farm Centre Bustling farm centre with decent indoor and outdoor play areas (inc an assault course for older children), as well as farm animals, nature trail, pedal tractors and quad bikes; special events throughout the year. Meals, snacks, farm shop, some disabled access; cl Mon-Tues in term-time, 25 Dec-beginning Jan; (01234) 771597; £2.95 adults, £4.50 children (less in term-time). In the village the Jackal has good food (inc garden barbecues on Sun in summer).

WHIPSNADE TL0018

Tree Cathedral Tucked just off the village road is this most unusual war memorial, trees planted in the plan of a cathedral in the 1930s, with plantings continuing even nowadays; although it's not consecrated several services are held here each year.

Whipsnade Wild Animal Park Altogether 2,500 animals roam the beautiful downs-edge parkland, from tigers, giraffes and rhinos, to monkeys, wallabies, peafowl and chinese water deer. It's an enormous place, and an open-topped tour bus can take you between the various stopping points (or you can take your car, £9), though it's more fun on their narrow-gauge railway, which chuffs past herds of asian animals; their 17-acre elephant paddock is the biggest in Europe. There's a hands-on children's farm, a big adventure playground, an indoor discovery centre and several daily demonstrations (inc sea lion feeding at the newly reworked Splashzone). Whipsnade has an excellent record in conservation and breeding, and their successes have led to several species being saved from extinction. Meals, snacks, disabled access; cl 25 Dec; (01582) 872171; £12.50, £3 extra car park. Children are very welcome at the Farmers Boy in nearby Kensworth.

WILDEN TL0954

Bedford Butterfly Park 🅰 (off B660 just N of town) Well organised place

with quite an emphasis on children, inc a very good adventure playground with a separate play area for younger children. The hothouse is full of exotic plants and flowers, as well as colourful butterflies and caterpillars, ponds with koi carp and water-lilies, and a cascading waterfall. Children like the bugs room with tarantulas, scorpions and other creepy-crawlies, and they've a british butterfly enclosure and butterfly garden. Hay meadow nature trail (most colourful in July), children's quiz sheets from the gift shop. Snacks, shop, disabled access; cl end Oct to mid-Feb; (01234) 772770; £4.50.

WOBURN SP9632

Woburn Abbey & Deer Park One of England's grandest stately homes - everything from the lovely english and french 18th-c furniture to the splendid range of silver seems to have the edge over most assemblages elsewhere, and the art collection, taking in sumptuous paintings by Rembrandt, Van Dyck and Gainsborough, is outstanding (where else can you see 21 Canalettos in just one room?). The 3,000 acres of surrounding parkland were landscaped by Humphrey Repton, and today are home to ten species of deer. Swans, ducks and other waterfowl on the lake; pottery and huge antiques centre. Meals, snacks, shop, mostly disabled access (stairs to gold and silver vaults); open wknds Jan-Mar and Oct, daily Apr-end Sept; (01525) 290666; £8.50. The drive into the park is attractive, with masses of rhododendrons in Jun. In the pretty village itself, Galloways restaurant (Market Pl) is well liked by those readers who have tried it.

Woburn Safari Park (off A4012, not far from M1 junction 13) Attractively set in 300 acres of Woburn Abbey's grounds, this well run park has a lot more to offer than simply its famous drive-through safari. As many activities and animals as at any comparable zoo, inc a splendid walk-through monkey enclosure, an aviary where birds swoop down and feed from your hand, Sea Lion Cove (a nicely landscaped breeding ground for californian sea lions) and the recently added Land of the Lemurs. Popular shows are based around the elephants or penguin-

feeding; Apr-Sept they have birds of prey displays. As you drive round the safari it's hard to beat the thrill of spotting a lion or a tiger through the car window, and you may spy zebra, rhinos, and various types of antelope not too far away. You can drive round as many times as you like, but bank hols and summer wknds can produce slow-moving traffic jams; no dogs, convertibles or soft-roofed cars. Various play areas inc an indoor one shaped like Noah's Ark, a soft play area for younger visitors, and an outdoor Treetop Trail rather like an assault course; you can boat on the lake. A train can take you between various points of the park. There's easily enough here to fill a whole day, with lots under cover - though you'll get more out of it in dry weather. Meals, snacks, shop, disabled access; cl wkdys Nov-Feb; (01525) 290407; £13 (£1 extra late July-early Sept).
Other attractive villages include

Aspley Guise SP9335, spacious Biddenham TL0249 (nice 12th-c church), Broom TL1743, Clophill TL0837, Eggington SP9525, Northill TL1546, Sharnbrook SP9959 (interesting specialist shops), Pulloxhill TL0634, Radwell TL0057, Toddington TL0028 and Turvey SP9452 (the interesting church has Saxon origins) and Woburn Sands (good wooded walks nearby) SP9235; all have pubs we can recommend for lunch. Carlton SP5555 is also pleasant. Ickwell Green TL1545 nr Northill is well worth a look, too, with its colourful thatched houses around a broad green; Stagsden SP9849 is attractive, with a good few thatched houses, and strolls in the woods nearby. Stevington SP9853 has a handsomely restored windmill, and a holy well opposite the handsome church. Other churches worth investigating include Chalgrave TL0027 and Potton TL2449 (it's the gravestones that are worth the visit).

Where to eat

HOUGHTON CONQUEST TL0441 **Knife & Cleaver** *The Grove (01234) 740387* Civilised 17th-c dining pub with welcoming comfortable bar, blazing winter fire, attentive friendly service, smartly stylish bar food (lovely fresh fish and shellfish), over two dozen good wines by the glass, well kept real ales, good choice of whiskies, no smoking conservatory restaurant, and neat garden; good bdrms; cl Sun pm, 27-30 Dec; disabled access. £22.95|**£6.50**

IRELAND TL1341 **Black Horse** *(01462) 811398* Busy and attractive beamed pub in lovely setting, with a good choice of imaginative food in sizeable lounge or family dining area, helpful friendly staff, and lots of tables in lovely front garden with play area; cl Sun pm, 25-26 Dec, 1 Jan; disabled access. £25|**£4.95**

KEYSOE TL0763 **Chequers** *Pertenhall Rd (01234) 708678* Friendly and unpretentious village local with two comfortably modernised beamed bars, consistently good food, well kept beer, and terrace and garden with children's play equipment; cl Tues; disabled access. £20|**£6.75**

MILTON ERNEST TL0156 **Strawberry Tree** *3 Radwell Rd (01234) 823633* 18th-c thatched cottage with low beams and open fires, very good interesting lunchtime and evening food using the best ingredients from a sensibly short menu in the no smoking dining room; cl Sun, Mon, Tues, 2 wks winter, 2 wks summer; disabled access. £45

WOBURN SP9533 **Paris House** *Woburn Park (01525) 290692* Lovely black and white timbered house in Woburn's deer park, with a neat garden for pre-meal drinks, and serving enjoyable modern french food with exotic touches and a mainly french wine list; cl Sun pm, Mon, all Feb; disabled access. £60|**£15**

Special thanks to Michael and Jenny Back, Judith Feline, Mrs Y Champion

BERKSHIRE

Windsor, with its Castle, Royal connections and the excellent Lego theme park, is the big draw; unique and appealing family attractions elsewhere, and the west of the county has possibilities for quiet breaks

The west of the county has a good range of walking possibilities, from gentle strolls to long hikes - with some comfortable and attractive places to stay in, and lots of good eating places. Its rolling downland and civilised small villages linked by pleasant minor roads make for scenic drives - the Lambourn Valley and Lambourn Downs, the B4009 and B4494, and the back road from Pangbourne to Aldworth are among the best.

There's plenty of boating activity, and easy towpath sauntering between Marlow and Henley - the best stretch of the Thames. The river does get very busy during the holidays, but is idyllic on a fine early summer or autumn afternoon. Away from the Thames, there are also boat trips in Hungerford, Newbury and Kintbury. Besides world-famous Ascot, fine racecourses can be found at Newbury and Windsor, and in Lambourn you can even watch the horses being trained.

Pretty Windsor has much to offer visitors. Home of the monarch for 900 years, Windsor Castle is a tourist honey-pot, while Legoland, continually improving, is an outstanding whole day out for families. Windsor Great Park is good for a pleasant stroll; peaceful Savill Garden and the Valley Gardens are also well worth a visit. Very close, Eton has an interesting museum on its famous school.

Our Family Attraction this year, Beale Park at Lower Basildon, has plenty of exotic birds and animals in lovely surroundings (and there's an interesting Palladian mansion nearby). Bucklebury Farm Park is a good place to take younger children, and the Look Out discovery park in Bracknell is a successful mixture of hands-on science with nature and outdoor adventure. Wellington Country Park at Riseley, and (more peacefully) Trilakes Country Park and Fishery are pleasant in fine weather, and the reconstructed rainforest at Hampstead Norreys is handy on a cold day. Bird-watchers recommend Thatcham Moor.

Where to stay

BRAY SU9179 **Monkey Island** *Old Mill Lane, Bray, Maidenhead, Berkshire SL6 2EE (01628) 623400* **£190***, plus wknd breaks; 26 comfortable rms. Set on an island in the River Thames and reached only by footbridge or boat, this peaceful 18th-c former fishing lodge, built by the 3rd Duke of Marlborough, is made up of two smart white buildings surrounded by beautifully kept gardens with peacocks, ducks and geese; some fine original features such as an original painted ceiling in the lounge showing monkeys in 18th-c sporting gear; helpful friendly staff, and enjoyable food in restaurant overlooking the water; disabled access

HAMSTEAD MARSHALL SU4165 **White Hart** *Hamstead Marshall, Newbury, Berkshire RG20 0HW (01488) 658201* **£80**; 6 comfortable beamed rms in converted barn. Civilised country inn in quiet village with a log fire open on both sides of the

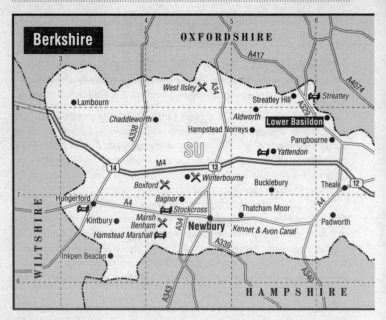

L-shaped bar, a partly no smoking restaurant, good italian food (the daily specials are the thing to go for), decent italian wines, friendly service, and very pleasant walled garden; cl 25-26 Dec, 1 Jan; disabled access

HUNGERFORD SU3369 **Bear Hotel** *41 Charnham St, Hungerford, Berkshire RG17 0EL (01488) 682512* **£93**, plus special breaks; 41 comfortable, attractive rms with antiques and beams in older ones, and some with views over the river. Civilised and carefully restored hotel with open fires, plentiful bar food and well kept real ales in Courtyard Bar (open all day), and a relaxing brasserie restaurant; dogs welcome in bedrooms

HUNGERFORD SU3268 **Marshgate Cottage** *Marsh Lane, Hungerford, Berkshire RG17 0QN (01488) 682307* **£60***; 10 individually decorated rms. Family-run little hotel backing on to Kennet & Avon Canal, with residents' lounge and bar, super breakfasts, a friendly atmosphere, and seats overlooking water and marsh, and in sheltered courtyard; plenty to see nearby; disabled access; dogs by arrangement

MAIDENHEAD SU8880 **Fredricks Hotel & Restaurant** *Shoppenhangers Rd, Maidenhead, Berkshire SL6 2PZ (01628) 581000* **£260**; 37 luxurious rms, many with garden views. Smart red-brick hotel next to the greens of Maidenhead Golf Club, with champagne on arrival in reception with its stylishly modern chandeliers and marble waterfall; plush cocktail bar, fine professional cooking in luxurious restaurant, and good formal service from long-standing staff; lush winter-garden conservatory, and terrace where you can take meals in warm weather; cl Christmas/New Year; disabled access

STOCKCROSS SU4468 **Vineyard** *Stockcross, Newbury, Berkshire RG20 8JU (01635) 528770* **£269**, plus special breaks; 31 lovely big elegant rms or suites with garden views. Old hunting lodge with lots of modern art out in the grounds and in the public rooms, opulent country house-style furnishings, plants, lovely flower arrangements, newspapers and books, excellent food in restaurant, two exceptional wine lists (one specialising in californian wines), and kind staff; indoor swimming pool and gym

STREATLEY SU5980 **Swan at Streatley** *High St, Streatley, Reading, Berkshire*

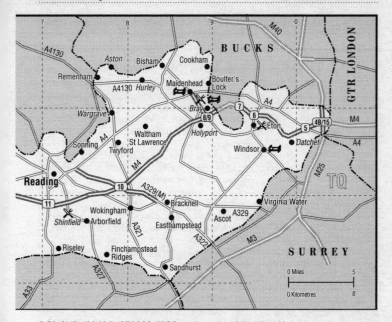

RG8 9HR (01491) 878800 **£129**w, plus special breaks; 46 attractive rms, many overlooking the water. Well run, friendly riverside hotel with comfortable, relaxed lounges, consistently good food in attractive newly refurbished restaurant, popular leisure club with indoor swimming pool, restored Magdalen College Barge, and flower-filled gardens; disabled access

WINDSOR SU9277 **Oakley Court** *Windsor Rd, Water Oakley, Windsor, Berkshire SL4 5UR (01753) 609988* **£250***, plus special breaks; 118 spacious, individually furnished rms. Splendid Victorian country-house hotel in 35 acres of grounds by the Thames with 9-hole golf course, croquet lawn, tennis, fishing, boating, and health club; log fires in the elegant lounges, a panelled library, and particularly good food in smart restaurant; used in 200 films, notably the St Trinians series and Hammer Dracula films; disabled access

YATTENDON SU5574 **Royal Oak** *The Square, Yattendon, Newbury, Berkshire RG18 0UG (01635) 201325* **£130**, plus special breaks; 5 pretty rms. Elegant and comfortable old inn in peaceful village, with fresh flowers and log fires in prettily decorated panelled bar and lounge, a relaxed atmosphere, interesting modern food, real ales, a good wine list, and a charming walled garden

---

To see and do

Berkshire Family Attraction of the Year

LOWER BASILDON SU6179 **Beale Park** 🖼 (Church Farm) Appealingly laid out over 400 acres of Thames Valley parkland and water meadows, this genuine and nicely undeveloped wildlife centre has lots of animals and birds to fascinate younger children - and plenty of space to picnic or simply let off steam. It was set up 45 years ago by benefactor Gilbert Beale, whose love of birds was such that his favourite peahen often rode round the estate with him in his Rolls Royce. Your editor well remembers being shown round by him that first year; since then the collection of birds has grown, and they've gained an impressive record in both breeding and returning rare species to the wild. They're continually improving and replacing aviaries (the huge new owlery is particularly impressive), as well as adding popular new features like the meerkat enclosure. There are also plenty of unusual farm animals, a pets corner, and some other enjoyable attractions such as the National Model Boat Collection, and a narrow-gauge steam railway (small extra charge). Plenty of good play areas too, with paddling pools and water slides. In fine weather it can easily fill a good chunk of a leisurely, undemanding day, and extra activities in school holidays include animal handling sessions. For a special treat, you can book their more elaborate outdoor children's activities, for example a fun, well supervised junior survival course that takes in everything from shelter-building to marshmallow toasting; these usually cost around £15, but check their website, www.bealepark.co.uk, for more details. Meals, snacks, shop, disabled access; cl Nov-Mar; (0118) 984 5172: £5.50 adults, £4 children over 3 (slightly less out of season). A family ticket for two adults and two children is £16.50; one adult and three children £15.50. They don't take credit or debit cards. You can get a boat to here from Caversham Bridge in Reading (two hours each way, (0118) 948 1088, £12 return).

ARBORFIELD SU7566
Henry Street Garden Centre
Specialist rose and bedding plant grower, with a well stocked garden centre. From Jun to Sept you can wander through the fragrant rose fields. Meals, snacks, shop, disabled access; cl 25-26 Dec, and Easter Sun; (0118) 976 1223; free. The George & Dragon at Swallowfield is a nice cottagey dining pub.

ASCOT SU9268
Royal Ascot Probably the most famous racecourse in the world, though most visitors spend as much time watching the people as the horses. The four-day Royal Meeting in mid-Jun (first held in 1711) is still one of the highlights of the english season; to try for admission to the Royal Enclosure, british citizens should apply to The Royal Enclosure Office, Ascot Racecourse, Ascot, SL5 7JN, foreign citizens to their embassy. For the other

stands contact the racecourse; tickets must be booked in advance and are available from 1 Jan. Plenty of other top-class races throughout the year, when ticket prices range from £7 to £33 depending on the enclosure (the Silver Ring is the cheapest). Meals, snacks, shop, disabled access; (01344) 876876 for dates. The Thatched Tavern at Cheapside is the best nearby place for lunch.

BISHAM SU8484
Bisham church Well worth a look; sitting on a seat in the churchyard by the Thames on a fine evening is rather special.

BOULTER'S LOCK SU9082
An excellent starting-point for leisurely strolls by the River Thames (head upstream).

BRACKNELL SU8666
Look Out 🖼 (3m from centre; Nine Mile Ride, off B3430) This busy centre should satisfy both lively minds and legs.

It's the starting-point for 2,600 acres of woodland, but the main feature is the under-cover hands-on science centre. Visitors can enjoy climbing through a giant mole hole, try the Puzzle Carousel, or have a go at launching a miniature hydrogen rocket or a hot-air balloon. Mainly conifer plantations, the forest is full of nature trails and wildlife; you can hire mountain bikes (school hols and wknds mid-Feb to Oct; (01344) 874611; around £8 for two hours), the many tracks, some based on Roman roads, allow long if not varied walks and rides (one leading to an Iron Age hill fort). There are good views from the 22-metre look-out tower. Meals, snacks, shop, disabled access; cl 25-26 Dec; (01344) 354400; £4.65 (half price after 4pm, but shuts at 5). For those with any energy left, across the road the Coral Reef swimming pool complex is great for younger members of the family; the Wild Water Rapids are the best bit (cl 2 wks before Christmas; (01344) 862525; £5.70).

BUCKLEBURY SU5570
Bucklebury Farm Park (on the edge of village, signed from Hermitage off A34) A good bet for under-12s into animals, this friendly and traditional little farm park is attractively set in the Pang Valley. All the animals you'd expect, plus a herd of red deer; a tractor-drawn trailer ride takes you right up to them (the calves are born in Jun). Children can handle rabbits and guinea pigs in the pets' corner, bottle feed lambs and calves in spring, and there's an adventure playground and a cable slide. Also five acres of woodland (awash with bluebells in spring), and a two-mile way-marked walk across an ancient common. Snacks, some disabled access, open daily mid-Mar to mid-Sept and autumn half-term, plus wknds mid-Sept to autumn half-term; (0118) 971 4002; £4.25 adults. The Rowbarge down at Woolhampton is a good waterside family dining place.

COOKHAM SU8985
The village, leading down to the Thames, is attractive, and has several decent pubs, of which the very smart if expensive Bel & the Dragon, and Uncle Toms Cabin at Cookham Dean, are our current favourites. There are plenty of opportunities in this area for **walks** combining the Thames with its hinterland, including great views from the chalk escarpment of Winter Hill. Cock Marsh (NT), by the Thames, is a fine lowland marsh, with breeding wading birds and wetland flora. Paths in this area are very well kept, and it is hard to lose the way seriously, although woodland walking sometimes means you have to keep your eyes skinned for arrow markers painted on trees.
Stanley Spencer Gallery (King's Hall) Cookham really made its mark on Spencer and his art: it was his birthplace and he spent most of his working life here. This rewarding little gallery has a good range of his unique work, with highlights including *The Last Supper* and the curious unfinished *Christ Preaching at Cookham Regatta*. Shop, disabled access; cl wkdys (exc bank hols) Nov-Easter; (01628) 471885; £1.
EASTHAMPSTEAD SU8667
Easthampstead church The church here has fine Pre-Raphaelite stained glass by William Morris, Edward Burne-Jones and others.
ETON SU9677
So close to Windsor it's pretty much part of it, this has a restrained and decorous High St with a mix of interesting old shops and houses. Its glory is **Eton College**, the famous public school, whose stately Tudor and later buildings in graceful precincts are marvellously calm during the school's holidays. The Chapel is an outstanding late Gothic building in the Perpendicular style, and a museum tells the story of the school from its foundation in 1440 up to the present, with fascinating videos on life for pupils here today. Bizarre information is turned up by the various historical documents - in the 17th c, for example, smoking was compulsory for all scholars as a protection against bubonic plague. The Brewhouse Gallery has some good changing exhibitions, and next door is a collection of Egyptian antiquities. Shop, some disabled access; cl am in term-time, and all Oct-Mar; (01753) 671177; from £3.70 (guided tours from £4.70). The college runs summer residential courses on a wide range of topics. Gilbeys (High St) does

good imaginative light meals.

FINCHAMPSTEAD RIDGES
SU7863

A steepish chunk of heather and pinewood, not big but with a good natural character, good views and sheltered picnic spots; the fine avenue of wellingtonias just above it is well worth seeing too. The Queens Oak in the village has good value food. To the N, Simons Wood is NT woodland, with a walk to Heath Pool and Devil's Highway Roman road, now a track.

HAMPSTEAD NORREYS SU5376
Living Rainforest (B4009 slightly out of village) Readers are most impressed with this unusual and quite fascinating tropical rainforest reconstructed under glass, with thousands of weird-looking plants. They're spread over two different areas, Lowland Tropical and Amazonica, each with its own climate and atmosphere. Particularly strange are the giant 8-ft lily pads (best from Jun-Oct), which start life the size of a pea, and the orchid collection is exceptional. Quite a few of these plants can't be seen anywhere else in Europe. Also rare monkeys, various fish, tarantulas, a chameleon and even a dwarf crocodile; special events throughout the year. As it's so warm, this is particularly handy on a cold day. Snacks, good shop (with plants for sale), mostly disabled access (though hard work in gravel car park); cl 25-26 Dec; (01635) 202444; £4.75. The White Hart has good value food.

HUNGERFORD SU3368
Attractive small town with some interesting antiques shops, inc a large arcade on the High St (01488) 683701; some general, others specialising in items as diverse as fireplaces and billiard tables. The Kennet & Avon Canal Trust run **canal trips** from the Wharf; phone (01488) 683389 for details. The John o' Gaunt (High St) has a good choice of food.

INKPEN BEACON SU3562
The high escarpment between here and Walbury Hill gives some dramatic ridgeway walking; best reached from the minor road S of Inkpen, where the Crown & Garter is an appealing country food pub. The gibbet on top of the hill is a macabre relic from highwayman days.

Immediately S lie some lovely rolling downlands laced with gentle and mostly well marked tracks, field paths and woodland paths.

KINTBURY SU3866
Horse-drawn barge trips 🖼 1½-hr trips along the restored Kennet & Avon Canal. Snacks, shop, disabled access by arrangement; open mid-Apr-Sept; phone (01635) 44154 for a timetable; £5.20. The waterside Dundas Arms has good food (not Mon evening or Sun).

LAMBOURN SU3278
Quiet streamside racehorse-training village below the downs. The parish **Church of St Michael and All Angels** is worth a look (originally Norman, with Perpendicular additions). **Lambourn Trainers Association** (Windsor House) Guided tours around this racehorse training centre; you meet individual horses and see them put through their paces. Wear suitable shoes, and you must make an appointment. Shop, disabled access; open around 10-12am, daily exc Sun and bank hols; (01488) 71347; £7; annual open day Good Fri £10. **Seven Barrows** Up on the downs off the Lambourn—Kingston Lisle rd (OS Sheet 174 SU329827) this Bronze Age cemetery has at least 32 barrows - a spectacle even for the uninitiated.

LOWER BASILDON SU6178
Basildon Park (off A329) Elegant Bath stone Palladian mansion, with delicate plasterwork on the ceilings and walls, unusual Octagon Room, and intriguing collection of rare sea shells in the Shell Room. Outside are old-fashioned roses, a pretty terrace, and pleasant grounds beyond. The classical frontage is particularly impressive. Meals, shop, disabled access to garden and grounds only; open pm Weds-Sun and bank hols Apr-Oct, best to check; (0118) 984 3040; £4.50, £2.10 grounds only; NT. **Beale Park** See separate family panel on p.12.

MAIDENHEAD SU9081
Boating on the Thames Though busy in summer, this is a lovely stretch of the river, flowing through lively towns and villages, past grand houses in imposing grounds. Some idyllic reaches by steep quiet woodland have islets where you can picnic. A particularly

pretty trip is from Wargrave to Henley to Medmenham Abbey to Hambleden, Hurley and Marlow Reach. A good shorter stretch is Cliveden Reach (the two miles between Cookham and Boulter's Lock). As well as motor launches, you can hire very attractive (not to mention silent and quite environmentally friendly) electric launches, though for the purists - and the energetic - only a rowing boat will do. Kris Cruisers in Datchet have 6- to 12-seater motor boats for hire ranging from £81 to £261 a day (good discounts mid-week); (01753) 543930.

NEWBURY SU4667

Busy shopping town with some nice old parts, and interesting older buildings among the High St shops (less traffic-plagued since the opening of the notorious bypass). **St Nicolas** is a fine early 16th-c Perpendicular church with a magnificent pulpit. West Mills is the best evocation of the town's 18th-c prosperity, and leads to the attractively rejuvenated canal. **Boat trips** run mid-Apr-end Sept from the old wharf, beyond the market square on the other side of the High St; phone (01635) 44154; around £5.70 return. The town has an excellent **racecourse**, with mid-week and wknd races all year; (01635) 40015 for dates, prices from £5. **Donnington Castle** (just N off B4494) is the tall ruined medieval gatehouse of a much larger fortress destroyed in the Civil War. The nicely set canalside Lock Stock & Barrel, with suntrap balcony, has decent food all day.

West Berkshire Museum (The Wharf) Handsome museum housed in a 17th-c Cloth Hall and an 18th-c granary, good on the Civil War battles fought here, and on the development of ballooning, also local archaeology and history. Shop, disabled access to ground floor only; cl Weds (exc school hols), Sun, bank hols, and maybe first two wks in Jan, best to check; (01635) 30511; free.

PADWORTH SU6067

Kennet & Avon Canal Visitor Centre (Aldermaston Wharf) In a nice little house beside the canal, exhibitions on the history and usage of the waterway, and useful information on things to do along its various stretches (of which some would say the Berkshire bits are the prettiest); good trails and walks. Snacks (in picnic garden), shop, limited disabled access; cl end Nov-end Feb; (0118) 971 2868; free. Nearby quietly placed **Padworth church** feels very ancient and peaceful, and the Round Oak has decent food. See also Hungerford, Kintbury and Newbury entries for boat trips. And besides other places we mention, there's good access from Marsh Benham SU4267, Thatcham SU5167 and Woolhampton SU5767, all of which have decent pubs. The railway makes a useful method of return, after a walk along the canal from Hungerford to Kintbury, for example.

PANGBOURNE SU6376

Pangbourne Meadow Pleasant wildflower meadow by the Thames; the attractive riverside Swan has food all day. The village has some decent shops, and was the home of Kenneth Grahame, who perhaps found inspiration around here for The Wind in the Willows.

READING SU7173

Berkshire's county town, largely 19th-c red brick, and not really a tourist town, but with museums worth visiting; the abbey ruins in Forbury Gardens are worth a look if passing. For the extravagant, a **balloon trip** gives a very different view of Berkshire; lift off from town-centre parks (weather permitting) in summer, dawn and dusk; (020) 8840 0108 for details; £145. Sweeney & Todd (Castle St) has excellent value home-made pies.

Museum of English Rural Life (University of Reading, Whiteknights Park; 2m SE on A327, so you don't have to go into the busy centre) You won't find a better exploration of life in the english countryside over the last couple of centuries than this, taking in farm tools, rural crafts, and domestic room settings. Shop, disabled access; cl 1-2pm, all day Sun and Mon, and 25 Dec-1 Jan; (0118) 931 8661; £1. A £5 million lottery grant has been awarded to the museum to help it move nearer the town centre, so it will be closed from Easter 2004, and reopen at its new location in St Andrew's Hall (which is currently being extended) early in 2005.

Museum of Reading (Blagrave St) In a showy neo-Gothic building, with hands-on displays, and a unique Victorian copy of the Bayeux Tapestry, exhibits range from biscuit tins back to Roman pottery; also changing exhibitions. Meals, snacks (not Sun), shop, disabled access; cl Mon exc bank hols, 25-26 Dec; (0118) 939 9800; free.

REMENHAM SU7682
A good start for gentle strolls along the Thames towpath, showing to full effect the river's nostalgic qualities of boating and Edwardian England. There are spectacular period riverside mansions towards Maidenhead. This reach is the course of the Henley regatta; you can instead start a walk from Henley itself (coming back over the bridge).

RISELEY SU7164
Wellington Country Park (off B3349 Reading—Basingstoke) Quite a bit for families in this big country park; the 350 acres of meadows, woodland and lakes include marked nature trails, a miniature railway, a collection of small domestic animals, a sandpit and an adventure playground. You can fish and hire rowing and pedal boats on the lake; caravan and camping facilities. Snacks, shop, disabled access; cl Nov-Mar; (0118) 932 6444; £4.60.

SANDHURST SU8262
Trilakes Country Park and Fishery (Yateley Rd) Not just for fishermen, these attractive lakes and surrounding park and woodland have lots of animals (including alpacas) and birds, some of which you can feed; also a model railway, remote control boats, and they plan to open a new indoor adventure playground. Meals, snacks, shop, limited disabled access; cl 25-26 Dec; (01252) 873191; £3, £8 fishing (licence required). The nearby Bird in Hand at Little Sandhurst is useful for lunch.

SONNING SU7575
A charming village, with a pleasant walk through the churchyard and past the lovely **church** to the River Thames, and to Sonning Lock. The attractive old Bull is open all day on wknds.

STREATLEY HILL SU5580
The NT car park below here gives access to NT downland for fine views over the Thames Valley. The long-distance downs-top Ridgeway Path, one

of the oldest tracks in England, follows surfaced farm roads in places hereabouts, but takes in some quiet countryside. The nearby Bell at Aldworth is a delightful country pub.

THATCHAM MOOR SU5066
(car park S of A4) Surprisingly, the largest area of inland freshwater reed beds in England; lots of birds (some rare), moths, and marshland and aquatic plants. The **Nature Discovery Centre** explains more about the environment with some hands-on exhibits, and has a good programme of special events; also two large adventure playgrounds. Snacks, shop, disabled access (limited inside); cl Mon all year, Sun am Nov-Feb, 25-26 Dec, and a few wks in Jan, best to check as they may also cl ams in term-time; (01635) 874381; free. The Sun in the Wood at Ashmore Green just N has good food.

THEALE SU6271
Englefield House (A340) This historic house is open only to groups of 20 or more by appointment, but the attractive surrounding woodland is open to individuals, with interesting trees, water and formal gardens, and deer park. Some disabled access; open Mon all year, plus Tues-Thurs Apr-Oct; (0118) 930 2221; £3. Both the Bull and the Old Boot over at Stanford Dingley are enjoyable for lunch.

TWYFORD SU7975
Valley Vineyard (Stanlake Park, B3018) English wines made by a pioneering blend of tradition and technology. Shop; usually cl Sun am, 25 Dec-2 Jan; (0118) 934 0176; free. The cosily old-fashioned Green Man (Hinton Rd, Hurst) has enjoyable food and a nice garden.

VIRGINIA WATER SU9768
Very beautiful, particularly in autumn; the Long Walk gives glorious perspectives of Windsor Castle. Best access via Valley Gardens or Savill Garden car parks.

WALTHAM ST LAWRENCE SU8377
Shottesbrooke church A magnificent 14th-c building, unusually set in a park just E of Waltham St Lawrence - itself an attractive quiet village with an ancient centre, and good value food in the handsome old Bell.

WINDSOR SU9676

Well worth an expedition (though a tremendous magnet for visitors), the town is dominated by its famous castle, the largest inhabited one in the world. The little streets to the S have many pretty timber-framed or Georgian-fronted houses and shops. The High St, by contrast, is wide and busy. You can walk by the Thames (for example, from Home Park, beyond the station); or across to Eton. The good evening racecourse is best approached by boat - shuttle services run from Barry Avenue Promenade; (01753) 498400 for race dates. The Two Brewers in pretty Park St is a good food pub. In the quieter nearby Thames-side village of Old Windsor the Union has good bar food, and the café at the Windsor Farm Shop (Datchet Rd) is good value.

Frogmore House (Home Park) This lesser known former Royal residence is definitely worth catching on one of its few open days (usually in May and Aug) - phone (020) 7766 7305; shop; £6.20, no under-8s. It was a favourite with Queen Victoria, who is buried in a mausoleum in the grounds, alongside her beloved Albert.

Guildhall (High St, opposite Tourist Information Centre) Over 300 years old, it was designed by Sir Thomas Fitz and, after his death, completed by Sir Christopher Wren. Notice how the central columns don't quite reach the ceiling (tradition has it that the councillors of the time insisted that columns were necessary for safety, so Wren added some - an inch short of the ceiling to prove his plans were correct). Open 10-2 Mon (or Tues after a bank hol); (01753) 796033; free.

Legoland (B3022, 2m SW of town centre; shuttlebus from the station at Windsor & Eton Riverside, which connects with London Waterloo) Ever-expanding and truly imaginative, for children under 12 this is one of the most exciting days out in the country. It isn't cheap, but considering how much there is to see and do it's really not bad value; you can save quite a bit off the entrance price and avoid the queues by visiting outside peak season, and booking in advance. The park is divided into eight differently themed areas, and

highlights include the driving school at Lego Traffic, the Rat Trap - a first-class labyrinth of wooden walkways, climbing nests and slides - a dragon-themed roller-coaster, and an excellent steep water chute. Children over 9 can create robots in the more sophisticated Mindstorms workshops (entrance is by timed ticket), colourful Lego Explore Land appeals to younger children, while My Town has some jolly fairground rides and a circus. There's a virtual reality racing game, but best of all is Miniland, where 35 million bricks recreate european capitals in miniature, with moving vehicles, people and animals, and wonderful attention to detail. You'll need a full day to stand even a chance of seeing everything. Meals, snacks, good shops, good disabled access; open daily Mar-early Nov (exc Tues-Weds Sept-Oct), phone for exact dates; (08705) 040404; £18.95 off peak, £22.95 peak.

Savill Garden (Wick Lane, Englefield Green - where the Fox & Hounds, no children, is a good lunch break) On the eastern edge of Windsor Great Park, 35 peaceful acres taking in woodland, a formal rose garden, a garden in honour of the Jubilee, rock plants, herbaceous borders and so forth, and punctuated with many rare trees, shrubs and perennials. Perhaps best in spring, when there's a dazzling range of colours, but quite stunning at any time of year. Meals, snacks, good shop, plant sales, disabled access; cl 25-26 Dec; (01753) 847518; £5.50 Apr-May, £4.50 Jun-Oct, £3.25 Nov-Mar.

Valley Gardens Lovely for a relaxing stroll, with over 200 acres of woodland - 50 of which are devoted to rhododendrons, making this the largest planting of the species in the world. Also an outstanding collection of trees and shrubs, a heather garden, waterfowl lakes and attractive landscaping. It's free for pedestrians (the mile-long walk from Savill Garden is pleasant), though cars can enter by a gate on Wick Rd, Englefield Green, for a fee of £4, £5.50 Apr-May - change needed for the automatic barrier.

Windsor Castle A mass of towers, ramparts and pinnacles, this awesome castle is one of the official residences of the monarch, though it's changed considerably since William the Conqueror built his original wooden fort here. Henry II constructed the first stone buildings, inc the familiar Round Tower, but for many the highlight is the magnificent **St George's Chapel**, a splendid example of Perpendicular Gothic architecture, with intricate carvings on the choir stalls, fine ironwork, an amazing fan-vaulted ceiling, and the arms and pennants of every knight entered into the Order of the Knights of the Garter. This is closed Sun and occasional other dates, often at short notice - best to check on the number below. The **State Apartments**, used for ceremonial and official occasions, are decorated with carvings by Grinling Gibbons and ceilings by Verrio, and full of superb paintings from the Royal Collection (inc Rembrandts, Holbeins, Canalettos and Van Dycks), porcelain, armour, and exceptionally fine furniture. This part may be closed when the Queen is in residence. Although everything is well signed, readers recommend buying a guidebook or audioguide (available at the entrance), and if you visit in one of their quieter periods the helpful staff take time to point out details you might not notice. Entrance to **Queen Mary's Doll's House**, an exquisite creation by Sir Edwin Lutyens, built for Queen Mary in the 1920s, with perfectly scaled furniture and decoration, is also included in the general admission price. When there are enough people they take groups round the new Royal garden, designed for the Golden Jubilee to grace the approach to the castle, rather than be an attraction in its own right - ask at reception when you arrive.

Shops, disabled access; occasionally closed for official events, so best to phone (020) 7766 7304; £11.50. The guards generally change daily Mon-Sat (alternate days only in winter), at 11 o'clock - again, phone for exact dates. **Windsor Great Park** Miles of well maintained and peaceful parkland, so sensitively landscaped that it takes the occasional surprising find (statues, even a totem pole) to remind you that it's not natural. It's the only real prospect in this eastern part of the county for walks that'll make you feel genuinely exercised.

WOKINGHAM SU7865
California Country Park (B3016 S of Wokingham, turning R at Wick Hill opposite B3430) These woods and open spaces are very useful for young children to let off steam in.
Holme Grange Craft Village (Heathlands Rd, just SE) Craft centre with everything from candles and pottery to rugs and traditional sweets; there's also an art gallery. Children like the pygmy goats and chipmunks, and there's an aviary. Snacks, shops, disabled access; cl 25 Dec-1 Jan; (0118) 977 6753; free. Heathlands Rd has a good farm shop with pick-your-own; the nearby Crooked Billet (Honey Hill) is a friendly place for lunch.
Other attractive villages, all with decent pubs and pleasant local walks, include Aldworth SU5579, Aston SU7884, Bagnor SU4569 (with a well regarded theatre in a lovely old watermill), Bray SU9079, Chaddleworth SU4177, Datchet SU9876, Holyport SU8977, Hurley SU8283, Wargrave SU7878, Winterbourne SU4572 and Yattendon SU5574.

Where to eat

BOXFORD SU4271 **Bell** *Lambourn Rd (01488) 608721* Civilised and neatly kept mock-Tudor village inn with long snug bar, a nice mix of racing pictures, smaller old advertisements and interesting bric-a-brac, a rather smart restaurant, thoughtful modern cooking, well kept real ales and great wines; bdrms; cl 26 Dec. £25|£8
BRAY SU9079 **Fat Duck** *1 High St (01628) 580333* Really innovative food cooked with immense care and based on traditional french cooking (some perfectly cooked more straightforward dishes as well) in this black and white former pub; a relaxed if slightly sophisticated feel, knowledgeable helpful staff, and a well chosen wine list; cl Sun pm, Mon, 2 wks Christmas; disabled access. £70/3-course lunch £29.75
BRAY SU9178 **Riverside Brasserie** *Bray Marina (01628) 780553* Unassuming

café-like building idyllically set on the banks of the Thames with simple furnishings, seats outside on the decked terrace, delicious, inventive cooking, reasonably priced wines, and cheerful service; cl Sun pm, Mon, Christmas/New Year. £35

BRAY SU9079 **Waterside Inn** *Ferry Rd (01628) 620691* In a lovely setting by the Thames, this enormously - and justifiably - popular restaurant is a very special place, and for many, the perfect dining experience; impeccable, classic french cooking beautifully presented inc superb puddings, wonderful petits fours, cosseting and helpful service, and a fine french wine list; a lovely place to stay, too; cl Mon, Tues (but open Tues evening during Jun, July, Aug); children over 12; disabled access. £39.50

ETON SU9677 **Gilbey's Bar and Restaurant** *82 High St (01753) 854921* Bustling wine bar with an airy and relaxed bar overlooking the High St, a restaurant and conservatory with bookable tables and friendly helpful staff, an elegant private dining room, imaginative modern food, and a super wine list; cl 4 days over Christmas; disabled access. Sister restaurants in Old Amersham and in Ealing, West London. £30/2-course set menu £10.95

MARSH BENHAM SU4267 **Red House** *(01635) 582017* Attractively set smart thatched dining pub with comfortable bar, no smoking dining room, and front orangery restaurant, good carefully cooked food, well kept ales, decent wine list, lots of malt whiskies, and quite a few brandies and ports; seats on terrace and long lawns that slope down to water meadows and River Kennet; cl pm Sun and Mon, 25-26 Dec, 31 Dec, 1 Jan; children must be well behaved and over 6 in restaurant; disabled access. £42|£9

SHINFIELD SU7268 **Ortolan** *Church Lane (0118) 988 3783* Recently completely refurbished, this ivy-clad former vicarage has a clubby lounge bar with suede and leather armchairs, a pale yellow conservatory, a restful dining room of beige and brown, especially good creative cooking, a wide-ranging wine list, and knowledgeable, friendly staff; cl Sun pm, 27-30 Dec, bank hol Mon; partial disabled access; the set meals, £27, are very good value. £60

WEST ILSLEY SU4782 **Harrow** *(01635) 281260* Popular white-tiled village inn overlooking duck pond and green, with enjoyable home-made bar food, no smoking dining area, real ales, a relaxed atmosphere, and big garden; no food winter Sun pm, Mon; children must be well behaved; disabled access. £35|£6

WINTERBOURNE SU4572 **Winterbourne Arms** *(01635) 248200* Well run and friendly country pub with interestingly decorated bars, a collection of old irons around the fireplace, early prints and old photographs of the village, and a log fire; little no smoking restaurant area with original bakers' ovens; good lunchtime snacks plus interesting, more substantial meals, well kept real ales, a decent wine list, and prompt, friendly service; peaceful view over the rolling fields, bright flowering tubs and hanging baskets, and picnic-sets in the garden. £25|£6.25

Special thanks to Paul Kennedy, B and K Hypher

We welcome reports from readers

This *Guide* depends on readers' reports. Do help us if you can - in return, we offer a discount on the next edition to people who've helped us with reports for it. Tell us what you think about places already in it, and anything extra you think we should say about them. And send us your ideas for inclusion in the next edition: places to visit, eat at or stay in, attractive drives or walks, maybe even unusual shops you know of. Use the card in the middle, the report forms at the end, or just write - no stamp needed: *The Good Britain Guide*, FREEPOST TN1569, Wadhurst, E Sussex TN5 7BR. Or log on to www.goodguides.co.uk

BUCKINGHAMSHIRE

Lovely Chilterns scenery, grand houses and gardens, plenty of enjoyable family outings, and some unusual museums

With endless scenic walking possibilities, the Chiltern Hills give the south of the county a special charm: quiet valleys, lovely tucked-away villages with pretty brick-and-flint houses. This scenery is at its best in spring and autumn through to November, when the beechwoods are at their most beautiful. Some of the most picturesque stretches of the Thames are in this area - the finest reaches of all are best seen from a boat. Coombe Hill, the highest point, is an excellent spot for kite-flying.

Buckinghamshire boasts a glittering array of stately homes, with two sumptuous Rothschild mansions, Waddesdon Manor and Ascott at Wing, and the splendidly lavish Claydon House at Middle Claydon. For a contrast head to 15th-c Chenies Manor House, or Benjamin Disraeli's Hughenden Manor. The gardens at Stowe and Cliveden are outstanding, and West Wycombe Park is good strolling ground - the Hell Fire Caves here are fun.

With intriguing displays on the role of its codebreakers in World War II, Bletchley Park is our Family Attraction award winner this year. The reconstructed buildings of the Chiltern Open-Air Museum at Chalfont St Giles are another highlight, and younger children like the rides at Gulliver's Land in Milton Keynes. Odds Farm Park at Wooburn Common and the Bucks Goat Centre at Stoke Mandeville will appeal to animal-lovers; Roald Dahl fans enjoy the displays in Aylesbury.

Where to stay

AYLESBURY SP7812 **Hartwell House** *Oxford Rd, Aylesbury, Buckinghamshire HP17 8NL (01296) 744444* **£275***, plus special breaks; 46 rms, some large and well equipped, others with four-posters and fine panelling, inc 10 secluded suites in restored 18th-c stables with private garden and statues. Elegant Grade I listed building with Jacobean and Georgian façades, wonderful decorative plasterwork and panelling, fine paintings and antiques, a marvellous Gothic central staircase, splendid morning room, and library, exceptional service, fine wines, and excellent food; 90 acres of parkland with ruined church, lake and statues, and spa with indoor swimming pool, saunas, gym and beauty rooms, and informal restaurant; tennis, croquet and fishing; children over 8; good disabled access; dogs in Hartwell Court

HAMBLEDEN SU7886 **Stag & Huntsman** *Hambleden, Henley-on-Thames, Oxfordshire RG9 6RP (01491) 571227* **£68**; 3 attractive rms. Peaceful brick-and-flint pub opposite church in very pretty village surrounded by Chilterns beechwoods; compact half-panelled lounge, large fireplace, attractively simple public bar and cosy snug, good food, well kept real ales, and spacious pretty garden (summer barbecues); cl 24-26, 31 Dec, 1 Jan; no children

KINGSEY SP7406 **Foxhill** *Risborough Rd, Kingsey, Aylesbury, Buckinghamshire HP17 8LZ (01844) 291650* **£54**; 3 beamed rms, 2 with showers. Neatly kept white house with heated swimming pool and wendy house in mature and pretty back garden, a pond in front, carefully furnished rooms, enjoyable breakfasts in breakfast/sitting room (nearby places for evening meals), and charming, helpful owners; cl Dec-Feb; children over 5

Buckinghamshire

NORTHANTS

BEDFORDSHIRE

HERTFORDSHIRE

OXFORDSHIRE

THE CHILTERNS

CHESS VALLEY

BERKSHIRE

Lavendon
Ravenstone　Olney
Weston Underwood　Emberton
Hanslope
Moulsoe
14
Stowe　Calverton　Milton Keynes
Buckingham　Beachampton　Woburn Sands
Westbury　Thornborough Bridge
Little Horwood　Bletchley
Chetwode　Stoke Hammond
Preston Bissett
Winslow　Stewkley　Soulbury
Middle Claydon　Wing
Quainton
Weedon　Mentmore
Boarstall　Waddesdon　Marsworth
Brill　Ivinghoe
Lower Winchendon　Pitstone
Shabbington Wood　Cuddington　Stoke Mandeville
Easington　Dinton　Bishopstone
Worminghall　Haddenham　Terrick
Long Crendon　Kingsey　Coombe Hill
Whiteleaf Cross　Little Hampden
Bledlow　Great Hampden　Great Missenden
Lacey Green　Hyde Heath
Speen　Little Missenden
West Wycombe　Bradenham　Hodgemoor Woods　Amersham
Ibstone　Hughenden　Chalfont St Giles
High Wycombe　Penn　Jordans
Forty Green　Beaconsfield
Turville　Northend　Fingest
Skirmett　Wooburn Common　Hedgerley
Fawley　Marlow　Church Wood　Fulmer　Denham
Hambleden　Bovingdon Green　Burnham Beeches
Taplow　Stoke Poges
Dorney

0 Miles　5
0 Kilomètres　8

MARLOW SU8586 **Compleat Angler** *Bisham Rd, Marlow, Buckinghamshire SL7 1RG (01628) 484444* **£203**w, plus special breaks; 64 pretty, individually furnished rms overlooking garden or river. Famous Thames-side hotel with comfortable panelled lounge, balconied bar, spacious beamed restaurant, imaginative food, and prompt service; tennis, croquet, coarse fishing, and boating; disabled access

TAPLOW SU9185 **Cliveden** *Taplow, Maidenhead, Berkshire SL6 0JF (01628) 668561* **£255** (plus £7 each paid to National Trust), plus special breaks; 39 luxurious, individual rms with maid unpacking service and a butler's tray. Superb

Grade I listed stately home with gracious, comfortable public rooms, fine paintings, tapestries and armour, and a surprisingly unstuffy atmosphere; lovely views over the magnificent NT Thames-side parkland and formal gardens (open to the public); imaginative food in the two no smoking restaurants with lighter meals in the conservatory, friendly breakfasts around a huge table, and impeccable staff; pavilion with swimming pool, gym, etc.; tennis, squash, croquet, and boats for river trips; they are kind to children; dogs welcome away from eating areas ☺

WESTBURY SP6235 **Mill Farmhouse** *Westbury, Brackley, Northamptonshire NN13 5JS (01280) 704843* **£50**; 3 pretty rms. Carefully restored miller's house (the mill itself is used as workshops) on large farm, and a colourful big garden with swimming pool; plenty of original features and open fire in comfortable sitting/dining room, oak furniture and plenty of hunting prints; charming owners and good light suppers if ordered; two self-contained flats, too; disabled access; dogs welcome in bedrooms

WINSLOW SP7627 **Bell** *Market Sq, Winslow, Buckingham, Buckinghamshire MK18 3AB (01296) 714091* **£64**; 43 rms. Carefully furnished and elegant black and white timbered inn with beams and open fires, plush hotel bar, all-day coffee lounge, enjoyable bar food, and good lunchtime and evening carvery in restaurant; disabled access; dogs welcome in bedrooms

WOOBURN COMMON SU9087 **Chequers** *Kiln Lane, Wooburn Green, High Wycombe, Buckinghamshire HP10 0JQ (01628) 529575* **£77.50**w, plus special breaks; 17 stripped pine rms in mock-Tudor wing. Popular inn with unchanging traditional atmosphere in cosy low-beamed bar, standing timbers and alcoves, log fires and comfortable sofas, well kept real ales, good daily-changing food in busy dining room, nice breakfasts, and spacious garden

To see and do

Buckinghamshire Family Attraction of the Year

BLETCHLEY SP8633 **Bletchley Park** 🏛 (turn off B4034 at Eight Bells pub, then right into Wilton Ave) Anyone with even a passing interest in wartime history can get a lot out of a visit to this Victorian mansion and its grounds. During World War II, 12,000 men and women worked here cracking german codes, so successfully that it's reckoned they shortened the war by two years. Their top-secret activities remained largely unknown until Robert Harris made them the focus of his best-selling novel *Enigma*. It's a fascinating story, told here in meticulous and intriguing detail: too technical perhaps for younger children, but with enough extra displays and exhibits for most older ones to find something that grabs their attention. Around the grounds are carefully preserved wartime huts and vehicles, collections of wartime fire engines, uniforms and vintage toys, and a fascinating exhibition tracing the development of computers, from seemingly ancient, lumbering machines to more familiar contemporary models. What some of the displays lack in sophistication they more than make up for in enthusiasm; it's a genuine, untouristy place, staffed by dedicated volunteers. For families it's perhaps best to visit at weekends, when you can wander the grounds and house freely, and either join one of the excellent guided tours, or try one of the well thought out children's trails, with recorded commentaries. During the week you'll need to stick with the tour (starting at 2pm), which some children may find a little long. Attractive landscaped grounds, and the house itself is worth a look. Meals, snacks, shop, disabled access; open all day wknds and bank hols Feb-Nov, wkdys pm only; (01908) 640404; £8 adults July/Aug, less at other times, children under 12 are free (12-16s get £1 off adult price). They may have summer discounts on their website, www.bletchleypark.org.uk.

AMERSHAM SU9597

The older part, especially the High St, retains a number of well preserved buildings from several periods inc the interesting Crown, fronted by a Georgian façade, but containing some 16th-c wall paintings and original beams inside; it has good value bar food, as does the slightly later Saracens Head.

AYLESBURY SP8113

Buckinghamshire County Museum and Roald Dahl Children's Gallery (Church St) Roald Dahl lived in Buckinghamshire for most of his life, and as well as having local history displays, this museum celebrates the connection with a gallery of hands-on displays that use Dahl's novels and characters to teach children about insects, light and any number of other topics; visitors can crawl through the tunnel of Fantastic Mr Fox, discover Willy Wonka's inventions, and even go inside the Giant Peach to find out what things look like under the microscope. Also a good collection of regional art and a walled garden. Snacks, shop, good disabled access; cl am Sun and 25-26 Dec (Dahl gallery cl until 3pm wkdys in term-time); (01296) 331441; museum free, £3.50 Dahl Gallery. The Kings Head is an almost unique Tudor inn around a courtyard, with a small crafts shop in the corner.

BEACONSFIELD SU9391

Bekonscot Model Village 🏰 (Warwick Rd) This miniature portrayal of rural Britain in the 1930s includes scaled-down churches, castles, zoo and even a racecourse, as well as a gauge-1 model railway; train ride and play area. Snacks, shop, disabled access; cl Nov to mid-Feb; (01494) 672919; £4.80. The Crown up at Penn (great views, interesting church) is a good family pub, with enjoyable food all day.

BLETCHLEY SP8633

Bletchley Park *See separate family panel on p.22.*
The Crooked Billet at Newton Longville (Westbrook End) has good food and wines.

BOARSTALL SP6214

Boarstall Duck Decoy Displays and working demonstrations of one of only four remaining 17th-c working duck decoys. Also woodland walks and nature trail. Open wknds and bank hols plus 4-7pm Weds, Apr-Aug bank hol; (01844) 237488; £2.10; NT. Brill is the nearest useful place for lunch.

BRADENHAM SU8396

This pretty village is surrounded by ancient woodland, with pleasant strolling possibilities.

BRILL SP6514

The **windmill** (usually open pm summer Suns) is in a magnificent position right on the edge of the Chilterns, with distant views across Oxfordshire; there's been a mill on this site for over 700 years. In the distinctive and quietly attractive village the Pheasant (with a view of the windmill) is useful for lunch. There's a decent walk up nearby Muswell Hill, or along the ridge and down to Boarstall.

BUCKINGHAM SP6933

Quite a lot of attractive early 18th-c brick buildings, and much of the nostalgic charm of a once important town that has been eclipsed by rivals (in this case Aylesbury and Milton Keynes). The White Hart (Market Sq) is handy for a snack or coffee.

Old Gaol Museum (Market Hill) Housed in an extraordinary early Gothic Revival gaol, this small local history museum has a good audio-visual show in an intact original cell and other exhibits in a glazed exercise courtyard; the Tourist Information Centre is in here too. Shop, partly disabled access; cl Sun, and a few days at Christmas; (01280) 823020; £1.50.

BURNHAM BEECHES SU9485

A supreme example of a Chilterns beechwood, splendid in spring and autumn colours, and with perhaps a glimpse of deer; maps are posted throughout the forest, but it is quite easy to lose one's bearings. The main starting-point is at East Burnham Common car park, opposite the W end of Beeches Rd at Farnham Common. There are several decent pubs dotted around the forest.

CHALFONT ST GILES TQ0193

Chiltern Open-Air Museum (Newland Park, Gorelands Lane) 30 or so buildings have been painstakingly dismantled and rebuilt here piece by piece to avoid demolition: you can look round structures as diverse as an Iron

Age house (its design based on excavations in the area), a Victorian farmyard complete with animals, intriguing oddities like the 18th-c well head and Edwardian public convenience, and a 1940s prefab, with useful displays on their original use. It's best in fine weather when the 45 acres of woods and parkland are a delight to explore, and there's a decent children's playground (and space for picnics); dogs are welcome on a lead. You can pick up themed guidesheets; lots of hands-on activities and demonstrations for children in the school hols. Snacks, picnic area, mostly disabled access; open Apr-Oct; (01494) 872163; *£6. Nearby, the smart Ivy House (London Rd) has good food.

Milton's Cottage 🅱 (Deanway) The writer brought his family to this timber-framed 16th-c cottage to escape the Plague in 1665, and while here completed *Paradise Lost* and began *Paradise Regained*. Displays of first editions, other rare books and memorabilia, and a charming cottage garden full of plants and flowers mentioned by Milton in his poetry. Shop, disabled access to ground floor; cl 1-2pm, all day Mon (exc bank hols), and Nov-Feb; (01494) 872313; £3. The nearby White Hart (Three Households) has decent food.

CHENIES TQ0198
Chenies Manor House Rewarding 15th-c house with Tudor rooms, tapestries, priest's hole and 16th-c cellars; the gardens include a physic garden, herbs and mazes. Home-made teas, shop (good for dried flowers and herbs), disabled access to gardens and tearoom only; open pms Weds, Thurs and bank hol Mons beginning Apr-Oct; (01494) 762888; £5.20 house and garden, £3 garden only. The neighbouring **church** has the rich family monuments of the Bedfords (viewed through a glass panel), 15th-c brasses and a Norman font. The Red Lion is good for lunch.

CHESS VALLEY TQ0298
Shared between Bucks and Herts, this is miniature and unspoilt, and handily reached from Chalfont & Latimer station on the Metropolitan Underground line; Chenies and Latimer

in Bucks, and Sarratt just over the Herts border, are the villages to head for.

CHETWODE SP6430
Chetwode church A handsome church, notable for its fine Early English windows.

CHILTERNS SU7295
The well wooded Chiltern Hills offer plenty of easy-going walks, with a good scattering of rural pubs and pretty villages, though sometimes you have to choose your path carefully to avoid the numerous suburban developments. Even so, it's easy to escape into idyllic landscapes which some rate above all others for wknd walks, and the soaring red kites, reintroduced here by the late Sir Paul Getty, add a touch of exotic wildness. The escarpment where the hills drop sharply down to the plain gives some very distant views, for instance from above Bledlow. The signposted Ridgeway takes in the most dramatic features.

CHURCH WOOD SU9786
On the edge of the immaculate village of Hedgerley (where the friendly old White Horse has decent food), this is a nature reserve managed by the RSPB, with over 80 species of birds in 34 acres.

COOMBE HILL SU8506
The highest point in the Chilterns, with its Boer War Memorial (an excellent place for views - and for kite-flying). Wendover Woods with some well marked nature trails are adjacent. The town of Wendover (the Red Lion Hotel here is walker-friendly) gives nearby access, or you can follow paths from Ellesborough and sneak views of Chequers, the Prime Minister's country retreat (emphatically private); an alternative path in is from Dunsmore.

DORNEY SU9279
Dorney Court 🅱 Engaging partly 15th-c timber-framed manor house with pleasant gardens and some very fine furniture, as well as the Elizabethan Palmer Needlework tapestry. The same family have lived here for over 450 years, and in the 16th c they grew the first pineapple raised in England. Plant centre, with plants from Blooms of Bressingham, snacks, shop, some disabled access (ground floor only); open pm bank hols and preceding Suns

in May, and daily pm in Aug exc Sat; (01628) 604638; £5.50. The village itself, the most southerly in the county, is known for its honey - its name means 'island of bumble bees'. The Palmer Arms is handy for lunch.

FAWLEY SU7684

Fawley Court Not the typical english stately home it appears to be; though it does boast some fine Wyatt interiors and an elaborate ceiling by Grinling Gibbons, it's owned by a polish religious order, and has a surprising museum dedicated to their homeland, particularly strong on polish military history. The grounds (landscaped by Capability Brown) run down to the river, and you can stay here, B&B or half and full board. Snacks, limited disabled access; open pm Weds, Thurs and Sun May-Oct (not Whitsun week or Easter); (01491) 574917; £4. The Walnut Tree has enjoyable food.

FINGEST SU7791

Fingest church This brick-and-flint church is famous for its huge Norman tower with a twin saddleback roof. The Chequers opposite in this picture-book village is nice for lunch, and, below the landmark windmill to the N, this is a particularly delectable valley - try the road round through Turville.

FORTY GREEN SU9291

Royal Standard of England The pub stands out as a quite remarkable old building, full of interesting furniture - crowded at wknds, it's well worth a quiet prowl during the week.

HADDENHAM SP7408

St Tiggywinkles Visitor Centre (Aston Rd) The expanding visitor centre at this wildlife hospital has a hedgehog museum, and a video system lets you watch the animals being treated without disturbing them. The gardens have enclosures for the animals that they can't release back into the wild, inc hedgehogs, ducks, badgers and foxes. Snacks, shop, disabled access; usually only cl wknds end Sept-Easter, and 25-26 Dec; (01844) 292292; £3.80. The Green Dragon (Church End; no under-7s) is a good dining pub.

HAMBLEDEN SU7886

Thames walk The footbridge over the weir below the charming Chilterns village of Hambleden is attractive, and is

the best starting-point on the Buckinghamshire bank for riverside walks. The Stag & Huntsman is a very pleasant food stop.

HANSLOPE SP8046

Hanslope church Attractive in its own right, but the most striking feature is its unusually tall spire. The White Hart over at Stoke Goldington is good value for lunch, with a footpath network on its doorstep.

HIGH WYCOMBE SU8693

Wycombe Museum (Castle Hill House, Priory Avenue) 18th-c house telling the history of the town's furniture industry, in pretty landscaped gardens, with local history displays and hands-on exhibits; changing exhibitions and special events. Snacks, shop; disabled access to ground floor; cl Sun am and all day bank hols; (01494) 421895; free.

HODGEMOOR WOODS SU9693 (W of Chalfont St Giles) This ancient woodland has three colour-coded nature trails, giving enjoyable walks of varying lengths.

HUGHENDEN SU8695

Hughenden Manor The home of Benjamin Disraeli until his death in 1881, this imposing house still has many of the Victorian Prime Minister's books and other possessions, as well as related memorabilia, portraits of friends, and formal gardens; he's buried in the grounds. Meals, snacks, shop, some disabled access; open pm Weds-Sun and bank hols Apr-Oct, wknds only in March; surrounding woodlands open all year; special events and performances throughout the summer (01494) 755565; £4.50, garden only £1.60, NT. The Red Lion at Great Kingshill does good fish lunches.

IVINGHOE SP9416

Attractive old village giving its name to the Beacon hill high above. The Rose & Crown does fresh bar lunches. This enclave is a fragment of Buckinghamshire almost encircled by Hertfordshire.

Ford End Watermill (Station Rd) 18th-c and well restored, the only remaining working watermill with original machinery in the county. Shop, limited disabled access; open pm Easter Mon, then first and second Suns and bank hols May-Sept, with milling (water level permitting) 3-5pm on bank hols and second Sun in May and July; (01582) 600391; £1.20.

Ivinghoe Beacon This is a protruding finger of the Chilterns, and the finish of the long-distance Ridgeway Path which begins in Wiltshire. The slopes, too steep for ploughing, comprise woodland, scrub and unspoilt downland, with an Iron Age earthwork on top. From the beacon itself you look down over eight counties; the best views are northwards.

JORDANS SU9791
Interesting as a quiet tree-filled village built mainly this century in honour of the first 17th-c Quaker meeting place here - a simple, evocative building. The nearby Mayflower Barn is built with timbers from the famous ship.

LACEY GREEN SP8100
Lacey Green Smockmill (off A4010) The oldest surviving smockmill in the country, and indeed the third-oldest windmill of any type, built around 1650. It's been well restored. Open pm Sun and bank hol Mons May-Sept; (01844) 343560; *£1. The Pink & Lily does good food - and has kept its little tap room much as Rupert Brooke enjoyed it.

LITTLE MISSENDEN SU9298
Pretty village with charming old timbered and tiled houses; the **church** has wall paintings from the 12th c and some pre-Norman traces. You can get good sandwiches at the attractive old Crown.

LONG CRENDON SP6909
The cottages in the High St are very pretty, some little changed since the village was a rich wool centre in the 15th c. The Angel (Bicester Rd) is a good restaurant, and the Churchill Arms has decent pub food.
Courthouse A particularly lovely timber-framed building, early 15th-c; probably built as a wool store. Open wknds and pm Weds (upper floor only), end Mar-Sept; (01494) 528051; £1; NT. Snacks in the nearby church house.

LOWER WINCHENDON SP7312
This secluded old place has carefully restored houses and a charming, simple church - the walk over the hill to Upper Winchendon gives interesting views. The Crown in Cuddington has good interesting food.

MARLOW SU8586
Thames boating Marlow Reach is lively and attractive, and a good centre for trips in either direction. Salters (01865) 243421 operate 40-min cruises May-Sept (and occasional fine days in Apr). Snacks, some disabled access (boats can take wheelchairs on deck but no facilities); £4.50, under-5s free. The Compleat Angler right on the river is a fine place for lunch; on a humbler plane the Two Brewers back over the bridge and the Hare & Hounds out towards Henley are good bets.

MARSWORTH SP9114
Canalside walk Marsworth gives good towpath access to an imposing **flight of locks**. The cheery Red Lion has good value food.

MIDDLE CLAYDON SP7125
Claydon House The wonderfully over-the-top rococo décor is the prime attraction of this mainly 18th-c house - quite a surprise given the classical simplicity of the exterior. Highlights are the carvings by Luke Lightfoot and the fantastic walls, ceilings and overmantels, though there are also portraits by Lely and Van Dyck. This year's exhibition marks the 150th anniversary of the Crimean War; Florence Nightingale was a frequent guest. The original owner's tastes were considerably richer than his pockets, and his ambitious plans for the house eventually bankrupted him, though his family still live here. Meals, snacks, secondhand bookshop, disabled access to ground floor; open pm Sat-Weds 27 Mar-Oct; (01296) 730349; £4.50; NT. The Old Thatched Inn over at Adstock has enjoyable food.

MILTON KEYNES SP8742
Britain's largest New Town is perhaps also the most successful example of the idea, with roads well laid out to keep traffic moving easily and well away from pedestrians, and plenty of greenery. Locals are proud of the remarkable number of public sculptures dotted around, from the endearing Wounded Elephant to the famous concrete cows in a field on the N side of the H3 road (Monks Way, or A422), nr the A5 junction. There's a swish shopping centre at Midsummer Boulevard, and in Avebury Boulevard a huge leisure and

16-screen cinema complex contains one of Europe's largest real-snow ski slopes; (01908) 230260. Tucked around the city are various villagey corners, and the Old Beams (Osier Lane, Shenley Lodge) and canalside Black Horse at Great Linford are both pleasant retreats for lunch.

City Discovery Centre (Bradwell Abbey) Tells you all you could need to know about the New Town development (lots of slides, maps and old photographs), in a 16th-c farmhouse in the 17-acre grounds of a former abbey. Also 14th-c barn and chapel, medieval fishponds, herb gardens and nature trail. Meals, snacks, shop, disabled access; open Mon-Fri and some Sun pms, but best to phone in advance to avoid large school groups; (01908) 227229; free.

Gulliver's Land (Newlands, M1 junction 14) Most under-12s will happily spend a day at this friendly family-run place. Like its sister parks at Matlock Bath and Warrington, it's loosely based on Jonathan Swift's tale of the shipwrecked surgeon taken prisoner by the pint-sized population of Lilliput. Most of the 30 or so rides and attractions are scaled-down versions of what you'd expect, but there are some unusual ones: you can travel on musical instruments and flying boots, or on a water ride that whisks you through waterfalls and whirlpools; good play area for the under-5s. Most rides are under cover, and they have special events. Restaurants, cafés, shops, disabled access; open wknds Easter-Jun and Sept-Oct and daily Jun-Aug; best to ring outside peak summer times as they may also be open other days; (01908) 609001; £9.95 adults and children, includes unlimited goes on everything all day. Free for children under 90cm (they may not be able to go on some rides).

Milton Keynes Gallery (900 Midsummer Blvd, Margaret Powell Sq) Contemporary art gallery with changing exhibitions, in a sleek modern building. Shop, disabled access; cl Mon and bank hols, and when they change their exhibitions; phone (01908) 676900 to check; free.

Milton Keynes Museum (McConnell Drive, H2 Millers Way) Includes Victorian and Edwardian room settings, a school-room, a steam tram, print shop and a transport hall; they have a Victorian Christmas festival (usually end of Nov). Snacks, shop, disabled access; usually open Weds-Sun and bank hols Easter-Oct, and wknds Nov-Easter but best to check; (01908) 316222; £3.50.

Willen Lakeside Park (Brickhill St) Two lakes - one with water sports, hotel and restaurant, and the other for bird-watching; also a japanese peace pagoda built by buddhist monks, turf maze, nature trail, and you can hire bikes.

OLNEY SP8951
Pleasant stone-built small town with a nice riverside stroll to the Robin Hood at Clifton Reynes, and a Thurs market. The Bull is HQ for the town's famous Shrove Tuesday pancake race, first run in 1445; the civilised old Swan (no under-10s) does good lunches.

Cowper and Newton Museum 🖼 (Market Pl) Enthusiastically run, in the former home of hymn-writer William Cowper. Several of his personal possessions, manuscripts and poems are on display, along with some belonging to his friend John Newton, curate of Olney and composer of 'Amazing Grace'. There's a notable textiles exhibition, a restored period summerhouse in the little garden, and local history displays. Shop, limited disabled access to building; cl 1-2pm, all day Sun (exc pms Jun-Aug) and Mon (exc bank hols), Good Fri and 23 Dec-Feb; (01234) 711516; £3.

PITSTONE SP9415
As well as a decent little **agricultural museum** (shop, disabled access; open 2nd Sun of month and bank hols May-Sept; (01582) 605464; £3) and an interesting old **church**, this small village has the oldest **windmill** in the country, built in 1627; open pm Sun and bank hols Jun-Aug; £1; NT. You can hire canal boats for a day from the Wharf (over the B489; phone (01296) 661920), and there are pleasant canal walks from there to the Red Lion or White Lion at Marsworth.

Attractive old village giving its name to the beacon hill high above. The Rose & Crown does fresh bar lunches. This

enclave is a fragment of
Buckinghamshire almost encircled by
Hertfordshire.

QUAINTON SP7419

Bucks Railway Centre (Quainton Rd
Station) One of the largest collections
of engines and rolling stock we know of,
with examples from all over the world
attractively displayed in a restored
country station; also vintage steam-
train rides, workshops, miniature
railway and small museum. Regular half-
day steam driving courses (not cheap at
£175, but people come away converted
for life). Meals, snacks, picnic area, shop,
disabled access; cl Mon (exc bank hols)
and Tues, all Nov-Mar; (01296) 655720;
£6 (£7 bank hols). Discount voucher
not valid for Thomas the Tank Engine
Events. Waddesdon is the closest good
place for lunch.

Quainton Hill This prominent
viewpoint is one of the main features on
the 30-mile North Bucks Way, a long-
distance footpath from Chequers Knap
above Great Kimble to Wolverton in
Milton Keynes; the Way also runs past
Waddesdon.

Quainton Tower Mill Particularly tall
19th-c mill on the edge of the village
green; you can watch the continuing
restoration work. Shop; open Sun
10am-12.30pm; (01296) 655348; £1.

SHABBINGTON WOOD SP6210
(nr Oakley) Designated a Site of Special
Scientific Interest because of its rich
butterfly habitats; a special butterfly
trail helps you to spot some of the
40-odd species here. The thatched
Clifden Arms over in the attractive
village of Worminghall has decent food
and pretty gardens.

STEWKLEY SP8525
The **church** in this unusually long
village has good examples of late
Norman work; the Carpenters Arms is
a useful lunch stop.

STOKE MANDEVILLE SP8309
Bucks Goat Centre (Layby Farm, just
off A4010) Goats galore as well as a pig,
poultry, llamas, wallabies, donkeys, pets
and a reptile and bird house; you can
feed the animals (they sell bags of cut-up
vegetables in the shop). Many animals
are under cover, so good for a rainy
day. Meals, snacks, farm shop, disabled
access; open daily; (01296) 612983;

£3.50. The rather swish Bernard Arms
at Great Kimble (photographs of recent
prime ministerial visits) has good food.

Oak Farm Rare Breeds Park (off
A41, E edge of Aylesbury) There's
more to see at this friendly little
working farm than you might think; you
can get close to some of the animals
(they sell bags of food), and there are
walks and trails, play and picnic areas,
and duck ponds. Snacks, shop, mostly
disabled access; open daily (weather
permitting) Easter-Oct; (01296)
415709; £3. The Bell at Bierton has
decent food.

STOKE POGES SU9783
Stoke Poges church The graveyard
inspired Thomas Gray's elegy (he's
buried here); the church itself has
17th-c stained heraldic glass in the
16th-c chapel. The Red Lion at Stoke
Green is a reliable food pub.

STOWE SP6737
Stowe Landscape Gardens Stunning
gardens stretching over 350 acres, first
laid out between 1713 and 1725.
Capability Brown was head gardener
for ten years, and the monuments and
temples that adorn the grounds are by
the likes of James Gibb, Sir John
Vanbrugh and William Kent. There's a
continuing programme of restoration
and in recent years they've planted
thousands of new trees and shrubs; a
new exhibition with audio-visual display
covers the evolution of the gardens.
Several suitably grand events
throughout the year, but at any time
this is a spectacular place to visit, the
scale of its artistry quite staggering.
Meals, snacks, shop, disabled access
(inc electric-powered cars at no extra
charge); open Weds-Sun Mar-22 Dec;
(01280) 822850; £5; NT. The house itself
(a public school since 1923) is open
during the Easter and summer hols, pm
Weds-Sun; (01280) 818000; £3 (less if
restoration work underway). You may
feel it's outclassed by its surroundings,
though it is very elegant from the outside.
The Wheatsheaf at Maids Moreton does
good lunches, and the Queens Head at
Chackmore is even handier.

TAPLOW SU9185
Cliveden ▥ Nearly 400 acres of
lovely formal gardens, woodland and
parkland overlooking the Thames. The

magnificent house used to belong to the Astors and is now a luxury hotel (and extremely enjoyable as such), although non-resident visitors can see some of the rooms with their family portraits and elegant furnishings and décor. Meals, snacks, shop, disabled access; gardens open daily mid-Mar-Dec, house open only Thurs and Sun Apr-Oct, 3-5.30pm; (01628) 605069; £6, house £1 extra; NT. The village too is attractive.

TERRICK SP8408

Chiltern Brewery Small and friendly with helpful staff, this traditional brewery has a little museum, and guided tours at noon every Sat (phone to book (01296) 613647; £3.50). Shop, disabled access; cl Sun, 25-26 Dec and 1 Jan; free.

THORNBOROUGH BRIDGE SP7433

(A421) A 4½-mile walk starting and ending here, and well described in a leaflet from Bucks County Council, takes in a mill, the site of a medieval village and the Buckingham Arm Canal. Leaflets from information centres or from the County Hall; (01280) 823020; 25p. The Lone Tree (A421) has decent food.

WADDESDON SP7316

Waddesdon Manor One of the spectacular mansions built for Baron Ferdinand de Rothschild at the end of the 19th c, and designed as a showcase for his french art collection rather than a home. Plenty of rooms to see, each as lavish as the last, and filled with a dazzling array of furnishings, porcelain, portraits and other objects, and there's an unrivalled display of Sèvres china; the Manor made the news in summer 2003, when 100 rare miniature gold boxes were stolen by burglars. The fabled wine cellars have huge vintage bottles, and a collection of labels designed or painted by some of the century's greatest artists. Quite splendid late Victorian formal gardens surround the house, and they still use the rococo-style aviary. An extremely satisfying place to visit, but it does get busy; they operate a timed ticket system for the house (can be bought in advance, but £3 booking charge), and recommend you get there by 2.30pm. Good meals, snacks, shops, disabled access; house open Weds-Sun and bank hol Mon 31

Mar-Oct, grounds Weds-Sun and bank hol Mon 3 Mar-Oct; special Christmas dates Nov-23 Dec, phone for details; (01296) 653226, £11 house and grounds, £4 grounds only; NT.

WEEDON SP8018

This is a lovely little village, well worth walking around for the variety of its 17th- and 18th-c houses. The White Swan in nearby Whitchurch has decent food.

WEST WYCOMBE SU8394

The whole village was bought by the NT in 1929 when it was threatened with road-widening. It's still beleaguered by traffic, and you risk getting run over as you step back to admire the architecture along the village street - all the sites we mention are just off street. The busy George & Dragon is popular for lunch. A visit to the caves and village here can be easily combined with a walk into the beechwoods just N; the pretty village of Bradenham makes a good objective for longer circular walks.

Hell Fire Caves 🖼 Great fun, these spooky old caves were extended in the 1750s by Sir Francis Dashwood to provide work for the unemployed. Legend has it that the Hell Fire Club he founded met in the tunnels for their drinking, whoring and sorcery. Once through the atmospheric Gothic entrance, the tunnels extend for about a third of a mile underground, and are filled with colourful models and tableaux. Underground café, shop; cl wkdys Nov-Feb (exc school hols); (01494) 533739; *£4.

St Lawrence church On the site of an Iron Age fort, adapted by Dashwood, and crowned with a golden ball so big (it can seat six people) that it too served as a meeting-place for the Hell Fire Club. The view from the top of the tower is impressive.

West Wycombe Park 300 acres of beautifully laid-out parkland surround this splendid 18th-c Palladian house, parts of which are currently being restored. The magnificent rooms have a good collection of tapestries, furniture and paintings, and the italianate painted ceilings are particularly notable. Disabled access to ground floor only, braille guide; house and grounds open pm Sun-Thurs Jun-Aug, grounds also open pm Sun-Thurs Apr-May; (01494) 513569; £5, grounds only £2.60; NT.

WHITELEAF CROSS SP8204
A large ancient hill cross dug out of the chalk on the Chilterns escarpment, above which is a neolithic barrow. The Red Lion below is useful for lunch.

WING SP8922
Ascott Another Rothschild mansion, its black and white timbers and jutting gables quite a contrast to the luxuriant opulence of nearby Waddesdon. Once again it's crammed full of treasures, but it feels more like a home and less like a museum; indeed it's still lived in. Ming and K'ang Hsi porcelain, paintings by Hogarth, Rubens and Gainsborough, dutch art by Hobbema, Cuyp and others, and french and Chippendale furniture. The 260-acre grounds have extensive gardens with rare trees and shrubs. House and grounds open pm Tues-Sun 16 Mar-Aug (exc Fri-Sun May-29 Jul); (01296) 688242; £5.60 (£4 garden only), NT. **All Saints church** has a fine monument to Sir Robert Dormer (died 1552), a 10th-c apse, crypt and nave, and 12th-c font. The Boot over at Soulbury has good food.

WINSLOW SP7627
Keach's Meeting House Fine example of a 17th-c dissenters' chapel; you'll need to get the key from Wilkinson's the estate agent on Market Sq; (01296) 712717. The Bell is useful for lunch.

WOOBURN COMMON SU9189
Odds Farm Park Everything at this well organised place has been carefully designed with children in mind. They can go right up to the cattle, pigs, sheep and poultry, and join in daily activities such as bottle-feeding the lambs, or collecting chickens' eggs. Good outdoor and indoor play areas (one for under-5s), and most pens and enclosures have signs written in a way that children can understand. In winter most bits are under cover, though there are some days when not every activity will take place; regular special events, and usually tractor and trailer rides in summer. Meals, snacks (and picnic area), shop, disabled access; cl mid Dec-beginning Jan; (01628) 520188; £5.50. The Falcon (Old Moor Lane) has decent food and an attractive garden.

Other attractive villages, all with decent pubs, include Beachampton SP7737 (stream along main street), Bishopstone SP8010 (pleasant country walks), Bledlow SP7702 (great views; Norman church with early wall-paintings), Calverton SP7939, Cuddington SP7311, Denham TQ0386, Dinton SP7611, Emberton SP8849, Fulmer SU9985, Great Missenden SP8901, Hedgerley SU9686, Hyde Heath SU9399, Ibstone SU7593, Lavendon SP9153, Little Hampden SP8503, Little Horwood SP7930, Northend SU7392, Penn SU9193, Preston Bissett SP6529, Ravenstone SP8450, Speen SU8399, Stoke Hammond SP8829, Turville SU7690 (perhaps the most lovely valley of all here), Weston Underwood SP8650, Woburn Sands (wooded walks nearby) SP9235 and Worminghall SP6308.

Where to eat

BOVINGDON GREEN SU8386 **Royal Oak** *Frieth Rd (01628) 488611* Well organised and civilised rambling country pub with several attractively decorated areas opening off the central bar; half-panelled walls variously painted in pale blue, green or cream, a mix of church chairs, stripped wooden tables and chunky wall seats, with rugs on the partly wooden, partly flagstoned floors, co-ordinated cushions and curtains, and a very bright, airy feel; a big, square bowl of olives on the bar, smart soaps and toiletries in the lavatories, and carefully laid out newspapers; excellent food from a changing blackboard menu, well kept real ales, and helpful, polite service; appealing garden. £31|**£5.75**

EASINGTON SP6810 **Mole & Chicken** *Easington (01844) 208387* Bustling country dining pub with very attractively furnished beamed bar, winter log fires, candles on tables and a relaxed atmosphere, particularly good imaginative food served by neatly dressed young staff, and a fine range of drinks; bdrms; cl 25 Dec; disabled access. £28|**£8.95**

GREAT HAMPDEN SP8401 **Hampden Arms** *(01494) 488255* Comfortable two-room country pub by cricket green with civilised atmosphere, interesting reasonably priced food, real ales, quietly obliging service, and a tree-sheltered garden; good for nearby walks; partial disabled access. £20.95|**£6.95**

HADDENHAM SP7408 **Green Dragon** *8 Churchway (01844) 291403* Civilised dining pub with imaginative food in its two attractively decorated high-ceilinged rooms, a french brasserie-type atmosphere, well chosen wines, real ales, a winter log fire, and seats out on the big sheltered terrace; cl Sun pm; disabled access. £25.50|**£6.50**

LITTLE HAMPDEN SP8503 **Rising Sun** *(01494) 488393* Secluded upmarket dining pub surrounded by fine walks, with interesting food, a short but decent wine list, real ales, and an attractive terrace; bdrms; cl Sun pm, Mon, Tues pm; disabled access. £25|**£4.95**

MARLOW Vanilla Pod *31 West St (01628) 898101* Bustling small restaurant - once T. S. Eliot's house - with tiny bar and reception area leading to a wood-floored dining room, peach and tangerine walls, boldly coloured paintings, hard-working mainly french staff, modern anglo-french cooking with classical undertones, and a modest little wine list; cl Sun, Mon, bank hols, 2 wks Sept, Christmas/New Year. £38

MENTMORE SP9019 **Stag** *The Green (01296) 668423* Pretty village pub with small civilised lounge bar, fresh flowers and open fire, well kept real ales in simple public bar, and friendly service; nicely presented enjoyable food; seats on pleasant flower-filled terrace and in neat sloping garden. £20|**£6**

MOULSOE SP9141 **Carrington Arms** *Cranfield Rd (01908) 218050* Well refurbished old brick house with comfortable traditional furnishings, meat and fish displayed in refrigerated glass case with friendly staff who guide you through what is on offer (it is then sold by weight and cooked on a sophisticated indoor barbecue), separate bar menu as well, an oyster bar, well kept real ales, and a good range of wines inc champagne by the glass; bdrms; disabled access. £30|**£4.95**

SKIRMETT SU7790 **Frog** *(01491) 638996* Brightly modernised country inn with the atmosphere of a smart rural local, a mix of comfortable furnishings and open fire in neat beamed bar area, good popular interesting food, efficient service, no smoking restaurant, real ales and a fair range of wines, and lovely garden; bdrms; cl Sun pm from Nov-Easter Sun; disabled access. £25.50|**£6.25**

SOULBURY SP8826 **Boot** *High Rd (01525) 270433* Brightly modernised and civilised village pub with a nice mix of smart and individual furnishings in the red-tiled bar, as well as sporting prints and houseplants, and neat blinds on the windows; a well chosen wine list with a dozen by the glass, well kept real ales, friendly, smartly dressed staff, and a couple of cosy rooms for eating; interesting well prepared food with fresh fish (not Sun); all eating areas are no smoking. £30|**£10**

WADDESDON SP7416 **Five Arrows** *High St (01296) 651727* Rather grand small hotel - part of the Rothschild estate - with an informally pubby bar made up of several open-plan rooms, a relaxed but civilised atmosphere, Rothschild family portraits and old estate-worker photographs on the walls, sturdy furnishings on parquet flooring, newspapers and magazines, delicious imaginative food, a no smoking country house-style restaurant, a formidable wine list, well kept real ales, efficient service, and sheltered back garden; good bdrms; cl 25 Dec pm, 26 Dec. £30|**£6.95**

WEST WYCOMBE SU8394 **George & Dragon** *High St (01494) 464414* Striking partly Tudor inn with a cheerful bustling atmosphere in rambling main bar, big log fire, popular food inc very good home-made pies, and big peaceful garden; bdrms (not Christmas, New Year or Easter); disabled access. £22.50|**£7**

WOBURN SANDS SP9235 **Spooners** *61 High St (01908) 584385* Smart, pretty restaurant with good value, highly enjoyable french and english cooking, and a welcoming atmosphere; good value snacks downstairs; cl Sun, Mon, 1 wk Aug, 1 wk Christmas; disabled access. £30 dinner|**£8.95**

Special thanks to Michael and Jenny Back, Mrs Y Champion, Mrs D E Reynolds

CAMBRIDGESHIRE

Cambridge is great for a short visit, with lots to see and bags of character; elsewhere, plenty for all ages and most tastes - if you know where to look

Heading a list of good animal attractions is Linton Zoo, our choice for Cambridgeshire Family Attraction this year. Shepreth Wildlife Park and Hamerton Zoo Park (handy when it's wet) are fun too, and Wimpole Hall and Home Farm has enough variety to keep families happy for most of the day. There are fine houses at Elton and Lode, while Waterbeach has a medieval abbey and farming museum; delving even further back in time is the well organised prehistoric site at Flag Fen.

Picturesque Cambridge is a charming place to visit, with beautiful colleges, gardens and churches to explore, and a cluster of free-of-charge world-class museums to browse around. The best time to go is during the university terms, as in summer (when it's host to foreign language students) its popularity with coach tours means that certain parts can get crowded. Worth a visit even if aviation is not something you're usually interested in, the Imperial War Museum Duxford is only a short bus ride away from the city.

This is a good county for pottering around picturesque villages and towns - some with fine churches; Barrington, Fulbourn, Ickleton and Hemingford Grey (the Norman house here is interesting) are among the best. The quiet city of Ely with its graceful cathedral (and unusual stained-glass museum) is well worth a trip too. The countryside, though, is a bit monotonous - especially the north's flat silt fens and vast level fields. But there are those who love the misty bleakness in autumn, and this area has a lot to offer bird-watchers (especially at Wicken Fen, parts of Grafham Water and Ramsey Heights). To the west, the land is drier and more rolling, with stone-built villages more reminiscent of Leicestershire.

Where to stay

BASSINGBOURN TL3145 **Finch Farmhouse** *28 Fen Rd, Bassingbourn, Royston, Hertfordshire SG8 5PQ (01763) 242019* **£49**; 3 light, pretty rms with views of river. Originally an alehouse for irish farm workers, this Victorian house has an open fire in the sitting room, delicious imaginative food in the boldly decorated dining room (lunches are available on request), and friendly owners; children over 5

CAMBRIDGE TL4459 **Arundel House** *Chesterton Rd, Cambridge CB4 3AN (01223) 367701* **£103.90**; 105 comfortable rms, some overlooking the river. Carefully preserved terrace of fine early Victorian houses overlooking the River Cam and parkland; comfortable, attractive bar with two fires, elegant restaurant, large and airy plant-filled conservatory, good imaginative food, and seats in the pleasant garden

CAMBRIDGE TL4359 **Cambridge Lodge** *139 Huntingdon Rd, Cambridge CB3 0DQ (01223) 352833* **£84**; 15 rms, 12 with own bthrm. Mock-Tudor house on the outskirts, with open fire in relaxed and comfortable lounge, friendly service, and good freshly prepared food in the popular oak-beamed restaurant; cl 27-30 Dec; dogs welcome in bedrooms

DUXFORD TL4845 **Duxford Lodge** *Ickleton Rd, Duxford, Cambridge CB2 4RU (01223) 836444* **£105**w; 15 good-sized, warm rms, 2 with four-posters. Carefully run late Victorian hotel in an acre of neatly kept landscaped gardens, with a welcoming, relaxed atmosphere, individually chosen modern paintings and prints, a restful little lounge, decent wines, enjoyable modern cooking in the airy no smoking restaurant, and good breakfasts; partial disabled access; dogs welcome in bedrooms

ELY TL5480 **Lamb** *2 Lynn Rd, Ely, Cambridgeshire CB7 4EJ (01353) 663574* **£95**; 32 comfortable rms. Pleasant, neatly kept old coaching inn (newly refurbished) near cathedral, with two smart bars, enjoyable food in an attractive restaurant, very friendly staff, and good car parking; dogs welcome in bedrooms

HUNTINGDON TL2471 **Old Bridge** *1 High St, Huntingdon, Cambridgeshire PE18 6TQ (01480) 451591* **£145**, plus wknd breaks; 24 excellent rms with CD stereos and power showers. Creeper-covered Georgian hotel with pretty lounge, log fire in panelled bar, imaginative british cooking and extensive wine list in the no smoking restaurant and less formal lunchtime room (nice murals), and quick courteous service; riverside gardens; partial disabled access; dogs welcome in bedrooms

NEEDINGWORTH TL3571 **Pike & Eel** *Overcote Lane, Needingworth, St Ives, Huntingdon, Cambridgeshire PE17 3TW (01480) 463336* **£70**, plus wknd breaks; 9 rms. 17th-c inn in very peaceful riverside spot with spacious lawns and grounds by marina, roomy plush bar, big open fire and easy chairs in smaller room, glass-walled restaurant, carvery, real ale, good breakfasts, and friendly staff; disabled access

SIX MILE BOTTOM TL5857 **Swynford Paddocks** *Six Mile Bottom, Newmarket, Cambridgeshire CB8 0UE (01638) 570234* **£135**; 15 individually furnished rms with good bthrms. Gabled country house in neat grounds overlooking stud paddocks; carefully furnished rooms with fresh flowers and log fires, bar decorated with Brigadier memorabilia (a tribute to the great racehorse who is buried in the hotel grounds), conservatory Garden Room, a relaxed atmosphere, good food and friendly service; tennis, putting and croquet; disabled access; dogs welcome in bedrooms

STILTON TL1689 **Bell** *7 High St, Stilton, Peterborough, Cambridgeshire PE7 3RA (01733) 241066* **£96.50***; 19 rms. Elegant, carefully restored coaching inn with attractive rambling bars, big log fire, generous helpings of good food using the famous cheese (which was first sold from here), and seats in the sheltered cobbled and flagstoned courtyard; cl 25 Dec

WANSFORD TL0799 **Haycock** *London Rd, Wansford, Peterborough, Cambridgeshire PE8 6JA (01780) 782223* **£110**, plus special breaks; 50 individually decorated rms. 16th-c golden stone inn with relaxed, comfortable and carefully furnished lounges and pubby bar; pretty lunchtime café, smart restaurant with good food, excellent wines and efficient friendly service; garden with boules, fishing and cricket; disabled access. The little village it dominates is attractive, with a fine bridge over the Nene, and a good antiques shop; dogs welcome in bedrooms

WICKEN TL5571 **Spinney Abbey** *Stretham Rd, Wicken, Ely, Cambridgeshire CB7 5XQ (01353) 720971* **£50**; 3 peaceful, no smoking rms. 18th-c house, built using stones from the original abbey (which was closed by Henry VIII); charming, friendly owner, comfortable sitting room, good, hearty breakfasts, big garden with tennis court, and nearby village pub for evening meals; children over 5

To see and do

Cambridgeshire Family Attraction of the Year

LINTON TL5546 **Linton Zoological Gardens** (B1052, just off A604) With everything from snakes and tarantulas to snow leopards and tigers, this friendly family-run zoo has enough animals to fascinate most children for at least half a day, with good close-up views of most of them. The emphasis is firmly on conservation and breeding, and the animals are all housed in enclosures as close to their natural habitats as possible. The latest project is a breeding centre for rare lemurs, in a carefully planned complex with a big, landscaped open area. In fact the landscaping of the whole site is one of its main draws: when the zoo first opened the area was little more than a big field, but it's been very appealingly and thoughtfully developed, with some unusual plants - in late summer, look out for the flowers of the chinese trumpet vine around the terrace of the café. Other residents include giant tortoises, a couple of grevy's zebras, and brazilian tapir; there are good talks and family quiz trails, as well as play areas for smaller children, a bouncy castle (weather permitting), and plenty of picnic areas, some under cover. Some activities may be seasonal. Snacks (summer only), shop, disabled access; cl 25-26 Dec; (01223) 891308: £6 adults, £4.50 children 2-13.

BARNACK TF0704
Barnack has interesting dotted-about clusters of stone-built houses, a windmill and a part-Saxon church.

BARRINGTON TL3949
Superb village green surrounded by pretty timbered houses, an interesting church and a pleasant food pub, the Royal Oak; the nearby village of Foxton is especially interesting if you know the book *The Common Stream* by Rowland Parker (an intricate account of the village through the ages).

BOURN TL3158
Bourn Mill The working windmill here is thought to be the oldest trestle post mill in the country. Open last Sun pm of the month Mar-Sept, or ask for key from cottage next door (01223) 243830. The Duke of Wellington has good food.

Wysing Arts (Fox Rd) Lively arts centre in 11 acres of farmland, with contemporary art exhibitions and a continuous programme of events and workshops. Snacks, shop, disabled access; cl Sun, and maybe Sat, phone to check; (01954) 718881; free, charges for workshops. The Duke of Wellington is a decent food pub.

BURWELL TL5866
Burwell church This handsome and airy building has a fine oak roof. The village also has a restored windmill. Nearby Swaffham Prior is another attractive village, and the Red Lion there does good fresh food.

CAMBRIDGE TL4458
Quieter than Oxford (which the colleges here were founded to escape), the centre is dominated by ancient and graceful university buildings, and you get a real sense of centuries of study. It still has the character of a small, old-fashioned market town; Cambridge's hi-tech light industry is kept firmly on the outskirts. Between the colleges and university buildings are numerous less imposing but attractive old buildings, often grouped together quite picturesquely. The architecture has a striking diversity (continuous development of the colleges means that most have much-loved or maligned modern blocks), though isn't always shown off at its best, thanks to layers of muck and grime that rather spoil some of the libraries and faculty buildings. Happily, one of the most delightful parts of town, **The Backs**, where the river snakes through the colleges, always looks charming, with its delightful lawns, trees, college gardens, punts gliding past the weeping willows and grazing cattle opposite King's. Don't try to drive around town; there isn't really

any parking, and apart from the pedestrianised centre there's a frustrating tangle of congested one-way streets. Head for one of the big out-of-town car parks and use the excellent park and ride system. If you don't plan to take a car at all, it's worth noting that the railway station is far from central, although there is a frequent bus service into the historic centre. For a first-time visit, the Tour Bus (about an hour) is a good introduction. Walking tours set off from the Tourist Information Centre (Wheeler St) four times a day in summer (£7.85 inc entrance to King's Chapel, last tour £6.50 inc entrance to St John's - best to book in advance; (01223) 457574). Cyclists will enjoy the towpaths here; nettle-free, and safe if you have children with you. Quite a few shops are that bit different and worth popping into. In term-time, there are countless events; any college notice-board will show what's on. West Road concert hall has outstanding acoustics, while a concert in one of the smaller college chapels can be a charmingly intimate experience.

Cambridge colleges The colleges look private, but you can usually wander into the courtyards (access limited at exam time, and expect to be charged by many during the summer). Be warned though, college porters will get extremely agitated if you even look at the grass let alone accidentally step on it. Several of the dining halls and chapels are worth seeking out. The largest, finest and richest college is Trinity, where the imposing Great Court is usually open to the public, and the Wren Library (open wkdys 12-2pm) in Neville's Court is definitely worth a visit. King's is probably the best known, with its magnificent chapel, and is pleasant to walk through. Gonville & Caius (pronounced 'keys') is small, but very pretty. Queen's has a half-timbered courtyard and an eye-catchingly gaudy painted hall, as well as the famous Mathematical Bridge. Peterhouse is the oldest, founded in 1284; the buildings carry their years very gracefully, although these days its deer park is devoid of deer. Opposite, Pembroke's chapel is one of Wren's first buildings. St John's has the very

photographed Bridge of Sighs. Jesus, a bit off the main beat, is huge and grandly impressive, and Emmanuel has notable gardens. Clare and Trinity Hall are smaller yet charming colleges, next to each other by The Backs.

King's College Chapel The annual Festival of Nine Lessons and Carols has made the interior and something of the atmosphere familiar to most visitors, but you're still not fully prepared for the grandeur and scale of the fan-vaulted ceiling, or the miraculously preserved 16th-c stained glass. The overall effect is marred slightly by the unique dark oak screen added by Henry VIII, but the chapel's other famous feature - Rubens's *Adoration of the Magi* - is quite breathtaking. In term-time try to attend choral evensong (5.30pm Mon-Sat, Sun 10.30am and 3.30pm). Shop, disabled access; cl most of Sun during term-time, Advent, Easter Sun and 23 Dec-5 Jan - phone to check other times; (01223) 331212; £4.

Cambridge churches Of the many churches here, it's worth noting **St Bene't's**, one of the city's oldest, the popular **Holy Sepulchre** or Round Church, and **Great St Mary's** with its fine roof and good city views from the tower.

Fitzwilliam Museum (Trumpington St) This is a wonderful place, a grand and impressive building, crammed with more dazzling treasures than you could hope to examine in one visit. Downstairs are Greek, Egyptian and Roman antiquities, while upstairs you'll find furniture, sculpture and paintings by Titian, Canaletto and the Impressionists. Until they finish redeveloping the courtyard around summer 2004, only the Founder's Building will be open, so displays are limited to the highlights of collections, and there won't be any temporary exhibitions; very limited disabled access till then. Shop opposite museum; cl 22 Dec 2003-Easter 2004, see website www.fitzmuseum.cam.ac.uk for details. Usually only cl Mon (exc bank hols), am Sun, Good Fri, and around a wk over Christmas and New Year; (01223) 332900; free.

Cambridge & County Folk Museum (2-3 Castle St) Useful

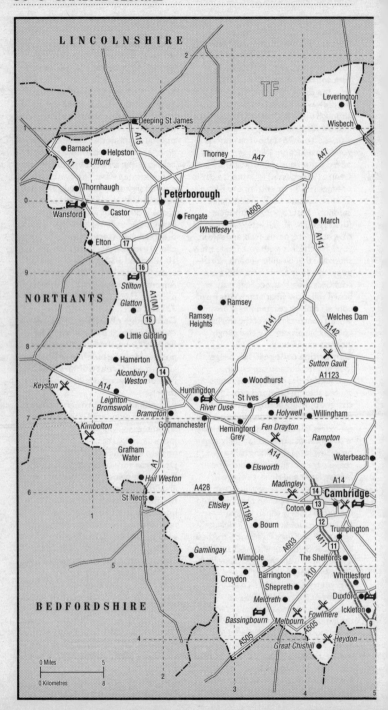

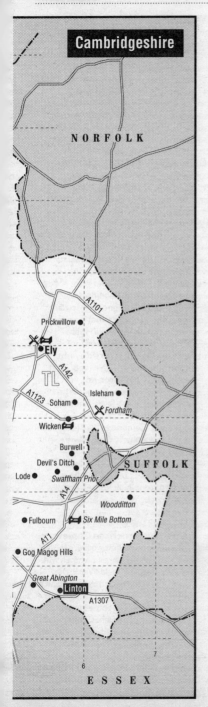

Cambridgeshire

NORFOLK

A1101

Prickwillow ●

✠ Ely

A142

TL

A1123   Soham ●   Isleham ●

✠ Fordham

Wicken

Burwell ●

Devil's Ditch

Lode ●   Swaffham Prior   SUFFOLK

A14

Woodditton

● Fulbourn   Six Mile Bottom

A11

● Gog Magog Hills

Great Abington

Linton

A1307

6   7

ESSEX

exploration of local life in a handsome
16th-c former inn near the river - a
touch-screen database includes
contemporary residents' diaries and
'virtual' city tours. Shop, disabled access
to ground floor only; cl till Easter
because of renovation work (so phone
to check). Usually cl Mon Oct-Mar
(exc school hols), am Sun, Good Fri,
23 Dec-2 Jan; (01223) 355159; £2.50.
University Botanic Garden (Cory
Lodge, Bateman St) Opened in 1846,
and now covering 40 acres, with some
marvellous mature trees, a rock garden
displaying alpine plants from the
mountains of every continent, scented
garden, autumn and winter gardens;
they've newly renovated the bog and
dry gardens, and have many rare plants
inc nine National Collections. Rarely
crowded, and very pleasant to stroll
through. Tearoom (wknds only in
winter), summer shop, disabled access;
cl 25 Dec-1 Jan, (01223) 336265; £2.50.
Other Cambridge museums Most
of the town's other museums have a
rather academic bent, but are no less
rewarding for that: the **Sedgwick
Museum** (Downing St) is the
university geology museum, with an
outstanding collection of fossils, and
rocks from Darwin's journey in HMS
Beagle. The curator once proved that
iguanadons were put together
differently from how scientists had
previously thought: the bones of his
museum's 6-metre (20-ft) specimen
have not been rearranged for historical
reasons although theoretically, he
claims, it is currently in agony. Shop,
limited disabled access; cl 1-2pm, Sat
pm, all Sun, Christmas-New Year,
Easter; (01223) 333456; free. Down the
same street is the **Museum of
Archaeology & Anthropology**,
home to a 15-metre (50-ft) totem pole
(open pm Tues-Sat, cl Christmas,
Easter; (01223) 333516; free) and a
Museum of Zoology, where a 21-
metre (70-ft) whale skeleton hangs
above the entrance inside (cl wknds and
1-2pm; (01223) 336650; free). The
Museum of Classical Archaeology
on Sidgwick Ave has one of the few
surviving collections of casts of Greek
and Roman sculpture (cl wknds;
(01223) 335153; free), while the

various scientific instruments and apparatus at the **Whipple Museum of Science** (Free School Lane) quickly make you thankful we need no longer rely on sundials and abacuses (open wkdys pm though best to check outside term; (01223) 330906; free). The **Scott Polar Research Institute** (Lensfield Rd) houses fascinating exhibits from the fateful polar expedition inc diaries, letters and clothing, also inuit carving. Shop, disabled access; open pm Mon-Fri (exc bank hols), but phone to check; (01223) 336540; free. The exhibition centre at the towering and austere **University Library** (West Rd) has occasional displays of rare and ancient manuscripts; open pm Mon-Fri; (01223) 333030; free.

Kettle's Yard (Castle St) Lively arts centre with temporary exhibitions in the gallery and permanent displays in the avant-garde yet surprisingly welcoming house (you may sit in any of the chairs - some of which are more than 300 years old), taking in 20th-c paintings and sculptures (interesting St Ives connections), lovely 18th-c furniture and oriental carpets, and collections of shells and stones. Lots of activities and workshops, several designed especially for the blind or hard of hearing; also concerts 1.10pm Fri during term-time. Shop, disabled access (limited in house, best to ring first); cl am, all Mon (exc bank hol Mon), Good Fri, 24-28 Dec and 1 Jan; (01223) 352124; free.

Punting The only way to travel, though if your skills in this department were picked up in Oxford you'll find they do things a little back to front here. You can punt right along The Backs, and even down to Grantchester, a pleasant little village still much as described in Rupert Brooke's poem of the same name, with the civilised Orchard Tea Gardens (lovely in summer - and does other drinks too, inc champagne) and three pubs. Hire punts from Scudamores on Mill Lane (cl wkdys Dec-Jan; (01223) 359750) or other stations along the water; prices are generally around £14 an hour per punt (£12 per person if you require a chauffeur). Bumps races (several rowing eights start off in a line and have

to catch up with the one in front) take place on the river in Feb, Jun and July.

Towpath walks From Magdalene Bridge right in Cambridge itself there's a pleasant walk by the towpath out into the meadows - tranquil, with only punts as far as the lock. Beyond that, you could walk as far as Ely, with oarsmen setting an altogether more vigorous tone - though the Ancient Shepherds at Fen Ditton might be a gentler target. Another pleasant stroll out from Cambridge - in the opposite direction - is along the Cam to Grantchester.

Snacks in Cambridge Many attractive snack places include the little Indigo Coffee House (St Edward's Passage - off King's Parade), Roof Garden (top floor of Arts Theatre - side entrance in St Edward's Passage), and the tiny Little Tea Room (All Saints Green); the eastern-european Cazimir's (King's St) does great coffee, lunches and cakes, Rainbow Café (King's Parade) has good vegetarian food, Dojo's (off Mill Lane) is a popular chinese restaurant, while Hobbs Pavilion (Park Terr) is good for pancakes. Decent **riverside pubs** include the Anchor (Silver St Bridge), Boathouse (Chesterton Rd), Fort St George (Midsummer Common) and Granta (Newnham Terr). The best pubs away from the river are the smoke-free Cambridge Blue (Gwydir St) and atmospheric Eagle (Bene't St).

CASTOR TL1298
Pleasantly relaxed ancient village with a fine **church** and several handsome thatched stone-built houses; Fratellis (Peterborough Rd) is an attractive italian restaurant.

COTON TL4059
Cambridge American Cemetery A beautiful and haunting tribute to the american servicemen and women who lost their lives in World War II, this covers 30 acres, framed by woodland to the west and south. The Portland stone memorial chapel has some intriguing features inc a map of air assaults over the Atlantic and stained-glass windows depicting the seals of the States arranged from left to right in the order that they entered the Union. Disabled access; cl 25 Dec and 1 Jan; (01954) 210350; free.

CROYDON TL3149
Croydon church Quietly charming, a proper country church with a timeless feel. The Queen Adelaide is a roomy and popular dining pub.
DEEPING ST JAMES TF1809
Exotic Pet Refuge Quite impressive pet sanctuary with animals ranging from jungle cats and lemurs to snakes and lizards; open a few wknds throughout the year, inc Easter, best to phone (01778) 345923; £3. The friendly Goat at nearby Frognall, with a good family garden, has decent food (all day on Sun).
DEVIL'S DITCH TL5765
This miles-long ancient embankment lets you fuel a walk with speculations on whether it was built to fight off the Romans, or some centuries later to protect the riches of East Anglia from Midlands warlords. It's not much of a topographical feature, and is crossed by one or two very busy roads. A good start or finish might be the Dykes End pub in Reach, at its N end, with a wide range of food.
DUXFORD TL4546
Imperial War Museum Duxford (just off M11, junction 10) Unmissable for anyone interested in aviation, this big former airfield is rewarding for children too. It's home to Europe's best collection of military and civil aircraft, nearly 200 in all, from flimsy-looking bi-planes to current state-of-the-art front-line fighters. Children can clamber into the cockpits of some of them, pick up helmets and gunpacks, and there's an adventure playground. They also have a huge collection of tanks and military vehicles, and a naval collection inc midget submarines and helicopters. There are several exhibitions with new ones all the time (2004 will have a temporary exhibition on D-Day), and a project to re-house their british aircraft should be completed in 2006. The American Air Museum, a collection of US combat aircraft, is in a remarkable building by Norman Foster. The site covers about a mile (a bus can take you between the different bits), and the preserved hangars, control tower and operations rooms have something of the atmosphere they must have had when this was a working base. Each year they have several dramatic air shows

(extra charge), and some planes still fly on other days. A free bus runs every hour from and to Cambridge Station; it takes about 20 minutes. Meals and snacks (and plenty of space for picnics), shop, good disabled access; cl 24-26 Dec; (01223) 835000; £8.50, children free. The Green Man close by at Thriplow is an interesting place for lunch.
ELTON TL0892
Elton Hall From the back a splendid 'gothick' fantasy, this is a fascinating lived-in house dating back to Tudor times, with lovely furnishings, porcelain and paintings, inc works by 15th-c Old Masters, Gainsborough and Constable. The library has a Prayer Book that belonged to Henry VIII (his writing is inside), and the gardens are especially pleasant in summer when the roses are in bloom. Shop, adjacent garden centre and tearoom, disabled access to garden only; open pm last bank hol in May and Aug bank hol, pm Weds in Jun, pm Weds-Thurs and Sun July-Aug (phone to check); (01832) 280468; £5, £3 garden. The Black Horse nearby has good interesting food, and the attractive stone-built village has a lovely Saxon church.
ELY TL5480
This busy little market town with good shops and some lovely old buildings well repays a leisurely stroll. A Passport to Ely ticket allows you to visit the cathedral, Oliver Cromwell's House, Ely Museum and the Stained Glass Museum for £9.
Ely Cathedral One of England's most striking, its distinctive towers dominating the skyline for miles; especially good views coming in on the Soham rd. Complete by the late 12th c, it was restored in a surprisingly sympathetic manner mainly in the mid-19th c. The façade, covered in blind arcading, is fantastic, but most remarkable perhaps is the Octagonal Tower, over 400 tons suspended in space without any visible means of support; it looks especially impressive from inside. The Lady Chapel has the widest medieval vault in the country, and the walls are carved with hundreds of tiny statues which were all brutally beheaded in the Reformation. The

splendid Norman nave seems even longer than it really is because it's so narrow. Also not to be missed are a couple of elaborately sculpted medieval doors. It's worth trying to catch the evensong here, 5.30pm daily exc Weds (Sun at 3.45pm). Meals, snacks, shop, disabled access to ground floor; (01353) 667735; £4.80.

Ely Museum (Old Gaol, Market St) Displays inc fossils, Roman remains, original gaol cells and brewing in Ely. Shop; disabled access; usually cl Tues Oct-Mar, and two wks over Christmas and New Year; (01353) 666655; £3, children free with adult.

Oliver Cromwell's House (St Mary's St) Next to the unexpectedly grand Church of St Mary, this fine old house was the home of Oliver Cromwell and his family from 1636 until shortly before he became Lord Protector. Period furnished rooms, useful videos (one on the draining of the Fens), and information centre in the downstairs front room. Shop; usually cl 25-26 Dec, 1 Jan, best to check; (01353) 662062; £3.50.

Stained Glass Museum In the cathedral's south triforium, this preserves fine medieval and modern stained glass, much of it rescued from redundant buildings and churches. Good displays on how the windows are made, and a bonus is the unusual view over the cathedral. Meals, snacks, shop; cl am Sun, 25-26 Dec and Good Fri; (01353) 660347; £3.50.

FENGATE TL2199
Flag Fen Bronze Age Excavation ▣ (Fengate, 2m E of Peterborough) Fascinating and well organised prehistoric site, centred on remains of a wooden platform which crossed a shallow lake; from it Bronze Age settlers appear to have thrown all sorts of deliberately broken bronze objects as part of a ritual - some of the best finds (inc England's oldest wheel) are in the very good adjacent museum, and there's an environmentally friendly Heritage Centre. In summer you should be able to watch archaeologists painstakingly uncovering more secrets, while reconstructed Bronze and Iron Age roundhouses help put the discoveries in context; peaceful lakeside walk and primitive breeds of

sheep and pigs. Snacks, shop, mostly disabled access; cl 24 Dec-2 Jan; (01733) 313414; £4.

FULBOURN TL5155
This is an attractive largely thatched village, with a windmill on the Cambridge rd, a good farm shop with pick-your-own fruit, and a pretty church; the picturesque Bakers Arms is a popular lunch spot. A path takes you eastwards to the wooded line of the Fleam Dyke, a miles-long Dark Ages defence earthwork.

GODMANCHESTER TL2668
Wood Green Animal Shelter ▣ (Kings Bush Farm) This well maintained rescue centre has wildlife and unwanted pets, water garden, oriental cattery, picnic site and playground; events most wknds. Meals, snacks, shop, disabled access; cl 25-26 Dec; (01480) 830014; free (donations welcome). In Godmanchester itself there are a few interesting buildings, the Exhibition has good food, and you can stroll along the river to the lock.

GOG MAGOG HILLS TL4953
Not exactly a towering range, these are worth a passing visit; among tall trees you can trace the main rampart and ditch of **Wandlebury Iron Age fort**, and there are good views of the city's distant towers and spires.

GRAFHAM WATER TL1667
A regular outing for some of our readers, this has fishing, sailing, cycle hire, and a nature reserve with bird-watching hides and trails (you'll see a lot more birds in winter). An attractive path follows the northern shore, and you can take wheelchairs the whole way round. Visitor centre and café; (01480) 812154; free, £2 (£1 in winter) parking charge (some car parks may be cl Nov-Mar). The Lion over in Buckden, an appealing coaching inn, has enjoyable food.

HAMERTON TL1481
Hamerton Zoo Park ▣ This dedicated centre is continually expanding, and has a splendidly varied collection of rare and endangered species from all over the world; readers who come here regularly tell us there is always something new to see. More than 100 different species are spread over 15 acres of pretty countryside,

from playful gibbons, wolves, boa constrictors and bengal tigers (one of them is white) to smaller animals such as tortoises and porcupines; they usually have plenty of birds, and you can feed and stroke some of the animals (listen out for the noisy miniature donkey). Talks from the keepers during feeding times at wknds and school holidays. Nearly a mile of covered walkways mean you can get between most of the animal houses without getting wet. Tearoom (cl in winter), small shop, disabled access; cl 25 Dec; (01832) 293362; £6 (honesty box in winter).

HELPSTON TF1205
Magnificent bluebell woods border the minor road that runs over to the A47 between Wansford and Ailsworth, a pleasant place for walking even out of bluebell season. In the village there's good food at the Blue Bell (where John Clare the early 19th-c poet, born next door, started work).

HEMINGFORD GREY TL2970
Charming village with a peaceful view of the church over the willow-bordered river (the odd church tower is the result of its spire being lopped off by an 18th-c storm); the Cock is a good dining pub, and nearby Hemingford Abbots is also pretty.

Manor This stone house, among the thatched brick ones, is Norman and said to be the oldest continuously inhabited house in Britain. It was the home of author Lucy Boston, and the setting for her Greene Knowe books; the pretty garden (open daily) has a fine collection of roses. Shop and plant sales; phone (01480) 463134 for an appointment; £4, garden only £2.

HUNTINGDON TL2371
After considerable recent growth the old centre now feels a bit sidetracked, but has one or two fine buildings such as the George, a particularly handsome Georgian coaching inn. The Old Bridge is a smart place for a very good lunch.

Cromwell Museum (Grammar School Walk) Two of Huntingdon's MPs can claim to have run the country for a while, and this commemorates the first. The restored Norman building is where the future Lord Protector went to school (as did Pepys), and many of his possessions are on display. Shop,

disabled access; cl 1-2pm, Mon, bank hols (exc Good Fri), plus am in winter (exc Sat), phone to check; (01480) 375830; free.

Hinchingbrooke Country Park (off B1514 W) Good for a walk, a run-about or picnic; guided walks or events throughout the year. Snacks (wknds and school hols), disabled access; (01480) 451568; free.

Hinchingbrooke House (B1514 W) Now a school, this is where some reckon Cromwell and Charles I met as children. Snacks, disabled access; usually open pm Sun May bank hol-Aug bank hol; (01480) 375678; *£3. The Exhibition in Godmanchester is the best nearby place for lunch.

ICKLETON TL4944
This attractive village has a fine church, with Roman columns as bases for its arches, and interestingly carved pews. The churchyard is lovely, and around the church and small green are several beautiful old houses - often a good deal older than their Georgian refacing suggests. The John Barleycorn in Duxford is a good food pub.

ISLEHAM TL6474
Isleham church Attractive from the outside, but its best feature is its wonderful roof.

LEVERINGTON TF4411
Leverington church The tower and its spire are noteworthy, as is the very unusual two-storey 14th-c porch. The Woodmans Cottage over at Gorefield has decent food.

LINTON TL5648
Chilford Hall Vineyard (towards Balsham) A friendly 18-acre winery with interesting old buildings and tours at 11.30am, 2.30pm and 4pm. Meals, snacks, shop, disabled access; cl 23 Dec-Feb; (01223) 895625; £4.25 (inc tastings).

Linton Zoological Gardens See *separate family panel on p.34.*

LITTLE GIDDING TL1281
Little Gidding church Archetypal small-village country church, well worth a look inside.

LODE TL5362
Anglesey Abbey, Gardens and Lode Mill 🖼 All that remains of the original priory is a medieval undercroft, but the handsome 17th-c house has an

engaging collection of clocks and eclectic range of furniture and paintings; it's definitely worth pausing at Constable's view of the Thames and the landscapes by Claude. The bookshelves in the library are made from Rennie's Waterloo Bridge. The lovely gardens were laid out from 1926 by the first Lord Fairhaven; a restored **watermill** still produces flour. Varied events and activities, inc highly regarded open-air jazz. Meals, snacks, shop, mostly disabled access; house open pm Weds-Sun and bank hols Apr-Oct, grounds open all year; (01223) 810080; £6.50, £4 grounds only (discount voucher not available on bank hols or special events days); NT. The White Swan at Stow cum Quy does enjoyable lunches.

MARCH TL4195
Pleasant country town, market day Weds and Sat; a good base for exploring the fens. **St Wendreda's church** with its wonderful angel roof was described by Betjeman as being 'worth cycling 40 miles in a headwind to see'. The Acre (Acre Rd) has good home cooking.

PETERBOROUGH TL1998
Has preserved much of its long history and fine old buildings, though it expanded hugely in the mid-1970s and is now a thriving industrial town (with a good pedestrianised shopping centre). Handily, a network of cycleways, footpaths and bridleways link tourist attractions and nature reserves with residential areas. Charters (by Town Bridge) is an enjoyable floating pub/restaurant in a converted barge.
City Museum and Art Gallery (Priestgate) Among other interesting exhibits are some unusual models made from fishbones by Napoleonic prisoners of war; children's activities and temporary displays. Shop, disabled access; cl Mon (exc bank hol Mon), am Sun, plus am wkdys in term-time, Good Fri, Easter Sun, 25-26 Dec, 1 Jan; (01733) 343329; free, charge when special exhibits shown.
Ferry Meadows Country Park (off A605 W of Peterborough) Useful for children to let off steam; 500 acres with play areas, two big lakes with water sports, fishing and boat trips, nature reserve, pony rides, miniature railway,

and two golf courses and pitch and putt nearby. Visitor centre; snacks, shop, disabled access; (01733) 234443; free, parking charge wknds and bank hols Apr-Oct, £2.60. The Cuckoo at Alwalton out this way is a reliable dining pub.
Longthorpe Tower (Thorpe Rd, W of centre) 13th/14th-c fortified house with rare wall paintings; phone (01733) 268482 for opening times and prices; EH.
Peterborough Cathedral One of the most dramatic in the country, its extraordinary west front a medieval masterpiece, with a trio of huge arches. Despite the damage inflicted by Cromwell, the richly Romanesque interior has preserved its original fabric to a remarkable degree; especially worth a look are the elaborately vaulted retro-choir and the fine early 13th-c painted wooden nave ceiling; an exhibition in the north aisle tells more about its history. Meals, snacks, shop, some disabled access; cl 25-26 Dec and am Sun (except for services); (01733) 345064; donations.
Railworld 🏛 (Oundle Rd) Friendly railway and environment exhibition centre with museum; wknd and bank hol snacks, shop, disabled access; cl wknds Nov-Feb, Good Fri and 25 Dec-1 Jan; (01733) 344240; £4.
St Margaret's church (Fletton) On the southern edge of Peterborough, this has some exceptionally fine little Anglo-Saxon sculptures.

PRICKWILLOW TL5982
Drainage Engine Museum The story of water, pumping and fen drainage in the area since the last Ice Age, especially interesting when the engines are running (phone for dates). Snacks, small shop, disabled access; usually open Fri-Tues May-Sept, wknds and bank hols Mar-Apr and Oct, best to check; (01353) 688360; *£2 (*£3 when engines running).

RAMSEY TL2984
Abbey Gatehouse The ruins of an ornate Gothic gatehouse with buttresses and friezes, along with the 13th-c Lady Chapel (all that's left of the abbey itself). Cl Nov-Mar; free. Some of the stone from the abbey is thought to have made up the nearby local history

museum (open Thurs and pm Sun, Apr-Sept, other times by appointment; (01487) 815715; £2). The Cross Keys at Upwood (where there's a windmill) has good value food.

RAMSEY HEIGHTS TL2384

Woodwalton Fen (off B1040 W of Ramsey) Quiet and peaceful nature reserve, developed around the overgrown remains of old brick pits and kilns; nature trails lead through several meadows and along a dyke, and you may spy some of the many small woodland birds from a hide over-looking a marshy area, with boardwalks over ponds for a closer look.

RIVER OUSE TL2772

The stretch between St Ives and Hemingford Grey is a popular wknd stamping-ground, with **Houghton Mill** as a charming set piece - a lovely building in a pretty setting. Nearby the Three Jolly Butchers has good food, and occasional barbecues in its huge garden.

SHELFORDS, THE TL4552

The interlinked villages of Great and Little Shelford will reward a slow stroll for those with an eye for architectural detail, and even a quick drive through will show up several delightful timbered houses.

SHEPRETH TL3847

Docwra's Manor Gardens Tranquil gardens, at their best Apr-Jun but always with a variety of unusual plants. The best bit is perhaps the lovely intimate walled garden. Disabled access (although gravel paths may be hard work); open Weds and Fri, plus pm first Sun of month Apr-Oct; (01763) 261557; £3.

Shepreth Wildlife Park (off A10, next to Shepreth railway station) Attractively laid out around three lakes, this genuine little animal centre started out as a wildlife sanctuary, and rescued animals and birds are still a major part of the mix, though these days you're as likely to find mountain lions, monkeys and prairie dogs as you are deer or squirrels. Particular favourites are the big cat house, the tropical house, and the fantastic collection of spiders, ants and all sorts of creepy-crawlies entertainingly presented in Bug City - there are over 2,000 creatures in here alone; this section, and its aquatic-

themed neighbour Waterworld, are £1.65 extra. Younger visitors can pet rabbits and feed horses and koi carp (they sell bags of feed), and there are several well organised play areas; pony rides at wknds. The entrance isn't that well signed so keep an eye out. Meals, snacks, picnic areas, shop, disabled access; cl 25 Dec; (01763) 262226; £4.95.

SOHAM TL5872

As well as a rather grand **church**, this has two surviving mills.

ST IVES TL3171

Pleasant little town, with a graceful church, small local museum (cl 11-2pm, plus winter Sat pm and Sun), and walks by the curving river. There's an unusual tiny chapel on the old bridge, rising straight out of the water; key from museum. In the town, the Royal Oak does generous food, and the riverside Pike & Eel out at Needingworth is attractively placed for lunch.

ST NEOTS TL1860

Pleasant town next to the River Ouse with a large market place and a pleasant landscaped park; the medieval church of St Mary's is worth a look, and the Chequers near it has good value food. An interesting little museum (New St), in a former police station and Magistrate's Court, has a rare example of a 1907 cell block; other displays include the story of St Neot, local crafts and trades, and changing exhibitions by local artists, with new interactive displays; shop, disabled access; open Tues-Sat (cl during Jan school hols), best to check; (01480) 388788; £2.

THORNEY TF2804

Rises from the flatlands like an island - which it was, when this was all half-submerged marsh. Much older than most villages in the area, it has a Norman-modified Saxon church on its green, and some interesting yellow-brick workers' houses put up by the Duke of Bedford.

Thorney Heritage Museum (144 Wisbech Road) Friendly with good displays, and organises tours of the village and abbey. Shop, disabled access (but no facilities); open pm wknds Easter-Sept; (01733) 270780; museum free; tours £2, by appointment only. The Rose & Crown does freshly made food.

THORNHAUGH TF0700
Sacrewell Farm and Country Centre (off A47/A1) Based around an old working watermill, with demonstrations and displays of rural crafts, tools and machinery and discovery centre, as well as gardens, children's maze and nature trails, lots of animals. Pleasantly simple and undeveloped, this is a friendly well organised place. Meals, snacks, shop, disabled access; cl Christmas wk; (01780) 782254; £3.50. Wansford is very handy for lunch.

TRUMPINGTON TL4454
Trumpington church Attractive in its own right, but perhaps most famous for having the second-oldest memorial brass in England.

WANSFORD TL0997
Nene Valley Railway 🚂 15-mile round trip on steam trains through quiet countryside to Peterborough. Also a fine collection of steam locomotives and rolling stock, and a small museum. The railway is a favourite with film-makers. Meals and snacks on steam days, shop, disabled access; phone for train times (01780) 784444; £2 site admission, £10 for the train. It's easy to extend this into an all-day trip by breaking your journey at one of the country parks alongside stations en route, or by taking a stroll around Peterborough. At the Wansford end (pretty village), the Haycock is particularly good for lunch.

WATERBEACH TL4868
Denny Abbey & Farmland Museum 🚂 (off A10) 12th-c Benedictine abbey with some impressive Norman remains and a 14th-c nuns' refectory. The museum focuses on farming and the county's rural history, with reconstructions of a village shop, kitchen and dairy, and there's a 1940s cottage; various workshops and events. Wknd snacks and picnic area, shop, disabled access (limited in the abbey and cottage), and they'll lend you a wheelchair; open pm Apr-Oct; (01223) 860988; £3.70; EH.

WELCHES DAM TL4786
Ouse Washes Reserve (via Manea, off B1093 SE of March) The best time to visit is in winter when this RSPB reserve floods, and you can watch some of the thousands of ducks and swans from hides (one is wheelchair accessible) along the banks of the River Ouse; picnic areas, and an information centre where you can hire binoculars (cl 25 Dec); (01354) 680212; donations.

WHITTLESFORD TL4748
Whittlesford church The interior is a rich testament to the former agricultural wealth of this area.

WICKEN TL5670
Wicken Fen (Lode Lane) The last of the undrained fens, sheathed underground in plastic to prevent its drying out, it is an outstanding area for bird-watching (there are hides); look out for otters too. The marshy and open fen landscape is one of the oldest nature reserves in the country, originally safeguarded in 1899 as an example of what the fens were like before they were turned over to intensive agriculture. Beautiful at all times of year, it's home to a remarkable range of plants, insects, birds and other wildlife; some good trails (one for wheelchairs), along with the last fenland windpump (moved here from elsewhere), and tiny fen cottage (open Sun and bank hols Apr-Oct and some Weds in Aug, phone to check). Reserve open every day, visitor centre with snacks, shop and disabled access; cl Mon exc bank hols, 25 Dec; (01353) 720274; *£3.90, £1.50 cottage only; NT. The Maids Head prettily set by the village green duckpond has good food.

WILLINGHAM TL4070
Willingham church Lots to notice here: outside are the fine tower and spire, and inside it has many early wall paintings and some fine early screens. The old Three Tuns has good value home cooking (not Mon).

WIMPOLE TL3350
Wimpole Hall and Home Farm (off A603) The varied attractions at this huge estate can easily fill most of a day. Children like the working stock farm best, its thatched and timbered buildings designed by Sir John Soane when it was at the forefront of agricultural innovation. A restored barn houses machinery and tools from those days, and there are plenty of farm animals (with younger ones to pet and feed) inc various rare breeds; separate play areas for older and younger

children. The mainly 18th-c house is one of the most striking mansions in East Anglia. Behind its imposing and harmonious Georgian façade is a lovely trompe l'oeil chapel ceiling, and rooms by James Gibbs and Sir John Soane. The gardens are good for spring daffodils, and vegetables grow in the restored walled garden. Best of all perhaps are the 360 acres of parkland, home to the National Walnut Collection, and designed by several different notable landscapers inc Capability Brown and Repton; the remains of a medieval village are under the pasture. Good programme of concerts and events in the hall or grounds. Meals, snacks, shops, some disabled access (not to house). Hall open pm Tues-Thurs and wknds 20 Mar-Oct, plus bank hols and Fri pm in Aug. Farm open same times plus am, wknds in winter, and Fri in July and Aug; (01223) 207257; *£9.80 hall and farm (*£6.60 hall, *£5.10 farm); NT. The surrounding park is open all year, with walkers welcomed free of charge to the extensive paths and tracks through its farmland and woodland, past a folly and up to a surprisingly elevated ridge path. The handsome Hardwicke Arms has decent food.

WISBECH TF4609

The North Brink along the River Nene has handsome Georgian houses (among them the Red Lion has decent food, and serves beer from the nearby brewery - see below - in fine condition).

Elgoods Brewery Museum and Gardens (North Brink) Watch traditional brewing methods in practice at this handsome 200-year-old brewery on the banks of the River Nene. Behind, four acres of gardens include a hot-house, lake and lawns leading to a maze (in the shape of a yard of ale). Snacks, shop, disabled access to gardens only; open pm Tues-Thurs, 27 Apr-end Sept, brewery tours 2pm; (01945) 583160; £6 brewery hall, £2.50 gardens only.

Octavia Hill Birthplace Museum (South Brink) Five rooms in this Georgian house document the considerable influence on us today of a Victorian woman many people have never heard of. Housing reformer Octavia Hill's vigorous public campaigns to save recreational open space led

among other things to the foundation of the National Trust. The highlight is probably the re-created slum dwelling of 1861, though there are also some interesting tales about Octavia's eccentric family (until she was 13 her father kept Jeremy Bentham's skeleton in the corner of one room). Shop; open pm wknds, Weds and bank hol Mon 17 Mar-Oct, or by appointment; (01945) 476358; £2.

Peckover House (North Brink) Lovely early 18th-c house with rococo decoration, restored Victorian library, and a two-acre Victorian garden with a pond, herbaceous borders, rose gardens, summer houses and glasshouses - where orange trees are still fruiting after 300 years. Meals and snacks when house open, shop, disabled access in garden; house and garden open pm Weds, wknds and bank hol Mon (plus Thurs May-Aug), garden open pm Sat-Thurs Apr-end Oct; (01945) 583463; *£4.25, *£2.75 garden only; NT.

Wisbech & Fenland Museum (Museum Sq) Honest and thorough local history museum, with several early manuscripts, an exhibition on Thomas Clarkson and the slave trade, and a display on former times in fenland; the museum itself is interesting, with original showcases and fittings from Victorian period. Shop, good disabled access; cl Sun, Mon; (01945) 583817; free.

WOODHURST TL3375

Raptor Foundation 🏠 Sanctuary and breeding centre for over 300 birds of prey inc owls, buzzards, hawks and falcons, with flying displays three times a day; take your camera. Meals, snacks, shop, disabled access; cl 25 Dec, 1 Jan; (01487) 741140; *£3.50.

Other attractive villages, all with decent pubs for something to eat, include Alconbury Weston TL1776, Brampton TL2170, Eltisley TL2659, Elton TL0893, Elsworth TL3163, Glatton TL1585, Leighton Bromswold TL1175, Gamlingay TL2452, Great Abington TL5348, Great Chishill TL4239 (well restored windmill), Hail Weston TL1662, Holywell TL3370, Meldreth TL3746, Rampton TL4268, Swaffham Prior TL5764, Ufford TF0904 (lovely area at bluebell time), Whittlesey TL2797 and Woodditton TL6659.

Where to eat

CAMBRIDGE TL4559 **Twenty Two** *22 Chesterton Rd (01223) 351880* Simple and pretty candlelit evening restaurant in Edwardian house with imaginative modern cooking from a set menu, a fine wine list, and friendly service; no smoking; cl Sun, Mon, 1 wk Christmas; children over 12. £32

ELY TL5380 **Old Fire Engine House** *25 St Marys St (01353) 662582* Former fire station next to the cathedral, with good hearty english cooking inc nice puddings, an interesting wine list, simple furnishings and a relaxed atmosphere; large walled garden, also an art gallery; cl Sun pm, bank hols, 25 Dec-6 Jan. £30

FEN DRAYTON TL3368 **Three Tuns** *High St (01954) 230242* Pretty thatched inn with two inglenook fireplaces and heavy Tudor beams and timbers in its unpretentious and cosy bar; well kept real ales, generous helpings of good reasonably priced food, and a neat back garden with children's play equipment; children until 8pm; disabled access. £22|**£5.95**

FORDHAM TL6270 **White Pheasant** *Market St (01638) 720414* Well converted, fresh-feeling dining pub with simple decorations, flowers in bottles on tables, farmhouse chairs and a cheerful log fire; creative food, super daily specials, good house wines and well kept real ales; cl 25-30 Dec. £30|**£5.95**

FOWLMERE TL4245 **Chequers** *High St (01763) 208369* Civilised old coaching inn with a carefully chosen menu in galleried restaurant, good puddings and thoughtful wine list; two comfortably furnished rooms downstairs with an open log fire, while upstairs there are beams, wall timbering and some interesting moulded plasterwork; airy no smoking conservatory overlooking the neat garden; cl 25 Dec; children in family room; disabled access. £25|**£5.20**

HEYDON TL4243 **King William IV** *Chrishall Rd (01763) 838773* Bustling village pub with nooks and crannies in rambling rooms, neatly kept agricultural implements and a log fire; notably interesting vegetarian dishes (plus some meaty dishes, too), well kept real ales, and friendly efficient staff; disabled access. £25.80|**£8.25**

KEYSTON TL0475 **Pheasant** *Village Loop Rd (01832) 710241* Pretty thatched former smithy, full of character, with a nice civilised atmosphere, a relaxed bar, a slightly more formal no smoking room with linen napkins, courteous, efficient young staff, delicious imaginative food from an innovative changing menu, a particularly good wine list and real ales; cl 25 Dec pm; partial disabled access. £31

KIMBOLTON TL0967 **New Sun** *20 High St (01480) 860052* Nice old pub with low-beamed front lounge, standing timbers and exposed brickwork, armchairs and sofa by fireplace, well kept real ales, and dining room and bright, busy conservatory; good food inc interesting daily specials, and seats in very pleasant garden; no food Sun and Mon pm; children must be well behaved and away from bar. £25|**£5.50**

MADINGLEY TL3960 **Three Horseshoes** *High St (01954) 210221* Thatched dining pub, smart and well run, with a relaxed and civilised atmosphere, open fire in the charming bar, and an attractive conservatory; very good imaginative food, well kept real ales, a thoughtful, but fairly priced wine list, and efficient attentive service; pretty summer garden; cl Sun pm. £33|**£9.50**

MELBOURN TL3844 **Sheene Mill** *39 Station Rd (01763) 261393* Lovely late 17th-c River Mel watermill owned by celebrity chef Steven Saunders, just 200 yards from its sister restaurant, the Pink Geranium; relaxed bar and conservatory, airy restaurant decorated in yellow and terracotta, and lovely gardens with terrace seating; delicious modern cooking inc vegetarian dishes, and light lunches or snacks; bdrms; cl Sun pm, 26 Dec, 1 Jan; partial disabled access. £50

SUTTON GAULT TL4279 **Anchor** *Bury Lane (01353) 778537* Very friendly, popular dining pub with gas lamps and candles in four heavily beamed rooms (two are no smoking), log fires and stripped pine furniture; delicious imaginative modern cooking, very good wine list (10 by the glass), well kept real ales, helpful service, and riverbank tables; bdrms; cl 26 Dec; disabled access. £30|**£7.50**

Special thanks to Michael and Jenny Back, Mrs C Dewell

CHESHIRE

A county of great charm; wonderfully varied countryside, pretty villages, and a real diversity of attractions - from the Romans to the Space Age

Cheshire does well for great houses, often with plenty of appeal to children: we've picked Tatton Park in Knutsford, with its lovely grounds and working historic farm, as our Cheshire Family Attraction this year. Arley Hall & Gardens (children like the tractor ride to nearby Stockley Farm) is enjoyable too. The hall and gardens at Lyme Park near Disley, splendid-looking Little Moreton Hall near Congleton and the unusual Adlington Hall have a great deal to offer adult tastes. Pretty Gawsworth Hall has outdoor plays and concerts, while Tabley House boasts an exceptional collection of paintings; Norton Priory in Runcorn and Capesthorne Hall are also rewarding. Lovely for summer strolls, there are gardens at Neston, Cholmondeley, Kettleshulme and Scholar Green (children prefer the busy water gardens in Nantwich).

Quarry Bank Mill & Country Park at Styal is an ideal family-friendly introduction to the Industrial Revolution, and other good heritage centres include the Salt Museum in Northwich, and the three silk museums in Macclesfield. Learning about chemistry becomes an adventure at Catalyst in Widnes, and a visit to Hack Green Secret Nuclear Bunker (Nantwich) is a haunting experience. The friendly motor museum at Mouldsworth has a splendid assortment of cars.

Where to stay

BEESTON SJ5559 **Wild Boar Hotel** *Whitchurch Rd, Beeston, Tarporley, Cheshire CW6 9NW (01829) 260309* **£105.75**, plus special breaks; 37 rms with appealing touches such as fresh fruit. Striking timbered 17th-c former hunting lodge, much extended over the years, with relaxed and comfortable bars and lounges, enjoyable bar meals and formal beamed restaurant, and friendly, professional service; disabled access; dogs in ground floor bedrooms only

BICKLEY MOSS SJ5450 **Cholmondeley Arms** *Cholmondeley, Malpas, Cheshire SY14 8HN (01829) 720300* **£60***, plus special breaks; 6 rms. Airy converted Victorian schoolhouse close to castle and gardens (famously, Cholmondeley is pronounced 'Chumley'), with lots of atmosphere, very friendly staff, interesting furnishings, open fire, excellent imaginative bar food and very good choice of wines; disabled access; dogs welcome anywhere

BROXTON SJ4754 **Egerton Arms** *Whitchurch Rd, Broxton, Chester, Cheshire CH3 9JW (01829) 782241* **£51.45**; 7 attractive rms. Welcoming neatly kept family inn with handsome big dark-panelled bar, enjoyable reasonably priced food in dining room, well kept real ales, decent wines by the glass, consistently friendly service, and garden with children's play area and pleasant country views

CHESTER SJ4065 **Castle House** *23 Castle St, Chester CH1 2DS (01244) 350354* **£52***, plus special breaks; 5 comfortable rms, 3 with own bthrm. Small carefully preserved 16th-c guest house in the middle of the city, with helpful friendly owners and fine breakfasts; dogs welcome in bedrooms

CHESTER SJ4066 **Chester Grosvenor** *56-58 Eastgate St, Chester CH1 1LT (01244) 324024* **£210**, plus special breaks; 80 large, pristine rms. Gabled and half-

timbered luxury hotel with antiques and oil paintings in drawing room, a club-like
library for light lunches and tea, two restaurants (one a brasserie) with imaginative
food, outstanding service, and use of country club; cl 25-26 Dec; disabled access

CHESTER SJ3965 **Mitchell's** *28 Hough Green, Chester CH4 8JQ (01244) 679004*
£56; 7 cottagey rms. Handsome Victorian house with open fire, old clocks, period
furnishings, and garden views in comfortable sitting room; helpful, friendly owners
and homely breakfast room with big central table; cl Christmas period

COTEBROOK SJ5765 **Alvanley Arms** *Cotebrook, Tarporley, Cheshire CW6 9DS
(01829) 760200* **£60**; 7 rms. Handsome 400-year-old sandstone inn with pleasant
beamed rooms (three areas are no smoking), big open fire, a chintzy little hall, shire
horse décor (pictures, photographs, horseshoes, horse brasses, harness and
bridles), generous helpings of good food, and a garden with lake and trout; shire
horse stud next door

FULLERS MOOR SJ4854 **Frogg Manor** *Nantwich Rd, Broxton, Chester CH3 9JH
(01829) 782629* **£125**, plus special breaks; 7 lavishly decorated rms with thoughtful
extras. Enjoyably eccentric Georgian manor house full of ornamental frogs and
antique furniture, open fires and ornate dried-flower arrangements, a restful
upstairs sitting room, cosy little bar, a large collection of 30s/40s records, and good
english cooking in elegant dining room which leads to conservatory overlooking the
gardens; disabled access; dogs welcome in bedrooms

HIGHER BURWARDSLEY SJ5257 **Pheasant** *Higher Burwardsley, Burwardsley,
Chester, Cheshire CH3 9PF (01829) 770434* **£70**, plus special breaks; 10 rms in
comfortably converted sandstone-built barn. Pretty, recently refurbished, half-
timbered 17th-c inn on top of Peckforton Hills with marvellous views, an attractive
bar with a huge log fire in the see-through fireplace, no smoking conservatory, and
good modern cooking; lots of walks nearby; disabled access

HIGHER WYCH SJ4943 **Mill House** *Higher Wych, Malpas, Cheshire SY14 7JR
(01948) 780362* **£44**; 3 rms, most with own bthrm. Very welcoming and friendly
B&B in former farmhouse on the Wales/England border, with relaxed atmosphere
and good breakfasts - evening meals by arrangement; self-catering cottage; cl
Christmas-New Year

HOOLE SJ4167 **Hoole Hall** *Warrington Rd, Hoole, Chester, Cheshire CH2 3PD
(01244) 408800* **£116**, plus special breaks; 97 well equipped rms, some no smoking.
Extended and attractively refurbished 18th-c hall with five acres of gardens, good food in
two restaurants, and friendly service; good disabled access; dogs welcome in bedrooms

KNUTSFORD SJ7479 **Longview** *51-55 Manchester Rd, Knutsford, Cheshire WA16
0LX (01565) 632119* **£89.50**; 26 rms. Friendly Victorian hotel with attractive
period and reproduction furnishings open fires in original fireplaces, pleasant cellar
bar, ornate restaurant, and good well presented food; cl Christmas and New Year;
dogs welcome in bedrooms

MACCLESFIELD SJ9271 **Sutton Hall Hotel** *Bullocks Lane, Sutton, Macclesfield,
Cheshire SK11 0HE (01260) 253211* **£90**; 9 marvellous rms. Welcoming and
secluded historic baronial hall, full of character, with stylish rooms, high black beams,
stone fireplaces, suits of armour and so forth, friendly service, and good food; can
arrange clay shooting/golf/fishing; partial disabled access; dogs welcome in bedrooms

MOBBERLEY SJ7779 **Laburnum Cottage** *Knutsford Rd, Mobberley, Knutsford,
Cheshire WA16 7PU (01565) 872464* **£57**; 5 pretty rms. Neatly kept and friendly no
smoking country guest house in an acre of landscaped garden; relaxed atmosphere
in comfortable lounge with books, a sunny conservatory, and very good food; dogs
by arrangement

MOLLINGTON SJ3869 **Crabwall Manor** *Parkgate Rd, Mollington, Chester CH1
6NE (01244) 851666* **£175***, plus special breaks; 48 very comfortable individually
decorated rms. Partly castellated, largely 17th-c hotel in landscaped grounds with
restful, attractive rooms, open fires, very good modern british cooking in elegant
restaurant, and friendly professional service; leisure club; disabled access

POTT SHRIGLEY SJ9478 **Shrigley Hall** *Shrigley Park, Pott Shrigley, Macclesfield,
Cheshire SK10 5SB (01625) 575757* **£130**, plus special breaks; 150 smart well

equipped rms, some with country views. In over 260 acres of parkland, this impressive country house has a splendid entrance hall with several elegant rooms leading off, enjoyable food in the orangery and restaurant, and good service from friendly staff; championship golf course, fishing, tennis, and leisure centre in former church building; plenty to do nearby; disabled access; dogs welcome in bedrooms

PRESTBURY SJ9077 **White House** *The Village, Prestbury, Macclesfield, Cheshire SK10 4HP (01625) 829376* **£123***, plus wknd breaks; 11 individual, stylish and well equipped rms with antiques, in separate manor just a short walk from the restaurant. Carefully restored Georgian house (partly refurbished this year) with an exceptionally friendly and pretty restaurant, imaginative modern british cooking, thoughtful wine list and a spacious bar; breakfast in small conservatory lounge or in room; cl 25-26 Dec; children over 10

ROWTON SJ4464 **Rowton Hall** *Whitchurch Rd, Rowton, Chester CH3 6AD (01244) 335262* **£150**, plus wknd breaks; 38 attractive rms. 18th-c country house in eight acres of award-winning gardens with tennis courts and croquet lawn; conservatory lounge, comfortable bar, log fires, a relaxed atmosphere, and smart oak-panelled restaurant; swimming pool, gym, sauna and solarium; children must be over 6 to use health club; disabled access

SANDBACH SJ7560 **Old Hall** *High St, Sandbach, Cheshire CW11 1AL (01270) 761221* **£70***, plus special breaks; 11 comfortable rms. Fine Jacobean timbered hotel with lots of original panelling and fireplaces, relaxing lounge, friendly welcome, and popular, attractive restaurant; disabled access; dogs welcome

SANDIWAY SJ5968 **Nunsmere Hall** *Tarporley Rd, Oakmere, Northwich, Cheshire CW8 2ES (01606) 889100* **£220**w inc dinner; 36 individually decorated rms. Luxurious lakeside hotel on wooded peninsula with elegantly furnished lounge and library, oak-panelled cocktail bar, very good modern cooking, and a warm welcome from courteous staff; children over 12 in evening restaurant; disabled access

TARPORLEY SJ5562 **Swan** *50 High St, Tarporley, Cheshire CW6 0AG (01829) 733838* **£78**; 16 rms. Well managed Georgian inn with a good mix of individual tables and chairs in attractive bar, well kept real ales, decent wines, and quite a few malt whiskies, good food from extensive menu, nice breakfasts, and friendly staff; limited disabled access; dogs welcome in bedrooms

TILSTON SJ4650 **Tilston Lodge** *Tilston, Malpas, Cheshire SY14 7DR (01829) 250223* **£70***; 3 thoughtfully equipped rms, 2 with four-posters. Warmly friendly and beautifully restored Victorian house in 16 acres of grounds that include award-winning gardens, ponds, and a collection of rare breed farm animals; comfortable and attractive public rooms with original features, open fire in dining room, and good breakfasts with home-made jams and marmalades

WESTON SJ7352 **White Lion** *31 Main Rd, Weston, Crewe, Cheshire CW2 5NA (01270) 500303* **£68**, plus wknd breaks; 16 comfortable rms. Pretty 17th-c timbered inn with low beams (several no smoking areas), a friendly relaxed atmosphere, well kept real ales and popular food; own bowling green, and they have a licence for civil marriages; cl Christmas and New Year; dogs welcome in bedrooms

WETTENHALL SJ6261 **Boot & Slipper** *Wettenhall, Winsford, Cheshire CW7 4DN (01270) 528238* **£48**; 4 attractive rms with showers. Cosily refurbished 16th-c coaching inn on small country lane, with low beams and open fire in quiet bars, a relaxed friendly atmosphere, and good breakfasts; children over 11

WORLESTON SJ6555 **Rookery Hall** *Main Rd, Worleston, Nantwich, Cheshire CW5 6DQ (01270) 610016* **£150**, plus special breaks; 45 individually decorated rms. Fine early 19th-c hotel in 38 acres of lovely parkland, with elegant lounges, log fires, intimate panelled restaurant with enjoyable food, and friendly service; disabled access; dogs in bedrooms in Coach House

---

Please let us know what you think of places in the *Guide*. Use the report forms at the back of the book, write us a letter or log on to www.goodguides.co.uk

To see and do

Cheshire Family Attraction of the Year

KNUTSFORD SJ7481 **Tatton Park** On Knutsford's northern edge, this busy estate has so much going on you may not be able to explore it all properly in one day - happily, a sensibly organised ticketing system means you pay only for the bits you want to see, so don't have to rush around trying to get your money's worth. You pay for parking, which includes entry to the grounds and to the adventure playground (these two alone can easily fill a couple of hours), then there are separate charges for the working farm, Tudor Old Hall, gardens, and the handsome neo-classical mansion at the heart of the estate. Children will probably want to head first for the Home Farm, which works as it did 80 years ago, with vintage machinery and rare breeds of animals. After that the magnificently opulent mansion is a high point, with a splendid collection of furnishings, porcelain and paintings (inc two Canalettos) in its State rooms, and tours of the restored kitchens and servants' quarters. The lovely grounds boast an Edwardian rose garden, italian and japanese gardens, orangery and fern house, and lead to a big country park with mature trees, lakes, signposted walks and deer and waterfowl; you can fish or take a carriage ride. Open only on summer weekends, the Tudor Old Hall hints at the long history of the site. In the summer holidays there may be extra activities, particularly on the farm, and among several appealing shops one specialises in produce from the estate. It's a delightful place to spend an undemanding day, whether you're headed for the attractions, or simply taking a carload for a picnic in the park. Meals, snacks, shop, disabled access; park and gardens open all year (exc winter Mons and 25 Dec), the rest open Tues-Sun (and bank hols) Apr-Sept, exc Tudor hall, which is open only pm wknds then (plus some wknds in Dec - best to check), and the farm, which is open pm wknds in winter too; (01625) 534400. Entry to the park is £3.80 per car (free for cyclists and pedestrians), then £3 for each of the mansion, gardens, farm or Tudor Hall. A ticket allowing entry for any two attractions is £4.60; NT (though as the site is managed by the county council, members still have to pay for all exc the mansion and garden; the Tudor Hall and farm are half price).

ADLINGTON SJ9080
Adlington Hall This unusual black and white timbered manor house with Georgian additions has been home to the Legh family since 1315. The impressive Tudor great hall has an original hammerbeam roof, huge Elizabethan windows and the largest 17th-c organ in the country; they'll show you the hunting song written by family friend Handel on a visit here. The Capability Brown-style 18th-c gardens have a fine yew walk, rose garden, maze and lime avenue. Snacks, limited disabled access; open pm Weds Jun-Aug, phone to check; (01625) 820875; £4.50. The Windmill over at Whiteley Green is a useful family pub.
ARLEY SJ6780
Arley Hall & Gardens and Stockley Farm The dramatic-looking house is Victorian Jacobean, but the same family

have lived on the estate for over 500 years, so there are older furnishings and mementoes. Outside, the charming grounds include walled, scented and herb gardens, shrub rose collection and a more informal woodland area; also an interesting private chapel. Meals, snacks, shop and nursery, disabled access; open Tues-Sun 9 Apr-26 Sept and bank hols (hall open pm Tues and Sun); (01565) 777353; £4.50 grounds and gardens, hall £2.50 extra. From the car park, tractor and trailer rides take you to nearby **Stockley Farm**, a friendly working dairy farm that's ideal for younger children; (01565) 777323; £4.50.
ASTBURY SJ8461
This is a delightful village, and its church is well worth a look - graceful detached spire, spectacular roofing, rich carving. The Egerton Arms is a charming pub.

AUDLEM WHARF SJ6543
For walkers, a good access point for the **Shropshire Union Canal** which threads through this area, giving interesting stretches for strolls; just outside the village is an impressive flight of over a dozen locks.

BARTHOMLEY SJ7752
This charming village has lots of thatch, black and white timbering, quiet up-and-down lanes, a fine church, and a delightfully unspoilt pub, the White Lion.

BEESTON SJ5459
Beeston Castle Well worth the steep climb, this ruined 13th-c fortress gives wonderful views from its perch on a dramatic crag; Richard II is said to have left treasure buried here. Good exhibition covers site's 4,000-year history; special events in summer. Snacks, shop; cl 24-26 Dec and 1 Jan; (01829) 260464; £3.20, EH. The pub of the same name, handy for the canal, does good value generous food.

BOLLINGTON SJ9377
Bollington is well worth a stroll: handsome stone milltown buildings, unchanged 19th-c shops and houses, and overhead a great stone aqueduct and its later rival the railway viaduct. The Church House is a useful pub, and on the E edge of town the Poachers (Ingersley Rd) or Redway (Kerridge) are good start points for the viewpoint Kerridge Hill (crowned by a curious folly known as White Nancy). You can also pick up the long-distance Gritstone Trail for walks among high stone-walled pastures.

BRIDGEMERE SJ7243
Bridgemere Garden World (A51) A garden-lover's paradise - 25 acres of gardens, plants, glasshouses and garden furniture, with more plants in more varieties than almost anywhere else in Britain (indoor and outdoor), and professional help on hand for any sort of query. There's an art and crafts shop and an aquatics area. Best to visit in the morning before the coach parties arrive. Good meals and snacks, excellent shop, disabled access; cl 25-26 Dec; (01270) 521100; free.

BUNBURY SJ5758
Bunbury has pretty cottages around its 14th-c church, a well restored 19th-c watermill, and an excellent dining pub, the Dysart Arms.

BURWARDSLEY SJ5257
Cheshire Candle Workshops
Popular demonstrations of candle-making and other crafts, and a big craft shop. Meals, snacks, disabled access; cl 24-26 Dec and Mon-Tues Jan-Feb; (01829) 770401; free. The Pheasant is good for lunch, with great views.

CAPESTHORNE SJ8473
Capesthorne Hall 18th-c family home of the Bromley-Davenports, who have lived on the site since Domesday; fine paintings include Lowry's unusual interpretation of the house's striking exterior, and there's a good collection of Roman and Greek busts and vases. Also lovely Georgian chapel and 60 acres of gardens and woodland. Snacks, disabled access; open pm Weds, Sun and bank hols Apr-Oct; (01625) 861221; £6.50, £4 garden and chapel only. The Blacksmiths Arms at Henbury (A537 towards Macclesfield) is a decent family dining pub, if you don't want the longer trip to the Dog over at Peover Heath.

CHESTER SJ4066
A great place to visit, Chester was the site of an important fort in Roman times, and later plentiful river traffic kept it rich. Nowadays, it's a cheerful bustling place with interesting shops, and a good variety of places to eat and drink. The old centre is ringed by a medieval **town wall** that's more complete than any other in Britain. You can walk the whole way round, enjoying marvellous views; there are usually summer exhibitions, and music festivals for you to visit along the way. Partly because of the limit set by the wall, the centre of town is easy to get around on foot, not too big, and with the main streets pretty much free of cars (there may be a few buses), although in summer the sheer number of tourists and shoppers can still make them appear congested. If you're driving in, you'll be shunted round to one of the big car parks, and you may have to queue a while to get a space, so it's best to use the park and ride on the major approach roads. Chester's racecourse, the Roodee, is the oldest in Britain; it still has fashionable races May-Sept, with lively family events in Aug; (01244) 304600. The quaint Albion (Park St) and

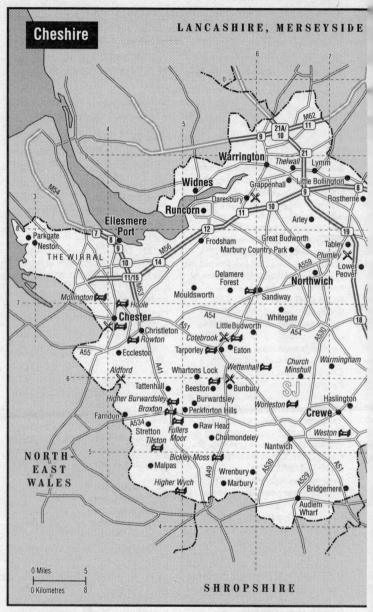

Cheshire

LANCASHIRE, MERSEYSIDE

THE WIRRAL

NORTH-EAST WALES

SHROPSHIRE

canalside Old Harkers Arms (Russell St) both have good food.
Chester Castle Though now largely moated by car parks and occupied by civil servants, the castle has some impressive buildings, both medieval and grand-manner late 18th-c, although only a few rooms are open to the public; free. The **Military Museum** here is worth a visit; it covers the history of the Cheshire Regiment, with interactive displays, re-creations and dioramas. Shop, disabled access; cl around 2 wks over Christmas and

& MANCHESTER

8   9

0

7   M56

Disley

Styal   Poynton

Middlewood Way

Mobberley   Kettleshulme

Adlington

A538

Knutsford   Prestbury   Bollington

Kerridge Hill

Nether Alderley   Pott Shrigley

A535   A537   Capesthorne   **Macclesfield**

Jodrell   Teggs Nose Country Park

Bank   A536

Lower Withington   Gawsworth   A54

Swettenham   A523

M6   A54

A50   Congleton   Macclesfield Canal

17   Cloud

Sandbach   Astbury

Hassall Green

Mow Cop

Scholar Green

16

Barthomley

STAFFORDSHIRE

New Year; (01244) 327617; £2.
Chester Cathedral Not unlike an
ordinary church at first glance, this is far
more impressive inside, with some
marvellous medieval carving in and
above the choir stalls, and some fine
vaulting. Many of the former abbey

buildings survived the Reformation, so
the precincts still include peaceful
arcaded flagstoned cloisters, a medieval
chapter house, and older Norman parts
inc a refectory - brought back into use
as an excellent café (they usually have a
pianist Tues, Fri lunchtimes). Handel
first rehearsed *The Messiah* here in
1742, and they show a copy of his
marked score. All the carved bosses
have been gilded, and a model of the
cathedral has a braille text. Shop,
disabled access; cl for Sun am services
(up to 12.30pm); (01244) 324756; free,
£3 suggested donation. There are quiet
cobbled Georgian lanes around Abbey
Sq, behind the cathedral a little way
down Northgate.
Chester Visitor Centre (Vicars
Lane) Lots of helpful information, and
an exhibition on the city's history (inc a
reconstruction of the Rows), brass
rubbings and a video. Tearoom, shop,
disabled access; cl 25-26 Dec, 1 Jan;
(01244) 351609; free. Guided walks
leave from here 10.30am daily, and also
2.15pm May-Oct; £3.50.
Chester Zoo (A41, 2m N) The biggest
and undoubtedly one of the best zoos in
Britain, constantly developing and
improving. Its several thousand animals
are housed in spacious near-natural
enclosures (their jaguar enclosure is the
best in Europe) spread over 80 acres of
glorious gardens, with 11 miles of
pathways. More than 200 of the species
here are classed as rare or endangered,
and they put a great deal of effort into
breeding, so there's usually quite a
range of baby animals. Highlights
include the splendidly laid out
Chimpanzee Island, the komodo
dragons and amazon parrots in the
Islands in Danger tropical habitat, and
the remarkable free-flying bat cave.
There's a full programme of feeding
sessions throughout the day, and
smaller children can pet the animals at
the well organised farm; they've
recently added a new play area. A
waterbus can ferry you between the
attractions, and an overhead train zips
around the grounds (£1.80 each mid-
July-Aug, £1.50 rest of year). Meals,
snacks, shops, good disabled access,
tactile maps and braille guides; cl 25
Dec; (01244) 380280; £11.

Dewa Roman Experience
(Pierpoint Lane, off Bridge St) Re-
creation of Chester's Roman heyday,
with the sights, sounds and smells of
streets, fortresses, and even
bathhouses. It starts off as though
you're on board a Roman galley, and at
the end is an exhibition of Roman,
Saxon and medieval relics found on the
site. Shop, disabled access; cl 25-26
Dec; (01244) 343407; £3.95.

Grosvenor Museum (Grosvenor St)
This interesting museum breathes life
into all sorts of detail about Chester
and its surroundings; an unexpected
highlight is the gallery of huge Roman
tombstones. A conservatory shop leads
to a Georgian house with restored
Georgian and Victorian rooms, an art
gallery and displays of locally made
silver and furniture; interactive
computers and good changing
exhibitions. Good disabled access -
touch-screen computers give
wheelchair visitors a virtual view of the
exhibits upstairs, and there are large
print and braille labels. Cl Sun am, Good
Fri, 25-26 Dec and 1 Jan; (01244)
402008; free.

Roman Chester Research has led to
speculation that Emperor Vespasian
foresaw a key role for Chester at the
heart of an enlarged province of
Britannia. This would help to explain
the city's grandiose walls, constructed
with unusually large sandstone blocks in
a manner designed to impress, with
imposing ornamental gateways. Other
remains include some broken Roman
columns from the fortress baths in a
neat and peaceful garden running
outside the city walls by the Newgate.
Nearby is the excavated part of a very
large Roman amphitheatre - probably
big enough to seat nearly 5,000 people.
Other relics can pop up in unexpected
places: Spud-U-Like (Bridge St) and
Miss Selfridge (Northgate St) show off
well preserved sections of hypocaust.

The Rows Giving Chester's heart a
magnificently Tudor look, these are sets
of timbered two-storey shops with
open upper arcaded galleries, radiating
from the central Cross (town crier
usually here 12pm Tues-Sat May-Aug).
Parts are thought to be at least 700
years old. Besides being attractive to

look at and charming to walk through,
they form the heart of the city's
shopping centre (and include a useful
pub, the Boot, on Eastgate Row N).
Watergate is one of the finest
stretches, with some of Chester's most
glorious timber-framed buildings,
though more fine buildings jetty out
over the pavement in Lower Bridge St
(for instance, the late 17th-c Falcon,
once a house used by the Duke of
Westminster's ancestors but now a
well restored pub), and in St Werbergh
St off Eastgate (built in the 1890s,
despite their Elizabethan look).

Waterside Chester The tree-shaded
Groves look out to the medieval bridge
over the River Dee - very photogenic
and a pleasant place for a stroll or
picnic. Several companies offer boat
trips on the river from here daily in
summer; around £5 for 45 mins in a
rowing boat or 15 mins in a motor boat.
The bridge at the N end of Northgate
gives a close view of the so-called
Bridge of Sighs over the canal far below.

CHOLMONDELEY SJ5351
Cholmondeley Castle Gardens
Very pretty to stroll through, with
acres of colourful ornamental gardens
around elegant castle buildings (not
open). Also fine woodland and lakeside
walks, llamas and entertaining pygmy
goats among the rare breeds, aviary,
play area, and an ancient private chapel.
Snacks, shop and plant centre, limited
disabled access (there's a new
wheelchair route); open Sun, Weds,
Thurs and bank hols (exc Good Fri)
Apr-Sept; (01829) 720383; £3.50. The
Cholmondeley Arms is good for lunch.

CHRISTLETON SJ4465
Though now almost part of Chester,
this is still very much a distinct village,
with a classic green, pond with a nesting
swan, pretty almshouses and medieval
packhorse bridges; you can walk along
the canal into the town centre. The
Plough has good value food.

CLOUD SJ9063
There are good hilly walks here, and the
craggy summit, with steep drops to the
Cheshire Plain, gives grand views; the
Coach & Horses at Timbersbrook is a
useful nearby pub.

CONGLETON SJ8562
Congleton Museum Good clear

displays at this interesting local history museum; highlights inc a prehistoric log boat and ancient burial urn, and you can see the Elizabethan royal town charter; also re-creations and touch-screen computers. Shop, disabled access; usually cl am (exc Sat), all Mon, Easter Sun, and a few days over Christmas; (01260) 276360; £2. Town walks leave from here on the last Sun of the month at 2pm (£2.50 inc refreshments).

Little Moreton Hall (Scholar Green; A34 S) One of Britain's best-preserved half-timbered buildings, its splendid black and white exterior pretty much unchanged since it was built in 1580, and covered with such a profusion of lines the effect is almost dizzying. The inside, though largely unfurnished, has some interesting features too, especially the wainscoted Long Gallery, Great Hall and chapel. There's a re-creation of a typical 17th-c knot garden - and make sure you don't miss the built-in dog kennel; phone for information about open-air theatre. Meals, snacks, shop, disabled access to ground floor only; usually open pm Weds-Sun and bank hols Apr-Oct, then wknds Nov to mid-Dec, but phone to check; (01260) 272018; £4.75, NT. The Brownlow Inn nearby is popular for lunch. **Heritage Narrow Boats** at Kent Green have electric narrow boats to hire by the day; (01782) 785700; £80 wkdys for up to 12 people (£95 wknds) - very satisfying, gliding along in silence.

CREWE SJ7055
A 19th-c railway town, smartened up a lot in the last decade or two (they're currently developing a new leisure area on the edge of the town) with bargains in the market, a pedestrianised centre, colourful Queens Park and useful foyer restaurant in the Victorian theatre.

Railway Age (Vernon Way) A museum with a wide range of locomotives from electric through to steam, along with models, miniature and standard-gauge railways and other displays. Shop (not always open), some disabled access; usually cl Nov to mid-Feb; (01270) 212130; £3.50 wkdys, £4.50 wknds (when there's more going on). The Crown (Earle St) is handy for something to eat, with a model shop nearby.

DARESBURY SJ5882
Daresbury church The 'Alice in Wonderland' stained-glass window commemorates Lewis Carroll, who was born here. There are attractive canalside strolls, and the Ring o' Bells is good for lunch.

DELAMERE FOREST SJ5571
Several square miles of mainly coniferous plantation, with some older oak and other woodland, inc plenty of open stretches and picnic places, and some small stretches of reedy water. A section of the 30-mile **Sandstone Trail** long-distance path takes in much of the best bits, with good access from several places inc Delamere and Hatchmere, and decent prettily placed pubs in both villages.

DISLEY SJ9682
Lyme Park The Hall at the centre of this wonderful country estate is a magnificent blend of Elizabethan, Georgian and Regency architecture and styles, and you can now explore two bedrooms, a dressing room and bathroom. Tours are unguided, so you can take your time looking at the intricate carvings, and lovely tapestries, paintings and furniture. There's a particularly grand staircase, and a fine collection of english clocks. Around the house are 17 acres of Victorian gardens with orangery, sunken dutch garden and wilderness garden, and a sprawling ancient park with a restored hunting tower, herds of red deer, and nature trails inc one suitable for wheelchairs; if you get a feeling of déjà vu, it'll be from the estate's starring role in the TV series *The Forsyte Saga*. Meals, snacks, shop, disabled access (to part of the house only); house open pm Fri-Tues Apr-Oct, garden open Apr-Oct, plus wknds Nov; the park is open all year; (01663) 766492; *£3.80 per car to go in the park, then *£5.80 house and garden, *£4.20 house only, *£2.70 garden only. NT. The White Horse in the pleasant hillside village is a useful food stop, with OAP lunch days. There's a pleasant walk down to the canal, and for more committed hikers the long-distance **Gritstone Trail** starts from the park and runs along the western flanks of the Peak District. It's well marked and offers a few days' walking of the highest quality.

EATON SJ5763

Eaton is a classic Cheshire village, with picture-postcard combinations of thatch, stone and timbering. The Alvanley Arms over at Cotebrook has good generous food.

ECCLESTON SJ4162

This romantically eclectic estate village was built for the Duke of Westminster, with a richly expansive sandstone church that's a culmination of Victorian ecclesiastical architecture.

ELLESMERE PORT SJ4174

Blue Planet (off A5117 nr M53 junction 10) One of Britain's most stunning aquariums, this includes a dramatic 71-metre (233-ft) viewing tunnel through sharks, stingrays and nearly 16,000 tons of water; a moving walkway lets you trundle along gawping. Knowledgeable staff (many of them marine biologists) are on hand to answer questions, and they give talks throughout the day. Good shows in the Aquatheatre, where you can watch divers feeding the creatures; they use underwater microphones to chat with the audience. The main displays re-create water environments from around the world, and touchpools give children the chance to handle starfish and the like. As well as fish they have reptiles, insects, and now otters too; their encounter sessions can introduce you to everything from toads and hissing cockroaches to toxic frogs. Also several film and slide shows, and free face painting. Meals, snacks, shop, good disabled access; cl 25 Dec; (0870) 4448440; £8.50 adults. Nearby on this S edge of town is the huge factory outlet shopping village, **Cheshire Oaks**, a great place to pick up bargains.

Boat Museum 🅕 (South Pier Rd) Nicely set in a historic dock complex, a huge floating collection of canal boats, as well as steam engines, a blacksmith's forge, workers' cottages, stables, big indoor exhibitions (inc one about the families that lived and worked on the waterways), and boat trips. Shop, mostly disabled access; cl Thurs and Fri Nov-Mar, and a few days over Christmas; (0151) 355 5017; £5.50. Parts of the surrounding dock have been redeveloped with craft workshops and the like. The

Woodlands (Chester Rd) is a useful pub/restaurant (with its own bowling green).

FARNDON SJ4154

Charming rustic two-mile riverside walk along welsh border from car park by arched medieval Dee bridge; the Nags Head is a useful place to pause for lunch.

FRODSHAM SJ5075

Foxhill Arboretum (off B5393, S of Frodsham) As we went to press, the future of this arboretum (which has a mix of rare conifer and broadleaf trees, from dawn redwood and spanish firs to native elms) was uncertain, so best to phone first; (01928) 739189.
Netherton Hall (A56 Frodsham—Helsby) has good food all day.

GAWSWORTH SJ8969

Gawsworth Hall Exceptionally pretty timbered manor house dating back to Norman times, the former home of Mary Fitton, possibly the Dark Lady of Shakespeare's Sonnets; plenty of fine furniture, stained glass, pictures and sculptures. In summer the open-air theatre has a well chosen range of concerts and plays; good gardens and park too. Snacks, shop, disabled access to gardens; open pm Sun-Weds and bank hols 8 Apr-3 Oct (pm daily early Jun-Aug), best to check; (01260) 223456; £4.50. The village has fine houses in parkland, ponds, an interesting church and an unusual unspoilt farm pub, while the Sutton Hall Hotel over at Sutton Lane Ends is quite handy for lunch.

GRAPPENHALL SJ6386

This attractive village is worth a visit for the grinning cat on its church tower, which inspired Lewis Carroll; the Parr Arms by the church has good home cooking, and there are peaceful canalside strolls here.

GREAT BUDWORTH SJ6677

In attractive rich countryside, this is a quaint purpose-built estate village; the church is imposing (as is the George & Dragon pub), and there are many pretty cottages.

HASLINGTON SJ7358

Lakemore Country Park (Lane End Farm) Readers enjoy this 36-acre country park (now with full zoo status), and animals range from miniature donkeys and endangered birds of prey to ring-tailed lemurs, wallabies and raccoons; they've recently added an otter sanctuary. Nature trails link five man-made lakes, and there are outdoor and indoor playgrounds - extra charge for donkey rides. Open Weds-Sun Apr-Oct and daily during school hols; (01270) 253556; £4.50. The friendly Fox nearby has decent food.

JODRELL BANK SJ7970

Jodrell Bank Observatory & Arboretum (off A535, nr M6 junction 18) The science centre is being knocked down and rebuilt over the next three years (there's a little exhibition in the café), but the huge radio telescope remains - the second largest in the world and as big as the dome of St Paul's; a new walkway is being built to let visitors view it from all angles. The 35-acre arboretum includes 2,500 varieties of tree and shrub, and there are several nature trails; special events and activities. Meals, snacks, picnic area, shop, good disabled access; cl Mon Nov to mid-Mar, and 23-27, 31 Dec, 1, 6-10 Jan; (01477) 571339; £5. The Olde Red Lion at Goostrey is quite handy for lunch.

KERRIDGE HILL SJ9477

Above Bollington, and with fine views, this is topped by the curious folly known as White Nancy. Good walks here, and to the E - where the quaint Highwayman pub (B5470 N of Rainow) also has good views, and is handy for the long-distance Gritstone Trail.

KETTLESHULME SJ9879

Dunge Valley Hidden Gardens 🔠 (off B5470) Colourful gardens in Peak District countryside, esp good for rhododendrons, acers, magnolias (May, Jun), roses and unusual perennials. Meals, snacks, plant sales, limited disabled access; cl Sept-Mar, Mon exc bank hols, plus Tues-Weds mid-Jun to Aug, best to check; (01663) 733787; *£3. The Crag at nearby Wildboarclough does decent food, and fits in well with a walk to the Three Shires Head and the summit of Shutlingsloe.

KNUTSFORD SJ7578

Despite obvious present-day prosperity and some rather heavy traffic, this has a pleasantly old-world feel, with lots of striking Georgian and

other period buildings. It might seem strangely familiar to you if you've read Mrs Gaskell's *Cranford* - its alias.

Tatton Park *See separate family panel on p.50.*

LITTLE BOLLINGTON SJ7286

This peaceful hamlet gives strolls by the Bridgewater Canal and in Dunham Massey deer park; the Swan With Two Nicks is a very pleasant refreshment stop.

LITTLE BUDWORTH SJ5867

Cheshire Herbs Specialist herb nursery growing and selling over 400 different varieties from agrimony to yellow melilot. Shop, disabled access; cl 24 Dec-3 Jan; (01829) 760578; free. The Shrewsbury Arms has good value food.

Little Budworth Common This country park is a strong (and oddly refreshing) contrast to most of this area's richly manicured countryside: poor wild heath with young bogs and scrawny birch woods.

LOWER PEOVER SJ7474

Many people's favourite Cheshire village: cobbled lanes, glorious 14th-c black and white timbered church, quiet watermeadows and an appealing pub, the Bells of Peover.

LOWER WITHINGTON SJ8169

Welltrough Dried Flowers (signed off A535) Helpful and friendly dried and silk flowers specialist based on a working arable farm. Snacks, shop, disabled access; cl 25-27 Dec, 1-3 Jan; (01477) 571616; free. The Black Swan is a pleasant country dining pub. Further along the A34 at Marton is a simple 14th-c shingle-roofed black and white timbered **church** in unpromising surroundings.

LYMM SJ6887

There are pretty cottages in The Dingle; the walk up to the lake at Lymm Dam is a pleasant stroll, and the Spread Eagle (Eagle Brow) has good value food.

MACCLESFIELD SJ9173

Away from the modern shopping streets are plenty of fine old buildings associated with the early industrial revolution and the silk industry; the weavers' cottages on Paradise St with their wide garret windows are of special note. You can buy a joint ticket to the two silk museums and Paradise Mill (£6.20 for three, £4.15 for two). Behind

St Michael's church is a more ancient core with quaint little cobbled alleys, the famous 108 steps, and fine views across the town to the Pennines. The tea shop at Arighi Bianchi furniture shop (Silk Rd) is highly recommended. The Sutton Hall Hotel just S is best for lunch.

Hare Hill (off B5087 NW) Acres of lovely parkland with walled garden, pergola, fine spring flowers, and rhododendrons and azaleas in May (when the garden is open daily - phone for dates). Some disabled access; usually open Weds-Thurs, Sat-Sun and bank hols Apr-Oct; (01625) 584412; £2.70 (car park £1.50 but refundable when you enter garden); NT. A footpath leads to Alderley Edge.

Paradise Mill (Park Lane) Enthusiastic guides, many of whom are former silk workers, take you around and demonstrate the silk production process on the mill's restored handlooms - room settings give a good idea of 1930s working conditions. Good disabled access; tours are 11.30, 1.00, 2.30 and 3.30; cl am Sun, 25-26 Dec and 1 Jan; (01625) 612045; £3.10. Nearby the **Park Green Silk Museum** is housed in what used to be the art school, where silk designers were trained; displays on the properties of silk and design, and lots of historic machinery. Cl am Sun, 25-26 Dec and 1 Jan; £3.10.

Silk Museum & Heritage Centre ▦ (Roe St) Formerly a Sunday school for children who worked in the silk mills, this heritage centre now houses a good silk museum with audio-visual displays, exhibitions and some fine examples of the end product. Meals, snacks, shop, some disabled access (and audio guides); cl 25-26 Dec, 1 Jan; (01625) 613210; £3.10.

West Park Museum (Prestbury Rd) Small museum with a decent range of decorative arts (inc works by local bird artist Charles Tunnicliffe), and some interesting Egyptian antiquities. Adjacent West Park is pleasant and has one of the largest bowling greens in the country. Shop, disabled access; cl am, all day Mon (exc bank hols), 24-26 Dec, 1 Jan; (01625) 619831; free.

MACCLESFIELD CANAL SJ8965 With good more or less level towpath

walks, this tracks through fine high countryside from the Cheshire county boundary nr Disley to pass Bollington, Macclesfield and Congleton, with plenty of access points. One of the most interesting places is S of the A54 just W of its junction with the A523, where a staggering flight of ten locks leads down to a sturdily elegant iron aqueduct.

MALPAS SJ4847 The most striking thing in this attractive place is the extraordinarily uplifting ceiling in its 14th-c hilltop **church**. There's also a fragmentary castle ruin nearby, as well as pretty cottages and almshouses, and some grander buildings.

MARBURY SJ5645 Some delightful landscapes open up in this village, with its attractive church, lake, wood and canal surroundings.

MARBURY COUNTRY PARK SJ6576 With some quiet short walks, this gives on to the extensive **Budworth Mere**, with sailing, and herons, ducks, grebes and coots pottering around the rushes. The George & Dragon at Great Budworth is good for lunch.

MIDDLEWOOD WAY SJ9482 A sort of linear country park near Macclesfield, this runs along a former railway; attractively bordered with wild flowers and trees, with cycle tracks, and horse riding (from around £12 an hour-long lesson (01625) 872656); several decent pubs in Bollington, one at Whiteley Green. The pleasant stretches around the Poynton inclines are underrated, and the Boars Head here has good value food (all day wknds).

MOULDSWORTH SJ5070 **Mouldsworth Motor Museum** (Smithy Lane) Splendid changing collection of cars, everything from vintage MGs to gleaming Ferraris. It's an especially friendly place, and you really don't have to be a car fiend to enjoy it - the 1930s art deco building and its grounds are very attractive in themselves, and there's plenty to amuse children, with quizzes, play areas and space to run around. There's also a collection of unusual teapots, many from the 1920s and 30s. Shop, disabled access; open pm Sun and bank hols Feb-end Nov, plus pm Weds July and Aug, best to check; (01928) 731781; £3. The Boot over at Boothsdale nr Willington is a good nearby dining pub (food all day wknds and bank hols).

MOW COP SJ8557
Right on the Staffs border is a shaggy steep hill with a castellated folly on top, and a rock pinnacle left by former quarrying; views over Cheshire (the village just behind, which is in Staffs, is a reminder of the contrast with Cheshire's richness). Worth a look if passing.

NANTWICH SJ6552
A pedestrian-only centre protects the splendid 14th-c **church**, with its exceptional carved choir-stalls; look out for the devil forcing open a nun's mouth, and the wife threatening her husband with a ladle. Much of the town, destroyed by a firestorm in 1583, was rebuilt then in intricate black and white timbering, and with countless window-boxes in flower in spring and summer it is a fine sight esp around the centre. Quite a few decent antiques shops, and the picturesque Crown (High St) has good value lunchtime food. As most of south Cheshire's roads seem to intersect at the town, traffic can be a problem. Just N of town **Reaseheath College** (B5074) has a huge annual maize maze; usually open daily in the school summer hols; (01270) 613215; £3.50; they also have lambing wknds in Mar.

Dorfold Hall 🏛 (Acton, A534 just W) Guided tours of this Jacobean country house take in eye-catching plaster ceilings and attractive oak panelling; four centuries of gardening fashions are reflected in the pretty gardens. Open pm Tues and bank hol Mon Apr-Oct; (01270) 625245; £5.

Firs Pottery (Aston; A530 towards Whitchurch) Friendly place organising one-day pottery workshops (half-days for children). Booking essential; (01270) 780345; £30 for a day course, inc lunch (£12.50 children, during school hols). Shop selling all sorts of useful pots; disabled access to ground floor only. A vast array of different flavours of ice-cream are available at **Snugbury's Ice-Cream Farm** (Hurleston, A51 N); cl 25-26 Dec and 1 Jan.

Hack Green Secret Nuclear

Bunker (off A530 S of Nantwich; Baddington) Built in the 1950s, this concrete labyrinth would have hidden civil servants and military commanders in the event of a nuclear war. An ordinary utility building on the surface, inside is crammed with gadgets and interactive displays conjuring up a picture of what life would be like during nuclear fall-out - you can even view the original TV broadcasts that would have been transmitted on all channels before a strike; children's trail. Meals, snacks, shop, disabled access; cl Dec; (01270) 629219; £5.30. The Bhurtpore at Aston (its name commemorating an earlier battlefield) is quite handy for lunch.

Stapeley Water Gardens (A51 about a mile SE) The country's largest and best-regarded water-garden centre, with display pools full of over 350 sorts of water-lily (at their best Jun-Sept), fountains and waterfalls, various gardens, and coldwater and tropical fish (eels, piranhas, stingrays and even black-tip reef sharks). A huge heated glasshouse has palms, parrots and toucans, and the animal room has monkeys, creepy-crawlies, a crocodile and lots of different frogs. Plenty for fishermen, a pet centre and frequent special events. Meals, snacks, shop, disabled access; cl 25 Dec and Easter Sun; (01270) 623868; gardens free; £4.35.

NESTON SJ3075
Ness Botanic Gardens Liverpool University's extensive collection of specimen trees and shrubs, herbaceous plants, renowned heather, rock, rose and water gardens; visitor centre, children's play area and picnic area. Meals, snacks, shop and plant sales (not over Christmas), wheelchair route; cl 25 Dec; (0151) 353 0123; £4.70. The Boathouse and Red Lion in nearby Parkgate are good for a light lunch.

NETHER ALDERLEY SJ8476
Nether Alderley Mill 🏛 Lovely 15th-c watermill with carefully preserved atmosphere, and restored working waterwheels. The Victorian machinery still grinds flour (water supplies permitting). Usually open pm Weds-Fri, Sun and bank hols Apr-Oct; (01625) 584412; £2.20; NT. Nearby Alderley Edge SJ8677 (not to be confused with the straggling suburban

settlement named after it) rises high out of the plain, with good walks through the woodland and fine views of the higher hills to the E.

NORTHWICH SJ6876

Anderton Boat Lift (just N of town) This is one of the great monuments of the canal era, a vast 1875 structure that was the only one of its kind ever built in Britain. Recently restored, it once again lifts crafts more than 15 metres (50ft) between sections of the Trent and Mersey canal; boats enter a water-filled tank (or 'caisson') counterbalanced by another, and gravity does most of the work. There's a new visitor centre (£2.50), and you can go up the lift in a specially designed glass-topped boat; £6.50 (£1 less off peak). Meals, snacks, shop, disabled access; cl beginning Nov-beginning Apr; (01606) 786777; free.

Salt Museum 🖾 (London Rd) Cheshire is the only british county to produce salt on a large scale, and much of it comes from this area. This interesting museum has the industry pretty well covered; microscopes let you see the intricacy of each crystal. Snacks, shop, limited disabled access; cl am wknds, all day Mon (exc bank hols and in Aug), 24-26 Dec; (01606) 41331; £2.25. You can follow the Salt Heritage Trail around some of the other buildings. The Smoker at Plumley (A556 E) is a reliable dining pub.

PARKGATE SJ2879

Once a more important port than Liverpool, this interesting village is the country's only inland seaside resort, the Dee estuary having retreated since its palmy days at the end of the 18th and early 19th c. There's an eerie charm in sitting in the Boathouse or Red Lion on the 'Promenade', looking out over the tussocky marshes to the distant waters and the welsh hills on the far side; there's a good ice-cream shop here too. A similar sense of stranded time can be had at the Harp by the ruined marshside quay near Little Neston; you can walk between the two (and on to Ness Gardens at Ness) along the Dee estuary 'coastal' path.

PECKFORTON HILLS SJ5256

These are tracked by a particularly fine section of the 30-mile **Sandstone**

Trail, with splendid views of real and real-looking romantic castles, and good pubs usefully placed at Bulkeley and Higher Burwardsley. The Trail offers very varied scenery, following the romantically wooded sandstone ridges, crags and outcrops stretching from Overton on the edge of Frodsham in the N (the church here is pretty, and the Ring o' Bells is a most attractive pub, with Mersey views) to the Shropshire border S of Malpas (the ancient Bell o' the Hill pub nr Tushingham down there is another useful stop).

POYNTON SJ9183

Brookside Garden Centre (Macclesfield Rd) A splendid miniature railway chuffs its way through an authentically detailed circuit in a pretty garden setting to a replica West Country station, packed with railway memorabilia; there's also a pottery. Parking is not always easy. Meals, snacks, shop, disabled access (limited on train, phone beforehand); railway runs wknds all year (exc in Christmas hols) plus Weds Apr-Sept and daily mid-July to Aug, best to check; (01625) 872919; train £1, garden centre free. A mile away at Higher Poynton, Coppice Fruit Farm has **pick-your-own**, and the Boars Head does enjoyable food (all day wknds).

PRESTBURY SJ9077

Very prosperous-feeling now, with leafy surroundings, good shops, and for refreshment the smart Legh Arms, doing well under new management. There are pleasant riverside walks to the S, along the Bollin.

RAW HEAD SJ5154

From the A534 nr Harthill a section of the 30-mile Sandstone Trail ascends Raw Head, the most spectacular natural feature of the central Cheshire ridge, with sandstone cliffs weathered into bizarre shapes, and a cave to explore. The Pheasant at Higher Burwardsley is a pleasant nearby haven.

ROSTHERNE SJ7483

As well as charming brick cottages along its quaint cobbled pavement, this picture-postcard village gives a lovely view over one of the county's broadest meres from the graveyard of its attractive timbered church.

RUNCORN SJ5481

Apart from Norton Priory, this New

Town has some enjoyable surprises - such as the Sunday-afternoon **miniature train rides** in the Park on Stockham Lane (Halton); Easter-Sept; 50p. There are views from the nearby ruins of **Halton Castle** up on its grassy hill.

Norton Priory Museum and Gardens ⚑ (Tudor Rd, Manor Park) Lovely 12th-c priory that developed into a now demolished Georgian country house, with exhibitions on medieval monastic life, and sculpture inc a twice-lifesize sandstone statue of St Christopher, said to be carved by an inmate of the priory 600 years ago. There are beautiful woodland gardens and an enchanting 18th-c walled garden. Meals, snacks, shop, disabled access; cl am, 24-26 Dec and 1 Jan, walled garden cl am, and Nov-Mar; (01928) 569895; £3.95.

SANDIWAY SJ6070

Blakemere Craft Centre (Chester Rd) Top-notch craft centre based around restored Edwardian stable block, with interesting range of goods in the 30 shops, aquatic and falconry centre, garden centre and indoor play area. Wknd craft fairs, meals, snacks, disabled access; cl Mon (exc bank hols); (01606) 883261; free.

SCHOLAR GREEN SJ8157

Rode Hall Gardens ⚑ In a Repton landscape, this fine house has been in the same family since it was first built in the early 18th c (though it's been extensively remodelled inside since then); the large gardens include a stylish rose garden, a working Victorian walled kitchen garden, and a grotto and ice-house. Snacks, poor disabled access (steps up to house, pebbled walkways in garden); house open pm Weds and bank hols, garden open pm Tues-Thurs and bank hols beginning Apr-Sept (also 2 wks in Feb for snowdrops); (01270) 873237; £5 house and garden, £3 garden only.

STRETTON SJ4453

Stretton Watermill Working watermill in lovely countryside, which still produces corn, powered by two ancient wheels. Drinks, shop, some disabled access; open pm wknds Apr and Sept, pm Tues-Sun and bank hols May-Aug; (01606) 41331; £1.90. The Cock o' Barton up on the A534 is quite useful for lunch, and a good base for walks.

STYAL SJ8383

Quarry Bank Mill & Styal Estate One of the best and most extensive places in the country to get to grips with the Industrial Revolution. The 18th-c cotton mill that's the centrepiece is still operational, and there's always plenty going on, with lively displays and demonstrations of cotton production spread over five floors; an astounding 50-ton waterwheel still turns every afternoon. The Power gallery has multimedia displays, a good film and interactive exhibits, with activities such as rope-making and dip-dyeing. The Apprentice House in the village outside is a highlight, and enthusiastic guides in period dress explain the lifestyle and 12-hour working days faced by the pauper children who worked here; children love discovering how grim their lives could have been back then, pumping water from the well, testing the straw-filled beds, and stirring the porridge in the kitchen (timed tickets are in operation). The surrounding village is nice to stroll around, with its carefully preserved workers' cottages, chapels and shop, and there are good woodland and waterside walks in the park, with plenty of space for picnics by the river. Meals, snacks, shop, disabled access; mill cl Mon Oct-Mar, Apprentice House cl Mon (exc summer hols), and am Tues-Fri in term-time; (01625) 527468; an all-in ticket is £7.30, mill-only ticket £5.20; free to National Trust members. Parking is £2.50.

SWETTENHAM SJ8067

One of Cheshire's tucked-away comfortable villages - rich paddocks with wrought-iron fences, daffodils in spring in a dell by an old mill, a good dining pub (the Swettenham Arms) behind the partly 13th-c church.

TABLEY SJ7177

Cuckoo Land (Old School House, Nether Tabley) The friendly owners will take you on a guided tour of this huge collection of cuckoo clocks, all made in the Black Forest. They currently have over 550 rare and beautiful clocks, most of them working; five working historic fairground organs are among the other mechanisms on show, as well as a collection of vintage motorcyles. Phone for an appointment; snacks, shop, disabled access; (01565) 633039; £4.50.

Tabley House (A5033, off A556 just S of M6 junction 19) The only Palladian house in the North-West, with a splendid collection of paintings. Sir John Fleming Leicester (whose family lived at Tabley for over 700 years) was the first great collector of british art, and though plans to turn his home into a National Gallery came to nothing, most of the works he assembled are still here, inc pictures by Turner, Reynolds, Henry Thompson and James Ward. Snacks, shop, very good disabled access (though they prefer notice); open pm Thurs-Sun and bank hols Apr-end Oct; (01565) 750151; £4. The Smoker at Plumley is good for lunch.

TARPORLEY SJ5562
Largely bypassed and quietly attractive, with very individual shops inc antiques shops, and a fine pub (the Rising Sun).

TATTENHALL SJ5059
Cheshire Farm Ice-Cream (Drumlan Hall Farm) Watch the cows being milked then sample over 30 flavours of the delicious end product. They've also a birds of prey rescue centre, play barn and rare breeds corner. Snacks, shop, disabled access; usually only cl 25-26 Dec and 1 Jan; (01829) 770995; free. The village is most attractive, and the Calveley Arms at nearby Handley has good imaginative food.

TEGGS NOSE COUNTRY PARK SJ9472
Cheshire's hilly eastern edge forms part of the Peak District, and offers some grand views westwards towards North Wales. This country park has a useful information centre, and good walks with far views, punctuated by relics of the former quarrying here. From the park, a well marked track - actually part of the long-distance Gritstone Trail - heads off S into the **Macclesfield Forest**, with steep deep green pine plantations around neatly walled small reservoirs; on the far side of this the isolated Leathers Smithy E of Langley is a welcoming moorside refuge with superb views, and the Stanley Arms tucked away at Bottom of the Oven is also good.

WARRINGTON SJ5990
Gulliver's World (Old Hall) Theme park very similar to its sister parks in Milton Keynes and Matlock Bath (see **Buckinghamshire** and **Derbyshire** chapters), with rides and entertainment aimed at the under-12s. Meals, snacks, shop, disabled access; cl Jan-Feb and Nov, and other days at the beginning and end of the season, phone for dates; (01925) 444888; £8.50.

Warrington Museum and Gallery (Bold St) The geology and botany galleries contain hands-on displays and a 'breathing' model dinosaur. Other weird and wonderful exhibits include a model mermaid, a cannibal's flesh hook, an Egyptian mummy, a toy-packed nursery, and lots of beetles and other creepy-crawlies. Snacks, shop, disabled access; cl Sun and bank hols; (01925)442392; free.

WHARTONS LOCK SJ5360
With a handy family dining pub nearby, this is a good place for walks along the **Shropshire Union Canal**; this is a charming section, winding through the richly wooded farming country below Beeston Castle.

WHITEGATE SJ6168
An interesting village, with thatched houses around the village green, fragmentary remains of what was once the biggest Cistercian monastery in the whole of England opposite its church, and a lakeside walk along a nearby derelict railway.

WIDNES SJ5183
Catalyst (Mersey Rd) This science discovery centre explores the role of the chemical industry in our lives. Put like that it doesn't sound too gripping, but children who like museums where you poke, press and push things will really get a lot out of it. It's all presented in an enormously enjoyable way, with over 100 interactive exhibits in four themed galleries; plenty of games, quizzes and re-created scenes. A glass lift whisks you up to a rooftop observatory with splendid views. An adjacent waterside park has wildlife and brightly coloured fishing boats. Meals, snacks, shop, disabled access; cl Mon exc bank and school hols, 24-26 Dec, 1 Jan; (0151) 420 1121; £4.95.

WRENBURY SJ5947
Canal walks The pretty **Llangollen**

Branch is a relaxing canal for gentle waterside walks, with access at Wrenbury for example; the good Dusty Miller dining pub here has an interesting lifting bridge by it.

Other attractive villages, all with decent pubs, include Church Minshull SJ6660, Thelwall SJ6587 and Warmingham SJ7161.

Where to eat

ALDFORD SJ4158 **Grosvenor Arms** *Chester Rd (01244) 620228* Sizeable but friendly Victorian pub, attractively decorated, with big panelled library and several quieter rooms, airy conservatory, good interesting food, well kept real ales, lots of New World wines (and malt whiskies), and large sun-trap terrace lawn; best to get there early; cl 25 Dec, 1 Jan pm; no children;disabled access. £25|**£6**

BUNBURY SJ5758 **Dysart Arms** *Bowes Gate Rd (01829) 260183* By the village church, this neat former farmhouse has a civilised, old-fashioned atmosphere, log fires, lots of antique furniture, cosy alcoves, a no smoking library area, well kept ales and house wines, interesting food, friendly service, and tables in lovely elevated big garden; cl 25 Dec; children over 10 in evenings; disabled access. £24|**£4.95**

CHESTER SJ4066 **Brasserie 10/16** *10-16 Brookdale Place (01244) 322288* Good modern brasserie food in light and airy, simply decorated two-floored restaurant; interesting mediterranean/british dishes, lovely puddings, good value wines, an open kitchen, and friendly helpful service; disabled access. £22|**£6.95**

CHESTER SJ4166 **Old Harkers Arms** *1 Russell St (01244) 344525* Attractive conversion of an early Victorian canal warehouse with lofty ceiling, tall windows and well spaced tables and chairs, efficient staff, a changing choice of nicely presented food inc interesting sandwiches, well kept real ales and New World wines; cl 25 Dec, 1 Jan; children until 7pm; disabled access. £20|**£6.50**

COTEBROOK SJ5765 **Fox & Barrel** *Foxbank (01829) 760529* Well run bar and restaurant with a lively friendly atmosphere, interestingly furnished snug areas, a very big log fire, extensive no smoking candlelit dining area, and huge helpings of tasty, interesting bar food; real ales, decent choice of wines, jazz Mon pm. £24.75|**£8.45**

DARESBURY SJ5782 **Ring o' Bells** *(01925) 740256* Roomy pub with plenty of places to sit including no smoking dining rooms and a down-to-earth part for walkers; reasonably priced and interesting daily specials, well kept real ales, a dozen malts, lots of wines by the glass, efficient, friendly service, and roaring fire; tables in long, partly terraced garden; disabled access. £22|**£6.90**

HASSALL GREEN SJ7758 **Brindley's Lockside Restaurant** *Canal Centre (01270) 762266* 200-year-old house with tearoom offering breakfasts, snacks, lunches, cream teas, and evening restaurant; you can watch narrow-boats going through the locks; gift shop and towpath walks; bdrms; cl 25-26 Dec. £26|**£5.95**

KNUTSFORD SJ7578 **Belle Epoque Brasserie** *60 King St (01565) 633060* Popular restaurant-with-rooms decorated in art nouveau style with lavish drapes, marbled pillared alcoves and smartly set tables, enthusiastic friendly staff and lovely modern cooking; cl Sun pm; children over 12. £30|**£7.95**

PLUMLEY SJ7176 **Smoker** *Chester Rd (01565) 722338* Popular thatched 16th-c pub with open fires and comfortable sofas in three well decorated connecting rooms, good swiftly served food, a wide choice of whiskies, well kept real ales, and friendly service; big garden; disabled access. £25|**£8.50**

PRESTBURY SU8976 **Legh Arms** *The Village (01625) 829130* Civilised 16th-c building with several distinctive areas: ladderback dining chairs, solid dark tables, elegant french steam train prints; also, brocaded bucket seats, staffordshire dogs on the stone mantelpiece, a good coal fire, and snug panelled back part; well kept real ales, good coffee and wine list, daily papers, and interesting daily specials plus excellent bread; more elaborate choice in attractive restaurant, and pleasant service by uniformed staff; hoping to add bedrooms. £23.50.|**£7.50**

Special thanks to E G Parish, Paul Kennedy, Michael and Jenny Back

CORNWALL

Ideal for holidays, from sandy resorts through picturesque creeks,
coves and quaint fishing villages to wild majestic cliffs and bleak moors;
masses of family attractions, some spectacular gardens, a fine
choice of places to stay in

The stunning Eden Project continues to impress its flood of visitors, and is worth seeing even if gardens aren't something that normally interest you. And if they are, you'll find this a great county; because of its climate Cornwall can produce exotic plants unlike those elsewhere in England. Among the many outstanding gardens, we pick out especially the Lost Gardens of Heligan in Mevagissey (combines nicely with a trip to nearby Caerhays Castle Gardens), the two great gardens at Mawnan Smith and Trewithen at Probus.

Lanhydrock, Bodmin, Calstock and Torpoint are also good places to head for lovely gardens, combined here with fine houses. The medieval castle at Marazion is magically set, and the Minack Open-Air Theatre at Porthcurno is an unforgettable place to see a play. Elsewhere, train enthusiasts have plenty to keep them occupied at Bodmin, Launceston and Newlyn East, and there are mines to explore at Pendeen and Wendron.

From a good choice of lively family outings, Dairyland near Newquay (masses to do, and good value too) is our Family Attraction award winner for the county this year. Flambards Theme Park near Helston, and Land's End also have enough to fill a busy day. The National Maritime Museum is proving a great draw in Falmouth, and Dobwalls Family Adventure Park has the twin attractions of miniature trains and good play areas. Animal lovers are very well catered for, with Newquay Zoo, Shires at Tredinnick (plenty going on here), a very long-established monkey sanctuary near Looe, a seal sanctuary at Gweek, an otter park at North Petherwin and an animal centre at Trecangate; colourful Paradise Park in Hayle is HQ of the World Parrot Trust.

Without a doubt, Cornwall's strongest attractions are its splendid beaches and delightful seaside villages and towns. With 500 miles of coastal walks (many carefully preserved by the National Trust), it's easy to find breathtaking beauty throughout the county. The pretty south coast is very sheltered, with some fine places to stay. East of the Lizard point are plenty of interesting little coves, winding estuaries and creeks rich in bird life, with boat trips from almost every harbour.

The north coast is ideal for family beach holidays, with an almost continuous line of resort developments and lots of attractions within easy travelling distance. The pretty harbour town of St Ives (with two good galleries), the quaint working fishing town of Padstow with its attractive slate houses, and Cornwall's biggest resort, bustling Newquay, are all superb for a lively holiday.

Some dramatic cliffy stretches of coast are interspersed with fine sandy beaches, especially on the Penwith peninsula (the bit on the extreme 'left', west of Marazion/St Ives), culminating in a spectacular range of cliffs from Treen to Land's End. Penwith, with its rugged windswept moorland, ruined tin mine buildings and overgrown stone walls, has lots of visible prehistoric remains - Bronze Age burial chambers and standing stones, Iron Age hill forts and village sites, and ancient stone crosses. Our pick of the best are Men an Tol, Chun Castle, Chun Quoit and Lanyon Quoit (all near Morvah), Ballowal (see Pendeen entries), the Iron Age village sites of Chysauster and Carn Euny (the latter near Sancreed), Zennor Quoit, and the Merry Maidens (near Lamorna).

Another stretch of wild Cornwall is up towards Devon, north of commercialised Tintagel - with high cliffs, dramatic surfing beaches and plenty of wildlife. Port Isaac and Boscastle are the pick of this part's few settlements.

The inland parts of the county are largely treeless, with rolling pastures and moorland. Windswept Bodmin Moor is the county's most untouched inland area (for a change of pace here, there's Lakeside Adventure Park). In the more exposed spots the towering alloy propellers of the new wind farms are a striking landscape feature.

In high summer, there's lots of traffic on the narrow roads (and some serious parking problems). Even then you can easily escape the hordes, and out of season, Cornwall comes into its own, with lots to do, a very relaxed pace and attractive prices. Late May and early June is an ideal time for a short break here, with relatively few other visitors. In spring (the best time for the gardens) and early summer, the tall hedged banks which block the view from many byroads compensate by being virtual walls of wild flowers. September and October is seal pup time.

It's worth noting that not many of the roads actually follow the coast - great for walkers, but disappointing for drivers and cyclists. A Cornish Rail Rover ticket is good value for eight days (which don't have to be consecutive) of unlimited train journeys throughout the county for around £40.50 (less out of summer); you can also get a ticket for three days; phone (0845) 748 4950 for details. Much of Cornwall is covered by a surprisingly good bus network, and for a county-wide bus timetable and map, contact the Cornish Tourist Board (01872) 322900.

The Isles of Scilly are great for a really quiet and relaxing holiday, with Penzance the quickest jumping-off point.

Where to stay

BODINNICK SX1352 **Old Ferry** *Bodinnick, Fowey, Cornwall PL23 1LX (01726) 870237* **£70**; 12 comfortable and spacious rms, most with own bthrm and river views. 400-year-old inn in lovely situation overlooking Fowey estuary; back flagstoned bar partly cut into the rock, real ales, comfortable residents' lounge with french windows opening on to a terrace, and decent food in both bar and little evening restaurant; quiet out of season; cl 25 Dec; dogs welcome away from restaurant

BOTALLACK SW3632 **Botallack Manor** *Botallack, St Just-in-Penwith, Penzance, Cornwall TR19 7QG (01736) 788525* **£54**; 3 rms. Blissfully quiet and friendly 17th-c

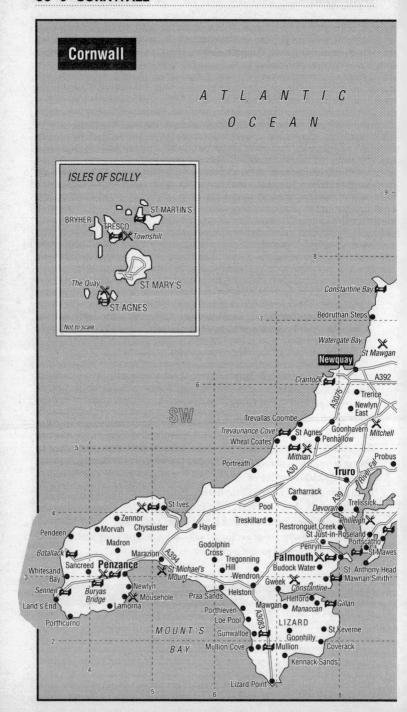

Cornwall

ATLANTIC
OCEAN

ISLES OF SCILLY

BRYHER
TRESCO
×Townshill
ST MARTIN'S

The Quay
ST MARY'S
ST AGNES

Not to scale

SW

Constantine Bay
Bedruthan Steps
Watergate Bay
St Mawgan
Newquay
A392
Crantock
Trerice
Newlyn East
Trevallas Coombe
Goonhavern
St Agnes
Penhallow
Mitchell
Trevaunance Cove
Wheal Coates
Mithian
Portreath
Probus
Truro
River Fal
Carharrack
A30
A39
Pool
Devoran
Trelissick
St Ives
Treskillard
Restronguet Creek
Philleigh
Zennor
Chysauster
Hayle
St Just-in-Roseland
Portscatho
Morvah
Penryn
St Mawes
Pendeen
Godolphin Cross
Falmouth
Botallack
Madron
Tregonning Hill
Budock Water
St Anthony Head
Whitesand Bay
Sancreed
Marazion
A394
Wendron
Gweek
Mawnan Smith
Penzance
St Michael's Mount
Constantine
Sennen
Newlyn
Helston
Helford
Gillan
Buryas Bridge
Mousehole
Praa Sands
Mawgan
Manaccan
Land's End
Lamorna
Porthleven
Loe Pool
LIZARD
St Keverne
Porthcurno
Gunwalloe
Goonhilly
Coverack
MOUNT'S
BAY
Mullion Cove
Mullion
Kennack Sands
Lizard Point

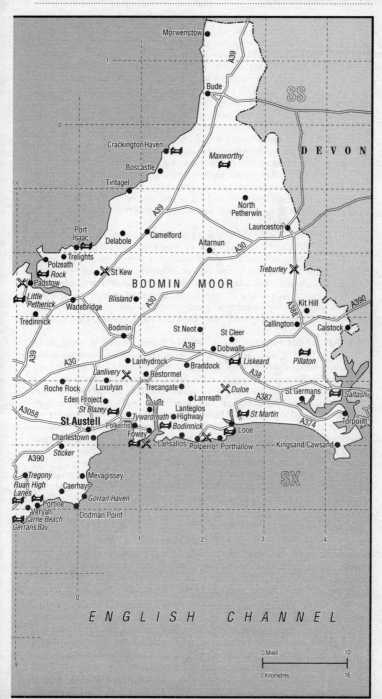

Morwenstow

A39

SS

Bude

DEVON

Crackington Haven

Maxworthy

Boscastle

Tintagel

North
Petherwin

A39

Port
Isaac

Delabole   Camelford   Altarnun   Launceston

A30

Trelights

Treburley

Polzeath   St Kew   BODMIN   MOOR

Rock

Padstow   Blisland   A30   Kit Hill   A390

Little
Petherick   Wadebridge   A388   Callington

Tredinnick   Bodmin   St Neot   St Cleer   Calstock

A38   Dobwalls

A30   Lanhydrock   Braddock   Liskeard   Pillaton

A38

Roche Rock   Lanlivery   Restormel

Eden Project   Luxulyan   Trecangate   Duloe   St Germans   Saltash

A3058   St Blazey   Golant   Lanreath   A387

St Austell   Lanteglos   St Martin   A374

Polkerris   Tywardreath   Highway   Torpoint

Charlestown   Fowey   Bodinnick   Looe

Lansallos   Polperro   Porthallow   Kingsand/Cawsand

A390   Sticker

SX

Tregony   Mevagissey

Ruan High   Caerhays
Lanes

Portloe   Gorran Haven

Veryan   Dodman Point
Carne Beach
Gerrans Bay

1   2   3   4

ENGLISH   CHANNEL

0 Miles   10

0 Kilometres   16

local granite manor on working farm, with a medley of furnishings in reading room, good breakfasts with home-baked bread, and safe walled garden; no pets; marvellous cliff walks, ruined mines and small coves

BURYAS BRIDGE SW4427 **Rose Farm** *Chyenhal, Buryas Bridge, Penzance, Cornwall TR19 6AN (01736) 731808* **£50***, plus winter breaks; 3 delightfully furnished rms. Relaxed, informal and friendly 200-year-old farmhouse tucked away down remote country lane, with excellent breakfasts around big table; can see lots of animals (working farm), and children love it; cl 24-25 Dec ☺

CARNE BEACH SW9138 **Nare Hotel** *Carne Beach, Veryan, Truro, Cornwall TR2 5PF (01872) 501279* **£326** inc afternoon tea and dinner, plus special breaks; 36 lovely rms to suit all tastes - some stylish ones overlook garden and out to sea. Attractively decorated and furnished hotel in magnificent clifftop position with secluded gardens, outdoor and indoor swimming pools, tennis, sailboarding and fishing; antiques, fresh flowers and log fires in the airy, spacious day rooms, very good food in two restaurants (one is new this year, with a more relaxed atmosphere), wonderful breakfasts, and run by staff who really care; ideal for quiet family hols, with safe sandy beach below; disabled access; dogs welcome in bedrooms ☺

CONSTANTINE BAY SW8674 **Treglos Hotel** *Constantine Bay, Padstow, Cornwall PL28 8JH (01841) 520727* **£178** inc dinner, plus special breaks; 42 light rms, some with balcony. Quiet and relaxed hotel close to good sandy beach, and in the same family for 30 years; comfortable traditional furnishings, log fires, good food, friendly helpful staff, sheltered garden plus playground and adventure equipment, indoor swimming pool, table tennis, table football and pool table and children's playroom with electronic games; lovely nearby walks; self-catering apartments; cl end Nov-beginning Mar; children over 7 in restaurant; disabled access; dogs welcome in bedrooms ☺

CRACKINGTON HAVEN SX1496 **Manor Farm** *Crackington Haven, Bude, Cornwall EX23 0JW (01840) 230304* **£60***; 3 pretty rms. Lovely Domesday-listed, no smoking manor surrounded by 25 acres of farmland and carefully landscaped gardens; antiques in four lounges, a log fire, a house-party atmosphere, big breakfasts, and a delicious 4-course dinner at 7pm; cl 25 Dec; no children

CRANTOCK SW7760 **Crantock Bay Hotel** *West Pentire, Crantock, Newquay, Cornwall TR8 5SE (01637) 830229* **£78.50**, plus special breaks; 33 comfortable rms, most with coastal views. In a lovely setting on the West Pentire headland, facing the Atlantic and a huge sheltered sandy beach, this relaxed and informal hotel has been run by the same friendly family for 50 years; four acres of grounds, an indoor swimming pool, toddlers' pool, sauna and exercise room, all weather tennis court, a putting course and children's play area; two lounges, bar lounge and restaurant, enjoyable food using local produce, and nice afternoon teas; cl Dec-Feb; families most welcome; lots to do nearby; disabled access and facilities; dogs welcome in bedrooms ☺

FALMOUTH SW8031 **Dolvean** *50 Melvill Rd, Falmouth, Cornwall TR11 4DQ (01326) 313658* **£80**; 11 individually decorated with plenty of extras rms. Built as a gentleman's residence, this smart cream house has views to Falmouth Bay and the Lizard; attractive lounge with carefully chosen antiques, fine china and books, traditional breakfasts using good local produce in neat room, and friendly owners; cl Christmas; children over 12

FALMOUTH SW7932 **Penmere Manor** *Mongleath Rd, Falmouth, Cornwall TR11 4PN (01326) 211411* **£108**, plus special breaks; 37 spacious rms. Run by the same owners for 34 years, this quietly set Georgian manor has five acres of subtropical gardens and woodland, heated outdoor swimming pool, giant chess, croquet, and leisure centre with indoor swimming pool, gym and sauna; particularly helpful friendly staff, an evening pianist, and enjoyable food in restaurant and informal bar; cl 24-26 Dec; disabled access; dogs welcome in bedrooms

FOWEY SX1251 **Fowey Hall** *Fowey, Cornwall PL23 1ET (01726) 833866* **£160** inc dinner; 24 rms inc 11 suites and 4 pairs of interconnecting rms. Fine Gothic-style mansion in five acres of grounds overlooking the harbour and run along the same lines as their other hotels - Woolley Grange, Bradford-on-Avon and Moonfleet Manor at Fleet; marble fireplaces, baroque plasterwork, panelling, antiques, big potted plants, two enjoyable restaurants, marvellous facilities for children inc supervised nursery, and covered swimming pool, croquet and badminton; dogs welcome in bedrooms ☺

FOWEY SX1251 **Marina Hotel** *17 Esplanade, Fowey, Cornwall PL23 1HY (01726) 833315* **£130**, plus special breaks; 13 rms, several with lovely views (some with balcony). Friendly Georgian hotel in fine position overlooking Fowey River and open sea (private access from secluded walled garden); refurbished, comfortable lounge/reading room, cheerfully decorated bar, attractive dining room overlooking the water, very good food (super fresh fish and shellfish) and helpful service; disabled access

GERRANS BAY SW8938 **Pendower Beach House** *Ruan High Lanes, Truro, Cornwall TR2 5LW (01872) 501241* **£180** inc dinner, plus special breaks; 11 rms. Family-run hotel dating back to 16th c in eight acres by lovely sandy beach, with superb sea and coastal views, and plenty of seats on sunny terrace; a relaxed, friendly atmosphere in attractive and comfortable rooms, good food in cosy restaurant (super fresh local fish and shellfish), and tennis court; cl Nov-Feb; disabled access; dogs welcome in bedrooms

GILLAN SW7825 **Tregildry** *Gillan, Manaccan, Helston, Cornwall TR12 6HG (01326) 231378* **£130*** inc dinner, plus special breaks; 10 attractive rms with fine views over Falmouth Bay. Elegantly furnished hotel in four acres of grounds with private access to the cove below; spacious comfortable lounges, fresh flowers, books and magazines, a restful atmosphere, very good food in attractive restaurant, enjoyable breakfasts, and kind, courteous service; cl Nov-Feb; children over 8; dogs welcome in bedrooms

GUNWALLOE SW6522 **Halzephron** *Gunwalloe, Helston, Cornwall TR12 7QB (01326) 240406* **£80***; 2 cosy rms. 500-year-old former smugglers' inn run by knowledgeable and friendly cornish landlady, with imaginative food in bar areas and bistro-style restaurant, open fire and fine views of Mounts Bay; lots of walks, nearby beaches and golf; cl 25 Dec; no children for accommodation (allowed in pub)

LISKEARD SX2460 **Well House** *St Keyne, Liskeard, Cornwall PL14 4RN (01579) 342001* **£115**, plus special breaks; 9 individually designed rms with fine views. Light and airy Victorian country house, recently redecorated, with warm, friendly owners, courteous staff, comfortable drawing room, cosy little bar, and particularly good food and fine wines in dining room overlooking terrace and lawns; three acres of gardens with hard tennis court, swimming pool and croquet lawn; children over 8 in evening restaurant; dogs welcome in bedrooms

LITTLE PETHERICK SW9172 **Old Mill Country House** *Little Petherick, Wadebridge, Cornwall PL27 7QT (01841) 540388* **£68***, plus special breaks; 4 rms. 16th-c corn mill in lovely riverside gardens with waterwheel and other original features, enjoyable breakfasts in beamed dining room, lounges, and attentive service; plenty of places nearby for evening meals; cl Nov-Mar; no children

LOOE SX2251 **Talland Bay Hotel** *Porthallow, Looe, Cornwall PL13 2JB (01503) 272667* **£130**, plus special breaks; 23 charming rms with sea or country views. Down a little lane between Looe and Polperro, this restful partly 16th-c newly refurbished country house has lovely subtropical gardens just above the sea; comfortable drawing room with log fire, smaller lounge with library, fresh flowers, courteous service, good food in pretty oak-panelled dining room, and pleasant afternoon teas; heated outdoor swimming pool, putting, croquet; children over 5 in evening restaurant (high tea for younger ones); dogs welcome in bedrooms

MAWNAN SMITH SW7828 **Meudon Hotel** *Mawnan Smith, Falmouth, Cornwall TR11 5HT (01326) 250541* **£200** inc dinner, plus special breaks; 29 well equipped comfortable rms in separate wing. Run by the same caring family for over 36 years, this is an old stone mansion with a newer wing, in beautiful subtropical gardens laid out 200 years ago by R. W. Fox; fine views from the dining room, comfortable lounge with log fire and fresh flowers, good english cooking, and old-fashioned standards of service; cl 3-31Jan; disabled access; dogs welcome in bedrooms

MAXWORTHY SX2492 **Wheatley Farm** *Maxworthy, Launceston, Cornwall PL15 8LY (01566) 781232* **£52***, plus special breaks; 4 attractive rms mainly with showers. In the same family for five generations, this working dairy farm has comfortable, pretty furnishings, log fires, good 4-course evening meals using local produce in spacious dining room, and hearty breakfasts; new indoor swimming pool, sauna and spa bath; cl Nov-mid Feb; self-catering cottages, children during school hols only; safe children's play area, animals to visit and pony rides

MITHIAN SW7450 **Rose-in-Vale Country House Hotel** *Mithian, St Agnes, Cornwall TR5 0QD (01872) 552202* **£129**, plus special breaks; 18 pretty rms inc 2 suites. Secluded and quietly set Georgian house in four acres of neatly kept gardens, with comfortable spacious day rooms, a friendly atmosphere, helpful, long-standing local staff, and good food in enlarged dining room; ducks on ponds, a trout stream, outdoor swimming pool, badminton and croquet, plus a sauna and solarium; children over 7 in evening in public rooms and restaurant (high tea for smaller ones); cl Jan-Feb; disabled access; dogs welcome in bedrooms

MULLION SW6818 **Meaver Farm** *Meaver Rd, Mullion, Helston, Cornwall TR12 7DN (01326) 240128* **£50***, plus special breaks; 3 individual rms with super bthrms. 17th-c stone farmhouse (no longer a working farm), with good Aga-cooked breakfasts in beamed kitchen, log fire, plants and antiques in sitting room, and friendly helpful owners; children over 12; dogs welcome

MULLION SW6718 **Polurrian Hotel** *Mullion, Helston, Cornwall TR12 7EN (01326) 240421* **£210** inc dinner, plus special breaks; 39 rms, some with memorable sea view. White clifftop hotel in lovely gardens with path down to sheltered private cove below, a restful atmosphere in the comfortable lounges and bright cocktail bar, fresh flowers, good food using fresh local ingredients (pianist and sea views in the dining room), enjoyable breakfasts, leisure club with heated swimming pool, and heated outdoor pool, badminton, tennis, mini-golf, squash and croquet; particularly good for families; disabled access; dogs welcome ☺

PENZANCE SW4730 **Abbey Hotel** *Abbey St, Penzance, Cornwall TR18 4AR (01736) 366906* **£110***, plus winter breaks; 8 charming rms. Stylish little 17th-c house close to harbour with marvellous views, a relaxed atmosphere in comfortable drawing room full of flowers, fine paintings and antiques, a good set menu in small Abbey Restaurant next door, and pretty garden; cl Jan; children over 7 in dining room; dogs welcome in bedrooms

PENZANCE SW4730 **Georgian House Hotel** *20 Chapel Street, Penzance, Cornwall TR18 4AW (01736) 365664* **£46**; 11 comfortable rms, most with own bthrm. Warmly friendly little hotel, once the home of the Mayor of Penzance and close to the harbour and shopping centre, with helpful owner and staff, very good breakfasts in attractive dining room, reading lounge, and private parking; cl Christmas; dogs welcome in bedrooms

PENZANCE SW4729 **Summer House** *Cornwall Terrace, Penzance, Cornwall TR18 4HL (01736) 363744* **£75**, plus winter wknd breaks; 5 charming rooms with fresh flowers and antiques. In a mews 50 metres from the sea, this Regency restaurant-with-rooms (flooded with light by a curving glass tower) has a relaxed, informal atmosphere, lots of cheerful yellows and blues, wooden floors, comfortable sofas and local paintings, and wonderful mediterranean-style food (the owner/chef worked in some top London restaurants); pretty walled garden; cl Jan/Feb; children over 13

PILLATON SX3663 **Weary Friar** *Pillaton, Saltash, Cornwall PL12 6QS (01579) 350238* **£55***, plus special breaks; 13 rms. Pretty 12th-c inn by church in pleasantly remote village; lots of character in its four knocked-together rooms (one no smoking), attractive furnishings, well kept real ales, and good food in both bar and restaurant

PORT ISAAC SX0080 **Port Gaverne Hotel** *Port Gaverne, Port Isaac, Cornwall PL29 3SQ (01208) 880244* **£100***, plus special breaks; 15 comfortable rms, several newly refurbished this year. Lovely place to stay and an excellent base for area (dramatic coves, good clifftop walks and lots of birds); big log fires in well kept bars, relaxed lounges, decent bar food, good restaurant food and fine wines; also, restored 18th-c self-catering cottages; cl 1st 2 wks Feb; children over 7 in restaurant; dogs anywhere except dining room

PORTLOE SW9339 **Pine Cottage** *Portloe, Truro, Cornwall TR2 5RB* (01872) 501385 **£80***; 2 rms. Charming old house in pretty garden just a few hundred yards from the harbour of this unspoilt fishing village; open fire, books and honesty tray in cosy sitting room, particularly good food using fresh local produce and a thoughtful little wine list in light, spacious dining room, super breakfasts (they will make up picnics and packed lunches, too), and warmly friendly owner; cl Christmas/New Year; babies welcome, but children over 9

ROCK SW9375 **St Enodoc Hotel** *Rock, Wadebridge, Cornwall PL27 6LA* (01208) 863394 **£180**, plus special breaks; 20 individually designed rms with lovely views. Quietly set hotel overlooking the Camel estuary and next to two 18-hole golf courses; stylish mediterranean décor with plenty of paintings and fresh flowers, delicious modern cooking in bar and split-level restaurant, a relaxed informal atmosphere, a gym, sauna and billiards room, and heated swimming pool in big garden; good for families with playroom, table tennis, table football, TV and video, and quite a few other facilities; lovely nearby beaches and walks; cl Jan-mid-Feb ☺

RUAN HIGH LANES SW9039 **Crugsillick Manor** *Ruan High Lanes, Truro, Cornwall TR2 5LJ* (01872) 501214 **£84**, plus special breaks; 3 rms. One of the loveliest houses in Cornwall, this Queen Anne manor is extended from a pre-Elizabethan farmhouse and surrounded by a big quiet garden with wooded valley views; log fire in drawing room with Napoleonic ceiling, candlelit dinners in 17th-c dining room using home-grown produce where possible, fine breakfasts, and charming owners; self-catering cottages in grounds - excellent disabled access, and children welcome (but must be over 12 in main house); house cl Christmas (self-catering open then); dogs anywhere in cottages, not in bdrms in house

SALTASH SX3957 **Erth Barton** *Elmgate, Saltash, Cornwall PL12 4QY* (01752) 842127 **£70**; 3 rms. Lovely old manor house with its own chapel, peaceful rooms with lots of books, pictures and big fireplaces, good enjoyable food, bird-watching in the surrounding estuaries, and riding (you can bring your own horse); children over 12; dogs welcome

SENNEN SW3425 **Lands End Hotel** *Sennen, Penzance, Cornwall TR19 7AA* (01736) 871844 **£150***, plus special breaks; 33 elegant airy rms, many with splendid sea views. Comfortable hotel right on the clifftop with fine sea views, good food in attractive conservatory-style restaurant, elegant seating areas, informal bar with lots of malt whiskies, and helpful staff; lots to do nearby; dogs welcome in bedrooms

ST BLAZEY SX0655 **Nanscawen Manor House** *Prideaux Road, St Blazey, Par, Cornwall PL24 2SR* (01726) 814488 **£88***, plus winter breaks; 3 spacious, pretty rms overlooking the garden. Extended 16th-c house in five acres of lovely grounds and gardens with an outdoor heated swimming pool and whirlpool spa, and a sunny terrace; big sitting room with honesty bar, friendly helpful owners, enjoyable breakfasts in light conservatory (plenty of places nearby for evening meals), and a relaxed atmosphere; no smoking; the Eden Project is close by; children over 12

ST IVES SW5437 **Countryman** *Old Coach Rd, Trink, St Ives, Cornwall TR26 3JQ* (01736) 797571 **£65***, plus special breaks; 6 rms. Small friendly no smoking hotel in two acres of gardens; comfortable lounge, bright flower-filled conservatory and cosy restaurant; walks, golf and Tate Gallery nearby; cl Dec and Jan; children over 5

ST IVES SW5040 **Garrack** *Burthallan Lane, St Ives, Cornwall TR26 3AA* (01736) 796199 **£136***, plus winter breaks; 18 rms, some in more modern wing. Friendly hotel in two acres of gardens with wonderful sea views, cosy lounges with antiques, books and open fires, a family room, good food inc fresh shellfish, helpful staff, and indoor leisure centre; disabled access

ST MARTIN SX2755 **Bucklawren Farm** *St Martin, Looe, Cornwall PL13 1NZ* (01503) 240738 **£55***, plus special breaks; 6 rms. Spacious farmhouse on 500-acre beef and arable working farm with coastal and sea views, croquet and putting in the big garden, large homely lounge, south-facing sun lounge, and enjoyable food in restaurant; cl Nov-Feb; children over 5; disabled access

ST MAWES SW8433 **Rising Sun** *The Square, St Mawes, Truro, Cornwall TR2 5DJ (01326) 270233* **£60***; 8 rms. Small attractive hotel in popular picturesque waterside village, with harbour views, large comfortable lounge with bustling bar area, airy conservatory, charming terrace; dogs welcome in bedrooms

ST MAWES SW8432 **Tresanton** *Lower Castle Rd, St Mawes, Truro, Cornwall TR2 5DR (01326) 270055* **£245**, plus special breaks; 29 rms all with individual furnishings and sea views. Hidden away behind a discreet entrance, with elegant terraces (heating for cool weather), little bottom bar, steps up to the main building and its stylish lounge with deeply comfortable sofas and armchairs, big bowls of flowers, log fire, daily papers and sophisticated but relaxed atmosphere; excellent food, a fine wine list and friendly informal service; several boats for hire inc the beautiful 48-ft yacht *Pinuccia*

TREVAUNANCE COVE SW7251 **Driftwood Spars** *Trevaunance Cove, St Agnes, Cornwall TR5 0RT (01872) 552428* **£80**; 15 attractive, comfortable bdrms, some with sea view, 8 in separate building. Friendly family-owned hotel dating from the 17th c and just up the road from the beach and dramatic cove; woodburner in comfortable lounge, main bar with large open fire, upstairs gallery, beamed ceilings, helpful staff and enjoyable food; live music wknds; cl 25 Dec; dogs welcome

To see and do

Cornwall Family Attraction of the Year

NEWQUAY SW8657 **Dairyland** (A3508 4m SE) A favourite with families for nearly 30 years, this bustling dairy farm is not only hugely entertaining, it's particularly good value too. There's masses to do, with plenty of play areas and children's activities; a huge new undercover play area, the Bull Pen, with climbing nets, slides and ball pools, is open at weekends and in school holidays throughout the year, even when the rest of the farm is shut. Other extras include trampolines, an assault course, play area for smaller children, go-karts, mazes, and displays on rural heritage and alternative energy. But first and foremost it's still a working farm, and the centrepiece remains the unique daily milking session (around 3pm), when cows step aboard a bizarre merry-go-round milking machine and are milked to a rousing musical accompaniment. This bit's had something of a makeover in recent months: it now looks rather like a space-age nightclub, complete with glitter balls. There are a good few other animals too, including paddocks of rheas, llamas and deer, and a petting area for small children, where they may be able to bottle-feed some of the animals. Well labelled nature trails take in quieter corners, with woodland and duck-filled lakes, and, for an extra charge, there are pony and hay rides. Like any farm this is best in dry weather, but there's enough under cover to make it a good bet on a wet day too. The clotted cream and ice-cream are made with their own milk; even if you're just passing you can pop in to buy some. Many visitors return every year, and it's one of the very best farm attractions in the country. Meals and snacks (made with mostly local ingredients), shop, disabled access; cl Nov-Mar; (01872) 510246; *£6.50 adults, *£5.50 children 3-15. The family ticket is excellent value: two adults and up to three children for £20. Better still, all tickets give you unlimited entry for the next week - very handy if you're staying nearby.

ALTARNUN SX2281
Altarnun church The church has an enchanting set of 16th-c carved bench ends, much humanity and humour. The unpretentious Rising Sun pub just N is good value. Nearby **Wesley's Cottage** just off A30 at Trewint, the world's smallest Methodist place of worship, has a room set out as it would have been in 1744.

BEDRUTHAN STEPS SW8469 (off B3276 Newquay—Padstow) The scenic highlight of this stretch of coast: gigantic rock pillars towering over a rocky beach; NT car park nearby.

BODMIN SX0766
Bodmin & Wenford Railway 🔄 (General Station, St Nicholas St) Restored steam locomotives take you back to the glory days of the Great Western Railway when thousands of holiday-makers travelled this route to the sun. As well as enjoying the view, you can stop off for pleasant woodland walks. Mainline connection at Bodmin Parkway station. Snacks, shop, disabled access; cl Jan-late Mar and Nov, with a limited service in Apr, May, Oct and Dec; runs daily Jun-Sept - best to phone for train times; (0845) 125 9678; from £5 (discount voucher not valid for special events).

Bodmin Gaol (Berrycoombe Rd) The former county prison, built in 1778, with spooky underground dungeons; the Crown Jewels were stored here in World War I. Meals and snacks (pub on site), shop; open daily in summer, phone in winter; (01208) 76292; £4.20. There's a sacred well in the churchyard of St Petroc's church.

Pencarrow (Washaway, 3m N of Bodmin off A389) Notable 18th-c house with fine paintings and furniture, rococo ceiling in the music room, and, perhaps the highlight, 50 acres of lovely formal and woodland gardens with over 700 different rhododendrons and an acclaimed conifer collection. Also marked trails, children's play area, peacocks, chickens and other birds, craft centre and ancient british encampment. Meals, snacks, shop, limited disabled access; house cl Fri-Sat, and Nov-Mar; gardens open daily; (01208) 841369; *£7, garden only £3.

On the way out, the Borough Arms is good value for lunch.
BODMIN MOOR SX1875
Cornwall's highest part, this granite upland is something like a miniature Dartmoor, though not as richly endowed for walking as its Devon counterpart. Although largely pathless and bleak, it does have its own character, with gnarled tors, wind-bent trees, prehistoric traces, granite walls and lonely lakes. Good views from the main A30 (generally better than the side roads). One of the most accessible bits is around Minions, on the south side of the moor. Amid disused quarries here, you can park near the Hurlers stone circles and stroll an old quarry track to a striking weathered rock formation, the Cheesewring (resembling a great stack of cheeses); excellent views E to Dartmoor and N over the centre of Bodmin Moor. Just S of Minions at Darite, Trethevy Quoit is the area's best antiquity - a megalithic tomb complete with capstone. Also grand views from the summit of Rough Tor (pronounced Row Tor), reached from a signed car park off the A39 nr Camelford, looking towards Brown Willy, the highest point in Cornwall. Riding is popular on the moor, and quite a few stables on or around it cater for all levels of riding ability.

Lakeside Adventure Park (off A30 just S) Red squirrels have successfully been reintroduced at this family-orientated place; also rare breeds of birds, poultry, indoor and outdoor pets, adventure play areas, under-cover assault course, museum and lakeside walks. Snacks, shop, some disabled access; cl end Sept-Easter; (01208) 821469; £5. About a mile away, Dozmary Pool is one of two cornish lakes that claim to be where a legendary arm rose from the depths and reclaimed Excalibur (the other is Loe Pool), and it's an easy starting-point for Bodmin Moor.

Smugglers at Jamaica Inn The little complex that has sprung up around Jamaica Inn (the pub immortalised by Daphne du Maurier) includes a **Smuggling Museum** in the former stables. As well as tableaux illustrating the story (with a video at the end), there's a room devoted to Daphne du Maurier (you can see her writing desk), and a display on smuggling past and present; usually cl 24-25 Dec, and around 3 wks from early Jan, best to phone; (01566) 86250; £2.50. The extraordinary collection of thousands of Victorian stuffed animals which made up Potters Museum of Curiosity here has now been sold.

BOSCASTLE SX0991
Pretty harbour with 16th-c pier squeezed into a rocky creek, cottages converted from warehouses, gift shops, a witchcraft museum; the Napoleon (a stiff climb) is nice for lunch. The cliffs nearby afford some fascinating views. Not far from here at Trevalga, Tredole Farm will arrange coastal or country **horse and pony trekking** (inc a 3-hr ride to a pub); non-riders welcome; (01840) 250495; from £15. Nearby **St Juliot church** was restored by Thomas Hardy in his career as an architect; he described the area later in *A Pair of Blue Eyes*.

BRADDOCK SX1662
Braddock church Hardly striking as a building, but well worth visiting for its handsome wood carvings.

BUDE SS2106
A popular area for surfing, with great beaches beyond the dunes; Sandy Mouth slightly N has clean water for bathing. Otherwise it's an unremarkable resort, though the Bude and Stratton Museum (the Wharf) is a decent rainy-day retreat (shop, disabled access; open daily Easter-end Oct; 50p, (01288) 353576) - placed by the lock at the seaward end of the Bude Canal (now navigable for only two miles to Helebridge). The Falcon Hotel does good value quick food. The carved bench-ends up at Poughill church (pronounced 'poffle') are entertaining; the Preston Gate is a decent pub there.

BUDOCK WATER SW7730
Penjerrick Garden 🖼 Peaceful 15-acre garden with some huge trees, created 200 years ago by the Fox family who were also responsible for Glendurgan at Mawnan Smith. The upper garden (good sea views from here) contains a notable collection of rhododendrons as well as camellias, azaleas, tree ferns and bamboos, while

the wilder valley garden has ponds and tree ferns dating back almost to the original planting of the garden; open pm Weds, Fri and Sun Mar-Sept; (01872) 870105; *£2.50.

CAERHAYS SW9741
Caerhays Castle Gardens Revered by gardening cognoscenti, these magnificent spring gardens are beautifully set around the back of a striking castle, with lovely coastal views. Renowned especially for their rhododendrons, magnolias and camellias, they're easily combined with a visit to the better known Lost Gardens of Heligan. Tearoom, limited disabled access; garden open 16 Feb-May, castle open pm wkdys 15 Mar-May; (01872) 501310; *£5.50. Depending on where you're coming from, the Crown over at St Ewe and the Kings Arms at Tregony up on the main road are handy for lunch.

CALLINGTON SX3769
Dupath Holy Well (off A388 S) In a 15th-c chapel, the best preserved of Cornwall's many holy wells, its unappetising water said to cure whooping cough. The town is not in itself remarkable, but the Coachmakers Arms is a good lunch stop.

CALSTOCK SX4268
Cotehele (1m W by footpath, 6m by road) Tucked away in a network of twisting roads high above the Tamar, this rambling granite house has hardly changed since being built in the late 15th c; there's no electricity, so the dark rooms - with fine furniture, armour and tapestries - have an authentically medieval atmosphere. Outside are lovely terraced gardens, a medieval dovecote, a restored working watermill and miles of peaceful woodland walks. Down at Cotehele Quay a National Maritime Museum outpost shows the quay's history, and the last of the Tamar ketch-rigged barges has been restored here; there's a little art gallery too. Tearoom in pleasant riverside setting with good cream teas, shop (selling flour ground at mill), some disabled access; house cl Fri and Nov-Mar, mill as house (but cl am and open Fri July-Aug), garden open daily all year; (01579) 351346; £6.60, £3.80 garden and mill only; NT. Pleasant

walks along the Tamar from the charming village. The comfortable Who'd Have Thought It at St Dominick is handy for lunch.

CAMELFORD SX1083
Locals will tell you this is the site of Camelot, and send you a mile N to the otherwise unremarkable Slaughter Bridge where Arthur supposedly fell at his last battle. The friendly Darlington does food at almost any time.

British Cycling Museum ▣ (The Old Station - B3266 N) Comprehensive collection of more than 400 bicycles, tricycles and even a five-wheeled Hen and Chickens bike, ranging from an original 1819 hobby-horse through boneshakers and penny-farthings to the hi-tech bikes of today. The couple who run it met through cycling, and really know their stuff. Outside is a sculpture made of old bicycles. Shop, disabled access; usually cl Fri and Sat, and 25 Dec; (01840) 212811; £2.90.

North Cornwall Museum and Gallery ▣ (The Clease) Good exploration of regional life over the past century, with displays of cider-making and farming, and collections of pottery and even early vacuum cleaners. Shop; cl Sun and Oct-Mar; (01840) 212954; £1.50.

CARHARRACK SW7341
Carharrack Methodist church Has an exhibition on Cornish Methodism and John Wesley, who preached at the octagon chapel that used to stand here; disabled access; open by appointment; (01209) 820381; free. Wesley preached more regularly at nearby **Gwennap Pit**, a spectacular grass amphitheatre, which still has services (usually spring bank hol, 3pm Sun in July and Aug and perhaps other times), and a visitor centre. Shop, snacks, disabled access; centre usually cl lunchtime, Sat pm and end Sept-Apr (though open occasionally then too), best to check; (01209) 821390. The peaceful grass amphitheatre itself is open all the time; free. The Fox & Hounds at Lanner is good for lunch.

CHARLESTOWN SX0351
A picturesque working china clay port, with sailing ships as well as modern cargo boats; it's much used as a film/TV setting. Two square-rigged sailing ships,

stars of many films, may be in the harbour. The **Shipwreck & Heritage Centre** (Quay Rd) has an exhibition about the *Titanic* and is good for local history (cl Nov-Feb; (01726) 69897; £4.95). The waterside Harbour Inn (Pier House Hotel) is useful for lunch.

CHYSAUSTER SW4735
Chysauster Ancient Village (off B3311 N of Gulval, where the Coldstreamer is a well run dining pub) Highly evocative Iron Age site, on a breezy hillside: remains of eight courtyard houses grouped beside what might be Britain's oldest village street give an idea of Celtic life almost 2,000 years ago. The site is also notable for its large untreated meadow, popular with wild birds, and, depending on the season, bright with bluebells, heather or unusual orchids. Snacks, shop; cl Nov-Mar; (07831) 757934; £2; EH.

COVERACK SW7818
A beautiful fishing village, with great views from the Paris, a nice pub. A rewarding walk takes you down to Black Head and beyond, or to Lowland Point, for dramatic views of the Manacles - striking offshore rocks.

CRACKINGTON HAVEN SX1496
A really nice beach here, with plenty of rock pools; the 'Crackington formation' creates fissures and arches in the rocks that were treacherous to sailors. With a superbly sited family dining pub, the Coombe Barton, to set you up (or reward you afterwards), there's also a good walk to **High Cliff**, Cornwall's loftiest.

DELABOLE SX0884
Gaia Energy Centre On the country's first wind farm, this hi-tech visitor centre promotes green issues; you can get a close-up look at the 30-metre wind turbines, and see lots of examples of alternative energy ranging from waterwheels and wave power to futuristic hydrogen fuel cells; cl 24-26 and 31 Dec and 1 Jan. Meals, snacks and picnic area, shop, disabled access; (01840) 213321; £4.95.

DOBWALLS SX2165
Dobwalls Family Adventure Park (off A38) This place started life as a miniature railway, and the two miles of scaled-down american-style railroad are still very much the hub of activity;

ten different steam and diesel trains chuff up and down the track. Active visitors may prefer to head straight for their extensive adventure play area full of ropes, aerial walkways and so on; in a pleasant woodland setting, it's got sections for children at both ends of the age range. The skydome, a complex climbing frame of latticed ropework, is particularly unusual. For an extra charge, a children's driving school lets over-5s drive a tiny London bus and take a driving test, and there are go-karts. Next door an art gallery specialises in birds and animals. Meals, snacks, shop, some disabled access; cl Fri May, Thurs-Fri Oct, and wkdys Nov-Easter, phone to check; (01579) 320325; £7.95.

DODMAN POINT SX0039
Reached from Gorran Haven (where the Llawnroc Hotel does good value food inc local fish), or one of the closer car parks - for instance, at Hemmick Beach - this allows a round walk mainly along clifftops.

EDEN PROJECT SX0554
This mammoth £86 million project is now fully opened, if not completely finished: several features will be better in the next few years when they have had the chance to grow a bit more. Originally intended to be the world's largest greenhouse, it's like a space-age version of Kew Gardens, focusing on how plants from around the world affect us all. The 35-acre site is a conversion of an old china clay pit: you start in a visitor centre, which will give you your first view of the place's most dramatic features, the huge conservatories (called biomes). Constructed with massive hexagonal panels that slot together like a giant Meccano set, these are interesting to walk through, particularly the bigger Humid Tropics Biome, which effortlessly fits in a re-created rainforest, lagoon and 25-metre waterfall, with all the plants you'd expect to find and perhaps some birds and insects too. The colourful Warm Temperate Biome features plants from the Mediterranean and California (which still need to grow a bit), while gardens outside show what you'd find in a temperate climate like that of Britain, or the Himalayas. Displays explain how people live in various climates, and how plants are used for food, medicine and to make everything from tyres to toothpaste. As well as on display boards, ecological points are also made with art, sculpture or music, and the friendly staff are ready to explain things in an accessible way; adventure trails have hands-on activities for children, but don't expect elaborate play areas or computer displays. Even if you are highly allergic to eco-correctness, the sheer spectacle of the plants themselves is always rewarding. Although it's very well organised, at peak times it does get extremely crowded, and they may shut the site to prevent overcrowding. Meals, snacks, interesting shops (one sells cornish wines), good disabled access and facilities (a train can take you from the entrance to the biomes); cl 24-25 Dec; (01726) 811911; £10, tickets are also available in advance from Tourist Information Centres, and even some hotels. The Kings Arms at Luxulyan is a handy retreat.

FALMOUTH SW8132
The huge natural harbour is full of sailing boats of every description, big sea-going ships and little passenger ferries (to St Mawes and Truro - great fun). There's a good choice of boat trips (ask at the tourist information centre or head for the Prince of Wales Pier); a summer road train stops at all the town's main attractions. It's also a busy but pleasant shopping centre, with some nice old-fashioned streets, ships' chandlers and a good bustling atmosphere. Broad avenues of spiky-leaved dracaena trees away from the centre give it quite a foreign feel; there's not just a park and ride, but also a park and float. The Quayside and Chain Locker by the inner harbour do useful food, and the Warehouse is an enjoyable waterside restaurant. The A39 here from Truro can be tiresomely slow.

National Maritime Museum Cornwall (Discovery Quay) In a spectacular building dominating the waterfront, this is a rewarding half-day out for boat enthusiasts and landlubbers alike. It sets out to explore all things relating to boats and the sea, and particularly the importance of the sea to Cornwall. The National Small Boat Collection is on permanent loan from the museum's better-known branch in Greenwich, and 40 different boats are shown each year. A definite highlight is the tidal gallery, built below sea level with big glass windows to show the dramatic patterns of the tide; you can get a good look at local sealife too. Many of the exhibits are hands-on: an interactive water science gallery is aimed at children, while other interactives explain aspects of navigation and meteorology. At the top of the building's lighthouse-like tower, telescopes and push-button exhibits reveal more about the surrounding area; talks, workshops and demonstrations of traditional ship-building techniques. Meals, snacks, shop, good disabled access; cl 25-26 Dec, plus 2-30 Jan for exhibition renewal; (01326) 313388; £5.90.

Pendennis Castle (1m SE of Falmouth) Superb views from this well preserved fort, one of Henry VIII's chain of coastal defences; displays of firearms and uniforms in the museum, a hands-on discovery centre and World War II guardroom with cells. Snacks, shop, limited disabled access; cl 24-26 Dec, 1 Jan; (01326) 316594; £4.20; EH.

FOWEY SX1251
(pronounced 'Foy') Steep, lively and bustling, in an exceptional riverside position, with pretty views from up the hill on either side, some interesting shops in its maze of quaint alleys and tiny lanes, and a choice of good value food pubs - King of Prussia, Ship and Galleon. The harbour has yachts to ocean-going ships, also car ferry to Bodinnick, and foot ferry to Polruan, the similarly steep little harbourside hamlet opposite - less interesting, but with lovely views of Fowey (both have decent pubs). **St Catherine's Castle** is a ruined stronghold built by Henry VIII, restored mid-19th c; free. The NT owns most of the coastline in these parts, so count on clean beaches; just around from the harbour, the secluded cove at Lantic Bay (reached by a steep coastal path) is particularly nice. A popular circular route takes walkers

across on the Bodinnick car ferry, then takes the path through the steep creekside woods round to Polruan, and comes back on the other foot ferry.

GODOLPHIN CROSS SW6031
Godolphin House You can watch restoration in progress at this 15th-c house of the Earls of Godolphin, well known for its colonnaded front; the gardens date back to Tudor times, and there's a display of wagons in the old stables. Snacks, shop; open Easter-Sept, phone for details; (01736) 762409; £6. There's free access to the estate, which is owned by the NT and has splendid views as well as over 400 archaeological features; open all year; £2. The Queens Arms down at Breage does decent food.

GOLANT SX1254
This waterside village has its attractions - particularly the **church**, unusual for its complete 15th-c fittings. The Fishermans Arms is a charming water's-edge local.

GOONHAVERN SW7853
World in Miniature The world's landmarks at a fraction of the normal size; and some much larger dinosaurs. Beautiful gardens with thousands of plants, children's fairground rides, a maze and an indoor play area. Meals, snacks, shop, disabled access; cl Nov-Easter; (01872) 572828; £6.

GOONHILLY SW7221
Goonhilly Satellite Earth Station
This eerily space-age international telecoms complex dominates the flat hinterland of the Lizard peninsula, a startling sight in the heart of Cornwall; the main 33-metre (108-ft) dish has recently joined the national list of buildings of architectural or historical importance. The visitor centre has a film show and free internet surfing, and lets you operate one of the tracking dishes; there are guided tours of the site, which is part of a national nature reserve. A well presented, interesting and genuinely exciting place, though probably not ideal for younger children. Meals, snacks, shop, disabled access; phone for opening times; (0800) 679593; £5. The B3293 past here and the byroad to Kuggar are unusual for cornish roads, in giving some quite distant views.

GUNWALLOE SW6620
St Winwaloe This romantic little
15th-c church is set among the sand
dunes in Church Cove; its detached bell
tower (usually half-buried in blown
sand) is actually built into the cliff.
North of here, the beach at Halzephron
has been the scene of many shipwrecks
(the name means 'Hell's cliff' in
Cornish); it's popular with treasure-
hunters.

GWEEK SW7027
National Seal Sanctuary Britain's
largest marine mammal rescue centre,
this provides a home for dozens of
injured or orphaned seals (all with their
own names and character traits) that
they hope to be able to release back
into the wild. They've underwater
observatories, a sea lion pool, and a pair
of otters too; also woodland walks and
a nature trail, play area, donkeys, ponies
and goats, and an audio-visual display.
Snacks and summer barbecues, shop,
disabled access; cl 25 Dec; (01326)
221361; £7.50. The Gweek Inn is a
handy nearby family pub, and the
Trengilly Wartha at Nancenoy is good
for lunch, with a nice walk down to
Scotts Quay on the creek.

HAYLE SW5536
Paradise Park Wildlife Sanctuary
The World Parrot Trust's HQ, with
some of the beautiful and sometimes
rare residents shown to spectacular
effect in the huge Parrot Jungle, a
splendid mix of waterfalls, swamps and
streams; they've recently added a
feeding station here for their hyacinth
macaws from Brazil. You can try feeding
lorikeets in the walk-through australian
aviaries (nectar for sale in the shop),
there's a toucan aviary, and lots of
other exotic birds and numerous
animals inc miniature horses, pygmy
goats, red pandas, and a recently gained
lemur, some of which you can feed at
the Fun Farm. Daily free-flying bird
show (usually at 12.30), summer bird of
prey displays (not Sat exc July- Aug),
entertaining penguin and otter feeding
shows, children's quiz trails, big play
area, and a narrow-gauge railway gently
rattling through the park. Adults may
prefer the tropical plants in the
Victorian walled garden, or the pub that
brews its own real ale. Meals, snacks,

shop (and plant sales), mostly disabled
access; (01736) 751020; £7.50.

HELFORD SW7526
The beautifully sited thatched
Shipwrights Arms here does a good fish
pie, and an undemanding coast path
heads E to **Dennis Head** and beyond.
This NE part of the Lizard is appreciably
leafier, with some intricate coves.

HELSTON SW6527
Pleasantly quiet, hilly town that livens
up for its famous annual Furry Dance in
early May. Worth a visit if passing, the
folk museum in the Old Market Place
has a costume gallery; shop, disabled
access; usually cl Sun and bank hols;
01326 564027; £2. The simple Blue
Anchor pub has a 15th-c working
brewhouse which you can usually look
around at lunchtime; the best food
nearby is at the Halzephron at
Gunwalloe, off the A3083 S - a good
road with views, and usually signs of
action from the Culdrose helicopter
base.

Flambards Village Theme Park (off
A394, S edge of village) A clear cut
above the average, this beautifully kept
leisure park appeals to adults as much as
children, and you could easily spend a
day here. One of the best parts is the
very good reconstructed Victorian
village, which now has over 50
authentically furnished and stocked
houses, shops and settings, complete
with cobbled streets, carriages and
other period pieces. Also a life-size
'Britain in the Blitz' street, a collection
of aircraft, adventure playground and
play areas, beautiful gardens, displays on
topics from wedding fashions to antique
prams, and rides to suit all ages. Meals,
snacks, shop, disabled access; usually cl
end Oct-wk before Easter, and some
days at the beginning and end of season,
phone to check ; (01326) 573404;
£12.25.

Trevarno Estate & Gardens (off
B3303 NW) There are some lovely
walks around a tranquil lake with
Victorian boathouse, through a yew
tunnel, and in a wood full of bluebells in
spring. Also here, the **National
Museum of Gardening** traces the
development of gardening from the
18th c; the collection includes lots of
antique gardening equipment and

memorabilia. The attractive conservatory has a fountain, and serves good value snacks and cream teas; various workshops inc soap-making, and they've recently reopened the bee centre (making beeswax can be fun for children). Meals, snacks, shop, some disabled access; (01326) 574274; £4.75.

KENNACK SANDS SW7316
(just E of Kuggar) One of the cleanest beaches in Britain, with beautifully clear water; it can get crowded.

KINGSAND/CAWSAND SX4350
Appealing seaside village with higgledy-piggledy charm, nr great cliff walks, notably S to Rame Head, which juts far out at the E end of Whitsand Bay; it is capped by a primitive hermitage chapel. Also easy access on foot to Mount Edgcumbe Country Park. The Halfway House in the village has good local fish.

KIT HILL SX3771
(off the A390 N of Callington) With a huge chimney stack and mine shafts, this gives breezy walks, and impressive views across to Dartmoor.

LAMORNA SW4424
The cove is pretty, with good walks along the coast path; there's a nice view of the Merry Maidens stone circle from the B3315 just W, a Bronze Age stone circle, reputedly 19 local girls turned to stone for dancing on Sunday. **Lamorna Pottery** also has a garden with acclaimed cream teas; meals, snacks, shop, disabled access; cl 25-26 Dec; (01736) 810330; free. The Lamorna Wink is pleasant for lunch, with interesting warship memorabilia.

LAND'S END SW3425
The most westerly point of England, with wild and blustery walks along dramatic clifftops, and on a clear day views out as far even as the Isles of Scilly. You'll be lucky if you're able to stand and contemplate it on your own, though - the 200-acre site has been extensively developed for families over the years; with 'multi-sensory experiences', farm animals, a sound and light show, amusement arcades, gift shops, craft centres, burger bars and plenty to amuse children. The exhibitions and hi-tech displays are a useful enough introduction to the folklore of the area; there's also a Wildlife Trust hut, and an RSPB

observation hide has information on the coastline's wildlife. Meals, snacks, shopping arcade, good disabled access; cl 24-25 Dec; (01736) 871501; £10 for all attractions. However, there's no need to go in or buy a ticket if you just want the views, as a public right of way goes through here to Land's End itself. The same goes for the fine cliff walks in both directions - the one to Sennen is short and sweet (good family beach at Sennen Cove), but it's even better in the other direction: the eight-mile clifftop walk to Treen encompasses two natural arches (one in Nanjizal, the first bay after Land's End), stupendous views and three wonderfully remote beaches (in Nanjizal, Porthgwarra and Porthcurno - this last has the best swimming opportunities).

LANHYDROCK SX0863
Lanhydrock House This splendid old house has a staggering 50 rooms to look at; the highlight is the Long Gallery, with its magnificently illustrated Old Testament scenes - it's one of the few original 16th-c parts left, as a disastrous fire in the 19th c resulted in major changes and refurbishments. Do leave time to explore the pretty formal gardens (glorious around May) and grounds with Victorian coach house stables; it's a lovely walk down to the river and back through the woods. Good meals and snacks, shop and plant sales, disabled access; house cl Mon (exc bank hols) and Nov-Mar; (01208) 73320; £7.20, £3.90 grounds only (free Nov to mid-Feb); NT. The Crown down at Lanlivery is most enjoyable for lunch, in a Jane Austen village setting.

LANREATH SX1856
Pretty village with some remarkable woodwork in its exceptional medieval **church**.
Folk & Farm Museum Most fun for its summer demonstrations and workshops: corn dolly making (Mon), pasty crimping (Weds) and egg decorating (Fri) - all activities 2-4pm; also farm animals to feed, a children's telephone exchange, and picnic area. Snacks, shop, disabled access; cl Nov-Easter; (01503) 220321; £2.50.

LANSALLOS SX1751
Lansallos church The attraction here is inside the church - the ancient carved

bench-ends, each individual but all sharing a style.

LANTEGLOS HIGHWAY SX1453
Lanteglos Highway church A curiosity, Perpendicular but not - subsidence has left the arches at drunken angles.

LAUNCESTON SX3285
Once Cornwall's capital, this is the most attractive inland town in Cornwall, with winding old hillside streets and an untouristy feel; the White Hart does popular food.

Launceston Castle On a Norman motte, the ruined 12th- and 13th-c hilltop castle is substantial and commanding - it was captured four times during the Civil War. Snacks, shop; cl Nov-Mar exc Fri-Sun, 24-26 Dec and 1 Jan; (01566) 772365; £2.10; EH.

Launceston Steam Railway 19th-c locomotives running on a 2-ft gauge line along the trackbed of the old North Cornwall Railway, through 2½ miles of scenic valley - open carriages on sunny days; also transport museum. A network of footpaths leads off from Newmills Station, where there's an extensive play area (handy for wearing out energetic children). Snacks, bookshop, disabled access; phone for a timetable; (01566) 775665; £5.50, 50p extra for dogs.

Lawrence House (Castle St) Georgian house with useful displays on the town's past; shop, disabled access to ground floor; cl wknds and Oct-Mar; (01566) 773277; free.

Trethorne Leisure Farm 🖾 (Kennards House, off A30 3m W of Launceston) 140-acre farm with plenty under cover; good for children, who can milk a cow, play with the rabbits, take a pony ride or bottle-feed the lambs. Also roller-blading, ten-pin bowling, good 18-hole golf course and driving range, assault course and big outdoor and indoor play areas. Meals, snacks, shop, disabled access; cl Sun (exc golf) and 25-26 Dec; (01566) 86324; £5.50.

LIZARD SW7012
This peninsula S of Helston is famous as the most southerly part of mainland Britain, and though the inland parts can be rather flat and dull and not really worth extended walks, the coastline is more attractive. The National Trust have improved the area around Lizard Point, the southern tip, in recent years, and it's a good start for bracing cliff walks in either direction, with uplifting views. Readers very much enjoy exploring the Lizard's dramatic western and eastern edges. The W side has mighty cliffs, with roads down to beautiful Mullion Cove and Kynance Cove. The E side is more sheltered and lusher, with wooded creeks: ensconced in a cove here, Cadgwith is a picturesque steep village with photogenic fish stores, thatched cottages, and a good pub. A rewarding short stroll on the coast path leads S to Chynhalls Point past the aptly named Devil's Frying Pan, where the waves foam into a spectacular collapsed cavern. Lizard village itself is pretty uninspiring (the Top House is a very civilised pub, and a shop has interesting local serpentine rock carvings), but is well placed for longer walks encompassing Church Cove to the E. It's also a lovely walk NW along the coast to Kynance Cove, a wonderful little tidal beach below the spectacular cliffs (or a shorter walk down from the Kynance Cove car park), with huge rocks, caves and sandy coves. On top and inland the Lizard is disappointing: a big flat peninsula, although the Goonhilly satellite station is a remarkable landmark.

Wireless Station (Bass Point - 10 mins walk from Housel Bay Hotel) The two wooden huts and aerial mast are thought to be the oldest surviving purpose-built wireless station in the world; in 1901 it was from here that Marconi proved that radio waves could travel around the curvature of the earth when he received signals from the Isle of Wight. Shop, phone for opening times; (01326) 290384; donations.

LOE POOL SW6424
Cornwall's largest lake, a haven for waterfowl, is blocked from the sea by a shingle bank called Loe Bar (only breeding place of the rare sandhill rust moth - and favourite place of worship of a german evangelical sect); a path leads round the lake and through the NT-owned Penrose estate. There's a coast walk from here to Gunwalloe fishing cove.

LOOE SX2553
Seaside resort packed with tourist
shops, teashops and pubs, but with a
nice easy-going atmosphere even in
high season. The old fishing village with
its picturesque harbour and narrow
little back streets is now immersed in
tourism, and is the main shark-fishing
place (on 'shark-fishing' trips you watch
others doing the catching). From the
quay there may be summer **boat trips**
to nearby St George's Island; phone the
tourist information for details; (01503)
262072. The Olde Salutation has plenty
of atmosphere and good simple food;
the Smugglers is a decent friendly
restaurant, and the quayside Trawlers
has very good unusual seafood.
Monkey Sanctuary (signed off B3253
at No Man's Land, just E of Looe) A
fascinating place, going strong now for
40 years, its wooded grounds home to a
colony of amazonian woolly monkeys.
All were born here, and talks by staff
give an intriguing insight into the
dynamics and politics of the monkey
community. Meals, snacks, shop,
disabled access (though some bits are
quite steep); cl Fri-Sat, and end Sept-wk
before Easter (exc perhaps autumn half-
term); (01503) 262532; *£5.
LUXULYAN SX0558
The village has an attractive church, and
from the village you can walk along the
valley to the S, and explore the area's
industrial archaeology, most of it
tucked away in the woods; 19th-c
granite quarrying left a huge viaduct,
inclines and water courses. The Kings
Arms has decent food.
MADRON SW4431
Trengwainton Garden (B3312) The
name in Cornish means 'Farm of the
Spring', and it does always seem to be
spring at this lovely place, the climate
favouring plants not usually found
outside in England. Magnolias, azaleas,
rhododendrons, unusual southern
hemisphere trees and shrubs inc a
delightful tree-fern grotto, walled
gardens, good views to Mounts Bay and
the Lizard. Cream teas, shop,
interesting plant sales, some disabled
access; open Sun-Thurs (and Good Fri)
mid Feb-Oct (01736) 362297; £4; NT.
MARAZION SW5130
St Michael's Mount There's

something particularly awe-inspiring
about this medieval castle, rising
majestically from the sea. On gloomy or
stormy days the picturesque silhouette
seems even more dramatic. The little
island is reached by ferry (it doesn't go
in bad weather), or at low tide on foot
along a causeway; the walk up to the
castle, still the home of the family which
acquired it in 1660, is quite steep. Fine
Chippendale furniture, plaster reliefs,
armour and paintings. Summer meals,
snacks, shop; open (tide and weather
permitting) wkdys and some wknds
Apr-Oct, and Mon, Weds and Fri only
Nov-Mar, phone to check; (01736)
710507; £5; NT (members have to pay
at wknds). The Godolphin Arms has
popular food.
MAWGAN SW7223
Trelowarren This manor house is
worth a look for its elaborate
Strawberry Hill 'gothick' chapel (open
by appointment), and the surrounding
estate (open all the time) has plenty
going on in summer inc woodland
walks, craft shops and pottery,
campsite, and good meals in the New
Yard Restaurant; parts may be cl over
winter, when there's no parking charge;
(01326) 221224; £1.50 per car.
MAWNAN SMITH SW7728
This sheltered coastal village is pretty,
and the Red Lion is good for lunch.
From nearby Mawnan a fine if blowy
stretch of the coast path takes you
around Rosemullion Head and on N to
Maenporth, where there's a sheltered
sandy cove with decent modern
pub/restaurant.
Glendurgan Garden Lovely
subtropical garden in valley above
Helford River, started by Alfred Fox in
1820; fine shrubs from all over the
world, mature trees, walled garden and
restored laurel maze. Snacks, shop; cl
Sun, Mon (exc bank hols), Good Fri, and
Nov to mid-Feb; (01326) 250906;
£4.10; NT.
Trebah Garden Next to Glendurgan,
this gorgeous steeply wooded ravine
garden is a favourite of many readers. It
can feel as if you've strayed into a
benign, exclusive jungle, with huge
subtropical tree ferns and palms, giant
gunnera, lots of blue and white
hydrangeas, 100-year-old

rhododendrons, and some fine rare trees. Several activities for children, and at the bottom end a private beach on the Helford River - good for a picnic or secluded swim. Restaurant with home-made snacks and meals, art gallery and shop (plants for sale), some disabled access (electric buggies are available); (01326) 250448; £5 (half price with a Truronian bus or King Harry ferry ticket).

MEVAGISSEY SX0144

This fishing village is great fun, and still packed with cornish character, despite commercialisation and sizeable modern outskirts. At its most fetching around the knot of streets at the little working harbour (which has a parking charge of £1.50 in winter and £2.50-£3 in the summer), with hillside cottages looking over it. The Fountain (down an alley by the post office) has a good harbourside atmosphere, and the local male voice choir enliven the Kings Arms (Fore St) on Mon (in Aug they sing on the harbour jetty instead); the waterside Mr Bistro and Sharks Fin do mainly fresh fish.

Folk Museum Run by enthusiastic staff, this decent local museum in an 18th-c boat-builder's shed on East Quay has a comprehensive wartime exhibition; shop, disabled access to ground floor only; cl Nov-Easter, also pm Sat, am Sun, best to check; (01726) 843568; £1.50.

Lost Gardens of Heligan (off B3273, just NW) The televised restoration of these gardens, neglected and forgotten from 1914 to 1991, made them among Britain's best known. Some very fine mature trees, Victorian walled gardens, lots of rhododendrons, lakes, and impressive collection of tree ferns, bamboos and palms. You can watch what's happening in numerous cameras set up in nesting boxes, and their latest project has been to restore the Home Farm. It's a friendly place, and they're more than happy to talk about their work; readers highly recommend the guided tours (£1.50). Meals, snacks, shop/nursery, disabled access; cl 24-25 Dec; (01726) 845100; £6. The Crown at St Ewe is good for lunch.

World of Model Railways (Meadow St) Over 50 model trains trundling

through a realistic little world that takes in cornish china clay pits, ski resorts, fairgrounds, towns and country. Shop, disabled access; open daily Mar-Oct, Sun and school half-term Nov-Feb; (01726) 842457; £3.25.

MORVAH SW4035

Wonderfully rugged scenery both inland and along the coast here: the moors nearly reach the sea, and in a few miles walkers can take in the cliff path, the moors close to the ruin of Ding Dong Mine, the prehistoric stone hoop of Men an Tol, the inscribed stone of Men Scryfa, and the Iron Age hillfort of Chun Castle (Cornwall's best preserved hillfort, with many stones still in place), which looks down to the mushroom-shaped Bronze Age burial chamber of Chun Quoit. Lanyon Quoit, a very photogenic prehistoric burial chamber sometimes called the Giant's Table, reassembled after a storm toppled it in the early 19th c, is beside the road from Madron. The Gurnards Head Hotel (B3306) is a good refreshment or meal stop; the eponymous headland, jutting dramatically into the Atlantic, gives bracing cliff walks.

MORWENSTOW SS2015

The **church**, in an idyllic setting, has Norman arches and 16th-c bench ends, with shipwrecked sailors' headstones in the graveyard. A driftwood shack built for contemplation by a Victorian parson over the impressive cliffs is preserved by the NT. The Bush is an interesting very ancient pub, and the rectory tearoom is delightful. Handy for restless children **Killarney Springs** has a variety of play areas and activities; also farm animals, an aerial slide, karting (£3) and bumper boats (£2.50). Meals, snacks, shop, disabled access; open Apr-Oct; (01288) 331475; £5.95.

MOUSEHOLE SW4626

Attractive working fishing village with steep little roads - too many summer visitors, but lovely out of season, with spectacular Christmas lights in the little harbour; the Old Coastguard has good interesting food and a lovely shoreside garden.

MULLION SW6719

This attractive village has a popular family pub (the Old Inn) and a possibly unique feature in its church - a dog flap. You can hire bicycles at Atlantic Forge; £5 half-day, £7 a day (and wetsuits too; £5); (01326) 240294 - open Easter-late Sept, phone to check at other times. This is a good way to explore the Lizard.

MULLION COVE SW6617
This dramatic fusion of rock, sand and sea is most rewardingly reached by a there-and-back walk along the cliff from Porth Mellin; for the energetic, the extension S to Kynance Cove is outstanding.

NEWLYN SW4629
Cornwall's busiest working fishing port - it's great fun watching the boats come in - and home to the last working **Salt Pilchard Works**, a tour of which passes a surprisingly entertaining hour or so; shop; cl wknds (exc by appointment) and Nov-Mar; (01736) 332112; £3.25. There's an excellent and occasionally rather avant-garde **Art Gallery** (New Rd) in a lovely coastal setting with fine views; changing exhibitions around every five weeks (cl Sun, 25-26 Dec and 1 Jan; (01736) 363715; donations). At Christmas the fishermen decorate the harbour and its boats with spectacular lights. The Tolcarne, with a sea wall terrace (and parking), is useful for lunch.

NEWLYN EAST SW8655
Lappa Valley Steam Railway and Leisure Park 15-inch gauge steam line through pretty countryside to an old lead mine. It's surrounded by parkland with lakes, woodland walk, a maze, and play areas; a section of the old branch line leads to a nine-hole golf course. Meals, snacks, shop, some disabled access; cl Nov-Easter, and some days in Oct - best to check train times; (01872) 510317; £6.80, covers fare and all attractions exc golf. The backstreet Pheasant has good home cooking.

NEWQUAY SW8261
England's surfing capital, this thorough-going seaside resort has a cheery young feel. It has excellent safe golden beaches below breezy cliffs; Crantock Beach is the best and least crowded, with great views from the Bowgie family pub up on West Pentire headland. Fistral Beach is reckoned by some to be the best surfing beach in Europe; a couple of surfing schools here can get beginners

started. There's no shortage of souvenir shops, an alcohol-free zone declared on the streets, theme parks on the edge, and older houses around the harbour. The sea-view Fort Hotel (Fore St) has decent family food all day, and up on the Pentire headland the newly rebuilt Lewinnick Lodge does good interesting food, with great views.

Blue Reef Aquarium (Towan Beach) Lots of fascinating living displays, and a centrepiece underwater tunnel running through a recreated caribbean tropical reef; bubble windows bring you face to face with fish, sea-horses and sharks. At Cornish Coastlines open-top tanks let you get close to friendly rays, an octopus exhibition has a host of mind-boggling facts, there's a mediterranean underwater display, and a new exhibition on crustaceans features some truly awesome crabs; regular talks and feeding displays. Meals, snacks, shop, disabled access; cl 25 Dec; (01637) 872134; £5.50.

Dairyland See separate famly panel on p.72.

Holywell Bay Fun Park 🔢 (off A3075 SW) Active children should enjoy the go-karts, bumper boats, rides, climbing wall, indoor play area, maze and crazy golf (pitch and putt course too). Meals, snacks, shop, mostly disabled access; cl Nov-Easter; (01637) 830095; separate charges for various attractions (discount voucher gives ten tokens free when you buy £20-worth of tokens). A short walk away, **Holywell Bay** is one of the area's more sheltered beaches, with a 70-year-old shipwreck, and a cave visible at low tide; the Smugglers Den at Cubert is a nice pub.

Newquay Zoo (Trenance Leisure Park, off A3075 Edgcumbe Ave) The emphasis is very much on conservation here, with many exotic animals in natural enclosures inc monkeys, penguins and lions, as well as gardens, and summer activities. Feeding displays are well timetabled so there's something to see throughout the day, and there's also a children's farm, play areas, and a maze. Meals, snacks, shop, disabled access; cl 25 Dec; (01637) 873342; £6.75. **Water World**, a lively fun pool, is just up the road; (01637) 853829.

Tunnels Through Time (St Michaels Rd) A 40-minute rainy day diversion, with recreated figures and scenes from history and myth inc King Arthur, smugglers and pirates, past punishments for drunken husbands and nagging wives, and some gory torture scenes. Snacks, shop; open Sun-Fri (plus Sat school and bank hols) Easter-autumn half-term; (01637) 873379. £3.90.

NORTH PETHERWIN SX2889
Tamar Otter Park Friendly place breeding otters, then releasing them back into the wild; it's fun to watch them playing. Three species of deer roam free, and there are waterfowl lakes, wallabies, and nature trails. The otters are fed at noon and 3pm. Snacks, shop, some disabled access; cl Nov-Mar; (01566) 785646; £5. The Countryman at Boyton is a handy lunch stop.

PADSTOW SW9175
Quaint streets, old buildings clustered around the working fishing harbour, and attractive slate houses. The quayside **Lobster Hatchery Visitor Centre** has viewing tanks and displays inc some interactive ones; shop, disabled access; cl Sun Sept-Apr plus 24-26, 31 Dec and 1 Jan; (01841) 533877; £2.50. Rick Stein's restaurant draws the crowds (you'll need to book well in advance), and the Golden Lion and London Inn are useful for lunch. The Camel estuary, popular for sailing, has gentle dreamy scenery with lots of little boats, while the Camel trail is good for walkers and cyclists. Plenty of lovely clean beaches near here (though no beaches in the town itself); Constantine Bay is the best, and well liked by surfers. The B3276 has the best roadside coastal views in this part of Cornwall.
Prideaux Place (NW outskirts) Still a lived-in family home, this fine old house has changed little since it was built in the late 16th c. Highlights include the elegant ceilings, atmospheric library and the intricate biblical tableaux in the Great Chamber. Notable concerts and special events in the grounds (which they are currently restoring), and there's a deer park. Snacks, shop, disabled access to ground floor only;

usually cl am, Fri-Sat, Oct-Easter, and around 2 wks after Easter to mid-May, best to check; (01841) 532411; £6, gardens only £2.
Shipwreck, Rescue and Heritage Centre (South Quay) A friendly museum not far from the town's little harbour, with relics and tales of the plentiful shipwrecks along this coast, and a decent collection of diving equipment with exhibits dating back to 1740; you can also clamber on board an old lifeboat, and have a go at remote-control boats (50p). Snacks, shop, disabled access; open Mar-Oct; (01726) 69897; £4.95.

PENDEEN SW3834
Geevor Tin Mine (Boscaswell) You get a good idea of what mining was really like at this nicely undeveloped tin mine, which was working until 1990; you can explore the mine's surface (the changing rooms are especially evocative), a guided tour takes you underground, and there's a museum. Meals (Easter-Oct), snacks, shop, limited disabled access; cl Sat Easter-end Oct; (01736) 788662; £6. The Radjel has good value food.
Levant Mine (B3306, 1m W) The coast path goes right through this ghostly wasteland of abandoned buildings, mine shafts and rubble; in the midst of it all is the clifftop engine house, restored and powered by the oldest steam engine in Cornwall (built 1840), all explained by knowledgeable and enthusiastic staff - if someone is available they'll take you on a tour of the site. Shop, limited disabled access; usually open Fri all year, Easter and May bank hol Mon, Weds (or perhaps Tues), Thurs and Sun in Jun, daily exc Sat July-Sept, Tues in May and Oct, phone to check (steamings Mar-Oct); (01736) 786156; £4; NT. The nearby Pendeen Watch lighthouse is worth a look, and not far down the coast (forking left to Carn Gloose off the Cape Cornwall road out of St Just) is Ballowal, an extraordinarily complex Bronze Age burial mound above the sea, with local tales of fairies and dancing lights.
PENHALLOW SW7650
Cornish Cyder Farm Working cider farm producing scrumpy, country wines and jam, with seasonal demonstrations,

and friendly horses, rabbits, goats, pigs and donkeys. Enjoyable guided tours inc a tractor trailer ride, and a visit to the cider museum (£5). Meals, snacks (inc cream teas), shop (with samples of everything they make), disabled access; cl 23 Dec-12 Jan, wknds mid-Jan to Mar; (01872) 573356; free. The Miners Arms at Mithian is handy for lunch.

PENRYN SW7834

Appealing waterside town, quite sizeable, with pretty Tudor, Jacobean and Georgian houses.

PENZANCE SW4730

The area's main shopping centre, a pleasantly relaxed town by the sea with appealing 18th- and 19th-c terraces and squares, and two palm-shaded parks. The prettiest part is Chapel St; the extravagantly designed early 19th-c Egyptian House deserves a passing look, and the Turks Head is a good pub. Harris's restaurant in New St has fresh local fish. On the promenade, Jubilee Pool is of the few operational lido swimming pools left in the country; filled with seawater, it's only a little warmer than the sea (cl mid-Sept to end May, and perhaps at other times for cleaning). In summer you can take boat trips around the coastline, and there are ferry trips to the Isles of Scilly (phone (08457) 105555; £57-£75 return (£30 day return), or you can take a helicopter flight across; best to book (01736) 362341; £117 return, from £81 day return - ask about special offers. You can't get to the islands on Sun.

National Lighthouse Centre (Old Buoy Store, Wharf Rd) Easy to spot thanks to the big buoys outside, this has an excellent collection of lighthouse equipment, and a good audio-visual display on what it was like to live in one; a typical room is reconstructed, with original curved furniture. There is a lighthouse opposite. Shop, mostly disabled access; open Easter-Oct, though best to check as they may cl for refurbishment; (01736) 360077; £3.

Penlee House Gallery & Museum £ (Morrab Rd) In pleasant Penlee Park, this Victorian house mainly shows paintings by the Newlyn School. Meals, snacks, shop, disabled access; cl Sun, and a few days over Christmas and New Year; (01736) 363625; £2 (free Sat).

POLKERRIS SX0952

Little seaside hamlet - scarcely more than the good waterside inn - with terrific view, almost even better in winter, across St Austell bay from well restored ancient quay.

POLPERRO SX2150

Almost unbelievably pretty, tiny streets around a very quaint sheltered fishing harbour, little cottages perched on rocks - once a busy smuggling place, now some enjoyable craft shops tucked away, one or two tourist attractions, oddities like the shell-encrusted Shell House, and unspoilt harbourside fishermen's locals (the Blue Peter and Three Pilchards); the Crumplehorn Mill does decent food. The beaches around here are some of England's cleanest. It gets very busy in summer, with little electric buses (or horse and cart) shuttling in from the out-of-village car park. A sensible alternative to sweating out summer traffic jams in the village itself is to park instead in Talland Bay, for an easy one-mile walk along the coast to enter this harbour feeling you've earned it.

Land of Legend & Model Village (The Old Forge, Mill Hill) A useful enough distraction for children, with four model railways (one brand new this year), and a scaled-down version of Polperro. Shop, some disabled access; cl Nov-Easter; (01503) 272378; £2.50.

POLZEATH SW9378

The village itself, facing the mouth of the Camel estuary, is unremarkably modern, but a lovely path N rounds the rocky headland at Rumps Point, all of which can be walked round in an hour or so. To the S the coastal path heads through the dunes beyond Brea Hill (worth diverting inland to St Enodoc church, burial place of John Betjeman) to Rock - with the option of walking along the beach at low tide. Useful foot passenger ferry from Rock to Padstow, call Padstow tourist information for details; (01841) 533449; £2 return.

POOL SW6741

Cornish Engines (A3047) Two big beam engines originally used for pumping water from tin and copper mines dominate this site - one of them is now working, powered by electricity, and they're in the process of restoring the other one. Visitor centre with interactive and audio-visual displays. Shop, disabled access; open Sun-Fri Apr-Oct plus Sat in Aug; (01209) 315027; £5; NT. The Cornish Choughs (at Treswithian, just off the far end of the Camborne bypass) has interesting food inc good fresh fish.

PORT ISAAC SX0080
Delightful steep fishing village, a favourite with many: tiny streets, and houses hanging high over the pretty harbour - the Golden Lion's terrace overlooks it. Park at the top and walk down (at low tide you can park on the beach). There are some particularly fine stretches of cliffs for walking around here, and just up the coast Port Gaverne is a beautiful NT cove.

PORTHALLOW SX2251
This is snugly set above a picturesque small fishing harbour. A friendly little **vineyard** here has self-guided tours, free samples of their wines, and a particularly tasty birch country wine; usually open Mon-Sat (cl 1-2pm) Easter-Oct; (01326) 280050; free.

PORTHCURNO SW3822
Porthcurno's lovely silver sands - among Cornwall's best beaches - are the property of the National Trust, in common with so much of the coastline round here. If you walk their length, be careful not to get cut off by high tide. There's no problem if you stick to the coast path, which is exciting in either direction. A mile E it reaches Treryn Dinas, arguably the most stunning of Cornwall's headlands, capped by the precariously balanced Logan Rock. From here, the Logan Rock pub at Treen is a short lunchtime diversion across fields.

Minack Theatre & Visitor Centre
There are few better backdrops for plays than the one at this famous little open-air theatre - dramatic cliffs and blue sea stretching into the distance make this a magical setting. Varied summer season, and an exhibition on the life of Rowena Cade, the remarkable woman who built the theatre, cut into these steep cliffs, with her own hands. Tickets go on sale in May, but aren't for particular seats - if you've booked you'll still need to get there early to bag the best. Evening shows are more atmospheric. Shows are cancelled only in extreme conditions, so take a waterproof. Meals, snacks, shop, disabled access to café and exhibition; performances May-Sept, exhibition cl during matinées, and 25-26 Dec; (01736) 810181; shows £7, exhibition £2.50.

Museum of Submarine Telegraphy Don't be put off by the name - this museum housed in the secret World War II communications centre in underground tunnels is a good deal more interesting than you'd think. Shop, disabled access, cl Sat Apr-Oct (exc July-Aug and before a bank hol), phone for winter opening times; (01736) 810966; £4.

PORTHLEVEN SW6225
Pretty working fishing village; the Ship, built into the cliffs, is a good pub, and the long stretch of rocky beach S is a good walk if the surf's not beating in too fiercely.

PORTLOE SW9339
Tiny unspoilt village wedged into a precipitous cove, with splendid cliff walks in rugged scenery, and stiffish climbs on to Nare Head; good teashop, and good value bar lunches in the Ship.

PORTREATH SW6545
A good base for long bracing clifftop walks, with enjoyable food at the Portreath Arms; along this whole section of coast, between St Ives Bay and Trevose Head (nr Padstow), the coast path is rich in rugged views, and very rewarding to those with sturdy legs. For walkers and riders, the 11-mile Coast-to-Coast Trail links Portreath to Devoran following two mineral tramways (once a vital communication and transport link between copper and tin mines in West Cornwall).

Cornish Goldsmiths (Tolgus Mill, B3300 towards Redruth) You can watch goldsmiths at work, and there are a few gold-related displays inc the chance to see what your weight in gold looks like; also James Bond car and a working pottery; children's activities in summer. Meals, snacks, large jewellery shop; cl 25 Dec, 1 Jan, Easter Sun; (01209) 218198; free. Tricky Dickies up on Tolgus Mount has good value food.

PORTSCATHO SW8735
Very sheltered fishing village with a

picturesque little harbour, good value food at the Plume of Feathers, and some fine nearby beaches - excellent for families. Virtually the whole of Gerrans Bay around here is good easy walking, with some lovely clifftop stretches; there's a good sandy stretch at Pendower Beach.

PRAA SANDS SW5828

A popular summer family beach. Worth strolling along the coast SE for half a mile to Rinsey Head (car park): here by the coast path are two magnificently sited ruined tin and copper mine buildings, Wheal Prosper and Wheal Trewavas, both now maintained as landmarks by the NT. The welcoming Lion & Lamb up on the A394 has a wide range of food.

PROBUS SW9047

Probus Gardens Worth popping into, and quite a contrast to the area's grander gardens, ex-local authority demonstration garden recently taken over and being restored by volunteers; includes useful ideas for your own garden, and a 60-ft long geological map of Cornwall using the relevant rocks. Snacks, shop, disabled access; cl wknds Nov-Feb and over Christmas and New Year; (01726) 882597; £4.

Trewithen 🏠 (off A390 between Probus and Grampound, where the Dolphin has good value food) Justly famous landscaped gardens, with many rare trees and shrubs. The early 18th-c house is a little unfairly overshadowed by what's outside, and is an interesting obviously lived-in family home. Snacks, plants sales, disabled access; gardens open Mar-Sept (cl Sun exc Apr and May), house open only Mon and Tues pms Apr-July (plus Aug bank hol); (01726) 883647; gardens £4.25, house another £4.50, combined £6.50.

RESTORMEL SX1060

Restormel Castle Very well preserved Norman castle with notable round keep and fine views over Fowey Valley; lots of flowers in spring. Shop; cl Nov-Mar; (01208) 872687; £2; EH. The Royal Oak in Lostwithiel (Cornwall's capital in the 13th c) is good for lunch.

RESTRONGUET CREEK SW8137

Though the waterside village is mainly of no great age, its pub the Pandora has a lovely location - you can park in Mylor

Bridge for a leisurely two-mile waterside walk there and back (though parking can be difficult in summer), or drive all the way.

ROCHE ROCK SW9959

This small but picturesque crag is worth the short walk from the B3274, with a 14th-c ruined ivy-covered chapel built into it (decent pub nearby, past the station).

SANCREED SW4129

Carn Euny Ancient Village

Substantial traces of a little village of stone courtyard houses lived in nearly 2,000 years ago, and a 'fogou' - a 20-metre underground passage leading to a circular chamber of unknown purpose; some very minor roads to get here, free access.

ST AGNES SW7150

A former mining town, now with a holiday role; some attractive steeply terraced cottages, fine cliff scenery nearby, and great views from the St Agnes Beacon hilltop, just W of town. The Railway Inn has some interesting collections, and there are good surfing beaches nearby at Trevaunance Cove and Chapel Porth (NT).

Presingoll Barns (Penwinnick Rd) Craft centre with demonstrations of glass painting, candle and fudge-making, good picnic areas. Meals, snacks, shop, limited disabled access; cl 25-26 Dec; (01872) 553007; free (99p for candle-dipping).

ST ANTHONY HEAD SW8431

On the E side of the Fal estuary, by the **Zone Point lighthouse**, this has superb views, and easy walks along low, level cliffs; parking at the head itself, or near Porth Farm on the way down.

ST AUSTELL SX0352

The centre of the china clay industry and a busy modern shopping town. Holy Trinity **church** has a fine tower and interesting font, and you can tour the **St Austell Brewery** on Trevarthian Rd (wkdys only, phone to book - (01726) 66022; £4, inc beer samples, children over 8 only); shop and visitor centre (free). **Pine Lodge Gardens** (Holmbush) are well worth a visit: the 30 acres include an arboretum, fernery, herbaceous borders, japanese garden, and several ponds and water features (the lake has black swans);

tearoom, plant sales, disabled access; open beginning Mar-Oct; (01726) 73500; £4.50. The area N is a strange bleak moonscape of whitish spoil heaps with metallic blue lakes dotted among them; the B3279 St Stephen—Nanpean gives some of the best views over this.

China Clay Museum (B3274 N - you don't have to go into the town) Interestingly restored 19th-c clayworks showing the 250-year history of china clay production. Working waterwheels and other equipment, steam locomotives, nature trails with a spectacular viewpoint over a huge clay pit, children's adventure trail and picnic areas. Meals, snacks, shop; cl 24-25 Dec; (01726) 850362; £5.50. The Bugle Inn (A391) does food all day.

ST CLEER SX2568

Trevethy Quoit This is a very photogenic megalithic tomb, its massive stones now left high and dry by a fall in the soil level over thousands of years. The Crows Nest down near Darite is handy for lunch.

ST GERMANS SX3657

St Germans church Wonderful Norman doorway and particularly fine east window; worth a look if you're passing this waterside village. There's a good view towards Port Eliot, a stately home designed by John Soane (not open).

ST IVES SW5039

A pretty place, despite the summer crowds, with its attractive working harbour and narrow streets and alleys (the cobbled Fore St is the prettiest). It has good wide beaches, and plenty of bird life along the Lelant Saltings (the Old Quay House there, sharing its car park with the RSPB reserve, has good value food). Besides the Blue Fish, the waterside Sloop (interesting pictures for sale) is reliable for lunch, and the Pedn Olva overlooking Porthminster beach has enjoyable modern food. The best beach for surfers is Porthmeor slightly N, while in the other direction the B3306 to Land's End has great coast and moorland views. Out of season, when the caravan and camp sites are empty, the magnificent sands around St Ives Bay are well worth walking, with good cliff walks to the west.

Barbara Hepworth Museum and

Sculpture Garden (Porthmeor Beach) This tranquil escape from the holiday hordes, devoted to the artist's work and life, has sculptures (including unfinished ones) in the house, studio and subtropical garden, which survive almost unchanged since her death in 1975, as well as photographs, letters and tools. Shop, disabled access by appointment; cl Mon Nov-Feb, and 24-26 Dec; (01736) 796226; £4.25. Other works by Hepworth are dotted about the town.

Tate Gallery St Ives (Porthmeor Beach) St Ives's famous popularity with artists is best explored at this gallery, which can take a lot of the credit for the town's tourism boom. Works by the familiar St Ives School names are regularly joined by displays of 20th-c art with a cornish connection. It's an impressive building, outside and in, fully exploiting its spectacular cliffside setting - views are best from the café. Meals, snacks, shop, disabled access; cl Mon Nov-Feb, 24-26 Dec, and perhaps other days for rehanging; (01736) 796226; £4.75.

ST JUST-IN-ROSELAND SW8435

An unspoilt spot, with its church in an idyllic creekside setting; the steep graveyard, described by John Betjeman as 'perhaps the most beautiful churchyard on earth', is like a lost subtropical garden - well worth a visit on a quiet sunny day, or in spring with the baby rooks blethering and the smell of wild garlic. The churchyard paths are full of stones inscribed with words of wisdom, which almost steal the show.

ST KEVERNE SW7921

Set around a little square, this is a pleasant village, with a lovely **working farm** just S at Tregellast Barton, undeveloped and tranquil, with pleasant walks through woods and meadows, afternoon milking (4.30), and a good farm shop with samples of their unusually flavoured ice-cream such as apricot or marzipan; (01326) 280479; free. New people at the Three Tuns are doing decent food, and there's a good walk to Lowland Point.

ST KEW SX0276

Delightful quiet leafy village with old-fashioned feel; the St Kew Inn is a nice place for a meal.

ST MAWES SW8433

Very pretty harbourside and estuary views, a long waterfront to stroll along, clean bathing waters, a foot-passenger ferry to Falmouth and other boat trips (full of yachtsmen and others in summer). The 16th-c **castle** is remarkably well preserved and has a decent audio tour (tours Jun and Sept; cl Mon and Tues Nov-Mar; £3; EH). On the hillside, and with good views out to sea, **Lamorran House Gardens** is a four-acre mediterranean garden with lots of different species inc a large collection of palms; open Weds, Fri and first Sat in month Apr-Sept; (01326) 270800; £4. The Victory, Rising Sun and Idle Rocks Hotel all do enjoyable food. The King Harry chain-drawn car ferry on the B3269 N of St Mawes is a favourite family crossing, and the ferry across to St Anthony-in-Roseland gives access to some remote and unspoilt views and walks.

ST NEOT SX1867

This attractive village shelters in a wooded valley below Bodmin Moor. The **church** is well known for its early stained glass, and also has an unusual stone vault in the south porch. Nearby ancient remains include the five impressive **Brown Gelly Barrows** and some hut circles, halfway to Bolventor. The London Inn is a good lunch spot.

TINTAGEL SX0588

King Arthur's Great Halls (Fore St) Far from being a light-hearted romp, Arthurian legends are treated very earnestly here, and there's no denying the impressive craftsmanship, esp in the 72 stained glass scenes. The best bit though is the tour's sound and light show, which outlines the legend. Decent shop, disabled access; cl 2nd Sat in Oct and 25 Dec, limited opening hours in winter; (01840) 770526; £3.

Old Post Office Full of character, one room in this small saggy slate-roofed 14th-c manor was used as a post office in the 19th c; shop; usually cl Nov-Mar; (01840) 770024; £2.40; NT.

Tintagel Castle Forgetting the myths and legends, these dramatic 12th- and 13th-c ruins have a spectacular setting and unrivalled views. A good start is from Rocky Valley, a craggy valley

leading from the B3263 to the sea. Try to come out of season, when the crowds are fewer and the mist and crashing waves add a touch of mystery. There's quite a lot of climbing involved, and the often steep steps among the crags can be slippery in wet weather. As for King Arthur, latest theories suggest he was a Shropshire lad, but a small exhibition makes the most of the cornish case, inc the recently found Arthnou stone, a 1,400-year-old inscribed slate naming the hero. Shop; cl 24-26 Dec and 1 Jan; (01840) 770328; £3.20; EH. In summer, a Land Rover can ferry you to the site from the village (a tourist trap since the 19th c) at regular intervals throughout the day; £1. The Old Malthouse is a useful food stop, and the parish **church** is worth a look.

TORPOINT SX4156

Antony House (2m NW) A pleasant ferry ride from Devonport in Plymouth, this is the finest Classical house in Cornwall, little changed since the early 18th c, with interesting contents and paintings in its panelled rooms; also riverside grounds redesigned by Humphrey Repton, a dovecote, topiary and woodland and knot gardens. Snacks, shop, disabled access to ground floor only; open pm Tues-Thurs and bank hols Apr-Oct, plus Sun Jun-Aug; (01752) 812191; £4.60, grounds only £2.40, woodland garden £3.60 (woodland garden and grounds £3.90); NT. If instead you go by road (it's a long way round), the B3247 takes you past the Finnygook at Crafthole, a useful dining pub.

Mount Edgcumbe (B3247 E of Kingsand) The family seat of the Edgcumbes, who left their old house at Cotehele and opted for a more fashionable pile here in the 16th c. The walls survived a direct hit by a stray World War II bomb, and the mansion is now faithfully restored. The main attraction is the surrounding spread of lovely gardens and parkland, featuring english, french and italian sections, with great views to Plymouth. Free bus running when house and gardens open. Meals, snacks, shop, disabled access; house cl Fri-Sat and Oct-Mar (but park and gardens open then, free); (01752) 822236; £4.50, £7 inc a cruise on the river Tamar. It's a short walk up from the Plymouth pedestrian ferry to Cremyll, where the attractive Edgcumbe Arms has decent food.

TRECANGATE SX1759

Porfell Animal Land 🔲 Unspoilt and friendly, this has deer, wallabies, raccoons, meerkats and a capybara called Bart, as well as rabbits, guinea-pigs, goats and chickens in 15 acres of sloping fields and woodland, all feeling delightfully peaceful and remote. Snacks, shop, disabled access; cl Nov-Mar; (01503) 220211; £4. The Ship over at Lerryn is fairly handy for lunch and often has good watercolours for sale; the stepping stones over the river there are a hit with children, and good circular walks are signposted from the car park.

TREDINNICK SW9270

Shires Far more to this busy complex than just the magnificent shire horses: there's a children's farm, a haunted castle, an exhibition of rural antiquities, nature trails, a train round the park, watermill and working craftsmen, and very big indoor and outdoor adventure playgrounds. Also animated animal shows, and the biggest ride in Cornwall - a double log flume. You can see the horses being groomed in their stables, along with shetland ponies. Lots for all ages, but ideal for children. Meals, snacks, shop, disabled access; cl Nov-Easter; (01841) 540276; £7. The Ring o' Bells at St Issey is handy for lunch.

TREGONNING HILL SW6029

Takes only a few minutes to climb but has an impressive view; here in 1746 William Cookworthy made the first discovery of china clay in England, and went on to make porcelain.

TRELIGHTS SW9879

Long Cross Victorian Gardens Slightly inland at Trelights (but with good views down to the sea), the prettily restored gardens by the Long Cross Hotel, intricately hedged against the sea winds, have interesting granite and water features, and a maze, and playground and pets' corner for children. Meals, snacks, plant sales (not Nov-Easter), disabled access; (01208) 880243; £2 (donations only in winter).

TRELISSICK SW8339

Trelissick Garden (B3289)

Woodland park with beautifully kept gardens of camellias, magnolias and hydrangeas, also subtropical garden and other unusual plants; good views of the King Harry Passage and over to Pendennis Castle. There's a pretty orchard, and good walks in the surrounding woodland. Meals, snacks, shop, disabled access; cl am Sun, 24-26 Dec and 1 Jan; (01872) 862090; £4.60; NT. The NT have four holiday cottages on the estate. The Punch Bowl & Ladle at Penelewey on the King Harry Ferry rd is popular for lunch.

TRERICE SW8458

Trerice House Pretty Elizabethan house with unusual dutch-style gables, and elaborate plasterwork ceilings in the magnificent Hall and Great Chamber. Fine furnishings from the 17th and 18th c, notable paintings, early embroideries, oriental and english porcelain, and in the grounds an unusual collection of lawnmowers; lovely colourful gardens with cornish fruit trees. Snacks (in a barn with activities for toddlers), shop, very good disabled access; cl Sat and Tues (exc cl Sat only 15 Jul-11 Sept), and Nov-Mar; (01637) 875404; £4.70; NT. The Two Clomes at Quintrel Downs is quite handy for lunch.

TRESKILLARD SW6739

Shire Horse Farm & Carriage Museum 🔲 Refreshingly uncommercialised; most displays are indoors, and there are working blacksmith's and wheelwright's shops. Cl Sat and Nov-Easter; (01209) 713606; £4.50.

TREVALLAS COOMBE SW7351

Blue Hills Tin Streams Tours of this family-run outfit include demonstrations of the tinner's craft. Shop, disabled access; cl Sun and 24 Dec-2 Jan, best to phone; (01872) 553341; £4. The ancient Miners Arms at Mithian is good for lunch.

TRURO SW8244

A busy but civilised city with good shops; Lemon St is a particularly fine Georgian street, and Boscawen St is cobbled. Bustling Lemon Quay has been developed into a pleasant piazza and shopping area; the adjacent covered farmers' market is open Weds and Sat. The **cathedral** is one of the newer

Anglican ones, designed in 1880 in Early English style and completed in 1910; the handsome three spires pop up dramatically from behind shops and houses; meals, snacks, shop; free. Just outside the centre, **Bosvigo** (Bosvigo Lane) is a charming plantsman's garden, with most colour Jun-Sept; small nursery; usually open Thurs-Fri Mar-Sept; (01872) 275774; £3. The City (Pydar St) and Old Ale House (Quay St) are popular for lunch.

Royal Cornwall Museum (River St) Cornwall's largest museum, this has archaeology, local and natural history, Egyptian and textile galleries, also paintings by the Newlyn School and Old Masters; changing exhibitions, and regular children's activities. Meals, snacks, shop, disabled access; cl Sun and bank hols; (01872) 272205; £4.

VERYAN SW9139
Lovely village famous for its five devil-proof thatched round houses; also a water garden sheltered by holm oaks. The New Inn has good value food.

WADEBRIDGE SW9673
The disused railway track between Wadebridge and Padstow is a level six miles along the edge of the Camel estuary, with banks of wild flowers, birds, and lovely views between cuttings - you can walk or cycle (bike hire at either end (01208) 813050; £6-£10 a day - best to book in summer), or picnic on the small beaches at low tide. Those with less energy could park at Wadebridge, walk to Padstow, have lunch and get the bus back. You might then walk on through scenic countryside beyond Bodmin (worth stopping at Helland pottery, just by the path at Helland Bridge).

WENDRON SW6831
Poldark Mine & Heritage Centre
The underground post box in this 18th-c tin mine is the deepest in Britain. Varied enough to interest most members of the family, with plenty of children's amusements, an underground tour of the mine, a working beam engine, a museum, a film on the history of Cornwall's mining, and gardens. Meals, snacks, craft shops, limited disabled access; cl Jan-Feb, but phone for opening hours; (01326) 573173; guided tour £5.95, entry free.

WHEAL COATES SW6949
One of the most photogenic **mine ruins** on the cornish coast; for walkers, the diversion up St Agnes Beacon is well worth it for the commanding views. Down on Porthtowan beach, Blue has good snacks and great surf views.

WHITESAND BAY SW3526
Long expanses of wonderfully clean sands below the cliffs here give good walks, stretching away N of Sennen Cove (very popular with surfers; the Old Success here has a great view).

ZENNOR SW4538
The church here is best seen in its granite landscape from the hills above. The Tinners Arms is useful for lunch, and the hostel in the adjacent former chapel doubles as a tearoom. Around here you can walk for miles without seeing another soul; a striking objective is Zennor Quoit, with its enormous leaning capstone, on the hillside to the SE.

Wayside Folk Museum Enjoyable little local history museum, with chatty descriptions and information scattered through the exhibits; children's quiz trails. Snacks, shop (specialising in cornish books and crafts); cl Nov-Mar; (01736) 796945; £2.75.

Other charming seaside or coastal villages, all with nice pubs, include Devoran SW7938 (cycle path from Portreath), Gorran Haven SX0141 and Manaccan SW7625; and inland Blisland SX0973, Sticker SW9750, Tregony SW9245 and Tywardreath SX0854.

Where to eat

CONSTANTINE SW7328 **Trengilly Wartha** *(01326) 340332* Well run tucked-away inn with a woodburner in relaxed and civilised bar, bright no smoking family conservatory, thoughtful wine list with 20 by the glass (they also operate a retail business), very good imaginative food, a fine range of changing real ales, 40 malt whiskies, and a pretty, landscaped garden; nice bdrms; no food 25 Dec. £32.50|£9

DULOE SX2358 **Olde Plough House** *(01503) 262050* Very neatly kept pub with lovely slate floor in both communicating bar rooms, three woodburners, a mix of pews and chairs, good interesting food inc fishy specials and steaks cooked on hot stones, real ales, sensibly priced wines, and attentive service; cl 25 Dec, pm 26 Dec; disabled access. £25|**£5.95**

FALMOUTH SW8135 **HMS Ganges** *Mylor Yacht Harbour (01326) 374320* Not actually a ship though obviously named after one, this friendly little restaurant looks across the River Fal and specialises in fresh fish and seafood - they also serve breakfast for the many yachtsmen who sail in; good choice of wines from around the world at reasonable prices, and helpful service; cl Mon-Tues Oct-Easter; no evening meals Jan; disabled access. £33|**£6.95**

FOWEY SX1251 **Food for Thought** *4 Town Quay (01726) 832221* Carefully run quayside evening restaurant with generous helpings of attractively presented food inc fine fish and some simple as well as other elaborate dishes, and lovely puddings; cl some Sun, cl Jan/Feb; children must be well behaved. Set 3-course meal £19.95|**£7**

LANLIVERY SX0759 **Crown** *(01208) 872707* Pretty 12th-c inn with friendly licensees, a rambling series of rooms with open fires and a chatty atmosphere, good food using home-grown and local produce (popular fish dishes), well kept real ales, and a nice garden; disabled access. £15|**£5.50**

MITCHELL SW8554 **Plume of Feathers** *(01872) 510387* Popular pub with friendly licensees, attractive bars, stripped old beams, an enormous open fire, pastel-coloured walls, plenty of seats for either a drink or a meal; a natural spring well has been made into a glass-topped table; no smoking restaurant with interesting paintings; nice garden; good, interesting and well presented food, well kept real ales, a comprehensive wine list, and fresh italian coffees; well liked bdrms. £22.95|**£5.50**

MITHIAN SW7450 **Miners Arms** *(01872) 552375* Secluded Tudor pub with lots of character, fine old furnishings and warm winter fires, popular food, a no smoking dining room, real ales, and friendly service. £24|**£8**

MOUSEHOLE SW4626 **Cornish Range** *6 Chapel St (01736) 731488* Very friendly and neatly kept restaurant with a relaxed atmosphere and carefully cooked food inc plenty of good local fish dishes and enjoyable puddings; smart bdrms; cl winter Mon, Tues; partial disabled access. £30

MOUSEHOLE SW4726 **Old Coastguard** *The Parade (01736) 731222* Attached to a comfortable hotel, this notable seaside bar is bright and spacious with a relaxed, cheerful feel, modern furnishings on the wood-strip floor, good modern paintings, fresh flowers and potted plants, and lower dining area overlooking Mounts Bay; good enterprising, mainly modern food, well kept real ales, a decent choice of wines, and thoughtful choice of juices; seats on decking by attractive garden that leads to the sea; cl 25 Dec. £25|**£8**

PADSTOW SW9175 **Seafood Restaurant** *Riverside (01841) 532700* Airy quayside restaurant so famous for its wonderfully fresh seafood straight from the boats that you have to book far in advance; good puddings, nice cheeses, a long, interesting and fairly priced wine list, and friendly service; conservatory for aperitifs; smart, comfortable bdrms; cookery school courses; they also own Rick Stein's Café; cl 1 May, 22-26 Dec; children over 4. £60|**£17.50**

PADSTOW SW9175 **St Petroc's Hotel & Bistro** *4 New St (01841) 532700* Attractive little hotel (under the same ownership as the Seafood Restaurant) with a cheerfully and informally decorated dining room, good quickly served food from a short bistro-type menu (plenty of fish), a sensible wine list, and friendly atmosphere; bdrms; cl 1 May, 22-27 Dec; children over 4. £35|£14.50

PENZANCE SW4730 **Harris's** *46 New St (01736) 364408* Long-standing and boldly decorated cosy restaurant in a narrow cobbled street, with good enjoyable food using local produce (the freshest fish and shellfish), well liked puddings, and a decent wine list; cl Sun, Mon in winter (open Mon pm in summer), cl 3 wks in winter. £27|£7.50

PHILLEIGH SW8739 **Roseland** *(01872) 580254* Friendly little 17th-c pub just up the hill from the King Harry ferry, with good popular home-made food, well kept real ales, several small interesting rooms, old photographs, helpful, efficient and friendly staff, and a good winter fire; disabled access. £20|£6.75

POLPERRO SX2051 **Kitchen** *The Coombes (01503) 272780* Cottagey, informal no smoking evening restaurant with really enjoyable interesting food inc vegetarian and daily-changing fresh fish dishes (lovely fresh lobster and crab), and good value wines; cl Mon, Oct-March; children over 12. £25

POLPERRO SX2051 **Plantation Café** *The Coombes (01503) 272223* Popular beamed teashop with good, totally home-made food inc lovely soups and cream teas, a wide choice of interesting teas inc herbal and fruit, lunchtime sandwiches, and evening meals (in season); cl Sat (but open then in July/Aug), cl winter wkdys (but open Christmas period), Jan/Feb (but open Feb half-term); disabled access.|£5

ST IVES SW5140 **Porthminster Beach Café** *(01736) 795352* Bustling, popular café open all day for morning coffee with home-baked pastries, cream teas, light lunches and more substantial evening meals offering good mediterranean-style cooking (nice daily specials) using local produce, and a wide choice of coffees and teas; kind to children; cl Nov-Mar. £25|£7

ST IVES SW5140 **Seafood Café** *45 Fore St (01736) 794004* Simply furnished and very popular new café with lots of blonde wood, chrome, pot plants, and modern art, and serving excellent fresh fish dishes - you choose the fish at the counter and it arrives beautifully presented; plenty of local meat too, and lovely puddings. £23.40|£5.95

ST KEW SX0276 **St Kew Inn** *(01208) 841259* Handsome stone-built pub with welcoming new owners, nice old-fashioned furnishings in neatly kept bar, good popular food, and peaceful garden; lovely church next door. £21|£6.25

ST MAWGAN SW8765 **Falcon** *(01637) 860225* Comfortable, friendly pub in a pretty village with neatly kept big bar, log fire, small modern settles, and large antique coaching prints and falcon pictures on the walls; no smoking restaurant with paintings and pottery by local artists for sale; well kept real ales, decent wine list, and efficient service; delicious fresh fish dishes plus other enjoyable meals, and nice garden with outdoor heaters and play equipment for children. £25|£6.25

ST MICHAEL'S MOUNT SW5130 **Sail Loft** *The Harbour (01736) 710748* Converted boat house with enjoyable home-made cakes, cornish cream teas, more substantial meals, and friendly service; no smoking; cl 31 Oct-mid-Mar; disabled access. £19|£4.50

TREBURLEY SX3477 **Springer Spaniel** *(01579) 370424* Bustling, popular pub with a relaxed and friendly bar, big fireplace with woodburning stove and pictures of olde worlde stage-coach arrivals at inns, attractively furnished no smoking restaurant, particularly good, interesting food, well kept real ales, and several wines by the glass. £25|£7.95

Isles of Scilly

Charmingly unspoilt, these islands, about 30 miles W of Land's End, are a great place for utter relaxation. They have beautiful scenery, an almost subtropical climate, and an intricate variety of shorelines giving excellent coastal walks. In a lazy day you can comfortably walk round the largest, St Mary's, which is just six square miles. Tresco and St Agnes are the other main populated ones, though that means small undeveloped communities rather than any towns or big settlements. There are over 100 islands in all, some just strange-shaped rocks jutting out of the sea, their only visitors seals, dolphins and puffins.

You can get there from Penzance by ferry or more spectacularly by helicopter, a 20-minute ride with really beautiful views of the Cornish coast and of the islands; for more detail and phone numbers see *Penzance, p.85*. The islands also have their own little airline Skybus which leaves from Land's End, Newquay or Exeter several times a day. The trip from Land's End is quickest and cheapest (from £68 return; no flights Sun). They also do combined air and rail tickets - (0845) 710 5555 for details.

Where to stay

ST AGNES SV8808 **Coastguards** *St. Agnes, Isles of Scilly, Isles Of Scilly TR22 0PL* (01720) 422373 **£69** inc dinner; 3 rms with views of the sea. Peacefully set former coastguard cottages with open fire, interesting artefacts, and sea views in the sitting room, enjoyable homely dinners and breakfasts, friendly, helpful owners, and big garden; no smoking; cl Nov-Mar; children over 12; dogs welcome in bedrooms

ST MARTIN'S SV9116 **St Martin's on the Isle** *Lower Town, St Martin's, Isles of Scilly TR25 0QW* (01720) 422092 **£160**, plus special breaks; 30 attractively decorated rms, most with fine sea views. Welcomed by the friendly manager as you step off the boat, you find this stone-built hotel set idyllically on a white sand beach, with stunning sunsets; comfortable, light and airy split-level bar-lounge with doors opening onto the terrace, lovely flower arrangements, genuinely friendly professional staff, sophisticated food in main restaurant (lighter lunches in the bar), and a fine wine list; they are particularly kind to children, with buckets and spades to borrow, videos, and high tea for under-12s (they must be over 12 in evening restaurant); fine walks (the island is car free), launch trips to other islands, and good bird-watching; small swimming pool; cl Nov-end Feb; disabled access; dogs welcome in bedrooms ☺

TRESCO SV8915 **Island Hotel** *Tresco, Isles of Scilly TR24 0PU* (01720) 422883 **£202**inc dinner; 48 rms, many with balconies and terrace overlooking gardens or sea. Tiny private island, renowned for its wonderful subtropical Abbey Gardens and reached by helicopter or boat - hotel tractor-drawn bus (no cars allowed though bike hire available) takes you to spacious, very friendly modern hotel with colonial-style bar, fine food and wine, panoramic views, swimming pool, and private beach; cl Nov-Mar; disabled access

To see and do

BRYHER SV8715
A tiny quiet place, even by Scilly standards. The South bay has lots of wild flowers, and Watch Hill has wonderful views. The Hell Bay Hotel is good value.

ST AGNES SV8708
The most south-westerly community in the British Isles, joined to a smaller island called Gugh by a sandbar, awash at high tide. The sheltered cove here is especially popular. The 17th-c

lighthouse is the second oldest in Britain. The views from here out to the rocks and islets are very atmospheric, especially when you remember the incredible number of ships which have been wrecked here.
ST MARTIN'S SV9315
A narrow rocky ridge with flowers stretching down to the main attraction - the extensive beaches, very popular for picnics. There's a diving school, and the St Martin's Hotel has lovely sunset views.
ST MARY'S SV9010
The hub of Scilly Isles life, though its centre, Hugh Town, is little more than a village by mainland standards. Most ferries and planes arrive here, and you can get **pleasure cruises** from the Quay out to the bird and seal colonies on the outer islets and islands; there are fishing trips from here too. There's a 9-hole golf course with fine views, and a local history **museum**; usually cl Sun, plus pm Oct-Easter; £2. The Bishop & Wolf is a pleasant pub, and the Atlantic Hotel has a good pub part. Up in the N at Bant's Carn there's a burial chamber and ancient village. Back down S, walk out to

Penninis Head for good views of the Wolf and Bishop's Rock lighthouses. Just along the coast is **Star Castle** Hotel.
TRESCO SV8915
The highlight here is the amazing **subtropical garden** around the grounds of the abbey, begun in 1834, which, despite storms, contains a magnificent collection of exotic plants, bananas even. Also in these grounds is **Valhalla**, a collection of carved figureheads from wrecked ships, many dating back to the 17th c. Helicopters from Penzance land just outside the garden gate, so it's possible (though not cheap) to come here just for a day. The southern parts of the island are mainly sandy, but in the north it's more wild and rugged, with the remains of the castles of both Charles I and Oliver Cromwell, and a cave known as the Piper's Hole. Cycling and walking are real pleasures - not least because there aren't any cars. The New Inn, embellished with a mystery cargo of pine planking which washed ashore a while back, has good food inc seafood; the Island Hotel also has good seafood.

Where to eat

ST AGNES SV8708 **Turks Head** *The Quay (01720) 422434* Idyllically placed pub (a pleasant place to stay) with outstanding views over sweeping bay, enjoyable food in simple pine-panelled bar inc legendary huge locally made pasties, afternoon teas, evening barbecues, real ales, and decent wines; you can walk down to the slipway and sit right on the shore - or enjoy the wonderful views from seats on the lawn; children must be well behaved; cl Nov-Mar. £18.50|£7.25
TRESCO SV8915 **New Inn** *Townshill (01720) 423006* Just up from the harbour, this popular inn has a chatty, cosy bar, a main room with comfortable old sofas, banquettes, planked partition seating, and farmhouse chairs and tables, a few standing timbers, boat pictures, a large model sailing boat, a collection of old telescopes, and plates on the delft shelf; an airy dining extension has plenty of seats and tables on the blue wooden floors, cheerful yellow walls, and doors to the terrace; enjoyable food (more elaborate at night) with daily specials and afternoon tea, well kept real ales, good wines, and proper coffee; bdrms. £28|£7.95

With special thanks to Dr Venetia Stent, Jenny and Brian Seller, Ian Downes, B and K Hypher, J Black, Prof R J Harrison

CUMBRIA

**Some of Britain's finest scenery, with outstanding access to the
countryside; plenty of outdoor activities, with lots of interesting
places to visit, and excellent places to stay**

The National Trust control over a quarter of the land in the Lake District
National Park, and this means that preservation of and access to the
countryside is first-class. You could stay here for weeks every year of your
life and never walk the same path twice - so our walks suggestions are just
initial pointers. Also, many of our places to stay (and there's an excellent
choice, with lots serving really good food) have been chosen for the grand
walks right from their doorsteps, and are strong on peace and quiet.

The most beautiful scenery is concentrated thickly around the central
area, especially around the towns of Ambleside and Windermere. Both
are quite intensively developed for visitors and very busy in summer;
Keswick too has lots going on for all ages. Cockermouth to the NW has
plenty of attractions to fill a rainy day.

Each lake has its own character, and the landscape around them varies
greatly too. Windermere, the longest and busiest, has always been a
favourite; it's picturesquely dotted with villas built by Victorian magnates,
and has masses of accommodation on its E side. Ullswater approaches the
grandeur of Scottish lochs, and has some excellent (if not cheap) places to
stay right by the lake shore. Buttermere and Crummock Water also have
scenery on the grand scale. Derwent Water wavers charmingly between
highland and lowland in flavour, and its islands and manageable proportions
make it a favourite for idle boating and bankside strolls. Coniston Water,
quite well wooded, also appeals to both boaters and walkers, with some
fine views - in some ways it's a smaller and quieter version of Windermere.
Wast Water, England's deepest lake, is austere, surrounded by towering
screes. Bassenthwaite is altogether gentler, lowland in feel. Some much
smaller lakes, notably Grasmere, Rydal Water and Elterwater, are idyllic.

Lakeland generally is at its best out of season. May (sheets of wild
flowers on the hills) and June are ideal: more sun, no crowds. The views
are often clearest (and the ground firm and dry for walkers) in October
and November. In the summer holidays and at other peak times crowds
make the best places less enjoyable. For all but the hardiest expert
outdoorsmen, winter up here is too bleak for pleasure - unless you plan to
stay indoors. Whenever you come bring something waterproof - the Lake
District has more annual rainfall than any other part of the country.

For a quiet break with plenty of walking on your doorstep, the
Langdales, particularly Great Langdale, and Borrowdale are outstanding.
The west is even quieter, separated from the central Lake District by high
ridges with tortuous roads over the few passes. British rock-climbing was
born over here, with England's highest mountain, Scafell Pike, surrounded
by other awesome peaks - serious walking country.

Public transport in the Lakes is good and works well for round-trip long walks. Local information leaflets offer plenty of choice of well guided walks; information too from National Park visitor services (015394) 46601. Many places offer horse riding, and bicycles can be hired by the day in the main towns (considering the scenic grandeur, you can cycle for a surprisingly long way, at least in the central area, without having to struggle up steep hills).

Another area where, even in summer, you can count on peace and quiet is the part east of the M6 - one of England's least-known areas. Though overshadowed by the Lake District proper it has a lot of charm, as well as some excellent value places to stay in. Quiet river valleys shelter below more awesome open country and high moors, and there are some attractive and untouristy places to visit. Much of the high country is too bleak and boggy for most walkers, but moorland roads give drivers good views (eg A683 Kirkby Lonsdale—Kirkby Stephen, B6260 Tebay—Appleby, B6413 Lazonby—Brampton, A689 Brampton—Alston). The railway crossing the moors between Carlisle and Settle is perhaps the best way of all for seeing this unusual part of England.

The best coastal scenery is around Morecambe Bay. The W coast is untouristy, with miles of unfrequented beaches. Hawkshead, Troutbeck (the preserved 'statesman's' farm here is interesting), Cartmel, and Hutton-in-the-Forest are all good wandering territory.

Though the great outdoors is Cumbria's special plus, there are also plenty of organised things to see and do here, especially for families. Our number one Cumbria Family Attraction this year is the South Lakes Wild Animal Park at Dalton-in-Furness. The Lakeland Sheep & Wool Centre in Cockermouth (an entertaining show), Trotters World of Animals at Bassenthwaite Lake (busy place, with a good range of animals), and Eden Ostrich World in Langwathby (lovely on a sunny day) are all great fun for families. The Lakeland Wildlife Oasis at Milnthorpe is a successful mixture of museum and zoo, and Newby Bridge has an interesting aquarium.

Many of Cumbria's great houses have the added appeal of having been in the same family for centuries. The ones that get top marks for children are Holker Hall & Gardens at Cark-in-Cartmel, and Muncaster Castle & World Owl Centre at Ravenglass; the conservation centre at Appleby Castle is great in fine weather. Mirehouse near Bassenthwaite, Dalemain at Dacre, Blackwell in Windermere, and Hutton-in-the-Forest at Skelton are fascinating too, while Sizergh Castle and Levens Hall will particularly interest gardeners.

A good selection of museums and heritage centres includes unusual ones such as the Rheged Centre near Penrith (the huge grass-covered building is quite a sight), Tullie House in Carlisle (absorbing for children), the lively Sellafield Visitor Centre in Seascale, and in Whitehaven the Beacon, where you can learn how weather forecasts are put together - the rum museum here is also worth popping into. Kendal has three interesting museums, and the local history museum in Barrow-in-Furness is good. You'll find a steamboat museum in Windermere, and one of

England's oldest and prettiest railways in Ravenglass; this year we've added the slate mine up on Honister Pass too.

The literary trail is very popular in summer, and Grasmere, Rydal and Cockermouth are magnets for Wordsworth fans. Admirers of Ruskin enjoy the museum at Coniston (his house Brantwood, across the water, has a more general appeal). If Beatrix Potter is more your style, you'll find her paintings in Ambleside and Hawkshead, and her house in Near Sawrey (and the re-creations at the World of Beatrix Potter in Windermere delight young children).

Where to stay

ALSTON NY7646 **Lovelady Shield Country House** *Nenthead Rd, Alston, Cumbria CA9 3LF (01434) 381203* **£200** inc dinner, plus special breaks; 12 rms. In a lovely setting with River Nent running along bottom of garden (tennis and croquet), this handsome country house has a tranquil atmosphere, courteous staff, log fires in comfortable rooms (no smoking in sitting room or restaurant), and very good food inc fine breakfasts; children over 7 in evening restaurant; dogs welcome in bedrooms

AMBLESIDE NY3703 **Rothay Manor** *Rothay Bridge, Ambleside, Cumbria LA22 0EH (015394) 33605* **£130**, plus special breaks; 17 attractive rms (many overlooking garden) inc 3 suites. Family-run Regency country house in neatly kept mature grounds, with open fires and fresh flowers in quietly civilised and comfortable day rooms, very good english food in no smoking dining room, a thoughtful wine list, super big breakfasts, and helpful friendly service; free use of nearby leisure club, and walking, cycling and sailing close by; cl 3 Jan-6 Feb; good disabled access

AMBLESIDE NY3703 **Wateredge Inn** *Borrans Rd, Ambleside, Cumbria LA22 0EP (015394) 32332* **£90**, plus special breaks; 21 good comfortable, recently refurbished rms. Beautifully placed, warmly welcoming inn with neat gardens running down to Lake Windermere (embarkation point for cruising the lake); light airy bar (with fine views) and lounge, good meals in no smoking beamed dining area (more lovely views and candlelit at night), and excellent service; cl 3 days over Christmas; disabled access; dogs welcome in bedrooms

APPLEBY NY6920 **Appleby Manor** *Roman Rd, Appleby, Cumbria CA16 6JB (01768) 351571* **£128***, plus special breaks; 30 well equipped rms in original house (the nicest), coach house annexe or modern wing. Very friendly family-run hotel with fine views over Appleby Castle and Eden Valley, log fires in two of the three comfortable lounges, relaxed bar with wide range of whiskies, excellent service, good interesting food in panelled restaurant, and leisure centre; enjoyed by families; cl 24-26 Dec; disabled access; dogs in coach house bedrooms only ☺

BARBON SD6282 **Barbon Inn** *Barbon, Carnforth, Cumbria LA6 2LJ (015242) 76233* **£65**; 10 simple but comfortable rms, some with own bthrm. Small friendly 17th-c village inn in quiet spot below fells, with relaxing bar, traditional lounge, good meals in candlelit dining room, and helpful service; lots of good tracks and paths all around; dogs by prior arrangement

BASSENTHWAITE LAKE NY2032 **Armathwaite Hall Hotel** *Bassenthwaite Lake, Keswick, Cumbria CA12 4RE (017687) 76551* **£150***, plus special offers; 42 rms. Turreted 17th-c mansion in 400 acres of deerpark and woodland; handsome public rooms with lovely fireplaces, fine panelling, antiques, paintings and fresh flowers, good french and english cooking, a super wine list, and helpful staff; snooker room, croquet, pitch-and-putt, tennis court, indoor swimming pool, gym and beauty salon, fishing, archery and clay pigeon shooting, jogging and mountain-bike tracks, and free children's club; disabled access; dogs welcome in bedrooms ☺

BASSENTHWAITE LAKE NY1930 **Pheasant** *Bassenthwaite Lake, Cockermouth, Cumbria CA13 9YE (017687) 76234* **£140**, plus special breaks; 16

comfortable rms. Civilised hotel with delightfully old-fashioned pubby bar, restful lounges with open fire, antiques, fresh flowers and comfortable armchairs, and interesting gardens merging into surrounding fellside woodlands; cl 25 Dec; children over 8; disabled access; dogs in bar and in Garden Lodge bedrooms

BRAMPTON NY5760 **Farlam Hall** *Hallbankgate, Brampton, Cumbria CA8 2NG (016977) 46234* **£250** inc dinner, plus special breaks; 12 comfortable rms. Charmingly Victorian (though parts are much older) and very civilised country house with log fires in spacious lounges, excellent attentive service, good 4-course dinner using fine china and silver, marvellous breakfasts, and peaceful spacious grounds with croquet lawn and small pretty lake; cl 26-30 Dec; children over 5; dogs welcome except in restaurant

BUTTERMERE NY1716 **Bridge** *Buttermere, Cockermouth, Cumbria CA13 9UZ (017687) 70252* **£116**, plus special breaks; 21 comfortable rms. Comfortable hotel surrounded by some of the best steep countryside in the county, with beamed bar, open fire and deep armchairs in sitting room, good food in bar and no smoking restaurant, real ales, decent malt whiskies, and a friendly atmosphere; self-catering also; cl 2 wks Jan; children over 7 in dining room; dogs welcome in bedrooms

CARLISLE NY4055 **Number Thirty One, Howard Place** *31 Howard Pl, Carlisle, Cumbria CA1 1HR (01228) 597080* **£85**; 3 well equipped individually decorated rms. Carefully restored no smoking Victorian townhouse with a relaxed informal atmosphere, open fire and plenty of books in the cosy lounge, delicious interesting food using the best local produce, breakfast with home-baked bread, home-made preserves and home-made cumbrian sausages, and helpful courteous owners; cl 1 Nov-1 Mar; no children

CASTERTON SD6279 **Pheasant** *Casterton, Carnforth, Lancashire LA6 2RX (015242) 71230* **£80**, plus special breaks; 11 comfortable, newly refurbished rms, most with countryside views, and several newly refurbished. Small civilised inn with pleasant atmosphere, good food in no smoking panelled dining room, cheerful staff, and small but sound wine list; cl 25-26 Dec; disabled access; dogs welcome

CROOK SD4395 **Wild Boar** *Crook, Windermere, Cumbria LA23 3NF (015394) 45225* **£118**, plus special offers; 36 rms. Comfortable well run extended hotel with period furnishings and log fires in its ancient core, attentive service, and good food in no smoking dining room; free access to nearby leisure club and discounts on watersports; children's club at sister hotel, The Lowwood; dogs welcome in bedrooms

CROSBY ON EDEN NY4459 **Crosby Lodge** *High Crosby, Crosby on Eden, Carlisle, Cumbria CA6 4QZ (01228) 573618* **£120***, plus special breaks; 11 spacious rms (2 in stable conversion). Imposing and carefully converted country house in attractive mature grounds, with comfortable and appealing individual furnishings, enjoyable home-made food using local produce in no smoking restaurant, friendly long-established owners, and nice surrounding countryside; cl Christmas/New Year; limited disabled access; dogs by arrangement

DENT SD7686 **Sportsmans** *Cowgill, Dent, Sedbergh, Cumbria LA10 5RG (01539) 625282* **£47**, plus winter breaks; 6 rms with shared bthrm. Unassuming comfortable pub notable for its wonderful position in Dentdale by the River Dee overlooking the Settle—Carlisle railway, and walks in all directions; open log fires, real ales, and good value home-made food; dogs welcome in bedrooms

DERWENT WATER NY2618 **Hilton Keswick Lodore** *Borrowdale, Keswick, Cumbria CA12 5UX (017687) 77285* **£163**, plus special breaks; 71 well equipped rms. Long-standing but well updated big holiday hotel with lots of facilities in 40 acres of lakeside gardens and woodlands, comfortable day rooms, elegant restaurant, leisure club, tennis and squash, outdoor swimming pool, and games room; particularly well organised for families with NNEB nannies and so forth; self-catering house too; children over 6 in evening restaurant (high tea is offered); dogs welcome in bedrooms ☺

DOCKRAY NY3921 **Royal** *Dockray, Penrith, Cumbria CA11 0JY (017684) 82356* **£68**, plus special breaks; 10 rms. Friendly family-run hotel with open fires in big modernised open-plan bar, good value hearty meals, and well kept beers; in fine spot between hills and lake with walks from the doorstep; children must be well behaved; dogs welcome in bedrooms

ELTERWATER NY3204 **Britannia Inn** *Elterwater, Ambleside, Cumbria LA22 9HP* *(015394) 37210* **£88**, plus special breaks; 9 rms. Simple charmingly traditional pub in fine surroundings opp village green, with a happy friendly atmosphere (it does get very busy at peak times), hearty home cooking inc superb breakfast, comfortable no smoking lounge and bustling bar, real ales, and Sun evening quiz; fine walks all around; cl 24-26 Dec; dogs welcome in bedrooms

ENNERDALE BRIDGE NY0615 **Shepherds Arms** *Ennerdale, Cleator, Cumbria CA23 3AR* **£59**; 8 rms. Set on the popular coast-to-coast path and with wonderful surrounding walks, this welcoming inn has a simple, convivial bar, a woodburning stove, carpeted main bar with coal fire and a homely variety of comfortable seats, and small brick-floored extension with director's chairs around teak tables; cheerful and obliging service, substantial bar food using local meat and fish and only fresh vegetables, well kept real ales, and a good choice of wines by the glass; a couple of daily papers; disabled access

FAR SAWREY SD3895 **Sawrey** *Far Sawrey, Ambleside, Cumbria LA22 0LQ* *(015394) 43425* **£83**, plus special breaks; 18 rms. Friendly hotel well placed at the foot of Claife Heights, with simple pubby and smarter bars, friendly staff, good straightforward food, and seats on pleasant lawn; cl Christmas; kind to children; partial disabled access; dogs welcome in bedrooms

GARRIGILL NY7441 **Ivy House** *Garrigill, Alston, Cumbria CA9 3DU* *(01434) 382501* **£44***, plus special breaks; 3 rms. 17th-c farmhouse in fine scenery on Alston Moor, with a comfortable guest lounge, open fire and plenty of books, games and newspapers, helpful welcoming owners, and good breakfasts plus packed lunches and evening meals (which must be booked in advance); they also offer llama treks with instructions on how to handle and befriend them (children must be over 12 for this); dogs welcome

GRASMERE NY3307 **Wordsworth Hotel** *Grasmere, Ambleside, Cumbria LA22 9SW (015394) 35592* **£140***, plus special breaks; 37 comfortable, pretty rms. Well run hotel, right in village next to the churchyard where Wordsworth is buried; stylish lounges and airy restaurant overlooking landscaped gardens, a relaxed conservatory and popular pubby bar, friendly service, enjoyable food inc super buffet lunch, and heated indoor pool, mini-gym, and sauna; good disabled access

HAWKSHEAD NY3501 **Drunken Duck** *Barngates, Hawkshead, Ambleside, Cumbria LA22 0NG (015394) 36347* **£135**, plus special breaks; 16 comfortable rms. Civilised and friendly 17th-c Lakeland inn alone in 60 hillside acres, with several cosy mainly no smoking beamed rooms, cases of fishing flies and lures, open fires, distant views of Lake Windermere, home-brewed ales, 20 wines by the glass, and good imaginative lunchtime food (more elaborate and restaurant-style in the evening); fishing in private tarn; cl 24-25 Dec; limited disabled access; dogs in bar only

KENDAL NY5401 **Low Jock Scar** *Selside, Kendal, Cumbria LA8 9LE (01539) 823259* **£62***; 5 rms, most with own bthrm. Relaxed and friendly small country guesthouse in six acres of garden and woodland, with residents' lounge, and good home cooking (picnic lunches on request); no smoking; cl Nov-mid-Mar; children over 12; dogs welcome in bedrooms

KESWICK NY2623 **Shu-le-Crow Cottage** *7 Penrith Rd, Keswick, Cumbria CA12 4HF (017687) 75253* **£50***; 3 attractive rms. Pink-washed no smoking 18th-c cottage with plenty of original features, cheerful owners who can advise on local walks, and super breakfasts (vegetarian options); plenty of places to eat nearby; cl Christmas

KESWICK NY2421 **Swinside Lodge** *Newlands, Keswick, Cumbria CA12 5UE* *(017687) 72948* **£120**, plus special breaks; 7 comfortable rms. Victorian hotel in own grounds surrounded by wonderful unspoilt scenery at the foot of Cat Bells, and a few minutes from shores of Derwent Water; hearty breakfasts and super home-made evening meals in candelit dining room, helpful friendly service, and two relaxing sitting rooms; children over 5

KIRKCAMBECK NY5269 **Cracrop Farm** *Kirkcambeck, Brampton, Cumbria CA8 2BW (016977) 48245* **£55***; 4 rms with showers, overlooking garden and open fields. Friendly Victorian farmhouse on 425 acres with very good marked farm trails (they are keen on conservation), comfortable homely rooms, good traditional breakfasts (other food arranged in advance) and games room and sauna; no smoking; children over 12; dogs welcome

LANGDALE NY2806 **Old Dungeon Ghyll** *Great Langdale, Ambleside, Cumbria LA22 9JY (015394) 37272* **£75**, plus special breaks; 14 rms, some with shared bthrm. Friendly, simple and cosy walkers' and climbers' inn dramatically surrounded by fells, wonderful views and terrific walks; cosy residents' lounge and popular food - best to book for dinner if not a resident; cl Christmas; dogs welcome away from dining room

LINDALE SD4180 **Greenacres Country Guest House** *Lindale, Grange-over-Sands, Cumbria LA11 6LP (015395) 34578* **£52***, plus special breaks; 4 appealing rms. Charming 19th-c cottage with friendly atmosphere, pretty sitting room, conservatory, log fire, big breakfasts in cosy dining room, and packed lunch on request; kind to families and will set aside the whole house for family parties; cl Christmas and New Year ☺

LITTLE LANGDALE NY3103 **Three Shires** *Little Langdale, Ambleside, Cumbria LA22 9NZ (015394) 37215* **£70**, plus special breaks; 10 rms. Family-run stone-built country inn with beautiful views, comfortable residents' lounge, separate walkers' bar with real ales, decent food, and pretty gardens; cl mid-week during Dec/Jan

LORTON NY1522 **New House Farm** *Lorton, Cockermouth, Cumbria CA13 9UU (01900) 85404* **£98**, plus special breaks; 5 rms with wonderful hillside views. Friendly no smoking 17th-c house (not a working farm) in 15 acres, with beams and rafters, flagstones, open fires, and three residents' lounges, very good food inc game and fish caught by owner, home-made scones and preserves, a thoughtful wine list - and lots of walks; children over 6; dogs welcome in bedrooms

MUNGRISDALE NY3630 **Mill Hotel** *Mungrisdale, Penrith, Cumbria CA11 0XR (017687) 79659* **£80**; 9 rms, most with own bthrm. Very friendly small streamside hotel beautifully placed in lovely valley hamlet hidden away below Blencathra, with open fire in cosy and comfortable sitting room, good imaginative 5-course evening meals, and a small carefully chosen wine list; cl Nov-beginning Mar; they are kind to children; disabled access; dogs welcome in bedrooms

POOLEY BRIDGE NY4521 **Sharrow Bay** *Pooley Bridge, Penrith, Cumbria CA10 2LZ (017684) 86301* **£320** inc dinner, plus special breaks; 25 lovely rms with antiques, books, and games. Country-house hotel in quiet idyllic spot by Ullswater with lovely views of the lake and mountains, and showing the years of loving care the owners put into its distinctive style, furnishings and décor; unobtrusively attentive service and excellent english cooking in the two contrasting dining rooms; cl mid Dec-end Feb; children over 13; disabled access

RYDAL WATER NY3406 **White Moss House** *White Moss, Ambleside, Cumbria LA22 9SE (015394) 35295* **£150** inc dinner, plus special breaks; 5 thoughtfully furnished and comfortable little rms in main house plus separate cottage let as one unit with 2 rms. Bought by Wordsworth for his son, this attractive stripped-stone country house - set in charming mature grounds overlooking the lake - is a marvellously relaxing place to stay, with owners who have been there for over 20 years, a comfortable lounge, excellent fixed-price 5-course meals in pretty no smoking dining room, a fine wine list, and exemplary service; free fishing and free use of local leisure club; cl Dec-Jan; no toddlers; dogs in cottage

SEATOLLER NY2413 **Seatoller House** *Borrowdale, Keswick, Cumbria CA12 5XN (017687) 77218*; **£60**; 10 spotless, comfortable rms. Friendly house-party atmosphere in 17th-c house that has been a guesthouse for over 100 years, with self-service drinks and board games in comfortable lounges (no TV), and good no-choice fixed-time hearty dinner (not Tues) served at two big oak tables; packed lunches; two acres of grounds and many walks from doorstep (house is at the foot of Honister Pass); cl Dec-Feb; dogs welcome in bedrooms

TALKIN NY5557 **Hullerbank** *Talkin, Brampton, Cumbria CA8 1LB (016977)*
46668 **£50***; 3 rms. Recently refurbished, comfortable and very friendly no smoking
Georgian farmhouse in unspoilt countryside, with a relaxed atmosphere and
inglenook fireplace in homely lounge, enjoyable breakfasts, and packed lunch on
request; cl Dec-Jan; children over 12

THIRLMERE NY3117 **Dale Head Hall** *Thirlmere, Keswick, Cumbria CA12 4TN*
(017687) 72478 **£90***, plus special breaks; 12 pretty rms, most with lake views, and
4 in new wing. Peaceful partly 16th-c country house in lovely lakeside grounds, with
comfortable lounges, log fire, cheerful owners, and home-cooked food using
produce grown in own walled garden; children over 10 for evening meals; cl Jan

TIRRIL NY5026 **Queens Head** *Tirril, Penrith, Cumbria CA10 2JF (01768) 863219*
£65*, plus special breaks; 7 lovely, recently refurbished rms. Bustling very
welcoming inn with flagstones and bare boards in the bar, spacious back restaurant
(mostly no smoking), low beams, black panelling, inglenook fireplace and old-
fashioned settles in older part, good interesting food inc snacks and OAP specials,
and well kept real ales (inc their own brews); babies welcome but older children
must be over 13; dogs welcome except in restaurant

WASDALE HEAD NY1607 **Wasdale Head Hotel** *Wasdale Head, Seascale,
Cumbria CA20 1EX (019467) 26229* **£98***, plus special breaks; 9 simple but warmly
comfortable pine-clad rms, with 3 more luxurious ones in farmhouse annexe. Old
flagstoned and gabled walkers' and climbers' inn in magnificent setting surrounded
by steep fells, with newly opened micro-brewery, civilised day rooms, popular
home cooking, good wine list, huge breakfasts, and busy public bar; steam room;
self-catering cottages; partial disabled access; dogs welcome in bedrooms

WATERMILLOCK NY4421 **Leeming House** *Watermillock, Ullswater, Penrith,
Cumbria CA11 0JJ (017684) 86622* **£174**, plus special breaks; 40 cosseting rms,
many with beautiful views. Well run extended hotel in 20 acres of quiet lakeside
grounds, with log fires in comfortable lounges, cosy panelled bar, fine food in lovely
no smoking dining room, and good courteous service; boating and fishing; high teas
for young children; good provision for disabled; dogs welcome in bedrooms

WATERMILLOCK NY4523 **Rampsbeck Country House** *Watermillock,
Penrith, Cumbria CA11 0LP (017684) 86442* **£100**, plus special breaks; 20 attractive
rms, some with balconies. 18th-c hotel in 18 acres by Lake Ullswater with extensive
lake frontage and seats on sunny terrace; open fire in the cosy sitting room, french
windows into the garden from the plush, comfortable lounge, friendly attentive
staff, and carefully prepared food in the attractive dining room; croquet; lots to do
nearby; cl Jan-mid-Feb; children over 8 in dining room; dogs welcome in bedrooms

WINDERMERE SD4097 **Fir Trees** *Lake Rd, Windermere, Cumbria LA23 2EQ*
(015394) 42272 **£68***, plus special breaks; 9 attractive spotless rms inc 2 family
ones. Well run and comfortable no smoking Victorian house with an informal
relaxed atmosphere, antiques, fine prints and fresh flowers, warmly helpful service
(detailed suggestions of what to do), and good hearty breakfasts and vegetarian
meals by prior arrangement; free use of leisure club; children over 5

WINDERMERE SD4295 **Gilpin Lodge** *Crook Rd, Windermere, Cumbria LA23
3NE (015394) 88818* **£200** inc dinner, plus special breaks; 14 marvellous rms with
lots of space, sitting areas, super bthrms, and fine views. Impeccably run country
house hotel with lovely gardens and grounds that take in ponds, woodlands and
moor; big peaceful sitting rooms with antiques, fresh flowers, magazines, and open
fires (no formal bar or reception desk), delicious food in three charming restaurant
rooms, exceptional breakfasts and afternoon teas, and genuinely friendly,
professional but unpretentious staff; free use of nearby Parklands Country &
Leisure Club; children over 7

WINDERMERE NY3801 **Langdale Chase Hotel** *Windermere, Cumbria LA23
1LW (015394) 32201* **£130**; 27 rms, many with marvellous lake view. Welcoming
family-run hotel in lovely position on the edge of Lake Windermere with water-
skiing and bathing from the hotel jetty; tennis, croquet, putting and rowing,
afternoon tea on the terraces, gracious oak-panelled rooms with antiques,

paintings, fresh flowers, open fires, very good food (huge breakfasts, too), and friendly service; disabled access; dogs welcome ☺

WITHERSLACK SD4384 **Old Vicarage** *Witherslack, Grange-over-Sands, Cumbria LA11 6RS* (015395) 52381 **£150** inc dinner, plus special breaks; 14 individually decorated rms - some in the modern Orchard House are more spacious and have their own woodland terraces. Late Georgian vicarage in five acres of peaceful gardens and woodland, with two comfortable lounges, a log fire, good interesting food in cosy restaurant inc home-made bread, cakes and preserves, and hearty breakfasts; tennis and lots of surrounding walks; dogs welcome in bedrooms

To see and do

Cumbria Family Attraction of the Year

DALTON-IN-FURNESS SD2273 **South Lakes Wild Animal Park** (Crossgates) Though this committed place is only ten years old, it's quickly established a reputation as one of Britain's very best zoos, achieving in that time greater success in breeding and conservation than some better-known places have managed over much longer periods. In recent months lemurs, kangaroos, wallabies and emus have all been born in the park, and, as part of international breeding programmes, they've also welcomed new tigers, a red panda, a very rare type of lemur, and a female babirusa (think of a cross between a pig and a hippo). The enclosures have been carefully designed with the animals' welfare in mind, and they work hard at developing the senses and skills the animals would use in the wild. For instance, the sumatran and amur tigers are encouraged to clamber up a 6-metre (20-ft) vertical pole, not for entertainment, but to hunt their meat; it's quite a spectacle (daily, at 2.30). Between Easter and Oct they have a busy schedule of interesting and informative afternoon talks and feeding displays; you may be able to join in feeding some of the lemurs. Among the other animals are giraffes, cheetahs, monkeys and rhinos, gathered together according to the continents they hail from. Also lots of smaller creatures such as meerkats, pandas, coatis and porcupines; they've recently acquired spectacle bears. There's a new aviary for the free-flying macaws, and as well as the animals, plenty to keep children happy, including a play area, and, in summer, a miniature railway. Good views of the entire Furness peninsula. Meals, snacks, shop, disabled access; cl 25 Dec; (01229) 466086; £7.50 adults, £5 children (less in winter). You'll get £1 off admission if you can prove you travelled by bus or train.

ABBEY TOWN NY1751
Holme Cultram (B5302 Wigtown—Silloth) Remains of formidably rich Cistercian abbey - extraordinarily grand for this quiet village.
ALSTON NY7146
This interesting little well weathered Pennine market town is the highest of its kind in England, with a surprising number of pubs up and down its very steep cobbled main street (the Angel is best), and a couple of craft shops; readers recommend Stokoe House Ceramics (Market Pl, usually open Easter-Oct) and Just Glass (Front St), also Blueberries restaurant nearby.

Gossipgate Gallery (The Butts) Local art and crafts, with changing exhibitions, a good big shop, and a garden with a tea terrace, and cultivated flowers planted alongside their wild ancestors; disabled access (though no facilities); cl 1-2pm wkdys, Jan-mid-Feb, Mon (exc bank hols) and Tues, and other days in winter, best to phone at beginning and end of season; (01434) 381806; free.
Hartside Nursery (A686 W of Alston) Beautifully placed alpine nursery with small streamside garden and rare plants for sale; it's quite a draw for birds and wildlife. Some disabled

access with notice; cl am wknds and bank hols, Nov to mid-Mar (exc by appointment); (01434) 381372; free.

South Tynedale Railway The chief attraction around here, giving leisurely rides through the beautiful scenery of the South Tyne valley, behind preserved steam and diesel locomotives from here and abroad. Snacks, shop, disabled access (you can book a wheelchair-accessible carriage); phone for a timetable; (01434) 381696; fares from £5.

AMBLESIDE NY3704

A busy holiday-orientated shopping town inc excellent outdoor equipment shops strung along its central one-way system, with the quaintest information centre in the Lakes - the little NT shop in the tiny stone Bridge House over Stock Ghyll by the main car park. Above Stock, the old milling quarter, lying just uphill from here, has cottagey charm and is at the beginning of the road up to Kirkstone; ½m farther is the entrance to verdantly set Stock Ghyll Force waterfall. Waterhead is the northern ferry terminal on Lake Windermere, and close by are the scant remains of Galava Roman Fort (free access). Traditional glass blowing at Adrian Sankey, Rydal Rd; good demonstrations and shop; (015394) 33039. Hayes Garden World (Lake Rd) is a big garden centre in landscaped gardens; café, disabled access (only on ground floor). The Wateredge Hotel (A5095) has good bar food and lots of tables in its lakeside garden.

Armitt Ambleside Museum Decent local history museum with the largest collection of Beatrix Potter's watercolours, plus works by local artists, photographers, several original manuscripts by local writers, numerous archaeological remains, and changing exhibitions. Shop, disabled access; cl 25-26 Dec; (015394) 31212; £2.50.

Brockhole (A591 S of Ambleside, or launch from town pier) National Park information centre in country house with well landscaped gardens and attractive lakeshore grounds; also audio-visual show, exhibitions, and adventure play area. Special talks and events all year. Meals, snacks, shop, disabled access; visitor centre cl Nov-Mar, gardens and grounds open all year;

(015394) 46601; free, but charge for parking (£4 all day, £3 for half day). In summer you can go on a 45-min circular cruises from here (£5).

Homes of Football (Lake Rd) Charts the changes in football since 1989, with masses of photos and memorabilia; interestingly, the emphasis is on the grounds and supporters. Good shop (all the photos are for sale); cl 2 wks Jan; (01539) 434440; free.

Stagshaw Garden (Waterhead, just S) Hillside woodland garden with lovely lake views, mature camellias, rhododendrons, magnolias and heathers; best in spring. Open daily Apr-Jun then by appointment July-Oct; (015394) 35599; honesty box £1.50; NT. Parking is very limited.

APPLEBY NY6820

An attractive riverside village; the main street, rising from the harmonious 12th-c church to the castle, is still a grand sight despite the cars, with a good few handsome buildings inc a lovely courtyard of almshouses. Pleasant strolls by the River Eden. The Royal Oak is enjoyable for lunch.

Appleby Castle Conservation Centre This interesting place has one of the best-preserved Norman keeps in the country (the rest of the buildings are later additions); terrific views from the ramparts. The Clifford family lived here for nearly 700 years, though they moved later to the grander house next door; the Great Hall has recently been renovated. Attractive grounds in a lovely setting above the river, with a big collection of birds, waterfowl and farm animals, and a children's play area. Meals, snacks, shop, limited disabled access; usually open Easter-end Sept but best to check; (017683) 53823; £5.

ARNSIDE SD4578

A good start for the 20-min train trip along the N shore of Morecambe Bay to Ulverston: long viaducts, stupendous views. Great views too from the elevated garden of the seaside Olde Fighting Cocks here, which attractively priced food.

ARNSIDE KNOTT SD4577

Medium-sized wooded limestone hill, easily walked up from Arnside, with a highly rewarding view across Morecambe Bay to the southern Lakeland fells.

ASKHAM NY5123

Idyllically dozy limestone village with greens and broad verges; actually in the Lake District, but more reminiscent of the Yorkshire Dales. Pleasant pastoral walk skirting the spooky ruin of Lowther Castle and heading along the River Lowther to Whale, then on to Helton and back to Askham. The Queens Head and recently reopened Punch Bowl are useful for lunch.

BARBON SD6282

An unpretentious village given appeal by its fine setting, just below the fells; the road from here to Dent via Gawthrop leads through lonely Barbondale, dominated by the Barbon Fell. The Barbon Inn is good.

BARROW-IN-FURNESS SD1969

The town shows the effects of the virtual collapse of shipbuilding in this country, on which it depended. The **railway** from here to Whitehaven hugs the coast and has good views, missed by the road, though in the other direction the A5087 to Ulverston has fine views across Morecambe Bay. The cheerful Black Dog out past Dalton-in-Furness is a good stop.

Dock Museum (North Rd) Modern-looking museum exploring how Barrow developed from a tiny hamlet to the biggest iron and steel centre in the world, before becoming renowned for shipbuilding. Displays range from simple fishing boats to model submarines and rare Vickers ship models; also interactive displays and an adventure playground. Snacks, shop, good disabled access; cl Mon (exc bank hols), plus Tues Nov-Easter and 25-26 Dec; (01229) 894444; free.

Furness Abbey (slightly NE, towards Dalton) Impressive warm sandstone Norman remains of the one-time second richest monastery in England, with lovely arched cloisters, peaceful lawns, and views of pretty valley. Small museum, shop, disabled access; cl Mon and Tues in Nov-Mar, 24-26 Dec, and 1 Jan; (01229) 823420; £3.00; EH.

Sandscale Haws (via Hawthwaite Lane, off A590 N towards Askam) These dunes are protected as a **nature reserve**.

BASSENTHWAITE NY2332

Attractive close-set little village - the

12th-c parish church is three miles S; the Sun is a decent pub.

Mirehouse (off A591 S) The family that still live in this modest 17th-c house once had excellent literary connections, so the fine rooms have mementoes of Wordsworth, Carlyle and Tennyson among others. They frequently have informal piano recitals (guests are welcome to sit by the fire and listen), and on Weds in Jun, July and Sept they usually have lace-making demonstrations. Interesting garden (bee/butterfly plants) with changing poetry exhibitions in the verandah, as well as peaceful lakeshore grounds, lakeside church, and woods with well thought-out adventure play areas. Lots to do, with a surprising number of activities for children, inc a trail, secret drawers, and dolls to play with. Generous cumbrian home cooking in ex-mill tearoom, disabled access; open Apr-Oct, house pm Sun and Weds, garden daily; (017687) 72287; £4, garden only £2.

BASSENTHWAITE LAKE NY1931

Curiously, the only body of water in the Lake District to be called purely a lake (the others, even Lake Windermere, are all 'waters', 'meres' or 'tarns'). The surrounding scenery lacks the grandeur of the better-known lakes, but in recent springs and summers it's been the hunting ground for England's only ospreys. You can hire rowing boats on it; the Pheasant (off A66 at N end) is an attractive place for lunch.

Dodd Wood (off A591 N of Keswick) Marked walks through the woods, or on open hillside, with views of the lake.

Trotters World of Animals (Coalbeck Farm, B5291, signed from A591 and A66 as Trotters and Friends) The range of animals at this 25-acre site really is wide, from rare breeds of pigs, cattle and goats, through birds of prey, lizards and snakes, to otters, llamas and gibbons. Throughout the day, at certain times, you might be able to bottle-feed a baby goat, cuddle the rabbits, or have a hawk fly down to your wrist, and helpful uniformed staff are on hand to answer questions. For an extra charge they usually have trailer, tractory and pony rides; there's an adventure

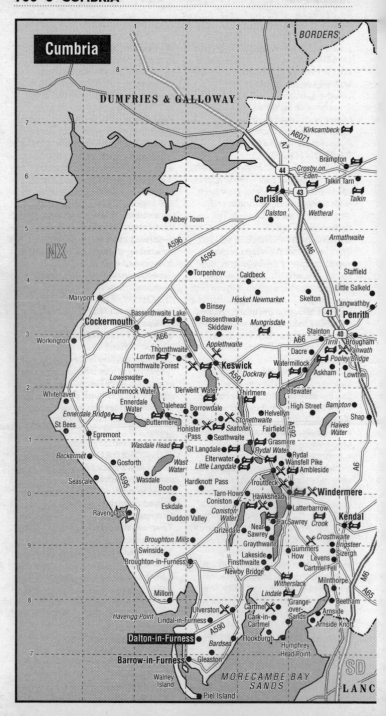

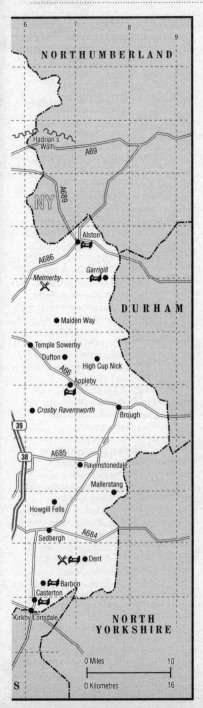

playground, and plenty of space for a picnic. Quite a few things are under cover, and in winter they keep up a full range of indoor activities. Their birds of prey centre has the region's only breeding golden eagles and caracaras. Meals, snacks, shop, disabled access; cl wkdys Nov-Jan, and 25 Dec, 1 Jan; (017687) 76239; *£5.25.

BEETHAM SD4979

Heron Cornmill and Papermaking
Well organised working watermill dating from 1096, though the current building is 18th c; baking exhibition. Displays about the paper-making industry are in a converted barn next door. Shop; cl Mon (exc bank hols), and Oct-Easter; (015395) 65027; £2. Beetham itself is attractive, with an interesting **church**, and the Wheatsheaf is good for lunch. A woodland walk leads to the Fairy Steps with rewarding views over the bay.

BINSEY NY2235
A pathless lump of a hill, but with splendid views of the Lakes and Solway Firth (and into Scotland) by virtue of its geographical isolation.

BOOT NY1801
The steam railway from Ravenglass ends here, at Dalegarth Station, and Dalegarth Falls here are lovely. The Burnmoor Inn, very well placed for walkers, has good value food; the Bower House further down Eskdale at Eskdale Green is also good.

BORROWDALE NY2517
Good views from the B5289 of what is many people's favourite Lakeland base for walks, with good paths along or just above the wooded River Derwent; impregnable-looking Castle Crag is a splendid mini-peak to head for, reached in about 30 mins from Grange (which has a useful teashop). Close to the road are the Bowder Stone (a huge boulder with a ladder up to the top), and the Lodore Falls (behind Lodore Hotel). For prized walks see Seathwaite entry, and Watendlath under Derwent Water. The Flock Inn tearoom at Yew Tree, Rosthwaite has good home-made food, and the Langstrath at Stonethwaite (run by a direct descendant of huntsman John Peel) makes a beautifully placed base.

BRAMPTON NY5563

Lanercost Priory (brown signs from town) Impressive and extensive remains of Norman priory, built with stone recycled from Hadrian's Wall; new audio-guides. Shop, some disabled access; cl Nov-Mar; £2.50; EH. The nave, picturesquely framed by an arch, was restored in the 18th c as a red sandstone church, and has stained glass by William Morris and Burne-Jones. The newly refurbished nearby Abbey Bridge Inn has decent food.

BROUGH NY7914

Brough Castle Classic ruined Norman fortress, in a romantic setting on moors above the village, with great views; free. The Golden Fleece is useful for lunch.

BROUGHAM NY5329

Brougham Castle (off A66 S of Penrith) A sturdy Norman ruin on steep lawns above riverside sheep pastures; climb to the top of the keep for the best view. Traces of Roman remains too, with a small exhibition of tombstones. Snacks, shop, disabled access; cl Nov-Mar; (01768) 862488; £2.20, EH. The Gate Inn at Yanwath has good food.

Brougham Hall Craft Centre 16 different craft workshops inc metal workers, furniture restoration, smoked foods and home-made chocolates, in the attractive stone courtyard of a 15th-c Hall. Plenty to see around the house and grounds inc Cromwellian chapel and a collection of dolls and doll's houses. Meals, snacks, disabled access; cl 25 Dec; (01768) 868184; £2.

BROUGHTON-IN-FURNESS SD2187

Small town with a villagey feel, and a handsome sloping square lined with Georgian houses; the Manor Arms does popular snacks. A handy base for exploring the Duddon and other quieter Lakeland valleys; for an exciting high-altitude drive, head NW over Corney Fell to Corney.

BUTTERMERE NY1815

A splendid varied flat walk circles the lake, with glorious views, plenty of safe opportunities for children aged 6 or more to let off steam, and even a tunnel; weather has to be really savage to spoil it. Parking at Gatescarth. The Bridge

Hotel in the village is good for lunch; in summer you can hire **rowing boats**; (017687) 70233; from £6.

Ceiling of the Lakes The green slatey fells N of Buttermere offer keen walkers superlative routes along high ridges: Whiteless Pike, Causey Pike, Crag Hill and Grasmoor are among the most exciting points.

Hay Stacks To the south of Buttermere and high above it, this is a challenging walk, but a rewarding one for the enjoyable views, continuing on to Fleetwith Pike.

Rannerdale Knotts Modest-sized hill reached via Low Bank from Buttermere village, a grand vantage point and a good alternative to the much loftier summits around it; splendid views of Crummock Water and the hills surrounding it.

CALDBECK NY3239

The grave of John Peel (of 'Do ye ken John Peel' fame) can be found in the churchyard here; the Oddfellows Arms has good generous food, and we have had a strong tip from readers for the vegetarian restaurant (and shops) at Priests Mill. There's a pretty drive to attractive Mungrisdale; alternatively, a pleasant stroll to a peaceful spot with a waterfall called the Howk.

CARK-IN-CARTMEL SD3577

Holker Hall & Gardens Plenty to keep families occupied at this busy estate. The opulently built and furnished mansion dates back to the early 16th c (and has been in the same family ever since), but the present building is mainly Victorian; despite its beauty, it has an appealingly unstuffy feel. The glorious 25-acre formal and woodland gardens are among the best in the county, with spectacular water features, a sunken garden, rhododendron and azalea arboretum, and rare plants and shrubs. A potting shed has an exhibition on garden history. The motor museum has a good collection of cars, bikes, tractors, and all sorts of related equipment and memorabilia, and a display on Donald Campbell's world record-breaking attempts. Children enjoy the 125-acre deer park, there's an adventure playground for under-12s, and a picnic area. Dogs on a lead are welcome in the park. Meals, snacks, shop, disabled access; cl Sat, and Nov-Mar; (015395) 58328; all-in ticket £8.75, house and garden £7.25, motor museum and garden £7.50, gardens £4.25; more during their May festival. The nearby Engine has good home-made food.

CARLISLE NY3956
Cumbria's only city, not an obvious holiday destination, but plenty to interest the visitor, with several quietly attractive old buildings (and a very helpful visitor centre in one of them, the Old Town Hall). **St Cuthbert's church** is remarkable for its mobile pulpit. The Kings Head (Fisher St) does good value snacks, and there's good home cooking in the Black Lion out at Durdar, where the attractively placed racecourse has meetings every month exc July; phone (01228) 522973 for dates.

Carlisle Castle This extensive medieval fortress, rather gaunt and forbidding, is surprisingly well kept considering its violent history. Interesting period furnished rooms, a portcullised gatehouse, lots of staircases and passages, and centuries of prisoners' carved graffiti in the dungeons; good views from the ramparts. Snacks, shop, limited disabled access; cl 24-26 Dec and 1 Jan; (01228) 591922; £3.50; EH.

Carlisle Cathedral This unpretentious abbey church, founded in 1122 and severely damaged in the Civil War, has fine stained glass; try to go on a bright morning when the sunlight comes streaming colourfully through the east window. Also medieval carvings inc the Brougham Triptych, painted panels and stonework, and crypt treasury. Meals, snacks, good shop (some tasty local foods), disabled access; during services access may be restricted; (01228) 535169; free, recommended donation £2.

Guildhall Museum (Green Market) A handsomely restored medieval timbered hall; worth a look inside if passing - some displays inc interesting Guild silver. Cl am, and Mon (exc bank hols) and all Nov-Mar; free.

Settle—Carlisle railway Running up Ribblesdale and into the Cumbrian Pennines, stopping at Dent Station, Garsdale Head, Kirkby Stephen, Appleby, Langwathby and other Eden

Valley villages, this is a memorable 72 miles of grand scenery, best from Appleby to Settle; (08457) 484950 for times and fares, or have a look at their website www.settle-carlisle.co.uk.

Solway Aviation Museum (Aviation House, Carlisle Airport; A689 towards Brampton) Exhibits inc several aircraft, Whittle's prototype jet engines and various displays on local airports used as World War II air bases. Meals, snacks, shop, disabled access (not to aircraft); open wknds early Apr-end Oct, and perhaps other days, best to check; (01228) 573823; £3.50.

Tullie House (Castle St) Great fun: dramatic displays of Border history, using state-of-the-art techniques of sight, sound and smell. Children especially find lots to do, from exploring mine tunnels to trying out a Roman crossbow; the ground floor has a more conventional art gallery/museum. The Millennium Gallery contains archaeology and mineral displays, a local art exhibition, and two discovery walls (one you explore by opening doors, windows and letterboxes, and when you crouch close to the other one you can hear local stories). Meals, snacks, shop, good disabled access; cl am Sun in winter, 25-26 Dec, 1 Jan; (01228) 534781; £5.20.

CARTMEL SD3778
Picturesque little alleys lead off the delightfully harmonious central square - esp the one out through the former **Priory gatehouse**. The **Priory church**, which towers massively over the village, is an interesting mix of architectural grandeur from 12th to 16th c, inc fine carving. Lots of arts and crafts in the village, and Cartyhing and Penrith fudge. The picturesque Kings Arms does reasonably priced food, and the Mallard has good cakes and coffee. The village can get particularly busy in summer.

CARTMEL FELL SD4189
In a wonderful tucked-away country location, **St Anthony's church** here has interesting early pews and a fine triple-decker pulpit. Arthur Ransome lived nearby when he wrote *Swallows and Amazons*. The Masons Arms is an appealing place for lunch, and the road here from Winster (where the Brown

Horse is a popular dining pub) is very pretty.

CASTERTON SD6279
Brontë fans will want to see **Casterton School**; attractive Pre-Raphaelite stained glass and paintings in the **church** result from enthusiastic Brotherhood holidays here. The Pheasant is good.

COCKERMOUTH NY1130
Quietly attractive riverside town, just outside the Lake District proper, but a good base for the western fells, with a distinctive character of its own and a good wide range of places to visit. The comfortable Trout does good food.

Castlegate House 💷 (Castlegate) Friendly lived-in Georgian house opposite the castle, home to changing exhibitions of modern art, with Adam ceiling, warming winter fires, and sculpture in the walled garden. Sales of paintings, disabled access; cl Thurs, am Sun, and all Jan-Feb; (01900) 822149; free.

Jennings Brewery Tours of traditional Castle Brewery, where the water for brewing is still drawn from the well that supplied the castle at the time of the Norman Conquest. Snacks, shop; tours 11am and 2pm Mar-Oct - booking advisable; cl Sun (exc July-Aug when they do extra tours), 25-26 Dec, 1 Jan; (0854) 1297185; £4.50. No under-12s.

Lakeland Sheep & Wool Centre (off A5086 slightly S) Along with an entertaining live show starring 19 different varieties of sheep (and sometimes a few geese), they also hold shearing demonstrations and sheepdog trials at this friendly place; the adjacent exhibition is a worthwhile introduction to the area. Meals, snacks, shop, disabled access; centre cl 2 wks in Jan, shows usually Mar-Oct, but best to phone first; (01900) 822673; show £4, exhibition free.

Printing House (next to Wordsworth House) This working print museum has a good range of historic presses and equipment; you can try out various printing methods. Shop, disabled access; cl Sun, bank hols and a few days over Christmas; (01900) 824984; £2.75.

Toy & Model Museum (Market Pl) Good expanding collection of mainly british toys (some you can operate yourself) from the 20th c; shop; cl Dec-Jan exc by appointment; (01900) 827606; £3.

Wordsworth House (Main St) This restored 18th-c town house, the poet's happy childhood home, should reopen in Jun following extensive work to improve disabled facilities and the indoor displays. With fine furniture, pictures by friends and contemporaries, and good original panelling, it's worth a visit in its own right as well as for its Wordsworth connections; interesting to see how different it is from the places he lived in later on. There are also plans to recreate the garden and to open a new visitor centre. Phone for opening times and prices; (01900) 824805; NT.

CONISTON SD2997
Unpretentious former mining village turned resort, at the foot of its mountain, the Old Man, and spreading towards Coniston Water. From Spoon Hall there's pony trekking on the fells above; cl Nov-Easter; (015394) 41391; from around £12 an hour. The Sun is good for lunch.

Brantwood Ruskin's rambling Victorian house round on the E side of the lake, with lots of his furniture, books and paintings. It's appealingly unstuffy, but the real attraction is the surroundings and setting, especially the very extensive informal hillside woodland gardens (best in late May/Jun); reaching the end of extensive structural restorations, the eight themed gardens (inc recently completed Zig-Zaggy and High Walk) reflect Ruskin's ideas. Good hour's walk on nature trail, and breathtaking views of lake and fells. Meals, snacks, good shop, limited disabled access (grounds steep in places); cl Mon-Tues mid-Nov to mid-Mar and 25-26 Dec; (015394) 41396; £4.75, £3 gardens only.

Coniston Water An opulent Victorian **steam yacht** sails daily usually Easter-Oct, from Coniston Pier and Brantwood; (015394) 41288 for times - best to ring between 9 and 10.30am or you're likely to get the answerphone; £5 for a 45-min round-trip. Or hire rowing or other boats from the boating centre run by the National Parks, 15 mins' walk from the village; usually cl Nov-Mar but worth ringing; (015394) 41366; rowing boats from £6 an hour (£1 each extra person), motorboats from £11.

Coniston Water walks A lovely path follows the W shore, S of Coniston; you can combine this walk with one on a higher-level route along the Walna Scar 'Road' (an ancient hard track closed to through traffic) beneath the **Old Man of Coniston**, the outstanding viewpoint of the vicinity. Climb the Old Man from Coniston, go up past the remains of copper mines, and return down the Walna Scar Road.

Ruskin Museum (A593 Yewdale Rd) Eclectic mix of displays inc some interactive ones in this friendly little museum, from local architecture and lace-making to a video of Donald Campbell's water speed record attempts, and a virtual tour of local copper mines; audio guides in several languages. Naturally, much is given over to the eponymous Victorian philosopher, inc a look at his watercolours, essays, and even his funeral pall. His elaborately biographical memorial is in the nearby churchyard. Shop, disabled access; cl Mon-Tues mid-Nov to mid-Mar, 24-26 and 31 Dec and 1 Jan; (015394) 41164; £3.50.

CRUMMOCK WATER NY1518 The scenery is less rewarding than around neighbouring Buttermere, but it's not to be sniffed at. A good start for a walk is the car park by **Lanthwaite Wood**, off the B5289 towards Loweswater at the N end; there's a pretty view from the hill above the wood. You can hire rowing boats on this lake (015394) 35599, and if you're keen to swim in one of the lakes this is probably the best.

DACRE NY4726 **Dalemain Historic House & Gardens** 🏛 A medieval, Tudor and Georgian house, so an appealing variety of periods and style. Some rooms are grand, others are charming, with splendid furnishings and paintings and some bits for children to enjoy too. Particularly interesting chinese Room with hand-painted wallpaper. There are deer in the carefully landscaped **park** with mountain views. Atmospheric restaurant in a medieval hall, shop, plant centre, limited disabled access; open Sun-Thurs 28 Mar-21 Oct; (017684) 86450; £5.50, £3.50 grounds; discount voucher not valid for special events. The village **church** has pre-Norman sculpture, and quaint medieval stone bears in the graveyard. The Horse & Farrier has good value food.

DALEHEAD NY2215 From Howtown there's a good walk up Martindale (where the **church** has attractive primitive stonework), then up over the fells to Bedafell Knott and down into Patterdale; hard work, but gorgeous views, also buzzards and ring ouzels.

DALTON-IN-FURNESS SD2273 The village has a rather austere square castle; the Black Dog (Broughton Rd) has good value hearty food (all day wknds, but cl winter wkdy lunchtimes). **South Lakes Wild Animal Park** See *separate family panel on p.103.*

DENT SD7087 Inside the modern outskirts is a delightful cobbled village, a rewarding end to an attractive drive - though now on the tourist trail, so busy in summer. During its heyday the town had a thriving knitting industry - Robert Southey even referred to the incessant knitters of Dent. The welcoming Sun has brewed its own beer (but was for sale as we went to press), and the church is well worth a look; the views from the churchyard are spectacular. Dentdale has easy to middling walks, in the shadow of Whernside.

DERWENT WATER NY2523 With all its inlets and islets, a pleasant place for pottering about in boats. It has gorgeous lakeside scenery, romantic little islets, ancient woodland, a variety of mountain backdrops. You can hire rowing boats and launches in Keswick (017687) 72263. Regular launches run all year from Keswick to half a dozen points around the lake. Walks along the lake's W shore, best reached from car parks off the back road between Grange and Swinside, can be combined with the more demanding walk up Cat Bells for the superb views of the lake. It looks equally magnificent from the E side at Friar's Crag (by the lakeside, a level stroll out from Keswick), Castlehead Wood (just S of Keswick), and Walla Crag (a more adventurous climb from the NT car park at Great Wood, an area teeming with red squirrels).

Watendlath This lovely lost village is little more than a tarn, a farm and a very modest café. A narrow road climbs from the B5289 by Derwent Water, but the village makes a very rewarding destination for a walk over the hills - for instance from Rosthwaite, where the Scafell Hotel has a popular walkers' bar.

DUDDON VALLEY SD2296
A favourite starting point for rather more demanding walks, either by the river or up into the heights, with the Newfield Inn at Seathwaite a good base (food all day). Outstanding scenic drives along the valley, and then along the Wrynose and Hard Knott passes.

DUFTON NY6926
High Pennines Over to the E of the Lakes, these have few walking routes and are extremely bleak: this is the reserve of the dedicated peat-bog enthusiast. An easy way to get an idea of the remoteness of these hills is to walk along paths encircling **Dufton Pike** from Dufton, where the Stag has good food.

EGREMONT NY0110
Dominated by its very ruined Norman **castle**; as so often, the gatehouse is the best preserved part. **Lowes Court Gallery** Georgian house with local arts and crafts for sale, disabled access; cl Sun, pm Weds and pm wkdys Jan-Feb, phone for opening times over Christmas; (01946) 820693; free.
Florence Mine Heritage Centre (A595 just SE of Egremont) Based around the last working iron ore mine in Europe. Tours of the pit (wknds and bank hols at 11am - phone for wkdy times), and visitor centre with reconstructions of pit life 100 years ago. Snacks, shop, disabled access to visitor centre; (01946) 825830; £6.50 pit tour, £2 visitor centre (£1 if you buy ticket to pit tour).

ELTERWATER NY3204
Idyllically placed village, with lake views. The Britannia is a favourite place for lunch; readers also recommend taking the recently improved footpath opposite, to Kirkstone Galleries (ceramics, glass, kitchenware, and a good café), good views along the way.

The B5343 past Elterwater gives awesome mountain views; you can keep on a poorer steeper road, passing pretty Blea Tarn, and coming back down through Little Langdale.

ENNERDALE WATER NY1016
One of the quietest lakes, with nearby slopes densely cloaked in conifer plantations, so it's not to everyone's taste. Gentle walks by the lake (no boating), with glimpses of high peaks above, and Ennerdale is virtually car-free. Under its new owners the Shepherds Arms at Ennerdale Bridge, packed with pictures, has good local food and a weather forecast blackboard. The road S from Ennerdale Bridge to Calder Bridge gives outstanding views of fells and coast.

ESKDALE NY1700
Excellent for walks, esp around Boot. Here, a prime objective is the **Stanley Ghyll Force** waterfall, approached by a series of bridges and visible from a dizzying view-platform high above. From Trough House Bridge car park nr the waterfall you can walk along one side of the river to Doctor Bridge, then return the other side, for an easy route - with delectable views throughout. Other walks take you up towards the open fells (the landlord of the Burnmoor Inn is helpful with route suggestions). You can use the Ravenglass & Eskdale railway as part of a round trip.

FAIRFIELD NY3511
Rewarding for determined fell-walkers, climbed by a horseshoe layout of ridges from Rydal.

FAR SAWREY SD3895
Between the ferry here and the Wray Castle estate to the N can be found the cream of Windermere's waterside strolls, along the lake's W shore. The estate is a large NT tract with public access. The forested slope rising from this shore has several well signposted routes, with Far Sawrey and Near Sawrey villages, and Latterbarrow, worthwhile objectives for circular walks. The beautifully placed Sawrey Hotel's character stable bar serves good value pubby food.

FINTHSWAITE SD3788
Stott Park Bobbin Mill (just N) In coppiced woodland, this former water-

and-steam mill made wooden cotton reels from 1835 right up to 1971; enthusiastic guides give excellent demonstrations of 19th-c industrial techniques. The mill is still powered by steam Tues-Thurs: the lathes look lethal. Snacks, shop, disabled access; cl Nov-Mar; (015395) 31087; £3.50; EH. The Swan at Newby Bridge is attractively set for lunch.

FLOOKBURGH SD3675
This peaceful village has excellent potted local shrimps. In Winder Lane **Lakeland Miniature Village** has over 100 buildings made from Coniston slate, and a developing Japanese garden; snacks (in the new Japanese-style tea house), disabled access; (015395) 58500; £3. The Engine in nearby Cark has good home cooking.

GLEASTON SD2671
Gleaston Watermill Well restored working watermill in peaceful surroundings, with a pleasant streamside walk and apiary tours (Sat, protective clothing provided, over 5s only), and you can watch bees in a new observation hive; it's also the site of archaeological digs. Enjoyable meals and snacks, shop specialising in all things piggy, some disabled access; cl Mon (exc bank hols), 25-26 Dec and 1 Jan; (01229) 869244; £2.50. The ruins of a partly built medieval castle are nearby, and the General Burgoyne at Great Urswick is a good refreshment stop.

GOSFORTH NY0603
The churchyard has a 10th-c carved **cross**, one of Britain's finest; there are more ancient carved hogback tombstones in the church. The working pottery has a good shop.

GRANGE-OVER-SANDS SD4077
This sedately old-fashioned resort, with several good cafés along the High St and a long promenade, is the start for summer guided walks over **Morecambe Bay Sands**, oddly other-worldly; glistening tidal flats, quick-stepping patrols of wading birds, distant hills, grisly tales of people and horses sucked under - a guide really is essential; phone Cedric Robinson (the official guide, appointed by the Queen), who's been doing it for almost 40 years, on (0153 95) 32165 for times.
Hampsfield Fell From the town, a

pleasant and not too steep walk up through the woods to the modest, flattish summit, giving terrific views over the Bay from its limestone pavements and summit 'hospice' inscribed with 19th-c words of wisdom.

GRASMERE NY3407
The pretty village swarms with visitors in summer, most of them here to see **Dove Cottage** - still much as Wordsworth had it in his most creative years (he completed *The Prelude* here), with sister Dorothy's journals and his extensive cottage garden. Informative guided tours cope well with the bustle, but in early morning (opens 9.30) out of season you may get some space to yourself. The place always was crowded; barely big enough for two, with the poets' children and friends it often had a dozen or more people living here. The adjoining **Wordsworth Museum**, included in the price, has changing exhibitions and possessions of the poet and his family and friends, as well as a reconstructed Lakeland kitchen and contemporary art gallery. Meals, snacks, shop, limited disabled access; cl mid-Jan to mid-Feb, 24-26 Dec; (015394) 35544; £5.80 museum and house, £3 museum only. Work on the £3m Jerwood Centre, which will house artefacts from the Wordsworth Trust collection, should be completed in spring. Wordsworth is buried in the graveyard of the pebbledashed old church, which is better inside than outside. Sarah Nelson's gingerbread shop by the church is wonderfully old-fashioned. The Travellers Rest (A591 N) is our current pick for lunch. The lake itself, with Rydal Water and Elterwater, is the very heart of picturesque Lakeland. All three are famous for their lovely settings, and there are pleasant walks all around; you can even link all three together in a long afternoon's walk filled with glorious views. The walk up the good track to Easedale Tarn from Grasmere quickly gets you away from the crowds, into a fine valley; the lake itself is romantically set below rocks.

GRAYTHWAITE SD3791
Graythwaite Hall Gardens ⊞ (2m N of Lakeside) Well kept late Victorian garden, strong on rhododendrons and

late-spring shrubs. Disabled access (though need a strong pusher); open Apr-Jun; (015395) 31248; £2.

GREAT LANGDALE NY2806

Dominated by the awesome Langdale Pikes, this is the area's main centre for more serious fell-walking in grand scenery. One very popular shorter walk here is up the good track to Stickle Tarn, from the car park by the Stickle Barn (useful for refreshments), and Bow Fell and Crinkle Crags are two longer fell walks. Wainwrights, in the not specially graceful settlement of Chapel Stile off the B5343, is another useful refreshment place and base for walks along here.

GRIZEDALE SD3394

Grizedale Forest Park Visitor Centre Woodland trails from short strolls to half-day walks, punctuated by 90 or so forest-based sculptures. These trails are good when rain cuts off more open views; the sculptures are set in various spots throughout the forest (map from visitor centre). Lots of other activities too: exhibitions, gallery, good information centre, orienteering, bike hire (it's an ideal area for cycling), and adventure play area. In all, six or seven square miles of mixed woodland to get lost in. Meals, snacks, shop, some disabled access; cl 24 Dec-1 Jan; (01229) 860373; parking from £2. The Eagles Head at Satterthwaite has been good value for lunch (changed hands 2003), and the back roads through this area are quiet and pleasant.

GUMMERS HOW SD3988

An easy 20-min climb from the road, for a fine lake view of Windermere.

HADRIAN'S WALL NY5664

Surviving traces of this far less known western section of the Roman wall can be reached on well signed paths from the lanes between the A69 and B6318 N of Brampton. For the Birdoswald Roman fort at Gilsland, see Northumbria chapter.

HARDKNOTT PASS NY2101

Hardknott Roman Fort Quite well preserved and interestingly restored, but most notable for its breathtakingly lonely position high in the mountains; magnificent views to sea and even the Isle of Man. The drive up here is not for the faint-hearted - it's very steep and twisting, through this pass and Wrynose Pass, but the scenery makes it worthwhile; the Woolpack Inn at Bleabeck just W is good value.

HAWKSHEAD SD3598

Don't miss this virtually unchanged Elizabethan Lakeland village, with sturdy outside walls, and sheltered flower-filled inner courtyards. Though very popular with summer visitors, even at its busiest it has a pleasantly foreign 'different' feel, and the fact that cars are kept out helps a lot. The church has some eye-catching early 18th-c murals. The Queens Head and Kings Arms both do enjoyable food (as does the upmarket Drunken Duck up at Barngates). Trout **fishing** and **boat hire** on nearby Esthwaite Water, the largest stocked lake in the region; (015394) 36541; day permit £19, plus boat hire £31.50.

Beatrix Potter Gallery (Main St) A generous annually changing selection of the original illustrations of *Benjamin Bunny* and other favourites, as well as rather different more acutely (almost acidly) observed drawings. A timed ticket system keeps it uncrowded - during holiday periods you may have to wait to get in. Shop; cl Thurs, Fri, and Nov-Mar; (015394) 36355; £3 (inc 50p off entry to Hill Top; NT).

Old Grammar School Museum Founded in 1585, this is now a museum worth poking your nose into, if only to see where Wordsworth carved his name on a desk (he attended 1779-1787). Shop, disabled access to ground floor only; cl 12.30-1.30pm, Sun am, and Nov-Mar; (015394) 36735; £1.

HELVELLYN NY3415

This famous Lakeland landmark is most easily (and crowdedly) tackled from Thirlmere, but much more exciting when reached from Glenridding and Striding Edge, where the path follows a narrow rocky edge (mild scrambling needed - best ascended rather than descended; return via Swirral Edge or one of the other paths) above a great post-glacial corrie; it's a day's hard walking, for perhaps the grandest and certainly the most popular of all Lakeland panoramas, with dramatic ridges leading off for miles.

HIGH CUP NICK NY7426

A great scoop in the ridge of the

Pennines, this is one of the most dramatic features in the whole of the range, well worth the long but easily followed walk from the pretty village of Dufton, where the welcoming Stag has good value food.

HIGH STREET NY4515
One of Lakeland's great fell walks, this is a Roman ridge road, reached best from Hawes Water reservoir (the hotel here is a useful stop).

HONISTER PASS NY2213
From the top of the pass, stout-hearted and well equipped walkers can tackle Brandreth, and perhaps head on via Windy Gap for the least taxing ascent of **Great Gable**. Even if you decide not to go the whole way, the views in clear weather are spectacular.

Honister Slate Mine Guided tours of the huge caverns at this dramatically set slate mine (the only one in England) show the interesting mixture of modern and traditional methods used to extract the slate. You can usually watch them preparing the slate in the visitor centre, which has a reconstruction of a slate mine entrance; also a slate stone garden. Snacks, shop, disabled access to visitor centre; tours 10.30am, 12.30 and 3.30pm, cl mid-Dec to mid-Jan, best to check; (017687) 77230; free, mine tour £7. Down at Stonethwaite, the beautifully set Langstrath does nice bar lunches.

HOWGILL FELLS SD6897
Bold 2,000-footers, tough going even for hardened walkers; the easiest walks into them are up Winder from Sedbergh, and from the A683 N of Sedbergh to majestic **Cautley Spout** waterfall.

HUMPHREY HEAD POINT
SD3874
This ¾-mile-long headland protruding into the sea gives walkers stunning views of Morecambe Bay.

KENDAL SD5192
A real town as opposed to a tourist centre, busy, with traffic streamed round a one-way system, but lots of small closes leading off the main street, some of them attractively restored to give a feel of what the place was like in the 18th-c heyday of the wool-weaving industry. The mint cake that takes its name comes in a surprising number of

varieties. A joint ticket to Abbot Hall Art Gallery & Museum and Lakeland Life is £4.50. **Brewery Arts Centre** (Highgate) has good changing events and exhibitions, café, bar, and landscaped garden; (01539) 725133 for what's on. The child-friendly Olde Fleece (Highgate) does inexpensive food all day, and Alexanders (Castle Green Hotel, high over the town) is good. **Webbs Garden Centre** (Burneside Rd) is big, with lots of plants; decent café, disabled access.

Abbot Hall Art Gallery & Museum (Kirkland) Beautifully restored Georgian house with an art collection that reflects Kendal's importance in the 18th c as the centre of an artists' school, inc works by Ruskin, Turner, Constable, and esp George Romney; also changing exhibitions. Meals, snacks, shop, disabled access; cl Sun, and Christmas-mid-Feb; (01539) 722464; £3.75.

Kendal Castle Ruin on a small hill on E edge of town, reputedly the birthplace of Henry VIII's wife Katherine Parr. There's little more now than parts of the outer wall with some towers - but children enjoy it, and there are fine views. A humble building associated with it is the **Castle Dairy** (Wildman St), an unspoiled Tudor house with some period furniture, inc the oldest bed the V&A have ever recorded. It's a restaurant but they are happy to let people look around.

Kendal Museum (Station Rd) One of the oldest museums in the country, this traditional place takes a comprehensive look at local and natural history, geology and archaeology; one display is devoted to the work of Alfred Wainwright, the walkers' guru. Shop, disabled access to ground floor only; (01539) 721374; cl Sun and 25 Dec to mid-Feb; £3.50.

Lakeland Life (behind Abbot Hall, Kirkland) Lovingly re-created period rooms, shops and workshops, and an almost palpable feel of the past. Subjects as diverse as shoemaking, Arthur Ransome, and the Arts and Crafts movement. Meals, snacks, shop, some disabled access; usually cl Sun, and end Dec to mid-Feb; (01539) 722464; £3.50.

Quaker Tapestry Exhibition 🖭 (Friends Meeting House, Stramongate) Bayeux-style tapestry history of the

Quaker movement, also embroidery demonstrations and video. Meals, snacks, shop, disabled access; cl Sun (plus Sat Nov-Dec) and end Dec-early Apr; (01539) 722975; £3.30.

KESWICK NY2623

The tourist centre of the northern lakes, handy for Derwent Water, with lots of Victorian villas (many of them now guesthouses and small hotels) outside quite a traditional centre, with small cobbled closes running off the main streets. It's full of breeches, boots and backpacks in high season, with good outdoor equipment shops, and is a routine stop on coach tours. The Dog & Gun and interesting old George Hotel are very popular for lunch, with the Pheasant out towards Crosthwaite also good value (and giving a pleasant walk up to the ancient church of St Kentigern). The **Wild Strawberry** (Main St) is a useful café in a quaint building, and further out on this road Greta Hall, now part of a school, is where the poets Coleridge then Southey lived. **Lakeside Tea Gardens** (Lake Rd) have home-baking, lots for children, pleasant modern furniture and crockery inside and in garden with trees and chaffinches; cl wknds in Jan. George Fisher (Borrowdale Rd) is a good big outdoors shop. The Theatre by the Lake seats 400 people; cl some Suns; box office (017687) 74411. The back road around Swinside is pretty (with the Swinside Inn a good stop), and in clear weather is worth following up the gauntly formidable Keskadale Pass.

Cars of the Stars Motor Museum (Standish St) Unusual collection of cars from film and TV dating back to Laurel & Hardy's Model T Ford, taking in Chitty Chitty Bang Bang, the Batmobile and cars used by James Bond, the Flintstones, Postman Pat and even Del Boy's van. Shop, disabled access; cl wkdys in Dec, all Jan-Feb, half-term, best to check; (017687) 73757; £3.50.

Castlerigg stone circle (just E) This neolithic monument is well preserved, and gives photogenic perspectives of the mountains (the best times for pictures are morning and evening); take a map to identify the peaks it aligns with. There's a brief explanation of the stones' history. NT.

Pencil Museum (Southey Works) Alongside the Derwent pencil factory, this surprisingly interesting museum has some unexpected exhibits inc, at 7.91 metres (26ft), the world's longest pencil. Shop, disabled access; cl 25-26 Dec, and 1 Jan; (017687) 73626; £2.50.

Puzzling Place (Museum Sq) Designed to challenge your concept of the world, there's a hologram gallery, various optical illusions inc an anti-gravity room (computers explain how it works), illusionary artwork, and puzzles for you to have a go at solving. Snacks, shop; cl 25-26 Dec, 1 Jan; (017687) 75102; £3.

Teapottery (Central Car Park Rd) Lots of extraordinary teapots to wonder at, a short video explains the process, and there's an exhibition on the history of tea. Café, shop, disabled access to ground floor only; cl 25-26 Dec, 1 Jan; (017687) 73983; free.

KIRKBY LONSDALE SD6178

Small and usually quiet town of considerable character, interesting old yards and ginnels, and good country shops and tearooms; it's more lively on Thurs country-market day. Behind the fine **church** of St Mary is a pretty stretch of the River Lune, good for walking or just lazing about - even swimming if it's hot (though watch out for currents). Along here 87 steps lead up to Ruskin's View, a beautiful panorama over the Lune Valley, appealing countryside little visited by tourists. The Snooty Fox has good food. The lovely Devil's Bridge over the River Lune just below the town dates from the 12th c.

LAKESIDE SD3787

Lakeside & Haverthwaite Railway A 3½-mile steam trip running up to Haverthwaite. There's a small collection of steam and diesel locomotives. Meals, snacks, shop, disabled access; cl Nov-Easter (exc Christmas special wknds in Dec); (015395) 31594 for times; £4.30 return. The White Hart at Bouth does good food (not Mon/Tues lunch).

LANGWATHBY NY5734

Eden Ostrich World (Langwathby Hall Farm) This friendly farm has quite a few animals to see, inc alpacas, wallabies, zebras, emus, rare breeds, and of course ostriches; you can feed some of the animals, and watch sheep being milked; also a maze, riverside walks, and indoor and outdoor play areas. Meals, snacks, shop, disabled access; open daily Mar-Oct, phone in winter; (01768) 881771; £4.50. By the big village green, the Shepherds has good value food.

LATTERBARROW SD3699
A mere hillock in comparison to the great Lakeland fells, but elevated enough above a relatively low-lying area to give views over Windermere and Langdale.

LEVENS SD4985
Levens Hall (A6) Impressive Elizabethan mansion based around older core, with fine carved oak chimney-pieces, ceiling plasterwork, spanish leather panelling, period furnishings and interesting paintings. The magnificent **topiary gardens** in their original layout of 1692 are perhaps the highlight, the fantastic shapes really standing out against the ancient grey stone of the house. Traction **steam engine** (in steam bank hols and summer Suns), play area, grand beech trees, and deer park. Snacks, plant sales, shop, disabled access to grounds only; open Sun-Thurs (house cl am) Apr to mid-Oct but best to ring to check; (015395) 60321; £7, £5.50 for grounds only. The Hare & Hounds is handy for lunch.

LINDAL-IN-FURNESS SD2576
Colony Country Store View the candlemakers at work then browse among the vast array of candles in the shop; disabled access; cl 25-26 Dec and 1 Jan; (01229) 461102; free. Chandlers Café next door has good value home-made food.

LITTLE SALKELD NY5737
Long Meg and Her Daughters There's access off the lane N to this quaintly named **stone circle**. Also worth a visit if you're passing, the **Watermill** is a bustling bright pink 18th-c watermill which produces 11 sorts of organic flour; they usually do guided tours Mon, Tues, Thurs and wknds (11am, 12, 2.30 and 3.30pm - best to check), and hold bread-making and cookery courses. Organic café; cl Christmas-beginning Feb; (01768)

881523; £3.50 for a tour. The Highland Drove in Great Salkeld does good inventive food.

LOWTHER NY5323
Lakeland Bird of Prey Centre Hawks, eagles, owls, buzzards and falcons in the huge Victorian walled garden at Lowther Castle, with flying displays at 12, 2 and 4pm. Teas, shop, disabled access; cl Nov-Mar; (01931) 712746; £5. English Heritage has provided a £65,000 emergency grant to prevent the collapse of the crumbling castle, and work is currently under way to consolidate the central tower. There are long-term plans to turn this fine example of the Gothic Revival once again into a visitor attraction - in its prime it used to draw the likes of Wordsworth and Hogarth.

MAIDEN WAY NY6433
The back road from Langwathby on the A686 through Skirwith to Kirkland leads to this **Roman road**, amazingly still sound for walkers after all those centuries. It plunges northwards into the bleak high Pennines, giving a great feeling of solitude. There are other walks from the clusters of farms along the foot of the Pennines between here and Appleby.

MALLERSTANG NY7800
This area, which the B6259 S of Kirkby Stephen runs through, has a lot of charm as a place for a short break. Lady Anne's Way, a lonely walk, runs down the valley passing the romantic ruin of Pendragon castle, supposedly once the home of King Arthur's father.

MARYPORT NY0336
There's a straightforward **maritime museum** on Senhouse St (the tourist information centre is also here); shop, disabled access to ground floor only; usually cl 1-2.30pm (exc Sun-Thurs in summer), winter Sun, but best to check; 01900 813738; donations. The B5300 N has good views across to Scotland.
Lake District Coast Aquarium 🔲 (South Quay) Local marine and freshwater life; you can gently touch some of the fish - check the board in the entrance for feeding times. Meals, snacks, shop, disabled access; cl 25-26 Dec; (01900) 817760; £4.50.
Senhouse Museum (The Battery, Sea Brows) Impressive collection of Roman

military altar stones and inscriptions, dug from the adjacent fort from the 1570s onwards, making it one of the oldest collections of antiquities in the country, also other artefacts inc a Celtic serpent stone; children's activities. Snacks, shop, disabled access; usually open Tues, Thurs-Sun and bank hols Apr-Jun, daily July-Oct, Fri-Sun Nov-Mar; (01900) 816168; £2.50.

MILLOM SD1779

Not much of a town, but there's an interesting **church**, and **ruined castle** around what's now a farm (A5093 N: ask at the house for permission to look round the ruins). The Duddon Pilot (Borwick Rails) has good value food. S of the town a broad lagoon built to protect former mineworks is now a bird reserve (also home to natterjack toads), the loneliness exaggerated out of season when the nearby unsmart but enjoyable little resort of Haverigg SD1678 (great beaches, good sailing and fishing) has closed down; the Harbour Inn has good cheap food, good walks in the wildflower dunes.

Haverigg Point This huge stretch of impressive **dunes** is a high point on this section of coast, but virtually the whole length from Ravenglass down to Hodbarrow Point is good for breezy seaside walks - lots of long beaches, deserted except in high season.

MILNTHORPE SD5078

Lakeland Wildlife Oasis 🏛 (Hale, A6 S) Millions of years of evolution flash before your eyes at this lively wildlife centre, a fascinating cross between zoo and museum. Interactive displays alongside the brightly coloured and unusual fish, birds, insects and animals, and woodland where children can crawl along tunnels overlooking the meerkat enclosure. Children's activities, and a chance to meet some of the animals. Meals, snacks, shop, disabled access; cl 25-26 Dec; (015395) 63027; £5.50. The B5282 to Arnside has quiet estuary and mountain views.

NEAR SAWREY SD3795

Hill Top Small-roomed typically cumbrian 17th-c farmhouse, kept exactly as it was when owned by Beatrix Potter, who wrote many of her stories here; with the royalties from her books, she bought a lot of Lake District land and gave it to the NT. Shop, disabled access to ground floor by prior arrangement; cl Thurs-Fri, and Nov to mid-Mar; (015394) 36269; £4.50 (inc 50p off entry to the Beatrix Potter Gallery; NT). The old-fashioned NT-owned Tower Bank Arms (with nicely furnished bedrooms) is pictured in *The Tale of Jemima Puddle-Duck*.

NEWBY BRIDGE SD3787

Aquarium of the Lakes By the steamer stop, this imaginatively laid out aquarium-style centre vividly demonstrates the story of a local river. You can walk in see-through tunnels along a re-created lake bed, with the area's animals (inc otters), insects, birds and plants all around, and a water lab has microscopes for close-up encounters with various forms of pond life; audio-visual display and good views of the lake. Snacks, shop, disabled access; cl 25 Dec; (015395) 30153; £5.95. The nicely set Swan Hotel is a very comfortable refreshment stop (snacks all day).

PENRITH NY5130

The biggest town in Lakeland, still a northern country town rather than a tourist place even though the livestock market has closed and the farmers' market is now just monthly (every 3rd Tues) rather than weekly. There are still weekly open-air markets Sat and Tues, and traditional Lakeland shops sell real fudge and toffee, rich cakes (Greggs), local cheeses (Grahams), tasty cumberland sausages (Cranstons), local antiquarian books, and cheap and sturdy country clothes. John Norris (Victoria Rd) is the outstanding fishing/outdoor-wear shop, with something for everyone at good prices. A **museum** on Middlegate is a useful introduction to the area, and the George does decent lunches.

Penrith Castle Built in the 14th c as a defence against scottish raids, and the home of Richard III when he was Duke of Gloucester. The ruins are surrounded by a park; free.

Rheged Discovery Centre (Redhills, A66/A592 W) Named after the Celtic kingdom which once stretched from Strathclyde to Cheshire, this vast development, set right into a hillside, is Europe's largest grass-covered building.

They show three different films a day (inc one on cumbrian myths and legends) on a cinema screen the size of six double-decker buses, while a separate video display takes a look at contemporary life through the eyes of six local people. Also a permanent mountaineering exhibition, changing exhibitions of local art (some of it for sale), pottery demonstrations, indoor children's play area (£2 an hour), and regular special events. Glass atriums and two huge windows give stunning countryside views. Meals, snacks, specialist shops, disabled access; cl 25 Dec; (01768) 868000; cinema or exhibition £5.50, £9.45 for both. The Kings Arms at Stainton is handy for a good lunch.

St Wilfred's church (B6262 E of Eamont Bridge) A striking exception to the usual Lakeland rule of simplicity in churches, filled with magnificent furnishings inc continental treasures; candlelit. The nearby Gate Inn at Yanwath has good food.

Wetheriggs Pottery (Clifton Dykes, signed off A6 S) Interesting and very smart working pottery - one of the oldest in the country - with 19th-c steam engine and equipment, and a new art gallery; children can try their hands at the wheel, and there's a play area. Meals, snacks, shop, disabled access; cl Tues (exc in Aug and cumbrian school hols), Tues-Weds end Sept-Easter, 25-26 Dec, and 1 Jan; (01768) 892733; free.

PIEL ISLAND SD2363
Small island shared by a basic inn and a grand 14th-c ruined fortress commanding Barrow Harbour and Morecambe Bay. It's reached by ferry (by arrangement only in winter) from Roa Island nr Barrow, subject to tides; (01229) 8335809.

RAVENGLASS SD0896
Pretty sailing harbour by the well sheltered Esk estuary; the Ratty Arms does interesting food. The so-called **Walls Castle** just outside the village is actually a Roman bath house; its walls stand taller than any other building of its age so far north.

Muncaster Castle & World Owl Centre (A595, 1m E) The same family have lived in the elegant house since 1208, and will continue to do so as long as a magical glass drinking bowl (left by

King Henry VI) remains intact. Extended over the centuries (esp the 19th) from its original tower, it still feels very lived-in, and the rich furnishings and décor include some fine Elizabethan furniture and embroidery. There's an entertaining audio tour, and young children will especially like the undercover maze (you can advance only by answering questions about the environment). Muncaster is the HQ of the World Owl Trust, and they have over 180 birds from 50 different species; an interpretation centre has CCTV of nesting owls. There are talks and flying displays at 2.30pm, and you can watch wild herons being fed (4.30pm Mar-Nov, weather permitting). The lovely 77-acre grounds are particularly rich in species rhododendrons and have unusual trees, nature trails, adventure play area and lots of rescued birds of prey. Various special events. Meals, snacks, shops, mostly disabled access; castle open daily (exc Sat) beginning Mar-Oct, garden and owl centre open all year; (01229) 717614; £7.58 for everything, £5.70 for the garden, owl centre and maze.

Ravenglass & Eskdale Railway Narrow-gauge steam trains, lovingly preserved, with covered or open carriages chugging seven miles through unspoilt valleys to Dalegarth station up near Boot; admirers say it's the most beautiful train journey in England. Cafés each end, and at Ravenglass a small museum, audio-visual display, and play area; free. Shop, disabled access; open daily end Mar-beginning Nov, trains many winter weekends, phone to check; (01229) 717171; £7.80 return. Plenty of enjoyable walks from stations along the line, or even right down from the top (booklet available from stations).

RAVENSTONEDALE NY7203
The village is notable more for its pleasant riverside scenery than for its buildings - apart from the unspoilt **church** which escaped Victorian refitting; longitudinal pews, three-decker pulpit, steeply pitched gallery (steep stairs up), and fine E window memorial to Fothergill family (one was last female Protestant martyr to be burned at the stake). Choose a bright day for best light.

RYDAL NY3606

Rydal Mount 🏛 (A591)

Wordsworth's sister Dorothy described Rydal as a paradise when the family moved here from Grasmere in 1813; they stayed for the rest of their lives. The house itself is quite modest, with family portraits and period furniture, and it's what's outside that really stands out - the good-sized garden is still much as the poet laid it out, consciously picturesque, with original ideas that people are still rediscovering today. The setting is lovely, overlooking mountains and lakes; they often have readings of the poetry it inspired. Shop, limited disabled access; cl Tues Nov-Feb, 25 Dec, last 3 wks in Jan; (015394) 33002; £4. Decent campsites nearby. The Glen Rothay Hotel does decent lunches, and Dora's Field beside it has lots of daffodils.

SEASCALE NY0204

Sellafield Visitor Centre (off A595) Children enjoy the lively hands-on approach to the industry at this nuclear power visitor centre, imaginatively redesigned by the Science Museum using the latest interactive technology. Meals, snacks, shop, disabled access; cl 25 Dec; (019467) 27027; free. Also here, the world's first commercial nuclear power station, Calder Hall, has recently been closed after 46 years in operation. Seascale itself has a pleasant beach, and a singularly scenic golf course, where every hole offers views of the sea or the mountains.

SEATHWAITE NY2109

Packhorse track Determined fell-walkers enjoy the unspoilt packhorse track from Seathwaite (just off the B5289 in Borrowdale) over **Styhead Pass** down into Wasdale. The summit of the pass is a start point for a fiercely dramatic route up Scafell Pike. More easily reached is the Taylorgill Force waterfall.

SEDBERGH SD6390

Hardy small town at the foot of the Howgill Fells, with a helpful Yorkshire Dales National Park Centre on Main St (wknds only Oct-Easter); (015396) 20125). The Dalesman is good for lunch.

Farfield Mill (A684 E) An attractively restored four-storey mill with working looms, craft workshops, and a good café. Shop, disabled access; cl wkdys 12 Jan-4 Apr, 25-26 Dec, 1 Jan; (015396) 21958; £2.

Holme Farm (Middleton, just SW) Tours of traditional hill farm, with plenty of young animals and nature trail; they do occasional evening tours with badger watch. Shop, disabled access; cl Oct-Feb exc by arrangement; (015396) 20654; £2.50. You can camp here (from £5).

SHAP NY5514

Shap Abbey (left towards Keld off A6 going N out of village) The best feature is the unspoilt and undeveloped riverside seclusion; the abbey itself is ruined, but you can trace the 13th-c layout in some detail. Nearby **Keld Chapel** is a lonely untouched shepherds' church in a riverside hamlet, and the gated Swindale road signed off the Bampton road nr Rosgill is pretty. The Greyhound has good unfussy food.

SIZERGH SD4888

Low Sizergh Barn Highly recommended by readers for its fresh farm foods, and other local produce inc damson beer and Morecambe Bay shrimps. A nature trail around the organic dairy farm highlights its conservation work. The tearoom, upstairs in a 17th-c barn well worth visiting anyway for its glorious array of local and organic produce, crafts (inc a potter) and clothes, overlooks the milking parlour and makes a fine place for lunch. Meals, snacks, shop; cl 25-26 Dec and 1 Jan; (015395) 60426; free.

Sizergh Castle Lovely country house surrounded by two lakes, over the centuries harmoniously extended from its original sturdy 14th-c tower by the family who have lived here for generations. Fine Tudor and Elizabethan carving, panelling and furniture, Jacobite relics, and terraced gardens surrounding a grand flight of steps down to the water. Lots to interest a gardener, inc an enormous rock garden, japanese maples, water garden, wild flowers, and daffodils in the apple orchard; the autumn colours are lovely. Snacks, shop, disabled access to garden and ground floor of house; open pm Sun-Thurs Apr-Oct; (015395) 60070; £5, £2.50 garden only; NT.

SKELTON NY4635
Hutton-in-the-Forest (B5305) Some say this formidable mansion was the castle of the Green Knight of Arthurian legend. Grandly extended in the 17th c from its 14th-c peel tower core, then castellated more recently, it has a magnificent panelled gallery. A terraced garden runs down to the lake; there's an 18th-c walled formal garden, and a more romantic Victorian garden with grand trees, dovecot and woodland nature walk. Tearoom, shop; open Thurs, Fri, Sun and bank hols 9-18 Apr, and 2 May-3 Oct; house cl am; (01768) 484449; £4.50, £2.50 garden only. Nearby in Unthank, readers like the **Upfront Gallery**: changing exhibitions, craft shop and good vegetarian café; cl Mon, and 25 Dec-25 Jan; disabled access; free.

SKIDDAW NY2629
One of Cumbria's four 3,000-footer peaks, but more accessible than many lesser ones - quite an easy haul up from Applethwaite (just N of Keswick), for far-ranging views.

ST BEES NX9712
In the old centre of this coastal village (the starting point for the popular 190-mile Coast to Coast Walk across three National Parks to Robin Hood's Bay in Yorkshire), St Bees Priory stands on a 7th-c Augustinian site; now just the church remains, rather done over in the 19th c but a magnificent Norman door-way survives. Close by, you can glimpse the 16th-c part of St Bees School, quite Oxbridgey in character. The Queens does good generous home cooking.
Cliffs and birds The cliff path between Whitehaven and St Bees is the best part of the cumbrian coast for walkers and bird-watchers (each town has a railway station). From the beach car park NW of St Bees an easy walk takes you up the nature-reserve sandstone headland, famous for its bird life, and with magnificent sea and hill views.

STAFFIELD NY5342
Nunnery Walks These private paths through old woodland take you through a lovely Eden Valley river gorge with waterfalls and quiet pools. The Crown over at Kirkoswald is now doing good food, and there are other good free walks in this delightfully wooded

sheltered valley, for instance from Armathwaite and Wetheral. The Eden Valley has the handy reputation of staying dry when it's pouring over in Lakeland.

STAINTON NY4827
Alpaca Centre The first centre for these fleecy andean animals in Britain; you can view them in their paddocks, from the tearoom, or get up close on a field walk and hear them humming (£1). Snacks, shop, disabled access; cl 25-26 Dec, 1 Jan; (01768) 891440; free. The Kings Arms is good for lunch.

SWINSIDE SD1688
Swinside Stone Circle Not that much visited, but definitely one of the best prehistoric sites in Lakeland: it's a bit of a trek to reach and worth combining with the drive over spectacular Corney Fell, which gives views of the coast and the Duddon Valley. Take the side turn to Millom, leading to a lone house called Cragg Hall, from where it's a 15-min walk.

TALKIN TARN NY5457
Lovely lake with partly wooded shores, peaceful mountain views, plenty of space for strolling; nature trail, orienteering and rowing boats; disabled access, teas. The village is pretty; the Blacksmiths Arms has good food.

TARN HOWS SD3299
So popular a beauty spot that it has its own one-way system to get to it; this is a gorgeously photogenic small lake, particularly beautiful on a still clear autumn day, or early in the morning before the crowds have arrived.

TEMPLE SOWERBY NY6128
Acorn Bank Garden (off B6412 N) Richly planted terraced and walled garden with 250 varieties of medicinal and culinary herbs, clematis, unusual old fruit trees, and herbaceous borders; the steep wild garden drops down to the stream. The wheel of the restored mill down here turns at wknds when there is a volunteer. This is a lovely spot at daffodil time (and woodland walks are organised at wknds, beginning Mar, to see early flowers). Meals, snacks, shop, disabled access; cl Tues, and Nov-Mar; (017683) 61893; £2.75; NT. The handsome Kings Arms does enjoyable food. The B6412 to Lazenby and then the back road through the Eden Valley

to Armathwaite and on up to Wetheral gives delicious quiet views.

THIRLMERE NY3213

At the geographical heart of the Lake District, a lake enlarged into a reservoir, but mostly naturalistic. Looks its best from the unclassified road around its W side; here short stretches of lakeside path look across to the massive slopes of Helvellyn. On the main road the Kings Head is a useful lunch spot.

THORNTHWAITE NY2225

Thornthwaite Galleries Fine art, sculpture, pottery and crafts, as well as teas, and a children's play area. Snacks, shop, disabled access; usually cl Tues, Mon-Thurs in Nov, and all Dec-Feb; (017687) 78248; free. The Coledale Inn at Braithwaite is useful for lunch.

THORNTHWAITE FOREST NY2124

The first-ever Forestry Commission plantation: walks through it, and to the fells above (with lake and mountain views), are best started with a visit to the Whinlatter Visitor Centre (B5292 above Braithwaite). This has good explanatory forestry displays, and the newly opened Osprey Experience (open Apr-Sept) has CCTV letting you watch the ospreys while they're in the forest (for the last couple of years they've nested around Mar-Aug); shop, forest maps, teas.

TORPENHOW NY2039

Torpenhow church A formidable Norman building, striking in itself but worth looking at closely, for the even older Roman masonry.

TROUTBECK NY4002

Townend The perfectly preserved home of a comfortably off, very traditional farming family who lived here for 300 years till the 1940s, the house showing little change over all that time. Solid simple unshowy comfort, and a sensible, down-to-earth and entirely self-sufficient layout. This is one of several such beautifully placed 'statesmen's' farms making up this lovely village strung along the steep valley below high fells. Braille guide; cl am, all day Mon (exc bank hols) and Sat, and Nov-Mar; (015394) 32628; £3; NT.

ULLSWATER NY4421

Here elegant Victorian steamers converted to diesel run between Pooley Bridge, Howtown and Glenridding; disabled access, cl Dec-Mar. Motor boats can be hired from Ullswater Marina at Watermillock, sailing dinghies too if you're experienced - (017684) 86415, cl Nov-Mar; the sailing school at Glenridding has a range of canoes and sailing dinghies for hire - some experience of sailing necessary to hire a sailboat, though they do give introductory lessons and courses - (017684) 82541; cl winter. Mountain bikes, rowing and other boats can be hired from Tindals in Glenridding - (017684) 82393; prices for two people, rowing boat £7, motorboats around £16, fishing boats £25 full day; mountain bikes from £10 for a half day.

Aira Force Waterfall This is the best-known walk on Ullswater's W side - a pleasant if rather populated stroll of a mile or so from the car park on the A592 just NE of the A5091 junction, through NT lakeshore woods to the waterfalls themselves, and the 'gothick' folly of Lyulph's Tower, with Wordsworth's daffodils a bonus in spring. Above here, Gowbarrow Park has the best lake views on this side. Aira Force is a 20-metre (65ft) waterfall, at its best after rain or on a misty morning; tearoom and shop, parking £3 for 4 hours. The Royal Hotel at Dockray (open all day) is a good refuge.

Ullswater walks The E shore is outstanding; there are many different views, with a rewarding combination of waterside stretches and higher ground giving more sweeping vistas. On the best and most popular stretch, Howtown—Patterdale—Glenridding, you will meet quite a few other people in summer (when it can be combined with the steamer for a round trip; best to take the steamer on the way out in case the service is cancelled). The Howtown Hotel is a useful stop, and Hallin Fell nearby gives an aerial view of the lake.

ULVERSTON SD2878

This town holds the bizarre double claim of being the birthplace of both pole-vaulting and the Quaker movement (no wonder it went on to produce Stan Laurel). The Farmers Arms (Market Pl) has good food and seems very much the welcoming heart of the town. The unusual-looking Lanternhouse arts centre (The Ellers) has changing exhibitions, and regular workshops.

Conishead Priory (Priory Rd) There's a unique Buddhist Temple in the grounds of this eye-catching early 19th-c Gothic mansion; guided tours of the mansion and temple £2.50; phone for opening times; snacks, shop, disabled access; (01229) 584029. A woodland walk goes down to Morecambe Bay.

Lakes Glass Centre (Oubas Hill) Watch the craftsmen blowing, cutting and engraving. The factory shop is good value, with cheap seconds. Meals, snacks, shop, disabled access; cl 25-26 Dec and 1 Jan (no glassmaking on Sun); (01229) 584400; £2.

Laurel & Hardy Museum (Upper Brook St) In Stan Laurel's home town, with delightfully informally presented mementoes and all-day films. Shop, disabled access; cl Jan; (01229) 582292; £2.50.

Swarthmoor Hall (off A590 SW of centre) Elizabethan manor known as the 'powerhouse of the early Quaker movement', after George Fox was sheltered here in 1652. The interior has been lovingly restored with 17th-c furnishings. They do good interesting guided tours (2.30pm Thurs, Fri and Sun mid-Mar to mid-Oct); (01229) 583204; £2.50.

WALNEY ISLAND SD1869 Over the bridge from Barrow, this has some long roads of low houses but is mostly a windswept sweep of duney grass, very offshore-feeling; nature reserves at both ends, with excellent bird-watching and interesting plants. The George has decent food.

WANSFELL PIKE NY3904 Gained by a path from Ambleside, this is toylike in size compared with the bigger fells, but the view is as good as from many more imposing peaks.

WASDALE NY1808 The start for many magnificent fell walks, inc the ascents of Great Gable and Scafell Pike; one less taxing walk is straight up the head of the valley to the summit of Black Sail Pass and back. Apart from around the interesting

churchyard, it's not so good for gentle strolls, and parking at Wasdale Head can be a problem in summer or at holiday times. Besides the Wasdale Head Hotel, the Strands lower down is a useful stop for food.

WATERMILLOCK NY4422 The **church** is worth stopping at for its evocative photographs of all its 1930s parishioners. The cheerful Brackenrigg overlooking the lake has imaginative food.

WHITEHAVEN NX9718 Planned as an 18th-c industrial town and major port, this has emerged full of interest from a major restoration project following economic decline; the harbour is attractive at high tide. Michael Moon's **bookshop** (Lowther St) has a vast and rewarding second-hand stock, the best in the Lakes (cl Sun, bank hols, and Weds Jan-Easter), and there's a pottery in the Market Place. There are some other interesting shops in side streets, and Sal Madges (Duke St) has cheap food; if you plan to visit the Rum Story and the Beacon, it's worth getting a joint ticket (£7.50). Just S at Sandwith, the Lowther Arms, with good homely food and accommodation, is handy for the coast-to-coast walk. The site of Haig Colliery (Solway Rd, Kells) now houses a developing mining museum (future plans inc a new café, mining experience and steam train trips from the town centre); ask for a guided tour. Shop, disabled access; cl Weds, 25-26 Dec, 1 Jan; (01946) 599949; free.

Beacon (West Strand) Whitehaven's history is well covered here, but what really makes this friendly museum worth a look is the Met Office Weather Gallery on the top floor, full of hi-tech monitoring and recording equipment, and excellent hands-on displays explaining how weather forecasts are put together. The building itself is striking, with good views from the top floor over the town and harbour and even across to Scotland. Snacks, shop, disabled access; cl Mon (exc school and bank hols), and 25 Dec; (01946) 592302; £4.25. A ground-floor gallery has changing exhibitions; free. They do heritage walks from here Tues and Sat afternoons; phone to book (01946) 852939; £3. Ask at the friendly Tourist

Information Centre about the Quest (you complete ten different trails and answer questions, and are then entered into a prize draw; £5.95).

Rum Story Covers the history of rum in a way designed to appeal to children, with some lively re-creations from a slave ship and rum store to a prohibition-era FBI office; also a film on rum-making in Grenada, various audio-visual displays, and an extraordinary kinetic clock. Meals, snacks, shop, disabled access; cl 25 Dec and 1 Jan; (01946) 592933; £4.95.

WINDERMERE SD4096

An extensive largely Victorian development of guest houses and small hotels spreads up between the older village of Bowness and the hillside station. It has a touristy feel right through the year, especially around the main street down to the steamer piers. Bowness itself has an inner core of narrower much older streets and buildings - one of the most ancient is the quaint Hole in t' Wall pub. The tourist information centre on Victoria St has a useful range of locally produced crafts if you haven't time to look properly, and the Birdcage (College Rd) is a good **antiques shop** - mostly small things, esp lamps. Lakeland Ltd (Alexandra Buildings, by station), a quality kitchenware shop, has a good café.

Blackwell Arts and Crafts House (Storrs Park, Bowness) This is one of England's most important surviving houses from the turn of the 20th c. It was designed by M H Baillie Scott as a holiday home for Mancunian brewer and twice Lord Mayor Sir Edward Holt, and is a fine example of Arts and Crafts movement architecture. Inspired by Lakeland surroundings, it has lots of attractive detail inc carved panelling, stained glass and intricate wrought ironwork. Upstairs are changing art and craft exhibitions, and they're replanted the small terraces outside. In a beautiful setting, the views from here are quite breathtaking. Good tearoom, shop, mostly disabled access; cl Christmas to mid-Feb; (01539) 722464; £4.50.

Holehird Gardens (A592 Kirkstone Pass rd) Lakeland Horticultural Society's hillside garden - ten acres of well grown plants, with three National Collections inc one of hydrangeas, extensive rock gardens, herbaceous borders and alpine houses; lovely lakeland views. Open all year, limited disabled access; (015394) 46008; £2 suggested donation (they rely on this to maintain the gardens).

Lake Windermere This is England's largest lake - the most popular boating lake in Cumbria, and the easiest place to hire rowing boats and other craft. Lots of launches, of all sorts of shapes and sizes, run cruises of varying lengths from Bowness Bay, Ambleside and (not Nov-Mar) Newby Bridge. The pick of the sightseeing boat trips is the 45-min tour on the silent steam launch *Osprey*, though it's available only to visitors to the Steamboat Centre (see separate entry). For a treat, readers like the Sail 'n' Dine cruises, phone to book (015242) 74255; £50 inc a five-course evening meal and drinks; lunch and breakfast deals also available, plus sailing lessons on board. The pier at the S end of the lake is the terminus for the Haverthwaite steam railway. Rowing boats can be hired from the Bowness Bay Boating Co; from £3 an hour. They also have motorboats, and a number of launches - at least one of which is equipped to take disabled people; (015394) 43360 to check. Lake Holidays Afloat do motorboats too; (015394) 43415; from £14 an hour. A pleasant place to hire rowing boats (not Nov-Easter) is **Fell Foot Park** nr Newby Bridge, an 18-acre park with plenty of room for lakeside picnics; café and shop (cl Nov-Mar), some disabled access; (015395) 31273; parking charges (from £2); rowing boats £5 per hour for two people; NT. They can provide details of boating and fishing on other NT waters. Maples (Marina Village, Bowness) do day, wknd or longer cruises and courses on large sailing yachts; from £135 a day. Waterskiing can be arranged at Low Wood Water Sports Centre, Windermere; (015394) 39441. The chain ferry linking the ferry road below Bowness with the Hawkshead road below Far Sawrey is a utilitarian way of taking to the water; but though it runs every 20 mins and saves miles of driving, queues mean that it saves time only out of season.

Orrest Head A short steep walk (half-hour each way) from opposite the station, this gives spectacular views over the lake and the Pennines, lovely at sunset.

Windermere Steamboats & Museum (Rayrigg Rd) Nearly three dozen gleamingly restored graceful antique steamboats and a collection of motorboats, inc the 1850 steam launch *Dolly*, the oldest mechanically powered boat in the world. Also Arthur Ransome and Beatrix Potter boats, and they hold quite a few events like vintage boat rallies and model boat regattas. Snacks, shop, disabled access; open mid-Mar to early Nov; (015394) 45565; £3.50. For an extra £5 and weather permitting, there are stately 50-minute tours of the lake on the silent steam launch *Swallow* or motor launch *Water Viper*.

World of Beatrix Potter 🖼 (Old Laundry, Crag Brow, Bowness) Much enjoyed by young children, delightfully detailed re-creations of characters and scenes from *Peter Rabbit* and other tales. Some bits have smells, so you can get more of the atmosphere of Mrs Tiggy-winkle's laundry or nasty old Mr McGregor's potting shed. Meals and snacks (in the Tailor of Gloucester's tearoom), shop, disabled access; cl 25 Dec, and 12 Jan-1 Feb; (015394) 88444; £3.75.

WORKINGTON NY0028
Heavily industrial and not at all a tourist town, but reaches a moment of unexpected cobblestone prettiness in Portland Sq, plus a few other streets of colour-washed terraced cottages; the Alamin indian restaurant (Jane St) is good. In Curwen Park (on the NE edge of town) you can still see the ruinous hulk of **Workington Hall**; mansion not open but the grounds are; free.

Helena Thompson Museum (Park End Rd) Some antique and Georgian costumes, as well as pottery, silver, furniture and local history, in period surroundings. Bookshop, disabled access to ground floor only; cl Sun; (01900) 326255; free.

Other nice villages or hamlets in fine scenery, all with good pubs, include Armathwaite NY5146, Bampton NY5118, Bardsea SD3074, Beckermet NY0207, Brigsteer SD4889, Broughton Mills SD2290, Crosby Ravensworth NY6215 (Maulds Meaburn is also pretty), Dalston NY3650, Garrigill NY7441, Hesket Newmarket NY3438, Langwathby NY5734, Stonethwaite NY2613 and Wetheral NY4654. The comfortable Kirkstile Inn at Loweswater NY1222 deserves a mention for its glorious setting.

Where to eat

AMBLESIDE NY3704 **Glass House** *Rydal Rd* (015394) 32137 Restored 15th-c mill, next to the owner's glass studio, with working waterwheel, lots of space, a relaxed and friendly atmosphere, imaginative food plus simpler set lunches, and a carefully chosen and reasonably priced wine list; cl Tues, cl 3 wks Jan; children over 5 in evening. £25|**£8**

AMBLESIDE NY3704 **Sheila's Cottage** *The Slack* (015394) 33079 250-year-old cottage and converted barn run by the same owners for over 30 years, with very good and enjoyable food served all day inc popular afternoon teas; cl Tues-Weds pms Nov-Easter, cl 2 wks early Jan; children over 8 in evening. £24|**£5.50**

APPLETHWAITE NY2725 **Underscar Manor** *(01768)* 775000 Italianate Victorian house in wonderful position with panoramic views, a comfortable sitting room, two pretty restaurants with ornate drapes and lovely fresh flowers, very good beautifully presented classical cooking, and a mainly french wine list; smart dress; no smoking; bdrms plus time ownership apts, and health spa; cl 3 days after New Year; children over 12. £28 lunch, £38 dinner

CARTMEL SD3778 **Enclume** *Cavendish St* (015395) 36362 Gastronomic restaurant-with-rooms in former 13th-c blacksmith's with many original features such as wooden beams, furnaces, and the eye-catching hooping block; local artefacts displayed and for sale, sophisticated modern cooking using fine local produce, an impressive wine list, a glass conservatory for breakfasts, morning coffee and afternoon tea, and delightful garden; luxurious bdrms; cl Mon; children over 10 in evening; disabled access. £29

CROSTHWAITE SD4692 **Punch Bowl** *(015395) 68237* Prettily set Lakeland inn with an interesting series of nicely furnished rooms, and concentrating very much on excellent food; well kept real ales, and friendly service; bdrms; cl Sun pm, Mon, last wk Nov, 1st wk Dec, 1 wk Jan. £30/£9.95 2 courses|**£6.95**

DENT SD7087 **Stone Close** *Main St (015396) 25231* Cottagey 17th-c teashop with pine furniture on the flagstones, cast-iron ranges, beams, and local crafts, home-made meals served from mid-morning until early evening inc delicious cakes and pastries, and a relaxed friendly atmosphere; bdrms, plus self-catering cottage next door; tea shop cl mid-Jan-early Feb (bdrms open then). £15|**£5**

HAWKSHEAD SD3598 **Queens Head** *Main St (015394) 36271* Lovely black-and-white timbered pub in heart of village, with pretty summer window boxes, a bustling low-ceilinged bar, heavy bowed black beams, lots of decorative plates on the panelled walls, and an open fire; interesting food, friendly, helpful staff, well kept real ales; bdrms and holiday cottages. £27.50|**£6.75**

KESWICK NY2623 **George** *3 St John's St (017687) 72076* Fine old inn with attractive traditional black-panelled side room with interesting Wordsworth connection, and a good log fire; open-plan main bar with old-fashioned settles and modern banquettes under Elizabethan beams; enjoyable, often interesting bar food, well kept real ales, and a no smoking restaurant. £21|**£6.45**

KESWICK NY2623 **Maysons** *33 Lake Rd (017687) 74104* Busy restaurant with an interesting range of highly enjoyable food inc good vegetarian dishes, nice salads, and yummy cakes; cl Weds in Jan/Feb, cl evenings Nov-Easter; partial disabled access. £15|**£5**

MELMERBY NY6137 **Village Bakery** *(01768) 881515* Converted stone barn selling wonderful organic bread and cakes for cream teas, super breakfasts (until 11am) and good home-made lunchtime restaurant food using organic produce; craft gallery upstairs; cl 25-26 Dec, 1 Jan; disabled access. £20|**£6**

SEATOLLER NY2413 **Yew Tree** *(017687) 77634* Set at the foot of a lovely valley, this restaurant was originally two 17th-c miners' cottages, and has fine oak beams, a slate floor, an open range and brick bread oven, lots of interesting old photographs and memorabilia, a super atmosphere, and good interesting food using local produce; cl Mon, Jan; disabled access. £22|**£6**

STONETHWAITE NY2613 **Langstrath** *(017687) 77239* Small civilised inn surrounded by beautiful steep fells; neat simple bar, log and coal fire in big stone fireplace, simple furnishings and local pictures, well kept real ales, enjoyable bar food, and separate back restaurant. £21|**£8.25**

TROUTBECK NY4103 **Queens Head** *(015394) 32174* Popular gabled 17th-c coaching inn with several rambling bar rooms, some fine antique carving, a log fire and woodburner, efficient staff, particularly good first-class bar food, and well kept real ales; bdrms; cl 25 Dec; disabled access. £23.75|**£6.25**

ULVERSTON SD3177 **Bay Horse Hotel and Restaurant** *Canal Foot (out Past Glaxo) (01229) 583972* Civilised and nicely placed inn overlooking Morecambe Bay, with attractively presented, interesting food, well kept real ales and good wine list; bdrms; children in bar lounge only; cl Mon am; children over 12; disabled access. £27.50/3-course lunch £17.95

WINDERMERE SD4096 **Porthole** *3 Ash St, Bowness (015394) 42793* Long-established bustling bistro with consistently good meals (mainly italian), genuinely personal service, simple furnishings, and decent wine; cl Sat am, Mon am, Tues, Weds am, Christmas-mid-Feb; limited disabled access. £30|**£6.25**

YANWATH NY5127 **Gate Inn** *(01768) 862386* Unpretentious village local with really good inventive food, well kept real ales, obliging service, log fire in simple chatty bar, and no smoking dining room; cl 2 wks Jan. £21|**£7.25**

Special thanks to T D Surgenor, Jonathan S Colman, Margaret Dickinson, Helen Wharton, Michael Doswell, Mrs Y Champion, Mrs D E Reynolds, Roger and Jenny Huggins

DERBYSHIRE

**Busy holidays for all ages, with great days out and glorious landscapes
to walk through; very good places to stay in**

It's not surprising that Derbyshire has so many magnificent stately homes -
it was one of Britain's richest pre-industrial areas. Topping the list is
Chatsworth, an excellent day out, with masses to keep all sorts of people
happy. Sudbury Hall has a good museum of childhood, and other
rewarding houses include the 18th-c Palladian mansion at Kedleston (a
fine example of Robert Adam's work), the well preserved medieval manor
house at Haddon Hall, Melbourne Hall (home to two prime ministers),
unusual Hardwick Hall, and Bolsover Castle. Eyam Hall, in an interesting
village, and Catton Hall in Swadlincote are still very much family homes.
Calke Abbey (and the manor at South Wingfield) is a fascinating contrast.
The gardens are what make Renishaw Hall special.

Derbyshire played an important role in the Industrial Revolution; the
mills between Cromford and Derby have been granted World Heritage
status. So there's plenty of industrial heritage to investigate, too. The best
places to start are the 18th-c cotton milling village of Cromford, and the
Derwent Valley Visitor Centre at Belper; children like the hands-on
displays in Derby's Industrial Museum, and, new for this year, we've added
Masson Mills textile museum in Matlock Bath.

Top Family Attraction this year is Gulliver's Kingdom at Matlock Bath (a
treat for younger children, and not too expensive), and there's another
good theme park at Ilkeston. Crich Tramway Village is enjoyable for
families; there's a developing railway museum at Ripley, and for wildlife,
there's the conservation centre at Chapel-en-le-Frith.

A quirky bonus for Derbyshire are the remarkable underground
caverns. For families we'd particularly pick out the Heights of Abraham in
Matlock Bath (the mining museum here too is worth a visit), and
spectacular Poole's Cavern in Buxton is Britain's longest show cave; for
more impressive caverns and interesting mines, head for Castleton.

The best of the scenery is in the central area, more or less S of the
A625, known as the White Peak. This limestone country, picturesquely
cut by the intricate channels of the dales, has an abundance of generally
gentle walking - it's rewarding for drivers too. High, flat pastures have
small fields of rich grassland enclosed by silvery stone walls, clusters of
often very photogenic pale stone farm buildings, and small old-fashioned
villages. In summer the loveliest dales do have almost a crocodile of
walkers snaking along them, though even then you can find quiet areas.
Further north, up in the High Peak, the scenery becomes bleaker and
more forbidding - daunting for all but the most committed walker, though
exhilarating for drivers - the A6024, A628 (rather slow), A57, A5002,
A624 and A625 all have outstanding views.

Where to stay

ASHBOURNE SK1746 **Callow Hall** *Mappleton Rd, Ashbourne, Derbyshire DE6 2AA (01335) 300900* **£130**, plus special breaks; 16 lovely well furnished rms, excellent bthrms. Quietly smart and friendly Victorian mansion up a long drive through grounds with fine trees and surrounded by marvellous countryside; comfortable drawing room with open fire, fresh flowers and plants, and period furniture, very good traditional food using home-grown produce in warmly decorated dining room, excellent breakfasts, and kind hosts; good private fishing; cl 25-26 Dec; disabled access; dogs welcome in bedrooms

ASHFORD IN THE WATER SK1969 **Riverside Country House Hotel** *Fennel St, Ashford in the Water, Bakewell, Derbyshire DE4 1QF (01629) 814275* **£135***, plus special breaks; 15 individually decorated pretty rms. Creeper-covered Georgian house in delightful village with attractive riverside gardens, a relaxed house party atmosphere, antiques and log fires in cosy sitting rooms, good modern english cooking, and professional service; children over 12; disabled access

BAKEWELL SK2272 **Hassop Hall** *Hassop, Bakewell, Derbyshire DE45 1NS (01629) 640488* **£94**, plus winter breaks; 13 gracious rms. Mentioned in the Domesday Book, in lovely parkland surrounded by fine scenery, this handsome hotel has antiques and oil paintings, an elegant drawing room, oak-panelled bar, good food and friendly service; tennis; no accommodation 3 nights over Christmas; partial disabled access; dogs welcome in bedrooms

BASLOW SK2572 **Cavendish Hotel** *Baslow, Bakewell, Derbyshire DE45 1SP (01246) 582311* **£159.80**, plus winter wknd breaks; 24 spotless, comfortable and individually furnished rms (varying in size). Charming hotel with magnificent views over Chatsworth estate, most attractive well furnished day rooms (some furnishings come from Chatsworth), an eclectic collection of the owner's pictures, open fires and fresh flowers, fine food in two restaurants, very courteous staff

BASLOW SK2572 **Fischer's Baslow Hall** *Calver Rd, Baslow, Bakewell, Derbyshire DE45 1RR (01246) 583259* **£150**, plus special breaks; 11 comfortable, pretty rms. Handsome Edwardian manor house with individually chosen furnishings and pictures, open fires, fresh flowers and plants, beautifully presented fine food using the best ingredients (some home-grown and lots of game and fish) in airy, no smoking dining room, and courteous attentive service; cl 25-26 Dec; no children

BIGGIN-BY-HARTINGTON SK1559 **Biggin Hall** *Biggin-by-Hartington, Buxton, Derbyshire SK17 0DH (01298) 84451* **£68**, plus special breaks; 20 spacious rms with antiques, some in converted 18th-c stone building and in bothy. Cheerfully run 17th-c house in quiet grounds with a very relaxed atmosphere, two comfortable sitting rooms, log fires, freshly cooked straightforward food with an emphasis on free-range wholefoods served at 7pm in the attractive dining room, and packed lunches if wanted; children 12 and over; limited disabled access; dogs welcome in bedrooms

BIRCH VALE SK0287 **Waltzing Weasel** *New Mills Rd, Birch Vale, High Peak, Derbyshire SK22 1BT (01663) 743402* **£78***; 8 lovely rms. Attractive traditional inn with open fire, some handsome furnishings, daily papers and plants in quiet civilised bar, very good food using the best seasonal produce in charming back restaurant (fine views), excellent puddings and cheeses, obliging service; children over 7 in restaurant; disabled access; dogs welcome away from restaurant

CASTLETON SK1582 **Bargate Cottage** *Market Pl, Castleton, Hope Valley, Derbyshire S33 8WQ (01433) 620201* **£50***; 3 well equipped rms. Lovely, beautifully restored old cottage with beams, an inglenook fireplace, delicious, hearty breakfasts, super packed lunches, and pretty terraced garden; no smoking; cl 24-26 Dec; children over 12

DOVE DALE SK1550 **Peveril of the Peak** *Thorpe, Ashbourne, Derbyshire DE6 2AW (08704) 008109* **£80***, plus special breaks; 46 rms. Relaxing hotel in pretty village amidst some of the finest scenery in the Peak District and with 11 acres of grounds; comfortable sofas and log fire in spacious lounge, modern bar and attractive restaurant overlooking the garden, friendly staff, and good english cooking; tennis; wonderful walking nearby; disabled access; dogs welcome away from restaurant

GRINDLEFORD SK2478 **Maynard Arms** *Main Rd, Nether Padley, Grindleford, Hope Valley, Derbyshire S32 2HE (01433) 630321* **£79***, plus special breaks; 10 rms. Comfortable hotel with log fire and good Peak District views from the first-floor lounge, smart welcoming bar, good choice of food, popular evening restaurant, and particularly attentive service; good walks nearby; disabled access; dogs welcome in bedrooms

HATHERSAGE SK2281 **George** *Main Rd, Hathersage, Hope Valley, Derbyshire S32 1BB (01433) 650436* **£110***, plus special breaks; 19 pretty rms (the back ones are quietest). Substantial and comfortably modernised old inn with attractive airy lounge, beamed friendly bar, popular food, and a neat flagstoned back terrace by rose garden; good walks all around

HOPE SK1783 **Underleigh House** *Edale Rd, Hope, Castleton, Derbyshire S33 6RF (01433) 621372* **£69***, plus special breaks; 6 thoughtfully decorated rms. In unspoilt countryside, this spotlessly kept converted barn has fine views from the comfortable sitting room, hearty breakfasts with good home-made preserves enjoyed around communal table in flagstoned dining room, friendly cheerful owners, attractive gardens; terrific walks on the doorstep, packed lunches can be arranged; cl Christmas and New Year; children over 12; dogs by arrangement

KIRK IRETON SK2650 **Barley Mow** *Kirk Ireton, Ashbourne, Derbyshire DE6 3JP (01335) 370306* **£50**; 5 rms. Tall, Jacobean, walkers' inn with lots of woodwork in series of interconnecting bar rooms, a solid fuel stove in beamed residents' sitting room, and well kept real ales; close to Carsington Reservoir; cl Christmas and New Year; dogs in one ground floor rm

MONSAL HEAD SK1871 **Monsal Head Hotel** *Monsal Head, Buxton, Derbyshire DE45 1NL (01629) 640250* **£51**, plus special breaks; 7 very good rms, some with lovely views. Comfortable and enjoyable small hotel in marvellous setting high above the River Wye, with horsey theme in bar (converted from old stables), freshly prepared decent food using seasonal produce, and good service; cl 25 Dec; dogs welcome in bedrooms

SHIRLEY SK2241 **Shirley Hall Farm** *Shirley, Ashbourne, Derbyshire DE6 3AS (01335) 360346* **£52**; 3 rms. Timbered and part-moated farmhouse on family-run dairy and arable farm, with homely sitting room, and good breakfasts with home-made bread, jam and marmalade, and local organic sausages; private coarse fishing and lots of walks; nearby pub for evening meals; self-catering cottages; children over 9

SHOTTLE SK3050 **Dannah Farm** *Bowmans Lane, Shottle, Belper, Derbyshire DE56 2DR (01773) 550273* **£79***, plus special breaks; 8 rms with old pine and antiques, and some with private sitting rooms, four-posters, and whirlpool baths. Carefully restored and newly refurbished, friendly Georgian farmhouse with two comfortable sitting rooms, popular imaginative cooking in attractive no smoking dining room, and super breakfasts; hens, a friendly english setter called Cracker, hairy kune-kune pigs and farm cats; cl 24-25 Dec; partial disabled access

---

We welcome reports from readers

This *Guide* depends on readers' reports. Do help us if you can – in return, we offer a discount on the next edition to people who've helped us with reports for it. Tell us what you think about places already in it, and anything extra you think we should say about them. And send us your ideas for inclusion in the next edition: places to visit, eat at or stay in, attractive drives or walks, maybe even unusual shops you know of. Use the card in the middle, the report forms at the end, or just write – no stamp needed: *The Good Britain Guide*, FREEPOST TN1569, Wadhurst, E Sussex TN5 7BR. Or log on to www.goodguides.co.uk

To see and do

Derbyshire Family Attraction of the Year

MATLOCK BATH SK2958 **Gulliver's Kingdom** (1m S, off A6) The original in what's now a small chain of three similar theme parks (the others are at Warrington and Milton Keynes), this is a well organised place, aimed at children between 2 and 13. It's not exactly Alton Towers, and children at the top of the age range may find it slightly less thrilling, but there's plenty to keep younger ones happy, and for families with small children it's quite a reasonably priced day out. All the required rides are here in some form, including log flumes, a gentle roller-coaster, chair lifts, and dodg'ems, as well as a small animal farm. They've recently reintroduced one of the original rides, the Jubilee Junior carousel. Plenty of rides for under-5s, and it's all in a pleasant setting, with good views of the valley. The live shows are similar to what you'd find at just about any other theme park, and none the worse for that - and in fact that's a fair summation of the place as a whole: no big surprises, but straightforward unadulterated fun, achieving all it sets out to, and keeping plenty of children happy in the process. They usually end the season with a spectacular firework display, but reopen for a few dates around Christmas. Meals, snacks, shop, limited disabled access; open wknds and school hols Easter-Sept, plus some days before Christmas; (01925) 444888; £7.50 adults and children over 90cm (covers everything except any coin-operated activities); children under 90cm are free but won't be able to go on all the rides.

ASHBOURNE SK1846
Southern gateway to the Peak District, though quite separate in character; a good few interesting Georgian and earlier buildings (inc almshouses and the 16th-c old grammar school) nr the market place and along Church St. This street leads to the elegantly proportioned church, which has a famous white marble statue of a sleeping child. The Gingerbread Shop sells the town's long-standing speciality, and Bramhalls (Buxton Rd) has good interesting food. The B5056 towards Bakewell and B5053 to Wirksworth have characteristic views. You can hire bicycles by the half day or day from Ashbourne Cycle Hire, Mapleton Lane; (01335) 343156; £8.50 for half a day. **Derwent Crystal Centre** (Shaw Croft) Quality glassworks and engravers, with demonstrations (9am-1.30pm Mon-Fri) and factory shop. Disabled access; cl Sun, 25-26 Dec, 1 Jan; (01335) 345219; free. **Tissington Trail** This path for walkers and cyclists follows a disused railway track from Ashbourne up to Parsley Hay on the A515, where it joins the similar **High Peak Trail** from Buxton

to near Cromford; branching off at Roystone Grange is an archaeological trail. You can hire cycles in Ashbourne, or from Parsley Hay Cycle Hire, Parsley Hay; (01298) 84493; 3 hours £8.50, full day £12.50. This has a particularly interesting finale from Middleton Top engine house (cycle hire here, too) to High Peak Junction, dipping down a great incline past old engine houses to reach the Cromford Canal.

ASHFORD IN THE WATER SK1969
An attractive main street in a village of three bridges, inc Sheepwash Bridge with its attached sheep enclosure; good food in the Bulls Head. **Magpie Mine** (2m SW, nr Sheldon) Surface remains of a mine last worked in 1958 and stabilised in the 1970s give a good idea of a 19th-c lead mine; free.

BAKEWELL SK2168
The only town inside the Peak National Park; once away from the traffic, this is a civilised place, especially around the church. You can still get those famous tarts here, though there has been some dispute over the original recipe - two shops have claimed rights to the authentic Bakewell Pudding, and the

case even went to court. The handsome Rutland Arms has enjoyable food in its bar and restaurant.

Old House Museum (Cunningham Pl) Folk collection in a 16th-c house, still with its original wattle-and-daub interior walls and open-timbered chamber. Limited disabled access; open pm daily Good Fri-Oct, plus am July-Sept (01629) 813642; £2.50.

BELPER SK3448

Derwent Valley Visitor Centre Though it looks quite simple from the outside, this early 19th-c cotton mill was the most technically advanced building of its time, and is now a World Heritage Site. An exhibition inside traces the evolution of the machines which developed the factory system with examples from hand spinning wheels and a spinning jenny right up to 20th-c machines of mass production. You can find out more about the Belper man who took Britain's industrial plans to America, and they've a fine collection of silk and cotton stockings. Shop, disabled access; cl am, Mon and Tues, plus Weds Nov-Feb and two weeks at Christmas; (01773) 880474; £2. The Holly Bush over in Makeney has just the right sort of atmosphere.

BIRCHOVER SK2362 Starting point for an extraordinary walk over Stanton Moor, where among quarry workings and prehistoric burial mounds are the Nine Ladies stone circle, a folly tower and a huge boulder known as the Cork Stone, equipped with metal steps for the courageous and adorned with at least four centuries' worth of graffiti (the earliest we found was 1613). There are good views into Darley Dale from the edge of the escarpment; honesty box in car park at start of walk. Behind the Druid Inn in Birchover are Rowtor Rocks, a gritstone outcrop into which a contemplative parson cut steps, benches and a stone armchair.

BOLSOVER SK4770 **Bolsover Castle** The original ruined castle dates back to the 12th c, but was rebuilt in 1613 as a spectacular mock castle - about 200 years ahead of this fashion. Battlements and turrets outside, and inside allegorical frescoes, fine panelling and ornate fireplaces;

visitor centre and restored fountain garden. Snacks, shop, some disabled access; cl Tues and Weds Nov-Mar, 24-26 Dec and 1 Jan; (01246) 823349; £6.20, inc Walkman tour. Just on the other side of the M1 at Sutton Scarsdale (and in fact looking down on the motorway) are the evocative ruins of a once-grand 17th-c hall.

BRADBOURNE SK2152 Appealing Dales village, with an ancient Saxon cross outside its **Norman church**.

BUXTON SK0572 England's highest market town, it's much changed but still has some handsome buildings dating from its days as a flourishing spa, with Georgian terraces (The Crescent is a noble Georgian streetscape), and a restored Edwardian opera house. St Ann's Well is the only direct reminder of its water-based heyday (you can take the water for free here, and it's naturally warm) though there are plans to revive the spa (which is underneath the tourist information centre) and The Crescent over the next few years. Many of the grander buildings come back to life during the town's excellent July festival. The Columbine (Hall Bank) and the Old Hall Hotel's wine bar (The Square) are good for food. An enjoyable self-guided walk takes you around the town's attractions inc the Pavilion Gardens, currently being restored; available from the Tourist Information Centre (The Crescent); 75p.

Buxton Museum & Art Gallery (Terrace Rd) A useful introduction to the area; shop, disabled access; cl Mon (exc bank hols) and winter Sun, 25-27 Dec and 1 Jan; free.

Grin Low Woods (just S) Well landscaped, with mature woodland and the Victorian folly of Solomon's Temple (good views from the top).

Poole's Cavern (Buxton Country Park, Green Lane; off A53 or A515 SW of centre) The best show cave in the Peak District and thought to be the longest in Britain, a spectacular natural limestone cavern in 100 acres of woodland, with well lit stalactites and stalagmites, and exhibitions on caves, woodland and Romans. As in other caverns, wrap up well. Snacks, shop,

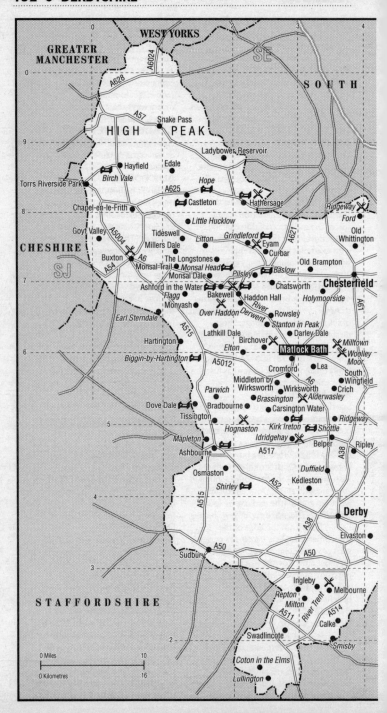

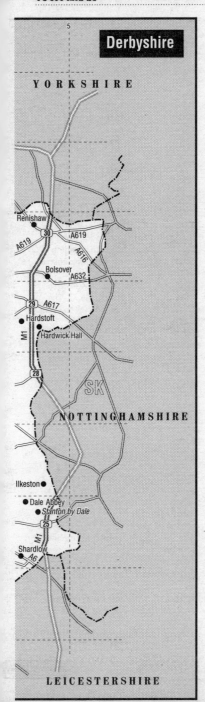

some disabled access with notice; cl
Nov-Feb; (01298) 26978; £5.40.

CALKE SK3622

Calke Abbey 🏛 This unusual
baroque mansion is one of the most
fascinating NT properties in Britain, still
in pretty much the same state as when
the last baronet died here in 1924. You
might expect the splendidly decorated
rooms with their absorbing displays (inc
an extensive natural history collection),
but it's quite a surprise to find the more
dilapidated corridors and areas where
possessions are just bundled together
in heaps (by the 20th c, with the army of
servants dispersed, the family had
shrivelled into the grand formal rooms).
This gives you a better appreciation of
how the abbey was once a much-loved
family home - and of how things
forgotten in the attic can quickly
become social history. Also extensive
parkland, pretty gardens, and the family
church. Meals, snacks, shop, phone for
disabled access; cl Thurs, Fri, and Nov-
Mar, plus house cl am; (01332) 863822;
£5.60, garden only £2.80 - there's a
£2.70 vehicle charge on entering the
park, refundable on entry to the house
(which has a timed ticket system on
busy days); NT.

CARSINGTON WATER SK2552
Britain's newest major reservoir,
already toning into the landscape as if
it's been a lake for ever, is developing
into a great place for inexpensive family
outings; good visitor centre with
interactive displays and a good safe play
area, easy waterside walks (even with
pushchairs or wheelchairs), bird hides,
fishing, cycling, watersports inc kayaks
and canoes. Meals, snacks, shop,
disabled access; cl 25 Dec; (01629)
540696; car park charge, £2 all day. The
Red Lion at Hognaston has good food,
and the Miners Arms in Carsington is a
useful stop.

CASTLETON SK1482
Very much geared to visitors, and filled
with walkers and cavers in summer;
plenty of cafés, and shops selling
expensive worked pieces of the Blue
John fluorspar that's found only in the
nearby mine workings. The village's
attractive dark stone buildings (one of
the most impressive now a youth
hostel) are dominated by the ruins of

Peveril Castle, built high above in the 11th c - magnificent views. Shop, snacks; cl Mon and Tues Nov-Mar, 24-26 Dec and 1 Jan; (01433) 620613; £2.50; EH. There's decent food at the Castle Hotel, Rose Cottage and George. The B6061 to Sparrowpit (where the Wanted Inn is good value) has fine views. The most varied **walks** in the High Peak are found around Castleton and Hope. The great walk here takes in Castleton, the Lose Hill/Mam Tor ridge, the caves, and Winnats Pass; Mam Tor is so shaly and prone to landslips that it's dubbed the Shivering Mountain - the abandoned section of the A625 is a testament to the victory of the mountain over man. Cave Dale is an optional side trip from the back of Castleton. Quarrying has had an unfortunate effect on the local landscape in the area, and limits walks further afield, though there are some pleasant walks to be had in the gentler high pastures of the limestone country to the south.

Blue John Cavern & Mine (Buxton Rd) Containing eight of the 14 known veins of Blue John, this has been the main source of the precious stone for nearly 300 years. It's an impressive example of a water-worn cave, over a third of a mile long, with chambers 45 metres (150 ft) high. Snacks, craft shop; cl 25-26 Dec, 1 Jan; (01433) 620638; £6.50.

Peak Cavern Right in the village, this is the biggest natural cavern in the country and really does seem huge - the entrance hall is so large it used to house an entire village; there are no significant stalactites or stalagmites. From there it's a half-mile walk along subterranean passageways to the Great Cave, 45 by 27 metres (150 ft wide, 90 ft long). By the time you reach the Devil's Staircase you'll be nearly 140 metres (450 ft) underground. Rope-making demonstrations; snacks, shop; cl wkdys Nov-Mar; (01433) 620285; £5.50.

Speedwell Cavern 🔲 (Winnats Pass - declassified continuation of A6187 W of Castleton) Very atmospheric former lead mine, with 105 steps down to a half-mile underground boat trip along floodlit passages, finishing in a cathedral of a cavern with an impressive 'bottomless pit'. Great fun; there may be a queue. Snacks, shop; (01433) 620512; cl 25 Dec; £6.00.

Treak Cliff Cavern (off declassified continuation of A6187 W) Informative tours of one of the first Blue John mines, worked since 1750, with rich veins of the mineral and quite staggering stalactites and stalagmites. Well placed lights create spooky shapes and atmospheric shadows. The entrance is narrow, and it's quite steep, but readers like this even more than many of the other caverns nearby, and they hold regular special events. Snacks, shop; cl 24-26 and 31 Dec, 1 Jan (weather permitting); (01433) 620571; £5.80.

CHAPEL-EN-LE-FRITH SK0580
Chestnut Centre (A625) Warmly recommended conservation park, concerned especially with breeding otters and barn owls, but other animals and birds of prey too; good observation platforms. Snacks, shop; cl wkdys Jan and Feb; (01298) 814099; £5.75. The Cross Keys has good food (all day Sun).

CHATSWORTH SK2670
(off B6012) This wonderful estate on the banks of the River Derwent has almost as much appeal for children as it has for adults. The first-class adventure playground is perhaps the highlight for younger visitors, and a working farmyard has plenty of opportunities to get close to cows, sheep, pigs and horses. The house itself has been home to the Duke of Devonshire's family for nearly 450 years. Sumptuously furnished, the 26 rooms on display show off a superb collection of fine arts, with memorable paintings by Rembrandt and Van Dyck, and a set of nine Regency bedrooms is usually open for a small extra charge. You can also arrange to book a good private guided tour (extra charge). The gardens cover 100 acres; brass bands play on summer Sun afternoons. The surrounding park was landscaped by Capability Brown, and covers 1,000 acres; well marked walks and trails. Good meals and snacks, shop, garden centre, disabled access to garden only; open 17 Mar-19 Dec; (01246) 582204; £8.50 house and garden, £4.50 garden only, and a further £3.60 for the farm and adventure playground. Entry to the park is free (open all year). Car parking is £1. Also

in the grounds, at Stud Farm, 1½ miles towards Pilsley, is one of England's best farm shops. Around Chatsworth, **Edensor** is a very attractive estate village, and walkers have free access to the park W of the River Derwent; there is a delightful riverside walk at Calton Lees car park, N to Chatsworth bridge and Edensor. The B6012 (busy in summer) has pleasant views, and the Devonshire Arms at Beeley has decent food all day.

CHESTERFIELD SK3871
Not a tourist town but, next to the tourist information centre, its mainly 14th-c **church** has a really striking leaning spire, and is a rich building inside; the town **museum** (Corporation St) has the full angle on it; cl Weds and Sun; free. The ancient Rutland (Stephenson Pl, by the church) has decent food. The Victorian market hall has flourishing indoor and outdoor markets Mon, Fri and Sat (flea market Thurs, street entertainment summer Sat). The first phase of ongoing renovation work on Chesterton Canal has so far yielded around five miles of towpath walks (forming part of the Trans-Pennine Trail), with a good Visitor Centre at Tapton Lock; cl wkdays (exc bank hols) Nov-Easter; (01246) 551035. From here you can take boat trips (disabled access), cl around Jan-Easter; £2.50, and they provide leaflets on walks, events and wildlife around the canal. Nearby **Grassmoor Country Park** is a pleasant place to stroll, with a fishing lake. The Derby Tup (Sheffield Rd) is an enjoyable ale house with good value simple food.

CRICH SK3455
Crich Tramway Village (Matlock Rd) When you enter this enthusiastically run place, you're given an old penny (or half-penny for children), which you use to pay for unlimited rides on the lovingly restored vintage trams that run up and down a one-mile period street and beyond, through lovely parts of the Derwent Valley (familiar to viewers of *Peak Practice*). A comprehensive exhibition has more trams, from all over the British Isles and further afield. There are plenty of play areas: a big one outside, with bridges, ropes and

balancing poles, and a tram-themed one inside with a section for under-5s. Nice walks through the surrounding woodland, and regular special events - it's particularly good fun in the run-up to Christmas. They've a workshop viewing gallery (where you can watch the trams being restored). Pub and restaurant, picnic areas, disabled access (one tram has been adapted for wheelchairs, and they have a guide book in braille); cl Jan, wkdys Feb-Mar (exc half-term hols), and Tues-Fri Nov-22 Dec (exc 2nd wk Dec), best to check; (0870) 7587267; £7. The Cliff Inn nearby has great views.

CROMFORD SK2956
A good example of an 18th-c cotton-milling village, little developed after its original building, and rewarding to stroll through. Carefully preserved North St (1777) is the first true industrial street in Derbyshire. The old-fashioned Boat Inn has good value basic food. The canal is a quiet and attractive early Industrial Revolution setting with a restored steam-powered pumping house and a fine aqueduct over the river. Good walks along the canal and the High Peak Trail (see Ashbourne). The A5012 to Grangemill gives evocative views.

Cromford Mill 🖾 (Mill Lane) Richard Arkwright established the world's first successful water-powered cotton mill here in 1771; the true beginning of the factory age, it's now a World Heritage Site. Meals, snacks, shops, limited disabled access; cl 25 Dec; (01629) 824297; site free, tours *£2.

High Peak Junction Workshops
Oldest surviving railway workshops in the world. The visitor centre includes exhibitions, a film and now an audio tour; snacks, shop; cl wkdys Oct-Mar; (01629) 822831; 60p.

CURBAR SK2575
The eastern edges of the Peak District include the abrupt ramparts of Curbar Edge and Froggatt Edge, popular with rock-climbers and easily accessible from the road. The Bridge Inn down at Calver has good value plain food and a big Derwentside garden. In this same area, Birchen Edge and Wellington's Monument are obvious objectives for walkers from the Robin Hood, on the A619 E of Baslow.

DALE ABBEY SK4338
Abbey ruins, Hermits Cave and remarkable All Saints church, part of which was formerly the village inn; the village is attractive, and the low-beamed Carpenters Arms has good value food.

DARLEY DALE SK2762
Carriage Museum (Red House Stables) Collection of vehicles and equipment, some of which you can ride in; also horses - they do carriage rides (booking essential). Teas, disabled access; cl 25 Dec; (01629) 733583; *£2.95.

Peak Rail 🚂 Private railway; trains run between here and Matlock, then on to Rowsley, and the eventual aim is to run as far as Buxton. Wknd restaurant car, shop, limited disabled access; usually open wknds all year, but best to check; (01629) 580381; £6.

DERBY SK3536
A big busy city, but not too daunting for a visitor to explore, with a pedestrianised centre, and several things worth visiting. It's got far more open spaces than you'd expect, including England's first public park, donated to the city by a local mill owner, and now enjoying a £5 million renovation.

Derby Cathedral The 16th-c tower is the second highest church tower in the country; the nave was built in the 18th c. Bess of Hardwick is buried in the vaults, and there's a delightful early Georgian screen. New visitor centre, meals, snacks, shop, disabled access; (01332) 341201; suggested donation £2. Nearby **St Mary's Chapel** is one of only six surviving bridge chapels still in use. The quaint nearby Olde Dolphin (Queen St) has bargain food all day.

Derby Museum & Art Gallery (The Strand) Stands out for its collections of porcelain, and paintings by local Joseph Wright. Shop, disabled access; cl Sun am and over the Christmas hols; (01332) 716669; free.

Heritage Centre (St Peter's churchyard) Once a Tudor grammar school, now the start for good ghost walks through the city's tunnels and other themed tours (also from Old Gaol, Friargate) 7pm; cl winter hols; booking essential, (01332) 299321; from £17 inc meal. Centre cl Sun and most bank hols; free.

Industrial Museum (Full St) This restored early 18th-c silk mill has a range of displays on local industries, a major collection of Rolls-Royce aero engines, and a Power Gallery with lots of hands-on displays. Shop, disabled access; cl am Sun and bank hols, 25-26 Dec; (01332) 255308; free. The nearby Old Silk Mill is an interesting pub, open all day.

Pickfords House Museum (Friargate) Gives a very good idea of 18th-c domestic life, with period furnished rooms and Georgian garden; also costume display and a collection of toy theatres. Shop, disabled access to ground floor only, and video with subtitles; cl am Sun and bank hols, and around a wk over Christmas and New Year; (01332) 255363; free.

Q Gallery (Queen St) City-centre gallery showing contemporary visual art, photography and new media; shop, disabled access; cl am (exc Sat), and Sun-Tues, around 2 wks over Christmas, and between exhibitions - best to phone; (01332) 295858; free.

Royal Crown Derby Visitor Centre (Osmaston Rd) Cheerfully informative tours four times a day of a bone-china factory, celebrating 250 years of porcelain production. A museum traces the industry's development from its origins. Meals, snacks, shop (lots of bargain seconds), disabled access (exc museum); open daily, no tours wknds, bank hols or factory shutdown weeks; advisable to book tours, (01332) 712800; £4.95 (£2.95 without tour) - no under-10s on tours.

DOVE DALE SK1452
Shared between Derbyshire and Staffordshire, with the River Dove as the boundary, this is the most popular of all the dales. Partly wooded, it has a beautifully varied mixture of water, trees and pastures, and is lined with crags and curiously shaped outcrops of rock. The main access point is at the S end, where the scenery is at its most spectacular. A less crowded approach is to start from the quiet village of Alstonefield and walk down to the hamlet of Milldale (handy refreshment places on the Staffordshire side of the river are the Watts Russell Arms at Hopedale and George at Alstonefield).

Or head further upstream towards Beresford Dale, Wolfscote Dale and Biggin Dale (nr Hartington). Useful nearby refreshment places are the Coach & Horses or Bentley Brook at Fenny Bentley, and on the Staffordshire side the Izaak Walton Hotel nr Ilam (cosier inside than it looks from out). Also try the Okeover Arms at Mapleton (with a domed church, and a nice riverside walk to Thorpe).

EDALE SK1285

Famous as the start of the 256-mile Pennine Way to Scotland's border, with a good information centre (01433) 670207, and decent food in the Old Nags Head. It tends to be packed with expectant long-distance walkers on Sunday mornings. For a taste of the Dark Peak proper, this can be the start for half-day walks that quite quickly take you up through the stone-walled pastures of the valley on to the edge of the dark plateau above. The track signed as the alternative Pennine Way route up Jacob's Ladder is easier to find than the official Pennine Way plod across a huge blanket bog; it also has more to see, inc some strange weathered rocks and an ancient cross.

ELVASTON SK4032

Elvaston Castle Country Park (B5010) 200 acres of lovely 19th-c landscaped parkland, with formal and old english gardens, wooded walks, and wildfowl on the ornamental lake. Snacks, shop, disabled access; (01332) 571342; car park 70p wkdys, £1.30 wknds. Shardlow is convenient for lunch.

EYAM SK2276

Attractive secluded village with a dark past: in the Great Plague sick villagers confined themselves here for fear of infecting people outside - plaques record who died where, and stones on the village edge mark where money was disinfected. The Miners Arms is very good for lunch. Just up the B6521 at Upper Padley, **Padley Chapel** is an interesting 15th-c revival, effectively restored in 1933.

Eyam Hall 🏛 Sturdy-looking 17th-c manor house, still very much a family home, with furniture, portraits and tapestries, fine Jacobean staircase and impressive flagstoned hall; there's a small craft centre in the stables. Meals,

snacks, shop, some disabled access; house open Weds-Thurs, Sun and bank hol Mon Jun-Aug, craft centre open daily exc Mon, and over Christmas and New Year; (01433) 631976; £4.50 - timed ticket system.

GOYT VALLEY SK0177

The well wooded valley with its three miles of reservoirs is a man-made landscape, but nonetheless charming for walks or picnics; sterner rambles up to the viewpoint of Shining Tor (also reached via a bracing ridge walk from a car park to the N). Reached off the A54 W of Buxton (one-way system operates; no access from A5002). The quaintly named Beehive at Combs has good value food (all day wknds).

HADDON HALL SK2366

One of the most perfectly preserved medieval manor houses in England, still with its 12th-c painted chapel, 14th-c kitchen, and banqueting hall with minstrels' gallery. Perhaps because nothing's been added to the original furniture and tapestries, some rooms can seem rather bare; a bright spot is Rex Whistler's painting of the house in the silver-panelled long gallery. It's a particularly pretty location in summer when the long terraced rose gardens are in full bloom. Several films and TV adaptations have had scenes shot here in recent years. Meals, snacks, shop; cl Mon-Weds in Oct, and all Nov-Mar; (01629) 812855; £7.25. The Lathkil Hotel up in Over Haddon is good for lunch, and nearby roads have attractive views.

HARDSTOFT SK4264

Herb Garden (B6039, not far from M1 junction 29) Big main garden with lots of herbs and old english roses, smaller gardens specialising in rare medicinal herbs, pot-pourri or lavender. Snacks, shop; cl Mon-Tues (exc bank hols and Easter) and mid-Sept to mid-Mar; (01246) 854268; £1.50.

HARDWICK HALL SK4663

The marriages of the redoubtable Bess of Hardwick couldn't necessarily be described as happy but she certainly did very well out of them, the fourth leaving her enough money to build this triumphant Elizabethan prodigy house. The beautifully symmetrical towers are crowned with the monogram ES, and there's an amazing expanse of glass (not just to show that she could afford that height of luxury - her sight was dimming, too). Also fine tapestries and needlework, large park, and gardens laid out in walled courtyard. They're restoring the huge and ancient Gideon tapestries which run the length of the 50-metre (167-ft) Long Gallery, a silk canopy, and the garden walls; a gazebo houses an exhibition on garden history; guided walks to stonemason's yard (Weds and Thurs at 11.30am, 1.30 and 3pm). Meals, snacks, shop, disabled access to ground floor only; open pm Apr-Oct, garden cl Tues, house cl Mon, Tues and Fri (exc bank hols), hall cl am; £2 vehicle charge to enter the grounds; £6.60 house and garden, £3.50 garden only; NT. Not far from this 'new' house is the shell of Hardwick Old Hall, Bess's birthplace; (01246) 850431; £3; EH. A joint ticket is available for both houses (£8.80). Also on the estate is a restored watermill (£2.10, NT). The park is attractive for walks, and nearby Hardwick Inn, also NT-owned, is good for lunch.

HARTINGTON SK1260
This attractive village has a good cheese shop selling local stilton, and the Devonshire Arms is a popular stop. Excellent valley floor walks into Beresford Dale and then on through Wolfscote Dale to the N end of Dove Dale; Hartington Hall youth hostel is one of the best, very family-friendly; (0870) 770 5848.

HATHERSAGE SK2281
Charlotte Brontë wrote *Jane Eyre* here, and Little John's supposed grave is in the churchyard. Though somewhat suburban in character, it's a good village for walkers and climbers, with fine routes along the River Derwent towards Grindleford, and E through the moors and woods of the Longshaw Estate (nr the reliable Fox House Inn up on the Sheffield road) and up to the dramatic Iron Age hill fort of Carl Wark. The riverside Plough (A622) is good for lunch.

HAYFIELD SK0387
This moorland village and its attractive nearby smaller sister Little Hayfield have good walks around them, both up towards Kinder Scout and to the Lantern Pike viewpoint in the opposite direction. There's also a popular walk or cycle ride - the Sett Valley Trail - along a hillside former railway to New Mills, looking down on the mill buildings by the River Sett. A handy bike shop does hire in Hayfield (Station Rd), and there's an information centre for the Trail; (01663) 746222. New owners are doing enjoyable food at the Lantern Pike (Little Hayfield).

ILKESTON SK4444
American Adventure Theme Park (off A6007, signed from M1 junction 26) A little overshadowed by better-known Alton Towers nearby, this is a good (and cheaper) alternative; a more manageable size, and easy to get round in a day. The rides and attractions are all as you'd expect, with a few good white-knuckle rides to keep thrill-seekers happy, and lots for younger children, from gentler roller-coasters and a scaled-down swinging boat to carousels, a helter-skelter and a huge indoor play area. Those with braver tastes will want to head for the Missile, a stomach-churning roller-coaster, Nightmare Niagra (a triple log flume), and the Sky Coaster freefall ride. There are live shows, and a big lake has pedaloes and a steamboat; a train travels between the various areas. A few things, like the crazy golf, have an extra charge. Meals, snacks, shops, good disabled access; open Apr-Oct; (0845) 330 2929; £14.99 adults and children over 12, smaller children are free, but can't go on as many rides.

Shipley Country Park (between Ilkeston and Heanor) Medieval estate developed and landscaped in the 18th c, with 600 acres of woodland, lakes and fields; it's a pleasant place to wander, with railway lines transformed into leafy walkways. Snacks, shop, disabled access; visitor centre cl 25 Dec; (01773) 719961; free.

INGLEBY SK3427
River Trent Good views of the formidable river from the big riverside garden of the John Thompson pub, which brews its own beer and has decent food.

KEDLESTON SK3140
Kedleston Hall This 18th-c Palladian mansion is thought by many to be the finest example of Robert Adam's work -

it's certainly the least altered. Interesting objets d'art, original furnishings, good collection of paintings, and a museum of items collected by Lord Curzon when he was Viceroy of India. Adam designed a charming boathouse and bridge in the park outside, which also has extensive formal gardens with marvellous rhododendrons, and long woodland walks. Meals, snacks, shop, disabled access; house and garden open 20 Mar–Oct, house cl am and Sun–Mon; park open daily; (01332) 842191; £5.80, £2.60 grounds only; NT. The Joiners Arms in Quarndon does good value wkdy lunches.

LADYBOWER RESERVOIR SK1788
One of a chain of impressive reservoirs, scenic enough to merit driving along; also the lane up to the car park by the Derwent Reservoir gives plenty of easy waterside-forest **walking** on the relatively sheltered stone-walled slopes of the upper parts of Derwent Dale, with access to the higher moors for better views - for example, up on to Win Hill, or on a kind day on to the formidable Derwent Moors to the E. The Yorkshire Bridge Hotel (A6013 towards Bamford) is a good refuge.

LATHKILL DALE SK1865
Charming combination of woods, steep pastures and well weathered signs of old mines; its short tributary Bradford Dale is also very attractive for walks. The large attractive village of Youlgreave makes a useful focal point for walkers; its church has windows by William Morris and Burne-Jones, and the 17th-c George has good home cooking.

LEA SK3258
Lea Gardens Beautiful woodland gardens with rhododendrons inc rare species and cultivars, azaleas and rock plants. Home-baked snacks, shop and garden centre, limited disabled access; open 20 Mar–Jun, other times by appointment; (01629) 534380; £3.50. The nicely placed White Lion at Starkholmes has good value imaginative food.

LONGSTONES, THE SK1871
Little Longstone (with its appealing 16th-c rustic pub the Packhorse) and nearby Great Longstone are charming steep stone-built villages, and the back

road from Baslow through here to Tideswell is a pretty drive.

MATLOCK BATH SK2958
Pleasantly busy place, with lots to do. A spectacular wooded cliff looks across the lower roadside town to pastures by the Derwent; up the side of the gorge, quiet lanes climb steeply past 18th- and 19th-c villas. The Temple Hotel (Temple Walk) has great views and decent food.

Gulliver's Kingdom *See separate family panel on p.130.*

Heights of Abraham 🄴 Derbyshire is full of stunning show caverns, but few are as good for families, and none can boast as thrilling an introduction as the one here: cable cars whisk you up from the Derwent Valley to a 60-acre hilltop country park, with dramatic views over the ancient limestone gorge (not to mention a railway and the busy A6). At the end of the 5-minute trip a multi-media show explains how the rock was formed 325 million years ago, then guides escort you into the two show caverns. Outside are nature trails, nicely laid out woodland walks, the Prospect Tower to climb, and a few play areas (inc a maze, and a new playground aimed at the under-5s); usually special events in summer. Good restaurant and café, limited disabled access; cl Nov–15 Feb and wkdys 8–23 March (01629) 582365; £7.50.

Masson Mills 🄴 Built in 1783 by Richard Arkwright ('father of the factory system'), this well preserved cotton mill now houses a working textile museum. You can see yarn being turned into cloth on some of the oldest looms in the world, and they've a massive collection of bobbins. Meals, snacks, shopping village, disabled access; cl 25 Dec and Easter Sun; (01629) 581001; £2.50.

Matlock Bath Aquarium & Hologram A useful family attraction if you're staying in the area. Shop; cl wkdys Nov–Easter (exc school hols); (01629) 583624; £1.80.

Peak District Mining Museum 🄴 (Temple Rd) Lively exploration of mining, with a unique early 19th-c water-pressure pumping engine, and interactive display on the pitfalls of working in a mine. Also tours of the old

Temple Mine workings (£5, £9 for tour of museum and mine), and the chance to pan for minerals - in the past they've even found a tiny amount of gold. Snacks, shop, disabled access; cl 25 Dec, plus mine cl wkdys Nov-Easter; (01629) 583834; without tour *£2.50, joint ticket to museum and mine £4.

MELBOURNE SK3825
This pleasant small town has a good relaxed feel and villagey lanes; the White Swan and Railway Hotel are good for lunch. The **church** of St Michael and St Mary is impressive, more like a cathedral than an ordinary parish church.
Melbourne Hall Behind its 18th-c façade, this grandly extended house dates back in part to the 13th c, and has been the home of two prime ministers; fine pictures and furnishings. Glorious formal gardens with fountains, pools, and famous yew tunnel; interesting craft centre (open all year). Meals, snacks, shop, limited disabled access; Hall open pm daily in Aug (exc first three Mons), plus gardens open Weds, Sat, Sun and bank hol Mon pm Apr-Sept; (01332) 862502; £3 (with gardens, £5).

MIDDLETON BY WIRKSWORTH SK2755
Middleton Top Engine House
Home to a beam engine built in 1829 to haul waggons up a steep incline on the Cromford & High Peak Railway. Snacks, shop; engine house open first wknd of month and bank hol wknds; visitor centre cl wkdys Oct-Easter; (01629) 823204; £1.20. The Olde Gate over at Brassington is a lovely place for a pub lunch (not Mon). And see Tissington Trail entry, under Ashbourne.
National Stone Centre 🖼 (Porter Lane) Surprisingly enjoyable centre, featuring 330-million-year-old tropical lagoons and limestone fossil reefs, as well as an exhibition, guided fossil trails, and, for an extra charge, activities like gem-panning or fossil-rubbing. Snacks, shop, disabled access; cl 25-26 Dec and 1 Jan; (01629) 824833; £1.80.

MILLERS DALE SK1573
The B6049 N off the A6 SE of Buxton gives access to Millers Dale, just past the little village of that name (the Anglers Rest is a decent pub with great gorge views); upstream of Monsal Dale, this is rather less visited but also a lovely

spot for walks - as is its continuation Chee Dale.
MONSAL DALE SK1771
This winding valley is the outstanding place for walks in this central part of the White Peak area, its pastoral quality emphasised by the disused limestone cotton mills along the way. It's especially lovely in May and June with wild flowers enriching the pastures along the broader stretches. Don't expect to have it to yourself. There's good access from the A6 a couple of miles towards Buxton from Ashford in the Water; and from Monsal Head (friendly hotel), where a disused railway viaduct, part of the Monsal Trail, adds interest.

MONSAL TRAIL SK1172
This outshines the other former railway-track walks in the Peak District, though like them is in parts more exposed to the winds than walks down in the dales. It runs from Wye Dale E of Buxton to Coombs Road viaduct S of Bakewell. W of Millers Dale Station, the trail leaves the old railway and takes a stepping-stone route along the river beneath the towering cliffs of Chee Tor before rejoining the railway track.

MONYASH SK1566
2m S of this quiet village (good value home cooking at the Bulls Head) is the mysterious **Arbor Low**, the finest prehistoric site in the Peak District - a henge monument with a circular bank enclosing a fallen stone circle and inner sanctum; access via adjacent farmyard (honesty box).

OLD BRAMPTON SK3371
The village itself is attractive, and has one special curiosity: count the minutes between one and two o'clock on its church clock.

OLD WHITTINGTON SK3874
Revolution House (High St) Innocuous-looking thatched cottage where three conspirators met to plan their powerful part in the Revolution of 1688. Good audio-visual display and period furniture. Shop; disabled access to ground floor; usually open Easter-Sept (exc perhaps Tues) plus two weeks over Christmas, but phone to check; (01246) 345727; free. Just behind, the Cock & Magpie is a handy dining pub.

OSMASTON SK2043
This village of pretty thatched cottages has a pleasant path through a lakeside park; the Shoulder of Mutton has good value food.

RENISHAW SK4378
Renishaw Hall Gardens Beautiful series of italianate gardens around a grand house, home to the Sitwell family since the mid-17th c. Laid out at the turn of the 20th c by Sir George Sitwell, grandfather of the present owner, they include sculptured yew hedges, carp-filled ornamental water features, a Gothic temple and hidden gardens. Below the gardens a lakeside walk leads past caves and through woodland. In the stable block, the **Museum of Sitwell Memorabilia** gives an insight into the colourful lives of Edith, Osbert and Sacheverell, the siblings who were at the centre of artistic developments in the 1920s; also a costume gallery, performing arts gallery, and an exhibition on the artist John Piper, whose 'sombre and fiery genius' Osbert found 'peculiarly suited' to the Renishaw landscape. Meals, snacks, shop, disabled access; open Fri-Mon Easter-end Sept; (01246) 432310; £6, gardens/galleries and museum only £3.50. The civilised Sitwell Arms has decent food.

RIPLEY SK3947
Denby Pottery Visitor Centre (B6179 S) Guided factory tours (11am-3pm), inc the chance to paint a plate and make clay souvenirs. Extensive factory shop, cookery demonstrations, small museum. Meals, snacks, shop and garden centre, disabled access; cl 24-26 Dec; (01773) 740799; free, guided tours £3.50. The Moss Cottage (A610 Nottingham rd) has a good carvery.
Midland Railway Centre 🎫 (Butterley Station, B6179 just N) Regular steam-train passenger service through country park, and developing railway museum. Meals, snacks, shop, disabled access; best to ring for train timetable (01773) 570140; £7.50 (£8.50 bank hols and special events). There are a few farm animals on the adjacent farm (you can visit here free without having to go on the railway). The Excavator on the A610 out at Buckland Hollow is a good value family dining pub (all day Sun).

ROWSLEY SK2565
Caudwell's Mill & Craft Centre Working 19th-c flour mill, powered by water turbines, with crafts such as glass-blowing, ceramics and wood-turning. Meals, snacks, shop; cl wkdys in Jan and 24-26 Dec, mill cl 24 Dec-1 Jan; (01629) 733185; mill £3, craft centre free. Rowsley also has an interesting **stone circle** called the Nine Ladies. Nearby Stanton in Peak is a lovely steep stone village overlooking this rich green valley; the Flying Childers has good value filled rolls (not Mon).
Peak Village Developing designer shopping village in the heart of the Peak District; also craft and other shops. Meals, snacks, disabled access; (01629) 735326; free. Also here (a useful reward for children after a tedious morning's shopping), the **Wind in the Willows** attraction is based on the classic adventures of Toad, Mole, Ratty and Badger. The characters are brought to life with films, interactive displays and re-creations - children can climb into Toad's caravan, wander through the Wild Wood and creep along the passage to Toad Hall; they can also learn about real voles, moles, badgers and toads. Shop, disabled access; cl 25 Dec and Jan 29-31; (01629) 733433; £3.75.

SHARDLOW SK4430
Shardlow - canal basin Attractive, with some handsome former wharf buildings - one now an antiques warehouse, another, the Malt Shovel, a good pub.

SNAKE PASS SK1092
(A57 Glossop—Hathersage) The car park at the top of the pass is near the centre of the biggest of the NT's moorland holdings here, giving free access to the miles of Hope Woodlands (there aren't actually many trees). The dark moors of the High Peak are one of England's great wildernesses. But they have few easy circular routes for walkers, are largely very bleak indeed, and often consist of private grouse moor, with future public access rights still to be thrashed out.

SOUTH WINGFIELD SK3754
Wingfield Manor (B5035) Substantial ruin with virtually complete banqueting hall, tower and undercroft. The 16th-c Babington Plot is thought to have been

hatched here, leading to the final downfall of Mary, Queen of Scots. Snacks, shop, some disabled access; cl Mon and Tues, best to phone (01773) 832060; EH; £3.20. The nearby Old Yew Tree does good value food.

SUDBURY SK1532
Sudbury Hall Individual but attractive Stuart mansion with elaborate carving, frescoes, murals and plasterwork in splendidly elegant rooms. It's worth a visit just for the excellent **National Trust Museum of Childhood**, which has a chimney climb for sweep-sized children, and a fine collection of toys and dolls; you can play with some exhibits, and at wknds the schoolroom is staffed by an Edwardian teacher. They've recently introduced a treasure hunt around the rooms; the staff are friendly. Snacks, shop, some disabled access (bear in mind, car park is 400 yds from Hall); museum and Hall open pm (grounds all day) Weds-Sun 20 Mar-Oct, plus museum open a few wknds in Dec for special events; (01283) 585305; £7 for everything, £4.50 house and grounds or museum only; NT.

SWADLINCOTE SK2015
Catton Hall You'll enjoy the guided tour of this classic Georgian house, designed by James Gibbs, and still with much of its original furniture and paintings. Catton has been in the same family since 1405, and you may even be taken around by one of the owners; it's right by the River Trent, with a formal garden and parkland, and a little chapel. Tours 2pm Mon Apr-Oct; (01283) 716311; £4.

TIDESWELL SK1575
In good walking country, this large and attractive village is almost a small town; its spacious 14th-c church is known as the Cathedral of the Peak. The George is good value, and the B6049 across Millers Dale has nice views.

TISSINGTON SK1752
The Peak District's most beautiful village, its broad main street wonderfully harmonious, with wide grass verges, handsome stone houses inc a Jacobean hall (open pm Tues-Thurs late Jun to late Aug; (01335) 352200; £5.50, gardens only, £2) and interesting church. The grey stone gardener's cottage is familiar from many

calendars; garden centre, decent homely café.

TORRS RIVERSIDE PARK SJ9984
This deep gorge below New Mills is a good place to potter among the ivy-covered remains of former mills and other industrial relics; the canal basin has been restored over at Buxworth - the Navigation here is an enjoyable pub. The Goyt Way is a track heading N towards and beyond Marple, partly following the Peak Forest Canal - a pretty walk.

WIRKSWORTH SK2854
Wirksworth Heritage Centre (Crown Yard, Market Pl) Attractive old silk and velvet mill, with displays on quarrying and local customs such as well-dressing and clypping the church, and children's activities. Meals, snacks, shop; cl Sun am, Mon (exc bank hols), plus Tues in Nov and mid-Feb-Easter, and all Dec-mid-Feb, but phone to check; (01629) 825225; £2. The town boasts a lot of restored old buildings; the Blacks Head (Market Pl) is a useful local pub.

Other attractive villages, all with decent pubs for something to eat, include Brassington SK2354, Coton in the Elms SK2415, Duffield SK3443, Earl Sterndale SK0967, Elton SK2261, Flagg SK1368, Ford SK4080, Holymoorside SK3469, Idridgehay SK2849, Kirk Ireton SK2650, Little Hucklow SK1678, Litton SK1675, Lullington SK2513, Mapleton SK1648 (domed church, nice riverside walk to Thorpe), Milton SK3126, Parwich SK1854, Pilsley SK2471, Repton SK3026, Ridgeway SK3551, Smisby SK3419, Stanton by Dale SK4638 and Stanton in Peak SK2464.

Decent country pubs perfectly placed for walkers include the Peacock at Barlow SK3474, Robin Hood at Baslow SK2572 (handy for the ridge of Baslow Edge), Barley Mow at Bonsall SK2858 (by the Limestone Way, landlord organises walks), Bowling Green at Bradwell SK1781 in Smalldale, Barrel on the ridge at Bretton SK2077, Church at Chelmorton SK1170, Beehive at Combs SK0478 (lovely valley), Packhorse at Crowdecote SK1065, Gate just W of Cutthorpe SK3273, Bridge at Ford SK4080,

Grouse nr Froggatt Edge SK2577, Queen Anne at Great Hucklow SK1878, Miners Arms at Milltown SK3561, Bulls Head in pretty Monyash SK1566, Grouse at Nether Padley SK2577, Fox in Brookbottom at New Mills SJ9886, New Napoleon by Ogston Reservoir SK3761, Little Mill nr Rowarth SK0189 (particularly for Lantern Pike), Moon at Stoney Middleton SK2375, Queens Arms at Taddington SK1472 and Bulls Head at Wardlow SK1874 (for well wooded Cressbrook Dale).

Where to eat

ALDERWASLEY SK3152 **Bear** *(01629)* 822585 Enchantingly unspoilt pub in peaceful setting with a delightful interior, several small dark rooms with low beams and bare boards, a great variety of old tables and seats, log fires in huge stone fireplaces, candles galore, plenty of Staffordshire china ornaments, several grandfather clocks, and canaries, talkative cockatoos, an african grey parrot and budgies; enjoyable daily-changing food using the best local ingredients, fine range of interesting wines, well kept real ales, and peaceful country views from well spaced picnic-sets out on the side grass. £22.20|**£7.95**

BAKEWELL SK2168 **Byways** *Water Lane* *(01629)* 812807 Olde-worlde tearoom with several separate areas, roaring log fire, well presented good value food from snacks and morning coffee or afternoon teas to meals, and warmly friendly staff. £9.50|**£3.30**

BAKEWELL SK2168 **Renaissance** *Bath St (01629)* 812687 Overlooking a little walled garden where fresh herbs are grown, this beamed restaurant serves imaginative french dishes inc gourmet specials and a fresh fish of the day, and delicious puddings; friendly service; cl Sun pm, Mon, 25 Dec-mid-Jan, first 2 wks Aug. £30.65|**£7.99**

BIRCHOVER SK2362 **Druid** *(01629)* 650302 Civilised and pleasantly remote creeper-covered dining pub with huge choice of very popular interesting food (best to book), well kept real ales, and friendly service; bustling little bar with big coal fire, no smoking Garden Room, and spacious and airy two-storey dining extension; children must leave by 8pm; may cl Mon. £24.30|**£9.90**

BUXTON SK0673 **Coffee Bean Café** *50 Spring Gardens (01298)* 27345 Small bustling café, long and narrow, with old tea and coffee advertisements, 15 types of coffee, all-day breakfasts, savouries and light lunches, and delicious cakes; cl evenings; partial disabled access.|**£4**

EYAM SK2276 **Miners Arms** *Water Lane (01433)* 630853 Newly refurbished this year, this cosy pub has a restful atmosphere in its three little plush beamed rooms, good interesting lunchtime food served by attentive staff, well kept ales, and decent nearby walks; bdrms; no food Sun pm; disabled access. £21|**£6.95**

HATHERSAGE SK2380 **Plough** *(01433)* 650319 Popular former farmhouse in lovely spot by River Derwent with seats in pretty garden next to the water; spotlessly kept, attractive bar on two levels with big log fire at one end and woodburning stove at the other, well organised, hardworking staff, well kept real ales, nine good value wines by the glass, and an excellent choice of imaginative food; super breakfasts. £24.50|**£7**

HOGNASTON SK2350 **Red Lion** *Main St (01335)* 370396 Carefully renovated open-plan oak-beamed dining pub with a friendly welcome and relaxed atmosphere, attractive mix of candlelit tables on ancient flagstones, three open fires, a collection of teddy bears, well presented imaginative food (book at wknds), well kept real ales, and attentive staff; attractive bdrms; cl Mon am; children over 12. £23|**£4.95**

IDRIDGEHAY SK2848 **Black Swan** *Wirksworth Rd (01773)* 550249 Open-plan dining pub with bright airy simple décor, a relaxed, unhurried atmosphere, cheerful paintings, no smoking lower garden room, and small bar area with daily papers and real ale; generous and enjoyable food and prompt, polite service. £22/ 2-course lunch £8.95

MELBOURNE SK3825 **Bay Tree** *4 Potter St (01332) 863358* Small family-run cottagey restaurant with beams and simple furnishings, carefully presented popular food (Sun lunch is booked up weeks ahead), and thoughtful relaxed service; cl Sun pm, Mon. **£25|£8**

MILLTOWN SK3661 **Miners Arms** *(01246) 590218* Impeccably kept and comfortable stone-built dining pub with L-shaped layout, a back bar, and no smoking dining room; particularly good home-made food, well priced, with especially good interesting vegetables (a choice of half a dozen), and three sorts of potato, well kept real ales, decent value wines, and friendly efficient service. **£21|£8.25**

OVER HADDON SK2066 **Lathkil** *(01629) 812501* Comfortable inn with stunning views and plenty of surrounding walks; open fires, beams, partly no smoking dining area which doubles as an evening restaurant, enjoyable food and well kept real ales, and helpful service; children lunchtime only; cl 25 Dec. **£20.70|£6.50**

RIDGEWAY SK4081 **Old Vicarage** *Ridgeway Moor (0114) 247 5814* Big Victorian house in lovely gardens with a marvellously relaxing welcoming atmosphere, cosy sitting room for pre-dinner drinks and beautifully presented, quite exceptional cooking using home-grown produce in candlelit dining room or light and airy less formal conservatory; cl Sat am, Sun pm, Mon (though they will open then for private parties of over 10 people); disabled access. **£50/3-course Sun lunch £34**

WOOLLEY MOOR SK3661 **White Horse** *Badger Lane (01246) 590319* Popular old pub run by very friendly people - and much liked by locals; very good food using best local produce, lots of daily specials, decent wines and beers, conservatory, lovely view from garden (pleasant Ashover Valley walks), good play area; disabled access. **£22.50|£7.50**

Special thanks to Peter Gondris, F Blanchard

DEVON

Devon has a tremendous range of really good holiday possibilities - so much, in fact, that we have divided it into three areas. East Devon is classic family holiday country, with Exeter a charming small city for a short break. South Devon, with Dartmoor, has the widest appeal of all, with a mass of interesting places to visit, and glorious vistas of coast and moor. North Devon, with Exmoor, is rewarding but less touristy than the other areas. There are some outstanding places to stay, at all price levels, and the food in this area is particularly good.

Some of the best views here are from trains, with vintage steam trains puffing through gorgeous river valleys. Standard train trips go through a wonderful variety of scenery, too. For these, the Devon Rover is a good deal, with unlimited journeys in the area at a reduced rate for either eight days out of fifteen (£46.50) or any three days out of seven (£30); phone (08457) 484950.

Exeter & East Devon

Plenty for family seaside holidays; Exeter city makes an appealing short stay

A rewarding small city with some unexpected highlights, Exeter is served by fast trains and the M5. Good roads bring other parts of Devon within comfortable reach of it, making it a fine base for day trips.

Family outings in this part of Devon often handily combine different things to do in a single package: Crealy Adventure Park at Clyst St Mary (rides, play areas and animals too) and the World of Country Life in Exmouth (from steam engines to safari rides through llama paddocks) both have all-round appeal for a day out. Other enjoyable family attractions include the Pecorama Pleasure Gardens at Beer (great if you like trains), and Escot Aquatic Gardens at Ottery St Mary (lovely in fine weather, with a combination of wild and tame animals). Gardeners should head for East Budleigh and Killerton (the house is worth popping into, too).

The coast has four main beach resorts, each quite different from the others. Doubling as a working port, Exmouth is the liveliest and biggest. Quieter Seaton is a more typical family resort, in an attractive setting, while Budleigh Salterton, the quietest, is rather retiring and genteel. Sidmouth has the broadest all-round appeal: it's slightly busier, with a good deal of character as well as plenty for families. The prettiest coastal village is Branscombe.

Inland, coastal downs give a gently varied landscape of charming wooded valleys with views and high pastures between, and several attractive villages. N of the A30/A35 is more self-contained farmland, still mainly well hedged traditional stock and dairy farms, though cattle numbers have been falling.

Where to stay

CULLOMPTON ST0305 **Upton House** *Cullompton, Devon EX15 1RA (01884) 33097* **£50**; 3 rms. Big, pink-washed 300-year-old farmhouse in large garden and surrounded by 180 acres of organic farm and lots of horses (the owners breed race horses); careful renovation has revealed beamed ceilings, panelling, and huge stone fireplaces, and there's a woodburning stove and fine furniture in sitting room, oak-panelled dining room and sunny conservatory, good breakfasts served around a big table, and welcoming hosts; pubs and restaurants nearby; cl Christmas/New Year; children over 12

EXETER SX9292 **Edwardian Hotel** *30-32 Heavitree Rd, Exeter, Devon EX1 2LQ (01392) 276102* **£56**, plus special breaks; 12 individually furnished rms, 4 with four-posters. Popular guest house, recently renovated, close to cathedral and city centre, with pretty lounge, enjoyable breakfasts in attractive dining rooms, and warmly friendly and knowledgeable resident owners; plenty of places nearby for evening meals; cl 25-26 Dec; partial disabled access; dogs welcome in bedrooms

EXETER SX9292 **Hotel Barcelona** *Magdalen St, Exeter, Devon EX2 4HY (01392) 281000* **£111**; 46 beautifully furnished rms with CD-player and video, and lovely bthrms. Stylishly modern, converted Victorian eye hospital filled with bright posters and paintings, a bar with 1950s-style furniture and fashionable cocktails, a smart but informal no smoking restaurant overlooking the big walled garden, with a woodburning oven for pizza cooking plus other good-value contemporary choices, a nightclub featuring 1950s films noir and live entertainment, and very helpful staff; disabled access; dogs welcome in bedrooms

GITTISHAM SY1497 **Combe House** *Gittisham, Honiton, Devon EX14 0AD (01404) 540400* **£138**, plus winter breaks; 15 individually decorated pretty rms with lovely views. Peaceful, Grade I listed, Elizabethan country hotel in gardens with 400-year-old cedar of Lebanon, and walks around the 3,500-acre estate; elegant day rooms with fine panelling, antiques, portraits and fresh flowers, a happy relaxed atmosphere, very good food in restaurant and faithfully restored Georgian kitchen, and fine wines; can use the house for special occasions and meetings; dogs welcome away from restaurant

MEMBURY ST2703 **Lea Hill** *Membury, Axminster, Devon EX13 7AQ (01404) 881881* **£70**; 4 individually furnished rms. Thatched, no smoking 14th-c longhouse in 8 acres of secluded grounds inc their own par 3, 9-hole golf course, and lovely views; comfortable beamed rooms, flagstones and beams, relaxed and friendly owners, and nice breakfasts, morning coffee, and afternoon tea with home-made cakes and cream teas; self-catering, too; no children; dogs welcome

SIDFORD SY1489 **Blue Ball** *Sidford, Sidmouth, Devon EX10 9QL (01395) 514062* **£70**; 6 rms, most with own bthrm, and with nice touches like free papers, fruit and fresh flowers. Welcoming thatched 14th-c inn run by the same family since 1912, with lovely winter log fire in low partly panelled lounge bar, heavy beams, lots of bric-a-brac, no smoking snug, very friendly service, and decent food inc hearty breakfasts

STOCKLAND ST2404 **Kings Arms** *Stockland, Honiton, Devon EX14 9BS (01404) 881361* **£60**; 3 rms. Cream-faced thatched pub with elegant rooms, open fires, first-class food in bar and evening restaurant food (esp fish), and interesting wine list; skittle alley, live music Sat, Sun pm; cl 25 Dec; dogs welcome

WHIMPLE SY0497 **Woodhayes Country House Hotel** *Whimple, Exeter, Devon EX5 2TD (01404) 822237* **£90**; 8 lovely spacious rms. Big Georgian country house in neat grounds, with comfortable quietly decorated lounges, open fires, flagstoned bar and pretty no smoking dining room, fine food, afternoon teas, and excellent breakfasts; croquet; cl 2 wks over Christmas and New Year

To see and do

BEER SY2289
Rather cottagey resort village, still with fishing boats pulled up on the shingle beach (summer boat hire, too; (01297) 20076), a stream channelled down the main street, and good local fish in the newly restyled Anchor. The village was famous from Roman times for its cavernous whitestone quarries (phone for information about guided tours - (01297) 680282; £4.75), and the B3174 inland passes lots of Bronze Age burial mounds. Fascinating coast path W to Branscombe Mouth, through the tumbled chalky mass of Hooken Undercliff.

Pecorama Pleasure Gardens Fun for railway lovers, with models and train collections in the exhibition, and outside a miniature steam and diesel passenger line with stunning bay views. Also crazy golf, aviary, wooden maze and assault course, a multi-themed garden, and live entertainment. Meals, snacks, shop, mostly disabled access; cl Sat pm, Sun (exc Jun-Aug), and outdoor features cl Oct-Easter (exc Oct half-term); (01297) 21542; £4.75.

BRANSCOMBE SY1988
The **church** has a magnificently carved oak gallery, and a Norman tower with distinctive stair-turret. The village is notably pretty - a series of largely unspoilt thatched hamlets strung along a lovely seaside valley. Branscombe, lying just inland, is linked to the coast path by other paths, and has the good Masons Arms in the main part of the village, as well as the NT Old Bakery tearoom opposite the unique NT thatched smithy.

BROADCLYST SX9897
Pretty thatch-and-cob village, with a marvellous old church, picturesque outside, interesting in; the Red Lion beside it is owned by the NT.

CLYST ST MARY SY0090
Crealy Adventure Park (Sidmouth Rd) There's plenty to amuse children of all ages at this bustling family complex. The Magical Kingdom, a delightfully constructed area aimed mostly at under-7s, has play areas and a soaring gondola swing, while among the attractions for older children are bumper boats, go-karts and a farm where you can milk the cows, and meet baby animals. Many of the attractions are indoors, inc some of the animals, and a good varied adventure playground. There's also a family roller-coaster, swingboat, a new carousel and log flume, toddlers' garden play area, multicolour meadow, splash zone, pony rides and lakeside walks (with an embryonic arboretum); lots of special events and activities (usually summer Suns). Meals, snacks, shop, disabled access; (01395) 233200; cl Mon and Tues during term-time Nov-Feb, 24-26 Dec and 1 Jan; £7.75. If you don't want to eat in the park, the Half Moon is good value.

CULLOMPTON ST0207
The church is notable for its remarkable painted screen; the busy little town is appealing, and the farmers' market (Station Rd, 2nd Sat each month) was the prototype for the hundreds which now exist. The Merry Harriers at Westcott (B3181 S) has enjoyable food.

CULMSTOCK ST1013
The village has a handsome **church**, good interesting food in the ancient waterside Culm Valley pub, and a pleasant riverside walk to Uffculme.

DALWOOD SY2499
Burrow Farm Gardens (half a mile or so off A35; turn off at Taunton Cross sign) Part of this 7-acre site has been created from an ancient Roman clay pit, with spacious lawns, borders and unusual shrubs and trees, as well as a woodland garden, pergola walk with old-fashioned roses, and super views; also a rill garden, and a wildlife lake. Cream teas, snacks, nursery, disabled access; cl Oct-Mar; (01404) 831285; £3.50. The pretty Tuckers Arms is good for lunch.

DOWLAND CLIFFS SY2889
The steeply tumbled brambly wooded wilderness of this undercliff 3m E of Axmouth has numerous small birds.

EAST BUDLEIGH SY0684
Attractive and quietly placed cob and thatch village; the pleasant **church** has fascinating Jacobean carved pew ends - some grotesque, some hilarious, some frankly rude. The Sir Walter Raleigh has decent food.

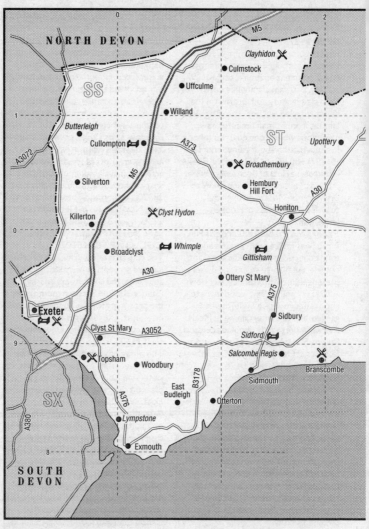

Bicton College The gardens here are of great if rather specialised appeal; long monkey-puzzle avenue through parkland, rich collection of magnolias, camellias and flowering cherries, national pittosporum and agapanthus collections, and 17-acre arboretum with woodland garden. Snacks, plant centre; cl wknds Nov-Mar, 25 Dec and Good Fri; (01395) 562353; £2.50.
Bicton Park 63 acres of lovely gardens, shrubs, lakes and woodland. A futuristic-looking glass Palm House turns out to be early 19th c, and has a

fine collection of tropical trees and plants; also fuchsia, geranium and orchid houses, bird garden, pinetum, magnificent italian gardens, miniature train rides and nature trails. There's a miniature golf course and two play areas. Meals, snacks, shop and plant centre, disabled access; cl 25 Dec; (01395) 568465; £4.95.
EXETER SX9292
Though large parts of the centre were devastated by World War II bombing, some choice streets and buildings survive, with picturesque partly Tudor

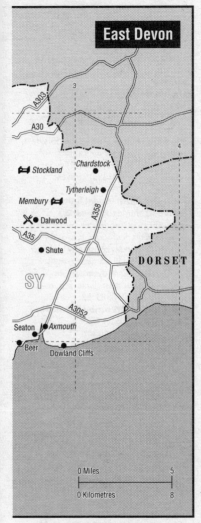

East Devon

Stockland

Chardstock

Tytherleigh

Membury

Dalwood

Shute

DORSET

SY

A303

A30

A35

A358

A3052

Seaton · Axmouth

Beer

Dowland Cliffs

0 Miles 5

0 Kilometres 8

narrow lanes leading from the mainly pedestrianised High St into the serene tree-shaded cathedral close. In the centre, modern shops are integrated into the old layout very discreetly. With many smaller churches, decent book and other shops, pubs and so forth nearby, this is a very pleasant part for browsing around, and there's a good easy-going atmosphere. Particularly attractive streets include Southernhay at the end of the close, and Stepcote Hill, a picturesque detour from Fore St. The Quay, beyond the streams of fast

traffic on the ring road (there are quiet underpasses), has become lively and entertaining, with handsomely restored buildings, resurgent cafés and pubs (the Prospect and Port Royal are worth knowing), and craft shops and the like; the Old Quay House has a visitor centre with audio-visual show; (01392) 265213. Civilised pubs and wine bars with decent food include the sumptuous Imperial (New North Rd), Ship (14th-c, Martins Lane), Well House (The Close - cathedral view and Roman well) and newly reopened waterside Port Royal (Weirfield Path, downstream from the Quay). There are **boat trips** down the ship canal to Turf Locks; or you can walk down, passing the easy-going Double Locks pub and ending at the Turf Hotel looking out over the estuary. A range of daily free guided tours leave the Royal Clarence Hotel (Cathedral Close) throughout the day (phone (01392) 265203 for details, or pick up a programme from the tourist information centre, Paris St); there are good cycle paths into the countryside. The quickest way into the city from either the M5 or the A38 is to keep on round to the westbound A30 and go into the city from the Alphington roundabout. A striking new HQ for the Met Office has recently been built on the outskirts of the city, which has a thriving university.

Bill Douglas Centre (Old Library, Exeter University, Prince of Wales Rd) Display of almost 1,000 cinema-related objects amassed by the late film-maker Bill Douglas; includes film-star dolls, 19th-c optical toys, and oriental shadow puppets. Shop, disabled access; cl wknds and bank hols, 24 Dec-2 Jan, and a wk over Easter; (01392) 264321; free (though you'll get more out of the good guided tour, *£2).

Exeter Cathedral England's finest example of Decorated Gothic architecture, with its magnificent nave soaring to the vaulted roof, and intricately carved choir stalls; the 13th-c misericords are thought to be the oldest set in the country. It also boasts the longest unbroken Gothic vaulting in Europe, superbly atmospheric. Lots of colourfully embroidered cushions, chronologically illustrating english and local history. The façade has three tiers of sculpted figures, inc the Apostles. Meals, snacks, shop, disabled access; guided tours 11am and 2.30pm (plus 12.30 July-Aug) wkdys, 11am Sat, 4pm Sun Apr-Oct, or by appointment; £3.50 suggested donation.

Guildhall (High St) This medieval municipal building with its ornately colonnaded Elizabethan façade is one of the oldest still in use; it has displays of civic regalia and so on. Disabled access to ground floor only; cl 1-2pm (exc Aug), Sat pm (all day Sat in winter), all day Sun and bank hols, during civic functions and over Christmas; (01392) 265700; free.

Royal Albert Memorial Museum (Queen St) Wonderful Gothic exterior, notable displays inside of regional silver, african carvings, archaeology, paintings, natural history and world cultures: three galleries include touch-screen computer displays and intriguing exhibits such as materials collected during Captain Cook's voyages; changing exhibitions, and special events. Snacks, shop, disabled access; cl Sun and bank hols; (01392) 665858; free.

St Nicholas's Priory (Mint Lane) 11th-c Benedictine monastery with unusual Norman undercroft, Tudor room and 15th-c kitchen. Shop, disabled access to ground floor only; open 2-4.30pm Mon, Weds and Sat Easter-Oct, occasionally cl for private functions; (01392) 665858; 50p.

Underground Passages (entrance via Boots Arcade in High St) An unusual medieval attraction is this atmospheric network, built in the 14th c to bring water into the city; an introductory exhibition and video is followed by a guided tour of the passages themselves, still much as they were centuries ago. The guides can be very entertaining, and clearly enjoy their work. Flat shoes are recommended. Shop; cl Sun Jun-Sept, plus Mon Oct-May; (01392) 665887; £3 (£3.75 in summer).

EXMOUTH SY0080
Good family seaside holiday town, worth a visit for its lively harbour and marina, its long sandy beach, and its stately church. Summer cruise trips go from the harbour up to Topsham, (01395) 222144 for details; there are

sea fishing trips from the landing stage (they supply rod and bait); (01395) 275882. The Seafood Restaurant (Tower St) has nothing but the freshest fish and shellfish; the Grove (attractive seafront garden and play area) is good value too.

A la Ronde ⊞ (A376 2m N) Extraordinary 16-sided house, built around 1795 and decorated in part with feathers, seashells, seaweed and sand. A charmingly whimsical place, the outside looking not entirely unlike a giant biscuit barrel. Snacks, shop; cl Fri, Sat, and all Nov-Mar; (01395) 265514; £3.80; NT.

Great Exmouth Model Railway (Sea Front) Home to the world's biggest 00 gauge model railway, nearly 1½ miles of track indoors. It took 14 years to build and is constantly updated - some of the detail is amazing, right down to the birds in the trees. Shop, some disabled access; cl mid-Sept to Easter; (01395) 278383; £2.

High Land of Orcombe Reached by the shore road E out of Exmouth and protected against campsite encroachment by its National Trust ownership, this gives walkers a short stroll with sea views.

World of Country Life (Sandy Bay) 40 acres of enjoyable family-based activities, with friendly animals (you can feed some of them, and there are usually babies to see), adventure playground and under-cover play areas, safari rides through deer and llama paddocks, and there's an owl centre; also reconstructed Victorian street, classic motorcycle collection, steam engines, crazy golf and quad bikes. Meals, snacks, shop, disabled access; cl Nov-Easter; (01395) 274533; £6.50.

HEMBURY HILL FORT ST1103
A walk up from the A373 NW of Honiton, for good views.

HONITON ST1600
Some handsome Georgian buildings along this country town's long High St, and some interesting shops. The Red Cow is good value for lunch. Fine views from the A375 S - Daniel Defoe considered this 'the most beautiful landscape in the world'.

Allhallows Museum (High St) This refurbished 13th-c building has displays of Honiton lace, and lace-making demonstrations Jun-Aug. Shop, disabled access; cl pm Sat, all Sun, and Nov-Mon before Easter; (01404) 44966; £2.

KILLERTON SS9700

Killerton House Best of all in spring, 15 acres of beautiful hillside gardens, shrub borders and planted beds, with an impressive avenue of beech trees. The 18th-c house has an annually changing costume exhibition in period furnished rooms, collection of paintings, and a recreated 1960s post office, but it's the gardens that really give the place its special appeal. Meals, snacks, shop and plant centre, disabled access to ground floor (with buggies round the grounds); house cl Tues (exc Aug), plus Mon in Oct and 3 Nov-13 Mar (garden open daily); (01392) 881345; £5.50, £3.90 garden only; NT. The Three Tuns in Silverton has well prepared food, esp vegetarian, and there's a rewarding antiques centre at nearby Hele (towards Bradninch).

OTTERTON SY0785

Otterton Mill Centre Working watermill still grinding flour for the bread, cakes and pies sold on the premises. Also craft workshops, display of local lace, and interesting evening events. Enjoyable meals and snacks, shop, garden centre, some disabled access; cl 3 days over Christmas; (01395) 568521; free. The village is pretty.

OTTERY ST MARY SY1095

Restrained small town - or extended village - with some attractive old buildings around its interesting twin-towered church. The circular **tumbling weir** by an 18th-c mill signed off Mill St is unusual, and photogenic. The London Inn is useful, and the Otter Nurseries (Gosford Rd) have good plants. **Cadhay** (just NW) Beautiful Tudor and Georgian manor house, with fine timbered 15th-c roof in its Great Hall, and unusual Court of Sovereigns - a pretty courtyard with statues of various monarchs. Disabled access to garden and downstairs; as we went to press the house had just gained a new owner, so best to phone for information; (01404) 812432; £4.50.

Escot Aquatic Centre & Gardens ♿ (Parklands Farm, Escot; off A30) Tropical and coldwater fish from koi

carp to piranhas, as well as rabbits and other pets, otters (fed at 11am and 3pm), Victorian walled rose garden, wild boar enclosures, walks, views and parkland. Also wetlands and waterfowl park, birds of prey, play area, and pet centre with all you'll need for any kind of pet, as well as the animals themselves. Meals, snacks, shop, some disabled access; cl 25-26 Dec; (01404) 822188; £4.95.

SEATON SY2589

Pleasantly restrained family resort, with quite a long beach, the amusements you'd expect, and an attractive setting, with cliffs on either side - see Dowland Cliffs for the interesting landslips to the E. Open-top trams (not wkdays Dec-Easter, exc school hols; £5.20 return) run up the Axe valley to Colyton, where the Kingfisher is a good pub; back in town, the Fishermans (Marine Crescent) has decent cheap food all day. On the other bank of the river, Axmouth has pretty cottages, a Norman church, and near it the Ship, a nice pub doubling as an owl rescue centre.

SHUTE SY2496

Lyme Bay Winery (Seaton Junction) Vintage equipment and free tastings of cider, country wines and traditional liqueurs; shop selling local food and drink. Cl winter wknds, best to phone first; (01297) 551355; free.

SIDBURY SY1391

A pretty village, with a charming **church**; the Hare & Hounds (3m N, A375/B3174) has enjoyable food all day.

SIDMOUTH SY1287

Attractive old streets, very 18th c, running back from the seafront, and grander Regency buildings facing the sea. It was a fashionable upper-class resort in the early 19th c, and many of the town's buildings show undoubted architectural verve - there's very little seaside tat. The pebbly beach has fishing boats pulled up on it, and the town is protected by warm red sandstone cliffs; it stretches back along the river valley, though away from the sea the buildings are less interesting. The partly 14th-c Old Ship is the best pub here, and Sue's Pantry (High St) has tasty cakes and pastries. Summer walking tours around the town (Tues and Thurs 10.15 am) are organised by the **Heritage**

Centre (in a fine Regency house on Church St); cl am Mon and Sun and all Nov-Easter; £1. The dedicated **Donkey Sanctuary** is a useful free attraction for families, with an incredible number of donkeys; meals, snacks, shop, disabled access; (01395) 578222. Space enthusiasts will enjoy the open days at the **Norman Lockyer Observatory** (Salcombe Hill Rd); exhibitions (helpful staff are on hand to answer any questions), guided tours and a planetarium; disabled access; (01395) 579941; £4.

Cliff walks The long stretch of **red sandstone cliff** between Sidmouth and Branscombe can be reached from either place (or, steeply but very prettily, from Salcombe Regis).

SILVERTON SS9502
An attractive village, with a particularly handsome **church**. The friendly old Three Tuns is good for lunch.

TOPSHAM SX9688
Old-world seaside village, good for a quiet potter. Its buildings show its past importance as a port - as do its large number of good pubs and inns. The Passage House and Galley restaurant have good fresh fish.

Topsham Museum (the Strand) On a pretty street with 17th-c dutch-gabled houses overlooking the Exe estuary, this friendly little museum is crammed full of local and maritime history, and, more unexpectedly, has some Vivien Leigh memorabilia, and an exhibition on Thomas Hardy's cousin; also model and full-sized boats, period room re-creations and touch-screen computers. Good tearoom (the riverside garden is a nice place to enjoy one of their popular cream teas), disabled access; open pm wknds, Mon and Weds Apr-Oct; (01392) 873244; free.

UFFCULME ST0612
A large pleasant village above the Culm River, with a magnificent carved screen in the attractive **church**. The B3397 to Culmstock and then the turn to Hemyock is a pretty drive; beyond at Clayhidon the Merry Harriers has good food, by a footpath to the Blackdown Hills visitor centre; (01823) 680280.

Coldharbour Mill Working Museum You can watch every stage in the production of wool at this well restored 18th-c mill building (it was operated as a woollen factory by the same family for almost 200 years and is now run by enthusiastic volunteers); there's also a crafts gallery. Meals, snacks, shop, and improved disabled access now; cl 24 Dec-Feb; (01884) 840960; £5.50.

WILLAND ST0309
Diggerland (B3181 N of Cullompton) Readers enjoy visiting this unusual adventure park: under close supervision, children from 5 upwards can operate and drive real excavation equipment inc JCB diggers, dumpers and a fork-lift truck. Rides or drives last around five minutes, and children complete various challenges such as fishing a duck from a pond or knocking down skittles. Also pedal-power diggers, computer games and a video, bouncy castle, and a good play area for under-6s. Meals, snacks, shop, disabled access. Cl wkdys in school term-time (exc bank hol Mon) and 25 Dec; (08700) 344437; £2.50 entrance fee, from £1.50 per ride or drive.

WOODBURY SY0387
Lonely heathland, fine views (off B3180 E) Miles of heath with some pinewoods, a place to get away from people even in high summer (red flags warn if there's firing on one section which is a shooting range). From the highest points, nr the road, there are far views along the coast and to Dartmoor. The wooded **hill fort** right by the road is worth a look, and it's a bit eerie tracing the ramparts through the beech trees. The village of Woodbury itself is attractive, and by the church the White Hart has good value food.

Other attractive villages, all with decent pubs, include seaside Axmouth SY2591, Broadhembury ST1004, Butterleigh SS9708, Chardstock ST3004, Lympstone SX9984, Otterton SY0684, Salcombe Regis SY1488, Tytherleigh ST3103 and Upottery ST2007.

Where to eat

BRANSCOMBE SY1988 **Masons Arms** *(01297) 680300* Popular, well run inn with open kitchen for new restaurant, no smoking bar, two-sided woodburner, stripped original pine woodwork, low beams in main bar with massive central hearth, no smoking restaurant, particularly enjoyable imaginative food inc spit roasts, well kept real ales inc summer beer festival, 14 wines by the glass, and outside tables under little thatched roofs; good bdrms, some with four-posters; self-catering cottages; disabled access. £31

BROADHEMBURY ST1004 **Drewe Arms** *(01404) 841267* Excellent fresh fish in charming 15th-c pub with carved beams and handsome stone-mullioned windows in the bar, several other interesting rooms, lovely puddings, fine wines, well kept beers, and charming garden in attractive village (church worth a visit, nearby craft centre); cl Sun pm, 31 Dec; disabled access. £34

CLAYHIDON ST1716 **Merry Harriers** *(01823) 421470* Warmly welcoming and charmingly laid out dining pub with comfortably cushioned pews and farmhouse chairs in several small linked areas, plenty of horsey and hunting prints and local wildlife pictures, lit candles in bottles, and a couple of warm woodburning stoves; good restauranty food using local venison, lamb, and duck, organic chicken, fresh fish from Brixham, and local cheeses and cream, ten enjoyable wines by the glass, well kept real ales, two pub dogs, and picnic-sets on a small terrace, with more in a sizeable garden; good walking area; cl Sun pm, Mon; children over 6 lunchtime, no children in evening. £25|**£7.50**

CLYST HYDON ST0300 **Five Bells** *(01884) 277288* Charming spotless thatched pub, with long bar divided by standing timbers, lots of plates on shelves, sparkling brass and copper, fresh flowers and candles in bottles, very good popular food, warmly friendly service, and lovely cottagey gardens. £28.|**£7.10**

DALWOOD ST2400 **Tuckers Arms** *(01404) 881342* Delightful thatched medieval longhouse with fine flagstoned bar, lots of beams, log fire in inglenook, woodburner, a good mix of dining chairs, window seats and wall settles, huge collection of miniature bottles, well prepared enterprising bar food and lots of colourful hanging baskets; bdrms; no children; disabled access. £27

EXETER SX9292 **Brazz** *10-12 Palace Gate (01392) 252525* Stylish, buzzy brasserie with elegant modern décor (inc interesting two-tier fish tank), enjoyable contemporary all-day food plus imaginative extras and rich puddings, a good range of drinks, friendly service, and a decent wine list; they are kind to children; cl 25 Dec; disabled access. £27.50|**£7.50**

EXETER SX9292 **Michael Caines at Royal Clarence** *Cathedral Yard (01392) 310032* Opposite the cathedral, this smart, no smoking and colourful restaurant in a historic hotel has a friendly relaxed atmosphere, helpful service, enjoyable artistically presented food inc good puddings, and a thoughtful wine list; there's also a stylish, airy café-bar; cl pm 25 Dec; disabled access. £35/2-course lunch £16.50

TOPSHAM SX9688 **Georgian Tea Room** *35 High St (01392) 873465* 18th-c house with pretty embroidered tablecloths and fresh flowers, and good food all day - breakfasts, morning coffee, snacks, lunchtime meals inc a popular roast on Tues, Thurs and Sun, cream teas with home-made cakes and cookies, and a wide range of teas and coffees with home-made lemonade; no smoking bdrms; cl Weds, 25-26 Dec; partial disabled access|**£4.95**

Please let us know what you think of places in the *Guide*. Use the report forms at the back of the book, write us a letter or log on to www.goodguides.co.uk

South Devon & Dartmoor

**The West Country at its very best - tremendous seaside charm
in great variety, contrasting Dartmoor, picturesque villages, plenty of
family attractions, and beautiful places to stay in**

The new Living Coasts, our pick for Devon Family Attraction this year, makes Torquay even more rewarding for visitors. Besides the lovely sandy beaches, other high points here range from tours of an ancient cave, to a carefully re-created Victorian street, and the county's largest art gallery. This whole area of Torbay and its English Riviera is lovely in summer, with spacious promenades, low cliffs, bright gardens and palm trees.

Very different but no less rewarding, Plymouth is particularly strong on family attractions (and a good bet when the weather's bad). The National Marine Aquarium (improving all the time, and now with a unique robotic shark), Plymouth Dome (the city's past presented in a way that children enjoy), historic gin distillery (good tours), and Crownhill Fort (exciting to explore) are just some of the options.

Pretty Paignton Zoo, and the bustling animal centre at Pennywell in Buckfastleigh, cater well for families. Young children very much enjoy the miniature horses at Moretonhampstead and, new to the *Guide*, we've added the developing farm park at Kingsbridge. The rides and animals at Woodland Leisure Park (Blackawton) and the industrial re-creations at Morwellham Quay are more than enough to occupy a whole day. Swapping steam trains for river boats between Dartmouth and Totnes, or catching a steam train to the enjoyable Butterfly Park & Dartmoor Otter Sanctuary at Buckfastleigh, are other suggestions for nicely varied days out.

Impressive houses include Saltram at Plympton, and the delightful modern impostor Castle Drogo at Drewsteignton. Okehampton is Devon's largest medieval castle, Compton at Marldon is picturesque, popular Buckfast Abbey has the bonus of an irresistible shop, and Buckland Abbey at Buckland Monachorum has interesting displays. Many would consider the gardens in Salcombe and Kingswear even more of a draw than the houses (you'll find rewarding and unusual plant places too at Newton Abbot). Appealing for adult tastes, in Newton Abbot there are tours of one of the few working maltings in the country; cider drinkers like the farm at Dunsford, and there's a vineyard at Sharpham.

Dartmoor is a splendid brooding wilderness, with complete walking freedom in most parts (you're not confined to footpaths), and all sorts of points of interest - especially its tors (weirdly shaped rock excrescences) and visible prehistoric remains. The National Park Authority website is useful (www.dartmoor-npa.gov.uk) for information about guided walks, transport and so forth; or you can phone (01822) 890414. Around its edges are delightful places to explore, from the dramatic scenery of Lydford Gorge to intimate and picturesque valleys and villages. There's a similar intimate appeal in the small coves, stretches of cliff, sheltered boating creeks and estuaries cut deeply into the hills of the S and W coast. Here, relaxed and welcoming small towns such as Dartmouth and Totnes have plenty to see and do. Some of England's best and cleanest beaches such as Slapton Sands are to be found here.

Away from Dartmoor, the inland landscape is made up largely of well hedged hilly pastures, steeply wooded valleys and occasional vivid red-earth fields.

Where to stay

ASHBURTON SX7270 **Holne Chase** *Ashburton, Newton Abbot, Devon TQ13 7NS* (01364) 631471 **£130**, plus winter breaks; 17 comfortable and individually furnished rms, many with views over the Dart Valley, and some split-level suites in converted stables. Marvellously peaceful ex-hunting lodge of Buckfast Abbey in 70 acres with sweeping lawns and plenty of woodland walks, a mile of Dart fishing, shooting and riding on Dartmoor; cheerful welcoming owners, comfortable public rooms with log fires, very good modern english cooking using home-grown vegetables, and enjoyable breakfasts and afternoon teas (home-made breads and so forth); children over 12 in evening restaurant; dogs welcome in bedrooms

BIGBURY-ON-SEA SX6544 **Henley** *Folly Hill, Bigbury-on-Sea, Kingsbridge, Devon TQ7 4AR* (01548) 810240 **£88**; 6 compact rms. Renovated Edwardian cottage with fine views of the Avon estuary, Burgh Island, and beyond; lounge and conservatory dining room with magnificent sea views, deep wicker chairs and polished furniture, binoculars and books, good, enjoyable food from a small menu, super breakfasts, and steep, private path down the cliff to a sandy bay; cl Nov-Mar; dogs welcome in bedrooms

BOVEY TRACEY SX8078 **Edgemoor Hotel** *Haytor Rd, Bovey Tracey, Newton Abbot, Devon TQ13 9LE* (01626) 832466 **£99.50**, plus special breaks; 16 charming rms. Ivy-covered country house in neatly kept gardens on the edge of Dartmoor, with comfortable lounge and bar, log fires, good food in elegant restaurant; cl 1 wk after Christmas; children over 10; limited disabled access; dogs welcome away from food areas

BURGH ISLAND SX6443 **Burgh Island Hotel** *Burgh Island, Bigbury-on-Sea, Devon TQ7 4AU* (01548) 810514 **£260** inc dinner; 21 suites or rooms all with sea views, most with balconies. Art Deco hotel (and 14th-c smugglers' pub) on private tidal island, reached by foot or hotel 4WD vehicles at low tide, by sea tractor at high tide; public rooms and suites all furnished in period style: 20s domed Palm Court with classic cocktail bar, glamorous 30s Ballroom, and sunny black and white Ganges Room and Terrace for enjoyable meals using the best local produce; Wednesday and Saturday evening dinner dances; tennis court, snooker and table tennis, sea-water bathing pool; cl 1st three wks Jan; children over 12 in public rooms in evening; disabled access

CHAGFORD SX7189 **Easton Court** *Sandy Park, Chagford, Newton Abbot, Devon TQ13 8JN* (01647) 433469 **£70***; 5 comfortable rms. Extended Tudor thatched longhouse in four acres of gardens and paddocks, with a relaxed and informal atmosphere, hearty breakfasts in guest lounge/breakfast room, helpful, friendly owners, and lots to do nearby; plenty of surrounding pubs and restaurants; cl Jan; children over 12; dogs welcome in bedrooms

CHAGFORD SX7087 **Gidleigh Park** *Chagford, Newton Abbot, Devon TQ13 8HH* (01647) 432367 **£430** inc dinner, plus winter breaks; 15 opulent and individual rms with fruit and flowers. Exceptional luxurious Dartmoor-edge mock Tudor hotel with deeply comfortable panelled drawing room, wonderful flowers, conservatory overlooking the fine grounds (40 acres, with walks straight up on to the moor), log fires, particularly fine cooking and a fine wine list, and caring staff; children over 7 in restaurant; dogs welcome in bedrooms

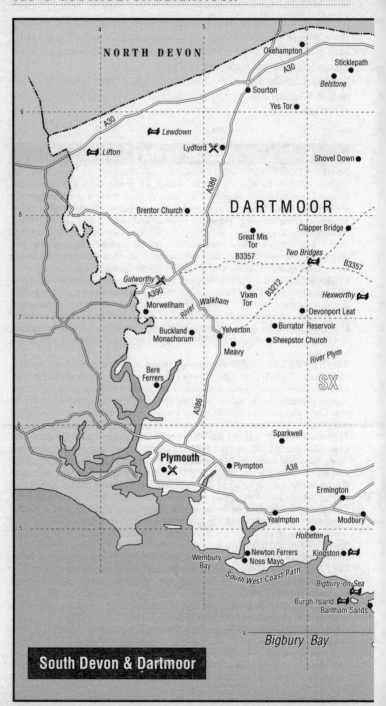

NORTH DEVON

Okehampton

Sticklepath

A30

Belstone

Sourton

Yes Tor

Lewdown

Lydford

Shovel Down

Lifton

DARTMOOR

Brentor Church

Clapper Bridge

Great Mis Tor

Two Bridges

B3357

B3357

Gulworthy

Vixen Tor

Hexworthy

A390

Morwellham

River Walkham

Devonport Leat

Buckland Monachorum

Yelverton

Burrator Reservoir

Sheepstor Church

Meavy

River Plym

Bere Ferrers

A386

SX

Sparkwell

Plymouth

Plympton

A38

Ermington

Yealmpton

Modbury

Holbeton

Newton Ferrers

Kingston

Wembury Bay

Noss Mayo

South West Coast Path

Bigbury-on-Sea

Burgh Island

Bantham Sands

Bigbury Bay

South Devon & Dartmoor

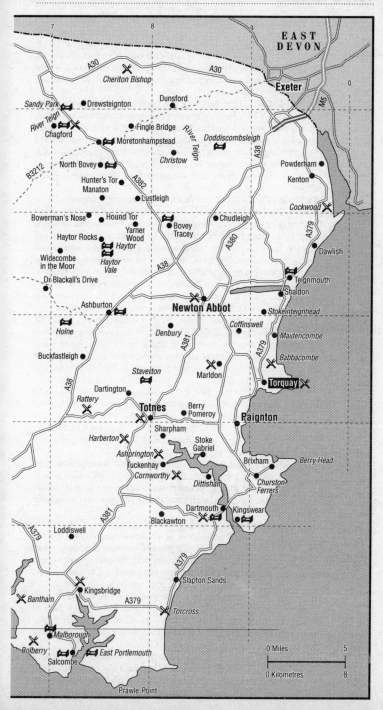

EAST
DEVON

7
8
9

0

A30

Cheriton Bishop

A30

Exeter

Sandy Park

Drewsteignton

Dunsford

M5

River Teign

Fingle Bridge

Chagford

Moretonhampstead

Doddiscombsleigh

A38

Powderham

Christow

Kenton

North Bovey

B3212

A382

River Teign

Cockwood

Hunter's Tor
Manaton

Lustleigh

Bowerman's Nose

Hound Tor

Chudleigh

Dawlish

Haytor Rocks

Yarner
Wood

Haytor

Bovey
Tracey

A380

A379

Widecombe
in the Moor

Haytor
Vale

A38

Teignmouth

Shaldon

Dr Blackall's Drive

Ashburton

Newton Abbot

Stokeinteignhead

Holne

Denbury

A381

Coffinswell

Maidencombe

Buckfastleigh

A38

Staverton

Marldon

A379

Babbacombe

Dartington

Rattery

Totnes

Berry
Pomeroy

Torquay

Harberton

Sharpham

Paignton

Ashprington

Stoke
Gabriel

A381

Tuckenhay

Brixham

Berry Head

Cornworthy

Dittisham

Churston
Ferrers

Loddiswell

Blackawton

Dartmouth

Kingswear

A379

A379

A381

Slapton Sands

Bantham

Kingsbridge

A379

Torcross

Malborough

Bolberry

Salcombe

East Portlemouth

Prawle Point

0 Miles   5

0 Kilometres   8

DARTMOUTH SX8751 **Royal Castle** *11 The Quay, Dartmouth, Devon TQ6 9PS* *(01803) 833033* **£169.90**, plus special breaks; 25 individually furnished rms. Well restored mainly Georgian hotel (part 16th c) overlooking the inner harbour - great views from most rooms; lively and interesting public bar with open fires and beams, quiet library/lounge with antiques, drawing room overlooking the quayside, winter spit-roasts in lounge bar, elegant upstairs seafood restaurant, decent bar food, and friendly staff; dogs welcome in bedrooms

DODDISCOMBSLEIGH SX8586 **Nobody Inn** *Doddiscombsleigh, Exeter, Devon EX6 7PS (01647) 252394* **£70***; 7 rms, some in a Georgian manor house 150 yds down the road, and most with own bthrm. Friendly 16th-c pub with beams, heavy wooden furniture, and inglenook fireplace in the attractively furnished two-roomed lounge bar, an outstanding cellar running to 800 (fairly priced) wines and 250 malts, and popular food in bar and restaurant inc huge range of Devon cheeses; good views from garden, and the church is worth visiting for fine stained glass; cl 25-26, 31 Dec; no children

EAST PORTLEMOUTH SX7537 **Gara Rock** *East Portlemouth, Salcombe, Devon TQ8 8PH (01548) 842342* **£140** inc dinner; 17 rms, some can convert to family suites, and 20 self-catering apartments. Originally a coastguard station and look-out, with its own beach at the foot of the cliffs; marvellous for families with daily clubs and rooms for every age, baby-listening and sitting, acres of grassy garden with heated outdoor swimming pool and paddling pool, tennis, an adventure playground with wooden boat, various pets, lots of entertainments, children's menus, early suppers, and so forth; enjoyable food all day inc barbecues, helpful friendly staff, and an informal and relaxed atmosphere; lots to do nearby (though so much in the hotel, you might not leave the grounds); cl Dec-Jan; disabled access; dogs welcome ☺

HAYTOR SX7777 **Bel Alp House** *Haytor, Newton Abbot, Devon TQ13 9XX (01364) 661217* **£120***, plus special breaks; 8 spacious rms. Handsome Edwardian country house with elegant drawing room, comfortable sitting room, log fires and lots of fresh flowers and plants, friendly atmosphere, and fine careful cooking in pretty restaurant; wonderful views and peaceful garden; cl 15 Dec-20 Jan; disabled access; dogs welcome in bedrooms

HAYTOR VALE SX7777 **Rock** *Haytor Vale, Newton Abbot, Devon TQ13 9XP (01364) 661305* **£86**, plus special breaks; 9 individual rms. Civilised old coaching inn on the edge of Dartmoor National Park, with good food (inc fresh fish), a nice mix of visitors and locals in the two rooms of the panelled bar, open fires, no smoking restaurant, courteous service, and big garden; walking, fishing, riding and golf nearby; cl 25 Dec; dogs welcome in bedrooms

HEXWORTHY SX6572 **Forest Inn** *Hexworthy, Princetown, Yelverton, Devon PL20 6SD (01364) 631211* **£65**; 10 cosy, comfortable rms, most with own bthrm. Country inn in fine Dartmoor setting, popular with walkers and anglers; varied menu in both bar and restaurant, local ales, good choice of wines, and welcoming staff; partial disabled access; dogs welcome

HOLNE SX7170 **Wellpritton Farm** *Holne, Ashburton, Devon TQ13 7RX (01364) 631273* **£45**, plus special breaks; 5 pretty rms. Small, recently refurbished friendly Dartmoor farm set in 15 acres with horses, goats and chickens and lovely views from terrace and garden; comfortable sitting room, good, completely home-made evening meals using local produce, and enjoyable breakfasts; cl Christmas week; children under 5 by arrangement; disabled access; dogs welcome in bedrooms

KINGSTON SX6347 **Dolphin** *Kingston, Kingsbridge, Devon TQ7 4QE (01548) 810314* **£55***; 3 rms. Peaceful 16th-c inn with several knocked-through beamed rooms, a warmly welcoming atmosphere, a small no smoking area, very good home-made food, and real ales; swings for children in extensive gardens, and tracks down to the sea

KINGSWEAR SX8850 **Nonsuch House** *Church Hill, Kingswear, Dartmouth, Devon TQ6 0BX (01803) 752829* **£85***, plus special breaks; 3 big, comfortable rms overlooking the river to Dartmouth. Two Edwardian villas in a lovely hillside spot, with open fires and books in elegant sitting room, an airy conservatory overlooking the lovely, carefully tended garden (the owners are serious gardeners), enjoyable food using the freshest local produce, nice breakfasts, and warmly welcoming owners; no smoking; children over 10

LEWDOWN SX4586 **Lewtrenchard Manor** *Lewdown, Okehampton, Devon EX20 4PN* (01566) 783256 **£170**, plus special breaks; 9 well equipped rms with fresh flowers and period furniture. Lovely Elizabethan manor house in garden with fine dovecot and surrounded by peaceful estate with shooting, fishing and croquet; dark panelling, ornate ceilings, antiques, fresh flowers, and log fires, a friendly welcome, relaxed atmosphere, and candlelit restaurant with very good imaginative food; children over 8; partial disabled access; dogs welcome in bedrooms

LIFTON SX3885 **Arundell Arms** *Fore St, Lifton, Devon PL16 0AA* (01566) 784666 **£130**, plus special breaks; 27 well equipped rms, 5 in annexe over the road. Carefully renovated old coaching inn with 20 miles of its own waters - salmon and trout fishing and a long-established fly-fishing school; comfortable sitting room, log fires, super food in both bar and elegant restaurant, carefully chosen wines, and kind service from local staff; new eating area in attractive terraced garden; cl 4 days over Christmas; disabled access; dogs allowed away from restaurant and river bank

MALBOROUGH SX7039 **Soar Mill Cove Hotel** *Malborough, Salcombe, Devon TQ7 3DS* (01548) 561566 **£228***, plus special breaks; 22 comfortable rms, some opening on to garden. Neatly kept single-storey building in idyllic spot by peaceful and very beautiful cove on NT coast (excellent walks), with lovely views, extensive private grounds, tennis/putting, and warm indoor pool; outstanding service, log fires, very good food (marvellous fish) in new restaurant and coffee shop, and they are particularly kind to children of all ages: microwave, fridge, and so forth for little ones, own high tea or smaller helpings of most meals, fully equipped laundry, a play room, table tennis and snooker, swings, and donkey and pony; cl Jan; disabled access; dogs welcome in bedrooms ☺

MORETONHAMPSTEAD SX7386 **Great Sloncombe Farm** *Moretonhampstead, Newton Abbot, Devon TQ13 8QF* (01647) 440595 **£50***; 3 rms - the big double is the favourite. Lovely 13th-c farmhouse on a working dairy and stock farm, with friendly owners, carefully polished old-fashioned furniture in oak-beamed lounge, decent food, hearty breakfasts, log fires, a relaxed atmosphere, and good nearby walking and bird-watching; no smoking; children over 8; dogs welcome in bedrooms

NORTH BOVEY SX7483 **Gate House** *North Bovey, Newton Abbot, Devon TQ13 8RB* (01647) 440479 **£62***, plus special breaks; 3 charming rms. 15th-c thatched cottage in picturesque village, with huge granite fireplace in attractive beamed sitting room, breakfasts and candlelit evening meals in beamed dining room, tea with home-made cakes, friendly owners, and outdoor swimming pool in peaceful garden; plenty to do nearby; no children; dogs welcome in bedrooms

SALCOMBE SX7338 **Tides Reach** *Cliff Rd, South Sands, Salcombe, Devon TQ8 8LJ* (01548) 843466 **£170** inc dinner, plus special breaks; 35 rms, many with estuary views. Unusually individual resort hotel run by long-serving owners in pretty wooded cove by the sea, with airy luxury day rooms, big sea aquarium in cocktail bar, good restaurant food using fresh local produce, friendly efficient service, and squash, snooker, leisure complex, health area, and big heated pool; windsurfing etc, beach over lane, and lots of coast walks; cl Dec-Jan; children over 8; dogs welcome in bedrooms

SANDY PARK SX7189 **Mill End** *Sandy Park, Chagford, Newton Abbot, Devon TQ13 8JN* (01647) 432282 **£90***, plus special breaks; 15 attractive rms with fine bthrms and views. Quietly set former flour mill with waterwheel in neatly kept grounds below Dartmoor with 600 yards of private salmon and trout fishing, access to miles of game fishing and still-water fishing on local lakes; comfortable lounges, carefully prepared interesting food, fine breakfasts, cream teas on the lawn, and good service; cl Jan; partial disabled access; dogs welcome in bedrooms

STAVERTON SX7964 **Sea Trout** *Staverton, Totnes, Devon TQ9 6PA* (01803) 762274 **£78**; 10 cottagey rms. Comfortable pub in quiet hamlet nr River Dart with two relaxed beamed bars, log fires, popular food in bar and airy dining conservatory, and terraced garden with fountains and waterfalls; cl Christmas; disabled access; dogs welcome away from restaurant

TEIGNMOUTH SX9372 **Thomas Luny House** *Teign St, Teignmouth, Devon TQ14 8EG (01626) 772976* **£80**, plus special breaks; 4 pretty rms with flowers and books. Lovely little no smoking Georgian house nr fish quay; open fires in spacious, comfortable drawing room and elegant dining room, a relaxed friendly atmosphere, enjoyable food (plus free afternoon tea with home-made cake), and sunny walled garden; children over 12

TWO BRIDGES SX6274 **Prince Hall** *Two Bridges, Yelverton, Devon PL20 6SA (01822) 890403* **£120***, plus special breaks; 8 attractive spacious rms. Surrounded by Dartmoor National Park, this tranquil, recently refurbished 18th-c country house is run by caring friendly owners and their helpful staff; lovely views from convivial bar, comfortable sitting room, and cosy dining room, open fires, very good evening meals, enjoyable breakfasts, and lots of fine walks; cl mid-Dec to mid-Feb; children over 10; dogs welcome

To see and do

Devon Family Attraction of the Year

TORQUAY SX9163 **Living Coasts** (Beacon Quay) Opening not long before we went to press, this ambitious and eagerly awaited £7million attraction offers a splendidly enjoyable and comprehensive look at life around the world's coastlines. Part of Paignton Zoo, it's been put together with real thought and flair, with lots of hands-on and interactive features, and carefully designed tunnels and underwater viewing panels giving fantastic views of the marine life. The creatures are in painstakingly reconstructions of their natural habitats, with re-created beaches, cliff tops and even an estuary, with sea water from Tor Bay (it eventually returns there, much cleaner than it was when it first arrived). For most children the stars of the show are the penguins and the cute little fur seals, but there are plenty of other species too, including puffins, sea ducks, and even black rats, with useful explanations of their effects on the environment. Birds fly free overhead in a big meshed aviary, and there's a good range of plant life. You'll probably need a good couple of hours to see everything properly. There's a full programme of keeper talks and feeding displays spread throughout the day; if you particularly want to see, say, the seals being fed but don't want to hang around, they'll stamp your hand so you can come back later. An appealing modern building on a busy but previously rather redundant part of the seafront, it boasts fine views along the bay, particularly from the terrace of the café. Meals and snacks (a good emphasis on local ingredients, and open in the evenings too), shop, disabled access; cl 25 Dec; (01803) 202470; £5.50 adults, £3 children 3-15. A family ticket (two adults, two children) is £16.90.

ASHBURTON SX7370
The most attractively individual of the ring of small towns around the edge of Dartmoor. The **River Dart Country Park** (Holne Park) is pleasant for walking or fishing, with adventure playgrounds for children. Snacks, shop; cl Oct-Mar; (01364) 652511; £5.95, dogs £2.
BANTHAM SANDS SX6643
Bantham has an excellent 16th-c pub,

the Sloop, and a gentle walk through dunes with good picnic spots takes you to this broad stretch of rivermouth sand facing Burgh Island. You can go on above the rocks S, for views of Bolt Tail and the coves between.
BERE FERRERS SX4563
Tamar Belle (Bere Ferrers Station) Unusual new heritage centre (tracked down for us by readers) in a vintage

railway carriage; various booths cover different areas of Tamar Valley history. Other converted carriages house a tearoom and restaurant, and you can even stay here overnight; limited disabled access; usually open wknds, but best to check as it's run by volunteers; (01822) 840044; donations. Down in the secluded waterside village the 16th-c Old Plough has good value food and an estuary-view garden.

BERRY POMEROY SX8361
Berry Pomeroy Castle (off A385 just E of Totnes; keep on past village) Reputedly Devon's most haunted castle, hidden away on a crag over a quiet wooded valley. Appropriately spooky medieval gatehouse and walls around the ruins of an imposing and unexpected Tudor mansion, with an interesting 15th-c fresco inside; an audio tour tells you more about the castle and its inhabitants. The lawns in front are ideal for a picnic. Snacks; cl Nov-Easter; (01803) 866618; £2.80; EH. The red sandstone 15th-c village **church** is worth a look on the way; odd monument in Seymour Chapel. The road through here from Ashburton via Littlehempston and on to Stoke Gabriel is a nice drive.

BLACKAWTON SX8052
Woodland Leisure Park (off A3122) Fairly traditional good value family fun, especially enjoyable for children up to around 12 who like to charge around. The highlight for children at the upper end of the age range is the spiralling and plunging water-coaster Twister (there are several similar waterchutes nearby), and an exciting toboggan run, the Tornado. There's also a nicely put-together Wild West town aimed at the under-5s, and a little zoo with wallabies, llamas and foreign and exotic birds. Stacks of well thought out play areas range from a commando-style assault course to imaginative under-cover areas for toddlers. Five floors of indoor rides and activities inc a ferris wheel, and the chance to drop well over 10 metres (40 ft) to experience weightlessness. Also a honey farm with millions of bees behind glass, a tractor yard, paddling pool, pedal karts; twice-daily falconry displays and special events all year. Woodland walks, boating lake, and they have an adjacent caravan park.

Meals, snacks, shop, disabled access but steep hills; cl Nov to mid-Mar exc wknds and school hols; (01803) 712598; £7.90 adults and children (less in winter, when the water rides aren't open). In the village the family-friendly George has enjoyable food.

BOVEY TRACEY SX8178
An unassuming small Dartmoor-edge town; the Devon Guild of Craftsmen have a good varied **craft centre** at Riverside Mill (cl 24-26 Dec and 1 Jan; free). The **House of Marbles and Teign Valley Glass** (Pottery Rd) has demonstrations of glass-blowing at a factory specialising in marbles; there are some interesting marble runs in its museum inc, they claim, the largest marble run in the world. Meals, snacks, shop, disabled access; cl 25-26 Dec, first two wks in Jan and Easter Sun; no glass-blowing Sat end Sept-Easter, but best to check; (01626) 835358; free. The Cromwell Arms does generous food.

BRIXHAM SX9256
Busy fishing port, perhaps the prettiest of the Riviera resorts, with some attractive narrow streets on the hill above. Lots of activity (and summer seaside shops and cafés) in the harbour, inc a full-size reconstruction of Drake's Golden Hind, and summer boats around Tor Bay. With something of a maritime emphasis, the local history **museum** (Bolton Cross) is well worth a look. Shop, disabled access to ground floor only; usually cl pm wknds (exc school summer hols), all Nov-Easter, best to check; (01803) 856267; £1.50. The harbourside Blue Anchor has decent food inc local fish, and Shoalstone beach nr here has some of the cleanest bathing water in the UK.
Berry Head Tremendous coast, sea and shipping views from ex-quarry country park; squat lighthouse, formidable Napoleonic War battlements with cannon (and guardhouse café), nature trail takes in kittiwakes and guillemots on cliffs, uncommon plants.
Scabbacombe Head A blowy but rewarding day's walk from Brixham to Kingswear, 12 miles of stunning wild scenery (and some steep climbs), passing the oasis of Coleton Fishacre gardens

BUCKFASTLEIGH SX7467
Buckfast Abbey Originally established in 1018, but after the Dissolution of the Monasteries left abandoned until 1882, when it was refounded by Benedictine monks. They then did most of the rebuilding work themselves, over a period of 32 years. It's now one of the most visited religious sites in Britain, with an interesting exhibition, and several services each day. Excellent shops sell not just their own famous tonic wine, but goods produced at other Benedictine monasteries around Europe, inc bavarian beer, french cakes, and irish linen; for many, this alone is worth a special journey. Good meals and snacks, disabled access; cl Good Fri and 24-26 Dec; (01364) 645500; free. A vintage bus does a loop around Buckfastleigh usually every 15 mins in summer, and the abbey can be viewed from the route; phone for times (01364 644522); free.

Butterfly Park & Dartmoor Otter Sanctuary (Dart Bridge Rd) You can watch otters swimming and playing from an underwater viewing tunnel, or see them on land in the six big landscaped enclosures; summer feeding times (readers enjoy this part most) 11.30am, 2 and 4.30pm. Also undercover tropical garden with free-flying butterflies and moths. Meals, snacks, shop; cl Nov-Mar; (01364) 642916; £4.95. Combined with a trip on the South Devon Railway (the trains stop here), this makes for a very pleasant day out. The nearby Dartbridge Inn is a popular family pub.

Pennywell (Lower Dean, off A38 just S) Friendly and unfussy, with over 750 animals in 80 acres, and a birds of prey centre, as well as lovely scenery, wildlife viewing hides, and barn owl demonstrations. Different events every half-hour so always something for children to get involved in, from milking and feeding to ferret racing and worm charming; there's a new miniature train (£1), as well as play areas, an assault course, go-kart ride, theatre, pony and donkey rides and an area where children can try out crafts like basket weaving. Meals, snacks, shop, disabled access; cl Nov-Feb half-term (phone for opening times over Christmas); (01364) 642023; £6.95.

South Devon Railway GWR steam train trips through lovely unspoilt scenery along the wooded River Dart (some of which is hard to see any other way). It stops at Totnes as well as at Staverton, and they do tickets combining it with a Dartmouth—Totnes river trip; also a small museum, play area and a chance to see the ongoing restoration of rolling stock. Shop, disabled access; trains normally run four times a day (more in the height of summer, less at other times); best to check dates; cl Nov-Mar (exc Santa trains at Christmas, booking essential); (0845) 345 1420 for timetable (or pick one up from local tourist information centres); £7.50. The Dartbridge opposite is a popular family dining pub.

Valiant Soldier (Fore St) A fascinating time-capsule, this former pub has hardly changed since it closed in the 1960s (even down to the money in the till); local history displays and an exhibition on the pub's restoration. Open Mon-Sat Apr-Oct, but best to check; (01364) 644522; £3.

BUCKLAND MONACHORUM SX4866
Buckland Abbey The home of Francis Drake until his death in 1596, and of his family until 1946. They've modernised the three museum rooms: one room explores the abbey's history, another has objects associated with Drake (inc the famous drum said to sound whenever England is in danger), while a third has various interactive displays designed to catch children's interest. Also craft workshops, a brass rubbing centre, herb knot and thyme gardens, an Elizabethan garden, good walks, and entertaining summer activities for children. Meals, snacks, shop, limited disabled access; cl Thurs, wkdays Nov-end Mar, plus 6 wks after Christmas; (01822) 853607; £5, £2.70 grounds only; NT. The Drake Manor pub is a really nice village archetype.

Garden House Profusion of unusual plants beautifully laid out in a warm walled garden surrounding the picturesque ruin of a medieval vicarage; also a spring garden, quarry garden and wildflower meadow. Interesting plant sales, meals, snacks, limited disabled access; cl Nov-Feb; (01822) 854769; £4.

BURGH ISLAND SX6544
Connected at low tide by a causeway to Bigbury-on-Sea (undistinguished for much save its clean sandy beaches); spectacular cliffs on the seaward side, a true island and quite remote-seeming when the tide's in. At high tide an odd giant tractor-on-stilts wades back and forth with passengers. The neatly refurbished Pilchard, in a great seaview setting, is open all day.

CHAGFORD SX7087
Appealing large village or small town right in the heart of Dartmoor, and an attractive jumping-off point for the moor; even the bank is thatched, and the two old-fashioned general stores are fun. The Ring o' Bells is good for lunch, and for non meat-eaters, the small vegetarian Courtyard Café is recommended. If you eat at the luxury country-house hotel Gidleigh Park, you can stroll around their lovely grounds, with colourful woodland walks and water garden, and immaculate more formal gardens.

CHUDLEIGH SX8678
Despite the 1807 fire which destroyed lots of the buildings, this is a pleasant old wool town with pretty cottages in narrow, winding lanes. In Fore St the Bishop Lacey and Old Coaching House both have decent food.

Rock Garden and Cave ⬚ Eight acres of wild gardens in an ancient quarry, populated by a good range of birds and wildlife. The cave has some interesting calcite formations, and they are still digging in search of legendary larger caverns. From the pretty neighbouring waterfall it's a short walk up Chudleigh Rock for dramatic vistas of the surrounding countryside and moors. Snacks, nursery, limited disabled access; cl 25 Dec-1 Jan; (01626) 852134; £3. You can arrange abseiling or caving on (01626) 852717.

Ugbrooke Park (off A380 just SE) An interesting early example of the work of Robert Adam, in lovely Capability Brown parkland. Delightfully informal guided tours (2pm and 3.45pm). Teas, disabled access; open pm Sun, Tues, Weds, Thurs and bank hols mid-July to early Sept; (01626) 852179; £5.50.

DARTINGTON SX7862
Dartington Cider Press Centre (Shinners Bridge) Cluster of 16th- and 17th-c buildings with craft shops, Dartington Crystal, farm foods, herbs and such, and restaurants, inc a good vegetarian one. The surroundings add a lot to the attraction, with nearby medieval great hall on photogenic lawned courtyard, sculpture gardens, street entertainers from jugglers to clog dancers, and a streamside nature trail. Disabled access; cl Sun (exc Easter-Christmas), 25-26 Dec and 1 Jan; (01803) 847500; free. The Cott Inn is useful for lunch.

DARTMOOR SX5880
The National Park covers two very contrasting landscapes. One is the moor itself, one of England's most untouched and wild-seeming areas, a vast expanse rising to the highest points south of the Pennines. Then further E and S are the deep lush valleys of the Teign, Dart and other rivers, where stone-built houses crouch among sycamores and oaks. It's not an area thick with indoor sights: the outdoors is the great attraction here (though unfortunately the massif is prone to sudden and prolonged bouts of mist and fog). The moor is punctuated with all sorts of interesting focal points and features (it's one of the most important areas for Bronze Age remains in Europe): strange wind-sculpted, eroded granite tors crowning many of the slopes; little streams threading over boulders; water-courses where leats (or miniature canals) curl carefully around the contours; abandoned and ruined tin-mine workings' wheel-houses; and shaggy ponies hoping for a hand-out (though it's an offence to feed livestock because it encourages them on to the roads). Good roads over the moor are the B3212 and B3357, and the back road towards Ashburton off the B3344 just NW of Manaton. Villages within the national park (such as Chagford, North Bovey, Lustleigh and Widecombe) are well worth exploring: typically thatched white-plastered stone cottages clustered around an ancient stone church beside its church-house inn. The towns ringing the moor (and just outside the national park) have

rather more facilities. A big chunk of NW Dartmoor is used by the Ministry of Defence for firing practice; during training the ranges are marked out by red flags and white posts by day and red lights at night; you can check times on (0800) 458 4868. Dartmoor is outstanding for walking, but mist can come down very suddenly, so on the open moor you must carry a compass, wear strong footwear, and carry spare clothing and food. A lot of the moor is a long way from the road, hence rather inaccessible. Guided walks are available and a bus network, inc an extensive Sunday service, takes people to the start of these walks; phone (01392) 382800 for bus details. For a programme of the guided walks, phone (01822) 890414; from £3, free with bus ticket into park. There are more paths for walkers than the right-of-way network suggests, but don't assume a right of way marked on the OS map will be visible on the ground (the black dashed lines on these maps are generally more reliable though not necessarily rights of way unless they are overprinted with a green line). Old mineral railways and cart tracks make for some good walkers' routes. There are plenty of things to head for, to give a moorland walk a sense of purpose - most obviously, one of the many tors of naked rock rising out of the moor (beware: the rounded rocks can be a good deal more slippery than they look). Villages and sights are described separately; the following is a list of scenic and archaeological highlights:

Bowerman's Nose SX7480 This quaint tor, looking snootily out over a patchwork of pastures, makes a pleasant objective for a Dartmoor walk.
Brentor church SX4780 (above back rd Lydford—Tavistock, just S of North Brent Tor) 12th-c St Michael de la Rupe is one of England's smallest churches, notable for its lonely hilltop position with remarkable coast and Dartmoor views. The Royal Standard over at Mary Tavy does good food.
Burrator Reservoir SX5568 This gives up to a five-mile walk in beautiful woodland and moorland surroundings.
Sheepstor church nearby has interesting memorials to the Brookes

family, former rajahs of Sarawak.
Clapper bridge SX6578 By the B3212 at Postbridge (enjoyable food from the East Dart Hotel) is a complete clapper bridge - an ancient stone packhorse bridge; there are other ruined examples nr Bellever (a mile S), and by the end of the B3357 at Dartmeet.
Devonport leat SX5975 This watercourse, still largely complete, was first engineered over 200 years ago to give Devonport a water supply. A path largely along the gently graded channel takes in some remote scenery in southern Dartmoor, and makes getting lost quite difficult; it's easily reached off the B3212 NE of Yelverton.
Dr Blackall's Drive SX7073 This old carriage drive from Bel Tor Corner to near Poundsgate (where the Tavistock Inn is a useful stop) gives splendid views of the Dart Valley, and is among Dartmoor's finest paths for walkers.
Fingle Bridge SX7489 Beautifully sited bridge over the Teign, at the end of a minor road. From the pleasant Anglers Rest café/pub the lovely Fisherman's Path winds along a wooded stretch of the valley; you can return at high level on the Hunter's Path, passing near Castle Drogo, and gaining tremendous views.
Great Mis Tor SX5676 In the lonely terrain NW of Princetown (and Dartmoor Prison), this gives walkers panoramic views over much of the moor - it's within the Ministry of Defence range areas so look out for the red warning flags.
Haytor Rocks SX7577 This fortress-like collection of rocks makes a striking and popular objective for walks. Nearby abandoned granite quarries were served by an unusual 19th-c tramway with grooved-granite rails, linked with a canal to the coast - now an 18-mile walk down to Teignmouth called the **Templer Way**.
Hound Tor SX7478 Majestically monumental and a good destination for a walk, with an interesting excavated abandoned **medieval village** nearby.
Hunter's Tor SX7682 The ridge path to this landmark gives panoramic views of Lustleigh Cleave and the Bovey Valley.
Plym Valley SX5866 The upper valley

of the Plym has numerous ancient sites, inc visible hut circles, stone rows and cairns.

Shovel Down SX6585 These open moorland expanses harbour some of Dartmoor's richest concentrations of **antiquities**. You'll need a map just to find the car park at Scorhill, SW of Gidleigh and W of Chagford; from there, a path brings you out on to the moor within sight of Scorhill stone circle. Close by are stone slab bridges over clear brooks; among the litter of rocks by one river is the Teign Tolmen, a natural boulder through which the water has gouged a perfectly circular hole. You can walk over to nearby Kes Tor, close to which is the Long Stone and a fine stone row of about 2500-1500BC.

Vixen Tor SX5474 Towering up from the bracken, this looks unclimbable, but is quite easily reached. This area of the **Walkham Valley** is relatively lush and green, and walkers can explore the old railway tracks which once served local quarries.

Yarner Wood SX7778 (nr Bovey Tracey) This National Nature Reserve has a good nature trail.

Yes Tor SX5890 On the NW of Dartmoor, this high landmark gives great views over Devon and Cornwall. This area of Okehampton Common is the highest terrain in southern England, though as in other Ministry of Defence areas, check for red flags.

DARTMOUTH SX8751
Charming waterside small town with many exceptional buildings, esp around the inner harbour. Though so popular, it's kept its own strong character, and stays very much alive through the winter. Cobbled Bayards Cove, with old fort and steep wooded hills behind, is particularly photogenic, as is pedestrianised Foss St. Old Market is picturesque with markets on Tues and Fri. The Royal Naval College is a striking building; the tourist information centre has details of guided tours; (01803) 834224. Interesting shops, plenty of waterside seats, lots of action on the river. Parking in summer can be trying: best to use good park-and-ride on B3207 Halwell Rd. Enjoyable boat trips run from here to Totnes; (01803)

834488; £5.50 single, £7 return.
Dartmouth Castle (slightly SE of town, off B3205) Classic late 15th-c battlemented fortress, virtually intact, with cannon and later gun batteries (a video display shows it firing), and great views out into the Channel. Shop, some disabled access; cl winter lunchtimes, and all day Mon and Tues Nov-Mar, and 24-26 Dec and 1 Jan; (01803) 833588; £3.20; EH. In summer a little ferry leaves the South Embankment for here every 15 mins or so (01803) 835034. Otherwise it's an enjoyable and fairly gentle 20-min walk from Dartmouth itself, though the immediate hinterland is unremarkable.

Dartmouth Museum (Duke St) Well restored 17th-c timbered house, with mainly nautical displays. Shop, some disabled access; cl Sun, 25-26 Dec, and 1 Jan; £1.50.

Newcomen Engine House (Royal Avenue Gdns) Housed in the tourist information centre, a huge steam-powered atmospheric beam-engine pump, thought to be the world's oldest, worked 1720-1913. Shop, some disabled access; cl Sun Nov-Mar, 25-26 Dec and 1 Jan; (01803) 834224; free, donations welcome.

River trip to Totnes 🎫 Passes some of Devon's prettiest scenery, much of which can't be seen on foot or by car (including where Agatha Christie lived); you can combine this with steam trains or a connecting bus back - which saves hearing the commentary a second time. You can also go on circular tours of the surrounding area, known as doing a 'Round Robin' (from £12, cl Nov-Easter) - an enjoyable way to spend an afternoon. Cl Mon, Fri and Sun Jan-Feb; limited sailings in winter, phone to check (01803) 834488; £7 return to Totnes. Also quaint car and pedestrian ferries to Kingswear and the A379 (can be 2-hr car wait at peak summer times) (01803) 752342.

St Saviour's (Church Close) Lots of charming detail, well worth a look, inc altar, pulpit, painted rood screen, brasses on chancel floor, elaborate 14th-c hinges on S door.

DAWLISH SX9576
Old-fashioned small resort with modern developments and camps

outside; red sandstone cliffs, waterside parks with black swans, small summer museum (open May-Sept; (01626) 888557; £2), prom and pier; the mainline railway cut through the cliffs right by the water is striking, and the Castle Inn at Holcombe has reliable food and lovely views.

Dawlish Warren Sandy grassy spit (with golf course) largely blocking in Exe estuary, with glistening tidal flats full of wading birds, and dunes with some rare plants. In summer get well out to the point, to avoid the crowds and caravan parks; in winter it's splendidly wild and blowy there, with thousands of ducks, brent geese and waders (even avocets) congregating at high tide to wait till the mudflats show again. Shop, disabled access to visitor centre; visitor centre cl 1-2pm and wkdys Oct-Mar; free; (01626) 863980 for times. The Boathouse is a good value family eatery in a big seafront complex at the station end, near a large amusement arcade.

DREWSTEIGNTON SX7290
Castle Drogo Impressive granite castle, designed by Lutyens and built early last century as a bizarre and brilliantly inventive mixture of medieval style and 20th-c luxury, with cunningly disguised radiators and amazing details even in the kitchen and lavatory. Lovely grounds with yew hedges form an outer barbican. Good guided walks through the surrounding woodland, and super views - it's 275 metres (900 ft) up overlooking the gorge of the River Teign. Meals, snacks, shop; cl Nov-Mar, plus castle cl Tues (though garden, shop and tearoom still open); (01647) 433306; £5.90, garden and grounds only £3; NT. Down on the village square nr the church, the unspoilt Drewe Arms does good lunches. A well signposted minor road W takes you to **Spinster's Rock**, a well preserved neolithic burial chamber and the most easily accessible prehistoric feature in the area.

DUNSFORD SX8389
Brimblescombe Farm Cider (Farrants Farm, off B3212 W of Exeter) Cider is made here in the traditional way, which visitors often find fascinating. Parts of the farm pre-date Saxon times; shop; cl Nov-Easter; (01647) 252783; free (inc sample). In

the village, the Royal Oak has generous home cooking.

ERMINGTON SX6353
Ermington church Notable for the crooked 14th-c stone spire above its tower - Victorian rebuilding kept the tilt. The Crooked Spire pub has enjoyable food, and the B3210 from Totnes is pretty.

KENTON SX9583
Kenton church A delightful church, its harmonious medieval sandstone masonry photographing well against blue sky; fine carving inside. In the pretty village the Dolphin does generous meals.

KINGSBRIDGE SX7344
Small town of character, with pretty cobbled lanes diving off steep Fore St, and arcaded shops; there are various markets (Mon-Thurs), and a farmers' market on the first Sat of the month. Interesting monuments in church, boats on tidal estuary (and ferry to Salcombe); the waterfront Crabshell is very popular for seafood. At the head of the nearby creek, pretty South Pool has a fairly interesting **church**, with a delightfully ghoulish story attached.
Cookworthy Museum of Rural Life (Fore St) Collection of rural artefacts from Victorian kitchen implements to 1930s farming equipment, housed in a 17th-c grammar school. A resource centre (open all year) houses local history and public access databases plus newspaper collection dating from 1835. Shop, some disabled access; cl Sun, and Nov-Mar; (01548) 853235; *£2.
Sorley Tunnel Adventure Farm (Loddiswell Rd, off A381 N) They've recently added miniature quad-bikes, go-karts, and a nature trail to this developing 200-acre organic farm; also indoor and outdoor play areas (inc one for the under-5s), peddle tractors, trampolines, and friendly animals from pigs and ponies (rides are £2.50) to rabbits and chipmunks. Organic meals, snacks, gift and farm shops, disabled access; cl wkdys Oct-Easter (exc Feb half-term), and 25-26 Dec and 1 Jan, best to check; (01548) 854078; £5. There's also a riding school here; (07974) 813389.

KINGSTON SX6347
There are several walks from the village

down to an unspoilt beach; the Dolphin has enjoyable food.

KINGSWEAR SX9051

Coleton Fishacre 🏛 (3m E, off Lower Ferry Rd at Tollhouse) D'Oyly Carte's romantic and lush subtropical garden, with 24 colourful acres dropping down to a pretty cove; formal terraces, walled garden with stream-fed ponds, unusual trees and shrubs and grassy woodland paths. Designed in the 1920s, the house reflects the Arts and Crafts tradition, but has a modern interior. Snacks, shop, limited disabled access to garden; open Weds-Sun and bank hol Mon Apr-Oct; (01803) 752466; £3.90 (house £1.10 extra); NT. More ambitious marked paths beyond the gardens take you along the cliffs, showing how wild this part was before the garden was planted. The Paignton and Dartmouth Railway (described under Paignton) runs from here; the Ship has decent food.

LODDISWELL SX7248

If you cross the river by the lane towards Woodsleigh, there's a quiet walk upstream by riverside pastures and woods towards Topsham Bridge. The Loddiswell Inn has generous home cooking.

LUSTLEIGH SX7881

One of England's most attractive villages, with charming riverside walks in utterly unspoilt woodland around it, or up to Hunter's Tor on Dartmoor. Primrose Cottage has great cream teas, and the Cleave Inn is good.

LYDFORD SX5084

Lydford Gorge 🏛 Spectacular gorge formed by the River Lyd cutting into the rock, causing boulders to scoop out potholes in the bed of the river. Walks along the ravine take you to dramatic sights such as the 27-metre (90-ft) White Lady Waterfall and the Devil's Cauldron whirlpool (summer crowds around this bit). Children like it but need to be watched carefully as paths can be narrow and slippery. Various family events are organised throughout the year (phone for details). Meals, snacks (in ingeniously designed tearoom), shop, special path for the disabled; open Apr-Oct (and perhaps Fri-Sun, when there's a Christmas shop, in Dec); (01822) 820320; £3.80; NT. The forbidding ruined **castle** has a

daunting 12th-c stone keep, its upper floor once used as a court, and the lower as a prison; free. The Dartmoor Inn has excellent creative food.

MANATON SX7580

An attractive village, with the private riverside woodland around **Becky Falls Woodland Park** (B3344 to Bovey Tracey) useful enough for undemanding family walks if you don't plan to take advantage of the countryside proper (also rescued owls and birds of prey, and animals for children to pet). Meals, snacks, shop, some disabled access; cl Nov-Feb (exc wknds); (01647) 221259; £3.50. The prettily placed Kestor has decent food.

MARLDON SX8664

Compton Castle (1m N, off A3022; or off A381 at Ipplepen turnoff) Formidably fortified and rather picturesque 14th-, 15th- and 16th-c manor around courtyard with portcullised entrance, particularly interesting for its completeness. Meals and snacks opposite main gate, very limited disabled access; open Mon, Weds and Thurs Apr-Oct, cl 12.15-2pm; (01803) 875740; £3; NT. The Church House Inn is good for lunch.

MEAVY SX5367

This clear wooded river has some pleasant spots for strolling. Meavy itself (pronounced Mewy locally) is an attractive village with one of the oldest oak trees in Britain, and where the parish still owns the (good) pub, whose locals dance around the tree on New Year's Eve. Another useful pub for people walking in this valley is the Skylark at Clearbrook.

MODBURY SX6551

Attractive buildings esp in steep Church St, with photogenic church at top and pretty Exeter Inn at bottom. Brownston St is quite interesting too, with an ornate water conduit at the top.

MORETONHAMPSTEAD SX7184

Miniature Pony & Animal Farm (B3212 W) Geared towards younger children, with sociable miniature ponies and donkeys (go in spring and you'll probably see foals), pigs, rabbits, goats, and other small animals. Carefully supervised activities inc pony rides and animal feeding sessions; also an adventure play area (and an indoor play area for toddlers), nature trail, trout lake, and picnic areas. Meals, snacks, shop (with various arts and crafts), disabled access; as we went to press the farm had just been sold - the new owners don't plan to make any changes, but best to phone for opening times; (01647) 432400; £6.00.

MORWELLHAM SX4470

Morwellham Quay Thriving and meticulously researched open-air museum in lovely countryside, with costumed guides convincingly re-creating the boom years when Morwellham was the greatest copper port in the Empire. You can watch the work of a blacksmith, assayer, coachmen and quay workers, and dress up in different Victorian dress. They've recently refurbished the model farm, and there's a tramway ride into the copper mine. Very popular in school hols - a visit can easily last all day. Meals, snacks, shop, disabled access limited (reduced admission price); cl Nov-Easter (exc for booked groups); (01822) 832766; £8.90. The Ship (part of the centre) is good, with period waitresses and drinks.

NEWTON ABBOT SX8670

A working town rather than a holiday centre, but several interesting places here or nearby.

Bradley Manor (off A381 S) Peaceful 15th-c house nr stream through extensive wood-fringed grounds, quiet walks. Open pm Tues-Thurs Apr-Sept; (01626) 354513; £3; NT.

Orchid Paradise (Forches Cross, A382 N) Colourful place, with lots of rare and endangered species in elaborate indoor reconstructions of their natural habitats. Snacks, nursery and shop; cl winter bank hols; (01626) 352233; £2.

Plant World (St Marychurch Rd; signed from Penn Inn roundabout) Unusual four-acre garden built and planted as a giant map of the world, with the countries containing their correct native plants, trees and flowers - many of them quite rare in this country, but flourishing in the mild Devon climate. Also plant centre (with seeds of some of the rarest plants), old-fashioned english garden and fine views from picnic area. Snacks; open Easter-Sept;

(01803) 872939; £2. The Linny in nearby Coffinswell is a charming old thatched pub.

Tuckers Maltings (Teign Rd) One of the few remaining working malthouses in the country, and the only one open to the public - every year they produce enough malt for 20 million pints of beer. Tours show all aspects of malting (you can touch the grain and taste the malt); they also have their own brewery. There's a hands-on section for children. Snacks, shop with over 200 speciality bottled beers (open all year); open Mon-Sat (plus Sun July-Aug) Good Fri-Oct, last guided tour starts 3.15pm; (01626) 334734; £5.25 (inc sample of beer).

NEWTON FERRERS/NOSS MAYO SX5548

Picturesque twin villages on very sheltered rocky wooded creek of Yealm estuary; besides modern development, there are some charming whitewashed cottages - and lots of yachting in summer. The riverside Ship is a good place for a meal; beware of rising tides if you park on the slipway. There are attractive walks from here along the estuary, then beyond to Gara Point and exposed cliff; largely NT. This can be reached in sections via the Noss Mayo—Holbeton coastal ridge rd.

NORTH BOVEY SX7184

A delightful peaceful Dartmoor village, not usually invaded by tourists: oak-shaded green with mounting block, stone cross, pump and ancient cottages - the 13th-c thatched Ring of Bells is a nice pub.

OKEHAMPTON SX5895

This bustling Dartmoor-edge working town has enterprising food in the Plymouth (West St), and a couple of things worth stopping for:

Museum of Dartmoor Life (West St) Due to reopen around May at the earliest, following extensive building work to improve disabled facilities, renovate the galleries and open a new restaurant. Well converted Victorian agricultural mill with interactive displays on local life, tourist information centre and working craft studios next door. Meals, snacks, shop, some disabled access; best to phone for opening dates; (01837) 52295; usually £2. The

Plymouth nearby has enterprising food.
Okehampton Castle The tower on a
steep grassy mound above the river is
remarkable above all for the way it stays
standing - a balancing act of ruined
masonry zigzagging up into the sky. It's
the biggest medieval castle in Devon,
with sections dating from 11th-14th c;
good woodland walks. Snacks, shop; cl
Nov-Mar; (01837) 52844; £2.60.
PAIGNTON SX8861
Largely a typical resort, with long
promenade between good sandy beach
and green; the little harbour is pretty,
with working fishing boats as well as
yachts. The original inland core has an
attractive red sandstone church with
some interesting buildings nearby, esp
Kirkham House, a handsome
sandstone Tudor merchant's house
with lofty hall. The formal and
subtropical lakeside gardens at
Oldway are colourful and free to
enter; in summer there are guided
tours of some rooms in the Versailles-
style colonnaded mansion (which now
serves as council offices) at their centre;
phone (01803) 557671; £1; (you can
also hire tennis courts here). Attractive
Elberry Cove between Paignton and
Brixham is altogether quieter. Decent
places for lunch include the Embassy
(Colin Rd), Inn on the Green (Esplanade
Rd) and Ship (Manor Rd, not far from
Preston beach).
**Paignton & Dartmouth Steam
Railway** (Queens Park Station, Torbay
Rd) One of the nicest such steam train
trips we know of - GWR steam trains
run from here right by the sea along the
spectacular Tor Bay coast; the front
Pullman coach is less crowded. You can
combine this with a boat Dartmouth—
Totnes, and bus Totnes—Paignton.
Dining train available on some Suns,
snacks, shop, disabled access; open
Mar-Oct (daily Jun-Sept) and selected
dates out of season; (01803) 555872 for
timetable; £6.60 return.
Paignton Zoo (St Michael's) Well run
and shown, with over 1,300 animals and
birds (many of them breeding) in 75 acres
of beautifully planted surroundings; it's
perhaps the country's most visually
appealing zoo, and lays a decent emphasis
on conservation. Also lakeside miniature
railway, play area and splendid hands-on

animal education centre for children.
Lots of events and feeding displays
throughout the day. Meals, snacks, shop,
good disabled access; cl 25 Dec; (01803)
697500; £8.25.
Quaywest Waterpark
(Goodrington Sands) Lively waterpark
(the water is heated so worth
considering even if the weather's not
that great) with a submarine themed
play zone and a play pool for the under-
5s, as well as 8 flumes and slides (inc the
highest and fastest flume in the
country); go-kart rides too (£3.50) and
regular Punch and Judy shows. Meals,
snacks, shop; open daily in summer (exc
in very bad weather); (01803) 555550;
£8.50. Across the road at Ski West you
can arrange jet ski rides, waterskiing,
pedalo and canoe hire and other
watersports; (01803) 663243.
PLYMOUTH SX4753
Apart from the area around the
Barbican most of the old parts of the
city were destroyed in World War II; in
parts it's like lots of other busy modern
towns. There are some interesting
escapes from the bustle, and in places
The Hoe has something of the feel of
smaller seaside promenades, with great
views out over the Sound, and for hardy
souls a newly reopened art deco
swimming lido at one end; decent food
from the Yard Arm (looking out in a
suitably nautical style) and the
Waterfront bar/restaurant. A statue of
Drake is a reminder that he's supposed
to have played his famous game of
bowls here; there's still a bowling green
close by. Cornwall St has an indoor
market. A tour bus can take you to the
main attractions, though it's perhaps
more fun on one of the **boat trips** run
by Tamar Cruises from Mayflower
Steps, off Madeira Rd, Barbican; (01752)
822105. There are also boats from here
to the **Mountbatten Peninsula**, a
former Ministry of Defence area now
open to the public; you can walk along
the breakwater, which goes right out
into The Sound with views back
towards the city. The ferries to
Torpoint in Cornwall put Antony
House and Mt Edgcumbe in very easy
reach. The Notte Inn (Notte St) has
enjoyable food, and the China House
(Sutton Harbour, with great views)

now has reliable food all day; or take a water taxi across to the cheerful 18th-c Boringdon Arms, set into the Turnchapel cliffs across the water.

Barbican Carefully restored since the war, a series of narrow twisty streets of old buildings W of working Sutton Harbour; photogenic - and evocative even in wet weather. New St is its oldest core. The Dolphin pub has original Beryl Cook paintings.

Black Friars Distillery (60 Southside St) Photogenic home of Plymouth Dry Gin, now the only english gin still made in its original distillery, founded in 1793. The building itself dates back much further, and has had periods as a monastery and a prison; they've recently expanded into adjacent buildings which were also originally part of the distillery. Tours include demonstrations of production, a film of the city's history and, of course, samples of the various gins made on the premises. Shop open all year; tours daily beginning Mar-24 Dec (limited opening over Christmas and New Year, phone to check), plus Sat Jan-Feb; (01752) 665292; £2.75, free if you visit the National Marine Aquarium. The nearby Queens Arms does excellent sandwiches.

City Museum & Art Gallery (Drake Circus) Friendly museum with well shown collections of mostly West Country interest; also changing exhibitions, and special events. Shop, good disabled access; cl Sun, Mon (exc bank hols) and 25-26 Dec; (01752) 304774; free.

Crownhill Fort 🅰 (Crownhill Fort Rd, just N) The biggest and least altered of Plymouth's Victorian forts, though from the road it looks little more than a wooded hill. Used by the Army right up to 1986, it's been well restored by the Landmark Trust, with barrack rooms, underground tunnels with new audio effects, secret passageways, and lookout towers to explore; children can run around quite freely. There's a new outdoor adventure area (and an indoor hands-on activity area) as well as a brass rubbings trail; the guns are fired daily at 1.30pm. You can stay here in a Victorian officer's flat (all year), and have the run of the place after dark. Meals, snacks, shop, partial disabled

access (lots of steep steps); cl Nov-Mar and Sat; (01752) 793754; £4.50.

Elizabethan House (32 New St) Splendid timber-framed Tudor sea-captain's house with period furniture. Shop; cl Mon and Tues, and Oct-Easter; (01752) 304380; £1.10. There's an Elizabethan garden just down the road at number 39.

Merchant's House 🅰 (St Andrew St) Well restored 16th-c jettied house, telling the city's day-to-day history in displays themed on tinker, tailor, soldier, sailor; also early Victorian apothecary's shop (open as a pharmacy Mon and Weds) and schoolroom. Shop; cl 1-2 pm, Sun, Mon (exc bank hols), and Oct-Easter; (01752) 304381; £1.10.

National Marine Aquarium (The Barbican) This enthralling, world-class aquarium goes from strength to strength - and it's now the first in the world to have a robotic shark (you can watch Roboshark swimming around recording the movements of the creatures around him). The centrepiece is an enormous walk-through tank, the size of a three-storey building and filled with two and a half million litres of water, to show off the sort of creatures you'd find in the Mediterranean: countless fish swirl above your head, below your feet and on either side, and, of course, there are sharks. There's plenty more to see: thousands of splendidly coloured and curiously shaped individuals are shown in elaborate indoor reconstructions of their natural habitats, starting with a moorland stream and bog, and passing through an estuary before arriving at the sea shore. A highlight is the largest collection of seahorse species in the world, and there are discovery pools for children to get a closer look at creatures like starfish. They've a good programme of talks and demonstrations. Meals and snacks (the café has nice views over Plymouth Sound), shop, disabled access; cl 25 Dec; (01752) 600301; £8 adults (tickets allow same day re-entry, and you can visit Black Friars Distillery free). The Thistle Park nearby in Commercial Rd has tasty food all day, and beers brewed next door.

Plymouth Dome (The Hoe) This state-of-the-art evocation of

Plymouth's past and present is interesting and fun. Using feel-part-of-it technology, you can stroll along lively Elizabethan streets, dodge press gangs, meet Drake and the Pilgrim Fathers, and come bang up to date with satellite and radar monitoring of current harbour action and weather. Their exhibition on the four Eddystone Rock lighthouses includes a virtual tour of Smeaton's Tower, and they've a popular film about the Blitz. Snacks, shop, good disabled access; cl Sun and Mon Nov-Easter; (01752) 603300; £4.50, £6 with Smeaton's Tower.
Prysten House (Finewell St) The city's oldest house: austere late 15th-c granite building with galleried courtyard. Unpretentious but quite atmospheric restored rooms feature a model of 17th-c Plymouth, and several yards of an ambitious tapestry showing american colonisation. Entry via neighbouring church, cl wknds; (01752) 661414; £1.
Royal Citadel (The Hoe) Unrivalled views of the city and sea from the ramparts of this magnificent 17th-c battlemented fortress. The gateway is striking, and the barracked parade-ground is still in use. Disabled access (though no facilities); admission by guided tour only, Tues 2.30pm May-Sept (01752) 266030; £3.
Smeaton's Tower (The Hoe) Colourfully striped 18th-c former Eddystone Rocks lighthouse, moved here 110 years ago, with a good view from the top if you like steps. Cl Sun and Mon Nov-Easter; (01752) 304849; £2, joint ticket with Dome available.
St Andrew's (St Andrew St) Bombed but lovingly restored, with stained glass by John Piper illustrating the city's history.

PLYMPTON SX5255
Saltram ☒ (2m W, off A38/A379 at Marsh Mills roundabout) Magnificent mostly 18th-c mansion still with pretty much all the original contents, and notable for its unaltered Robert Adam rooms. George II furnishings, decoration and paintings (strong on Reynolds, who as a regular guest advised on which other pictures to buy), interesting period kitchen, stately garden with orangery, and parkland by wooded Plym estuary. Tearoom, shop

and local art/crafts gallery (cl 21 Dec-Mar), disabled access; house cl Fri and all Nov-Mar (gardens open all year, exc Fri), best to check; (01752) 333500; £6.30, garden only £3.30; NT. The old town around Plympton St Maurice church is worth a look if you're here: attractive partly arcaded streets, very ruined motte and bailey castle, decent food at the George.

POWDERHAM SX9684
Powderham Castle ☒ The ancestral home of the Earls of Devon, badly damaged in the Civil War but elaborately restored in the 18th and 19th c. The richly decorated state rooms were used in the film adaptation of *The Remains of the Day*. Spectacular rose garden, home to Timothy the tortoise (who's more than 160 years old), spring woodland garden, a secret garden designed for children with ducks, rabbits, guinea-pigs and chinchillas, and broad deer park with views over Exe estuary; also tractor and trailer rides around the castle. Good guided tours, and lots of special events. Meals, snacks, a country store, some disabled access; cl Sat, and Nov-Mar; (01626) 890243; £6.90. The ancient waterside Anchor at Cockwood has good seafood.

PRAWLE POINT SX7735
Impressive scenery: wind-blasted gorse, grass and thrift above low but fierce cliffs, lending itself to a round walk, with a useful network of green lanes leading inland to the village of East Prawle, where the cheery Pigs Nose is a nice stop.

SALCOMBE SX7438
Steep narrow-streets fishing village, full of enjoyable holiday bustle in summer, with lots of souvenirs, bric-a-brac, boating shops, teashops and pubs overlooking sea; nearby beaches and coves. For **boat trips** and boat hire phone (01548) 843818, and there's a little maritime museum in Market St (cl 12.30-2.30pm, and Nov-Mar). The Fortescue is our readers' current favourite here for pub lunches.
Bolt Head/Bolt Tail Six miles of one of the best coast-path sections, with remote exposed clifftops, glorious coves, far views, well preserved Iron Age earth ramparts on Bolt Tail; all NT. Best access is via Overbecks, Soar Mill

Cove or Hope Cove.

Overbecks (South Sands; signed from Salcombe and Malborough) Named after the eccentric research chemist who lived here until 1937; among his possessions and inventions you can still see the Rejuvenator which he claimed 'practically renewed' his youth. For most the chief attraction is the luscious subtropical gardens, with terraced plantings among woodland, many rarities and plenty of palms and citrus fruits; outstanding late May-Jun for the magnolias, but worth a trip any time of year. Glorious views out to sea, also colourful statue garden, picnic belvedere and collections of dolls and lead soldiers. Snacks, shop; cl Sat (exc Aug), Fri in Oct, and all Nov-Mar (garden open all year); (01548) 842893; £4.60, £3.40 garden only; NT. Mill Bay nr here has one of the area's safest bathing beaches.

SHALDON SX9372
Interesting and colourful mix of seaside houses spanning 200 years of architectural fancy; some lovely corners esp down by water away from the centre, also much older cottages in Crown Sq. The London Inn and Shipwrights Arms, both under new management, have decent food. High grassy sandstone Ness overlooks the sea and Teignmouth, with a tunnel cut by the 19th-c landowner to a sheltered beach; the beautifully set Ness House up here is useful for food, too. There's a ferry from Teignmouth (exc 25 Dec, and times limited in winter), and the A379 to Maidencombe has sea views.
Wildlife Trust (Ness Drive) Specialist breeding centre for rare and endangered foreign birds, and small mammals inc monkeys. Shop; cl 25 Dec; (01626) 872234; £4.

SHARPHAM SX8158
Sharpham Vineyard & Cheese Dairy ⌂ Two self-guided trails (one alongside a river) take you through the vineyard at this attractive 500-acre estate that also includes a Jersey dairy farm (not open to the public). Shop; cl Sun (exc Jun-Aug), and Jan-Feb; (01803) 732203; £3.50 (inc wine and cheese tasting).

SLAPTON SANDS SX8343
One of the finest beaches in the country, six miles of almost straight shingle N of the lighthouse at Start Point, backed by hills in the S and by road, shingle bank, lake (Slapton Ley nature reserve, marked nature trail) and marsh, then low cliffs, in the N. Good for out-of-season desolation, sheltered from W winds, with a storm-ruined village at Hallsands, and salvaged tank memorial to a US Normandy landings practice disaster at Torcross.

SOURTON SX5390
Highwayman An extraordinary pub, one bar recalling a galleon, the other a sort of fairy-tale fantasy, and the garden demonstrating yet more exuberant imagination - all meticulously done by the owners, not some brewery theme pub.

SOUTH WEST COAST PATH SX5446
The finest part of Devon's S coast for walkers is between Plymouth and Brixham - much of it quite unspoilt. In summer ferries cross the rivers (exc the River Erme S of Ermington, which you have to cross at low tide); phone (01752) 896237 for details.

SPARKWELL SX5858
Dartmoor Wildlife Park & Westcountry Falconry Centre ⌂ A variety of animals inc big cats (feeding time 3.30pm) in 30 acres of countryside. Also falconry centre with displays at 12pm and 4pm (Easter-Oct exc Fri, weather permitting), adventure playground and picnic area. Meals, snacks, shop, disabled access; (01752) 837209 (info line); £7.95. The Treby Arms has reliable modestly priced food.

STICKLEPATH SX6494
Finch Foundry No longer producing the sickles, shovels and tools for which it was known in the 19th c, but the waterwheels and machinery all still work, with regular demonstrations throughout the day. Snacks, shop; cl Tues, and Nov-Mar; (01837) 840046; £3; NT.

STOKE GABRIEL SX8457
Steep village above a sheltered side-pool of the Dart estuary, with 14th-c church (with ancient yew) and Church House (pleasant for lunch) perched prettily on a high cobbled terrace.

TEIGNMOUTH SX9473
A popular resort for family holidays, with good beaches, windsurfing and so on, some handsome 19th-c streets and active docks, and on French St a decent

local history **museum** (cl Sun, and Nov-Apr (exc Easter Fri, Sat and Mon); (01626) 777041; £1). The riverside Ship (Queen St) has good food, all day in summer.

TORQUAY SX9163
The busiest of the area's resorts, good for evening strolling, with palm trees and rocks, promenades, colourful gardens, decorous guesthouses and huge hotels, broad Victorian streets and upmarket shops. The sheltered beaches around here are cleaner than many along this coast. Summer bustle centres around the attractive harbour, with lots of shops, cafés, boat trips, and an aquarium. In summer a **cliff railway** takes care of a dizzy swoop from Oddicombe Beach to the high wooded clifftop; (01803) 328750; £1.35 return. The quaint Hole in the Wall (Park Lane) does good value food. The waterfront between Princess Pier and Beacon Cove is currently undergoing a £21 million rejuvenation which includes new bridges to let visitors walk around the whole harbour; it's on track for completion by the spring.

Bygones 🖼 (Fore St, St Marychurch) Enthusiastically reconstructed life-sized Victorian street, with well stocked period shops and rooms, model railway, and re-created World War I trench with sound effects and cooking smells. Open till 9.30pm (6pm Fri-Sun) July-Aug. Snacks, shop, disabled access to ground floor only; cl 24-25 Dec; (01803) 326108; £4.50.

Cockington Winding lanes of olde-worlde thatched cottages and bric-a-brac/craft shops in sheltered village with millpond etc, well preserved by Torbay Council; adjoining 500-acre park. The Drum pub (a useful stop) was designed to match by Lutyens in 1934. Terribly pretty, and very touristy in season, with open horse-drawn carriages.

Kents Cavern Showcaves 🖼 (Ilsham Rd, Wellswood) The oldest directly dated archaeological site in Britain; continuing excavations often make scientists reconsider their theories about prehistoric life. Good guided tours really bring out the history of the caves, and colourful stalagmites and stalactites add to the eerie atmosphere. Very well presented, and

definitely worth an hour or so if you're in the area; in summer they do spooky evening tours (booking essential), and there are special visits at Christmas. The facilities are currently being modernised, and it's the only cave in the UK to have a licensed bar. Summer meals, snacks, shop, disabled access (with prior notice); cl 25 Dec; (01803) 215136; £6, evening tours £6.30.

Living Coasts See separate family panel on p.160.

Model Village (Hampton Ave, Babbacombe) Hundreds of one-twelfth scale buildings in four acres of miniaturised landscape, beautifully done and continually expanding. Try coming at dusk between Easter and Oct, when the scenes are prettily floodlit. Meals (a new bar was added in 2003), snacks, shop, good disabled access; cl 25 Dec; (01803) 315315; £6.20 - a little pricey, but it's probably the best of its type (you may also have to pay for parking). The beach here has safe bathing water, and the Cary Arms (Beach Rd) is good, with great views.

Torquay Museum 🖼 (529 Babbacombe Rd) The county's oldest museum, this includes galleries on the Devon farmhouse, and Agatha Christie (the author was born in Torquay), plus finds from ancient local caves and local history. Shop; cl Sun (exc pm Easter-Oct), and Christmas wk, best to phone in winter; (01803) 293975; £3.

Torre Abbey 🖼 (Kings Drive) Torquay's oldest building; some of the earlier parts of the abbey remain, inc the medieval barn, gatehouse, undercrofts and ruined Norman tower, but they've been eclipsed by the later house with its 18th- and 19th-c period rooms. The main feature is Devon's largest art gallery, and there's an Agatha Christie room full of her possessions; also garden and palm house. Meals, snacks, shop; open wk before Easter-Oct; (01803) 293593; £3.50.

TOTNES SX8060
Busy in summer, but still keeping most of its charm then, particularly early in the morning. The picturesque Elizabethan area known as **The Narrows** is very atmospheric, esp along the High St down to the arch at the top of Fore St, with quaint pillared

arcades (on Tues mornings May-Sept there's a little Elizabethan and craft market). There's a working harbour, and you can walk some way downstream on either side of the River Dart. Behind the church of St Mary's (which has a super rood screen), several rooms in the 11th-c **guildhall** may be open (wkdys mid-Oct-Easter); it was originally part of a Benedictine priory. Perhaps unexpectedly, Totnes has quite a New Age flavour: there's even a flotation tank to wash away city stresses. The Kingsbridge Inn (Leechwell St) has enjoyable food. The **South Devon Railway**, which stops here, is described under Buckfastleigh, and the highly recommended river trips are described under Dartmouth.

Devonshire Collection of Costume (43 High St) Period costumes and accessories from the 18th c to the present, from ordinary work clothes to high fashion, with changing annual exhibitions. Shop; cl wknds, and Oct-May (open by appointment in Oct); (01803) 862857; £2.

Totnes Castle Part Norman, part 14th c, these classic circular remains were lucky enough to avoid any battles, so the keep is pretty much intact. There's a tree-shaded inner lawn, and lovely views of the town and down to the river. Snacks, shop; cl Nov-Mar; (01803) 864406; £1.80.

Totnes Museum (Fore St) Elizabethan merchant's house with galleried courtyard, herb garden, and display on the inventions of Totnes boy Charles Babbage, creator of one of the earliest computers. Shop; cl wknds, and mid-Oct-Easter; (01803) 863821; £1.50.

TUCKENHAY SX8156
This gives a pretty one-mile stroll E along wooded Bow Creek, from the Maltsters Arms - good food here.

WEMBURY BAY SX5148
A walk here gives good views, starting from Wembury past the church at the start of NT clifftops; woods and pastures on opposite shore, Plymouth shipping in the distance. The Odd Wheel (Knighton Hill) has decent food.

WIDECOMBE IN THE MOOR SX7176
One of the most visited villages on Dartmoor, immortalised by the trip of

Uncle Tom Cobbleigh and all to Widecombe Fair (the granite-carved village sign shows them all crowded on to their old grey mare); get here before lunchtime to avoid the coach parties. The **church**, known as the Cathedral of the Moors, has a distinctive disproportionately high tower. The adjoining 16th-c **church house**, now the church hall, is worth a look. Next door, the **Sexton's Cottage** is a NT and Dartmoor National Park information centre and gift shop; cl 24 Dec to mid-Feb. The Post Office Stores has good ice-cream and local honey. The well run reconstructed Olde Inne in the village is very popular with tourists, but for more of a Tom Cobbleigh flavour try the Rugglestone Inn just S. The finest view over the village is from **Honeybag Tor**, to the north. The **Shilstone Rocks Riding Centre** organises horse-riding over Dartmoor, beginners welcome. Disabled access; (01364) 621281; from £18 an hour.

YEALMPTON SX5751
They open the stunning illuminated **Kitley caves** here only to small groups or individuals with a special interest in the subject; phone (01752) 880885 to book a free guided tour. Above ground 50 acres of pretty woodland and riverside walks with many varieties of plants, shrubs and trees. The Volunteer does good food. Nearby is a good **farm shop**; (01752) 880925, and seasonal **pick-your-own** fruit and veg; (01752) 880688.

YELVERTON SX5167
Paperweight Centre (Buckland Terrace) Private collection of hundreds of glass paperweights, all sizes and designs, inc collectors' pieces. Extensive paperweight shop, disabled access; open daily Apr-Oct, by appointment in winter; (01822) 854250; free. The Rock (A386) is a good family pub.

Other attractive villages, all with decent pubs, include Belstone SX6293, Christow SX8384, Churston Ferrers SX9056, Coffinswell SX8968, Denbury SX8168, waterside Dittisham SX8654, Holbeton SX6150, seaside Maidencombe SX9268, Malborough SX7039 and Stokeinteignhead SX9170.

Where to eat

ASHPRINGTON SX8157 **Durant Arms** *(01803) 732240* Friendly gable-ended dining pub opposite the church, with two attractive bar rooms, several open fires, good enjoyable bar food, well kept beers, and friendly service; disabled access. £21|**£6.95**

BABBACOMBE SX9265 **Tea Rose Tea Rooms** *49 Babbacombe Downs Rd (01803) 324477* Charming and very popular small tearoom with inside and outside tables in a garden opposite the sea, with waitresses in period dress, generous cream teas and snacks, and proper leaf tea; disabled access.|**£4.20**

BANTHAM SX6743 **Sloop** *(01548) 560489* Near a sandy beach (good for surfing), this 16th-c nautical village inn has good bar food inc lots of fish, hearty breakfasts, and decent beers and wines; comfortable bdrms, self-catering cottages; cl pm 25 and 26 Dec. £24|**£6.50**

BOLBERRY SX6939 **Port Light** *(01548) 561384* Popular even on dismal winter wkdys, this clifftop former RAF radar station (easy walk from Hope Cove) is warmly friendly, with good home-made food in attractive bar and restaurant, super sea views, woodburner, and good outdoor children's play area; bdrms; cl 1-8 Dec, and all Jan; disabled access. £23|**£6.95**

CHAGFORD SX6987 **22 Mill Street** *22 Mill St (01647) 432244* Cheerfully decorated little restaurant with a relaxed, friendly atmosphere, plenty of loyal customers, highly enjoyable modern cooking, lovely puddings, and a carefully chosen wine list; cl Sun, am Mon and Tues, 2 wks Jan, 1 wk late May; children must be well behaved. £20 lunch, £27 dinner

CHERITON BISHOP SX7695 **Old Thatch** *(01647) 24204* Bustling 16th-c inn with good bar food from big menu, interesting puddings, beamed bar and big open stone fireplace, real ales from small independent breweries, and friendly service; bdrms; cl Sun pm Nov-Feb, 25 Dec. £19.95|**£5.95**

COCKWOOD SX9780 **Anchor** *(01626) 890203* Friendly and very popular pub by the harbour with small low-ceilinged rambling rooms and lots of good fresh fish dishes - 30 ways of serving mussels, 12 of serving scallops, 10 of oysters, and so forth, no smoking restaurant, well kept real ales, 10 wines by the glass, and 50 malt whiskies; cl 25 Dec pm; disabled access. £27|**£6.95**

CORNWORTHY SX8255 **Hunters Lodge** *(01803) 732204* Welcoming and popular country local with a two-roomed low-ceilinged bar, cottagey restaurant with 17th-c fireplace, tasty lunchtime food and imaginative evening meals, well kept real ales, decent wines, and plenty of seats outside; disabled access. £18|**£5**

DARTMOUTH SX8751 **Café Alf Resco** *Lower St (01803) 835880* On three levels (the one on street level is partly open-air), this is a bustling, popular café with a friendly easy-going atmosphere, people dropping in all day to read the papers over a cappuccino, simple wooden furnishings, old newspapers decorating the ceiling, regular live jazz, a heated marquee with plenty of seats, and good hearty breakfasts (served all day), morning coffee and lunchtime snacks; bdrms; cl Mon, Tues, end Jan/beg Feb; disabled access. £29|**£4**

DARTMOUTH SX8751 **Carved Angel** *2 South Embankment (01803) 832465* Black and white timbered restaurant, airy and attractive, overlooking the quay, with delicious meals using carefully chosen absolutely fresh produce - superb fish, impressive puddings and fine cheeses, wines in every price range, and a smart yet friendly atmosphere; no smoking; the cheerful (and much cheaper) **Carved Angel Café** at 7 Foss St, under the same owners, has very good simpler but imaginative food in the form of morning coffee, light lunches, afternoon tea, and wknd evening meals (they've just opened a new branch in Exeter, by the cathedral); main restaurant cl Sun pm, Mon am, 3 days Christmas; children welcome lunchtime (over 10 in evening); partial disabled access. £39.50/2 courses £18.50

DARTMOUTH SX8751 **Cherub** *10 Higher St (01804) 832571* Dartmouth's oldest building (already 300 years old when Sir Francis Drake used it), this has a bustling bar, liked by locals, an upstairs dining room, decent food, and well kept ales; no children. £24|**£7.25**

GULWORTHY SX4473 **Horn of Plenty** *(01822) 832528* On the edge of Dartmoor in quiet flower-filled gardens, this relaxed, refurbished Georgian no smoking restaurant-with-rooms has excellent carefully cooked food using top-quality local produce inc lovely puddings and cheeses (wonderful breakfasts, too), a good wine list, and vine-covered terrace for aperitifs; comfortable bdrms; cl Mon am, 24-26 Dec; disabled access. £35

HARBERTON SX7758 **Church House** *(01803) 863707* Ancient village pub with magnificent medieval panelling, attractive old furnishings, generous helpings of interesting daily specials, well kept beers, and decent wines; bdrms; children in family room; cl pm 25 and 26 Dec and 1 Jan. £22|**£5.95**

KINGSBRIDGE SX7443 **Crabshell** *The Quay, Embankment Rd (01548) 852345* Famous old dining pub, very popular for its lovely waterside position and fresh local fish and shellfish - they also do picnics and take-aways; quick friendly staff, well kept real ales, decent wines, warm winter fire, and live music Thurs; cl 25 Dec pm; disabled access. £17|**£5.50**

LYDFORD SX5285 **Dartmoor Inn** *(01822) 820221* The overall feel in the small bar here is of civilised but relaxed elegance: matt pastel paintwork in soft greens and blues, naïve farm and country pictures, little side lamps supplemented by candles in black wrought-iron holders, basketwork, dried flowers, fruits and gourds, and perhaps an elaborate bouquet of fresh flowers; limited choice of lunchtime bar snacks plus creatively cooked and beautifully presented restauranty food using top-notch local produce; well kept real ales, an interesting and helpfully short wine list, and polite young staff; tables on terrace, with a track straight up on to the moors. £28

MARLDON SX8663 **Church House** *(01803) 558279* Well run bustling pub with several different attractive bar areas and restaurant, candles on tables, bare boards, hops and dried flowers, imaginative daily-changing food, well kept real ales, ten wines by the glass, and seats outside; bdrms; no children. £30|**£8.50**

NEWTON ABBOT SX8468 **Two Mile Oak** *(01803) 812411* Old coaching inn with relaxed atmosphere, beamed lounge and an alcove just for two, a mix of wooden tables and chairs, and fine winter log fire; traditionally furnished, beamed and black-panelled bar , well kept real ales, decent wines, and enjoyable food; picnic-sets on terrace. £28.|**£6.25**

PLYMOUTH SX4754 **Chez Nous** *13 Frankfort Gate (01752) 266793* Classic informal french evening bistro with long-serving owners, a red, white and blue colour scheme, careful cooking of fresh local produce, esp fresh fish and fine puddings, some distinguished wines, and friendly atmosphere; cl Sun, Mon, 3 wks Feb, 3 wks Sept; children over 12; partial disabled access. £50

RATTERY SX7461 **Church House** *(01364) 642220* One of Britain's oldest pubs, with big open fires, friendly customers and staff, good bar food, decent wines and beers, fine malt whiskies, and nice dog and cats; peaceful setting; disabled access. £19|**£6.75**

TORCROSS SX8241 **Start Bay** *(01548) 580553* Notable and very popular fresh seafood generously served in busy thatched pub overlooking three-mile pebble beach; farm cider; family room; cl 25 Dec pm ; partial disabled access. £18.70|**£5.95**

TORQUAY SX9064 **Mulberry Room** *1 Scarborough Rd (01803) 213639* Popular no smoking restaurant-with-rooms, with good innovative food using local produce, and very enjoyable home-made cakes and scones for afternoon tea; cookery demonstrations; bdrms; cl Mon, Tues (exc to residents); disabled access. £25

TOTNES SX8060 **Greys Dining Room** *96 High St (01803) 866369* No smoking Georgian house with pretty china on a handsome dresser and partly panelled walls, lots of teas plus herb and fruit ones, sandwiches, salads and omelettes as well as lots of cakes and set teas; cl Weds and Sun; no pushchairs and children must be well behaved; partial disabled access|**£6.50**

North Devon & Exmoor

**Outstanding coastal scenery, particularly below Exmoor;
plenty of peace and quiet, but some good family outings too**

Exmoor is full of interest for walkers (and drivers), and far less visited than
Dartmoor. Though part lies in Somerset, we've covered the whole of the
moor area in this chapter (some places such as Dunster within the
boundary of the National Park but outside the moor itself are described in
the Somerset chapter). Some of the best parts of the Tarka Trail, a popular
route for walkers and cyclists, are on and around the moor. Other inland
areas are largely secluded farmland. The twisty wooded Taw Valley is
pretty; the A377 gives drivers some good views here, though not quite so
outstanding as the Exeter—Barnstaple rail journey, one of England's finest.

Aside from the few resorts and the famously pretty Clovelly and
Combe Martin, much of this area is still untouched by tourism, and long
stretches of coastline remain almost empty all year round. Even
Ilfracombe, the main resort, is not too touristy; pleasant and distinctive,
with plenty for families, it stays alive even out of season. In contrast the
lower-key beach resorts such as Woolacombe and Westward Ho!
virtually shut down when the season's over, making their amazing beaches
perfect for lonely wanderings then. A magnificent coastal path includes
some sensational cliff walks. Lundy Island is a windswept offshore
wilderness, and getting there adds to the fun.

Alongside its appeal to people who like getting away from organised
tourism, the area also has plenty of well orchestrated family
entertainment. The Milky Way in Clovelly is a good rainy day excursion,
and the sheep races and duck trials at the Big Sheep at Bideford are
tremendous fun. Watermouth Castle at Ilfracombe, with its captivating
fairy-tale world, and its sister park Once Upon A Time at Woolacombe
(lots of rides and activities), are delightful for small children. At Combe
Martin you'll find an excellent blend of wildlife and dinosaurs, and Exmoor
Zoological Park (South Stowford) and Exmoor Falconry & Animal Farm
(Allerford) are other appealing outings for animal-lovers.

History is brought to life by the enthusiastic guides at the Torrington
heritage centre. With its eccentric collections, Arlington Court is
fascinating to look round, the gardens at lavish Knightshayes Court in
Bolham are glorious, and the RHS Rosemoor gardens near Torrington are
full of interest.

Where to stay

BISHOP'S TAWTON SS5928 **Halmpstone Manor** *Bishop's Tawton,
Barnstaple, Devon EX32 0EA (01271) 830321* **£100***; 5 pretty rms. Quietly relaxing
small country hotel with log fire in comfortable sitting room, enjoyable food in
panelled dining room, good breakfasts, caring service, an attractive garden, and nice

views; plenty to do nearby; cl Christmas, New Year, and Feb; dogs welcome away from restaurant

BRAUNTON SS4437 **Saunton Sands Hotel** *Saunton, Braunton, Devon EX33 1LQ (01271) 890212* **£166**; 75 light airy rms inc family rms, many with lovely sea views. Family-run hotel with stunning views over five miles of sandy beach and grounds with outdoor swimming pool (there's also an indoor swimming pool), and squash and tennis courts (Saunton Golf Club is on the doorstep); cocktail bar, comfortable terraced lounge, very good imaginative food and a thoughtful wine list in elegant dining room, and helpful polite staff; live music and entertainment; gym, sauna, and solarium; very good for families with full-time nursery, a full programme of entertainments, games room and junior putting green, and adventure area; partial disabled access ☺

BUCKLAND BREWER SS4220 **Coach & Horses** *Buckland Brewer, Bideford, Devon EX39 5LU (01237) 451395* **£60**; 2 rms above bar (so could be noisy for children until 11.30pm). Welcoming well preserved 13th-c thatched village pub with cosy beamed bar, log fires in inglenook fireplaces, enjoyable food, dining room, and pleasant garden; partial disabled access; dogs in bar on lead

CADBURY SS9005 **Beers Farm** *Cadbury, Exeter, Devon EX5 5PY (01884) 855426* **£44**; 2 rms. Set in several acres with lovely views across to the Raddon Hills, this non-working farm is quiet and comfortable (and no smoking) with friendly, helpful owners and good breakfasts; packed lunches on request; garden plants for sale; lots to do nearby

CHITTLEHAMHOLT SS6520 **Highbullen** *Chittlehamholt, Umberleigh, Devon EX37 9HD (01769) 540561* **£140***, plus special breaks; 40 comfortable and elegant, often spacious rms in main building and various attractively converted outbuildings. Victorian 'gothick' mansion in huge wooded parkland and gardens with lots of wildlife, fishing (several beats), 9-hole golf course, indoor tennis court and swimming pool, table tennis, and squash court; consistently good food in intimate restaurant overlooking the valley, busy little bar, library, and relaxed informal service (no reception, you ring a bell and wait); children over 8

CLAWTON SX3499 **Court Barn Hotel** *Clawton, Holsworthy, Devon EX22 6PS (01409) 271219* **£70***, plus special breaks; 8 individually furnished rms. Charming country house in five pretty acres with croquet, 9-hole putting green, small chip-and-putt course, and tennis and badminton courts; comfortable lounges, log fires, library/TV room, good service, imaginative food and award-winning wines (and teas), and a quiet relaxed atmosphere; cl first 2 wks Jan; dogs welcome in bedrooms

LYNMOUTH SS7249 **Rising Sun** *Mars Hill, Lynmouth, Devon EX35 6EG (01598) 753223* **£98***, plus special breaks; 16 comfortable and cosy rms, plus 3 new suites. Thatched 14th-c inn with lovely views over the little harbour and out to sea, oak-panelled dining room, beamed and panelled bar with uneven oak floors, enjoyable food and wines, charming terraced garden, and lots of nearby walks; children over 7; dogs welcome in bedrooms

LYNTON SS7249 **Highcliffe House** *Sinai Hill, Lynton, Devon EX35 6AR (01598) 752235* **£56***, plus special breaks; 6 well equipped attractive rms. Carefully decorated no smoking Victorian house with wonderful views over Lynton, the sea, and wooded countryside; two comfortable sitting rooms, good food in candlelit dining conservatory, and kind staff; cl Dec-Jan; no children

NORTHAM SS4528 **Yeoldon House** *Durrant Lane, Northam, Bideford, Devon EX39 2RL (01237) 474400* **£95***, plus special breaks; 10 individually decorated rms. Quietly set hotel in two acres by the River Torridge, with a warmly friendly and relaxed atmosphere, a comfortable lounge, good food using local produce in the attractive dining room, and helpful service; lots to do nearby; cl Christmas; dogs welcome in bedrooms

OAKFORD SS9122 **Newhouse Farm** *Oakford, Tiverton, Devon EX16 9JE (01398) 351347* **£54***, plus special breaks; 3 rms. 17th-c longhouse on edge of Exmoor, with a cottagey sitting room, beams, and country dining room serving home-made food inc their own bread, pâtés and puddings, and using the best local ingredients; bring your own wine; cl Christmas; no children

PORLOCK SS8846 **Oaks** *Doverhay, Porlock, Minehead, Somerset TA24 8ES (01643) 862265* **£110***, plus special breaks; 8 airy and pretty rms. Particularly welcoming and spotless Edwardian country house looking down from Exmoor to Porlock Bay, with surrounding lawns and oak trees, a relaxed atmosphere and log fire in attractive lounge, and good unpretentious cooking in attractive no smoking restaurant; cl Nov-Mar; children over 8; dogs welcome in bedrooms

PORLOCK SS8846 **Seapoint** *Redway, Porlock, Minehead, Somerset TA24 8QE (01643) 862289* **£54***, plus winter breaks; 3 rms. Surrounded by the Exmoor hills and with views of Porlock Bay, this no smoking Edwardian guesthouse has a comfortable sitting room with winter log fire, a friendly and relaxing atmosphere, enjoyable home-made food in candlelit dining room, and fine breakfasts; cl Dec/Jan; they are kind to children; dogs welcome in bedrooms

SELWORTHY SS9346 **Hindon Farm** *Selworthy, Minehead, Somerset TA24 8SH (01643) 705244* **£50***; 3 rms. Organic Exmoor hill farm of 500 acres with sheep, pigs, cattle, donkeys and ducks; lovely walks from the door including award-winning conservation trail, adjoining heather moors; fine breakfasts using their own organic bacon, sausages, eggs and fresh baked bread; self-catering farmhouse wing plus cottage, and free organic produce hamper on arrival; organic farm shop also; dogs welcome

SHEEPWASH SS4806 **Half Moon** *Sheepwash, Beaworthy, Devon EX21 5NE (01409) 231376* **£80**, plus special breaks; 14 rms inc some in converted stables. Civilised heart-of-Devon hideaway in colourful village square with 10 miles of private salmon, sea trout and brown trout fishing on the Torridge, a neatly kept friendly bar, solid old furnishings and big log fire, good wines, lovely evening restaurant, lunchtime bar snacks; cl 20-27 Dec; limited disabled access; dogs welcome away from dining room

WEST BUCKLAND SS6630 **Huxtable Farm** *West Buckland, Barnstaple, Devon EX32 0SR (01598) 760254* **£60***, plus special breaks; 6 rms. 16th-c farmhouse surrounded by carefully converted listed stone buildings, open fields, fine views, sheep, chickens, and pigs; candlelit dinner with wholesome home-made food using home-grown produce, home-made wine and bread, a relaxing sitting room, and beams, open fireplaces with bread ovens, and uneven floors; sauna, fitness room, tennis court, games room, and play area with swings, sandpit and wendy house; good for families; cl Dec/Jan (but open New Year) ☺

WEST PORLOCK SS8746 **Bales Mead** *West Porlock, Somerset TA24 8NX (01643) 862565* **£75**; 3 comfortable rms with thoughtful little extras. This quiet and relaxing no smoking Edwardian house has lovely Exmoor views towards the sea, a particularly pretty garden, charmingly decorated sitting room with log fire and baby grand piano, super breakfasts (no evening meals), and friendly helpful new owners; cl Christmas/New Year; no children

WOOLACOMBE SS4543 **Woolacombe Bay Hotel** *Woolacombe, Devon EX34 7BN (01271) 870388* **£120**, plus special breaks; 64 rms. Carefully extended Victorian hotel in six acres of gardens running down to a splendid three-mile Blue Flag beach; quiet comfortable lounges, elegant high-ceilinged restaurant with chandeliers, bustling bistro for light lunches, two bars, and splendid facilities for children: indoor and outdoor pools and paddling pools, a children's club plus teenage activities, a crèche, discos and bands, board games and books, and billiard room, pool tables and table tennis; 9-hole approach golf, tennis, squash, and gym, sunbed, jacuzzi, and steam room; golf, riding and surfing nearby, and lovely unspoilt surrounding countryside; cl Jan-mid Feb; dogs in mews apartments ☺

Please let us know what you think of places in the *Guide*. Use the report forms at the back of the book, write us a letter or log on to www.goodguides.co.uk

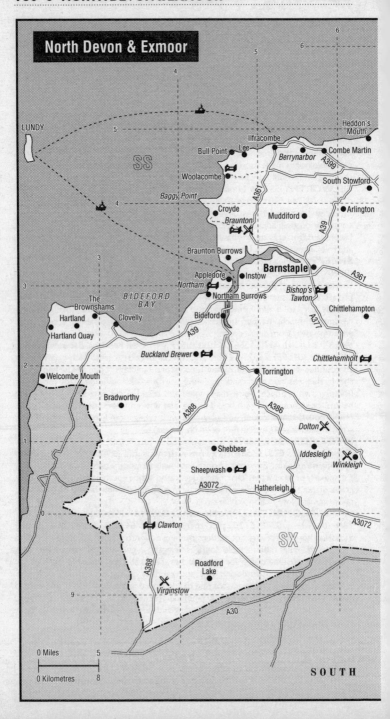

North Devon & Exmoor

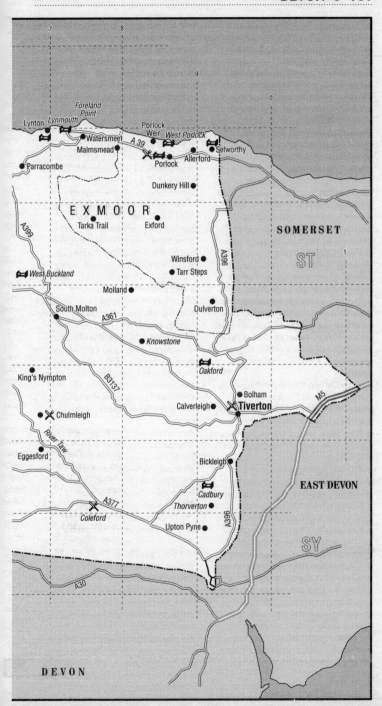

DEVON

To see and do

ALLERFORD SS9047

Pretty stone-built village with lovely packhorse bridge, and enthusiastic **West Somerset Rural Life Museum** with occasional summer craft demonstrations; open wkdys Easter-end Oct; (01643) 862529; £1.50.

Exmoor Falconry & Animal Farm Friendly 15th-c farmstead with animals to feed, twice-daily animal handling with snakes, lizards, rabbits, ferrets and parrots, and flying displays; special events all year such as hawk walks and clay-pigeon shooting. B&B in the 15th-c farmhouse, meals, snacks, shop, disabled access; cl Tues-Thurs Nov-Feb; (01643) 862816; £5.50.

APPLEDORE SS4630

A pretty centre of narrow cottagey streets off the quayside road which looks out over the Taw estuary, and ship- and boat-building in the yard just upstream. There's a pedestrian ferry over to Instow (depending on the tide) run by Tarka Cruises; (01237) 476191. Good value food and superb estuary views in the Royal George and the Beaver.

North Devon Maritime Museum (Odun House, Odun Rd) Good museum exploring a different topic in each room. Shop, disabled access to ground floor only; cl 1-2pm, am Apr and Oct, am wknds, and Nov-Mar; (01237) 422064; £1.

ARLINGTON SS6140

Arlington Court (A39) From its Victorian heyday up to 1949 Rosalie Chichester filled this early 19th-c house with model ships, stuffed birds, holiday souvenirs - in fact anything she could get her hands on; her assemblages have been watered down since, but there's still quite a fascinating medley (look out for Tom Thumb's miniature carriage and suit). The grounds have attractive landscaped gardens and a number of shetland ponies and sheep, along with Victorian garden and conservatory, woodland and lakeside nature trails, and an unusual collection of carriages (in a new wing) and horse-drawn vehicles; rides available. There is also a batcave (you can watch rare lesser horseshoe bats on CCTV, and use a joystick to zoom in on particular ones). Meals, snacks, shop, disabled access to ground floor only; usually cl Nov-Mar, but as we went to press opening days were undecided, so phone for details; (01271) 850296; *£6.20, garden only £4; NT. The Pyne Arms at East Down is nice for lunch.

BARNSTAPLE SS5533

The main regional shopping centre: pedestrianised, with a good deal of unforced charm in the older parts. Interesting buildings include an imposing 18th-c colonnaded arcade on the Great Quay, a lofty Victorian market hall (markets every day exc Sun), almshouses behind the church, more off the square by the long old stone bridge, and some interesting shops. It's still a working port, though in a very small way now. Panniers (Boutport St) has decent food all day. In summer you can hire bikes at the main railway station (01271) 324202; £9.50 a day; a good ride is the one along the disused rail track up to Torrington. The surviving mainline **Exeter—Barnstaple** line (known as the Tarka Line), mostly tracking along closer to the River Taw than the road does, is one of the finest of all train rides for scenery.

Art Hotel (off B3230 towards Ilfracombe) There's an appealing blend of old and new at this friendly late Victorian hotel surrounded by woodland. Inside, the house is decorated with antiques and contemporary art, while new works are continually added to the evolving sculpture garden; they also run a programme of lectures, music recitals and poetry readings. Meals, snacks; garden and gallery cl am and Mon-Tues pm (plus Weds pm Nov-Apr), and 15 Dec-15 Jan; (01271) 850262; £4.50. The hotel has a tennis court and heated outdoor swimming pool; B&B £29.50 (wknd £34.50).

Barnstaple Heritage Centre ⊞ (Queen Anne's Walk) You pass through an ornate Queen Anne colonnade to reach this centre, which relates the 1,000-year history of the town with the help of computer and hands-on displays. Shop, disabled access; cl Sun, 25-26 Dec, 1 Jan; (01271) 373003; £2.50.

Disused railway paths Down at sea level sections of the former track from Barnstaple and Bideford can be walked or cycled (Tarka Trail Cycle Hire at the railway station; (01271) 324202; £9.50 a day for an adult). The best section is the one from Barnstaple through Instow and Bideford up to the Puffing Billy at the former Torrington Station. In autumn and winter particularly this gives close views of the wading birds massed on the tidal sands of the estuary, and year-round the section up to Torrington is very attractive. The longest cycle ride here is 28 miles without touching a road.

Marwood Hill Gardens (Marwood; off A361 towards Braunton) 18 well kept and colourful acres inc rare trees and shrubs, small lakes, extensive bog garden, clematis, camellias, alpines and eucalyptus, and national collections of astilbes (best in July) and tulbaghias. Snacks, plant centre, some disabled access; cl 25 Dec; (01271) 342528; £3. The Ring o' Bells at Prixford is very handy for lunch.

Museum of North Devon (The Square) Local history museum with interactives for children, and temporary exhibitions upstairs. Disabled access; cl wknds, a wk over Christmas and New Year, and winter bank hols; (01271) 346747; free.

BICKLEIGH SS9306

Bickleigh Castle Charming moated and fortified manor house, and its 11th-c chapel is said to be Devon's oldest complete building; it has been well worth visiting, with a fair bit to amuse children, but as we went to press was changing hands, so may possibly no longer be open for visits - phone for details; (01884) 855363. The big riverside Fishermans Cot is a useful food stop.

Bickleigh Mill and Maize Maze (Bickleigh Mill Farm) Bustling family-run place with a working waterwheel, resident potter, and an 11-acre maize labyrinth which can grow over head-height; you can also fish for trout (£10 inc rod hire and bait). Meals, snacks, shops, limited disabled access; open daily exc 25-26 Dec (maze late Jun-end Sept only); (01884) 855419; free (exc maze; £2.50).

BIDEFORD SS4526

Quiet hillside town now bypassed, with notable medieval bridge and some pleasant old streets, partly pedestrianised, behind the Quay. The day-trip boat for Lundy (a good long day) sails from here year round, though not every day, and only rarely in March; phone (01271) 863636 for times. One of the oldest streets is Bridgeland St, and up towards the top of Bridge St are a couple of antiques or antiqueish shops. The Joiners Arms (Market Pl) has decent food, and the Vagabond Cavalier (Cooper St) does good value italian meals.

Big Sheep 🖼 (Abbotsham, off A39 2m W) Exuberant sheep centre, with splendidly entertaining sheep steeplechasing (usually around 3.45pm), when sheep with knitted jockeys on their backs race 200 yards from their field towards the prize of extra food. Even better are the duck trials at midday, miniature sheepdog trials with the sheep replaced by ducks; there are more traditional sheepdog demonstrations too. Other displays take in everything from shearing and bottle-feeding to milking, with plenty of opportunities to get close to the animals (lambs are born throughout the year). Decent adventure play area, lots under cover. Home-made meals and snacks (good teas), shop, disabled access; usually open daily Easter-Dec, wknds Dec-Easter exc 3 wks over Christmas and New Year - but best to check; (01237) 472366; £6.50, tickets are valid for unlimited return visits for a week for £2. The nearby Thatched Inn is an enjoyable family dining pub.

BOLHAM SS9615

Knightshayes Court Lovely woodland garden with acres of unusual and even unique plants, esp lovely in spring but a glory at any time of year. Alpine and more formal gardens, ancient yew topiary, attractive walks, and good Exe Valley views; they've recently restored the walled garden too. The spooky-looking house itself is extravagantly ornate Victorian Gothic, with elaborate painted ceilings and décor, and a restored minstrels' gallery. The original plans were even more over-the-top, but when the horrified owner saw them he sent the architect William Burges packing, though one room has been reconstructed as Burges intended it. Meals, snacks, shop and plant centre, disabled access; cl Nov-Mar (house cl Fri); (01884) 254665; £5.70, garden only £4.10; NT.

BRADWORTHY SS3213
A pleasant jumping-off point for walks, with some quiet local strolls on the common, or over by the Tamar Lake a couple of miles SW. The thatched Bradworthy Inn has good food.
Gnome Reserve 🖼 (West Putford, 2m E) One of the most delightfully silly places in the area, woodland and wildflower meadows populated by hand-painted and individually modelled pixies. They lend you gnome hats and fishing rods so that resident gnomes will think you're one of them. The setting is pretty (flowers and plants are labelled), and very small children love it. Shop, snacks, disabled facilities but limited access; cl Nov-20 Mar; (0870) 8459012; £2.45.

BRAUNTON BURROWS SS4532
This vast nature reserve expanse of great swelling dunes, grazed by little soay sheep, is easily reached from the B3231 W of Braunton (red flags warn if there's shooting on the range in the southern part here). The Mariners Arms in South St in Braunton itself is a pleasantly untouristy pub, and the Seafood Bistro (Caen St/Chalenors Rd) has friendly service and good fresh locally caught fish.

BROWNSHAMS, THE SS2825
These isolated farmhouses, recent NT acquisitions, give walkers good quiet access to the woods, cliffs and clifftop farmland W of Clovelly.

BULL POINT SS4646
There's a lighthouse here, and dramatic cliff walks between here and Morte Point; Mortehoe makes a good start point, with an interesting church, and enjoyable food in the Ship Aground.

CALVERLEIGH SS9214
An attractive village with a fine **church** and decent pub.

CHITTLEHAMPTON SS6127
Cobbaton Combat Collection 🖼 (off A377) Private collection of british and canadian World War II vehicles which always has something new, quite tightly packed under cover but looking ready for action; also mock-ups of wartime scenes, and wartime memorabilia. Summer snacks and picnic area, shop, some disabled access; cl Sat exc July and Aug, and wknds Nov-Easter, but phone to check; (01769) 540740; £4.50. The Exeter Inn at Chittlehamholt has good food.

CHULMLEIGH SS6814
Lovely unspoilt village, and a good base for touring the coast and Taw Valley. The Globe has attractively priced home cooking.

CLOVELLY SS3124
One of Devon's most famous views, down the very steep old cobbled street, free from traffic and with flower-covered cottages either side, to the tiny harbour below. It's a delightful village, best appreciated out of season. At any time of year you'll have to park up at the top, outside the village, then pay £4 to pass through a turnstile, and walk down. The Red Lion is pleasantly placed down by the quay; if you can't face the climb back up, a Land Rover can drive you back from behind here (summer only, £2.50). Up towards the A39 is a big Iron Age hill fort, Clovelly Dykes, and along the coast the beachside hamlet of Bucks Mills is well worth a visit. The woods, cliffs and clifftops farmland W of Clovelly is attractive walking country. The moorland road down from Stibb Cross on the A388 via Woolfardisworthy is good, and the woodland Hobby Drive toll road is the area's best coast drive.
Clovelly Court These parkland gardens have tranquil sea views, and a fine walled garden and restored Victorian greenhouse. Meals, snacks, shop, disabled access. Cl 25 Dec; (01237) 431200; £1.50 (Land Rover ride to Court, return £2.50).
Milky Way (Downland Farm) Plenty of action for families in this adventure park, and as it's one of the biggest covered attractions in the region it's handy for a rainy day. Games and rides are based on the theme of alien life -

one of them, the fun Clone Zone ride, is interactive. Good big indoor and outdoor play areas (inc one for toddlers), an assault course and archery as well as mini golf, laser target shooting, new dodg'ems, birds of prey (twice-daily displays), and a little railway. There's also an animal barn with lambs and kids for children to bottle feed, a chick hatchery, and you can watch ferret racing too; cl wkdys Nov-Mar (exc school hols), 25-26 Dec and 1 Jan; (01237) 431255; £7.50, may be reduced in winter when less is open.

COMBE MARTIN SS5846
A string of former smallholdings and cottages scattered down a lovely sheltered valley, with an odd pub, the Pack of Cards, built to celebrate a cards win - four floors, 13 doors, 52 windows. There's a little fishing harbour in the shingly cove between the cliffs, and the Fo'csle is useful for lunch.

Combe Martin Wildlife & Dinosaur Park 🖼 (A399) A good place for children, with plenty of animals and birds in acres of woodland, inc sea lions, a pair of rare snow leopards, and meerkats in a huge desert enclosure. Also a dinosaur museum, and meticulously researched life-size dinosaurs, some of which move and roar - like the towering *Tyrannosaurus rex*. A themed train ride runs through the 26 acres of gardens, which have rare and tropical plants; there are wallabies to feed, daily falconry displays, and a tropical butterfly house. Meals, snacks, shop; cl Nov-22 Mar; (01271) 882486; £10.

CROYDE SS4439
A magnet for surfers, this clean-sand village has a good family pub, the Thatched Barn. Baggy Point W of here has a path good enough for wheelchairs.

EGGESFORD SS6811
This quiet Taw Valley village has a 14th-c **church**, and a garden centre set in the walled garden of a ruined house; refreshments on a terrace with lovely views. A good base for inland walks (and a stop on the Barnstaple—Exeter rail line): in Flashdown Wood, up wooded Hayne Valley to Wembworthy, or through Heywood Wood, where the mound of the former

castle gives good views (and there are picnic sets).

EXMOOR SS7739
(We include the Somerset part of the park here; Allerford and Lynton are listed separately, and Dunster is in the Somerset chapter.) Excellent walking, both inland and along the coast, and less busy than Dartmoor in summer. In some places it's been more tamed than Dartmoor - drained and resown with richer-growing grasses for better pasture. But it's still a wild place, with hawthorns and low oak trees bent and gnarled by the winds, and (unlike Dartmoor) wild deer; Exmoor is probably the part of Britain where hunting traditions are most deeply rooted. Where it drops away sharply to the sea, fast streams and rivers cut deeply into beautiful wooded valleys. Note that some of Exmoor's moorland paths have a disconcerting habit of fizzling out without warning. It's also rewarding territory for drivers, with plenty of good views; the B roads are generally less congested than others.

Dulverton SS9127 The main town for Exmoor is a civilised place, with a handsome old stone market house, and a fine bridge over the river which has cut this steeply wooded valley. The Lion Hotel is useful for lunch, and the area's main information centre is at the S end of Fore St; (01398) 323841.

Dunkery Hill SS8941 Exmoor's great ridge walk, with Dunkery Beacon as its high point surveying a huge chunk of SW England and S Wales (as tramping boots have worn three feet off the top of the Beacon, walkers are asked to take a bag of stones and earth up to deposit there). It is easily walked from the nearby road; a handy place to leave the car is Webbers Post (which is also good for local pottering). It can also be incorporated into longer walks from Horner Woods or Luccombe.

Exford SS8538 Prettily set in a sheltered valley by a small streamside green; the church up the hill a bit is well worth a look. The Crown, with a delightful water garden, is good for lunch, and satisfying walking is to be had along the Exe to Winsford.

Heddon's Mouth Cleave SS6548 A secretive wooded combe running between rugged hills from the beautifully placed Hunters Inn to the sea - an easy walk which can be extended along the cliffs at two levels to Woody Bay to the E. W of Hunters Inn is the terraced walkway known as the Ladies Mile, along a charming valley nr Trentishoe.

Malmsmead Natural History Centre SS7947 Badgworthy Water is the focus of a walkers' path from Malmsmead which takes you into the very heart of Lorna Doone country - it gets wilder and more remote with every step southwards (the surrounding moors provide a handful of return routes). From the **Malmsmead Natural History Centre**, the Exmoor Natural History Society run leisurely two-hour strolls through the striking scenery every Weds mid-May to mid-Sept, plus Tues and Thurs July-Aug, at 2pm; very enthusiastically done, and free (you can get a cup of tea afterwards for a small donation); Mr and Mrs Cornish have full details on (01984) 631859. The Exmoor Sandpiper at Countisbury up towards Lynton is a useful food stop.

Parracombe SS6644 A lovely little village worth visiting in its own right, but particularly interesting is **St Petroc's church**, one of the few churches to have an unspoilt medieval fabric completely untouched by Victorian restoration, all flagstones and Georgian box pews; this may be locked Nov-Easter, but key from custodian then. The interesting Fox & Goose has good food using local ingredients.

Porlock SS8846 Hilly village, with a lot of traffic, but some attractive thatched cottages; the Ship with its distinctive lighthouse-like chimney and nice garden is a good stop here, and near it is a nature trail to Dunkery Beacon.

Porlock Weir SS8647 This harbour tucked below wooded cliffs is much quieter than nearby Porlock, though it does get a lot of summer visitors; decent food at the thatched pub (like the one up at Porlock, also called the Ship). It has a pebbly beach and wooded cliffs to the W - you can walk this way to remote **Culbone church**, the smallest complete church in the country.

Selworthy SS9146 Gloriously unspoilt village, rated by some readers as the most attractive they've ever seen, with groups of white thatched cottages around a prettily planted hillside green looking out over Exmoor. The church is a gem, with a fine waggon-roof; Selworthy Beacon, some way above the village, is a four-way viewpoint nr a minor dead-end road that climbs steeply up from Minehead.

Tarka Trail This long-distance figure-of-eight signed path runs nearly 200 miles, linking Exmoor, Dartmoor and the N Devon coast, following the route of Henry Williamson's *Tarka the Otter* - and is most enjoyable with a copy of the book. One beautiful section is the route around **Pinkworthy Pond** and The Chains, reached from the car park a couple of miles along the B3358 E of Challacombe. It's even more popular with cyclists than walkers.

Tarr Steps SS8632 The River Barle's most famous feature, the finest of all the stone-and-slab clapper bridges for packhorses. The path along the river, which runs between Simonsbath and Dulverton, is uneven and surprisingly slow-going in places.

Watersmeet SS7448 Paths run eastward out of Lynton along the Lyn River to Watersmeet (1½m E), where the Hoaroak Water tumbles down to meet the East Lyn in a series of rocky cascades among steeply picturesque oak woods. There's a discreet NT refreshment pavilion here, cl Nov-Mar. Don't miss the wonderful return route on the Tarka Trail/Two Moors Way high above the valley to the S (some steep sections). Riverside paths head on further upstream, to the prettily set Rockford Inn (a good base for walks - food finishes at 2pm). Just N of Watersmeet, the Foreland Cliffs are the highest in the country and have dramatic views.

Winsford SS9035 A quiet and attractive village below high hills, with the River Exe lacing through its countless bridges. The Royal Oak is good for lunch.

HARTLAND SS2424

Hartland Abbey ⌨ Fine old (and still lived in) house on the site of an Augustinian abbey, with elegant rooms (the drawing room is modelled on the

House of Lords), paintings by Gainsborough and Joshua Reynolds among others, several interesting historic documents, exhibition of old photography, woodland walks and peacock-filled parkland. There's a restored Victorian fernery and shrub gardens, an 18th-c walled garden, and a wild-flower walk leading to a peaceful cove. Cream teas, shop; house open pm Easter Sun and Mon, pm Weds, Thurs, Sun and bank hols (plus pm Tues July-Aug) Apr-Oct, garden open pm Sun-Fri Apr-Oct, best to check; (01237) 441264; £6, grounds only £3. The village has **craft shops** inc working potter, and windsor chair-maker (children's sizes too).

HARTLAND QUAY SS2324
Grand isolated spot at foot of toll road (no fee winter), on jagged coast which looks a dramatic cross between illustrations for geology textbooks and ones for a shipwreckers' manual. Down by the sea is a wonderfully maritime old inn (cl winter), and the **museum** covers four centuries of smuggling and shipwrecks - even big ships still go down here; cl Oct-Easter; phone Hartland Quay Hotel for details, (01273) 441218; £1. For walkers, the cliffs around here are much more dramatic than those at nearby Hartland Point (which also has a toll gate). Just S at Spekes Mill Mouth the sea-eroded valley leaves the river spewing down the cliff in a **seaside waterfall**.

Docton Mill 🔢 (Milford) Extensive and interesting sheltered streamside garden and recent woodland plantation, largely naturalised, beside an ancient restored watermill. It's particularly attractive in spring. Snacks inc good cream teas, plant sales; cl Nov-Feb; (01237) 441369; £3.50 They have a couple of bedrooms you can stay in.

HATHERLEIGH SS5404
An attractive hillside village - even the church slopes - with a handsome inn (the George) and a good **pottery** (20 Market St).

ILFRACOMBE SS5147
Picturesque resort around busy harbour sheltered by high cliffs, with terraces of late Victorian boarding houses and small hotels looking out over it from their perches among the trees of the steep bay. There are period resort buildings and gardens, and even tunnels cut through the rock to a former Victorian bathing place. The 14th-c chapel above the harbour mouth has doubled as a lighthouse for over 450 years; the **lifeboat station** can be visited (donation requested). **Holy Trinity church** (Church St) is worth a look for its richly carved 15th-c waggon-roof, one of the most striking in the area. The ancient George & Dragon is a nice spot for lunch. In summer the newly restored paddle steamer *Waverley* or the traditional cruise ship *Balmoral* run cruises from the pier to Lundy, Minehead, and other places - even as far as Swansea. Bicclescombe Park (A361 just S) has a restored 18th-c **cornmill**. The best cliff walks are to the W of the town, towards Lee Bay.

Ilfracombe Museum (Runnymede Gardens) Enthusiastic town museum, a bit like looking through someone's attic (cl pm and wknds Nov-Mar; £1.50).

Old Corn Mill & Pottery 🔢 (A399 just E) Well restored early 16th-c mill; pottery demonstrations, and the chance to throw your own pot. Snacks, shop, disabled access to pottery and tearoom only; cl Nov-Mar; (01271) 863185; £2.50.

Old Railway This disused railway trail above Ilfracombe is popular with walkers and cyclists, with a tunnel, interesting plants, and attractive scenery inc the lakes of Slade Reservoirs. For a one-way walk it's best to do it in reverse, for better views - and it's downhill all the way; Red Bus 31 or 31A to Lee Bridge or Lee Cross (or to the Fortescue Hotel for a preliminary bracer); (0870) 608 2608 for bus information.

Watermouth Castle 🔢 This fine 19th-c structure overlooking the bay has been transformed into a world of gnomes, goblins, trolls and fairy-tales, with slides, carousels and a musical water show; also miniature golf, various rides, swingboats, carousel and a maze. Very much for families with young children (the ones who'll enjoy it most). Snacks, picnic area, shop, disabled access; open Easter-Oct, but phone for times as they vary each week; (01271) 867474; £8.50.

INSTOW SS4728
At the mouth of the Torridge estuary, this has an expanse of tidal sands, with dozens of moored boats beached on them at low tide. The Boathouse has good food and views.
Tapeley Park 🏛 The very pretty italianate garden with rococo features and walled kitchen garden is the main draw, though there's also a pets corner, play area, and woodland walk. Lovely views down to the sea. Teas and snacks in period dairy, plant sales, some disabled access; cl Sat, and Nov-Mar; (01271) 342558; £4 (house tours £2.50 - you need to give a week's notice).
KING'S NYMPTON SS6819
An attractive village with a fine **church** and decent pub.
LEE SS4846
This pretty village in a sheltered woody valley has an attractive ancient pub, the Grampus. There are good cliff walks between Lee Bay and Ilfracombe.
LUNDY DAY TRIPS SS1344
(boat from Bideford or, in summer, Ilfracombe) Well worth considering if you're in Devon for more than just a few days. The island's best known for the migrant birds that come here in spring and autumn, but the remoteness and loneliness are also a powerful draw - the permanent population is around a dozen. Lovely walks along its seven miles of formidably high cliffs, windswept rough pastures, small church, evocative castle ruins, two lighthouses (one the highest in Britain), wandering goats, small soay sheep and ponies, and the chance of seeing seals (especially in autumn), the introduced small sika deer, and, in Apr and May, the island's trademark puffins. Accommodation can be arranged through the Landmark Trust; (01628) 825925. The Marisco Tavern is the place to eat. The return boat trip (1-2 hrs each way) is £25; (01271) 863636 for sailing times.
LYNTON SS7249
This beautifully placed hilltop village tucks into the wooded seaside gorge where the East and West Lyn tumble down to the sea. One way of getting down to its pretty harbourside extension, Lynmouth, is a 19th-c funicular cliff railway; £2.75 return. The

most delightful walks in N Devon are around here. Lynton clearly shows its origins as a Victorian resort in one of the many areas then known as Little Switzerland, with hillside villas (now quiet boarding houses), photogenic corners and some older cottages. Craft shops and so forth; lots of trippers during the day in summer. The Bridge Inn (B3234 - lovely walk up The Lynway from Sinai Hill) has good food under its new landlady, and the Rising Sun down by the harbour has a good restaurant. The Valley of Rocks is an easy (and enjoyable) walk from the village; Watersmeet is also within reach.
Exmoor Boat Cruises Informative boat trips, with talks about sea birds and coastal geography, leave the harbour from 11am daily, but very much dependent on weather and tide, Apr-Oct; check when rough (01598) 753207; from £6 for a 40-min trip.
Glen Lyn Gorge Carefully restored after the tragic flood of 1952, with pretty walks and an exhibition on water power (the village uses hydro-electricity). Some disabled access. Exhibition cl Nov-Mar (reduced admission £2), gorge open most winter days, circumstances permitting; (01598) 753207; £3. They have decent holiday flats and cottages in a peaceful setting.
Lyn & Exmoor Museum 🏛 (Market St) In the old part of the upper village, this engagingly simple museum of local history is in an 18th-c cottage. Usually cl 12.30-2pm, Sat, am Sun, and Nov-wk before Easter; (01598) 752225; £1.
Valley of Rocks A great valley bowl with steep crags and pinnacles of rock dividing it from the sea (and a dreadful unscreened car park smack in the middle). It's reached by an easy coast path from Lynton, or by paths over Hollerday Hill (wooded, but opens out dramatically on top). The cliff-skipping goats here are ancient feral stock.
MOLLAND SS8028
An attractive village with classic box pews in its wonderfully untouched **church**, and good value food in the London Inn beside it - a classic archetypal Exmoor-edge unspoilt pub.
MUDDIFORD SS5535
Blakewell Trout Farm Working

trout fishery, fish farm and watergarden with ornamental fish; good for experts and beginners, with friendly, knowledgeable staff. Snacks and picnic area, good shops, disabled access; cl 25-26 and 31 Dec, 1 Jan; (01271) 344533; free, £1 for fun fishing in the little pool. The Muddiford Inn is an inexpensive family pub.

NORTHAM BURROWS SS4430
Dunes, sand slacks and meres behind a pebble ridge, with the Atlantic rollers swinging in along the rock-strewn Saunton Sands beyond - deserted out of season and stimulating then for lonely walks; in summer a popular family beach.

ROADFORD LAKE SX4290
Trout fishing Serious trout fishing in this carefully landscaped reservoir; cl 13 Oct-21 Mar; £13.50 day permit. Full watersports centre, meals, snacks, shop, disabled access for fishing from bank; if you want a boat you will have to book 24hrs in advance; (01409) 211507.

SHEBBEAR SS4409
An interesting and attractive tucked-away village, with the odd Devil's Stone by the green (and a decent pub named after it), and a working wood-fired pottery; (01409) 281271.

SHEEPWASH SS4806
Quiet village with cob-and-thatch houses around the green; the Half Moon is useful for lunch. A mile N is Duckpool Cottage traditional wood-fired **pottery**.

SOUTH MOLTON SS7126
An attractive central square and imposing church - and its farming roots show in the Thurs cattle market. The 18th-c Town Hall has a local history **museum** (opening dates were undecided as we went to press, phone for details; (01769) 572951; free), and monthly art-and-craft shows. The Corn Dolly (East St) is nicely decorated with its namesakes and is ideal for afternoon tea, while the Mill (cl Weds; off A361 at Bish Mill roundabout) is a pleasant family food pub.

Quince Honey Farm (North Rd) The biggest wild-bee farm in the world, with observation hives looking right into the centre of the colonies. Meals, snacks, shop (lots of honey and their own beeswax skin and hair care products); cl Nov-Easter (though shop stays open); (01769) 572401; £3.50.

SOUTH STOWFORD SS6540
Exmoor Zoological Park (off B3226 N of Bratton Fleming) Good-sized collection of rare and endangered creatures, many of which breed successfully throughout the year. Children can feed the smaller animals or play on the assault course, and there are good views from the well landscaped grounds; regular activities in summer inc wallaby and guinea-pig feeding, face painting and birds of prey displays. Snacks, shop, disabled access; cl 21 Dec-1 Jan; (01598) 763352; £5.95. The Old Station House at Blackmoor Gate is a pleasant dining pub.

TIVERTON SS9512
Formerly prosperous wool town, well worth wandering around; **St Peter's church** is magnificently decorated with rich carving, and other grand buildings include the Jacobean council offices. The four showrooms of the **Tiverton Craft Centre** showcase the work of over 170 local craftsmen (cl Sun). The White Ball (Bridge St) is useful for food all day. In summer there are 2½-hr **horse-drawn boat trips** along the attractively restored canal from the wharf; booking advisable (01884) 253345; open Apr-Oct; £7.30. They also hire out rowing boats and motor-boats.

Tiverton Castle ⊞ The handsome castle was built in 1106 as a Royal fortress dominating the River Exe, and still has its Norman tower and gatehouse, as well as one of the best assemblages of Civil War armour and arms; pretty gardens too. You can stay in apartments in the oldest parts of the building. Shop, disabled access to ground floor and garden; open pm Sun, Thurs and bank hol Mon Easter-Jun and Sept, pm Sun-Thurs July and Aug; (01884) 253200; £4.

Tiverton Museum of Mid-Devon Life ⊞ (Beck's Sq) A mid-19th-c school houses this large local history museum, with two waterwheels, an excellent railway gallery, a display on the work of the wheelwright, and a collection of farm waggons; shop, disabled access; cl Sat pm, Sun, and

Christmas-Jan; (01884) 256295; £3.50.

TORRINGTON SS4919

Quiet dairy-farming town on a ridge above the River Torridge, with some attractive buildings inc 14th-c Taddiport Chapel (for a former leper colony), the imposing Palmer House, and a rather grand church built to replace the original blown up in the Civil War. There are good views from the neatly mown hill above the river, and other nearby strolls on the preserved commons surrounding the town. The Black Horse is useful for lunch.

Dartington Crystal 📷 (Linden Cl) You can tour the factory (last tour 3.15pm); there's a useful visitor centre, and reputedly the biggest glass shop in the country. They get very busy on wet days in summer - best to phone and check tour availability. No tours wknds and bank hols, shop cl 25-26 Dec, Easter Sun; meals, snacks, disabled access (not to tour); (01805) 626242; £4.50 (discount voucher allows two for the price of one).

Downes 📷 (A386 Torrington—Bideford, nr Monkleigh) Fine big woodland garden with interesting flowering trees and shrubs, lovely landscaped lawns, and great views. Plant sales; open daily Easter to mid-Jun, then by appointment till Sept; (01805) 622244; £2.

RHS Garden Rosemoor 📷 (off A3124 just S) A wonderful place, constantly being developed and updated by the Royal Horticultural Society; marvellous rare trees, shrubs, and other plants in charmingly landscaped sheltered woodland setting, rose, stream and bog gardens, foliage and plantsman's garden, and trails for children. Meals, snacks, picnic area, shop, disabled access; cl 25 Dec; (01805) 624067; £5.

Torrington 1646 (South St car park) This lively heritage centre brings to life one of the lesser-known battles of the Civil War, fought here in February 1646. Actors, all in period clothes, and rarely stepping out of character, work hard to get children involved. The scene-setting first part is a fairly

traditional exhibition of Civil War history, where you can try on a helmet or find out from touch-screens whether you'd have been a Cavalier or Roundhead. Then you're taken back to a reconstruction of the town on the night of the battle; a 17th-c local ushers you away from the battle to safety, taking you through various situations, until you get to the church. Outside, army stragglers will try to sell you their armour and weapons, and they'll show you how to charge into battle, and let you examine their swords; they've introduced daily weaponry displays, and you can watch musket balls being made in the traditional way. There's a reconstructed 17th-c garden, and they now do tours of the real town. Snacks, and picnic area, shop, disabled access; cl Sun, and a few days over Christmas; (01805) 626146; £6.95.

UPTON PYNE SX9197

Appealingly unspoilt village, the basis of Barton in *Sense and Sensibility*. The Agricultural in Brampford Speke is a good dining pub, brewing its own beer.

WELCOMBE MOUTH SS2118

Rather a rough drive down, but an attractive spot, and the cliffs around have possibilities for wild coast walks.

WOOLACOMBE SS4843

The clean beach here is one of the best in Britain, and its Atlantic breakers draw quite a few surfers. The Rock at Georgeham has good value food and a great conservatory for children, and the back road to Mortehoe is scenic.

Once Upon a Time (Old Station, B3343 inland) Run by the same people as Watermouth Castle in Ilfracombe, this is a super place for children up to about 11, with lots of rides and other activities; there's a driving school that even offers tests. Snacks, shop, disabled access; open Apr-end Sept, but times and days vary so phone to check; (01271) 867474; £3.50, £5.75 children.

Other attractive villages with decent pubs include Berrynarbor SS5646, Buckland Brewer SS4220, Iddesleigh SS5708, Knowstone SS8223, Thorverton SS9202 and Winkleigh SS6308.

Where to eat

BRAUNTON SS4836 **Squires Fish Restaurant** *Exeter Rd (01271) 815533* First-class fish and chip take-away and restaurant with really excellent fish, good wines, friendly service and attractive airy surroundings; cl Sun (but open school summer hols then), 25-26 Dec; disabled access. £12.50|**£3.80**

CHULMLEIGH SS6814 **Old Bakehouse** *South Molton St (01769) 580137/580074* Thatched 16th-c merchant's house with lots of beams, a flower-filled courtyard, and dining room serving morning coffee, light lunches and afternoon teas (plus breakfast and dinner for residents); no smoking; charming bdrms; cl Sun pm, Mon; children over 5; disabled access. £25.50|£6

COLEFORD SS7701 **New Inn** *(01363) 84242* Comfortable thatched 14th-c inn with good interesting food, an extensive wine list, well kept real ales, four nicely furnished areas, winter log fire, and attractive garden with seats on decking along the stream; bdrms; cl 25-26 Dec. £24.95|**£6.95**

DOLTON SS5712 **Union** *Fore St (01805) 804633* Relaxed and friendly old pub with good interesting genuinely home-made food using first-class produce, well kept real ales, and decent wines; comfortable little lounge, characterful lower bar with chatty drinking area and tables for eating, and charming owners; bdrms; cl Weds, 1st 3 wks Feb; children over 12. £23|£5

PORLOCK SS8647 **Andrews on the Weir** *(01643) 863300* Victorian villa housing a restaurant-with-rooms overlooking the harbour; country house-style décor, imaginative modern british cooking using first-class local produce (the Exmoor hill lamb, fish freshly landed on the nearby quay, and West Country cheeses, are excellent), lovely puddings, and a well chosen wine list; cl Sun pm, Mon, all Jan; children over 12; dogs welcome in bedrooms £43.50/2-course lunch £11.50

TIVERTON SS9512 **Four and Twenty Blackbirds** *43 Gold St (01884) 257055* Friendly teashop with beams, a mix of old tables and chairs, lots of interesting things to look at, and delicious food (all home-made); cl Sun.|£4

VIRGINSTOW SX3892 **Percy's Country Hotel and Restaurant** *(01409) 211236* Carefully renovated and interestingly designed restaurant-with-rooms in 16th-c longhouse set in 40 acres (which provide quite a bit of the organic produce used in the no smoking evening restaurant); good imaginative seasonal modern cooking (super bread and puddings) and a well chosen wine list; comfortable spacious bdrms; children over 12; disabled access. £37.50/2 courses £20

WINKLEIGH SS6308 **Pophams** *Castle St (01837) 83767* Tiny bustling place for morning coffee and lunch - bring your own wine - with particularly good interesting food, and relaxed happy atmosphere; cl Sat-Weds, and Feb; no children. £30

Special thanks to Mrs K L Anderson, Dave Irving, B and K Hypher, Tamsin Shelton, Derek and Sylvia Stephenson, Yvonne Rogers, E G Parish, M G Hart, Karen Scott

We welcome reports from readers

This *Guide* depends on readers' reports. Do help us if you can – in return, we offer a discount on the next edition to people who've helped us with reports for it. Tell us what you think about places already in it, and anything extra you think we should say about them. And send us your ideas for inclusion in the next edition: places to visit, eat at or stay in, attractive drives or walks, maybe even unusual shops you know of. Use the card in the middle, the report forms at the end, or just write – no stamp needed: *The Good Britain Guide*, FREEPOST TN1569, Wadhurst, E Sussex TN5 7BR. Or log on to www.goodguides.co.uk

DORSET

Great for families, with a really varied seaside, from bustling Bournemouth to spectacular fossil-packed coastal scenery; interesting and unusual attractions, rewarding towns and untouched countryside

The classic seaside resort of Bournemouth has seven miles of good beaches, and a civilised and spacious spread of comfortable resort areas and leafy suburbs. Its close neighbours Poole (beautiful gardens, lively harbour and fun waterpark) and Christchurch (interesting buildings, and an engagingly eclectic museum) have much to offer in their own right. Weymouth has a great range of attractions: highlights for families include the excellent Sea Life Park and Victorian fort. Elegant Lyme Regis is smaller and more individual.

Dorchester has a good deal to offer too, from teddies to Tutankhamun (and this year we've added the Terracotta Warriors Museum). There's plenty for Thomas Hardy fans here and elsewhere in the county; his books (and films of them) are vividly conjured up by particular Dorset villages and tracts of countryside. Sherborne (some attractive buildings including Sherborne Castle), Shaftesbury and Blandford Forum (the Royal Signals Museum is lively) are smaller towns well worth visiting. Wimborne Minster is rewarding - impressive 17th-c Kingston Lacy (superb paintings) and beautiful Knoll Gardens particularly stand out; the model village is worth a look, and there's a new farm and nature park.

Forde Abbey at Thorncombe is on the must-see list, combining a lovely house with beautiful gardens; Chickerell, Beaminster and Minterne Magna are other worthwhile destinations for plant-lovers. The tank museum at Bovington Camp has quite a bit for families (Lawrence of Arabia's Clouds Hill is nearby), and in Tolpuddle you can learn more about the eponymous martyrs. Bird-lovers find the centuries-old swannery at Abbotsbury enthralling (there are interesting subtropical gardens here too).

Monkey World at Wool is our Dorset Family Attraction this year, and other animal-based treats include Putlake Adventure Farm at Langton Matravers and well run Farmer Palmers at Organford - best for younger children, who also like the theme park at Hurn. Moors Valley Country Park on Ashley Heath is great for letting off steam and, in contrast, Stapehill Abbey is ideal for a laid-back afternoon.

Ninety-five miles of coast between Orcombe Point in Devon and Old Harry Rocks (see Studland) in Dorset has been declared a World Heritage Site, because of its geological importance; this 'Jurassic Coast' gives Dorset some spectacular scenery. Striking coastal features include Lulworth Cove, the rugged Isle of Purbeck, Portland Bill, and the tremendous sweep of Chesil Beach and its great lagoon near East Fleet. A coastal path, often with magnificent views, runs the length of the county. Ask in the Tourist Information Centres about the Explorer ticket - a good buy here if you're going to be doing much travelling on buses.

Inland, the countryside has a subtle understated appeal, with secluded valleys, narrow lanes threading through peaceful farmland, and tucked-away villages (Milton Abbas best of all - a good day out). The central area's chalk uplands cut by intricate valleys give some splendid high viewpoints - not to mention the prehistoric giant cut into the hillside north of Cerne Abbas. In May the bluebells of Bere Wood and Delcombe make for lovely walks. The west's intimate farming country feels untouched by time, with ancient monuments such as the impressive earth ramparts of Eggardon Hill. The heathland W of Poole Harbour, partly planted with conifers, has a quite different character - largely flat tank training ground W of Weymouth, a more interesting roaming ground for nature-lovers towards Studland Bay with its fine beach. Off Poole, Brownsea Island is a good place to run around and explore, with lots of wildlife.

Where to stay

ABBOTSBURY SY5785 **Abbey House** *Church St, Abbotsbury, Weymouth, Dorset DT3 4JJ (01305) 871330* **£65***; 5 pretty rms. Partly 15th-c house (said to have been the Abbey infirmary) with 17th and 18th-c additions, and set in gardens which slope down to the mill pond, behind which stands the impressive Abbey Tithe Barn, the largest in England; in the corner of the garden stands the only surviving Benedictine water mill in this country; comfortable, homely sitting room, reasonably priced and enticing lunches and teas in attractive country-style dining room, and friendly, efficient service

BOURNEMOUTH SZ1091 **Langtry Manor** *26 Derby Rd, Eastcliff, Bournemouth, Dorset BH1 3QB (01202) 553887* **£139**, plus special breaks; 25 pretty rms, some in the manor, some in the lodge. Built by Edward VII for Lillie Langtry, with lots of memorabilia, relaxed public rooms, helpful friendly staff, and good food inc Edwardian dinner every Sat evening; no children; disabled access; dogs welcome in bedrooms

BRIDPORT SY4691 **Britmead House** *West Bay Rd, Bridport, Dorset DT6 4EG (01308) 422941* **£60**, plus special breaks; 8 rms. Extended Victorian hotel with lots to do nearby, comfortable lounge overlooking garden, attractive dining room, good food, and kind helpful service; disabled access; dogs welcome in bedrooms

CHURCH KNOWLE SY9380 **Bradle Farmhouse** *Bradle, Wareham, Dorset BH20 5NU (01929) 480712* **£50**, plus special breaks; 3 spacious rms. Fine Victorian stone-built house on 550 acres of working farmland with long views, good breakfasts in homely dining room with its woodburner, helpful owners, and a relaxed friendly atmosphere; good nearby pub for meals; cl 25-26 Dec; children over 8

CORFE CASTLE SZ0080 **Knitson Old Farmhouse** *Knitson, Corfe Castle, Wareham, Dorset BH20 5JB (01929) 422836* **£40***, plus special breaks; 2 no smoking rms, 1 with shared bthrm. Big ancient cottage on working farm with sheep and Jersey cows, large garden with hens and horses and children's play area; comfortable sitting room with flagstones and woodburner, and good evening food by arrangement using home-reared pork and lamb and free range eggs served in the spacious kitchen; they are kind to families

CORFE CASTLE SY9681 **Mortons House** *45 East St, Corfe Castle, Wareham, Dorset BH20 5EE (01929) 480988* **£124**, plus special breaks; 17 individual rms inc 2 suites. Fine, recently refurbished Elizabethan manor house in walled garden, with an oak-panelled drawing room, log fire, nice prints, and carved wooden friezes, the original stone fireplace in the entrance hall, very friendly, helpful staff and owners, delicious modern evening meals, and plenty to do nearby; no smoking; children over 5 in restaurant

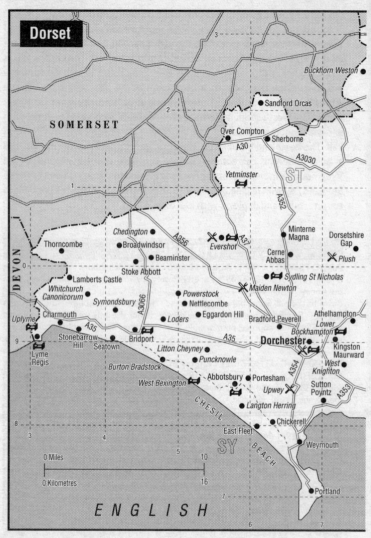

DORCHESTER SY6990 **Casterbridge** *49 High East St, Dorchester, Dorset DT1 1HU (01305) 264043* **£85**, plus wknd breaks; 14 individually decorated, pretty rms. Small Georgian hotel in town centre with modern annexe across little courtyard; elegant drawing room, cosy library, attractive dining room and conservatory, and generous breakfasts; no evening meals (lots of nearby restaurants); best to book early as they are very popular; cl Christmas; disabled access

DORCHESTER SY6889 **Maiden Castle Farm** *Dorchester, Dorset DT2 9PR (01305) 262356* **£60***; 4 rms. Victorian farmhouse in 2 acres of gardens in the heart of Hardy country and set beneath the prehistoric earthworks from which the farm takes its name; views of the hill fort and countryside, nice breakfasts, afternoon tea with home-made cakes, and comfortable traditionally furnished sitting room which overlooks the garden; disabled access; dogs welcome in bedrooms

EAST KNIGHTON SY8185 **Countryman** *East Knighton, Dorchester, Dorset DT2*

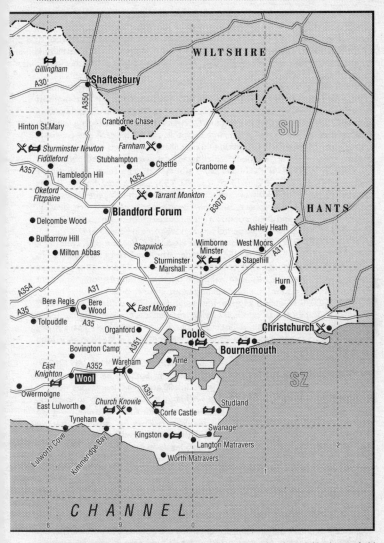

8LL *(01305) 852666* **£75***; 6 rms. Attractively converted and much liked pair of old cottages with open fires and plenty of character in the main bar which opens into several smaller areas, no smoking family room, half a dozen real ales, imaginative, generously served food inc nice breakfasts and a hot carvery in large restaurant, and courteous staff; cl 25 Dec; dogs welcome

EVERSHOT ST5704 **Summer Lodge** *Evershot, Dorchester, Dorset DT2 0JR (01935) 83424* **£265**, plus special breaks; 17 big, individually decorated rms. Beautifully kept, peacefully set former dower house with lovely flowers in the comfortable and elegantly furnished day rooms, excellent food using the best local produce in most attractive restaurant overlooking pretty garden, delicious breakfasts and afternoon tea, and personal caring service; outdoor swimming pool, tennis and croquet; children over 7 in evening restaurant; partial disabled access; dogs welcome in bedrooms

GILLINGHAM ST7827 **Stock Hill Country House Hotel** *Wyke, Gillingham,*

Dorset SP8 5NR (01747) 823626 **£240** *inc dinner, plus special breaks; 8 lovely very comfortable rms.* Marvellously relaxing carefully run Victorian manor house in 11 acres of wooded grounds, with antiques and paintings in opulent day rooms, particularly welcoming service, and excellent food in the no smoking restaurant using home-grown herbs and vegetables, local meat and fish; all-weather tennis court, croquet; children over 7

KINGSTON *SY9579* **Kingston Country Courtyard** *West St, Kingston, Corfe Castle, Wareham, Dorset BH20 5LH (01929) 481066* **£60**; 10 rms in most attractive farm building conversion. A collection of stylish suites and apartments in beautifully decorated houses keeping much original character and charm, and with wonderful views over Corfe Castle, Arne Peninsula, and the Isle of Wight; enjoyable full english or continental breakfasts in Old Cart Shed dining room; self-catering too; lots to do nearby; cl Dec/Jan; good disabled access; dogs welcome in bedrooms

LOWER BOCKHAMPTON *SY7290* **Yalbury Cottage** *Lower Bockhampton, Dorchester, Dorset DT2 8PZ (01305) 262382* **£93**, *plus special breaks; 8 rms overlooking garden or fields.* Very attractive family-run 16th-c thatched house with a relaxed friendly atmosphere, and low beams and inglenook fireplaces in comfortable lounge and dining room; carefully cooked often imaginative food, good wines, and attractive mature garden; cl Jan; dogs welcome in bedrooms

LYME REGIS *SY3392* **Charnwood Guest House** *21 Woodmead Rd, Lyme Regis, Dorset DT7 3AD (01297) 445281* **£55***, *plus special breaks; 8 rms with showers.* No smoking Edwardian house with covered verandah, recently modernised rooms, friendly owners who will help with walks and other local information, and decent breakfasts; best to phone for winter opening times; children over 5

POOLE *SZ0090* **Mansion House** *Thames St, Poole, Dorset BH15 1JN (01202) 685666* **£120***, *plus special breaks; 32 stylish rms with lots of added touches.* Close to the vibrant quayside, this civilised old merchant's town house has a lovely sweeping staircase, antiques in the elegant lounge, convivial cocktail bar, good food in the attractive restaurant, and friendly service

STUDLAND *SZ0383* **Knoll House** *Studland, Swanage, Dorset BH19 3AH (01929) 450450* **£260** *inc lunch and dinner; 80 comfortable rms.* Spacious, very well run hotel owned by the same family for over 40 years, in 100 acres with marvellous views of Studland Bay and direct access to the fine 3-mile beach; relaxed friendly atmosphere, particularly helpful staff, super food in dining room with windows overlooking the gardens, cocktail bar, TV lounge, and excellent facilities for families: attractive children's dining room (with proper food and baby food, microwave, own fridge, etc.), well equipped play room, table tennis, pool and table football, heated outdoor pool and health spa, tennis courts, small private golf course, marvellous adventure playground, and nearby sea fishing, riding, walking, sailing and windsurfing; cl end Oct-Easter; children over 8 in evening dining room; disabled access; dogs welcome ☺

STURMINSTER NEWTON *ST7711* **Plumber Manor** *Hazelbury Bryan Rd, Plumber, Sturminster Newton, Dorset DT10 2AF (01258) 472507* **£160***, *plus special breaks; 16 very comfortable rms, some in nearby period buildings;* many in the house itself overlook the peaceful, pretty garden and down the stream with herons and even maybe egrets. Handsome 17th-c, family-run house in quiet countryside, with warm fires, a convivial well stocked bar, attractive writing room/lounge, resident black labradors, good interesting food inc tempting puddings in three dining rooms, nice breakfasts, a relaxed atmosphere, and exceptionally friendly, helpful service; tennis; cl Feb; children welcome by prior arrangement; disabled access; dogs welcome in bedrooms

SYDLING ST NICHOLAS *SY6399* **Lamperts Cottage** *Sydling St Nicholas, Dorchester, Dorset DT2 9NU (01300) 341659* **£44**; *3 little rms under the eaves, shared bthrms.* Charming mainly no smoking 16th-c thatched cottage in unspoilt village, with friendly welcome from helpful owner, good breakfasts in beamed dining room with huge inglenook fireplace and bread oven, and pretty garden; children over 8; dogs welcome in bedrooms

UPLYME *SY3194* **Amherst Lodge Farm** *Uplyme, Lyme Regis, Dorset DT7 3XH*

(01297) 442773 **£80**; 3 rms. Comfortable longhouse surrounded by 140 acres of gardens, woodlands, fields and seven lakes - rod room, trout fishing; relaxed friendly country-house atmosphere, oak-panelled lounge with fire, books and magazines, and enjoyable breakfasts; self-catering also; cl Christmas; no children; disabled access

WAREHAM SY9287 **Priory Hotel** *Church Green, Wareham, Dorset BH20 4ND (01929) 551666* **£220**, plus special breaks; 18 very comfortable rms - the best being in the converted boathouse with its own landscaped gardens. Beautifully converted medieval buildings in four acres of carefully kept riverside gardens; two elegant lounges with antiques, delicious english cooking served in the converted Abbot's Cellar (exceptional english cheese board), and genuinely welcoming service; children over 8

WEST BEXINGTON SY5386 **Manor** *Beach Rd, West Bexington, Dorchester, Dorset DT2 9DF (01308) 897616* **£120***, plus special breaks; 13 cottagey rms. Handsome and civilised old stone hotel mentioned in Domesday Book in a pleasant setting not far from beach; relaxed informal atmosphere, comfortable lounges, popular pubby cellar bar, log fires, good bar food, excellent restaurant, and friendly service

WIMBORNE MINSTER SZ0199 **Beechleas** *17 Poole Rd, Wimborne, Dorset BH21 1QA (01202) 841684* **£79**, plus special breaks; 9 attractive, comfortable rms. Carefully restored Georgian house with open fires in cosy sitting room and charming dining room, airy conservatory overlooking walled garden, enjoyable Aga-cooked food using organic produce, nice breakfasts, and friendly helpful owners; lots to do and see nearby; cl 24 Dec-mid-Jan; disabled access; dogs welcome in bedrooms

YETMINSTER ST5910 **Manor Farmhouse** *High St, Yetminster, Sherborne, Dorset DT9 6LF (0800) 0566761 - free in UK* **£70**; 4 rms. Fine, carefully modernised, no smoking 17th-c building, with beams and oak panelling, inglenook fireplaces, homely sitting room, helpful owners, and good fresh traditional cooking; cl 24 Dec-6 Jan; disabled access; children over 12

To see and do

Dorset Family Attraction of the Year

WOOL SY8589 **Monkey World** (off A352 towards Bere Regis) As enjoyable as it is worthwhile, this exemplary rescue centre for apes and monkeys delights visitors of all ages with its enthusiasm and dedication. Founded in 1987 to rehabilitate abused or injured chimps, it now looks after all kinds of primates as it gradually reintroduces them to natural surroundings. As well as the biggest group of chimpanzees you'll see outside Africa, residents include ring-tailed and ruffed lemurs, barbary macaques, capuchins and woolly monkeys, orang-utans and gibbons, all roaming and climbing in decent-sized open enclosures spread over 65 acres. Some of the experiences the animals have been through are heartbreaking. Keepers give useful talks, and you can see baby chimps playing in their nursery. Plenty of thought has been put into developing the site for visitors, without over-commercialising it or spoiling its appeal; extensive play areas, some under cover, include a 15-stage obstacle course (climbing frames offer plenty of opportunities for children to ape the monkeys), and there's a pets corner. Also woodland walks, a well placed viewing tower, and space for picnics. It's a very satisfying fine weather half-day out for families; you'll find special events most bank hols. As we went to press the site was expanding, with a new animal hospital about to be built. Meals, snacks, shop, disabled access (a few steep paths); cl 25 Dec; (0800) 456600; £7 adults, £5.50 children 3-15. A family ticket for two adults and two children is good value at £21; usefully, they also do a ticket for one adult and two children, for £16.

ABBOTSBURY SY5982

Delightful village of golden stone and thatch, beneath a breezy chalk escarpment (itself excellent walking country, with wide coastal views), and with several worthwhile places within easy walking distance - most famous are the unique ancient swannery and the gardens (see separate entries, a joint ticket is available for £11). On prominent Chapel Hill, the green hillock grooved with the patterns of ancient field systems, stands 14th-c **St Catherine's Chapel** (always open), with a bare earth floor; it belonged to the abbey, of which there are a few medieval fragments around the church. A huge medieval thatched **tithe barn** built for the abbey has children's play areas, some animals and a video on smugglers. Shop, disabled access; cl Nov-Mar and wkdys Sept-Oct; (01305) 871817; £4.80. The Ilchester Arms (open all day) is useful for lunch. From Abbotsbury you can stroll around Chapel Hill and on to the massive shingle bank of **Chesil Beach** (see East Fleet entry; swimming here is dangerous). Paths leading N from the village get lovely views from the chalk downs. The B3157 W also has fine views.

Abbotsbury Subtropical Gardens 20 acres of beautiful woodland with the very mild coastal climate letting rare and record-breaking plants and trees flourish. The central walled garden in spring is a mass of azaleas, camellias and rhododendrons. Also woodland trail, owls, and children's play area. Pleasant tearoom, shop and plant centre, some disabled access; cl Christmas-New Year; (01305) 871387; *£6.20 summer.

Abbotsbury Swannery (Newbarn Rd) Another legacy of the former abbey, this is home to the only sizeable colony of swans in the world that can be seen during nesting time. The swan families quite happily come right up to visitors, and during the cygnet season (late May-Jun) you might see some of the hundreds of eggs hatching right next to you. All year there are mass feedings of the flock at noon and 4pm; they sometimes choose a visitor to help, and it can be rather dramatic - certainly a far cry from the average trip to feed the swans. An ugly duckling trail keeps younger children amused, and the reed

bed walks are interesting; also the country's oldest duck decoy, and an audio-visual show. No dogs. Restaurant (reached by a little bridge), shop, good disabled access; cl Nov to mid-Mar; (01305) 871858; *£6.20.

ARNE SY9788

Tucked away above the inlets of Poole Harbour, this backwater of a village is home to a good **Toy Museum** (Arne House), with over 40 working vintage amusement machines, and antique and collectors' toys. Snacks (there are plans to expand the tearoom into a restaurant), shop; cl am, all Oct-Easter, and Mon Apr-Jun and Sept; (01929) 552018; £3.50. There's also a quiet beach and a nature trail.

ASHLEY HEATH SU1006

Moors Valley Country Park A great place for family adventures, with nearly 988 acres of forest. Plenty to do here when it's sunny, with river and lakeside walks, and nature trails inc a play one that children really enjoy, with various activities such as jumping across stepping stones and climbing into and sliding out of the snake pit, or exploring the giant ant hill; there's also an unusual treetop walkway. Also cycle hire, narrow-gauge steam railway, and 18-hole golf course. Meals, snacks, shop, disabled access; cl 25 Dec; (01425) 470721; £5 car parking charge (less after 4pm), 50p winter wkdys (£2.50 wknds then and also off-peak outside winter). The park now also has a new tree-top rope-based assault course; over 10s only, book in advance (0870) 4445562; £14.50. The Old Barn Farm at Three Legged Cross is good value for family meals.

ATHELHAMPTON SY7794

Athelhampton House and Gardens ⌨ (old A35) This magnificent 15th-c house is built on the legendary site of King Athelstan's palace. The great hall has a fantastic roof, and throughout are beautiful furnishings and contents, with some fine panelling. An added bonus are the acres of wonderful formal and landscaped gardens with rare plants, topiary and fountain pools. Meals, snacks, shop, disabled access; open daily (exc Fri-Sat) Mar-Oct, and Sun only (cl 1-2pm) Nov-Feb; (01305) 848363; £7 house and gardens, £4.95 garden only (voucher admits two adults for the price of one). The young Thomas Hardy helped design the church across the road. The Martyrs at Tolpuddle has decent home cooking.

BEAMINSTER SY5199

Mapperton Gardens ⊞ (off B3163 E) Several delightful acres of terraced hillside gardens in grounds of a 17th-c manor house; specimen trees and shrubs, fountains, grottoes, fishponds, orangery, good walks and views. Occasional musical events in summer. Snacks, shop, some disabled access; cl am, and Nov-Feb; (01308) 862645; £4. In the town Pickwicks (The Square) has good food.

BERE REGIS SY8494

Bere Regis church This boasts the finest timbered roof in Dorset, with extraordinary carved figures; 20p in a slot lights these up to remarkable effect. It also contains the Turberville tomb and window mentioned in *Tess of the D'Urbervilles*. The Drax Arms has good home-made food.

BERE WOOD SY8794

At the W end of Bloxworth, this is a fine bluebell wood, at its best in May; the track can be followed right through to Bere Regis.

BLANDFORD FORUM ST8806

Georgian market town, rebuilt in 1731 after the older buildings were destroyed by fire - very interesting to walk round. The Crown Hotel (West St) does good value bar meals. At nearby Blandford St Mary, you can go on a tour of the **Hall & Woodhouse Badger Brewery**, followed by a browse around their visitor centre. Meals, snacks, shop, disabled access (not on tour); tours 11.30am and 2pm Mon-Sat, phone to book; 01258 452141; £4.50 inc a pint.

Cavalcade of Costume Museum ⊞ (The Plocks) 250 years of fashion housed in Georgian Lime Tree House, very well done, with good clear information and pleasant staff. Snacks, shop, disabled access to ground floor only; cl Tues, Weds, and early Dec to mid-Feb; (01258) 453006; £3.50.

Royal Signals Museum (Blandford Camp) A lively look at the history of army communications, with an exhibition on SAS codes and code-breaking, plus several interactive displays and fun trails for children; the staff are friendly. Snacks, shop, disabled access; cl wknds exc Mar-Oct, and 3 wks at Christmas - phone to check; (01258) 482248; £4.50.

BOURNEMOUTH SZ0890

A classic beach resort with neatly kept streamside gardens in the centre (various bands in summer), a pier (though they charge you 40p to stroll along it - the theatre at the end is quaintly old-fashioned), long promenades below the low cliff, and seven miles of well organised sandy beaches. The best beaches, with water safe for swimming and good wrist-band schemes to prevent children from getting lost, are from Durley Chine to Southbourne; regular boat rides leave from next to the pier. All this, along with a mild climate, has made the town a favourite place to retire to, though it's also very popular with foreign language students and families; the town is working hard to attract younger visitors. Though it's a big, busy place surrounded by suburbs, with tall buildings and monumental traffic schemes, down by the sea all that seems far away, with features such as the IMAX cinema (Pier Approach), palm trees, Edwardian street furniture, and a camera obscura (Bournemouth Sq). Tethered balloon flights in Lower Gardens are a nice way to take it all in; (01202) 314539; £10; also here are miniature golf (queues in summer), and children's activities in summer. The western residential suburbs, where Bournemouth merges imperceptibly into Poole, are quiet, with pinetree valleys winding down to the sea. The West Beach Restaurant (Pier Approach) and Moon in the Square (Exeter Rd) are good value, and the Durley Inn (Durley Chine) is a very well run beachside pub.

Hengistbury Head By far the best place close to Bournemouth for a stroll: not a long walk, but the feeling of space and views over Christchurch harbour and beyond are outstanding. It has traces of an Iron Age hill fort, and a good beach below.

Oceanarium (Pier Approach, West Beach) Well liked by readers, with an impressive range of fish from all around the world, friendly staff, and plenty to keep children entertained. There's an emphasis on the environment and conservation, and they've recently added a reptile sanctuary. Meals, snacks, shop, disabled access; cl 25 Dec; (01202) 311993; £6.25.

Russell-Cotes Art Gallery & Museum Victorian mansion with a good collection of 17th- to 20th-c paintings, ceramics and furnishings as well as exhibitions on japanese art, and a story-telling gallery aimed at children. Café, shop, disabled access; cl Mon, 25 Dec, and Good Fri; (01202) 451858; free.

BOVINGTON CAMP SY8288
A military area, with army vehicles and the distant sound of firing practice much in evidence.

Tank Museum Enjoyed by a wider spectrum of readers than you might guess (and good on a wet day as it's all under cover), over 150 armoured fighting vehicles from 26 countries, some of which you can go inside; also costumes, medals, weapons and videos, and a reconstructed World War I trench. Many of the tanks are put through their paces, complete with simulated gunfire (Tues and Thurs in summer hols); there are armoured vehicle rides on summer wkdys. There's an exhibition on Lawrence of Arabia, and a family activity trail. Meals, snacks and picnic areas, shop, disabled access; cl around a wk over Christmas; (01929) 405096; £7.50.

Clouds Hill A mile or so up the road is this cottage where Lawrence of Arabia lived in relative obscurity as a private in the Tank Corps after his famous desert exploits. His sleeping bag, furniture and other memorabilia can be seen in the four ascetic little rooms on display (the re-created bathroom is covered in cork tiles, while the walls of a room upstairs are lined with aluminium foil). An information centre and video will tell you more. Shop, disabled access to ground floor only, open Thurs-Sun pm and bank hols Apr-end Oct; (01929) 405616; £2.90; NT.

BRADFORD PEVERELL SY7191
New Barn Field Centre 🖼
Authentic re-creation of Iron Age

homestead, complete with animals and so on; also working potter, wildflower reserve and nature trails. Summer meals and snacks, shop, some disabled access; open Aug; (01305) 268865; £3.50.

BRIDPORT SY4692
Still the country's main rope producer, and its old harbour is now the busy fishing port of nearby West Bay, a restrained small resort (where the West Bay Hotel has good local seafood).

Bridport Museum (South St) Usually has displays of rope- and net-making and loom weaving, while a display on the Romans teaches you how to wear a toga. Free activity sheets for children; shop, disabled access to ground floor only; cl Sun, and Nov-Mar; (01308) 422116; £2.

BROADWINDSOR ST4302
Craft & Design Centre Good centre in former farm buildings. Meals, snacks, shop, disabled access; cl 25-26 Dec, 1-2 and last wk in Jan; (01308) 868362; free. The White Lion has generous home cooking.

Pilsdon Pen Not a place for long walks, but ideal for those who want a rewarding view in a very short stroll - Dorset's highest point, capped by a hill fort, and looking over Lyme Bay and N towards the Mendips. It is reached within minutes from the layby on the B3164 2m SW. This road to Birdsmoorgate and then the B3165 through Marshwood is an unspoilt scenic drive through a little-known valley.

BULBARROW HILL ST7705
Memorable viewpoint on the narrow lanes just S of Woolland, esp on a summer evening with the sun going down over Somerset. Around here, a scenic drive runs from Piddletrenthide through Plush (the Brace of Pheasants is a good lunchtime stop) and Mappowder to Hazelbury Bryan, then through Ansty and Melcombe Bingham, to turn right at Cheselbourne for Piddletrenthide again.

CERNE ABBAS ST6701
The village itself is most attractive in its own right: a fine church, fragments of the old abbey, and a very good pub, the Royal Oak. There's a working **pottery** (cl Sun and Mon, phone Nov-Easter (01300) 341865) on the way up to the

giant; above it, the old Dorchester—Middlemarsh ridge road has some bracing views.

CHARMOUTH SY3693

The beach here is famous for fossil-hunting. A small museum exhibits locally found relics; open Easter-Sept, plus Oct half-term; (01297) 560772; free; good shop, hammers for hire.

CHETTLE ST9513

Chettle House Fine baroque country house, with beautifully laid out gardens, and various craft wknds. Snacks, disabled access to garden only; open 1st Sun of month Easter-Oct and for special events, tours by appointment; as we went to press the owners were considering extending the open days, phone to check; (01258) 830209; £3.50. The Museum Hotel over in Farnham does good lunches.

CHICKERELL SY6580

Bennetts Water Gardens (Putton Lane) Eight acres of landscaped lakes renowned for their summer water-lilies - over 150 varieties, plus a replica of Monet's famous bridge at Giverny; also a tropical house, and a museum covering the gardens and local history. Home-made teas, shop, disabled access; cl Mon, Sun in Sept (exc bank hols), and all Oct-Mar; (01305) 785150; *£5.50. The Red Barn on working Bagwell Farm (B3157 NW) does enjoyable lunches.

CHRISTCHURCH SZ1592

The E end of the Bournemouth complex, and the oldest part, with attractive Georgian brick buildings in its centre, a restored watermill, and a quay looking out over the yachting harbour, busy in summer. Beyond the harbour mouth, long beaches stretch off into Hampshire from the vast Mudeford car park; the Haven House family pub has an unrivalled spot by the sea here, there's an excellent fishmonger nearby, and the Ship in Distress is a good dining pub specialising in local seafood. Pleasant walking out of season.

Stewarts Gardenlands (A35 E of A337 roundabout) has a giant maize maze from around July until the first frost, plus bouncy castle, go-karts and puzzles; (01425) 272244; £4.75.

Christchurch Castle & Norman House All that remains is a ruined keep, and the ruins of the Norman house probably used by the castle constable. It's quite well preserved, with one of the earliest chimneys in the country, and an ancient midden by a millstream; free; EH.

Christchurch Priory Magnificent medieval monastic church, at well over 90 metres (300 ft) the longest parish church in the country; very striking inside, with remarkable carving. The 'Miraculous Beam' apparently fitted in the roof only with divine assistance, so prompting the renaming of the borough to Christchurch (it used to be called Twynham). Shop, mostly disabled access; cl 25 Dec and Sun during services; (01202) 485804; donations. The church has a small museum open in the summer, and good views from the tower (£1, only when a member of staff is available) - though with 176 spiral steps you certainly earn them.

Highcliffe Castle 🏛 Originally built in the 1830s using large quantities of medieval stonework from France. Externally restored, this fine example of Romantic Picturesque architecture could almost fool you into thinking it's still a stately home. Inside, any decorative features have been destroyed after two fires left it vulnerable to the weather, and it now houses a friendly exhibition centre with displays that change every three weeks. Snacks, shop; house cl end Dec-Mar; (01425) 278807; £1.50 (discount voucher admits one adult free for every adult paying full entry price).

Museum of Electricity (opposite Castle's Ironmongers, Bargates) In an Edwardian power station, this has a range of electrical exhibits from antique washing machines to power generators. A transport gallery houses vehicles as diverse as a 90-year-old Bournemouth tram, a 1970s electric car, and Sir Clive Sinclair's over-hopeful Sinclair C5; interactive displays, and demonstrations of early electrical experiments. Shop, some disabled access; cl am, wknds (exc bank hols), and Oct-Easter (exc half-terms); (01202) 480467; £2.50.

Red House Museum & Gardens (Quay Rd) Georgian house with local history and archaeology, Victorian bygones, costumes, and a walled herb garden. Snacks, shop, disabled access to ground floor and herb garden only; cl Sun am, Mon (exc bank hols), Good Fri, and 25 Dec-1 Jan; (01202) 482860; £1.80.

CORFE CASTLE SY9681

One of the most spectacular ruins in England, the spiky remains of the castle rise on a hill in a breach in the Purbeck ridge, above the village of the same name; superb views from its dramatic hilltop position. Until it was seized in the Civil War and blown up it was a veritable skyscraper; its demolition has left the masonry leaning at unlikely looking angles, with remnants of portcullises and menacing murder holes. Much of the stone was reused in buildings in the village. Meals, snacks, shop; cl 25-26 Dec; (01929) 481294; *£4.50; NT. The Swanage Railway runs to here; a joint ticket is available (worth walking along **Nine Barrow Down**, the Purbeck ridge from Swanage, for wonderful two-way views, then getting the train back); phone for a timetable (01929) 425800; £9.90, cl wkdys Oct-Easter. Readers like the craft workshops and gallery opposite the station (Sandy Hill Lane). The bustling ancient Greyhound has popular food, all day in school hols. Parking can be a problem here in summer; it's best to use the castle car park on the edge of the village. The road W through Church Knowle is pretty.

Corfe Castle Model Village 🖼 In attractive gardens, with a faithful reconstruction of how the Norman castle looked before the Parliamentarians destroyed it in 1646. Meals, snacks, shop, disabled access (but no facilities); cl Mon-Thurs Nov-beginning Apr; (01929) 481234; £2.75.

CRANBORNE SU0513

A peaceful place, with the Fleur-de-Lys a good pub well known to Hardy and the subject of an entertaining poem by Rupert Brooke (framed inside).

Cranborne Manor Gardens Delightful 17th-c gardens originally laid out by Tradescant; Jacobean mount garden, herb garden, lovely river garden and avenues of beech and lime. Particularly attractive in spring. Snacks, shop and garden centre (open all year),

disabled access (limited in gardens); gardens open Weds Mar-Sept; (01725) 517248; *£3.50. The B3078 has good country views, as does the minor rd crossing it to Three Legged Cross and the Gussages.

CRANBORNE CHASE ST9116

Shared between Dorset and Wiltshire, this offers good walking with some fine views, especially around Ashmore.

DELCOMBE WOOD ST7805

A lovely bluebell wood, sheets of colour in May; but the only public track just skirts the W edge of the wood.

DORCHESTER SY6990

Thriving county town (which features as Casterbridge in Hardy's novels), with busy shopping streets inc a pedestrian zone, Weds market, and several worthwhile antiques and print shops. Though most of the more attractive Georgian buildings are just out of the bustle, there are a few distinguished buildings on the main streets, inc the timbered building of **Judge Jeffreys' Lodgings** in High West St; he stayed here during his notorious Bloody Assizes (the Oak Room tearoom in Antelope Walk, with good teas and cakes, is the courtroom where the Monmouth rebels were tried). The trial of the Tolpuddle Martyrs also took place on High West St, in the **Old Crown Court**, preserved as a memorial; for an extra £1.50 you can look round some of the cells (open wkdy pms in summer). There are traces of the Romans' occupation, inc the fragmentary remains of a town house behind the County Hall (which has a booklet on its history), and of an amphitheatre (Maumbury Rings), rather tucked away on Weymouth Ave. The Napper's Mite restaurant (South St), a former almshouse, is good value, and the Blue Raddle (Church St) does good attractively priced pub lunches.

Dinosaur Museum (Icen Way) The best of Dorset's dinosaur-related exhibitions, a well displayed and entertaining collection designed with younger visitors very much in mind. There are full-size skeletons and reconstructions, lots of opportunities to handle bones, fossils and the like (not many exhibits have barriers), and fun activities such as Dinosaurs and You, where you put in your height and weight and the computer works out how you compare with a couple of dinosaurs. Look out for the intriguing Dinosaurid - a canadian expert's idea of what dinosaurs would have evolved into if they hadn't become extinct. Shop, disabled access to ground floor only; cl 24-26 Dec; (01305) 269880; £5.50.

Dorset County Museum (High West St) Hardy's study from Max Gate has been reconstructed at this comprehensive museum, the largest Thomas Hardy collection in the world. The writer's gallery looks at the lives of Hardy and other Dorset novelists such as Sylvia Townsend Warner, with touch-screen computer displays. Also, dinosaur footprints and fossils in the geology gallery, and a gallery devoted to the town. Shop, disabled access to ground floor only; cl Sun Nov-Apr, plus 24-26 Dec and Good Fri; (01305) 262735; £3.90. The nearby Old Tea House is popular (good welsh rarebit), and in High East St the Kings Arms Hotel is full of Hardy associations.

Dorset Teddy Bear Museum (Antelope House, off South St/Trinity St) Tucked away in an old coaching house behind a good teddy shop, a family of human-sized bears dwell in blissful oblivion to the outside world. You can snuggle up next to a dozing Grandpa on the chair, go upstairs to see Mother and her ever-increasing brood of baby bears, or head downstairs to the cellar, where the Dorset Teddy Bear Museum collection includes every kind of teddy imaginable; enthusiastically run, this is a must for all teddy lovers. Shop; cl 25-26 Dec; (01305) 263200; £2.95.

Hardy's Cottage (Higher Bockhampton, just off A35 3m E) All alone by a sandy track inside the edge of a forest, the thatched cottage where Thomas Hardy was born in 1840 hasn't changed much since. Shop, disabled access to ground floor only; cl Tues and Weds, and all Nov-Mar; (01305) 262366; £2.80; NT. The forest was heath in Hardy's day, but you can walk through the plantations SE of the cottage to find open heathland much as he knew it on Black Heath and Duddle Heath, parts of the 'untamed and untameable' Egdon Heath of his novels. From the Hardy's Cottage car park, it's a shortish walk to the cottage; a nature trail takes a slightly longer but prettier route via Thorncombe Wood. The 16th-c thatched Wise Man at West Stafford has good value food. See nearby Stinsford and Max Gate for more Hardy associations.

Keep Military Museum (Bridport Rd) More interesting than most military museums, in handsome Victorian barracks gatehouse, with interactive displays and videos; splendid views from the battlements. Shop, disabled access; cl Sun (exc July-Aug), plus 3 wks at Christmas; (01305) 264066; £3.

Maiden Castle (off A354 S; no access from bypass) Europe's most famous Iron Age fort, a series of massive grassy ramparts covering 47 acres, and once home to some 200 families; the Romans captured it after a particularly bloody battle. It's so vast that the tour of its grassy ramparts almost qualifies as a fully fledged walk; free.

Max Gate (Alington Ave, A351 1m E) Among the places associated with Thomas Hardy (who lived in Dorchester for most of his life), this is the house he designed and lived in from 1885 to his death in 1928, and where he wrote *Tess* and *Jude the Obscure*. You can see only the dining and drawing rooms (the study has been moved to the County Museum), but the gardens are fascinating, not least because they inspired so much of Hardy's poetry. Shop, disabled access; open pm Sun, Mon and Weds early Apr-end Sept; (01305) 262538; £2.40; NT.

Stinsford (off A35 at E end of bypass) On the Thomas Hardy trail: he featured the village as Mellstock, and at the church his heart is buried beside the body of his first wife.

Terracotta Warriors Museum (High St) The only museum outside China dedicated to the terracotta warriors; interactive displays of armour and costumes as well as life-size replicas of the warriors, and multi-media presentations. Shop, disabled access; cl 23-26 Dec; (01305) 266040; £4.75.

Tutankhamun Exhibition (High West St) Impressive exhibits recreating the discovery of ancient treasures using a mix of sights, sounds and smells. Shop, disabled access; cl 24-26 Dec; (01305) 269571; £5.50.

DORSETSHIRE GAP ST7403
The downland W of Melcombe Bingham is attractive for walkers; the dry ground of the Gap comes as a pleasant surprise on those days when it seems as if all Dorset is turning to chalky mud. Despite the ultra-english charm of much of inland Dorset - chalk downs, sleepy thatched villages, clumps of beechwoods and fine views - the area is surprisingly little walked, so field routes are often not obvious and careful map-reading is needed.

EAST FLEET SY6380
Interesting, particularly for the tiny ruined church which was wrecked by a legendary 1824 storm. The vicinity's pleasant walks are especially interesting if you've read J M Faulkner's *Moonfleet*, and the Elm Tree food pub at Langton Herring is a useful stop for lunch. Nearby **Chesil Beach**, its pebbles and boulders immaculately graded by millennia of storms, is emphatically not for swimmers - the undertow will suck you straight down - but with its long lagoon behind is fascinating for beachcombers and nature-lovers. Swans nest on the great lagoon, which was used for trying out the World War II dam-busting bouncing bomb; now a peaceful spot, with lots of other birds too. The beach itself is tiring to walk any distance along.

EAST LULWORTH SY8280
Lulworth Castle 🏛 Restored 17th-c hunting lodge with splendid views over the wooded park from its SE tower; the formal gardens are a nice spot for a picnic. The Roman Catholic chapel was the first to be built in England after the Reformation, and an Anglican church was built in part by Thomas Hardy (there's an exhibition about him inside); also children's summer farm and play area. Snacks, shop, limited disabled access; cl Sat and 24 Dec to mid-Jan; (01929) 400352; £6.

EGGARDON HILL SY5494
On the summit, this prehistoric hill fort has wonderful views and - still after thousands of years - impressive earthen ramparts. New owners are doing enjoyable food in the charming Spyway

at Askerswell; good views here too.

HAMBLEDON HILL ST8412
In a commanding position above the peaceful village green of Iwerne Courtney (where the welcoming Cricketers has good food), this hill fort has a winning view, and still gives a strong sense of how formidable it must have been thousands of years ago.

HINTON ST MARY ST7816
This attractive village has a superb manor house and a striking medieval tithe barn. The White Horse is a useful food stop.

HURN SZ1197
Alice in Wonderland Family Park (opposite Bournemouth Airport; signed from A338 Christchurch junction) Children up to about 10 love this theme park based around the Lewis Carroll books. It's grown quite a lot in the last few years, starting out as just the big, elaborate maze that still remains the centrepiece, with 5,200 bushes shaped into characters from the two Alice books. Around that several gentle fairground rides have sprung up, such as spinning teacups, a caterpillar train, flying elephants, and a new runaway train roller-coaster; other attractions include croquet lawns of course, and play areas (a huge new indoor one is planned). For many the highlight is the half-hour show that adapts the stories into something close to a pantomime; extra events and activities in the summer hols. Meals, snacks, picnic area, shop, some disabled access; open wk before Easter to mid-Sept; (01202) 483444; £6.50 adults and children. The Avon Causeway Hotel does decent food.

Bournemouth Aviation Museum Well worth a visit if you're interested in aviation, with an increasing collection of aircraft inc vintage planes and helicopters, a large display of aircraft models, and occasional flying. Snacks, shop, disabled access; (01202) 580858; cl over Christmas and New Year, phone to check; £5.

KIMMERIDGE BAY SY9179
A lovely spot with intriguing rock strata, kept quieter than it might be by the toll. The New Inn up at Church Knowle is good for lunch. On the E side of the bay, the **Marine Centre** has displays on the

rich marine life of the rocky ledges that run across the bay; also a live underwater camera, re-created rockpool, interactive computer, and microscope close-ups of what you find on the beach; cl Sept-Easter; free but donations welcome.

KINGSTON SY9579
An easy level path runs from here to Hounstout Cliff; fortify yourself beforehand at the Scott Arms, a good family pub with superb views of Corfe Castle. Turn left at the end and you are into Dorset fossil country, presided over by the primitive hermitage chapel on St Aldhelm's Head, with an excellent picnic place in the quarried ledge just below, looking down the undercliff; the path here is of the switchback sort (decidedly vertiginous), and the sticky mud can make it tough going in wet seasons. The walk down to Chapman's Pool is steep and exciting; some of the paths have disappeared and you can scramble down to the beach.

KINGSTON MAURWARD SY7191
Kingston Maurward Garden and Animal Park 🖼 This feels like the heart of the countryside despite its proximity to Dorchester, with peaceful woodland and lakeside walks, visitor centre, farm park (children can feed the rare-breed animals), and plenty of garden variety spread through its 35 acres, inc Elizabethan and Edwardian gardens, penstemon and salvia national collections. The agricultural college, based in an elegant square-cut mansion built for George Pitt in 1720, holds some good special events. Meals, snacks, shop, plant sales, disabled access; cl around 10 days over Christmas and New Year, phone for details; (01305) 215003; *£4.

LAMBERTS CASTLE SY3799
This unspoiled hill fort above Marshwood (B3165) is charming for strolls, especially in late summer when the heather is out; it's quite hard to spot the turning from the road. The 16th-c thatched Bottle has enjoyable food.

LANGTON MATRAVERS SZ0078
Putlake Adventure Farm (B3069) Children are encouraged to join in the lively activities at this unspoilt farm (best for the under-8s); they can help hand-milk the cows, collect eggs from the chickens, or bottle-feed the lambs and goats, and the staff are friendly and professional. They do pony and tractor rides, and there are plenty of delightful small animals to fuss over; a more novel feature is the daily ferret racing. Plenty of things to play on, from miniature or full-sized tractors to scramble over, to an adventure playground and indoor play area, also a walk-through aviary and little maze. On wet days most of the attractions move under cover. Good café, indoor and outdoor picnic areas, shop, disabled access; open daily Apr-Oct, plus some wknds in Nov, Dec and Mar, phone to check; (01929) 422917; £4.40.

LULWORTH COVE SY8279
One of the great natural sights on the south coast, this is a gigantic scoop, with rock strata exposed and displaying all manner of rock types and contortions. Best appreciated out of season, this beauty spot, a magnet for summer visitors and geologists (especially now that it's been designated a World Heritage site), has a classic mini-walk W along the cliffs to Durdle Door, a natural arch eroded by the sea; the unusually shaped rocks are surrounded by particularly good beaches. Exhibitions on smuggling and country wines, and a Bronze Age display in the Lulworth Heritage Centre (cl 24-25 Dec). E of Lulworth Cove is army training land, which means high-security fences and dire warning notices, but you are allowed in most wknds and daily July-Aug and during Easter (keep to the paths; firing times are published in local papers). Information boards by road junctions off the A351 and A352 nr Wareham give opening times; or ring (01929) 404819. The coast walk between Lulworth Cove and Kimmeridge Bay is very strenuous but excellent, heading to Mupe Bay past the surreal 'fossil forest' (formed of petrified algae that once clung to tree-trunks; turn right after passing into the ranges from Lulworth Cove, and take steps down on to the undercliff). Another path ascends Bindon Hill, looking down over the semicircular cove. Inland, at West Lulworth the thatched Castle Inn is useful for lunch; the Lulworth Equestrian Centre can

arrange **horse-riding**; (01929) 400396; £15 an hour.

LYME REGIS SY3492

Enchanting old seaside town, with rather an elegant, steep main street and interesting side streets; the esplanade is pretty, and there's a lively little fishing and yacht harbour. A coast path snakes W through an intriguing nature-reserve undercliff, still subject to landfalls; this is a celebrated area for fossils and flora (several shops sell fossils, with show collections too). There are pleasant walks in the valley. The Pilot Boat on the front has popular food all day; the Royal Standard has a suntrap terrace (lit at night) right by the broadest part of the beach. The town gets very busy in summer, but it is worth braving the crowds. The Jane Austen cliffside gardens have peaceful sea views, and the cleaned-up sea here now tempts some quite varied creatures to make the occasional visit.

Dinosaurland (Coombe St) An excellent collection of fossils, and they can tell you about any you may have at home; they also do two-hour fossil walks along the beach (£5, booking recommended). Shop; cl 25-26 Dec; (01297) 443541; £4.

MILTON ABBAS ST8001

Lovely thatched estate village, all white walls and grass verges, built in the 18th c to replace an earlier one which had spoilt the view from the big house; the 17th-c almshouses were moved here at the same time. For the best views, drive in from Hilton. Pleasant stroll past the lake through the Capability Brown park to the fine 15th-c **abbey church** of a former Benedictine monastery (it now serves the public school in the nearby house). There's an attractive signed walk over the lane to a former chapel in the wood. Another pleasant walk through the abbey estate leads into Green Hill Down Nature Reserve, and a longer walk continues NW to Bulbarrow Hill. The road through the Winterbornes to Okeford Fitzpaine has good downland views.

MINTERNE MAGNA ST6604

Minterne Gardens 🖼 (Minterne House, A352) Beautiful landscaped gardens, with lakes, cascades, streams, rare trees and impressive spring shows

of azaleas, rhododendrons and bulbs; the autumn colours can be quite spectacular. Open 28 Feb to mid-Nov; (01300) 341370; £3. The road W up Gore Hill and Batcombe Hill to Holywell has memorable views.

NETTLECOMBE SY5295

This sleepy village is in charming walking country, little touched by agricultural improvement - delectable downland and valley landscapes, with a reasonably good path network. The Marquis of Lorne does good food.

ORGANFORD SY9392

Farmer Palmers (Organford, between A35 and A351 W of Poole) Highly regarded by readers, this superbly organised place appeals to under-8s, who enjoy the hands-on animal barn (the staff show them how to handle and feed a range of animals), straw mountain, indoor and outdoor play areas, bouncy castles and pedal tractors; daily milking demo, tractor trailer rides (50p), and a woodland walk (not in wet weather). Meals, snacks, shop, disabled access; cl Jan to mid-Feb and wkdys Oct-Mar (exc Feb half-term), phone to check; (01202) 622022; £4.50. The Old Post Office tearoom (Wareham Rd) and the St Peters Finger (B3067 E) are both good value for food.

OVER COMPTON ST5916

Worldlife & Lullingstone Silk Farm 🖼 Superb collection of butterflies, flying free in reconstructions of their natural habitats in the grounds of Elizabethan Compton House. The silk farm (the only one in Britain) demonstrates production of english silk used for coronations and royal weddings. Shop, some disabled access; usually cl Oct-Mar, best to check; (01935) 474608; £4.50. The Rose & Crown prettily set by a medieval church over in Bradford Abbas has enjoyable food.

OWERMOIGNE SY7685

Mill House Cider Museum and Dorset Clock Collection Cider museum with fully restored 18th- and 19th-c equipment, and video demonstrating the process. Also collection of locally made 18th- and 19th-c clocks. Shop with local ciders, some disabled access; usually cl 25 Dec-2 Jan; (01305) 852220; £1.50 cider museum, £2 clocks, £2.90 both. The beautifully placed Sailors Return at East Chaldon is good value for lunch.

POOLE SZ0190

Merging indistinguishably into Bournemouth on its well heeled residential edges, its centre is more lively, especially around the Quay (special events in summer, and a good factory outlet mall inc a Poole Pottery shop). The broad harbour, the second largest natural harbour in the world, with a busy yacht marina and flourishing luxury motor-cruiser boatyard, is still busy with the comings and goings of boats and ships (several decent pubs to watch them from - the nautical Portsmouth Hoy is best for lunch); launch ferries around the harbour, and out to wooded Brownsea Island. There are interesting old buildings along here; the streets behind, some pedestrianised, are well worth strolling through. A big regeneration project is adding new public spaces to the harbourside parks of Whitecliff and Baiter, and opening up another ¾m of waterfront. Dolphin Quays, a new luxury apartment development with shops and restaurants, should be open by the time we go to press, and the town's art centre, the **Lighthouse** (Kingland Rd), has recently undergone a radical £8.5m refurbishment. There are miles of good sandy beaches, with boats for hire at Sandbanks. Poole is well served for cyclists, with plenty of signed routes; the tourist information centre has leaflets on the town trail. Run by a friendly french couple, the Guildhall restaurant (Market St) has good local fish, and the Inn in the Park (Pinewood Rd) and Crown (Market St) are also useful for lunch.

Brownsea Island In the middle of Poole's huge natural harbour, this unspoilt 500-acre island is famous as the site of the first scout camp in 1907. It's a splendid place to explore, with uncrowded beaches, heath and woodland, and the whole island is good for spotting birds and wildlife; they have a burgeoning population of red squirrels, as well as a neat little bird-watching hide, and a large heronry. The nature reserve at the northern end is run separately by the Dorset Wildlife

Trust and is well worth a look; it costs £2 extra, with self-guided tours in Apr, May, Jun, Sept and Oct, and guided walks (2-3.45pm daily) in July-Aug; (01202) 709445. The visitor centre has a video, and in summer holidays activities like painting and clay-making. Free walking trails and occasional special events for children. In summer an open-air theatre has Shakespeare or opera; tickets go fast, so apply well in advance; (01202) 251987. Ferries go from Poole Quay (twice hourly, takes around 20 mins, £5.50 return fare for adults; (01202) 669955), Sandbanks (twice hourly, takes 10 mins, £3 return for adults; (01929) 462383), Bournemouth Pier (two a day, takes 25 mins - only Mon, Weds, and Fri outside summer, £6 return adults; (01202) 558550), and, less often, from Swanage; (01929) 424152. Decent restaurant and shop, and some disabled access; open Apr-Oct (cl 15 mins before last boat leaves); (01202) 707744; the landing fee (free to NT members) is £3.70 adults, £1.70 children 5-17, family tickets available. No dogs or bikes. There's a holiday cottage - the island's very quiet indeed after the last boat leaves.

Chain ferry This runs from Sandbanks, by the harbour mouth, to the Studland side - a spectacular entrance to Dorset proper; you can go as a foot passenger, or on a bus; (01929) 450203; car £2.20, foot 90p. The beach at Sandbanks is lauded as one of the best in Britain.

Compton Acres Gardens (Canford Cliffs) Perhaps Poole's outstanding attraction, with lovely statuary among fine plants landscaped in an eclectic variety of styles - the japanese garden is the foremost in Europe, and a wildlife walk has models of canadian animals; the italian garden has recently been renovated. Good views of the hills and Poole Harbour. Sat is the least busy day to visit. Meals, snacks, new shop and plant sales, disabled access; cl 25 and 26 Dec, 1 Jan; (01202) 700778; £5.95. The Inn in the Park (Pinewood Rd, off B3065 E) has good value food.

Splashdown (Tower Park, 2m NE on A3049) Fun for children, a water park with 11 rides and slides (indoor and out), inc a near-vertical drop in total darkness, and a new learner pool.

Snacks; cl ams outside school hols (in peak periods they may have limits on how long you can stay), best to phone; (01202) 716123; £6.80.

Waterfront Museum (High St) Four floors of well laid out local history. Disabled access; (01202) 262600; cl 25-26 Dec (reduced hours in winter); free. In Aug, you can go next door to **Scaplen's Court**, a well restored medieval merchant's home with exhibitions upstairs.

PORTESHAM SY6086
The high heathland above here is good walking territory, with a view covering the entire sweep of the West Dorset coast.

Hardy Monument As hideous as it is prominent, this commemorates Nelson's admiral, not the Dorset author; it has tremendous views. A track along Bronkham Hill SE from the car park feels truly ancient, with prehistoric burial mounds flanking it. If you don't feel like leaving the car, the Black Down road passing the Monument towards Martinstown also gives fine views.

PORTLAND SY6973
This odd, much-quarried promontory with its narrow neck and long naval connections gives tremendous views from its peak. Nearer at hand, the remarkable sea defences of Portland Harbour laid out below are a fine sight - and you may glimpse Britain's first prison ship for generations moored off here. The George (not Weds), Pulpit, and the Lobster Pot (usually open Mar to mid-Nov - good crab sandwiches) are useful for lunch, and handy for a stroll to the cliffs. Here, **Portland Bill Lighthouse** is worth a look - you must be at least 1.1m tall; cl Sat, and winter exc Sun; (01305) 861233; tours £2.

Climbing With over 900 climbs, the Isle of Portland is the main centre for sports climbing in the south of England, with bolted climbs from easy to hard. Restrictions for nesting birds on some crags Mar-July, phone the Portland Ranger to check (01305) 266920; for equipment the Climbing Shop (01305) 826666 is useful.

Portland Castle You can try on armour and soak in the views at this fortress, built under Henry VIII to defend the south coast; the recently opened Governor's Garden is part of the English Heritage contemporary gardens scheme - at its heart is a 200-seater circular amphitheatre. Audio tour, snacks, shop, disabled access; cl Mon-Thurs Nov-Mar, 24-26 Dec and 1 Jan; (01305) 820539; £3.50; EH.

Portland Museum (Wakeham) A cottage used by Hardy in *The Well-Beloved* is now a local history **museum** which was founded by Dr Marie Stopes, the birth control pioneer. Shop, disabled access to ground floor; cl 1-1.30pm, Weds and Thurs (exc school hols), and all Nov-Easter; (01305) 821804; £2.

SANDFORD ORCAS ST6221
Manor House Interesting inhabited Tudor manor house, largely unaltered since 16th c, with fine furnishings and family portraits, and pleasant gardens. Open Easter Mon, then pm Sun and Mon May-Sept (exc Jun); (01963) 220206; £3. The Mitre has decent food.

SEATOWN SY4291
This seaside hamlet has some charming stone cottages and a perfectly placed seaside pub, the Anchor. A steep walk leads up to the **Golden Cap**, the highest point on the county's coast, and another good walk along to the New Inn at Eype. Just inland, the village of Chideock is pretty - or would be, if it weren't sadly ripped in half by the busy A35.

SHAFTESBURY ST8623
Hilltop town with good views from Castle Hill and Park Walk; there are several craft shops and workshops. The most famous street is Gold Hill - thatched cottages stepped down a steep cobbled street, familiar from those old Hovis TV advertisements and more recent hanky-panky revelations. At the bottom, St James (where the Two Brewers is a good family food pub) is attractive.

Shaftesbury Abbey Museum & Garden You can see some of England's most ancient graves at this abbey founded by Alfred the Great in AD888 (for 700 years this Benedictine community for women was the most important in the country). An adjacent museum has excavated remains, and there's an Anglo-Saxon herb collection; a good audio tour sets the abbey's history in a national context. Shop, disabled access and facilities; cl Nov-Mar; (01747) 852910; *£2.

Shaftesbury Town Museum At the top of Gold Hill, the local history museum includes an 18th-c fire engine and a collection of old farm implements. Limited disabled access to ground floor only; cl Oct-Easter and Weds; (01747) 852157; £1.

SHERBORNE ST6316

An attractive town to wander through, given a feeling of unchanging solidity by the handsome stone medieval abbey buildings that mix in with later ones of the public school here, and by many other fine old buildings in and nr the main st. The **abbey** itself is a glorious golden stone building with a beautifully vaulted nave; at the Dissolution the townspeople raised the money to buy it, and it's been the parish church ever since. The West Window is beautiful, as is the Laurence Whistler engraved glass reredos in the Lady Chapel, and for 20p you can illuminate the fan vaulting of the roof; (01935) 815191; suggested donation £2. The unspoilt Digby Tap (handy for the abbey but no food Sun), smart Half Moon (Half Moon St) and cheerfully foody Skippers (Horsecastles) are useful for lunch. Several craft shops include a working saddlery (Cheap St).

Sherborne Castle (just E of town) This striking old house, which has been in the same family for almost 400 years, was built by Sir Walter Raleigh in 1594. Its wonderful period furnishings are the highlight, and there are interesting paintings and porcelain. Outside are gardens designed by Capability Brown, and beautiful parkland with an enormous lake. Meals, snacks, shop, limited disabled access; open Apr-Oct exc Mon (exc bank hols) and Fri; castle cl Sat am; (01935) 813182; £6 castle and gardens, £3.25 grounds only, children free.

Sherborne Museum (Abbeygate House, Church Lane) An eclectic collection includes a reconstruction of the old castle in its heyday, as well as a Victorian doll's house and Roman remains. Shop, disabled access to ground floor only; cl Sun am, Mon (exc bank hols), and Nov-Mar; (01935) 812252; £1.

Sherborne Old Castle (Castleton) Facing Sherborne Castle across the lake is the original 12th-c castle, now a beautifully evocative ruin. Good for a picnic, and especially appealing in Apr when the dry ditch is full of wild primroses. Shop, disabled access; cl Oct 1-2pm, and Nov-Mar; (01935) 812730; £2.

STAPEHILL SU0500

Stapehill Abbey 🔲 Just right for a relaxed afternoon, a 19th-c Cistercian abbey (the nuns moved out in 1989, although the chapel has been preserved) now houses craft workshops and exhibitions on monastic life; acres of park and landscaped grounds inc a Japanese garden, with waterfalls and woodland walk, a play area, and farm animals for children. Snacks, shop, disabled access to ground floor only; cl Mon and Tues Oct-Easter, Christmas hols-Jan; (01202) 861686; £7.50. The Barley Mow at Colehill is a good food pub.

STOKE ABBOTT ST4500

With thatched houses, a good deal of charm, and a good pub (the New Inn), this offers walkers attractive undisturbed surrounding countryside, with a reasonably good path network.

STONEBARROW HILL SY3893

Reached by a steep narrow road just E of Charmouth, this has good easy walking, fine sea and inland views, and a disabled lavatory. Below in Morcombelake, biscuits have been baked at family-owned **Moore's Dorset Biscuit Factory** since 1880; you can watch part of the process (not lunchtime), and there are free samples. Shop and little local art gallery; cl wknds (exc Sat am in summer), bank hols and over Christmas; (01297) 489253; free.

STUBHAMPTON ST9214

In good weather the bridleway from here along Ashmore Bottom to Ashmore is well worth exploring; but it can be muddy in a wet spring.

STUDLAND SZ0482

The scattered village has an interesting Norman church (more French than English), and is the start point for one of most varied short walks on the south coast. In a couple of hours you can take in the Agglestone (a rock standing solitary on Dorset's largest surviving heath), Ballard Down (huge views over Poole Harbour) and Old Harry Rocks (tooth-like chalk pinnacles detached from the cliff), before ending by the coloured sands on the miniature cliffs at the lovely South Beach, which has two areas set aside for dog owners - and a summer parking charge (expensive exc for NT members, less after 2pm). Decent food at the very popular Bankes Arms with its huge sea-view garden, or the Manor House Hotel (where Churchill and Eisenhower watched D-Day rehearsals). Next to the Sandbanks ferry, the simple Shell Bay is good for seafood.

STURMINSTER MARSHALL
ST9500

White Mill 🏠 Rebuilt in 1776 and restored over 200 years later, this waterside corn mill still has its original wooden machinery (too fragile to operate); delightfully set on the banks of the River Stour, it's a very pleasant spot for a picnic. Disabled access; open pm wknds and bank hols Easter-end Oct; (01258) 858051; £2.60; NT. Opposite the handsome church, the Red Lion has good value food.

SUTTON POYNTZ SY7083
This attractive thatched village has a good path to the nearby village of Osmington (also thatched, pretty and with a nice pub). The path gives views of the **White Horse** - an equestrian portrait of George III etched into the hillside. You can walk back along the Dorset coast path, which here leads along the top of the downs rather than along the coast itself. The Spyglass family dining pub (Bowleaze Coveway, off A353 S) gives great views over Weymouth Bay.

SWANAGE SZ0278
Fairly quiet 19th-c resort, with a clean, sandy beach; the seaview Mowlem Theatre restaurant (Shire Rd) is good. On Church Hill, the **Tithe Barn Museum & Art Centre** has local history displays inc an exhibition on quarrying (the town was once very important to the stone trade), a re-created 1930s chemist, dinosaur footprints and a huge ammonite; there's also a little summer art and craft gallery. Shop, mostly disabled access; cl 12.30-2.30pm, am wknds, and Oct-May (exc

Easter wk); (01929) 423174; free. This is a popular area for diving; the Pier Diving School does a 3-hour course for beginners (£40), and for more experienced divers there are boat trips to nearby wrecks (£15); (01929) 423565.

Durlston Country Park On the edge of Swanage, this has spectacular clifftop scenery and unspoilt countryside, with fine views from the headland, the **Great Globe** (a 40-ton global representation in Portland stone), a new pond by the visitor centre, and good spots to watch seabirds, butterflies or deer (let staff know if you see dolphins, seals or whales). Snacks, shop, some disabled access; information centre cl wkdys Nov-Mar, park open all year; (01929) 424443; free, though there's a parking charge of £3 in summer (£1 in winter).

Swanage Railway Steam trains run along six miles of track to Corfe Castle (a joint ticket is available): a nice way of approaching the ruins - or you could walk there via Ballard Down and Nine Barrow Down (far-ranging views on all sides) and ride back. Corfe Castle station has an exhibition of old railway memorabilia, while a travel agency in Swanage station helps towards the railway's upkeep. Parking is easier at the Norden end of the line. Snacks, shop, disabled access; cl 25 Dec, and wkdys Nov-Apr; (01929) 425800 for train times and prices.

THORNCOMBE ST3504
Forde Abbey and Gardens The extensive gardens here really are special, with glorious trees and shrubs, a fine collection of asiatic primulas, many other interesting plants, and sweeping lawns, as well as a visitor centre and Ionic-style temple. The striking abbey buildings still retain many of the features of the original 12th-c Cistercian monastery, but it was modernised in 1520 by Abbot Chard, and his great hall and tower remain. Cromwell's Attorney-General later turned the abbey into a house, and the interior has changed little since, with magnificently furnished rooms, unusual plaster ceilings and a set of Mortlake tapestries. Meals and snacks (in 12th-c undercroft), shop, disabled access to gardens and ground floor only, dogs on

lead welcome; house open pm Tues-Fri,
Sun and bank hol Mon Apr-Oct, garden
and nursery all year; (01460) 221290;
£7, £5.25 garden only, under-15s free.
Thorncombe Wood is awash with
bluebells in spring; dogs on lead.

TOLPUDDLE SY7894
Famous for the agricultural workers
who were transported to Australia after
they united to improve their working
conditions and terms of employment.
The Martyrs' Tree under which they
supposedly met still remains, and more
of their story is explained in interactive
displays in a little museum between the
six cottages built by the TUC as a
memorial. Shop, disabled access; cl Mon
(exc bank hols), and usually 1 wk over
Christmas, phone for details; (01305)
848237; free. The Martyrs pub (open all
day) has good food.

TYNEHAM SY8880
On the army's Purbeck firing ranges
(open holidays and most wknds; call
(01929) 404819 for details), this
abandoned village is quite poignant; the
former church has an explanatory
exhibition. The army presence has
meant the landscape has been
preserved remarkably well; this is the
best starting point for walks through
the Lulworth Ranges - taking in
Kimmeridge and Lulworth Cove,
through some of the wildest coastal
scenery in southern England. It's quite
relentlessly tough going, with nearly
1,000 metres (about 3,000 ft) of ascent
if you do the whole thing, but makes a
marvellous day's walking.

WAREHAM SY9287
This largely modern town has a few
striking old buildings, inc the church of
St Martin, with a finely carved memorial
to Lawrence of Arabia (a little local
history museum in East St has a display
of his photographs; usually open Mon-
Sat; (01929) 553448; free). The church
of Lady St Mary not far from the Quay
has the coffin of Edward the Martyr,
murdered at nearby Corfe Castle in
978; in contrast, the 1920s Rex cinema
(West St) is a period gem, still gas-lit,
and there are two very traditional old
inns, the Black Bear and Kings Arms.
Still surrounding the old town, massive
grassy banks mark the Anglo-Saxon
town wall. The attractive road over the

West Creech Hills may sometimes be
closed for army firing practice.
Blue Pool (Furzebrook, 3m S) Bluest
on an overcast day, the water in this
former claypit changes colour with the
weather, depending on how the light
strikes diffracting particles in it; the
surrounding 25 acres of heathland in this
beauty spot are peaceful. There's a small
play area and museum. Snacks, shop,
plant sales, some disabled access; site
open Mar-Nov; (01929) 551408; £3.20.

WEST MOORS SU0704
Aurelia Gardens (Newmans Lane, off
B3072 Bournemouth—Verwood, N of
West Moors) Appealing little garden
mostly made up of heather and conifers
no more than four feet high, laid out in a
labyrinth of curving beds; also small
ponds, and around a dozen enclosures
with rare breeds of poultry. Snacks,
plant sales; as we went to press opening
times for 2004 were still under
discussion, so phone for details;
(01202) 870951; £2.50.

WEYMOUTH SY6878
Elegant 18th- and 19th-c terraces along
its curving esplanade, and some older
buildings in the narrower partly
pedestrianised streets behind. The
harbour is lively, with big ferries leaving
from the outer quay, and the town's
inner ring road running one-way
around the inner harbour. There's
decent cheap food in the lively Red Lion
(opposite Brewers Quay, with lots of
tables outside) and the seafront
Dorothy and Old Rooms (both all day
in summer); the Café Royal (Esplanade)
is also recommended, and the enjoyable
Sea Palace chinese restaurant has an
unusual location - the pier bandstand.
On the far side of the harbour the
narrow streets of the old town are
worth exploring; you can go on a guided
tour of one of the town's few remaining
Tudor buildings (Trinity St), furnished
as the home of an early 17th-c middle-
class family; Tues-Fri pm Jun-end Sept,
1st Sun pm of month Oct-May (exc Jan);
(01305) 779711; £2.50. The resort has
a good beach, and lots of lively family
attractions. Overlooking Weymouth
Bay (in summer a landtrain leaves from
near the tourist information centre, and
there's a park and ride), Lodmoor
Country Park has a miniature railway,

go-kart track and bumper boats, as well as an RSPB nature reserve, and plenty of space to run around. Abbotsbury Oysters (Ferrybridge, towards Portland) does good fresh seafood.

Brewers Quay In the heart of the Old Harbour, this is a skilful conversion of a harbourside Victorian brewery into shopping complex, with plenty of good year-round activities. **Timewalk** imaginatively re-creates scenes from the town's history, and an interactive gallery takes an interesting look at its brewing heritage (£4.25). There's also a craft centre, bowling, microbrewery, and lively hands-on science centre. Several places to eat, and good specialist shops, disabled access (exc to Timewalk); cl 25-27 Dec, and last two weeks in Jan; (01305) 777622; free admission to centre.

Deep Sea Adventure 🖼 (Custom House Quay) Fascinating look at underwater exploration, shipwrecks, and the search for buried treasure, with lots of interactive displays. Meals, snacks, shop, disabled access; cl 25-26 Dec and 1 Jan; (0871) 2225760; £3.75. Also here, **Sharky's** is the biggest indoor play area in the county (£3.30 per child).

Model World 🖼 (Lodmoor Country Park, Preston Rd) In landscaped gardens, this miniature world includes a model airport, funfair, miniature dino-land, zoo and 0 gauge railway (runs daily, weather permitting); also plenty of models to operate yourself, all with special sound effects. Snacks, shop, disabled access, dogs welcome on a lead; cl Oct-Apr; (01305) 781797; *£3.50.

Nothe Fort 🖼 (Barrack Rd) Interesting Victorian fort on three levels, with displays spread over a staggering 70 rooms. Children can clamber over some of the vehicles and guns, and there are fine views of the harbour and coast. Snacks, shop, limited disabled access; open daily May-Sept, Easter hols and Oct half-term, plus Sun rest of year; (01305) 766626; *£3.50. Good views too from the garden of the Nothe Tavern (with tasty fresh fish), and from the pleasant nearby Nothe Gardens.

Sea Life Park 🖼 (Lodmoor Country Park, A353) One of the most elaborate in the excellent Sea Life Centres chain. As well as the stunning marine displays and touch pools, features include a Shark Academy, with fun interactive games and quizzes leading to a Scholarship, seal, penguin and otter sanctuaries, and a splendid outdoor play area. Meals, snacks, shop, disabled access; cl 25 Dec (reduced hours in winter); (01305) 788255; *£8.95.

WIMBORNE MINSTER SZ0199 Georgian houses (and decent little independent shops) in the narrow central streets around the Minster - a fine, well preserved, largely Norman church with contrasting red and grey masonry, twin towers, and a brightly coloured jack carved as a grenadier striking the clock bell every quarter. Inside, an interesting Norman crypt, a distinctive astronomical clock and the original chained library. The low-beamed White Hart nr the Minster, Dormers (Hanham Rd) and the Cross Keys (Victoria Rd, W) are all useful for lunch. Just W of town at Pamphill is a good big farm shop, and just E there are pleasant country walks around the Fox & Hounds at Little Canford.

Honeybrook Country Life (Stanbridge, B3078 N) New farm and nature park with farm animals, gypsy camp, kitchen garden and restored early Victorian farm house; also riverside trails, play area, swing boats, and pony and dray rides (£1 and £1.50). Snacks (good cream teas), shop, disabled access; cl Oct-Easter, best to check; (01202) 881120; £4. The Stocks just S at Furzehill does enjoyable meals.

Iron Age hill fort The once formidable hill fort of **Badbury Rings**, just off B3082 NW of Wimborne, is associated by some with King Arthur. It's a good strolling ground with an impressive range of wild flowers - and if you feel more energetic, a **Roman road** lets you strike out for miles N.

Kingston Lacy House (B3082 NW) Impressive 17th-c mansion later remodelled by Charles Barry, with grand italian marble staircase and superb venetian ceilings; outstanding paintings such as the *Judgement of Solomon* by Sebastiano del Piombo, and others by Titian, Rubens and Van Dyck. The enormous grounds have landscaped gardens and a herd of red devon cattle in the park; lovely snowdrops in Feb and early Mar. There's easily enough here to fill a good day out. Meals, snacks, shop, disabled access to park and gardens; open Apr-Oct, house cl Mon-Tues; (01202) 883402; £6.80, £3.50 grounds only; NT. The Anchor at Shapwick is fairly handy for a good lunch (not Mon).

Knoll Gardens (Stapehill Rd) Rare and exotic plants in various colourfully themed well developed gardens, with over 6,000 different well labelled species, many of which can be bought in the expanding nursery (which specialises in grasses and hardy perennials); they've recently added a gravel garden. They maintain a good working relationship with the Dorset Wildlife Trust. Snacks, disabled access; cl Mon and Tues, and 3 weeks over Christmas; (01202) 873931; £3.50. Adjacent Trehane Nurseries have a great range of camellias, and the Angel at Longham (A348) has good value food.

Priest's House Museum (High St) Historic townhouse with carefully researched period rooms, a gallery on local villages, a new costume gallery, and a charming walled garden. Summer teas, shop, disabled access to ground floor; cl Sun and Nov-Mar (exc special 2-wk exhibition from 27 Dec); (01202) 882533; £2.50.

Walford Mill 🏠 (Stone Lane) Converted 18th-c flour mill with exhibitions and crafts. Meals, snacks, shop, disabled access; cl Sun am, 25 Dec, 1 Jan, and Mon Jan-Mar; (01202) 841400; free.

Wimborne Model Town & Gardens 🏠 (King St) This entertaining 1950s model town is so accurate that it's used to assess the impact of planning applications here. Also well maintained gardens with some interesting plants, and an indoor miniature railway; young children enjoy visiting, and there's a little play area with wendy houses, and a children's trail. Good value tearoom and picnic area, plant sales, disabled access; cl Oct-Mar; (01202) 881924; (01202) 881924; *£3.

WOOL SY8486
This attractive village was used by Thomas Hardy as the ancient seat of the D'Urbervilles; the Ship is a pleasant family pub with generous food all day. **Monkey World** *See separate family panel on p.197.*

WORTH MATRAVERS SY9677
In this prettily set coastal hamlet the interesting old Square & Compass has lovely views, and is a good base for coast walks. Near here, the rock pool at Dancing Ledge is said to have been cut by a local schoolmaster.

Other attractive villages with decent pubs include Buckhorn Weston ST7524, Burton Bradstock SY4889, Chedington ST4805, Church Knowle SY9481, Evershot ST5704, Farnham ST9515, Fiddleford ST8013, Kingston SY9579, Langton Herring SY6182, Litton Cheyney SY5590, Loders SY4994, Okeford Fitzpaine ST8011, Powerstock SY5196, Puncknowle SY5388 (pronounced Punnel), Shapwick ST9302, Sydling St Nicholas SY6399, Symondsbury SY4493, Tarrant Monkton ST9408, West Knighton SY7387 and Whitchurch Canonicorum (fine church) SY3995.

Where to eat

CHRISTCHURCH SZ1592 **Splinters** *12 Church St (01202) 483454* Fine old building nr priory with three attractively decorated rooms, international modern cooking, lovely puddings, a fine british cheese choice, good value wines, and friendly helpful owners; also run Pommery's (next door) with delicatessen and lively upstairs café-bar; cl Sun, Mon. £31|**£8.25**
CHURCH KNOWLE SY9481 **New Inn** *(01929) 480357* Very attractive partly thatched old pub with two nicely furnished main bar areas, lots of bric-a-brac, log fires, and relaxing dining lounge; very good fresh fish (and other food), well kept ales, decent wines including interesting bin ends, and skittle alley (private hire only); camping in field behind (need to book). £20

DORCHESTER SY6990 **Oak Room** *Antelope Walk (01305)* 250760 Genteel tea shop in a 1930s time warp and once the courtroom where Judge Jeffreys tried the Monmouth rebels in the Bloody Assizes; excellent sandwiches with interesting fillings, light hot meals and super clotted cream teas; cl Sun.|**£4.50**

EAST MORDEN SY9194 **Cock & Bottle** *(01929)* 459238 Popular dining pub with several beamed communicating areas, a nice mix of old furnishings, good log fire, enjoyable food inc interesting daily specials with plenty of fish and seasonal game, well kept beers and good wines; cl 25-26 Dec; disabled access. £28.50|**£5.75**

EVERSHOT ST5704 **Acorn** *28 Fore St (01935)* 83228 Well run old coaching inn with a comfortable L-shaped bar, two fine old fireplaces and copies of the inn's deeds going back to the 17th c; imaginative daily specials, well kept ales, and a thoughtful wine list; nice village and good nearby walks; bdrms. £29|**£7**

FARNHAM ST9514 **Museum Inn** *(01725)* 516261 Odd-looking thatched building with various effortlessly civilised areas - flagstoned bar with big inglenook fireplace, light beams and good comfortably cushioned furnishings, dining room with a cosy hunt-theme, and what feels rather like a contemporary version of a baronial hall, soaring up to a high glass ceiling, with dozens of antlers and a stag's head looking down on to a long wooden table and church-style pews; excellent food, three real ales, a fine choice of wines, and very good attentive service; lovely bdrms in back stable block; cl 25 and 31 Dec; children lunchtime only; disabled access. £33|**£7**

MAIDEN NEWTON SY6097 **Petit Canard** *Dorchester Rd (01300)* 320536 Welcoming little restaurant (they prefer you not to smoke) with simple furnishings, good very interesting food inc fine puddings, and a well chosen wine list; cl Mon, some Suns; children over 12. £38

PLUSH ST7102 **Brace of Pheasants** *(01300)* 348357 Long low 16th-c thatched cottage with a civilised but relaxed atmosphere, good solid furnishings, fresh flowers and a good log fire in the airy beamed bar; interesting food, well kept real ales; swings in the garden; children in the family room; cl Mon. £28|**£7**

STURMINSTER NEWTON ST7814 **Red Rose** *Market Cross (01258)* 472460 Long-standing and very popular family-run lunchtime restaurant with proper english cooking using their own lamb and local produce, and with a very relaxed and happy atmosphere; cl most evenings (open Fri and Sat); disabled access. £18|**£7**

TARRANT MONKTON ST9408 **Langton Arms** *(01258)* 830225 Charmingly set and welcoming 17th-c thatched pub with beams and an inglenook fireplace, no smoking bistro restaurant in an attractively reworked barn, no smoking family room with play area in skittle alley, well kept interesting real ales, popular enjoyable bar food, and garden with another play area; good nearby walks; bdrms; bar open 7 days a week, restaurant cl Mon, Tues, Weds-Sat am, Sun pm; disabled access. £20|**£7**

UPWEY SY6684 **Wishing Well** *Church St (01305)* 814470 Nice little restaurant, popular locally, with good interesting lunchtime food and afternoon teas, and friendly service; bring your own wine; cl Mon-Tues Mar, cl mid-Dec to beginning Mar; disabled access. £16|**£6.50**

WIMBORNE MINSTER SZ0199 **Cloisters** *40 East St (01202)* 880593 Friendly restaurant with pleasant décor and enjoyable food inc breakfast with home-made marmalade, lunchtime snacks and meals, and afternoon tea; cl 4 days over Christmas; disabled access. £19.50|**£3.50**

Special thanks to Peter Neate, Dave Morgan, M G Hart, Paul Kennedy, B and K Hypher, Jo and Michel Hooper-Immins, Dave Morgan, Tamsin Shelton

Please let us know what you think of places in the *Guide*. Use the report forms at the back of the book, write us a letter or log on to www.goodguides.co.uk

ESSEX

Some nice surprises in this low-key area, from quirky museums to ancient forests; some good family fun, too

Saffron Walden is the finest small town in the region, lovely to potter around, with the extra draw of magnificent Audley End House. Of the many beautiful villages in Essex, especially worth picking out are Finchingfield, Thaxted and Great Bardfield (all of which have windmills). Coggeshall has some fine medieval buildings, and waterside Burnham-on-Crouch (friendly railway museum) is lively in summer. Many of the churches are well worth a look.

Southend-on-Sea is good for traditional seaside fun: the Central Museum & Planetarium and Sea Life Adventure are among rainy-day treats for children here. A great zoo (with well thought out play areas as well as animals), and lively museums with hands-on displays (the one at the castle is outstanding), make Colchester another worthwhile place to aim for. In Waltham Abbey, you'll find a friendly farm park and interesting nearby gardens, and you can visit a historic gunpowder mill. Stansted has the double attraction of the House on the Hill Toy Museum (lots of the displays are aimed at children), and Mountfitchet Castle (an enthusiastic introduction to life 1,000 years ago).

Our Essex Family Attraction of the Year (excellent value traditional family fun) is Old Macdonalds Farm Park. South Woodham Ferrers has the double draw of a working farm, and one of the largest tropical houses in the country; Mole Hall Wildlife Park at Widdington offers animals and butterflies too. The striking Tudor Layer Marney Tower has a rare breeds farm, and there's a farm museum at Billericay.

Gardeners can choose between the magnificent gardens at Little Easton, the RHS Garden at Rettendon, Beth Chatto Gardens at Elmstead Market and the Gibberd Garden in Harlow. Elsewhere, tours of the nuclear bunker at Kelvedon Hatch are memorable, and there's a good railway museum (and castle) at Castle Hedingham. Walton Hall Museum at Linford has an appealingly eclectic mix of memorabilia, and, a newcomer to the guide this year, we've added the Motorboat Museum in Pitsea.

Driving through North Essex, you pass lots of attractive houses right by the road, often with fine old timbering and distinctive colour-washed plasterwork - the intricate patterning is known as pargeting. Constable's Stour Valley still enchants, with its unspoilt landscapes still very much as millions of us know them from prints of his paintings. The Blackwater/Crouch coast has a surprisingly remote feel, given the closeness of densely urban South Essex. Further north, there are good coastal walks at Walton-on-the-Naze; Brightlingsea has the best beach.

Where to stay

BROXTED TL5827 **Whitehall** *Church End, Broxted, Dunmow, Essex CM6 2BZ* *(01279) 850603* **£125**, plus special breaks; 26 pretty rms. Fine Elizabethan manor house in lovely walled gardens, with restful spacious lounge, a smaller cosier one with log fire, pleasant bar, good food in big, heavily timbered restaurant, and friendly service; cl 26-31 Dec

BURNHAM-ON-CROUCH TQ9595 **White Harte** *The Quay, Burnham-on-Crouch, Essex CM0 8AS (01621) 782106* **£59**; 19 rms, 11 with own bthrm. Old-fashioned 17th-c yachting inn on quay overlooking the River Crouch with its own jetty; high ceilings, oak tables, polished parquet flooring, sea pictures, panelling, residents' lounge, and decent food in bar and restaurant; dogs welcome

DEDHAM TM0433 **Maison Talbooth** *Stratford Rd, Dedham, Colchester, Essex CO7 6HN (01206) 322367* **£160**, plus special breaks; 10 luxuriously furnished rms. Tranquil Victorian country house in fine Constable country, with deeply comfortable seating and fresh flowers in elegant lounge, very good imaginative food in lovely timber-framed restaurant overlooking river and gardens, and marvellous breakfasts; restaurant cl winter Sun pm; disabled access

TOPPESFIELD TL7437 **Ollivers Farmhouse** *Yeldham Rd, Toppesfield, Halstead, Essex CO9 4LS 01787 237642* **£50**; 2 rms, 1 with own shower. Historic, no smoking 17th-c farmhouse in particularly pretty gardens with attached vineyard; lots of original beams and fireplaces, big sitting room with piano and large collection of modern paintings, and breakfasts with home-made brown bread and jam, free range eggs and locally cured bacon (and light suppers if ordered) in antique-filled dining room; cl 23 Dec-2 Jan; children over 10; disabled access

WIX TM1429 **Dairy House Farm** *Bradfield Rd, Wix, Manningtree, Essex CO11 2SR* *(01255) 870322* **£47**; 2 comfortable bdrms. No smoking Victorian farmhouse on 700 acres of arable land and fruit farm with fine country views, many original features, a cosy sitting room, home-made cake on arrival, and enjoyable breakfasts with home-made preserves in elegant dining room (no evening meals); garden with croquet; children over 12

To see and do

Essex Family Attraction of the Year

SOUTH WEALD TQ5992 **Old Macdonalds Farm Park** A trip to this friendly working farm will cost a family of four only a little over £10 - great value, even if you just stay for a couple of hours. It's a nicely undeveloped place, with no gimmicks or added-on attractions, just the animals, and plenty of them. They specialise in rare breeds of sheep, cattle, pigs and poultry, with 30 different breeds of sheep alone. Children can get close to many of the animals, buy food to feed them with, and in spring and summer watch chicks hatching in their incubators. There's also a breeding colony of red squirrels, and they've recently introduced some otters. Picnic sites are spread around the 16 acres; next to one of them at the top of the farm is a small play area. The helpful staff are always happy to answer questions, and there are good views of the whole site from the mound next to the cafeteria. They have walks and nature trails, and craft displays. Meals, snacks, shop, disabled access; cl 25 Dec, 1 Jan (but best to check); (01277) 375177; £3.25 adults, £2 children between 2 and 15.

Please let us know what you think of places in the *Guide*. Use the report forms at the back of the book, write us a letter or log on to www.goodguides.co.uk

ABRIDGE TQ4897
Crowther Nurseries (off A113 E)
Working garden with decorative shrub
beds, flower borders, a vegetable plot,
greenhouses and over 600 varieties of
clematis; also pets corner inc goats,
donkey, rabbits and ducks, and a Lego
corner. Snacks, plant sales, disabled
access; cl 25-27 Dec; (01708) 688581;
free. The Maltsters Arms in the village
has bargain food.
BASILDON TQ6688
Langdon Nature Reserve (Lower
Dunton Rd, Langdon) During the early
1900s little pieces of land, known as
'plotlands', were auctioned off mainly to
East Enders who spent their free time
here. The land gradually grew into a
scattered settlement of some 200
homes, before being compulsorily
purchased by the council after World
War II. Almost all the homes have gone
now, leaving 460 acres of ancient
woodland and meadows, lakes and
ponds to wander through. One of the
few surviving plotland homes, The
Haven, has been restored in 1930/40s
style, and you can learn more about the
social history of the reserve in the
museum. Visitor centre with displays,
snacks, shop, disabled access; cl Mon
(exc bank hols), and 25-26 Dec; (01268)
419103; free.
BATTLESBRIDGE TQ7894
Attractive village, with popular antiques
and crafts centre, walks to head of
Crouch estuary; the Barge is useful for
food all day.
BILLERICAY TQ6991
**Barleylands Farm Museum &
Visitor Centre** ▦ (A129 SE) An
exercise in diversity, from farm animals
and rural life displays to working
glassworks, craft studios and miniature
railway (summer Sun and daily (exc Sat)
in Aug), also picnic and play areas.
Meals, snacks, shop, disabled access; cl
Nov-Feb; (01268) 290229; £2.50. The
nearby Duke of York (South Green) has
good value food.
BLAKE END TL7023
Original Great Maze ▦ (A120
Dunmow—Braintree) Each year they
try to outgrow the previous year's crop
labyrinth with more than ten miles of
pathways in around ten acres; children's
play area. Meals, snacks, shop, disabled

access; open daily mid-July to early Sept;
£4. **Blake End Craft Centre** is also
here; open daily; (01376) 553146. The
15th-c Three Horseshoes over in
Bannister Green has good value food.
BOCKING TL7524
Windmills As well as the one here in
Churchstreet, good examples can be
found in Aythorpe Roding TL5815, and
Mountnessing TQ6397.
BOXTED TL9931
Carter's Vineyard You can go on a
tour of this 7-acre vineyard, which is
powered by alternative energy (£3.50
inc samples), or just wander round
yourself. A few interactive displays on
alternative energy and a video, also
nature trail, picnic area and you can fish
for carp (£5, booking essential). Snacks,
shop, disabled access; cl Mon, and end
Oct-Easter; (01206) 271136; free. The
Anchor over at Nayland (just off A134,
S of main village turn) does good food.
BRADWELL-ON-SEA TL9907
Worth the long drive for the sense of
being right out on the edge of things - the
timeless emptiness if anything
exaggerated by distant views of vast
industrial installations. The walk E down
the old Roman road across the marshes
takes you to a little restored **Saxon
chapel** of St Peter right on the sea wall,
the scene of an annual pilgrimage in July.
The Green Man is a good traditional pub.
BRIGHTLINGSEA TM0816
Surrounded on three sides by water,
this is a classic South-East seaside
resort; the beach here is probably the
county's best.
BURNHAM-ON-CROUCH
TQ9595
Attractively old-fashioned yachting
station, lively in summer (packed
around the Aug bank hol for its regatta),
but nice in winter too with rigging
clacking forlornly against the masts of
those yachts left to ride at anchor. The
quayside local history museum has
recently been refurbished; cl am, plus
Mon, Tues, and Fri (exc school hols);
£1. Pleasant walks along the banks of
the River Crouch, and the waterfront
White Harte is good for lunch.
Mangapps Farm Railway Museum
(B1021 towards Southminster) Friendly
and growing collection of vintage rolling
stock and railway memorabilia. They

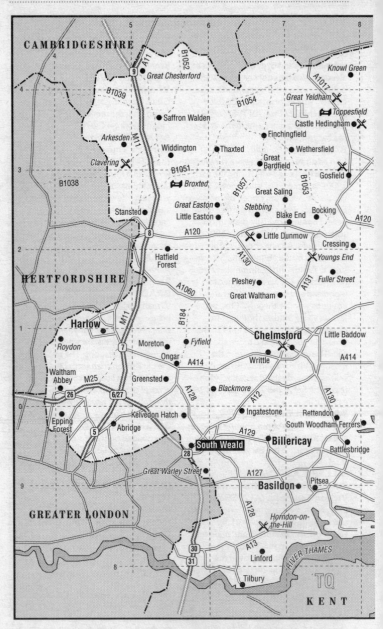

Knowl Green

Great Chesterford

B1052

A1017

B1039

Great Yeldham

B1054

TL

Toppesfield

Saffron Walden

Castle Hedingham

Finchingfield

Arkesden

M11

Widdington

Thaxted

Wethersfield

Great Bardfield

Clavering

B1051

Broxted

B1057

B1063

Gosfield

B1038

Great Saling

Great Easton

Stebbing

Blake End

Bocking

Stansted

Little Easton

A120

8

A120

Little Dunmow

Cressing

2

Hatfield Forest

A130

Youngs End

Fuller Street

HERTFORDSHIRE

A1060

Pleshey

A131

Great Waltham

1

Harlow

B184

Chelmsford

Little Baddow

Roydon

M11

7

Moreton

Fyfield

A414

Ongar

A414

Writtle

Waltham Abbey

M25

Greensted

A128

Blackmore

A12

A130

26

6/27

0

Kelvedon Hatch

Ingatestone

Rettendon

Epping Forest

Abridge

South Woodham Ferrers

5

A129

Billericay

Battlesbridge

28

South Weald

Great Warley Street

A127

Pitsea

9

Basildon

A128

GREATER LONDON

Horndon-on-the-Hill

A13

30

Linford

RIVER THAMES

31

TQ

Tilbury

KENT

have a station formed from railway buildings from sites all over East Anglia, and steam/diesel rides along ¾ mile of track. Mostly under cover, snacks, shop, limited disabled access; open pm wknds, daily in Aug and Easter school

hols (cl Jan); (01621) 784898; £4.50 (£1 extra when the steam trains are running - usually bank hols and special events, and higher charges on other special days). Further along, the Limes is a decent **farm shop**, with nature trails

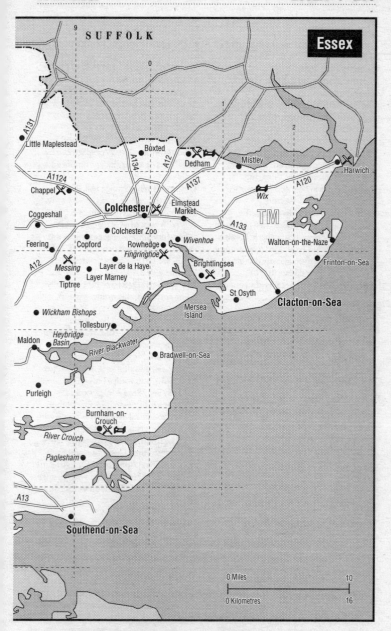

and **pick-your-own**; (01621) 782051.
CASTLE HEDINGHAM TL7736
£ The town, which has some
attractive buildings, is named for the
Norman **castle** which dominates it, the
magnificent four-storey keep towering

above the surrounding trees.
Exceptionally well preserved, it still has
its roof, banqueting hall and minstrels'
gallery. Teas, shop; cl Sat, Mon and Tue,
and Nov–week before Easter; (01787)
460261; £4 (may be more if there are

special events on). The **church** has grand Norman masonry and interestingly carved choir seats; the Bell is good for lunch. The B1058 towards Sudbury then left through Gestingthorpe and the Belchamps is a pleasant excursion.

Colne Valley Railway and Museum ⊞ (A1017 N) Lovingly restored Victorian railway buildings with collection of vintage engines and carriages; short steam-train trips Sun pm Mar to Oct, and Weds and Thurs pm in hols; diesel rides Tues, and Thurs-Sat pm in hols - best to ring for timetable, or check website (www.colnevalleyrailway.co.uk). Admission price includes train rides and entry to rare breeds farm park. Meals on Pullman coaches (you need to pre-book these). Snacks, shop, mostly disabled access; cl Nov-end Mar; (01787) 461174; £6, £3 when trains not running (vouchers not valid for special events).

CHAPPEL TL8927
The prettily sited Swan has good food, in sight of the Chappel Viaduct (reputedly the biggest brick structure in Europe), and there's a decent **railway museum**, and perhaps rides on a short demonstration line, usually first and last wknd of month Apr-Sept - best to ring for timetable. Wknd snacks, shop, some disabled access; cl 24-25 Dec; (01206) 242524; £6 (£3 non-steam days).

CHELMSFORD TL7007
A big busy city with little for visitors, but its 15th-c **cathedral**, consecrated as such only in 1914, has particularly harmonious Perpendicular architecture. The Alma (Arbour Lane) has good food in nice surroundings.

Chelmsford Museum (Oaklands Park, off Moulsham St) Local, social and natural history museum in a Victorian mansion, with a live beehive, room reconstructions and changing exhibitions; the friendly staff will have a go at identifying any objects you bring in. Adjoining is a museum devoted to the Essex Regiment; children's playground and picnic area in the park. Shop, disabled access to ground floor; cl am Sun, 25-26 Dec and Good Fri; (01245) 615100; free.

CLACTON-ON-SEA TM1714
Roomy family seaside resort, with long stretches of gently shelving sandy beach and all the usual amusements. The pier has an aquarium, reptile house and various rides (cl winter, exact dates depend on weather; (01255) 421115); and watching the fishing at its end has a curiously mesmerising charm. The Robin Hood (London Rd) is the best family dining pub in the area.

COGGESHALL TL8422
Attractive small town with a good few antiques shops. The Woolpack out by the church is a magnificent timbered building.

Grange Barn (Grange Hill; B1024 S edge) 12th-c, one of the oldest surviving timber-framed barns in Europe, originally part of a Cistercian monastery. Disabled access; hours as Paycocke's (see entry below); (01376) 562226; £1.70, or joint ticket with Paycocke's £3.40; NT.

Marks Hall ⊞ (B1024 N) Gradually being restored, this estate is pleasant for an undemanding stroll. There's a massive 13th-c oak, a developing arboretum, and a 17th-c walled garden recently reopened after five years of renovation . Meals, snacks and picnic area, shop, disabled access; cl Mon (exc bank hols), and wkdys Nov-Mar; (01376) 563796; £3.50 per car.

Paycocke's (West St) A fine timber-framed medieval merchant's home with unusual panelling and carvings, and pretty garden behind. Disabled access; open pms, Tues, Thurs, Sun and bank hols beginning Apr to mid-Oct; (01376) 561305; £2.30 (joint ticket with Grange Barn £3.40); NT. The Fleece next door has decent food.

COLCHESTER TL9925
Britain's oldest recorded town, the capital of Roman Britain. You can trace the Roman wall (the Hole in the Wall, Balkerne Gdns, is a decent pub built into the one surviving fragmentary gatehouse). The High St has handsome buildings, some extravagantly timbered, and plenty more historical buildings inc **St Botolph's**, the oldest Augustinian priory in the country. The good **Minories Art Gallery** (High St), has innovative changing exhibitions in a converted Georgian townhouse, with events for all ages; (01206) 577067; free. Town tours usually leave the

tourist information centre (Queen St) at 11am (Jun-Sept; £2.50), and they also do themed tours (6pm Sat; £3.50), with costumed guides, best to check; (01206) 282920. The Tudor Rose & Crown (East St) is good for lunch.

Bourne Mill (just off B1025 S) Delightfully quaint restored watermill by pretty millpond, worth a look from the outside even when it's not open. Usually open pm bank hol Sun and Mon, plus pm Sun and Tues Jun-Aug, but best to check; (01206) 572422; £2; NT.

Colchester Castle Museum (Castle Park, off High St) Great for families: they let you try on Roman togas and helmets, or touch 2,000-year-old pottery excavated nearby; also splendid collection of Roman relics from jewellery to military tombstones (they've a new display of rare Roman coffins, and burial urns). The castle stands on the site of a colossal Roman temple (you can still see the vaults), and the museum itself is housed in the biggest Norman keep in Europe. They go to some lengths to bring grisly moments in its history to life: you can hear a dramatisation of one of the forced confessions of the suspect witches incarcerated here. For £1.50 extra a guided castle tour takes you up on the roof as well as to the vaults and chapel. Snacks, good shop, mostly disabled access (to castle museum but not to vaults or castle roof); cl 5 days over Christmas; (01206) 282939; £4.25.

Colchester Zoo 🆒 (Maldon Rd, Stanway, 2m E by B1002) One of the country's most satisfying animal collections, with over 200 rare and endangered species kept in enclosures as close to their natural environments as possible. The zoo is particularly good on cats and primates, they've a breeding herd of african elephants, and have recently opened a £2m sea lion facility, but one enclosure has shire horses, pigs, rabbits and other tame animals for children to get close to. Several good play areas (our favourite is the Kalahari Capers under-cover complex), and an activity centre with changing animal-related or native american crafts; activities such as face-painting and brass-rubbing included in the price. Meals, snacks, shops, indoor and

outdoor picnic areas, mostly disabled access (reduced admission); cl 25 Dec; (01206) 331292; £10.99.

Hollytrees Museum (High St) With hands-on and audio displays, this Georgian townhouse has displays on its history and famous local figures, as well as a collection of toys, costumes and curios from the last two centuries, inc a doll's house modelled on Hollytrees. Shop, disabled access; cl 25-26 Dec and 1 Jan; (01206) 282940; free.

Natural History Museum (All Saints church, High St) Lots of hands-on displays and a children's quiz, with an emphasis on man's impact on the environment; shop, disabled access; cl 25-26 Dec and 1 Jan; (01206) 282941; free.

Rollerworld (Eastgates) Children like this place, Britain's only international-standard roller-skating rink; opening arrangements change regularly, so best to check online (www.rollerworld.co.uk), or phone; (01206) 868868; from £3.90; also Quasar and ten-pin bowling.

Tymperleys Clock Museum (Trinity St) A particularly unusual selection in a lovely 15th-c house; there's something very special about coming here and hearing all the ticking; also recon-structed Tudor herb garden. Shop, disabled access; cl 1-2pm, Sun-Mon, and Oct-Apr; (01206) 282931; free.

COPFORD TL9222

Copford church Originally built around AD1130, and worth a visit particularly for its well restored 12th-c wall paintings.

CRESSING TL7918

Cressing Temple Barns 🆒 (Witham Rd) Two impressively large medieval barns built by the Knights Templar, plus a Tudor walled garden; special events in summer. Meals, snacks, shop, disabled access; cl Mon (exc bank hols) Tues and Sat (plus Weds-Fri Mar-Apr and Oct), and all Nov-Easter; (01376) 584903; £3.50.

DEDHAM TM0533

Several fine old buildings, especially the 15th-c flint **church**, its pinnacled tower familiar from so many Constable paintings. There's also the school Constable went to, and good walks through the protected riverside meadows to his father's mill at Flatford (across the river lock, so in Suffolk, and described in that chapter). The partly medieval Sun has decent food, and the handsome Marlborough Head, formerly a wool merchant's house dating from 1475, is well worth a look.

Dedham Art & Craft Centre (High St) A number of crafts in this converted church, such as floristry, glass-engraving and wood-turning, as well as a toy museum. Vegetarian meals, snacks, shop; cl 25-27 Dec; (01206) 322666; free.

Gnome Magic (Ipswich Rd) This attractive garden extends into woods where 500 gnomes live; picnic site; open Apr-Sept; (01206) 231390; £3.50.

Sir Alfred Munnings Art Museum (Castle House, Castle Hill) The house itself is a mix of Tudor and Georgian, and inside the artist's own furniture gives a real sense of how it would have looked when he and his wife lived here. His horsey paintings are hung throughout the house, and you can also view his studios and stroll through the pleasant gardens. Shop, disabled access to ground floor only; open pm Weds and Sun Easter-beginning Oct, plus Thurs and Sat in Aug; (01206) 322127; £4.

ELMSTEAD MARKET TM0623
Beth Chatto Gardens 🔲 A riot of colour in spring and summer, with lots of gardening ideas, and unusual varieties of plants for sale. It's hard to believe that these attractive gardens were once four acres of wasteland. Snacks during summer, plant shop, disabled access; cl Sun (plus Sat Nov-Feb), and 2 wks over Christmas; (01206) 822007; £3.50. At Great Bromley the Old Black Boy has good food.

EPPING FOREST TQ4197
A magnificent survival, an expansive tract of ancient hornbeam coppice, mainly tucked between the M25 and outer London; the 6,000 acres have remained free from developers since 1878. There are miles of leafy walks (and rides - you can hire horses locally), with some rough grazing, and occasional distant views; they've recently introduced Longhorn cattle. There are so many woodland paths that getting lost is part of the experience; the long-distance Forest Way is,

however, well marked. On the W side is a pleasant diversion to High Beach, from where a few field paths lead SW; the Owl at Lippitts Hill is a useful refreshment stop.

Queen Elizabeth's Hunting Lodge (A1069 just NE of Chingford) Well preserved timber-framed hunting lodge, actually built for King Henry VIII; great views from the top. Explore the kitchen and shooting gallery, and there are children's dressing up clothes and brass rubbings. Shop, disabled access to ground floor only; open pm Weds-Sun and bank hols, phone over Christmas; (020) 8529 6681; free.

FEERING TL8620
Feeringbury Manor (Coggeshall Rd) Fine big riverside garden with ponds, streams, a little waterwheel, bog gardens and a range of plants. Disabled access; open Thurs and Fri Apr-July and Sept; (01376) 561946; £2.50. The Sun towards Kelvedon is a friendly refreshment stop.

FINCHINGFIELD TL6734
The county's prettiest village, with charming houses spread generously around a sloping green that dips to a stream and pond; just off stands a pristine-looking small windmill. The Tudor Red Lion opposite the churchyard and the 15th-c guildhall has sensibly priced food. There's a pleasant, easily followed path along the Finchingfield Brook to nearby Great Bardfield.

FRINTON-ON-SEA TM2419
A pleasant, unspoilt family seaside resort, with long stretches of gently shelving sandy beach; it's a quieter place than its neighbour Clacton (it acquired its first pub ever, the Lock & Barrel, only in 2000). Beyond, the blowy open space of the Naze is pleasant for strolling, especially out of season when you're likely to have its 150 acres virtually to yourself.

GOSFIELD TL7729
Gosfield Hall 🔲 Famous visitors to this Tudor house, built around a courtyard, include Elizabeth I, Louis XVIII of France and Horace Walpole. Open pms Weds and Thurs May-Sept (tours 2.30 and 3.15pm); snacks, disabled access; £3.50. The Green Man has good food.

GREAT BARDFIELD TL6730
Known as the Montmartre of Essex
because of the group of artists who
once lived here, this has several
attractive pargeted houses, a village
green, a church with a rare 14th-c
carved stone screen, and a windmill.
GREAT SALING TL7025
Saling Hall Gardens 🔢 12 acres of
tranquil gardens created over the last
50 years. There's a fine walled garden
and water features, but the aboretum is
the main draw here. Disabled access;
open pm Weds May-July; (01371)
850243; £2.50 (which goes to charity).
The ancient White Hart has decent
food.
GREAT WALTHAM TL6913
Pleasant village, with an attractive and
interesting church. The Dog & Gun in
nearby Little Waltham is a good dining
pub.
GREENSTED TL5302
St Andrew's church Tests have
established that it was probably built
around the time of the Norman
Conquest - the oldest wooden church
in the world; shop, disabled access. The
nearby Green Man at Toot Hill has
enjoyable food (and fine wine).
HARLOW TL4611
A New Town, and not perhaps top of
most itineraries, but it does have a
surprisingly good museum (cl Sun and
Mon; free). A large part of the town
around the town hall is being redeveloped in order to create new gallery
space and a playhouse as well as council
buildings - work should finish this spring.
The Marquis of Granby (Market St, Old
Harlow) is an attractive old pub.
Frederick Gibberd Collection On
the first floor of the civic centre, this
surprisingly fine collection of british
modern art includes works by Graham
Sutherland, Elizabeth Blackadder and
John Nash. Disabled access; cl wknds
and bank hols; (01279) 446763; free.
Gibberd Garden (Marsh Lane, Gilden
Way) The master planner of Harlow
New Town designed these gardens in
the late 1950s and continued to develop
them until his death in 1984. Planned as
a series of individual 'rooms', the glades,
groves, pools and allees provide
settings for sculpture, architectural
salvage, a gazebo and even a moated

castle. Snacks, shop, disabled access;
open wknd and bank hol pms Apr-end
Sept; (01279) 442112; £4.
Museum of Harlow (Muskham Rd)
Local museum with an important
Roman collection, a bicycle collection
and period landscaped gardens, which
include a Tudor herb garden and three
walled gardens; shop, disabled access;
museum cl 12.30-1.30pm Sat, and all Sun
and Mon; (01279) 454959/439680; free.
HARWICH TM2430
The Redoubt here is a circular fort built
in 1808 in case of invasion by Napoleon,
with three small museums. Shop; cl
Sept-Apr (exc Sun); (01255) 503429;
£1. Harwich's two lighthouses both
have small museums, one a **Maritime
Museum** (times as above; 50p), the
other a collection of vintage radios and
TVs (wknds only; £1). Also a little
lifeboat museum (times as above, 50p),
and a foot ferry to Felixstowe and
Shotley. The A120 W gives an unusual
sight for this part of Essex - a tall narrow
windmill (actually an interloper, as it
was brought from Suffolk).
HATFIELD FOREST TL5320
(just S of Stansted Airport) This NT
medieval Royal hunting forest is an
unexpected survivor, with ancient
mainly hornbeam woodland, not on
quite the same scale as Epping Forest
but still extensive enough, with nature
trails, cycle paths, and a lake where you
can fish (mid-Jun to mid-Mar; around
£4.50 - phone to check). Look out for
the unusual shell grotto built in the
1750s by the family that once owned
the forest. A new boardwalk around
the forest is opening in Mar;
information centre and café; (01279)
870678; car park £3.20.
INGATESTONE TQ6598
Ingatestone Hall 🔢 Interesting old
house, not too grand and given life by
enthusiastic tours guided by the family
that live here, and lovely grounds. Teas,
shop; open pm wknds, bank hols and
Weds-Fri in school hols Easter-Sept;
(01277) 353010; £4. The Cricketers out
at Mill Green is a prettily set food pub.
KELVEDON HATCH TQ5599
Secret Nuclear Bunker (off A128)
Who'd have thought that a three-storey
Cold War underground complex lay
beneath this innocuous 1950s

bungalow? It's eerily quiet when you enter (not even a member of staff in the bungalow, you pay at the end of the visit); knowledgeable tours take you through all parts of this clinically self-sufficient little world, and are done with real relish, so you can't help feeling relieved when you're back in the surrounding woodland. Very atmospheric, it's as much a vision of what the future might have been like as a grim memento of the Cold War. Audio tour, various videos (one showing what you needed to do in case of a nuclear bomb alert), wknd meals, snacks, well-stocked shop; cl Mon-Weds Nov-Feb and 25 Dec, best to check; (01277) 364883; £5. The Black Horse in Pilgrims Hatch is a good handy dining pub.

LAYER DE LA HAYE TL9517
Abberton Reservoir Wildlife Centre (B1026, Layer de la Haye) Popular wetland stop for wildfowl; observation room and hides, nature trails, and events for families in summer. Snacks, shop, disabled access; cl Mon (exc bank hol) and 25-26 Dec; (01206) 738172; £1 suggested donation (more for special events). The Donkey & Buskins (B1026) is handy for a meal.

LAYER MARNEY TL9217
Layer Marney Tower The mansion here was never completed, but its eight-storey Tudor gatehouse is very impressive - one of the most striking examples of 16th-c architecture in Britain. Around it are formal gardens, a rare breeds farm, medieval barn, farm shop, parkland and a play area. Tearoom, shop, disabled access (new lift); cl am, all day Sat, and Oct-Mar; (01206) 330784; £3.50.

LINFORD TQ6881
Walton Hall Museum 🎟 Private collection of memorabilia in restored farm buildings, with a bit of everything from a decent collection of farm machinery and engines, tricycles and a 19th-c gypsy caravan, to military items and Victorian and Edwardian toys. Also children's play area, picnic and barbecue areas. On some summer days you can watch blacksmiths, saddle-makers, printers and wheelwrights, and they often bake bread. Snacks, shop, disabled access; cl Mon-Weds (exc school and bank hols), and Dec 24-Easter; (01375)

671874; £3. The Bell at Horndon-on-the-Hill is fairly handy for lunch.

LITTLE BADDOW TL7707
Blakes Wood Ancient woodland of hornbeam and chestnut coppice, with lovely bluebells in spring. The newly refurbished Generals Arms is useful for lunch.

LITTLE DUNMOW TL6521
Little Dunmow church Unusually stately for such a relatively small village - it's the surviving part of a priory founded in 1106. The Flitch of Bacon is a good pub.

LITTLE EASTON TL5924
Gardens of Easton Lodge 🎟 Queen Elizabeth I once owned the 14th-c deer park in which these charming gardens are set. Handed down through generations of the Maynard family, who lived in the apparently doomed Easton Lodge (both the original and its Jacobean wings were destroyed by fires), the gardens were redeveloped by the current owners in the mid-1990s, and are a nice reflection of changing tastes in gardening. Harold Peto possibly left the biggest impression in the early 1900s, with his sunken italian garden, unique courtyard and adults' tree-house (now a ruin). The most recent development is a flower bed with every plant mentioned in Shakespeare's works. Snacks and cream teas, shop, disabled access (can be tricky in wet weather); open pms Fri-Sun and bank hols Feb-Oct (open daily when the snowdrops are out, phone to check); (01371) 876979; £3.80. The ancient Green Man at Mill End Green NE of here has good food.

Little Easton Manor 🎟 Pleasant summer gardens with topiary and lakes - you can fish here (from £3). Snacks, disabled access; open Thurs pm Jun-Sept; (01371) 872857; £2.50 (inc a deck chair). Little Easton church just beside the manor is also worth a visit. Nearby Great Easton is attractive for strolling through, with good plain food at the Swan.

LITTLE MAPLESTEAD TL8234
Little Maplestead church Very different from most in the area - an unusual round building modelled on the Holy Sepulchre in Jerusalem.

MALDON TL8506
The **Maeldune Heritage Centre**

(junction Market Hill/High St) houses a 13-metre (42 ft) tapestry commemorating the 1,000th anniversary of the crucial Battle of Maldon. Art gallery, shop, disabled access; cl am and Sun, plus Weds Nov-Mar; (01621) 851628; free. The **Millennium Gardens** are named for the same event, and recreate what a garden might have looked like at the time of the battle. Also a **church** with an unusual triangular tower, some decent shops, a couple of small museums, and a riverside stroll past the golf course to the pretty weir by Beeleigh Abbey. You can pick up guided walk leaflets from the Tourist Information Centre in Coach Lane, and go on a tour of the Moot Hall (High St), which has an unusual brick newel staircase, courtroom and good views from the roof; Sat 2 and 3.30pm Mar-Oct or by appointment; (01621) 857373; £1. The interestingly furnished Blue Boar (Silver St), open all day, is a good civilised port of call.

Hythe Quay Full of life, and the best chance to see one of the classic Thames barges with its ox-blood sails in action. At the quayside Jolly Sailor (Church St) you can eat looking out over the water.

MERSEA ISLAND TM0012
Much of the coast is a National Nature Reserve for its shore life, and there's a bracing coastal walk from East Mersea along the sea dyke overlooking the Colne estuary. It does feel very much an island (the highest tides cover the little causeway which links it to the mainland), and away from the extended village of West Mersea, popular for retirement homes, there are few people about out of season (in summer the caravan parks bring in lots of families). The Company Shed serves huge platters of shellfish in simple surroundings, and you can take your own wine and bread; the Willow Lodge has good food, and the Blackwater and Fox are good value too.

MISTLEY TM1031
Environmental & Animal Centre (New Rd) Very friendly animal rescue centre with over 2,000 inmates: Ping and Pong the white vietnamese pot-bellied pigs may roll out to greet you as you go in. Snacks (wknds only in winter), shop, disabled access; cl Mon and in bad weather during winter - phone to check; (01206) 396483; £3. The village has the remains of a Robert Adam church (known locally as Mistley Towers). If you come by train, don't miss the splendid station buffet at Manningtree.

MORETON TL5306
This is an attractive village, with an interesting circular walk from the White Hart (which has enjoyable food).

ONGAR TL5305
Blake Hall Gardens 🏠
(Bobbingworth, off A414 W) A peaceful garden walk takes in an ornamental wood, ice house and bog garden, herbaceous borders, rose garden, sunken garden and large tropical house; in the south wing of the house is a little aviation museum. Snacks and picnic area, shop; open Sat-Weds Easter to end Sept; £3. The White Hart at nearby Moreton has generous italian-leaning food all day.

PITSEA TQ7387
Motorboat Museum (Wat Tyler Country Park) The evolution of the motorboat with exhibits from 1823 to the present (inc rare examples and record breakers); remote control boats for children (20p). Snacks, shop, disabled access; cl Tues and Weds (exc school hols), and 23 Dec-2 Jan; (01268) 550077; free. The 125-acre country park also contains a play area, miniature railway and craft shops.

PLESHEY TL6614
This attractive village has a ruined castle, charming churchyard, country walks - and a good pub, the White Horse.

PURLEIGH TL8302
New Hall Vineyards Covering 97 acres, this 30-year-old vineyard is the largest in East Anglia; free tastings, guided group tours (by arrangement May-Sept). They host an annual english wine festival (craft fair, live music, art exhibitions) on the first wknd in Sept. Snacks, shop, disabled access; cl wknd pms, 25-26 Dec and 1 Jan ; (01621) 828343; free.

RETTENDON TQ7899
RHS Garden (Hyde Hall) Twenty acres of year-round hillside colour, with woodland garden, big rose garden, a dry garden (this is one of the UK's driest areas), ornamental ponds, shrubs,

trees, national viburnum collection, and a millennium avenue with wildflower meadows. Meals and snacks in thatched barn, plant centre, visitor centre and shop, garden library, disabled access; cl 25 Dec; (01245) 400256; *£4.50. The Windmill over at East Hanningfield has enjoyable food.

RIVER CROUCH WALKS TQ8596
The Ferry Boat Inn down nr the River Crouch at the end of the lane through North Fambridge is a good base for lonely waterside walks.

ROWHEDGE TM0221
The village itself is well worth a visit, with enjoyable food and good views from the recently reopened waterside Anchor, and a pedestrian ferry to Wivenhoe - phone Colchester visitor centre for times; (01206) 282920. Nearby is a nature reserve among former gravel workings at Fingringhoe, where the Whalebone (beside the county's oldest oak) has good inventive food.

SAFFRON WALDEN TL5438
The finest small town in the region, with prime examples of warmly colour-washed pargeting throughout. Walking around looking at buildings, you'll find it difficult to avoid being tempted into one of the many antiques shops (or David Prue, the fine cabinet-maker in Radwinter Rd; cl Sun and am Sat; (01799) 522558). The grand airy **church** has a magnificent spire, the very ruined **castle** up on a grassy mound is worth prowling around, and children will enjoy the maze on the Common. The Eight Bells is an appealing food pub, and the Crown just N at Little Walden is very nice for lunch. The town has a goodish network of tracks for walks around it, extending into the parkland of nearby Audley End House. Longer rambles can take in Newport, where the houses have characteristic pargeted plaster walls, and Wendens Ambo. The B184 to Chipping Ongar is a pleasant country drive; about 4m along, Grace's Farm Shop at Wimbish is good, with **pick-your-own** in summer; (01371) 830387. Another good drive is the B1053 to Braintree.

Audley End House (B1383, 1m W)
Spectacular Jacobean mansion and former Royal palace remodelled by Robert Adam. This is serenely surrounded by splendid gardens landscaped by Capability Brown. Nothing inside can compete with the quite breathtaking façade, but it's not for want of trying - there are around 30 rooms to see, crammed with fine furnishings inc a magnificent doll's house, and art. There are also suitably grand concerts and other events in the grounds. Meals, snacks, shop, disabled access to gardens and ground floor; cl Mon (exc bank hols), Tues, wkdys Oct, and Nov-Mar; (01799) 522842; £8, £4 grounds only; EH.

Bridge End Gardens (Bridge St)
These early Victorian gardens spread over 3½ acres, with rose garden, formal dutch garden, kitchen garden and an atmospheric wilderness leading to a little grotto, are often closed, and they keep the yew maze locked anyway. So book ahead to collect a key from the tourist information centre (Market Pl). Limited disabled access; cl 25 Dec; (01799) 510444 to book; £10 refundable deposit.

Saffron Walden Museum (Museum St) Notable natural history section in this town museum, as well as social history, archaeology, ethnography, toys and dolls, and a new furniture gallery. Shop, good disabled access; cl am Sun and bank hols, 24-25 Dec; (01799) 510333; £1.

SOUTH WEALD TQ5992
In this attractive village, the Tower Arms is an enjoyable food pub.

Old Macdonalds Farm Park See *separate family panel on p.216.*

SOUTH WOODHAM FERRERS TQ8096

Marsh Farm Country Park You can get close to some of the animals at this working farm, and there are play areas, tractor rides and a farm trail. Meals, snacks, shop, disabled access; open daily Feb half-term to Oct half-term then wknds till middle of Dec, best to check; (01245) 321552; £5.20. Surrounded by the River Crouch on three sides, the 350-acre park also has a nature reserve attracting a variety of wild birds to its marshes and freshwater lakes.

Tropical Wings Butterfly and Birds (Wickford Rd) Lots of free-flying exotic butterflies and birds in this 560-sq metre (6,000-sq ft) tropical house, as well as a collection of creepy-crawlies and reptiles; outdoor aviaries inc a walk-through one, and a children's play area; also special events and encounter sessions in summer. Tearoom, good farm shop and plant centre, disabled access; cl wkdys Nov-Feb, 24-26 Dec, 1 Jan; £4.25.

SOUTHEND-ON-SEA TQ8885
Traditional seaside resort long favoured by East Londoners, with the attractions you'd expect. Most famous is the pier, the longest in the world, excellent for fishing, with its own museum housing, amongst other things, a collection of slot machines (open wknds, Tues-Weds and bank hols); (01702) 611214. A restored train service runs the length of the pier - it's a long walk there and back. Like many such resorts, Southend in winter has a special appeal for people who wouldn't like it in summer - seafront shops by the endless promenade looking closed for ever, the sea itself a doleful muddy grey. The Westcliff part of town is pleasant, with a decent art gallery (cl 1-2pm; Sun and Mon; (01702) 347418; free), and on the Eastern Esplanade, the Kursaal, first opened in 1901, was the world's first theme park (now a bowling alley and amusement arcade). The Victorian cliff gardens (Prittlewell Sq) have now been restored with the help of a lottery grant. Summer **boat trips** include occasional runs on a vintage paddle-steamer; (01634) 827648 for dates (usually Jun-July, and Sept-Oct). The Last Post (Weston Rd) has decent food all day.

Central Museum & Planetarium (Victoria Ave) The only planetarium in the South-East outside London, with a local history museum and a hands-on discovery centre. Shop, disabled access to museum; cl Sun, Mon, inc bank hols (planetarium cl Sun-Tues); (01702) 215131; planetarium £2.30, museum and discovery centre free.

Leigh-on-Sea Adjoining Southend, this has a quite distinct character, altogether more intimate, with wood-clad buildings and shrimp boats in the working harbour; Ivy Osborne's cockle stall here is justly famous, and the Crooked Billet overlooking the water has real old-fashioned character.

Prittlewell Priory Museum (Priory Park, slightly N of centre) 12th-c Cluniac priory in nice grounds, with eclectic collections of local and religious history. Shop, disabled access to ground floor only; usually cl 1-2pm, all day Sun, Mon and bank hols; (01702) 342878; free. Repairs to the museum will take place probably early 2004, so phone for information, or check their website (www.southendmuseums.co.uk).

Sea Life Adventure (Eastern Esplanade) The highlight is the walk-through tunnel along a reconstructed sea bed with sharks; you can watch shoals of piranhas being fed, and there are regular daily talks. Meals, snacks, shop, disabled access; cl 25 Dec; (01702) 601834; £5.25. Also here is a three-storey children's play centre (£3 or joint ticket £4.75).

Southchurch Hall Museum (Park Lane) An unexpected find, a medieval moated manor house in an attractive park, with period room settings, and fun talks on Tudor life; occasional lute demonstrations. Shop, limited disabled access; cl 1-2pm, all Sun and Mon and bank hols, plus a few days over Christmas; (01702) 467671; free (small charge for talks).

ST OSYTH TM1215
This pretty village is distinguished by the remarkable crenellated flint gateway leading to **St Osyth Priory** (the lovely buildings and grounds behind are not open to the public). The White Hart towards Point Clear has good value food.

STANSTED TL5125
House on the Hill Toy Museum (Grove Hill (B1051)) Home to an awesome privately owned toy collection, with over 50,000 toys, games and playthings from Victorian times to the 1970s. Quite a few toy museums attract parents more than children, but this one avoids that by making its very well thought out displays entertaining to look at; lots of them are animated, and it's great fun watching the soldiers, trains and Meccano in action. There are a few coin-operated slot machines and puppet shows, and a collection of celebrity memorabilia. All indoors, so good in any weather. Good shop, cl Mon Nov-Mar, plus a few days over

Christmas; (01279) 813237; £4 (discount if you visit the castle in the same day). The Three Willows over at Birchanger is a good food pub.

Mountfitchet Castle & 1066 Village (Grove Hill) Intriguing, an authentically reconstructed Norman castle and village, complete with thatched houses, and deer, sheep, goats and chickens wandering around among them. The castle includes a small chunk of the original, and dummies display gruesome tortures and punishments. Cheerful and enthusiastic rather than particularly sophisticated, it's a good introduction to life a thousand years ago, though you will need to visit on a dry day. Snacks (and space for picnics), shop, some disabled access; cl mid-Nov to mid-Mar; (01279) 813237; £6. It's under the same management as the toy museum five mins' walk up the hill, with a discount if you visit both on same day.

Stansted Mountfitchet Windmill The well preserved 18th-c windmill still has much of its original equipment (though isn't working). Shop; open pm first Sun of month Apr-Oct, and pm bank hol Sun and Mons; 50p.

THAXTED TL6131
This engaging small town has a graceful, airy church (where Holst was organist) with a tremendous spire, several handsome buildings inc nearby almshouses, a fine 600-year-old guildhall (occasional craft markets), and the restored John Webb windmill. The Raven Armoury (B184 towards Dunmow) does hand-forged steel and weaponry. The 15th-c Swan has decent food.

TILBURY TQ6475
Tilbury Fort Well preserved 17th-c fort with unusual double moat, and good views of the Thames estuary. The most violent episode in its history was a 1776 cricket match that left three dead. Snacks, shop, some disabled access; cl Mon-Tues Nov-Mar, also 24-26 Dec and 1 Jan; (01375) 858489; £3; EH. For an extra £1.30 you can fire a 1943 anti-aircraft gun. There is a pleasant 3-mile walk along the Thames to **Coalhouse Fort** (off A1013 Orsett—Stanford-le-Hope; open last Sun of month and bank hols Mar-Oct, plus 11 July, 11-12 Sept and 29-30 Oct; park around the fort open all year; (01375) 844203; £2.50.

TIPTREE TM8915
Tiptree Visitor Centre Readers tell us this famous jam firm's well set out little jam museum, popular tearoom, and shop are worth popping into if you're in the area; they do occasional factory tours, phone for details. Cl Sun (exc pm May-Aug), plus a wk over Christmas; (01621) 814524; free.

TOLLESBURY TL9510
This inland village is the ideal starting point for one of the best circular coastal walks in Essex, where linking paths head out to the sea wall skirting a breezy peninsula jutting into the Blackwater estuary; excellent for bird-watching, and lots of flora and insect life in the surrounding marshes. You can also start nr the marina and Edwardian sail lofts E of the village.

WALTHAM ABBEY TL3800
Despite the surrounding housing developments, the centre has some handsome buildings - especially the **Abbey church** with its famous peal of 12 bells. Shop (in the crypt), disabled access ground floor only; cl am Sun, 25-26 Dec, Good Fri, and during church services; (01992) 767897. There are claims that King Harold was buried here after the Battle of Hastings, and there's a memorial to him E of the church. Associated ruins include part of a Norman cloister, and the bridge dates back to the abbey's time.

Capel Manor College 🎫 (Bullsmoor Lane, off A10 just S of M25) Plenty of useful tips for would-be gardeners, with over 30 acres of themed gardens, and lots of good special events; animal corner and holly maze. Cl wknds end Oct-beginning Mar and over Christmas; (020) 8366 4442; £5. Though officially in Enfield, this fits well with a Waltham Abbey visit. The nearby Pied Bull has well priced food.

Epping Forest District Museum (Sun St) Lively holiday activities for children, archaeological displays, Tudor room and Victorian gallery in two timber-framed old houses, and also a herb garden. Snacks, shop, limited disabled access; cl am (exc Sat), Weds-Thurs, and also Sun Oct-Mar; (01992) 716882; free.

Lee Valley Park Farms 🎫 (B194, 2m N) Takes in Hayes Hill children's farm with plenty of traditional animals, a pet centre and play area, and Holyfield Hall working farm and dairy, with 150 cows milked every afternoon around 3pm, and seasonal events such as sheep-shearing and harvesting. Meals, snacks and picnic area, shop, disabled access; (01992) 892781; £3.50.

Royal Gunpowder Mills (Beaulieu Drive, off A121) These former gunpowder works, established in the 17th c, had an international reputation because of their superior production methods, and in World War I 5,000 people were employed here. Many of the restored old buildings are open, and there are good displays on the evolution of explosives and development of the mills, with a film, and a nice mix of traditional and hands-on exhibits; changing displays too. It's a massive site, with 175 acres of surrounding parkland, and part of this is now a well laid out nature reserve, with a colony of herons, muntjac deer and otters; good views from a tower. For £1 extra, they usually have guided tractor trailer rides throughout the day. Meals, snacks, shop, disabled access; open wknds 24 Apr-26 Sept, and for special events round Christmas; (01992) 707370; £5.50 adults.

WALTON-ON-THE-NAZE TM2623

There's a nice coast walk N from this quiet seaside town. Rounding the tip of the Naze, with views of ships entering and leaving Harwich and Felixstowe, you come to a nature trail through a reserve harbouring migrant birds. You can fish from the long pier (£5), and there are amusement arcades, various rides in summer, and a soft play area. Two-hour wildlife spotting boat trips (you'll see seals) leave from Foundry Slip, signposted from Hall Lane; (01255) 671852.

WETHERSFIELD TL7229

Boydells Dairy Farm [£] Working dairy farm where you may be able to

join in milking - cows, even goats and sheep. Also working beehive, various other animals, and ice lollies made from their own sheep yoghurt. Snacks, shop, disabled access; cl am, Mon-Thurs (exc school hols) and end Sept-Easter; £3.50; (01371) 850481. The Bull over at Blackmore End is a popular dining pub welcoming children.

WIDDINGTON TL5431

Mole Hall Wildlife Park Family-run place with wide variety of animals around moated manor house. Otters a speciality, but also free-roaming wildfowl, deer paddock, a butterfly house, and a summer maize maze. Summer snacks, shop, some disabled access; park only cl 25 Dec, but butterfly house cl Nov to mid-Mar; (01799) 540400; £5, less in winter. The low-beamed Fleur de Lys has tasty home-made food.

WRITTLE TL6700

Hylands House and Gardens [£] (Hylands Park) Six rooms in this neo-classical villa have been restored, inc the gilded Victorian drawing room and Georgian entrance hall, and they've also recently finished restoring the West Wing and basement. Outside are pleasure gardens and over 500 acres of landscaped park; guided tours by arrangement; tearoom on Sun, shop, disabled access; open Sun and Mon (cl 25 Dec, and during its annual pop festival); (01245) 496800; £3.20 (free to park and garden). The Red Lion at Margaretting is a popular food pub.

Other attractive villages, all with decent pubs, include Arkesden TL4834, Blackmore TL6001 (big antiques/crafts shop), Fuller Street TL7416, Fyfield TL5606, Great Chesterford TL5143, Great Easton TL6126, Great Warley Street TQ5890, Knowl Green TL7841, Paglesham TQ9293, Roydon TL4109, Stebbing TL6624, Wickham Bishops TL8412, and (both waterside) Heybridge Basin TL8707 and Wivenhoe TM0321.

Where to eat

BURNHAM-ON-CROUCH TQ9595 **Contented Sole** *80 High St (01621) 782139* Long-standing, family-run evening restaurant (though they do Sun lunch), very popular for consistently good imaginative food with emphasis on fine seafood; popular wine tastings all year; cl Sun pm (open for lunch), Mon, Jan; disabled access. £28

CASTLE HEDINGHAM TL7835 **Bell** *St James's St (01787)* 460350 Run by the same family for over 30 years, this interesting old coaching inn has a log fire in the beamed lounge bar, a traditionally furnished public bar, no smoking area, enjoyable traditional bar food, and lovely big walled garden behind; cl 25 Dec pm; disabled access. £20|£5

CHAPPEL TL8928 **Swan** *The Street (01787)* 222353 Popular old timbered pub, splendidly set, with the River Colne running through the garden on its way downstream to impressive Victorian viaduct, and big overflowing flower tubs and french street signs give the sheltered suntrap cobbled courtyard a continental feel; spacious, low-beamed rambling bar with standing oak timbers dividing off side areas, plenty of dark wood chairs around lots of dark tables for diners, one or two swan pictures and plates on the white and partly panelled walls; big fireplace, and pubby central bar; no smoking lounge, well kept real ales, wines by the glass, and excellent range of deliciously cooked fresh fish (and other dishes, too). £23|£6.95

CHELMSFORD TL7107 **Alma** *37 Arbour Lane (01245)* 256785 Attractively laid out place with a civilised country-pub feel, beamed bar, a comfortable mix of furniture and central brick fireplace, a nice collection of old advertising posters, well kept real ales and decent house wines; good friendly service, no smoking dining area and prettily decorated restaurant, and good, imaginative food; picnic-sets out on a crazy-paved front terrace and in a small back garden; cl 26 Dec. £25|£6

CLAVERING TL4832 **Cricketers** *(01799)* 550442 Run by the parents of TV chef Jamie Oliver, this smart comfortably modernised 16th-c dining pub has an L-shaped beamed bar with standing timbers on new brickwork, gleaming copper, dried flowers in big fireplaces, and a wide choice of interesting and elaborate food inc super puddings; pretty bdrms; cl 25-26 Dec; partial disabled access. £30|£10

COLCHESTER TL9925 **Warehouse Brasserie** *12 Chapel St North (01206)* 765656 Bustling bistro with friendly relaxed atmosphere, pine settles and chairs, an upper gallery area, prints on warm red walls, real ales, enjoyable interesting food, and decent wines; cl Sun, Mon; disabled access. £25|£5.95

DEDHAM TM0433 **Milsom's** *Stratford Rd (01206)* 322795 Stylish place with ties to Le Talbooth and the Pier at Harwich; scrubbed wooden tables on wooden floors in two dining areas, contemporary bistro-style food, a good wine list, and smart, casual staff; open for morning coffee; disabled access. £25|£6.50

FINGRINGHOE TM0220 **Whalebone** *Chapel Rd (01206)* 729307 Garden with a peaceful valley view, three opened-up room areas inside with a pleasant mix of chairs and cushioned settles around stripped tables on unsealed bare boards, a coal fire, and especially good changing daily specials cooked inventively and nicely presented; they do a good breakfast until 11.30am; good service, well kept real ales and decent house wines and coffee; partial disabled access. £22|£5.50

GOSFIELD TL7829 **Green Man** *The Street (01787)* 472746 Smart dining pub with a relaxed chatty atmosphere, two little bars and no smoking dining room, good daily changing food inc marvellous lunchtime cold buffet and delicious puddings, well kept real ales and decent wines, many by the glass; no food Sun pm; partial disabled access. £24|£6.95

GREAT YELDHAM TL7637 **White Hart** *Poole St (01787)* 237250 Striking black and white timbered building with beams, oak panelling, and stone or wooden floors, successfully ambitious food which can be eaten in bar or restaurant, a fine range of wines inc 12 by the glass, real ales; best to book; seats in the attractive garden. £25.50/2-course lunch £10.50

HARWICH TM2532 **Pier at Harwich** *The Quay (01255)* 241212 Attractive restaurant overlooking the Stour and Orwell estuaries, with particularly good fresh fish dishes (and lobsters from their salt-water tanks); more informal, brightly decorated Ha'penny Pier downstairs, and first-floor dining room with more ambitious dishes; thoughtful choice of wines; attractive bdrms; cl pm 25-26 Dec. £36/2-course lunch £16

HORNDON-ON-THE-HILL TQ6783 **Bell** *(01375)* 673154 Flower-decked medieval inn with welcoming licensees, open-plan beamed bar with polished oak floorboards and flagstones, carefully prepared imaginative food that changes twice daily, five real ales, good choice of wines; restaurant cl 25-26 Dec, bank hol Mon; disabled access. £28|**£6.95**

LITTLE DUNMOW TL6521 **Flitch of Bacon** *(01371) 820323* Friendly pub with a good mix of customers, a small attractively furnished timbered bar, decent reasonably priced food, several wines by the glass, and real ales; comfortable bdrms; children away from bar area; disabled access. £19.50|**£6.75**

MESSING TL8918 **Crispin's** *The Street (01621) 815868* Friendly Elizabethan restaurant with open fire in beamed lounge, candles on the walls and tables, good food inc fish and vegetarian choices, monthly themed evenings, a good wine list, helpful service, and quiet back garden; bdrms; cl Mon, Sun pm; children over 5. £35

YOUNGS END TL7319 **Green Dragon** *London Rd (01245) 361030* Well run dining pub with attractive understated barn theme in no smoking restaurant area, extensive range of good interesting bar food inc lots of fish, well kept real ales, and plenty of seats in back garden; disabled access. £21|**£6.50**

Special thanks to Michael and Jenny Back, Roy and Lindsey Fentiman

GLOUCESTERSHIRE

Perfect Cotswold countryside, the very different Forest of Dean, some of Britain's prettiest villages, and a good mix of places to visit, from farm parks to elegant gardens; though there are good family places, this is an outstanding area for older people

Flanked by a spectacular stretch of the Wye Valley, the hilly woodland of the Forest of Dean is punctuated by all sorts of interesting features often connected with the living people have made here in past centuries. Plenty of space is not the only attraction though: if you're after more structured entertainment, there's the Dean Heritage Centre (now even more family-friendly), Puzzle Wood and the Perrygrove Railway (great for little ones), and you can go on interesting tours of Hopewell Colliery, and explore atmospheric caverns nearby at Clearwell. Symonds Yat is very beautiful.

On a different note, the Cotswolds are a highly rewarding if rather grown-up place for a relaxing break, with their broad landscapes, charming stone-built villages and handsome towns. All filled with sightseeing possibilities, Chipping Campden, Cirencester, Northleach (the mechanical music museum is a favourite), Painswick (a cheery garden) and Stow-on-the-Wold are towns of real individuality. Villages such as Lower and Upper Slaughter, Bibury and Eastleach are perfect for an afternoon spent sauntering. The best place for families is bustling Bourton-on-the-Water, where you can choose between a maze, a motor museum, exotic birds, and a collection of amazingly detailed models.

Two drawbacks to the Cotswolds are that they tend to be expensive, and that in season they can get very crowded. Also, away from the villages, the countryside (with long stretches of unchanging arable farmland) can be a bit monotonous for serious walkers - though great for cyclists. The long-distance Cotswold Way between Chipping Campden and Bath goes through much of the best scenery. Cheltenham, still with a considerable degree of Regency elegance, is a good base for exploring the area, and the tourist information centre does a useful leaflet explaining how to get to most Cotswold attractions by public transport.

Away from the Cotswolds, some less well known parts are delightful (and generally cheaper): the tortuously steep hills and valleys around Stroud, the quiet water-meadows of the upper Thames, the unspoilt orchard and farming countryside around the Severn Valley (so few river crossings that the little villages down by the W bank, with few people passing through, have a very secluded and unchanging feel).

Gloucestershire has quite a bit to offer bird-lovers. The place with the most appeal for families is the Wildfowl & Wetlands Trust at Slimbridge (lots to see, even in winter). Bourton-on-the-Water has more than 50 aviaries, there are flying demonstrations at Moreton-in-Marsh, and at Prinknash Bird Park they have tame animals as well as birds. If you prefer animals, we recommend the farm park at Kineton (well organised, and handy on a wet day), friendly Butts Farm in South Cerney, and the country park at Tockington (good adventure play areas).

Favourite houses are topped by Berkeley Castle (our Gloucestershire Family Attraction), Sudeley Castle near Winchcombe (splendid inside and out), Dyrham Park (hardly changed since the 17th c), and Stanway House (a picturesque 16th-c manor in interesting grounds). Quite a contrast are the well preserved Roman villa at Yanworth, and the never-finished Gothic mansion at Nympsfield. There are magnificent arboretums at Moreton-in-Marsh and Westonbirt (lovely for a walk). If you prefer roses, a visit to Mickleton or North Nibley is a must; Lydney Park is more of a spring garden. The art collection inspired by nature at Twigworth has some interesting surprises.

Among other attractions in busy Gloucester, the National Waterways Museum in the docks is especially worth mentioning. For a change of pace, attractive Tewkesbury, with its outstanding abbey, makes a nice objective for a peaceful day trip.

Where to stay

ASHLEWORTH SO8125 **Ashleworth Court** *Ashleworth, Gloucester, Gloucestershire GL19 4JA (01452) 700241* **£50***; 3 rms, shared bthrms. By a small elegant church and NT tithe barn, this striking ancient house is part of a working farm and has a homely kitchen with an Aga, a comfortable sitting room, enjoyable breakfasts served in what was originally part of the Great Hall, and chickens in the back garden; trampoline and wooden climbing frame for children; two good pubs in the village; cl Christmas

BIBURY SP1106 **Bibury Court** *Bibury, Cirencester, Gloucestershire GL7 5NT (01285) 740337* **£130**, plus special breaks; 18 individual rms. Lovely peaceful mansion dating from Tudor times, in beautiful gardens, with an informal friendly atmosphere, panelled rooms, antiques, huge log fires, conservatory, a fine choice of breakfasts, and good interesting food; disabled access; dogs welcome in bedrooms

BIBURY SP1106 **Swan** *Bibury, Cirencester, Gloucestershire GL7 5NW (01285) 740695* **£130**, plus special breaks; 20 very pretty individually decorated rms. Handsome creeper-covered hotel on the River Coln, with private fishing and attractive formal gardens; lovely flowers and log fires in carefully furnished comfortable lounges, a cosy no smoking parlour, good food in opulent dining room, nice breakfasts, and attentive staff; disabled access; dogs in cottage

BLOCKLEY SP1634 **Lower Brook House** *Lower St, Blockley, Moreton-in-Marsh, Gloucestershire GL56 9DS (01386) 700286* **£80*** ; 7 attractive rms with fresh fruit and chocolates. 17th-c Cotswold stone building with beams, flagstones and open fires, antique furniture and interesting bric-a-brac, good modern british cooking using home-grown produce and enjoyable breakfasts in cosy dining room, a comfortable drawing room, and helpful staff

BUCKLAND SP0835 **Buckland Manor** *Buckland, Broadway, Worcestershire WR12 7LY (01386) 852626* **£235***; 13 sumptuous rms. Really lovely 13th-c building in 10 acres of beautifully kept gardens, comfortable lounges with magnificent oak panelling, flowers and antiques, and elegant restaurant with fine food using home-grown produce; outdoor swimming pool, riding, tennis, croquet, putting; children over 12

CHELTENHAM SO9523 **Hotel on the Park** *Evesham Rd, Cheltenham, Gloucestershire GL52 2AH (01242) 518898* **£136**, plus special breaks; 12 lovely rms. Warmly welcoming and handsome Regency house with elegantly furnished drawing room and dining room, pretty flowers and antiques, and imaginative food in stylish restaurant - good breakfasts, too; children over 8; dogs by special arrangement

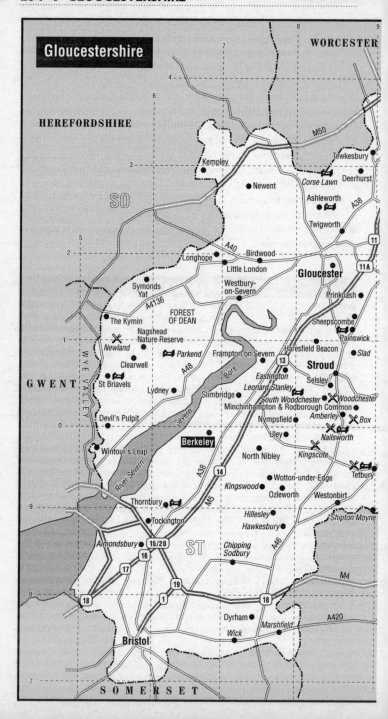

Gloucestershire

WORCESTER

HEREFORDSHIRE

SO

Kempley

Newent

Corse Lawn   Deerhurst
Tewkesbury

Ashleworth

Twigworth

M50

A38

11

11A

A40   Birdwood
Longhope   Little London   **Gloucester**

Symonds   Westbury-
Yat   on-Severn   Prinknash

A4136   THE KYMIN   Sheepscombe
The Kymin   FOREST   Painswick
OF DEAN   Slad
Nagshead   Haresfield Beacon
Nature Reserve   13   **Stroud**
Newland   Parkend   Frampton on Severn
Clearwell   A48   Eastington   Selsley
St Briavels   Leonard Stanley   Woodchester
Lydney   Slimbridge   South Woodchester
Minchinhampton & Rodborough Common
Devil's Pulpit   Nympsfield   Amberley   Box
Uley   Nailsworth
Wintour's Leap   **Berkeley**   Kingscote   Tetbury
North Nibley
14   Wotton-under-Edge
Kingswood   Ozleworth   Westonbirt
Thornbury   Hillesley   Shipton Moyne
Tockington   Hawksbury

GWENT

WYE VALLEY

River Severn

Severn Bore

A38

M5

Almondsbury   15/20
16   ST   Chipping
Sodbury
17   A46
19
18   1   18   M4
Dyrham
A420
Wick   Marshfield

Bristol

SOMERSET

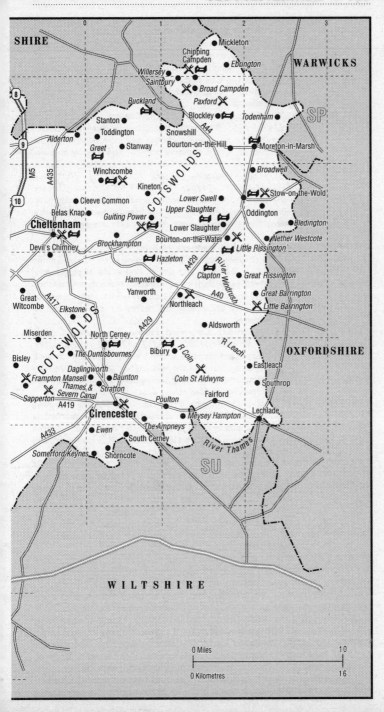

CHELTENHAM SO9421 **Kandinsky Hotel** *Bayshill Rd, Cheltenham, Gloucestershire GL50 3AS (01242) 527788* **£90**; 48 large, stylish and well equipped rms. White-painted Regency hotel with an interesting mix of old and new furnishings, antiques and modern paintings, big pot plants, lots of mirrors, unusual collections on walls, tiled or wooden floors, and a relaxed, informal atmosphere; enjoyable modern food in bustling Café Paradiso, friendly bar, willing young staff, downstairs cocktail bar, and seats out on decked terrace; they are kind to families; disabled access; dogs anywhere ☺

CHELTENHAM SO9421 **Lypiatt House** *Lypiatt Rd, Cheltenham, Gloucestershire GL50 2QW (01242) 224994* **£75**; 10 attractive rms. Carefully restored Victorian house in its own grounds, with an open fire, books and fresh flowers in light, comfortable drawing room; attractive conservatory bar, and friendly personal service; cl 2 wks Christmas

CHELTENHAM SO9421 **Wyastone Hotel** *Parabola Rd, Montpellier, Cheltenham, Gloucestershire GL50 3BG (01242) 245549* **£79.50**, plus special breaks; 13 pretty rms. Quietly set Victorian house with a panelled bar and cosy pink-coloured lounge, plenty of period features, warmly friendly owners, enjoyable breakfasts, and traditional french evening meals; charming little terraced garden; cl Christmas-New Year

CHIPPING CAMPDEN SP1539 **Badgers Hall** *High St, Chipping Campden, Gloucestershire GL55 6HB (01386) 840839* **£75**; 2 beamed rms. Opposite the historic market hall, this fine old stone and timber house has friendly helpful owners, a relaxed atmosphere, particularly good breakfasts plus a thriving teashop with home-made lunches and afternoon teas, and a display of local artists' work for sale; no smoking; plenty of pubs and restaurants nearby for evening meals; cl Christmas/New Year; no children

CHIPPING CAMPDEN SP1539 **Cotswold House** *The Square, Chipping Campden, Gloucestershire GL55 6AN (01386) 840330* **£175**; 20 rms. Imposing Regency house in lovely town and run by warmly friendly 'hands-on' owners; beautiful central staircase, relaxing drawing room with log fire, good british cooking in modern brasserie or restaurant, a cossetting atmosphere, sunny terraces, and formal garden; plenty to see nearby; disabled access; dogs welcome in bedrooms

CHIPPING CAMPDEN SP1539 **Eight Bells** *Church St, Chipping Campden, Gloucestershire GL55 6JG (01386) 840371* **£70**, plus winter breaks; 4 rms. Neatly restored heavy-beamed 14th-c pub by church, with a newly refurbished bar, three log fires, interesting food with fresh local produce, friendly staff, decent wines and beers, a new terrace, and pleasant courtyard; cl Nov-Mar; dogs anywhere

CLAPTON SP1617 **Clapton Manor** *Clapton, Cheltenham, Gloucestershire GL54 2LG (01451) 810202* **£80***; 2 charming rms. Fine 16th-c Cotswold stone house in lovely interestingly planted gardens with marvellous views across the Windrush Valley; large inglenook fireplaces, heavy beams, mullioned windows, antiques, and a relaxed, informal family atmosphere; log fire and TV in residents' sitting room, and good breakfasts with home-made jams and their own eggs served in the dining room or on the terrace; no smoking; several restaurants and pubs nearby for dinner; cl Christmas and New Year's Eve

CORSE LAWN SO8330 **Corse Lawn House** *Corse Lawn, Gloucestershire GL19 4LZ (01452) 780771* **£135***, plus special breaks; 19 pretty, individually furnished rms. Magnificent Queen Anne building with comfortable and attractive day rooms, a distinguished restaurant with imaginative food and excellent wines (there's a less pricey bistro-style operation too), warmly friendly staff, a relaxed atmosphere, and an indoor swimming pool, tennis court, croquet, and horses in 12 acres of surrounding gardens and fields; cl 24-26 Dec; disabled access; dogs welcome away from restaurant

GREET SP0230 **Manor Farm** *Market Lane, Greet, Cheltenham, Gloucestershire GL54 5BJ (01242) 602423* **£60***; 3 rms. Carefully restored 16th-c manor house on mixed farm with nice breakfasts, fine views, and a big garden with a fish pond and croquet; steam train just 150 yards away; also, camp and caravan site; cl Christmas

GUITING POWER SP0924 **Guiting Guest House** *Post Office Lane, Guiting*

Power, Cheltenham, Gloucestershire GL54 5TZ (01451) 850470 £70; 7 pretty rms with thoughtful extras. 16th-c Cotswold stone guest house with inglenook fireplaces, beams, and rugs on flagstones, two sitting rooms, enjoyable evening meals by candlelight, attentive owners, and a very relaxed atmosphere; cl Christmas week; dogs in self contained annexe

HAZLETON SP0818 **Windrush House** *Hazleton, Cheltenham, Gloucestershire GL54 4EB (01451) 860364 £56**; 4 rms, 2 with own bthrm. Warmly friendly and neatly kept no smoking guest house, with exceptionally good imaginative food, lovely breakfasts, log fire, and traditional furnishings; cl mid-Dec to mid-Feb; no children; dogs welcome

LEONARD STANLEY SO8003 **Grey Cottage** *Leonard Stanley, Stonehouse, Gloucestershire GL10 3LU (01453) 822515 £67**; 3 rms overlooking garden or countryside, with flowers, fruit and biscuits. Carefully restored 170-year-old cottage with a pretty garden, really kind and thoughtful owner, interesting furnishings and fresh flowers, comfortable sitting room, marvellous breakfasts, and enjoyable meals by prior arrangement; children over 10

LITTLE RISSINGTON SP1919 **Touchstone** *Little Rissington, Cheltenham, Gloucestershire GL54 2ND (01451) 822481 £45**; 3 rms with thoughtful extras. Attractive traditional Cotswold stone house with very friendly owners, good breakfasts in dining room with doors on to terrace, and lots of nearby walks; cl Jan; no children

LOWER SLAUGHTER SP1522 **Lower Slaughter Manor** *Lower Slaughter, Cheltenham, Gloucestershire GL54 2HP (01451) 820456 £220*; 16 luxurious rms. Grand 17th-c manor house in four neatly kept acres with a 15th-c dovecot, all-weather tennis court, and croquet; lovely flower arrangements, log fires, fine plaster ceilings, antiques and paintings, excellent modern cooking and most enjoyable wines in the new restaurant, and attentive welcoming staff; children over 12; partial disabled access

MORETON-IN-MARSH SP2032 **White Hart Royal** *High St, Moreton-in-Marsh, Gloucestershire GL56 0BA (01608) 650731 £90*; 19 good rms. Busy and comfortable, partly 15th-c inn with interesting Civil War history, oak beams and stripped stone, big inglenook fire in lounge area just off main bar, friendly helpful staff, well kept real ales, and decent food in bar and pleasant restaurant; attractive courtyard; disabled access

NAILSWORTH ST8599 **Egypt Mill** *Stroud Rd, Nailsworth, Stroud, Gloucestershire GL6 0AE (01453) 833449 £75*, plus special breaks; 17 comfortable airy rms. Carefully converted 16th-c watermill with original millstones and lifting equipment in the spacious lounge, a split-level restaurant, ground floor bar where two waterwheels can be seen, enjoyable food, friendly service, and seats in the waterside gardens

NORTH CERNEY SP0107 **Bathurst Arms** *North Cerney, Cirencester, Gloucestershire GL7 7BZ (01285) 831281 £65*; 5 pleasant rms. Civilised and handsome old inn with lots of atmosphere, a nice mix of polished old furniture and a fireplace at each end of the beamed and panelled bar, small no smoking dining room, imaginative food, quite a few well chosen wines by the glass, well kept real ales, and an attractive garden running down to the River Churn; lots of surrounding walks

PAINSWICK SO8609 **Painswick Hotel** *Kemps Lane, Painswick, Stroud, Gloucestershire GL6 6YB (01452) 812160 £130**, plus special breaks; 19 individually furnished, comfortable rms with views of the village or countryside. 18th-c Palladian mansion - once a grand rectory - with fine views, antiques and paintings in the elegant rooms, open fires, good food using the best local produce, a thoughtful wine list, and a relaxed, friendly atmosphere; garden with croquet lawn; they are kind to families; dogs welcome away from restaurant ☺

PARKEND SO6108 **Edale House** *Folly Rd, Parkend, Lydney, Gloucestershire GL15 4JF (01594) 562835 £57**, plus special breaks; 5 rms, most with own bthrm. Georgian house opposite cricket green and backing on to Nagshead Nature Reserve; comfortable, homely sitting room, little bar, very good food in attractive no smoking dining room (overlooking the garden), and a relaxed atmosphere; children over 12; dogs welcome away from dining room

ST BRIAVELS SO5504 **George** *St Briavels, Lydney, Gloucestershire GL15 6TA (01594) 530228* **£55**; 4 rms. Pleasant old pub in particularly interesting village overlooking 12th-c castle, with three rambling rooms, big stone fireplace, a Celtic coffin lid dating from 1070 (found in a fireplace here and now mounted next to the bar counter), cosy dining room, real ales, and good food; outdoor chessboard; dogs in bar areas

STOW-ON-THE-WOLD SP1925 **Grapevine** *Sheep St, Stow-on-the-Wold, Cheltenham, Gloucestershire GL54 1AU (01451) 830344* **£130**, plus special breaks; 22 individually decorated, attractive, no smoking rms. Warm, friendly and very well run hotel with antiques, comfortable chairs and a relaxed atmosphere in the lounge, a beamed bar, and imaginative food in the attractive, sunny restaurant with its 70-year-old trailing vine; partial disabled access

STOW-ON-THE-WOLD SP1925 **Old Stocks** *The Square, Stow-on-the-Wold, Cheltenham, Gloucestershire GL54 1AF (01451) 830666* **£80**, plus special breaks; 18 rms. Well run 16th/17th-c Cotswold stone hotel with cosy welcoming small bar, beams and open fire, comfortable residents' lounge, good food, friendly staff, and sheltered garden; cl 18-28 Dec; disabled access; dogs welcome away from restaurant

TETBURY ST8494 **Calcot Manor** *Calcot, Tetbury, Gloucestershire GL8 8YJ (0666) 890391* **£180**, plus special breaks; 28 attractive rms inc 10 super family ones and suites in old Granary Barn. Charming former farmhouse with country house décor and log fires in comfortable lounges, extremely helpful friendly staff, imaginative food in conservatory restaurant and Gumstool brasserie, enjoyable breakfasts, and smallish outdoor swimming pool in enclosed courtyard; new spa with indoor pool and hot tub, exercise studio, gym, and 50 beauty treatments; they are particularly kind to families, with a qualified nanny in the playroom (stuffed with toys and games), computers and Playstation, tasty high teas, two tennis courts, an outdoor play area with bikes and lots of equipment, and plenty to do nearby; disabled access ☺

THORNBURY ST6390 **Thornbury Castle** *Castle St, Thornbury, Bristol BS35 1HH (01454) 281182* **£195**; 25 opulent rms, some with big Tudor fireplaces or fine oriel windows. Impressive and luxuriously renovated early 16th-c castle with antiques, tapestries, huge fireplaces and mullioned windows in the baronial public rooms, three dining rooms (one in the base of a tower), fine cooking, extensive wine list (inc wine from their own vineyard), thoughtful friendly service, and vast grounds inc the oldest Tudor gardens in England; cl 4 days Jan; partial disabled access; dogs by arrangement

UPPER SLAUGHTER SP1523 **Lords of the Manor** *Upper Slaughter, Cheltenham, Gloucestershire GL54 2JD (01451) 820243* **£155**, plus special breaks; 27 rms carefully furnished with antiques, Victorian sketches and paintings. Warmly friendly hotel with mid 17th-c heart (though it's been carefully extended many times), lovely views over eight acres of grounds from very comfortable library and drawing room, log fires, and fresh flowers; fine modern english cooking in attractive candlelit restaurant overlooking the original rectory gardens, good breakfasts, and kind service; children over 7 in restaurant (high tea available); partial disabled access

WINCHCOMBE SP0327 **Sudeley Hill Farm** *Sudeley Rd, Winchcombe, Cheltenham, Gloucestershire GL54 5JB (01242) 602344* **£50***; 3 comfortable no smoking rms. Friendly 15th-c farmhouse on working mixed farm of 800 acres, with log fires, a guest sitting room, and dining room overlooking the large garden; cl Christmas

WINCHCOMBE SP0228 **Wesley House** *High St, Winchcombe, Cheltenham, Gloucestershire GL54 5LJ (01242) 602366* **£75**, plus special breaks; 5 pleasantly furnished rms with individual antiques and showers. Pretty, half-timbered 15th-c town house with quiet friendly atmosphere, log fire in comfortable front lounge, very good attractively presented food inc lovely puddings in beamed restaurant, enjoyable breakfasts, and friendly informal service; old-fashioned garden furniture on small back terrace with pretty view; cl 25 Dec; babes in arms and children old enough to have their own room

To see and do

Gloucestershire Family Attraction of the Year

BERKELEY ST6899 **Berkeley Castle** (off A38) One reason why this excellently preserved castle seems to stimulate children's imaginations is because it's still very much a family home, and that lived-in feel makes it so much easier to picture the sometimes dark events that have occurred here. Indeed the same family has lived here for nearly 900 years, and the story of their castle's transition from Norman keep to the more elegant stately home of today is essentially the story of Britain; King Edward II was murdered here in 1327, Elizabeth I hunted and played bowls here, and it was where *A Midsummer Night's Dream* was first performed in the 16th c. There's masses to see, including impressive paintings, china and silver, furniture from Sir Francis Drake's *Golden Hind*, the splendid Great Hall, and the huge medieval kitchens. A breach in the wall of the still impressive original keep lets you see just how sturdy the original building was. Outside, the terraced gardens are full of interesting plants, as well as a notable collection of roses. Younger visitors enjoy the Butterfly House in the old walled kitchen garden, with lots of free-flying exotic species - and the world's largest moth; there's a good plant centre in here too. Special events might include extra activities for families, as well as occasional days when the castle's past is brought vividly to life by costumed actors, or when tours are conducted by the heir to the estate. Snacks, shop, limited disabled access (to Inner Courtyard and Butterfly House only); open Weds-Sat and pm Sun, Apr-Sept, plus bank hol Mon, and some summer Tues for special events (www.berkeley-castle.com for dates); (01453) 810332; £6.25 adults, £3.25 children over 5; a family ticket (two adults, two children) is good value at £16.25. The Butterfly House is an extra £2 for adults, £1 children.

ALDSWORTH SP1412
Sherborne Estate Covering 4,000-acres, this is a good example of a traditional Cotswold estate, with three deer parks and working water meadows; open all year; free. At **Lodge Park**, a rare 17th-c deer coursing park, you can visit the recreated grandstand; disabled access to ground floor; open Mon-Fri and am Sat Apr-end Oct; (01451) 844130; £4.40. Much of pretty Sherborne village is owned by the National Trust too.

ASHLEWORTH SO8125
A **tithe barn** of some note, a good dining pub, the Queens Arms, and a splendidly traditional pub, the Boat, right on the River Severn - in the same family for centuries.

BELAS KNAP SP0125
There's a pleasant walk up to Belas Knap, a massive 4,000-year-old barrow - one of England's best-preserved prehistoric burial sites, complete with original dry-stone walling enclosing four internal chambers. Great views from

the Craven Arms in Brockhampton (a good pub, with a nice garden in a lovely setting); this could be tied in with a walk past some very surprising ruins of a Roman villa tucked away in the woods.

BERKELEY ST6899
Berkeley Castle See *separate family panel above.*
Cattle Country Adventure Park £ (off B4066 E) Various cattle inc american bison, as well as birds of prey, miniature golf, willow maze, splash pool, and a giant zip wire; they've also a farm trail and indoor and outdoor adventure playgrounds - the staff are very friendly. Meals, snacks, shop, disabled access; open daily school hols (exc Christmas), plus Sun Feb half-term to Easter, and end summer hols to autumn half-term, best to phone; (01453) 810510; £5.50 (less out of season).
Jenner Museum £ (High St) Largely unchanged Georgian home of Edward Jenner, who discovered the principle of vaccination here, and after developing the smallpox vaccine gave free

vaccinations from the thatched hut in the attractive grounds. Shop, some disabled access; cl am, all day Mon exc bank hols, Oct exc Sun, and all Nov-Mar; (01453) 810631; £3. The Berkeley Arms (Market Pl) is a pleasant country town hotel.

BIBURY SP1106

One of the most popular villages in the area (William Morris thought it the most beautiful in England), with lovely golden streamside houses (owned by the NT). Nowadays, summer crowds can rather blunt its appeal. The **River Coln** lets you approach Bibury more quietly and prettily, along the path from the toll-house just S of Coln St Aldwyns. This route takes you in by the mill and bridge over the Coln itself. The beautifully placed Swan Hotel has a reasonably priced brasserie.

Arlington Mill Museum The 18th-c machinery of this well restored watermill is demonstrated on some days (staff will often work the machinery if asked), with guided tours by arrangement; at the back, a developing herb garden overlooks the river. Meals, snacks, shop, disabled access to tearoom; cl 25 Dec; (01285) 740368; £2.

Bibury Trout Farm ⊞ Long-established working farm breeding rainbow trout in 40 ponds and tanks. You can feed the fish, or try to catch your own (summer only). Summer snacks, good shop, limited disabled access; limited opening hours in winter, best to phone; (01285) 740215; £2.50.

River Coln villages By the same trout-stream as over-visited Bibury, a pleasant drive links other villages that are just as engaging, but bypassed by most visitors, particularly Coln St Aldwyns (the New Inn is good) and Quenington (decent food at the Keepers Arms). On the far side of Bibury the back road tracking along the river passes through a string of pleasant little villages such as Coln Rogers, Coln St Dennis and Yanworth, eventually reaching the pretty village of Withington (the Mill Inn is delightfully set right on the stream).

BIRDWOOD SO7418

Old Ley Court (Chapel Lane) Working farm producing double and single Gloucester cheese - you can

normally watch them make it on Tues and Thurs, best to phone. Ask about their home-cured bacon, sausages and ham; some disabled access (but no facilities); (01452) 750225; £2.

BISLEY SO9106

Selsley Herb Nursery (Hayhedge Lane, E of centre) This friendly garden has a wide range of herbs and garden plants; cl Mon (exc bank hols) and am Sun; (01452) 770073; free. The ancient Bear has enjoyable food.

BLOCKLEY SP1635

Mill Dene Garden ⊞ Lovely 2½-acre garden surrounding a Cotswold stone watermill with an orange stream (turned that colour by the rusted waterwheel), also shell grotto, water features and lots of scented plants; 78 species of bird have been seen in the garden, inc kingfishers and dippers. Meals, snacks, shop; open Weds-Fri Apr-Oct, plus occasional Sun pm, phone to check; (01386) 700457); £4. The village is attractive, and the Great Western Arms has good value food and nice views.

BOURTON-ON-THE-HILL SP1732

Bourton House ⊞ Unusual plants inc tender ones in attractive garden around fine old house (not open). Art and craft gallery in 16th-c tithe barn (where they serve teas), shop; open Weds-Fri 26 May-Aug, Thurs-Fri Sept-Oct; *£4.50, children free; (01386) 700754.

Sezincote House and Garden (off A424 about 1m S) Exotic onion-domed forerunner of Brighton Pavilion, stunning from the outside, less interesting inside. Also classic early 19th-c water garden, and a more recent indian-style garden to match the building. Garden open pm Thurs, Fri and bank hols (cl Dec), house Thurs and Fri pm May-July and Sept; £5, £3.50 garden only. Children are not allowed in the house.

BOURTON-ON-THE-WATER SP1620

One of the best-known Cotswold villages, but submerged in sprawly crowds in summer unless you get there very early in the morning - when it's enchanting. There are all sorts of visitor attractions. The Mousetrap (Lansdown) and Old Manse (Victoria St - tables out by river) have decent food. The best walk from the village heads out W past the church and school and over the old railway line, then following the lanes and tracks S of Upper Slaughter to rejoin the River Windrush and back to Bourton. **Birdland** 🏛 (Rissington Rd) A bird fanciers' favourite, with all its rarities and exotics on the banks of the meandering River Windrush, inc a large colony of penguins and over 50 aviaries. Also a play area, tropical and desert houses, and picnic areas. Meals, snacks, shop, disabled access; cl 25 Dec; (01451) 820480; £4.75.

Cotswold Motor Museum and Toy Collection (Sherbourne St) In an old watermill, the collection here includes cars and motorcycles from vintage years to the 1950s, along with advertising signs, Dinky cars, automobilia, and a toy collection (inc Brum the children's TV character); also interactive displays for children in a converted van, and a new blacksmith exhibition. New shop, disabled access; cl Dec-Jan; (01451) 821255; £2.75.

Dragonfly Maze (Rissington Rd) Imaginative and stimulating for children and grown-ups. There's an interesting maze and puzzle to solve - if you find the dragonfly, the children get a little prize at the end. Shop, disabled access; usually open daily (exc 25-26 Dec, and in bad weather); (01451) 822251; £2.

Miniature World (High St) Readers love this incredible collection of miniature scenes and figures made by over a hundred of England's leading model-makers. Detailed dioramas, full of life and drama, from a fruit and veg stall to a wartime italian street - look out for the ghosts in the Victorian chemist's shop. Disabled access; open daily Easter-Oct, wknds only in winter; (01451) 810121; £2.95.

Model Village (High St) It won't take you long to look around this replica of the village, modelled from Cotswold stone in the 1930s to a scale of one-ninth; snacks, shop; cl 25 Dec; (01451) 820467; £2.75. Good home-made food (and lovely river view) in adjacent welcoming Old New Inn.

Perfumery Exhibition (Victoria St) Includes the origins of perfume, a cinema with smells, and perfume quiz and garden. Shop, disabled access; cl 25-26 Dec; (01451) 820698; £2.

CHELTENHAM SO9523
Beautiful spa town useful for exploring Cotswolds, shopping, or admiring the elegant Regency architecture of its tree-lined avenues. These days Cheltenham is best known for its races, and the racecourse at Prestbury Park (N on A435) has an exhibition on Gold Cup winners; (01242) 513014; cl wknds; free. Lots of antiques shops, esp around the Montpellier area. Tailors (Cambray Pl), the Montpellier Wine Bar (Montpellier St), Mitres (Sandford St) and Belgian Monk (Clarence St) have decent food. The well run café in the beautiful Imperial Gardens is good for families, and readers recommend the Muffin Man restaurant in Crescent Terrace.

Art Gallery & Museum (Clarence St) Excellent Arts and Crafts collection inspired by William Morris, fine paintings inc 17th-c dutch works, rare porcelain and ceramics, and special exhibitions. Meals, snacks, shop, disabled access; cl am Sun, bank hols, and Easter Sun; (01242) 237431; free.

Holst Birthplace Museum (Clarence Rd) A 10-min walk from the Pump Room, this interesting Regency house is where the composer was born in 1874; you can see the piano on which he composed *The Planets*. Worthwhile even if you're not mad about Holst, as the rooms are all carefully furnished in period style. Shop; cl Sun, Mon and all Jan; (01242) 524846; £2.50.

Pittville Pump Room (Pittville Park) A short walk from the centre, this is the town's finest building, 19th-c Greek Revival with a colonnaded façade and balconied hall. It's easy to imagine the place's Regency heyday, especially strolling around the super park and gardens, or during concerts in the July music festival. On some summer Sun they may have teas accompanied by live music, also occasional art and craft exhibitions. You can still sample the spa water. Shop, disabled access to ground floor only; cl Tues and bank hols; (01242) 523852; free. A 19th-c chapel (North Pl) now houses a spa and gym; phone for information about day passes; (01242) 518075; from £30.

CHIPPING CAMPDEN SP1539
Extremely attractive town, with

interesting old buildings inc an ancient covered open-sided market hall, a grand Perpendicular church typical of the area's rich 'wool churches', enjoyable shops, and fine old inns. Many of our contributors would put it among the country's most delightful small towns, though until they get the cars out of the centre not all would agree. The Eight Bells, Volunteer, Kings Arms, Noel Arms and Lygon Arms are all good for lunch. The **Cotswold Way**, a 100-mile path from here all the way to Bath, carefully picks out some of the choicest Cotswold scenery - a worthwhile aid for those planning a shorter stroll.

CIRENCESTER SP0202

A busy country town, particularly on its Mon and Fri market days, with a succession of fine Cotswold stone streets off the long market place (plans to pedestrianise this, which would make it much more visitor-friendly, have been held up by local authority cash shortages). It has many attractive buildings, and interesting antiques and other shops inc traditional country saddlers' etc. Though one of the most handsome of all the Cotswold towns, it isn't too touristy. The **church** of St John the Baptist (Market Pl) is wonderfully grand, with a striking late Gothic tower (and an unusual medieval wall painting of the martyrdom of St Thomas à Becket). **Brewery Arts** has independent craft businesses and shops in former brewery (cl Sun and some bank hols), along with theatre, gallery and café. Also worth a look are the 12th-c remains of **St John's Hospital**, the **Norman arch**, and the various well preserved wool merchants' houses. Cecily Hill, one of the town's most attractive streets, gives on to **Cirencester Park** (open daily, free) a vast 3,000-acre forested country estate abutting the town. Nearby is the town's heated **open-air swimming pool** (May-Sept, £2.50; (01285) 653947), with the backdrop of the castle-like 19th-c former barracks. Decent places for lunch include the Corinium Hotel (Gloucester St), Somewhere Else (Castle St) and Twelve Bells (Lewis Lane).
Corinium Museum (Park St) Cirencester was one of the most important cities in Roman Britain, and

this spacious museum has one of the finest collections of antiquities from the period (all clearly displayed and labelled). The museum will be closed for major refurbishments (inc larger gallery space and new education facilities) until around February; so phone for opening times; (01285) 655611.

CLEARWELL SO5708

Clearwell Caves [£] (off B4228) You find your own way around the nine caverns, reckoned to be some of the oldest underground workings in Britain. Generations of miners worked the site for iron ore, but today the very small-scale mining produces pigments used in allergy-free paints. In places, artificial pools make it seem as if you're in a natural cave, and the years of work down here have resulted in some unique shapes and colourful patterns. It's quite a labyrinth, so stout shoes are recommended, and wrap up well. Also displays of mining equipment and engines, and special events inc a Christmas walk-through grotto. Snacks, shop, phone for disabled access; usually open Mar-Oct, and the run-up to Christmas plus wknds Jan-Feb; (01594) 832535; £4 (discount voucher not valid for bank hols and end of Nov-Dec). The partly 13th-c Ostrich over at Newland has good interesting food.

CLEEVE COMMON SO9924

The steep grassy slopes of the W escarpment of the Cotswolds make for some of the area's best walking. This, the highest point of the Cotswolds, has breezy, unkempt grassland on its open expanses, and can either be reached from the nearby village of Cleeve Hill on the A46 (where the Rising Sun has decent food and lovely views to the Malvern Hills), or integrated into a circular walk past Belas Knap long barrow and through the Sudeley Castle estate into Winchcombe.

COTSWOLDS SP0912

It's the countryside above all which delights here - especially the rolling hills themselves, with their traditional dry-stone-walled fields, occasional beechwoods, meandering streams, and beautiful villages of warm golden-tinted stone picturesquely roofed in heavy stone slabs. Many villages have handsome medieval churches, and their cottages and houses don't hide away behind gardens and high walls, but tend to be right by the road. Often, there's a strip of daffodil-planted grass between pavement and road (the area is particularly attractive in spring), and sometimes a little stream. *The Romantic Road*, a guide to the prettiest villages in the area, is available from Visit Cheltenham (01242) 522878, or from tourist information centres in the area. For cyclists, the Cotswolds are great - quiet village-to-village lanes with ever-changing views. Compass Holidays not only hire bikes (£12 per day) but can arrange your route and accommodation too; (01242) 250642.

DEERHURST SO8729
Ancient remains here include **Odda's Chapel**, a restored 11th-c chapel discovered as part of a farmhouse, and the **Priory Church of St Mary**, a mainly Saxon church with a lovely atmosphere and some intriguing original carvings and features. The riverside Coal House at Apperley does substantial food.

DEVIL'S CHIMNEY SO9418
On the Cotswold Way, a viewpoint rock pinnacle amid old quarries on Leckhampton Hill, perched above Cheltenham.

DYRHAM ST7475
Dyrham Park 🏛 In an ancient park grazed by fallow deer, this fine William and Mary house has hardly changed since the late 17th c. The interiors have dutch-style furnishings, Delftware, dutch bird paintings and a remarkable trompe l'oeil by Hoogstraten. Victorian domestic rooms inc a bakehouse, larders, kitchen and dairy are also open. Meals, snacks, shop, disabled access to ground floor; house cl am, Weds and Thurs, and Nov-Mar, park open all year exc 25 Dec; (0117) 937 2501; *£8.30, garden and deer park only *£3.20; NT. The Bull at Hinton Dyrham is an attractive nearby place for lunch.

EASTLEACH SP2005
Delightful Cotswold village; a lovely ancient clapper bridge links the two Norman churches, very photogenic when the daffodils are out. The Victoria, looking down on it all, has enjoyable food.

FAIRFORD SP1501
Pleasant riverside meadows, and a wonderful 15th-c Perpendicular **church**, which has Britain's only intact set of medieval stained-glass windows (inc a fascinating depiction of Hell), and comical misericords. The Bull Hotel has good value food.

FOREST OF DEAN SO6212
The Forest of Dean has a unique landscape: hilly woodland that shows many traces of the way it has provided a livelihood for the people living around it. The scenery has most impact on those prepared to delve into its past a bit - a good start is the **Heritage Centre** at Upper Soudley. You can find ancient iron workings, the tracks of abandoned railways and tramways, and still one or two of the freeminers, who've been digging coal by hand from surface seams for hundreds of years. Still largely ancient oak woodland despite encroaching pine plantations, the forest rolls over many miles of hilly countryside, giving plenty of space - even in summer you can often have much of the woods to yourself. There are ponds, streams with stepping stones, cattle and perhaps fallow deer; its woodland colours are at their best in late May and autumn. The forest is well equipped with car parks, picnic sites and forest trails. The **Sculpture Trail** takes a four-mile route passing nearly 20 specially commissioned sculptures hidden deep in the forest (from picnic site nr the comfortable Speech House Hotel). The **Kidnalls Forest Trail** is a good way of tracking down some early industrial sites. The **Foundry Wood Trail** passes Soudley fish ponds and gains some fine views. The **Wench Ford Forest Walk** leads past a series of quite interesting rock outcrops. Signed paths ensure easy route-finding up to the open summit of May Hill, where on a clear day you can see the Cotswolds, Malverns, Welsh Marches and Severn estuary. Around the edges of the forest the scenery changes to a patchwork of steep pastures - also very attractive. It's well worth getting a forest map, either from the Dean Heritage Centre or direct from the Forestry Commission in Coleford (01594) 833057; these outline walks (inc the sculpture trail), and mark the best spots

for views or picnics. The information centres can also provide details of canoeing, caving, cycling or fishing in the forest. The B4432 to Symonds Yat gives some good views, the B4228 down past St Briavels is a pleasant country road, and the little lanes around the edges of the forest are rewarding drives - but need a large-scale map.

Conifer arboretum SO6212 This makes an interesting change from the forest's predominantly broad-leaved trees; nr Speech House.

Dean Heritage Centre 🏛 SO6513 Recently reopened after a £½m refurbishment (with new galleries, and improved disabled access), this provides a very good introduction to the history and culture of the Forest of Dean. Displays cover everything from freemining to the Horlick family (inventors of the famous drink), and it has changing costume and art displays. You can see a reconstructed forester's cottage, as well as replicas of a charcoal burner's hut, and a free mine; agricultural displays, Gloucester Old Spot pigs, craftshops, an adventure playground, maze and a picnic area. It's a starting point for several woodland walks, and they hold special events including traditional charcoal burns. Meals, snacks, shop, disabled access; cl 24-26 Dec and 1 Jan; (01594) 824024; £4.

Hopewell Colliery ((B4226 E of Broadwell)) SO5911 45-min underground tours of the 'free' mine guided by ex-miners; the privilege of free mining may date back to the time when King Edward I asked the miners to undermine a castle wall and blow it up, and freeminers must be born in the forest. You'll need sturdy shoes and warm clothing. New picnic area with swings and train ride (£1); snacks, shop; cl Nov-Easter (exc wk leading up to Christmas for special events); (01594) 810706; £3.50 for tour, entry free.

Nagshead Nature Reserve SO5909 (off B4234 S of Parkend, where the Woodman has enjoyable food) A good place to see deer and other wildlife.

Puzzle Wood ((just off B4228 S of Coleford)) SO5808 Wooded paths arranged as a stroll-along puzzle, landscaped in the 19th c nr remains of Roman iron mines; they've added a new

indoor wood puzzle too. Snacks, shop; cl Mon (exc bank hols), and Nov-Easter (may be open Feb half-term); (01594) 833187; £3.25. Across the road is the **Perrygrove Railway** Steam trains run along a ¾-mile stretch of narrow-gauge track, with children solving clues that lead to treasure along the way. There are four stops, with footpaths through the woods nearby. Snacks, disabled access; open Sat July, wknds Aug, and bank hol wknds Easter-Aug; (01594) 834991; £3.50 for unlimited train journeys, plus £1.80 for the children's treasure trail. The Dog & Muffler at Joyford is a pretty place for lunch; good walks nearby.

Roman road SO6508 You can track the paving, still in good nick after nearly 2,000 years, just off the Cinderford—Nibley rd (B4431 on older maps) at Blackpool Bridge.

Symonds Yat Rock SO5615 Perhaps the Forest of Dean's most spectacular feature, where the River Wye rolls around a monumental wooded cliff barrier, a favourite spot with peregrine falcons; tremendous views in all directions from the top, and at the bottom a ferry runs between two inns (you can hail it from the opposite bank); (01600) 890435; 80p.

FRAMPTON ON SEVERN SO7407
Frampton Court 🏛 Elegant lived-in Georgian house, with original furniture, porcelain, tapestry and paintings, and fascinating gardens. Disabled access to gardens; personal tours all year by appointment, (01452) 740267; £4.50. The village green is said to be the longest in the country, with the 18th-c orangery (now self-catering holiday accommodation) on one side, and the Bell (a comfortable dining pub, open all day) on another. Just outside the village the Gloucester & Sharpness Canal passes grand colonnaded lock keepers' houses by pretty swing bridges.

GLOUCESTER SO8318
A busy modern city despite its long history - you have to search out the old buildings among today's big shops (for instance the splendid timber-framed house tucked down a passageway off 26 Westgate St). Tours leave from the tourist information centre (28 Southgate st) at 2.30pm Jun-Sept; £2.50;

(01452) 421188. The Black Swan (Southgate St, close to docks) and - all handy for cathedral - Fountain, 15th-c New Inn and Tailors House (Westgate St) are useful for a quick lunch.

City Museum and Art Gallery (Brunswick Rd) Local history (inc a very old backgammon set) and an art gallery. Shop, disabled access; cl Sun-Mon; (01452) 396131; £2. Guided tours of the ancient **City East Gate** leave here on Sat May-Sept, and by arrangement; (10.15am, 11.15, 2.15pm, 3.15, 4.15); free.

Docks Interesting to walk around, the revitalised waterfront deserves much of the credit for the city's tourism renaissance (this year they're addding new shops); there are guided walks, and summer boat trips along the canal or up the river as far as Tewkesbury (contact the National Waterways Museum). Attractions here include the unusually interesting **Soldiers of Gloucester Museum** which has life-size reconstructions inc a World War I trench (cl winter Mon; (01452) 522682; £4.25); and a big **antiques centre**, with 110 antiques shops in Dickensian arcades (limited disabled access; cl am Sun; free wkdys, 50p wknds and bank hols; (01452) 311190).

Folk Museum (Westgate St) Social history in a group of Tudor and Jacobean timber-framed houses; Victorian classroom, reconstructed ironmonger's, wheelwright's and carpenter's shops, toy gallery, interactive displays and cottage garden. Shop, disabled access to ground floor only; cl Sun-Mon; (01452) 396467; £2, children and Gloucester residents free.

Gloucester Cathedral Towering majestically over the city's more recent buildings, this has lovely fan-vaulted cloisters, the second-largest medieval stained-glass window in the country, and a fine collection of church plate in the Treasury. In 1330 the Abbot astutely purchased the remains of murdered Edward II, and the resulting stream of pilgrims paid for elaborate rebuilding, an early example of Perpendicular style. The cloisters' temporary transformation into parts of Harry Potter's Hogwarts school for wizards has recently boosted younger

visitor numbers. Meals, snacks, shop, some disabled access; (01452) 508210; £3 recommended donation. Not far from here are what's left of 9th-c **St Oswald's Priory**, the city's oldest structure, and other ecclesiastical remains inc **Greyfriars** and **Blackfriars**, the latter pretty much unchanged since the 13th c, with a rare scissor-braced roof.

House of the Tailor of Gloucester (College Court) Inspiration for Beatrix Potter's story, with an exhibition and shop; cl Sun, 25-26 Dec and some other bank hols (phone to check); (01452) 422856; £1.

National Waterways Museum 🖼 (Llanthony Warehouse, Gloucester Docks) Focusing on the history of Britain's network of inland waterways, this puts quite an emphasis on hands-on exhibits, with lots of touch-screen activities ranging from building your own canal, to an infuriating share certificate game where you're allocated a company and then follow its fortunes. One gallery looks at the way boats have been decorated from ancient times. Most displays are under cover, though there are some historic boats outside; special events during the school holidays, and from Easter to Oct you can take 45-min boat trips along the canal (£3 extra). A traditional forge is usually in full operation. Snacks, shop, disabled access (not to floating exhibits); cl 25 Dec; (01452) 318200; £5.

Over farm shop (1m W) A good one, with local produce and pick-your-own in summer (plus, depending on the harvest, a PYO pumpkin festival in Oct half-term). Also farm animal centre with ostriches, rare sheep, and a water buffalo; disabled access; cl 25-26 Dec; (01452) 521014.

Robinswood Hill Country Park (2m S) A little outcrop of the Cotswolds, with 250 acres of walks and trails, new rare breed farm animals, a wildlife information centre (fun talks and events), and wonderful views of the city from the summit. Snacks, shop, disabled access; (01452) 303206; free. Not far away is a dry ski slope.

GREAT WITCOMBE SO9316 **Crickley Hill Country Park** (just N of village) Has a few ancient sites, as well as nature trails, lovely clearly marked woodland walks, and fine views. Some disabled access; visitor centre cl am (exc Sun), and Oct-Mar; (01452) 863170; free. The Air Balloon is a handy family dining pub.

Roman villa The outlines of a substantial Roman villa can still be traced here, around a courtyard, with several mosaics and evidence of an underfloor heating system; free; EH. The Golden Heart at Brimpsfield nearby is good for food.

GUIDED HORSE-RIDING SO8412 Ongers Farm at Brookthorpe run this, (01452) 813344, from £10 an hour.

HARESFIELD BEACON SO8108 (3m NW of Stroud) 450 acres of NT woodland and grassland on the Cotswold escarpment, with spectacular views; free, and just a short ascent from the road.

KEMPLEY SO6731

Kempley church Remote and ancient-feeling Norman church, miraculously untampered with over the passing of the centuries and retaining one of the best-preserved sets of medieval wall paintings in the country, as well as an ancient timber door some 900 years old. The original timber roof, unfortunately concealed by a later ceiling, is said to be one of the finest of its kind in Europe; open daily; free; EH. N of the village, the church is signposted off the main roads around Dymock (where the Beauchamp Arms has decent food) and Much Marcle.

KINETON SP0926

Cotswold Farm Park 🏕 (off B4077) This friendly place, the original pioneer in rare breeds, is full of delightfully odd-looking species of sheep, cattle, pigs, goats, horses and poultry. It's very much a working farm rather than a more developed leisure attraction, but is particularly well organised as far as children are concerned, and excellent value too. Rabbits and guinea-pigs to cuddle or feed, tractor and trailer rides, battery-powered tractors for 3- to 12-year-olds, good safe rustic-themed play areas, and even a designated children's shop. Audio tours are available for adults; nature trails and woodland walks, and plenty of space for a picnic. Lots under cover, so still good when the

weather isn't perfect (best to wear wellies then); seasonal demonstrations inc lambing, shearing, and milking. Meals, snacks, shop, disabled access; open mid-Mar to Oct; (01451) 850307; £4.80. The unpretentious Halfway House nearby does good traditional food.

LECHLADE SU2199 Graceful village with one or two decent antiques shops, pleasant walks, and access to the quiet reed-fringed Thames for footpath walks - especially along to Kelmscot in Oxfordshire. The New Inn, with a Thames-side garden, is good value.

LITTLE LONDON SO6918

Mohair Countryside Centre (Blakemore Farm) Countryside centre in 100 acres of parkland with indoor and outdoor play areas (there's one for toddlers), various friendly farm animals to meet inc lots of goats, picnic areas and nature trails; a new exhibition on Dick Whittington is due to open in spring, and there's a toy corner. Snacks, shop selling clothes made from goat and other fleeces, and disabled access; cl Mon-Tues during term-time and 25-26 Dec, best to check; (01452) 831137; £2.50, £4 children. The Red Hart at Blaisdon is attractive for lunch.

LONGHOPE SO6818

Harts Barn Craft Centre (A4136 W) Smart craft workshops inc furniture, jewellery and ceramics, in an attractive Norman hunting lodge with landscaped grounds and lake; there's also a play area and history trail. Courtyard tearoom, picnic area, disabled access; cl Mon exc bank hols and 25 Dec-2 Jan; (01452) 830954; free.

LOWER SLAUGHTER SP1622 With its sister village Upper Slaughter, this is one strong candidate for the title of prettiest village in Britain - a perfect harmony of stone, water, grass and trees. It's not as overwhelmed by summer visitors as its nearby rival Bourton-on-the-Water, though it certainly gets its fair share. The riverside stroll from Lower to Upper Slaughter is a leisurely mile or so; to make a longer walk for a circuit of a couple of hours, you can follow the signposted Warden's Way.

LYDNEY SO6304

Dean Forest Railway (New Mills, slightly N) Lots of locomotives, waggons and equipment at the Norchard Railway Centre station (free parking), and steam and diesel trips run through here from Lydney Junction. An extension into the Forest to Parkend (where the Woodman has decent food and good nearby walks) should be fully completed by the spring. Snacks, shop, disabled access; static displays open all year round; best to ring for train times; (01594) 843423; or check the website (www.deanforestrailway.co.uk); fares from £5.50 a day for unlimited train trips.

Lydney Park Extensive sheltered spring garden rich with flowering shrubs, rhododendrons, azaleas and magnolias; also lakes and deer park. On an adjoining hilltop are the remains of a Roman temple; a museum has finds from the site, inc the astonishingly intricate Lydney dog. Snacks, shop, limited disabled access; plant sales; open Sun, Weds and bank hol Mon late Mar to mid-Jun, but best to check; (01594) 842844; £4 (£3 Weds). The 17th-c coach house and courtyard now houses Taurus Crafts, with a working pottery, art studios, workshops and exhibition; the 4-acre vegetable garden provides for the organic food shop and restaurant (01594) 844841.

MICKLETON SP1743

Hidcote Manor Garden (off B4081) Series of small gardens separated by walls and hedges of different species, with rare shrubs, trees and roses, and some interesting topiary. Very popular even midweek. Meals, snacks, good shop, some disabled access; cl Thurs-Fri and Nov-Mar; (01386) 438333; £6.20; NT. The Kings Arms is good for lunch, with OAP bargains.

Kiftsgate Court Garden (off B4081) Renowned for its old-fashioned roses (best Jun and July), this has many other rare plants, shrubs and trees, good views across the Vale of Evesham, and that special feel that comes from generations of care by a gifted gardening family. Snacks, rare plant sales; open pm Weds, Thurs, Sun and bank hols Apr-Sept, plus Mon and Sat pm Jun and July; (01386) 438777; £5.

MINCHINHAMPTON & RODBOROUGH COMMON ST8898

900 acres of open land with fine views and a wide range of wildlife; NT, free. The Halfway Inn at Box on the N edge has good food, and the steep lanes all around are interesting drives.

MISERDEN SO9308

Misarden Park 🖼 Views over the wooded Golden Valley from handsome gardens of 17th-c manor house (not open), with Lutyens topiary, mature shrubs and trees, and colourful walled garden. Nursery, some disabled access; open Tues-Thurs Apr-Sept; (01285) 821303; £3.50. The quiet village is charming, with good food in the Carpenters Arms.

MORETON-IN-MARSH SP2032 Attractively bustling old place, former linen-weaving centre and coaching town, with popular Tues market. For food, the Inn on the Marsh and Redesdale Arms are pleasant.

Batsford Arboretum 🖼 (Batsford Park, just NW) Well grown private collection of over 1,500 rare and beautiful species of tree and flowers spread over 55 acres; hundreds of maples, 90 different magnolias, and national collection of japanese flowering cherries (there's also a Japanese Rest House). Best in May and autumn, but relaxing any time. Meals, snacks, garden centre, limited disabled access; open daily Feb to mid-Nov, and wknds in winter; (01386) 701441; £5. The park is home to many deer.

Cotswold Falconry Centre 🖼 (Batsford Park, just NW) Flying demonstrations of eagles, hawks, owls and falcons throughout the day, with a chance to handle some of the birds; you can also look round the breeding aviaries, and CCTV cameras have been installed in many of the nests. Snacks, shop; open mid-Feb to mid-Nov; (01386) 701043; £5.

Wellington Aviation Museum (Broadway Rd) Collection of RAF memorabilia, and local history displays. Shop, disabled access; cl 12.30-2pm, all day Mon, 25 Dec, and Jan-Feb (exc wknds); (01608) 650323; £2.

NEWENT SO7225

Small country town with some timbered buildings which have a bit of a Worcestershire or Herefordshire look.

Shambles Museum of Victorian Life Enthusiastic re-creation of a Victorian town, with display shops, workshops and furnished houses. Summer snacks, shop; cl Mon (exc bank hols), wkdys Nov-Dec, and all Jan to mid-Mar; (01531) 822144; £3.85. The George, a friendly old coaching inn opposite, has inexpensive lunchtime food.

St Annes Vineyard (Oxenhall, off B4221 W) They grow and sell 100 varieties of vine, and make wines; open pm Weds-Fri, and all day wknds and bank hols Mar-Oct, wknds only in winter; (01989) 720313; free.

Three Choirs Vineyard (off B4215 towards Dymock) One of the six largest vineyards in England; you can go on a self-guided tour, which now includes the new Whittington microbrewery; nature trail and video. Summer meals and snacks, shop, disabled access; cl 25 Dec and 1 Jan; tastings free, tour and exhibitions £5; (01531) 890223. The Vineyard Restaurant also has accommodation.

NORTH CERNEY SP0207
Cerney House Gardens 🖼
Expansive old garden behind 13th-c church, with old roses, trees, shrubs, walled and herb gardens, a few animals (they make tasty goat's cheese), and a water garden. The surrounding woods are lovely at bluebell time. Teas, plant sales, some disabled access; open Tues, Weds and Fri Easter to July; (01285) 831300; £3. The village is attractive, and the Bathurst Arms is good for lunch.

NORTH NIBLEY ST7496
Hunts Court Informal gardens with over 400 varieties of old roses, plus unusual shrubs and other plants, and a developing mini arboretum; fine views. Plant sales, disabled access; cl Sun-Mon, all Aug, Good Fri and 25 Dec-1 Jan; (01453) 547040; £2. The walk up to the Tyndale Monument gives even better views, and the Black Horse is handy for lunch.

NORTHLEACH SP1114
Fine example of an unspoilt small wool town, with handsome stone-built streets and a particularly interesting **church**, renowned for its collection of brasses. The Wheatsheaf (West End) is a rather stylish dining pub.

World of Mechanical Music (Oak House, High St) Readers are really taken with this quite captivating collection of clocks, musical boxes and automata,

demonstrated by enthusiastic and knowledgeable guides in period settings in an old wool merchant's house. It's quite spooky watching the instruments work themselves. Snacks, shop, good disabled and blind access; cl 25-26 Dec; (01451) 860181; £5. Don't miss it if you're nearby.

NYMPSFIELD SO8000
Woodchester Mansion (B4066) Construction of this splendid unfinished Gothic mansion was inexplicably abandoned virtually overnight in 1870. It's being repaired but not finished, and you can usually see traditional building techniques such as stonemasonry. Readers have high praise for the guided tours. Five species of bat have made this their home, and infra-red CCTV in their colonies (the only such installation in Britain) lets you watch them. Snacks, shop, disabled access to ground floor only; open Sun, bank hol wknds, plus first Sat in month (all Sats July-Aug) Easter-Sept, park open all year; (01453) 750455; £5. The walk up Coaley Peak gives tremendous views over the Severn Valley. In the village the Rose & Crown is a good value dining pub.

ODDINGTON SP2325
Charming Cotswold village; the 11th-c **church** has an interesting mural, and there are pleasant walks, especially from the Fox at Lower Oddington. This and the very welcoming Horse & Groom at Upper Oddington both have good food.

OZLEWORTH ST7992
This valley, not far from Wotton-under-Edge, has a nostalgically forgotten quality about it, giving an interesting walk between Lasborough Manor and Ozleworth Park, with its unusual Norman church endowed with a hexagonal tower.

PAINSWICK SO8609
Readers really enjoy this delightful little town, sometimes referred to as 'Queen of the Cotswolds'. There's been a settlement here since Celtic times, and **Painswick Beacon** has the remains of the earliest structures; it's a short ascent from the road, with great views towards the Malvern hills. Plenty of old buildings to look at, such as the 15th-c **Post Office**, and several craft workshops. The **church of St Mary**

has fine interesting tombs and a fascinating churchyard where 99 immaculately clipped yews form gateways and canopies. The Falcon opposite is good for lunch.

Rococo Garden ⊞ (B4073) Careful restoration of sizeable 18th-c garden to match a 1748 painting showing its fanciful mix of precisely trimmed hedging, paths and shrubs with unrestrained trees; also a maze and slightly zany garden buildings. Pleasant vistas, children's walks - a cheery-feeling place. Snacks, shop, plant sales; cl Nov-Dec; (01452) 813204; £3.60.

PRINKNASH SO8713

Prinknash Abbey Visitors Centre (off A46) Unusual 20th-c Benedictine monastery and earlier house; sadly they no longer produce their famous pottery, but they do still sell it in the shop. Meals, snacks, some disabled access; cl 25-26 Dec, Good Fri; (01452) 812066. The abbey buildings aren't to everyone's taste but the grounds are attractive, with good views over the Severn Vale; picnic areas. The Black Horse in the very steep village of Cranham has enjoyable food.

Prinknash Bird Park ⊞ (Prinknash Abbey) Exotic pheasants, peacocks and other birds, as well as deer, goats and waterfowl - most animals feed from your hand (the fallow deer are particularly friendly); there's also a fishpond, wendy house and play castle. Snacks, shop; cl 25 Dec, Good Fri; (01452) 812727; £3.80.

SELSLEY SO8203

Strung-out Cotswold village in the steep country just S of Stroud; William Morris, Maddox-Brown, Burne-Jones and Rossetti all worked on the **church windows**. The Bell has reasonably priced home cooking and is well placed for walks.

SEVERN BORE SO6904

Tidal wave surging upstream at high tide, which can sometimes reach up to two metres (6ft) in height around the spring and autumn equinox. The Environment Agency produce a calendar listing the best times and places to catch the phenomenon, with a rating of how spectacular it's likely to be; (01684) 850951. A good quiet spot to get down to the river is from Purton.

SEVERN ESTUARY ST6196

This makes for some lonely walks along the sea wall, with power station cooling towers and the vast Severn bridges emphasising the emptiness of the tidal flats. The White Hart in Littleton-upon-Severn, Anchor in Oldbury-on-Severn and right by the embankment the Windbound at Shepperdine are useful starting points. Further upstream Arlingham is locked within a big bend of the Severn, about a mile from the river, with the river path looking across to the Forest of Dean; the Ship at Upper Framilode nearby is a good family dining pub.

SHEEPSCOMBE SO8910

Delightful Cotswold village, clinging to picturesque hillsides; the cricket ground's so steep that fielders can scarcely see the bowler. The friendly Butchers Arms has good food.

SHORNCOTE SU0296

Cotswold Water Park 2,000 acres of lakes, country park and nature reserves, with facilities for fishing, windsurfing, sailing and other watersports, cycle hire and walks, and bird-watching; lots of activities for children in the summer hols. Meals and snacks at some lakes, shop, disabled access; some activities cl winter; (01285) 861459; car parking charge for some lakes. On the E edge of the park the Crown in Cerney Wick is a useful food stop.

SLIMBRIDGE SO7204

Wildfowl & Wetlands Trust (off A38) The original and best of the Trust's nine centres, this enormous place is one of the most visitor-friendly bird reserves in the country. Showing off a comprehensive collection of geese, swans and ducks, it's the only place in Europe where you can see six species of flamingo, as well as plenty of other rare and wild birds, and a tropical house that re-creates the sights, sounds and smells of a rain forest. In the Pond Zone children can take part in pond-dipping and see the things they fish out of the water magnified on TV screens. Lots of touch-screen computers, video displays and games, and extra events and activities in the school holidays; there's also a small play area. Other highlights include a discovery centre, a tower with a telescope (great views of the River Severn), and a wildlife art gallery. It's unusual in being somewhere that you might get more out of visiting in winter, when up to 30,000 wild birds fly in. Meals, snacks, shop, good disabled access; cl 25 Dec; (01453) 891900; £6.40, free to WWT members. The Tudor Arms by the swing bridge across the canal is useful for food, and the village Post Office has details of pleasant little walks.

SNOWSHILL SP0933
The Manor itself will be closed until Spring 2005 for essential reservicing work and for restoration of the collection; they hope to run temporary exhibitions about the restoration work while the manor is closed, as well as activities and events, phone for details; (01386) 852410. The charming organic cottage garden will remain open, and you can still stay in one of three cottages. Meals, snacks, shop and second-hand books by the entrance, disabled access to garden only; open Weds-Sun and bank hols Easter-Oct; £3.80; NT. The nearby Snowshill Arms is popular for lunch (busiest 12-1.15pm), and the drive along the River Windrush to Ford, Kineton and Naunton is delightful.

SOUTH CERNEY SU0698
Butts Farm 🏠 (1m NE, on A419) Unpretentious farm with a good range of animals for children to feed; there's a play area, and pets corner with bunnies and chinchillas to cuddle, and activities include goat milking. Special events one wknd every month; bring wellies when it's wet. Snacks, shop, disabled access; cl Mon and Tues outside school hols and all Nov-Easter (exc Feb half-term); (01285) 862205; £3.75 The largely 16th-c village is prettily preserved.

SOUTHROP SP2003
Charming Cotswold village that really comes into its own when the daffodils appear, with a delightful riverside church. The Swan has good food.

ST BRIAVELS SO5504
Attractive and unusual small village centred on the ruins of its 13th-c castle (the inhabited part is a youth hostel), with a steeply grassy former moat and views from the ramparts of the curtain wall. The George is good for lunch, and

there are various circular walks around the parish, devised by Mr McGubbin in the craft shop, available from there and the post office; (01594) 530201.

STANTON SP0734
One of the prettiest Cotswold villages, very small - and rarely overrun with visitors. The best views over it are from the Mount pub, up the steep no through road beyond the village centre. This is the start of a trio of timeless villages on the **Cotswold Way**, a well marked track that conveniently picks out some of the best scenery for walkers. The next two are Stanway and Buckland; field paths and farm track let you detour to Snowshill, and from there it's a pleasant 3-mile walk to Broadway just over the Worcs border.

STANWAY SP0632
Stanway House and Water Garden
One of the most beautiful 16th-c manor houses in the country, a cluster of gabled buildings popping up unexpectedly from the countryside, with charming and clearly lived-in rooms. The early 18th-c grounds have fine trees, a restored canal and cascade, and interesting buildings inc a folly pyramid on a steeply wooded hill; their new 50-metre (165ft) fountain is the tallest in Britain. Open Tues pm and Thurs July-Aug; (01386) 584469; £6 house and garden, £4 garden only. The Old Bakehouse in the picturesque village does teas.

STOW-ON-THE-WOLD SP1925
Handsome market town with fine stone buildings around its square and in the narrow lanes around, and a good few antiques shops, book shops and so forth - it's a good place to buy presents. It's something of an antidote to the more sweetly pretty Cotswold villages, on quite a high plateau and altogether more austere in style - not for nothing was it known as 'Stow-on-the-Wold, where the wind blows cold', and the ancient stocks on the village green add a touch of quaint severity. The **Toy Museum** on Park St has toys from Victorian times to the present. Shop; usually cl 1-2pm, Sun-Tues, May, and Nov-Jan, worth checking; 01451 830159; £2.50. The Queens Head and Talbot are both good for lunch.

STROUD SO8405
Museum in the Park (follow signs to

Stratford Park Leisure Centre)
Surrounded by parkland, this local
history museum has a surprising amount
for children, with interactive displays,
various trails, and a play area for younger
children, as well as the world's first
lawnmower; one gallery has changing
exhibitions. Shop, disabled access; cl Mon
(exc bank hols), ring for opening times in
Dec; (01453) 763394; free, charge for
some exhibitions. The Bear, on
Rodborough Common up on the other
side of the valley, has good value food.

TETBURY ST8993
A splendid raised **market house**, some
interesting little lanes, quite a few
antiques shops and craft workshops,
and good food in the Snooty Fox
(Market Pl). The old Court House (Long
St) houses a police museum with
memorabilia inc handcuffs, uniforms,
batons and photographs; you can peer
into one of the old cells and look round
the courtroom upstairs (partly disabled
access; cl wkdys, bank hols, 2 wks over
Christmas and Easter; free). The House
of Cheese (Church St) offers about 120
cheeses in their tiny shop.
Chavenage ⊞ (2m NW) Friendly
unspoilt 16th-c manor house with
entertaining tours by the owner. It's a
popular location for TV programmes,
providing a backdrop for characters
from *Poirot* to *Casualty*. Shop, disabled
access to ground floor only; open pm
Easter Sun and Mon, then pm Thurs,
Sun and bank hols May-Sept; (01666)
502329; £5. Out this way the Gumstool
(A46/A4135) has very good food.

TEWKESBURY SO8832
Severnside town, site of the last battle
in the Wars of the Roses in 1471, still
full of attractive half-timbered medieval
buildings in a maze of little alleyways.
Most impressive is the **abbey**, its
massively confident Norman tower one
of the finest in existence. Also splendid
vaulting, some 14th-c stained glass, and
regular concerts; guided tours available,
phone for details; (01684) 850959. In
Church St, the attractive **John Moore
Countryside Museum**
commemorates the work of the local
naturalist/writer. Shop, usually open
Tues-Sat and bank hols (exc 1-2pm)
Apr-Oct; (01684) 297174; £1.25. The
historic Bell Hotel and (simpler) ancient

Black Bear are good for lunch.
THAMES & SEVERN CANAL
SO9303
The rich, steeply sheltered valleys
around Stroud make up a complicated
landscape, seen to best advantage for
example between Chalford and
Sapperton. British Waterways and the
Cotswolds Canal Trust are working to
restore the first nine miles of this 36-
mile canal; its towpath forms an
attractive wooded walkway, and they
now do boat trips from Sapperton
tunnel; (01285) 643440. The Crown at
Frampton Mansell, Butchers Arms at
Oakridge Lynch or Daneway at
Sapperton are useful jumping-off points.
TOCKINGTON ST6187
Oldown (B4461) Lively country park
with good adventure play areas for
older children - lots of rope bridges,
tube slides and climbing nets. Play area
for younger children too, who'll
probably get the most out of the
animals and demonstrations at the farm.
Miniature steam railway running
through woodland and garden (£1),
several picnic areas, pleasant walks, and
summer **pick-your-own**. Snacks,
shop, disabled access; cl Mon (exc in
school hols), and Nov to mid-Feb;
(01454) 413605; £5. The quiet village
itself is attractive, with good value food
in the Swan.
TODDINGTON SP0432
**Gloucestershire—Warwickshire
Railway** Well liked by readers, this well
organised railway now runs through ten
miles of quiet countryside all the way to
Cheltenham racecourse. Steam and
some diesel train trips depart from
restored GWR stations either here, in
Winchcombe, or at the racecourse.
Snacks, shop, good disabled access
(though parts of the car park are
uneven); usually cl wkdys (exc July-Aug
and Easter), and all Jan-Feb, phone for
timetable (01242) 621405; from £9. The
Pheasant is useful for lunch.
TWIGWORTH SO8223
Nature in Art ⊞ (Wallsworth Hall,
A38) In an imposing Georgian mansion,
this collection of art from 60 countries
includes well displayed paintings,
sculpture, and mosaics inspired by
nature; more interesting than you'd
expect - besides David Shepherd,

artists represented include Picasso, Henry Moore and they've flemish masters. Good meals and snacks, shop, disabled access; cl Mon (exc bank hols), 24-26 Dec; (01452) 731422; *£3.60.

ULEY ST7898
Attractive former weaving village with some 18th-c or older stone houses. The Old Crown has enjoyable home cooking.

Owlpen Manor (B4066, just E) Charming Tudor manor house, with lovely formal gardens and woodland. Restaurant; cl am, all Mon (exc bank hol), and Oct-Mar; (01453) 860261; £4.80. Good views from this road.

WESTBURY-ON-SEVERN SO7114
This village is a good spot for catching the Severn Bore. The church is unusual, for its detached tower; beside it, the Red Lion has good generous food.

Westbury Court Formal dutch garden with canals, yew topiary, etc. restored to its 1700s layout using pre-1700 cultivars inc old fruit varieties. Disabled access; open Weds-Sun Mar-Jun and Sept-Oct, daily July-Aug, phone for winter opening; (01452) 760461; *£3; NT.

WESTONBIRT ST8588
Westonbirt Arboretum 🖼 Over 18,000 numbered trees and shrubs fill the 17 miles of pathways at this magnificent national collection, begun in 1829. Outstanding in spring and autumn, but interesting any time, with lots of wildlife hidden away among the trees; you'll need more than one visit to see it all; Jun-Sept they host the international festival of contemporary garden design (£1.50 extra). Restaurant, picnic areas, shop, disabled access; open all year, though visitor centre cl winter bank hols; (01666) 880220; £6. The Hare & Hounds is handy for food.

WINCHCOMBE SP0228
Very peaceful and photogenic - once the capital of Mercia, now worth a stop for a look at the **church** with its grotesque and sometimes rather rude gargoyles, or just to soak up the tranquil atmosphere. The White Hart (High St) handily has food all day, and there are interesting craft and other shops here.
Folk & Police Museum In the Victorian Town Hall, this has a

sometimes surprising collection of british and international police uniforms and equipment, as well as local history displays; shop; cl Sun, and Nov-Mar; (01242) 609151; £1.

Hailes Abbey (Hailes, B4632) Graceful ruins of 13th-c Cistercian abbey, once a centre for pilgrims who flocked to see a phial containing what they believed to be Christ's blood. Audio tour, snacks, shop, disabled access; cl Nov-Mar; (01242) 602398; £3; EH (NT members free too). Hayles Fruit Farm down the road is good for snacks, and has **pick-your-own**; (01242) 602123.

Railway Museum & Garden (Gloucester St) Victorian garden full of lovingly rescued railway memorabilia inc booking office, working signals and signal box. Snacks, shop, disabled access; open pm Weds-Sun Easter-Oct, and 2nd Sun of month in winter; (01242) 609305; £2.25.

Sudeley Castle & Gardens 🖼 (off B4632) Once home to Katherine Parr, the luckiest of Henry VIII's wives, the remains of the original medieval castle were skilfully blended into a 19th-c reconstruction. Rich furnishings, porcelain and tapestries, and notable paintings by Turner, Van Dyck and Rubens; dotted round the castle you can also see mannequins of Henry VIII's six wives and other important Tudor figures wearing sumptuous replica costumes. The ten gardens are splendid, and include a knot garden constructed using plants shown on a 16th-c tapestry on view in the library; displays in a former workshop show the life of Emma Dent, the woman responsible for the most attractive of the Victorian improvements, and an exhibition tracks the history of the garden; also adventure playground and picnic area. Meals, snacks, shop and specialist plant centre, disabled access to garden; house open Apr-Oct (gardens from Mar); (01242) 602308; £6.70 (extra charge Sundays and bank hols May-Aug), £5 grounds and exhibition only. A working pottery is nearby (cl winter Suns); (01242) 602462.

WOTTON-UNDER-EDGE ST7693
More small town than village, and full of

charm, with a fine Schneider organ in its church, a little **heritage centre** (open Tues-Fri (exc 1-2pm), and am Sat; free) and some handsome old buildings; the Swan Hotel (Market St) is useful for bar lunches, and the B4058 is a good drive.

WYE VALLEY SO5309

The lower Wye Valley on the W side of the Forest of Dean cuts through a gorge giving some very picturesque views. As there are few crossing points, and the scenery away from the gorge is relatively unspectacular, walks along it are generally of the there-and-back sort. The valley is tracked by the Offa's Dyke Path on the Gloucestershire side; the Wye Valley Walk takes in the western bank. S of Monmouth, the A466 threads through the valley below the paths.

Devil's Pulpit ST5499 A great viewpoint on the Offa's Dyke Path, where trees frame a perfect vista of Tintern Abbey far below on the opposite bank of the Wye (see South Wales section for Tintern).

The Kymin SO5212 Can be climbed from May Hill just inside the England/Wales river border opposite Monmouth; at the summit is the Naval Temple, a quaint rustic conceit put up in 1800 to commemorate admirals of the Napoleonic Wars. A couple of miles S at Redbrook a footbridge from the A466 crosses the Wye to a beautifully set walkers' pub called the Boat.

Wintour's Leap ST5496 A highlight of the Offa's Dyke Path: a sheer cliff over the Wye N of Chepstow with dizzy views downwards.

YANWORTH SP0713

An attractive village, especially at daffodil time.

Chedworth Roman Villa The best example of a 2nd-c Roman house in Britain, excavated in 1864 and nicely set in secluded woodland. Well preserved rooms, bath houses, 4th-c mosaics, and a water shrine, with smaller remains in the deliberately Victorian-feeling museum. Snacks, shop, some disabled access; cl Mon (exc bank hols), and mid-Nov to Feb; (01242) 890256; *£4.10; NT. The Mill at Withington and Seven Tuns in Upper Chedworth are quite

handy for lunch, and the walk from each is very picturesque and unspoilt, with Chedworth Woods providing further scope for short walks.

Other attractive villages, all with decent pubs, include Alderton SP0033, Almondsbury ST6084, Amberley SO8401, Bisley SO9005, Bledington SP2422, Broad Campden SP1637, Broadwell SP2027, Brockhampton SP0322, the Duntisbournes SO9709, Eastington SO7805, Ebrington SP1840, Ewen SU0097, Frampton Mansell SO9201, Great Barrington SP2013 (good cheap bedrooms at the Fox, lovely walks), Great Rissington SP1917, Guiting Power SP0924, Kingswood ST7491, Lower Swell SP1725, Marshfield ST7773, Meysey Hampton SU1199, Nether Westcote SP2120, Poulton SP1001, Shipton Moyne ST8989, Slad SO8707 (the setting for Laurie Lee's *Cider With Rosie*), Somerford Keynes SU0195, South Woodchester (particularly for the views) SO8302, Todenham SP2436, Wick ST7072 (pleasant walks) and Willersey SP1039. Though there's no pub to recommend there, Saintbury SP1139 is a winner when the daffodils are out. The B4060 N of Chipping Sodbury ST7282 and the side roads through Hawkesbury ST7786 and Hillesley ST7689 take you through attractive Cotswoldy scenery.

Many villages have most **attractive churches**, few of them as yet locked. Cirencester is a good base for planning circuits of these. One such group E of the town consists of Ampney Crucis SP0602, Ampney St Peter SP0801, Ampney St Mary SP0802, Down Ampney SP1097 (Vaughan Williams was the vicar's son), Hampnett SP1015 and Northleach SP1114. Another group, NW of Cirencester, has Elkstone SO9612, Duntisbourne Abbots SO9707, Duntisbourne Rouse SO9806, Daglingworth SO9905 (with its finely preserved Saxon carving of Christ on the cross), Stratton SP0103, Baunton SP0204 and North Cerney SP0208.

Where to eat

BOURTON-ON-THE-WATER SP1620 **Vernes** *Riverside* (01451) 822005
Pretty 17th-c cottage with enjoyable lunch, early evening meals, and Sunday roasts, all-day savouries, cream teas, and good choice of coffees and teas; cl Mon; limited disabled access. £16|£5.50

BOX SO8600 **Halfway Inn** (01453) 832631 Extended tall house on edge of the Common with attractive open-plan bar, simple but sturdy chairs and tables, fresh flowers and décor, and enjoyable food in bar or no smoking restaurant; well kept real ales, well chosen wines, and helpful service. £28|£7

BROAD CAMPDEN SP1537 **Bakers Arms** (01386) 840515 Atmospheric ex-granary in tranquil village with good value bar food (inc children's menu), a fine range of real ales, cosy beamed bar, log fires, friendly cats, pleasant service, and nice garden; open all day in summer; cl 25 Dec, pm 26 Dec. £19.45|£6.25

CHELTENHAM SO9421 **Champignon Sauvage** 24-26 *Suffolk Rd* (01242) 573449 Exquisite french cooking in quietly and simply decorated restaurant with a cheerful blue and yellow colour scheme, helpful service, an unstuffy atmosphere, and good thoughtful wine list; cl Sun, Mon, 10 days Christmas, 3 wks summer; partial disabled access. £27 lunch, £48 dinner

CHIPPING CAMPDEN SP1539 **Hicks Brasserie Bar** *Cotswold House Hotel, The Square* (01386) 840330 Fine 17th-c hotel, stylish and attractive brasserie with good interesting meals and light snacks, plus morning coffee and afternoon tea - more formal restaurant, too; pretty bdrms; no children. £22.50|£5

CIRENCESTER SP0202 **Swan Yard Café** 6 *Swan Yard, W Market Pl* (01285) 641300 Popular with shoppers, this small simple family-run café has friendly service, and very good value totally home-made food (inc vegetarian choices); cl Sun; disabled access. £11|£5.25

COLN ST ALDWYNS SP1405 **New Inn** (01285) 750651 Under a new licensee, this is a civilised ivy-covered inn with imaginative restaurant-standard food served in a relaxed pubby atmosphere; attractively decorated rooms, a central log fire, well kept real ales and good wines, a no smoking restaurant, and split-level garden; nice surrounding countryside and walks; comfortable bdrms; children over 10 in eating area of bar. £28.50|£8.50

FRAMPTON MANSELL SO9201 **White Horse** (01285) 760960 Excellent modern english cooking in this smart, friendly dining place with attractive furnishings in the main part, a cosy bar area with large sofa and comfortable chairs for those who want to pop in just for a relaxing drink; a well chosen wine list and well kept real ales; cl Sun pm, 24-25 Dec; disabled access. £32|£5.95

GUITING POWER SP0924 **Hollow Bottom** (01451) 850392 Snug old cottage with a homely atmosphere, beamed bar full of horse-racing memorabilia, winter log fire, flagstoned public bar, well kept ales, enjoyable food in bar and restaurant, and pleasant service; nice walks; disabled access. £22.65|£5.95

KINGSCOTE ST8196 **Hunters Hall** (01453) 860393 Civilised old creeper-covered inn with some fine furniture and big log fires in high-beamed connecting rooms, good bar and restaurant food, enjoyable breakfasts, and quite a few wines by the glass; big garden with play area; bdrms; disabled access. £20.95|£7.50

LITTLE BARRINGTON SP2012 **Inn For All Seasons** (01451) 844324 Handsome and civilised old inn with an attractive, mellow lounge bar, low beams, stripped stone and flagstones, a big log fire, particularly good fresh fish and other food, well kept real ales and wines, lots of malt whiskies; a pleasant garden surrounded by lots of walks; cl 1 wk Jan; disabled access. £27.50|£7.95

NAILSWORTH ST8699 **Weighbridge** (01453) 832520 Bustling pub with particularly friendly, chatty licensees, a relaxed bar with three cosily old-fashioned rooms, black beams festooned with country bric-a-brac, raftered no smoking hayloft with an engaging mix of rustic tables; very popular 2-in-1 pies (half the bowl has the filling of your choice and the other is full of home-made cauliflower cheese), and other enjoyable food, 16 wines (and champagne) by the glass, well kept real ales, and a sheltered landscaped garden with picnic-sets under umbrellas; good disabled access. £18.50|£6.20

NEWLAND SO5509 **Ostrich** *(01594) 833260* Unspoilt country pub with friendly pubby atmosphere, spacious but cosily traditional low-ceilinged bar, creaky floors, uneven walls, window shutters, candles in bottles on the tables, comfortable furnishings, and fine big fireplace; properly home-made and very popular food (you can eat from the restaurant menu in bar, too), eight real ales, and nice wines; no smoking restaurant. £25.95|£7.50

NORTHLEACH SP1114 **Wheatsheaf** *West End (01451) 860244* Handsome and civilised 16th-c stone-built dining pub on a quiet street of similarly attractive buildings, and with new licensees this year; three light and airy big-windowed rooms, flagstones, bare boards and carpet matting, modern horse-racing oil paintings, and log fires; appealing choice of imaginative food, good interesting wines, and well kept real ales; pretty back garden with picnic-sets on tiers of grass among flowering shrubs; bdrms. £26|£8.50

PAXFORD SP1837 **Churchill** *(01386) 594000* Bustling and friendly dining pub with restaurant extension off simply furnished flagstoned bar - low ceilings, assorted old tables and chairs, and a snug warmed by a good log fire in its big fireplace; well kept real ales, eight good wines by the glass, and constantly changing interesting food; in the best pub tradition, they don't take bookings, but your name goes on a chalked waiting list if all the tables are full; seats outside; bdrms; disabled access. £25|£8.50

SAPPERTON SO9403 **Bell** *(01285) 760298* Carefully renovated 250-year-old pub with a nice mix of wooden furniture in three separate cosy rooms, country prints on stripped stone walls, log fires and woodburners, fresh flowers, newspapers and guidebooks, imaginative bar food using local produce when possible, well kept real ales, up to ten wines (and champagne) by the glass, tables out on small front lawn and partly covered back courtyard; good surrounding walks, tether for horses; cl 25 and 31 Dec; children lunchtime only; disabled access. £30|£7.50

STOW-ON-THE-WOLD SP1925 **Eagle & Child** *Digbeth Street (01451) 830670* Appealing pub with flagstone floors, dark low beams and joists, terracotta pink walls with a modicum of horsey prints and old school photographs, woodburning stove, perhaps a friendly black labrador - and a thriving bustling atmosphere; nice mix of individual tables in the main part and a back conservatory, and french windows onto small courtyard; good interesting modern cooking from the hotel's australian chef, well kept real ales, good wines by the glass and friendly staff in smart black and white; bedrooms in interesting and ancient adjacent hotel. £26.45|£7.75

TETBURY ST9195 **Trouble House** *(01666) 502206* (A433 2m NW) Popular newish dining pub in attractively reworked ancient building, lots of hops in three relaxed rooms, chesterfield by a good fire in one big stone fireplace, a mix of stripped pine or oak furniture; imaginative food, a nice choice of wines by the glass, well kept real ales, friendly service; smaller helpings for children, and they sell quite a few of their own preserves; one room is no smoking; picnic-sets on the gravel behind or in a back paddock; cl Sun pm, Mon, 2 wks Jan, bank hols; no children in bar; disabled access. £32|£6.75

WINCHCOMBE SP0228 **White Hart** *High St* Café-bar with big windows giving on to the village street - passers-by knock on the glass when they see their friends inside; food usefully served all day inc quite a few swedish dishes (staff and landlady are swedish), newly opened pizzeria, good choice of wines by the glass, well kept real ales; smaller no smoking back area, daily papers, a good relaxed mix of all ages, and laid-back piped music; comfortable bdrms. £19.95|£7.50

WOODCHESTER SO8402 **Ram** *Station Rd (01453) 873329* Bustling cheerful pub with spectacular valley views from terrace, attractive beamed bar, very enjoyable bar food inc interesting daily specials, prompt friendly service, and lots of real ales; children must be well behaved; partial disabled access. £15|£4.95

Special thanks to Roy and Lindsey Fentiman, Brian and Anna Marsden, Derek and Sylvia Stephenson

HAMPSHIRE

Portsmouth's maritime bustle, plenty of enjoyable historic places to visit, and attractive countryside - especially the New Forest

Naval and military museums have been one of the great beneficiaries of modern presentational techniques. In the last few years many have become really exciting and intriguing, for all ages - and Hampshire has some of the very best. Portsmouth (and nearby Gosport) now have some terrific attractions based round the city's naval heritage. Head of the list is Hampshire's top Family Attraction, the Historic Dockyard - more than enough to occupy an action-packed weekend. Explosion! (lots to see, with lively hands-on displays), and the Royal Navy Submarine Museum (interesting tours bring it all to life) are great for families too. Southsea, Portsmouth's resort part, boasts an outstanding aquarium, a lively museum and a castle, as well as beachfront amusements.

Among the multitude of military museums, especially worth mentioning are Fareham's Fort Nelson (a bit like a huge adventure playground) and the Museum of Army Flying at Middle Wallop. For places with a more specialised appeal head to Aldershot and Winchester. Hampshire County Council publish *Defence of the Realm*, a brochure detailing discounted entry to over 40 military-linked attractions; available from individual sites and most tourist information centres.

The energetic re-creations at Milestones Living History Museum in Basingstoke make a first-class day out, and younger children find the attractions and rides at Paultons Park in Ower a delight. The Watercress Line steam railway (Alresford) has good special events, and there's a huge steam collection near Liphook. Enjoyable animal-related attractions include Marwell Zoo at Colden Common (all sorts of exotic species in carefully thought out surroundings), and for tame animals there's Finkley Down Farm Park (near Andover), and the country park at Bursledon, based around a working farm. The birds of prey centre at Weyhill is very good. Busy Southampton has quite a bit to keep families occupied for a day.

Fine houses include elegant Broadlands in Romsey, and the Tudor mansion at Sherborne St John. On a humbler scale, you can visit Jane Austen's house in Chawton, and Dickens' birthplace in Portsmouth. Houghton Lodge at Stockbridge and Mottisfont Abbey have much to appeal to garden-lovers, and the grounds of waterside Exbury are quite gorgeous in late spring; the more recent gardens at Boldre are a magnet for people interested in uncommon plants. At Stansted Park in Rowland's Castle (the glimpse of life downstairs is thought-provoking) there's a falconry centre, and lots of space for strolling. The ruins of Basing House are evocative, and the memorial chapel at Burghclere is moving.

Mainly rolling heathland, the New Forest is great for free-form wandering among ponies and deer, and ideal for children to romp around in (the New Forest website has lots of useful information:

www.thenewforest.co.uk). The coast close to it has sheltered yachting harbours, the pleasant waterside town of Lymington with warm Georgian buildings (the rest of Hampshire's coastline is largely built up), and the interesting Bucklers Hard. Excellent places to visit in and around the New Forest include Beaulieu Abbey with its most enjoyable subsidiary attractions, and the farm and wildlife centre at Ashurst.

Central Hampshire has a broad belt of gentle countryside stretching from Andover, Stockbridge and Romsey along the Test Valley in the W, through Winchester (a lovely city for a relaxed trip, with quite a few attractions including a new science centre) and Alresford, to Alton and Petersfield in the E. This is a quietly charming mix of rolling blowy chalk downland, a patchwork of hedged fields and clumps of steep beechwood, the rich valleys of the clear chalk streams, and attractive small villages often of brick and flint, with plenty of peaceful walking opportunities.

Where to stay

BEAULIEU SU3902 **Montagu Arms** *Palace Lane, Beaulieu, Brockenhurst, Hampshire SO42 7ZL (01590) 612324* **£145**, plus special breaks; 23 individually decorated pretty rms. Attractive creeper-clad hotel with lovely terraced garden, comfortable sitting room, conservatory lounge, very good food in beamed restaurant and more informal brasserie, and attentive staff; their health club is in the nearby village of Brockenhurst

CHERITON SU5828 **Flower Pots** *Cheriton, Alresford, Hampshire SO24 0QQ (01962) 771318* **£65**; 4 rms. Unspoilt and quietly comfortable village local run by very friendly family, with two pleasant little bars, log fire, decent bar food, super own-brew beers, and old-fashioned seats on the pretty lawns; no credit cards; no accommodation Christmas and New Year; no children; dogs welcome

DROXFORD SU6018 **White Horse** *South Hill, Droxford, Southampton, Hampshire SO32 3PB (01489) 877490* **£50**; 3 rms, 1 with own bthrm. Rambling 16th-c inn with a relaxed atmosphere, small cosy lounge bars, log fires, a sizeable public bar, good reasonably priced bar food, no smoking restaurant areas, well kept real ales, and seats in a flower-filled courtyard; no accommodation over Christmas

HURSTBOURNE TARRANT SU3954 **Esseborne Manor** *Hurstbourne Tarrant, Andover, Hampshire SP11 0ER (01264) 736444* **£120***, plus special breaks; 15 individually decorated rms. Small stylish Victorian manor with a relaxed, friendly atmosphere, comfortable lounge and snug little bar, good modern cooking, log fires in elegant dining room, and courteous staff; neat gardens with tennis, and croquet; special arrangement with local golf club and health and leisure centre; disabled access; dogs welcome in bedrooms

LYMINGTON SZ3094 **Efford Cottage** *Milford Rd, Everton, Lymington, Hampshire SO41 0JD (01590) 642315* **£60**, plus winter breaks; 3 comfortable rms. Spacious Georgian cottage near New Forest, and in an acre of garden, with marvellous breakfasts inc home-baked bread and home-made jams and preserves, enjoyable evening meals using home-grown produce (only as part of winter special breaks), and good parking; no children; dogs by arrangement and away from dining room

LYMINGTON SZ3295 **Stanwell House** *High St, Lymington, Hampshire SO41 9AA (01590) 677123* **£110***, plus special breaks; 28 pretty rms. Handsome town house with comfortable attractively furnished lounge, cosy little bar, good imaginative food, and pretty walled back garden; dogs welcome

LYNDHURST SU3107 **Poussin at Parkhill** *Beaulieu Rd, Lyndhurst, Hampshire SO43 7FZ (023) 8028 2944* **£110**, plus special breaks; 19 carefully furnished, spacious and comfortable rms. 18th-c former hunting lodge reached by a long drive

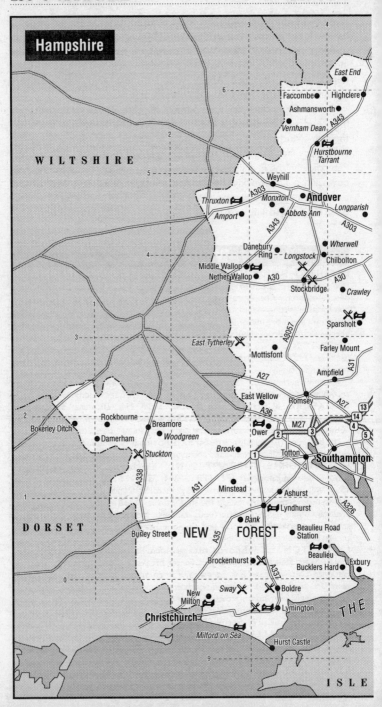

Hampshire

WILTSHIRE

East End

Faccombe Highclere

Ashmansworth

Vernham Dean

Hurstbourne
Tarrant

Weyhill

Thruxton Monxton **Andover** Longparish

Amport Abbots Ann A303

Wherwell

Danebury
Ring Longstock Chilbolton

Middle Wallop Nether Wallop A30 Stockbridge Crawley

Sparsholt

Farley Mount

East Tytherley Mottisfont Ampfield

A27

East Wellow Romsey A27 13

A36 14

Rockbourne Breamore Ower M27 4

Bokerley Ditch Woodgreen 2 3 5

Damerham Stuckton Brook Totton **Southampton**

Minstead Ashurst

Lyndhurst

DORSET Bank Beaulieu Road
Station

Burley Street **NEW** **FOREST**

Brockenhurst Beaulieu

Bucklers Hard Exbury

New
Milton Sway Boldre

Christchurch Lymington

Milford on Sea Hurst Castle THE

ISLE

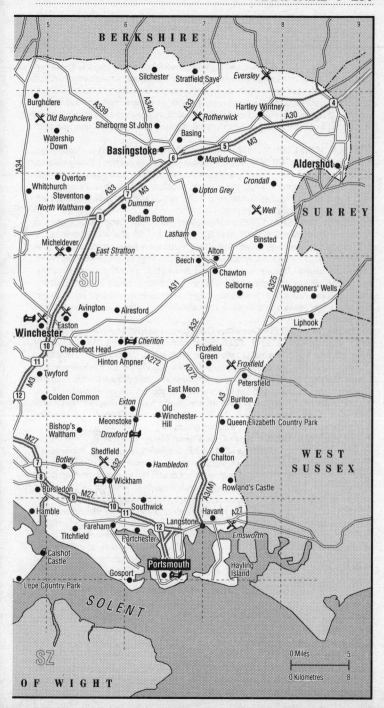

BERKSHIRE

Silchester
Stratfield Saye
Eversley
Burghclere
Old Burghclere
A339
A340
Rotherwick
Hartley Wintney
Sherborne St John
A30
Aldershot
Basing
A34
Watership Down
Basingstoke
M3
Mapledurwell
Overton
A33
Crondall
Whitchurch
Steventon
Upton Grey
North Waltham
Dummer
Well
SURREY
Micheldever
Bedlam Bottom
Lasham
Binsted
East Stratton
Alton
SU
Beech
Chawton
Avington
Alresford
A31
Selborne
Waggoners' Wells
Easton
A32
Liphook
Winchester
Cheesefoot Head
Cheriton
Froxfield Green
Hinton Ampner
A272
Froxfield
Twyford
A272
Petersfield
Colden Common
East Meon
Buriton
M3
Exton
A3
Old Winchester Hill
Queen Elizabeth Country Park
Meonstoke
Bishop's Waltham
Droxford
WEST SUSSEX
Shedfield
Chalton
Botley
A32
Hambledon
Burseldon
Wickham
Rowland's Castle
M27
Hamble
Southwick
Havant
A27
Fareham
Langstone
Titchfield
Portchester
Emsworth
Calshot Castle
Portsmouth
Hayling Island
Gosport
Lepe Country Park
SOLENT
SZ
OF WIGHT

0 Miles 5
0 Kilometres 8

through wood-flanked New Forest pastures; a nice, informal, family-run atmosphere, big welcoming peaceful lounge/hall with sofas, easy chairs, a writing desk, a good log fire and daily papers, and an inner hall with a grand piano and longcase clock; the pink-carpeted lounge has another big log fire, lots of sofas and deep easy chairs and low tables, and big windows looking over a narrow flagstoned terrace and pond-side lawn; a little library with lots of books, smallish cosy bar, and pretty, formal restaurant with conservatory-style extension; quite excellent, beautifully presented food, a good wine list with an exceptionally good choice of wines by the glass, and enjoyable breakfasts with home-preserved fruits and home-made jams and marmalade; children over 8 in dining room; dogs in one bedroom only

MIDDLE WALLOP SU2837 **Fifehead Manor** *Middle Wallop, Stockbridge, Hampshire SO20 8EG* (01264) 781565 **£130**w, plus special breaks; 17 spacious rms, some in the garden wing. Friendly and comfortable old brick manor house in several acres of lovely gardens; a restful atmosphere, pleasant small no smoking lounge and bar, fine food in candlelit restaurant, enjoyable breakfasts, and friendly staff; croquet; dogs in some garden rooms

MILFORD ON SEA SZ2891 **Westover Hall** *Park Lane, Milford on Sea, Lymington, Hampshire SO41 0PT* (01590) 643044 **£150***, plus winter breaks; 12 individually furnished rms, 6 with fine views. Victorian mansion in marvellous spot nr peaceful beach, views of Christchurch Bay, Isle of Wight and the Needles rocks; impressive original features inc dramatic stained glass, magnificent oak panelling, and ornate ceilings, very good food using the best local produce in grand (but not stuffy) candlelit restaurant overlooking garden and sea, lighter lunches in lounge bar also with water views, sunny terrace, and helpful friendly staff; children over 8; dogs welcome in bedrooms

NEW MILTON SZ2294 **Chewton Glen** *Christchurch Rd, New Milton, Hampshire BH25 6QS* (01425) 275341 **£260** inc dinner; 59 really beautiful, individually designed rms. Luxurious hotel (a member of Relais & Chateaux) in immaculate grounds with fine antiques, paintings and an abundance of fresh flowers in sumptuous day rooms, the relaxing atmosphere of a large private house, excellent modern french cooking, and impeccable service; gardens inc nine-hole par 3 golf course, swimming pool, tennis (two indoor courts too) and croquet; health club with gym, sauna, steam room, hydrotherapy spa, and indoor and outdoor swimming pools; children over 6; disabled access

NEW MILTON SZ2497 **Yew Tree Farm** *Bashley Common Rd, New Milton, Hampshire BH25 5SH* (01425) 611041 **£70***; 2 lovely spacious rms. Marvellously warm and comfortable, well run traditional thatched smallholding on forest edge; small cosy hall, friendly welcome, extensive breakfasts (taken in bedroom on tables laid with fine china and crisp napery), and enjoyable home-made dinners (if required) using top-quality produce; riding nearby; no smoking and no children

OWER SU3318 **Ranvilles Farm House** *Pauncefoot Hill, Romsey, Hampshire SO51 6AA* (023) 8081 4481 **£55***; 4 attractively decorated rms with antique furniture. Dating from the 13th c when Richard de Ranville came from Normandy and settled with his family, this Grade II* listed house is in five quiet acres of gardens and paddock, with warmly friendly owners and enjoyable breakfasts; no evening meals; cl 25 and 31 Dec, 1 Jan; disabled access; dogs welcome in bedrooms

PORTSMOUTH SZ6299 **Fortitude Cottage** *51 Broad St, Portsmouth, Hampshire PO1 2JD* (023) 9282 3748 **£50**; 4 neat and attractive rms. Comfortable B&B in cottage named after an old ship, with pretty beamed breakfast room overlooking fishing boats; no evening meals but places nearby; cl Christmas; children over 10

PORTSMOUTH SZ6399 **Sally Port** *High St, Portsmouth, Hampshire PO1 2LU* (023) 9282 1860 **£65**, plus special breaks; 14 rms, most with own bthrm. Beautifully kept inn (built using 16th-c timbers from an old building) in quiet spot opposite cathedral, with good food and very friendly efficient service; said to have been a favourite of Nelson; disabled access

SPARSHOLT SU4431 **Lainston House** *Sparsholt, Winchester, Hampshire SO21 2LT (01962) 863588* **£185**, plus wknd breaks; 50 spacious, individually decorated rms. Close to Winchester, this elegant William and Mary hotel stands in 63 acres of fine parkland, with tennis court, croquet, fishing, archery, and clay pigeon shooting; fresh flowers and paintings in relaxing, elegant lounge, panelled bar and restaurant, a fine wine list, and good british cooking; gym; disabled access; dogs in some ground floor rooms

THRUXTON SU2945 **May Cottage** *Thruxton, Andover, Hampshire SP11 8LZ (01264) 771241* **£70***; 3 rms. Creeper-clad early Georgian house in quiet village (two decent inns with good food), with friendly owners, residents' sitting room, good breakfasts, and afternoon tea with home-made cake in pretty garden; no smoking; cl Christmas

WICKHAM SU5711 **Old House** *The Square, Wickham, Fareham, Hampshire PO17 5JG (01329) 833049* **£90***, plus special breaks; 8 rms. Lovely ivy-clad early Georgian house fronting the village square, with beamed and panelled rooms, antiques, fresh flowers and open fires, reliably good french cooking in the restaurant (once the timber-framed outhouse and stables), and pretty back garden

WINCHESTER SU4729 **Hotel du Vin & Bistro** *14 Southgate St, Winchester, Hampshire SO23 9EF (01962) 841414* **£105**; 23 rms of real quality, each sponsored by a well known wine company with relevant paintings, labels and old photographs. An engaging early 18th-c town house with enthusiastic owners and hard-working staff, deeply comfortable sitting room, two relaxed and pretty eating areas with imaginative bistro-style cooking and an exceptional wine list, and a lovely walled garden for summer dining; disabled access

WINCHESTER SU4828 **Wykeham Arms** *75 Kingsgate St, Winchester, Hampshire SO23 9PE (01962) 853834* **£90**; 14 well equipped attractive rms (half refurbished this year). Very well run, smart old town inn, close to cathedral, with interestingly furnished bustling bars, two small dining rooms serving delicious daily-changing food (very good breakfasts, too), fine wines (lots by the glass), and prompt friendly service; several no smoking areas; cl 25 Dec; children by arrangement

To see and do

Hampshire Family Attraction of the Year

PORTSMOUTH SU6300 **Portsmouth Historic Dockyard** Perhaps best described as the home of the Royal Navy, this extraordinary complex has over the last few years considerably widened its appeal, with the addition of new exhibitions, attractions and lively interactive displays; if you allow enough time to see it properly, it's now one of the most rewarding places to visit in the whole country. HMS *Victory*, the *Mary Rose*, HMS *Warrior* and the Royal Naval Museum are all based here, along with the excellent Action Stations, a hi-tech examination of the Navy in modern times. Entry into the dockyard itself, and its shops and restaurants, is free (after a security check), but entry is charged for all the attractions. Even if you're relatively short of time, don't be tempted to buy individual tickets - the all-inclusive one is much better value, and covers not only the attractions listed above but a 40-minute boat trip round the harbour. And don't worry if you feel you won't fit everything in: any unused parts of the ticket are valid for life, so you can always come back to see the rest another time. First stop for most visitors, at the opposite end from the main entrance, is the spectacular HMS *Victory*, which is still in commission; guided tours (not in school holidays) bring those Trafalgar days very close, and include the spot where Nelson died. Next to here, the Tudor *Mary Rose* is displayed inside a huge hall where she's sprayed constantly to prevent the timbers from drying out. When the ship was raised from The Solent silt after 437 years, she provided a wealth of material and information about the Tudor period; the discoveries are well shown in a museum on the other side of the dockyard. Housed in handsome 18th-c dockside buildings, the Royal Naval Museum has lively displays on the history of the Navy up to and beyond the Falklands War (or as it's called here the South Atlantic Campaign); the four main interactive galleries focus on Nelson, HMS *Victory*, a re-creation of the Battle of Trafalgar, and a vivid illustration of daily life on board an 18th-c warship. Back near the main entrance of the dockyard is HMS *Warrior*, which when launched 140 years ago was the most fearsome battleship in the world; she's been immaculately restored. Then finally in a converted Victorian boathouse is Action Stations, with dramatic hands-on displays looking at current naval deployment; highlights include an extraordinarily vivid IMAX-style film, and a simulator ride in either a Sea Harrier or Lynx helicopter. This section is a big hit with children, and there can be long queues in school holidays, when around the whole site you'll find extra activities and costumed actors. If you can, try to visit out of season, when it's easier to enjoy things at your own pace. Meals, snacks, shops; disabled access is generally very good but is limited in some of the ships; cl 24-25 Dec; (023) 9272 7562; the all-inclusive ticket is £14.85 for adults, or £11.90 for children, with a family ticket for two adults and two children costing £47.55. Individual tickets for the attractions are £9.50 for adults, and £8 for children, with the family ticket £33; the one for HMS *Victory* also covers the Royal Naval Museum, but see above. Leave your car somewhere else if you can: a full day in the adjacent car park will cost £6.

ALDERSHOT SU8651
Airborne Forces Museum 🆓
(Browning Barracks) One of the best of Aldershot's many military museums (most of which have been of rather specialist appeal), looking at the parachute forces. Lots to take in, with very traditional displays. Shop, some disabled access; cl over Christmas hols; (01252) 349619; *£3.
Military Museum (Queens Ave) Galleries look at early flying experiments, vehicles, and the development of the local military camps

and their impact on civilian and military life; quite a few hands-on activities inc the chance to try out a Victorian soldier's bed. Snacks, shop, disabled access; cl 25-26 Dec and 1 Jan; (01252) 314598; £2.

ALRESFORD SU5832

A charming little town, from the Roman ponds teeming with wildfowl in Old Alresford to the so-called New Alresford founded around 1200; good antiquarian bookshop here. The Globe overlooking the ponds does decent lunches. The Itchen road W through Ovington and Easton is pretty, the B3046 N shows high Hampshire farmland well, and the old road E past Ropley and Monkwood to Steep gives a fine downland impression.

Watercress Line 🖾 One of the nicest steam railways in the country, with 10-mile trips between Alresford and Alton through wonderful countryside and its watercress beds. They try to create a pre-war feel, with stations decked out accordingly. Their Thomas the Tank Engine weeks around Easter and in Aug are extraordinarily popular (the Thomas here is built to the design and proportions in the books). Properly called the Mid-Hants Railway, it runs special main-line monthly trips to places as far away as Brighton and Bristol. A visitor centre houses a museum and shop, meals, snacks, disabled access; phone for timetable; (01962) 733810, cl Mon and Fri, no trains Nov to mid-Jan (exc Dec Santa specials); £9 for unlimited rides all day.

ALTON SU7139

Allen Gallery (Church St) Superb collection of pottery, and a little herb garden. Snacks, shop, disabled access to ground floor only; cl Sun-Mon and 2 wks over Christmas; (01420) 82802; free. Across the road (and open the same times) is an engaging local history museum. The town is the other terminus of the Watercress steam line (see *Alresford*). Coors Brewery (Turk St - formerly Bass) offers wkdy tours inc snacks and beer tasting 11.30-3pm and 7.30-10pm (not Fri), cl all Aug; phone first; (01420) 520158; £11. The church bears scars from one of the last battles of the Civil War. The French Horn (The Butts) is a friendly food pub.

AMPFIELD SP3824

Sir Harold Hillier Gardens and Arboretum (Jermyns Lane, off A31) Impressive collection of trees and shrubs, the biggest of its kind in Britain, covering 180 beautifully landscaped acres. Full of colour and surprises all year, but particularly delightful in spring; good seasonal walks and events. A new £3.5m visitor and education pavilion opened in 2003 with a shop, exhibition centre and a larger restaurant. Nursery, disabled access; cl 25-26 Dec; (01794) 368787; *£5.50. The White Horse nearby is a comfortable lunch break.

ANDOVER SU2744

Fast Helicopters (Thruxton Airport) The most exciting - and expensive - way to take in the local sights, with a chance to test your piloting potential; (01264) 772508; half-hour flight £139.

Finkley Down Farm Park (just NE) Well laid out working farm with wide range of animals and poultry inc rare breeds; they encourage you to touch the tamer animals, and there are varied activities every half-hour. Also countryside museum, adventure playground and picnic site. Readers rate this very highly, and it has lots for children (inc space for them to run around). Meals, snacks, shop, disabled access; cl Nov-Mar; (01264) 352195; £4.75. The Hare & Hounds, on Charlton Down a mile or two up the nearby Roman Icknield Way, does good meals, and on the other side of town (A343 at Abbotts Ann) Poplar Farm is a useful family food stop, with an indoor play area. There are well stocked trout fishing lakes around Andover, inc Rooksbury Mill.

Museum of the Iron Age Near the church at the top of the impressive High St of this very extended country town, the museum looks particularly at finds from nearby Danebury Ring, giving a vivid impression of life for the pre-Roman Celts. Snacks, shop; cl Sun, Mon, and Christmas; (01264) 366283; free. The same building has a more general local history museum (open same hours, free).

ASHMANSWORTH SU3758

Hampshire's high country There are fine views from many of the lanes around Ashmansworth and Linkenholt - best explored by car, though there are good walks too. The Plough does simple home cooking.

ASHURST SU3510

Longdown Dairy Farm (Deerleap Lane) This friendly place has plenty of animals to feed, and lots of hands-on activities; their herd of friesian cows is milked from 2.30pm every day. There's an indoor and outdoor play area. Snacks, shop, disabled access; usually cl 22 Dec-Jan, but best to check; (023) 8029 3326; £4.75. The Happy Cheese (A35) is a useful all-day dining pub.

New Forest Otter, Owl and Wildlife Park (Longdown, off A35) Large collection of otters, owls and other indigenous or previously indigenous wildlife such as pine martens, polecats, wild boar and even lynx; woodland nature trails. Meals, snacks, shop, disabled access; cl 25-26 Dec, plus wkdys Jan-Feb half-term; (023) 8029 2408; £6.50. The Pilgrim (Hythe Rd) is an attractive thatched dining pub.

AVINGTON SU5332

Avington Park Georgian mansion with Tudor origins, set in lovely parkland; the church too is worth a visit. Teas in the orangery; open pm Sun and bank hols May-Sept, plus Mon in Aug; (01962) 779260; £3.75. The Bush at Ovington is a good nicely placed pub (as we went to press, all talk there was of the oilfield just discovered below the village).

BASING SU6652

Basing House Ruins Peaceful ruins of what was once the country's largest house, destroyed during a two-year siege in the Civil War. Also remnants of a Norman castle, a 16th-c barn, dovecotes, an exhibition explaining the eventful history of the site and a re-created 17th-c garden. Nice walks from here along the River Loddon. Shop, some disabled access; open pm only, Weds-Sun and bank hols Apr-Sept; (01256) 467294; £2. The Gamekeepers at pretty nearby Mapledurwell is handy for lunch.

BASINGSTOKE SU6252

Milestones Living History Museum ⊞ (Leisure Park, off B3400, Churchill Way W) A network of streets and authentically assembled buildings has been constructed to re-create the sights and sounds of local life since Victorian times, with factories, a railway station, brewery with attached

pub, fire station, and shops; staff in period clothes explain things. The whole thing is indoors, in a splendid very modern-looking glass building, and there's an interactive post office for under-5s, a big toy area where activity trucks compare today's toys and games with those from the past, and a hands-on history section for 7- to 11- year-olds, with a fun old-fashioned photographer's studio (on some wknds you can have your picture taken). There is some emphasis on local industries, with vehicles and collections inc steam engines, and early clothing from Burberrys, who first opened in Basingstoke in 1856. Good value meals (1-2pm only) and snacks, shop, disabled access; cl Mon (exc bank hols), 25-26 Dec, and 1 Jan; (01256) 477766; £6.50. The surrounding leisure park has ice-skating, cinemas and ten-pin bowling.

Viables Craft Centre (Harrow Way, off A30 and via Grove Rd off A339) Sixteen craft workshops on an old Victorian farm; ceramics studio, art and craft gallery, miniature railway, model car racing circuit, and various courses all year. Indian restaurant, disabled access; cl Sun and Mon; (01256) 473634; free.

BEAULIEU SU3802

Beaulieu Abbey ⊞ A great day out, its centrepiece is the ever-growing National Motor Museum, a collection that from humble beginnings has become one of the most comprehensive in the world, from stately horseless carriages to breathtaking racing cars. Wheels is probably the highlight for children - you sit in a pod-like vehicle and trundle through 100 years of motoring; for an extra charge a simulator ride gives you a more robust driving experience. A monorail whizzes round the grounds, and in summer you can ride on a replica 1912 London bus. Also radio-controlled cars and in summer go-karts. Palace House is a fine old mansion based around the gatehouse of the huge Cistercian Abbey that stood here until the Reformation (still with what are thought to be the original monastic fan-vaulted ceilings). The surrounding lakeside parkland and themed gardens are rewarding to explore, with ruins of other abbey buildings, and an exhibition on the monks who lived here. Meals, snacks, shops, disabled access; cl 25 Dec; (01590) 612345; £13. In the village facing the Palace House gates, Montys is popular for lunch, and a marked trail leads from here down to Bucklers Hard.

BEAULIEU ROAD STATION SU3506

New Forest walks A good starting point, for its surrounding remote-feeling heaths.

BEDLAM BOTTOM SU6246

Pleasant partly wooded valley walks, particularly pretty in spring; just W of Ellisfield SU6345 (where the Fox has good food), with more downland walks above.

BEECH SU6838

Alton Abbey (signed off A339) The home of a community of Benedictine monks, in peaceful woodland so a relaxing place for a stroll. The grounds have mature specimen trees and shrubs, especially rhododendrons and azaleas; donations. The traditional Sun at Bentworth does good food.

BINSTED SU7740

Binsted church Where Field Marshal Montgomery is buried; after the war he lived a mile away at Islington Mill - a pretty spot. The Cedars has decent food.

BISHOP'S WALTHAM SU5517

Bishop's Waltham Palace 🏛 Impressive ruins of Bishop of Winchester's majestic 12th-c palace, with the remains of state apartments round a cloister court, and William of Wykeham's great hall and tower. Snacks, shop, disabled access to ground floor and grounds; cl Nov-Mar; (01489) 892460; *£2.50; EH. The White Horse (Beeches Hill, off B3035 just NE) does nice meals, and the downs N of here between Owslebury, Beauworth and Warnford give scenic drives.

BOKERLEY DITCH SU0419

This acted as a bulwark from raiders into Dorset in the 4th c; still impressive to walk along, it marks the county boundary and can be reached by walking up from Martin. Towards Pentridge Hill is a nature reserve.

BOLDRE SZ3298

Spinners (School Lane) Wonderful gardens created since the 1960s. The nursery is famed for its rare trees

(especially maples and magnolias), shrubs and woodland plants. Plant sales; gardens open Tues-Sat mid-Apr to mid-Sept, or by appointment, nursery open all year exc Sun-Mon; (01590) 673347; *£2. The Red Lion (no children) is good for lunch.

BREAMORE SU1519

Breamore House 🏛 Late Elizabethan manor house, with fine furnishings, tapestries and paintings (mainly 17th- and 18th-c Dutch School), and better than average countryside museum with displays of Roman artefacts found within the estate, and a rare 16th-c bavarian turret clock. Children aren't left out - there's a maze and adventure playground. Meals, snacks, shop, disabled access; cl am, all Mon and Fri (exc Aug and bank hols), and all Sept-Easter (though open Tues and Sun in Apr); (01725) 512468; *£6. The village has many thatched houses, and is within a pleasant walk of Breamore House - and the mysterious Mizmaze, cut in the turf. The Cartwheel at Whitsbury has enjoyable food.

BROCKENHURST SU2902

New Forest trails The village is well placed for walks, or if you prefer you can hire bicycles at Country Lanes Cycle Hire (the Station); (01590) 622627; from £12 a day.

BUCKLERS HARD SZ4099

Bucklers Hard Maritime Museum Very pretty little waterside village, with 18th-c cottage rows flanking a wide, grassed street leading to the Beaulieu River. It was once an important centre for shipbuilding, and the Maritime Museum tells the story of the industry, right up to the voyages of Sir Francis Chichester. You have to pay to come into the village, though admission includes entry to the museum and the various other exhibitions and reconstructions dotted around, inc the carefully restored 18th-c homes of a shipwright and labourer, and a typical inn scene complete with costumed figures, smells and conversation. Meals, snacks, shop; cl 25 Dec; (01590) 616203; £5. There are summer boat trips, and the Master Builders House is useful for lunch. A pleasant 2½-mile riverside walk takes you to Beaulieu, run by the same people.

BURGHCLERE SU4660
Sandham Memorial Chapel (Harts
Lane) Stanley Spencer's moving
masterpiece, dedicated to the memory
of H W Sandham, killed in World War I.
The final resurrection scene is
especially dramatic, best on a bright day
as there is no artificial lighting. Open
Weds-Sun and bank hols Apr-Oct,
wknds only Nov and Mar, and by
appointment in winter; (01635)
278394; £3; NT. The Carpenters Arms
opposite is pleasant for lunch, with
superb views.
BURITON SU7320
Quiet village below the South Downs
N-facing scarp slope nr Petersfield;
enjoyable walks in all directions, and
handy for the Queen Elizabeth Country
Park and Butser Hill. The Five Bells is an
interesting old pub.
BURLEY STREET SU1904
New Forest walks A good area, with
a mix of wooded parts and more open
country; the White Buck is a
comfortable food pub.
BURSLEDON SU4911
Manor Farm Country Park (Pylands
Lane) Woodland and riverside walks
based around traditional working farm,
with lots of animals, crafts and activities
inc a forge and a wheelwright; maps
show the various paths (80p). Meals,
snacks, shop, mostly disabled access;
park open all year, farm cl Nov-Apr exc
Sun; (01489) 787055; £4.60, free entry
to park, parking £1.50 (refundable
against ticket to farm). There are **boat
trips**, and a river bus from here along
the Hamble, phone for details; (023)
8045 3542. Bursledon also has a
windmill; open Sun, plus Sat May-Sept;
£1.50. The Jolly Sailor is a beautifully
placed food pub.
CALSHOT CASTLE SU4802
Down past the oil refineries and power
stations, this Tudor fort stands on the
end of the spit of land out over the tidal
mudflats at the end of Southampton
Water; splendid views of the shipping
and the Isle of Wight. Shop, some
disabled access; cl Nov-Mar (023) 8089
2023; £2.50; EH. The Jolly Sailor at
Ashlett Creek nr Fawley is a pleasant
waterside food pub.
CHALTON SU7117
Butser Ancient Farm 🔲 (Bascombe

Copse) Using archaeological evidence,
the farm aims to give you a feel of what
life was really like in prehistoric and
Roman times, with period crops,
animals and crafts. There are some
good hands-on activities for children,
and they are currently working on a
reconstruction of a Roman villa. Shop,
disabled access; open last wknd in
month Mar-Sept; (023) 9259 8838; £5.
The ancient Red Lion is good for lunch.
As there is hardly enough at the farm
itself to justify a journey, you could tie
this in with a visit to Butser Hill, a steep
chalk hill that was once a large Iron Age
fort (by the A3 towards Petersfield); it's
a good place for kite flying and picnics,
and you can walk from here to Queen
Elizabeth Country Park.
CHAWTON SU7037
Jane Austen's House Enjoyable
unpretentious 17th-c house where the
author lived and worked 1809-17, still
with some of her letters and
possessions. Rooms are furnished in
period style, and the pleasant garden is
good for picnics. Good bookshop,
disabled access to ground floor and
garden; cl wkdys Dec-Feb, and 25-26
Dec; (01420) 83262; £4. The Greyfriar
opposite has good food, and there are
good walks here. Just up the road,
Chawton House, the former home of
Jane Austen's brother Edward, is now
the Centre for the Study of Early English
Women's Writing.
CHEESEFOOT HEAD SU5327
(locally pronounced Chesford) Good
for walks; a natural amphitheatre where
Eisenhower and Montgomery
addressed the troops before the
Normandy invasion.
CHILBOLTON SU3940
An attractive village where the
common is being carefully preserved;
River Test and other walks. The Abbots
Mitre (open all day Sun) is a decent pub.
COLDEN COMMON SU5121
Marwell Zoo (off A333 towards
Bishop's Waltham) Undoubtedly one of
Britain's best zoos, and one which
doesn't just pay lip-service to its
conservation message. It's beautifully
laid out, with plenty of space for
residents, and well conceived viewing
areas include a glass wall at the end of
the tiger enclosure, underwater

windows into the big penguin world, and covered walkways for watching the playful lemurs. Though many of the species aren't familiar names, children will see all the types of animal they'd want to, from giraffes and flamingoes to rhinos and bats; they've recently added a new leopard enclosure. Particularly impressive are the Into Africa house, the outstanding collection of primates, and the Desert Carnivores house. Children enjoy the nicely sheltered Encounters Village, where in summer holidays they might be able to handle a snake or ride a camel, and there's a good adventure playground; regular special events during the hols. Road and rail trains can whisk you between the different enclosures. Meals, snacks, shop, good disabled access; cl 25 Dec; (01962) 777407; £11 adults. On the downs above, the Ship at Owslebury is good for a family lunch - quieter than nearby Fishers Pond.

DAMERHAM SU1016
Damerham churchyard Well worth a February visit, to see the carpet of snowdrops. The prettily set Compasses has good food, and there are downland walks nearby.

DANEBURY RING SU3237
Iron Age hill fort rich in (excavated) remains. The Peat Spade at Longstock to the E does interesting food.

EAST MEON SU6822
This appealing village has a splendid Norman church; the George is a good pub.
Snowdrop woods Many of the woodlands in this part of Hampshire fill with snowdrops in Feb, and are famous for their bluebells in Apr/May.

EAST WELLOW SU3020
St Margaret's Florence Nightingale is buried in the churchyard of this peaceful 13th-c church; there are pleasant walks nearby.

EASTON SU5031
This attractive village is well placed for pleasant Itchen Valley walks; the Chestnut Horse is very good for lunch.

EXBURY SU4200
Exbury Gardens 🏛 Wonderful 200-acre landscaped woodland gardens on E bank of the River Beaulieu, with splendid rock garden, heather garden and river walk, and above all the Rothschild collection of rhododendrons, azaleas, magnolias and camellias - one of the world's finest, at its best Apr-May. A 12½ inch gauge steam railway runs through the summer garden (from £2). Meals, snacks, shop, disabled access; cl wkdys Nov-Dec, and all Jan-Feb; (023) 8089 9422; price varies with the season, from £3.50 in summer to £5.50 in spring. The Bridge Tavern (Ipers Bridge, Holbury) has above-average food.

FACCOMBE SU3957
Bright with daffodils in spring, this neatly attractive village in idyllic countryside has great views from Pilot Hill; the Jack Russell has enjoyable food.

FAREHAM SU6007
Fort Nelson (Downend Rd) You don't have to be interested in weaponry to enjoy a trip to this restored 19th-c fort, built in response to fears of an attack from France, and now part of the Royal Armouries Museum. It has been known as the noisiest museum in the world, thanks mainly to the roar of the two huge cannons fired twice a day, at 12 and 3pm, and the lingering smell of gunpowder adds to the atmosphere. With plenty of underground tunnels to investigate, it's not unlike an enormous adventure playground. Occasional battle re-enactment days (ring for dates), and regular guided tours. Good views of Portsmouth Harbour from the ramparts. Meals, snacks, shop, disabled access; cl 25-26 Dec; (01329) 233734; free. The Osborne View (Hill Head) has superb views, and is handy for the beach and walks in Titchfield Haven nature reserve, where you can see wildfowl and waders plus rare wetland flora; cl Mon-Tues, 25-26 Dec; £3.30.

FARLEY MOUNT SU4229
An attractive area of downland and woodland, with good views - good for walks.

FROXFIELD GREEN SU7124
Bluebells In May much of the woodland around Froxfield Green is carpeted with bluebells, as are woods elsewhere in the area - for example at East Tisted and Ropley.

GOSPORT SZ6199
Dominated by its navy base; several millennium grant-funded attractions have come to fruition here, inc a

gigantic sundial by the harbour, and the Millennium Promenade (see also *Portsmouth*) which takes in some of the town's naval heritage.

Explosion! (Priddy's Hard, Heritage Way) Small boys of all ages will be particularly excited by this splendid museum of naval firepower, but it has a much wider appeal than that; the often lively displays offer a look at not just how weaponry has been made and used over the years, but also the effect it has on those who produce it - and the people on the receiving end. Housed in 18th-c naval stores, there's plenty to see from old muskets to Exocet missiles. There are rooms devoted to small arms, mines, big guns, submarines and torpedoes; most have some kind of interactive feature or touch-screen displays (from quizzes to explanations of how a rifle works), and children are able to handle lots of the hardware. A highlight is the well laid out and awesome Grand Magazine, where films put the building and its history nicely in context. They've taken pains to make it relevant to girls as well, with displays on the lives of female munitions workers. There may be extra activities in school holidays. The best way to get there in fine weather is the three-minute ferry from Portsmouth, and stroll along the Millennium Promenade (if you show your Gosport ferry ticket you get a 10% discount). Waterside meals and snacks, shop, disabled access; open Thurs and wknds Nov-Mar (exc 24-26 Dec), daily April-Oct and school hols; (023) 9250 5600; £5, £7.60 joint ticket with the Royal Naval Submarine Museum (free shuttlebus between the attractions). Nearby, the friendly harbourside Jolly Roger has reasonably priced food.

Fort Brockhurst A good overview exhibition of how the various forts protected Portsmouth. Shop; opening days were undecided as we went to press, so best to phone (023) 9258 1059; £2.20. The Dolphin (Fort Rd) has popular food, good views and a huge play area.

Gosport Museum (Walpole Rd) Imaginative geology and local history display. Snacks, shop, disabled access; cl Sun-Mon, and a few days over Christmas and New Year (best to phone then); (023) 9258 8035; free.

Royal Navy Submarine Museum (Haslar Jetty Rd) As well as *Holland 1*, a 100-year-old fully restored submarine (the Royal Navy's first, with an exhibition on how she was recovered), highlights include a tour (often by an ex-crewman) of beached World War II submarine HMS *Alliance*, still in full working order, and fascinating inside to boys of any age, with lots to fiddle with. More conventional features include an audio-visual show giving the flavour of diving into the depths, and you can look through two periscopes - one from the submarine that sunk the argentine *Belgrano*. A waterfront extension to the museum, to increase space for exhibits, is planned for this year, but shouldn't affect visitors too much. Snacks, shop, some disabled access; cl 24-25 Dec, and 1 Jan; (023) 9252 9217; £4. You can get a Waterbus across to Portsmouth (Apr-Oct), and the sea at Stokes Bay is probably Hampshire's cleanest for swimming in; the Alverbank House by the prom there has enjoyable food and a nice big seaview garden. The Clarence (A32) is a good pub brewing its own beer.

HAMBLE SU4806
This pleasant village in *Howards Way* country has interesting views of the yachts, and you can walk a long way up river or towards The Solent. There's a friendly little ferry to Warsash taking about ten people at a time, with a wildfowl nature reserve just N; (023) 8045 4512 for ferry times. The Olde Whyte Harte is good for a pub lunch. Nearby Netley has a coastal **country park** and the extensive ruins of a 13th-c abbey.

HARTLEY WINTNEY SU7456
West Green House Garden 🏛
(Thackhams Lane) This restored formal 18th-c garden is adjacent to a neo-classical park, its lake surrounded by follies, monuments and ornamental fruit cages. Meals, snacks; usually open Weds-Sun May-Aug, but phone to check; (01252) 844611; £5. The Phoenix (A30) has decent food.

HAVANT SU7208
Staunton Country Park (off B2149 N) 1,000 acres of landscaped parkland, created in the 1830s for botanist and explorer Sir George Staunton,

containing the only remaining ornamental farm in England (you can buy animal feed, and there are children's trails and a play area). A walled garden has an impressive restored glasshouse; there's also a maze and puzzle garden. Meals, snacks, shop, disabled access; cl 25-26 Dec; (023) 9245 3405; £4.10.

HAYLING ISLAND SU7201
Readers enjoy this holiday resort popular for watersports. The Inn on the Beach (it is indeed right on the shingle) is good value.

HIGHCLERE SU4360
Highclere Castle 🔳 (best approached from A34 rather than Highclere itself) Magnificent pastiche of a medieval castle, impressively grand inside and out. Elaborate saloon and main staircase, a desk that belonged to Napoleon, and a Van Dyck of Charles I. Exhibitions of Egyptian relics (the 5th Earl of Carnarvon discovered Tutankhamun's tomb with Howard Carter), and horse racing. The lovely gardens and grounds include a Victorian tropical conservatory and walled garden. Meals, snacks, shop and plant centre, disabled access; usually open July-Aug, but phone to check as they hadn't confirmed their opening days before we went to press; (01635) 253210; £7, £3 gardens only. The Yew Tree (A343 S of village) is a good value dining pub.

HINTON AMPNER SU5927
Hinton Ampner Garden Attractive Georgian house, but it's the splendid grounds that impress most, with tranquil 20th-c shrub gardens. Teas, disabled access; gardens open pm Sat-Weds Apr-Sept, house open pm Tues-Weds Apr-Sept, plus pm wknds in Aug; (01962) 771305; £5.50 house and garden, £4.50 garden only; NT. The neighbouring Hinton Arms has good food.

HURST CASTLE SZ3189
One of the most sophisticated fortresses when built by Henry VIII, on a long spit commanding The Solent, and best reached on foot or by summer ferry from Keyhaven (there's a pleasant walk from the 17th-c Gun pub - good value food). Fortified again in the 19th c, it still has two huge 38-ton guns.

Summer snacks, shop, disabled access to ground floor; cl wkdys Nov-Mar, and 25-26 Dec; (01590) 642344; £2.80.

LANGSTONE SU7104
Thatched cottages, an old tidal mill, and the nice Royal Oak looking out over the thousands of acres of silted harbour - winter sunsets are memorable. Swans float up at high tide, oystercatchers and droves of darting dunlins on the low-tide mud flats. Interesting walks along the old sea wall.

LEPE COUNTRY PARK SZ4598
A pleasant spot for mild saunters along the coast.

LIPHOOK SU8330
Bohunt Manor Lovely woodland gardens owned by Worldwide Fund for Nature, with water garden, roses and herbaceous borders, lakeside walk, unusual trees and shrubs, and wildfowl. Disabled access; (01428) 727936; suggested donation £1.50. The nearby Links Hotel restaurant is handy for lunch.
Hollycombe Steam Collection 🔳 (Midhurst Rd, S) Huge collection of steam-driven equipment, from paddle-steamer to an entire Edwardian fairground, inc the big wheel. Occasional open evenings when the fairground is delightfully lit. Traction engine rides, and woodland steam train trips. Snacks, shop, some disabled access; open pm Sun and bank hols Easter to mid-Oct, and pms daily end July-Aug bank hol; (01428) 724900; £7.50. The nearest place for a good lunch is the Kings Arms on the A286 S of Fernhurst.

LYMINGTON SZ3295
Handsome and relaxed if rather steep waterside town, very popular in summer with yachting people; it has quite a number of attractive Georgian buildings and some good shops. The 17th-c Kings Head on pretty cobbled Quay Hill, Chequers (Ridgeway Lane, off A37 W) and Fishermans Rest (All Saints Rd) have good food. You can get ferries to the Isle of Wight from here (phone (0870) 5827744 for times), and the B3054 to Dibden Purlieu is a pretty road.
St Barbe Museum and Art Gallery 🔳 Aimed at families, with quite a few hands-on exhibits (children can try on World War II uniforms, climb into a pilot boat, or weigh produce in the re-

created shop), this local history museum has displays on subjects such as boat-building, smuggling, and salt-making. Two art and craft galleries have changing exhibitions. Shop, disabled access; cl Sun, 25-26 Dec, and 1 Jan; (01590) 676969; *£3.

LYNDHURST SU2908
The tourist centre of the New Forest, as well as the main shopping town for people living here, so lots of tearooms, cafés, etc. Traffic tends to bottle-neck here, so it's worth parking on the edge of town and walking in. The car park, with walks straight into the forest, has a good information centre for the area; (023) 8028 2269. The Crown Hotel (High St) has good value food and a cosy log-fire bar.

New Forest Museum (High St)
Recently reopened after extensive building work, this good museum (the tourist information centre is in the same building) has interesting themed displays on the Forest's history and wildlife, with new interactive displays on its geology; there's also an audio-visual display and a 7½-metre (25-ft) embroidery. New resource library and shop, disabled access; cl 25-26 Dec; (023) 8028 3914; £3.

MEONSTOKE SU6119
An attractive riverside village, with decent food at the Bucks Head. The road from here down past the cheerful White Lion at Soberton runs by the River Meon, and is quiet enough to suit walkers; the old Meon Valley railway line nearby is now open as a walkway.

MICHELDEVER SU5138
Village of lovely thatched cottages and colourful gardens. There are fine walks in open countryside to the S, and up the River Dever valley to the E. The Half Moon & Spread Eagle has good food.

MIDDLE WALLOP SU3038
Museum of Army Flying 🏛 This exemplary military museum has plenty to interest, celebrating over 100 years of army aviation with kites, balloons, vintage aircraft, World War II gliders, helicopters, and a science centre; frequent special events too. Meals, snacks, shop, disabled access; cl Christmas wk; (01980) 674421; £5.

MINSTEAD SU2711
Furzey Gardens 🏛 Eight peaceful

acres, with developing young arboretum, sensory garden and lake, around charming 16th-c thatched cottage and local craft gallery (cl Nov-Feb). Snacks, plant sales, limited disabled access; cl 25 Dec; (023) 8081 2464; £3.50 (£1.50 winter). The village is quiet and pretty, with a fine old church at the top of the hill; the Trusty Servant by the green has good food.

MOTTISFONT SU3227
Mottisfont Abbey 12th-c priory salvaged from the Reformation as a charming family house, in wonderful peaceful surroundings. The gardens are a delight, housing a national collection of old-fashioned roses (largely scented). You can usually see a few of the rooms, inc one richly decorated by Rex Whistler. Meals, snacks, shop, good disabled access; open Sat-Weds Mar-Oct (plus Thurs July-Aug), and daily during the rose season (9-29 Jun); (01794) 340757; *£6.50 rose season; NT. The Bear & Ragged Staff up on the A3057 does good value food all day, and the road along the Test through Houghton and on to the attractive village of Wherwell is pretty.

NETHER WALLOP SU2936
An attractive sleepy thatched village with an interesting Saxon church; surprisingly Leopold Stokowski died here, not in Hollywood. The Five Bells is a nice place for lunch. Just E of the village, you can look around **Danebury Vineyards**.

NEW FOREST SU2605
The New Forest countryside has great charm. Only parts of it are in fact wooded; the rest is unspoilt rolling heathland. Walkers can head off in virtually any direction without worrying about trespassing. Once away from the roads, it does give a great feeling of untrammelled space. Children like it: there are free-running wild ponies (don't feed them, they can be aggressive), even the occasional pig, and plenty of scope for generally running riot without coming to grief. This unchanging blend of woodland and heath covers nearly 150 square miles, designated a Royal hunting preserve by William the Conqueror not long after the Battle of Hastings. The two best drives are the slow back rd from

Brockenhurst N through Bolderwood and then round past Linwood to Rockford, and the road from Brockenhurst to Burley; main roads can get very busy around the more popular areas, especially on summer wknds. Still with quite a medieval feel, the ancient woodlands are very atmospheric to stroll through, especially when you come across an unexpected sunlit leafy glade. It's most fun just to potter around, but you'll also get a lot out of a guided tour with people who've lived or worked in the forest all their lives; (023) 8028 3141 for details. Many of them have ancient forest rights and privileges, such as letting their pigs forage for acorns, or one of the newer licences to harvest the great variety of wild mushrooms. The path network in the New Forest is remarkably comprehensive, and in most places there's no obligation to stick to rights of way (of which there are very few). The lack of major objectives can be a problem for purists: there are no obviously defined hills, and long walks in the eastern woodlands, many of which are coniferous, can become monotonous. Further W, the scenery is more intricate and a touch more varied. It is often a good idea to use routes that have plenty of landmarks to guide the way; the heath and forest can be fiendishly disorientating. Besides the ponies, you may see fallow deer, especially at the Bolderwood Deer Sanctuary (and in the woods, very occasionally, the smaller, shyer roe deer; even in some places red deer). The best walks alternate mixed forest with heathland; isolated ponds and country pubs provide focal points. The Museum and Visitor Centre at Lyndhurst is a good place to start, and has details of watersports, riding and campsites (we recommend the Forestry Commission ones; (0131) 314 6505). Handy pubs include the Oak Inn at Bank, Red Lion at Boldre (nr Roydon Woods nature reserve), White Buck at Bisterne Close just E of Burley, Green Dragon in the pretty village of Brook, New Forest at Emery Down, Royal Oak at Fritham, Foresters Arms at Frogham, High Corner Inn or Red Shoot nr Linwood, Trusty Servant at Minstead,

Royal Oak at North Gorley, Sir Walter Tyrell at Upper Canterton and Rockingham Arms at Canada Common nr West Wellow.

NEW MILTON SZ2396
Sammy Miller Museum (Bashley Manor) Well regarded changing collection of 300 fully restored motor cycles, many the only surviving examples of their type in the world; farm animals too and a play area. Snacks, shop, disabled access; cl 25-26 Dec; (01425) 620777; £3.50. There's an adjacent craft shop, and the Rising Sun (Bashley Common Rd) has a good choice of food all day (with more animals and a good play area in its garden).

OLD WINCHESTER HILL SU6420
This hill fort gives wide views of Hampshire, The Solent and Isle of Wight, with nature trails through natural downland that's never been ploughed and resown; fairly busy on fine wknds, wonderfully remote on a blustery spring or autumn weekday. The George & Falcon at Warnford is popular for food.

OVERTON SU5149
There's a charming **drive** along the B3400 to Hurstbourne Priors and B3048 to Wherwell; Overton though quite large is an attractive stop along the way, with a good pub - the Bush.

OWER SU3116
Paultons Park Agreeable family leisure park with over 40 attractions and rides, gardens, birds and wildfowl, as well as model dinosaurs in marshland, a 10-acre lake with working waterwheel, hedge maze, animated *Wind in the Willows* scenes, and unique Romany Experience with the sights, sounds and smells of traditional gypsy life. The mini log flume and digger ride for younger children join rides such as the Raging River log flume, swingboat, tea-cups, and go-karts (the only thing with an extra charge), roller-coaster and several good play areas, many ideal for toddlers. Meals, snacks, shop, disabled access; cl wkdys Nov and Dec (exc Christmas specials), and all Jan to mid-Mar; (023) 8081 4455; £12.50.

PETERSFIELD SU7423
(Dragon St) The **church** on Market Sq is interesting, and you can browse around the nearby **Flora Twort**

Gallery. Meals, snacks, shop; cl Sun-Mon, and over Christmas; (01730) 260756; free. The 16th-c Good Intent has decent food.

PORTCHESTER SU6204
Portchester Castle The imposing high walls and towers stretching right down to the waterfront were originally part of a 3rd-c Roman fort - they're the best example of their type in Europe, and from the top give good views across The Solent. Other remains include a 12th-c church and 14th-c great tower, and what's left of a palace built by Richard II. Snacks, shop, disabled access to ground floor only; cl 24-26 Dec, and 1 Jan; (023) 9237 8291; £3.50 to visit the tower (inc audio tour); EH. The nearby Cormorant has good value food all day.

PORTSMOUTH SZ6299
The £86 million harbour redevelopment includes several interesting places to visit, and has opened up parts of the city which have been closed to the public for centuries. Portsmouth is at the heart of English naval history, and the city's rejuvenation focuses on this. The ongoing project, the **Millennium Promenade**, forms part of a trail linking the two areas most interesting to visitors: the Old Town and the Historic Dockyard, on either side of the ferry berths and well away from the traffic. Overlooking the narrow harbour neck, Georgian buildings on an old-fashioned cobbled hard give a good feel of the old days, and the little inner Camber Harbour still has fishing boats. The naval base has been revitalised in recent years, and now includes **Gunwharf Quays** - a huge waterfront factory outlet and leisure complex inc a cinema, bowling alley, bars and restaurants with waterfront tables, and an occasional craft market. The landmark **Spinnaker Tower**, a graceful 165 metres (540 ft) tall, is now due for completion towards the end of this year; views from the decks at the top should be tremendous. A lot of development is also under way across the harbour in Gosport (see separate entry), and a Waterbus service links the two towns; £1.60 return. A passport ticket (ferry fare included) covers all the

new attractions, £25 for a day. The Still & West and Spice Island family pubs have great harbourside positions, and the Dolphin's a nice old place in the old High St behind. The **cathedral**, dating from the 13th c to the present, is a delightful departure from the traditional layout. Portsmouth is an island city, with just two roads and the motorway bridging it and its residential/resort part Southsea to the mainland - traffic can be very slow indeed on the main approaches.

Blue Reef Aquarium (Clarence Esplanade, Southsea) A most enjoyable treat for families; the huge coral reef display is the centrepiece, and from an underwater walk-through tunnel you can spot black-tip reef sharks among the colourful shoals of fish. A freshwater display has asian otters (they recently made the news when their keeper started feeding them fish ice-lollies), and the hands-on rock pools are a big hit with children; there are regular talks and feeding demonstrations, and special events. Snacks, shop, disabled access; cl 25 Dec; (023) 9287 5222; £5.95 (they'll stamp your hand and let you come back later in the day). **Boat trips** round the harbour from nearby; Easter-Oct, hourly; (023) 9282 0564; from £4 (length of tour depends on which ships are in harbour). The nearby Wacky Waves swimming pool complex (Pyramid Centre) is useful on a wet day; flumes, toddlers' pool; open all year, but phone in winter; (023) 9279 9977; £4.95.

City Museum (Museum Rd) Very good displays on the city's history, in an astonishing former barracks that looks rather like a french chateau. Also decorative art and crafts. Snacks, shop, disabled access; cl 24-26 Dec; (023) 9282 7261; free.

Cumberland House Natural History Museum (Eastern Parade, Southsea) As well as its good conventional natural history displays, this little museum has a butterfly enclosure, and an aquarium. Shop, very limited disabled access; cl 24-26 Dec; (023) 9282 7261; £2, £2.50 in butterfly season.

D-Day Museum (Clarence Esplanade, Southsea) The most notable of the museums devoted to Portsmouth's fighting history; it vividly recalls and explains the Normandy landings from the point of view of both sides. There's a remarkable 84-metre (272-ft) D-Day embroidery inspired by the Bayeux Tapestry. Snacks, shop, disabled access; cl 24-26 Dec; (023) 9282 7261; £5, free on 6 Jun.

Dickens' Birthplace Museum (Old Commercial Rd, in the main town) Restored to the modest middle-class style it had when the author was born here in 1812. Still has various Dickens-related objects such as the couch on which he died. Shop; cl Nov-Mar (exc 7 Feb, his birthday); (023) 9282 7261; £2.50.

Guildhall (Guildhall Sq) Contains what's said to be the world's biggest glass mural. Snacks, disabled access; free tours by appointment; (023) 9283 4560.

Portsmouth Historic Dockyard *See separate family panel on p.262.*

Royal Garrison church (French St) This once-grand place was where Charles II was married in 1662; left roofless after german bombing raids which devastated much of the city, it now stands as a memorial. The 13th-c chancel is still intact, and modern stained glass tells the story of its history; open wkdys Apr-Sept; (023) 9237 8291; free; EH.

Royal Marines Museum 🖼 (Eastney Esplanade, Southsea) This vigorous place couldn't be more different from the usual military exhibitions - lively re-creations of major amphibious actions, a junior commando assault course, and a jungle room with a real snake and scorpion. Also lots of changing exhibitions and special events. Snacks, shop, disabled access; cl a few days over Christmas; (023) 9281 9385; £4.75.

Southsea Castle The fortifications in defence of Portsmouth Harbour, here, around Gosport, and up on Portsdown, give a remarkably complete picture of the development of defensive strategy from Tudor times to the fears of french invasion in the 1860s, though they have more appeal to people interested in warfare than to those who like the romantic idea of a regular 'castle'. Southsea Castle and Museum is the best place to start, built in 1545 as part of Henry VIII's coastal defences. Good

displays on Portsmouth's military history, and a time-tunnel experience of the history of the castle; special events (esp summer). Shop; cl Nov-Mar; (023) 9282 7261; £2.50. On the seaward side of Southsea are sturdy Tudor and later towers, bastions and batteries, alongside the resort's gardens and entertainments, giving interesting sea views. Good guided walks around the Tudor fortifications and the best parts of the Old Town leave the Square Tower at 2.30pm on Sun (mid-Apr to late Sept); (023) 9229 4282; £2.

Southsea Model Village (Lumps Fort) Developing Victorian-style model village, with around forty $\frac{1}{12}$ scale buildings, a miniature railway, even a prettily-lit waterfall; there's also a little toy museum, and doll collection. Snacks, shop, limited disabled access; open daily Apr-Sept, and most days in winter (exc Mon), depending on weather, best to check; (023) 9229 4706; £3.

Spitbank Fort Wind up an exploration of Portsmouth's naval past with the boat trip from the Naval Base to this granite, iron and brick fortress a mile out to sea. Its two floors are linked by a maze of passages, and there's a 130-metre (420-ft) deep well which still draws fresh water. The inner courtyard is now a sheltered terrace for summer refreshments from the café and bar. Open Sun in summer for day visits which include the boat trip (£8, ferries leave from the Historic Dockyard and Gunwharf Quay in Portsmouth). They also do popular pub nights with - of course - a spit-roast (£16, ferries leave from Gosport ferry terminal and the Hard in Portsmouth); phone for more information; (023) 9250 4207.

Treadgold Industrial Heritage Museum (Bishop St) A good insight into early industrial town life: the focus points are the restored 19th-c ironmonger's and blacksmith's shops, and handling areas include a Victorian kitchen and scullery with full cupboards and drawers to explore. Shop, disabled access; open Weds and Thurs Apr-Sept, (023) 9282 4745; free.

QUEEN ELIZABETH COUNTRY PARK SU7117 (Gravel Hill, NE of Clanfield) Lots going on all year, with woodland walks and rides (stables at the park), open downland, an adventure play trail, and events such as Easter egg rolling. You can arrange horse-riding; (023) 9259 9669. Disabled access; park open all year, visitor centre, shop and café cl wkdys Jan-Mar; (023) 9259 5040; £1.50 parking charge Sun and bank hols, £1 rest of wk. The good Five Bells at Buriton is not far.

ROCKBOURNE SU1117

Rockbourne Roman Villa (off B3078) Remains of largest known Roman villa in the area, found by chance 50 years ago by a farmer digging out a ferret. Interesting mosaics in the museum. Shop, disabled access; cl end Sept-beginning Mar; (01725) 518541; £1.95. In the charming thatched village, the Rose & Thistle is pleasant for lunch.

ROMSEY SU3520

Broadlands (just S) Elegant Palladian mansion on banks of the River Test, surrounded by beautiful landscaped grounds. Fine furnishings and paintings, and good exhibition on former resident Earl Mountbatten. Snacks, shop, limited disabled access; open pm early Jun-early Sept; (01794) 505010; £5.95. The nearby Dukes Head (A3057) is an attractive dining pub. Mountbatten is buried in the interesting 13th-c **abbey**, bought by the townspeople as their parish church at the Dissolution; it has some notable Saxon crosses and a 16th-c panel painting.

Romsey Heritage and Visitor Centre This includes King John's House, once the focus of a large 13th-c complex, with some interesting medieval graffiti and a rare bone floor, and period garden (open Mon-Sat Apr-Oct); the visitor centre has local history displays and re-creations of a Victorian parlour and old gunshop. Tearoom, shop, disabled access to visitor centre; cl Sun; (01794) 512200; £2.50 Apr-Sept, £1.50 Oct-Mar. Close by, the Abbey Hotel has an enterprising food choice.

ROWLAND'S CASTLE SU7610

Stansted Park (2m E) This fine Caroline revival-style house was actually built in 1903 (the original burnt down a few years earlier). The bit most visitors like best is the re-created Edwardian servants' quarters in the basement - quite a contrast to the fine

furniture and paintings upstairs. The surrounding parkland (no formal gardens but ancient woodland, an arboretum, a chapel and a maze) is pleasant for a leisurely stroll. Tearoom in a restored Victorian glasshouse, disabled access to grounds only; house open pm Sun and Mon Easter-end Sept, plus pm Tues and Weds July-Aug, grounds open daily (exc 25-26 and 31 Dec and 1 Jan); (023) 9241 2265; £5.50 house and chapel. Also here, a falconry centre has flying demonstrations (cl Thurs and perhaps in winter, phone garden centre to check; £3), craft workshops inc a pottery and glassblower, and a popular garden centre set around a walled garden; (023) 9241 3090. In the village, the Castle Inn does good lunches.

SELBORNE SU7433

Gilbert White's House (The Wakes) Impressive 18th-c home of naturalist Gilbert White, recently refurnished in period style; the extensive gardens have also now been restored to their original form. A temporary exhibition celebrates the life of the explorers Captain Oates and Frank Oates, while work continues on the Oates Museum here. Impressive teas and 18th-c style snacks, good shop, plant sales, disabled access to ground floor and garden; cl 25-31 Dec; (01420) 511275; £4.50. The Selborne Arms (with collectables for sale) is handy for lunch. There are good pockets of scenery nearby - the countryside White recorded in such detail. The zigzag path he created with his brother in 1753 still climbs Selborne Hanger (the hangers hereabouts are beechwoods which cling to the abrupt escarpments). Noar Hill close by has been designated a nature reserve for its chalkland flora, and from Selborne churchyard, a path leads into the Lythe, a wooded hillside that was another favourite haunt of White's.

SHERBORNE ST JOHN SU6356

The Vyne Tudor mansion with splendid 17th- and 18th-c embellishments: see if you can spot the stonemason's error which grafted a parrot's beak on to an eagle. The gardens include a 19th-c walled garden and a summerhouse garden (the restored summerhouse is due to open in Apr), and there are pleasant woodland walks. Meals, snacks, shop, disabled access; cl Thurs and Fri, and all Nov-Mar (grounds also open wknds Feb-Mar); (01256) 881337; £7, grounds only £4; NT. The Plough over at Little London does good value pub lunches.

SILCHESTER SU6262

Calleva Museum (Bramley Rd) The site of Roman town Calleva Atrebatum has been excavated nearby; the vestiges of 1½ miles of city wall to walk along (tricky in places), as well as a 9,000-seat amphitheatre, 12th-c church on the site of the Roman temples, and a small **museum** giving a pictorial account of the site; visitors can watch the six weeks of annual excavation work every year from mid-July to Aug, with explanations from archaeologists - last year two ladies' rings were found. Some disabled access; cl 25 Dec; free. The Calleva Arms, and Red Lion over at Mortimer West End, are both good food stops, and sell a guide to the site. Over at Little London the Plough (good snack lunches) is handy for Pamber Forest walks.

SOUTHAMPTON SU4111

Known early last century as the Gateway to the World because of its shipping importance then, this huge bustling city rather unexpectedly has one of the three best-preserved medieval town walls in the country. The best stretch is along the western side of the old core, around from the magnificent partly Norman **Bargate**; there are usually guided walks along here at 10.30am Sun and bank hol Mon (10.30am and 2.30pm daily in summer hols), (023) 8086 8401; or you can walk it on your own at any time. Lots of other old buildings are dotted around the less appetising modern townscape, though if you're short of time it's best to concentrate your efforts on the area around St Michael's Sq, Bugle St and perhaps the old High St. At the opposite end is the huge West Quay shopping complex - serious shopping, with lots of cafés, and work due to start this year (to finish by Sept 2005) on an Olympic-sized ice rink and an open plaza. You can take trips from Southampton to the Isle of Wight with Red Funnel Ferries (foot and car ferries leave regularly all year); (0870) 444 8898.

City Art Gallery (Civic Centre, Commercial Rd) Extensive and distinguished collection of british and european paintings and sculptures from the last 600 years, with particular emphasis on the 20th c. Meals, snacks, shop, disabled access; cl Mon, 25-26 Dec, 1 Jan and Good Fri; (023) 8083 2277; free.

God's House Tower (Winkle St) An early 15th-c prototype gun battery, now housing an archaeology museum with displays on the city's Saxon forebear, Hamwic. Shop, disabled access to ground floor only; usually cl 12-1pm, Sun am, all Mon, Good Fri, and a few days over Christmas and New Year; (023) 8063 5904; free. The nearby bowling green is said to be the oldest in the world.

Hall of Aviation 🖼 (Albert Rd S) Various aircraft of local interest - inc prototype helicopters and the Spitfire. Snacks, shop, some disabled access; cl Sun am, all day Mon (exc bank and school hols), 25-26 Dec; (023) 8063 5830; *£4.

Maritime Museum (Bugle St) Fine 14th-c warehouse with an impressive timber roof, and useful displays on the history of the port - especially good on the great liners, and there's a display on the Titanic. Shop, disabled access to ground floor only; cl 1-2pm, Sun am, Mon, Good Fri, and a few days over Christmas and New Year; (023) 8022 3941; free. The ancient Duke of Wellington nearby has decent food.

Medieval Merchant's House (French St) Fine timbered building ½m from city centre, splendidly refurbished with period furnishings which vividly re-create what life must have been like for a wealthy merchant's family; free audio tour. Shop, disabled access; cl Nov-Mar; (023) 8022 1503; £2.50; EH.

SOUTHWICK SU6208

This attractive village, with a decent pub, is well placed for good walks on Portsdown Hill - fine views (where Eisenhower and Montgomery saw off the troops before D-Day).

SPARSHOLT SU4331

Attractive village very close to Farley Mount, with good woodland and downland walks, and good food at the Plough.

STEVENTON SU5447

Steventon church 12th c, with a

memorial to Jane Austen, who was born in the village.

STOCKBRIDGE SU3433

Houghton Lodge Gardens 🖾 (just SW) Pretty and very peaceful gardens running down to River Test, with fine trees and lawns, a peacock statue made from recycled car metal, a herb garden, and a topiary dragon that breathes 'steam'. An intriguing hydroponicum demonstrates how to grow plants without soil, and there is a restored 18th-c shrubbery. Plant sales, disabled access; open all day wknds and bank hols and pm wkdys (exc Weds) Mar-Sept; (01264) 810912; £5 (children free). The Boot in Houghton has decent food; walks by this lovely stretch of the Test, or up on the Downs. The nearby town of Stockbridge has good art and antiques shops, with pleasant little waterways and ducks alongside its broad High St; the Greyhound and Three Cups facing each other across it both have good food.

STRATFIELD SAYE SU6962

Stratfield Saye House (off A33) Bought for the Duke of Wellington by a grateful nation after Waterloo, this 17th-c house has recently reopened after restoration work. Perhaps surprisingly, the Duke had a taste for french furniture, lots of which is still here, as is his splendid funeral carriage, and his hearing aid - needed after prolonged exposure to cannons. Snacks, shop, disabled access; phone for opening times, admission by guided tour only, £6; (01256) 882882. The elegant Wellington Arms has good food. There are pleasant walks on Heckfield Heath E of the estate, and Wellington Country Park in Berks is nearby.

TITCHFIELD SU5406

Titchfield Abbey (Mill Lane) Ruined 13th-c abbey, almost overshadowed by the grand Tudor gatehouse built after the Dissolution. Some of Shakespeare's plays were reputedly first performed here. Disabled access; cl 25 Dec; (01329) 842133; free; EH. The Titchfield Mill, a nearby converted watermill, caters well for families, and there's a fine walk by the old canal to the coast at Meon Shore nr Hill Head.

TOTTON SU3612

Eling Tide Mill (Eling Toll Bridge)

There's been a mill on this causeway for over 900 years, and the present one still uses tidal energy to produce flour. Snacks, shop (selling their own flour), disabled access to ground floor only; cl Mon (exc bank hols), Tues, and 25-26 Dec - ring for milling times, which of course depend on the tide; (023) 8086 9575; £1.90. There's also a Heritage Centre; usually open same days as mill, but phone to check; (023) 8066 6339. In unpromising surroundings, the Anchor on Eling Quay is a good cheap place for something to eat.

TWYFORD SU4925

Waterworks Museum (Hazeley Rd) Worth a stop if you're at all interested in engines, this remarkably intact Edwardian waterworks was built to supply water to rural areas around Southampton (5m gallons of water are still extracted from here every day). Follow the evolution of water supply over the 20th c from steam engines (in steam 1st Sun in month in summer) to huge diesel engines to electric. You can still see the lime kilns (quick lime used to be added to the water to soften it), and the volunteers are enthusiastic and knowledgeable. Snacks, open Sun May-Oct; (01489) 784545.

WAGGONERS' WELLS SU8534

A series of hammer ponds, a legacy of the medieval Wealden iron industry, in a valley of charming heathy woodlands, perfect for a picnic. Paths skirt these NT-owned ponds, which are a haven for wildlife.

WATERSHIP DOWN SU4957

(just S of Kingsclere) The home of the rabbits in the novel by Richard Adams - their final adventure was down at Freefolk, where the eponymous pub often has live rabbits. Pleasant wooded walks through this area.

WEYHILL SU3046

Hawk Conservancy One of the best birds of prey centres we've come across; you can handle some of the birds, and there are three daily flying displays (the best at 2pm). Wildflower meadow, ferret- and duck-racing in school hols, adventure playground and toddlers' play area. Meals, snacks, shop, disabled access; cl Nov to mid-Feb; (01264) 772252; £6.95. The Weyhill Fair is handy for lunch, and the lanes N take you into a particularly unspoilt corner of Hants.

WHITCHURCH SU4648

Whitchurch Silk Mill (Winchester St) Interesting working silk mill, producing fabric for theatrical costumes, interior designers and historic houses using Victorian machinery and traditional processes. There's a self-guided audio tour, and visitors have a chance to work on a loom. Prettily set on an island in the River Test, where you can watch the trout or feed ducks. Helpful staff, good value snacks, shop; cl Mon exc bank hols, and 25 Dec-1 Jan; (01256) 892065; £3.50. The Red House (London St) is the best pub here, and you can get a good cup of coffee at the White Hart Hotel (The Square).

WICKHAM SU5711

An attractive village despite the traffic, notable for its huge village square, where the Kings Head and more upmarket Greens do enjoyable food.

WINCHESTER SU4829

The compact and fascinating medieval centre still has two city gates intact; it was England's capital in Saxon times. The most attractive part is the glorious and peaceful Cathedral Close, surrounded by a very harmonious and distinguished collection of buildings; the handsome old Eclipse Inn nr the NE edge is a useful refreshment break. The Brooks Shopping Centre has a few jolly dioramas and displays on the city's history (free), with the chance for children to make their own Roman mosaic; the good farmers market is held near here on Middle Brook St (usually the last Sun in month from 10-2pm). Guided walks around the sights leave from the tourist information centre at 11am Mon-Sat (plus 2.30pm Sat in Apr, 2.30pm Sat and Sun May-Jun, and 2.30pm Mon-Sun July-Oct, exc Sun in Oct), Sat only Nov-Mar; £3, themed tours in spring and autumn, phone to check (01962 840500). Nearby (off Hyde St) a new garden commemorates the burial place of King Alfred. There's a multi-storey car park at the top of the High St, or a Park & Ride nr the junction with the M3. There are pleasant walks up rounded St Catherine's Hill, which has a small medieval turf maze and

traces of a hill fort, or up Giles Hill (good for picnics).

City Mill (Bridge St) Restored and working 18th-c watermill, with timbered and raftered ceilings and a pretty little island garden; there's a video and children's quiz. Shop, disabled access; open wknds in Mar, Weds-Sun Apr-Jun and Sept-Oct, daily July-Aug; (01962) 870057; £2.20; NT.

City Museum (The Square) This well organised museum is good for local history and archaeology, with a telling Roman mosaic. Shop, good disabled access; cl Sun am, Mon Nov-Mar, and 25-26 Dec; (01962) 848269; free.

Great Hall of Winchester Castle All that now remains is its huge 13th-c great hall, where Raleigh was tried and condemned to death; hanging on one wall is a round table they call King Arthur's (actually much the same date as the castle, and painted with its Arthurian scenes later). Restored roof, stone parapets and stained glass, and a small recreated medieval garden S of the hall is interesting. Visitor centre, shop; disabled access; cl 25-26 Dec; (01962) 846476; free.

Guildhall Gallery (Broadway) 19th-c building with changing exhibitions of fine art, crafts and photography. Snacks, shop, disabled access; cl Sun am, all Mon Nov-Mar, 25-26 Dec, and 1 Jan; (01962) 848289; free.

Hospital of St Cross 🄳 Very attractively set around two quadrangles, the quaint 15th-c almshouses still provide bread and ale to travellers who ask at the massive gate (you have to ask for 'wayfarer's dole'). 19th-c scandals here inspired Trollope's *The Warden*. Summer snacks, shop, disabled access; cl Sun, Good Fri and 25 Dec; (01962) 851375; £2. The Bell here is useful for lunch, and the stroll out from the city centre, along the water-meadows by the River Itchen, is one of the nicest short walks in southern Britain.

Intech (Telegraph Way, off A272/A31 just E) New science centre housed in a unique futuristic-looking pyramid, with 100 interactive exhibits, inc the chance to create your own vortex and tornado, and there's a giant Newton's cradle; changing exhibitions, lectures, workshops and special events. Meals, snacks, shop, disabled access; cl 25 Dec and 1 Jan; (01962) 863791; *£5.50.

Peninsula Barracks Anyone interested in military history will enjoy the four military museums here (Romsey Rd), and a new one on the Adjutant General's Corps is due to open (after we go to press) with a new visitor centre. The Gurkha Museum, though, has the most general appeal; shop, disabled access; cl Sun am, 25-26 Dec, and 1 Jan; (01962) 842832; £1.50. A sixth museum in the Lower Barracks on Southgate St is due to re-open around Apr.

Westgate Museum (High St) Local history above a formidable medieval city gate, which was a debtors' prison for 150 years (the walls are still covered in prisoners' graffiti); brass rubbings here too, and an interesting Tudor ceiling. The panorama of the city and surrounding countryside is rewarding. Shop; cl Sun am, Mon in Oct and Feb, and all Nov-Jan; (01962) 848269; free.

Winchester Cathedral Awesome and full of interest - one of Europe's finest, and quite a mixture of architectural styles. Among many rare books and manuscripts in its library is a wonderful 12th-c illuminated Bible, while the sculpture gallery contains some outstanding late Gothic work. William of Wykeham paid for much of the rebuilding, so his tomb is appropriately the finest; also memorials and monuments to Jane Austen, King Canute and St Swithun. The cathedral hosts changing exhibitions of modern art through the summer, and a sculpture by Antony 'Angel of the North' Gormley beautifully exploits reflections in the winter flood waters of the crypt. Good guided tours, and first-rate visitor centre in 16th-c coach house, with very good meals and snacks (not cheap) and distinguished shop, disabled access; £3.50 suggested donation. The Dean Garnier Garden between the deanery and the cathedral

reflects the cathedral's architecture; open all day; (01962) 857202; free. Close by are the appreciable remains of Wolvesey Castle, the original Bishop's Palace begun in the 12th c, and beside it (not open, but a handsome sight), the present Bishop's Palace of 1684. The best way out of the Close is through the medieval King's Gate, which includes the upper-floor church of St Swithun. This takes you into Kingsgate St, calm and old-fashioned, with an excellent dining pub, the Wykeham Arms. Down on the left a lovely riverside path takes you along to the City Mill and a mighty statue of King Alfred.

Winchester College (College St) All along Kingsgate St are buildings connected with this, the oldest school in the country. Most of the original school buildings remain intact, especially around the grand 14th-c chapel and its calm, tilting cloisters with a delightful two-storey chantry in their centre, and a glimpse of the warden's garden through one gate. Good shop in former Tuck Shop, limited disabled access; guided tours, cl Sun am, pm Tues and Thurs, 24 Dec-1 Jan (but best to check then); (01962) 621209; £3.50.

Other attractive villages with decent pubs include Abbots Ann SU3243, Amport SU2944, Bank SU2807, Botley SU5112, Brook SU2713, Buriton SU7320, Cheriton SU5828, Crawley SU4234, Crondall SU7948, Dummer SU5846, East End SU4161 (the one nr Highclere), East Stratton SU5439, Exton SU6120, Hambledon SU6414 (Broadhalfpenny Down just E was the birthplace of cricket), Hurstbourne Tarrant SU3853, Lasham SU6742, Longparish SU4344, Mapledurwell SU6851, Monxton SU3144, North Waltham SU5645, Rowland's Castle SU7310, Upton Grey SU6948, Vernham Dean SU3456, Wherwell SU3840 and Woodgreen SU1717.

Where to eat

BOLDRE SZ3198 **Red Lion** *Boldre Lane* (01590) 673177 Very busy, friendly pub with four black-beamed rooms, interesting bric-a-brac and bygones, generously served, well liked bar food, prompt service, a fine choice of wines by the glass, and well kept beer; worth getting there early; fine area for walking; cl 25 Dec; no children; disabled access. £26.55|£8

BROCKENHURST SU2902 **Simply Poussin** *The Courtyard, Brookley Rd (01590)* *623063* Popular little simply furnished restaurant, run by the son of the former owners, with carefully cooked interesting food using the best local produce, good cheeses and puddings, a short wine list, and friendly service; cl Sun pm, Mon, 6-20 Jan; children over 7; disabled access. £25/2 courses £10

BROCKENHURST SU3002 **Thatched Cottage** *16 Brookley Rd (01590)* *623090* Charming 400-year-old thatched cottage with cosy beamed lounge, good dried and fresh flower arrangements, pretty no smoking restaurant, and enjoyable well presented imaginative food served by friendly staff; super cream teas in neat garden, morning coffee too; individually decorated bdrms; cl Sun pm, Mon, Tues am, Jan; children over 12. £55/2 courses £12

EAST TYTHERLEY SU2927 **Star** *East Tytherley Rd (01794)* *340225* 16th-c dining pub with stylish menu of imaginative food (you can eat the same menu in the bar or restaurant), well kept real ales, a thoughtful wine list with ten by the glass, pretty no smoking restaurant, and a mix of comfortable furnishings; log fires, horse brasses and saddlery, and skittle alley; seats on smartly furnished terrace, play area; comfortable cottage-style bdrms overlook the village cricket pitch; cl Mon (exc bank hols); disabled access. £25|**£7.50**

EASTON SU5132 **Chestnut Horse** *(01962)* *779257* Smart but cosy 16th-c pub, candlelight even at lunchtime, dark comfortable furnishings, black beams and joists hung with all sorts of china, lots of attractive country pictures, some panelling, log fires in cottagey fireplaces; good generous creative food and Sunday brunch in no smoking restaurant areas, decent wines inc champagne by the glass, well kept real ales, nicely served coffee, a buoyant yet relaxed atmosphere, friendly efficient service; tables out on a smallish sheltered back terrace with pretty flower tubs and baskets; this sleepy village is handy for Itchen valley walks; cl winter Sun pm; disabled access. £35|**£9**

EMSWORTH SU7405 **36 On The Quay** *47 South St (01243)* *375592* Charming cheerfully decorated quayside restaurant with exceptional modern cooking, friendly helpful service and a sound wine list; new bedrooms; cl Sat am and Mon am, all Sun, 3 wks Jan, last week Oct; disabled access. £21.95

EVERSLEY SU7861 **Golden Pot** *(0118)* *973 2104* Little brick pub with a comfortable easy-going atmosphere in the different spreading areas, bowls of lilies, candles in bottles, fireside sofa; pretty no smoking restaurant, and good interesting food inc special Mon evening rösti menu with lots of different toppings; well kept real ales and decent wines by the glass; picnic-sets out in front; disabled access. £23.50|**£695**

EVERSLEY SU7662 **New Mill Restaurant & Grill Room** *New Mill Rd (0118)* *973 2277* 16th-c watermill by the Blackwater River with working waterwheel and grinding equipment; big windows overlooking the river and its wildlife, open fires and candlelit tables, a good range of interesting carefully cooked food, and a thoughtful wine list with many by the glass; the beamed Grill Room is more informal and cheaper; cl 24-29 Dec; partial disabled access. £28|**£7.25**

FROXFIELD SU7227 **Trooper** *(01730)* *827293* (NW of Steep) Interesting pub transformed by very jolly landlord, big windows looking across rolling countryside, airy feel, little persian knick-knacks, lit candles all around, fresh flowers, and log fire; attractive raftered restaurant, popular, enjoyable food from a sensibly short menu, well kept real ales, and decent house wines; lots of picnic-sets on lawn and partly covered sunken terrace; the horse rail in the car park ('horses only before 8pm') does get used; good bdrms; disabled access. £28.50|**£8.25**

LONGSTOCK SU3537 **Peat Spade** *(01264)* *810612* Popular dining pub with airy attractive bar, toby jugs around the fire, an elegant little dining room, no smoking area, good interesting food, well kept real ales, and decent wines; bdrms; cl Sun pm, all Mon, 25 Dec, 1 Jan; disabled access. £27|**£7.50**

LYMINGTON SZ3295 **Egan's** *Gosport St (01590)* *676165* Cheerfully decorated and friendly new bistro just off bustling high street, with well presented and reasonably priced food - fish is the speciality with plenty of blackboard specials and tip top produce; long mainly french wine list; no smoking dining room; cl Sun, Mon. £30/2 courses £8.95

280 ● HAMPSHIRE

Where to eat

MICHELDEVER SU5138 **Half Moon & Spread Eagle** *Winchester Rd (01962) 774339* Attractive country pub with a simply decorated beamed bar, woodburners each end, and solid furniture, generous helpings of interesting food inc lots of good daily specials, well kept real ales, and decent wines; seats on terrace and by cricket green; disabled access. £25|**£7**

OLD BURGHCLERE SU4658 **Dew Pond** *(01635) 278408* Beautiful 16th-c country house with log fires, friendly atmosphere, and imaginative attractively presented evening meals using fresh local produce on a frequently changing small menu - good game, fish and lovely puddings; no smoking; cl Sun, Mon, 2 wks Jan/Aug; no under-5s; disabled access. £34

ROTHERWICK SU7156 **Falcon** *The Street (01256) 762586* Quietly placed and relaxed country pub with a light and fresh open-plan layout, informal mix of furnishings on varnished boards, sunny window seats, fresh décor, log fires; rather more formal no smoking back dining area, interesting, enjoyable food, well kept real ales, good coffee, and very friendly helpful service; tables and benches on front and back terraces, and picnic-sets in sizeable informal back garden with a pair of swings and pasture views; good easy walks nearby. £20|**£7.95**

SHEDFIELD SU5413 **Wickham Vineyard** *Botley Rd (01329) 832985* Modern red brick restaurant overlooking the vineyard (you can take an audio tour round them), with modern pictures on the walls, wooden rafters in the high pitched ceiling, good modern cooking on classic french lines, friendly, informed service, and of course, Wickham wines; cl Mon, Tues, 1st 2 wks Jan; disabled access. £37.50/2 courses £15.50

SPARSHOLT SU4331 **Plough** *(01962) 776353* Busy, neatly kept dining pub in attractive countryside, with a bustling atmosphere in the main bar, farm tools on the walls, winter log fire, friendly staff, enjoyable, popular and interesting food (best to book), well kept real ales, and thoughtful wine list; plenty of seats outside, children's play area; cl 25 Dec; disabled access. £25|**£8.95**

STOCKBRIDGE SU3535 **Three Cups** *High St (01264) 810527* Enticing-looking 15th-c pub with little dormer windows in a very low tiled roof, low beams, soft lighting, an engaging mix of furnishings, dark red walls packed with old engravings, fishing gear and taxidermy, and a relaxed and easy-going atmosphere, with daily papers, logs blazing in the woodburner, and friendly staff; good interestingly cooked fresh bar food, several decent wines by the glass and well kept real ales; no smoking restaurant. £26.45|**£5.95**

STUCKTON SU1613 **Three Lions** *(01425) 652489* Warmly welcoming restaurant with informal atmosphere, a neat airy bar, fresh flowers, very imaginative food inc local fungi and lovely puddings, a fine wine list, superb breakfasts, and charming owners; good atmosphere and friendly efficient service; cl Sun pm, Mon, 2 wks Feb; disabled access; comfortable bdrms. £40/2-course lunch £15.75

SWAY SZ2798 **Nurses Cottage** *Station Rd (01590) 683402* Small, immaculately kept no smoking restaurant-with-rooms with emphasis on personal service by the resident chef/owner; outstanding breakfasts in Garden Room restaurant (which can be enjoyed by non-residents, as can afternoon tea), imaginative food using herbs and vegetables from the neat garden, and an exceptional wine list; booking essential; cl 2 wks Mar, 3 wks Nov; children over 10; disabled access. £30/2 courses £18.25

WELL SU7646 **Chequers** *(01256) 862605* Well liked pub with low-beamed cosy rooms, winter log fire, lots of alcoves, panelled walls hung with 18th-c country-life prints and old sepia photographs, relaxing atmosphere and friendly, attentive staff, enjoyable food, real ales and decent wines; water and biscuits for dogs. £24|**£6.95**

WINCHESTER SU4829 **Cathedral Refectory** *Visitor Centre, Inner Close (01962) 853224* Excellent totally home-made food in bright airy modern conservatory, lovely breads and soups, afternoon cream teas, good children's menu, a friendly informal atmosphere, and nice staff; cl 25-26 Dec, 1 Jan, Good Friday; disabled access. £17.85|**£6.95**

Special thanks to Michael and Jenny Back, B and K Hypher, Paul Kennedy, Margaret Ross, Phyl and Jack Street, James Avery

HEREFORDSHIRE

Classic unspoilt english countryside, with beautiful black and white villages, good food too - great for peaceful short breaks

This relaxing county is great for adults. And we've picked out quite a few places which cater well for children. At the Shortwood Family Farm in Pencombe (Herefordshire's Family Attraction of the Year) children really feel part of the action; the farm parks in Kington, Little Marcle and Kentchurch also offer opportunities to get really close to the animals. The Neo-Gothic castle at Ledbury (spacious grounds, a yew maze and good play areas) and elegant 18th-c Berrington Hall at Ashton (children's orienteering course, an adventure playground and fun trails) are other family favourites.

Also well worth visiting is the 14th-c manor at Lower Brockhampton, and Croft and Goodrich Castles. Inspiring gardens range from Hergest Croft, the product of several generations in Kington, to the recently planted gardens at Hope-under-Dinmore, and from the spacious arboretum in Queenswood Country Park (Bodenham) to a lively little cottage garden near Ross-on-Wye. Cider-drinkers like the tours and tastings at Weston's Cider Mill (Much Marcle), and you can also visit Dunkerton's Cider Farm (Pembridge); for other local produce, head for the expanding craft centre at Bishop's Frome.

It's a scenic county, and driving or walking here is rewarding. The well signposted Black and White Villages Trail (a 40-mile self-guided car tour) takes in five of the county's timeless villages - Eardisland, Pembridge, Lyonshall, Weobley and Dilwyn. As you head W the peaceful countryside becomes almost bewitchingly untouched. Not many tourists or second-homers have reached here, even at the height of summer, and yet the civilised small towns have an abundance of art galleries and bookshops.

Attractive towns ideal for an unhurried afternoon include Hereford (worthwhile little museums including one on cider, as well as the interesting cathedral), Ledbury, Kington, Leominster and Ross-on-Wye. Picturesque Symonds Yat is a popular place for lovely Wye Valley walks.

You can stay in Herefordshire in great comfort for a modest price, and there is an enviable range of pocket-friendly places for enjoyable meals.

Where to stay

BRIMFIELD SO5267 **Roebuck** *Brimfield, Ludlow, Shropshire SY8 4NE (01584) 711230* **£70**; 3 rms. Smart country dining pub with an impressive inglenook fireplace in the quiet, old-fashioned locals' snug, two other civilised bars with small open fires, a cosy no smoking dining room, excellent food, well kept real ales, carefully chosen wines, and courteous staff; dogs welcome in bedrooms

BROMSBERROW HEATH SO7333 **Grove House** *Bromsberrow Heath, Ledbury, Herefordshire HR8 1PE (01531) 650584* **£79***; 3 spacious rms with bowls of fruit and home-made biscuits, 2 with four-posters. Wisteria-clad 15th-c manor house with dark panelling, open fires, beams, fresh flowers and polished antiques, and good evening meals at huge dining table using home-grown produce; 13 acres of fields and garden, hard tennis court, and neighbour's outdoor swimming pool; cl Christmas

GRAFTON SO4936 **Grafton Villa Farm** *Grafton, Hereford HR2 8ED (01432) 268689* **£52***; 3 pretty rms. Beautifully kept early 18th-c farmhouse with an acre of lawns and garden, panoramic views, and lots of animals; an open fire in lounge, enjoyable hearty breakfasts in large dining room using their own free-range eggs and home-made bread, and friendly owners; no smoking; nearby inn for evening meals; cl Christmas and New Year; self-catering; disabled access

HOARWITHY SO5429 **Old Mill** *Hoarwithy, Hereford HR2 6QH (01432) 840602* **£46**; 6 cottagey rms. Cream-painted 18th-c building with the mill-race flowing through the flower-filled garden; log fire and books in beamed sitting room, good breakfasts and enjoyable evening meals, friendly helpful owners, and lots to do nearby; no smoking; disabled access; dogs allowed if well behaved

KIMBOLTON SO5461 **Lower Bache House** *Kimbolton, Leominster, Herefordshire HR6 0ER (01568) 750304* **£67**; 4 charming rms. Carefully renovated half-timbered 17th-c farmhouse surrounded by 14 acres of grounds, with antiques and flagstones in the sitting/dining room, lots of prints and interesting books, delicious food using organic produce, super breakfasts with home-made jams, marmalade and honey, home-baked bread, home-smoked fish, and free range eggs, and a relaxed atmosphere; no smoking; children over 8; lots to see nearby; limited disabled access

KINGTON SO3156 **Penrhos Court** *Lyonshall, Kington, Herefordshire HR5 3LH (01544) 230720* **£95**, plus special breaks; 19 elegant rms. Beautifully restored 13th-c Hall in six acres, with fine beams and flagstones, a magnificent hall for dining, a huge wood fire, and very good carefully cooked food using seasonal organic home-grown herbs and vegetables; they run regular food and health courses; cl Jan; disabled access

KINNERSLEY SO3349 **Upper Newton Farmhouse** *Kinnersley, Hereford HR3 6QB (01544) 327727* **£60***, plus special breaks; 3 prettily decorated rms with hand-crafted items and their own kitchen and sitting rm. Attractive 17th-c farmhouse in the middle of a working farm, with a particularly welcoming helpful landlady, log fires, beams, sloping floors, good food (inc vegetarian) using fresh farm veg, colourful garden, and lots of walks; no smoking; self-catering cottage; partial disabled access

LEDBURY SO7137 **Feathers** *25 High St, Ledbury, Herefordshire HR8 1DS (01531) 635266* **£99**, plus special breaks; 19 carefully decorated rms making the most of the old beams and timbers. Very striking, mainly 16th c, black and white hotel with a relaxed atmosphere, log fires, comfortable lounge hall with country antiques, beams and timbers, particularly enjoyable food and friendly service in hop-decked Fuggles bar, a good wine list, and a fine mix of locals and visitors; health and leisure spa with indoor swimming pool; dogs welcome in bedrooms

LEOMINSTER SO4757 **Highfield** *Newtown, Ivington Rd, Leominster, Herefordshire HR6 8QD (01568) 613216* **£52**, plus special breaks; 3 no smoking rms. Edwardian house in large garden with open farmland views, two sitting rooms - one with television and french windows opening onto the terrace, the other with helpful books - and open fires; enjoyable home-cooking using local produce in charming dining room, full english breakfast, and helpful, attentive owners; cl Dec-Feb; no children

LEYSTERS SO5762 **Old Vicarage** *Leysters, Leominster, Herefordshire HR6 0HS (01568) 750574* **£70***; 2 rms. Comfortable and friendly 17th-c farmhouse with Victorian additions in 18 acres with a two-acre garden, all-weather tennis court, and surrounded by the unspoilt north Herefordshire hills; antiques, enjoyable dinner on request, often using home-grown produce, and eaten around a big dining table; cl Christmas and New Year; children over 12

LLANGARRON SO5321 **Trecilla Farm** *Llangarron, Ross-on-Wye, Herefordshire HR9 6NQ (01989) 770647* **£55***; 3 rms. Charming 16th-c farmhouse in extensive pretty gardens with croquet lawn, fishing and riding, and free range chickens and geese; beams and an inglenook fireplace in snug, comfortable sitting room, good Aga-cooked breakfasts and evening meals, and friendly owners; no smoking; cl Christmas-New Year; children over 12

STOKE LACY SO6149 **Dovecote Barn** *Stoke Lacy, Bromyard, Herefordshire HR7 4HJ (01432) 820968* **£55***; 2 rms. Carefully converted 17th-c barn on edge of peaceful village with lovely country views; beams and latched doors, comfortable sitting room, super breakfasts with home-made bread, jams and marmalade, enjoyable meals (by arrangement; dining pubs nearby also), and friendly owners; no smoking; lovely walks
WEOBLEY SO4051 **Salutation** *Market Pitch, Weobley, Hereford HR4 8SJ (01544) 318443* **£74**; 4 comfortable, pretty rms. Friendly 500-year-old inn with enjoyable bar food, elaborate restaurant meals using local produce and nice breakfasts, quiet lounge with standing timbers and log fires, and small public bar; the restaurant is no smoking; children over 6; partial disabled access

To see and do

Herefordshire Family Attraction of the Year

PENCOMBE SO5951 **Shortwood Family Farm** Children particularly enjoy the unique two-hour animal feeding tours at this working organic farm. Starting at 2pm on weekdays, and 11am at weekends and bank holidays, they're great fun, and a truly hands-on experience, with the opportunity to collect eggs, join in feeding the hens, pigs, calves and lambs and milking the cows and goats, and holding some of the smaller animals. The tours alone would be worth the entry price, but there's plenty more, with good indoor and outdoor play areas, farm trails, and a new area, Mini Farm World, ideal for younger children, with the farm's smallest animals and birds, including rabbits, guinea-pigs, and miniature shetland ponies. They usually do trailer rides in dry weather, and some parts of the farm give views across four counties. Snacks (plus organic meals at weekends and summer hols), shop; (01885) 400205; open Easter-Oct; £4.50 adults, £2.90 children. The village is attractive; the Three Horseshoes over at Little Cowarne is a charming place for lunch.

ABBEY DORE SO3830
⊞ Primarily the impressive surviving part of a once-huge 12th/13th-c Cistercian abbey church, with Early English features and an awesome stone altar. **Abbey Dore Court Gardens** is an attractive plantsman's garden, with a pleasant river walk; they've recently replanted the walled garden. Meals and snacks (in 17th-c stables), disabled access; cl Mon, Weds and Fri, and Oct-Mar; (01981) 240419; £3. The Neville Arms has good food these days (cl Mon/Tues lunchtimes).
ALMELEY SO3351
Early 18th-c half-timbered Quaker Meeting House, contemplative feel; key in porch
ASHTON SO5164
Berrington Hall ⊞ (A49) This elegant 18th-c house has a few activities that make it a reliable bet for families, inc quiz sheets and trails to follow going round the house (50p extra), as well as

an I Spy sheet (10p) for the beautifully laid out grounds. The house itself has lots of interest; the finely painted ceilings and Regency furnishings are memorably elegant, and the main stairway is splendid. Many rooms are furnished in a way that lets you think they are still in use: there's a fully equipped Victorian nursery and a tiled dairy. Also a good adventure playground and a children's orienteering course, and plenty of walks and pathways. Capability Brown laid out the grounds (the house was built by his son-in-law); the most famous feature is the 14-acre lake with picturesque views, and there's also an attractive woodland garden, rows of yew trees, and a walled garden with some venerable apple trees. Meals, snacks, shop, some disabled access; open pm Sat-Weds from Apr-Dec; (01568) 615721; £4.60. The picturesque old Stockton Cross Inn (off

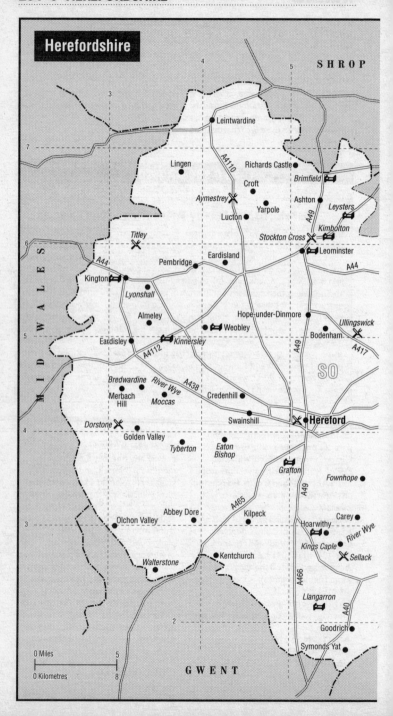

Herefordshire

SHROP

Leintwardine

Lingen

Richards Castle

Brimfield

Croft

Aymestrey

Ashton

Leysters

Lucton

Yarpole

Kimbolton

Titley

Stockton Cross

Leominster

Eardisland

Pembridge

A44

Kington

Lyonshall

Almeley

Hope-under-Dinmore

Ullingswick

Weobley

Bodenham

A417

Eardisley

Kinnersley

SO

A4112

Bredwardine

River Wye

A438

Credenhill

Merbach Hill

Moccas

Swainshill

Hereford

Dorstone

Golden Valley

Tyberton

Eaton Bishop

Grafton

Fownhope

A465

Abbey Dore

Kilpeck

Carey

Olchon Valley

Hoarwithy

River Wye

Kings Caple

Sellack

Kentchurch

Walterstone

A466

Llangarron

A40

Goodrich

2

Symonds Yat

0 Miles 5

0 Kilometres 8

GWENT

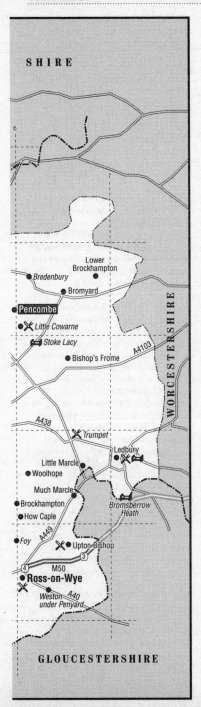

A49 S) has good food.

BISHOP'S FROME SO6647

Hop Pocket Craft Centre
Traditional hop farm, its 100 acres a
hive of activity in the harvest season,
with pretty gardens and a plant centre.
The recently expanded craft centre
includes wine, jewellery, antiques, and
delicatessen - you can also buy lots of
hop-related products inc hop bines.
Restaurant, tearoom, disabled access; cl
Sun am, Mon (exc bank hols and Nov-
Dec), plus Tues Jan-Feb, and 25-26 Dec,
1 Jan; (01531) 640323; free.

BODENHAM SO5151

Queenswood Country Park
(Dinmore Hill) 170 acres of woodland
and arboretum with over 500 tree
varieties; also wildlife displays and good
views. Meals, snacks, shop and
infomation centre, disabled access;
(01568) 798320; free. The heavy-beamed
Englands Gate has enjoyable food.

BROCKHAMPTON SO5931
Extraordinary turn-of-the-century Arts
and Crafts church designed by Lethaby;
note that this is in the little village
between Hereford and Ross-on-Wye.

BROMYARD SO6554
Some pretty black-and-white houses,
and a Norman church; the Heritage
Centre (Rowberry St) has an exhibition
on hop-growing (cl Sun and Nov-
Easter; free). On the Square, the
Teddy Bear Museum has six rooms
of displays inc hundreds of dolls, trains,
toys and, of course, teddies; TV
memorabilia too, inc a Thunderbirds
puppet exhibition, and Dr Who dalek.
Shop, disabled access; cl Tues, Sun, and
end Oct-Mar; (01885) 488329; £5.50.

CAREY SO5630
Delightful tucked-away village, with a
charming pub, the Cottage of Content.

CREDENHILL SO4443
Escargot Anglais (A480) Part of the
National Snail Farming Centre, with
snail trails showing various species (you
may even see hairy ones) and
exhibitions. You can buy snails here;
open Thurs, Fri and wknds by
appointment only; (01432) 760218;
£2.70. The Bell at Tillington does more
orthodox food.

CROFT SO4565
Croft Castle The walls and turrets
date from the 14th and 15th c, but the

inside is mostly 18th-c, with an interesting staircase and plastered ceilings. Attractive parklands with avenue of 350-year-old chestnuts. Tearoom, disabled access; open Weds-Sun and bank hols Apr-Sept, plus wknds Mar and Oct; (01568) 780246; £4.40, £3.10 gardens only; NT. The Bell at Yarpole is handy for lunch. The brackeny expanse of Leinthall Common, scattered with cottages, is a quiet corner of Herefordshire where you can walk around the castle's estate, and scale the modest heights of Croft Ambrey, an Iron Age hill fort with a view into Shropshire.

EARDISLAND SO4158

A gorgeous riverside black and white village, with lovely views along the river. Outside the Cross Inn (which has decent food) is one of Britain's oldest AA boxes, restored as a landmark (though not in its original location), and you can peep inside; there's a display on it in the Georgian dovecote across the road (free). The well signposted Black and White Villages Trail takes you 40 miles round the lanes via Pembridge and Weobley.

Burton Court ▣ (A44 just S) Interesting old house with 14th-c great hall, collections of ship models, costumes, and natural history specimens; also working model fairground, and in season pick-your-own. Snacks, disabled access; open pm Weds, Thurs, wknds and bank hol Mons end May-Sept; (01544) 388231; *£3.50.

EARDISLEY SO3149

Eardisley church 12th-c font with wonderfully vivid carvings of sinner being wrested from clutches of evil.

GOLDEN VALLEY SO3141

The B4348/B4347 Golden Valley road is a pretty drive, with particularly satisfying walks in the surrounding hills; the tucked-away village of Dorstone has an impressive prehistoric burial mound nearby (and the county's oldest pub, the Pandy). The remoter roads parallel to this, to the W, are also well worth the drive, through Clodock (delightful church) and Michaelchurch Escley (another good pub down by the river), or passing Craswall, with its enjoyably old-fashioned Bulls Head pub.

GOODRICH SO5719

Goodrich Castle This proper-looking

12th-c castle (built using the same red sandstone rock it stands on, so that it seems almost to grow out of the ground) appeals a lot to readers. Still plenty to see, with towers, passageways, dungeon and marvellous views of the surrounding countryside. Snacks (summer only), shop; cl 1-2pm, Mon-Tues in Nov-Mar, 24-26 Dec, and 1 Jan; (01600) 890538; £3.70. These formidable ruins are a feasible objective for stout-hearted walkers from Symonds Yat, or could be a start point for Wye Valley gorge walks. The partly Norman Spread Eagle at Walford, back to its original name now after a spell as the Mill Race, has good value food.

HEREFORD SO5039

Grew as a regional market centre, and still has its livestock and general market every Weds. For the rest of the week it feels very quiet-paced and old-fashioned, its streets, mostly pedestrianised, lined with handsome Georgian and other buildings; Church St is almost wholly medieval. Guided walks leave the tourist information centre every day mid-May to mid-Sept at 11am (2.30pm Sun); they also do a ghost walk (7.15pm Weds Jun-Sept; £2). The arts centre on Edgar St has changing exhibitions, and occasional craft fairs (cl Sun). Wye-side walks give a pleasing view of the city, its spires and towers. The Bay Horse (Kings Acre Rd), Gilbies bistro (St Peters Close) and Stagecoach (West St) are all useful for lunch, and, in an imaginatively converted church, the Café @ All Saints is very good.

Cider Museum and King Offa Distillery ▣ (Pomona Place, next to Sainsburys) Cider-making through the ages, with huge 17th-c french press, original champagne-cider cellars, and a working cider-brandy distillery - offering free samples. Snacks, shop, audio guides, disabled access to ground floor only; cl Mon Jan-Mar, 25-26 Dec, 1 Jan; (01432) 354207; *£2.80.

City Museum and Art Gallery (Broad St) Natural history and archaeology, with an interesting bee-keeping display, and changing art displays; hands-on displays inc a dressing-up box, and various special events. Disabled access; cl Mon (exc summer bank hols), plus Sun Oct-Mar, 25-26 Dec, 1 Jan and Good Fri; (01432) 260692; free.

Hereford Cathedral Nicely placed on the bank of the Wye, this largely Norman building has a lovely 13th- and 15th-c chapel, as well as the country's biggest chained library, and the famous Mappa Mundi, the largest surviving 13th-c map of the world. There's a splendid interpretative exhibition; the map itself is shown in an environmentally controlled room to preserve it. Meals, snacks, shop, disabled access; cl winter Sun, most of Jan, Good Fri, 25 Dec (tower only open July-Aug); (01432) 374200; Mappa Mundi exhibition and chained library £4.50, suggested donation for cathedral £2. Guided tours at 11am and 2.30pm Mon-Sat Easter to end Sept (£2.50).

Old House (High Town) Glorious Jacobean house with period furnishings and paintings; there's a new virtual tour if you can't manage the stairs, and hands-on displays. Shop; open Tues-Sat, plus Sun and bank hols Apr-Sept; (01432) 260694; free.

St John Medieval Museum and Coningsby Hospital (Widemarsh St) Little museum and chapel dating back to 13th c, with armour and relics relating to the Order of St John and the Crusades, and a display on the pensioners who lived at the hospital in the 17th c; in the rose garden you can see the ruins of Black Friars Monastery, and a rare preaching cross. They usually do guided tours, ask the friendly staff; disabled access; cl am, Mon and Sat, all Oct-Easter; (01432) 267821; £2.

Waterworks Museum (Broomy Hill) This Victorian pumping station with its impressive steam pumps and smaller hand engines (you can work some yourself) is undergoing a £½m renovation, but should be open again by Sept; the refurbishment will improve existing museum facilities, and will add a new engine room and visitor centre; best to phone for opening times; (01432) 344062; £3.

HOARWITHY SO5429

Glenda Spooner Farm Centre for the International League for the Protection of Horses, offering care and rehabilitation for equine victims of maltreatment; it's a friendly place. Snacks, shop, some disabled access; open Sat and Weds 11-4pm or any time by appointment; (01432) 840253; free.

Hoarwithy church Remarkably italianate, full of mosaics, etc. The village, nr the River Wye, is attractive.

HOPE-UNDER-DINMORE SO5252

Hampton Court Gardens ⊞ (A417 S of Leominster) In the grounds of a romantic-looking castle (actually a grandly fortified medieval manor), these organic gardens mix old-fashioned formal planted walks interspersed with bridges to little follies, with carefully contrived wilder areas (woods, waterfalls in rocky grottoes), and a classic maze around a small tower. The surrounding parkland gives river walks. Meals and snacks (with produce from the new ornamental kitchen garden), shop, disabled access; cl Mon exc bank hols, and 24 Dec-4 Jan; (01568) 797777; £5. The interesting 16th-c Englands Gate over at Bodenham has enjoyable food.

HOW CAPLE SO6130

How Caple Court Eleven acres of peaceful formal and woodland Edwardian gardens overlooking the river. Snacks; open daily Easter-Sept; (01989) 740626; £2.50. Also interesting medieval church. The 15th-c Green Man at Fownhope is popular for food.

KENTCHURCH SO4126

Barton Hill Animal Centre ⊞ Most of the animals here have been hand-reared, giving plenty of opportunities for getting close to the residents; also indoor and outdoor play and picnic areas. Snacks, shop, disabled access; open wknds Apr-Aug, plus Mon-Weds during school hols, and 1-23 Dec, best to check; (01981) 240749; £2.70.

KILPECK SO4430

Kilpeck church This small Norman church in a delightful little hamlet has amazing sandstone carving inside and out, beautifully preserved (except for the more uncomfortably pagan bits which prudish Victorians tried to remove).

KINGTON SO2956

Attractive border town by the River Arrow, well placed for walks. Antiques and bric-a-brac are noticeably cheaper here than - say - in Gloucestershire; there's a livestock market on Thurs (and a general market on Tues). On Mill St is a little local history museum (cl Sun, and Oct-Mar; (01544) 231486; free). The town is overlooked by St Mary's Church, which has a massive Norman tower; the nearby mound is all that's left of Kington Castle. The unassuming Queens Head (Bridge St) brews its own good beers and has good value snacks. The long-distance Offa's Dyke Path passes through town, descending into it from Hergest Ridge, NW Herefordshire's answer to the Malverns; at the far end across the welsh border the ridge tapers into horseback width above Gladestry, while N of Kington the path goes along one of the best-preserved stretches of Offa's Dyke.

Hergest Croft Gardens 🅱️ (just W, off A44) The splendid result of inspired work by several generations of keen gardeners; some of the centenarian rhododendrons in the woods are of incredible size. Famous kitchen garden with colourful flowerbeds, and the national collections of birches, maples and zelkovas. Snacks, shop, limited disabled access; cl am, and Nov-Mar (exc wknds Mar); (01544) 230160; £4, children under 16 free.

Small Breeds Farm Park and Owl Centre (Kingswood, off A4111 S) Plenty of opportunities to get close to the animals at this welcoming little park; there's a genuine enthusiasm for both residents and visitors, and the atmosphere is particularly relaxed and friendly. What's especially nice for children is the number of miniature breeds that can be fed by hand. There's also a nicely laid out owl centre (the highlight for some visitors, it includes rare species all looking frightfully wise), and an attractive waterfowl enclosure with ducks, geese and swans. In bad weather most of the animals are shown under cover, and a heated barn is handy for picnics (good outdoor picnic areas too). The views and setting are a bonus. Snacks, shop, disabled access; open daily Feb half term, and Easter-end Oct, plus most winter wknds; (01544) 231109; £4.50.

LEDBURY SO7137
The spaciously leisured High St has some fine buildings: the old Market House, the Feathers Hotel and Ledbury Park House are famous for their well balanced 15th- and 16th-c timbering, and there are plenty of similar structures. From the Market House an exceptional alley (Church Lane) of ancient jettied buildings leads to the partly Norman church of St Michael and All Angels, with an unusual spire tower detached from the main building, its carillon ringing out a well known hymn every third hour. On Church Lane too, the Old Grammar School has been restored as a heritage centre (cl Nov-Easter; (01531) 636147; free), and there's a friendly local history museum in Butcher Row House (usually open Good Fri-end Oct; free); unusual locally made ice-creams at Mrs Muffins Tearoom. The council offices (Church St) must be the only ones in the country decorated with medieval wall paintings; you can see these summer wkdys between 11am and 4pm; donations. There are antiques shops, and the Feathers has good food. The road N towards Mathon has some fine views.

Eastnor Castle (just E on A438) Just what you want a castle to look like, with stirring battlements, exaggerated towers, and some breathtakingly extravagant rooms. Built 1810-24 by Robert Smirke (architect of British Museum), it's a wonderful marriage of mock medievalism (Norman revival) and creature comforts (it's still very much a family home), with a huge warren of rooms. The entrance hall, originally austerely medieval, was converted to a cosy if still high-ceilinged sitting room, giving a much gentler impression as soon as you walk in; this part was redecorated in italian style in 1860. Pugin was responsible for the highly ornate Gothic drawing room, evidently the inspiration for Lord Irvine's recent use of those notoriously pricy Pugin wallpapers in his official apartment. The attractive grounds have an arboretum, 300-acre deer park, and plenty of space for a picnic, but what younger visitors enjoy most is the growing yew maze, which has three trails to make it more fun. They also have a rope maze, a new assault course, and nine men's morris. You can stay in the house for the full castle experience.

The outside looks especially dramatic in autumn, when the virginia creeper that all but envelops the walls turns a fiery red. Dogs are welcome on a lead in the castle and grounds. Snacks, shop; open Sun and bank hols Easter-early Oct, daily (exc Sat) July and Aug; (01531) 633160; £6.50 adults, £4.50 garden only.

LEINTWARDINE SO4074
This appealing riverside village is notable partly for its church - much bigger than usual for this county. The Lion has good food and a nice waterside garden.

LEOMINSTER SO4958
An attractive centre, the medieval streets almost lined with black and white timbered houses; plenty of antiques and speciality food shops to browse around, and a Fri market. The red priory church still has many of its original Norman features; inside you can see a ducking stool. There's a little local folk museum in Etnam St (cl Sat pm, Sun, and Nov-Easter; (01568) 615186; free). The handsome old Talbot Hotel has decent food.

Herefordshire Cheesemaking 🏛 (A44, 2m W) You can watch cheese being made by hand using traditional methods. Snacks (inc ploughman's with their own cheese), shop, disabled access; shop and café cl winter Sun and Mon, and 25 Dec-8 Jan (cheesemaking Mon, Weds and Fri 10-2pm only); (01568) 720307; £2.

LINGEN SO3667
Attractive village prettily set among hills, with Kim Davis's renowned alpine nursery and garden (snacks, entry to garden £2).

LITTLE MARCLE SO6637
Newbridge Farm Park 🏛 (A4172 W of Ledbury) Friendly family-run farm park with rare and traditional animals, and large indoor and outdoor adventure play areas; there's also a pets barn, free tractor and trailer rides, and activities such as bottle feeding and pig racing. Snacks and picnic areas, shop, mostly disabled access; open Mon-Sat Easter-Sept; (01531) 670780; £3.50, £1.50 for pony rides.

LOWER BROCKHAMPTON SO7055
Brockhampton Idyllic moated and timber-framed 14th-c manor house in attractive secluded countryside. Particularly interesting 15th-c gatehouse, and the ruins of a 12th-c chapel. Tearooms, shop, disabled access to ground floor only; cl am and Mon (exc bank hols), Tues, and Nov-Mar; (01885) 488099; £3.20; NT. The Trust also own the surrounding Brockhampton Estate, covering nearly three square miles, with splendid views from its park and woodlands, marked trails and a sculpture trail. The individualistic Talbot at Knightwick (B4197/A44), a favourite of many readers, is an interesting place for lunch.

Garden at Bannut (A44 Bromyard Rd) Developed over the last 20 years, 2½ acres of formal and informal gardens rooms, with plenty to interest gardeners. Tearoom, plant sales, disabled access; open pm Weds, wknds and bank hols Apr-Oct; (01885) 482206; £2.50. The Royal Oak at Bromyard Downs (over towards the B4203) is a pleasant place for lunch.

LUCTON SO4263
Mortimer's Cross Mill Charming watermill on banks of River Lugg, still in working order, with exhibition on the decisive Wars of the Roses battle fought here in 1461. Open Thurs pm Apr-Sept; (01568) 708820; *£2. The Riverside at Aymestrey has good food.

MERBACH HILL SO3143
Reached by driving up from Bredwardine, and then walking from the top of the lane, this gives a view right over the Black Mountains, Herefordshire and Radnorshire. A short stroll along the lane SE brings you to Arthur's Stone, a prehistoric burial chamber. Across the Wye Valley at Letton the Swan (A438) has good value food.

MUCH MARCLE SO6433
Hellens 🏛 Unspoilt manor house dating from the 13th c, with a bedroom (said to be haunted) where Bloody Mary slept, the portrait of Catherine of Braganza that convinced Charles II to marry her, and a coach and carriage collection. Teas; tours at 2, 3 and 4pm, open pm Sat, Sun, Weds and bank hols Easter-Sept; (01531) 660504; £5 (£1 gardens only). The memorial monuments in the village church are unrivalled in the area.

Weston's Cider Farm Still alongside

the family house, this has an engaging combination of modern equipment and old-fashioned atmosphere. Enthusiastic guided tours (2.30 wkdys, best to check), and liberal tastings; they've recently opened a rare breeds farm (Easter-Sept; £2), and have re-created an Edwardian garden. Meals, snacks, good shop with interesting ciders and perries; cl Sun Sept-Easter, and 25 Dec-1 Jan; (01531) 660108; free, £3.50 for tours. The nearby Slip is a useful food stop, with lovely gardens.

OLCHON VALLEY SO3029
Perhaps the remotest place in Herefordshire, a magnificent dead-end valley beneath the E flank of the Black Mountains. From the well signed picnic site nr Longtown a path heads up the Black Hill, an exciting knife-edge ridge, its end-on aspect strikingly triangular - this bit is known as the Cat's Back; after the trig point you can make a circuit by dropping down from the very head of the Olchon Valley, or carrying on over peaty terrain to join the Offa's Dyke Path.

PEMBRIDGE SO3958
One of Herefordshire's most striking black and white villages, full of fine timbered buildings inc a medieval market hall, the ancient New Inn (good bar food), a craft gallery in a former chapel (East St; cl 25-26 Dec; (01544) 388842; free), and a lovely church with an unusual detached belfry where you can watch the clock mechanism.
Dunkerton's Cider Mill (Luntley, 1m S) Uses ancient traditional local cider-apple and pear cultivars, for distinctive organic ciders and perries; welcoming atmosphere, free tastings, and good restaurant (Easter-Sept). Shop, disabled access; cl Sun, 25-26 Dec, and 1 Jan; (01544) 388653.

PENCOMBE SO5951
Shortwood Family Farm See *separate family panel on p.283.*

RICHARDS CASTLE SO4969
St Bartholomew There's little left of the Norman castle which gave this village its name. The nearby church, dedicated to St Bartholomew, is a magnificent medieval structure with a detached tower which probably doubled as a look-out for the castle; the views from here stretch over three counties.

ROSS-ON-WYE SO5924
Picturesquely perched on a sandstone cliff by the river, with markets on Thurs and Sat at the striking 17th-c market hall, which also has a little heritage centre; disabled access; cl Sun Nov-Mar; free. The lower riverside part has attractive waterside walks; the Hope & Anchor here is good value for family lunches, and on Broad St the Eagle does interesting bistro dishes, while Oat Cuisine has substantial vegetarian food. On Copse Cross St is a little miniature railway museum; shop; usually open Thurs, Sat and bank hol Mon, phone in winter; (01989) 563394; free. Penyard Park, SE of town, has woodland walks.
Kingstone Cottages (Kingstone; off A40 E at Weston under Penyard, towards Rudhall) Charming, exuberant cottage garden, not to be missed at midsummer for its profusion of old-fashioned pinks and border carnations. Also fine views, and tucked-away little grotto - looking out, it seems as though you're waist-high in water. Unusual plants for sale; open Sun-Fri 6 May to 5 July, or by appointment; (01989) 565267; *£2.

SWAINSHILL SO4341
Weir Gardens Delightful riverside gardens at their best in spring, with displays of bulbs along woodland walks, and fine views from clifftop walks. Paths can be steep in places. Open every day in Mar, Weds-Sun (and bank hols) Feb and Apr-Sept, plus wknds Oct and Jan; (01981) 590509; *£3.50; NT.

SYMONDS YAT SO5517
Shared with Gloucestershire on the other side of the river, this is a spectacular bend of the River Wye through a steep wooded rock gorge, where peregrine falcons nest (the RSPB have an information area with a telescope; cl Sept-Mar); splendid Wye views, nature trails. Two inns on either side of the river are linked by a hand-pulled ferry (see Symonds Yat entry in Gloucestershire chapter for times and prices), and there's ample (walkers would say over-generous) parking. It's a big tourist draw. The gorge has potential for more ambitious walks, following an old railway line along the river; to the SW an entertainingly rickety wire-mesh suspension bridge at

the Biblins gives access to the W bank.
Jubilee Park Centres on a hedge maze
created for the Queen's Silver Jubilee; a
lively maze museum tells the history of
similar creations. Meals, snacks, shop,
disabled access; open daily Good Fri-
Oct, wknds only in Mar and Oct;
(01600) 890360; £3.50.
UPTON BISHOP SO6327
Wobage Farm Craft Workshops
Several potters, a furniture-maker,
wood-carver and jeweller. Open wknds
all year plus Thurs-Fri Apr-Sept;
(01989) 780233; free. The Moody Cow
is a good individual lunch stop.
WEOBLEY SO4051
In the very top rank of the county's
black and white villages, with its long
sloping green, and idyllic stroll out past
the bowling green to the church; the
Olde Salutation is good for lunch.
WOOLHOPE SO6135
The elevated country around here has a

good variety of scenery for walkers; the
views from Ridge Hill E and the more
densely wooded hills nr Mordiford are
among the highlights.
YARPOLE SO4765
The church of this attractive streamside
village has an uncommon free-standing
medieval bell tower. The picturesque
Bell Inn has good food.
Other attractive villages, all with
decent pubs, include Bredenbury
SO6156 (despite the main rd), Little
Cowarne SO6051, Lyonshall SO3355,
Walterstone SO3425 (peaceful walks)
and Weston under Penyard SO6323.
Quiet country drives can link several
attractive **churches**, such as
Bredwardine SO3344, Moccas SO3543,
Tyberton SO3839 and Eaton Bishop
SO4439; or perhaps Fownhope
SO5834, Kings Caple SO5528 and even
Foy SO5928 with Brockhampton and
Hoarwithy.

Where to eat

AYMESTREY SO4265 **Riverside Inn** *(01568)* 708440 Black and white timbered
riverside inn with rambling beamed bar, some fine furniture, log fires and a relaxed
atmosphere; enjoyable food, well kept beers, and decent wines; seats by the water
and in steep garden; comfortable bdrms and fly-fishing for residents; does get very
busy at peak times; cl 25 Dec. £23.75|**£7.25**
DORSTONE SO3141 **Pandy** *(01981)* 550273 Ancient half-timbered pub
(Herefordshire's oldest), with a good mix of customers in the heavily beamed and
neatly kept main room, a no smoking area, huge fireplace, and side extension;
enjoyable bar food, well kept real ales, and lots of malt whiskies; picnic-sets and a
play area in the neat side garden, and pretty surrounding countryside; cl Mon am
(open bank hols); children must be well behaved; disabled access. £22|**£6.50**
HEREFORD SO5139 **Castle House** *Castle St (01432)* 356321 Smart hotel near
the cathedral with elegant La Rive restaurant and terrace that overlooks the river
and garden; beautifully presented ambitious food using first-class ingredients, some
produce from their own farm, an extensive wine list, and courteous formal service;
fine bdrms; disabled access. £35
LEDBURY SO7137 **Market Place Restaurant** *I The Homend (01531)* 634250
Pleasant bustling restaurant open all day for morning coffee, lunch and afternoon
tea with home-made cakes, flans and puddings; partial disabled access. £12|**£4**
LITTLE COWARNE SO6050 **Three Horseshoes** *(01885)* 400276 Civilised
place set in deep country with peaceful views from the terrace or pretty lawn area;
quarry-tiled bar with sturdy old kitchen tables, old local photographs above the
corner log fire, and hops on the black beams in the dark peach ceiling; no smoking
sun room with wicker armchairs, games room, decent wines, well kept real ales,
and obliging service; good bar food using local gamekeepers and fishermen, local
eggs and vegetables (though they grow summer salads themselves), and their own
chutneys, pickles, and jams; interesting food including noteworthy sandwiches, and
popular OAP Thursday lunch; attractive stripped stone raftered restaurant
extension with lunchtime carvery. £22.45|**£7.95**
ROSS-ON-WYE SO5924 **Pheasants at Ross** *52 Edde Cross St (01989)* 565751
Attractive little restaurant with hard-working owners, simple furnishings,

particularly good food using the best local produce, an interesting wine list, and relaxed atmosphere; open Thurs-Sat evenings only; cl 22 Dec-2 Jan; well behaved children welcome. £36

SELLACK SO5526 **Lough Pool** *(01989) 730236* Attractive black and white timbered cottage in lovely countryside, with a log fire at each end of the beamed central room, flagstones and bunches of dried flowers, other individually decorated rooms leading off, interesting food, well kept real ales, several malt whiskies, local farm ciders, and a well chosen wine list; cl winter Sun pm, pm 26 Dec; well behaved children in snug or restaurant only. £25|**£7.50**

STOCKTON CROSS SO5161 **Stockton Cross Inn** *(01568) 612509* Neatly kept black and white timbered pub with an old-fashioned atmosphere in its heavy-beamed long bar, a huge log fire and woodburner, solid furnishings, a wide choice of enjoyable food, well kept beer, and good welcoming service; seats in garden; cl Sun and Mon pm; children over 6. £28|**£7.25**

TITLEY SO3359 **Stagg** *(01544) 230221* Attractive old pub with main emphasis on the two dining rooms, one quite big, the other intimate; well kept real ales, up to ten wines by the glass from a carefully chosen list, a fine collection of malt whiskies, and particularly good, imaginative food inc a formidable cheese range; helpful service; tables out in the garden, and lovely surrounding countryside; bdrms; cl Sun pm, Mon (exc bank hols and then they close Tues), first 2 wks Nov, 1 wk Feb, 25-26 Dec, 1 Jan. £35|**£7.50**

TRUMPET SO6639 **Verzons** *Hereford Rd (01531) 670381* Charmingly reworked roadside country hotel with good interesting food in the linked rooms of its pleasantly informal restaurant, a nice mix of country pub furniture and log fire in its civilised bar, cheerful young staff, good house wines and well kept real ales; tables out in extensive neatly kept gardens with broad views to the Malvern Hills; bdrms. £25|**£7.50**

ULLINGSWICK SO5948 **Three Crowns** *(01432) 820279* As well as a place for local farmers to enjoy their well kept ales, this bustling pub is very popular for its good imaginative food from an extensive seasonally changing menu (the choice is smaller at lunchtime); charming, cosy traditional rooms with hops on low beams, open fires, some no smoking areas, and carefully chosen wines; tables outside; cl Mon, 2 wks from 24 Dec; children must be well behaved; disabled access. £30.75/2-course meal £10.50

UPTON BISHOP SO6326 **Moody Cow** *(01989) 780470* In a quiet village, this cheerful and friendly pub has several snug separate areas, a pleasant medley of stripped country furniture, a big log fire, no smoking rustic candlelit restaurant and second small dining room, a good choice of enjoyable food, and well kept beers; children must be well behaved; partial disabled access. £27.95|**£8.95**

HERTFORDSHIRE

Beyond London's overspill are some nice finds - great houses, cheery children's outings, some unusual attractions, peaceful country walks

Willows Farm Village at London Colney is our choice for Hertfordshire's top Family Attraction - a busy place, with very well thought out activities. Another highlight for younger children is Standalone Farm on the edge of Letchworth (learning about animals here is fun), and the Paradise Wildlife Park in Broxbourne has a good mix of wild and tame animals. In the same family for 500 years, lavish Knebworth House is a reliable bet for an absorbing outing, with an excellent adventure playground, miniature railway and maze. At the fine Jacobean house in Hatfield you'll find the national collection of model soldiers.

Peaceful dry-weather excursions include Aldenham Country Park and the uncluttered expanses of the Ashridge Estate (Ringshall); the ruins of Berkhamsted Castle are nice for a picnic (interesting remains too at Hoddesdon). The sculpture garden in Much Hadham is a favourite with readers, and Cheslyn Gardens provide a pleasing contrast with the modern developments of Watford. More unusual attractions include the outstanding zoological museum at Tring, the intriguing decorative caverns in Ware and Royston, and a motorway-edge Roman bath near Welwyn.

An important Roman city, St Albans has enough variety to fill a day (some interesting museums, and the gardens of the Royal National Rose Society). Although Hertfordshire is one of the victims of the seeping urbanisation from London, there are still some very pretty villages dotted about, and clearly waymarked footpaths allow good escapes into protected countryside.

Where to stay

CHIPPERFIELD TL0401 **Two Brewers** *Chipperfield, Kings Langley, Hertfordshire WD4 9BS (01923)* 265266 **£69.50**w; 20 pleasant rms. Comfortable and very neatly kept country hotel with relaxing views of pretty village green, dark beams, bow windows, antique settles, log fires, and good bar and restaurant food; pleasant nearby walks; partial disabled access

KNEBWORTH TL2420 **Homewood** *Knebworth, Hertfordshire SG3 6PP (01438) 812105* **£70**; 2 rms. Lovely Lutyens-designed house in six beautiful acres; elegant rooms with antiques and tapestries and interestingly decorated by the owner, good breakfasts, evening meals by prior arrangement, and five cats and a friendly dog; cl 20 Dec-5 Jan; dogs welcome in bedrooms

ST ALBANS TL1407 **White Hart** *Holywell Hill, St Albans, Hertfordshire AL1 1EZ (01727)* 853624 **£45**w; 11 rms, most with own bthrm. Civilised former coaching inn with two bar areas, antique panelling, handsome fireplaces and furnishings, residents' lounge reached by barley-twist staircase, courteous friendly service, and good restaurant; children over 5

WIGGINTON SP9310 **Rangers Cottage** *Tring Park, Highfield Rd, Wigginton, Tring, Hertfordshire HP23 6EB (01442)* 890155 **£63**; 3 individually decorated rms, each with mini fridge. Built in 1880 by the Rothschild family for their estate manager, this attractively extended, no smoking cottage has fine country views, a pretty garden with seats on a sunny terrace, helpful friendly owners, enjoyable breakfasts using eggs from their own hens and home-made marmalade, and nearby pubs and restaurants for evening meals; good bird-watching and walks

To see and do

Hertfordshire Family Attraction of the Year

LONDON COLNEY TL1803 **Willows Farm Village** (Lowbell Lane, off A1081 just N of M25 junction 22) Lots to do at this busy working farm, particularly at weekends and in school holidays when younger children will find plenty to fill a happy afternoon. Some farms are undoubtedly cheaper, but it's probably fair to say that they don't always have quite so much going on, and what's particularly nice about this one is that the entry price covers everything inside: no extra charges for the tractor rides or boat trips. Loads of sheep, pigs and other traditional animals of course, with the usual farmyard activities, but this place really scores with its busy schedule of well thought out events, from falconry displays to their very popular duck trials and sheep racing (both repeated several times during the day). At weekends and holidays they have shows in an indoor theatre, and there's no shortage of ways to let off steam, from trampolines and mini tractors to old-fashioned fairground rides and bouncy haystacks. A decent play area has spiral slides and climbing frames, and under-5s have a separate one. In summer they add a maize maze, and you'll also find shire horses, boat trips, and lakeside walks. Younger children enjoy meeting the baby animals in their animal nursery, and the guinea-pig village is splendid, with 300 very friendly residents. Many of the main attractions are under cover. Meals, snacks, shop, disabled access; cl Nov-Mar; (01727) 822444; £7.95 adults, £6.95 children.

ALDBURY SP9612
A perfect village green, with attractive houses, village stocks, two good pubs; fine walks nearby (also see Ringshall, and - in Buckinghamshire chapter - Ivinghoe Beacon.

ALDENHAM COUNTRY PARK TQ1695
Plenty of space for children to run around in, with adventure play area, nature trails, and a rare breeds centre. Snacks, disabled access; cl 25 Dec; (020) 8953 9602; free, parking charge £3. You can also go sailing here (020) 8207 3782; or fishing (020) 8953 4978; £5 for a day.

ARDELEY TL3027
Attractive thatched village with good food at the Jolly Waggoner, and a pleasant quiet drive along the lane down through Wood End, Haultwick and Dane End. This rolling countryside is very rural, with quite an East Anglian flavour - some of Hertfordshire's best walking territory. Between Dane End and Great Munden, the Plough has a full-size cinema organ, usually playing on Sun lunchtime.

Cromer Windmill 🔢 (just NW)
Partly 13th c, lovingly restored, the last remaining post-mill in the county, its sails turning again after standing idle for nearly 80 years. Snacks, shop, disabled access to ground floor only; open Sun pm, bank hols and the second and fourth Sat mid-May to mid-Sept; (01438) 861662; £1.50.

ASHWELL TL2639
Attractive village with some fine houses and an unusually tall church tower; the Bushel & Strike just beside it and the Three Tuns are both pleasant for lunch.

AYOT ST LAWRENCE TL1916
Delightful little backwater, with a very picturesque 12th-c ivy-covered ruined church nr the appealingly old-fashioned Brocket Arms; the existing church is an incongruously grand Greek Revival affair. The village is conveniently close to link to a walk along the River Lea, which has been dammed at Brocket Hall to form a lake (in view from the public right of way). Shorter walks can start from Ayot Green, where the

Waggoners has good enterprising food, and an abandoned railway line, open to walkers, forms a useful link.

Shaw's Corner Much as it was when GBS lived here, 1906-1950; Shaw devotees will enjoy seeing his exercise machine, pen, spectacles, and even the soft homburg he wore for 60 years. The tiny writing shed at the bottom of the garden was designed to revolve and so maximise sunlight. Shop, phone to arrange disabled access; open pm Weds-Sun and bank hols 20 Mar-Oct; (01438) 820307; *£3.80; NT.

BERKHAMSTED SP9908
Berkhamsted Castle (next to railway station) The remains of this Norman castle boast a proud history - William the Conqueror acceded to the english throne here in 1066, and it lays claim to some of the finest earthworks from that time, the only double moat for a Norman castle in Europe, quite striking when flooded. When the sun is shining, it's a pleasant spot for a picnic. Shop, disabled access; cl 25 Dec, and 1 Jan; (01442) 871737; free; EH. The busy Old Mill (A4251, Hemel end) has at least some food all day.

BRAUGHING TL3924
(pronounced Braffing) Attractive village with pretty 14th-c riverside church; the low-beamed Brown Bear has decent food.

BROXBOURNE TL3306
Paradise Wildlife Park (White Stubbs Lane, W of town) Younger children should find plenty to keep them amused at this friendly little zoo and leisure park. Residents include brazilian tapirs, red pandas, even long-nosed potoroos, and a small woodland railway passes big fibreglass dinosaurs. There's a busy schedule of live shows and displays, from their jolly themed parrot displays to feeding the lions and cheetahs (a highlight worth watching). Children can feed the camels, zebra and other creatures in the paddocks, and go right up to the usual farmyard animals. A good collection of bugs and creepy-crawlies, falconry displays and undemanding rides and amusements inc a bouncy castle, slides, helter-skelter, roundabouts, and crazy golf. Most is outdoors, so better in fine weather. Meals, snacks, shop, disabled access;

open every day, inc Christmas Day (no shows then but it's free); (01992) 468001; *£10 adults. The Farmers Boy nearby at Brickendon has popular food all day.

ESSENDON TL2708
The mildly hilly partly wooded country around here is popular with wknd walkers, with pleasantly varied village-to-village paths. The Beehive over in Epping Green is a good refuelling stop for walkers.

GREAT AMWELL TL3612
Pretty conjunction of church, pre-Norman Emma's Well and pool with islets; the Waggon & Horses is a useful lunch break.

Van Hage Garden Co (A1170) A popular place with an excellent range of plants, and animal gardens with monkeys and owls. They have a miniature railway most summer wknds, and good special events at Christmas. Meals, snacks, shops, disabled access; cl Easter Sun, 25-26 Dec and 1 Jan; (01920) 870811; free. The Waggon & Horses just S has enjoyable food.

GREAT HORMEAD TL4029
An attractive village, plenty of thatch and timbering. The old Three Tuns has good imaginative food.

GREAT WOOD TL2704
(off B157 N of Northaw, where the Two Brewers is a good stop, with a view of the ancient church from its garden) Pretty woodland walks.

HATFIELD TL2308
Hatfield House A great Jacobean house built in 1611 on the site of a childhood home of Elizabeth I; the splendid State Rooms include portraits of that Queen, and even her gloves. Also the National Collection of Model Soldiers, with over 3,000 exhibits. The scented garden and knot garden contain plants that were typical in the 15th and 16th c. Alongside is an extensive park. Meals, snacks, shop, disabled access; open Easter Sat-Sept, house cl am. Guided tours wkdys only; (01707) 287010; £7.50, park only £2. The nearby church has a window by Burne-Jones, and the attractive village of Old Hatfield has a handsome old pub (the Eight Bells). Beyond is the extensive modern built-up area that has now taken the Hatfield name.

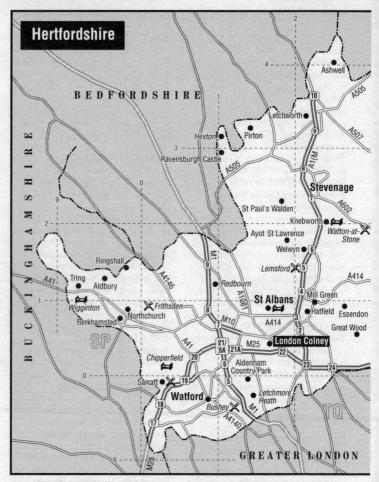

HERTFORD TL3212

Some quiet older parts include the old main Fore St, which has handsomely pargeted buildings. St Andrew St has several antiques shops (one in a fine 15th-c house). So-called **Hertford Castle** is in fact the 15th-c gatehouse for Edward IV's original moated castle, carefully restored and now occupied by the council; open for guided tours by arrangement, and for special events May-Sept; (01992) 552885; free. The partly Tudor White Horse opposite is good value, and the extensive riverside castle grounds (with the massive flint walls of Henry II's castle) are always open. McMullens Brewery is a striking Victorian building on the river. The Old Barge with tables out by the Lee Navigation Canal has decent food. Nearby Hertingfordbury is an attractive village, between river and beechwoods.

Hertford Museum (Bull Plain) Cheery local history museum, in an elegant 17th-c building; it has a graceful Jacobean knot garden. Shop, disabled access to ground floor; cl Sun, Mon, 25-26 Dec, 1 Jan and Good Fri; (01992) 582686; free.

HODDESDON TL3809

Rye House Gatehouse (Rye Rd) The Gatehouse, a rare and fine example of early brickwork, is all that remains of this 15th-c manor which, in Victorian

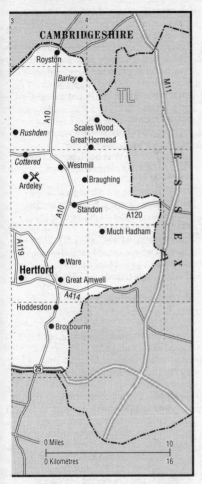

CAMBRIDGESHIRE

Royston
Barley
Rushden
Scales Wood
Great Hormead
Cottered
Westmill
Ardeley
Braughing
Standon   A120
Much Hadham
Hertford
Ware
Great Amwell
Hoddesdon
Broxbourne

0 Miles   10
0 Kilometres   16

waterside Fish & Eels (Dobbs Weir Rd)
has decent food; long riverside walks
from here.

KNEBWORTH TL2220

Knebworth House (Old Knebworth)
This historic estate appeals to children
as much as it does to adults, thanks to
its splendid adventure playgrounds;
there's also a miniature railway, and
Victorian maze. The house is a magnificent confection of turrets, domes and
gargoyles; the same family have lived
here for 500 years, so the guided tours
take in rooms and exhibits from a
variety of periods; highlights include the
marvellous Jacobean great hall, an
exhibition on the glory days of the Raj,
and mementoes of former guests like
Dickens and Churchill. A huge draw in
themselves, the well restored gardens
were designed by Lutyens, and include a
herb garden, and a delightful rose
garden. The 250-acre park also has
lovely woodland walks, and a church
with a nave and chancel dating back to
the 12th c. Meals, snacks, limited
disabled access; open wknds Easter-
Sept, and daily in July, Aug, and spring
and summer school hols; house cl am;
(01438) 812661; £7.50, grounds-only
£5.50. Along the outer edge of the park
is the pretty little hamlet of Old
Knebworth; the Lytton Arms here is a
useful pub.

LETCHWORTH TL2232

**First Garden City Heritage
Museum** The world's first garden city,
begun in 1903. The First Garden City
Heritage Museum (Norton Way S), in
the architects' charming Arts and Crafts
thatched building (arts and crafts style
furniture inside too), shows the thinking
behind this uniquely 20th-c idea;
temporary exhibitions too. Shop; cl Sun,
25-26 Dec and 1 Jan; (01462) 482710;
£1 (50p residents). The nearby Three
Magnets (Leys Ave) is a decent pub.

Standalone Farm (Wilbury Rd) This
farm has got something of an
educational bent, so it appeals most to
younger children with a genuine
interest in animals. Plenty of animals to
enjoy from shire horse and shetland
ponies to rabbits, chipmunks and
guinea-pigs. Pigs and rare breeds of
poultry wander around the farmyard,
and two friendly jersey cows take part

times, attracted so many Londoners to
the banquets held in its malthouse that a
station was built near it. You can climb
the steep spiral staircase to the roof
(there are displays inside for people
who can't manage the stairs), and inside
is an exhibition on the Rye House Plot,
an attempt to assassinate Charles II.
Canalside picnic area, shop, disabled
access to ground floor; open wknds and
bank hols Easter-Sept, best to check;
(01992) 702200; £1.30. Along the same
road, you can visit the RSPB **Rye
Meads Nature Reserve**; visitor
centre, shop, disabled access to most of
the ten bird-watching hides; cl 25-26
Dec; (01992) 708383; free. The nearby

in daily milking demonstrations at 2.30pm (1.30 during school term). An exhibition farm has a working beehive, model dinosaurs and various creepy-crawlies, and there's an outdoor play area. Most animals and displays are under cover on a wet day, and there are indoor and outdoor picnic areas. There's a play tractor to clamber on, and around 170 acres of farmland to explore, with walks and an arboretum. Snacks, shop, disabled access; open daily Mar-Sept, and Oct half-term; (01462) 686775; £3.80.

LONDON COLNEY TL1902
De Havilland Aircraft Heritage Centre (adjacent to Salisbury Hall, off B556) The Mosquito aircraft were developed here in secret from 1939, and the site houses a collection of 20 different De Havilland aircraft, as well as engines and other memorabilia, and a display outlining the history of the aircraft company. Snacks in verandah-style area in main hangar, shop, disabled access; open pm Tues, Thurs and Sat, all day Sun and bank hols first Sun in Mar to last Sun in Oct; (01727) 822051; *£5. The Green Dragon (Waterside) has good value food, and there are pretty riverside gardens nearby.
Willows Farm Village *See separate family panel on p.294.*

MILL GREEN TL2309
Mill Green Museum and Mill Well restored working watermill with craft demonstrations most Suns Apr-Sept and Sats July-Aug, from straw-plaiting to love-spoon carving; there's a new Jubilee garden too. Shop; cl am wknds, all day Mon and 25 Dec; milling Sun pm, Tues and Weds; (01707) 271362; free.

MUCH HADHAM TL4219
Forge Museum and Cottage Garden (High St) Based around a working blacksmith, the story of such craftsmen through the ages, with an unusual bee shelter in the Victorian-style garden. Shop; usually open Fri-Sun and bank hols Apr to mid-Dec; (01279) 843301; £1. The village is attractive, with fine Tudor and Georgian houses, and well presented food in the old Bull; Hopleys is a good specialist nursery; (01279) 842509.
Henry Moore Foundation (Dane Tree House, Perry Green; just SE) Several

works are displayed in the studios where they were made, while the larger ones are shown off against a backdrop of woodland, pasture and hedgerows. Shop, disabled access; open by appointment only, wkdys (exc bank hols) and Sun Apr-Sept; 90-min guided tour (wkdys only); (01279) 843333; £7. The Hoops opposite has good food (all day on Sun).

NORTHCHURCH SP9609
Largely swallowed up in Berkhamsted, but notable for the ancient church where Peter the Wild Boy is buried; the George & Dragon is handy for lunch.

PIRTON TL1431
Attractive village; the village green is actually the remains of a Norman motte and bailey. The Live & Let Live over at Pegsdon has good food.

RAVENSBURGH CASTLE TL1029
Up in the woods above Hexton (where the Raven is a good family dining pub), this is an easily traced Iron Age hill fort - a pleasant stroll.

RINGSHALL SP9912
Ashridge Estate Right on the Buckinghamshire border and near Whipsnade Zoo in Bedfordshire, eight square miles of unspoilt woodlands and open spaces. Plenty of deer and other wildlife (inc dormice, though you won't see them in daylight), and up on the escarpment a monument to canal mogul the 3rd Duke of Bridgewater; also an attractive toll drive through the estate. Snacks, shop and information centre, disabled access; cl am wknds, mid-Dec to Mar (monument also cl wkdys); (01442) 851227; monument £1.20; NT. The Greyhound and Valiant Trooper at Aldbury just below are good for lunch.

ROYSTON TL3540
Royston Cave (Melbourn St) Tucked beneath the pavement, this cave is thought to have been cut into the chalk which underlies the town by the Knights Templar in the 13th c; fascinating figures of saints and kings are carved into the walls. Shop; open wknd and bank hol pms Easter Sat-end Sept (otherwise by appointment); (01763) 245484; *£2.

SARRATT TQ0498
Long and attractive village green; the church is partly Saxon, and the Cock near it and Boot on the green are both good. There are pleasant unspoilt walks

from here into the Chess Valley in Buckinghamshire.

SCALES WOOD TL4133 (nr Anstey) A pleasant strolling ground; the thatched Woodman at Nuthampstead (open all day Sat) has generous home cooking.

ST ALBANS TL1407 Though modern shops dominate your first impressions, corners of real antiquity are tucked away between and behind them. This was one of the most important Roman towns in northern Europe, and has some fine well excavated remains in peaceful surroundings. A stroll in search of other notable buildings (the tourist information centre in the Town Hall, Market Pl, has helpful guide maps) is rewarded by the surprisingly large number of decent pubs here. Down between abbey gate and park, the Fighting Cocks is based on an ancient building which had some connection with the abbey, and its interesting layout includes the clearly discernible shape of a cockpit. In the quietly attractive largely Georgian St Michael's St, the Rose & Crown is very civilised, and the Six Bells is on the site of a Roman bath house, though not visibly so. The Cock (Hatfield Rd) is worth looking out because of its bizarre history; its floors were found to rest on thick foundations of human bones. Worth a look if you're nearby are the museum (Hatfield Rd), covering the town's post-Roman history (shop, disabled access to ground floor; cl Sun am, 25-27 Dec, and 1 Jan; (01727) 819340; free), and Grebe House in the wildfowl-filled park nr Verulamium, a regional wildlife trust HQ with a woodland garden (cl wknds and bank hols; (01727) 858901; free). The B651 N towards Hitchin is quite a scenic country drive.

Clock Tower This handsome free-standing stone building has a bell, striking on the hour, even older than the tower itself. Exhibitions on the way up, and fine views from the top; shop; open wknds and bank hols Good Fri to mid-Sept; (01727) 860984; 30p. Nearby, French Row is a narrow alley of timbered buildings jettied out over the street, right by a modern shopping centre. The Fleur de Lys pub here is a remarkable medieval building.

Gardens of the Rose (B4630 S) The showgrounds of the Royal National Rose Society, with over 30,000 roses on display. Plenty of interesting cultivar trials going on, new roses from all over the world, lots of clematis, and an iris garden. They do free guided tours pm wknds. Snacks, shop, good disabled access; open Jun-end Sept; (01727) 850461; £4. The Hollybush at nearby Potters Crouch has decent food (not Sun).

Gorhambury Two miles out (the other side of Verulamium's park) but peaceful enough to make you think it's the heart of the country, an 18th-c house with extensive assemblage of 17th-c family portraits, and some 16th-c enamelled glass. Open Thurs pm May-Sept; (01727) 855000; £6.

Kingsbury Watermill (St Michael's St) 16th-c watermill half a mile from the city on the banks of the River Ver, still with one working waterwheel and a museum. Good meals and snacks, shop, disabled access; cl 25-26 Dec, 1 Jan; (01727) 853502; £1.10.

Organ Museum (Camp Rd, 2m E of centre, off A1057/B691 junction) Tuneful collection of automatically operated dance organs and other musical instruments, inc Wurlitzer and Rutt theatre pipe organs. Commentary and recitals every Sun 2-4.30pm, and Sat evening concerts once a month. Snacks, shop, disabled access (but no facilities); open Sun pm only; (01727) 869693; £3.50.

Roman Theatre of Verulamium Most impressive; not large by the standards of some others in England (room for over 2,000), but taking into account its good state of preservation it's unique. Shop; cl 25-26 Dec, 1 Jan; (01727) 835035; £1.50.

St Albans Cathedral Up on a mound, this has good views; its 11th-c reddish exterior uses bricks recycled from the Roman remains. Once the country's premier abbey, it suffered a little after the Reformation, and its fortunes didn't revive until Victorian times. The refurbishments then changed a lot, but the majestic building does have many earlier features, inc 13th- and 14th-c wall paintings in the long nave, the Norman central tower, and some Saxon

transept pillars. Meals, snacks, shop, disabled access; cl 25 Dec, Good Fri, and during services Sun am; cathedral and audio-visual show free. The great 14th-c abbey gatehouse beyond leads down to a neat park, its lake and willow-edged stream packed with ducks.
Verulamium Museum This was the name of the Roman city; its remains are down in the SW corner of town, past the cathedral and attractive park (coming from outside, most easily reached by the A4147 off the Hemel Hempstead exit from M1 junction 7). The place to start is the excellent Verulamium Museum (St Michael's) with its lively interpretation of everyday Roman life, as well as jewellery, wall paintings and domestic items found nearby. Shop, disabled access; cl am Sun, 24-26 Dec and 1 Jan; (01727) 751810; £3.30. The best site outside, a carefully restored mosaic floor and hypocaust underfloor, should reopen in 2004, sheltered by a new anti-vandal building; signs also take you to a well preserved section of the Roman town wall.
ST PAUL'S WALDEN TL1922
A quiet village which, with the rolling rather East Anglian feeling surrounding countryside, offers some of Hertfordshire's most pleasant walking. The late Queen Mother was born at **St Paul's Walden Bury**, and a few times a year you can visit the Grade I landscaped gardens there. Snacks, disabled access; phone for dates; (01438) 871218; £3.
STANDON TL3822
Has some good timbered buildings in its curving High St. The Nags Head over in Wellpond Green does nice fresh food.
TRING SP9211
Walter Rothschild Zoological Museum (Akeman St, off High St) Part of the Natural History Museum, this is made up primarily of the remarkably eclectic collections of the second Lord Rothschild, started when he was a little boy; thousands of preserved mammals, insects, birds, fish and reptiles. Snacks, shop, disabled access to ground floor only; cl Sun am, and 24-26 Dec; (020) 7942 6171; free (under-5s might find the displays slightly startling). The olde-worlde Robin Hood (Brook St, B486) has good food, particularly fresh fish.

Tring has a choice of canal towpath walks from nr the Grand Junction Arms pub (B488 at Bulbourne), where the Grand Union Canal branches into a part-abandoned offshoot, the Wendover Arm, and the still-operational Aylesbury Arm. (There's also canal access from the Boat down Ravens Lane in Berkhamsted, and the Fishery at Boxmoor.) For more ambitious walkers, the nearby Ridgeway long-distance path heads off W right across southern England.
WALKING IN HERTFORDSHIRE TL3206
Large areas of this county are taken up by the northwards spread of London with continuous swathes of development, and also by the first early 20th-c New Towns, the garden cities of Letchworth and Welwyn, and their more modern successors Hatfield, Hemel Hempstead and Stevenage. But between and beyond these are good green windows of carefully preserved farmland and some more wooded countryside. These yield pockets of good walking terrain, though there is little that is really outstanding. A good point is that even in the prairie-like arable farmland that characterises large chunks of the county, the field paths are often in remarkably good condition and very adequately waymarked. Pubs handy for walks include the Crown & Sceptre at Bridens Camp TL0411 above Hemel Hempstead, Clarendon Arms at Chandlers Cross TQ0698, Two Brewers on Chipperfield Common TL0401, Black Horse at Chorleywood TQ0295, John Bunyan at Coleman Green TL1812, Three Blackbirds at Flamstead TL0714, Bricklayers Arms at Flaunden TL0100, Alford Arms at Frithsden TL0110, Silver Fox at Hertford Heath TL3510, Plough between Great Munden and Dane End TL3523, Cross Keys at Gustard Wood nr Wheathampstead TL1716, Five Horseshoes at Little Berkhamsted TL2908, Bridgewater Arms at Little Gaddesden SP9913, Crown at Newgate Street TL3005 (for Northaw Great Wood), Cabinet at Reed TL3636 and Half Moon at Wilstone SP9014.
WARE TL3513
Scott's Grotto (Scotts Rd) Built in the 1760s by the poet John Scott, this is one of the finest bits of romantic gothickry

in the world, extending 20 metres (67 ft) into the hillside by a modern housing development, with underground passages and chambers decorated with flints, shells, stones and minerals. Wear flat shoes and bring a torch. Open Sat and bank hol pms Apr-Sept, or by appointment; (01920) 464131; suggested donation £1.

WATFORD TQ1097
Cheslyn Gardens An unexpected pleasure in this largely modern urban area, with 3½ acres of woodland and formal gardens, a pond and an aviary; cl 25 Dec; free. The local museum (High St) has a display on the Watford Home Guard, the basis for the old TV series *Dad's Army*. Shop, disabled access; cl Sun-Weds; (01923) 232297; free.

WELWYN TL2315
Welwyn Roman Baths 🏛 (just off A1(M) junction 6 - towards Welwyn on A1000, and counting M-way slip roundabout as 1st roundabout go nearly all way round 2nd roundabout -

car park through two five-barred gates) Excavated before the construction of the A1 and since then rather ingeniously preserved within the motorway embankment, this Roman bath house is all that remains of a 3rd-c villa. Very good condition, with explanatory displays. Shop, disabled access (but no facilities); open pm wknds and bank hols Jan-Nov, and pms daily during school hols (exc Dec); (01707) 271362; £1. The Red Lion (B197 S) has decent food all day.

WESTMILL TL3627
A happy combination of neat green-tiled cottages and fine old church; there are pleasant walks nearby.
Other attractive villages, all with decent pubs, include partly thatched Barley TL3938, Cottered TL3129, Hexton TL1230, Letchmore Heath TQ1597, Redbourn TL1012 (despite motorway noise Church End with its workhouse and Norman church is pretty) and Rushden TL3031.

Where to eat

ARDELEY TL3027 **Jolly Waggoner** *(01438) 861350* Cream-washed dining inn in pretty, tucked-away village, with lots of nooks and crannies, plenty of woodwork, beams and an open fire, an extended restaurant, and a relaxed and civilised atmosphere; well presented food using local produce, a good range of wines, well kept Greene King ales, and attractive garden; cl Mon (exc bank hols when cl Tues); children over 7; disabled access. £30|**£6.50**

BUSHEY TQ1395 **St James** *30 High St (020) 8950 2480* Modern, airy bistro with parish church nearby, and church-themed decorations; enjoyable food inc daily specials, and reasonably priced wines; cl Sun; disabled access. £35

FRITHSDEN TL0109 **Alford Arms** *(01442) 864480* Fashionably refurbished and secluded country pub with imaginative changing food, well kept real ales, and good wines; airy interior, simple prints on pale cream walls with dark green or deep red areas, and an appealing mix of good furniture from Georgian chairs to old commodes on bare boards and patterned tiles; cl 25-26 Dec; limited disabled access. £25.95|**£5.75**

LEMSFORD TL2013 **Auberge du Lac** *Brocket Hall, Brocket Park (01707) 368888* 18th-c former hunting lodge on a lake, in the magnificent parkland of Brocket Hall; big windows give charming views of the water and terrace, tables are beautifully set, innovative cooking is based on classical french principles (lunch is particularly good value), and service is courteous; bdrms in the former stables for Brocket Hall; cl Sun pm, all Mon; disabled access. £60/3-course lunch £28

SARRATT TQ0398 **Cock** *Church Lane (01923) 282908* Cosy white 17th-c country pub, with a carpeted snug, oak-panelled lounge, and inglenook fireplaces; no smoking restaurant in a nicely restored thatched barn, elaborate food under new licensees, and real ales; benches in front, and seats on a pretty back lawn with country views; disabled access. £34|**£8.50**

WATTON-AT-STONE TL2919 **George & Dragon** *82 High St (01920) 830285* Civilised pub first licensed in 1603, with a relaxed atmosphere, antiques, open fires, and efficient service; enjoyable food in bar and no smoking restaurant, and good house wines; cl Sun pm; children must be well behaved. £23|**£7.25**

ISLE OF WIGHT

*Good beaches and weather, plenty of entertaining visits,
attractive prices, and appealing countryside including dramatic
coastal scenery - a great island for family holidays*

Getting here, of course, is part of the fun. The sea crossing takes about 30 mins - half that for the Portsmouth—Ryde catamaran, even less for the Southsea Hovercraft. The Lymington—Yarmouth trip is the most rewarding (you'll need to book in summer). Foot fares start at around £10.60 for a period return. A typical summer car return fare (inc up to six people) is around £105, with cheaper day trips, offers and bargains: (08705) 827744 for Portsmouth to Fishbourne or Ryde (passengers only), and Lymington to Yarmouth; (023) 8033 4010 for Southampton—Cowes; (023) 9281 1000 for Hovercraft Southsea—Ryde.

Prices are quite low compared to the mainland, and for longer stays some hotels do good value package deals that include the ferry fare.

The most attractive scenery is in the W, the largest concentration of things to do in the E. The coastal walks are the finest in SE England. Inland are long curving chalk ridges (tracks often follow the crests) and forestry plantations with many signposted woodland trails. The island bus service is excellent, and a week's bus pass is good value, as is a daily Rover road/rail ticket. In high summer the main resorts and places to visit get very busy. Even then, away from the main tourist haunts, much of the island is surprisingly unspoilt and little visited. Out of season the island feels fresh, uncrowded and leisurely - in winter many places aimed at children close for six months.

A bonus for families is the free return visit, within four days, to Blackgang Chine and its Downend counterpart (both have good rides and play areas), or to Brickfields Horse Country in Binstead (a must for horse-lovers, pig-racing too). Other enjoyable outings are headed by the excellent Sandown zoo, the island's top Family Attraction this year. At Flamingo Park in Seaview you can get really close to the birds, Amazon World Zoo Park in Newchurch offers a tantalising glimpse of the jungle, while ruined Appuldurcombe House (at Wroxall) is an atmospheric setting for the owl and falconry centre; there's a friendly farm in Porchfield. You'll find a nice medley of attractions at Fort Victoria Country Park in lively Yarmouth.

Elsewhere, striking Osborne House in East Cowes was Queen Victoria's favourite residence (absorbing anecdotes from the enthusiastic guides), and Dimbola Lodge at Freshwater Bay has a fascinating photography museum; at Brading, there are appealing houses. Dinosaur Isle in Sandown is the country's only purpose-built dinosaur museum (there's also a dinosaur museum at Brighstone), and Ventnor has a smuggling museum, and sun-trap subtropical gardens.

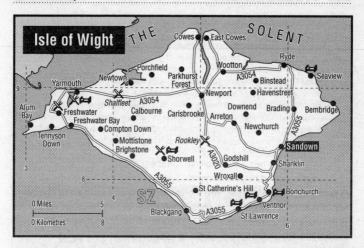

Where to stay

BONCHURCH SZ5777 **Lake Hotel** *Bonchurch, Ventnor, Isle of Wight PO38 IRF* (01983) 852613 **£64***, plus special breaks; 20 rms. Early 19th-c country house in two acres of pretty gardens, 400 metres from beach; lots of flowers and plants in three light and airy lounges (one is an attractive conservatory), a well stocked bar, and good food in neat restaurant; cl Nov-Jan; children over 3; partial disabled access; dogs welcome in bedrooms

SEAVIEW SZ6390 **Priory Bay Hotel** *Priory Croft, Priory Rd, Seaview, Isle of Wight PO34 5BU* (01983) 613146 **£130**, plus special breaks; 18 individually furnished rms with 10 more in cottages. Former Tudor farmhouse with Georgian and more recent additions in grounds leading to a fine sandy private beach with a beach bar (good for lunch); lovely day rooms with comfortable sofas, books and magazines on coffee tables, pretty flower arrangements, imaginative food in restaurant with charming Georgian murals and elaborate plasterwork, and an informal, relaxed atmosphere; outdoor swimming pool, tennis, croquet, and a nine-hole par three golf course; disabled access; dogs in cottages in grounds ☺

SEAVIEW SZ6291 **Seaview Hotel** *High St, Seaview, Isle of Wight PO34 5EX* (01983) 612711 **£95**, plus special breaks; 16 attractively decorated rms, some with sea views and private drawing rooms. Small, friendly and spotlessly kept hotel with fine ship photographs in the chatty and relaxed front dining bar, an interesting old-fashioned back bar, good imaginative bar food, and a highly regarded evening restaurant; cl 3 days over Christmas; proper high tea for children (must be over 5 in evening restaurant); partial disabled access; dogs welcome in bedrooms

SHORWELL SZ4582 **Westcourt Farm** *Shorwell, Newport, Isle of Wight PO30 3LA* (01983) 740233 **£50**; 3 rms. Fine Elizabethan manor connected to a farm of 200 acres, with comfortable lounge/dining room, and a restful atmosphere; no smoking; lots of surrounding walks; children over 10

ST LAWRENCE SZ5476 **Lisle Combe** *Bank End Farm, Undercliffe Drive, Ventnor, Isle of Wight PO38 IUW* (01983) 852582 **£50***; 3 rms, shared bthrm. Friendly, family-run Elizabethan-style farmhouse in five-acre coastal garden with sea views, and lovely paintings and furniture - it was once the home of poet Alfred Noyes and is still owned by the family; they keep their own rare breeds and farm, and are close to coves and beaches; must book months ahead (so popular with return customers); cl Nov-Mar ☺

VENTNOR SZ5577 **Royal Hotel** *Belgrave Rd, Ventnor, Isle of Wight PO38 IJJ*

(01983) 852186 **£135***, plus special breaks; 55 well equipped rms. Friendly Victorian hotel with fine sea views, neat gardens with heated outdoor pool, spacious and comfortable day rooms, cosy candlelit bar with open fire, good food in attractive restaurant, and helpful service; cl 1st 2 wks Jan; disabled access; dogs welcome in bedrooms

YARMOUTH SZ3589 **George Hotel** *Quay St, Yarmouth, Isle of Wight PO41 0PE* *(01983) 760331* **£175**; 17 comfortable rms. 17th-c house by the harbour, with gardens leading to little private beach; a fine flagstoned hall, fresh flowers and open fires, a convivial bar and attractive residents' sitting room with marvellously relaxing atmosphere, imaginative enjoyable food in informal brasserie and smart restaurant, hearty breakfasts, and prompt courteous service; motor yacht for hire; dogs welcome in bedrooms

To see and do

Isle of Wight Family Attraction of the Year

SANDOWN SZ6084 **Isle of Wight Zoo** (Seafront, Yaverland) This well established place focuses on big cats, with the main draw the collection of around 20 tigers; there are few places in the world where you can see as many, or learn so much about them. Many were born and raised at the zoo, and it's hard not to be impressed by the dedication and enthusiasm of the family that run the place, or their determination to raise awareness of the species and its plight. A mix of bengal, siberian, and chinese-blooded tigers, each of the cats has its own distinctive personality; excellent talks by staff help bring these out. Look out for the rare white tigress Zena, and the unusual ginger tiger, Diamond. There are plenty of other big cats too, including lions, leopards, jaguars, and a black panther, and in recent years they've also begun to focus on lemurs, with around a dozen of the fascinating little primates housed in a re-creation of their natural habitat in Madagascar. You'll also find a number of insects, snakes and other creepy-crawlies, with a good display of huge, hairy tarantulas; again, there are useful keeper talks. The zoo is built around the remains of a 19th-c granite fort, one of the chain built by Lord Palmerston as a defence against the French; there's a children's play area near the entrance. Ambitious plans to improve the tigers' enclosures are well under way. Meals, snacks, shop, disabled access; open Mar-Oct, plus wkds in Nov; (01983) 403883; £5.95 adults, £4.95 children over 5. They do a number of family tickets, depending on how many children you bring: two adults and two children is £19.25.

ALUM BAY SZ3085
The beach here is famous for its multi-coloured sands from the different rock strata in the cliff that runs down to it; 20 shades of pinks, greys and ochres, showing up most vividly after rain. The High Down Hotel towards Totland has decent food.
Needles Old Battery From Needles Park it's just under a mile's walk to this 19th-c Palmerstonian fort (you can't go by car but there's a half-hourly bus (01983) 532373); the parade-ground shows off two 12-ton gun barrels salvaged from the sea, and there's a World War I exhibition. A 60-metre (200-ft) tunnel leads to a look-out spot that gives stunning views of the Needles themselves, a group of wave-battered chalk pinnacles, and their lighthouse. Good views too from the 1940s-style tearoom; disabled access; cl Fri and Sat (exc July-Aug and Good Fri), all Nov-Mar, and in gale force winds; (01983) 754772; *£3.60; NT.
Needles Park Clifftop park with spectacular chairlift down to the beach, giving wonderful views along the way; also crazy golf, a simulator ride, and you can create your own geological work of

art by carefully layering differently coloured local sands in a glass tube. Meals, snacks, shop, disabled access; cl Nov-Easter; (01983) 752401; park entry free (though car parking is £3), then individual charges for attractions (£7.75 for saver ticket covering main attractions). Glass-blowing demonstrations at adjacent Alum Bay Glass, and tours of the Sweet Manufactory (cl over Christmas; £1.25 each, or free with saver ticket); both have good factory shops.

ARRETON SZ5386

A pleasant place with a delightful 13th-c **church** (which has a brass-rubbing centre (01983) 527553), and a lovely mellow stone Elizabethan manor house (not open to the public). Arreton Barn's Craft Village nearby has craft workshops, pub, and restaurant with home baking. The White Lion is good for lunch, and the cross-island Wootton Bridge—Niton back road through here has quietly attractive views.

BEMBRIDGE SZ6488

Even in summer this is quiet for a coastal place, though with plenty going on in its yachting harbour, and a lifeboat station nearby; there's a little local heritage centre in a former school on Church Rd. Though most of Wight's E coast is heavily developed, with the coastal path sometimes following roads and skirting large residential areas, Bembridge has the best opportunities for walks. Out on the Foreland the magnificent rock pools would keep any beachcomber happy for hours. Chachalot Charters (Fisherman's Wharf) run sea-fishing trips; Apr-Oct; from £8.50 for a 2-hr trip for mackerel. The clifftop Crab & Lobster (Forelands), an easy walk up from the beach, has good food and fabulous views. There's also a good walk S to Culver Cliff, for more views.

Shipwreck Centre Maritime Museum 🎫 (Sherbourne St) Six galleries of salvage and shipwreck items, and tales of pirates and mermen. Shop, disabled access ground floor only; cl Nov-Mar; (01983) 872223; £2.95.

Windmill Built in 1700 and used until 1913, this is the only surviving windmill on the island - much of its wooden

machinery is intact. Shop; cl Sat (exc Easter Sat) and all Nov-Mar; (01983) 873945; *£1.90; NT.

BINSTEAD SZ5792

Brickfields Horse Country 🎫 (Newnham Rd) Daily parades of horses in high season, shire-powered waggon rides, tractor and pony rides, carriage and museum tours, porkers' paradise with the Lester Piglet Derby three times a day (Jun-Sept), and a farm corner. Informal show-jumping on Weds evenings (car boot sales Mon evenings). Restaurant and bar, picnic area, saddlery, shop, disabled access; cl 25-26 Dec; (01983) 566801; £5.50 (free return visit within four days). There's a BHS approved riding school here. The old White Hart at Havenstreet is fairly handy for lunch.

BLACKGANG SZ4876

Blackgang Chine Fantasy Park This 40-acre family leisure park has an excellent policy on return visits: each ticket allows free re-entry for a second visit within four days. The liveliest attraction is an enjoyable high-speed water chute and wild west town, and they've recently added a new roller-coaster; there are plenty more gentle rides to suit younger children. The most interesting parts are the maritime museum at the restored quayside, and the complete replica of a Victorian sawmill, inc working steam and oil engines. Lots of models of dinosaurs, goblins, and nursery rhyme scenes dotted around the gardens (illuminated on summer evenings). Also fossils and gemstones, a hedge maze, and several play areas, inc one for toddlers. Meals, snacks, shop, disabled access (some steep hills); open Apr-Oct; (01983) 730330; *£7.50. The Wight Mouse at Chale is a popular family pub, and the A3055 in both directions gives fine sea and coast views.

BONCHURCH SZ5778

Much quieter than nearby Ventnor, with leafy lanes hugging the slopes and passing an unexpected tree-shaded pond; steep steps connect the different levels, and there's a quiet cove down below the cliff. The small 13th-c church has a lovely peaceful graveyard, and above the cliff St Boniface Down has tremendous views. The Bonchurch Inn is rather unusual, with its italian landlord and food. For several miles along this section of coast, the cliffs have been and to some extent still are subject to massive landslides.

BRADING SZ6086

🖼 Busy and attractive, with interesting monuments in its Norman church, and a pretty graveyard. The Bugle food pub is well organised for families. The remains of a **Roman villa** has good mosaics; shop; currently cl (they're adding a new cover building, Roman garden, shop, and restaurant) but due to re-open around May; (01983) 406223; £2.95. The road out over Bembridge Down to Culver Cliff gives fine views, especially from the Culver Haven pub at the end, nr the Yarborough Monument.

Isle of Wight Waxworks 🖼 In the partly 11th-c Ancient Rectory Mansion, this gives you what you'd hope for from a wax museum, with an adjacent natural history museum. Candle-carving demonstrations and shop open Easter-Sept (till 10pm summer hols), usually cl some weeks Dec-Jan, phone for details; (01983) 407286; £5.25.

Lilliput Doll and Toy Museum Excellent private collection, with over 2,000 exhibits, some up to 4,000 years old, and examples of almost every seriously collectable doll in Britain. Shop, some disabled access; cl 25 Dec; (01983) 407231; £1.95.

Morton Manor (off A3055 S) Friendly partly 13th-c manor house, in lovely landscaped gardens with ornamental ponds and Elizabethan turf maze. The little vineyard has an exhibition of wine-making relics. Tearooms, shop, some disabled access; cl Sat, and Nov-Mar; (01983) 406168; £4.50.

Nunwell House and Gardens 🖼 (Church Lane, off A3055 NW) Lovely lived-in 16th-c house with later additions, interesting furniture and military and family memorabilia, and five acres of charming gardens. Charles I spent his last night of freedom here. Shop; open pm Mon-Weds July-Aug, plus late May bank hol; tours 1.30, 2.30, and 3.30pm; (01983) 407240; £4 (inc guide book), £2.50 garden only.

BRIGHSTONE SZ4282

Dinosaur Farm (A3055 SE) An enthusiastic working museum where you can watch and chat to the experts as they prepare dinosaur bones for scientific research and display. One of the most important dinosaur skeletons to be found in the UK was discovered in this area in 1992. Snacks, shop, disabled access; open Tues, Thurs and Sun Easter-Oct and every day July-Aug; (01983) 740401; £2.30. The Three Bishops has decent food.

Inland walks Inland, the island is characterised by long curving chalk ridges (tracks often follow the crests) and forestry plantations (with many signposted woodland trails). The hills N of Brighstone represent some of the pick of the scenery. The Countryman on Limerstone Rd is a good refreshment break, with fine views down to the sea.

CALBOURNE SZ4186

Attractive village with photogenic streamside thatched cottages and 13th-c **church**. It's worth getting here early to avoid the coach tours.

Watermill and Rural Museum 🖼 (B3401) A six-metre (20-ft) waterwheel still powers this 17th-c mill, and the grounds have tame peacocks, a fire station, little World War and rural museums, and a putting green (£1); you can punt on the stream (£5 a punt for 30 mins) and feed the fish. Home-baked snacks (milling 3pm, Sun-Fri), shop with stone-ground flour, some disabled access; cl Nov-Mar; (0845) 6448720; £4.

CARISBROOKE SZ4888

Carisbrooke Castle Ruins of the only medieval castle on the island, between 1647 and 1648 home to the imprisoned Charles I (his daughter died here in 1650). Some later buildings behind the imposing gatehouse and walls, and entertaining demonstrations of how donkeys drew water from one of the medieval wells. Shop, summer café, disabled access to ground floor; cl 24-26 Dec, 1 Jan; (01983) 522107; £5; EH. The Eight Bells above the waterfowl lake has decent food and good Solent views.

COMPTON DOWN SZ3785

Another good place for walks on this S coast, a hogsback grassy hill E of Freshwater Bay; circular walks can take in the coast path along Compton Bay - one of the island's best beaches, not touristy, with impressive cliff views (NT car park).

COWES SZ4995
Stylish and lively, very much centred on its yachting connections, with interesting buildings and shops inc fascinating ships' chandlers in the long narrow High St, and the battery of over 20 brass cannons used to start the yacht races down by the harbour. The Boat Trail is a new self-guided tour around the town's highlights; maps from shops and tourist information centre (Fountain Quay). The Duke of York (Mill Hill Rd), Globe (The Parade) and Union (Watch House Lane) have enjoyable food inc lots of seafood. Seafaring collections at the small Maritime Museum in the public library on Beckford Rd (cl Thurs, Sun and bank hols; (01983) 823847; free), and at the pretty Sir Max Aitken Museum (open Tues-Sat May-Sept; (01983) 292191; £1).

DOWNEND SZ5387
Robin Hill Country Park A very useful retreat for families, particularly those with younger children who want to run around. Like its stablemate Blackgang Chine, it has a few rather dated-looking representations of trolls and the like, but scores more highly for rides such as the pirate ship, the 400-metre toboggan run (best for older children, £1 extra) and the motion-platform cinema. Boasting good play areas, with underground tunnels and assault course equipment, the park also has a pitch and putt course, look-out tower, wooden maze, and plenty of space for football and basketball. There's also an interactive wildlife area; paths and trails wind through the woodland. Meals, snacks, new shop, disabled access but rather hilly in parts; cl Nov-Mar; (01983) 527352; £6.50; ticket allows a free second visit within four days. The nearby Hare & Hounds is a useful family dining pub, open all day.

EAST COWES SZ5194
Osborne House (1m SE) Queen Victoria's favourite residence, where she died in 1901; the state and private apartments haven't changed much since. Designed to resemble an italian

villa, by Prince Albert with professional help from Thomas Cubitt, it's a striking place. Albert and his wife were also responsible for the original layout of the fine formal gardens, which seem filled with every conceivable english tree, masses of roses and clematis. The refurbished Durbar Wing is filled with opulent gifts to Victoria from the people of India. Swiss Cottage is where the Royal children learnt cooking and gardening (with furniture made especially for them). The house featured in the film *Mrs Brown*. Snacks, shop, some disabled access; cl Nov-Mar, best to phone for winter opening; (01983) 200022; £8, £4.50 grounds only; EH. Down on the River Medina, the beautifully placed Folly Inn has an appropriately nautical atmosphere.
Whippingham church Said to have been another of Prince Albert's designs, and a good deal more eccentric than Osborne House: a bizarre mix of different styles.

FRESHWATER SZ3386
A very extended rather sprawling village, with a charming quiet core. The picturesque 20th-c thatched church includes quite a few Tennyson family memorials, and beyond it a causeway crosses the head of the Yar estuary. The Red Lion has good food, and the Vine has a pleasant terrace for warm days. There are fine walks nearby, and Hill Farm has riding; (01983) 752502.
FRESHWATER BAY SZ3485
Dimbola Lodge (Terrace Lane) When the photography pioneer Julia Cameron lived here in the 1860/70s regular guests (and sitters) included Edward Lear, Lewis Carroll, Ellen Terry and her next-door neighbour Alfred Lord Tennyson. Vacant for years (and very nearly demolished), the restored house now proudly displays her ground-breaking portraits, with changing exhibitions by contemporary artists; summer music recitals. Tearoom (good vegetarian meals), shop, disabled access; cl Mon (exc bank hols and summer hols), and five days over Christmas and New Year; (01983) 756814; *£3.50.

GODSHILL SZ5281
Best appreciated in winter, when the coach parties that descend on the

tearooms and quaint little streets have gone home. Plenty of famously pretty thatched cottages, and a good 15th-c church, with interesting 15th-c wall painting (Shanklin Rd). The Old Smith and Gardens is a little gift centre based around a former blacksmith's forge with an aviary of exotic birds, and a garden in the shape of the island itself (meals, snacks, disabled access; (01983) 840364; cl 25-26 Dec, gardens cl Oct-Mar; free).The Griffin is a decent family pub with a good play area (and maze), and the village is an inland starting point for a good walk via the Worsley Trail on to Stenbury Down (radio masts, but redeemed by wide views), then back via the atmospherically ruinous Appuldurcombe House and passing through a huge estate gateway.

Model Village (High St) Painstakingly re-creates old Shanklin, its Chine Valley, and Godshill in miniature (there's even a model model village). Shop, disabled access; cl Nov-Feb; (01983) 840270; £2.95.

Natural History Centre (High St) Decent collection of fossils and minerals, and lots and lots of different sea shells. Jewellery shop, disabled access; cl Jan and first 2 wks Feb; (01983) 840333; *£1.50.

Nostalgia Toy Museum (High St) Lots of post-war toys and die-cast model cars; fans of Dinky, Corgi and Matchbox toy cars will be happy here; cl Nov-Easter; (01983) 840181; £1.50.

HAVENSTREET SZ5589
Isle of Wight Steam Railway Well restored railway with very pleasant 10-mile trip from Wootton to Smallbrook Junction nr Ryde (where you can change directly on to the main line). Vintage engines and rolling stock, and related memorabilia displayed in the old gasworks at Havenstreet Station. Meals, snacks, shop; open Mar-Oct (daily Jun-Sept); phone for timetable; (01983) 882204; £7.50. The Island Liner day ticket (£10) includes the steam railway and travel on all regular trains on the island. The White Hart (with lots of loco prints) does good generous food.

MOTTISTONE SZ4083
Charming old village with a well in the centre of the green; even the bus

shelter is stone-built. The Bluebell Wood opposite the church is lovely in spring, and the picture-book thatched Sun over at Hulverstone has imaginative food.

Mottistone Manor The fine gardens with sea views are open pm only Sun and bank hols and all day Tues and Weds Apr-Oct; Teas, shop, some disabled access; (01983) 741302; £2.90; NT. The manor house, medieval with Elizabethan additions, is open Aug bank hol only.

NEWCHURCH SZ5685
Amazon World Zoo Park (A3056 S) Among the 200 species are everything from anteaters to marmosets, tree porcupines, and crocodiles, through toucans and flamingos, to tarantulas and terrapins. Some of the bigger animals are outdoors, but as most of the exhibition is under cover, it's enjoyable in any weather. Divided into several areas, it starts with the story of the rain forests (the damage that's been done to them, and how we can reverse it), with free-flying birds. As well as twice-daily falconry displays (weather permitting) at 12.30 and 3.30pm, you can now watch them feeding the penguins every morning too; meet-the-animal sessions, where keepers show off three animals at a time, are daily at 2pm. An adventure playground includes a separate area for under-5s. Meals, snacks, picnic areas, shop, disabled access; cl 25 Dec; (01983) 867122; £5.75.

NEWPORT SZ5089
The island's capital, with a good deal of character, some fine old Georgian houses, and warm red brick 18th-c buildings down by the quay. It's the main place on the island for antiques shops. The parish church of St Thomas is worth a look - it has an interestingly carved Jacobean pulpit and a 19th-c memorial to Charles I's daughter. The 17th-c Wheatsheaf nearby is good for lunch. Designed by John Nash, the Guildhall (High St) now houses the tourist information centre, and the Museum of Island History (with touch-screen computers, and some hands-on exhibits); cl 25-26 Dec and 1 Jan; £1.80. The Quay Arts Centre (Sea St) has changing exhibitions and craft fairs

monthly on Sat; cl bank hols; (01983) 822490. The back road to Brading has pleasant views.

Classic Boat Museum (The Quay) Vintage motor and sailing boats inc the oldest lifeboat in the country, and a 1910 wooden launch used for Thames cruises; you can watch some of the boats being restored. Shop, disabled access; cl Mon, and Oct-Apr exc Tues and Sat; (01983) 533493; £3.

Roman Villa 🖼 (Cypress Rd) Well preserved baths and reconstructed rooms on the site of 3rd-c Roman villa, with an informative museum; also Roman garden. Shop, limited disabled access; cl Sun (exc Jul and Aug), and all Nov-Mar; (01983) 529720; *£2.

NEWTOWN SZ4290

For a while this was the island's capital, but it began a slow decline after a disastrous fire in 1377, and eventually faded out altogether - what used to be rich merchants' streets are now just grassy tracks. The Old Town Hall, rebuilt in 1699 but now left stranded and unusually isolated from any houses, is all that's left to mark the once thriving town. Shop; open pm Mon, Weds and Sun Apr-Oct, plus pm Tues and Thurs in July and Aug, Good Fri and Easter Sat; (01983) 531785; *£1.70; NT. Rewarding walks for bird-watchers at the nearby nature reserve. The New Inn at Shalfleet has good seafood.

Newtown Nature Reserve On the N coast, this has walks around the tranquil Norfolk-like creeks of the Newtown/Clamerkin estuaries, but there are few circular routes; from the village a boardwalk leads out into the heart of the reserve within a few minutes.

PARKHURST FOREST SZ4891

Just W of the prison, this is a couple of miles across, with plenty of signposted paths and a good chance of seeing red squirrels.

PORCHFIELD SZ4590

Colemans Animal Farm Pet and farm animals to handle and feed (they've a rabbit and guinea-pig village), straw fun barn, adventure play area, mini farm, aviary and pedal tractors; daily events, and milking demonstrations. Tearoom and barbecue area in 16th-c courtyard, shop, disabled access to most areas; cl

Mon (exc bank and school hols), and Nov-Feb; (01983) 522831; £3.95.

RYDE SZ5992

Now the biggest town here, with a long triple pier, good sandy beaches, and a full set of holiday-resort amusements - just right for a straightforward family holiday. Free tours and tastings at Rosemary Vineyard on Smallbrook Lane; (01983) 811084. At the Westbridge Centre, you can watch an unusual 40-min water, light and music show; cl mid-Dec to end Jan; (01983) 811333; £4.

National Wireless Museum (Puckpool Hill, off Seaview rd) This tells the story of broadcasting from 1922 onwards, inc demonstrations of how the first radio sets sounded. Snacks, shop; usually open pm wknds Oct-Apr and pm daily in summer; (01983) 567665; free.

SANDOWN SZ6084

All the usual things for a family beach holiday - pier, boat trips, canoeing lake, discos - and a fine beach. The Ocean Deck (Esplanade) has tasty food inc seafood from their own boat. You can tour the partly underground winery of **Adgestone Vineyard** on Upper Rd (01983) 402503; best to phone, and may close one day a week in winter; £3.50 for self-guided tour.

Dinosaur Isle 🖼 (Culver Parade) In a building shaped like a pterosaur, this is the country's only purpose-built dinosaur museum. Displays include dinosaur skeletons, full-size models (inc an animatronic one), experts at work on dinosaur bones in an open laboratory, hands-on activities, and fossil and rock collections; also special events inc guided fossil walks (must be booked) and temporary exhibitions. Shop, disabled access; cl 25-26, and 31 Dec, best to ring in Jan; (01983) 404344; £4.60.

Isle of Wight Zoo See *separate family panel on p.304.*

SEAVIEW SZ6291

A timelessly quiet retreat, with sedate streets of unassuming villas; the Seaview Hotel does very good lunches.

Flamingo Park Wildlife Encounter (B3330) Attractively laid out in spacious landscaped grounds, this friendly and nicely unspoilt place has far more than just flamingos. Events and demonstrations throughout the day include feeding penguins, pelicans, macaws and parrots; there's a free-flying display of brightly coloured exotic birds (some tame enough to feed from your hand), owls, and a penguin pool. As well as a wallaby walkabout (as the name suggests you can walk with them), there are beavers and red squirrels, and the new enchanted forest area has interactive exhibits. You can usually feed their koi and huge mirror carp. Good keepers' talks try to bring out the birds' individual characteristics, as well as passing on a conservation message. Snacks and picnic areas, shop, disabled access; cl Nov-Feb; (01983) 612153; £6.25.

SHANKLIN SZ5881
Shanklin Chine 🖭 Walk along quite glorious verdant natural gorge, illuminated at dusk, with magnificent 14-metre (45-ft) waterfall. A heritage centre gives details of rare flora, nature trails and life in Victorian Shanklin. Snacks, shop; cl Nov-Mar; (01983) 866432; *£3.50. Down on the beach, the thatched Fishermans Cottage is charmingly placed for lunch (cl Nov-Mar), and up at the top the Chine Inn is a good family pub (no food Sun evening or Mon).

SHORWELL SZ4583
One of the few really pretty villages on the island to have escaped a flood of tourist interest, with charming streamside thatched cottages and a fine church; the attractive Crown, open all day in summer, is very good for lunch.

ST CATHERINE'S HILL SZ4978
Capped by the ruins of a 14th-c oratory, a short walk up from the coast path further E; you can walk on along a ridge to the prominent Hoy's Monument at the far end of St Catherine's Down. The coast path meanwhile skirts the undercliff of St Catherine's Point, the isle's S tip, which has a modern working lighthouse; usually open pm Easter-Oct, guided tours only, phone to check; (01983) 867979; £2. There are several other paths through the undercliff here.

ST LAWRENCE SZ5276
Isle of Wight Studio Glass (Old Park Rd) You can watch glass-making (not

wknds), lovely displays, and shop. Disabled access; cl winter wknds and for 3 wks at Christmas; (01983) 853526; £1. The nearby St Lawrence Inn has enjoyable food, and brews its own beer.

TENNYSON DOWN SZ3285
On Wight's W tip, the best place of all for walkers here: a friendly grassy ridge and cliff walk rolled into one, with views over most of the island and across to the mainland. You pass the monument to Alfred Lord Tennyson (who lived nearby and loved this place), and the walk culminates in spectacular fashion above the Needles. You can walk the entire ridge from Freshwater Bay (an open-top bus service runs Apr-Oct from Alum Bay to bring you back; (01983) 532373), or make a round walk from Alum Bay car park, past the Needles Old Battery and along to the monument, then up on to Headon Warren before going down to Alum Bay. The High Down Hotel (B3322) is another start point.

VENTNOR SZ5476
Relatively untouristy little town up on the cliff (with a new harbour which welcomes temporary moorings). The fairly restrained and decorous seafront down below is linked to it by a tortuously steep loop of road; between them perched on ledges among the trees are quite a number of Victorian villas - many of them still private houses rather than guesthouses. Its great pride is the Botanic Garden, where an exceptional collection of subtropical plants make the most of the mild climate (visitor centre, meals, snacks; free); the Garden Tavern here has decent food and sea views. A nice walk from the garden is to Steephill Cove just below, a safe beach for children, and you can buy lobster and crab here. The Heritage Museum on Spring Hill is good for local history (cl 12.30-2pm, Weds and Sat pm, all Sun, and Nov-Apr; 75p). The Spyglass is an interesting pub with superb sea views, and the seafront Mill Bay is good too.
Bonchurch Down Above Ventnor, this has unsightly radar installations but gives walkers fine views.
Museum of Smuggling History 🖭 In the Botanic Garden (or more

correctly under it), this demonstrates the tricks smugglers past and present have used to sneak in wool, brandy, tobacco or drugs. Shop; cl Oct-Mar; (01983) 853677; £2.80.

Undercliff Formed from the irregular masses of earth which have come to rest below, with often rocky chasms between each other and the cliff itself. Sometimes planted and sometimes with profuse natural vegetation, the resulting scenery is unlike anything else on the island, with quite a subtropical aspect.

WOOTTON SZ5290

A terminus for the steam railway (see Havenstreet entry). It has an attractive partly Norman church. The Sloop down overlooking the creek is a reliable food pub.

Butterfly World & Fountain World ⊞ (Staplers Rd) Tropical butterfly house, italian and japanese gardens, and Small World with fairylit animated scenes and jumping-jet fountains, next to a five-acre garden centre with water gardens. Snacks, shop, disabled access; cl Nov-Mar; (01983) 883430; £4.75.

WROXALL SZ5480

Appuldurcombe House ⊞ (off B3327 W) Intriguing shell of Palladian house, nestling among grounds beautifully landscaped by Capability Brown. You can still catch something of the atmosphere of the days when this was one of the grandest houses on the island. The stables have been converted into holiday cottages, and the old laundry and brewhouse into an owl and falconry centre (daily flying displays at 11am, 1pm and also 3pm in summer) - Henry VIII is said to have stayed here with his falconers. Snacks, shop, some disabled access, though gravel paths may prove difficult for wheelchairs; cl mid-Dec to mid-Feb; (01983) 852484; £5.75 for house, grounds and falconry centre, £2.50 house, grounds only, £4.75 falconry only. The Four Seasons (B3327 S) has enjoyable food. Nearby Lower Winstone Farm (St John's Rd) has a donkey sanctuary, with over 200 residents; shop; open daily Easter-Oct,

and perhaps other times; (01983) 852693; free.

YARMOUTH SZ3589

A lively place, its old harbour busy with yachts in summer. The **castle** was built as part of Henry VIII's coastal defences; it's in an excellent state, and you can see the Master Gunner's surprisingly homely parlour and kitchen. Outside, the open gun platform has good views of the harbour. Shop, disabled access to ground floor; cl Nov-Mar; (01983) 760678; £2.50; EH. The Wheatsheaf serves popular food all day.

Fort Victoria Country Park (Westhill, Norton) The various attractions in the grounds of this 19th-c fort make a nice, traditional family day out. Best reached on foot with lovely sea views along the way, the park has good picnic spots, and 50 acres of woodland to explore, though the mile or so of pebbly beach isn't ideal for swimming (strong currents). The attraction with the widest appeal is perhaps the aquarium. Don't expect showpiece walk-through tanks, but the displays are just as absorbing; disabled access; (01983) 760283; £1.90. Next door's model railway is one of the biggest layouts we've seen; unusually, it's all digitally controlled. Good shop; disabled access; (01983) 761553; £3.50. Another highlight is the planetarium, with half-hour multimedia shows throughout the day; (01983) 761555; £3.50; they usually do longer presentations Tues-Thurs evenings at 8.45 (£7), followed on clear nights by the chance to stargaze through the centre's telescopes. There's also a maritime heritage exhibition; lots on local wrecks, and a replica of one of the 'First Fleet' ships that carried convicts to Australia. Disabled access; £1.90. The attractions are open Easter-Oct, but the park itself is open free of charge all year round.

Yar estuary The unspoilt reed-fringed estuary is skirted by a footpath along the former railway line S from Yarmouth.

Where to eat

FRESHWATER SZ3487 **Red Lion** *Church Pl (01983) 754925* Civilised white-painted house with a comfortable open-plan bar, lots of local pictures and photographs, open fires, and extremely popular very imaginative food - best to book ahead; well kept real ales, a fine choice of 16 wines by the glass, and tables on a grassy back area (behind which is the kitchen's herb garden); walks nearby, especially around the River Yar; no food 25 Dec; children over 10; disabled access. £22|£7.50

ROOKLEY SZ5083 **Chequers** *Niton Rd (01983) 840314* Former customs and excise house that's marvellous for families, with a large no smoking family room, a large play area outside with toboggan run and bouncy castle, and mother and baby room; cottagey ornaments and log fire in comfortable carpeted lounge bar, lively locals' bar, well kept real ales, and generous helpings of interesting bar food; disabled access. £21|£6.95

SHALFLEET SZ4089 **New Inn** *(01983) 531314* Welcoming former fishermen's pub with a partly panelled flagstoned public bar, yachting photographs and pictures, scrubbed deal tables, Windsor chairs, and a roaring log fire in a big stone hearth, a carpeted beamed lounge bar with more boating pictures and a coal fire; popular crab or lobster salads and up to 16 good fresh fish dishes (the fish is bought from the quay only a short walk away) plus other enjoyable food, well kept real ales, and a decent wine list. £28|£7

SHORWELL SZ4583 **Crown** *(01983) 740293* Friendly and very popular old pub in an attractive rural setting, with a traditional atmosphere in four bustling rooms, individual furnishings, winter log fires, lots of houseplants, and several no smoking areas; enjoyable food (nicely presented daily specials), well kept real ales, and efficient service; picnic-sets and white garden chairs in the peaceful tree-sheltered garden, and decent play area; disabled access. £16.50|£6.50

YARMOUTH SZ3589 **Jireh House** *The Square (01983) 760513* 17th-c guest house with friendly owners, a relaxed atmosphere, and a range of home-made meals, snacks and afternoon tea inc daily specials and fresh fish; bdrms; cl Nov-Easter; disabled access (restaurant only). £17/special afternoon tea £4.40

Special thanks to Mrs Rita Cox, Miss Sharpe

KENT

Excellent mix of family attractions, wonderful castles and gardens, seaside resorts with traditional appeal, some charming countryside

Canterbury is a powerful draw for visitors, with many fine buildings besides the cathedral, and a few good museums (including some which appeal to children). Rochester with its dramatic castle is another worthwhile destination, especially if you like Dickens. Dating from pre-railway Victorian days, the NE seaside resorts have kept a certain dignified charm. Broadstairs (Dickens connections here too) is a fine example.

Inland, the Weald (roughly W of the M20) has peaceful and intimate landscapes of little hills and valleys, small pasture fields and oak woods, timeless windmills and villages with attractive tile-hung and weather-boarded houses, early medieval stone-built churches, and a good smattering of antiques shops, tearooms and so forth - pleasant territory for roaming about by car. The North Downs between the M20 and M2, also N of the M25/M26, are more open; the best parts are above Wye. The flatlands of Romney Marsh have a certain bypassed-by-time charm.

Fine houses and well preserved castles are one of Kent's specialities. The ones which children like best are Hever Castle (fun maze, and adventure playground), lively Leeds Castle, and magnificent Penshurst Place (toy museum); atmospheric Dover Castle has underground tunnels to explore. Enjoyable for adults are Knole in Sevenoaks (the grandiose home of the Sackvilles), the medieval manor at Ightham, and Squerryes Court in Westerham. Darwin's Down House in Downe, and Churchill's Chartwell (Westerham), have interesting displays on their former owners.

Magnificent gardens are another strong point here. Magical Groombridge manages to delight both adults and children; you'll find other beautiful gardens at Sissinghurst, Lamberhurst and Doddington. Gardeners will also find plenty to interest them at Hadlow, and for trees head to Bedgebury Pinetum. There's an enormous fruit forest at Brogdale (Faversham), and unusual organic gardens at Yalding. Several vineyards include Barham, Tenterden at Small Hythe, Penshurst, Lamberhurst and Sandhurst.

Chatham's fascinating Historic Dockyard (a lively working museum with lots going on - Kent's Family Attraction of the Year), and Hop Farm Country Park in Beltring (well organised, especially nice in summer), both have enough to keep families happy for the whole day, and Maidstone's Museum of Kent Life has more than enough for a laid-back afternoon. Elsewhere, there are unusual collections at Birchington's Powell-Cotton Museum and Quex House, and at Goudhurst's Finchcocks.

Kent's top wildlife parks are not just enjoyable - they have a strong conservation message too: the zoo at Bekesbourne, wildlife parks at Lympne, Wingham, and Wildwood in Herne Bay are all well worth visiting. If you prefer tamer animals, the good value South of England Rare Breeds Centre at Woodchurch and friendly Farming World at Boughton are good bets.

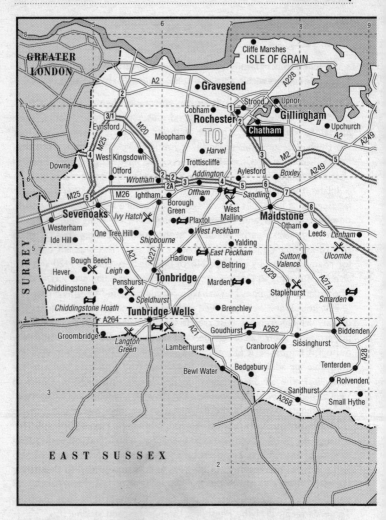

ASH TR2959 **Great Weddington** *Weddington, Ash, Canterbury, Kent CT3 2AR* *(01304) 813407* **£85**; 3 pretty bdrms. Regency country house surrounded by farmland and extensive gardens, with log fire in drawing room, enjoyable breakfasts and evening meals, and a relaxing atmosphere; no smoking; cl Christmas and New Year; children over 8

BOUGHTON LEES TR0147 **Eastwell Manor** *Eastwell Park, Boughton Lees, Ashford, Kent TN25 4HR (01233) 219955* **£200**, plus special breaks; 62 prettily decorated rms in hotel and 19 courtyard cottages (some cottages have their own garden and can also be booked on self-catering basis). Fine Jacobean-style manor (actually rebuilt in the 1920s) in 62 acres with croquet lawn, tennis court, two boules pitches and putting green; grand oak-panelled rooms, open fires, comfortable leather seating, antiques and fresh flowers, courteous helpful service,

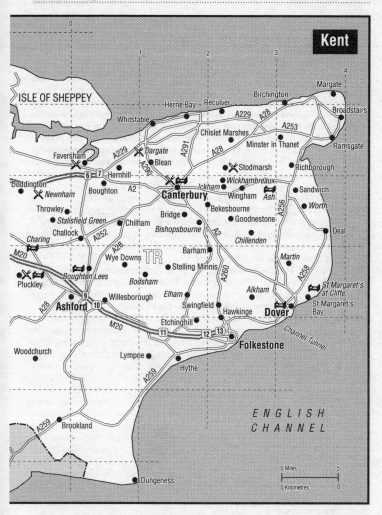

and extremely good food; health and fitness spa with 20-metre indoor pool and 14 treatment rooms, and lots of walks; disabled access; dogs welcome in bedrooms ☺
CANTERBURY TR1557 **Cathedral Gate** *36 Burgate, Canterbury, Kent CT1 2HA (01227) 464381* **£104**, plus special breaks; 27 rms, 12 with own bthrm and some overlooking cathedral. 15th-c hotel that predates the adjoining sculpted cathedral gateway; bow windows, massive oak beams, sloping floors, antiques and fresh flowers, continental breakfast in little dining room or your own room, and a restful atmosphere; municipal car parks a few minutes away; dogs welcome but bring own bedding
CANTERBURY TR1457 **Thanington Hotel** *140 Wincheap, Canterbury, Kent CT1 3RY (01227) 453227* **£76***, plus winter breaks; 14 rms, 5 large ones in the original house, 10 purpose-built ones linked to main building by Georgian-style conservatory. Thoughtfully run and warmly welcoming hotel with elegant little rooms, good-sized bar and cosy residents' lounge, enjoyable breakfasts, a games room, sun-trap walled garden, and indoor swimming pool; partial disabled access
CHARING TQ9247 **Barnfield** *Barnfield Rd, Charing, Ashford, Kent TN27 0BN*

(01233) 712421 **£50***; 6 beamed rms, shared big bthrm. Delightful early 15th-c farmhouse with fine beams, big open fires, comfortable sitting rooms, lots of books, antiques and homely knick-knacks, good breakfasts, friendly owners, and fine views over garden and lake; cl Christmas

CHIDDINGSTONE HOATH TQ4842 **Hoath House** *Penshurst Rd, Chiddingstone Hoath, Edenbridge, Kent TN8 7DB (01342) 850362* **£55**; 4 rms , 2 with own bthrm. Wonderful medieval house - added to over the years - with huge beams and plastered walls in the sitting room, family portraits, open fire in the library, heaps of interest and atmosphere, homely suppers, welcoming owners, and a big garden with fine views; they are kind to children; cl Christmas; disabled access☺

DOVER TR3241 **Churchill** *Waterloo Crescent, Dover, Kent CT17 9BP (01304) 203633* **£82**, plus special breaks; 66 comfortable rms, several with balconies. Above the harbour, this Regency terrace hotel has a congenial bar, sun lounge and terrace, friendly staff, and enjoyable food (lots of fresh fish) in brasserie-style restaurant overlooking the Channel; health club; disabled access

EAST PECKHAM TQ6651 **Roydon Hall** *East Peckham, Tonbridge, Kent TN12 5NH (01622) 812121* **£50***; 20 rms, some with own bthrm. Fine Tudor manor with many original features inc fine panelling in many of the public rooms, a peaceful atmosphere, and 10 acres of woodland and garden; vegetarian lunch and light supper by arrangement, and regular meditation courses; no smoking; cl Christmas/New Year/Easter; children over 4

GOUDHURST TQ7237 **Star & Eagle** *High St, Goudhurst, Cranbrook, Kent TN17 1AL (01580) 211512* **£80***; 10 character rms, 9 with own bthrm. Striking medieval inn with comfortable Jacobean-style furnishings in heavy-beamed day rooms, pretty views, polite staff, good food, and well kept ales; cl pm 25 Dec

MARDEN TQ7341 **Tanner House** *Goudhurst Rd, Marden, Tonbridge, Kent TN12 9ND (01622) 831214* **£50***; 3 rms (showers). Quietly set Tudor farmhouse on 150-acre, family-run mixed farm, with residents' lounge, inglenook dining room, large garden, and walks and picnic areas around farm; they breed shire horses, and have a quiet, secluded touring caravan and camping park with small play areas, and a shop; cl Christmas; children over 12

PLAXTOL TQ6054 **Jordans** *Sheet Hill, Plaxtol, Sevenoaks, Kent TN15 0PU (01732) 810379* **£68***; 3 rms, 2 with own bthrm. 15th-c no smoking house with leaded windows, beams, and an inglenook fireplace, good breakfasts, and pretty garden; the helpful owner is a qualified tourist guide, and can tell you about the many historic houses and lovely gardens nearby; cl mid-Dec to mid-Jan; children over 12

PLUCKLEY TQ9145 **Elvey Farm** *Pluckley, Ashford, Kent TN27 0SU (01233) 840442* **£69.50***; 10 rms, some in the oast house roundel, some in original barn and stable block. 15th-c farmhouse in secluded spot on 75-acre working family farm, with timbered rooms, inglenook fireplace, and french windows from lounge on to sun terrace; ample play areas for children; cl Christmas; partial disabled access; dogs welcome in bedrooms

SMARDEN TQ8842 **Chequers** *The Street, Smarden, Ashford, Kent TN27 8QA (01233) 770217* **£70**; 4 rms. Neatly kept 14th-c inn with friendly hard-working owners, a no smoking restaurant (and new one in fine barn conversion), lots of beams, flagstones and an enormous fireplace, a dining area with elegant reproduction tables and chairs, and a cosy, comfortable bar with a good relaxed atmosphere and plenty of chatty locals; enjoyable food, huge breakfasts, well kept real ales, and a decent wine list; in a very attractive village; cl 25 Dec

ST MARGARET'S AT CLIFFE TR3444 **Wallett's Court** *Dover Rd, Westcliffe, Dover, Kent CT15 6EW (01304) 852424* **£99**, plus special breaks; 16 rms, some in converted stable block with gentle views. Fine old manor house with 13th-c cellars, beams, antiques, comfortable seating and open fires, particularly friendly and helpful service, charming owners, and marvellous food; swimming pool and leisure facilities; they are kind to children; very close to ferries; cl 24-26 Dec; disabled access

TUNBRIDGE WELLS TQ5839 **Hotel Du Vin and Bistro** *Crescent Rd, Tunbridge Wells, Kent TN1 2LY (01892) 526455* **£136**; 36 very attractive individually decorated rms with CD players, satellite TV and power showers. Handsome sandstone building, extended in the 19th c, with a relaxed atmosphere in the two rooms of the bar, comfortable sofas and chairs in the lounge rooms, good modern cooking in the airy, high-ceilinged and informally french-feeling restaurant, and particularly good wines; seats on the terrace; disabled access

TUNBRIDGE WELLS TQ5739 **Spa Hotel** *Langton Rd, Tunbridge Wells, Kent TN4 8XJ (01892) 520331* **£138.50**, plus wknd breaks; 69 individually decorated rms. Run by the same family for three generations, this Georgian hotel stands in 14 acres of landscaped gardens; comfortable and quietly decorated, partly no smoking lounge, a popular and attractive bar with equestrian paintings and photographs, good enjoyable food in Regency-style restaurant, a carefully chosen wine list, and friendly long-serving staff; leisure centre with indoor heated swimming pool and well equipped gym; tennis court and pony riding; disabled access

WEST MALLING TQ6857 **Scott House** *High St, West Malling, Kent ME19 6QH (01732) 841380* **£79***; 5 pretty little rms. No smoking Georgian town house (from which the family also run an antiques and interior design business) with big comfortable lounge, good breakfasts in dining room, a friendly atmosphere, and helpful owners; cl Christmas/New Year; children over 10

To see and do

Kent Family Attraction of the Year

CHATHAM TQ7569 **Historic Dockyard** This excellent 80-acre working museum is very different from the historic dockyard we've highlighted in Portsmouth; though there are again several old ships to explore, the focus here is much more on the history of the site itself, with very well put together presentations and displays on the actual process of how those ships were built. Anyone even vaguely interested in maritime history could happily spend a good chunk of the day here. Family members who don't think it's their thing needn't despair: the Harbourmasters House in the dockyard, with seats out by the river wall, is a nice pub with Flagship beers brewed nearby, and a big new outlet shopping centre with waterside restaurant has just opened next to the dockyard. Tours of the various parts are exemplary, with costumed characters bringing vividly to life the days when this was one of the most important Royal dockyards in the country. A highlight is Wooden Walls, where a carefully researched story well illustrates how wooden warships like HMS *Victory* were built here. Over the last year they've considerably livened up tours of the ropery; this might not sound an instant must for children, but the new approach is great fun, and you can have a go at making your own rope, using traditional methods. Children also enjoy the extra activities laid on in the summer holidays, such as quiz trails and a very lively Air Raid drill, when at 11am and 3pm a siren sounds and everyone has to head for a shelter. Most visitors to the site go straight for the tours of the restored 1944 destroyer HMS *Cavalier* and the Cold War submarine *Ocelot*; there's also a Victorian sloop *Gannet*, the restoration of which was nearing completion as we went to press. Other exhibitions cover such diverse topics as the RNLI, with a collection of 16 lifeboats, and the role of beer in the Navy. The most complete Georgian dockyard in the world (though it dates back much further), it's a big site, and you can travel between the attractions on heritage buses similar to those that would have taken workers to the dockyard in the 1960s. Meals, snacks, shop, mostly disabled access (but not to ships); cl Dec/Jan, and some dates in Nov and Feb - best to check first then; (01634) 823800; £9.50 adults, £6 children 5-15. A family ticket for two adults and two children is £25; additional children are £3. You can get a ticket that includes boat trips on the paddle steamer *Kingswear Castle*.

ASHFORD TQ9843

Godinton House & Gardens 🖼 (off A20 N) An interesting mix of styles and tastes from the 14th c onwards; guided tours take in the fine panelling, and stunning collections of porcelain, pictures and furniture. Outside, you can see Blomfield's first garden design, enclosed by the country's longest yew hedge; also wild garden, 1920s italian garden and an 18th-c walled garden. Snacks, disabled access to gardens only; cl Oct-Good Fri, house cl Mon-Thurs, gardens cl Tues-Weds; (01233) 620773; £6 house and gardens, £3 gardens only.

AYLESFORD TQ7258

Friars These carefully restored 13th/14th-c buildings are once again home to a group of Carmelite friars. Fine cloisters and chapels, sculptures and ceramics by modern artists, working pottery, and beautiful grounds. Meals, snacks, shop, disabled access; cl 25 Dec-1 Jan (but grounds open); (01622) 717272; free. The Little Gem pub is very quaint and ancient.

Kits Coty House (towards A229) This massive Stone Age tomb chamber 'mightily impressed' Pepys; free.

BARHAM TR1947

Elham Valley Vineyard (SW of village, towards Elham) You can look around this friendly little vineyard, in a pretty and sheltered valley, and run by the Vale of Elham Trust which provides work for adults with learning disabilities. Pottery (demonstrations wkdys only), cream teas, wine sales, good craft shop; excellent disabled access; cl am wknds, best to check; (01227) 831266. The former B2065 through this valley is a pretty drive, and the Duke of Cumberland in Barham and Rose & Crown in Elham have enjoyable food.

BEDGEBURY TQ7233

Bedgebury Pinetum Lakeside landscaped valley full of an expanding collection of magnificent conifers, with walks up through forest plots designed to try out the commercial possibilities of all sorts of little-known species; walks vary from dragonfly surveys and early morning bird call walks to moth hunts. They're carrying out a programme of heathland restoration, and there's a new man-made lake; work on a new visitor and education centre is under way, too. Snacks, shop; open all year round; (01580) 211781; £3.50.

BEKESBOURNE TR1956

Howletts Zoo 🖼 (signed off A2) The first of the excellent wildlife parks founded by the late John Aspinall. Pleasantly spread over lovely grounds, it's well known (along with its bigger sister park at Lympne, see below) for its genuinely dedicated approach to looking after the rare or endangered animals and - more controversially, because of the danger - the bonds developed between the keepers and the animals. Highlights include the world's largest colony of breeding gorillas (over 100 have been been born here), and a herd of breeding elephants; the new glass-fronted tiger enclosure is good. Other animals include deer, antelope, leopards and gibbons; there's a new children's playground, and work has just begun on a model Saxon village. Meals, snacks, shop, disabled access; cl 25 Dec; (01227) 721286; *£11.95.

BELTRING TQ6746

Hop Farm Country Park (off A228) The conical Victorian oast houses used for drying hops are a distinctive feature of Kent and East Sussex; this is the largest surviving group, now converted into a popular and very well organised family outing. A couple of the galleried barns have comprehensive exhibitions, one on the hop industry, bringing to life with sounds and smells the experience of working on a hop farm, and the other an entertaining social history collection. Another barn has a big under-cover play area, and there are plenty of animals, and a pets corner (feeding sessions throughout the day). They also have an impressive collection of shire horses, stables tours and dray rides. Other areas include an aquarium, a collection of tanks and other military vehicles, and a working potter - you can have a go at making and painting your own creation (from 50p extra). Also an outdoor adventure playground, paddling pools, sandpits and a bouncy castle. Special events most summer wknds. Meals, snacks, picnic areas, some disabled access (not into oast houses); cl 24-26 Dec; (01622) 872068; £7.50 adults.

BEWL WATER TQ6733

The reservoir, dissected by the Kent/Sussex boundary, is skirted by a 13-mile path, and is surrounded by attractive partly wooded pasture. They have summer events, and it can be very busy on bank hols. Boat trips (Easter-Sept, wknds only in Oct; (01892) 890661; £3.50 wkdys, 50p more at wknds); trout fishing (01892) 890352; from £10.60; picnic areas, cycle hire (summer only; (01323) 870310; from £4 for an hour), and a great adventure play area. Interactive displays and videos about the reservoir, and interesting dry garden, overlooked by a glazed walkway. Meals, snacks, shop, disabled access; cl 25 Dec; £5 parking charge summer wknds and bank hols, £4 at other times.

BIDDENDEN TQ8538

Attractive village with several interesting old houses on the S side of the High St, and a handsome 13th-c **church** with a bold tower. The picturesque old Three Chimneys just W has good food.

Biddenden Vineyard and Cider Works (Benenden rd) Thriving wine- and cider-producing vineyard, reputedly Kent's oldest. All-year tastings, harvesting in late Sept and bottling in Mar. Snacks, shop, disabled access (but no facilities); cl Sun Jan-Feb and 24 Dec-1 Jan; (01580) 291726; free.

BIRCHINGTON TR3068

Powell-Cotton Museum and Quex House (off A28) Fascinating museum attached to fine Regency house with furnished period rooms. Eight galleries show the collections of the late Victorian explorer and naturalist Maj Powell-Cotton, with hundreds of well mounted african animals, ethnic artefacts and oriental art. The gardens include a Victorian walled garden with restored glasshouses, lawns, mature specimen trees, herbaceous borders and a woodland walk. Meals, snacks, shop, disabled access; open Tues-Thurs, Sun and bank hols Apr-Oct (house open pm only), plus gardens and museum open Sun only in Mar and Nov; (01843) 842168; £4, £3 in winter. The Minnis Bay beach is good, and just off the A28 W the 16th-c Bell at St Nicholas has enjoyable food.

BLEAN TR1161

Druidstone Park & Art Park 🖼 (A290) Farmyard, woodland trails, sculpture park and a couple of adventure playgrounds (one for under-5s). Snacks, shop, disabled access; cl end Nov-Mar; (01227) 765168; £4.10. Nearby Blean Woods are protected as a nature reserve, with well signed walks in the RSPB area.

BOROUGH GREEN TQ6356

Great Comp Garden (St Mary's Platt, 2m E) Interesting collection of trees, shrubs, herbaceous plants and heathers with fine lawns and paths. Snacks, plant shop, disabled access; cl Nov-Mar; (01732) 886154; £4. The Plough at Ivy Hatch a few miles S is a good restaurant.

BOUGH BEECH TQ4846

Bough Beech Nature Reserve At the N end of the reservoir, with wildlife exhibitions in a 19th-c oast house. Snacks, limited disabled access; open Weds, wknds and bank hols Apr-Oct; (01732) 750624; free. The Wheatsheaf has good food, and there are pleasant walks around here.

BOUGHTON TR0459

Farming World 🖼 (Nash Court) Friendly farm with traditional and rare breeds and heavy horses, tractor and waggon rides, nature trails, adventure playgrounds inc a new indoor one, walled garden, and seasonal fruit and veg. A hawking centre has daily flying displays and bird handling (summer only), and an incubation and conservation room where you can see baby birds hatching, and there's a new glass-fronted bee-keeping exhibition room. Meals, snacks, farm shop, disabled access (sensory garden specially designed for the disabled); cl Nov-Feb; (01227) 751144; *£4.75. The White Horse at Boughton Street has decent food all day.

BRENCHLEY TQ6840

Marle Place 🖼 Pretty garden around a fine 17th-c house (not open), with interesting plants, a walled scented garden, artists' studios and gallery, mosaic terrace, woodland walk, and ponds. Teas, picnic area; cl Oct-Mar, they hadn't decided their opening days for 2004 as we went to press, so best to phone; (01892) 722304; £4. The village has some attractive old houses, and the Bull does enjoyable lunches.

BRIDGE TR1953

Higham Park 🏠 It is claimed that this restored Palladian manor was the first house in the world to have a wireless set. The friendly owners are more than willing to pore through albums celebrating the house's colourful history with their visitors. The grounds are pleasant to stroll around: a highlight is the yew-lined italian water garden with water-lilies, secret garden, and extensive terraced rose garden. You can also see a replica of the classical temple built here by Harold Peto, and the renovated music room in the Victorian carnation house; seating 150, it's one of the largest in the country. Meals, snacks, shop, some disabled access; cl Fri and Sat, and Oct-Mar; (01227) 830830; £3.50 garden, £2.50 for tour of the house. In the attractive village, the White Horse has decent food.

BROADSTAIRS TR3967

The most attractive of the NE Kent seaside resorts, much of it dating from pre-railway Victorian days, when well-to-do Londoners came by boat. With its bathing huts, neat gardens and fishing boats, this is still tranquilly old-fashioned. There's a lively little harbour (where the Tartar Frigate has good views from its upstairs restaurant), plus seven small sandy bays (Joss Bay, slightly E from the centre, is excellent for families), refreshing clifftop walks, and lots of Dickens connections ('Our watering place', he called the town). Bandstand concerts usually 2.30pm on summer Suns. The arts centre on Crow Hill includes a developing local museum; free, charges for various special events and exhibitions. A pleasant way of approaching the town is to start from Ramsgate and walk along the coast - an easy 30-min stroll.

Bleak House Dickens Museum (Fort Rd) Dickens's favourite seaside residence, where he wrote *David Copperfield*, and which he used as the title for another novel. Lots of his belongings and related memorabilia, plus displays on local wrecks and smuggling. Shop, some disabled access; cl mid-Dec to mid-Feb exc wknds in Jan; (01843) 862224; £3.

Dickens House Museum (Victoria Parade) Former home of Miss Mary Strong, the basis for Betsey Trotwood in *David Copperfield* - the parlour is furnished as in the book. Also more of Dickens's letters and possessions. Shop; open Apr-Oct, and during Dec for special Christmas events, phone to check; (01843) 863453; £2.

BROOKLAND TQ9626

Fairfield church Standing quite alone in Romney Marsh NW of Brookland, this is a tent-roofed brick-and-timber building, remarkable for its utterly lonely surroundings - and attractive inside.

Philippine Village Craft Centre (A259 SW) Unique centre selling crafts from the Philippines, with some special events. Meals, snacks, limited disabled access; open wknds Easter-Whitsun, then daily till end Sept, other times by arrangement; (01797) 344616; free. The Walland Marsh here is an extension of Romney Marsh; the sign off the A259 to the Woolpack leads you to a particularly good pub with the right sort of atmosphere for the area.

CANTERBURY TR1457

At its most impressive out of season, as its compact and easily walked historic centre does get almost unpleasantly packed in summer. The most rewarding area is in the cathedral precincts, and the admission charge brings a measure of peace to one of Britain's greatest religious sites; the choicest parts elsewhere need a bit of seeking out. Good guided walks leave from the helpful visitor information centre on Sun St (2pm Apr-Oct, plus 11.30am July-Aug; (01227) 459779; £3.75), and every Fri and Sat at 8pm there are Ghost Tours (meet opposite Alberrys Wine Bar, Margaret St; (07779) 575831; £5). Summer boat trips leave daily from Kings Bridge; (07790) 534744; £5. If you're making your own way, don't miss Palace St, Burgate with the Buttermarket Sq, and St Peter's St, all of which have fine buildings, and you can follow quite a lot of the ancient city wall on a walk passing the remains of the Norman castle (some info panels, usually open). The city's Roman and ecclesiastical heritage is well known, but there are other remains here too, notably a prehistoric tumulus in Dane

John Garden. The Whitefriars area of town is currently being redeveloped to include a new shopping centre and library. There are good car park and ride sites at Wincheap, Sturry and New Dover Rd (£1.70 per car). The Olde Beverlie, part of a 16th-c almshouse block (St. Stephens Green), has enjoyable food, and the more central White Hart (Worthgate Pl, off Castle St, with a tree-shaded park opposite) is useful for its big garden.

Canterbury Cathedral Dramatically floodlit at night, this spectacularly lives up to expectations. The earliest parts are Norman, with much added in the 12th and 15th c. Rewarding features are everywhere - an airily impressive nave, fascinating stained glass, the Bell Harry Tower, lovely cloisters, and the shrine of Thomas à Becket, murdered here in the 12th c. The crypt has some wonderfully grotesque carvings, full of strange animals and fantastic fighting monsters. The precincts are particularly rewarding, containing buildings connected to the cathedral, inc the ruins of the former monastery in Green Court, the impressive Norman Staircase and the medieval King's School. Summer snacks, shop, disabled access; may be closed for services at certain times, limited opening Sun; (01227) 762862; £4 - note this isn't a donation, you'll be charged this just to enter the precincts. There are additional charges for guided tours, audio tours, audio-visuals, and photo permits. Entry to the services is free, and the choir's singing is then a bonus.

Canterbury Tales 🏛 (St Margaret's St) Well put together, Chaucer's characters brought enthusiastically to life with smells, sound effects and lively celebrity voices. Snacks, very good unusual shop, disabled access (prior notice preferred); cl 25 Dec; (01227) 479227; £6.75. They also have special events during most school hols.

Museum of Canterbury (Stour St) In the medieval Poor Priests Hospital with its magnificent oak roof, this is a splendid interpretation of the city's history, told with the deft use of up-to-date display technology - particularly rewarding; hands-on activities include looking at gold thread and medieval poo

under a microscope, and deciding how Christopher Marlowe died. There's also a gallery devoted to Rupert Bear, a wartime blitz experience, and displays on Joseph Conrad, and Bagpuss and the Clangers. Shop, good disabled access; cl Sun Oct-May, Good Fri and Christmas wk; (01227) 475202; £3. Hidden away through an arch beside the building is the charming Greyfriars, above the River Stour.

Roman Museum (Longmarket) Splendid underground museum, incorporating the remains of a Roman town house; lively reconstructions of a market and kitchen, as well as lots of hands-on and hi-tech displays. The mosaic floor is very well displayed. Shop, disabled access; cl Sun (exc Jun-Oct), Good Fri and Christmas wk; (01227) 785575; £2.70.

Royal Museum and Art Gallery (High St) Fine porcelain, and art collections, with the city's picture collection inc Victorian animal paintings by T S Cooper; the Buffs Regimental Museum is also here, telling the story of one of England's oldest regiments. Shop; cl Sun, Good Fri and Christmas wk; (01227) 452747; free.

St Augustine's Abbey (Longport) Founded at the end of the 6th c, but most of the remaining ruins date from the Benedictine rebuilding in the 11th c. A free audio tour takes you around the ruins and adjacent museum. Snacks, shop, disabled access; cl 24-26 Dec, 1 Jan; (01227) 767345; £3; EH.

St Martin's church (North Holmes Rd) The country's oldest church in continual use; the Venerable Bede wrote 1,300 years ago that it had been built by the Romans, and there are certainly Roman bricks in the walls.

West Gate Towers (where St Peter's St meets St Dunstan's St) The city's last remaining fortified gatehouse, built in the late 14th c, with interesting cells, and excellent views from the battlements. Children can do brass rubbing or try on replica armour. Shop; cl 12.30-1.30, all day Sun, Good Fri, Christmas wk; (01227) 789577; £1.

CHALLOCK TR0152
Beech Court Gardens 🏛 Peaceful gardens surrounding a medieval farmhouse, with lots of spring and

autumn colour; the firs and pines reflect the designer's admiration for Inverewe in Scotland. There are also a few farm animals, and a children's trail. Teas and snacks in oast house, picnic areas, plant sales and craft shop, disabled access; cl Fri and wknd am, and Nov-late Mar; (01233) 740735; *£3.75. The 17th-c Chequers by the pretty village green has good value food.

CHATHAM TQ7568

Fort Amherst (Dock Rd) Perhaps the finest surviving 18th-c fort in the country, with massive ditches, gun emplacements, a warren of tunnels and a firing gun battery. 18 acres of parkland, and occasional live re-enactments on Sun. Meals, snacks, shop; cl Jan-Feb, Mon-Tues Apr-Aug (exc school summer hols) and all wkdys Sept-Dec and Mar; (01634) 847747; £5. The Command House just below by the water does limited but decent food.

Historic Dockyard See *separate family panel on p.317.*

CHIDDINGSTONE TQ5045

A favourite kentish village, an unspoilt cluster of Tudor houses and buildings owned by the NT, in lovely countryside. The church and the mysterious stone which one story claims gives the village its name are worth a look. The Castle Inn has decent food all day.

Chiddingstone Castle 17th-c house rebuilt in castle style at the start of the 19th c; renowned paintings and antiquities from England, Egypt and the Orient, inc fine collections of japanese swords and buddhist art. Attractively restored landscaped grounds, and you can fish in the lake (£10 a day for two rods). Tearoom, shop, disabled access to ground floor only; open Thurs pm and Sun Jun-Sept, plus bank hols Easter, May and Aug; (01892) 870347; £5.

CHILHAM TR0653

The lovely village square is the prettiest in Kent, and several antiques shops reflect its popularity with visitors - in summer, get there early to catch it at its most photogenic. The Woolpack just down the hill is useful for lunch.

Badgers Hill Farm (New Cut Rd - towards Selling) Cheerily unspoilt spot, with cider-making, local crafts, a barrel merchant, free-roaming pigs, wallabies and other animals, play area and an old

little model village. Snacks, farm shop, disabled access; cl 24 Dec-Feb; (01227) 730573; free. Further towards Selling, the Rose & Crown at Perry Wood is a nice pub, with a lovely garden and woodland walks nearby.

CHISLET MARSHES TR2366

Thousands of geese and ducks; duck food by the bag from the nice little Gate Inn at Boyden Gate.

CLIFFE MARSHES TQ7279

N of Rochester, these are bounded by a long sea wall cum footpath which feels (and is) extraordinarily remote and not a little surreal - perhaps the best Thames Estuary walk in N Kent, an internationally important wildlife site (it's home to 200,000 birds in winter). The area is a fairly hot candidate for a new airport (among other factors the decision will balance the unpopular damage to wildlife, and very small but increased risk of bird-related air accidents, against the far smaller number of nearby people than would be adversely affected by expansion of Heathrow or Gatwick).

COBHAM TQ6570

Another attractive village, with a good mix of unspoilt buildings from various centuries - an excellent place to walk round (as Dickens liked to do). The partly 13th-c church is worth examining, with its magnificent brasses and tombs, as is the 14th-c **New College**, like a miniature Oxford college but far less known to visitors (open daily, disabled access; (01474) 812503; free). The Leather Bottle has decent food, interesting Dickens memorabilia and a good garden.

Cobham Hall 🏛 The Earls of Darnley once lived in this impressive place, now a girls' school. The décor is quite splendid in parts (some notable marble fireplaces), and there are lovely grounds. The outside of the building is currently being restored with the help of heritage lottery funds. Snacks, shop; open pm on selected Weds and Sun in the school hols; (01474) 823371; £3.50.

CRANBROOK TQ7736

This attractive miniature town has largely unspoilt lanes of tile-hung and weatherboarded buildings; also a friendly local history museum (open pm Tues-Sat and bank hols Apr-Sept;

£1.50), enjoyable up-to-date food at the White Horse, and for picnics Perfect Partners (Stone St) is the best delicatessen for many miles. The field walk to Sissinghurst and back is a pleasant way of joining two interesting places.

Cranbrook Union Mill Recent refurbishment to this working windmill included replacing its dutch-style sails (the mill was once owned by a dutch miller) with traditional kentish ones. The restored workshop has visual displays, while upstairs you can discover the history of the mill and its owners. Shop, open Sat and bank hols Apr-Sept, plus Sun mid-July to Aug; (01580) 712256; donations.

DEAL TR3752
Once the busiest harbour in SE England, and Caesar's landing point in 55BC; now a pleasantly understated seaside resort, full of pretty little streets and alleys - but beware of vigilant traffic wardens. The seaview Kings Head (Beach St) has good value food (and bedrooms).

Deal Castle The biggest in Henry VIII's chain of coastal defences, uniquely shaped like a Tudor rose with every wall rounded to deflect shot. Snacks, good audio tour, shop, disabled access to ground floor only; cl Mon and Tues Nov-Mar, and 24-26 Dec and 1 Jan; (01304) 372762; £3.50, EH.

Walmer Castle (just S) Another of Henry VIII's coastal defence fortresses, later the official residence of the Lord Warden of the Cinque Ports (one was the Duke of Wellington, who left behind his famous boot). It became more stately home than fortress, with rooms furnished in 18th-c style, and pretty gardens laid out mainly by a niece of William Pitt, and enlivened more recently. Snacks, shop, some disabled access; cl Mon and Tues Nov-Dec and Mar, wkdys Jan and Feb, 24-26 Dec, 1 Jan and whenever the Lord Warden is in residence; (01304) 364288; £5.50; EH.

DODDINGTON TQ9357
Doddington Place Gardens Grand 10-acre garden with formal plantings, some massive topiary, Edwardian rock garden, rhododendron woodland, broad views, folly and delightfully peaceful atmosphere. Snacks, plant sales, disabled access; open Sun pm Easter-July; (01795) 886101; *£3.50.

The George at Newnham is nice for lunch, with good walks nearby.

DOVER TR3241
The busiest passenger port in Europe, Dover is not in itself an attractive town but has several extremely interesting places to visit, reflecting the fascinating history it owes to its strategic importance; Blakes (Castle St) is a pleasant wine bar, and the seaview Mogul (Chapel Pl, off York St south roundabout) has simple food all day. The new De Bradelei Wharf factory outlet shopping complex at Wellington Dock is a useful place to pick up bargains.

Crabble Corn Mill (Lower Rd) Beautifully restored working 19th-c watermill. Fairs held year round. Meals, snacks (made with their own flour), shop, limited disabled access; open daily Apr-Oct, wknds only Nov and Feb-Mar, but best to check; (01304) 823292; £2.50, 50p extra for a tour guide.

Dover Castle Not to be missed, an excellently preserved magnificent Norman fortress with its original keep, 74-metre (242-ft) well, and massive walls and towers. There's a lot to see inc the atmospheric complex of underground tunnels that played a vital role in World War II, and an exhibition which dramatically re-creates an early 13th-c siege. Also included are the Pharos Tower (a Roman lighthouse using a 4th-floor flaring brazier as a guide-light), and a restored Saxon church. A walk round the battlements gives bird's-eye views of the comings and goings down in the harbour (something which captivates small children); the audioguide adds interest to your stroll. Meals, snacks, shop, disabled access; cl 25-26 Dec, 1 Jan; (01304) 211067; £8; EH.

Dover Museum (Market Sq) Excellent local history museum with three floors of displays. A highlight is the Bronze Age Boat Gallery, where you can see the world's oldest seagoing boat; other displays concentrate on Victorian Dover, the Romans and Saxons, and coal mining in Kent; also town models, touch-screen computers, hands-on displays and a film. New café, shop, disabled access; cl Sun, and 25-26 Dec, 1 Jan; (01304) 201066; £2, Dover residents free.

Dover Transport Museum (Whitfield, just off A2) All different kinds of road vehicles from bikes to buses (you might see some being worked on), a 1930s garage, model railway and tramway, and some maritime history. As we went to press they were moving across the rd, so best to phone for details; (01304) 822409; £2.

Grand Shaft An unusual Napoleonic spiral stone staircase which links top and bottom of Dover's famous cliffs; as we went to press, the local authority was looking for a private investor to take on the running of Grand Shaft, so best to phone Dover tourist information centre for opening days and price - should be £1.50 or less; (01304) 205108.

Roman Painted House £ (New St) Well preserved remains of Roman hotel with unique wall paintings, and elaborate underfloor heating system, fort wall and bastion. Brass rubbing, shop, disabled access (though no facilities); cl Mon, and Oct-Mar; (01304) 203279; £2.

Samphire Hoe (W of Dover, off A20 via steep road tunnel) Created from the spoil from the Channel Tunnel, this is Britain's newest land. Wild flowers have been encouraged, and a short walk around the site gives privileged views of the cliffs from beneath (something previously possible only from the sea); sea-angling here, day and season tickets available from teashop; (01304) 225688; charge for car park.

Western Heights Carved into the hillside are the remains of one of the largest Napoleonic fortresses in the country, now part of a local nature reserve, and surrounded by chalk meadows (wildflowers and butterflies in summer). One part of the fortress is now an immigration removal centre - ironic, given the fort's original purpose of repelling invaders. There are three circular walks, and trails with information panels; footpaths may be muddy and steep in places; free.

White Cliffs of Dover These provide an exhilarating walk (and interesting views of the harbour - you can even see France on a clear day) from Dover Castle to St Margaret's at Cliffe, passing the Roman lighthouse above Dover,

and a curious scaled-down windmill at St Margaret's. An open-top bus brings you back to Dover (no point making a circuit, as the inland scenery here is not worth while); (01304) 205108; £6, or you can press on to Kingsdown (the Rising Sun is a handy stop) or to Deal. The National Trust visitor centre at Langdon Cliffs is a good place to find out a bit about the area's history and wildlife. Snacks, shop, disabled access; cl 24-26 Dec; (01304) 202756; £1.60 car parking all day.

DOWNE TQ4464
Surprisingly rural village on the North Downs, technically in Greater London but quite kentish in character. Decent, though unspectacular, walking area, with very clearly marked paths inc the varied Cudham Circular Walk; a good starting point is High Elms, 1m NE, where from the car park you can stroll through the wooded High Elms estate. The Queens Head is a good pub.

Down House (Luxted Rd, out towards Westerham) Attractive restored house, former home of Charles Darwin who lived here with his family for 40 years, during which he wrote most of his major works inc *On the Origin of Species*. Filled with his personal belongings, notes and journals, the ground floor is much as it was when the Darwins were in residence, while upstairs is an interactive exhibition on Darwin's life and work; the gardens have also been restored. Snacks, shop, disabled access; cl Mon (exc bank hols), Tues, and 24 Dec-1st Weds in Feb; best to pre-book in Aug; (01689) 859119; £6; EH.

DUNGENESS TR0817
Fascinatingly odd, a real curiosity and quite foreign-feeling, its acres of shingle colonised by fishing shacks and railway carriages converted into homes (Derek Jarman used to live here). There are more pebbles than you could ever imagine. It's a terminus for the little steam railway described under New Romney, and the Britannia has good local fish.

Dungeness Nature Reserve RSPB, on the shingle headland, interesting for its unusual plants and variety of nesting and migrating birds. Snacks, shop, disabled access; cl 25-26 Dec; (01797) 320588; £3,

RSPB members free (informative guided walks from £2 extra).

Old Lighthouse Fine views from the top of its 167 steps; shop; open daily July–Sept, wknds only Mar-Jun (exc bank hols and school hols); (01797) 321300; £2.50.

ETCHINGHILL TR1638

Saxon Shore Way This long-distance path gives some good views and interesting walks. A section starting here crosses under an old railway line, heads up an unspoilt dry valley, and leads along the top of the slope for sightings of Dungeness and the french coast (Cap Gris Nez in Picardy).

EYNSFORD TQ5365

Eagle Heights Informative birds of prey centre, good in any weather as many displays are indoors (outdoor ones at 12 and 3.30pm). There's also a reptile house with some incredibly large pythons. You can meet snakes and reptiles (1.45pm) as well as the owls (2.15pm). Snacks, shop, disabled access; cl wkdys Nov-Feb; (01322) 866466; £6.30.

Eynsford Castle Norman fortress with impressive 9-metre (30-ft) walls, and remains of the hall and ditch; cl 24-26 Dec, and 1 Jan; (01322) 863467; free; EH. There are organised trails from the nearby countryside centre at Lullingstone Park, with various special events such as nature rambles, moth evenings and pond dipping; phone to book; (01322) 865995; from £5. The Malt Shovel has good seafood.

Lullingstone Castle Historic family mansion with fine state rooms, great hall, staircase and library, and beautiful grounds. The 15th-c gate tower was one of the first buildings to be made entirely of brick. Shop, disabled access; open pm wknds and bank hols May-Aug; (01322) 862114; £5.

Lullingstone Roman Villa (just SE off A225) Remains of 1st- and 2nd-c family's villa, with exceptionally well preserved floor mosaics and an extensive bath complex. Also an early Christian chapel - the only one so far found in a private house of that period. Shop, limited disabled access; cl 24-26 Dec and 1 Jan; (01322) 863467; £3.

FAVERSHAM TR0161

Delightfully photogenic small town ideal for a stroll: plenty of colour-washed timbered old buildings such as the Elizabethan grammar school and the Guildhall (one of the few raised market halls still to shelter stallholders in the pillared market court beneath it - Tues/Fri/Sat). The Sun in picturesque West St does good value lunchtime food, and by the riverside walkway (part of Saxon Shore long distance path) the Albion (Front Brents) has decent food inc summer cream teas. The **Shepherd Neame Brewery** in Court St has guided tours and tastings (no children under 14, and wear comfortable shoes as there are some steep staircases; booking essential, phone (01795) 542016; £5.20). Just N of the town, a track off the road to Oare leads to a remote waterside pub, the Shipwrights Arms: a charming setting on summer evenings.

Brogdale Orchard 🏛 (Brogdale Rd, S of A2) This mammoth fruit farm, inc the National Fruit Collection, is beautiful but baffling to stroll through (guided walks available), its 40 acres of orchards housing hundreds of distinct varieties of every hardy fruit imaginable; there are 2,300 variants of apple alone. The shop sells trees, bushes and flowering plants, as well as crops from pears, plums and cherries to cobnuts, quinces and medlars. Snacks, shop, disabled access; cl Dec-Mar; (01795) 535286; free (exc for special events), £4 for a guided tour.

Chart Gunpowder Mills (Westbrook Walk) Well restored gunpowder mill, one of the last left in the world (for another, see Waltham Abbey in Essex chapter), plus self-guided trail around Faversham's gunpowder heritage sites. Open pm wknds and bank hols Apr-Oct, by appointment at other times; (01795) 534915; donations.

Fleur de Lis Heritage Centre 🏛 (Preston St) This enthusiastically run museum has recently expanded; there are various colourful display and reconstructions, a gunpowder room, working vintage telephone exchange, and a Georgian town garden. Shop (good for books on Kent), mostly disabled access; cl 25 Dec-1 Jan; (01795) 534542; £2. The tourist information centre (limited hours Sun) is also here, and walking tours of Faversham leave at 10.30am every Sat Apr-Sept (£2).

FOLKESTONE TR2335

Despite much development of this port (now home to the Channel Tunnel), there's an intact pre19th-c area called the Bayle around the interesting old church - very pretty and kentish, with the British Lion a nice old pub. The part around the harbour, previously a picturesque warren, was badly bombed in World War II, but the fish stalls there contribute authentic local colour, the Old High St has a cornish-type quaintness, and Carpenters (The Stade) has good fresh fish. They're currently smartening up the town centre with new street furniture and paving and better lighting; a new shopping centre is on its way, and conference facilities have just been built. Just E of the harbour is the only sandy beach for miles (cramped at high tide but otherwise safe and popular). Particularly pleasant is a stroll along The Leas, a clifftop expanse of lawns and flower gardens with good views. For a longer walk carry on beyond The Leas down to Sandgate, an older village beneath the cliffs, somewhat picturesquely faded and with a cluster of antiques shops; the Clarendon, up a steep cobbled lane on the way, has enjoyable food. Return along the cycle path beneath the cliffs to a children' s adventure playground, where you can zigzag back up through a mock grotto to the top. A water-balanced Victorian cliff-lift operates between The Leas and the seafront. You can usually watch sweet- and rock-making on summer afternoons (exc Weds and Sun) at Rowlands Confectionery on the Old High St; (01303) 254723; free. A controversial 80-metre (265ft) Celtic-style white horse, recently cut into Cheriton Hill at a cost of £250,000, may have to be filled in after the European Commission said the project breached wildlife laws.

Battle of Britain Memorial (just W on B2011) The huge stone figure looking out in contemplation across the Channel gives this an extraordinary air of calm solemnity. Conservatory and Memorial Wall engraved with

Churchill's unforgettable tribute to the airmen. Snacks, shop, disabled access; cl Oct-Mar; (01303) 276697; free.

Folkestone Museum and Sassoon Art Gallery (Grace Hill) Brings the town's local and natural history to life through audio-visual displays and hands-on activities. A contemporary art gallery shows works by local and international artists. Meals, snacks, crafts shop, disabled access; cl bank hols; (01303) 850123; free.

Martello Tower Visitor Centre 🖼 (East Cliff) One of 74 towers built to defend the south coast from Napoleon's advances in the early 1800s, and later used as a World War II command post; it has various local history displays inside, and rewarding views from the top. Shop; open daily Apr-end Sept, cl 12.30-1.30pm; (01303) 852277; *£1.

Warren This intriguingly jungly tumbledown undercliff is reached from the East Cliff by a walk out past the Martello Tower; once there you can cross a railway footbridge and reach the shore, or go up a flight of steps and on to the clifftop, to return along the cliffs past the Battle of Britain Memorial. The cliff path also makes for a good bracing walk all the way to Dover, for the train or bus back.

GILLINGHAM TQ7669

Royal Engineers Museum 🖼 (Brompton Barracks, Prince Arthur Rd) More appealing than you might think, with sound effects, art and oddities brought back from various countries, a Harrier jump jet, and Wellington's battle-map from Waterloo. Snacks, shop, disabled access; cl Fri, and Christmas wk; (01634) 822839; £5. The town has a partly Norman church. Off the A2 between here and Boughton Street village, any of the little lanes take you deep into orchard country, with foody pubs at Dargate, Selling and Eastling; blossom-time Apr and early May, many farm shops with local apples Sept onwards. Covering a big swathe of former farmland, **Capstone Farm Country Park** (Capstone Rd) is typical of the rolling landscape of the North Downs. Visitor centre, pet area, picnic and play areas, fishing permits; (01634) 812196; free.

GOODNESTONE TR2653
Goodnestone Park ⊞ Old-
fashioned roses in traditional walled
garden recalling Jane Austen's stays in
the 18th-c house (not open). Also
woodland garden with fine trees. Teas,
nursery, some disabled access; cl Tues,
Sat, Sun am and Oct-Mar; (01304)
840107; £3.50. The Fitzwalter Arms has
good value food.

GOUDHURST TQ7237
Charming Wealden village, with quite a
few antiques shops and so forth, and
spectacular views from the graveyard of
the 14th-c hilltop church (but during
the day too much traffic for comfort).
Next to it the striking medieval Star &
Eagle, open all day, is a good stop.
Finchcocks ⊞ (off A262 W of
Goudhurst) The early Georgian house
and its lovely gardens are attractive, but
the main draw is the important
collection of working keyboard
instruments from the 17th c onwards.
Some of these are played whenever the
house is open, the well organised
recitals really adding to the
atmosphere; special events. Snacks,
shop, some disabled access; open pm
Weds-Thurs Aug, and pm Sun and
some bank hols Apr-Dec (otherwise by
appointment) - phone to check;
(01580) 211702; £7.50. The Green
Cross Inn up by the main road is good
for fish.

GRAVESEND TQ6573
New Tavern Fort (Milton Ave)
Originally built in the 1780s to defend
the Thames against the threat of a naval
attack from France, it was extensively
rebuilt in Victorian times (the huge guns
date from then); you can explore the
underground magazine complex, and
there's an exhibition on Gravesend
during the Blitz. Open Sat pm, Sun and
bank hols May-Sept, gardens open all
year; (01474) 323415; £1.50. Along by
the Tilbury ferry pier, the New Falcon
has decent food. Also in the gardens, a
14th-c Chantry now houses a local
history museum. Shop, limited disabled
access; usually open pm Weds-Sun
May-end Sept, pm wknds Oct-Dec, Mar
and Apr; (01474) 321520; £1.

GROOMBRIDGE TQ5337
Groombridge Place Gardens
(B2210) The glorious formal gardens

are still very much the main attraction,
but much has been done to make this
site more appealing to a younger
audience. The Enchanted Forest is a
series of quirky gardens designed by
Ivan Hicks, with surprises around every
corner, inc mirrors suspended from
trees above ponds, a formidable raised
walkway through the treetops with
rope slides, bridges and giant swings,
and a Celtic Forest with hidden snakes
and spiders. There's also a burgeoning
yew hedge maze, a giant rabbit
enclosure, and a birds of prey centre
(flying displays 11.30am, 1, and 3.30pm).
Many of the gardens date back 300
years, as do the famous peacocks;
highlights include the white rose
garden, and the pretty little secret
garden. Quite a few species flower
earlier than they do elsewhere, as the
gardens are walled and south-facing.
Beautifully arranged around a 17th-c
moated mansion (not open), the
gardens have inspired generations of
artists and writers: Sir Arthur Conan
Doyle set a scene in his Sherlock
Holmes novel *The Valley of Fear* here,
and there's a re-creation of his study.
You can take a canal boat trip between
the formal gardens and the Enchanted
Forest. Meals, snacks, shop, some
disabled access (to formal gardens, but
not Enchanted Forest); open Apr-6
Nov; (01892) 863999; £8.30. At wknds
and school holidays (though not usually
Mon or Tues), a particularly enjoyable
way to get here is on the Spa Valley
Railway, from Tunbridge Wells (see
entry below); a combined ticket is
available. Nr the entrance, the prettily
placed Crown does good food, and the
Junction Inn (Station Rd) is now also
good for food.

HADLOW TQ6249
Broadview Gardens A good mix of
traditional and imaginatively themed
gardens put together by students at
Hadlow College; the dramatic Heaven
and Hell Garden is one of our
favourites. National collections of
hellebores and japanese anemones, and
a well stocked plant centre. Meals
wkdys only, snacks, shop, disabled
access; cl 25-26 Dec; (01732) 850551;
£2; free car parking. Hadlow's church
has an interesting memorial dedicated

to the 30 hop pickers who one wet day
in 1853 drowned on their way back
from the fields; the enormously tall folly
of Hadlow Tower is worth a look.

HAWKINGE TR2039

Kent Battle of Britain Museum
Plenty of aeroplanes, and extensive
collection of relics and memorabilia of
british and german aircraft involved in
the fighting, inc relics of more than 600
crashed aircraft. Snacks, shop, disabled
access but no facilities; cl Mon, and
Nov-Easter; (01303) 893140; £3.50.
The Valiant Sailor at Capel-le-Ferne
(A20) saves you going into Folkestone
for lunch.

HERNE BAY TR1868
Decorous and spaciously laid-out
19th-c resort, with one or two pleasant
diversions. There's a decent art gallery
on William St; shop, disabled access;
open Mon-Sat, plus Sun pm July-Aug;
(01227) 367368; free. The working
windmill on Mill Lane is also worth a
visit; shop; open pm Sun and bank hols
Easter-Sept, plus Thurs in Aug; (01227)
361326; £1. Mike Turner runs boat
trips around the bay and out to see
seals, May-Oct; best to book for the
seal trip (01227) 366712. There are
band concerts on summer Sun, and a
Sat market all year. The Rose
(Mortimer St) is good value for lunch.
Wildwood (Herne Common) Decent
woodland wildlife park, strong on
conservation, which has just introduced
konik horses, and has the only breeding
pack of european wolves in Britain;
other animals to spot include deer,
badgers, and polecats. Costumed artists
demonstrate ancient crafts in the re-
created Saxon village, and there's an
enjoyably varied programme of events
throughout the year; also picnic and
play areas. Meals, snacks, shop, disabled
access; (01227) 712111; £7 summer, £5
winter, £6.60 rest of year. The First &
Last (A291 just N) has decent food.

HERNHILL TR0659
Mount Ephraim Gardens 🔲 Eight
acres of pleasant gardens, with
japanese-style rock garden, topiary
garden, water garden, woodland walk, a
rose garden, and a developing grass
maze; good views. Teas, shop; cl am,
Tues, Fri, and Oct-Easter; (01227)
751496; *£3.50. There's a craft centre

on Sun pm. By the church and small
green of this charming village, the
ancient Red Lion has decent food.

HEVER TQ4745
Hever Castle & Gardens In 30
beautiful acres, double-moated 13th-c
castle little changed externally since
Anne Boleyn lived here as a child. Inside
it's a different story, as the rooms were
magnificently restored by the Astor
family in the early 1900s. Antiques,
furnishings and art mostly from 16th c,
plus a room dedicated to Henry VIII's
wives. Another building is home to an
exceptional collection of astonishingly
detailed miniature houses, furnished
and decorated in authentic period
styles. The council chambers in the
gatehouse (the oldest part of the castle)
are also open to visitors; various
gruesome instruments of torture are
on display, and new information boards
cover the castle's history. The grounds
are a draw in their own right, with a 35-
acre lake, italian garden with antique
sculptures, walled rose garden and
maze; also very popular summer
splashing water maze, and adventure
playground. There are frequent Tudor
costume events in summer. Meals,
snacks, shop, good disabled access to
gardens, but to ground floor only of
castle; cl Nov-Feb, castle cl am; (01732)
865224; £8.40, £6.70 gardens only. The
Henry VIII is popular for lunch.

HYTHE TR1634
A hillside town full of attractive
corners: above the narrow High St,
steep paths and lanes lead up towards
the church, and there are numerous
pleasant old houses. A path from the
junction of Station Rd (B2065) and Mill
Lane enters parkland and continues up
to Saltwood Castle (not open to the
public), which still has its impressive
medieval curtain wall. You can extend
the walk W to Lympne Castle and the
Royal Military Canal at West Hythe. On
the seaward side, beyond the Royal
Military Canal, Hythe is quite different
in character, though still distinctly quiet,
with a beach stretching to Sandgate,
also pleasant to stroll through.
**Romney, Hythe & Dymchurch
Railway** 🔲 Well run and friendly, this
is the world's smallest-scale public
railway, and the longest miniature

railway in Europe. Opened in 1927, its 13½ miles of 15in-gauge track run between Hythe and Dungeness, through the little seaside resort of Dymchurch. The station has a toy and model museum with two magnificent model railways. Engines are often changed en route, and the carriages are comfortable. Meals, snacks, shop, disabled access (they prefer notice); trains usually daily Apr-Sept, wknds Oct and Feb, Mar - phone for timetable; (01797) 362353; £9.60 full fare (but wide range of lower ones).

St Leonard's Church The crypt houses an amazing collection of 2,000 skulls and 8,000 thigh bones, dating from before 1500 and all neatly arranged on shelves or carefully stacked in a large heap; Shop, disabled access (exc to crypt); cl Sun am (exc for services), and Oct-Apr; 50p.

IDE HILL TQ4851
With its pubs and picture-book green, this is on the scarp slope of the lower greensand escarpment, and on the Greensand Way: a good walking area. Views from the eponymous wooded rise, Ide Hill, reached from behind the church, just to the S.

Emmetts Garden (Toys Hill, 1m NW) Charming hillside shrub garden with magnificent views - it's one of the highest gardens in Kent. Full of bluebells in spring and a riot of colour in autumn. Snacks, shop, some disabled access; open wknds, Weds and bank hols Apr-Oct (Weds-Sun Apr-Jun); (01732) 868381; *£4; NT.

IGHTHAM TQ5853
Ightham Mote (off A227, 2m S) Lovely medieval manor house, still with its surrounding moat, a unique survival that looks esp beautiful on a sunny day. Fascinating restored great hall, Tudor chapel and 14th-c crypt; the drawing room has a striking Jacobean fireplace, frieze and windows. You can look around a Victorian housekeeper's room and, if there are enough staff, visit the tower; restoration of the South-West Quarter should be complete by spring. Pretty courtyard, garden and woodland walks. New restaurant, shop, disabled access; cl Tues, Sat, and 7 Nov-28 Mar; (01732) 810378; *£6.50; NT. The early 16th-c George & Dragon in

the village is a good all-day dining pub (just lunchtime on Sun).

ISLE OF SHEPPEY TR0469
Walkers may enjoy the E end, with a path along the sea dyke S from Leysdown-on-Sea to Shell Ness, at the mouth of the Swale.

LAMBERHURST TQ6436
Bayham Abbey (2m W, just over Sussex border) Impressive ruins of 13th-c Premonstratensian abbey and gatehouse in pretty wooded valley. Occasional outdoor theatre and special events. Snacks, shop, disabled access; cl wkdys Nov-Mar, and 24-26 Dec, 1 Jan; (01892) 890381; £2.50. The Elephants Head at Hook Green is a useful nearby pub.

Lamberhurst Vineyard
(B2100/B2169 just S) One of the biggest vineyards in SE England, no tours but you can wander round, and there are free tastings; play area and garden centre. Meals (in the vineyard's pub), snacks, shop, limited disabled access; cl 25 Dec-2 Jan; (01892) 890412; free.

Owl House Gardens 🖾 (off A21 NE) 16 acres of sweeping lawns, flowers, shrubs and fruit trees around timber-framed 16th-c wool smugglers' house; sunken water gardens and woodlands. Snacks (exc Sept-Apr), shop, some disabled access; cl 25 Dec, 1 Jan; (01892) 891290; £4 (free for wheelchair users).

Scotney Castle Garden (A21 just S) Beautiful 19th-c gardens surrounding the ruins of a small 14th-c moated castle, with impressive rhododendrons, azaleas and roses - a really romantic place. Shop, some disabled access (they recommend a strong pusher); open Weds-Sun and bank hols 20 Mar-Oct (exc Good Fri), castle open same hours May to mid-Sept, but best to check; (01892) 891081; *£4.40; NT. A public footpath strides through the estate's woods and pastures, which can form a basis for circular walks from Kilndown to Lamberhurst and back. The Brown Trout, on B2169 nearly opposite the main entrance, has good fish. The attractive village is at last likely to gain a sorely needed bypass in the next few years (it got the original go-ahead back in 1992, but endless delays have included most recently a costly redesign to add a 'land bridge' to the castle).

LEEDS TQ8353

Leeds Castle Long renowned as one of the loveliest castles in the country, perfectly placed on two little islands in the middle of a lake in 500 acres of landscaped parkland. It dates from the 9th c, and was converted into a Royal residence by Henry VIII. Lots of paintings, furniture and tapestries, and a unique dog-collar museum in the gatehouse. The enormous grounds have gardens (inc a mediterranean one), a maze and grotto, duck enclosure and aviary (well liked by readers), and a golf course. It's a busy place, not quite as idyllic as it appears from a distance, but very satisfying for a day out. Special events from food and wine festivals to open-air concerts. Meals, snacks, shop, good disabled access; cl 26 Jun, 3 July, and 25 Dec; (01622) 765400; around £11, but seasonal changes to prices. The Windmill at Eyhorne Street is good value for lunch.

LYMPNE TR0935

Port Lympne Wild Animal Park In wonderful ornamental parkland around a well restored house, Port Lympne and its sister park Howletts are well known for their genuinely dedicated approach to looking after the rare or endangered animals in their care; animals are kept in enclosures as close to their natural habitat as possible, with an aim to return them to the wild if they can, and in their turn the animals seem to treat their keepers almost as honorary members of their own species. There's a lot to see, paths can be steep, and there are 300 acres altogether - safari trailers run between attractions (£2). The gorilla-breeding programme (shared with Howletts) of 65 lowland gorillas is the most successful of its kind in the world. The park is also home to the country's largest breeding herd of black rhino. Other animals include tigers, elephants, lions and tapirs, and they hold occasional special talks and events. The house has unusual features, inc the Hexagonal Library used to sign the Treaty of Paris after World War I, Rex Whistler's incredible Tent Room, and one room entirely covered by a mural showing south-east asian animals and birds.

Meals, snacks, shop, disabled access; cl 25 Dec; (01303) 264647; £11.95.

Royal Military Canal Built along the N fringe of Romney Marsh as a defence against Napoleon, this forms a section of the Saxon Shore Way long-distance path. You can combine it with a path along the escarpment at Lympne Castle; the Botolphs Bridge Inn just S has decent home cooking.

MAIDSTONE TQ7555

Busy modern town, worth penetrating for its good museums. There are daily boat trips between here and the Malta Inn at Allington, hourly from 11.45am, wknds (and daily during school hols) Apr-Oct; (01622) 661064; £3. The Pilot (Upper Stone St) has good value food.

Maidstone Museum and Bentlif Art Gallery (St Faiths St) Handsome Elizabethan manor house with original period room settings, and an earth heritage gallery with life-size model dinosaurs. Snacks, shop; cl 25-26 Dec; (01622) 602838; free.

Museum of Carriages Notable collection of horse-drawn vehicles housed in the palace stables. Shop, disabled access to ground floor only; cl 25-26 Dec; (01622) 754497; £2. The site also includes the old parish church of All Saints.

Museum of Kent Life 🅰 (Sandling) The story of the Kent countryside, entertainingly told over 27 acres, taking in farming tools, crafts, gardens, animals, and an oast house; recent additions are a 1950s house and a 19th-c chapel. There are also two historic cottages, rescued from the path of the Channel Tunnel rail link at Lenham Heath; Old Cottage tells the story of the rescue, while Waterstreet Cottage has been reconstructed in World War II style. Children's play area, barrel-making at the new cooper's shop, and lots of special events. Meals, snacks, shop, disabled access; cl Nov-Feb (exc wknds); (01622) 763936; £5.50. Nearby, the well restored 17th-c Tyland Barn on Bluebell Hill is the HQ of Kent Wildlife Trust, with information on the area's nature reserves; cl 22 Dec-beginning Feb; (01622) 662012; free. The 16th/17th-c Kings Arms in the pretty neighbouring village of Boxley has decent food (all day Sun), with pleasant walks nearby.

MARDEN TQ7444
This attractive village has a 12th/14th-c ragstone church with a unique white weatherboarded tower, and other buildings going back to the 14th c. **Marden Meadow** (Staplehurst Rd) is a lovely unimproved hay meadow, alive with wild flowers and butterflies in late spring and early summer. The Wild Duck just S (Pagehurst Lane) has good food.

MARGATE TR3571
Often rather brash seaside resort, but with excellent sandy beaches (this was the first resort to introduce donkey rides and deck chairs). It's become a bit run down, but huge EC grants are going some way towards restoring its glory days, and a controversial £20m Turner gallery (critics argue it will destroy the view that he immortalised) is planned for 2007 - the artist visited the town regularly, and it inspired more than 100 of his paintings. You can find out more about Turner and the regeneration of the Old Town (which they'd like to turn into an artists' quarter) at Droit House in the harbour; cl Mon, free. The Old Town Hall (Market Pl) has a local history museum (cl Mon Easter-Sept, plus Tues-Weds in winter, and usually 3 wks over Christmas, but phone to check; (01843) 231213; £1), and nearby is the well preserved Tudor House, open only on special occasions, but worth a look from outside. It is not yet known what will replace the Dreamland theme park, which was about to close as we went to press. The Spread Eagle (Victoria Rd) has popular food. To the E of town on College Rd is a working windmill (usually open Sun pm May-Sept and Thurs eve Aug, but best to check; (01843) 226227; £1).
Margate Caves 🖼 (Northdown Rd) These huge caverns are atmospheric - with wall paintings and spooky shapes and shadows. Shop; open Easter-Oct; (01843) 220139; £2.
Shell Grotto 🖼 (Grotto Hill) An unexpected puzzle is this 185 sq metre (2,000 sq ft) of winding underground passages and exquisitely decorated tunnels leading to a mysterious ancient shell temple, thought to be the only one in the world. No-one knows its origins or what it was for, but a museum shows all the different theories, so you can make up your own mind. Gallery with exhibitions, art workshops, craft fairs, and Santa's grotto wknds in Dec. Snacks, shop; grotto cl wkdys Nov-Easter, plus 25-26 Dec and 1 Jan; (01843) 220008; *£2.

MEOPHAM TQ6365
Meopham windmill 🖼 Unusual both for its six sides and for the fact that its base is a meeting place for the parish council; it has recently undergone a substantial restoration, and is now fully working. Shop; usually open pm Sun and bank hols May-Sept, plus wkdys by arrangement; (01474) 813518; £1. The Cricketers prettily set on the green is a useful food pub.

MINSTER IN THANET TR3164
Minster Abbey (Church St) Site of one of the earliest nunneries in the country; founded in 670, with ruins and cloisters dating from the 11th c. The present house is still run by Benedictine nuns. Shop, some disabled access and facilities; open 11am-noon, then 2.30-4pm, am only Oct-Apr, cl Sun and Sat pm; (01843) 821254; free. The Bell (High St) has enjoyable fresh food.

ONE TREE HILL TQ5653
Reached from a NT car park S of Godden Green (where the old Bucks Head facing the duck pond is useful for lunch), this gives walkers a grand view over the Weald. From here the Greensand Way (look for GW markers) follows the very edge of the Lower Greensand escarpment which dips gently down to Ightham Mote, two miles E; Ivy Hatch and Stone Street have handily placed pubs to make this into a circuit.

OTFORD TQ5159
This charming village has a ruined archbishop's palace, food all day in the attractive Tudor Bull, and pleasant walks along an easy track to the attractive and largely unspoilt nearby village of **Shoreham**, which has a lovely church and several decent pubs. The downlands to the E give scope for longer walks across Magpie Bottom and past Romney Street.

OTHAM TQ7953
Stoneacre Lovely half-timbered 15th-c manor house, restored in 1920s, with charming cottage garden. Open pm Weds and Sat 24 Mar-17 Oct;

(01622) 862157; £2.60; NT.

PENSHURST TQ5243

A pretty village, with antiques shops, teas and so forth. The Leicester Arms now has good food all day. This attractive area has some of the Weald's most luscious lowlands, predominantly pasture, the cottages characteristically tile-hung, and the paths just elevated enough to gain charming views. As with much of the rest of the area, route-finding for walks is fiddly and patient map-reading is in order. One of the best circular routes, passing the Bottle House on Coldharbour Rd past Smarts Hill and the Rock at Chiddingstone Hoath (both good pubs), loops between Penshurst and Chiddingstone. **Penshurst Place** A great medieval manor house, unchanged since the Sidney family first came here centuries ago. Interesting combination of architectural styles, huge chestnut-beamed baronial hall, extensive collections of portraits and furnishings, toy museum, and marvellous formal gardens with woodland trail and adventure playground; special events. Snacks, shop and plant centre, disabled access to grounds (inc a garden for the blind); house cl am, wkdys in Mar, and Nov-Feb; (01892) 870307; £7, grounds only £5.50.

Penshurst Vineyard (Grove Rd, off B2188 S) Self-guided tours, tastings and various animals inc wallabies and exotic waterfowl. Cl 24 Dec-2 Jan, and wknds Jan and Feb; (01892) 870255; £1.50 to see the animals (children free).

PLAXTOL TQ6154

Old Soar Manor An ancient oak door at this 13th-c knight's dwelling has graffiti spanning the ages, and there's also a very well preserved chapel and barrel-vaulted undercroft; cl Fri, and late Sept-early Apr; (01732) 810378; free; NT. This general area is attractive orchard country, not too hedged, with good value apples from the farm shops, from Sept onwards; many here also have fresh cobnuts in Sept. The Tudor Kentish Rifleman (Dunks Green) has good food and an appealing garden.

PLUCKLEY TQ9245

This attractive estate village saw the filming of *The Darling Buds of May*, and has good pubs for refreshment, and

pleasant if not well marked walks.

RAMSGATE TR3864

Quietly civilised seaside resort, with some elegantly colonnaded Georgian buildings and other fine houses up on the cliffs (Pugin, the architect of parts of the Houses of Parliament, designed the church - where he's buried - and the house next door), and a historic harbour with a bustling yacht marina. On Harbour Parade the Ramsgate Royal Harbour Brewhouse is an unusual belgian-style café-bar doing its own brewing and baking all day.

Maritime Museum (Pier Yard) Good collection of historic ships and boats in a handsome early 19th-c harbour clock-house. Shop; cl Mon Easter-Sept, phone for winter opening; (01843) 587765; £1.50.

Motor Museum 🖾 (West Cliff Hall, The Paragon) Vintage cars, motorbikes and bicycles in cheerful period settings. Shop, disabled access; open daily Apr-Sept, and Sun only in winter; (01843) 581948; £3.50.

RECULVER TR2269

Reculver Towers & Roman Fort Built in the 3rd c, this was well preserved until the early 19th c, when cliff erosion collapsed some of it into the sea; some parts remain, though it's the proud pair of tall Saxon towers of the former church on the mound above the beach that stay in the memory. Surrounding these remains is a **country park**, with a visitor centre. Meals, snacks, shop, disabled access; site open all year round, visitor centre cl Mon exc bank hols, plus Tues in Sept, and Mon-Sat Oct-Mar; (01227) 740676; free; EH.

RICHBOROUGH TR3260

Richborough Castle In Roman times, this was Britain's port of entry, and a sizeable town grew up here. You can still see the base of a vast triumphal arch which started people on their Watling Street journey inland, and there are appreciable relics of the Roman castle curtain wall and other foundations; plus a small museum. Snacks, shop, disabled access; cl Mon and Tues Mar, all wkdys Nov-Feb, 25 Dec, and 1 Jan; (01304) 612013; £3 (inc audio tour); EH.

ROCHESTER TQ7468

This busy town is well worth walking

round, with several attractive buildings besides those we mention; one of the quaintest is Kent's oldest pub, the Coopers Arms (St Margaret's St; cheap lunches), and many of those on the High St feature in Dickens's novels. Casa-Lina (High St) has nice italian family cooking.

Charles Dickens Centre (High St) Late Tudor house used in both *Pickwick Papers* and *Edwin Drood*, with scenes and characters from the author's books brought vividly to life using impressive hi-tech effects. Shop; cl 24-26 Dec, and 1 Jan; (01634) 844176; £3.90.

Gad's Hill School (Higham, A226 NW) Dickens fans should also try to visit this, the only house the writer ever owned. He wrote many of his novels here, and his first sight of the house, many years before he lived there, is described in *A Christmas Carol*. Cream teas; open pm first Sun of month, plus bank hol Sun, during Rochester's summer and Christmas Dickens festivals, and other times - out of school hours - by arrangement; (01474) 822366; £3.50.

Guildhall Museum (High St) The highlight is a three-tier life-size replica of a late 18th-c convict hulk which was once moored on the Medway. There are also re-created Victorian and Edwardian drawing rooms, lots of Victoriana, 18th-c portraits, local history, hands-on exhibits for children, and a new 1900s kitchen. The decorated plaster ceilings are impressive; changing exhibitions. Shop, disabled access to ground floor only; cl 25-26 Dec; (01634) 848717; free.

Restoration House ⌂ (Crow Lane) From Tudor beginnings to recent conservation work, you can trace the development of this city mansion where Charles II stayed and Dickens reputedly found inspiration for the home of Miss Havisham in *Great Expectations*; fine furniture and pictures inc works by Kneller, Reynolds and Gainsborough. Pepys kissed a shopkeeper's wife in the very english interlinked walled gardens. Open Thurs and Fri Jun-Sept, phone to check; (01634) 848520; £5.50 (inc a guidebook), £2 gardens only.

Rochester Castle One of the best examples of 12th-c military architecture - dramatic too; the great square keep is one of the tallest in England. Shop; cl 25-26 Dec and 1 Jan; (01634) 402276; £3.90, audio tour 50p; EH.

Rochester Cathedral Spectacularly Norman, with original richly carved door, vaulted crypt, St Gundulf's tower, tombs and effigies, and huge 15th-c window. This year is the cathedral's 1400th anniversary and lots of special events are planned; phone for details. The new fresco here is the first to be painted in an english cathedral for 800 years; by contrast the Gundulf Door is England's oldest, with wood dating from 822. The choir sings Evensong at 5.30pm wkdys, 3.15 wknds. Snacks, shop, good disabled access; (01634) 401301; £3 suggested donation.

ROLVENDEN TQ8331
Good walking territory, with consistently appealing Wealden scenery, a **windmill** (not open to the public) and oast houses gracing the landscape; the Star has enjoyable food.

C M Booth Collection of Vehicles ⌂ (High St) Some unusual features inc a unique collection of 3-wheeled Morgans and a 1930s caravan; also toy and model cars and other automobilia. Shop; cl Sun, and 25-26 Dec; (01580) 241234; £2.

SANDHURST TQ7828
Sandhurst Vineyard ⌂ (Hoads Farm, Crouch Lane) Tours of vineyard and hop gardens (£2.50 with guide, otherwise free); hop-picking in Sept. Tastings and shop; cl am, and Jan-Easter exc by arrangement; (01580) 850296; free. They do B&B in a 16th-c farmhouse. The village has a fine 14th-c **church** with good views from the churchyard.

Tile Barn Nursery (Standen St, Iden Green) The only nursery in the world to specialise in wild cyclamen, with four greenhouses filled with over two dozen miniature species, most of them hardy, in flower Sept-Apr, also other rare bulbs. Cl Sun-Tues; (01580) 240221; free. The 17th-c Woodcock signed nearby has decent food.

Wealden walk E of the village (which has a fine 14th-c church with good views from the graveyard) a pleasant round walk runs from Burnt House Farm on the A268, via Cledge Wood and Marsh Quarter Farm to the Kent Ditch and the River Rother, to take you round to Bodiam Castle in Sussex, and back via Northlands Farm and Silverden.

SANDWICH TR3358

One of the best-preserved old towns in South-East England, and surprisingly untouristy: in many of the quiet old streets there's not a jarring note, with fine timbered buildings in Strand St and by the attractive former quay on the River Stour, nr the photogenic Bargate. You can go on a guided tour of the handsome Elizabethan guildhall in New St (11.30am and 2.30pm Tues-Thurs exc mid-Dec to Feb, or by arrangement; (01304) 617197; £1). The numerous medieval remains include some sections of the old town wall and three handsome medieval churches, one part-Norman. In its day it was one of England's main commercial ports; the sea's now left it far behind. The Admiral Owen (High St), Kings Arms (Strand St) and Red Cow (Moat Sole) all have decent food and long histories, and the St Crispin in the pretty village of Worth just S is also pleasant for lunch.

White Mill ⊞ (A257 just outside) A cheerful developing place around an 18th-c smock mill, with a little rural history museum and a cottage furnished in pre-1939 style. Shop, limited disabled access; open all year am Fri and Sun, plus pm Sun and bank hol Mon Easter to mid-Sept; (01304) 612076; £2.

SEVENOAKS TQ5453

Although there's little to see in this commuters' town apart from the handsome old buildings of Sevenoaks School, the area around it has more walk potential than a glance at the OS map might suggest. The terrain is complicated, the Wealden villages unspoilt to a remarkable degree, and the path network dense and very well kept. Orchards, hop gardens, tile-clad timber-framed cottages and oast houses set the kentish theme. Newcomers may be surprised to find such attractive and deeply rural countryside so close to London.

Jeffery Harrison Reserve (Bradbourne Vale Rd) 135 acres of lakes, ponds, woodland and reedbeds, several viewing hides and a satisfying nature trail. Snacks, shop, disabled access; open Weds, wknds and bank hols (exc over Christmas, phone to check); (01732) 456407; £4.

Knole (just E) Originally a simple medieval manor house, this was transformed into a palace by a 15th-c archbishop, Henry VIII, and several generations of the Sackville family. It's now a magnificent set piece, the largest - some would say the grandest - still lived-in private house in the country. It's a calendar house, with 365 rooms, 52 staircases and 7 courtyards. Wrap up well: some of the beautifully furnished rooms can get a little chilly. Outside are 26 acres of attractive grounds and a 1,000-acre deer park. Meals, snacks, shop, some disabled access; open pm Weds-Sun and bank hol Mon Apr-Oct (the garden is usually open only on the first Weds of each month May-Sept) - best to check, park open daily; (01732) 450608; £6, £2.50 car park; NT. The park is criss-crossed with public paths and tracks encompassing the deer park, as well as the great house itself.

Riverhill House Gardens (A225 S) Hillside gardens with rose and shrub terraces, woodland walks among fine trees, rhododendrons, bluebells in spring, and fine views. Teas, plant sales; open pm Weds, Sun and bank hol Sat and Mon Apr-Jun; (01732) 458802; £3.

SISSINGHURST TQ8037

Sissinghurst Garden Created by Vita Sackville-West and her husband Sir Harold Nicolson, these several charming gardens are themed according to season or colour, all offset by the lovely Elizabethan tower (not open). Meals, snacks, shop, disabled access; cl Weds, Thurs, and Nov-Mar, best to check; (01580) 710700; £6.50; NT. The Three Chimneys on the way to Biddenden is nice for lunch.

SMALL HYTHE TQ8930

Smallhythe Place (B2082) Handsome half-timbered house, now a museum of the life of former resident, the actress Dame Ellen Terry; charming rose garden. Open Sat-Weds Apr-Oct; (01580) 762334; *£3.75; NT.

Tenterden Vineyard Acres of vines, attractive lake ideal for picnics, winery, herb garden, agricultural museum and children's adventure trail; guided tours May-Oct £4. Meals, snacks, shop with free tastings, some disabled access; cl 25-26 Dec and 1 Jan; (01580) 763033; free.

Wittersham windmill (B2082 S) The tallest post mill in Kent, with good views over Romney Marsh and the Isle of Oxney. Shop; open pm Easter Sun-Mon, plus pm Sun and bank hols May-Sept; £1.

ST MARGARET'S BAY TR3844

Pines Garden 🏛 (Beach Rd) Six acres of trees, shrubs, flowers, an ornamental lake and waterfall and a Romany caravan; there's also an interesting little local history museum (£1). Summer snacks, shop, disabled access; gardens open daily, museum cl am, Mon and Tues and beginning Sept-end May (exc Easter wknd); (01304) 852764; £3.50.

South Foreland Lighthouse 🏛 You can go on a guided tour of this 19th-c lighthouse, used by Marconi in his early radio experiments; this was the first lighthouse to have an electrically powered beam, and the views from the top are excellent. The nearest parking is a mile away at St Margaret's Bay. Shop; cl Tues, Weds (exc school hols), and all Nov-Feb; (01304) 852463; £2; NT.

STAPLEHURST TQ7842

Iden Croft Herbs (Frittenden Rd) Peaceful walled herb gardens, with national collections of nepeta, mint and origanum, and gardens designed for the blind and disabled. Snacks, plant sales, disabled access; cl winter wknds; (01580) 891432; £2. The Lord Raglan (Chart Hill Rd) has good food.

STELLING MINNIS TR1446

Stelling Minnis windmill Working mill with small museum; usually open pms; donations welcome. The Tiger over at Stowting has good food.

STODMARSH TR2260

National Nature Reserve Huge expanse of watery marshland, with water channels and reedy lakes; wellingtons advisable at wetter times, when the paths may be flooded. Wild konik horses have recently been introduced to graze the marsh and reeds; they can be viewed from several hides and pathways. Beautiful walking country at any time of year, and a prime site for bird life, inc wild ducks,

kingfishers and migrants such as avocets and sandpipers; also mammals inc weasels, stoats and very occasionally otters. Good disabled access at Stodmarsh end. Free descriptive map from car park just N of Stodmarsh (where the Red Lion is a delightful place for a good lunch).

STROOD TQ7469

Diggerland (Whitewall Rd, via Anthonys Way off A289 by Medway Tunnel) Under close supervision, children over 5 can work real excavation equipment inc JCB diggers, dumpers and a fork-lift truck. Rides or drives last around 5 mins, and there are various challenges such as fishing a duck from a pond. Also pedal-power diggers, computer games and a video, bouncy castle, and a play area for under-6s. Meals, snacks, shop, disabled access. Open wknds, bank hols and school hols (exc Dec to mid-Feb); (08700) 344437; £2.50 entrance fee, from £1.50 per ride or drive.

SWINGFIELD TR2142

Butterfly Centre (MacFarlane's Garden Centre) Family-run garden centre and butterfly house; snacks, plant sales, shop; open Apr-Sept; (01303) 844244; £2.

TENTERDEN TQ8833

Busy but attractive small town with lots of charming 17th- and 18th-c weather-boarded buildings ranged along its broad High St (which could almost be somewhere in New England). A few antiques and reproduction shops, and the White Lion has enjoyable food.

Kent & East Sussex Railway 🏛 (A28 W) Steam trains now run for 10½ miles to Bodiam Castle in Sussex; lovely Wealden views. Meals, snacks, shop, disabled access; cl Nov and Jan to mid-Feb, phone (01580) 765155 for timetable; £9 return. Over the crossing, a Nissen hut houses a little museum on the history of the railway (open pm, when trains running Apr-Oct; £1). There's a small local history museum further up the road too; phone for opening times; (01580) 764310; £1.

THROWLEY TQ9856

Belmont 🏛 Pleasant 18th-c mansion in well placed parkland, with a sizeable collection of unusual clocks, and a walled garden inc a restored period

kitchen garden. Snacks at wknds, shop, disabled access to gardens and ground floor only; open pm wknds and bank hols (gardens open daily exc Fri) Apr-Sept; (01795) 890202; £5.25, £2.75 garden only. The Alma in Painter's Forstal has good value home cooking.
TONBRIDGE TQ5946
Tonbridge Castle (just off High St) Splendid Norman castle, with interactive displays, audio tours and re-created medieval scenes. Shop; cl 25-27 Dec and 1 Jan; (01732) 770929; £4.50 (free to motte and bailey castle site). The Chequers nearby has good value food. The commuter town is perked up a bit by the distinguished buildings of Tonbridge School, and with an outdoor area the swimming pool is a cut above the average municipal baths. In summer you can hire rowing boats on the river; (01732) 360630; £7.
TROTTISCLIFFE TQ6561 (pronounced Trosley) There's a good walk E to the **Coldrum Stones**, a 4,000-year-old burial chamber, with an extension on to the North Downs (Trosley Country Park), densely wooded exc on the steep slope itself. A problem for walkers elsewhere around here is that as you head E the farmland soon gets arable, with tedious slogs over ploughed fields. The unspoilt George has reasonably priced food.
TUNBRIDGE WELLS TQ5838 Very much a commuters' shopping centre nowadays (and popular with foreign language students in summer), but parts still show its former character as a genteel spa town. The allegedly health-restoring water still trickles through the Pantiles, the former centre of the town, full of elegant buildings and interesting shops. You can try the water at the Chalybeate Spring here, 40p a glass; cl end Oct-Mar. The **church** of King Charles the Martyr is an interesting chapel built in the late 17th c for the gentry visiting the Pantiles; it has a remarkable plaster ceiling. Signor Franco, along the old High St from here, is a good smart italian restaurant. Above the Pantiles the hillside Common is pleasant for strolls, with plenty of trees and rocks; out past there on Tea Garden Lane (off A264) the Beacon has enjoyable bar food.

A Day at The Wells (The Pantiles) The town's Georgian heyday elaborately brought to life using up-to-date display technology and re-creations. Shop, disabled access (prior notice preferred); cl 25 Dec; (01892) 546545; £5.50.
High Rocks (off A264 just W) On the edge of town, this former Stone Age camp has acres of impressive sandstone formations interlinked with bridges which give woodland walks; no unaccompanied children, and take care when wet. Meals, snacks; cl 25-26 Dec and 1 Jan; (01892) 515532; £2.
Spa Valley Railway (West Station, by Sainsburys, off A26 just S of centre) Runs steam train trips to Groombridge. Snacks, shop, disabled access; cl Nov, Jan and Feb, best to ring for a timetable; (01892) 537715; £4 return.
Tunbridge Wells Museum and Art Gallery (Civic Centre, Mount Pleasant Rd) Examples of Tunbridge ware, the area's speciality small-scale woodware, as well as local and natural history, historic costume, toys and dolls, and frequently changing art exhibitions. Shop, limited disabled access; cl Sun, bank hols, and Easter Sat; (01892) 554171; free.
UPCHURCH TQ8467
Upchurch church 13th c, with a unique 'candle snuffer' tower. An attractive village, with a decent pub.
UPNOR TQ7570
Upnor Castle Well preserved Elizabethan castle notorious for failing to protect the Medway from the Dutch in 1667; attractive turrets, gatehouse and windows. Snacks, shop; open Apr-Oct; (01634) 718742; £3.90. In this pretty sailing village, the Kings Arms has inexpensive pub food.
WEST KINGSDOWN TQ5763
Saxon church Largely Saxon, given great appeal by its unique tranquil setting, secluded in the middle of a wood; notice the ancient yew tree by the W door.
WEST MALLING TQ6857 Attractive village, most of which is a conservation area thanks to its many old timbered houses and wells; lots of nice alleyways to explore. Particularly worth a look are the **abbey,** one of the country's oldest ecclesiastical buildings, and **St Leonards Tower,** a fine

Norman tower from an 11th-c castle. The Swan has good modern food.

WESTERHAM TQ4454

This small country town is perhaps best known to visitors for Chartwell nearby; there are pleasant walks in the surrounding countryside, notably through the Squerryes estate and SE towards Chartwell, French Street and Toys Hill. The Grasshopper is our current choice for lunch.

Chartwell (off B2026 S) The home of Winston Churchill until his death. Still much as he left them, the rooms are full of his possessions and reminders of his career, and the gardens are attractive, with the famous black swans on the lakes. This is one of the NT's most popular houses, enjoyable to browse around even if you've no particular interest in the statesman; entry is by timed ticket. Meals, snacks, shop, disabled access (phone first); house and garden cl Mon (exc bank hols) and Tues (exc July-Aug), and 7 Nov-20 Mar; (01732) 866368; *£7 house and garden, gardens and studio only £3.50; NT. This is good walking country.

Quebec House Gabled boyhood home of General Wolfe, with exhibitions on his life and the battle that made his name. Shop, disabled access; open pm Tues and Sun 4 Apr-Oct; (01372) 453401; *£3; NT.

Squerryes Court Overshadowed by its more famous neighbour Chartwell but for some people more satisfying, this fine 17th-c manor house (home to the Warde family since 1731) overlooks attractive grounds and has excellent collections of paintings, china and furniture. The formal gardens, originally laid out in 1700, were relandscaped in the mid-18th c. Snacks, shop, limited disabled access (prior arrangement preferred); open pm Weds, wknds and bank hol Mon Apr-end Sept; (01959) 562345; £4.80, grounds only £3.20.

WHITSTABLE TR1066

Whitstable Museum and Art Gallery The focus of the town is still very much the busy working harbour; and the Museum and Art Gallery (Oxford St) explores its maritime history and traditions. Shop, disabled access; cl Sun (exc pm July-Aug), Good

Fri, and a few days over Christmas; (01227) 276998; free. The Native Oyster House (Sea Wall) and Crab & Winkle (Harbour) make the most of the famed local seafood.

WILLESBOROUGH TR0342

Willesborough windmill Working mill and heritage museum, open pm wknds and bank hol Mon beginning Apr-Sept, plus pm Weds July-Aug; snacks, shop, disabled access; (01233) 661866; £1.50. The Blacksmiths Arms has good value food.

WINGHAM TR2558

Wingham Wildlife Park 🖼 Endangered birds from all over the world, with the emphasis very much on breeding and conservation; they have a large walk-through aviary. Also meerkats, monkeys, wallabies and other animals, and a good adventure playground (made from recycled materials). Meals, snacks, shop, disabled access; cl 25-26 Dec; (01227) 720836; £4.90. The village is attractive, with decent food in the lovely medieval Red Lion.

WOODCHURCH TQ9534

South of England Rare Breeds Centre 🖼 (B2067) Particularly well organised and good value, this 90-acre working farm has a huge collection of rare farm breeds. Younger visitors may be able to cuddle baby pigs, meet the goats or get close to the animals in the children's barn. It's amazing seeing the different varieties of one species: the biggest type of rabbit is about 15 times as heavy as the smallest. Under-5s are well catered for, with paddling pool and sandpit; older children too have a good playground, nr a picnic area; lots of walks and trails, and some fine views of the kentish countryside. A Georgian farmstead has been rebuilt here; also trailer and tractor rides, and indoor play area. Good disabled access (they do a lot of work with people with physical or learning disabilities). Meals, snacks, shop, plant centre; cl Mon Oct-Mar, and 24-25 Dec; (01233) 861493; £4.

WYE DOWNS TR0746

Some of Kent's nicest walks are on the North Downs - not that high, but steep enough along the escarpment to give some great views. The Wye Downs, designated a nature reserve for their chalkland flora that includes a variety of orchids, look across the orchards below to both the Thames estuary and the Channel. The road above Wye through Hastingleigh, Bodsham Green, Sole Street (where the Compasses is a pleasant stop-off) and along the Crundale Downs is a nice drive.

YALDING TQ6949

Yalding Gardens (B2162 just S) Interesting series of gardens maintained by the Henry Doubleday Research Association, the organic farming and gardening organisation (see also Ryton Gardens in Warwickshire); each looks at how people have cultivated land in a given period, from medieval physick gardens to modern organic vegetable plots. Meals, snacks, shop, disabled access; open wknds Apr and Oct, Weds-Sun May-Sept, and Easter and bank hols; (01622) 814650; £3. In the attractive village, the Walnut Tree has good value food.

Other attractive villages, all with decent pubs, include Addington TQ6559, Alkham TR2542, Bishopsbourne TR1852, Bodsham TR1045, Boughton Lees TR0247, Boxley TQ7758, Chillenden TR2653, Elham TR1743, Harvel TQ6563, Ickham TR2257, Leigh TQ5446, Lenham TQ8952, Martin TR3346, Offham TQ6557, Sandling (despite the M20) TQ7558, Shipbourne TQ5952, Smarden TQ8842, Speldhurst TQ5541, Stalisfield Green TQ9553, Sutton Valence TQ8149, West Peckham TQ6452, Wickhambreaux TR2158, Worth TR3356 and Wrotham TQ6158.

Pubs useful for walkers include the Woolpack at Benover TQ7048, Pepper Box at Fairbourne Heath above Ulcombe TQ8550, Woodman on Goathurst Common TQ4952, Bucks Head at Godden Green TQ5555, Rock at Hoath Corner TQ4943, Cock at Ide Hill TQ4851, Cock at Henley Street nr Luddesdown TQ6667, Kentish Horse at Markbeech TQ4742, Horns and Bull in Otford TQ5359, Harrow at Warren Street TQ9253 and Rising Sun at Woodlands TQ5560.

Where to eat

BIDDENDEN TQ8238 **Three Chimneys** *Hareplain Rd (01580) 291472* Ochre-coloured country pub with rambling, low oak-beamed small rooms, interesting old furniture on flagstones and coir matting, some harness and sporting prints on exposed brick walls, and good winter log fires; well kept real ales, good wines, and good, interesting food (there may be a wait if they are busy); smart garden terrace area with seats by outdoor heaters; Sissinghurst Gardens nearby. £27|**£7.95**

BOUGH BEECH TQ4846 **Wheatsheaf** *Hever Rd (01732) 700254* Lovely old pub - thought to have started life as a hunting lodge belonging to Henry V - with oak timbers in unusually high ceilings, several bars and some interesting decorations, a massive stone fireplace, and piles of smart magazines to read; nice nibbles, chestnuts to roast and mulled wine in winter, summer Pimms, and popular interesting bar food (served all day); real ales, decent wines, and lovely gardens; children in Long Bar only; partial disabled access. £25|**£5.95**

CANTERBURY TR1556 **Bonne Cuisine** *Canterbury Hotel, 71 New Dover Rd (01227) 450551* Run by the same family for over 20 years, this neat little hotel is warmly friendly and comfortable and serves beautifully presented very good french food in the cheerfully yellow dining room; attractive bdrms; children over 6. £36

DARGATE TR0861 **Dove** *Plum Pudding Lane (01227) 751360* Tucked-away dining pub with charmingly unspoilt rambling rooms, plenty of seats on bar boards, a winter log fire, and exceptionally good restaurant-style food; well kept real ales, fine wines, and a pretty sheltered garden. £31|**£7.25**

FAVERSHAM TR0260 **Read's** *Macknade Manor, Canterbury Rd (01795) 535344* Restaurant-with-rooms in Georgian manor house with neat surrounding gardens that provide home-grown vegetables and herbs for the kitchen; exceptionally good innovative english cooking including fine fish dishes and lovely puddings, a marvellous wine list, and neat young staff; cl Sun, Mon; disabled access. £19.50 lunch, £42 dinner

IVY HATCH TQ5854 **Plough** *High Cross Rd (01732) 810268* Relaxed and friendly tile-hung house with a wide choice of consistently good french food (using french produce), carefully chosen wines and well kept beers, and efficient service; front dining bar with dark panelled walls, an old brick fireplace, and dining chairs and settles, separate little room to left of door, and popular conservatory restaurant; nearby walks; best to book; disabled access. £28|**£7.50**

LANGTON GREEN TQ5439 **Hare** *Langton Rd (01892) 862419* Popular, civilised dining pub with light, airy knocked-through rooms, a chatty atmosphere, imaginative generously served food from a menu that changes twice daily, attentive waitress service, real ales, and a good choice of wines; outside terrace; children before 7pm; partial disabled access. £27|**£7.50**

NEWNHAM TQ9557 **George** *44 The Street (01795) 890237* Distinctive 16th-c pub with a spreading series of attractive and interesting rooms with lots to look at, open fires, friendly staff, nicely presented, imaginative food using fresh local produce, well kept beers, and good wines; cl 25 Dec. £25|**£8.95**

PENSHURST TQ5142 **Bottle House** *Coldharbour Lane, Smarts Hill (01892) 870306* Relaxed and friendly 15th-c pub with huge beams, stone pillars, and big windows in the unpretentious bars, quite a collection of china pot lids and old paintings and photographs, very good interesting food, efficient service, and well kept local ales; cl 25 Dec. £26|**£7.95**

PLUCKLEY TQ9243 **Dering Arms** *The Grove (01233) 840371* Striking old building, originally a hunting lodge, with a variety of good solid wooden furniture on stone floors and a roaring log fire in a huge fireplace in the stylishly plain high-ceilinged bar, and a smaller panelled bar with similar furnishings; particularly good imaginative fish dishes, well kept real ales, an extensive wine list, and quite a few malt whiskies; bdrms; monthly vintage-car rally; cl 26-27 Dec. £28.50|**£7.85**

STAPLEHURST TQ7844 **Lord Raglan** *Chart Hill Rd (01622) 843747* Unpretentious yet quite civilised country inn with hops along low beams, comfortably worn dark wood furniture on nice parquet flooring, a coal fire, a pleasantly relaxed atmosphere, and charming licensees; very generous attractively presented food (the imaginative daily specials are the thing to choose), well kept real ales, and a good wine list; small french windows lead to an enticing little sheltered terrace; wooden picnic-sets in side orchard; cl Sun; partial disabled access. £24.50|**£6.50**

STODMARSH TR2160 **Red Lion** *(01227) 721339* Interesting food in delightful little pub with several idiosyncratic rooms full of bric-a-brac, friendly landlord, a big log fire, well kept real ales, good wine list with several by the glass; pretty little back garden with chickens; partial disabled access. £29.50|**£9.95**

TUNBRIDGE WELLS TQ5739 **Mount Edgcumbe Hotel** *The Common (01892) 526823* Bustling tucked-away hotel on one of several large rocky outcrops; small cosy bar with lots of exposed brick and grotto-like rock, enjoyable very popular brasserie food in big-windowed restaurant, cheerful staff, well kept real ales and a good wine list; bdrms; book at wknds; disabled access. £27|**£6**

TUNBRIDGE WELLS TQ5839 **Thackeray's House** *85 London Rd (01892) 511921* Civilised detached white clapper-board house with stylishly revamped beamed rooms, oak floors, crisp white tablecloths, friendly but carefully professional service, beautifully presented contemporary cooking, lovely puddings, and very good house wines; cl Sun pm, Mon, Christmas. £35

ULCOMBE TQ8550 **Pepper Box** *Windmill Hill (01622) 842558* Cosy old country inn with timbers and low beams hung with hops in friendly homely bar, copper kettles and pans on window sills, two armchairs and a sofa by the splendid inglenook fireplace, several cats, and a snug little no smoking dining room; good food (esp the daily specials), well kept real ales, and courteous service; nice country views from terrace and garden; no children. £25.50|**£7**

WEST MALLING TQ6857 **Swan** *35 Swan St (01732) 521910* Stylish brasserie/bar in most attractive little town; open-plan and very light and airy with stripped pale wood flooring, elegant modern furniture and fittings, efficient young staff, interesting fruity beers, good wines, and contemporary, enjoyable food. £30|**£6.95**

Special thanks to Jackie Sandford, Dave Irving

LANCASHIRE
(including Greater
Manchester and Merseyside)

**Good value and great variety: two cities full of interest,
vibrant seaside resorts, lots of places to visit - and a quiet side,
with marvellous unspoilt countryside and coast; friendly people too**

Manchester (home to our Lancashire Family Attraction, the outstanding Imperial War Museum North), and Liverpool (recently named European Capital of Culture for 2008) combine grand Victorian cityscapes with striking visitor-friendly modern developments - both cities have a good deal of character. A wealth of continually improving world-class museums and galleries (many of them are free), together with a lively nightlife, give them a wide-ranging appeal. They're within easy reach of each other, and have good public transport.

With plenty to entertain families and young adults, brassy Blackpool is the classic seaside resort: the Pleasure Beach, Tower, Illuminations, zoo and aquarium (quite aside from the lively nightclubs and bars) are just some of the attractions on offer. Southport is a good place for a day at the seaside, and attractive Lancaster has quite a few things to keep visitors occupied.

Especially worth picking out among a rich variety of family-friendly attractions are Wigan Pier (an irresistible mix of museum and theatre) and the imaginative theme park at Charnock Richard; Prescot has an enjoyable safari park. You'll find friendly farms at Fleetwood and Martin Mere (bird-lovers enjoy the nearby Wildfowl & Wetlands Trust, and Rockwater Bird Conservation Centre near Burnley). Leighton Hall is a pleasant spot for a relaxed afternoon. And as we've said, both Manchester and Liverpool have plenty of fuel for enjoyable family outings.

From a good choice of industrial heritage museums (often more fun than you'd imagine), we pick out Hat Works in Stockport and the World of Glass at St Helens as especially worth a mention. There are fine houses at Bramhall, Hoghton (lovely gardens too) and Chorley. On a completely different note, you can explore the warships at Birkenhead, and in Preston the National Football Museum is now free.

Glorious countryside is not something Lancashire is short of, either. Out of season Lancashire's long stretches of beach and dune are empty, with a lonely charm for walkers; the treacherous tidal sands of Morecambe Bay continue to fascinate. Even just outside the big cities, the moors have plenty of scope for exhilarating drives and walks. Bewitched Pendle Hill still captures the imagination. Other areas of fine countryside include the great whaleback of Longridge Fell, the wooded Beacon Fell country park, the magnificent Pennine moorland of the Forest of Bowland, and the equally peaceful Silverdale/Arndale area.

Where to stay

ASHWORTH VALLEY SD8512 **Leaches Farm** *Ashworth Rd, Rochdale, Lancashire OL11 5UN (01706) 41117* **£40**; 3 rms, shared bthrm. Creeper-clad 17th-c hill farm with really wonderful views, massive stone walls, beams and log fires; self-catering too; cl 22 Dec-2 Jan; children over 8; dogs by arrangement

BILSBORROW SD5039 **Guy's Thatched Hamlet** *St Michael's Rd, Bilsborrow, Preston, Lancashire PR3 0RS (01995) 640010* **£56.70**, plus wknd breaks; 53 smartly modern rms. Bustling complex of thatched buildings by the canal, comprising a restaurant and pizzeria, a tavern, and the accommodation part, Guy's Lodgings; craft shops and outside entertainment, a play area, all-weather cricket pitch, and crown green bowling; a useful base for exploring the area; open all day; cl 25 Dec; disabled access; dogs welcome in bedrooms ☺

BLACKPOOL SD3037 **Imperial Hotel** *North Promenade, Blackpool, Lancashire FY1 2HB (01253)* 623971 **£114**, plus special breaks; 181 well equipped pretty rms, many with sea views. Fine Victorian hotel overlooking the sea, with spacious and comfortable day rooms, lots of period features, enjoyable food and fine wines, and a full health and fitness club with indoor swimming pool, gym, sauna and so forth; children's club during summer, Christmas and Easter; lots to do nearby; disabled access; dogs welcome in bedrooms ☺

BLACKPOOL SD3033 **Old Coach House** *50 Dean St, Blackpool, Lancashire FY4 1BP (01253)* 349195 **£72**; 11 attractively furnished rms. Carefully restored 19th-c hotel, the oldest remaining house in Blackpool's South Shore; lots of original features, airy conservatory, enjoyable food in no smoking, little pine-furnished restaurant, very good service, and pretty landscaped gardens; disabled access

BROMLEY CROSS SD7213 **Last Drop Village Hotel** *Hospital Rd, Bromley Cross, Bolton, Lancashire BL7 9PZ (01204)* 591131 **£95**; 128 rms. Big well equipped hotel complex cleverly integrated into olde-worlde pastiche village complete with stone-and-cobbles street of gift and teashops, bakery, etc, even a spacious creeper-covered pub with lots of beamery and timbering, popular one-price hot and cold buffet, and heavy tables out on attractive flagstoned terrace; disabled access; dogs welcome in bedrooms

CAPERNWRAY SD5371 **New Capernwray Farmhouse** *Capernwray, Carnforth, Lancashire LA6 1AD (01524)* 734284 **£70**; 3 comfortable rms. Pretty 300-year-old ex-farmhouse with helpful friendly owners, cosy lounge, stone walls and beams, and candlelit dinner in what was the dairy with an informal house-party atmosphere; cl Nov-Feb; children over 9; dogs welcome in bedrooms

CHIPPING SD6343 **Gibbon Bridge Hotel** *Green Lane, Chipping, Preston, Lancashire PR3 2TQ (01995)* 61456 **£110**, plus special breaks; 29 spacious individual rms, inc 22 split-level suites, most with views of the Bowland Hills. Country hotel on the edge of the Forest of Bowland, with beautiful landscaped gardens (plus a popular bandstand which can be used for civil weddings or for music events), and old-fashioned values of quality and personal service; attractively presented food using home-grown produce in airy restaurant and conservatory, a quiet relaxing atmosphere, and fine wines; health and gym area; tennis court; a good base for walking and short driving trips; good disabled access; dogs in two restricted bedrooms

COLNE SD8741 **Higher Wanless Farm** *Red Lane, Colne, Lancashire BB8 7JP (01282)* 865301 **£50**; 3 rms, two with own bthrm. Warmly welcoming farmhouse with beams, log fires and lovely surrounding farmland used mainly for breeding of shire horses, as well as sheep; cl mid-Dec to mid-Jan; children over 10

COWAN BRIDGE SD6475 **Hipping Hall** *Cowan Bridge, Kirkby Lonsdale, Carnforth, Lancashire LA6 2JJ (01524)* 271187 **£96***, plus special breaks; 7 pretty rms, 5 in main hotel, 2 cottage suites across courtyard (with self-catering facilities). Relaxed country-house atmosphere and delicious food in handsome small hotel with help-yourself drinks in conservatory, an open fire, a lovely beamed Great Hall with minstrels' gallery, and four acres of walled gardens; fine walks from front door; cl Christmas and New Year; children over 12; dogs in cottage suites

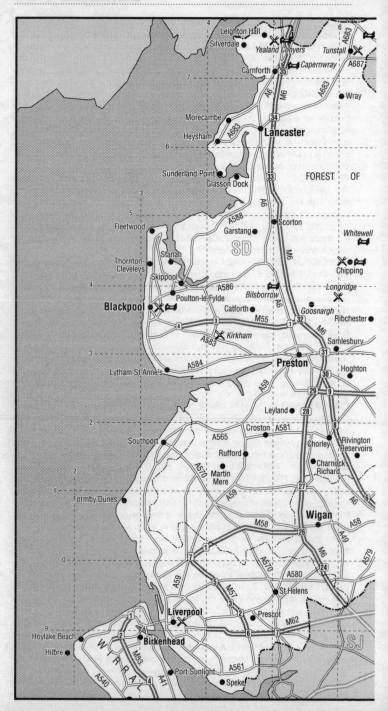

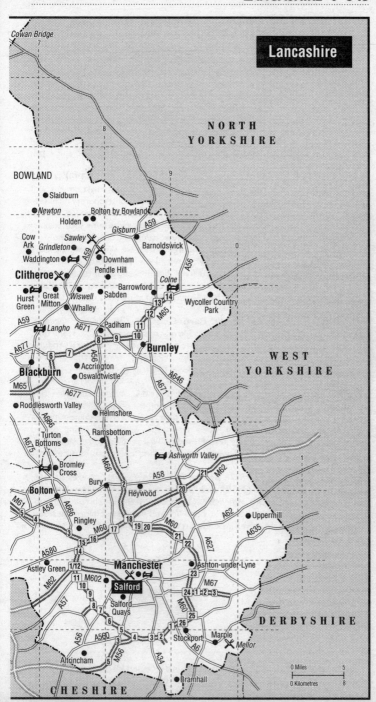

Lancashire

Cowan Bridge

7

NORTH
YORKSHIRE

8

BOWLAND

9

● Slaidburn
● Newton   ● Bolton by Bowland
Holden   A59
                    ● Gisburn
Cow   Sawley
Ark   Grindleton   ● Barnoldswick
Waddington ● Downham
                    Pendle Hill   A56
Clitheroe   0
                    ● Barrowford   Colne
Hurst   Great   Wiswell Sabden   14
Green   Mitton   13   Wycoller Country
         Whalley   Padiham 12   Park
A59   11
    Langho A671   8   9   10
A677   Burnley
    6   7
         ● Accrington   A646   WEST
Blackburn ● Oswaldtwistle   YORKSHIRE
M65
    A677   A671
● Roddlesworth Valley   ● Helmshore

         ● Ramsbottom
Turton
Bottoms   ● Ashworth Valley
    Bromley   1
    Cross   M66   A58   21   M62
Bolton   ● Bury   2
M61   Heywood   20
  5   A58 A666
  4   18   A62   ● Uppermill
    Ringley   19 20
  3   M60 17   M60   A635
    15 16   21
    14   22   A627
         Manchester ● Ashton-under-Lyne
Astley Green 1/12   23
    11   M602   M67
M62 10   Salford   24 1 2 3
  9   M60
A57 8   7   Salford   25
    6   Quays   1   26
    5   3   4 2 Stockport Marple
A56 A560 3   A6   ● Mellor
    Altrincham M56   A34
                                DERBYSHIRE
              ● Bramhall
                                0 Miles   5
CHESHIRE   0 Kilometres 8

HURST GREEN SD6938 **Shireburn Arms** *Whalley Rd, Hurst Green, Clitheroe, Lancashire BB7 9QJ (01254) 826518* **£70**, plus special breaks; 18 rms. Lovely 17th-c country hotel with a refined but friendly atmosphere, an airy modernised bar, comfortable lounge, open fires, well presented enjoyable food, good service, and fine view of the Ribble Valley from the conservatory; disabled access; dogs welcome in bedrooms

LANGHO SD7034 **Northcote Manor** *Northcote Rd, Langho, Blackburn, Lancashire BB6 8BE (01254) 240555* **£130***, plus special breaks; 14 attractive rms with antiques and board games, reached up a fine stairway. In pretty countryside, this neatly kept red brick Victorian house is more of a restaurant-with-rooms, with beams and oak panelling, big log fires, and two comfortable lounges, wonderful breakfasts, and delicious food in the civilised dining room; cl 25 Dec and 1 Jan; partial disabled access

MANCHESTER SJ8498 **Malmaison** *Piccadilly, Manchester M1 3AQ (0161) 278 1000* **£148.50**; 167 chic rms with CD player, in-house movies, smart bthrms, and really good beds. Stylishly modern hotel with comfortable contemporary furniture, exotic flower arrangements, bright paintings, very efficient service, french brasserie, generous breakfasts, and free gym; other hotels in the same small chain in Birmingham, Edinburgh, Glasgow, Leeds, and Newcastle; good disabled access

WADDINGTON SD7243 **Backfold Cottage** *The Square, Waddington, Clitheroe, Lancashire BB7 3JA (01200) 422367* **£55***; 3 rms. Tiny 17th-c cottage in cobbled street, attractive millennium clock on the front, beautiful antique furnishings (inc a doll's house in the lounge); very good service, all-day snacks, and candlelit evening meals (bring your own wines); nearby walks; children at owner's discretion; dogs welcome in bedrooms

WADDINGTON SD7144 **Peter Barn** *Cross Lane, Waddington, Clitheroe, Lancashire BB7 3JH (01200) 428585* **£56***; 3 lovely rms. Converted old stone tithe barn with beamed sitting room, antiques, lovely home cooking using local produce, home-made jams and marmalade, warmly welcoming owners and a gentle atmosphere; surrounded by a delightful garden in fine walking country; cl Christmas and New Year; children over 12

WHITEWELL SD6547 **Inn at Whitewell** *Whitewell, Clitheroe, Lancashire BB7 3AT (01200) 448222* **£98**; 17 rms, some with open peat fires. Civilised Forest of Bowland stone inn on the River Hodder, with seven miles of trout, salmon and sea trout fishing, and grounds with views down the valley; interesting period furnishings, plenty of room, highly praised food (as well as coffee and cream teas all day), fine wines (they house a wine merchant), and courteous service; dogs welcome

YEALAND CONYERS SD5074 **Bower** *Yealand Rd, Yealand Conyers, Carnforth, Lancashire LA5 9SF (01524) 734585* **£62**; 2 attractive rms. Charming no smoking Georgian house in big garden with views of Ingleborough and the surrounding hills; friendly owners (keen bridge players), open fire and piano in comfortable sitting room, and enjoyable food served around a large table in the kitchen or dining room; children over 12

Please let us know what you think of places in the *Guide*. Use the report forms at the back of the book, write us a letter or log on to www.goodguides.co.uk

To see and do

Lancashire Family Attraction of the Year

SALFORD SJ7997 **Imperial War Museum North** (Trafford Wharf Rd)
Displaying the same sure-handed approach as the London original, this new
branch of the Imperial War Museum impresses with its fascinating and thought-
provoking displays (all of which are completely free), but what really makes it
stand out is the extraordinary building. Covered in aluminium, it's designed to
resemble three shards of a shattered globe, representing conflict on land, in the
air, and on water. Look out for touches such as the black curved floor meant to
reflect the earth's curve. A viewing platform in the air shard has spectacular
views across the Manchester Ship Canal to the city centre. The museum's focus
isn't at all militaristic - if anything, it's the opposite, with the emphasis very
much on how war has affected us all from 1900 right up to the present. The first
things you see are the large-scale objects such as a T34 russian tank, and the
artillery piece that fired the first british shell in World War I. But it's the smaller
items in the six main galleries that leave the deepest impression: clothing,
diaries and art, all carefully displayed to illustrate topics such as the role of
women in wartime, and scientific and medical advances as a result of conflict.
Every hour a stunning 360-degree audio visual presentation called The Big
Picture projects sounds and pictures from the museum's archive all around
you. And there are plenty of activities for younger children, particularly at
weekends and school holidays, when they may have story-telling, quiz trails,
opportunities to handle things from the collections and learn who owned them,
and fun presentations on how children entertained themselves in wartime. You
can find the schedule on their website, www.iwm.org.uk/north. With plenty of
interactive displays and several big changing exhibitions, there's lots to see: it's
a hugely worthwhile place to visit. Café and waterfront restaurant, shop,
disabled access; cl 25-26 Dec; (0161) 836 4000; free. The museum is linked by a
footbridge to the Lowry (see Salford, in main text).

ACCRINGTON SD7627
Haworth Art Gallery (Haworth
Park, Manchester Rd) Notable for its
collection of Tiffany glass, the biggest in
Europe (an Accrington man used to
manage the Tiffany studios). Café, shop,
disabled access; cl am, and all Mon-Tues
(exc bank hols); (01254) 233782; free.
ALTRINCHAM SJ7387
**Dunham Massey Hall, Garden and
Park** (off B5160 W) Early Georgian
manor house extensively remodelled in
the early 20th c, with impressive
silverware, paintings and furnishings,
and restored kitchen, pantry and
laundry. The largely unaltered grounds
have plenty of deer, formal avenues of
trees, and a working Elizabethan saw
mill. Friendly staff give free tours daily;
concerts and events even in winter
when the house is closed. Meals, snacks,
shop, disabled access to ground floor of
hall; open Sat-Weds Apr-Oct, house cl
am; (0161) 941 1025; £5.80 house and

garden, £3.80 garden only; NT. The
Axe & Cleaver (School Lane) is a roomy
nearby family dining pub.
ASHTON-UNDER-LYNE SJ9399
**Museum of the Manchester
Regiment** (Town Hall, Market Pl)
Tells the story of the Manchester
Regiment, with displays inc a
reconstructed World War I trench
with special effects and a World War II
air-raid shelter, also interactive
computers, Home Front exhibition and
a recently expanded medal collection.
Shop, disabled access; cl most Sun and
bank hols; (0161) 343 2878; free.
Portland Basin Museum
Enthusiastic local history museum
overlooking the Ashton Canal, with a
re-created 1920s street and displays on
Tameside's crafts and trades; quite a
few hands-on displays for children.
Good value snacks, shop, disabled
access, baby-changing facilities; cl Mon
(exc bank hol), 25-26 Dec and 1 Jan;

(0161) 343 2878; free. There's a
heritage trail around the town, and
plenty of places for a picnic.

ASTLEY GREEN SJ7099

Astley Green Colliery Museum
(Higher Green, just off A580) The only
visible reminder of Lancashire's mining
heritage, with its 30-metre (100-ft)
steel headgear still intact, plus the
largest steam winding engine in Europe,
a narrow-gauge railway, working
stationary steam engines, and displays
on coal mining inc an exhibition of
photography from 1908 to 1970. Shop;
museum open pms only Sun, Tues and
Thurs, engines in steam pm 1st Sun of
month Mar-Oct; (01772) 553478; free
(exc special events).

BARNOLDSWICK SD9046

Bancroft Mill Engine Museum 🖭
The last working steam mill in the area -
not that long ago Barnoldswick had 13.
Snacks, shop, disabled access; open Sat,
and various Sun pms for steaming,
phone for dates; (01282) 865626; £2.
The Fanny Grey (B6251 towards
Colne) has decent food.

BARROWFORD SD8639

Pendle Heritage Centre Growing
local history centre, with an 18th-c
walled garden, woodland walks, and an
unusual cruck barn with friendly farm
animals. The museum, recently
refurbished (and due to re-open just
before the *Guide* comes out), has an
exhibition on the Pendle witches, and
there's also an art gallery (and the
tourist information centre). Meals,
snacks, shop, disabled access (they've
added a new lift); cl 25 Dec; (01282)
661704; admission price undecided as
we went to press. This is picturesque,
evocative countryside; the **church** at
nearby unspoilt Newchurch has the
witches' grave, and there's good food at
the Forest Inn at Fence and Bay Horse
at Roughlee - a stone's throw from
Alice Nutter's home. A few miles
upstream from here, just below Blacko,
the Water Meetings is an ideal place for
a picnic and a paddle.

BIRKENHEAD SJ3288

Waterfront views over to Liverpool, of
course, but a surprise in **Birkenhead
Priory** (Priory St), a ruined 12th-c
Benedictine priory with notable visitor
centre. Shop, mostly disabled access;

open pm Tues-Sun; (0151) 666 1249;
free. Good views from the tower of the
neighbouring church. The local history
museum is housed in the impressive
former Town Hall (snacks, shop,
disabled access; cl Mon and a wk over
Christmas and New Year; free). The
rejuvenated town centre has various
craft and art galleries. Laid out in 1853
and now being restored, Birkenhead
Park was the world's first public park,
and Europe's first tramway was built
here in 1860 - today various restored
trams, one from as far away as Hong
Kong, still run (£1 return). The
Shrewsbury Arms out in Claughton Firs
is the best place for lunch.

Historic Warships (Birkenhead
Docks) HMS *Plymouth* and the
Submarine *Onyx* both took part in the
Falklands War, and a recent addition is
HMS *Bronington*, once commanded by
Prince Charles. You can peep up the
periscope on the *Onyx*, and there's
plenty for children to fiddle with. A few
ladders to negotiate, but don't be put
off - readers find this a very satisfying
afternoon out. Snacks, shop, disabled
access to visitor centre and one deck
on *Plymouth* only; cl 24-26 Dec, 1 Jan
and wkdys Jan-mid Feb; (0151) 650
1573; £5.50. Adults can look around a
german U-boat alongside, which spent
50 years on the seabed (phone to book
a tour).

Shore Road Pumping Station
(Woodside, nr ferry terminal) This
unusual **steam pumping station** has
an adjacent small transport museum
with a working tram. Best to contact
tourist information centre for open
days; (0151) 647 6780; free.

**Williamson Art Gallery &
Museum** (Slatey Rd) English
watercolours and other art by the
Liverpool school, sculpture and
ceramics, model ships, and a collection
of cars and motorcycles in period
garage setting. Shop, disabled access; cl
Mon, 24 Dec-2 Jan; (0151) 652 4177;
free. On summer Suns in Jun-July and
Sept there are generally free concerts
here, and in Aug at the priory.

BLACKBURN SD6828

Put firmly on the map by the Industrial
Revolution, this has bustling shops and
market, some fine buildings, and lots of

beautiful unspoilt countryside around. The parish **church** (actually now a cathedral) is very handsome - grand yet elegant. The Royal Oak (B6233, nr A6119 ring rd) has popular home cooking. **Witton Country Park** has 480-acres of attractive countryside to explore.
Blackburn Museum & Art Gallery (Museum St) Newly refurbished galleries show english watercolours, japanese woodblock prints, greek and russian icons, and illuminated manuscripts; they also have some interesting temporary exhibitions. Shop, disabled access; cl Sun, Mon and bank hols; (01254) 667130; free.
BLACKPOOL SD3036
Britain's most loved and loathed (and most popular) seaside resort. The atmosphere in summer is unashamedly lively, especially at wknds when it's popular with young adults. Most families love it too, with plenty to do from donkey rides (not Fri) along the beaches (Blackpool South and Bispham are the cleanest), to days at the **Sandcastle** leisure complex; open wknds and school hols (plus daily Jun-Oct); (01253) 343602; £6.25. The tramway here was the first permanent electric tramway in the world and has regular summer historic tramcar rides; phone (01253) 473001 for information. A Hopper Pass (£42) allows you entrance to the Blackpool Tower and Circus, Zoo and Sandcastle complex and Pleasure Beach. An ambitious 20-year project aiming to modernise and smarten up the town is about to begin, and if gambling laws are altered, it will include a showy strip of hotel casinos along the seafront.
Blackpool Model Village Created by a landscape gardener, so the gardens are as much an attraction as the models. Very well done: tableaux range from a cricket match in a Tudor village to a scottish castle, there are two miniature railways, they've recently added model boats, and there's even a replica Blackpool tram. Snacks, shop, disabled access; cl Nov-Jan, and wkdys Feb-Easter; (01253) 763827; £2.75.
Blackpool Pleasure Beach Founded in 1896, this is still Britain's most popular attraction. Altogether more

than 145 rides and attractions are squeezed into the park's 42 acres, inc several roller-coasters that can whiz you through 360 degrees, backwards, or in the dark, bungee trampolines, ice-skating, and traditional rides such as ghost trains, River Caves and dodgems. Highlights inc the dizzying roller-coaster Spin Doctors where riders spin 360 degrees, 37 metres (120 ft) off the ground at up to 60 mph, and one of the best rides is the hi-tech water ride Valhalla, full of drops and effects that include real fire. At six minutes, it's also currently the longest dark ride in the world. There's still nothing to top the Big One though, a monster roller-coaster that climbs to 72 metres (235 ft) at speeds of up to 85mph. Most of the more exciting rides have height restrictions, so smaller children have their own section of the park, which includes a fine miniature wooden roller-coaster, the Zipper Dipper. Meals and snacks, shops, disabled access; open daily Easter-early Nov, plus wknds in Nov, Dec and Mar; (0870) 444 5566. Free entry to the park, then tickets for rides range from £1.30 to £5, or you can get a wristband offering unlimited rides on everything for £26.
Blackpool Tower This outstanding landmark has several lively attractions geared towards families, inc a circus, laser shows, aquarium, dinosaur dark ride, a lift to the top, and the Walk of Faith - a 5-cm thick glass floor 116 metres (380 ft) above the ground. Perhaps most fun at night (they're open till 11pm in summer). You can try old-fashioned ballroom dancing (they've an impressive organ), and there's non-stop cabaret music. Meals, snacks, shop, limited disabled access; cl winter wkdys (exc during Feb half-term), best to check; (01253) 292029; £11.50, £8.50 after 7pm. Those famous autumn light displays are the best of their kind, and they're continually adding new features - though you'll have to travel at a snail's pace along the Golden Five Hundred Yards (or Mile as they call it here) if you decide to drive.
Blackpool Zoo (East Park Drive) This enjoyable zoo has recently taken over by new owners (it used to be run by the council) who have plans for expansion.

There are more than 400 animals in 32 acres of landscaped gardens, inc a walk-through lemur wood, and gorilla island, and they've rare red pandas. The big cats are usually fed at 3.30pm (not Fri), the sea lions at 11am and 2.30pm, and there is an animal handling session at 4pm; there are plenty of animals to stroke in the children's zoo. A train chugs around the grounds, and there's a good playground; it's a pleasant place to take a picnic. Meals, snacks, shop, disabled access; cl 25 Dec; (01253) 830830; *£7.95.

Grundy Art Gallery (Queen St) This decent gallery away from the crowds is proof that there's more to Blackpool than rollicking seasidery. Shop, disabled access but no facilities; cl Sun and bank hols; (01253) 478170; free.

Sea Life Centre (Golden Mile Centre) Enjoyable for families, and broadly similar to others in the chain, but with a bonus: one of the biggest displays of tropical sharks in Europe, with a walk-through tunnel underneath so you feel you're in there with them. The touch-pools with crabs and starfish are another highlight, and there's a seahorse aquarium; experts are on hand to answer questions. Meals, snacks, shop, disabled access; cl 25 Dec; (01253) 622445; £8.

BOLTON SD7109
Quite a few places to visit here; the Kings Head (Junction Rd, Deane), with a bowling green behind, is useful for lunch, as is the restaurant of the Bolton Moat House (Higher Bridge St), an interesting church conversion.

Bolton Museum & Art Gallery (Le Mans Crescent) Quite good, with Egyptian mummies, lots of watercolours and 20th-c sculpture. Shop, disabled access; cl bank hols (and maybe Sun); (01204) 332211; free.

Hall i'th' Wood (Crompton Way) 15th-c, where Samuel Crompton developed his Spinning Mule in 1779; it was refurbished by the first Lord Leverhulme in 1902. Shop, disabled access to ground floor; cl Mon (exc bank hols), Tues, phone for winter opening times; (01204) 332370; £3.

Smithills Hall 🏛 (Smithills, Dean Rd) Interesting (though much restored) old manor house with 14th-c Great Hall

and splendid panelled drawing room. Snacks, shop, disabled access to ground floor only; cl Sun am, Mon (exc bank hols), and Oct-Easter, but best to check; (01204) 332377; £3.

BOLTON BY BOWLAND SD7849
Attractive streamside Forest of Bowland village, with a fine **church**, and quaint cottages leading off its two village greens. The Coach & Horses has good fresh food.

BRAMHALL SJ8886
Bramall Hall One of the finest houses in the area (particularly from the outside), a splendid timber-framed 14th-c hall with rare 16th-c wall paintings and furniture, and extensive parkland; attractively restored in the 19th c. Meals, snacks, shop, disabled access to ground floor; open pm Mon-Sat, and all day Sun and bank hols Good Fri-Sept, pm Tues-Sat, and all day Sun Oct-Dec (exc 25-26 Dec), and pm wknds the rest of the year; (0161) 485 3708; £3.95, small parking charge. The Davenport Arms at Woodford does decent lunches.

BROMLEY CROSS SD7213
Last Drop Village (N of Bolton) Pastiche of an 18th-c village, very rustic and quaint, with courtyard, shops, and a decent pub. The B6391 and old Roman road through Edgworth N of here are fine moorland roads, as are the A675 N of Bolton itself (good detours off at Belmont), and A666 to Darwen.

BURNLEY SD8530
The **canal wharf** (Manchester Rd) allows short towpath walks along the Leeds & Liverpool Canal, giving a vivid impression of the towering old weaving mills; the raised canal embankment across the valley is a remarkable sight. The Inn on the Wharf here has good value food.

Queen Street Mill (Harle Syke, NE outskirts) When it closed in 1982, this was the last surviving steam-powered cotton textile mill; its 300 Lancashire looms are quite a sight, some of them still in action. Meals, snacks, shop, disabled access; cl Sun and Mon (exc bank hols) and Dec-Feb; (01282) 412555; £2.50.

Rockwater Bird Conservation Centre (Foxstones Lane, Cliviger - above Mereclough SE) Expanding collection taking in waterfowl, pheasants, foreign birds and owls, as well as rabbits and chipmunks. Children can feed some animals. Snacks, limited disabled access; cl Mon (exc bank hols), and Oct-Mar; (01282) 415016; £3.

Towneley Hall (A646 S) Home of the Towneley family from the 14th c until 1902; you can look around an Elizabethan long gallery, Regency rooms, and a Victorian kitchen. There's also an art gallery and a craft museum, a natural history centre and an aquarium. Woodland trails and space for picnics in the park. Shop, disabled access; cl Fri, am wknds, and around 2 wks over Christmas and New Year; (01282) 424213; free.

BURY SD8010

East Lancs Railway 🚃 (Bolton St Stn) Well regarded by enthusiasts, a scenic 17-mile steam journey along the pretty Irwell Valley; you can get on or off along the way. Meals, snacks, shop, disabled access; open wknds, bank hols, and Weds-Fri May-Sept, phone for a timetable; (0161) 764 7790; £7 full return. The Lord Raglan up at Nangreaves (off A56/A666 N) has great moorland views, good food, and brews its own beer.

CARNFORTH SD4970

The station (once voted the worst in England) at this otherwise unremarkable little town starred in *Brief Encounter* in 1945. A £1.75m project to restore it to its cinematic heyday has recently been completed (and the famous clock is working again), the restaurant and bar have been refurbished with 1945 furniture and décor, and a new heritage centre has opened with exhibitions on the town's history. Ask at the visitor centre about maps for self-guided walks around Carnforth; shops, disabled access (and facilities); (01524) 720333. A mile or so N are the ruins of a 14th-c manor house, **Warton Old Rectory**, and the County Hotel (A6) has reliable traditional food.

Warton Crag (just N) Fine views over Morecambe Bay and the coast, and enjoyable walking.

CATFORTH SD4735

Lancaster Canal Between Preston and Carnforth, this is ideal for boating -

40 miles without a single lock; often through quiet countryside, with herons and even occasional kingfishers - best in spring or early summer, with ducklings and cygnets bobbing about, and lambs in the fields alongside. This is also a good departure point for pleasant towpath walks, largely through quiet countryside.

CHARNOCK RICHARD SD5415

Camelot Theme Park They've really stuck with the Arthurian theme at this imaginative park (which has recently added the popular whirlwind, a spinning roller-coaster). There is a spectacularly dizzying ride in the shape of Excalibur, the monorail round the place looks like a tamed dragon, and even the animals in their farm aren't out of place - they live in thatched and cobbled enclosures. A highlight is the splendid half-hour jousting display - twice a day in peak periods, and once at the start and end of the season. Dozens of other attractions include something for most age groups. You can bottle-feed lambs or help with milking at the farm, and there's a big indoor play area; also log flume and other water rides, a magician and jester, and a quirky show. The go-karts and the driving school have an extra charge, and there are lots of arcade games. A fair bit is under cover, but if it rains continuously for two hours you can get a half-price return ticket. Meals, snacks, shop, disabled access; open wknds and school hols Apr-Oct, daily Jun-Aug; (01257) 452100; £14.

CHIPPING SD6445

Bowland Wild Boar Park (Leagram, towards Dunsop Bridge) Deer, llamas, and longhorn cattle as well as wild boar at this good-value park; in summer children may be able to feed lambs and other small animals; woodland walks, picnic and play area. Shop with wild boar meat and dry cured bacon, disabled access; park open all year, shop and café (with good bacon sandwiches) open Easter-Oct; (01995) 61554; £3. The village is picturesque, with one of the oldest continuously trading shops in the country, the Chipping Craft Centre; and there's very good food in the Derby Arms at Thornley down towards Longridge.

CHORLEY SD5718
Astley Hall (Astley Park) This
unusual-looking timber-framed 16th-c
house has particularly elaborate
carvings and plasterwork, interesting
pottery and paintings, and extensive
gardens and woodland. Shop, disabled
access to ground floor only; cl am, Mon
(exc bank hols), and wkdys Nov-Mar;
(01257) 515555; £3, free for Chorley
residents. The Farmers Arms at
Eccleston over towards Southport is a
good value dining pub. Chorley has a
busy Tues market.
CLITHEROE SD7441
Bustling old market town: hundreds of
poultry and small livestock enthusiasts
normally come to the Weds evening
auctions, some from as far away as
Scotland. The High St is dominated by
the **castle** perched on its limestone
rock: one of the oldest buildings in
Lancashire, it has one of the smallest
Norman keeps in the country. The
Castle Museum has an extensive
geology exhibition, re-creations of a
Victorian kitchen, cloggers' workshop,
printing press, and good views of the
Ribble Valley. Shop, limited disabled
access; cl Thurs and Fri Oct-Mar, and all
Jan; (01200) 424635; £1.65. Cowmans
on Castle St has over 70 varieties of
traditional and speciality sausages, and
Byrne's on King St stocks a remarkable
range of wines. The **Platform Gallery**
(Station Rd) has good changing
contemporary craft exhibitions; regular
workshops and special events; shop,
disabled access; cl Sun and bank hols;
01200 443071; free. The Swan & Royal
(Castle St) is handy for lunch, and the
Apricot Meringue (15 King St) does
tasty home-made dishes at reasonable
prices. Readers enjoy the sculpture trail
in Bungerley Park; there's a lovely drive
through Bashall Eaves (where there's a
very good farm shop), the Trough of
Bowland and Quernmore.
COW ARK SD6845
Browsholme Hall ⌨ This
unpretentious-looking Tudor house, on
the edge of the Forest of Bowland, has a
surprisingly rich range of contents and
good guided tours. Snacks, shop,
disabled access to ground floor only; cl
Mon (exc late summer bank hol), mid-
July to mid-Aug, and Oct-late Jun exc

spring bank hol wknd, best to check;
(01254) 826719; £4. The Inn at
Whitewell in one direction and Red
Pump at Bashall Eaves in the other offer
a choice of good places to eat.
CROSTON SD4918
A good village to visit, with a very old
(and well preserved) church
surrounded by cobbled paths. The
Memory Lane tearoom (Town Rd) is a
pleasant place for lunch.
DOWNHAM SD7844
Below Pendle Hill, carefully preserved
by the Assheton estate and
outstandingly pretty, on the side of a
steep pasture valley with a stream
winding along the bottom; the
Assheton Arms is good.
FLEETWOOD SD3448
Behind some decay, you can easily trace
the elegance of its original 19th-c resort
development (there was even
landscaping by Decimus Burton). It still
has plenty of smart buildings, a lively
harbour, excellent market (in winter
Tues, Fri and Sat, daily in summer exc
Weds and Sun), two elegant lighthouses
(the one in the middle of the street did
serve a practical purpose, believe it or
not), Freeport factory shopping centre
(indoor and outdoor play areas), and
trams from Blackpool right through the
town. Worth a look, **Fleetwood
Museum** (Queens Terrace) has
displays on the fishing industry, a
reconstructed salt mine, some
interactive displays and touch-screen
computers; cl Sun am, and mid-Nov to
Mar; (01253) 876621; £2. In Fish Dock
(Fleetwood Marina) you can go on a
guided tour (often led by an ex-
fisherman) of *Jacinta* a restored
icelandic fishing vessel, in service till
1994. Open daily Easter-Oct but best to
check; (01253) 885642; £2. The
architecturally interesting North
Euston Hotel by the terminus is a safe
bet for food, and the Marine Hall
exhibition centre on the front has a
decent bar (the Wyre - no food) with
excellent views of the harbour and
Morecambe Bay.
Farmer Parr's Animal World ⌨
(Wyrefield Farm (B5409, between
A585 and A587 S)) This small farm has
over 200 animals inc llamas, wild boar,
emus and owls; pony and tractor rides,

children's play area, a pottery (run by
the charity Autism Initiatives), and a
rural heritage centre. Meals, snacks,
shop, disabled access; cl 25-26 Dec;
(01253) 874389; £3.50.

FOREST OF BOWLAND SD6650
Magnificent countryside, less visited
than most areas of comparable scenery,
as much of the moorland, privately
owned, is closed to walkers. Only a few
paths cross the impressive massif that
forms some of the county's most
significant scenery; Ramblers
Association has often organised mass
trespasses as demonstrations against
denial of access, and hopes for big
changes here from right-to-roam
legislation. Development in some of the
villages (also in private hands) is
controlled too strictly for any
significant expansion of holiday
accommodation - let alone a
proliferation of camp sites and so forth.
These restrictions make the area
particularly appealing for people who
want peace and quiet, and it's not
impossible to find good walks. There
are some fine ones on rights of way - for
instance, up Clougha Fell from
Quernmore; above Tarnbrook Wyre;
up Dunsop Fell from Slaidburn or
Dunsop Bridge; up Fairsnape and Wolf
Fell from Chipping or Bleasdale. Beacon
Fell Country Park is an atmospheric
place to wander through, and there are
some pleasant walks around the
Coronation Arms at Horton. Don't be
confused by road signs by the Rivers
Ribble and Hodder claiming some of the
territory for Yorkshire (as in the past
indeed it was).

FORMBY DUNES SD2808
Reached from the NW edge of Formby,
a large tract of sweeping sandy dunes
which in some areas is being stabilised
by pine plantations; broad beaches and
good walks through the adjacent
pinewoods, made interesting by the
chance of seeing and even feeding red
squirrels (you can buy nuts here); £3
per car, though you may be able to park
free within comfortable reach. Best in
spring and autumn - can be busy in
summer, cl 25 Dec; NT.

GARSTANG SD4945
Quite an attractive small market town
with a good deal of canal activity, and a

fine aqueduct crossing the River Wyre.
The waterside Owd Tithebarn, with
food all day, is fun (they boast one of the
largest collections of farming
implements in the country). From here
a wheelchair-accessible footpath to
Scorton gives panoramic views over the
River Wyre.

GLASSON DOCK SD4456
Once an important port for Lancaster,
this still has the occasional coaster
berthing, but is mainly a lively summer
boating place now, in pleasant
countryside. The Victoria on the dock
(with lots of fresh fish) is a popular
dining pub, as is the 17th-c Stork up on
the A588.

GREAT MITTON SD7139
Great Mitton church Attractive,
with an outstanding range of memorial
tombs. This is a nice spot by the River
Ribble, and the Aspinall Arms has
enjoyable food.

HELMSHORE SD7821
Helmshore Textile Museums
(Holcombe Rd) Two stone mills with a
comprehensive collection of textile
machinery, much still in working order,
and a new gallery with interactive
displays on the textile industry. One of
the best textile museums in the
country, though of course if social
history and machinery leave you cold
it's unlikely to convert you. Snacks,
shop, disabled access; cl am, and Nov-
Mar; (01706) 226459; £3. The nearby
White Horse is useful for lunch, and the
Duke of Wellington on the B6232 W of
Haslingden is a reliable family dining pub
in fine surroundings, with more views
further on.

HEYSHAM SD4160
A tremendous contrast with the power
station here is the quaint squint-walled
little village **church**, partly Saxon, with
Norse-carved hogback tombstone
inside. Look out too for the unusual
weighing machine, and the nearby
Heritage Centre is worth popping into,
with local history displays and a new
Viking-theme children's room; shop,
limited disabled access; cl wkdys, and
am wknds end Sept-Easter; (01524)
859517; free. You can also once again
buy non-alcoholic nettle beer, the
village's traditional drink. The Royal,
dating from 1502, has enjoyable food,

and the waterside Golden Ball at Heaton with Oxcliffe off the Lancaster road (may be cut off by very high tides) is fun for lunch.

HEYWOOD SD8510
Corgi Heritage Centre (York St) Hundreds of die-cast model vehicles from pre-war cars to James Bond's Aston Martins - even a turning Magic Roundabout; of course it's all a huge plug for the company that makes them, but fascinating for collectors. Shop, limited disabled access; cl Sun and bank hols; (01706) 365812; free. The Egerton Arms off the B6222 Bury rd is a good moorland dining pub.

HILBRE SJ1887
The biggest of three tidal islands which you can reach on foot at low tide from West Kirby; Hilbre is a **nature reserve**, once popular with sunbathers, now visited mainly by birds and occasional seals. Make sure you know the tide times - (0151) 648 4371 - as it's easy to be stranded out here.

HOGHTON SD6226
Hoghton Tower ⌖ (A675) This splendid 16th-c fortified hilltop mansion has grand state rooms, a Royal bedchamber, and a collection of dolls' houses; Shakespeare lived here for over a year. The gardens are lovely (particularly the rose garden), and the surrounding grounds offer wonderful views of the sea, moors, Lakeland hills and welsh mountains. Tearoom, shop; open Mon-Thurs and Sun pm July-Sept, and bank hols (pm Sun and Mon) rest of year (exc Good Fri, 25 Dec, and 1 Jan); (01254) 852986; £2 parking and grounds, £5 house inc guided tour. The Royal Oak at Riley Green, with a footpath to the tower, does reliable meals.

HOLDEN SD7749
Holden Clough Nursery Old-fashioned nursery with thoroughly up-to-date approach to raising interesting plants in Victorian kitchen garden of Holden Clough; beds of alpines, trough gardens, herbaceous perennials, shrubs and rhododendrons and sometimes special events. Shop, disabled access; cl 12-1pm, Sun (exc pms Easter and May bank hols), Good Fri, and 25 Dec-1 Jan; (01200) 447615; free. The friendly Copy Nook has good food, and is a useful stop for walkers.

HOYLAKE BEACH SJ2088
These sweeping sands are beautiful, with an unusual partly tidal **nature reserve** at Red Rocks N of the golf links. The Hilbre Court Hotel (Banks Rd) has decent food.

HURST GREEN SD6939
Stonyhurst College Magnificent 16th-c manor house, now home to the famous Roman Catholic boarding school. You can see the library, chapel, other historic rooms and the extensive grounds. Tolkien wrote most of his *Rings* cycle while working here (and some like to believe that Hobbiton is based on Hurst Green). Shop, limited disabled access; open pm mid-July - Aug exc Fri, gardens usually open July-Aug - phone to check; (01254) 826345; £5. The village is attractive, the Punch Bowl and Bayley Arms are handy for lunch, and there are fine Ribble Valley walks nearby.

LANCASTER SD4761
Friendly and relaxed despite the grandeur of many of its stone buildings; ambling down the cobbled streets and alleyways (much is pedestrianised), it's hard to believe this was once a major West Indies shipping port; these days the water traffic is more sedate. Riverside paths have been improved; there's now a 10-mile footpath and cycle route that follows the river from Lancaster to Lune Valley at Caton - along the way are various sculptures and other art works. The Lancastrian (Scale Hall Farm, A589 Morecambe rd) has good food, and other places worth knowing for lunch include the Brown Cow (Penny St) and canalside White Cross.
Ashton Memorial & Butterfly Park (Williamson Park) A magnificent folly clearly visible from the motorway (Pevsner rated it the best in Britain), in 54 acres of lovely landscaped parkland; splendid views from the upper galleries. The butterfly house has a good collection of plants and lepidoptera, as well as free-flying birds, various creepy-crawlies, and small mammals. Snacks, shop, disabled access; cl 25-26 Dec, 1 Jan; (01524) 33318; £3.50.
Judge's Lodging (Church St) Enjoyed by readers, this 17th-c house (the town's oldest) has well restored period

rooms, lots of Gillow furniture, a fine Regency billiard table, and museum of childhood. Shop; open pm mid-Mar to Jun and Oct, plus am wkdys July-Sept (cl lunchtime); (01524) 32808; £2. Other decent collections at the firmly traditional **City Museum** on Market Sq, in a very grand Georgian former town hall (shop, disabled access; cl Sun, 24 Dec-1 Jan; free), and at the **Cottage Museum** opposite the castle, furnished in the style of an early 19th-c artisan's house (open pm Easter-Sept; 75p).

Lancaster Castle Dramatic 12th-c Norman fortress famous for hangings and witch trials, owned by the Queen as Duke of Lancaster. Part of it is still used as a prison, but the dungeons, tower and 18th-c Gothic Revival Shire Hall can all be visited. Shop; cl 2 wks over Christmas and New Year; (01524) 64998; £4.

Lancaster Maritime Museum (St George's Quay) In an 18th-c Customs House, this is an up-to-date look at the local maritime trade and fishing industry; the audio-visual show is good fun. Snacks, shop, disabled access; cl am Nov-Easter, 24-26 and 31 Dec, and 1 Jan; (01524) 382264; £2 (free to local residents).

Lancaster Priory Dates back to before the Conquest, though the present hilltop building is mainly 14th and 15th c; very interesting medieval choir-stalls, needlework and Anglo-Saxon cross fragments. Refectory and book shop, some disabled access; priory cl winter lunchtimes, refectory and shop cl Oct-Easter; (01524) 65338; free. Nearby are the remains of a Roman bath house.

LEIGHTON HALL SD4874
A notably friendly welcome at this neo-Gothic mansion (more restrained inside), still the home of the Gillow family and with early examples of their furniture. The grounds have a collection of birds of prey, nature trails, and beautifully kept gardens. The setting is lovely, with Lakeland hills rising behind. Snacks, shop, disabled access; cl am, all day Sat and Mon (exc bank hols), and Oct-Apr; (01524) 734474; £5. The nearby New Inn at Yealand Conyers has enjoyable food.

LEYLAND SD5422
British Commercial Vehicle Museum (King St) Jazzed up with sound effects, this has over 90 perfectly restored british waggons, buses, trucks, vans, fire engines and even a Popemobile, shining so much you'd think they were new. Snacks, shop, disabled access; open Sun, Tues-Thurs and bank hols Apr-Sept, Sun only Oct; (01772) 451011; £4. The Midge Hall (Midge Hall Lane, about 2m W of here) is a popular food pub. Leyland also has a pleasant little town trail, and the medieval church has some fine stained glass.

South Ribble Museum (Church Rd) The sturdy 16th-c former school has changing local history displays; open Tues, Fri, pm Thurs and am Sat; (01772) 422041; free. **Worden Park** has art displays and nine craft workshops, walks, gardens, a maze, arboretum, and miniature golf; cl 25 Dec; (01772) 421109; free.

LIVERPOOL SJ3590
Recently declared European Capital of Culture for 2008, to follow such distinguished cultural hotbeds as Graz (2003), Genoa and Lille (this year), Cork (2005), then Patras and Luxembourg, Liverpool is full of character, with an increasing amount to offer visitors. The many fine 19th-c buildings recall Liverpool's past as one of the world's great ports - it's got more listed buildings than any other city except London (inc the landmark Radio City Tower). The Philharmonic (Hope St) is probably the country's grandest late Victorian pub; nearby the Everyman Bistro has good value food. The city's trademark Liver Building is best viewed from one of the famous ferries across the Mersey, which leave regularly from Pier Head (50-minute cruises with a commentary are £4.50); the real commuter ferries operate half-hourly during rush-hours (£2 return). The city's 'Three Graces' (made up of the Liver, Cunard and Port of Liverpool buildings) are to be joined by a fourth building, a futuristic structure known as the Cloud (due for completion around 2007, critics claim it looks like a deflated football). Very lively at night, Mathew Street is the place to head if you like the

Beatles, and Concert Sq is a popular place for a drink in summer with lots of cafés and bars. The main shopping street is pedestrianised; interesting for browsing, Quiggles (School Lane) has lots of stalls with vintage clothes, jewellery and the like. The chinese community here is one of the oldest in Europe, and the Arch in Chinatown is the largest outside China; nearby at the top of Bold Street look out for the remains of St Luke's church, bombed out in World War II, now with trees growing inside it.

Albert Dock Spectacular restoration of previously redundant warehouse buildings by the river, now a lively complex of shops, cafés and exhibitions, with regular events, boat trips. The Baltic Fleet, a majestically restored Victorian dockside pub, is handy for lunch. The next four attractions are housed in the complex - you can easily base a whole day around a visit here.

Beatles Story (Albert Dock) Bouncy tribute to the local boys made good and the sights and sounds of the 60s, inc a reconstruction of the Cavern Club. Shop, disabled access; cl 25-26 Dec; (0151) 709 1963; *£7.95. Devoted Beatles fans might want also to go on a 2-hour tour of related city sites; the bus leaves the Beatles Story daily at 12, 2.30 and 4pm, best to book in advance (0151) 709 1963; £10.95. A joint ticket to the Beatles Story and Football Museum is available; £11.

Merseyside Maritime Museum (Albert Dock) Huge (and growing) museum spread over six floors, with boats, ships, craft demonstrations and a lively interpretation of what it was like for the millions who travelled from here to the New World. The excellent Museum of Liverpool Life vividly re-creates social history from the last century or so; good interactive displays. The Customs and Excise museum, Anything To Declare, is much more fun than it sounds. It takes an intriguing look at concealment techniques, with demonstrations by sniffer dogs, and there's an interesting assortment of items seized by customs inc a guitar made from a turtle, a tiger-skin waistcoat, and a host of illegal weapons. A gallery on transatlantic slavery has

divided local historians, who disagree on Liverpool's true role in the slave trade. Also galleries on the *Titanic* and *Lusitania*, and an art gallery; in summer they display some of their larger exhibits outside, and you may be able to board one of the ships at the preserved dockside. Meals, snacks, shop, disabled access; cl 23-26 Dec, 1 Jan; (0151) 478 4499; free.

Tate Liverpool 🖼 (Albert Dock) In a converted warehouse, this is the largest collection of contemporary art outside London - all very well presented with especially good use of natural light; they give interesting half-hour talks most afternoons. Meals, snacks, shop, disabled access (and audio and Braille guides); cl Mon (exc bank hols), Good Fri, 24-26 Dec, 1 Jan; (0151) 702 7400; free, £4 for special exhibitions.

Yellow Duckmarine 🖼 A fun way of getting to know Liverpool is this hour-long city tour and river experience. Bright yellow amphibious vehicles, built in World War II to land troops and supplies, drive you along the waterfront and through the streets taking in the city's main sites, then splash down into the Mersey to continue the tour by water. Tickets are available from the Anchor Courtyard (Albert Dock), hourly tours leave daily 13 Feb-23 Dec; (0151) 708 7799; £9.95.

Bluecoat Arts Centre (School Lane) Attractive Queen Anne building housing changing art exhibitions and a programme of performances, plus art, craft and book shops. Meals, snacks, disabled access to ground floor only; gallery cl Sun and Mon, centre cl Sun and bank hols; box office (0151) 709 5297; free (exc for events).

Cains Brewery (Stanhope St) Evening tours of red brick brewery, inc buffet and tastings; tours start at 6.30pm and must be booked in advance (over-18s only); shop; no tours Fri-Sun, brewery cl wknds; (0151) 709 8734; £3.75. The splendidly restored Brewery Tap pub is good.

Cathedrals Unusually, both Liverpool's cathedrals were built last century, in widely differing styles. Walk along Hope St (the heart of the city's 18th-c area, with many Georgian brick terraces) to the impressive and more obviously modern Metropolitan Roman Catholic cathedral on Mount Pleasant, designed by Frederick Gibberd after a vast earlier scheme by Lutyens ran out of money; blue light from the 16-sided glass tower reflects evocatively on the marble inside. The Anglican cathedral looks much older, but was completed only in 1978. Britain's biggest, it's undeniably powerful, though its soaring proportions and cavernous scale make it impersonal. Both have good concerts.

Conservation Centre (Whitechapel) Intriguing glimpse of the world of museum and gallery conservation; interactive displays and demonstrations explain how various objects are preserved, and exhibits range from a mummified Egyptian crocodile to two Beatles' gold discs; good programme of events. Meals, snacks, shop, disabled access; cl Sun am, 24-26 Dec, 1 Jan; (0151) 478 4999; free.

Croxteth Hall & Country Park (5m NE) Period displays in Edwardian house, and working farm, Victorian walled garden, miniature railway, and country walks in the grounds - a pleasant family trip out. Meals, snacks, shop, some disabled access; house cl end Sept-Easter, farm cl winter wkdys, and 25 Dec-1 Jan, park open all year; (0151) 228 5311; park free; hall, farm, and garden £4, hall or farm only £2, walled garden only £1.20.

FACT (Wood St) Costing £10m, this is the first purpose-built arts project in Liverpool for over 60 years. Two galleries feature work by international artists working with film, video and new media; there are three comfortable cinemas (mostly independent films), and a good café (and bar). Shop, disabled access; galleries cl Mon, and a few days over Christmas; (0151) 707 4450; galleries free, cinema £5.50.

Grand National Experience 🅔 (Aintree Race Course) Takes you behind the scenes of the world's most famous steeplechase. A visitor centre has memorabilia charting the history of the race from its origins in 1839, while in the weighing room you can try on the silks of past winners, test out the scales and experience a steward's enquiry. Perhaps the highlight is the simulator ride - find out what it's like to jump a

National fence; guided tours of the course (11am and 2pm Tues-Fri, at other times by appointment) include a look around the stables. Shop, disabled access; cl Mon, end Oct-end May, and all race days, phone to check; (0151) 522 2921; visitor centre £3 (with simulator ride and tour £7).

Joseph Williamson Tunnels (Smithdown Lane) Built by an eccentric local philanthropist to create work for unemployed soldiers returning from the Napoleonic Wars, a small section of these intriguing underground tunnels are open (though there are plans to open more tunnels in the near future); you can find out more at the new heritage centre, and there are guided tours throughout the day; they plan to hold regular special events. Meals, snacks, shop, limited disabled access to tunnels; cl Mon-Weds Nov-Mar, 24-26 Dec and 1 Jan; (0151) 709 6868; £3.50.

Liverpool Museum (William Brown St) Although they're in the middle of a big expansion, there's still a lot to do at this top-class museum. A couple of galleries are currently closed (their aquarium for example), but the popular dinosaur gallery, and the excellent Natural History Centre, are still open (you can handle specimens and use video microscopes to get a closer look at some of the exhibits - staff are on hand to answer questions). Another highlight is the Space and Time gallery, with its rockets, chunks of moon rock, and interactive displays; children can get a free activity booklet, and the collection of time-keeping devices is interesting, from ancient sundials to the latest gadgets. The planetarium (£1), has an excellent half-hour journey between the planets, with some stunning images from the Hubble telescope and robotic spacecraft. Shows are usually at 3.15pm Tues-Fri (no show Mon, exc in school hols), and hourly in the afternoon at wknds and school hols. Snacks, shop, disabled access; cl am Sun, and all day 23-26 Dec, 1 Jan; (0151) 207 0001; free.

National Wildflower Centre (off A5080, nr M62 junction 5) In 35-acre Court Hey Park, this conservation centre for endangered british wildflowers was formerly a home of the

Gladstones. Made up of traditional stable buildings and a 150-metre (500-ft) 'working wall' with big display panels and a rooftop walkway, it has hands-on activities and exhibitions about conservation, demonstration areas, sculpture garden, and a play area. You can also see how wildflower seed is harvested and cleaned; special events. Meals, snacks, shop and garden centre, disabled access; open Apr-Sept; (0151) 737 1819; £3.

Open Eye Gallery (Wood St) Good changing photography exhibitions. Shop, disabled access; usually cl Sun, Mon, over Christmas, and Easter wknd; (0151) 709 9460; free.

Princes Road Synagogue Consecrated in 1874, this is one of Europe's finest examples of High Victorian Moorish Revival synagogue architecture; guided talks cover the Jewish community in Liverpool, the history and architecture of the building, and give an introduction to Jewish traditions. Shop; tours Thurs pm (exc Jewish hols), phone in advance to book (0151) 709 3431; free, donations welcome.

Sudley House (Mossley Hill Rd) Former home of Victorian ship-builder George Holt, this interestingly unspoilt private Victorian house has good gardens, attractive furniture, and paintings by Turner and Pre-Raphaelites. Shop, disabled access to ground floor only; cl Sun am, 23-26 Dec, 1 Jan; (0151) 207 0001; free.

University of Liverpool Art Gallery Highlights of this growing collection include paintings by JMW Turner and Lucien Freud, early porcelain, stained glass cartoons by Edward Burne-Jones, sculpture by John Foley, and a fine collection of clocks, all housed in an elegant Georgian terrace; free lunchtime talks and temporary exhibitions. Cl am, wknds and bank hols, plus all Aug; (0151) 794 2348; free.

Walker Art Gallery (William Brown St) One of the finest art collections outside London, this outstanding place now has two new galleries for temporary exhibitions, inc a new craft and design gallery. Especially notable italian, dutch and Pre-Raphaelite works (a blockbuster Rossetti exhibition runs

until 18 Jan), and, a highlight for many, W F Yeames's *When Did You Last See Your Father?*, plus, amongst the masters, the gallery houses a painting by Stu Sutcliffe, member of the Beatles in their pre-fame days. Meals, snacks, shop, disabled access; cl 23-26 Dec, and 1 Jan; (0151) 478 4199; free (may charge for special exhibitions).

Western Approaches (Rumford St) Evocatively restored underground command centre for the World War II Battle of the Atlantic; a labyrinth of rooms covering 4,650 sq metres (50,000 sq ft) under the city's streets. Shop; cl Fri, Sun, and Nov-Feb; (0151) 227 2008; £4.75.

The following attractions are all further out from the centre - a bit more of an expedition:

20 Forthlin Rd & Mendips 🔄 (Allerton) You can visit these Beatles landmarks only together, on a guided tour. First is **20 Forthlin Rd**, a 1950s terraced council house, the former home of the McCartney family. John, Paul and George met, rehearsed and wrote many of their earliest songs here, inc 'Love Me Do' and 'I Saw Her Standing There'. **Mendips**, a semi-detached 1930s house, is John Lennon's childhood home; he composed early songs in his bedroom and the front porch. Open Weds-Sun and bank hols Apr-Oct, best to phone; (0151) 427 7231; access is by minibus from Albert Dock (am) or Speke Hall (pm) - see Speke entry; £12, children free; NT members £6 for bus.

Liverpool Football Club Museum 🔄 (Anfield Rd) The visitor centre and Anfield tours are a must for the faithful. There are cups, trophies, programmes and other treasured memorabilia as well as films of the club's finest hours. The tour takes in the grounds, dressing room and pitch - you can even sit on the manager's bench. Snacks, shop, disabled access; visitor centre cl a few days over Christmas, no tours on match days and booking essential; (0151) 260 6677; £8.50 (museum only £5).

Sefton Park Palm House Magnificent 25-metre (82-ft) high three-tiered domed glasshouse, built 1896 but derelict and then unglazed for years. Now restored, with palms, cycads, orchids and tree ferns, it's surrounded by life-size statues of explorers and naturalists. Disabled access; cl for events and performances (usually Thurs and Fri), phone for details; (0151) 726 2415; free.

LYTHAM ST ANNE'S SD3228 Decorous conjoined seaside towns that seem a world away from nearby Blackpool. Lytham has a splendidly restored **windmill** by the promenade in the centre of its breezy green (shop; usually open Tues-Thurs and wknds (cl 1-2pm) May-Sept), and a small **Lifeboat Museum** next door (usually same times, exc open Weds July-Aug only); (01253) 730155; donations. St Anne's has traditional seaside activities inc Pleasure Island (a beachside family entertainment complex), and a café quarter on Wood St. The Taps is a good real ale pub.

MANCHESTER SJ8398 Manchester is packed with interesting places to visit, and exciting central developments add to its considerable attraction for visitors, such as the architecturally stunning **Urbis**, the centrepiece for the hugely ambitious new city-centre Millennium Quarter. On a fine summer evening, strolling around the impressive buildings is a real pleasure; Albert Sq is one of the finest areas, with the great Albert Memorial (predating London's). The Town Hall is a massively impressive piece of Victoriana; guided tours leave from the visitor information centre most Sats, phone to check (0161) 941 7620; £4. At the heart of the Millennium Quarter lies the very wide 15th-c **cathedral** which has notable choir stalls, and an interesting new visitor centre. The small medieval centre around it is now protected by a park, and nearby the reconstructed 18th-c Sinclairs Oyster Bar (Cathedral Gates) is good value (not just oysters). In front is the pedestrian Exchange Sq (big sporting events etc are shown here on a large screen), the Triangle (a shopping centre in the former Corn Exchange), and a group of tall post-modern stainless steel windmills. Opposite the Triangle is the Printworks entertainments complex (which has an IMAX cinema). The Castlefield area by the basin where

the Bridgewater and Rochdale canals meet is interesting: restored warehouses, viaducts and the like, lots of lively redevelopment inc a tramway and wonderfully light and airy footbridge. Dukes 92 is a good pub (may be street theatre outside). Not far off, on the other side of the GMEX exhibition centre, is the very smart Bridgewater Hall (box office (0161) 907 9000). By contrast, the Rochdale canal towpath is a fascinating seamy-side walk. Chinatown here has lots of authentic restaurants, and there's a Chinese Arts Centre in Edge St. Manchester's vibrant gay scene is based around the gay village on Canal St, with outdoor bars and cafés in summer. Afflecks Palace on Church St is good for antique clothing and records, and for more mainstream shopping, there's a huge shopping centre with a 20-screen cinema at Trafford Park to the S. The major revamp of Piccadilly Station is now complete, and Piccadilly Gardens, the old heart of the city, has been redeveloped into a public square, dramatically lit at night. Metrolink trams are a good way to get round the city centre, and there are plans to expand the area they cover. See also separate entries for Salford and Prestwich. Manchester also boasts Britain's only Olympic standard indoor cycle track (Stuart St, Clayton, E of the centre); they cater for all abilities (inc training sessions for beginners); phone for more information; (0161) 223 2244.

Chetham's Library (Long Millgate) Nestled among the modern developments of the Millennium Quarter, this is the oldest public library in Britain, founded in 1653. The attractive building itself dates from the 15th c and was originally a college for priests. Many of the original features remain, inc fellows' dormitories and 17th-c reading tables (still used). Cl 12.30-1.30pm, wknds, bank hols, and 25 Dec-1 Jan; (0161) 834 7961; free.

Manchester Art Gallery (Mosley St) An excellent place to visit, with a tremendous collection of fine and decorative art. Aside from outstanding Pre-Raphaelites, and a very good 20th-c british gallery, an interactive gallery has multi-media displays and hands-on activities for children. The Manchester Gallery is another highlight, and a vast high-ceilinged room on the top floor houses an arts and crafts gallery; three spaces are given over to temporary exhibitions. The staff are friendly, and you can pick up an audio-guide to help you round. Meals, snacks, shop, good disabled access; cl Mon (exc bank hols), Good Fri, 24-26 Dec, 1 Jan; (0161) 235 8888; free.

People's History Museum (Bridge St) Takes a comprehensive look at the way ordinary folk toiled and struggled to change society. Lots of well put together displays inc the largest collection of political banners in the world, plus quizzes and games to entertain children; an upstairs gallery hosts changing exhibitions. Meals, snacks, shops, disabled access; cl Mon (exc bank hols), Good Fri, 25-26 Dec, and 1 Jan; (0161) 839 6061; £1 (free on Fri).

Urbis (Cathedral Gardens, Corporation St) Another ambitious attraction for the city, housed in a futuristic glass structure (supposed to conjure up a huge early 20th-c cruise-liner). This ultra-modern museum aims to explore life in different cities of the world, with interactive displays and audio-visuals, focusing especially on Manchester, Los Angeles, Sao Paolo, Singapore, Paris and Tokyo. A glass elevator (unique in Europe for its 45-degree ascent) whisks you to the top, to work your way down the four themed floors. Restaurant, café (great views), shops, temporary exhibitions, disabled access; cl 25 Dec; (0161) 907 9099; *£5.

Manchester Jewish Museum (Cheetham Hill Rd, A665 1m N) In a former synagogue, the story of Manchester's Jewish community over the last 200 years, with fascinating recorded recollections of life early last century. Shop, disabled access to ground floor only; cl Fri, Sat, Jewish holidays, 24-28 and 31 Dec, plus 1 Jan; (0161) 834 9879; £3.75. The nearby Derby Brewery Arms is a classic Mancunian pub, good value snacks.

Manchester Museum (Oxford Rd) Excellent family-friendly museum with an interactive science gallery (test your memory and blood pressure, and see if you can fit all the organs into a model torso) as well as Egyptian and natural history galleries; there are also displays on dinosaurs and archery. Several galleries have recently been refurbished and expanded, inc the vivarium (the poisonous frogs are fascinating), and there are new ethnology and money galleries; they've a lively programme of special events. Meals, snacks, shop and disabled access; cl Good Fri, 25-26 Dec and 1 Jan; (0161) 275 2634; free.

Museum of Science & Industry in Manchester (Castlefield) One of Britain's most impressive and imaginative museums, built on the site of the oldest passenger railway station in the world. There are hours of things to do, and plenty to touch and fiddle with. The main galleries take a broad and accessible look at power, industry and transport (going right up to space travel), with highlights inc an exciting simulator in the air and space gallery, a big hands-on interactive science area, and a fascinating exhibition on sanitation. The vast power hall has working engines and railway locomotives, and there's an absorbing exhibition on the history of photography, and a comprehensive look at Manchester's development. The changing exhibitions are particularly good. Meals, snacks, shop, disabled access; cl Dec 24-26; (0161) 832 2244; free, charges for temporary exhibitions.

Pankhurst Centre (62 Nelson St) Emmeline Pankhurst launched the Suffragette movement from this Georgian semi, with period-furnished parlour and interestingly planted garden, now surrounded by University of Manchester buildings. Shop, disabled access to ground floor only; cl wknds and bank hols; (0161) 273 5673; free.

Royal Northern College of Music (Oxford Rd) Regular concerts, recitals and exhibitions. Meals, snacks, disabled access; cl Aug; box office (0161) 907 5555.

Whitworth Art Gallery (Oxford Rd) British watercolours from Sandby to Turner, plus modern paintings and sculpture, and unusual collections of textiles and wallpaper. In 2003 a thief stole then returned three valuable paintings, claiming he did it just to prove how easy it was. Meals, snacks, shop, disabled access; cl am Sun, Good Fri, and 25 Dec-1 Jan; (0161) 275 7450; free.

Gallery of Costume (Platt Hall, Rusholme - a mile S of the University area) Georgian mansion, with comprehensive displays of fashion over the last 400 years. Disabled access to ground floor only, but there's a video of the other areas; open last Sat in month, or by appointment; (0161) 224 5217; free.

The following attractions are also some way out from the centre:

Manchester United Museum 🏛 (Old Trafford, W of centre) Purpose-built football museum, covering the club's history from its foundation in 1878 to the more recent glory days. Hundreds of exhibits (changing almost as frequently as their strip) and tours of the ground (must book in advance, not match days, and limited on the days before). Meals, snacks, shop (not unjustifiably they call it a megastore), disabled access; cl a few days over Christmas; (0870) 442 1994; £8.50 tour and museum, £5.50 museum only.

Museum of Transport 🏛 (Boyle St, Cheetham, N of centre) Around 80 vintage local buses and other vehicles, as well as photographs, tickets and memorabilia - even historic bus stops. Snacks, shop, disabled access; open Weds, wknds and bank hols (exc over Christmas); (0161) 205 2122; *£3.

Heaton Hall 🏛 (Prestwich, northern suburbs) Splendidly decorated 18th-c neo-Classical house in extensive well used public parkland; fine paintings, plasterwork and furniture, and an unusual circular Pompeiian room. Shop, disabled access; usually cl Mon (exc bank hols) Tues and Weds, and Oct-Easter; (0161) 773 1231; free. The handsomely Victorian Woodthorpe by the main gate has decent food.

Wythenshawe Hall (southern suburbs) A few rooms in this attractive half-timbered Tudor house are open to the public, and it now houses some of the paintings and furniture from the Manchester Art Gallery. Disabled access to ground floor only; best to phone for opening times; (0161) 998

21171; free. The 110 hectares (270 acres) of surrounding parkland include woodland, a horticultural centre (with a café), and a farm (with farm shop).

MARPLE SJ9688

Peak Forest Canal Reached from Marple, the towpath soon leaves suburbia for green countryside; N is the famous set of Marple locks and aqueduct over the River Etherow. To the S, you can leave the canal at Strines and climb on to Mellor Moor.

MARTIN MERE SD4214

Wildfowl & Wetlands Trust 🏛 (off A59) Thousands of wild geese, swans, ducks and flamingos regularly visit the recreated natural open water habitats at this important 150-hectare (376-acre) centre. Some birds will feed straight from your hand. Good visitor centre, an adventure playground, well organised walks, lively activities for children, and plenty of events, such as watching the return of an increasing number of migratory swans; phone for details. Meals, snacks, shop, disabled access; cl 25 Dec; (01704) 895181; £5.50. The canalside Ship at Lathom is very popular for lunch.

Windmill Animal Farm (Fish Lane, Holmeswood; just N) This friendly 16-hectare (40-acre) place has animals and their babies to feed (inc rare breeds), pedal tractors, miniature railway, indoor play area and an adventure playground. Snacks, shop, disabled access; cl wkdys mid-Sept to Easter; (01704) 892282; £3.50.

MORECAMBE SD4264

Five miles of promenade and more of beaches to stroll along at this cheery resort, with pretty sunsets over the bay, and enjoyable guided walks across the sands (Cedric Robinson, the Queen's official guide, has been doing the job for more than 30 years); phone (01539) 532165; free. A lovely seafront statue commemorates the town's funniest son, Eric Morecambe, who so loved the place, adopted its name. The Dog & Partridge (Bare) has decent fresh food.

Morecambe Bay Sands Vast mudflats and sands, home to 200,000 wading birds. Walks over them are easiest from the Cumbria side, though guided walks are also available from

Hest Bank; phone (01539) 532165 or ask at local tourist information centres - the galloping tides and quicksand do make a guide essential. The pleasant Hest Bank Hotel does enjoyable food all day.

OSWALDTWISTLE SD7428
Oswaldtwistle Mills (Moscow Mill, Colliers St) This popular shopping village also has various craft workshops inc a sweet factory (£1), and a textile museum (free); also gardens, wildfowl reserve, nature trail, an outdoor play area, and summer events such as donkey rides; there's an indoor play centre too (£2.50). Meals, snacks, disabled access; cl 25-26 Dec and 1 Jan; (01254) 871025.

PADIHAM SD8034
Gawthorpe Hall Early 17th-c country house with fine panelling and moulded ceilings, minstrels' gallery, Jacobean long gallery, and some mid-19th-c alterations. Important collections of costume, embroidery and lace, and paintings from the National Portrait Gallery. Snacks, shop; house cl am, Mon (exc bank hols), Fri, and Nov-Mar, grounds open all year; (01282) 771004; £3; NT. The hilly cobbled alleys in the town's centre are now a conservation area. The Red Rock (Sabden Rd) has good value food, with fine views from its garden.

PENDLE HILL SD8240
An excellent network of paths lets you walk round and almost all over it. Although Pendle's witch-persecuting days are happily over, the place still has a haunting elemental appeal. The view that enraptured George Fox, the founder of the Quakers, is as good as ever. The quickest way up is from Barley village.

PORT SUNLIGHT SJ3384
Lady Lever Art Gallery Lord Leverhulme, who had built his Sunlight Soap factory here, donated this outstanding gallery to the village. It has interesting Victorian paintings inc Turners and Pre-Raphaelites - many adapted for use in soap ads, to the fury of the artists. Meals, snacks, shop, disabled access; cl Sun am, 23-26 Dec, 1 Jan; (0151) 478 4136; free.
Port Sunlight Heritage Centre Sets the scene for this most famous of the

garden villages built by 19th-c philanthropists, contriving something better than the appalling squalor of northern England's factory towns. Historically important as the precursor of garden cities, garden suburbs and New Towns, it's perfectly preserved, with swathes of greenery and parkland between groups of mock-Tudor cottages for the soap factory workers: no two groups of houses are alike. Useful village trail leaflets. Shop, good disabled access; cl Christmas wk; (0151) 644 6466; 80p. Nearby Thornton Hough was also built by Lord Leverhulme, as a mock-Tudor estate village - Port Sunlight on a much smaller scale; the Seven Stars there is useful for lunch.

POULTON-LE-FYLDE SD3439
Quite an attractive pedestrianised market square, with a lovely church (as others in Lancashire, looking a good deal older than in fact it is), and several useful places to eat - the Old Town Hall is particularly good value. Readers like Charlotte's Tearoom and giftshop in nearby Great Eccleston; (01995) 671108 (The Square); a small popular café where the food is served on Spode crockery.

PRESCOT SJ4793
Knowsley Safari Park Five-mile drive through very natural-looking reserves of lions, tigers, rhinos, monkeys and other animals; they have the biggest herd of african elephants in Europe. There's a roller-coaster and a pirate ship ride; also pets' corner, miniature railway, and an information centre. Meals, snacks, shop, disabled access; cl 25 Dec; (0151) 430 9009; £8. If you have to pass through the town, the **museum** (Church St) has an interesting collection relating to the area's former clock-making industry; cl 1-2pm, Sun am, Mon (inc bank hols), Good Fri, 25 Dec-1 Jan; (0151) 430 7787; free. The Clock Face (Derby St) is a pleasant old mansion-house pub here.

PRESTON SD5329
The city has some decent museums: the impressive if rather dour greek revival **Harris Museum and Art Gallery** on Market Sq (cl bank hols; (01772) 258248; free), and the **Museum of Lancashire** on Stanley St (cl Thurs

(exc school hols), Sun, and bank hols; (01772) 264075; £2) are worth a visit, and Fulwood Barracks (B6241/B6242) has a military heritage centre (cl bank hols; free). There's a good big market (the space is used for car-boot sales instead on Tues and Thurs). Decent food at Wall Street (Fishergate) and the Black Horse (Friargate); readers recommend the popular Chaps café (Cheapside). Phone for information about visiting **Moor Park Observatory** (01772) 257181. On the W side of the city, Haslam Park (A5085/B6241) is nice for a stroll. **Church of St Mary** (Penwortham) 4th-c chancel, and the scant remains of a motte and bailey castle in the churchyard; nearby the Fleece (A59) is useful for lunch.

Millennium Ribble Link The first new canal to be built for over a century, completing an ambitious scheme begun in the 18th c, this connects the Lancaster Canal to the national canal network. Nine new locks had to be built, inc a stairflight lock at Tom Benson Way (nr Preston Sports Arena) and a sea lock; this linear water park includes an arts trail, cycle paths, and picnic and play areas; disabled access; cl Nov-Easter; (01524) 751888; free. Phone for information on where you can fish; (01606) 723800.

National Football Museum (Sir Tom Finney Way, Deepdale) Fans will be fascinated by this museum, and even if you go just to keep company with an enthusiast you'll find lots to interest you. The 'first half', with an incredible collection of footballing memorabilia, covers the evolution of the game; it also places football in its wider social context showing what was happening in the world off the pitch. The 'second half', which examines different aspects of football such as rules, tactics and equipment, is more hands-on: you can play table football and then watch your game on screen, or have a go at commentating on *Match of the Day*, and the new interactive 'goal striker' exhibit gives you a chance to record the speed of your goals and compete with famous players (£2.50). Meals, snacks, disabled access; cl Mon (exc bank hols), 25 Dec; (01772) 908442; free.

RAMSBOTTOM SD8017
Lovely village with a Saturday market, overlooked by Holcombe Hill and crossed by the River Irwell. Down by the Twine Valley trout lakes, the Fishermans Retreat has interesting food served with proper chips.

RIBCHESTER SD6535
Attractive little town, many of its buildings incorporating masonry plundered from the former Roman town here: the White Bull pub, with decent food, has a couple of Tuscan pillars for its porch and an excavated Roman bath house behind. The 15th-c **church** stands on the site of the Roman fort, and looks as if it uses much salvaged material from it.

Ribchester Roman Museum On the site of a fort occupied between the 1st and 4th c, with lots of coins and pottery, weaponry, jewellery and leatherwork; they've also got some interactive exhibits, and various replicas. There are Roman remains outside inc a Roman granary. Shop, disabled access; cl 25 Dec; (01254) 878261; £2.

RINGLEY SD7605
Unexpected corner so close to urban areas, with village stocks and ancient bridge over the Irwell; the Horseshoe (off A667 at Kidds Garden Centre sign) has good food.

RIVINGTON RESERVOIRS SD6215
These attractive waters just outside Horwich make good walking territory. Lower Rivington Reservoir has a waterside path along its eastern edge, and a curious mock-up of Liverpool castle built in 1912 as an adornment to the vast and atmospherically decayed gardens of Lever Park, which cover the hillside. A trail guides you around the undergrowth and up to the Pigeon Tower, within a few minutes of Rivington Pike, the summit. The Great House Barn is the place to start, with information centre, maps and guides; (01204) 691549. The Millstone (A673, Anderton) has good food.

RODDLESWORTH VALLEY SD6622
Good woodland walks from the Royal Arms at Tockholes, and perhaps on to the ruins of Hollinshead Hall and its restored curative well.

RUFFORD SD4616
Rufford Old Hall Lovely timber-framed Tudor house built by the Hesketh family in the 16th c, with an intricate hammer-beam roof in the Great Hall, and impressive collections of 17th-c Lancashire oak furniture, and 16th-c arms, armour and tapestries. Some later rooms too; audio tour. Meals, snacks, shop, disabled access to ground floor and grounds; house cl am, Thurs-Fri, and Nov-mid-Apr, garden and tearoom cl Thurs-Fri, and 25 Dec to mid-Apr; (01704) 821254; £4.50, £2.50 garden only; NT. The Red Lion over in Mawdesley has good food.

SABDEN SD7737
Attractive village, with a decent antiques centre, on the slopes of Pendle Hill; linked by a scenic drive to another charming Pendle Hill village, Pendleton, where the Swan With Two Necks is a handy stop.

SALFORD SJ8198
Merging almost imperceptibly into Manchester, this owes its distinct place in the popular consciousness mainly to the works of L S Lowry, and one of its two stunning and iconic new buildings is dedicated to Lowry's work. (The other is the Imperial War Museum North.)
Imperial War Museum North See *separate family panel on p. 345.*
Ordsall Hall Museum (Ordsall Lane) Timbered Tudor manor house with local history and Victorian farmhouse kitchen. Shop, some disabled access; cl Sun am, Sat, Good Fri, Easter Sun, 25-26 Dec, 1 Jan; (0161) 872 0251; free.
Salford Museum and Art Gallery (Peel Park) Five temporary exhibition areas, a gallery of Victorian art, a reconstructed Victorian street, and a new gallery charting Salford's history from Victorian times to the present; you'll need to book for their school hol children's activities. Meals, snacks, shop, disabled access; cl am wknds, 25-26 Dec, 1 Jan, and Easter Sun; (0161) 736 2649; free.

SALFORD QUAYS SJ8398
Lowry (Salford Quays) This shimmering much-praised steel building houses the largest collection of works by the eponymous artist; other galleries have changing exhibitions, and Artworks is a creative interactive

gallery; it also has two theatres, and a plaza with bars and restaurants. Disabled access; cl 25 Dec; box office (0161) 876 2000; free, Artworks £3.75. There's a factory outlet shopping centre nearby too.

SAMLESBURY SD6130
Samlesbury Hall (A677) Well restored half-timbered 14th-c manor house, with good changing exhibitions and craft demonstrations, and sales of antiques. Meals, snacks, disabled access to ground floor only; cl Sat, 25-26 Dec, and 1 Jan; (01254) 812010; £3. There's a good farm shop at Huntley Gate Farm (A59), with around 46 different flavours of home-made ice-cream; cl Mon (exc bank hols). The New Hall Tavern (B6230) has enjoyable food.

SCORTON SD5048
This appealing village is the gateway to the Trough of Bowland, and has scenic walks through the Grizedale Valley and over Nicky Nook; the Barn (The Square) is a popular plant centre and gift shop. The Bay Horse off A6 N of here has good food.

SILVERDALE SD4875
A little-visited peaceful oasis, up beyond the attractive town of Lancaster: hilly countryside well suited both to walkers and to drivers, and a coastline that's particularly interesting to bird-watchers and naturalists. The small town looks out over the tidal sands to the Cumbrian hills, with streets of quiet houses and a church that looks 14th-c but was built barely a century ago. Various crafts are sold at the Georgian buildings of the **Wolf House Gallery** (Gibraltar), so named because a former occupant of the house was reputed to have killed the last wolf in England. It also has an adventure playground and a courtyard garden. Café, some disabled access (with notice); cl Mon Apr-Dec, and all wkdys Jan-Mar; (01524) 701405; free. There are good woodland walks behind the town, and the Waterslack tearooms (past the station) and Silverdale Hotel (Shore Rd) are useful stops. The coastal train ride from here to Ulverston gives good views.
Leighton Moss Nature Reserve 🔣 (off Yealand Redmayne Rd) RSPB reserve with several roomy hides looking out on to reedbeds where

bitterns, bearded tits and marsh harriers breed; good walks and views and a visitor centre. Events and guided walks throughout the year. Meals, snacks, shop, disabled access; cl 25 Dec; (01524) 701601; *£4.50 (RSPB members free). The Moss is also crossed by a (free) public footpath.
Yealand Conyers Friends' Meeting House Unobtrusively charming, in a quiet and pleasant village; the New Inn here is a popular dining pub.
SKIPPOOL SD3540
Lots of yachting activity in an attractive boating area.
SLAIDBURN SD7152
A perfectly preserved Forest of Bowland village: charming stone cottages, a green with the River Hodder running by, and at the opposite end an early 18th-c schoolhouse and a church with a very 18th-c feel inside. The Hark to Bounty (named after a former squire's dog) is pleasant for lunch and has comfortable bedrooms. The B6478, and the narrow road N past Stocks Reservoir, have appealing views. This second road passes **Gisburn Forest**, the county's largest, with picnic areas and cycle paths.
SOUTHPORT SD3217
Smartish Victorian seaside resort, long famed as the most pleasant shopping town in the area, and as the place where the sea doesn't come in. In fact it comes in as often as anywhere else, but doesn't stay quite as long; in recent years, they've made an effort to clean up the beach, and there are walkways for visitors and other improvements to the seafront. The promenade is set back quite a way from the sea, and looks over a man-made lake with boat; they've restored the pier. Lord St is the elegant main shopping street; the Bold Hotel here has bargain food all day, and there's an excellent antiquarian bookshop down the Wayfarers Arcade just off it. **Pleasureland** is a typical fairground, adding new attractions every year, its wooden roller-coaster and gut-wrenching Traumatiser ride well regarded by connoisseurs; usually cl Nov-Feb, and wkdys in Mar; (08702) 200204; £16 wristband for all rides.
Atkinson Art Gallery (Lord St) Specialises in 19th- and 20th-c watercolours, oil paintings, prints and sculpture, inc work by L S Lowry and Henry Moore. Snacks, shop, disabled access; cl Sun and bank hols; (0151) 934 2110; free.
British Lawnmower Museum (Shakespeare St) Over 300 fully restored and often bizarre machines from the 1840s to the present, inc robot mowers, racing lawnmowers, and celebrity lawnmowers; you can book a guided tour. Shop; cl Sun and bank hols; (01704) 501336; *£1.
Churchtown Southport's villagey oldest part, with a number of pretty thatched cottages, and the lakeside **Botanic Gardens**, which are very attractive as well as being interesting to plantsmen; boating lake, fernery, pets' corner, and local history **museum** (open Tues-Fri and pm wknd and bank hols; (01704) 227547; free). Just opposite, **Meols Hall** is worth a look for its paintings, inc works by Ramsey, Reynolds, Romney and Poussin. Disabled access; open pm mid-Aug to mid-Sept; (01704) 228326; £3. The Hesketh Arms across from the main gate is handy for lunch.
Model Railway Village Children (and train enthusiasts) enjoy watching the miniature trains meander around this 1/18 scale english-style model village, set in 1.5 acres of landscaped gardens. Snacks and picnic area, shop, disabled access; usually open daily Easter-early Sep; (01704) 214266; £3.50.
SPEKE SJ4282
Speke Hall Built around a square courtyard, this is one of the most beautiful and richly timbered black and white houses in the country; the inside is mainly Victorian, though there's a vast Tudor Great Hall. Restored Victorian garden. Hard to believe the centre of Liverpool is just six miles away. Meals, snacks, shop, disabled access; house open pm exc Mon and Tues mid-Mar to Oct, plus wknds Nov to mid-Dec, garden open exc Mon all year (house and garden open bank hols); (0151) 427 7231; £6, £3 grounds only; NT.
ST HELENS SJ5195
World of Glass (Chalon Way E) This brings a lot of sparkle to the world of glass, through a wide range of

informative and entertaining displays. The stylish modern building is fronted by a reconstructed traditional conical glasshouse, and includes several themed areas. Children enjoy the hands-on displays and crazy mirror maze in Glass Magic, while the Glass Revolution show takes a lively look at the importance of glass today. Earth Into Light includes a re-created glassmaker's parlour, and the evolution of glass from ancient times to the present day is studied in Glass Roots. An unexpected highlight is the labyrinth of tunnels to explore beneath the oldest Victorian furnace in Europe. Plenty of activities and demonstrations inc glass-blowers in action. Meals, snacks, shop, disabled access; cl Mon, 25-26 Dec, and 1 Jan; (08707) 444777; £5.80. The Carr Mill (E Lancs Rd) is a good value family dining pub.

STANAH SD3542

Out on the Wyre estuary, this has a stretch of waterside country with reedbeds, birds and views, attractive despite the chemical works in the background. On the opposite bank, over the toll bridge past Poulton, the Shard Bridge Inn at Hambleton is nicely placed for lunch.

STOCKPORT SJ8990

Hat Works 🏛 (Wellington Mill, Wellington Rd S) Fun look at the town's hat-making heritage, with lots of millinery exhibits from early 19th-c fur hats to fully restored machines. There's quite a lot aimed at children, inc occasional story-telling in a mock-up of a felt tent (recalling the town's trading links with central Asia); tours run on the hour, and you get to see a milliner and textile designer giving demonstrations. Meals, snacks, shop, disabled access; cl 25-26 Dec, and 1 Jan; (0161) 355 7770; *£3.95.

Stockport Air-Raid Shelters (Chestergate) Displays include a reconstructed canteen, tool stores and first aid post, re-creating a wartime atmosphere in this labyrinth of tunnels which protected thousands of people during World War II; guided tours around the more remote tunnels first Weds of month at 7pm (£4.50). Shop, disabled access; cl Sun am, 25-26 Dec and 1 Jan; (0161) 474 1940; £3.95. The

Arden Arms (Millgate St) has good value food - and a great collection of working grandfather clocks.

SUNDERLAND POINT SD4255

This unique hamlet is cut off by the tide twice a day; the local legend of Sambo the slave recalls how he was brought to the point by his master who then went away for such a length of time that Sambo died of a broken heart. He died at Upsteps cottage, and a short path leads to his grave on the other side of the peninsula, which has become a shrine that is still tended to this day. The route passes a cottage which sells a publication about the area. The Globe at Overton, with a popular carvery, is handy for a family lunch.

THORNTON-CLEVELEYS SD3342

Marsh windmill (B5412) One of the largest in Europe, this working windmill has tours to the top (£1.25, no under-5s), demonstrations, a good range of craft shops alongside, and wknd entertainment in summer. Shop, disabled access to ground floor; cl 25-26 Dec and 1 Jan; (01253) 860765; free to ground floor, 65p to 1st floor. Twelve (an imaginative conversion of a former dance studio here) has good inventive food; cl Mon. The nearby Burnside Garden Centre (New Lane) is worth a visit, with a nice café.

TURTON BOTTOMS SD7315

Turton Tower 15th-c Renaissance house with Elizabethan buildings and earlier peel tower; mostly a museum inside, but there are a couple of period rooms, and a major collection of carved wood furniture. It was interestingly extended by followers of the Romantic and later Arts and Crafts movements in the 19th c. Victorian woodland gardens. Tearoom, shop; open daily (exc Fri) May-Sept (cl am wknds), pm Sat-Weds in Mar, Apr and Oct, and just pm Sun Nov and Feb; (01204) 852203; £3. The Black Bull (Bolton Rd) has good value food, all day wknds.

UPPERMILL SD9905

This whole area of mill settlements in steep valleys cut through the moors is full of interest, and Uppermill itself is one of the most attractive places. Up above the town is a lonely moorland church, with good walks around it and an ancient pub opposite. Fine drives around here include the A635 over Saddleworth Moor, and B6197 Delph—Grains Bar then A672 or A640 over the moors.

Saddleworth Museum and Art Gallery 🖼 (High St) Based around an old mill, and volunteers occasionally dress up in appropriate garb. Shop, limited disabled access, cl am Nov-Mar and am Sun, 24-25 and 31 Dec and 1 Jan; (01457) 874093; *£2.

WADDINGTON SD7243
Forest of Bowland village, with a fine **church**, attractive memorial gardens, and a lovely drive from Longridge. The Lower Buck has popular home cooking.

WHALLEY SD7336
Whalley Abbey Striking remains of 14th-c Cistercian abbey - the monks' quarters, rather than the church which has virtually disappeared - in grounds of 16th-c manor house used as a religious retreat (they do B&B). Two gatehouses are intact, and there's a visitor centre. Good snacks, shop, disabled access; cl 22 Dec-3 Jan; (01254) 828400; £2. The separate 13th-c parish **church** has interesting woodwork and three ancient Celtic-Scandinavian crosses. In the Freemasons Arms at Wiswell just NE, the landlady's cooking is good.

WIGAN SD5908
Haigh Hall Country Park (2m N) 250-acre country park with guided walks, nature trails, beautifully set golf course, craft centre, walled gardens, play area, crazy golf, model village and miniature railway. Occasional tours of house - phone for dates, and a good programme of events. Meals, snacks, shops (one good for golfers), some disabled access; (01942) 832895; park free, charges for parking and attractions. The Boars Head over at Standish (A5106) has bargain food.
Wigan Pier 🖼 (Wallgate) Rather different from when Orwell knew it (and a great favourite with readers), this is now a dynamic and entertaining wharfside centre demonstrating local life in the early 1900s, with actors performing in a reconstructed mine, pub, school, music hall, houses and even seaside. An ingenious mix of museum and theatre, it's an enormously enjoyable family day out, and you do get

a tangible impression of what life was really like at the turn of the century. A museum takes a nostalgic look at each decade of the 20th c; you can see a Victorian schoolroom, mill steam engine and textile machinery hall, and take a canal boat trip. Meals, snacks, shop, disabled access; cl Fri, 25-26 Dec, and 1 Jan; (01942) 323666; £7.95.

WIRRAL SJ2484
Its Merseyside parts aren't on the whole that appealing to visitors, especially on the built-up E side (with the notable exception of Port Sunlight). The NW corner can be rather more attractive, particularly along the edges of the Dee, looking across to the mountains of N Wales. The more interesting bits, inc unusual National Trust heathland, are linked by a 12-mile footpath, best joined at the **Wirral Country Park** at Thurstaston, and running down to the Cheshire parts of the Wirral. The Fox & Hounds at Barnsby has good value food.

WRAY SD6067
Charming small backwater with venerable cottages, and an increasingly popular annual Scarecrow Festival (events for the week leading up to the May bank hol). The welcoming George & Dragon, with an attractive garden, has decent food. From here a spectacular drive over Tatham Fells leads to Slaidburn.

WYCOLLER COUNTRY PARK SD9339
Lancashire Brontë country (the ruined hall at Wycoller may have been the base for Ferndean Manor in *Jane Eyre*), with walks along a beck to Clam Bridge, an Iron Age slab, and up to Foster's Leap, a finely placed crag. The Herders has hearty home cooking.

Other attractive villages, all with decent pubs and great surrounding scenery, include Goosnargh SD5537, Hurst Green SD6838, Tunstall SD6173 (Brontë church) and Wiswell SD7437. Particularly pretty ones in or on the edges of the Forest of Bowland are Gisburn SD8248, Grindleton SD7545 and Newton SD6950.

Pubs well placed for walks include the Hare & Hounds at Abbey Village SD6422, Pack Horse at Affetside SD7513, Bay Horse at Arkholme

SD5872, Black Dog at Belmont SD6716, Dog at Belthorn SD7224, White House on Blackstone Edge SD9716, Owd Betts at Cheesden on Ashworth Moor SD8316, Edisford Bridge on the B6243 W of Clitheroe SD7241, Diggle Hotel at Diglea Hamlet above Diggle itself SE0008, Wright Arms at Egerton SD7114, Strawbury Duck by Entwistle Station SD7217, Bulls Head on Grains Bar SD9608, Duke of Wellington on the B6232 W of Haslingden SD7522, Egerton Arms off the narrow Ashworth Rd above Heywood SD8513, Green Man at Inglewhite (nr Beacon Fell) SD5440, New Drop on Longridge Fell SD6439, Romper at Ridge End above Marple SJ9686, Kettledrum at Mereclough SD8632, Highwayman at Nether Burrow SD6275 (pretty stretch of the Lune Valley), Old Rosins at Pickup Bank, Old Hoddlesden SD6922, Roebuck on Roebuck Low SD9606 and Railway at White Coppice SD6118. Up on the moors, many of these are closed during lunchtime Mon-Thurs.

Where to eat

BLACKPOOL SD3036 **September Brasserie** *15-17 Queen St (01253) 623282* Not far from the seafront and above a hairdresser's, this busy little airy restaurant's open-view kitchen does particularly good inventive food from a short menu with ideas from all over the world (inc lovely puddings), and a thoughtful wine list; cl Sun, Mon, 2 wks summer, 2 wks winter. £28|£7

CHIPPING SD6241 **Dog & Partridge** *Hesketh Lane (01995) 61201* Spotlessly kept and relaxed dining pub with comfortable main lounge, winter log fire, good choice of enjoyable food (inc fine home-made chips), real ales, and quite a few wines and malt whiskies; disabled access. £21|£9

CLITHEROE SD7441 **Café Emporia** *The Emporium, Moor Lane (01200) 427166* Restored and refurbished ex-Methodist chapel and now two floors of coffee shop, wine bar and brasserie, all with different looks, styles and atmospheres, and serving a fine choice of coffees, cookies, cakes and pastries, and enjoyable meals; the lower ground floor is the shop with all manner of furnishings and furniture - all the furniture in the restaurant areas is also for sale; cl Sun pm, 25 Dec; disabled access. £22|£6

DOWNHAM SD7844 **Assheton Arms** *(01200) 441227* Charmingly set dining pub in prettily preserved village, with rambling beamed bar, a massive stone fireplace, no smoking area, popular bar food (lots of good fresh fish dishes), well kept real ales, and decent wines; cl 1st wk Jan; disabled access. £27|£7.25

KIRKHAM SD4232 **Cromwellian** *16 Poulton St (01772) 685680* Tiny evening restaurant in 17th-c house with consistently good interesting food from a fixed-price menu - thoughtful wine list, too; cl Sun, Mon, 2 wks Easter, 2 wks Sept. £19.50

LIVERPOOL SJ3589 **60 Hope Street** *60 Hope St (0151) 707 6060* Listed Georgian double-fronted house with basement café bar and ground floor restaurant, relaxed modern décor, interesting contemporary european cooking, good puddings (try the popular deep-fried jam sandwich with Carnation ice-cream), friendly knowledgeable service, and a good wine list; cl Sun, bank hols. £38 restaurant, £20.25 in bar|£5.95

LIVERPOOL SJ3490 **Simply Heathcotes** *Beetham Plaza, 25 The Strand (0151) 236 3536* Chic modern restaurant with a curved plate-glass frontage, smart simple furnishings, contemporary british brasserie-style food, a varied wine list, and helpful, suited young staff; other branches in Manchester, Preston and Longridge; cl 25-26 Dec, 1 Jan; disabled access. £30|£10

LONGRIDGE SD6137 **Longridge Restaurant** *104-106 Higher Rd (01772) 784969* Three cottages knocked into one restaurant, completely refurbished this year, with smartly clothed tables and stylish dining chairs on the stripped wooden floor, cream walls and some exposed stone, exceptionally good food using tip-top local produce, a thoughtful wine list, and relaxed atmosphere; partly no smoking; cl Mon, Sat am, 1 Jan. £44/2-course lunch £14

MANCHESTER SJ8398 **Petit Blanc** *55 King St (0161) 832 1000* Stylishly renovated former bank, with smartly presented brasserie-style food from a diverse menu, helpful service, a good short wine list, and lovely flower arrangements; they offer set children's menus with proper food; other branches in Birmingham, Cheltenham, and Oxford; cl 25 Dec; disabled access. £40/2-course lunch £13.50

MANCHESTER SJ8398 **Restaurant Bar & Grill** *14 John Dalton St (0161) 839 1999* Ground-floor bar and firsT-floor restaurant with a lively atmosphere, leather chairs around wooden tables, big windows, efficient polite service from chic staff, and enjoyable international cooking from an open kitchen, with particular emphasis on north african and asian dishes; cl 25-26 Dec; disabled access. £35|£10

MANCHESTER SJ8398 **Simply Heathcotes** *Jackson Row, Deansgate (0161) 835 3536* Stylish modern restaurant with high ceilings, polished wood floors, bright paintings on coloured walls, and contemporary furniture, up-to-the-minute brasserie-style cooking inc very good value set lunches, thoughtful wine list, and efficient service; other branches, such as Liverpool; cl bank hol Mon, 25-26 Dec; disabled access. £34/2-course menu £13.50

MANCHESTER SJ8497 **Yang Sing** *34 Princess St (0161) 236 2200* Exceptionally good sophisticated chinese food using the best fresh ingredients (tanks of live fish, too), wonderful dim-sum (the widest choice in Europe), some unusual dishes among traditional cantonese specialities, good value set meals, a bustling atmosphere, and efficient service; must book ahead; cl 25 Dec; disabled access. £22|£8.60

MELLOR SJ9888 **Oddfellows Arms** *73 Moor End Rd (0161) 449 7826* Fine old building with low ceilings, open fires and a chatty atmosphere in two flagstoned rooms, no smoking restaurant, and a wide range of interesting food inc lots of different types of fresh fish; cl Sun pm, Mon, 25 Dec, 31 Dec, 1 Jan; children must be well behaved; disabled access. £25|£7.45

SAWLEY SD7746 **Spread Eagle** *(01220) 441202* Proficiently run dining pub with light and airy continental-feeling main bar (partly no smoking), comfortable banquette seating, plenty of paintings and prints and lovely photographs of local views, a roaring winter coal fire, big picture windows overlooking a pretty stretch of the River Ribble, and well kept real ales and well chosen wines; highly thought of imaginative food, and attentive, smartly dressed staff; 12th-c Cistercian abbey ruins opposite, and pub is handy for Forest of Bowland; cl Sun pm, Mon. £27.30/2-course mid-week set menu £8.50|£6.95

TUNSTALL SD6073 **Lunesdale Arms** *(01524) 274203* Civilised and brightly opened-up dining pub with enjoyable interesting food using home-baked bread, meat from local farms, and a lot of local organic produce; big unframed oil paintings (some for sale and often of bluebells) on yellow walls, cheerful bustling atmosphere, a couple of woodburners; well kept real ales, sensibly priced wines by the glass (in a choice of sizes), and good cafetière coffee; pretty Lune Valley village; cl Mon (exc bank hols), 25-26 Dec; disabled access. £22|£5.50

YEALAND CONYERS SD5074 **New Inn** *(01524) 732938* Ivy-covered stone dining pub with log fire in little beamed bar, two communicating cottage dining rooms, novel daily specials, fine salads served with meals, friendly professional service, decent wines, well kept ales, and a sheltered side lawn. £25|£7.95

Special thanks to Helen Wharton, Margaret Dickinson, Steve Chambers, T D Surgenor, Roy and Lindsey Fentiman

LEICESTERSHIRE AND RUTLAND

A get-away secret - some surprising attractions in this little-visited area, with its stately houses and castles, and sweeping country views

Families find lots to enjoy at Twycross Zoo Park (our choice for Leicestershire Family Attraction this year), and at lively Snibston Discovery Park in Coalville (plenty of variety, and engaging interactive displays). Newcomer Twinlakes Park, near Melton Mowbray, has an excellent range of play areas (plus animals and birds of prey), and in Desford you'll find tropical bird gardens. There is a farm park at Mountsorrel (a little collection of vintage cars here too).

Swinford has an unusual mix, with its combination of motorcycle museum and elegant 17th-c house. Among the county's several castles, Belvoir is the grandest, and at Donington le Heath the medieval house is worth a visit. More specialist attractions include the exceptional collection of single-seat racing cars at Donington Park (summer motor sport meetings at Mallory Park too), and Cottesmore, Loughborough and Market Bosworth all have something for train enthusiasts.

The outstanding National Space Centre, along with an eclectic mix of attractions (from a gas museum to Roman remains), make Leicester a good choice for day-trippers. Fine-weather excursions include Conkers at Moira (developing centre, with enough for a relaxed day), and Rutland Water (pleasant walking, with quite a lot of varied things to see and do around it).

The sweeping countryside particularly suits scenic drives or cycle rides, especially in the east: graceful patches of woodland, plenty of charming stone-built villages to potter through, delightful churches. Many of the less busy roads stride along old coach routes, with broad views. There are quite a few good walks, too - and you get out into unspoilt countryside very quickly from the built-up areas.

Where to stay

EMPINGHAM SK9408 **White Horse** *Main St, Empingham, Oakham, Rutland LE15 8PR (01780) 460221* **£65***, plus special breaks; 13 pretty rms, some in a delightfully converted stable block. Attractive, bustling old inn, handy for Rutland Water; a relaxed and comfortable atmosphere, a big log fire and fresh flowers in open-plan lounge, big helpings of very enjoyable food inc fine breakfasts, coffee and croissants from 8am, and cream teas all year; attractive no smoking restaurant, well kept real ales, and efficient friendly service; cots/high chairs; cl 25 Dec; good disabled access; dogs welcome in bedrooms

MEDBOURNE SP7992 **Nevill Arms** *Waterfall Way, Medbourne, Market Harborough, Leicestershire LE16 8EE (01858) 565288 wkdys* **£55**; 8 rms, 6 in separate cottage and barn conversion. Well run, bright and busy old mullion-windowed inn just across footbridge over stream, with open fires in inviting main bar, spacious back room with toys for children, excellent food, nice breakfasts in conservatory, and friendly prompt service; cl pm 24-26 and 31 Dec

PACKINGTON SK3514 **Champneys Springs Health Resort** *Measham Rd, Packington, Ashby-de-la-Zouch, Leicestershire NE65 1TJ (01530) 273873* **£170** inc full use of all facilities, plus special breaks; 89 rms. Britain's first purpose-built health resort with all the amenities, good healthy food, and friendly staff; cl 21-26 Dec; no children; disabled access

ROTHLEY SK5712 **Rothley Court** *Westfield Lane, Rothley, Leicestershire LE7 7LG (0116) 237 4141* **£95**; 32 rms (the ones in the main house have more character). Mentioned in the Domesday Book, this carefully run manor house with its beautifully preserved 13th-c chapel has some fine oak panelling, open fires, a comfortable bar, conservatory, and courteous staff; seats out on the terrace and in the garden; disabled access; dogs welcome in bedrooms

STAPLEFORD SK8118 **Stapleford Park** *Stapleford, Melton Mowbray, Leicestershire LE14 2EF (01572) 787522* **£232.65**; 51 individually designed rms, plus cottage. Luxurious country house, extravagantly restored, in lovely large grounds with riding and stabling, tennis, croquet, putting green, 18-hole championship golf course, trout fishing, falconry, and clay-pigeon shooting; lots of mahogany, opulent furnishings, fine oil paintings and an impressive library, delicious restaurant food, enthusiastic american owner, and warmly welcoming staff; health spa and indoor swimming pool; cots/babysitting; disabled access; dogs welcome away from restaurant

STRETTON SK9415 **Ram Jam Inn** *Great North Rd, Stretton, Oakham, Rutland LE15 7QX (01780) 410776* **£70.90**; 7 comfortable and well equipped rms. Actually on the A1, this civilised place has a comfortable airily modern lounge bar, a café bar and bistro, good interesting food quickly served all day from open-plan kitchen, and useful small wine list; large garden and orchard; cl 25 Dec

UPPINGHAM SP8699 **Lake Isle** *16 High St East, Uppingham, Oakham, Rutland LE15 9PZ (01572) 822951* **£80**, plus special breaks; 13 newly refurbished rms with home-made biscuits, sherry and fresh fruit, and three cottage suites. In a charming market town, this 18th-c restaurant-with-rooms has an open fire in the attractive lounge, a redecorated bar (once a barber's where the schoolboys had their hair cut), good, imaginative food in refurbished restaurant (enjoyable breakfasts, too), a carefully chosen wine list, and a small and pretty garden; dogs welcome in bedrooms

To see and do

Leicestershire and Rutland Family Attraction of the Year

TWYCROSS SK3305 **Twycross Zoo Park** (A444) Feeling nicely low-key and perhaps more friendly than some bigger zoos, this committed place specialises in primates, with an enormous range of apes, gibbons, orang-utans and chimpanzees. They look after every shape, size and species, from pygmy marmosets to big silverback gorillas, and it's the only UK zoo to keep what's now generally considered man's closest relative - the bonobo. Plenty of other animals include giraffes, sea lions, elephants and penguins; three-quarters of the residents here are from endangered species. It's an easy place to explore at a leisurely pace, but can get crowded on summer afternoons. That's probably because there's so much more going on then, with a good programme of talks and feeding displays, donkey rides, and a miniature railway. It's a little quieter out of season, though at weekends before Christmas they have an enthusiastically put together grotto. The keepers are helpful and knowledgeable, and there's lots of space for picnics (they don't mind you making use of the grass). Younger children enjoy the pets corner, and the adventure playground. Meals, snacks, shop, disabled access; cl 25 Dec; (01827) 880250; £6.50 adults, £4.50 children.

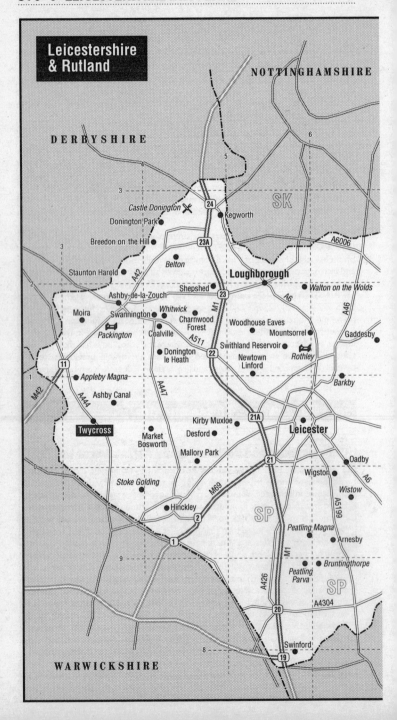

Leicestershire & Rutland

NOTTINGHAMSHIRE

DERBYSHIRE

SK

Castle Donington
24
Kegworth
Donington Park
23A
Breedon on the Hill
A6006
Belton
Staunton Harold
Loughborough
A42
Shepshed
23
Walton on the Wolds
Ashby-de-la-Zouch
A6
Moira
Whitwick
A46
Swannington
Charnwood
Woodhouse Eaves
Packington
Forest
Mountsorrel
Gaddesby
Coalville
A511
Swithland Reservoir
Donington
22
Rothley
le Heath
Newtown
Linford
11
Barkby
Appleby Magna
A444
A447
Ashby Canal
21A
Kirby Muxloe
Leicester
Twycross
Desford
Market
Oadby
Bosworth
Mallory Park
21
A6
Wigston
Stoke Golding
Wistow
M69
A5199
Hinckley
SP
2
Peatling Magna
1
Arnesby
Bruntingthorpe
9
Peatling
M1
Parva
SP
A426
A4304
20
Swinford
8
19
WARWICKSHIRE

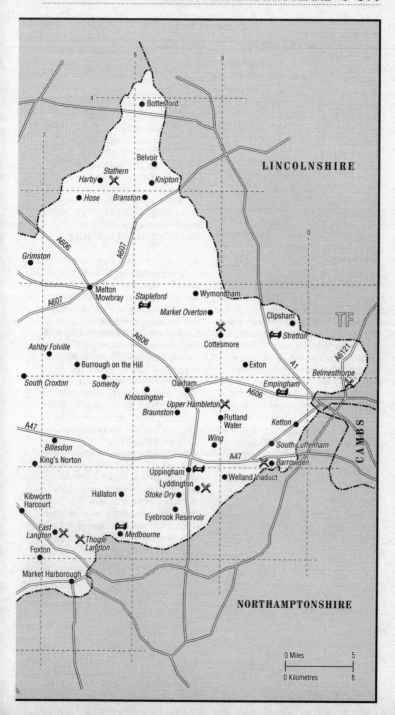

ARNESBY SP6192
Arnesby windmill Handsomely preserved, well worth a look. The Chandlers Arms over in Shearsby has interesting food.

ASHBY CANAL SK3707
The towpath has good countryside walking, with green fields and stone-arched bridges, as well as coots, moorhens, herons and perhaps even the flash of a kingfisher. The best parts run from the tunnel under Snarestone past Gopsall Park, and then on through Shackerstone and Congerstone to pass Shenton Park on an embankment, before heading into Warwickshire and its junction with the Coventry Canal. It also makes an ideal walking link between Bosworth battlefield and the steam railway to the N.

ASHBY-DE-LA-ZOUCH SK3516
Ashby-de-la-Zouch Castle The Norman core and its 15th-c extension were largely destroyed in the Civil War, but the ruins are impressive (inc an illuminated underground passage), and the adjoining fields were the setting for Sir Walter Scott's *Ivanhoe*; all much improved by the opening of the new bypass. Snacks, shop, limited disabled access; cl Mon, Tues Nov-Mar, and 24-26 Dec, 1 Jan; (01530) 413343; £3.20; EH. Next to the tourist information centre on North St, a little **museum** has local history displays; cl 1-2pm and Oct-Easter; (01530) 560090; free admission if you've been to the castle first, otherwise 50p. The Thirsty Millers (Mill Lane Mews) has fresh local food - and a reputed tunnel to the castle.

BELVOIR SK8133
Belvoir Castle 🏠 Pronounced Beaver, this has some impressive rooms, but is even better from the outside, a glorious fantasy of turrets and battlements, pinnacles and towers, surrounded by terraced gardens. Meals, snacks, shop, disabled access; cl Nov-Mar, Mon-Sat Apr and Oct, plus Mon (exc bank hols) and Fri Apr-Jun and Sept, best to check; (01476) 871002; £8. The Chequers at Woolsthorpe has good food. Good drives on fine old coach roads centre on Belvoir: for instance, from Long Bennington (Lincs) through Bottesford, Harby and Hose, or via Knipton down through Eastwell and past Grimston all

the way to Barrow upon Soar, where the canalside Navigation (Mill Lane) has good value food.

BOTTESFORD SK8139
Bottesford church Packed with elaborate monuments to the Earls and Dukes of Rutland, two by Grinling Gibbons; they had to raise the roof to fit them all in. The welcoming church has informative displays. The Windmill over at Redmile has enjoyable food.

BREEDON ON THE HILL SK4023
Breedon on the Hill church On an interesting partly quarried Iron Age hill fort, this is unrivalled in Britain or abroad for its Anglo-Saxon carvings, over 1,100 years old. The Three Horse Shoes has a popular restaurant.

BURROUGH ON THE HILL SK7510
Burrough Hill has an enjoyable path along its escarpment. The summit has splendid views, and an imposing Iron Age hill fort, its ramparts still largely intact (£1 parking for a day). The Stag & Hounds has good value food.

CHARNWOOD FOREST SK4515
Charnwood Forest views The friendly Bulls Head (former B587 Whitwick—Copt Oak), with a big garden and lots of animals, has fine views over surviving remnants of this former hunting park, popular for walks; the Copt Oak pub itself, over on the B591, is also a useful base for walks.

CLIPSHAM SK9716
Yew Tree Avenue (just E, off Castle Bytham Rd) Delightfully quirky avenue of 150 yew trees, clipped in sometimes bizarre shapes to represent animals, characters and events; free. The surrounding woods are full of deer (not to mention bluebells in spring). In the attractive stone-built village, the Olive Branch has very good food.

COALVILLE SK4114
Snibston Discovery Park 🏠 (Ashby Rd) Busy 100-acre site based around a former colliery (the first shaft was sunk by George and Robert Stephenson), with a huge outdoor science play area, a nature reserve, and historic mine buildings. At its centre an exhibition hall houses six (mostly interactive) galleries - children like the Science Alive gallery best, with plenty of experiments and hands-on activities, even the illusion of

cycling with a skeleton. Similarly
organised galleries look at transport,
mining and fashion, and they've recently
added a new gallery divided into Toy
Town (for children under 5) and Toy
Box (for the under-8s); there's also
space for temporary exhibitions.
Evocative tours of the old colliery are
taken by former pitmen. Snacks, shop,
disabled access; cl 25-25 Dec, 1 and
12-16 Jan; (01530) 278444; £5.50. The
charming old New Inn over at Peggs
Green (off A512 Ashby—Shepshed)
has lots of interesting old local
photographs, inc colliery ones.
COTTESMORE SK8913
Rutland Railway Museum Nearly 40
industrial steam and diesel locomotives,
and 60 other waggons and vehicles used
in the iron ore quarries and industry;
work should begin this year on a building
to house more of the engines, but
currently many are kept outdoors.
Occasional steam rides, and quite a nice
lineside walk to the old Oakham Canal.
Snacks, shop, disabled access; open most
wknds - best to phone (01572) 813203
for dates of steam days; free (£3 on
steam days). In the attractive village, the
thatched Sun is good for lunch.
DESFORD SK4704
Tropical Bird Gardens (Lindridge
Lane) This pleasant five-acre woodland
garden has over 50 different species,
many in walk-through aviaries; the free-
flying macaws are particularly
spectacular - they may even perch on
your shoulder. Meals, snacks, shop,
disabled access; cl Nov-Jan and any
inclement weather days till Mar;
(01455) 824603; £4. The Greyhound
over in Botcheston has good food.
DONINGTON LE HEATH SK4212
Donington le Heath Manor House
Except for some 17th-c refurbishment,
this medieval house has remained
practically untouched since it was built
in the 13th c. The developing 17th-c
style gardens include a decorative maze
and orchards with traditional trees and
ornamental beehives. Meals, snacks,
shop; disabled access to tearoom and
ground floor only, cl 25-26 Dec;
(01530) 831259; free.
DONINGTON PARK SK4225
Donington Grand Prix Collection
🖼 This includes the largest collection

of Grand Prix racing cars in the world,
with vehicles driven by all the greats,
and related memorabilia; the price
means it's never too crowded, and
enthusiasts find it all fascinating. Meals,
snacks, shop, disabled access; cl 24-26,
31 Dec, and 1 Jan; (01332) 811027; £7.
The Nags Head (A453, S end of town) is
a very good dining pub.
EXTON SK9211
Handsome collection of thatched
houses around a tree-studded green,
with pleasant walks around; the
attractive **church** is beautifully placed
in a park, and the Fox & Hounds has
decent home cooking.
Barnsdale Gardens (The Avenue,
SW of village) Familiar to viewers of
Gardeners' World: they were developed
on the programme by the late Geoff
Hamilton. The interesting plants are
grown using peat-free compost, and
there are plenty of useful ideas and
techniques. Licensed coffee shop,
nursery, disabled access; cl 23 and 25
Dec; (01572) 813200; *£5. S of here
towards the A606 the Barnsdale Lodge
Hotel has good food and comfortable
bedrooms, with an antiques centre next
door.
Rutland Falconry & Owl Centre
(W of village) Small woodland centre
with 100 or so birds of prey, and the
chance to handle some of the birds;
daily flying displays (depending on
weather). Snacks and picnic area, shop,
disabled access; (07778) 152814; £4.
EYEBROOK RESERVOIR SP8595
Rewarding for bird-watchers and
fishermen, although as it has no hides or
facilities it will appeal mainly to true
enthusiasts.
FOXTON SP6989
Foxton Canal Museum 🖼 Next to
an interesting staircase flight of ten
locks, and based around the
extraordinary Victorian steam-
powered boat lift built to avoid using
the lock and so save water - now being
restored, but it will take years. Shop,
some disabled access (some steep
slopes); cl some wkdys in winter, phone
to check; (0116) 279 2657; site free,
museum £2.50 (voucher enables one
adult free with another paying adult).
The Black Horse a short walk away has
good value food, sheep and goats in its

big garden, and evening vintage car rallies (last Thurs Apr-Aug). The locks are a good focus for Grand Union Canal towpath walks. The reservoir over at Saddington is also a pretty spot.

GADDESBY SK6812
Gaddesby church Notable for its elaborate 13th-c external workmanship (and see the squire's heroic Waterloo statue inside). The Golden Fleece over at South Croxton has good value fresh food.

HALLATON SP7896
Picturesque village, with an Easter Monday tradition of bottle kicking and hare pie scambling; you can find out more about these curious ancient customs at the little local history museum in Hogg Lane; open pm wknds and bank hols May-Oct; (01858) 555416; free. The Bewicke Arms has decent food.

HINCKLEY SP4594
Burbage Common & Woods (off A47 just E) Ancient woodland with lots of footpaths (some accessible by wheelchair), observation hides, and spectacular ground flora. Visitor centre usually open Sun, pm only Sat, plus some wkdys Apr-Nov, but phone to check; (01455) 633712; free. The Chequers (Lutterworth Rd) has home-cooked lunches (not Sun/Mon) and a nice family garden.

KEGWORTH SK4826
Country drive The Cap & Stocking in Kegworth is an interesting old tavern, at the start of a pleasant drive through the Leakes, Wysall, Widmerpool, Kinoulton, Colston Bassett (just over the Notts border - the Martins Arms is a good if not cheap lunch stop), Granby and Orston.

KIBWORTH HARCOURT SP6894
Kibworth Harcourt windmill The county's only remaining post mill, a fine example from the early 18th c. The old coach road through here from Uppingham and on to Kilby, Countesthorpe and Cosby is a fine long-striding drive.

KING'S NORTON SK6800
King's Norton church A graceful Gothic Revival building; the thatched Queens Head over in pretty Billesdon has enjoyable home-made food.

KIRBY MUXLOE SK5204
Kirby Muxloe Castle 15th-c ruins,

peaceful despite the sight of the M1 just under ½ mile away; the castle's original owner was executed before it was completed. Shop, disabled access; open pms Sat, Sun and bank hols Apr-Oct; (01162) 386886; £2.20; EH. The Royal Oak has good food.

LEICESTER SK5804
In this busy city's mix of a little ancient and a lot of modern, a bit of digging around among the shops, office blocks and traffic schemes does turn up reminders of its long and varied past. Most notable among some fine old buildings is the 14th-c Guildhall; (0116) 253 2569; cl Sun am; free. The strikingly modern National Space Centre at Abbey Meadows is a vivid contrast. Besides the museums described individually, several others are worth a look. **Newarke Houses** (The Newarke), in two historic houses with a quiet period garden, includes a Victorian street scene and the clothes of Daniel Lambert, Britain's heaviest man; cl Sun am and Christmas-New Year; (0116) 225 4980; free. The **City Gallery** (Granby St) has temporary exhibitions of contemporary visual arts and crafts; cl Mon-Sun and bank hols; (0116) 254 0595; free. **New Walk Museum and Art Gallery** (New Walk) includes an Ancient Egypt gallery with mummies, a natural history section, an art gallery with a notable collection of Expressionist and european art from the 15th c to the present day, and a discovery room where children can try on replica clothes. The Royal Tigers exhibition covers the story of the Royal Leicestershire Regiment; (0116) 225 4900; cl Sun am; free. The **Jain Centre** has fantastic examples of traditional indian architecture; disabled access; open pm wkdys; (0116) 254 3091; donations. Towpath walks along both the Grand Union Canal and the River Soar give a relatively tranquil back view of the city's industrial life, and Gorse Hill City Farm is a friendly little community farm in Anstey Lane; (0116) 253 7582; £1.50 suggested donation. Useful refreshment places include Café Bruxelles (High St), r/bar (Granby St) and Croques (Loseby Lane). N of the centre, Belgrave Rd is Leicester's asian

shopping district, with colourful saree shops and indian restaurants.

Abbey Pumping Station (Corporation Rd) With the largest working steam beam engines in the country, and a museum of public health, these former sewage pumping works have some bizarre displays inc the Flush With Pride exhibition, where you flush imitation faeces down a see-through loo and follow their movements through the drains; also regular events. Shop, mostly disabled access; cl Sun am, 24-26 and 31 Dec, 1 Jan; (0116) 299 5111; free, charges for special events.

Belgrave Hall (Church Rd, Leicester's N edge) A fine example of 18th-c Queen Anne architecture, furnished with Victorian and Edwardian pieces; charming gardens. Shop, disabled access to ground floor and gardens; cl 25-26 Dec and 1 Jan; (0116) 266 6590; free.

Eco House (Western Park, Hinckley Rd) This extended 1920s house is a showcase for environmentally friendly living, with interactive displays in every room, and an organic garden. Snacks, shop, disabled access; cl ams, all Mon and Tues and 25 Dec-1 Jan; (0116) 254 5489; free (donations).

Jewry Wall Museum and Site (St Nicholas Circle) Site of 2nd-c Roman baths; the courtyard has been excavated to reveal porticoes sheltered by the remains of a massive stone wall (the largest free-standing Roman structure in the country). Excellent collections of mosaic pavements and painted wall plaster. Shop, disabled access; cl Sun am, 25-26 Dec, 1 Jan; (0116) 225 4971; free.

National Gas Museum Trust 🔲 (Aylestone Rd) Housed under a Victorian clock tower in what used to be the gatehouse to the gas works, this comprehensive study of the industry includes one of the largest collections of gas and gas-related artefacts in the world, from lighting and cookers, to fires and washing machines. Shop, disabled access to ground floor only; open Tues-Thurs pm (exc 24 Dec-1 Jan); (0116) 250 3190; free.

National Space Centre (Exploration Drive, off Corporation Rd) Everything in space, from stars and planets to rockets and satellites, with the latest museum technology and hundreds of interactive and hands-on displays (though some may be out of action). A striking 41-metre (135-ft) tower visible for miles around houses their biggest rockets, Blue Steak and Thor Able. The glass lifts give a dramatic look at the rockets; good views of the city too. A planetarium has better shows than you'll see elsewhere inc a film exploring Mars, and one for under-5s (though in general it's older children who like the centre best). You'll get a timed ticket when you go into the main centre. The first of the four main galleries, Into Space, looks at astronauts. Exploring the Universe concentrates on how things began and the possibility of extra-terrestrials. The Planets examines our own solar system, and Orbiting Earth looks at how space technology affects our everyday lives. Along the way you can feel what it's like to be blasted into space, launch your own rocket, design your own alien, see pieces of the moon or Mars, and try forecasting the weather. A final section looks at the latest space happenings. Meals and snacks, shop, disabled access; cl Mon in term-time, Dec 25-26 and Jan 1; (0870) 607 7223; £8.95.

LOUGHBOROUGH SK5419
Bell Foundry Museum (Freehold St) Part of the largest working bell foundry in the world (bell-casting Thurs pm - you must book ahead if you want to watch), with a quite remarkable array of bells in the tuning room. Best not to wear light colours (they coat the moulds with graphite). Shop; open Tues-Sat 10am-12.30, 1.30-4.30pm, cl around Christmas-New Year; (01509) 233414; £2. The Swan in the Rushes (A6) has good home cooking.

Great Central Railway 🔲 (Great Central Rd) Main line steam railway to Leicester, with a museum and engine sheds this end. Meals, snacks, shop; disabled access is better at other stations on this line (phone in advance); limited service wkdys Sept-May (exc Easter and bank hols), phone for a timetable; (01509) 230726; £11, museum only £3.

Queen's Park With well organised local history, the little **Charnwood Museum** here has a couple of interactive displays inc a computer game about Loughborough. Snacks, shop, disabled access; usually only cl am Sun, and 25 Dec; (01509) 233754; free. The Carillon Tower here reflects the town's importance as a bell-founding town; carillon recitals Thurs 1pm and Sun 3.30pm; inside is a small war museum, and you can climb the spiral staircase to the top of the 46-metre (151-ft) tower; cl am Sun-Weds and Fri; (01509) 263370; 50p.

LYDDINGTON SP8796

Bede House This handsome 15th-c house was until the Reformation a residence of the Bishops of Lincoln. Notable carved ceilings, 15th-c glass, and tranquil garden. Shop, disabled access to ground floor only; cl Nov-Mar; (01572) 822438; £3.20. The stone-built village is attractive, and the Old White Hart is good for lunch.

MALLORY PARK SK4500

Mallory Park Circuit Motor sport meetings each wknd Mar-Oct; meals, snacks, shop, disabled access; (01455) 842931; from £10. The Windmill over at Brascote, Newbold Verdon, has good value food.

MARKET BOSWORTH SK3706

Battlefield Steam Railway Line Runs from Shackerstone through Market Bosworth to Shenton by Bosworth Battlefield, a rather nice return trip of just over nine miles. A Victorian tearoom is open when trains run, and the Shackerstone end has some displays; the Belper Arms at nearby Newton Burgoland is a very interesting old pub. Trains usually run wknds and bank hols Mar-Oct, plus Weds pm July-Aug; (01827) 880754 for timetable; £7 return.

Bosworth Battlefield Site of the deciding action in the War of the Roses, when Henry VII's 1485 victory over Richard III led to the Tudors' seizing the english throne. The visitor centre has explanatory films and exhibitions, as well as a detailed trail through the country park, following the sites of the fighting (now thought to be ever so slightly out). Meals, snacks, shop, disabled access; cl Mon-Sat Nov-Dec, all Jan-Feb, Mon-Fri in Mar; (01455) 290429; £3 entry, plus £1 for parking. The Royal Arms at nearby Sutton

Cheney has good food. Market Bosworth village itself is interesting to walk through, and the Black Horse (by the Market Pl almshouses) is good value.

MARKET HARBOROUGH SP7387 An attractive market town which used to specialise in the production of corsets; bizarre, florid and even agonising examples of which can be seen alongside many other aspects of the town's history in the **museum** (shop, disabled access with notice; cl Sun am, Good Fri, 25-26 Dec, 1 Jan and last full wk in Jan; (01858) 821085; free). The centre has some fine old Georgian buildings (don't miss the Old Grammar School, built on stilts), and above them the gracefully soaring 14th-c spire of the church. The handsome Three Swans Hotel (High St) has good value bar lunches. You can walk a mile along the river to nearby Welland Park.

Little Bowden church (outskirts, nr Sainsburys) Handsome 12th-c church, set off charmingly by its fine old rectory. The adjacent thatched Cherry Tree has good value food.

MELTON MOWBRAY SK7519 This little town is the home of Stilton cheese and pork pies; Dickinson & Morris (Nottingham St) still make the pies to a traditional recipe. **St Mary's church** (Burton St) is handsome, and the Anne of Cleves nearby (a former chantry for the monks) has popular food.

Melton Carnegie Museum (Thorpe End) Local history inc a look at Melton Mowbray's fashionable 19th-c days, with interactive displays; shop, disabled access; cl Good Fri and 25-26 Dec; (01664) 569946; free.

Twinlakes Park (Melton Spinney Rd, towards Scalford off A607 NE) Due to reopen as we go to press after substantial redevelopment, this busy centre has a splendid range of play areas from an assault course suitable for adults to a soft play area designed for toddlers (lots under cover, too). They also have a farm (activities every 30 minutes, from feeding the lambs to egg collecting), and now a falconry centre too, with daily flying displays. As well as a boating lake (with three different types of boat), there are zip slides, pedal-karts, a few fairground rides, and you can even paint your own pottery. Meals, snacks, shop, disabled access; cl 24-26 Dec; (01664) 567777; £6.49.

Websters Dairy (Saxelbye) A good place to buy Stilton cheese; (01664) 812223. The Black Horse in nearby Grimston is pleasant for lunch.

MOIRA SK3115

Conkers 🏰 (B586) This developing site grew out of the former visitor centre for the embryonic National Forest; it's a mix of indoor and outdoor activities, ideal for finding out about trees and the creatures that live in them. Children particularly enjoy the indoor Discovery Zones, with imaginatively conceived displays; you can crawl through a living leaf and see the world through the eyes of a spider, and multimedia shows have speeded-up footage of the seasons. Outside are 120 acres with lakeside walks, nature and sculpture trails, bird hides, mazes, play areas, a good assault course (aimed at adults), and a new indoor play area (£1.50); a steam train takes you round. Meals and snacks in two lakeside restaurants, shops, good disabled access; cl 25 Dec; (01283) 216633; £5.50.

Moira Furnace and Craft Workshops 🏰 Along the same road as Conkers above; guided tours take you around this 19th-c blast furnace, which has interactive displays about how it worked, a few craft workshops, woodland walks, and a children's play area. Meals, snacks, shop, disabled access; cl Mon (exc bank hols), plus Tues in winter, 25-26 Dec and 1 Jan; (01283) 224667; £3. The towpath beside the canal (the first stretch of the Ashby Canal to be reopened in the county) links the furnace to the attractions listed under Market Bosworth, and the museum runs boat trips; Weds-Sun; £2 (inc to Conkers on Sun).

MOUNTSORREL SK5715

Stonehurst Family Farm & Motor Museum (Bond Lane) Traditional farm with animals to handle, pony rides, play barn, trailer rides, nature trail, and a small collection of vintage cars with a recreated 1920s garage. Meals, snacks, farm shop, disabled access to farmyard and tearoom; cl 25 Dec-2 Jan; (01509) 413216; £3.95. The waterside Swan (Loughborough Rd) does good lunches.

NEWTOWN LINFORD SK5210

Bradgate Country Park This extensive tract of the former Charnwood Forest hunting park has changed little over the last 750 years. At its heart are the ruins of the 15th-c home of Lady Jane Grey, and a visitor centre tells her sad story. Shop, limited disabled access; visitor centre cl Mon (except bank hols), and Dec-Feb; (0116) 236 2713; parking from £1.50, visitor centre £1.20. Fallow and even red deer still roam these heathy slopes among the rock outcrops, and there's general access, plenty of waymarked paths, and lots of opportunities for picnics. Nearby Cropston Reservoir has waterfowl. The Pear Tree in Woodhouse Eaves has a wide choice of food.

OADBY SK6101

University Botanic Gardens (Stoughton Drive S) Around student halls of residence, these university gardens are 16 acres filled with a wide variety of plants in different and delightful settings, with a few national collections inc hardy fuchsias. Some disabled access; cl wknds and bank hols mid-Nov to Mar, 25-26 Dec and 1 Jan; (0116) 271 7725; free. The Cow & Plough (B667) has decent snack lunches Fri-Sun.

OAKHAM SK8608

Rutland's pint-sized county town is attractive, with a good sense of country bustle about it, and one or two interesting shops. The Whipper In (Market Pl) and 17th-c Wheatsheaf (Northgate, nr church) have enjoyable food, and there's a handsome drive through Ashwell, Wymondham and Waltham on the Wolds to Harby.

Oakham Castle The magnificent Norman great hall is all that's left of the building, but earthworks, walls and the remains of a motte give a good idea of what it must have been like. The hall itself is decorated with a quirky collection of extraordinary horseshoes, some grossly opulent, some enormously oversized. Shop, disabled access; cl 1-1.30pm, Sun am, Good Fri and 25-26 Dec; (01572) 758440; free.

Rutland County Museum (Catmose St) In a late 18th-c riding school, this puts the emphasis on rural life, though there are some Roman and Saxon finds,

and a new gallery on the history of
Rutland. Snacks, shop, disabled access;
cl Sun am, Good Fri and 25-26 Dec;
(01572) 758440; free.

RUTLAND WATER SK8707
Europe's biggest man-made lake, oddly
shaped, with a number of attractions.
On the N side are nature trails, an
unusual drought garden created by the
late Geoff Hamilton, places to hire bikes
(01780) 460705 or 720888, and pm
hourly **boat trips**; Apr-Sept; (01572)
787630; £5 . You can fish in various
parts of the water, and a visitor centre
down at Normanton has a small
museum in a church modelled on
London's St John's, Smith Sq; open
Easter-Sept, and wknds Oct. The
refreshingly informal Normanton Park
Hotel in waterside grounds here has
good food, as do the White Horse at
Empingham and - looking down on the
water - the Finches Arms at Upper
Hambleton (what was Lower
Hambleton is now under water).

Butterfly & Aquatic Centre ▣ (off
A606 Empingham—Whitwell) Next to
the main Rutland Water information
centre, a huge butterfly house with a
good water feature, free-flying birds,
and various insects and reptiles; also a
video on the reservoir's construction in
the 1970s. Snacks, shop, disabled access;
cl Nov-Mar; (01780) 460515; £3.95.

**Egleton Reserve and Birdwatching
Centre** This part of the nine-mile
reserve includes 14 hides and an interactive interpretation and observation
centre, with something for beginners
and more serious bird-watchers; varied
talks, walks and events. Snacks, shop,
excellent disabled access; cl 25-26 Dec;
(01572) 770651; £4.

Lyndon Reserve (off Lyndon—Manton
rd) Plenty of birds and wildlife, gentle
trails through mixed habitat. Snacks,
shop, disabled access to visitor centre
and some hides; reserve usually open all
year, useful visitor centre cl Nov-Mar exc
wknds, and some Mon exc bank hols, 25-
26 Dec; (01572) 737378; £3.

SHEPSHED SK4618
Shepshed windmill Handsomely
preserved, well worth a look.

STAUNTON HAROLD SK3720
Ferrers Centre for Arts and Crafts
(off B587 N of Ashby) Seventeen

workshops with everything from
furniture to ceramics and jewellery, in a
striking Georgian courtyard; tearoom,
craft shops, disabled access; cl Mon, and
25-26 Dec, and 1 Jan; (01332) 865408;
free. In attractive parkland, the **church**
out here, owned by the NT, was one of
the few built during the 1649-60
Commonwealth (its builder died in the
Tower of London for his defiance);
open pm only Weds-Sun and bank hols
Apr-Sept, plus wknds in Oct; (01332)
863822; £1 donation suggested.

SWANNINGTON SK4117
Hough Windmill Restored but not a
working windmill; picnic area and
nature trail; (01530) 832704; open pm
Sun Apr-Sept; free.

SWINFORD SP5879
**Stanford Hall and Motorcycle
Museum** 5,000 books line the library
of this handsome 17th-c house, an
elegant place that still keeps a cosy
lived-in atmosphere. Highlights are the
painted ceiling in the ballroom, the
portraits that accompany the winding
grand staircase, and a good costume
collection. The excellent motorcycle
museum (open pm most Suns and bank
hol Mon; £1 extra) is in the grounds,
which also have a lovely 14th-c church
with splendid stained glass, walled rose
garden, Sun craft centre, and a replica of
the country's first more or less
successful flying machine - it flew, but
crashed fatally. Snacks, shop, limited
disabled access; open pm Sun and bank
hol Mon Easter-end Sept; (01788)
860250; house and grounds £5, grounds
only £3. The Chequers (Swinford High
St) is useful for lunch.

SWITHLAND RESERVOIR
SK5713
Picturesque reservoir in natural woody
surroundings, with the embankment of
the Great Central Railway framing it
along one side; you can feed the ducks
and swans from the quiet Rothley—
Swithland lane which crosses the water.
The Griffin has enjoyable food.

TWYCROSS SK3305
Twycross Zoo Park *See separate
family panel on p.369.*

UPPINGHAM SP8699
Charming small town with an interesting
square (Fri market) and curving
18th/19th-c High St. The Falcon Hotel

does nice light lunches and teas. On most Weds lunchtimes in term-time, musicians from the famous local school (tours by arrangement (01572) 821264) give free concerts in the parish church; the Vaults next to it does decent food.

WELLAND VIADUCT SP9197
One of the county's most striking sights: nearly a mile long, swooping across the pastures of the valley, it is the country's longest viaduct. In the unspoilt nearby village of Seaton the George & Dragon has good value food (and viaduct views).

WIGSTON SP6099
Framework Knitters Museum (Bushloe End) A restored 18th-c knitters' house and workshop, with original hand frames. Shop; open Sun pm and pm first Sat in month, plus most bank hols; (0116) 288 3396; £1. The Royal Oak has cheap food.

WOODHOUSE EAVES SK5114
Beacon Hill Country Park This is a good surviving chunk of the former vast Charnwood Forest hunting park. The hill itself (above Woodhouse Eaves and the site of a Bronze Age fort) is one of the best viewpoints in the area - an intriguing mix of the industrial and the very rural; it's a popular local beauty-spot, rising almost like a volcano above its lower woodland slopes. From the 245-metre (800-ft) summit, a Jubilee Walk heads N and E through partly wooded country. A trail S makes a small circuit around Broombriggs Farm, with boards along the way explaining farming methods. Over 30,000 trees have been planted on the West Beacon Fields area in the last few years, with paths, a woodland craft trail, viewing platform and straw shelter; £1 car park charge. The Wheatsheaf is handy for lunch.
Long Close Garden 🅴 (Main St) Hidden behind a high wall, these gardens have been lovingly restored and extended since 1925; many rare plants thrive unexpectedly so far north,

and the wildflower meadow contains hedges thought to be 700 years old. Open Mar-July and autumn, cl Sun and usually Aug, best to check; (01509) 890616; tickets from Pene Crafts Gift Shop opp at No 53 (cl 1-2pm); *£3.

WYMONDHAM SK8518
Wymondham windmill One of only four six-sailed mills in the country, with tearoom, craft shop and children's play area. Disabled access; cl Mon (exc bank hols in summer), all Jan, and Mon-Thurs Sept-Dec and Feb-Easter; (01572) 787304; free. The attractive old Berkeley Arms does enjoyable fresh food.

There are many charming villages here. Ones with decent pubs include Appleby Magna SK3109, Ashby Folville SK7011, streamside Barkby SK6309, Barrowden SK9400, Belton SK4420, Billesdon SK7202, Branston SK8129, Braunston SK8306, Bruntingthorpe SP6089, East Langton SP7292, Grimston SK6821, Harby SK7531, Hose SK7329, Ketton SK9704 (good walks), Knipton SK8231, Knossington SK8008, Market Overton SK8816, Medbourne SP7993 (interesting church too), Peatling Magna SP5992 and Parva SP5889, Somerby SK7710, South Croxton SK6810, South Luffenham SK9402, Stoke Golding SP3997, Walton on the Wolds SK5919, Whitwick SK4316, and Wing SK8902, notable for its small medieval turf maze. Stoke Dry SP8596 and Wistow SP6496 have fine churches.

Pubs useful for walks here include the Bricklayers Arms in Thornton SK4607 (reservoir walks) and Pear Tree and Bulls Head in Woodhouse Eaves SK5214; and, all handy for canals, the Navigation or Soar Bridge in Barrow upon Soar SK5717, Griffin at Congerstone SK3605, Dog & Hedgehog at Dadlington SP4097, Navigation at Kilby Bridge SP6097, Rising Sun at Shackerstone SK3706 and George & Dragon at Stoke Golding SP3997.

Where to eat

BARROWDEN SK9400 **Exeter Arms** 28 Main St (01572) 747247 Tranquil 17th-c coaching inn with a cheery yellow open-plan bar, straightforward furnishings on bare boards or carpet, own-brewed beers, enjoyable, generously served good food inc interesting daily specials, and picnic-sets on a narrow terrace in front overlooking the pretty village green, ducks on the pond, and broader views stretching away beyond; boules in back garden; cl Mon am. £23.25|**£7.50**

BELMESTHORPE TF0410 **Blue Bell** *Shepherd's Walk (01780) 763859* Homely atmosphere in village pub, particularly in the first little beamed cottagey room with its open fire in huge stone inglenook and fresh flowers; originally three cottages, so it's on two levels: peer down into the bar counter, and a slope winds down round the counter to another area with similar cottagey furniture; well kept real ales, a good choice of wines by the glass, and imaginative seasonally changing bar food; disabled access. £25|**£5.75**

CASTLE DONINGTON SK4326 **Nags Head** *Hill Top (01332) 850652* Civilised low-beamed no smoking dining pub with a simple little bar area, an intimate room with three chunky old pine candlelit tables on seagrass and a pretty slate art deco fireplace, and a much bigger similarly decorated yellow-washed dining area; through an opening to the kitchen you can watch the chefs preparing the beautifully presented imaginative food; very attentive staff and conscientious landlord, well kept ales, 20-30 malt whiskies, and quite a few wines by the glass; handy for Donington Race Track; no food Sun; cl 26 Dec-2 Jan; children over 10; disabled access. £30|**£5.50**

COTTESMORE SK9013 **Sun** *25 Main St (01572) 812321* 17th-c stone-built thatched village pub with a few tables in the rooms off the bar (best to get there early, or even book), a warm fire in the stone inglenook, sunny yellow walls with some nice sporting prints and other pictures, and stripped pine furnishings; imaginative food, real ales, decent wines, and friendly helpful service; tables and boules in garden, and a new terrace. £21|**£6.50**

EAST LANGTON SP7292 **Bell** *Main St (01858) 545278* Pretty creeper-covered inn with a warm inviting atmosphere, a log fire and plain wooden tables in the long stripped stone bar, imaginative food from a seasonally changing menu, OAP wkdy lunches, Sunday carvery, and a no smoking dining room; own-brewed beers, decent wines, and friendly efficient service; cl 25 Dec; children must be well behaved; partial disabled access. £24|**£7.50**

LYDDINGTON SP8796 **Old White Hart** *Main St (01572) 821703* Warmly welcoming 17th-c village inn with just three tables in front of the log fire, heavy bowed beams, and dried flowers in the cosy softly lit bar; an attractive no smoking restaurant with corn dollies and a big oak dresser, and a tiled-floor room with some stripped stone, cushioned wall seats and mate's chairs, and woodburner; very popular imaginative bar food, well kept ales, and picnic-sets and boules in the pretty walled garden; good nearby walks, and handy for the Bede House; cl Sun pm, 25 Dec. £21.90|**£9.95**

STATHERN SK7731 **Red Lion** *2 Red Lion St (01949) 860868* Though it looks ordinary from the outside, this is a thriving village pub with a particularly laid-back feel to the yellow room on the right, a relaxing lounge with sofas, a fireplace, and a big table with books, paper and magazines; there's a smaller, more traditional flagstoned bar, with terracotta walls, another fireplace with a pile of logs beside it, and lots of beams and hops; dotted around are various oddities picked up by one of the licensees on visits to Newark Antiques Fair; excellent food with an emphasis on local produce, well chosen wines, local ales, and no smoking dining room; big play area for children. £24.95|**£8.25**

THORPE LANGTON SP7492 **Bakers Arms** *Main St (01858) 545201* Extended thatched pub with a warm friendly welcome, simple country furnishings, well presented interesting food changing daily (need to book well ahead), helpful service, well kept beer, an extensive wine list, and no smoking snug; cl wkdy lunchtimes, Sun and Mon pm; children over 12. £30

UPPER HAMBLETON SK8907 **Finches Arms** *Oakham Rd (01572) 756575* Delightfully placed pub looking over Rutland Water, with stylish cane furniture in both the bar and more modern no smoking restaurant, super imaginative upmarket food, and real ales; bdrms; no children. £22.40|**£6.75**

Special thanks to Jenny and Michael Back, F Blanchard, Mrs Y Champion

LINCOLNSHIRE

**Classic seaside family holidays, plus some interesting but
little-known holiday prospects elsewhere - grand country houses,
interesting towns, a good mix of wildlife attractions; a good value
corner of England largely off the tourist trail**

Many of Lincolnshire's family attractions are animal-orientated, and this
year the Natureland Seal Sanctuary in Skegness tops the list, as our
Lincolnshire Family Attraction; Mablethorpe has another good seal
sanctuary. The Butterfly & Wildlife Park at Long Sutton has lots to occupy
families, with birds of prey and animals as well as a huge tropical house, and
children can join in with the activities at the Great Steeping heavy horse
centre. Rand and Louth have farm parks, and in Langworth there's a
falconry centre; Elsham Hall Country & Wildlife Park has craft
demonstrations as well as animals.

The string of traditional resorts along Lincolnshire's sandy coasts are
great for families, and there are lively seaside fairgrounds at Cleethorpes
(a few good rainy-day attractions here as well) and Ingoldmells. Away from
the coast though, this is a county more for adults than children.

Lincoln is an interesting city with plenty to see (good museums as well
as the cathedral and castle). Stamford (with grand Burghley House) is a
particularly attractive town, and Boston is a pleasant place to spend a
leisurely afternoon.

N and E of Lincoln, the rolling Wolds countryside makes for enjoyable
drives on uncrowded roads, punctuated by attractive villages and
charming small towns, and by soaring church spires. The huge fields can be
rather tedious for walkers - and around The Wash and up the coast
towards Wainfleet and Coningsby it's very flat. The flatness made this
prime country for bomber airfields in World War II: for aircraft head to
Coningsby and East Kirkby (and there's a vintage vehicle collection at
North Hykeham). Lincolnshire is also classic windmill territory:
Claythorpe Watermill & Wildfowl Gardens (at Aby) are picturesque, the
windmill at Heckington is the only one in Britain with eight sails, and
Boston has Britain's tallest working windmill.

Mansions and castles well worth seeing include striking Tattershall
Castle, Normanby Hall (farming museum here too), Grimsthorpe Castle
(an interesting mix of styles, and you can go on tours with the ranger) and
Woolsthorpe Manor (Isaac Newton's former home, with an interactive
discovery centre). There's a medieval manor in Gainsborough, and the
ruins at Thornton Curtis are atmospheric.

Please let us know what you think of places in the *Guide*. Use the report forms
at the back of the book, write us a letter or log on to www.goodguides.co.uk

Where to stay

BOURNE TF0922 **Cawthorpe Hall** *Cawthorpe, Bourne, Lincolnshire PE10 0AB* *(01778) 423830* **£70**; 4 rms most with own bthrm. Georgian house surrounded by three acres of rose fields from which Mr Armstrong produces english rose oil and water; huge studio extension leading off grand entrance hall with wicker armchairs, sofas and big contemporary artwork; interesting furniture, a very relaxed atmosphere, charming friendly owners, and enjoyable breakfasts and afternoon tea; pubs nearby for evening meals; cl Christmas; partial disabled access

BUSLINGTHORPE TF0985 **East Farm House** *Middle Rasen Rd, Buslingthorpe, Lincolnshire LN3 5AQ (01673) 842283* **£50***, plus special breaks; 2 rms. 18th-c farmhouse surrounded by family farm, with beams, stripped pine, log fires, relaxed atmosphere, and good breakfasts (evening meals by arrangement); tennis and lots of walks; self-catering cottage; cl Christmas and New Year

DYKE TF1022 **Wishing Well** *Main St, Dyke, Bourne, Lincolnshire PE10 0AF (01778) 422970* **£65**; 12 rms with showers. The wishing well is at the dining end of the long rambling bar - heavy beams, dark stone, brassware, candlelight and a big fireplace; good value food, no smoking restaurant, helpful service, friendly atmosphere; gardens and grounds with play area; disabled access

EAST BARKWITH TF1581 **Bodkin Lodge** *Grange Farm, Torrington Lane, East Barkwith, Lincoln, Lincolnshire LN8 5RY (01673) 858249* **£58***; 2 pretty ground floor rms. Run by the same warmly friendly family as the Grange, this carefully extended bungalow has a comfortable sitting room with books, fresh flowers, open fire and baby grand piano, good breakfasts in big dining room with home-made bread and jams (light suppers by arrangement), award-winning wildlife farmland trails from the door, and marvellous country views; cl mid-Dec to New Year; children over 10; disabled access

EAST BARKWITH TF1581 **Grange** *Torrington Lane, East Barkwith, Lincoln, Lincolnshire LN8 5RY (01673) 858670* **£48***; 2 attractive, airy rms. A friendly welcome in Georgian farmhouse on immaculate family-run farm with views of Lincoln Cathedral and the Wolds; good cooking using local produce, guest sitting room, and mature gardens with grass tennis court, farm trail, trout lake, and conservation areas; cl Christmas and New Year; disabled access ☺

HOLBEACH TF3426 **Pipwell Manor** *Washway Rd, Saracens Head, Holbeach, Spalding, Lincolnshire PE12 8AL (01406) 423119* **£48***; 3 comfortable rms. Handsome 18th-c farmhouse, welcoming and spotless, with log fire in comfortable sitting room, pretty panelled dining room, afternoon tea with home-made cakes on arrival, good breakfasts with their own eggs and home-made preserves, and a conservatory; miniature railway in large gardens, and free bikes; no smoking; cl 23 Dec-1 Jan; children over 10

LINCOLN SK9771 **Carline** *1-3 Carline Rd, Lincoln LN1 1HL (01522) 530422* **£46***, plus special breaks; 8 well equipped rms. Spotlessly kept and comfortable double-fronted no smoking Edwardian guest house 5 mins from the cathedral, with helpful and cheerful owners, quiet dining/sitting rooms, and fine breakfasts; cl Christmas and New Year; children over 2

LINCOLN SK9871 **D'Isney Place** *Eastgate, Lincoln LN2 4AA (01522) 538881* **£89**, plus special breaks; 17 charming rms. Friendly 18th-c hotel with lovely gardens (one wall of the cathedral close forms its southern boundary), a relaxed and homely atmosphere, good breakfasts using free-range eggs served on bone china in your room (there are no public rooms), and friendly owners; partial disabled access; dogs welcome

STAMFORD TF0306 **George** *71 St Martins, Stamford, Lincolnshire PE9 2LB (01780) 750700* **£105**, plus special breaks; 47 individually decorated rms. Ancient former coaching inn with a quietly civilised atmosphere, sturdy timbers, broad flagstones, heavy beams and massive stonework, and open log fires; good food in Garden Lounge, restaurant and courtyard (in summer), an excellent range of drinks inc very good value italian wines, and welcoming staff; well kept walled garden and sunken croquet lawn; disabled access; dogs welcome in bedrooms

WINTERINGHAM SE9322 **Winteringham Fields** / *Silver St, Winteringham, Scunthorpe, Lincolnshire DN15 9ND (01724) 733096* **£120**; 10 pretty, chintzy rms with period furniture (3 off courtyard). Thoughtfully run restaurant-with-rooms in 16th-c manor house with comfortable and very attractive Victorian furnishings, beams and open fires, really excellent, inventive and beautifully presented food (inc a marvellous cheeseboard) in no smoking dining room, fine breakfasts, exemplary service, and an admirable wine list; cl 2 wks Christmas, last wk Mar, 1st wk Aug, last wk Oct; disabled access; babes in arms and children over 8; dogs welcome in bedrooms

To see and do

Lincolnshire Family Attraction of the Year

SKEGNESS TF5663 **Natureland Seal Sanctuary** 🏛 (North Parade) An entertaining and particularly rewarding place to spend at least a couple of hours, this very genuine seal sanctuary is now almost 40 years old. It's renowned for its success in rescuing baby pups found stranded on beaches around The Wash, and eventually returning them to their natural environment. Sick seals are treated in their seal hospital, then moved to the rearing pool outside. Friendly staff explain their work during the enjoyable feeding displays at various times throughout the day (announced over the public address system), and it's clear from the way they talk about each animal that they're very much treated as individuals. It's fun watching the seals perform: they aren't trained, they just love showing off. A pool has underwater viewing areas. They also have a good few penguins (they make a wonderful braying noise), an aquarium, and a tropical house with crocodiles, snakes, tarantula, and insects. A 52-metre (170-ft) greenhouse shows off free-flying tropical birds, flamingos and a splendid range of flowers and plants, with butterflies between May and Sept. You can feed the goats, rabbits, and guinea-pigs in the pets corner, using food on sale in the shop; in summer these are joined by calves from a nearby farm. Fine days are best, but a series of covered walkways mean if it rains you can see almost everything without having to venture into the open. Dogs allowed, on a lead. Snacks, shop, disabled access; cl 25-26 Dec, 1 Jan; (01754) 764345; £4.75 adults, £3.10 children 3-15. A family ticket (two adults, two children) is £14.10. The beach is directly opposite.

ABY TF4179
Claythorpe Watermill & Wildfowl Gardens 🏛 Pretty spot around 18th-c watermill with reconstructed early 1900s bread shop, the grounds full of ornamental birds, and animals such as wallabies and otters. Fun to wander through the picturesque woods. Meals, snacks, shop, mostly disabled access; cl Nov to mid-Mar; (01507) 450687; £4.40. The Vine at South Thoresby is a civilised place for lunch.

ALFORD TF4575
Pleasant town with some attractive brick and thatch buildings, and a summer market (Tues and Fri). The White Horse Hotel and the Half Moon (both West St) are useful for lunch. W of here, just N of the A16/A1104 junction, the Bluestone Heath hill rd past S Ormsby and on to the A157 W of Louth is a splendid scenic drive.
Five-sailed windmill 🏛 Tall mid-19th-c five-sailed **windmill** on the A1104 towards Mablethorpe, restored, with Victorian and Edwardian antiques in an old engine house. Tearoom, shop selling their own flour, disabled access; open every Tues and wknd, plus Fri Apr-Oct, and daily July-Sept (cl 24 Dec-1 Jan); (01507) 462136; £2.75.
ALKBOROUGH SE8821
Overlooks the confluence of the Trent and Humber from a high (for this area)

scarp called The Cliff; walks along it on a path leading S to the attractive village of Burton upon Stather.

ASWARBY TF0639

Aswarby church Delightfully set in a well tended park, by a pretty hamlet.

BARTON-UPON-HUMBER TA0321

Baysgarth House Museum (Caistor Rd) This handsome 18th-c house has well displayed local history, especially good on rural crafts. Snacks and shop wknds and school hols, disabled access to ground floor only; cl Mon (exc bank hols), 25-26 Dec, 1 Jan; (01652) 632318; free.

BELTON SK8844

Belton House Splendid Restoration-period mansion with wonderful carvings, ornate plasterwork, and sumptuous furnishings, paintings and ceramics, as well as a 1,000-acre deer park (picturesque public road through here on the E side), orangery and formal italian garden. Meals, snacks, shop, limited disabled access to house (best to phone); open pm Weds-Sun and bank hol Mon 31 Mar-Oct; (01476) 566116; *£6.50; NT. The Brownlow Arms in picturesque Hough-on-the-Hill is a good restaurant.

BOSTON TF3243

Once the country's second-largest seaport, this little town has a number of pretty spots and handsome historic buildings. Most famous is the **Boston Stump**, the graceful tower of the magnificent 14th-c church St Botolph's. Climb to the top for far views over this flat landscape - it's the second-tallest parish church in the country (the tallest is in Louth); the inside is spectacular too. Another prominent feature of the skyline is the waterside **Maud Foster Mill**, the tallest working windmill in the country, and one of the most photogenic (you can climb all seven floors); café (specialising in vegetarian food), shop with organic flour; open Weds, Sat and pm Sun, plus Thurs and Fri July-Aug; (01205) 352188; £2.50. Goodbarns Yard (Wormgate) is a popular central pub/restaurant, and the Eagle (West St) has good value food. The surroundings (and the Lincolnshire coast generally) are too flat for driving to be very interesting around here, and

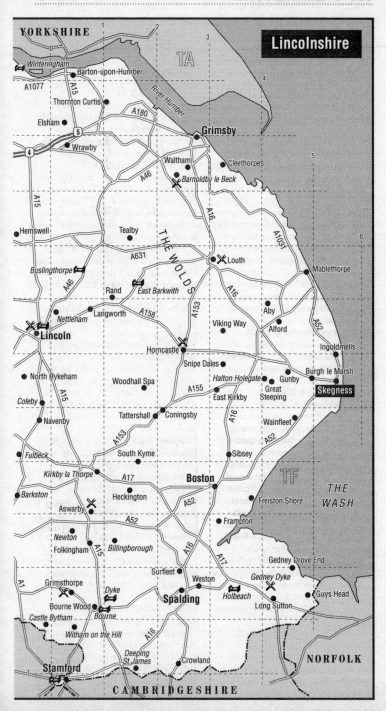

Lincolnshire

YORKSHIRE

Winteringham
A1077
Barton-upon-Humber
Thornton Curtis
River Humber
Elsham
Wrawby
Grimsby
A180
Waltham
Cleethorpes
Barnoldby le Beck
Hemswell
Tealby
THE WOLDS
A631
Louth
Buslingthorpe
Mablethorpe
A46
Rand
East Barkwith
A16
A158
Langworth
Nettleham
Aby
Viking Way
Alford
Lincoln
Horncastle
Ingoldmells
Snipe Dales
North Hykeham
Woodhall Spa
Halton Holegate
Gunby
Burgh le Marsh
A155
Great
Steeping
Skegness
Coleby
East Kirkby
Tattershall
Coningsby
Navenby
Wainfleet
A153
Fulbeck
South Kyme
Sibsey
Kirkby la Thorpe
A17
Boston
Barkston
Heckington
THE WASH
Aswarby
A52
Frampton
Freiston Shore
A52
Newton
Folkingham
Billingborough
A16
A17
Gedney Drove End
Surfleet
Weston
Gedney Dyke
Grimsthorpe
Dyke
Guys Head
Bourne Wood
Spalding
Holbeach
Long Sutton
Castle Bytham
Bourne
Witham on the Hill
A16
Deeping
St James
Crowland
NORFOLK
Stamford
CAMBRIDGESHIRE

side roads which look clear on a map can turn out to be tryingly slow in practice, with muddy agricultural vehicles trundling along; the B1183 and B1192 aren't bad.

BOURNE WOOD TF0721
(A151 just outside Bourne) Sheltered woodland good for a gentle stroll, esp welcome as so much of the country here is flat, treeless fen. Plenty of bird life, busy at wknds with locals exercising their dogs; parking charge. In the town's market place, there's decent food in the Angel Hotel, opposite an interesting antiques shop.

BRANSBY SK8979
Home of Rest for Horses Home to more than 250 rescued horses, ponies and donkeys; readers tell us it's a nice place for a wander and a picnic. Shop, disabled access; open daily; (01427) 788464; free.

BRANT BROUGHTON SK9154
Brant Broughton church spire Elegant and very tall, a landmark for miles around.

BURGH LE MARSH TF4965
Has a notable **church**; a five-storey working **windmill** nearby has unusual left-handed sails, and a little museum. Snacks; open pm Sun and bank hols May-Sept; (01754) 766658; 50p.

CLEETHORPES TA3108
Big traditional seaside resort with extensive gently shelving tidal sands, and a surprisingly ancient **church** among some attractive older houses in its original core. Some of the seafront buildings (inc the tourist information centre) have recently been restored to their Victorian/Edwardian elegance, thanks to a generous English Heritage scheme. The newish road in from the A16 is a big help. Willys (which brews its own beer) is useful for lunch.

Cleethorpes Coast Light Railway ⊞ (Kings Rd) Gentle mile through local scenery between Kingsway and Lakeside. Meals, snacks, shop, disabled coach; cl wkdys Oct-Easter (exc school hols); (01472) 604657; £2.20.

Humber Estuary Discovery Centre (Kings Rd) Unusual spiral-shaped building inspired by seashells on the edge of the boating lake, with an interactive journey through time (Cleethorpes lies on the Prime

Meridian) looking at local natural and social history; also aquarium and telescopes for bird- and ship-spotting on the Humber estuary, as well as paddling pool and sandpit. Snacks, shop, disabled access; cl 25-26 Dec, 1 Jan; (01472) 323232; £1.95.

Jungle (Lakeside, Kings Rd) Tropical wildlife from giant snakes and iguanas to meerkats and parrots, also llamas, raccoons and an alligator, plus a guinea-pig village. Shop, disabled access; cl Dec-Jan; (01472) 291998; £3.

Playtowers Very handy for wet days, this is one of the biggest indoor children's amusement complexes in Europe, with over 60 different activities on six floors. Meals, snacks, some disabled access; cl a few days over Christmas and New Year; (01472) 211511; £4.50 children 5-12 (£1 less for children under 5), £1 adults for 2 hours.

Pleasure Island (Kings Rd) Enough to keep a family entertained for the day, this theme park has lots of suitably scary rides; the terrifying Hyper Blaster shoots you up and down a 27-metre (90-ft) tower, and they've recently added Pendulas, which swings passengers 80 ft up, while rotating. Also children's rides, cabaret and various animal shows. Meals, snacks, shop, disabled access; cl wkdys Sept-Oct (exc autumn half term) and cl Nov-Mar; (01472) 211511; £11.50.

CONINGSBY TF2257
Battle of Britain Visitor Centre (A153) Subject to operational commitments you can see the aircraft of the Battle of Britain Memorial Flight, inc the only flying Lancaster in Europe. Snacks, shop, disabled access; cl wknds, bank hols, and 2 wks at Christmas, best to check; (01526) 344041; £3.50. The **church** has what's said to be the biggest dial of any clock with just a single hand. Just out of town, the interesting old Lea Gate Inn (B1192 NW) is good for lunch.

CROWLAND TF2410
Crowland church The imposing remains of a once-great abbey, part still used as the parish church - the village also has a three-legged bridge.

DODDINGTON SK9070
Doddington Hall ⊞ (B1190) Striking lived-in Elizabethan mansion,

unchanged externally since it was built, and still with its original walled gardens, gatehouse and family church. The elegant rooms are mostly Georgian; regular concerts in the Long Gallery. Teas, shop, disabled access to ground floor and gardens; open pm Weds and Sun May-Sept; (01522) 694308; £5, garden only £3.50. The Stones Arms prettily placed in nearby Skellingthorpe has good value food.

EAST KIRKBY TF3563

Lincolnshire Aviation Heritage Centre (A155) Enthusiastic World War II collection on a wartime airfield. The highlight is *Just Jane*, the famous Avro Lancaster NX611 lovingly restored by two brothers as a memorial to their brother who died during the Nuremberg Raid in 1944. They hope that one day it will fly again but for the moment are content with taxiing it around the airfield in summer. There is also an original Dambusters' bouncing bomb on display. Meals, snacks, shop, disabled access; cl Sun and Christmas wk; (01790) 763207; *£5. The Red Lion, handy for lunch, has quite a collection of bric-a-brac itself (some interesting tools for sale behind).

ELSHAM TA0311

Elsham Hall Country & Wildlife Park Arboretum, woodland garden, and plenty of space to let off steam, also barn theatre, sheep, goats and donkeys, some of which you can stroke or feed, and an unusual carp-feeding jetty, where monster-sized fish will feed straight from your hand. They have a wildlife or country talk and demonstration every day at 1 o'clock, and a craft centre has blacksmith demonstrations (Sun). An adventure playground has sections for different age groups. Special events include lambing days in spring. Meals and snacks (good Sun lunch), picnic area, shops, garden centre, disabled access; cl Mon and Tues (exc bank and school hols), and all mid-Sept to Mar; (01652) 688698; £4.50.

EPWORTH SE7803

Old Rectory (Rectory St) The childhood home of John and Charles Wesley, built in 1709 by their father. Restored in 1957, with rooms furnished in period style. Shop, disabled access to ground floor; cl Nov-Feb and 12-2pm Mar, April, Oct; (01427) 872268; £3. Thanks to the Wesley connection, the whole of this pleasant village, which is the centre of the Isle of Axholme with Georgian houses around the market place, has become something of a Methodist centre. The White Bear has enjoyable food.

FOLKINGHAM TF0733

Picturesque village with a fine market place. The Fortescue Arms over at Billingborough, a pleasant short drive away, is good for lunch.

FRAMPTON TF3239

Perhaps the prettiest fenland village. The Moores Arms has good traditional food.

FREISTON SHORE TF3942

(off A52 via Freiston) Good paths to the sea wall, with desolate views of myriad birds and even seals on the marshes and banks beyond - don't be tempted out among them, the tides are lethal.

GAINSBOROUGH SK8189

Old Hall (Parnell St) Restored medieval manor house with interesting Great Hall and original kitchen; good Walkman tour. Snacks, shop, disabled access to ground floor only; cl Sun Nov-Easter and am Sun all year, 24-26 and 31 Dec, 1 Jan; (01427) 612669; £2.60. The Elm Cottage (Church St) has good cheap food, and new walkways along the Trent embankment give views of the flood plain of this powerful brooding river; the Jenny Wren along at Susworth has good seafood and some tables out by the water. Delicious ice-creams at nearby Blyton Dairy (Old Hall Farm, off A159) include Turkish delight and marshmallow dream.

GEDNEY DROVE END TF4828

Sea walk A good way of seeing The Wash is by following the dyke forming the sea wall; access is from a car park nr Gedney Drove End, from which you can follow the dyke to the mouth of the Nene, with its twin lighthouses either side. When the red flag is flying walks on part of the sea wall are banned. This area is sprinkled with pillboxes, and other remnants of World War II defences.

GRANTHAM SK9136

Two rarities The unusually tall spire of the splendid parish church is commemorated in an early 19th-c jingle: 'Grantham, now two rarities are thine, A lofty steeple and a living sign'. The living sign is the hive with living bees - descended from those of that time - still used as an inn sign by the good value Beehive pub on Castlegate here.

Grantham Museum has local archaeology and history inc displays on Margaret Thatcher and the Dambusters; temporary exhibitions and special events for children. Shop, disabled access; cl Sun, and 24-26 and 31 Dec, 1 Jan; (01476) 568783; free.

GRANTHAM CANAL SK8435 Though largely derelict, its towpath is kept in very good condition throughout, and makes for easy interesting walks, with plenty of wildlife. Strolls or longer walks can be based at Woolsthorpe (for instance from the Rutland Arms, known locally as the Dirty Duck), or from several other villages along the canal in this and neighbouring counties, all of which have pubs with food; examples are Redmile SK7935, Plungar SK7633, Hose SK7329, Hickling SK6929 (the basin here is very popular, with its waterfowl) and Kinoulton SK6730.

GREAT STEEPING TF4364
Northcote Heavy Horse Centre Supervised by friendly staff, a full programme of activities and demonstrations throughout the day could include grooming, harnessing and waggon rides. Snacks, shop, disabled access; as we went to press dates were unconfirmed, best to phone for details; (01754) 830286; £5, waggon rides £2.25 extra. The Bell at Halton Holegate has good home cooking.

GRIMSBY TA2609
With nearby Immingham, this is Britain's busiest port, with a flourishing chemicals industry, and despite the decline of its own trawler fleet still the main english fish trading and processing centre. It's also making considerable strides towards attracting visitors, with improved road access. The Abbeygate Centre has reasonably priced antiques shops, also upstairs craft workshops inc lace-making and a café. Alfred Enderby's smoked fish house (Fish Docks Rd) demonstrates traditional methods of smoking salmon, haddock and cod

(usually 10-noon, not wknds). St James Sq has a farmers' market (third Fri of month). Cyclists are well catered for by routes both here and in adjoining Cleethorpes.

National Fishing Heritage Centre (Alexandra Dock) Displays recalling the experiences of a trawlerman of the mid-1950s take you from the back streets of Grimsby to the fishing grounds of the Arctic Circle and back. Everything in the main centre is under cover, but outside there are enjoyable guided tours of a real trawler, the *Ross Tiger*, led by a former trawlerman. Meals, snacks, shop, disabled access (not to *Ross Tiger*); as we went to press, opening times had not been decided, best to phone; (01472) 323345; £4.95. There's good value food on the *Lincoln Castle*, a former Humber paddle steamer moored nearby at Fishermans Wharf.

Time Trap In the prison cells of the Town Hall the town's social history gets a lively treatment; displays cover the building of the docks and the struggle for women's suffrage - and you can see what it's like to be locked in a prison cell; cl Fri-Sun and bank hols; (01472) 324109; free (donation recommended).

GRIMSTHORPE TF0422
Grimsthorpe Castle A patchwork of styles from its medieval tower and Tudor quadrangle to the baroque N front by Vanbrugh; the state rooms and galleries have especially fine furnishings. Outside are formal gardens and parkland with lake (you can take a tour with the ranger in his Land Rover), and red deer tame enough for children to feed, also play and picnic areas. Meals, snacks, shop, some disabled access; house, park and garden open Sun and Thurs Apr-Sept, Sun-Thurs in Aug, house cl am; (01778) 591205; £6.50 all-in, £3 park only. The Black Horse is a good dining pub.

GUNBY TF4666
Gunby Hall 🏛 (off A158 nr Spilsby) Interesting neat red brick William III house, with fine oak staircase and clock collection; especially worth visiting for the nine acres of splendid gardens, said to be Tennyson's 'haunt of ancient peace'. Disabled access to garden only; house and garden open pm Weds,

garden also open pm Thurs Apr-Sept; (01909) 486411; *£4, £2.80 garden only. The Willoughby Arms over in the quiet village of Willoughby does pleasant lunches.

GUYS HEAD TF4925

Peter Scott Walk A 10-mile walk E from the mouth of the Nene, with its twin lighthouses either side. Scott used to come here to study and paint wildfowl. It leads along the dyke into Norfolk, with access from a car park on the Nene's E bank.

HECKINGTON TF1443

Windmill In an understated but pleasant village, this well restored windmill is the only one in Britain with eight sails; (01529) 461919. The **church** still has many of its original 14th-c fittings, and is a delight.

HEMSWELL SK9590

Antiques, Craft & Design Centre (signed off A631) One of the largest craft centres in Britain, with thousands of antiques and bric-a-brac crammed into 270 shops; also a small aircraft museum (wknds only; donations). Good meals and snacks, disabled access; cl 25-26 Dec; (01427) 667066; free, 50p wknds for antiques centre.

HORNCASTLE TF2569

Attractive market town popular for antiques, with around 30 shops in the Bridge St Antiques Centre. You can still see parts of the town's **Roman wall**. The Admiral Rodney (North St) has a decent carvery, and the Fighting Cocks (West St) is also good value. Some 3m N the 'High Street' forking off the A158 is a good drive, following an Iron Age trackway up to Caistor. The A153 to Louth gives some good rolling Wolds views. Another good drive here includes Scrivelsby and its vast deer park, Belchford (the Blue Bell, with enjoyable food, is a nice base for Wolds walks), Fulletby (perhaps a stroll on the footpaths here), Somersby (Tennyson's birthplace - his bust is in the church), Old Bolingbroke (castle ruins, and the Black Horse is a useful food stop), Spilsby, and, if you've made good time, Wainfleet and Boston.

INGOLDMELLS TF5666

Fantasy Island (Sea Lane - beach just opposite) More elaborate than your average fairground and, unusually, most of the rides and other features are inside, with thatched buildings and palm trees nestling under a giant pyramid, though a number of rides are springing up outside too. The most exciting ride is the Millennium roller-coaster, which goes through 360-degree loops around the outside of the pyramid, at heights of 46 metres (150 ft) and a speed of around 100 mph. The £28 million suspended roller-coaster Odyssey has the longest drop in Europe, and a new ride called Absolutely Insane is an exaggerated inverted bungee; other highlights include a SiEmex virtual voyage theatre, and water-rides. Plenty for younger children, inc a train ride through the world of the Jellikins, and live shows with TV characters. Outside are a big play area for the under-5s, and a huge market, with up to around 780 stalls. Lots of places to eat, shops, disabled access; open daily Mar-Oct; (01754) 872030; free admission to park, rides charged separately, and tokens are 60p. Here our discount offer is a special one - if you buy £18 worth of ride tokens, on production of the voucher you'll receive a further £18-worth free (this offer excludes Odyssey, G-Force, Millennium, International Go-Karting and Absolutely Insane, not valid bank hols). It's open very late in the main season - till 11pm Fri and Sat.

Hardys Animal Farm (Anchor Lane) Working farm, recommended by readers for a relaxing sunny afternoon, with friendly farm animals (you can buy feed), and an adventure playground. Café, shop, disabled access; open wk before Easter-3 Oct; (01754) 872267; £3.50.

LANGWORTH TF0875

Woodside Falconry and Conservation Centre 🖾 (off A158 towards Apley) Pleasant for a sunny afternoon, with quite a lot for a small place; there are flying demonstrations at 12pm and 3pm (in summer they also have pig and ferret racing), and they have plans to add a tropical butterfly house. There's a children's play area and woodland trail (they usually do guided walks), and the fun fishing lake is a hit with budding young anglers (£2, plus £2.50 per fish). Good café and shop, some disabled access; open Feb half-term to Oct; (01522) 754280; £4.25.

LINCOLN SK9771

The cathedral and castle, both very striking, share the central hilltop, with enough old buildings around them to keep a sense of unity. There's a lot to appeal up here, and in Steep Hill and Strait St ancient buildings run steeply down to the 15th-c Stonebow Gate at the top of the High St. This lower part of the town is a more normal bustling shopping and working centre, though even here are a good few interesting old buildings - inc several Saxon churches and the Norman guildhall. The Time Travel Pass (from the Tourist Information Centre on Castle Hill, giving unlimited access for a week) lets you visit the cathedral, castle, Museum of Lincolnshire Life, Ellis Mill, and medieval Bishop's Palace for £20. Guided tours leave from the tourist information in Castle Sq (11 am, 2.15 pm wknds (daily July-Aug); phone (01522) 873213; £3). The **Greyfriars Exhibition Centre** (Broadgate) is in a lovely 13th-c Franciscan building (open Weds-Sat (exc 1-2pm) and Tues July-Aug; (01522) 530401; free). The Wig & Mitre and Browns Pie Shop (both on Steep Hill) and Victoria (Union Rd, behind the castle) are all good for lunch. Brayford Pool, the heart of the Waterfront Quarter, has boat trips, a multi-screen cinema, and lots of places to eat (bargain food at the riverside Royal William IV, for instance). There are some good views from the A607 to Grantham.

Ellis' Mill (Mill Rd, just NW of centre) Guided tours by volunteer millers take you right to the top of this 18th-c four-sailed mill, and when there's enough wind, you can see it working. Shop (inc their own wholemeal flour); open pm Sun, plus pm Sat May-Sept; (01522) 523870; 70p.

Lincoln Castle In beautiful surroundings on a formidable earthwork, this was originally built in 1068 for William the Conqueror, but only two towers and two impressive gateways date from then. One of only four remaining originals of Magna Carta is on display, and there are super views

from the ramparts. A 19th-c prison has suitably gruesome exhibits; its chapel is unusually designed so that none of the congregation could see each other. Special events such as medieval re-enactments, and open-air theatre (phone for details), and they do free guided tours (exc winter wkdys). Meals, snacks, shop, limited disabled access; cl 24-26 and 31 Dec, 1 Jan; (01522) 511068; £3.50.

Lincoln Cathedral Many people reckon that this is England's finest. The original building was largely destroyed in an 1185 earthquake, but the magnificent W front survived, and after nearly a century of rebuilding it was complete by 1280. The triple towers rise spectacularly above the nearby rooftops, and are beautifully lit at night. Inside, the carvings and stained glass are stupendous, and the architecture gracefully harmonious. Meals, snacks, shop, disabled access; (01522) 544544; £4. The impressive ruins of the once formidable medieval Bishop's Palace are close by, with a visitor centre containing displays, and two videos on its history; audio tour, snacks, shop; cl wkdys Nov-Mar (exc for a few days at the beginning of Dec for the Lincoln market festival); (01522) 527468; £3.20. There are also heritage gardens (their design was influenced by the cathedral), and even a small vineyard - supposedly one of the most northerly in Europe. The Adam & Eve, facing the gate to the cathedral close, has good value food, and the nearby Morning Star (Greetwellgate) also does enjoyable cheap lunches.

Museum of Lincolnshire Life 🆓 (Burton Rd) County life over the last couple of centuries, well illustrated in big former barracks, inc galleries on the Royal Lincolnshire Regiment, and a community gallery. Snacks, shop, disabled access; cl am Sun Nov-Apr, 24-26 and 31 Dec, 1 Jan; (01522) 528448; £2. A lawn in the courtyard makes a good picnic area.

Roman remains These include the high wall along Westgate, and the largely reconstructed Newport Arch N of the cathedral (it had survived intact until a 1964 disagreement with a lorry); the Fossdyke canal between Lincoln and the River Trent is also Roman - you can walk out into the country along it from the city (or go by boat), and the Pyewipe Inn out by the Saxilby road there makes a good destination.

The Lawn (Union Rd) In 1820 this was the county's first lunatic asylum; now its landscaped grounds include hands-on archaeology, an aquarium and exotic glasshouse, and a restaurant, coffee shop and bar. Disabled access; cl 25-26 Dec, 1 Jan; (01522) 873627; free.

Usher Gallery (Lindum Rd) Attractive gallery with fine watches, porcelain and miniatures, Tennyson memorabilia, Peter de Wint watercolours, and temporary exhibitions. Meals, snacks, shop, disabled access; cl Mon (exc bank hol), 24-26 Dec, 1 Jan; (01522) 527980; free.

LITTLE REEDNESS SE8022
Attractive village with 14th-c **church**, Ouse walks; RSPB **nature reserve** just E at Blacktoft Sands marshes.

LONG SUTTON TF4324
Butterfly & Wildlife Park 🖼 (Little London) Much more at this well organised place than simply the butterflies: they have everything from goats and pigs through llamas and wallabies to snakes and crocodiles. The walk-through tropical house is one of the country's biggest, with hundreds of butterflies flying free, and outside are lots of pretty wildflower walks to attract native species. The Reptile House is fun, as is the splendid collection of insects and creepy-crawlies. They have the only UK colony of breeding possums, and a birds of prey centre has twice-daily flying displays (usually noon and 3pm, weather permitting). Many of the farmyard animals can be stroked, inc the new water buffalo. There's also an adventure playground, a separate area for toddlers, and mini golf and tractor rides (extra charges). Snacks, shop, disabled access; open Easter-Oct; (01406) 363833; £5. This small town is pleasant to potter around, especially on market day (Fri).

LOUTH TF3186
Hubbard's Hill A walk SW; not in fact a hill, but a river valley - surprisingly deep for the Wolds.
Louth church Elegant 16th-c building

with the tallest spire of any parish church in Britain. The tower can be climbed on summer afternoons; hundreds of steps for a fabulous view. The market town is a pleasant stop, with lots of bustle on Weds, and some interesting shops; besides Chuzzlewits, the Masons Arms (Cornmarket) has enjoyable food.

Rushmoor Country Park 🖼 (NE, towards N Cockerington) Around 40 different kinds of poultry inc rare breeds in the grounds of an attractive farmhouse. Friendly, strokeable animals inc rabbits, chinchillas, ponies and lambs, and there are play and picnic areas (phone to book the barbecue), a herb garden and wildlife pond, and a new ornamental garden with a fish pond; regular special events. Snacks, shop, disabled access; usually cl wkdys Nov-Easter; (01507) 327184; *£2.25.

MABLETHORPE TF4987
Seal Sanctuary (North End) Rescued seals and seabirds unable to return to the wild find a permanent home here, along with lynx, wildcats and many other animals. It's right by the beach. Snacks, shop, disabled access; cl Oct-Mar; (01507) 473346; £4.

NAVENBY SK9957
Mrs Smith's Cottage 🖼 (East Rd) Built in the mid-19th c, this simple brick cottage has remained almost unchanged for the last 100 years; a ladder is the only way to get to the first-floor bedrooms, the range was used for cooking until the 1990s, and there's an outdoor privy and wash-house. Starting at the little visitor centre, volunteers show you around the house, and you can learn more about its unique owner, Hilda Smith, who lived here till she was 102, and first married at the age of 64. Shop, disabled access to ground floor only; open pm Sun and bank hol Mon mid-Mar to Nov, plus pm Fri-Sun Jun-July and Sept, plus pm Weds and Thurs in school hols; pre-booking is recommended as only five people allowed in at a time; (01529) 414294; £1. The Bell over at Coleby is a friendly dining pub.

NORMANBY SE8816
Normanby Hall Country Park 🖼 (B1430) Pleasant spot with grazing deer, lots of wildfowl, nature trails,

some interesting sculptures, colourfully and imaginatively restored entirely organic Victorian kitchen garden, other Victorian-style plantings, and a farm museum in its 350 busy acres. There are period rooms in the Regency mansion. Meals, snacks, shop, disabled access to ground floor only; house and museum open pm Apr-Sept, park open all year; (01724) 720588; £4. The Sheffield Arms at Burton upon Stather has decent food.

NORTH HYKEHAM SK9368
Road Transport Museum (Whisby Rd, off A46 bypass) Over 45 well restored vintage cars, buses and commercial vehicles; free classic bus rides on special open days. Disabled access; open all day Sun and wkdy pms May-Oct, and Sun pm Nov-Apr, best to phone; (01522) 500566; free (donations welcomed). The nearby Pride of Lincoln is a useful family food pub.

RAND TF1078
Rand Farm Park They encourage you to get close to the animals at this working farm, best for younger children who may even be able to help with feeding. Mostly under cover, so useful in wet weather, with a good heated play area; also go-karts, tractor rides and an outdoor adventure play area. Snacks, shop, disabled access; cl 25-26 Dec and 1 Jan; (01673) 858904; £4.50. In Wragby the Turnor Arms has good value food.

SIBSEY TF3551
Trader Mill 🏛 (A16 N of Boston) A splendidly restored six-sailed tower windmill with fine views from the top. Tearooms, shop, some disabled access; Open Tues, wknds and bank hol Mon Apr-Oct; (01205) 750036; *£2. EH. The village's second windmill is now a private house.

SKEGNESS TF5663
Archetypal 19th-c holiday resort, with the first Butlin's Holiday Camp just up the coast; the beach has clean bathing water (and there's also an outdoor swimming pool, at the Embassy Centre which has indoor attractions too). It's a very popular holiday spot, so traffic can be very slow in summer. The comfortable old Vine Hotel on the southern edge of the town was here long before the resort, welcoming

Tennyson among others; it's pleasant for lunch.
Church Farm Museum 🏛 (Church Rd S) Cluster of restored farmyard buildings and cottage provide a good re-creation of daily farm life at the end of the 19th c, also craft demonstrations and special events. Snacks, shop, limited disabled access; cl Nov-Mar; (01754) 766658; £1.
Gibraltar Point Nature Reserve (Gibraltar Rd) 1,000 acres of sandy and muddy seashore stretching 3m S to the mouth of The Wash. The impressive complex of sand dunes and saltmarsh is good for bird-watching (skylarks are more common here than anywhere else in the country), and home to a wide variety of wildlife; guided walks and events. Summer and bank hol snacks, shop, disabled access to visitor centre and some hides; reserve open all year, visitor centre cl wkdys Nov-May; (01754) 762677; parking from 50p to £2 depending on season.
Natureland Seal Sanctuary *See separate family panel on p.383.*

SNIPE DALES TF3368
Country park and nature reserve, managed by the county council, covering 210 acres rich in bird and plant life; the country park is a 90-acre area of pine woods, while the adjacent nature reserve has a trail leading through two valleys and to a viewpoint over the Wolds. The George & Dragon in Hagworthingham now has good value food.

SOUTH KYME TF1650
A fine 14th-c battlemented tower stands alone in a meadow quite nr the road.

SPALDING TF2422
The centre of England's bulb-growing industry, with a spectacular flower parade on the May bank hol wknd, the town is currently trying to build a reputation for good food, for example with the new farmers' market (first Sat of month). A remarkable fenland drive runs S from Spalding: turn left off B1172 in Little London, keeping alongside the Welland New River. Lagoons and reclaimed land on the right have water birds, with more on the river - perhaps even a seal, and on the pastures great percheron horses. At the B1116 a short

diversion left takes you to Crowland (see p.394). Back towards Deeping the road has more river views.

Springfields Gardens Home of the UK flower bulb industry since 1966, they've now extensively remodelled the gardens (features include gardens designed by celebrity gardeners, woodland walks and a carp lake), and there's a new factory outlet shopping village with around 40 shops (inc a garden centre); indoor and outdoor play areas, and regular special events. Meals, snacks, disabled access; due to open around Easter; (01775) 724843; free.

STAMFORD TF0307
Many would support John Betjeman's verdict that this is England's most attractive town. Within the medieval walls are no less than 500 listed buildings, inc a good number of attractive medieval **churches** - particularly All Saints in the centre, St George's with excellent 15th-c stained glass, and St Mary's nearby. There are riverside strolls and quite a few craft and antiques shops. The George, one of the town's grandest buildings with some parts going back to Saxon times, is excellent for lunch (and has food all day); the Crown (All Saints Pl) does traditional english country dishes.

Burghley House 🖼 A 20-min walk from Stamford's centre leads to this splendid mansion, built by William Cecil and still the home of his family. The exterior is Tudor at its most solidly showy, but the state rooms inside are largely baroque, with wonderful frescoes by Antonio Verrio - the Heaven Room is astonishing. The peaceful grounds, where the Burghley Horse Trials are held, were landscaped by Capability Brown; there's a sculpture garden, and the deer park is pleasant for strolling. Meals, snacks, shop, disabled access; cl end Oct-Mar; (01780) 752451; £7.50.

Stamford Museum (Broad St) Local history inc Stamfordware pottery and life-size figures dressed in replica clothes of Tom Thumb (only one metre - 3 ft 4 in - tall) and Daniel Lambert, a portly visitor to the town who weighed 218 kg (50 stone) when he died on a racing outing here; also a six-metre

(20-ft) tapestry depicting the town's history. Shop, disabled access to ground floor only; cl Sun am Apr-Sept, all day Sun Oct-Mar, 24-26, 31 Dec and 1 Jan; (01780) 766317; free.

Tolethorpe Hall (off A6121 N) Home to the Stamford Shakespeare company, this has Europe's finest **open-air theatre** in its grounds, with a covered auditorium and a good Shakespeare season of three plays Jun-Aug. Meals, snacks, shop, disabled access; cl Sun, and Sept-May; box office (01780) 756133; £10-£16. The Blue Bell nearby at Belmesthorpe has good food.

STOW SK8881
Stow church Notable for its fantastic Saxon arches, with plenty more of interest in this imposing building inc Viking ship graffiti; the attractive village has a decent food pub, the Cross Keys.

SURFLEET TF2528
Leaning spire The tower and spire of **Surfleet church** lean alarmingly. The riverside Mermaid has good food.

TATTERSHALL TF2056
Tattershall Castle 15th-c red brick castle with magnificent 30-metre (100-ft) turreted keep, with fine heraldic chimneypieces and stained-glass windows on each of the four storeys; there's a double moat, waterfowl and peacocks, and children can try on medieval costumes. Snacks, shop, disabled access to ground floor; open Sat-Weds Apr-Oct (exc Good Fri), wknds Mar, Nov-Dec; *£3.50; NT. Also built by same man, the airy 15th-c **church** is attractive, and just off the market place, you can see the ruins of **Tattershall College**, school for the church choristers. Just off the A153 towards Sleaford, on the left before you reach Tattershall Bridge, is a preserved steam engine which worked at keeping this area of fens drained for nearly a century. The Abbey Lodge Hotel (B1192 towards Woodhall) has good food.

TEALBY TF1590
The best example of that Lincolnshire speciality - colourful **village cottage gardens**, easily seen from the road. Here, a great variety of neat and charmingly planted gardens front the stone-built cottages, some thatched, on the main street running down from the

12th-c **church** to a watersplash nr a watermill, and there is more colour in the quaintly named side lanes. The 14th-c Kings Head has popular food.

THORNTON CURTIS TA1118
Thornton Abbey (E Halton rd) Ruins of 12th-c Augustinian abbey, very atmospheric with its worn spiral stone stairs and dark corridors, well worth a visit. Also small exhibition in magnificent 14th-c gatehouse. Disabled access (not into gatehouse); grounds open daily, gatehouse open only pm third Sun in month, plus pm first Sun Apr-Sept; (01904) 601901; free; EH.

VIKING WAY TF3072
Long-distance path helping village-to-village walks, with 'Tennyson country' a popular focus (Tennyson was born at the rectory in Somersby, when his father was rector at Bag Enderby); the Black Horse at Donington on Bain TF2382, Bell at Coleby SK9760 and the Kings Head at Tealby are handy stops.

WAINFLEET TF4958
Batemans Brewery Displays, models and an audio-guide take you through the brewing process, and there's a collection of thousands of beer bottles from all around the world. You can also go on a guided tour of this classic family-run traditional brewery (3pm daily, no disabled access). A games room has traditional pub games such as quoits, ring the bull and skittles, while outdoors you can have a go at croquet, giant draughts, and Connect Four. Meals, snacks, shop, disabled access to visitor centre; cl 25 Dec and 1 Jan; (01754) 882009; £2 visitor centre and games room (£4.95 with brewery tour, £8.95 in the evening).

WALTHAM TA2503
Waltham windmill This late 19th-c six-sail tower mill with its traditional Lincolnshire ogree (onion-shaped cap) has displays on the different types of mills, and occasional milling demonstrations. Also here, in a Nissen hut, is a museum with exhibits mostly from the 1930s/40s, and various special events such as RAF displays and classic car rallies (usually open pm wknds). Meals, snacks, shops (inc herb and old-fashioned sweet shops), some disabled access; open wknds (and usually Tues-Sun high season) Easter-Oct; (01472)

752122; £1.50. The Ship at nearby Barnoldby le Beck has good food in very interesting surroundings.

WESTON TF2924
Baytree Owl Centre (A151) Good value expanding collection of around 70 owls and other birds of prey such as the snake-killing secretary bird, with displays in a big arena (1.30 pm Mar-Oct, depending on weather and breeding season); some birds can be handled, and everything's well labelled. Good meals and snacks, shop, disabled access (and parking); cl 25-26 Dec, and Easter Sun; (01406) 372840; £2. It's part of a busy little complex, with ducks and rabbits in a landscaped glasshouse, meerkats, good garden centre, and play area.

WOODHALL SPA TF1963
Surrounded by woods, with a few interesting shops, and a little local history museum on Iddesleigh Rd (usually open daily; disabled access; £1).

WOOLSTHORPE SK9224
Woolsthorpe Manor 🏚 (the Woolsthorpe nr Colsterworth) Birthplace of Isaac Newton, who conducted some of his more important experiments here: geometry workings said to be in his handwriting are scratched into the plasterwork - and of course the garden has a venerable apple tree. An interactive discovery centre exhibits his work. Snacks, shop, disabled access to ground floor; open pm only, Weds-Sun and bank hol Mon Apr-Sept, Good Fri, and wknds Mar and Oct; (01476) 860338; *£4; NT.

WRAWBY TA0208
Wrawby post mill 🏚 Working windmill with snacks and a shop; open bank hols and some Sun Apr-Aug - phone Mrs Day to check; (01652) 653699; £1.

Other attractive villages, all with decent pubs, include Allington SK8540 (despite the nearby A1), Barkston SK9341, Barnoldby le Beck TA2303, Billingborough TF1134, Brant Broughton SK9154, Carlton-le-Moorland SK9058, Castle Bytham SK9819, Coleby SK9760, Deeping St James TF1609, Denton SK8632, Fulbeck SK9450, Halton Holegate TF4165, Kirkby la Thorpe TF0945, Nettleham SK9975, Newton TF0436,

Skillington SK8925, Witham on the Hill TF0516 and Woolsthorpe SK8435 (the one nr Belvoir). The woods at Stapleford SK8857 are pleasant for picnics (especially when the rhododendrons are in bloom). Langton by Partney TF3970 has an attractive church, and stone-built streamside Easton SK9226 is also pretty.

Where to eat

ASWARBY TF0639 **Tally Ho** *(01529) 455205* Handsome 17th-c stone inn with beams and open fire in country-style bar, a gently civilised atmosphere, and newspapers to read; good enjoyable food inc fine puddings, well kept real ales, decent house wines, and an attractive pine-panelled restaurant (best to book); bdrms; cl 26 Dec; disabled access. £20|£7

BARNOLDBY LE BECK TA2303 **Ship** *Main Rd (01472) 822308* Carefully run home with charming Edwardian and Victorian bric-a-brac - stand-up telephones, violins, a horn gramophone, bowler and top hats, old rackets, crops and hockey sticks, stuffed birds and animals, and grandmotherly plants in ornate china bowls; a truly tempting choice of very reasonably priced fresh fish from Grimsby, plus meaty dishes and lovely puddings, too; well kept ales, an extensive wine list with plenty by the glass, tables outside; children in restaurant only; disabled access. £20|£6.95

GEDNEY DYKE TF4126 **Chequers** *Main St (01406) 362666* Stylishly unassuming but friendly and spotlessly kept fenland pub with beautifully presented food (super fresh fish and seafood), an open fire, and elegant no smoking dining conservatory; well kept beer, decent wines, and helpful service; cl winter Mon. £27.70|£7.95

GRIMSTHORPE TF0423 **Black Horse** *(01778) 591247* 18th-c coaching inn with log fires, beams, exposed stone and plenty of brass, excellent, beautifully presented food, an intimate candlelit dining room, real ales, an impressive wine list with helpful notes, and friendly staff; pretty bdrms; cl Sun pm, Mon am. £23.45|£8.50

HORNCASTLE TF2669 **Magpies** *73-75 East St (01507) 527004* Popular well run restaurant with a relaxed atmosphere and good, enjoyable food using top-quality fresh local ingredients; cl Sun, Mon, Christmas and New Year; disabled access. £30|£6.95

LINCOLN SK9771 **Browns Pie Shop** *33 Steep Hill (01522) 527330* Bustling, popular place serving generous helpings of good, interesting pies (and lots of other good food), helpful staff, comfortable seats and pleasant traditional atmosphere; cl 1 Jan. £23|£5

LINCOLN SK9771 **Wig & Mitre** *30/32 Steep Hill (01522) 535190* Ancient, attractive pub with plenty of period features; simpler beamed downstairs bar with exposed stone walls and Gothic furniture on oak floor boards, with sofas in a back area, and a civilised upstairs dining room, light and airy, with views of the castle walls and cathedral; shelves of old books, an open fire, antique prints and more modern caricatures of lawyers and clerics, plenty of newspapers and periodicals; enjoyable food served all day, starting with full breakfast menu; well kept real ales, and an excellent choice of wines. £28|£8.50

LOUTH TF3287 **Chuzzlewits** *26 Upgate (01507) 611171* Family-run no smoking tearoom with a civilised atmosphere, little glass chandeliers, dining chairs around pretty print glass-covered table-clothed tables, potted palms, and big shop-front windows; wide choice of speciality teas and coffees, home-made cakes, pastries and biscuits, a good range of interesting snacks and light meals, and young waitresses in long black dresses with white frilly aprons and little lacy white caps; cl Sun, Mon and Tues; disabled access. £15|£4.50

Special thanks to Michael and Jenny Back, Mrs M E Moody

NORFOLK

Birds and seals on the endless sands of the unspoilt north coast,
lots of interesting outings, historic towns and villages, Broads boating,
a nice range of family beach resorts; smashing places to stay,
and good food too

A treasure-trove of family attractions is topped by Lenwade's Dinosaur Adventure Park (tremendous fun for younger children), this year's Family Attraction for Norfolk. Other excellent days out include the Norfolk Wildlife Centre in Great Witchingham (lots of european wildlife and a birds of prey centre), prettily set Banham Zoo, Pettitts Animal Adventure Park in Reedham (plenty of things to do here), and busy Country World in Fritton. Thrigby Hall Wildlife Gardens near Filby is another good choice, there's a working farm in Snettisham, and we really liked the seal-spotting trip from Blakeney. The Village at Burgh St Margaret offers pleasantly old-fashioned entertainment.

Sandringham is a must for royalists. There are magnificent 17th-c houses at Blickling and Felbrigg, and the Palladian mansions at Holkham and Houghton are just as impressive. If you want a contrast, you'll find interesting ruins at Castle Rising, Castle Acre and Baconsthorpe.

Gardeners enjoy the Fairhaven Garden Trust (listed under the Broads), Mannington Gardens in Saxthorpe (lovely summer roses), and Peter Beales's rather special rose collection near Attleborough. In Heacham you can go round the UK's largest lavender-growing and distilling operation. At Bressingham you'll find steam engines as well as glorious gardens. Also of interest to steam enthusiasts are the engines at Aylsham, Sheringham, Wells-next-the-Sea and Forncett St Mary; there's an unusual collection of organs (as well as steam engines) at Thursford Green.

The best of many bird sanctuaries and reserves here is the Wildfowl & Wetlands Trust in Welney. For something a bit different you can explore Grimes Graves, where neolithic people mined their flint, and Glandford has an unusual shell museum.

Hunstanton (with a good aquarium) and popular Cromer are civilised seaside resorts, and there are many attractive smaller places. Further down, the coast is dotted with beach resorts, some relaxed and individual, and some large and full of life - most obviously Great Yarmouth (quite a bit for families, even in wet weather). Inland, bustling Norwich (with a range of attractions from a science centre to a puppet theatre) is a good destination for families, and King's Lynn is pleasant for a day trip.

North Norfolk has a charmingly traditional feel, with a real sense of place from its dutch-gabled buildings, flint walls, broad sweeps of sea, saltings and sky, and the odd windmill. A path runs the length of the coast, with often hundreds of sizeable and colourful birds in sight at a time. In summer the twisty coastal A149 is a bumper-to-bumper crawl, but it's a pleasant drive out of season, with a real get-away-from-it-all feel. Inland too, this part then has the same sort of untouristy appeal (though the weather is often kinder on the coast).

Much of the inland countryside is flat and repetitive - better for cyclists than walkers, with quiet lanes, attractive villages and country churches, and fair views. We've found some good bits of the Norfolk Broads for land-lubbers, but these winding rivers and reed-fringed meres are of course best seen from a boat - and for many people that's what Norfolk's all about.

Where to stay

BLAKENEY TG0243 **Blakeney Hotel** *Blakeney, Holt, Norfolk NR25 7NE (01263) 740797* **£154**, plus special breaks; 59 very comfortable rms, many with views over the salt marshes and some with own little terrace. Overlooking the harbour with fine views, this friendly hotel has comfortable and appealing public rooms, good food, very pleasant staff, indoor swimming pool, saunas, spa bath, billiard room, and safe garden; very well organised for families, with plenty to do for them nearby; good disabled access; dogs welcome in bedrooms ☺

BURNHAM MARKET TF8342 **Hoste Arms** *Market Pl, Burnham Market, King's Lynn, Norfolk PE31 8HD (01328) 738777* **£102***, plus special breaks; 36 comfortable rms. Handsome inn on green of lovely Georgian village, with a smartly civilised atmosphere, attractive bars (the main bar has been renovated this year), some interesting period features, big log fires, conservatory lounge, stylish food (plus morning coffee and afternoon tea), well kept real ales and good wines, and professional friendly staff; big new awning covering a sizeable eating area in the garden; partial disabled access; dogs welcome

GRIMSTON TF7022 **Congham Hall** *Lynn Rd, Grimston, King's Lynn, Norfolk PE32 1AH (01485) 600250* **£185**, plus special breaks; 14 individually decorated rms. Warmly welcoming and handsome Georgian manor in 30 acres inc herb, vegetable and flower gardens (herbs for sale and garden open to public), outdoor swimming pool, tennis court, paddock and orchards - also, walks leaflets; lovely drawing room, a pretty orangery formal restaurant with excellent modern cooking (lighter lunches in bar), and exemplary service; children over 7 in restaurant

HOLKHAM TF8943 **Victoria** *Park Road, Holkham, Wells-next-the-Sea, Norfolk NR23 1RG* **£140**; 11 rms decorated in colonial style or with a more Victorian theme. Transformed into a stylish hotel, beautifully and individually decorated throughout, with an engagingly cosmopolitan bar with eclectic mix of furnishings and décor - sprawling sofas, chunky candles, flowers and fruit, colourful wall-hangings, nice fireplace; dining room with plenty of contemporary art and piped jazz; enjoyable food with emphasis on game or seafood, good range of wines with plenty by the glass, well kept real ales; friendly hard-working young staff; tables on the terrace and lawn, and a play area; disabled access

MELTON CONSTABLE TG0433 **Burgh Parva Hall** *Holt Rd, Melton Constable, Norfolk NR24 2PU (01263) 862569* **£50***; 2 rms. Lovely, partly 16th-c longhouse with lovely country views, friendly, helpful owners, a relaxed atmosphere in the big rooms, rugs, pictures and nice old furniture, home-grown produce for evening meals (if arranged in advance), and marvellous breakfasts using their own eggs; dogs welcome

MORSTON TG0043 **Morston Hall** *The Street, Morston, Holt, Norfolk NR25 7AA (01263) 741041* **£220** inc dinner, plus special breaks; 7 comfortable rms with country views. Attractive 17th-c flint-walled house in tidal village, with lovely quiet gardens, two small lounges, one with an antique fireplace, a conservatory, and hard-working friendly young owners; particularly fine modern english cooking (they also run cookery demonstrations and hold wine and food events), a thoughtful small wine list, and super breakfasts; croquet; cl Jan; partial disabled access; dogs welcome in bedrooms ☺

MUNDFORD TL8093 **Crown** *Crown St, Mundford, Thetford, Norfolk IP26 5HQ (01842) 878233* **£59**; 30 good rms (they've created quite a few new ones this year). Friendly small village pub, originally a hunting inn and rebuilt in the 18th c, with an attractive choice of reasonably priced straightforward food, very welcoming staff, a happy atmosphere, and well kept real ales; disabled access; dogs welcome

NORWICH TG2208 **Beeches** *4-6 Earlham Rd, Norwich, Norfolk NR2 3DB (01603) 621167* **£87**, plus special breaks; 36 quiet rms. Three separate listed Victorian mansions and an extension only 10-min stroll from city centre but with access to three acres of English Heritage Victorian gardens; relaxed informal atmosphere, friendly staff, enjoyable food in semi-formal restaurant, and good breakfasts; children over 12; disabled access

NORWICH TG2308 **By Appointment** *25-29 St Georges St, Norwich, Norfolk NR3 1AB (01603) 630730* **£95***; 4 exotically decorated comfortable rms. 15th-c merchant's house, very much a restaurant-with-rooms (you enter through the kitchen), in fine central location; there's a warren of rooms crammed with Victoriana and theatrical furnishings, beautiful dining rooms, delicious meals, excellent breakfasts, and particularly helpful, charming owners; cl 1st 2 wks Aug; children over 12

PULHAM MARKET TM1986 **Old Bakery** *Church Walk, Pulham Market, Diss, Norfolk IP21 4SL (01379) 676492* **£60**; 3 large rms. No smoking 16th-c house with lots of beams and timbers, an inglenook with a fine log fire in lounge, good breakfasts, enjoyable evening meal using local produce, and friendly atmosphere; cl Christmas and New Year; no children

SOUTH LOPHAM TM0381 **Malting Farm** *Blo' Norton Rd, South Lopham, Diss, Norfolk IP22 2HT (01379) 687201* **£50**; 3 well furnished rms, 1 with own bthrm. Welcoming no smoking Elizabethan farmhouse on working dairy farm, with inglenook woodburners in sitting and dining rooms, big breakfasts with home-baked bread and preserves around a large table, and a small play area with toys; the owner's passion is embroidery, patchwork, spinning and quilting and she holds winter classes; cl Christmas and New Year

STOKE HOLY CROSS TG2302 **Salamanca Farm** *Norwich Rd, Stoke Holy Cross, Norwich, Norfolk NR14 8QJ (01508) 492322* **£52**; 4 rms. Mainly Victorian farmhouse (parts are much older) just a short stroll from the River Tas, with guest lounge, spacious dining room, a flower arranger's garden, and farm shop; no smoking; cl 15 Dec-15 Jan; children over 6

SWAFFHAM TF8109 **Strattons** *Ash Close, Swaffham, Norfolk PE37 7NH (01760) 723845* **£100***, plus special breaks; 8 interesting, pretty rms, some recently restored. No smoking and environment-friendly Palladian-style villa run by charming warmly friendly owners with comfortable individually decorated drawing rooms, family photographs, paintings, lots of china cats (and several live ones), antiques, patchwork throws, fresh and dried flowers, and open fires; delicious highly imaginative food using local (and home-grown) organic produce, a carefully chosen wine list illustrated with Mrs Scott's own watercolours, and super breakfasts; big cupboard full of toys and games for children; garden with croquet; cl 24-26 Dec; dogs welcome but must be supervised ☺

THORNHAM TF7343 **Lifeboat** *Ship Lane, Thornham, Hunstanton, Norfolk PE36 6LT (01485) 512236* **£74**, plus special breaks; 14 pretty rms, most with sea view. Rambling old white-painted stone pub, well placed by coastal flats, with lots of character in the main bar - open fires, antique oil lamps, low settles and pews around carved oak tables, big oak beams hung with traps and yokes, and masses of guns, swords and antique farm tools; several rooms lead off; enjoyable popular food in bar and elegant restaurant and well kept real ales; sunny conservatory with steps up to terrace with seats and playground; marvellous surrounding walks; children welcomed rather than tolerated; partial disabled access; dogs welcome away from eating areas ☺

THORPE MARKET TG2434 **Elderton Lodge** *Cromer Rd, Thorpe Market, Norwich, Norfolk NR11 8TZ (01263) 833547* **£95**, plus special breaks; 11 rms. 18th-c shooting lodge for adjacent Gunton Hall, with lots of original features, fine panelling, a relaxing lounge bar with log fire, an airy conservatory where breakfast and lunch are served, and Langtry Restaurant with good food using fresh fish and game; six acres of mature grounds overlooking herds of deer; children over 6 or under a year; partial disabled access; dogs in bedrooms and lounge

TITCHWELL TF7543 **Titchwell Manor Hotel** *Main Rd, Titchwell, King's Lynn, Norfolk PE31 8BB (01485) 210221* **£70**, plus special breaks; 15 light, pretty rms. Comfortable hotel, handy for nearby RSPB reserve, and decorated in pretty soft lemon and beige colours; roaring log fire, magazines and good naturalists' records of the wildlife, a cheerful bar, attractive no smoking brasserie restaurant (lots of seafood) with french windows on to lovely sheltered walled garden, and particularly helpful licensees and staff; lots of walks and footpaths nearby; high tea for younger children; disabled access; dogs welcome in bedrooms

WARHAM TF9441 **Three Horseshoes** *The Street, Warham, Wells-next-the-Sea, Norfolk NR23 1NL (01328) 710547* **£52***; 5 rms, one with own bthrm. Basic but cheerful local with marvellously unspoilt traditional atmosphere in its three friendly gaslit rooms, simple furnishings, a log fire, very tasty generous bar food, decent wines, home-made lemonade, and very well kept real ales; bdrms are in the Old Post Office adjoining the pub, with lots of beams and a residents' lounge dominated by an inglenook fireplace; cl 25-26 Dec; no children; dogs welcome

WELLINGHAM TF8722 **Manor House Farm** *Wellingham, King's Lynn, Norfolk PE32 2TH (01328) 838227* **£70**; 3 rms. Attractively converted self-contained annexe in old stables attached to a lovely farmhouse, with log fire in big sitting room and small kitchen area; good breakfasts served in the main house using home-produced or local ingredients, and charming helpful owners; immaculate gardens with a well stocked carp pond; places to eat nearby; children over 10 by arrangement; stabling for horses available; disabled access

WINTERTON-ON-SEA TG4919 **Fishermans Return** *The Lane, Winterton-on-Sea, Great Yarmouth, Norfolk NR29 4BN (01493) 393305* **£70**; 3 rms reached by a tiny staircase. Traditional 300-year-old pub in quiet village, close to the beach, with warmly welcoming and helpful owners, a relaxed lounge bar with well kept real ales, open fire, good home-made food inc fresh fish (fine crabs in season), enjoyable breakfasts, and sheltered garden with children's play equipment; dogs welcome

To see and do

Norfolk Family Attraction of the Year

LENWADE TG1017 **Dinosaur Adventure Park** (Weston Park, off A1067) We've highlighted this enjoyably silly place before, and while it's true to say that there are cheaper, more instructive places to visit in the area, for sheer unadulterated fun, this is hard to beat. It probably won't have the same appeal for children over 9 or 10, but will delight small children who like dinosaurs (which of course is pretty much all of them) more than you'd expect or understand. Put together with some style, it has acres of woodland and space to run around, with life-size (and often furiously vocal) dinosaurs lying in wait at every turn. As you explore the Dinosaur Trail and walk beneath the legs of the brachiosaurus, you really appreciate just how big some of these ferocious beasts were. There are several cleverly themed play areas, with the most ingenious the Climb-a-Saurus, a 23-metre (75ft) brontosaurus replica with slides, ladders and so on tucked away inside; under-5s have a separate play area. Other features include a woodland maze, suitably themed crazy golf, and plenty of real-life, somewhat tamer farmyard animals and pets; you can get close to many of these, with regular feeding times and demonstrations. There's an extra charge for their deer safari. Staff are very friendly, and there are nice touches throughout: look out for the towering tyrannosaurus made out of bicycle frames. The picnic area has barbecues for hire. Meals, snacks, shop, disabled access; open Easter-Oct (they may close some wkdys either end of the season); (01603) 876310; £6.75 adults, £5.75 children over 3. You'll usually be given discount vouchers for a return trip.

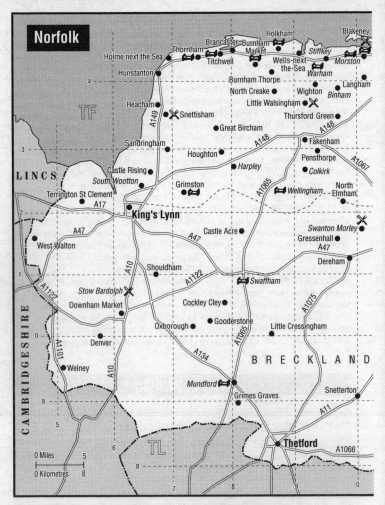

Norfolk

Blakeney
Holkham
Brancaster Burnham
Thornham Market
Holme next the Sea Stiffkey
Titchwell Wells-next Morston
Hunstanton the-Sea Warham
Burnham Thorpe Langham
North Creake Wighton Binham
Heacham Little Walsingham
Snettisham Thursford Green
Great Bircham A148 Fakenham
Sandringham Houghton Penshorpe
A1067
LINCS Harpley Colkirk
Castle Rising North
South Wootton Grimston A1065 Wellingham Elmham
Terrington St Clement
A17
King's Lynn Swanton Morley
A47 Castle Acre Gressenhall
West Walton A47
Shouldham Dereham
A1122
Stow Bardolph Swaffham A1075
Downham Market Cockley Cley
Oxborough Gooderstone Little Cressingham
Denver
BRECKLAND
Welney A10
A134
Mundford Snetterton
Grimes Graves
A11
TL Thetford A1066

0 Miles 5
0 Kilometres 8

ACLE TG3910
Acle windmill A fine example; the
Kings Head has good generous home
cooking.
ATTLEBOROUGH TM0292
Peter Beales Rose Nursery
Specialist in roses, inc old-fashioned
classics and others you won't find for
sale elsewhere - the owner is President
of the Royal National Rose Society; you
can wander around the 2½ acres of
gardens, and staff are on hand to answer
questions; snacks, disabled access;
cl over Christmas and New Year,
phone for details; (01953) 454707;
free.

AYLSHAM TG1926
Bure Valley Railway Friendly steam
train trips along nine miles of narrow-
gauge track between here and
Wroxham; you can combine the
journey with a 1½-hour Broads cruise.
Meals, snacks, shop, disabled access; cl
Nov-Mar, best to ring for timetable;
(01263) 733858; £8.50 return, £13.50
inc Broads cruise.
BACONSTHORPE TG1336
Baconsthorpe Castle The
gatehouses, curtain walls and towers
are all that's left of this moated and
semi-fortified 15th-c house, but displays
show what it looked like in its glory. A

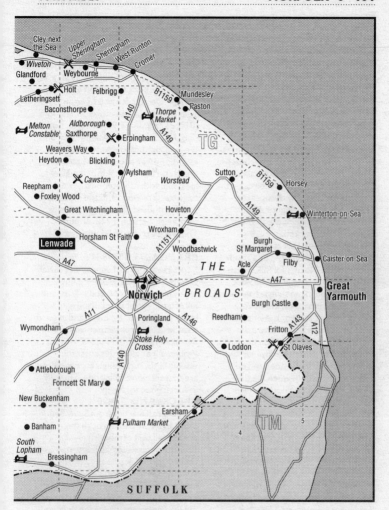

very pretty peaceful spot, with swans on the lake adding to its charm; free; EH. Light lunches and teas are served in Margaret's Tearooms (usually cl Mon-Tues, wkdys Nov and Dec-Mother's day), and the reopened Hare & Hounds over towards Hempstead has enjoyable food.

BANHAM TM0587

Banham Zoo (B1113) This well established and splendidly organised zoo is beautifully laid out, with hundreds of animals spread over 35 acres of parkland. There's everything from kangaroos to colobus monkeys, with particularly good enclosures for

their siberian tigers and ring-tailed lemurs, and an underwater viewing window into Penguin World. Talks and feeding sessions throughout the day, taking in fur seals, meerkats, tigers, and, in summer, bird of prey displays (their vulture Foster made the news in summer 2003 when he escaped; a mother and child found him on a Cornish beach and fed him hula-hoops until help arrived). Children can wander among the guinea-pigs, miniature donkeys, goats and sheep in the Farm Barn, and there's an adventure play area. Meals, snacks, shops, disabled access; cl 25 Dec and 1 Jan; (01953)

887771; £8.95, less out of season. It's run by the same people as Suffolk Wildlife Park at Kessingland (see Suffolk chapter). Across the road is a craft shop in a converted barn, as well as a working cider mill; there's an adjacent campsite.

BLAKENEY TG0443
Crabbing is fun from here, and surprisingly successful. Also a (free) collection of waterfowl down by the harbour, long breezy walks, unspoilt flint cottages, broad sky and sea vistas, perhaps even a seal pup on the beach in spring. There's a good dyke walk to Cley next the Sea, with the birds on the mudflats for company. Besides the Blakeney Hotel, the Manor, White Horse and Kings Arms are all good. In summer it gets packed.

Blakeney Point This NT-owned **nature reserve** is edged by a good stretch of the North Norfolk Coast Path, which gets better as you walk along it, although the shingle bank needs patience and is hard on the ankles; pleasant dunes await at the far end.

Seal boat trips Boats leave from Morston Quay slightly W on the A149 coast rd once or twice a day Mar-Oct (times depend on the tide), and on some winter wknds, when the tide allows. Most last two hours, which takes in an hour or so exploring the NT-owned bird reserve at **Blakeney Point**. The highlight comes just before that, when the boat goes past the sandbanks at the end of the Point, where dozens of grey and common seals lie basking happily in the sun. Several different operators run boats, with the smaller ones owned by the Beans, our favourites. Cl Dec-Jan, booking a few days in advance is recommended (esp in summer, when crowds of visitors wait on the quay; in winter they usually run only at wknds or in good weather), on (01263) 740038; £6. Local information centres have full details of operators and times.

BLICKLING TG1728
Blickling Hall (B1354) Magnificent house dating mainly from early 17th c, though the hedges that flank it may be older. Dramatic carved oak staircase and splendid paintings (inc a famous Canaletto), but best of all is the 38-metre (125-ft) Long Gallery with its

ornate Jacobean plaster ceiling, and the chinese bedroom, still lined with 18th-c hand-painted wallpaper. The gardens and grounds are lovely, with several miles of footpaths. Meals, snacks, shop, plant centre, good disabled access (a lift in the house); house open Weds-Sun pm Apr-Oct, garden also open am, Tues-Sun in Aug and winter Thurs-Sun; (01263) 738030; £6.90, £3.90 garden only; NT. There's a pleasant walk from the Buckinghamshire Arms (useful for lunch), and free public access to the **parkland** on the W side of the pike-filled lake with its water birds, with large tracts of woodland and pasture, as well as a disused railway line, perhaps even kingfishers on the River Bure. There are circular walks within the park.

BRANCASTER TF7944
Scolt Head Miles of dunes, flat coastal saltings, broad tidal beaches: a fine lonely place, largely National Trust and full of birds - Scolt Head island is an important breeding ground, and in good weather a ferry runs Easter-Sept from Burnham Overy; (07776) 302413; £2. Incidentally all along this coast the wading birds, surprisingly approachable, are best seen on a falling tide. The Jolly Sailors is good for lunch.

BRECKLAND TL9496
Pingo Trail Starting from Stow Bedon, this is an 8-mile path through the unforested part of the adjacent Breckland grasslands, largely army training ground. It passes through several Sites of Special Scientific Interest (inc Cranberry Rough, an alder swampland), taking you along a disused railway line before joining the Peddars Way at Hockham Heath. The picturesque 15th-c thatched Chequers at Thompson has good food.

Thetford Forest Park (off A1075 NE of Thetford) The largest lowland forest in England, with plenty of wild flowers, nature trails, a bat hibernaculum and hides for watching birds and four types of deer. Though there are picnic sites and car parks across the forest, a good starting point is **High Lodge** - you can pick up maps and hire cycles, there's an adventure playground (and a giant play sculpture trail), and an unusual maze formed by young pine trees. Meals, snacks, shop, mostly disabled access; visitor centre cl 25 Dec; (01842) 815434; car park from around £3.50. Great for the adventurous, **Go Ape** nearby is an unusual tree-top assault course - it takes around 2½ hours to complete with rope swings and bridges, zip slides and so forth; open in summer, phone to book (07736) 774 818; £14.50 (no under-10s, and you need to be at least 4ft 7ins or 1.4 metres). Elsewhere at Breckland they are currently re-creating 300-hectares of heathland; to show how the region of poor flat sandy heathland looked originally, with scattered shallow meres and scrubby mixed woodland; there are forest walks, for example from car parks on the A134 NW of Thetford, where you may disturb roe deer. The Crown at Mundford is the best nearby lunch place.

BRESSINGHAM TM0880
Bressingham Steam Museum & Gardens (A1066) The founder, Alan Bloom, has effectively combined his two interests at this rewarding site. The six acres of informal gardens are planted with 5,000 species and cultivars of alpines and perennials in island beds, with lots of the dwarf conifers Bloom has done so much to popularise. Then there's the excellent steam collection, inc 50 road and rail engines, some restored to working order, and a charming fairground carousel. Three steam-hauled trains run through the countryside and parts of the garden (all may not be in steam out of high season). An exhibition is dedicated to that enduring TV favourite, *Dad's Army*. Meals, snacks, shop, disabled access; cl Nov-Easter, phone for train times; (01379) 687386; £7 (£11.50 on full steam days). The Old Garden House is handy for lunch.

BROADS TG3017
Norfolk's network of linking waterways (formed in the Middle Ages when peat was dug for fuel) is not easy to visit on foot or by car; few paths get close enough to the Broads themselves, often tantalisingly out of sight, and once away from the waterside and fenny woodlands you are immediately into the flat, humdrum agricultural landscapes found in much of the rest of the area. There is some scope for

strolling along rivers, with pumping-mills, birdlife and the boating scene being the principal features. There's bike hire throughout the area, but the best way to see the Broads is undoubtedly by boat - see below. For a quick taste you can combine a boat trip with the trains on the **Bure Valley railway** at Aylsham.

Berney Arms windmill TG4605 Across the water from Burgh Castle and amazingly remote, this and its nearby pub can be reached not by road but by either boat or train from Great Yarmouth, or as a worthwhile objective for a long walk with a real sense of adventure, across the marshes from Wickhampton or Halvergate, passing other former windpumps. The seven-storey mill dates from the 19th c, when it was used to drain water from the marshes. Cl 1-2 pm and all Nov-Mar; (01493) 700605; £2. There's also scope for walking by reedy Breydon Water, the estuarine channel of the River Yare between here and Great Yarmouth.

Boat cruising Broads cruising is generally a week-long affair, but could be worked into a short-stay holiday; the boats nowadays have every mod con and are easy for even a novice to handle, but it's a chilly pastime until summer's well established. Wroxham is the main centre for this, with several boat hire firms. So it's a good place to watch the boating activities from dry land, or to use as the start of a longer cruising holiday. It can be very congested in summer.

Day boating The more northern Broads with their relatively quiet reaches are good for short boat trips; Stalham TG3724, Barton Turf TG3522 and Wayford Bridge TG3424 are possible bases.

Fairhaven Garden Trust TG3713 Charming wooded water gardens beside the private South Walsham Inner Broad, the waterways linked by little bridges. Rare plants, masses of rhododendrons, azaleas and candelabra primulas among the flowers, and a tree - the King Oak - said to be 950 years old. It's an extensive place, running to some 180 acres, inc a big **wildlife sanctuary** - to visit this part you need to get a key (£1 extra charge); perhaps also boat trips. Tearoom, shop, disabled access; cl 25 Dec; (01603) 270449; £3.50. The Ship (B1140) has good home cooking.

Hickling TG4122 It's normally possible to hire a boat for just the day or perhaps an even shorter period here. And walkers have a pleasant path along the N shore; the Pleasure Boat (building, not boat) up at the quiet end has a fair-sized dining room, with good parking and lots of birds to watch.

Horning TG3417 One of the main centres for Broads boat hire, chiefly for longer spells afloat; there are also paddle-boat cruises. So it's a good place to watch the boating activity, perhaps from the Swan or the Ferry, busy dining pubs. There's also some scope for walking along the canalised parts of the River Bure.

Neatishead TG3520 This attractive village gives access to the **Barton Broad** nature reserve, and a little museum at RAF Neatishead (down towards Horning) traces the development and operational use of air defence radar; snacks, shop, disabled access; usually open 2nd Sat of month, bank hol Mon, plus Tues and Thurs Apr-Oct, best to check (01692) 633309; £4. The White Horse has popular food (and lots of pictures of old Broads boats).

Ranworth Broad TG3514 One of the few Broads the cruise boats can't get to. The **conservation centre** here has interpretations of local and natural history; snacks, shop, disabled access; cl Nov-Mar; (01603) 270479; free. The village **church** has the best painted rood screen in the county, and a tower giving fantastic views over the Broads.

River Thurne TG4117 The towpath by the canalised parts gives one of the relatively few opportunities for waterside walks in Broadland.

Strumpshaw Fen 🔤 TG3306 Partly drained water meadows and fen between woodland and River Yare, with hides for watching marsh birds inc harriers and bearded tits, winter geese, and perhaps midsummer swallowtail butterflies. Disabled access to one viewing platform (and facilities); cl 25 Dec; (01603) 715191; £2.50 (RSPB members free). On the other side of the river, approached by a pleasant walk

from Rockland St Mary (where the New Inn is a nice food stop), there are more bird hides around Rockland Broad.

Toad Hall Cottage (How Hill, Ludham; off A149) Learn about the life of a family living and working on the marshes around 150 years ago at this little cottage; re-created rooms, and an information centre. Disabled access; cl end Oct-Easter; (01692) 678763; free. You can also be guided around the marshes in an Edwardian-style boat; wknds and school hols Easter-Jun, daily Jun-end Sept, best to check; £4 (no under-2s). A nature trail is open the same time as the cottage; 80p.

Watching the boats There aren't a great many places where it's easy to get down to the water by car. Among them are the attractive village of **Coltishall** TG2719, where the Rising Sun pub overlooks a pretty bend of the River Bure; **Ormesby St Michael** TG4715 (attractive waterside lawns at the Eels Foot pub); **Sutton Staithe** TG3823, a lovely quiet spot, with a useful pub; **Surlingham** TG3006, which has a rowing-boat ferry alongside the Ferry House pub, and lovely riverside lawns at the Coldham Hall pub; **Stokesby** TG4310, with another Ferry House pub overlooking quite a busy stretch of the River Bure; and **Bramerton** TG2905 (the Woods End pub is useful), and **Dilham** TG3325 (the Crown is a handy refreshment place here). **Geldeston** TM3891 is at the navigable head of the River Waveney; down a long track from the road, the Lock, a remote candlelit pub, gives a flavour of how the Broads were 50 years ago - at least out of high season.

BURGH CASTLE TG4705

You can still see sections of the massive walls of this coastal Roman fortress, built in the 3rd c to guard against Saxon marauders. The Church Farm Inn overlooking the Yare and Waveney has decent food.

BURGH ST MARGARET TG4513

Village (A1064) Restoration and making old rides work again is a theme of this rosy look at the past, set in over 30 acres. Expect to find restored fairground rides (inc traditional Victorian gallopers) and a working cinema organ collection. They also have a narrow-gauge railway, working sawmill, bear collection, swinging chairs, woodland walks, and decent indoor and outdoor adventure play areas. Meals, snacks, shops, mostly disabled access; cl Jan-Mar, plus wkdys Oct, phone for Christmas opening Nov-Dec; (01493) 369770; £6.50.

BURNHAM MARKET TF8342
Handsomely opulent village with a fine green, gatehouse and 13th-c priory remains; the Hoste Arms is a good dining pub.

BURNHAM THORPE TF8541
This hamlet's strong Lord Nelson connections include a good pub named after him, with interesting related memorabilia. The lectern in the village church uses wood from HMS *Victory*, and the church has other Nelson mementoes.

CAISTER-ON-SEA TG5012
Caister Castle Car Collection This moated ruin is set back from the town, a little way inland. Falstaff (the original behind Shakespeare's creation) built it on returning from Agincourt; its walls surround a 30-metre (98-ft) tower. The grounds contain a **motor museum** with a good collection of vehicles from 1893 onwards. Snacks, some disabled access; open Jun-last Fri in Sept, cl Sat; (01572) 787251; £6. The Ship (Victoria St, off Tan Lane) has a remarkably colourful pub garden, and the beaches are wide and sandy.

CASTLE ACRE TF8115
A delightful village, with an 18th-c feel along the tree-shaded walk of Stocks Green. The sparse ruins of a great **Norman Castle** are still awe-inspiring. The site is on the Peddars Way, a Roman road following the track of an earlier herding way. West Acre, just W, has a few further priory remains, and (like Castle Acre itself) picturesque fords over the River Nar.
Castle Acre Priory Extensive ruins of a Cluniac building by William the Conqueror's son-in-law include the fine arcaded W front of the 11th/12th-c church, and a chapel and 15th-c gatehouse; good interpreter tour, some special events. Well laid out, and very picturesque. Snacks, shop, some disabled access; cl Mon-Tues Nov-Mar, 24-26 Dec, 1 Jan; (01760) 755394; £4; EH.

CASTLE RISING TF6624
Castle Rising Castle Massive earthworks surround this fine 12th-c keep. Shop, limited disabled access; cl Mon-Tues Nov-Mar, 24-26 Dec; (01553) 631330; £3.75. The village is attractive, with an almshouse by the church.

CLEY NEXT THE SEA TG0443
Handy for the bird-sanctuary marshes towards the Blakeney Point sandspit, with excellent hides and plenty of avocets. The pleasant village has an imposing **church** with a fine tower, and the Three Swallows next door is a cheery food stop. The neatly restored **windmill** is an even more obvious landmark, and has great views from the top (open pm Easter-Oct; (01263) 740209; £1.50), as well as very good accommodation. There's a long pebbly beach.

COCKLEY CLEY TF8004
Iceni Village Lots of interesting historical things to see around this village (pronounced to rhyme with 'sly'). There's a **museum** in a 17th-c cottage, nature reserve, carriage collection, and 7th-c Saxon church, but most unusual is the **Iceni Village**, built as and where it was believed to have existed 2,000 years ago. Snacks, shop, disabled access; open Apr-Oct; (01760) 724588; £4 covers all attractions. The Twenty Churchwardens is good for lunch.

CROMER TG2242
Popular seaside resort since Victorian times, with lovely sandy beaches, more sun than the average, bustling markets, golf courses, interesting shops and galleries, and lots of entertainments. The pier is one of the last in the country to have an end-of-pier theatre - very popular, so worth booking early. The tower of the imposing **church** on Church St - Norfolk's tallest - gives spectacular views of the surrounding countryside. A good local history **museum** next door is spread over five 19th-c fishermen's cottages (shop; cl Mon lunch, Sun am, Good Fri, 23-26 Dec, 1 Jan; (01263) 513543; £1.80), and on the prom a small **Lifeboat Museum** looks at local lifeboatman Henry Blogg, who over 53 years saved 873 lives (shop, disabled access; (01263)

512503; cl Oct-Apr; free). Nearby you often find dressed crabs for sale; the crab boats still work from here, and Cromer crabs are the best on England's east coast. The restaurant of the comfortable Victorian seafront Red Lion Hotel has a good choice of fresh seafood.

Beacon Hill The only place of any height on the north Norfolk coast (a humble 90 metres, 300 ft); the Coast Path here detours over the sandy heath and through woodlands.

DENVER TF5800

Denver Sluice (S of Downham Market) These towering hydraulic sluice gates control water levels in these parts - quite a sight; it's a good place for watching birds too. The riverside Jenyns Arms is a pleasant lunch stop nearby, and the road from the village is pretty.

Windmill 🏚 (Sluice Rd) Daily guided tours go right to the top of this fully restored windmill, and you can regularly see flour being made in the traditional way; their visitor centre has displays and a video on milling. Craft workshops, teashop and bakery (with cakes made using their own flour); cl am Sun, 24-26 Dec and 1 Jan; (01366) 384009; £3.

DEREHAM TF9813

William Cowper is buried in the churchyard of the partly Norman St Nicholas's church, which has an unusual detached bell tower.

DOWNHAM MARKET TF5903

Collectors World & Magical Dickens Experience (Hermitage Hall, A1122 just W) Based around an old chapel and retreat centre used by pilgrims on their way to Walsingham, the eclectic displays include mementoes of local boy Nelson (letters, birth certificate and death mask), re-creations of Dickensian scenes, a pink room devoted to Barbara Cartland, and a car museum; they've also a replica of the 1st-c shrine at Ephesus. There's a wildlife sanctuary, riverside walk and picnic area. Tearoom, shop, some disabled access; cl 25 Dec; (01366) 383185; £3.50. In town, the old-fashioned Castle Hotel (High St) has above-average food.

EARSHAM TM3188

Otter Trust 🏚 (off A143) Charitable trust which has scored considerable success in reintroducing otters to rivers from which they had disappeared. The information centre has an exhibition on their work, but it's obviously seeing the friendly little creatures themselves that children enjoy most, and there are plenty of them, in big semi-natural enclosures prettily set on the banks of the River Waveney. The british ones tend to be fairly shy, so watching the slightly more extrovert asian short-clawed otters can be more rewarding; the best time to see them is around one of the feeding displays, at 12 and 3pm. Other wildlife inc lots of deer, and free-roaming wallabies, and their three lakes attract plenty of waterfowl. Nature trails and walks and a decent children's playground. Snacks, shop, disabled access; open Apr-Sept; (01986) 893470; £5 adults.

ERPINGHAM TG2032

Alby Crafts & Gardens 4½ acres of interesting shrubs, plants and bulbs, with a museum devoted to bottles (over 2,000 of them, mainly from regional brewers), and eight working craftsmen inc sculpture, wood-turning and cane work. Crafts gallery, tearoom, shop, some disabled access; cl Mon (exc bank hols), and 23 Dec-mid Jan; (01263) 761590; free, gardens £2, bottle museum 30p. The Ark, and the Saracens Head out at Wolterton, are both very good for lunch.

FAKENHAM TF9429

A pleasant market town; the comfortable Wensum Lodge Hotel has decent food (as does the prettily set Sculthorpe Mill off the A148 just W, recently rebuilt after a fire), and the roads N pass through attractive villages.

FELBRIGG TG1939

Felbrigg Hall Magnificent 17th-c house in splendid grounds, inc an orangery with fine collection of camellias, and a colourfully restored walled garden overlooked by a dovecot. The house is decorated with paintings and furnishings from the 18th c, and has a wonderful Gothic library. Meals, snacks, shop, second-hand bookshop, disabled access to ground floor; hall and gardens cl Thurs, Fri, and Nov-Mar; (01263) 837444; *£6.30, garden only *£2.60; NT. There's public access all year to the 1,700-acre wooded grounds

with their fine mature trees and lake.
FILBY TG4612
Thrigby Hall Wildlife Gardens
Popular 18th-c park filled with asian
animals and birds, with tropical and bird
houses, tree walk, willow pattern
garden, and ornamental wildfowl on the
lake. Also a huge jungly swamp hall
where crocodiles doze under water.
Snacks, shop, disabled access; (01493)
369477; *£6.90.
FORNCETT ST MARY TM1694
Industrial Steam Museum Unusual
collection of eight giant stationary
steam engines and over 20 smaller ones
rescued from all over the country, inc
one that used to open Tower Bridge.
Snacks, shop, disabled access; open
every Sun May-Nov (in steam first Sun
in month); (01508) 488277; £4 steam
days (two children free with each
adult), donations suggested on static
days. The Bird in Hand over at
Wreningham is a good value dining pub.
FOXLEY WOOD TG0522
(signed from Foxley village) A big block
of ancient woodland, mainly deciduous
and grown naturally for many centuries;
lovely woodland spring flowers.
FRITTON TG4700
Country World (Church Lane) Plenty
to keep families amused for most of the
day at this assortment of activities
based around a big lake. A children's
farm has opportunities to get close to
rabbits, chickens, ducks, ponies, sheep
and pigs, and the adjacent heavy horse
stables have splendid-looking suffolk
punches and shires, with regular
harnessing displays. A falconry centre
has twice-daily flying displays, at 12 and
3pm. You can go out on the water, in
guided tours or on pedaloes, and there
are plenty of gentle walks around the
edges and surrounding woodland, or in
the formal Victorian gardens. Several
trails for children, inc one for mountain
bikes (which you can hire), and play
areas. Extra charges for mini tractors
(£1), a miniature railway (80p), pony
and waggon rides, and miniature golf.
You can fish on the lake. Meals, snacks,
shop, disabled access; open daily Apr-
Sept, then wknds and half-term in Oct;
(01493) 488208; £5.80.
GLANDFORD TG0441
Shell Museum Curious little museum

built by Sir Alfred Jodrell (who lived in
nearby Bayfield Hall), housing his
collection of often very beautiful sea
shells and other interesting objects
such as a sugar bowl used by Elizabeth I,
and a 4¼ metre (14-ft) tapestry of the
north Norfolk coast. Shop, disabled
access; cl 12.30-2pm, all Sun and Mon
(exc bank hols), and Nov-Easter Sat;
(01263) 740081; £1.75. The Three
Swallows at Cley next the Sea is useful
for lunch.
GOODERSTONE TF7602
Attractive village with decent pub,
ancient church and nearby
watergardens.
GREAT BIRCHAM TF7632
Windmill Not far from Houghton Hall,
this striking mill is on that Norfolk
rarity, a hill - so one of the few places
with views. They sell bread baked at the
mill's own bakery. Tearooms, shop,
some disabled access; open Easter-Sept;
(01485) 578393; £2.75. You can hire
bikes (from £4). The village is attractive,
with a new crafts centre; the Kings Head
Hotel (unpretentious despite being a
favourite with Sandringham shooting
parties) is handy for lunch.
GREAT WITCHINGHAM TG0818
Norfolk Wildlife Centre 🖾
(A1067) In attractive parkland, this
dedicated centre (with a strong focus
on conservation) has a good range of
mostly british and european wildlife,
with everything from lynxes and otters
to tortoises, iguanas and snakes.
There's a walk-through subtropical
parakeet aviary, and birds of prey
centre with twice-daily flying displays,
and a farm and pets' pavilion, with
animals that younger children can fuss
and stroke. Good play areas include an
adventure playground and monkey slide
for older children, and a toddlers' play
area in a fenced-off section next to the
tearoom. Snacks and picnic area, shop;
open daily Apr-Oct, wknds and school
hols Nov, mid-Feb to Mar; (01603)
872274; £6.50 adults.
GREAT YARMOUTH TG5307
A cross between working town and
resort, this still has a busy fishing
harbour - used too as a port of call by
the Broads cruising boats. There are
lots of holiday entertainments,
particularly good for families, inc a

decent summer fairground. The town itself is in the second of a four-year regeneration project to encourage more visitors; currently the council are concentrating on traffic flow improvements and renovating the esplanade. The 14th-c church of St Nicholas at the top end of the market place has an exceptionally wide nave, and an impressive W front. The smart quay-view Star Hotel has good value bar food, and the backstreet Red Herring (Havelock Rd) is also worth knowing. On nearby Middle Scroby Sands Britain's largest offshore wind farm is now fully operational.

Amazonia (Seafront) Indoor tropical paradise with reptiles, insects, butterflies and birds; they have a 4-metre (13-ft) alligator, and a python well over 5 metres (16ft) long. Shop, disabled access; cl Nov-Feb; (01493) 842202; £4.50.

Elizabethan House Museum (South Quay) This is a patchwork of historical detail - built in 1596, it has a Georgian façade, 16th-c panelled rooms and, among features from later periods, some rooms decorated and furnished in 19th-c style, and a functional Victorian kitchen. Shop, open wkdys and pm wknds Apr-Oct; (01493) 745526; *£2.70. The 13th-c **Tolhouse Museum** (Tolhouse St) is a local history museum, housed in the town's former gaol and courthouse (you can still see the dungeons); times and price as above. A new museum is due to open this summer with displays on the town's maritime history; phone number above for more information.

Merrivale Model Village (Wellington Pier Gardens) Attractive landscaped gardens with the exceptionally detailed village - featuring a railway, radio-controlled boats and cars, and over 200 other models. Meals, snacks, shop, disabled access; cl Nov-Easter; (01493) 842097; £3.50.

Old Merchant's House (South Quay) 17th-c house among the narrow lanes or Rows nr the waterfront, with some well restored rooms. Close by and open with it is a group of the original 17th-c houses (Row 111). And admission includes the nearby ruin of 13th-c Greyfriars Cloisters. Shop; cl

Nov-Mar and maybe 1-2pm, phone to check; (01493) 857900; tours available £2.50; EH.

Sea Life Centre (Marine Parade) Displays of the kinds of marine life found on the Norfolk coast, as well as underwater tunnels through shark-infested oceans and colourful tropical fish. They've also touch-pools, and tanks with seahorses (they're very strong on breeding, and you may see baby ones), rays, and now an octopus too; talks throughout the day. Meals, snacks, shop, disabled access; cl 25 Dec; (01493) 330631; £6.95 (keep your receipt and you can go in and out).

GRESSENHALL TF9716

Norfolk Rural Life Museum There's more than enough for a pleasant afternoon at this good museum of local and rural life, housed in a former workhouse (children enjoy the exhibition on life in the workhouse, with games and hands-on activities). The 50 acres also contain a 1920s working farm with rare breeds and suffolk punch horses, gardens, trails, picnic areas and an adventure playground. There's a re-created 1930s post office, grocer and forge, steam engines (and the oldest car in Norfolk), special events and demonstrations. Meals, snacks, shop, disabled access; open Tues-Sun (plus Mon in school hols and bank hols) Mar-Oct, Sun only in Nov, though best to check; (01362) 860563; £5.45. Darbys over at Swanton Morley is a good family food pub.

GRIMES GRAVES TL8189

The strange pitted landscape in an open heathland area within Thetford Forest is the result of intensive flint mining during the neolithic period. Originally these 433 hollows were mine shafts, and equipped with a highly necessary hard hat you climb a ladder down into one that has been excavated: at the bottom, be prepared to get on your hands and knees to get a view into the openings of the galleries where the flint was mined. In 2002 excavations in the area showed that much earlier, in the last Ice Age, neanderthal men were using flint tools to butcher woolly mammoths around here. No lavatories at the site, but there are some within a mile. Snacks, shop, disabled access; cl

1-2pm, all day Mon and Tues Nov-Mar, 24-26 Dec, 1 Jan; (01842) 810656; £2.50; EH. From the woodland track across the road, you may see little muntjac deer.

GRIMSTON TF7022

Congham Hall Herb Garden In summer this has around 500 different herbs, in traditional layouts, with many unusual varieties for sale. Meals, snacks; (01485) 600250; free.

HEACHAM TF6837

Norfolk Lavender (Caley Mill) The largest lavender-growing and distilling operation in the country, along with a national collection of lavender species and cultivars. The guided tour (daily spring bank hol-Sept) really adds interest - it's best to go at harvest time (mid-July to mid-Aug) when they may drive visitors out to the fields. Also fragrant meadow and herb gardens. Meals and snacks (inc their lavender scones), shop, disabled access; cl 25-26 Dec, 1 Jan; (01485) 570384; tours £1.75, £3.95 at harvest time. The Gin Trap at Ringstead (with a decent nearby art gallery) and Rose & Crown at Snettisham both have good food.

HEYDON TG1127

Delightfully unspoilt tucked-away village, with a green that time seems to have passed by.

HOLKHAM TF9143

Holkham Hall Splendid Palladian mansion in delightful and very extensive tree-filled grounds with an ornamental lake and 18th-c walled garden. Sumptuously furnished state rooms, with fine paintings by Claude, Rubens, Van Dyck and Gainsborough. An ancestor of the present owner was Thomas Coke, whose revolutionary farming techniques are described in an exhibition in the pottery yard. Meals, snacks, shop, limited disabled access; open pm Thurs-Mon May-Sept; (01328) 713103; £10 for everything, £6.50 hall, Bygones museum £5. Walkers have free access to this coastal estate's driveways; the parkland is a bit sombre, but impressively landscaped with the lake, a temple and obelisk. The estate's Victoria Hotel is a smart place for lunch. The beach has a bird reserve (and a nudist section). There is a car park quite close to the beach, where pine trees

meet the sands; this coastal section of the North Norfolk Coast Path is good for lonely walks - westwards any summer crowds rapidly thin out.

North Norfolk Coast Path From **Overy Staithe** a particularly fine stretch of the path follows a zigzag dyke - saltmarsh on one side, neat farmland on the other - to the dunes and sandy beach, which never quite looks the same from one day to the next.

HOLME NEXT THE SEA TF6943

From the sandy beach a two-mile walk passes a rewarding **bird sanctuary** and saltings to Thornham - another good bird-watching place. Another more serious walking possibility is the **Peddars Way** which starts here - an inland link from the Coast Path, running from Holme down through Castle Acre and then in a strikingly straight bee-line right across the county to Knettishall Heath nr Thetford, following ancient-feeling green ways and quiet lanes. Earnest walkers may find there is a little too much road-walking to sustain interest.

HOLT TG0738

Pleasant little town with some handsome Georgian buildings; the friendly market-place Feathers Hotel has good value food and decent bedrooms. This is the terminus of the **North Norfolk Steam Railway** from Sheringham.

HORSEY TG4622

A quiet corner of the coast, below sea level - among the places most at risk of flooding if the sea defences are breached. There's a good path to the dunes and the sea from the lane past the Nelson Head (enjoyable homely food here). On the other side of the main road, **Horsey windpump** is a restored drainage windmill, now in full working order. Teas, small shop; cl Nov-Mar; (01493) 393904; £1.50; NT. There's a good varied round walk, along quiet reed-fringed Horsey Mere (NT, with wildfowl and otters) and the New Cut to another former drainage windmill - the marshes on the far side of the cut seem alive with birds. Then you can either walk straight back to the village, or for a total contrast join the beach for sea views nr Horsey Corner. Alternatively, it takes 1½ hours or so to walk down the beach to Winterton-on-Sea, and in autumn you may see seals sunbathing or playing in the surf.

HORSHAM ST FAITH TG2114

Norwich Aviation Museum 🏛 (Old Norwich Rd) Enthusiastic displays of local aeronautical history, with aircraft (inc Vulcan bomber), engines, and other paraphernalia; on the edge of Norwich Airport, so a good view of the live article too. Snacks, shop, some disabled access; cl Mon (exc late July-Aug), plus am Sun Apr-Oct, and Weds, wknds Nov-Mar, also cl 20 Dec-5 Jan; (01603) 893080; £2.80. The thatched Chequers prettily placed at Hainford has popular food.

HOUGHTON TF7928

Houghton Hall Built for Robert Walpole and obviously designed to impress, this is a spectacularly grand Palladian mansion in charming parkland, with a large walled garden. The state rooms were decorated and furnished by William Kent, and house an important collection of 20,000 model soldiers and other militaria. Meals, snacks, shop, disabled access; open Weds, Thurs, Sun and bank hol pms Apr-Sept; (01485) 528569; £6.50. Driving along the C road nr North Pole farm you may spot brown, white or red deer. The Rose & Crown in Harpley has good value home cooking.

HOVETON TG3120

Hoveton Hall Gardens 🏛 Large attractive woodland garden with daffodils and rhododendrons, lakeside walk, kitchen garden and old-fashioned herbaceous walled 'spider garden'. You can stay in a wing of the house. Teas, plant sales; open Weds, Fri, Sun and bank hol Mon (plus Thurs in May) Easter-end Aug; (01603) 782798; £3.75. The Black Horse is useful for lunch.

Wroxham Barns Craft Centre (Tunstead Rd) Good for families, with craft workshops in 18th-c restored farm buildings, as well as a children's farm and traditional fair; play area too. Meals, snacks, shop, disabled access; cl 25-26 Dec, 1 Jan; (01603) 783762; £2.50 for farm, otherwise free.

HUNSTANTON TF6740

An East Coast resort which actually faces west, this is a clean, fresh and well kept place with gently shelving tidal sands (summer pony rides, boat trips

and adventure golf), and pleasant dune walks past the golf course up to the **bird reserve** on Gore Point. On a clear day you can see Boston's Stump across The Wash. The low cliffs around the town are quite colourful, with different rock strata. The Le Strange Barns (Golf Course Rd) is an interesting craft gallery, and the bar of the Marine Hotel (St Edmunds Terr) has decent food all day.

Oasis Standing out among the typical resort entertainments is this giant leisure park on the prom, with tropically heated indoor and outdoor pools, and both towering and toddler aquaslides. Meals, snacks, disabled access; usually cl am in term-time and all Dec; (01485) 534227; £3.60.

Sea Life Aquarium (Southern Promenade) An ocean tunnel at this excellent place brings you face to face with under-water creatures inc toothy conger eels, sharks and rays; you can touch some of the inhabitants, there are hands-on displays (and a children's quiz), and plenty of talks and feeding sessions throughout the day. Also seals, otters, and penguins in their marine sanctuary. Meals, snacks, shop, disabled access; cl 25 Dec; (01485) 533576; £6.

KING'S LYNN TF6120

Once England's fourth-largest town, it's quieter now, with pleasant corners, some attractive Georgian brick buildings, and a few much older places such as the 17th-c Custom House on the quay by the River Purfleet (now home to the Tourist Information Centre), the 15th-c church of St Nicholas (Chapel Lane; attractive for Festival concerts), the South Gates, Red Mount Chapel and the two medieval guildhalls. The first of these, the 15th-c **St George's Guildhall** (King St), is now the town's theatre, and home of the King's Lynn Festival (usually open 10-2pm Mon-Fri, cl bank hols and on concert days so best to ring (01553) 764864). At **Caithness Crystal**, you can watch them making glass. Tearoom, factory shop, disabled access; cl Easter Sun, 25-26 Dec, 1-2 Jan; (01553) 765111/123; free. Guided walks leave from the Old Gaol House; May-Sept, best to check for details of times and days; (01553) 763044; £3. On Tues the main market-place has some good crafts stalls; the Olde Maydens Heade there does popular lunches inc OAP bargains.

Green Quay (South Quay) Housed in the Tudor Marriott's Warehouse, this discovery centre provides a solid introduction to The Wash, with interactive displays explaining how it was formed, and other exhibits on the wildlife that lives in and around it today. Though the aquarium has closed, there's a fair bit else to interest children, inc the chance to make rubbings of animal footprints in the floor, and the Mussel Game, based around the mollusc's daily struggles with local currents. Snacks, shop, disabled access; cl 25 Dec-3 Jan; (01553) 818500; £1.

Lynn Museum (Old Market St) Local history, archaeology and natural history inc a skeleton of a Saxon warrior, a surprisingly interesting collection of medieval pilgrim badges, and Victorian fairground gallopers. Shop, disabled access; usually cl Sun, Mon, bank hols, and a few days over Christmas and New Year; (01553) 775001; £1.

Tales of the Old Gaol House ⊞ (Saturday Market Pl) Lively journey through the town's rich history; with spirited models, and spooky sights, sounds and smells this is particularly good for children. Shop, disabled access; usually cl Weds and Thurs Nov-Easter, 25-26 Dec and 1 Jan, but phone to check; (01553) 774297; £2.50 (inc audio tour). The tour includes the 14th-c King John Cup and other fabulous examples of civic paraphernalia housed in the Undercroft of the handsome medieval Trinity Guildhall.

Town House Museum (Queen St) Social history told through reconstructed room settings from the Middle Ages to the 1950s, inc Victorian kitchen, nursery and town garden. Shop; usually cl Sun am (all Sun Oct-Apr), bank hols, 25-27 Dec and 1 Jan; (01553) 773450; £1.80.

Trues Yard (North St/St Anns St) Restored old fishermen's cottages giving a good picture of life here in the last century, when families of up to 11 were often squeezed into two little rooms. Snacks, shop, disabled access; cl

Sun and Mon Nov-Apr, and around 25 Dec-1 Jan; (01553) 770479; £2.25.

LANGHAM TG0041

Langham Glass (North St) Watch craftsmen making glass in the traditional way; feel free to ask any questions. There's a little museum, walled garden, play area, and from around mid-July to mid-Sept there's usually a maize maze (£3.50). Meals, snacks, shop, disabled access; cl 25-26 Dec, 1 Jan; (01328) 830511; £3.75. The Bluebell, with a charming garden looking up to the church tower, has good value food.

LENWADE TG1017

Dinosaur Adventure Park *See separate family panel on p.399.*

LETHERINGSETT TG0638

The **church** has an unusual round tower. A restored **watermill** in a pretty setting still mills flour from local wheat. Usually cl Sat pm and all Sun (exc summer bank hols), with demonstrations pm Tues-Fri (less in winter); (01263) 713153; £3 during demonstrations, otherwise £2. The Kings Head is a great place for families.

LITTLE CRESSINGHAM TF8600

Little Cressingham windmill A fine example - and the pub called the Windmill over at Great Cressingham is an attractive place for lunch.

LITTLE WALSINGHAM TF9336

Once as popular a centre of pilgrimage as Canterbury, thanks to a replica of the Virgin Mary's home in Nazareth. Things tailed off when Henry VIII destroyed the priory and its shrine in 1538, but have picked up again in the last few decades. The Bull Inn is a good place (with masses of clerical visiting cards). The village is the terminus of the **Wells & Walsingham Light Railway**, described under Wells-next-the-Sea.

Shirehall Museum Displays on pilgrimages and the history of Walsingham, in an almost perfect Georgian courtroom complete with original fittings. Shop, limited disabled access; cl wkdys Nov-Dec and all Jan; (01328) 820510; £3 (includes entry to abbey).

Walsingham Abbey Grounds Remains of the Augustinian Priory, inc the Abbey Gates, Great Arch, part of the refectory and the Holy Wells. Pleasant gardens and woodland walks, with masses of snowdrops in early spring. Open via the Shirehall Museum and tourist information centre in summer, or the estate office in winter (office hours only). Shop, limited disabled access; open daily end Mar-end Oct, and when the snowdrops are out, plus wknds Nov-Dec, best to check; (01328) 820259; ticket is joint with Shirehall Museum £3. Round the corner, the Black Lion has a wide choice of decent bar food.

LODDON TM3695

Reads Nursery (Hales Hall, off A146 SE) Specialising for over a century in unusual conservatory plants, inc a good range of lemon, orange and other citrus fruits, also nut trees, etc. Disabled access; cl two weeks over Christmas; (01508) 548395; nursery free, barn and garden £2. The village is attractive, and the 17th-c Swan has home-made food.

MUNDESLEY TG3136

Peaceful seaside resort with a clean sandy beach, a well preserved windmill, a church without a tower, and a tiny local history museum housed in the old coastguard lookout point. The Ship and the Seaview House Hotel both have decent food.

NEW BUCKENHAM TM0890

A fine village, largely medieval; the 16th-c Gamekeeper at Old Buckenham has good seasonal food.

NORTH CREAKE TF8539

Creake Abbey All that remains of this early 13th-c Augustinian priory is the crossing and E arm, but it's still worth a passing look, and the village is charming. The Jolly Farmers has good gently upmarket food.

NORTH ELMHAM TF9821

North Elmham church An attractive 13th-c building, odd in that there's a step down into it; a little further N are the interesting ruins of a **Saxon cathedral**, and there are pleasant walks. The Kings Head has decent food.

NORWICH TG2308

Busy but civilised, the old centre has quite a concentration of attractive buildings (literally dozens of churches, in great variety, are one of the city's joys), with all sorts of surprises in the narrow streets and lanes that still follow its medieval layout. One such surprise is the **Forum**, a sleek

horseshoe-shaped, glass-covered building between Bethel St and Theatre St; as well as one of Britain's most advanced public libraries, this has **Origins**, a good heritage centre with interactive displays on local history, several cafés, and a tourist information centre; cl 25 Dec; (01603) 727290; £4.95. Elm Hill is especially handsome, and there are plenty of antiques shops and so forth. Even the more commercial/industrial centre N of the River Wensum has fine patches (such as Colegate), and the main shopping areas are closed to traffic. Fortunately the visually disappointing university is hidden away out on the W edge, though in term-time its students do bring a good bit of life into the centre. Much of the nightlife is centred around Prince of Wales Rd, which leads down to the developing Riverside Quarter. Norwich is the home of Colmans Mustard, and the Mustard Shop (Royal Arcade) has some varieties you may not have come across before. There's a lively spring arts festival (first half of May). The ancient Adam & Eve (Bishopgate) is good for lunch, the Gardeners Arms (Timber Hill - also known as the Murderers) is interesting, and two pleasant riverside pubs are the Gibraltar Gardens (Heigham St) and Ribs of Beef (Wensum St).

Assembly House (Theatre St) Across the road from the library, this is one of the few so-called Assembly Houses that actually still houses assemblies. In its time it's been much more, too: founded as a hospice in 1248, it has served as priests' college, family home, 18th-c cards house, girls' school and wartime camouflage school. Although the chapel was completely destroyed in 1548, and, more recently, a fire ravaged the building in 1995, all the 18th-c buildings have now been restored, and a brick-vaulted medieval cellar still lies beneath the restaurant. Meals, snacks, shop, disabled access; cl Sun; (01603) 626402; free.

Boat trips From the River Wensum you can clearly see how some of the city's older buildings were designed for water-borne traffic, rather than road transport. City Boats do all sorts of different river trips; (01603) 701701.

Bridewell Museum (Bridewell Alley)

14th-c building used as a prison 1583-1828, with exhibits on the city's trade and industries, and reconstructed late 19th-c shops. Cl Sun, and Feb-Oct; (01603) 493625; £2.

Dragon Hall 🏛 (King St) Well preserved medieval merchant's hall, with splendid timber-framed roof, intricate carved dragon, cellars, vaulted undercroft, and some finely painted roundels. Shop, limited disabled access; cl Sun, wknds Nov-Mar, bank hols, and 20 Dec-2 Jan; (01603) 663922; £2.50.

Inspire Hands-on Science Centre 🏛 (Coslany St) In medieval St Michael's church (hence the punning name) this lively centre aims to make science enjoyable, even fun, with over 40 hands-on displays; they have an under-5s play area, and science shows during school hols. Snacks, shop, disabled access; cl 24 Dec-1 Jan; (01603) 612612; £4.20.

Norwich Castle (Castle Meadow) This impressive four-square Norman fortress dominates the city from the hill. Built as a Royal palace, it now houses a museum and art gallery. As well as displays of art (with particular emphasis on the Norwich school), silverware (for which the town was famous), and ceramics (inc a huge collection of teapots), a gallery traces the history of Boudicca and the Iceni-Roman conflict, while another has displays on Egyptian mummies; there are regular exhibitions from the Tate. Hands-on exhibits, interactives and a model give an idea of what life was like in Norman times; ask about guided tours of the battlements and dungeons. Snacks, shop, disabled access, cl am Sun, 23-26 Dec, and 1 Jan; (01603) 493625; *£4.95.

Norwich Cathedral The modern city is firmly shut out by the great medieval gateways of the close. Basically Norman/Romanesque, the church has some fine features from later periods - the flying buttresses for example, and the late 15th-c vaulted roof, spire and west window with Victorian glass. The Norman cloisters are the largest in the country, rebuilt after a serious riot between city and cathedral in 1272, and remarkable for the 400 bosses carved with scenes of medieval life; there are hundreds more in the cathedral itself (you can see close-up pictures of the

ones on the roof on touch-screen computers). Meals, snacks and shop (not Sun), disabled access; (01603) 218321; suggested donation £3. Free guided tours leave the Welcome Desk Mon-Sat Jun-Sept, but there's often someone available who will be happy to show you around; they have children's activities too. The extensive precincts make an awe-inspiring impression: medieval alleys and secluded gardens, with all sorts of varied buildings from the cottages of Hooks Walk through the finer houses in the Upper Close to the buildings of Norwich School. The best view of the cathedral is from the river by Pulls Ferry; it's not easy to see from other parts of the town.

Norwich Puppet Theatre 🏛 (St James's Church, Whitefriars) Unusual diversion for families, with performances and puppet-making workshops; phone for details. Snacks, shop, disabled access; cl Sun; (01603) 629921; £5.50.

Plantation Garden In an abandoned chalk quarry, this peaceful Victorian garden is enjoyable for a stroll, with some interesting detail. Snacks Sun p'm in summer, some disabled access; usually open daily; (01603) 455223; £2 (honesty box).

Sainsbury Centre for Visual Arts (University of East Anglia, off B1108 W) Striking Norman Foster building with notable 19th- and 20th-c european art and a fascinating range of ethnographic art, inc african tribal sculpture, and egyptian and asian antiquities. Meals, snacks, shop, disabled access; cl Mon (inc bank hols), 2 wks over Christmas and New Year; (01603) 593199; £2.

Stranger's Hall Classic example of a wealthy merchant's house, and one of the oldest buildings in Norwich; room re-creations show how the occupants would have lived from Tudor to Victorian times, and highlights include a Tudor Hall and Georgian dining room. Tours leave Weds and there's an open day Sat, phone to book, or ask at the castle or Bridewell Museum; (01603) 493636; £2.50 tour, £2 entry on Sat.

OXBOROUGH TF7401

Oxburgh Hall Henry VII stayed in this pretty moated manor house in 1487, which shows hangings worked by Mary,

Queen of Scots. Most of the house was thoroughly refurbished during Victorian times, but the gatehouse remains as an awe-inspiring example of 15th-c building work, 24 metres (80 ft) high. The garden has a colourfully restored french parterre, and there are pleasant woodland walks. Meals, snacks, shop, disabled access to ground floor only; cl Thurs, Fri, and early Nov-Mar, garden also open some wknds Mar, house cl am (exc bank hols), best to check; (01366) 328258; £5.50, £2.80 garden only; NT. The Bedingfeld Arms opp has decent food.

PASTON TG3135
Stow Windmill A fine example; snacks, shop; £1 suggested donation.

PENSTHORPE TF9429
Pensthorpe Waterfowl Park
(A1067) Good collection of wild and exotic waterfowl; the visitor centre has wildlife art and photography. Also woodland, meadow, lakeside and riverside nature trails, adventure playground, and talks and events. Meals, snacks, shop, disabled access; cl wkdys Jan-Mar, 25-26 Dec; (01328) 851465; £5.50. The Boar nicely set opposite Great Ryburgh church does enjoyable lunches.

PORINGLAND TG2601
Playbarn (Shotesham Rd, off B1332) Great for children under 7, with a range of indoor and outdoor play and activity areas; Easter-Oct they've also got farm animals, and there are pony and tractor rides; special events during the hols. It's a well organised place, and a CCTV system in the indoor play area lets parents keep an eye on children from the adjoining café areas. Shop, disabled access; cl Sat, 25-26 Dec, 1 Jan; (01508) 495526; £4 children under 8 (adults £1).

REEDHAM TG4202
Pettitts Animal Adventure Park
(Church Rd) A good variety of attractions here, inc aviaries and a reptile house, gnome village, miniature railway, tractor rides, big adventure playground (and an indoor play area for toddlers). Also a roller-coaster and pirate ship, crazy golf, a miniature horse stud, and an animal petting area; daily children's entertainment. Meals, snacks and picnic area, shop, some disabled access; cl Nov-Easter; (01493) 701403; £7.75.

REEPHAM TG0922
Attractive large village or small town with some worthwhile shops and a fine old inn (the Old Brewery House); the unusual churchyard with two churches (and a fragment of a third) is worth a look.

SANDRINGHAM TF6928
Sandringham House Many people come to this part of the county for its connection with the Royal Family. The house and 20,000-acre estate was bought by Queen Victoria for her son Edward in 1862, and has become famous as the family's Christmas residence; the 19th-c building is filled with their portraits and those of their continental counterparts, and has various gifts presented to the family over the years. Unlike at their other homes, you can see most of the rooms they actually use, so there's a much more intimate feel than you'd get at Windsor or Buckingham Palace, and the staff are particularly pleasant; there may be queues. The grounds and surrounding country park are lovely, with lakes, streamside flowers, handsome trees, sweeping lawns, and the colourful North Garden (the late Queen Mother's favourite); also nature trails, adventure playground, and the parish Church of St Mary Magdalene. Lovely rhododendrons in the woods May/Jun. Meals, snacks, shop, very good disabled access (a train runs between the grounds' entrance and the house); open Easter-Oct, exc during summer Royal visit (mid-July to early Aug); (01553) 772675; £6.50, £4.50 grounds and museum only. There's free access to **Sandringham Country Park** with its majestic trees and glades, a notable parkland walking area (readers recommend coming when the daffodils are out). The Feathers towards Dersingham is useful for lunch.

SAXTHORPE TG1332
Mannington Gardens The most beautiful feature of these gardens is the summer rose display, but 20 miles of footpaths around the hall and woodland are open all year (£1 parking), and there's a children's playground. Snacks, shop, disabled access; gardens usually open pm Sun May-Sept, plus Weds-Fri Jun-Aug; (01263) 584175; £3. Paths lead to the pleasant grounds of Wolterton

Park. The Walpole Arms in the pretty nearby village of Itteringham has good food.

SHERINGHAM TG1543

The working fishing harbour has some old buildings around it, though there's a lot of more modern building up behind. The beach is nice, and this is a town many of our readers enjoy. The Robin Hood (Station Rd) is a useful family food pub, the low-beamed Wyndham Arms (Wyndham St) has fresh local fish, and the Lobster (High St) is strong on seafood.

North Norfolk Railway Full-size steam railway, chugging through over five miles of lovely coastal scenery to Holt. Plenty of railway memorabilia at the Sheringham station, and a collection of steam engines and vintage rolling stock. Meals, snacks, shop, disabled access; (01263) 820800 for timetable; £8 all day ticket.

Sheringham Park Extensive parkland, gloriously landscaped by Humphry Repton (it was his favourite work), with excellent coastal views from its waymarked walks and viewing towers. Also mature trees and fine azaleas and rhododendrons (best late May/Jun), and good walks to the coast. Snacks, disabled access; (01263) 823778; free, but parking £2.80; NT.

Upper Sheringham The 14th-c **church** in this quiet flintstone village is very attractive, and the Red Lion is a pleasant stop. Footpaths from here lead to Sheringham Park.

SHOULDHAM TF6709

Just N of this attractive unspoilt village, which has a decent pub, are **nature trails** in pleasant woods; as well as lots of rabbits, you may be lucky enough to spot red deer.

SNETTERTON TL9991

Hall Farm HQ of the International League for the Protection of Horses; learn more about their work, and meet some of the residents. Snacks, shop, disabled access; open Weds and wknds (exc 25 Dec-2 Jan); (01953) 717309; donations.

SNETTISHAM TF6833

Park Farm Working farm offering good insight into seasonal farming operations, with lambing and red deer calving. Lots of animals, plus impressive adventure playground, and a small craft centre. Snacks, shop, disabled access; open daily Mar-Oct, phone for winter opening times; (01485) 542425; £4.75 for either farm or 45-min guided ride around deer park, £7.95 for both. Pretty walks nearby, as well as a nature reserve along the beach (which is a couple of miles from the village). The Rose & Crown (Old Church Rd) is a good dining pub.

ST OLAVES TM4599

St Olaves Priory Ruins of 13th-c Augustinian priory; you can still see the fine brick undercroft in the cloister - a remarkable early use of this material; free. Priory Farm is very handy for lunch, and the riverside Bell is worth a look - very old indeed, though much modernised.

SUTTON TG3923

Sutton windmill The most striking mill in Norfolk and the tallest in Britain, nine floors high. Shop, limited disabled access; cl Oct-Mar; (01692) 581195; *£4. The Crown in Catfield has attractively priced food.

TERRINGTON ST CLEMENT TF5519

African Violet Centre Wide range of plants besides the african violets it's developed so successfully as house plants; play area and visitor centre. Good tearoom, shop, disabled access; cl 25-26 Dec, 1 Jan; (01553) 828374. The Woolpack at Terrington St John has good food.

THETFORD TL8683

Ancient House Museum Early Tudor house with fine oak ceilings, now a local history museum with small period herb garden behind. Shop; cl 12.30-1pm, Sun Sept-May (exc pm Jun-Aug); (01842) 752599; free, exc July and Aug £1. At **Thetford Priory**, the ruins of a 12th-c Cluniac monastery, you can easily make out the full ground plan of the cloisters, and the 14th-c gatehouse still stands; disabled access; free.

Warren Lodge, a 15th-c flint former hunting lodge, is also worth a look. This is a quiet low-key town, and the Bell, Dolphin and Thomas Paine are civilised places for lunch.

THORNHAM TF7243

Walks along the coastline here give marvellous views, and this is good bird-watching terrain, with wading birds, the occasional marsh harrier and perhaps even seals. The Lifeboat is a favourite place for lunch. Beware of tides if parking on the seafront, as the lower road can be flooded.

THURSFORD GREEN TF9734
Thursford Collection 🏛 Bouncy collection of barrel, street and fairground musical organs and a Wurlitzer cinema organ, most demonstrated every day. Also showmen's steam engines, adventure playground, and Venetian Gondola switchback ride. Meals, snacks, shop, disabled access; cl am, Sat, and Jan-Mar; (01328) 878477; *£5.30.

TITCHWELL TF7544
Bird-watching Pleasant coastal village with good RSPB reserve nearby; the Briarfields has good value food and comfortable bedrooms.

WEAVERS WAY TG1531
This long-distance path can be used as part of a link from the parkland of Blickling Hall to take in walks through and around the **Wolterton Park** and **Mannington Hall** estates, both owned by the Walpoles, who have opened up a network of paths in the area extending NW to **Holt Country Park**. The Saracens Head on the edge of Wolterton Park is a very civilised dining pub.

WELLS-NEXT-THE-SEA TF9142
Pleasant rather gracious little village-sized town; don't be fooled by the name - the sea is a mile away these days, though there's a particularly good stretch of the North Norfolk Coast Path from here to **Overy Staithe**, where the sandy beach never looks quite the same from one day to the next.
Wells & Walsingham Light Railway Passing through quietly attractive scenery, this railway is remarkable for being the longest in the world to use a 10¼-inch gauge track, with a steam locomotive built specially for it. Snacks, shop; cl Nov-Good Fri; (01328) 711630 for times; £6 return.

WELNEY TL5393
Wildfowl & Wetlands Trust (Hundred Foot Bank) Excellent 1,000-acre wild bird reserve, with numerous hides, spacious observatory, and floodlit lagoon. During the summer there's a nature trail, while in winter the sights include 4,000 migratory bewick's swans and all sorts of ducks; try and get there for feeding time (12pm 26 Dec-Feb). It can be busy then, and you'll need to wrap up well. When the marshes are flooded (quite a striking sight) so are the paths to the other hides - readers recommend relaxing in the comfortable chairs in the observatory and watching what flies in; you can hire binoculars. Snacks, shop, part disabled access; cl 25 Dec, though best to check in very wet weather; (01353) 860711; £3.65, less when the marshes are flooded. In wet winters some local roads (watch out for birds from here too) can be flooded, and then you can approach it only from the E.

WEST RUNTON TG2042
Norfolk Shire Horse Centre Extensive collection of draught horses with working demonstrations. You can hire riding horses by the hour, and there's a children's farm and rural museum. Meals, snacks, shop, disabled access; cl Sat (exc bank hol wknds and in Aug), and Nov-Mar; (01263) 837339; *£5.50. The seaside village itself is attractive.

WEST WALTON TF4713
West Walton church A textbook example of early Gothic architecture; just about all of it dates from the mid-13th c, and there's a cool elegance throughout; get the key from the butchers shop. The King of Hearts (which does good lunches, inc OAP bargains).

WEYBOURNE TG1043
Muckleburgh Collection 🏛 (A149) Around 3,000 military items inc World War II fighting vehicles, on the site of a former military camp, once the lynch-pin of defences on this coast. You can ride in a Gama Goat (a six-wheel US personnel carrier), and there are usually tank demonstrations pm every Sun, plus pm bank hols and wkdys during school hols. Meals and snacks (in NAAFI-style café), shop, disabled access; open daily Feb half-term, then Sun only until Easter, then daily until end Oct; (01263) 588210; *£5.50. The old-fashioned Maltings Hotel has a pleasant restaurant. Nearby Salthouse and Kelling back heathy hinterlands, allowing walkers a mix between this and

the unvaryingly straight coast; the Dun Cow overlooking the Salthouse marshes has decent food all day.

WIGHTON TF9439
Pleasant village in attractive coastal area, once home to the sculptor Henry Moore. The School House is a good art gallery, and the Wells & Walsingham Light Railway stops here. The Three Horseshoes over at Warham is the best pub in these parts.

WINTERTON-ON-SEA TG4919
One of the quieter seaside resorts on this coast, with a gentle villagey feel, and a particularly good beach over the dunes - nice for a wander by the sea, and you may even spot seals. The 17th-c Fishermans Return is very pleasant for lunch.

WOODBASTWICK TG3215
Picturesque thatched estate village, home to Woodfordes Brewery, one of Britain's best microbreweries; the Fur & Feather dining pub is the brewery tap.

WROXHAM TG3017
Barton House Railway (Hartwell Rd) Miniature railway through a big riverside garden. Snacks, shop; open pm third Sun of month Apr-Oct; (01603) 782470; 50p. Boats leave for here from Wroxham Bridge; £1 inc entry to miniature railway.

WYMONDHAM TG1001
Mid Norfolk Railway Heritage diesel trains run from here through 11 miles of countryside to the market town of Dereham (where there's a little railway museum; snacks, shop, disabled access); it stops at some pretty villages on the way. Special events throughout the year, phone for timetable (01362) 851723; £5 return.

Wymondham Abbey The parish church is all that's left of this once majestic abbey, but its twin towers dominate the countryside for miles around, and there's plenty to interest inside, with helpful guides on hand to talk you round the features. Originally founded as a priory in 1107, it became an abbey less than a century before the monastic buildings were destroyed as part of the Dissolution. The nave is a scaled-down version of that of Norwich Cathedral, and its 15th-c roof is dotted with over 70 carved angels. Other things to spot include the delicate golden altar screen begun in 1919, and a 1904 Arts and Crafts triptych behind the Lady Chapel. Shop, disabled access; cl Sun during services; (01953) 607062; free (donations welcome). The picturesque 14th-c Green Dragon nearby has good food. At the other end of the small town, housed in a former prison, a lively **Heritage Museum** has plenty of well shown bygones of the area, and interactive displays on prison life in the old days; cl am Sun, and Dec-Feb; (01953) 600205; £2.

Attractive villages here, all with decent pubs, include Aldborough TG1834, Binham TF9839, Colkirk TF9126, Harpley TF7825, Mundford TL8093, South Wootton TF6422, Stiffkey (pronounced Stewkie) TF9743, Swanton Morley TG0116 (leaflet of pleasant walks), Wiveton TG0342 and Worstead TG3025.

Where to eat

BLAKENEY TG0243 **White Horse** *4 High St (01263) 740574* Small friendly hotel nr harbour (if that's not too grand a word), with a good mix of chatty customers in the attractively decorated long bar, enjoyable food inc local fish, real ales, up to 11 wines by the glass, small no smoking area and conservatory restaurant, and efficient friendly service; bdrms; cl 2 wks Jan. £30|**£7.50**

CAWSTON TG1422 **Ratcatchers** *Easton Way, Eastgate (01603) 871430* Bustling, warmly welcoming dining pub with open fire and nice mix of wooden tables and chairs in L-shaped beamed bar, quiet and cosy no smoking candlelit dining room and no smoking conservatory, huge choice of good freshly prepared food inc interesting fresh fish dishes, real ales, and a nice wine list; cl 26 Dec; disabled access. £25|**£8**

ERPINGHAM TG1732 **Saracens Head** *Wolterton (01263) 768909* Comfortably civilised inn with simple but stylish two-room bar, a nice mix of seats, log fires and fresh flowers, excellent inventive food, very well kept real ales, interesting wines, and a charming old-fashioned gravel stableyard; good bdrms; cl 25 Dec; limited disabled access. £24.75|£8

HOLT TG0738 **Owl Tea Rooms** *White Lion St (01263) 713232* Georgian building with bakery and tearooms behind, serving home-made bread, scones, quiches and pies on plates made by the owners; organic local veg, daily specials and vegetarian choices, home-made preserves, and good cream teas; cl Sun, bank hols; disabled access. £15|£4

LITTLE WALSINGHAM TF9336 **Old Bakehouse** *33 High St (01328) 820454* In an attractive medieval village, this Georgian-fronted house has high beams in the main restaurant, a smaller dining room with a brick oven dating from 1550, and downstairs bar; enjoyable cooking every evening for residents (open to non-residents Fri and Sat evenings only) with plenty of choice, and reasonably priced french wines; bdrms; cl 2 wks Jan, 1 wk Jun, 1 wk Nov. £30

NORWICH TG2208 **Adlards** *79 Upper St Giles St (01603) 633522* Warmly friendly and quietly decorated restaurant serving delicious, carefully thought out food from a menu that changes daily, lovely puddings, fine service, and good wine list; cl Sun, Mon am, 1 wk after Christmas; disabled access. £45/2-course lunch £15

SNETTISHAM TF6834 **Rose & Crown** *Old Church Rd (01485) 541382* Pretty white cottage with boldly decorated no smoking Cellar Bar, cheerfully painted Garden Room, and unchanging back bar; log fires, several real ales, around 20 wines by the glass, and very good imaginative food (super puddings); lovely walled garden with wooden play fort, guinea-pigs and chipmunks; lovely bdrms; well behaved dogs welcome; partial disabled access. £30|£7

ST OLAVES TM4599 **Priory Farm** *Beccles Rd (01493) 488432* Good interesting food inc fresh fish and children's menu; right by St Olaves Priory; open all day Jun-Sept (normal hours the rest of the year), but cl 26-30 Dec; disabled access. £17|£4.95

STOW BARDOLPH TF6205 **Hare Arms** *Lynn Rd (01366) 382229* Pretty, creeper-covered pub with old advertising signs, fresh flowers, plenty of tables around its central servery, and a good log fire in welcoming bar; maybe two friendly ginger cats and a sort of tabby; spacious, heated and well planted no smoking conservatory, good interesting food, well kept real ales, a decent range of wines, and quite a few malt whiskies; pretty garden with picnic-sets and wandering peacocks and chickens; cl 25-26 and 31 Dec; children in conservatory and family room only. £26|£8.45

SWANTON MORLEY TG0217 **Darbys** *Elsing Rd (01362) 637647* Cosy beamed country pub (carefully converted farm cottages) decorated with lots of farm tools and so forth, up to eight very well kept real ales, and good, generously served, often interesting bar food; log fire, friendly staff, children's room and adventure playground; also bdrms, self-catering, camping, caravan site, horse facilities, country trails; cl pm 25 Dec; disabled access. £22|£6.75

UPPER SHERINGHAM TG1542 **Red Lion** *The Street (01263) 825408* Relaxing little flint cottage with two quiet small bars, simple furnishings, a big woodburner, newspapers to read, and no smoking snug; good enjoyable food and well kept real ales; a new dining conservatory and bdrms; disabled access. £22|£5

Special thanks to Michael and Jenny Back, Ian Martin, Ben Dyson

NORTHAMPTONSHIRE

The big draws here are great mansions, fine churches and pretty villages, in appealing countryside - all rather grown-up, though families can track down some entertaining outings

Northamptonshire has more than its fair share of grand houses in beautiful surroundings - we've even chosen one as our Northamptonshire Family Attraction, mainly on the strength of its lively bank holiday special events: Holdenby House, Gardens & Falconry Centre. Also appealing for all ages including children are Sulgrave Manor, and richly furnished Boughton House. For other fine houses and gardens head for Althorp, Canons Ashby, Cottesbrooke, Coton and Lamport. Lyveden New Bield near Oundle and Rushton's Triangular Lodge (designed by the same man) are unique, and Prebendal Manor House in Nassington is impressively old. Opening in spring, 78 Derngate in Northampton will please fans of Rennie Mackintosh. There are interesting ruins at Kirby Hall near Deene.

Children enjoy the amusement park in Kettering; families who like animals can choose between the Old Dairy Farm Centre in Upper Stowe and the West Lodge Rural Centre in Desborough. Stoke Bruerne with its canal museum is the place to head for boat trips. Rockingham Forest is good for letting off steam (don't miss the castle).

The countryside of this archetypal shire is very relaxing, with gently appealing partly wooded landscapes, villages built of red or honey-coloured stone, and the fine churches of the Nene Valley.

Where to stay

BADBY SP5558 **Windmill** *Main St, Badby, Daventry, Northamptonshire NN11 3AN (01327) 702363* **£69.50**, plus special breaks; 10 rms. Carefully modernised and warmly welcoming thatched stone inn with beams, flagstones and huge inglenook fireplace in front bar, a cosy comfortable lounge, a relaxed and civilised atmosphere, good generously served bar and restaurant food, and decent wines; fine views of the pretty village from car park; disabled access; dogs welcome

CRANFORD SP9277 **Dairy Farm** *12 St. Andrews Lane, Cranford, Kettering, Northamptonshire NN14 4AQ (01536) 330273* **£50**; 4 comfortable rms. Charming 17th-c manor house of great character on an arable and sheep farm, with oak beams and inglenook fireplaces, good homely cooking using home-grown fruit and vegetables, kind, attentive owners, and garden with charming summer house and ancient dovecote; no smoking; cl Christmas; partial disabled access; dogs in annexe ☺

EAST HADDON SP6668 **Red Lion** *Main St, East Haddon, Northampton, Northamptonshire NN6 8BU (01604) 770223* **£75**; 5 rms. Rather elegant and substantial golden stone hotel with a smart, well heeled feel in the neat lounge bar, a nice mix of furniture, recessed china cabinets, old prints and pewter, and small public bar with well kept real ales and decent wines; pretty restaurant, high quality daily-changing food, and enjoyable breakfasts; attractive walled garden; 25 Dec

OLD SP7873 **Wold Farm** *Harrington Rd, Old, Northampton, Northamptonshire NN6 9RJ (01604) 781258* **£56**; 5 rms. No smoking 18th-c farmhouse in a quiet village, with spacious interesting rooms, antiques and fine china, hearty breakfasts in the beamed dining room, attentive welcoming owners, snooker table, and two pretty gardens; dogs welcome in bedrooms

OUNDLE TL0488 **Talbot** *New St, Oundle, Peterborough, Cambridgeshire PE8 4EA (01832) 273621* **£95**, plus special breaks; 39 most attractive rms. Mary, Queen of Scots walked to her execution down a staircase that's now in this carefully refurbished 17th-c hotel; attractive cosy lounge, big log fire, good food in timbered restaurant, and garden

PAULERSPURY SP7245 **Vine House** *100 High St, Paulerspury, Towcester, Northamptonshire NN12 7NA (01327) 811267* **£85***; 6 individually decorated rms. 300-year-old building with carefully preserved original features, a relaxed welcoming atmosphere, cosy bar with open fire, and very good modern english cooking (inc home-made bread and petits fours) in attractive restaurant; pretty cottage garden; cl 1 wk over Christmas; partial disabled access

To see and do

Northamptonshire Family Attraction of the Year

HOLDENBY SP6967 **Holdenby House, Gardens & Falconry Centre** With the exception of reliable old Wicksteed Park, most of the attractions in this county have perhaps most appeal to adults rather than children, so the very well organised bank holiday activities at this splendid former palace are quite a surprise. On the other days when parts of the estate are open (quite limited, see below), younger visitors will probably get most enjoyment from the falconry centre, but on bank holiday Sundays and Mondays they'll find special events with lots geared specially to them. These are generally fairly large-scale historical reconstructions, with costumed characters bringing various periods to life. As we went to press the timetable for 2004 hadn't been finalised, but was expected to follow the pattern of previous years: a Victorian theme on Easter Sunday and Monday, a return to the time of the Wars of the Roses over the first May bank holiday, a big plant fair with children's activities on the second, and a falconry festival in August; best to ring for exact details. On the afternoon of bank holiday Mondays you can look around the house, with its collection of rare and unusual pianos. At one stage Holdenby was eight times the size it is now, and the largest house in Elizabethan England. It was a Royal palace for part of the 17th c, and subsequently a prison, holding the captured King Charles I at the end of the Civil War. It's been at the heart of national affairs for centuries; the family that live here (the Lowthers) have produced more MPs than any other clan. The 20-acre gardens are lovely, with an Elizabethan-style garden laid out by Rosemary Verey that includes only plants that would have been grown in 1580. They've a splendid collection of birds of prey, with regular flying displays of buzzards, owls and kestrels. Teas and shop; (01604) 770074. The gardens and falconry centre are open Sun pm Easter-Sept, and pm daily mid-July to Aug. On non-event days admission is £4.50 for adults, £3 for children and £12 for a family ticket (two adults, two children); on bank holiday Sun event days it's £5 adults, £4 children and £16 families, and on bank hol Mons (when the house is open too) it's £6 adults, £4 children and £18 families.

ALTHORP SP6864

The home of the Spencer family since 1508, remodelled several times, especially in the 17th and 18th c, with a splendid collection of furnishings and porcelain, paintings by Rubens, Van Dyck and Lely; three rooms have been newly opened inc the chapel. The staff are particularly pleasant and helpful. It is of course the resting place of Diana, Princess of Wales. You can't see the grave itself (it's on an islet in the Oval Lake in a small arboretum just NE of the house), but you can view the lake, and the former stable block is now a museum/memorial filled with her personal possessions, favourite clothes inc bridal gown, and audio-visual displays.

Snacks, shop, good disabled access in many parts; open daily July-Sept (cl 31 Aug), but advance booking recommended; (0870) 167 9000; £10.50. The attractive **church** is on the edge of the park; its graveyard has fine views. On the far side of the estate there's public access to a sandy-floored area of wildlife-filled pine woods and heathland known as Harlestone Firs, pleasant for walking. The village of Great Brington is charming, and the Fox & Hounds here has lots of character; there's enjoyable food at the Old Saracens Head in Little Brington.

ASHBY ST LEDGERS SP5768
This village is quite a gem: fine manor house, Lutyens almshouses, and a remarkable church with wall paintings, pre-Reformation pews and triple-decker pulpit (few signs of interference by the Reformers, Cromwell or even the Victorians). The Olde Coach House is an interesting food pub.

BADBY SP5559
Knightley Way This path takes a pleasant 12-mile course from the attractive village of Badby, through an area where gorgeous orange-coloured stone adds to the charm of buildings; it's well waymarked to Greens Norton. The finest part is between Badby Wood and Fawsley Park, where the path drops to landscaped lakes by the hall and estate church. In May the Badby Wood bluebells are lovely. The Windmill is a good food stop.

BLISWORTH SP7253
Grand Union Canal The towpath is popular for country walks, with access among other places from the thatched Royal Oak here and the New Inn at Buckby Wharf SP6065.

BOROUGH HILL SP5962
This gives the best views in the region, from above the golf course; an Iron Age hill fort shares the top with a formidable array of television and telecommunications masts, but on a clear day the views are tremendous.

BOUGHTON SP8981
Boughton House 🏛 (SE of Geddington) Impressively grand old place, sometimes compared to Versailles (some of its treasures were in fact made for there). Richly furnished and decorated, with gorgeous mythical scenes painted on the ceilings, and

works by El Greco, Van Dyck, Murillo and Caracci lining the walls. Excellent armoury, beautiful parklands, and adventure playground and plant shop. Snacks, shop, disabled access; grounds open pm Sat-Thurs May-July (daily pm Aug), house pm Aug only, or by appointment; (01536) 515731; £6, grounds only £1.50.

BRIGSTOCK SP9485
The **church** has a Saxon tower, and a bell that used to be rung three times a day to help anyone lost in the woods; the Green Dragon is useful for food.
Fermyn Wood Country Park is good for a wander, especially around the wildlife-filled woods on the edge; it can be a little muddy; a visitor centre and shop are usually open pm school hols and wknds; (01536) 373625; £1 parking charge.

BRIXWORTH SP7471
Brixworth church Particularly fine Anglo-Saxon church, one of England's oldest - mostly 7th-c with much reused Roman material. It's an attractive village, and the Coach & Horses has enjoyable food.
Pitsford Water (just E) Praised for bird-watching, esp in winter when wildfowl flock to the N part of the lake; the S part is popular for fishing. The partly thatched White Swan across at Holcot has decent food.

CANONS ASHBY SP5750
Canons Ashby House (B4525) Exceptional little manor house, more northern-looking than Midlands, beautifully restored with Elizabethan wall paintings and glorious Jacobean plasterwork. The formal gardens have also been carefully restored over the last 20 years, and now closely reflect the layout of the early 18th c. A reasonably sized park has a hilltop 12th/14th-c priory church. Cottage garden tearoom, shop; house open pm Sun-Weds Apr-Oct (plus Sat Oct), garden open Sat-Weds Apr-Oct, plus wknds Nov-19 Dec; (01327) 860044; *£5.60, *£2 garden only; NT. The Royal Oak at Eydon is handy for lunch (not Mon).

CASTLE ASHBY SP8659
Castle Ashby House Only the gardens can be visited, but the house is well worth seeing from outside - a splendidly palatial Elizabethan building

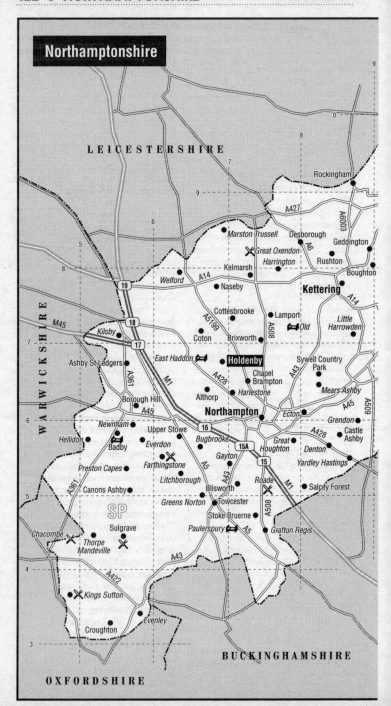

Northamptonshire

LEICESTERSHIRE

9

0

8

Rockingham

A427

7

A6003

9

Marston Trussell   Desborough   Geddington

Great Oxendon   Harrington   Rushton

Kelmarsh   Boughton

6   Welford   A14   Naseby   **Kettering**   A14

Cottesbrooke   Lamport   Little Harrowden

A5199   A508   Old

5   Coton   Brixworth

8   Kilsby   Sywell Country Park

M45   East Haddon   **Holdenby**

WARWICKSHIRE   18   A43   A509

19   Ashby St Ledgers   Chapel Brampton

17   A361   Althorp   Harlestone   Mears Ashby

Borough Hill   M1   A428   A45

A45   **Northampton**   Ecton   Grendon

6   Newnham   Upper Stowe   Bugbrooke   Great Houghton   Castle Ashby

Hellidon   16   A428   Denton

Badby   Everdon   15A   Gayton   Yardley Hastings

Preston Capes   Farthingstone   A5   15   Salcey Forest

A361   Litchborough   A43   Roade   M1

5   Canons Ashby   Blisworth

SP   Greens Norton   Towcester   A508

Sulgrave   Stoke Bruerne

Chacombe   Paulerspury   A5   Grafton Regis

Thorpe Mandeville

A43

4   A422

Kings Sutton

Evenley

3   Croughton

BUCKINGHAMSHIRE

OXFORDSHIRE

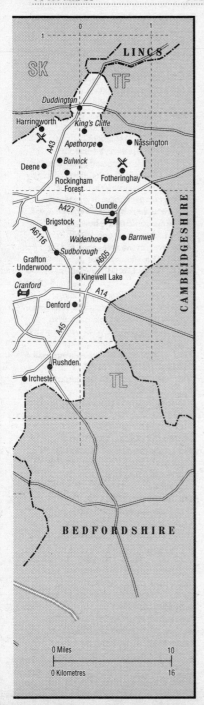

at the end of a magnificent mile-long avenue planted nearly 300 years ago. The gardens include grand Victorian terraces, sweeping lawns, italianate gardens with an orangery, and lakeside parkland that counts among Capability Brown's finest achievements. Plant centre; cl 25 Dec; (01604) 696187; £2.50. The **church**, within the park, is very attractive; there's a public path to it. Restored farm buildings nearby house a **Craft Centre and Rural Shopping Yard** with a good food shop (lots of different beers), and tearoom; cl Mon exc bank hols. The Falcon in the handsomely preserved estate village has nice food and bedrooms, and the drive through Cogenhoe, Whiston, Grendon and Easton Maudit is pleasant.

CHAPEL BRAMPTON SP7366 **Northampton & Lamport Railway** (Pitsford Rd) Enthusiastic little railway, static viewing pm, and usually short train rides Sun and bank hols (not Jan-Feb). Snacks in a restored buffet car, shop; (01604) 820327; £3.30, £6 special events. Its name is a proud commitment to growth northwards, but for the time being the 14-mile walk and cycle way through pretty countryside by the line is a very pleasant foretaste. The Brampton Halt here has decent food.

COTON SP6771 **Coton Manor** (off A428) Attractive views from charming gardens around 17th-c stone-built manor house (not open); interesting plantings, and water gardens with flamingos, cranes and ornamental waterfowl wandering freely. The wood is lovely at bluebell time. Grooms Cottage in the converted stables does really good light lunches, there are interesting plant sales, and disabled access; open pm Tues-Sat Apr-Sept; (01604) 740219; *£4.

COTTESBROOKE SP7174 **Cottesbrooke Hall** Very attractive Queen Anne house, reputedly the model for Jane Austen's Mansfield Park, with a renowned collection of mainly sporting and equestrian paintings. The lovely garden has formal borders, venerable cedars, a statue walk and extensive wild gardens. Teas, unusual plant sales, disabled access to gardens only; open pm Weds, Thurs 5 May-Jun, pm Thurs July-Sept, and bank hol Mons;

(01604) 505808; £6, garden only £4.

CROUGHTON SP5433

Croughton church Handsome church well worth a visit for its unusual murals, dating from the 14th and 15th c. The Cartwright Arms over in the pleasant village of Aynho does good food.

DEENE SP9592

Deene Park (off A43) Lord Cardigan who led the Charge of the Light Brigade used to live in this beautifully kept partly Tudor house; there's a high-spirited contemporary portrait of him in full attack gallop, and other memorabilia from the Crimean War. Rooms shown are used by family and friends. Extensive parklands with woodside and lakeside walks, and gardens reflecting continuing interest by the owners over the generations. Cream teas, shop, disabled access to ground floor and garden; open Sun pm Jun-Aug, plus Sun and Mon of bank hol wknds Easter-Aug; (01780) 450278/450223; £5.50, £3 gardens only. The Queens Head opposite the church in the pretty village of Bulwick has good food.

Kirby Hall (W) This splendid ruined Elizabethan mansion has a bizarre mix of styles and design; from some angles it still looks intact - even close up. The 17th-c garden was restored fairly recently, and it's a tranquil spot for a picnic. Shop, disabled access; cl wkdys Nov-Mar; (01536) 203230; £3.50 (inc audio tour); EH.

DENFORD SP9976

Denford church Charming in any event (like so many other churches along this river valley); doubly worth a visit for its nature-reserve churchyard by the River Nene, with waterside walks from here. The Cock is an attractive place for lunch.

DESBOROUGH SP8184

West Lodge Rural Centre Based around a working farm (so you can watch them at work) with a pets corner, indoor and outdoor play areas, tractor rides and a little museum; the nature trail has a few interactive sculptures for children. Meals, snacks, shop, disabled access; cl 24 Dec-Feb half-term; (01536) 760552; £3.50.

FOTHERINGHAY TL0793

Lovely village with interesting historical displays in the charming if slightly out-of-proportion 14th-c **church** across a watermeadow from the River Nene. It was part of a small pre-Reformation college and doubles as a memorial to the House of York, with some interesting heraldry. There's only a fragment left of the **castle** where Richard III was born, and 135 years later Mary, Queen of Scots was executed. The Falcon is excellent for lunch.

GEDDINGTON SP8982

The very well preserved elaborate 13th-c cross was erected by Edward I where Queen Eleanor's funeral cortège rested on its way to Westminster. The photogenic packhorse bridge is even older, and there's a 12th-c church. There are some pretty buildings made of the brown ironstone once quarried extensively in the area - look out for tracks of old railway lines.

GRAFTON UNDERWOOD SP9280

Pretty street of old stone buildings, roadside stream with seats for watching (or feeding) its ducks; pleasant drive from here to Oundle, via Brigstock and then the woods and open parkland of Fermyn Woods around the ancient Hall.

HARRINGWORTH SP9197

This attractive village is famous for its 82-arch **railway viaduct**. The imposing Tudor White Swan has good food and comfortable bedrooms.

HOLDENBY SP6967

Holdenby House, Gardens & Falconry Centre See separate family panel on p.420.

The civilised Red Lion over in East Haddon has good food.

IRCHESTER SP9265

Irchester Country Park (Gypsy Lane, Little Irchester) 200 acres of lovely woodland with nature trails, picnic sites, children's play area and even a railway museum (Sun only). The visitor centre has snacks, shop, disabled access and is open school hols and wknds; (01933) 276866; £1.50 all-day parking.

KELMARSH SP7379

Kelmarsh Hall (A508) James Gibbs designed this splendid Palladian-style house in the early 18th c; the most interesting features are the chinese room and double storey entrance hall. In the charming grounds the lake and triangular kitchen garden walls date from the 18th c, with other formal features added in the 20th, inc an 18th-c orangery that was moved here in the 1950s. A former owner bred the famous british white cattle whose descendants still graze the parkland. Tearoom, disabled access; house and gardens open pm Sun Easter-5 Sept, Thurs in Aug and bank hol Mons; *£4.50, gardens open Mon-Thurs pm Easter-Sept; *£3.50. The Stags Head at Maidwell (A508 S) is a pleasant food stop.

KETTERING SP8678

Manor House Museum (Sheep St) Worth a look if passing, with free monthly family event days, children's activities in school hols, and a famous mummified cat. Meals and snacks, shop and disabled access; cl Sun and bank hols; (01536) 534219; free. The adjacent **Alfred East Gallery** has a private collection and works for sale; cl Sun and bank hols; (01536) 534274.

Wicksteed Park (off A6, S outskirts) Big amusement park, one of the first of its type, set up in 1921 when they introduced boating on the lake. While several other original features still remain, in recent years they've tried to bring the park more up to date without spoiling its character - it's still relatively low-key compared to some leisure parks: though they have a roller-coaster, thrill rides here are mainly of the dodg'ems and pirate ship type. Lots of good rides for under-12s (some have height restrictions), inc a ladybird roller-coaster. The grounds are very pleasant for a stroll, with a pitch and putt course, various well laid out gardens, and an aviary. Younger children have a good big playground. Meals, snacks, shop, disabled access; open Easter-Oct, and for special events; (01536) 512475; £5 parking charge (less out of season, or after 3pm), then you buy vouchers for the rides (from 90p each), or a wristband for a day's unlimited rides for £12.50 children, £8.50 adults.

KINEWELL LAKE SP9979

Well managed local **nature reserve** around former gravel-pit lakes by the River Nene; pleasant walks. The Woolpack at Islip is an attractive food pub.

LAMPORT SP7574

Lamport Hall (A508) Mainly 17th-

and 18th-c house in spacious park, with tranquil gardens containing a remarkable alpine rockery - the home of the first garden gnomes, only one of which now survives. Frequent antiques fairs, concerts and other events. Snacks, shop, disabled access to ground floor and gardens; open pm Sun Easter-Oct; guided tours 2.30, 3.15 and 4pm, plus daily at 2.30pm in Aug, and on bank hols; (01604) 686272; £4.50. The Swan, with great views, has had good value food (we've had no reports since its recent management change).

NASEBY SP6877

Battle of Naseby Model Model of the crucial Civil War battle set out by the owner of Purlieu Farm, using many hundreds of model soldiers, with a 10-minute commentary; open bank hol Sun and Mon pms, and by appointment, (01604) 740241; £2. The nearby Fitzgerald Arms is a good value dining pub. One battle monument (Sibbertoft Rd) marks the position of Cromwell's New Model Army before his devastating counter-attack; there's another on the B4036 towards Clipston (this road from W Haddon and on to Market Harborough in Leics gives a good feel of rural Northants).

NASSINGTON TL0696

Prebendal Manor House The oldest surviving dwelling in the county, dating from the early 13th c, the manor forms the focus of a group of stone buildings inc a dovecote and tithe barn. Standing on the site of one of King Cnut's Saxon halls, it was used as a residence for influential prebends of Lincoln Cathedral. The six-acre re-created medieval garden has herbers, turf seats, arbours, fishponds, a vineyard and a nut walk; also medieval vegetable and pleasure gardens. A medieval model farm has geese, hens, ducks, pigs and sheep. Activities for children, inc dressing up, quill pen writing and medieval games. Good views of the village and River Nene. Snacks, shop, some disabled access; open pms Weds and Sun Easter Mon-Sept and bank hols; (01780) 782575; *£5. The Black Horse is a civilised dining pub.

NORTHAMPTON SP7560

This prosperous town these days owes much more to service industries such as Barclaycard, and the transport firms whose huge warehouses now ring it, than the declining shoemaking industry for which it has been famous. There are several fine **churches**, most notably the 12th-c Holy Sepulchre (one of only four remaining round churches in the country), the very grand central All Saints, and the ornate Norman St Peter's in Marefair right by the dual carriageway. The Welsh House and Hazelrigg House also recall the long-gone time when Daniel Defoe was able to call this one of the most handsome towns in England. A social history museum in Abington Park is set in the 15th-c home of Shakespeare's granddaughter; cl am and Mon, plus bank hols; (01604) 631454; free. The Malt Shovel (Bridge St) has good value food, though its forte is beer.

78 Derngate Charles Rennie Mackintosh's last completed project; he transformed this little Georgian house for W J Bassett-Lowke in 1916/17. Next door are displays on the house, its owner and Charles Rennie Mackintosh. Shop, partial disabled access. It's due to open around Mar, and entrance will be by timed ticket (you need to book in advance); phone for more information, or visit their website www.78derngate.org.uk; (01604) 603407.

Northampton Museum (Guildhall Rd) Home to an enormous collection of boots and shoes, inc an elephant's boot, Margot Fonteyn's ballet shoes, Roman sandals, and Queen Victoria's wedding slippers; they've recently added two new galleries - one has displays on shoe fashions, and the other concentrates on shoe-making. Also local history and arts, and the tourist information centre is here too. Shop, disabled access; cl Sun am, 25-26 Dec, 1 Jan; (01604) 838111; free.

OUNDLE TL0488
Charming and elegant stone-built town with a graceful church, a fine old public school, a busy Thurs market day, and a farmers' market (2nd Sat in month). The comfortable Rose & Crown (Market Pl) has imaginative food.

Barnwell Country Park (just S) A good spot for a walk, with a variety of birds; disabled access on gravel paths; parking £1.50 (free for disabled drivers, who can drive right up to the lake). The waterside Mill is a pleasant place for lunch.

Lyveden New Bield 🔢 (out towards Brigstock) This incomplete Elizabethan garden lodge was abandoned in 1605 after the owner, Sir Thomas Tresham, died in debt. Intriguing and unusual, it was intended to celebrate the Passion of Christ, and is shaped like a greek cross. The moated Elizabethan garden, thought to be one of Britain's oldest, includes a young orchard which has recently been planted with period varieties following the details of a letter written by Sir Thomas Tresham from prison. Snacks, shop; cl Mon (exc bank hols), and Tues, plus Weds-Fri Nov-Mar; (01832) 205358; *£2.50; NT. It's a half-mile walk from the car park, but has disabled parking next to the house.

ROCKINGHAM SP8691
Rockingham Castle 🔢 (A6003) Henry VIII granted the fortress to Edward Watson (ancestor of the present owner), who converted it into a comfortable Tudor house. It's a lovely old place, tucked away behind the original Norman curtain wall - obviously quite an effective defence, as the castle was able to resist repeated assaults in the Civil War. The outline of the two baileys and the drum towers survive, and the later building has a good range of furnishings and art inc 20th-c pictures. With fine views of five counties, the ramparts enclose 12 acres of lawns, formal and informal gardens, a circular rose garden on the site of the old keep, and a wild garden in the ravine below containing over 200 species of trees and shrubs, many rare. Meals, snacks, shop, limited disabled access; open pm Sun and bank hols Apr-Sept, plus pm Tues and Thurs July-Aug; (01536) 770240; £6, garden only £4. The Sondes Arms has enjoyable food and super views.

ROCKINGHAM FOREST SP9892
Pleasant back roads through the former Forest of Rockingham give quiet views of a particularly attractive area of the county. This part is good for walks, too, with enough country houses scattered around it to spice interest, the odd red kite now and then, and grey-stone cottages - a local feature. If you follow the yellow signs you'll get the best kite views, and a visitor centre at Fineshade Woods has CCTV viewing (and usually a warden on hand to answer questions); also guided walks and events, and a

good range of leaflets; (01780) 444098. Forest Enterprise is gradually recreating what the forest would have looked like when it was a Royal hunting forest by taking out the conifers and putting back indigenous trees. Around the edges the Queens Head in attractive Bulwick (interesting church) and White Swan at Woodnewton are well worth knowing for their food.

RUSHDEN SP9567

Rushden Station Transport Museum Steam trains run along the 400 yards of track on occasional special event wknds Jun-Sept. There's a little museum and a newly restored signal box, with Ginger the station cat keeping his eye on things; summer Sun 10-3; donations. If you ask nicely they may sign you into the charming member's bar, which is authentically lit by gas lamps and full of Victorian memorabilia. (01933) 318988.

RUSHTON SP8388

East Carlton Country Park 100 acres with pleasant strolls, children's play area and café.

Triangular Lodge (1m W) One of England's most unusual buildings, this 16th-c oddity was designed and built by Sir Thomas Tresham (also responsible for Lyveden New Bield nr Oundle). Purposely intriguing and infuriating, it's covered in the symbolism of Tresham's Roman Catholic beliefs - notably three levels, three walls, three windows, three triangular gables and a three-sided chimney, to represent the Holy Trinity. Shop, limited disabled access; cl Nov-Mar; (01536) 710761; £2; EH. In the attractive village, opposite the cricket green, the Thornhill Arms has good value food inc OAP bargains.

SALCEY FOREST SP8051

A couple of miles of ancient forest, largely oak, now managed for nature conservation, with well marked trails inc one good for wheelchairs. The thatched White Hart in nearby Stoke Goldington has good value food.

STOKE BRUERNE SP7449

Canal Museum 🎫 Close to a flight of locks on the Grand Union Canal, with fine old canal buildings (inc a popular pub, the Boat), and lots happening on the water, this handsome former corn mill houses a good collection of canal memorabilia, inc a reconstructed tradi-

tional narrowboat cabin complete with immaculately packed-in colourful furniture and crockery. Shop; cl Mon Oct-Easter; (01604) 862229; £3. Boat trips run from the museum to a nearby tunnel; cl Nov-Mar, phone for times (01604) 862107; £2.

SULGRAVE SP5545

Sulgrave Manor (off B4525) The ancestral home of George Washington's family, this modest manor is exceptional for families during their regular living history events, when the whole place returns to how it would have been during a particular period - Viking or Stuart, say. People in period costume go about their daily business, and there are regular special events (phone for details). Worth a visit too on non-event days, when they do guided tours. As well as elegant rooms and well kept gardens, there are several relics of Washington, though he never lived here - it was his great-great-grandfather who emigrated to America; outdoor theatre in late July. Snacks, shop, some disabled access; open pm Apr-Oct and wknds Dec, cl Mon and Fri (exc bank hols or during events); (01295) 760205; £6.50 on event days, otherwise £5. Just down the road, the Star is enjoyable for lunch.

SYWELL COUNTRY PARK SP8365 (off A4500) Woodland and lakeside walks, play areas, and a little wildlife display; you can fish on the lake - in fact a reservoir - with tickets in advance (01904) 479797; £8 for a day. An information foyer (open all year) leads into a small visitor centre (usually open pm wknds and school hols) with snacks and shop; (01604) 810970; £1.50 car park. The Griffins Head on the edge of Mears Ashby has bargain food.

TOWCESTER SP6948

This small town (pronounced Toaster) has quite a pleasantly villagey feel, and some attractive Georgian and Victorian buildings. Peggottys (Fosters Booth, A5 N) is an enjoyable food stop.

UPPER STOWE SP6456

Old Dairy Farm Centre Peacocks, ducks and donkeys, as well as craft workshops, galleries, antiques, plant nursery, gift and farm shop, and wool collection. Well organised, and decent views - though be prepared for it to be mpogue##

muddy. Restaurant, snacks, shop, disabled access; cl two wks from 25 Dec; (01327) 340525; free, exc special wknds. **Other attractive villages**, all with decent pubs, include Apethorpe TL0295, Barnwell TL0484, canalside Bugbrooke SP6757, Bulwick SP9694 (interesting church), Denton SP8358, Duddington SK9800, Ecton SP8263, Evenley SP5834, Farthingstone SP6155 (Knightley Way walks), Gayton SP7054, thatched Grafton Regis SP7546, Great Houghton SP7958, Greens Norton SP6649 (Grafton Way walks), Grendon SP8760, Harlestone SP7064, Harrington SP7779, Hellidon SP5158 (pleasant walks nearby), Kilsby SP5671, Kings Sutton SP4936, Litchborough SP6353, Little Harrowden SP8671, Marston Trussell SP6985, Mears Ashby SP8466 (narrow lanes of thatched cottages), Nassington TL0696, Newnham SP5859, Sudborough SP9682, Thorpe Mandeville SP5344, riverside Wadenhoe TL0383, Welford SP6480 and Yardley Hastings SP8656. We'd also recommend rather Cotswoldy King's Cliffe TL0097, and Preston Capes SP5754 and Everdon SP5957.

Where to eat

CHACOMBE SP4943 **George & Dragon** / Silver St (01295) 711500 Handy for the M40, this charming village pub has a tidy spacious bar with comfortable seats, beams, flagstones, and logs burning in a massive fireplace, real ales, a wide range of good imaginative food from a changing blackboard (also, afternoon snacks and teas), and friendly and attentive service; bdrms; cl Sun pm. £24|**£5.50**

FARTHINGSTONE SP6155 **Kings Arms** Main St (01327) 361604 In a pretty village, this handsome 18th-c stone building has comfortable sofas and armchairs, lots of decorative plates and pictures, spacious dining area, a good choice of cheeses (the only food they serve apart from winter soup), well kept real ales, decent wines and friendly licensees; nearby walks; cl Mon, Weds; disabled access.|**£6.50**

FOTHERINGHAY TL0793 **Falcon** (01832) 226254 Stylish but relaxed old country dining pub with a good mix of customers, no smoking conservatory and dining room, and little tap bar for locals; excellent food from a varied menu, well kept real ales, and a fine wine list; neat garden; disabled access. £27.50|**£8.50**

GREAT OXENDON SP7383 **George** Harborough Rd (01858) 465205 Though rather gaunt-looking, inside this carefully decorated dining pub is really cosy and convivial; two opened-together rooms of the main beamed bar have attractive prints and engravings, and there's a no smoking conservatory overlooking the shrub-sheltered garden; very good food (well liked by older lunchers especially), well kept real ales, decent wines; cl Sun pm; disabled access. £25.50|**£8.50**

HARRINGWORTH SP9197 **White Swan** Seaton Rd (01572) 747543 Neatly kept stone-built Tudor pub with generous helpings of enjoyable food, and friendly licensees; bdrms; cl Mon am, 25 Dec, 1 Jan; disabled access. £27|**£8.95**

KINGS SUTTON SP4936 **White Horse** 2 The Square (01295) 810843 Attractive village pub, stylishly modernised, with beams, timbers and some exposed brickwork around the fireplace, chunky tables and chairs and good pictures; two no smoking rooms for eating in, both with flagstoned floors and wooden tables with thick candles; particularly good elaborate food as well as some pubby dishes, obliging service, well kept real ales and a carefully chosen wine list with ten by the glass; picnic-sets overlooking village green. £24.75|**£6.95**

ROADE SP7551 **Roade House** 16 High St (01604) 863372 Smart and popular restaurant-with-rooms with comfortable surroundings, courteous service, reliably enjoyable food using first class ingredients, and reasonably priced wines; cl pm Sun, Sat am, 1 wk Christmas; disabled access. £35/2-course lunch £16

SULGRAVE SP5545 **Star** Manor Rd (01295) 760389 Hospitable, creeper-covered pub with small pews, cushioned window seats and wall benches on polished flagstones, good seasonal food, friendly staff, lots to look at, well kept real ales, and no smoking restaurant; bdrms; cl Sun pm, 26 Dec; disabled access. £25|**£6.95**

Special thanks to Michael and Jenny Back

NORTHUMBRIA

**Great holiday opportunities, excellent value: magnificent
untouched scenery, formidable castles and England's Great Wall,
and some outstanding family attractions**

If you're interested in the visible past, you'll find an awful lot to keep you busy in Northumbria. The awesome 73½-mile, 2,000-year-old Hadrian's Wall is the most obvious draw, and the Roman forts, museums and visitor centres along the way add greatly to its appeal (the ones we like most are lively Segedunum and the full-scale reconstructions at Vindolanda). If you prefer more recent history, the North of England Open-Air Museum at Beamish is an astonishing reconstruction of North of England life a century or two ago - a great day out. The interesting historic quay at Hartlepool has enough for a whole day's outing, too.

The most impressive of an abundance of fine castles are massive Bamburgh (the stately home is a nice surprise), Alnwick (the second-largest inhabited castle in the country), perfect-looking Raby in Staindrop, striking Chillingham with its ancient half-wild white cattle, and Bishop Auckland (the main residence of the mighty medieval Prince Bishops of Durham). The massive ruins in Embleton are haunting, and Warkworth Castle is pretty. Fine houses (and gardens) we'd highlight are magnificent Cragside in Rothbury (spectacular rooms), Belsay Hall and Gardens (in the same family for 600 years), and Washington Old Hall (17th-c furniture and paintings). At pleasant Barnard Castle you'll find a treasure-trove of fine arts in a beautiful french-style chateau, and an elegant 18th-c villa (some interesting ruins too).

Newcastle has some excellent child-friendly museums (the Newcastle Discovery centre is this year's top Family Attraction), and can be a lively place for adults, too; across the water, Gateshead benefits from some worthwhile rejuvenation projects. The beautiful ancient city of Durham has plenty of sightseeing possibilities. With its National Glass Centre and Sunderland Museum and Winter Gardens, Sunderland is good for an afternoon visit.

Animal-orientated outings include farm parks near Stannington and Berwick-upon-Tweed and, for wilder creatures, there's the Otter Trust near Bowes. More specialist attractions include the profusion of railway centres scattered around George Stephenson's homeland, and we've this year added a fishing museum in Alnwick. If Britain's emergence from the Dark Ages holds any fascination for you, tracing Christianity's early steps through this area will lead you to lots of interesting and beautiful places; good places to begin are the island of Lindisfarne, and Bede's World in Jarrow.

The coast has majestic stretches, with a path along the finest sections. If beaches as fine as these had mediterranean sunshine, you'd never be able to drag yourself away. Even the miles of extraordinary black sand beaches in the south of the area have been cleaned up, and graced with sculptures and visitor facilities: this coast is cleaner than it's been for centuries. Inland are great sweeps of largely unspoilt upland scenery, quiet and uncrowded even in summer; Kielder Water and the forest around it have plenty to fill active days out. Peaceful lower landscapes are enlivened by streams and woodland, solid stone country buildings, and unhurried small market towns. The area is very good both for walking and for driving, with the least traffic in England (outside the Tyneside/Teesside industrial areas).

May and June are the best months to visit, with long evenings (stay away from inland waters in later summer, unless you're midge-proof). September can be delightful, but autumn tends to set in quite fiercely in October. Low prices are helped along by saver schemes such as the Power Pass, jointly developed by the Northumbria Tourist Board and Northern Electric: with various special offers, it's available from their electrical shops and tourist information centres throughout the area; £2.

Where to stay

CAMBO NZ0584 **Shieldhall** *Wallington, Morpeth, Northumberland NE61 4AQ (01830) 540387* **£60***; 5 well equipped suites, each with its own entrance. 18th-c stone house and carefully converted farm buildings around a courtyard, with antiques and other interesting furnishings (Mr Robinson-Gay is a fine cabinet-maker), a library, bar, and cosy lounge with french windows opening on to the neatly kept big garden; enjoyable freshly produced food in candlelit beamed dining room; cl Christmas and New Year; children over 12

CHESTER-LE-STREET NZ2851 **Lumley Castle** *Chester-le-Street, County Durham DH3 4NX (0191) 389 1111* **£155**w, plus special breaks; 59 wonderfully atmospheric rms. Splendid 14th-c castle with Norman origins standing above the river Weir; plenty of gothic character in atmospheric rooms, tapestries, rugs and statues, carved wood and chandeliers, dimly lit corridors and spiral staircases, billiards room and library, good modern cooking in vaulted no smoking restaurant (they hold Elizabethan banquets), and 9 acres of grounds; cl 24-26 Dec, 1 Jan; partial disabled access

CHOLLERFORD NY9170 **George** *Chollerford, Hexham, Northumberland NE46 4EW (01434) 681611* **£120**, plus special breaks; 47 well equipped rms. Quiet hotel with fine gardens sloping down to the river, and the 17th-c bridge over North Tyne visible from the candlelit restaurant; thoughtful attentive service; swimming pool and leisure club; fishing, putting green, and mountain bike hire; limited disabled access; dogs welcome in bedrooms

CORNHILL-ON-TWEED NT8842 **Tillmouth Park** *Cornhill-on-Tweed, Northumberland TD12 4UU (01890) 882255* **£135**, plus special breaks; 14 spacious, pretty rms with period furniture. Solid stone-built country house in 15 acres of parkland, with comfortable relaxing lounges, open fires, a galleried hall, good food in bistro or restaurant, and a carefully chosen wine list; fishing, nearby golf, and shooting; lots to do nearby; cl 2 wks Feb; dogs welcome in bedrooms

CROOKHAM NT9138 **Coach House** *Crookham, Cornhill-on-Tweed, Northumberland TD12 4TD (01890) 820293* **£50**; 9 individual rms with fresh flowers and nice views, 7 with own bthrm. 17th-c farm buildings around a sunny courtyard, with helpful and friendly long-serving owner, an airy beamed lounge with comfortable sofas and big arched windows, good breakfasts with home-made preserves (which you can also take home), afternoon tea, and enjoyable dinners using own-grown vegetables; lots to do nearby; cl 31 Oct-Easter; good disabled access; dogs welcome in bedrooms

GATESHEAD NZ2560 **Eslington Villa** *8 Station Rd, Low Fell, Gateshead, Tyne & Wear NE9 6DR (0191) 487 6017* **£79.50***, plus wknd breaks; 18 rms. Comfortable, extended Edwardian house in quiet residential area with some original features, a lounge with comfortably modern furniture and bay windows overlooking garden, good food in conservatory restaurant, and a friendly atmosphere; cl 4 days over Christmas; disabled access; dogs welcome in bedrooms

GREENHEAD NY6667 **Holmhead** *Greenhead, Carlisle, Cumbria CA8 7HY (01697) 747402* **£60**, plus special breaks; 4 cosy rms with showers. No smoking family home, built of Wall stones, once a farmhouse but now a comfortable B&B with moorland, wildlife, Hadrian's Wall and Roman castles all nearby; airy lounge with TV at one end, small bar at the other, games and children's toys, good freshly prepared food using organic farm and local produce eaten family-style around candlelit oak table at 7.30pm, and pretty garden with a stream and games (table tennis and snooker in garage); Mrs Staff is a Hadrian's Wall tour guide, and there's a clue trail for children and special learning tour ; new self-catering and bunk/camping barn; cl 18 Dec-18 Jan; disabled access winter only ☺

GRETA BRIDGE NZ0813 **Morritt Arms** *Greta Bridge, Barnard Castle, County Durham DL12 9SE (01833) 627232* **£87.50**, plus special breaks; 23 rms. Smart, old-fashioned coaching inn where Dickens stayed in 1838 to research for *Nicholas Nickleby* - one of the interesting bars has a colourful Dickensian mural; comfortable lounges, fresh flowers, good open fires, and pleasant garden; coarse fishing; pets allowed; attractive garden with children's play area; disabled access; dogs welcome away from bistro and restaurant

HEADLAM NZ1818 **Headlam Hall** *Headlam, Darlington, County Durham DL2 3HA (01325) 730238* **£90**, plus special breaks; 36 pretty rms, in the main house and adjacent coach house, plus 2-bedroom cottage in village. Peaceful Jacobean mansion in four acres of carefully kept gardens with a little trout lake, tennis court, and croquet lawn; elegant rooms, a fine carved oak fireplace in the main hall, stylish food in the four individually decorated rooms of the restaurant, and courteous staff; indoor swimming pool, snooker and sauna, and gym; cl 25 and 26 Dec; disabled access; dogs welcome in bedrooms

KIRKWHELPINGTON NY9684 **Cornhills** *Kirkwhelpington, Newcastle upon Tyne, Tyne & Wear NE19 2RE (01830) 540232* **£50***; 3 rms. Big no smoking Victorian farmhouse on large stock-rearing farm, with marvellous views towards the coast and Tyne Valley; lots of original features, a comfortable lounge, good breakfasts (local pubs for evening meals), and indoor and outdoor games for children; self-catering also; cl Apr

LONGFRAMLINGTON NU1301 **Embleton Hall** *Longframlington, Morpeth, Northumberland NE65 8DT (01665) 570249* **£95**; 13 comfortable, pretty and individually decorated rms. Charming hotel in lovely grounds surrounded by fine countryside, with a particularly friendly relaxed atmosphere and courteous staff; neat little bar, elegant lounge, log fires, excellent value bar meals, and very good food in the attractive dining room; disabled access; dogs welcome in bedrooms

LONGHORSLEY NZ1596 **Linden Hall** *Longhorsley, Morpeth, Northumberland NE65 8XF (01670) 516611* **£115**, plus special breaks; 50 individually decorated rms. Georgian hotel in 450 acres of landscaped park with clay pigeon shooting, mountain biking (bike hire available), 18-hole golf course, pitch and putt, croquet, lots of leisure facilities inc a swimming pool, and health and beauty treatments; pubby bar, elegant drawing room, and good food in attractive restaurant; children in main restaurant early evening only; disabled access; dogs welcome in bedrooms

NEWCASTLE UPON TYNE NZ2564 **Malmaison** *Quayside, Newcastle upon Tyne, Tyne & Wear NE1 3DX (0191) 245 5000* **£129**; 116 individually decorated and well equipped rms. In a former Co-op warehouse and overlooking the river, this stylish hotel (part of a small chain with others in Birmingham, Edinburgh, Glasgow, Leeds, London and Manchester) is boldly decorated throughout, with contemporary furniture and artwork, genuinely friendly staff, modern cooking in fashionable brasserie, and decent breakfasts; disabled access

ROMALDKIRK NY9922 **Rose & Crown** *Romaldkirk, Barnard Castle, County Durham DL12 9EB (01833) 650213* **£96**, plus special breaks; 12 rms - those in the main house have lots of character. Smart and interesting old coaching inn by green of delightful Teesdale village, with Jacobean oak settle, log fire, old black and white photographs, and lots of brass in the beamed traditional bar; cosy residents' lounge, very good imaginative food in bar and fine oak-panelled restaurant, and well kept real ales and wines; cl Christmas; disabled access; dogs welcome in bedrooms

SEAHOUSES NU2232 **Olde Ship** *Main St, Seahouses, Northumberland NE68 7RD (01665) 720200* **£88**, plus special breaks; 18 rms, inc 4 apartments. Thriving harbourside inn with small rooms full of nautical items and fishing memorabilia, windows looking out towards the Farne Islands, comfortable residents' lounge and sun lounge, popular bar food, five real ales, and good service; ideal for coastal walks; cl Dec-Jan; children over 10

STANNERSBURN NY7286 **Pheasant** *Stannersburn, Hexham, Northumberland NE48 1DD (01434) 240382* **£65***, plus special breaks; 8 rms. Beautifully located unpretentious 17th-c stone inn close to Kielder Water and its quiet forests; traditional, comfortable lounge, simple public bar, a happy mix of customers, good food inc excellent fresh veg and enjoyable Sun lunch, well kept real ales, a fine choice of malts, good welcoming service, and nice breakfasts; picnic-sets in streamside garden; cl 25-26 Dec; disabled access; dogs welcome in bedrooms

SWINBURNE NY9374 **Hermitage** *Swinburne, Hexham, Northumberland NE48 4DG (01434) 681248* **£70**; 3 large rms with big baths, overlooking the garden or vegetable patch. Lovely 17th-c country house reached through a grand arch and down a long drive with woodland on either side; graceful rooms with family portraits, prints and antiques, friendly owners, and generous breakfasts; no smoking upstairs; several nearby pubs for meals; cl Oct-Feb; children over 10

To see and do

Northumbria Family Attraction of the Year

NEWCASTLE UPON TYNE NZ2464 **Newcastle Discovery** (Blandford Sq) Nearing the end of a £12¼ million refurbishment as we went to press, this thriving complex should be bigger and better than ever in 2004. It's an enthralling place, with a huge range of galleries covering a broad range of topics; there's something here to appeal to everyone, and it's all free. For families the best bit is the interactive Science Maze, with masses of hands-on displays and activities offering plenty of opportunities to push, press and poke. TV effects create the illusion of flying down the Tyne, there's a soft play area for very young children, and lots of mirrors, magnets and microscopes to fiddle with. The galleries on the history of the area are another highlight, well illustrating the development of the city and with the chance to handle chain-mail and try on a Norman helmet. They recently opened a new gallery about life on the River Tyne, while elsewhere are displays on fashion, shipbuilding and local inventors. The building has been well converted to its current use, and the central atrium provides a fitting home for the remarkable 30-metre (100-ft) Turbinia, once the fastest ship afloat. At weekends and during the Easter and summer school holidays they have lots of extra activities for children, from trails and crafts to storytelling: the website, www.twmuseums.org.uk, has the latest schedule. Meals, snacks, shop, disabled access; cl am Sun, and all day 25-26 Dec, 1 Jan; (0191) 232 6789; free.

Please let us know what you think of places in the *Guide*. Use the report forms at the back of the book, write us a letter or log on to www.goodguides.co.uk

ALLENDALE NY8352

The B6305/B6295 is a great scenic drive; lots of walks up there, and the Kings Head in Allendale Town (really a village) is a good stop.

ALNMOUTH NU2410

A pleasant town with attractive beaches, good coastal walks, and a lot for summer visitors. The Saddle has good food.

ALNWICK NU1813

Busy town at the heart of prosperous farming country (farmers' market last Fri of month), with some attractive old streets nr the market square - it was used in the film *Elizabeth*. The hillside **church** of St Michael and All Angels above the river is a perfect example of a complete Late Gothic building. A new local history museum housed in a former church, **Bailiffgate**, has a mix of interactive and more traditional displays; shop, disabled access; cl Mon Nov-Easter and 24 Dec-1 Jan; (01665) 605847; £2.20. An impressive number of second-hand books are on sale in the converted Victorian station, and the Market Tavern has bargain food.

Alnwick Castle The 'Windsor of the North' dates back to the 11th c, and is the second-largest inhabited castle in the country. Stone soldiers stand guard on the battlements, and inside all is Renaissance grandeur, with a magnificent art collection taking in works by Titian, Van Dyck and Canaletto, and an outstanding Claude. Also a famous collection of Meissen china, Roman remains, refurbished museum with displays on the Duke of Northumberland's own private army and local archaeology, and children's playground. Meals, snacks, shop, some disabled access; open Apr-Oct; £7.50, joint ticket with garden £10.

Alnwick Garden Exciting for gardeners, this new 12-acre sloping walled garden is a magnificent partnership of water, topiary, and precision plantings, designed by the Wirtz family of Belgium. Water displays, ornamental garden, water tower walk, rose garden, and woodland walks. Meals, snacks, shop; disabled access; cl 25 Dec; (01665) 511133; £4, joint ticket with castle £10.

House of Hardy (Willowburn Trading Estate, just off A1068) Fascinating for fishermen, who can trace the development of fishing tackle and techniques (and, of course, the history of the company) from the end of the 19th c up to today; you can even book a factory tour. Shop (with the latest rods and reels), disabled access (not on tour); cl Sun, and 24 Dec-2 Jan; (01665) 510027; free.

Hulne Park Excellent for gentle parkland walks; dogs not allowed. Don't miss the whimsical Brizlee Tower and hermit's cave, also some abbey and priory remains.

AMBLE NU2604

This attractive small town has a solid old fishing harbour, a modern yacht marina, and a new town square; Sun is market day. There are **boat trips** around nearby RSPB nature reserve, Coquet Island, with its colourful eider ducks and possibly puffins (bafflingly, the puffins snubbed twitchers by staying away last year; in 2002 there were 18,700 breeding pairs, but under 100 in 2003); (01665) 711975; £5 for an hour-long trip. Coquet Enterprise Park has a large children's indoor play centre; (01665) 714888.

AYDON NZ0066

Aydon Castle (just N of Corbridge) 13th c, and remarkably well preserved, in a lovely setting. Snacks, shop, some disabled access; cl Nov-Mar; (01434) 632450; £2.50; EH.

BAMBURGH NU1835

Bamburgh Castle Stunning huge square Norman castle on a cliff above the sea, its clock serving as timekeeper for the cricket green in the attractive village below. Despite the forbidding exterior, and a collection of armour from the Tower of London, the inside is very much a lived-in stately home. Snacks, shop; cl Nov to mid-Mar; (01668) 214515; *£5. There's a neo-Gothic shrine to Grace Darling the local shipwreck heroine in the yard of the interesting 13th-c **church**. The Lord Crewe Arms is well placed for lunch.

Grace Darling Museum (Radcliffe Rd) Pictures and mementoes of the local heroine, inc the boat in which Grace and her father rescued nine survivors from the wrecked SS *Forfarshire*. Shop, disabled access; cl am

Sun, and Nov-Easter; (01668) 214465; free (donations to RNLI).

BARNARD CASTLE NZ0416
Pleasant market town, which still comes to life on Weds market day, with several attractive buildings. The Old Well (The Bank), with a terrace over the town walls, has good food and bedrooms. There's charming gorge scenery nearby, here wooded, romantic and unmistakably lowland in character, making for good walks. The valley path W eventually climbs above the river and follows field routes as it leads towards Cotherstone.
Bowes Museum A beautiful french-style chateau in 9 hectares (23 acres) of parkland with a parterre garden, as lovely in the frosts of winter as it is in summer. The 40 rooms are filled with sumptuous fine arts and an outstanding display of paintings of national importance; also local history section, and a display of 1950s toys; a new interactive exhibition opens this year telling the romantic story of how the museum was founded. They hold temporary exhibitions, concerts, and events throughout the year. Relatively few people find their way to this knock-out treasure-house, though it's one of the most worthwhile places to visit in the entire country. Meals, snacks, shop, disabled access; cl 25-26 Dec, 1 Jan; (01833) 690606; £6.
Castle These dramatically set 12th-c ruins include the original keep and the 14th-c hall. Shop, disabled facilities; cl 1-2pm, Mon and Tues Nov-Mar, 24-26 Dec, and 1 Jan; (01833) 638212; £2.60 (inc audio tour); EH.
Eggleston Abbey Downstream from Barnard Castle, this is reached by a couple of miles of enjoyable riverside walk - or by car. Substantial remains inc gracefully arched windows, and some remnants of the monastic buildings; disabled access; free. Nearby is a fine medieval packhorse bridge.
Rokeby Park 🏛 (just SE) Elegant 18th-c villa in a fine setting, most famous for its *Rokeby Venus* by Velasquez (though the original is now in the National Gallery). The best of the other pictures is probably Pellegrini's *Venus Disarming Cupid*. Open May bank hols and the following Tues, then pm only

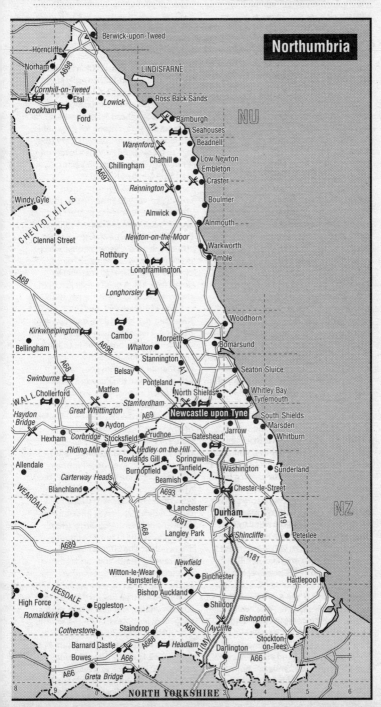

Northumbria

Berwick-upon-Tweed
Horncliffe
Norham
A698
LINDISFARNE
Cornhill-on-Tweed
Etal
Crookham
Lowick
Ross Back Sands
NU
Ford
Bamburgh
Seahouses
Warenford
Beadnell
Chillingham
Chathill
Low Newton
Embleton
Rennington
Craster
A1
A697
Boulmer
Windy Gyle
CHEVIOT HILLS
Alnwick
Alnmouth
Clennel Street
Newton-on-the-Moor
Warkworth
Rothbury
Amble
Longframlington
A68
Longhorsley
Woodhorn
Kirkwhelpington
Cambo
Morpeth
Bellingham
Whalton
Bomarsund
A696
Stannington
A68
Swinburne
Belsay
Seaton Sluice
WALL
Cholleford
Matfen
Ponteland
Whitley Bay
Haydon
Bridge
Great Whittington
Stamfordham
North Shields
Tynemouth
A69
Newcastle upon Tyne
South Shields
Hexham
Aydon
Corbridge
Stocksfield
Prudhoe
Gateshead
Jarrow
Marsden
Riding Mill
Hedley on the Hill
Whitburn
Allendale
Rowlands Gill
Springwell
Carterway Heads
Burnopfield
Tanfield
Washington
Sunderland
WEARDALE
Blanchland
Beamish
A693
Chester-le-Street
NZ
Lanchester
Durham
A691
A19
Langley Park
Shincliffe
Peterlee
A689
A68
A181
Newfield
Witton-le-Wear
Binchester
Hamsterley
Hartlepool
High Force
TEESDALE
Bishop Auckland
Eggleston
Shildon
Romaldkirk
Bishopton
Cotherstone
Staindrop
A68
Aycliffe
Stockton-
on-Tees
Barnard Castle
A688
Headlam
Darlington
A1(M)
Bowes
A66
A66
Greta Bridge
NORTH YORKSHIRE

Mon and Tues Jun to 1st Tues in Sept, but best to check; (01833) 637334; £5. The Morritt Arms nearby does good meals. The B6278 to Stanhope and Edmundbyers is a fine drive.

BEADNELL NU2329

On Northumberland's underpopulated coast, this attractive village has boats on the beach, and an interestingly restored waterside lime kiln; Benthall, above the harbour, is also a pleasant part.

BEAMISH NZ2154

North of England Open-Air Museum (A693) An amazingly ambitious 300-acre museum exhaustively re-creating life in the North of England in the early 1800s and 1900s. There are five main sections: a town with streets, shops, houses and businesses (inc a horse-drawn vehicle collection in a new carriage house), a colliery village (the shallow mine trips are fun if you don't mind stooping), chapel, cottages and school, a manor house with formal gardens, orchard and heavy horses, a railway station, and a home farm with animals and exhibitions (ducks and geese wander around for extra authenticity, and local Teeswater sheep graze on the ridge-and-furrow corrugations which were the rule in the english landscape before steam ploughs). Costumed staff bring the place to life, answering questions and showing off period crafts and skills. What's nice for children is that they can wander around touching everything and joining in most of the activities - learning how to play hoops and hopscotch for example, or taking part in lessons in the schoolroom. The sweet factory and the dentist offer demonstrations, and a Victorian fairground has rides and a proper Hall of Mirrors (the only bit that has a small extra charge). A re-created engine shed has a magnificent 1822 locomotive, and a full-scale replica of Stephenson's *Locomotion No. 1*, which carries visitors down a ¼-mile track, and an engaging new full-size replica of another early locomotive, the Steam Elephant. Extra activities most wknds, from vintage car rallies to Meccano-building or quilting, and in summer there may be brass bands or choirs. Working trams and buses link the different areas (though there may be queues even on a fairly quiet day), and there's plenty of space for picnics (dogs are allowed on a lead). Meals and snacks (some in a period pub), good shops, some disabled access; cl Mon and Fri Nov-Mar, and mid-Dec to early Jan; (0191) 370 4000; £12, £4 in winter, when only the town and tramway are open. The Shepherd & Shepherdess not far from the gate is useful for lunch, as is the more individual Beamish Mary (the sign to follow from A693 is a lovely one - 'No Place & Cooperative Villas').

BELLINGHAM NY8383

(pronounced Bellingjum) A small country town with an attractive 13th-c church, stone-roofed to protect it against arson-minded Border raiders; Black Middens Bastle House, a 16th-c stone-built defensive farmhouse which is 180 metres' walk from the road, is open to the public at all reasonable times; free; EH. A pretty walk just N of the town leads to the 9-metre (30-ft) cascade of Hareshaw Linn. The Riverdale Hall Hotel does interesting bar food. This is the main town in North Tynedale, one of the least known and most unspoilt parts of Northumberland, with good scenic drives. Between the Pennines and the Cheviots, it's a peaceful river valley surrounded by wild moorland. The riverside Riverdale Hall Hotel (W edge of town) has interesting bar food.

BELSAY NZ1078

Belsay Hall and Gardens (A696) The same family lived here for nearly 600 years, first in a medieval castle, then a Jacobean manor house, and finally a grand mansion designed to look like a greek temple. All can still be seen, but the mansion is strangely eerie: there's no furniture, and in some rooms no floors either. The 30 acres of landscaped grounds and parkland are spectacular, with rhododendron garden, formal terraces, woodland walks, and a fascinating garden quarried into the underlying rock. Meals, snacks, shop, disabled access; cl 24-26 Dec, and 1 Jan; (01661) 881636; £4.50; EH.

Bolam Lake Country Park (2m N of A696/B6524 junction) has lakeside walks, a variety of birds (take your binoculars), a summer visitor centre, and fishing (£4 day licence); readers find it magical when there's snow or frost. Home-made snacks, disabled access on surfaced paths; (01661) 881234; free. The Highlander (A696 S) is a good dining pub.

BERWICK-UPON-TWEED
NT9953

Captured or sacked 13 times before it finally came under english rule for good in 1482, the town's quieter more recent centuries have left it largely unspoilt, with some handsome 18th-c buildings and a fine 17th-c church. In Marygate, the handsome Georgian town hall with its soaring spire houses the **Cell Block Museum**; unusual in being upstairs, the gaol here was used between 1761 and 1849. Hour-long guided tours leave 10.30 and 2pm Easter-end Sept; (01289) 330900; £1.50. Most people who come here seem to while away at least a bit of time watching the swans on the River Tweed, or alternatively, look out over the sea from the Rob Roy restaurant (Spittal Rd), which has good local fish. Other places we can recommend for food are Barrels (Bridge St) and Foxtons (Hide Hill). The town has an impressive track record for hospitality: in the early 19th c it boasted a formidable total of 59 pubs and three coaching inns. Today, a more striking feature is its extraordinary trio of bridges, best appreciated by walking along the Tweed: there are paths on both banks, starting from the East Ord picnic site by the A1 road bridge. The town ramparts, impressively intact, were a masterpiece of 16th-c military planning. Partly grassed over and easy to walk, they give good views (though stick to the path - there are sudden drops).

Berwick Barracks (The Parade) Britain's oldest surviving purpose-built barracks, now a local history museum and gallery, with an interesting exhibition on the british soldier, another on early maps, and a contemporary art gallery. Snacks, shop, disabled access; cl Mon and Tues Nov-Mar, 24-26 Dec, 1 Jan; (01289) 304493; £2.80; EH.

Conundrum Farm (signed just off A1 N) The last farm in England (it reaches right up to the scottish border). A trail takes you through various animal paddocks with traditional farm animals

inc rare breeds to a pond where you can feed the trout; there's a pets corner, and you can usually see chicks hatching in the summer, and lambing at Easter and in May. Also fly-fishing, pedal tractors, playbarn, and play area. Meals, snacks, shop, disabled access; cl 24 Dec-Feb, but best to check; (01289) 306092; £2.95.

BINCHESTER NZ2332

Binchester Roman Fort Quite a lot left of this 1st-c 10-acre fort, inc the best-preserved military baths in the country, with an exceptional hypocaust system. Interesting events include days when you may be able to sample Roman food. Shop, disabled access; open cl Oct-Easter; (01388) 663089; £1.60. Nearby Escomb church is interesting, built in the 7th c from stone from the fort. A 3rd-c fort can be seen a few miles S at Piercebridge (where the riverside George, with its famous grandfather clock which stopped when the old man died, is useful for lunch), and finds from both sites are shown at the Bowes Museum in Barnard Castle.

BISHOP AUCKLAND NZ2130

Auckland Castle (N outskirts) The main country residence of the Bishops of Durham, a grand series of buildings entered through a splendid Gothic gatehouse in the town's market place. Some rooms are relatively stark, but a highlight is the chapel, splendidly transformed from a 12th-c aisled hall by Bishop John Cosin in the 17th c. The attractive grounds have an unusual 18th-c deercote. Shop, limited disabled access; open pms Mon and Sun Apr-Sept, plus pm Weds in Aug; (01388) 601627; £4. 2 or 3m N of here, the Fox & Hounds in Newfield does a good lunch (not Mon).

BLANCHLAND NY9650

The archetypal border village, every house looking a stronghold, alone in a great bowl of magnificent scenery; the Lord Crewe Arms here is an interesting hotel, in parts very ancient indeed.

BOMARSUND NZ2784

Earth Balance (signposted off A189 N of Bedlington) Enjoyable place spread over 260 acres, showcasing environmentally friendly living, with organic food and drink made on the premises, a green garden centre, and

Re-Dress, where new clothes and textiles are made out of recycled products. A trail takes you around eco-buildings, a willow maze, a nature reserve, and a fishing lake that provides power for the complex. Café and shop (good choice of locally made food and crafts); disabled access difficult in some parts of the trail; cl two wks over Christmas, phone for details; (01670) 821000; free.

BOULMER NU2613
One of several attractive villages and small towns dotted down Northumberland's scenic and underpopulated coast, this has active fishing boats.

BOWES NY9913
Bowes Castle Within the earthworks of a Roman fort, these remains include the great Norman keep, three storeys high; free; EH. The comfortable Ancient Unicorn, with *Nicholas Nickleby* connections, has good food.

Otter Trust North Pennine Reserve (off A66 W) As well as having british otters (bred for release into the wild) in large semi-natural enclosures along the River Greta (feeding times 12 and 3), this appealingly wild upland reserve is rich in birds. Two shallow lakes have hides for watching wildfowl; in spring five species of waders breed here. There's a rabbit and guinea-pig village for childen, a nature trail, model farm with asian otters, picnic area, and a visitor centre explaining the work of the Trust. Snacks, shop, disabled access; open Good Fri-Oct; (01833) 628339; £4.50.

BURNOPFIELD NZ1857
Gibside Chapel and Grounds
Marvellous Palladian mausoleum for the Bowes family in 18th-c landscaped park, with the rather sad ruins of a hall and other estate buildings dotted around. Miles of pleasant walks. Snacks, shop, disabled access; cl Mon (exc bank hols) and 23 Dec-2 Jan, chapel open by appointment only Nov-Mar; (01207) 542255; *£3.50; NT. The Harperley Hotel in Harperley Country Park, down past Tantobie, has good home cooking (and more nice walks).

BYRNESS NT7702
Chew Green Roman Camps Little-visited spectacular earthworks alone in

wild country, well repaying the stiff walk up the Pennine Way through the Redesdale Forest. The Pennines up here contain a great many more unspoilt prehistoric and other archaeological remains - useful goals for walkers in these magnificent hills, often yielding remarkable views. Some areas N of the A68 (which as it approaches the scottish border is a remarkably dramatic drive) and W of the B6341 may temporarily be put out of bounds by army training. The welcoming Redesdale Arms at Rochester has enjoyable food and comfortable bedrooms.

CAMBO NZ0283
Wallington House Built in 1688 and altered in the 1740s, with fine plasterwork and porcelain, and works by the Pre-Raphaelite circle often found here in the house's 19th-c cultural glory days; the house is due to reopen in spring after work on a new roof and the electrical supply. The gardens include over 40 hectares (100 acres) of lawns, terraces, lakes and woodland (with a woodland walk and wildlife hide) landscaped by Capability Brown. Also showpiece fuchsias in the conservatory, and an adventure playground. Meals, snacks, shop, plant centre, some disabled access; (01670) 773600; £7, £5 gardens only; NT. There is free access to the huge surrounding estate, which is laced with footpaths and includes prehistoric sites and more parkland.

CAULDRON SNOUT NY8128
Beyond High Force, the Pennine Way rewards walkers with some truly wild landscape as the Tees rushes along a gorge beneath Cronkley Scar and tumbles down Cauldron Snout, a 60-metre (200-ft) cascade which can be reached from the dam at Cow Green Reservoir (where there is also a nature trail). The pleasant Langdon Beck Hotel is a short drive or walk below the dam.

CHATHILL NU1825
Preston Tower (Preston) Built by the Sheriff of Northumberland as a tower house during the border raids of the late 14th c; half the building was later pulled down to provide stone for surrounding cottages and farm buildings. A scale model shows what it would have looked like originally, and furnishings in the remaining quarters

give an idea of what it must have been like to live there in the 15th c; open daily; (01665) 589227; £1.50.

CHESTER-LE-STREET NZ2751
St Mary & St Cuthbert and Ankers House Museum One of the oldest in the North, this church is on the site of a cathedral established in 883 by the monks of Lindisfarne, and this was where the Gospels were first translated into english. Adjoining the church is a little anchorite museum with a sobering re-creation of an anchorite's living quarters. Cl Sun, and Nov-Easter; (0191) 388 3295; free. The Chester Moor Inn (A167 S) has good value food.

CHEVIOT HILLS NT9716
Part of the Northumberland National Park, the Cheviots are strikingly empty and solitary, with only hardy upland sheep for company in most places - an area that suits walkers who really want to get away from other people.

CHILLINGHAM NU0525
Chillingham Castle Striking old castle dating back to 12th c, full of antiques, tapestries, arms and armour. Formal gardens, woodland walks, lake, and splendid views of the surrounding countryside; occasional concerts and special events. Brave souls can rent one of their haunted apartments (self-catering). Snacks, shop; cl am, Sat, and Oct-Easter; (01668) 215359; £5. The Tankerville Arms over in Wooler cooks with good local meat and fish.
Chillingham Wild White Cattle Park 🐂 The famous large-horned white cattle have been here for the last 700 years, the only animals of their kind still pure and uncrossed with domestic breeds. As they're potentially aggressive, tours are led by a warden. Bring binoculars for a closer view. Shop; open Apr-Oct (exc 12-2, Sun am and Tues); (01668) 215250; £3. Above the park, Ross Castle hill fort has great views.

CHOLLERFORD NY9070
Chesters Walled Garden (Hexham Herbs) (B6318, nr Chesters) Over 800 varieties of herbs beautifully laid out in an attractive walled garden; lots of other plants, a woodland walk, formal garden, and a restored greenhouse. Snacks, shop, plant sales, some disabled access; cl Nov-Mar (exc occasional open days;

phone for details); (01434) 681483; £2.
CLENNEL STREET NT9207
This ancient drove road leading from Coquetdale is a good walking route into the Cheviots - lonely grassy moors (boggy in parts when it's wet), dry stone walls, sheep, dark conifer plantations. You can pick up the route nr Alwinton, and there's a pretty way back, along a track by the River Alwin.

CRASTER NU2519
A pleasant place to visit, with its tidal fishing harbour, good kippering factory, nice pub (the Jolly Fisherman), and magnificent clifftop walk to Dunstanburgh Castle. Just down the coast at Howick, the gardens of **Howick Hall** (former home of Earl Grey, not open) will interest gardeners; cl am and Nov-Mar; (01665) 577285; £3. From the gardens, there's a pleasant walk to the little cove at Howick Haven.

DARLINGTON NZ2815
Railway Centre & Museum Interesting museum in carefully restored North Rd Station, part of which is still used for train services. Exhibits inc Stephenson's *Locomotion*, built in 1825, which pulled the first passenger steam train on a public railway. Snacks, shop, disabled access; cl 25-26 Dec and 1 Jan; (01325) 460532; £2.20. An extraordinary brickwork locomotive, a 40-metre (130-ft) approximation of the 1930s record-breaking *Mallard* complete with clouds of bricky steam, lies beside Morrisons supermarket (Morton Park Way). In the centre, St Cuthbert's (Church Row) is an interesting Early English church, and Old Yard Tapas Bar (Bondgate) has decent food.

DURHAM NZ2742
The ancient core of the town stands on a crag defended by an almost complete loop of the River Wear, with a rewarding riverside path going from Prebends Bridge up to South St (with some of the best views of the cathedral's magnificent pinnacled towers), recrossing the river by Framwellgate bridge. The old part of town, already largely pedestrianised, has become even more pedestrian-friendly, with a new £2 charge on vehicles entering its citadel core (10-4 exc Sun). It has attractive cobbled alleys

and narrow medieval lanes, and fine medieval buildings among the Georgian and later ones, particularly around the 12th-c pedestrians-only Elvet Bridge (comfortably overlooked by the big-windowed Swan & Three Cygnets). There are several medieval churches, and interesting little shops. You can hire rowing boats (summer only) nr Elvet Bridge, which is also the departure point for the Prince Bishop River Cruiser; (0191) 386 9525. The £29 million Millennium City development at the bottom of Claypath, includes a new theatre, tourist information centre, and an IMAX-style giant-screen cinema (with a film on the city's past); there are craft workshops nearby. Work has started on redeveloping the adjacent Walkergate area into a new leisure quarter to include restaurants, bar, hotel and multi-storey car park. Ghostly guided walks leave from outside the tourist information centre at various times throughout the summer - phone to check; (0191) 386 1500. The 'Cathedral' bus service linking station, coach and car parks to the city centre and cathedral now runs more frequently. Bistro 21 out at Aykley Heads (off B6532 N) and the Seven Stars just out at Shincliffe are our firm food recommendations (see *Where to eat*), and the Court Inn (Court Lane) is useful for decent food all day.

Crook Hall & Gardens 🏠 (Frankland Lane, Sidegate) Medieval manor surrounded by delightful themed gardens, moat pools and waterfalls, with fine views of the castle and cathedral; you can look into their eerie Jacobean room, and they've a summer maze. Special events such as Easter egg hunts and popular ghost tours. Teas in the pretty courtyard, disabled access; usually open pm Easter wknd, pm bank hols and Sun Easter-Sept, pm daily Jun-Aug and summer half-term; (0191) 384 8028; £4.

Durham Castle Developed from an early Norman motte and bailey. Still a proud building, with original chapel and 13th-c great hall, it's now used for university accommodation, and you can stay here. Shop; guided tours daily (usually every 30 mins in summer, less frequently in winter) - phone to check; (0191) 374 3800; £3.50.

Durham Cathedral Huge, and probably England's finest, a fiercely beautiful and unusually well preserved Norman building, breathtaking and very masculine inside; it was the first in Britain to use pointed arches. Bede's tomb and St Cuthbert's shrine are here; Benedictine spin doctors used to say that the Lady Chapel owes its odd position at the W end to his hatred of women; every time they tried to build it in the right place his spirit apparently caused the foundations to collapse (the truth is that the foundations were simply rotten - Cuthbert got on perfectly well with women and was great friends with St Hilda). Look out for a unique bronze knocker that seems to have a cheery grin. Rare books and manuscripts in the 15th-c monks' dormitory, and an exhibition on the cathedral's 900-year history; the Treasures of St Cuthbert Exhibition has a new state-of-the-art copy of the gloriously illuminated Lindisfarne Gospels. Meals, snacks, shop, disabled access; monks' dormitory open Mon-Sat, Sun pm Apr-Sept (£1), Treasury cl Sun am (£2), tower cl Sun, during services and inclement weather (£2); entry to the cathedral is free, but a donation of £4 is suggested. The Close behind the cathedral has some handsome old houses (a shame about the cars).

Durham Heritage Centre (North Bailey) St Mary le Bow Church now houses exhibitions and audio-visuals on the city's history, and you can have a go at brass rubbing (from 80p). Shop, some disabled access; cl am (exc July-Aug), wkdys (exc bank hols and Jun-Sept), and all Nov-Mar; (0191) 384 5589; £1.20.

Durham Light Infantry & Durham Art Gallery (Aykley Heads, just off B6532) This incorporates a museum with imaginative displays on Durham's illustrious light infantry regiment, and a gallery with unusual changing exhibitions. Snacks, shop, disabled access; cl 25 Dec; (0191) 384 2214; £2.50.

Finchale Priory (3m NE, minor rd off A167) St Godric chose this site in 1110 as a place to meditate, and it's still a pleasant spot for contemplation, beside the graceful ruins of the 13th-c church.

Snacks, shop, mostly disabled access; cl Oct-Mar; (0191) 386 3828; £2.

Houghall College Gardens (Shincliffe Rd) The county's main horticultural training centre, with four hectares (ten acres) of hardy plants, a water garden, woodland garden, alpine rock garden, parterre and arboretum. This area records some of the lowest temperatures in the country, so if it grows here, it'll grow anywhere. Snacks (some days), plant sales, disabled access; cl 25-26 Dec, but best to check; (0191) 386 1351; free.

Oriental Museum 🏛 (Elvet Hill) Exceptional collections of everything from ceramics, carvings, and paintings to costumes and mummies; also an activity room, plus a chinese and egyptian gallery. Snacks, shop, disabled access; cl am wknds, and 24 Dec-2 Jan; (0191) 334 5695; *£1.50.

University Botanic Garden (Hollingside Lane, off A167 S) Hugely enjoyable 7-hectare (18-acre) garden in mature woodland with exotic trees from America and the Himalayas, tropical house, cactus house, visitor centre, and unusual sculpture garden. Snacks, plant sales, disabled access; cl two wks over Christmas and New Year; (0191) 334 5524; £1.75.

University Museum of Archaeology On the river bank below the cathedral's SW corner, a former fulling mill with finds from the city and surrounding area. Snacks, shop; cl Tues-Thurs Nov-Mar, and 23 Dec-2 Jan; (0191) 334 1823; £1.

EGGLESTON NY9923

Eggleston Hall Gardens 🏛 A good example of an updated 19th-c country-house garden, with rare and unusual trees, shrubs, perennials and other plants. You can look around the early 17th-c chapel ruins, with photographs showing what it used to look like - a most tranquil place. They sell plants, organically grown herbs, and fruit and vegetables from the walled kitchen garden. Café and shop (cl Mon Oct-Easter), some disabled access; open daily; (01833) 650115; £1. The sloping moorside village is attractive; the Rose & Crown at Romaldkirk is the best nearby place for lunch.

EMBLETON NU2522

Dunstanburgh Castle Screeching gulls add to the atmosphere at these huge ruins, standing imposingly on the cliff above the North Sea. Turner painted the scene three times. Snacks, small shop; cl Mon and Tues Nov-Mar, 24-26 Dec, 1 Jan; (01665) 576231; £2.20; EH (NT members also free). The Dunstanburgh Castle Hotel does good meals. The NT owns much of this stretch of coastline, inc the pleasantly bracing walk to Craster - one of the finest sections of the Northumbrian coast path.

ETAL NT9239

Pretty row of white cottages running down to a ford across the river, with a working forge and pleasant thatched pub, the Black Bull.

Etal Castle Good Walkman tours guide you round these evocative 14th-c ruins; also exhibition on Border history. Shop, disabled access to exhibition area; cl Nov-Mar; (01890) 820332; £3; EH.

FORD NT9338

Built as an estate-workers' model village, for Ford Castle; very attractive, with one or two craft workshops, and a well restored working corn mill (cl Oct-Mar; (01890) 820338; £3); the friendly Heatherslaw Bakery making good use of the resulting corn.

Heatherslaw Light Railway Steam journeys on narrow-gauge railway to Etal, along the pretty valley of the River Till valley (recently extended, so even better views now). Meals, snacks, shop, disabled access; cl Nov-Mar; (01890) 820244 for times; £5 return.

Lady Waterford Hall Well worth a look: used till 1957 as the village school, with murals showing the village children and their families as characters from well known Bible stories; cl 12.30-1.30pm, and Nov-Mar (exc by appointment); (01890) 820503; £1.75.

GATESHEAD NZ2162

Exciting quayside regeneration projects are giving the town a much more positive image these days; the Gateshead Quays Visitor Centre in 13th-c St Mary's church (Oakwellgate) will tell you more about the quays, their history and current development, and includes a contemporary crafts gallery. The monumental Baltic Centre (see below) will soon be joined by a Norman Foster-designed £60 million music centre, the Sage Gateshead (due for completion in winter 2004/05). Another striking landmark, the graceful curved steel and aluminium Gateshead Millennium Bridge (winner of the Stirling top architecture prize), a pedestrian bridge which opens like a giant eyelid blinking up to form an arch under which ships pass, links Gateshead with Newcastle. The **Metro Centre** (A1 just W) is a useful rainy-day outing, a vast modern shopping and leisure complex with several different themed covered areas, all sorts of fairground attractions (better for younger children than teenage thrill seekers), even a Roman Catholic church; a massive extension is due to be completed in the autumn. Don't forget where you put your car - there are 12,000 parking spaces. In the town itself, the **Shipley Art Gallery** (Prince Consort Rd) is worth a look (cl am Sun; free), the Keelmans Way riverside walk & cycle path (off South Shore Rd) is quite pleasant.

Angel of the North (towering over the A1) With a 54-metre wing span (177-ft) and 20 metres high, it is the tallest sculpture in the country, its wings outstretched in blessing of the supplicant procession of some 90,000 motorists who stream past each day. For a more peaceful view, use the Angel View Hotel (A167, Low Eighton).

Baltic Centre for Contemporary Arts (Quayside) In the gargantuan frame of a derelict 1950s grain warehouse (Rank Hovis who built it named their mills after various seas), this major contemporary arts centre - the biggest of its kind outside the capital - is meant to be a focal point of Gateshead's quayside regeneration. It aims to be not so much another art gallery, but a place for artists to work in, with various exhibitions inc the cavernous 'high art gallery', lit naturally from above. It houses a range of changing exhibitions (see their website www.balticmill.com) from giant sculpture to performance art. Despite some reservations about business planning they've recently been granted £550,000 by the Arts Council, but as we went to press weren't able to tell us what it would be used for. The centre also has a lecture theatre, studios, a

library and archive, a café, bookshop and rooftop restaurant; good views of the river. Open daily; (0191) 478 1810; free (exc special exhibitions).

HADRIAN'S WALL NY7868
An amazing sight, if you've never seen it before. It's extraordinary to imagine those Roman military engineers, so far from their warm homeland, building this remarkable construction through such inhospitable surroundings. Many of its 73½ miles run along the natural hard rock ridge of the great craggy Whin Sill, making it that much more formidable; the overall sense of grandeur is a definite part of the appeal. The stone Wall itself, with its turret watchtowers, milecastles and more sporadic forts, defines the N side of a narrow frontier zone, bounded on its S side by an equally remarkable ditch between turf ramparts; a military road runs between wall and ditch. It was this whole installation rather than just the Wall which the Romans used to control trade and cross-border travel. The B6318 following the military road is a fine drive, with some of the best views of the Wall. This road also gives walkers easy access to the line of the Wall, with numerous car parks on the way. There's not a lot of point trying to make walks into circuits: all the interest is along the Wall itself, although in places you may prefer to drop down beneath the switchback Whin Sill, which itself can be quite tiring. The views are bleak and exhilarating. Even in fine summer weather the wind can be chilly on the Wall, so go well wrapped up. English Heritage have been cutting back on the publicity for some sites - thousands of marauding tourists have caused more damage than centuries of harsh weather and unstable politics ever managed. However, an environmentally friendly path will let you follow the Wall from beginning to end. In summer a tourist bus runs between Hexham and several of the main sites (and even as far as Carlisle), and you can get on or off at any of the stages along the way; check with the information centre on (01434) 652220 for times.
We list the following attractions working along the Wall from W to E:
Birdoswald Roman Fort 🏛
NY6166 (Gilsland) Overlooking the

Irthing Gorge (and in fact just over the Cumbrian border), this is one of the most impressive sites on Hadrian's Wall, partly because it has so many features in such a small area, and partly for its grand views; good visitor centre. Snacks, shop, some disabled access; visitor centre cl Nov-Feb; (01697) 747602; £3. There's enjoyable food down the valley in the Abbey Bridge Inn at Lanercost.

Greenhead Roman Army Museum NY6767 (Carvoran) Entertaining and informative intrepretation of what it was like to be a Roman soldier, with everything you could possibly want to know about his training, pay, and off-duty hobbies. Snacks, shop, disabled access; cl mid-Nov to mid-Feb; (01697) 747485; £3.30.

Cawfield Crags NY7166 One of the best-preserved sections of the Wall.

Cuddys Crag NY7567 Perhaps the most beautiful section of the Wall, very photogenic and giving glorious views. The nearby Milecastle Inn does good lunches.

Once Brewed National Park Centre NY7567 Very useful Northumberland National Park Information Centre, handy for Housesteads and Vindolanda, with exhibitions and audio-visual presentations. Guided walks leave from here (though not every day). Snacks, shop, disabled access; cl wkdys Nov to mid-Mar; (01434) 344396; free; EH. The nearby Twice Brewed pub, open all day, serves hearty food. The walk from here to Housesteads offers some of the best views of the Wall; it's only 3 miles but its ups and downs can take up to 2½ hours.

Vindolanda NY7766 Started well before the Wall itself, this Roman fort and frontier town soon became a base for 500 soldiers. Full-scale reconstructions, lots of well preserved remains, and further excavations in progress (weather permitting Sun-Fri Apr-Aug). The adjacent museum has a fascinating selection of hand-written letters and documents found on the site, inc party invitations, shopping lists and a note that could have been written by many a modern mother: 'I have sent you socks and two pairs of underpants'. Meals, snacks, shop, disabled access to

museum but not whole site; cl Mon-Tues mid-Nov to Feb, plus cl two weeks in Jan, phone for details; (01434) 344277; £4.10.

Housesteads Roman Fort and Museum NY7969 (B6318) The best-known and most visited section of the Wall (and also one of the best-preserved), pretty much slap bang in the middle. It owes its fine state of preservation partly to the fact that while other stretches were being used as a handy source of free recycled quality masonry, this fort was base camp for a powerful group of Border bandits; woe betide anyone who tried to use their fortifications as material for cowsheds or churches. A museum has altars, inscriptions and models, and there are good walks in either direction. Snacks, shop; cl 24-26 Dec, 1 Jan; (01434) 344363; £3.10; EH.

Carrawbrough Mithraic Temple NY8571 Three 3rd-c altars to Mithras were found here, on the line of the Roman wall nr the fort of Brocolitia. They're now in Newcastle's Museum of Antiquities, but you can see replicas in their original setting.

Chesters Roman Fort NY9170 (B6318, slightly W of Chollerford) The best-preserved example of a Roman cavalry fort in Britain, in an attractive riverside setting. In the bath house you can see exactly how the underfloor heating system worked, and a museum has sculptures and inscriptions from here and other sites. Summer snacks, shop, some disabled access; cl 24-26 Dec, 1 Jan; (01434) 681379; £3.10; EH. The Crown nearby at Humshaugh has enjoyable home cooking.

Corbridge Roman Site NY9864 (slightly NW) Granaries, portico columns and what may be the legionary HQ survive among these 3rd-c remains. The adjacent museum has the magnificent Corbridge Lion. Shop, limited disabled access; cl 1-2 pm, and Mon and Tues Nov-Mar; (01434) 632349; £3.10; EH. The village, above the Tyne, is attractive; the Angel, Black Bull (popular all-day Sun lunch) and Wheatsheaf are all good for lunch, and Brocksbushes Farm (2m E) has **pick-your-own** fruit and a farm shop; (01434) 633400.

Segedunum NZ3066 (Station Rd, Wallsend; A186/A187) The museum is a lot bigger than others along Hadrian's Wall: well put together displays give an excellent idea of everyday life in the fort that once stood here, and take an intriguing look at how the site developed over the centuries that followed. The remains of this great terminal fort lay buried under Victorian housing until the 1970s, after which they were excavated more thoroughly than just about any other site in the Roman Empire: you can see plenty of the finds. The most striking feature of the complex is the spectacular 35-metre (115-ft) viewing tower, which superimposes virtual reality reconstructions on the actual excavations. Another unique feature is a completely functional reconstructed Roman bath house. Elsewhere are videos, more reconstructions, and plenty of hands-on and touch-screen activities. There are also galleries on mining (there was once a colliery here) and shipbuilding (Swan Hunter are based next door). Children under 6 aren't going to be engaged for long, but older ones can be happily distracted for an hour or two, particularly if they know something about the Romans from school. Meals, snacks, shop, disabled access; cl 25-26 Dec, 1 Jan; (0191) 295 5757; £3.50. Visitors who arrive by metro will notice that several of Wallsend's shops and the station have been subject to a latin rebranding; Woolworths is now 'Domus Lana Dignorum' (the house of those worthy of wool).

Walltown Crags NY6766 One of the best-preserved sections of the Wall.

HAMSTERLEY NZ1231
Hamsterley Forest Miles of fellside forest with good walks, cycle routes, four-mile forest drive, and visitor centre with local wildlife exhibitions and a tearoom. Meals, snacks, shop, disabled access; cl Nov-Mar; (01388) 488312; forest drive around £2 a car. The Cross Keys in Hamsterley is a useful base.

HARTLEPOOL NZ5132
The re-created 18th-c Historic Quay and stylish next-door Designer Room shopping mall (The Marina, with decent food in its 18th-c-style Jacksons Wharf

pub) are tourist landmarks in the town's wholesale regeneration - half a billion pounds spent in the last decade. The historic Headland area with its medieval town wall remains and Abbey Church is benefiting from careful restoration thanks to lottery funding (the Harbour of Refuge up here, with great coast views, does nice lunches inc local fish). The town centre is becoming much more a place to visit, with plenty of bars, restaurants and some interesting shops around Church St. Just S are miles of clean sandy beaches backed by dunes, around the low-key resort of Seaton Carew.

Historic Quay Full-scale re-creation of an 18th-c port, with ships in the harbour, costumed characters, and painstakingly reconstructed houses, market, prison, and shops. It's very well done, and so realistic that it's often used as a location for period dramas. Behind some of the shop fronts are several well put together exhibitions and films: best (and certainly noisiest) is the one on Fighting Ships, and there's an eye-opening explanation of the press gangs who so dubiously drummed up volunteers to earn their sea legs. The highlight for younger visitors is the big, interactive Maritime Adventure Centre with themed areas exploring life at sea. You can plot a ship's course using the stars, take a turn at wiping out rats, or design your own seaman's tattoo. There's an adventure playship, and games such as skittles, shove ha'penny, or fishing for 'frenchies'; special events. Quite a lot is under cover. Meals, snacks and picnic area, shop, disabled access; (01429) 860888; £5.50.

HMS *Trincomalee* (Jackson Dock) This well restored frigate is the oldest ship afloat in Britain; you can climb aboard, and the re-created rooms (watch out for the low ceilings) give a good idea of what life must have been like almost two centuries ago; there's an audio-guide, a children's trail, and they do guided tours. Shop, mostly disabled access (not to the hold); cl 25-26 Dec, 1 Jan; (01429) 223193; £4.

Museum of Hartlepool & PSS *Wingfield Castle* (The Marina) Excellent local history, with something of a maritime emphasis; the well restored 1934 paddle steamer *Wingfield Castle* is used in part as a café. Shop, disabled access; cl 25-26 Dec, 1 Jan; (01429) 222255; free.

HEXHAM NY9364

A pleasant market town, not too big, with some attractive stone buildings. The Tap & Spile (Eastgate) does good filling lunchtime food.

Border History Museum Housed in the country's first purpose-built prison, this museum is due to reopen in July with revamped displays and a new lift. It colourfully charts the chequered contacts between the English and Scots, with waxwork scenes of border raids, and activities at wknds (inc dressing up in Tudor clothes). Shop; open daily Apr-Oct, then Mon-Tues and Sat only Nov, Feb-Mar, phone to check; (01434) 652349; £2.

Hexham Abbey Founded around 674 by St Wilfrid, once the largest church N of the Alps. The bulk of what is seen today dates from the 12th c, though there are two splendid Saxon survivals - the superbly atmospheric crypt, and the throne of the Bishop (St Wilfrid's Chair or Frith stool). The choir still descend the unique Night Stairs for services. Summer snacks, shop, disabled access; cl Good Fri; free, but £3 suggested donation.

Warden church (just N) Down a lane by the Tyne, this is a fine example of the sturdy northern churches that had to do double duty as holy places and watch-towers to warn of scottish raiders.

HIGH FORCE NY8828

High Force waterfall England's most powerful waterfall, this drops into a craggy cauldron at the end of a striking wooded gorge - though you'll have to pay (on top of parking) for the short path from the B6277 for the best view. From Bowlees Visitor Centre you can make more of a walk of it, first detouring N to Gibson's Cave, a pretty waterfall at the top of a gorge, and then heading S to cross the Tees for an easy two miles upriver, passing Low Force on the way. The nearby High Force Hotel has decent food (and the highest brewery in England).

HORNCLIFFE NT9450

Chain Bridge Honey Farm Over 1,500 colonies of bees, and a good visitor centre with an observation hive. Shop with honey-based products, limited disabled access with notice; cl am Sun, wknds Nov-Mar, and around 2 wks over Christmas; (01289) 386362; free.

JARROW NZ3365

Bede's World The Venerable Bede lived here for most of his 7th/8th-c life, producing the 37 books that encompass much of what is known of life in early Christian England. Along with the other half of the monastery, St Peter's, at nearby Monkwearmouth, the site is still a major Christian shrine. Very little remains of the original monastery, but there's Saxon stained glass in the church, and the chancel incorporates one of the earlier chapels. A museum next to Georgian Jarrow Hall has finely carved Anglo-Saxon stones, more stained glass, and excavated relics. There's an authentically re-created 11-acre period farm, and a herb garden too. Meals, snacks, shop, some disabled access; cl Sun am and Good Fri, 24-26 Dec and 1-2 Jan; (0191) 489 2106; £4.50.

KIELDER WATER NY6293

This huge reservoir has done a lot to open up a remote part of the Borders; an attractive drive from Bellingham. It's an interesting shape, modelled by the steep folds of the land, and already looks as if it's always been tucked away in these pine-blanketed hills. You can hire rowing boats for around £8 an hour; (01434) 250217. Visitor centres supply fishing permits for the lake, and you can rent **log cabins** around it by the week; (01502) 500500. The Pheasant at Stannersburn by the E end has enjoyable food.

Bakethin Conservation Area Up at the top of the Water, this is particularly rewarding for wildlife.

Kielder Castle Visitor Centre This 18th-c hunting lodge built for the Duke of Northumberland is now a very good Forest Enterprise visitor centre, with exhibitions, CCTV bird-watching, interactive sculptures, a maze and a play area. Meals, snacks, shop, disabled access; cl wknd before Christmas to wk before Easter, and wkdys Nov-wknd before Christmas; (01434) 250209; free. Regular guided walks and mini-bus safaris from here into the great surrounding tract of Kielder Forest - miles of pine trees with a chance of seeing red squirrels and deer. There are also 15 self-guided walks and cycle routes (easy to follow); the splendidly remote 12-mile toll drive right across to the Redesdale Forest is picturesque. **Kielder cycling** The forest surrounding Kielder Water has been well developed for cycling - the very friendly Kielder Bikes Company 🏧 hire bikes from Kielder Castle (weather depending out of season), and are good for repairs too; cl Christmas and at other times for staff holidays; (01434) 250392; a good all-terrain bike costs £17.50 a day.

Leaplish Waterside Park (slightly round to the W) Another good starting point for Kielder Water, with lots to do in summer, inc plenty of walks and cycle trails, mini golf and a swimming pool. Restaurant and bar, shop, disabled access; (01434) 250312; park free, charges for some activities, Kielder ferry £5.

Tower Knowe Visitor Centre Down at the eastern foot of the Water, with an exhibition and useful information about the area and its wildlife. Meals, snacks, shop, disabled access; cl Nov-Mar; (01434) 240398; free. **Cruises** start from here too, and call all around the lake (takes about 90 mins); £5.

LANCHESTER NZ1244
Hall Hill Farm (B6296 SW) Friendly working farm with lots of animals, riverside walk and trailer rides. Snacks, shop; usually cl wkdys Sept-Oct and all Nov-Mar exc Santa wknds in Dec - though best to check; (01388) 730300; £3.75. The Queens Head is good for food.

LANGLEY PARK NZ2145
Diggerland (Riverside Industrial Estate) Another in this unusual chain of adventure parks where children from 5 up can operate and drive real excavation equipment. Meals, snacks, shop, disabled access; open daily during school hols, wknds and bank hols only in term-time; cl 25 Dec; (08700) 344437; £2.50 to enter, from £1.50 per ride or drive.

LINDISFARNE NU1242
Otherwise known as Holy Island, this important centre for Christian pilgrims is linked to the mainland by a causeway which you can drive (or walk) over at low tide. Tide tables are posted at each end, or phone (01289) 330733; it really is worth checking these carefully - the causeway is impassable for around two hours before high tide and four hours after. If you want to visit a particular attraction, make sure that the tide and the opening times match on the day you want to go. There are nature-reserve dunes, fishermen's huts made of upturned former boats, old lime-kilns, a small extended village with tourist cafés and pubs (the Ship has good value food inc local seafood), and good views from the close-grazed grassy crags. The 3-mile walk around the island's shores is easy and fascinating.

Lindisfarne Castle The rather lonely and austere exterior belies what's within; the 16th-c fortress was restored by Lutyens for the editor of *Country Life* in a suitably monolithic quasi-medieval style. Sumptuous furnishings include a fine collection of antique oak furniture, and the walled garden was designed by Gertrude Jekyll as a protective retreat from the North Sea winds. Cl Weds, and Nov-Mar (exc Feb half-term), but varies according to tides, best to check; (01289) 389244; £4.50; NT. It's a mile's walk fom the car park.

Lindisfarne Priory From here St Aidan and monks from Iona replanted the seeds of Christianity in 7th-c England. These early monks were driven out by Vikings, so it's the extensive remains of a later 12th-c church you can see today; a very peaceful and romantic spot, with graceful red sandstone arches bordered by incongruously neat lawns. Shop, disabled access to visitor centre; cl 24-26 Dec, and 1 Jan; (01289) 389200; £3.

St Aidan's Winery Home of Lindisfarne Mead, a fortified wine made from grapes, honey, herbs, and water from an artesian well. They make preserves too, and the shop has british beers, ciders and cheeses, as well as local pottery and jewellery. Snacks, shop; cl 25 Dec-1 Jan, and other times according to tide - best to phone; (01289) 389230; free.

LONGFRAMLINGTON NZ1199
Brinkburn Priory Well preserved

12th-c church (thanks to unusually restrained Victorian restoration), still with medieval grave slabs, font and double piscina; occasional services and concerts. Shop, some disabled access; cl Nov-Mar; (01665) 570628; £2; EH. The Granby has good food.

LOW NEWTON NU2325
A charming seaside village on a fine stretch of little-visited coast, with a sloping square of old cottages facing a spectacular seascape above the beach and its off-shore seal rocks, and a **bird reserve** nearby. The Ship has good snacks.

MARSDEN NZ3964
Grotto (A183) The Grotto here is unique: a lift (or a hundred or so steps) down to a pub cut into the seaside cliffs.

MATFEN NZ0370
One of the prettiest inland villages in Northumbria, carefully laid out in the 18th c around a riverside village green.

MORPETH NZ2086
The clock tower here is one of only eight non-church bell towers in Britain, and still rings the curfew every night, exc Weds. The Tap & Spile (Manchester St); open all day, has good value food.

Morpeth Chantry Bagpipe Museum (Bridge St) Harmonious collection of small pipes and bagpipes from around the world. Headphones explain the difference between a rant and a reel. Shop; cl Sun (exc in Aug and Dec), Easter Sun and Mon, and 25-26 Dec; (01670) 500717; free. Good craft centre next door with occasional demonstrations (open same as museum).

NEWCASTLE UPON TYNE NZ2563
This big industrial conurbation is far from being conventionally pretty, but has a strong personality and lively, heady atmosphere - and several excellent free museums. Its best parts are grouped very compactly high above the River Tyne with its seven great bridges - the city's trademark is the majestic arch of the Tyne bridge, the largest bridge of its kind when it opened in 1928. The Metro system makes it quick and straightforward to get around, and to the attractions noted under North and South Shields, Tynemouth and Whitley Bay; a Day Rover ticket (available from stations or the tourist information centre) costs £4 and is good for all Metro trips (and the ferry between North and South Shields). You can still trace some stretches of the medieval **city wall**, especially from St Andrew's Church along the cobbled lane W of Stowell St - the city's Chinatown - and past the Heber Tower along Bath Lane. Steep alleys and steps lead from the centre down to the Quayside, the centre of Newcastle's nightlife, and also the oldest part of town, with several unexpected and quaintly attractive timber-framed medieval buildings; one of the oldest, the Cooperage, is a decent pub, and a good warehouse bar conversion here is Lloyds.

Downstream, E of the Tyne Bridge, the area around the old customs house and shipping offices provides an enjoyable stroll, with a traditional market on Sun, and a useful pub for food - the Bonded Warehouse. This quayside area has been rejuvenated, with impressive developments taking shape on the other side of the river, too. Another stylish quayside warehouse conversion, the Waterline (by Law Courts) has good food, as does the Fog on the Tyne overlooking St Peter's Basin marina. By 2005, the Ouseburn/Lime St areas will be regenerated, ready for the opening of the Centre for the Children's Book (a gallery with original manuscripts and illustrations). It's becoming an area for working artists and craftspeople; a trendy pub and live music place here is the Head of Steam @ The Cluny (Lime St), the Tyne (Maling St, at the end of the quayside walk) has exotic sandwiches all day, and the Free Trade (St Lawrence Rd) has awesome river views. From this part it's a short walk N to the Biscuit Factory (Stoddart St), a new contemporary art gallery where all the works are for sale.

Bessie Surtees House (Sandhill) Well renovated timbered Jacobean house, with elaborate plaster ceilings and carved panelling. Cl wknds, bank hols, 24-26 Dec, and 1 Jan; (0191) 269 1200; free; EH.

Hancock Museum 🎫 (B1318, Barras Bridge) Very good natural history museum, with magnificent traditional collections of stuffed birds and mammals, as well as Egyptology displays, fossils and minerals; lively temporary exhibitions, and plenty for children. Meals, snacks, shop, disabled access; cl am Sun, 25-26 Dec, and 1 Jan; (0191) 222 6765; £3.50.

Laing Art Gallery (New Bridge St) Notable temporary exhibitions, and excellent children's gallery, the activities well designed to encourage young children to think about shapes, texture and patterns. Free guided tours of the main galleries by appointment. Meals, snacks, shop, disabled access; cl Sun am, Good Fri, 25-26 Dec, and 1 Jan; (0191) 232 7734; free.

Life Science Centre 🖼 (Times Sq) In a dramatic building beside the city's main railway station, this innovative visitor centre explores the origins of life. You'd think anywhere setting out to explain DNA in an accessible way would be on to a loser, but the main exhibition areas put across serious science in a surprisingly entertaining way. A visit starts with the River of Life, a trip back through billions of years of evolution, tracing how mankind has got to where we are today. One highlight is the Crazy Motion ride, a simulator ride designed to make you feel you're surfing, roller-blading, and even bungee-jumping, and among numerous other interactive attractions is the chance to score against a virtual goalie. A live show in the Secret of Life explains what we have in common with everything from dinosaurs to daffodils, and a multimedia spectacle (shown in a theatre resembling a giant brain) aims to illustrate the range of emotions and activities going on in our heads. Meals, snacks, shop, disabled access; cl 25 Dec; (0191) 243 8223; £6.95.

Military Vehicle Museum 🖼 (Exhibition Park Pavilion, just off B6388 by A167(M) Over 50 military vehicles, plus a World War I trench and Anderson air raid shelter, dioramas and lots of World War I and World War II memorabilia. It's in the only remaining pavilion of the 1929 North-East Coast Exhibition, erected using the principles used in shipbuilding at the time; an interesting structure - designed to stand for six months, it's lasted for 75

years. Shop, disabled access; cl wkdys Nov-Mar, and Aug bank hol Sun and Mon; (0191) 281 7222; £2.

Museum of Antiquities (The University, B1318) Particularly good on Roman remains, with reconstructions of various points along Hadrian's Wall. The displays are organised in a very user-friendly fashion. Shop, disabled access with notice; cl Sun, Good Fri, 24-26 Dec, 1 Jan; (0191) 222 7849; free.

Newcastle Castle 🖼 This is the building which gave the city its name; much still remains - it's one of the finest surviving examples of a Norman keep and chapel in Britain. Panoramic views from the roof, and there's a small museum inside. Shop; cl Good Fri, 25-26 Dec, and 1 Jan; (0191) 232 7938; £1.50. The nearby Bridge Hotel has decent lunchtime food.

Newcastle Cathedral This 14th/15th-c cathedral, dedicated to St Nicholas, is worth a look; a dramatic stone sculpture occupies the Chapel of the Incarnation. Refectory open wkdy lunchtimes only, shop (cl Sun), disabled access; cl pm Sun; (0191) 232 1939; free. The civilised nearby Crown Posada (The Side) is a classic Victorian pub.

Newcastle Discovery See separate family panel on p.432.

NORHAM NT9148

Norham Castle A key fortress commanding a ford over the Tweed right on the scottish border, this has some interesting Tudor masonry, and was used by Scott as the setting for *Marmion*; the ruins high over the river dominate this pleasant village, whose church was founded by a bishop of Lindisfarne in 830. Snacks, shop; cl Oct-Mar; (01289) 382329; £2; EH.

NORTH SHIELDS NZ3568

Stephenson Railway Museum (Middle Engine Lane) Excellent, with steam train trips along a short section of the North Tyneside Railway, as well as displays on the development of steam and a collection of rolling stock, inc George Stephenson's *Billy*. Tearoom, good disabled access; centre cl late Sept-Apr, trains usually in steam pm Sun and bank hols May-Sept, plus some days in Aug - best to check; (0191) 200 7146 for details; site free, £2 steam trips. The Magnesia Bank

(Camden St) has good value food.
Wet 'n' Wild (Royal Quays) Children like this well heated indoor water park, with exciting flumes and slides (one has a very steep drop). Meals, snacks, disabled access; cl 25-26 Dec and 1 Jan; (0191) 296 1333; £7.35.

NORTHUMBERLAND COAST NU2615
This has much to interest walkers along its sandy and rocky shores, but the hinterland is rather dull, so it's better for pottering and for there-and-back walks than for round ones. A coast path covers the finest sections, which we pick out individually on the map.

PETERLEE NZ4338
Castle Eden Dene Nature Reserve The biggest of Durham's wooded coastal ravines, now a picturesque nature reserve with 12 miles of footpaths over 550 acres; free.

PONTELAND NZ1577
Kirkley Hall Gardens (2m N towards Morpeth) Attractive and thoughtfully maintained, with big collection of herbaceous perennials, Victorian walled garden, pretty sunken garden, woodland garden and unusual trees and shrubs. Plant sales, disabled access; cl Oct-Mar; (01661) 841200; free. On the other side of Ponteland, the Badger (A696 SE) has decent food all day, with good disabled access (and a next-door garden centre).

PRUDHOE NZ0963
Prudhoe Castle 12th/14th-c ruined castle on an impressive mound (the name means 'proud hill') overlooking the Tyne, once the stronghold of the powerful Percy family. Remarkable restored gatehouse, and exhibition in nearby 19th-c manor house. Snacks, shop, disabled access; (01661) 833459; cl Nov-Mar; £2; EH. The Feathers at Hedley on the Hill does good wknd and evening food.
Stephenson's Birthplace (Wylam) The single room open here is the NT's least visited property; tearoom; open pm Thurs-Sun, Good Fri and bank hol Mon Apr-Oct; (01661) 853457; £1. The Fox & Hounds (a short walk along the old railway track) and Boathouse (open all day, impromptu Sat afternoon music sessions) have good value food.

ROSS BACK SANDS NU1339
One of the finest sections of the Northumbrian coast path - splendid windswept solitude, looking out to Holy Island.

ROTHBURY NY9799
Coquetdale Northumberland's most scenic drive is the B6344 following the river past Brinkburn Priory to Rothbury, then W on the B6341 past Hepple, then turning right on the unclassified road past Holystone and Alwinton. Picturesque walks around Holystone (where the Salmon is a useful stop), increasingly desolate up towards Blindburn.
Cragside Opulent Victorian mansion of Lord Armstrong, the armaments king, with spectacular rooms and some of the amazing gadgets he designed. Best of all are the miles of well wooded landscaped grounds, with lakes, rhododendrons (glorious in Jun), showy formal garden, and a walk illustrating the various elements of the hydro-electric scheme he devised to light the house; there's also a children's play area. Meals, snacks, shop, some disabled access; house open pm Tues-Sun and bank hol Mon Apr-Oct, estate and gardens open daily Apr-Oct; (01669) 620333; *£8, £5.50 grounds only; NT. The Newcastle Hotel (open all day) has good value food inc Apr-Oct high teas. The Rothbury Terraces nearby are excellent for gentle parkland walks.

ROWLANDS GILL NZ1456
Derwentcote Steel Furnace (A694 towards Hamsterley, where the Cross Keys does good value food) The earliest and most complete steel-making furnace to have survived, with an exhibition on steel production. Shop, disabled access; open pm Sun Apr-Sept; (01207) 562573; free. There are good nearby forest walks, and past Hamsterley over on Ebchester Hill the Derwent Walk pub is a friendly food stop by the Gateshead—Consett river-valley walk for which it's named.

SEAHOUSES NU2232
An unpretentious seaside resort, with amusement arcades and so forth - and a busy fishing harbour, overlooked by a good interesting pub, the Olde Ship.
Farne Islands From Apr to Sept, weather permitting, boat trips from Seahouses let you see the eider ducks, thousands of other seabirds, and grey

seals. Breeding season for the birds is usually around May-July, though perhaps a little later for the seals, whose plaintive-voiced pups stay on shore for only a few weeks. Most boats cost £10. Landing on the NT-owned islands is extra (from £3.50, £4.50 breeding times); a shrine commemorates St Cuthbert, who came here to die in 687. The NT has a shop with information about the islands on Main St, cl Mon and Tues Nov-Mar (and Jan for refurbishment); (01665) 721099.

Marine Life Centre & Fishing Museum 🏛 (Main St) This enthusiastic museum looks at various aspects of the fishing trade, with re-created scenes such as a fisherman's kitchen, cooper's workshop, and smokehouse. You can compare early and modern methods of fishing, and feed fish in the trout pond; there's also a seawater aquarium, a little cinema room, and the atmospheric **Haunted Kingdom**, which has some gruesome reconstructions. Shop; open daily Easter-end Oct; (01665) 721257; £3 museum or Haunted Kingdom, £5 both.

SEATON SLUICE NZ3276

Seaton Delaval Vanbrugh's Palladian masterpiece, a splendid design of central porticoed main block and massive outer wings. Not all the interior has survived unscathed, and much of the original park and grounds has been submerged by surrounding developments. Snacks, shop; open pm Weds, Sun and bank hols May-Sept; (0191) 237 1493; £3. The buildings around the Norman **church** are attractive, and the Waterford Arms nr the low-key seafront does generous fresh fish.

SHILDON NZ2326

Shildon Railway Village (Hackworth Cl, just SE) Based around the restored home of early railway pioneer, Timothy Hackworth, this centre is being expanded as part of a £7m project to house the reserve collection of the National Railway Museum down in York. By the summer, a new building will house over 60 coaches, waggons and locomotives, and there'll be a new conservation centre. Snacks, shop, disabled access; usually cl Mon (exc bank hols), Tues, and Nov-Easter, best

to check; (01388) 777999; £2.10. The Flag & Whistle (Strand St) has enjoyable food.

SOUTH SHIELDS NZ3667

Arbeia Roman Fort (Baring St) Huge variety of remains and reconstructions of a fort gateway, a barrack block, and part of the commanding officer's house; there's also a museum with excellently displayed finds, and plenty for children to enjoy. Snacks, shop, some disabled access; cl Sun (exc pm Easter-Sept), 25-26 Dec, 1 Jan and Good Fri, phone to check; (0191) 456 1369; free, £1.50 for Time Quest (splendid hands-on archaeology exhibition). In a great beach-edge spot, the Littlehaven Hotel (River Dr) does good bar meals in its conservatory, and the Marsden Rattler (South Foreshore) is an enjoyable seafront bar complete with two original railway carriages.

Marsden Bay The **nature reserve** here gives one of the few good coastal walks in industrial Tyneside. The spectacular coast stretches 2½ miles from Trow Rocks to Lizard Point; Marsden Rock's birds include colonies of kittiwakes and cormorants.

South Shields Museum and Art Gallery (Ocean Rd) With good displays, this museum is due to reopen in Feb after work to extend the galleries and improve disabled access; a new gallery puts Catherine Cookson's life in the context of Tyneside social history, and a hands-on art gallery has jigsaws, and light and perspective experiments; cl Sun am Easter-Sept, all Sun Oct-Easter; (0191) 456 8740; free.

SPRINGWELL NZ2858

Bowes Railway On certain days throughout the summer, well restored steam trains tow passengers in brake vans as far as Blackham's Hill, where you can see two working electric-powered inclines designed by George Stephenson. The railway was developed to carry coal between local mines and on to Jarrow for shipment, and the centre itself houses many of these locomotives and coal waggons, in use until the last colliery closures in 1974. Snacks and shop when staff available; centre open Mon-Fri, trains in steam monthly Suns and some bank hol Mons in summer, phone to check; (0191) 416

1847; free (£2 on steam days). The Waggon (Galloping Green Rd, Eighton Banks), with a conservatory overlooking the old railway, has decent food.

STAINDROP NZ1221
Raby Castle Imposing fortress with Saxon origins; vast medieval hall, 14th-c kitchen, and dazzling octagonal drawing room, restored to its Victorian splendour. From the outside, where there are walled gardens and a deer park, it looks just as a castle ought to. Guided tours (wkdy ams; £8.50 inc tea). Meals, snacks, shop (selling oven-ready game and venison from the estate), disabled access to grounds only; open bank hol wknds Sat to following Weds, Weds and Sun only May and Sept, and Sun-Fri Jun-Aug, though best to check (castle open pm only); (01833) 660202; £6, £4 park and gardens only. The village is pretty. Up at Butterknowle the Malt Shovel has good value food, evenings and wknd lunchtimes.

STANNINGTON NZ1981
Whitehouse Farm Centre (2m N, towards Tranwell) Bustling place with a good variety of animals from chinchillas, snakes and mice to llamas, 15 different breeds of sheep, and a shire horse. In an under-cover area, children can touch lots of the smaller animals (often piglets, lambs and other baby animals here). Also soft play area, adventure playground, pedal tractors (50p for proper tractor rides), go-kart track, toboggan slide, and activities such as candle-making and face-painting. A few craft stalls inc a blacksmith, candle-maker and embroiderer. Meals, snacks, shop, disabled access; cl Mon in term-time, wkdys Nov and Jan; (01670) 789998; *£4.50. The Ridley Arms has good value family food all day.

STAWARD GORGE NY8063
Part of the Allen Banks estate (NT), with year-round access to the paths along the wooded River Allen - frequented by roe deer - and a ruined peel tower. The moorland Carts Bog Inn (A686E) has good food.

STOCKSFIELD NZ0762
Cherryburn (slightly E at Mickley) Well preserved 18th-c farm, the birthplace of artist and naturalist Thomas Bewick, with an exhibition on his life. A nice spot, with farm animals running about the yard, occasional craft demonstrations, and good valley views. Annual special event 1st May bank hol, traditional music or dance Sun pms. Shop, some disabled access; cl am, all day Tues and Weds, and Nov-Mar; (01661) 843276; *£3.20; NT. The Blue Bell (Mount Pleasant) has popular low-priced food.

STOCKTON-ON-TEES NZ4419
Green Dragon Museum (Theatre Yard) Local history displays, and a photograph gallery with changing exhibitions. Disabled access to ground floor only; cl Sun, bank hols, 1-2pm Sat, and 25 Dec-2 Jan; (01642) 393938; free. There's a railway heritage trail around town. Slightly E along the river, the surprisingly graceful Tees Barrage keeps polluted tidal water from mixing with water from the hills, moors and valleys, encouraging watersports in the area.

HM Bark *Endeavour* (Castlegate Quay) Full-size replica of Captain Cook's famous vessel with re-created cabins and exhibits from surgeons' knives to telescopes. Shop, disabled access to main exhibition area; open Mon-Weds Easter-Oct; (01642) 676844; £3.

Preston Hall Museum (A135 Stockton—Yarm) Very well constructed Victorian high street and various period rooms, plus working craftsmen, aviary, and woodland and riverside walks. Snacks, shop, disabled access to ground floor only; cl Sun am Oct-Mar, Good Fri, 25-26 Dec, and 1 Jan; (01642) 781184; £1.20. On the same site **Butterfly World** has a re-created jungle environment with hundreds of exotic butterflies flitting between the trees, rocks and waterfalls. Shop, disabled access; open Mar-Sept; (01642) 791414; £3.30. **Riverside Cruises** on the *Teesside Princess* sail from here to the attractive village of Yarm; it takes 3½ hours return, with a bar and café on board; no cruises Mon all year, or Tues, Thurs, Fri Oct-Apr; (01642) 608038; £3.50 single, £6 return. In Yarm you can also get something to eat at the George & Dragon, where the Stockton & Darlington Railway Co held their first historic meeting, which set modern mass transport rolling.

SUNDERLAND NZ3957

**Monkwearmouth Station
Museum** (North Bridge St) As well as
trains, the chance to play in a bus and
explore a Victorian station. Snacks,
shop, disabled access; cl Sun am, 25-26
Dec, and 1 Jan; (0191) 567 7075; free.

National Glass Centre (Liberty
Way) This dazzling place is a fascinating
cross between gallery and factory visit.
It focuses on how glass is made and
used all around the world, in a striking
glass structure on a sloping site on the
N bank of the River Wear - you can
walk along the glass roof, looking down
on the exhibitions below. They have
glass-blowing demonstrations, and the
Kaleidoscope Gallery explores the
more imaginative ways glass is used,
from time-lapse photography to a hall
of mirrors. Several exhibits are
interactive, with computer displays, and
there's a changing exhibition
programme. Meals, snacks, good shop,
disabled access; cl 25 Dec, 1 Jan; (0191)
515 5555; £5.

Roker church The interesting church
was designed by leading members of the
Arts and Crafts movement.

St Peter's church (St Peters Way)
Sister church of St Paul's at Jarrow, its
early years equally well documented by
the Venerable Bede. Much of the
original Saxon church still remains, inc
the west wall and tower. A striking
Colin Wilbourn sculpture outside
commemorates the church's 7th-c
founder Benedict Biscop.

**Sunderland Museum and Winter
Gardens** This takes a lively look at the
city's history. Themes range from
shipbuilding to geology, and, not for the
squeamish, in the natural history
section you can find out about all the
tiny creatures that live on our bodies
and in our homes. Lots of interactive
and hands-on displays; children can
crawl down a mine shaft, touch fossils,
and try on Victorian clothes. An art
gallery contains quite a few works by
Lowry, who often visited the town. The
Winter Gardens (access through
museum only) feature around 1,500
plants from different climate zones.
Meals, snacks, shop, disabled access; cl
25 Dec and 1 Jan; (0191) 553 2323; free.

The surrounding Victorian park has a
children's play area with giant chess
pieces, sculpture trail and duck house.
For good food in a welcoming
contemporary setting, we'd
recommend 11 Tavistock Place.

TANFIELD NZ2057

Tanfield Railway (A6076) The
world's oldest surviving railway, built in
1725 to carry coal to the Tyne. Steam
trains still chuff along the route through
a picturesque wooded valley, and you
can get off by a wooden gorge spanned
by **Causey Arch**, the earliest railway
bridge. There's a collection of
locomotives, and they often have a
blacksmith forging new parts for
restoration work. Summer snacks,
shop, disabled access; trains usually run
every Sun and bank hol Mon, plus Weds
and Thurs in summer hols; (0191) 388
7545 for timetable; fares from £4.50
(unlimited journeys). The friendly
Peacock (Tanfield Lea) has decent food.

TEESDALE NY9425

The best of County Durham's scenery;
the B6277 below its moors and on to
Alston in Cumbria is one of the finest
drives in England. Upper Teesdale has
much of the best walking in the Durham
Pennines, and is famous for its
limestone flora, inc rare arctic alpine
species and the unique Teesdale violet;
Widdybank Fell is a National Nature
Reserve. There are attractive villages
with good pubs or inns, notably
Eggleston, Cotherstone, Romaldkirk
(there's an esp distinguished church
here), and Middleton-in-Teesdale (soon
to gain a new visitor attraction based
around a typical family living here in the
1850s; phone for information (01833)
641000). There's good fishing on the
river or the reservoirs above it, and fine
landscapes all the way along. The no
through road on the other side of the
valley to Holwick is a nice detour; the
Strathmore Arms there is open all day,
at least in season.

TYNEMOUTH NZ3670

Blue Reef Aquarium ☒ (Grand
Parade, Beaconsfield) The best bit of
this enjoyable place is the spectacular
coral reef - you can see sharks, stingrays
and shoals of brightly coloured fish
from the underwater tunnel; also
hands-on rock pools, daily talks and

feeding demonstrations, and regular special events. Meals, snacks, shop, disabled access; cl 25 Dec; (0191) 258 1031; £4.95.

Castle and Priory (Priors Park, Pier Rd) Evocative clifftop ruins, high above the Tyne estuary. Little remains of the once-rich 11th-c Benedictine priory beyond its stirring nave and chancel, and the spooky gravestones outside. Even less is left of the 11th/14th-c castle, but it's unusual to find two such ruins next to each other, and it's a great spot for picnics. Shop, disabled access; cl 1-2pm and Mon and Tues Nov-Mar, 24-26 Dec, 1 Jan; (0191) 257 1090; £2.50; EH. The Grand Hotel (Grand Parade) does good bar lunches.

WARKWORTH NU2405
The main st of this quietly picturesque little town rises attractively from the riverside 12th-c Norman church with its finely vaulted chancel to the striking **Warkworth Castle** on its hill (beautifully covered in daffodils in spring) above the River Coquet. It's virtually complete, so wandering around the crooked passageways and dark staircases is wonderfully atmospheric. Events here were immortalised in Shakespeare's *Henry IV*. Shop, limited disabled access; cl 1-2pm Nov-Mar, plus 24-26 Dec, 1 Jan; (01665) 711423; £3; EH. Prettily placed a short way upstream, the **Hermitage** is a 14th-c cell of retreat, cut into the sandstone cliff, with some crude wall carvings and a tiny vaulted chapel; usually on Weds, Sun and bank hols Apr-Sept a boat can take you; (01665) 711423; £2, free to EH members. The Masons Arms, Hermitage Hotel and Warkworth House Hotel are good for lunch, there are one or two antiques shops, and this stretch of coast has some beautiful clean beaches.

WASHINGTON NZ3156
Washington Old Hall (The Avenue) Well restored stone-built manor dating from the 12th c, for several hundred years the home of George Washington's family, though his ancestors had been established elsewhere (notably Sulgrave Manor in Northants) for quite a while by the time his great-grandfather emigrated to America. The house is filled with 17th-c

furniture and paintings; there's an exhibition on the hall's spell as a tenement in the 19th c, and a re-created Jacobean garden. Snacks, shop, disabled access to ground floor only; open Sun-Weds Apr-Oct; (0191) 416 6879; £3.50; NT. The unspoilt old village comes as a real surprise when you've penetrated the surrounding New Town. The Washington Arms is good value for lunch.

Wildfowl & Wetlands Trust ⊞ (District 15, off A1231 E) Forty hectares (100 acres) with hides, well laid out walks, adventure play area, and very good visitor centre. Some birds will feed from your hand (you can buy birdseed). Meals, snacks, shop, disabled access; cl 25 Dec; (0191) 416 5454; £5.50.

WEARDALE NY8242
This gave much of County Durham's wealth, with lead- and iron-mining along its length and in the moors above. There's little reminder of those days now, but the A689 is a memorable drive. A **riding centre** at Low Cornriggs Farm has lessons, and guided rides along scenic former packhorse routes; (01388) 537089; also farmhouse B&B (01388) 537600. Along the dale is a string of attractive villages such as Wolsingham (good value food at the Black Bull), as well as pleasant waterside and moorland walks. The Golden Lion at St John's Chapel, open all day in summer, is another useful stop.

Durham Dales Centre (Castle Gardens, Stanhope) A good start for finding out more about the area, with a tourist information centre, craft workshops, tearoom, and you can wander round a typical dales cottage garden. Disabled access; visitor centre cl 24-26 and 31 Dec, 1 Jan; (01388) 527650; free.

North of England Lead Mining Centre ⊞ Probably the best-preserved lead-mining site in Britain, and unmissable if you're at all interested in industrial history. Equipped with hard hat and lamps, you're led through the mine's dark, chilly passageways to a huge underground waterwheel; there's also a woodland walk, and a play area for the under-7s. Meals, snacks, shop, disabled access; open daily Apr-Sept, wknds and half-term only in Oct; (01388) 537505;

£3.40 for surface exhibitions, £5 inc mine trip. In the nearby woods, a hide has been set up to let visitors watch a colony of red squirrels.

Weardale Museum (Ireshopeburn) Near the source of the river, this re-creates life in this high valley's heady lead-mining days, and has an exhibition on John Wesley, who often preached in the adjacent chapel; the chapel itself is the oldest still in continuous weekly use. Shop; cl am, Mon-Tues, and Oct-Apr; (01388) 537417; £1.50.

WHITBURN NZ4064

Souter Lighthouse Built in 1870, this was the most advanced lighthouse of its day, and the first to be powered by electricity; it still has period rooms and equipment. Meals, snacks, shop, disabled access (but not to tower); cl Fri (exc Good Fri), and Nov-Mar, phone to check; (0191) 529 3161; £3; NT. The Trust also own the Leas, the spectacular stretch of coastline around here, leading to Marsden Rock with its seabird colonies; bracing clifftop walks. The Jolly Sailor has decent food.

WHITLEY BAY NZ3575

St Mary's Lighthouse Out on St Mary's Island, reached by a causeway at low tide. Good views from the top - for those unable or unwilling to climb the 137 steps, a camera at the top relays the image to a colour TV at the bottom. Snacks, shop; cl wkdys Nov-Mar (exc school hols and occasional days in Feb), and possibly other times depending on the tide; (0191) 200 8650; £2. When the lighthouse is closed the island is worth a visit for the rock pools alone, and is visited all through the year by a wide range of birds.

WINDY GYLE NT8515

High summit by a fine ridge section of the Pennine Way, along the scottish border - the best of the Way's long, lonely plod over the Cheviots' grassy moors. You have to walk some way from the road to reach this main ridge: start from Barrowburn in Coquetdale and walk along The Street, an ancient drovers' track. Gradients are mild but the peaty ground can get boggy after rain; not all routes are defined on the ground, but stone boundary walls and forest plantations are useful guides.

WITTON-LE-WEAR NZ1631

Low Barns Nature Reserve 100-acre reserve with nature trails, woodland, grassland, lake and lots of interesting wildlife. Snacks, shop, good disabled access; cl wkdys Oct-Mar, and 25-26 Dec, 1 Jan; (01388) 488728; free. The village is attractive, with a tree-lined sloping green. The Red Lion over in North Bitchburn has good food.

WOODHORN NZ2889

Woodhorn Colliery Museum (Queen Elizabeth II Country Park) Former colliery buildings re-creating life in the pit and the communities around it. Also short trips on narrow-gauge railway, displays of art by local miners, interactive exhibition on the Lindisfarne Gospels, and woodland walks. Meals, snacks, shop, some disabled access; cl Mon (exc bank hols), Tues, and around 10 days over Christmas and New Year; (01670) 856968; free, though charge for railway.

Attractive or beautifully placed villages, with decent pubs for something to eat, include Bishopton NZ3621, Cotherstone NZ0119, Eggleston NY9924, Lowick NU0139, Rennington NU2118, riverside Riding Mill NZ0161, Romaldkirk NY9922, Stamfordham NZ0772 and Whalton NZ1382.

Where to eat

AYCLIFFE NZ2822 **County** *13 The Green (01325) 312273* Stylish pub with furnishings in the extended bar and no smoking bistro that are light and modern, definitely geared to dining; minimalist décor, a friendly and civilised atmosphere, exceptionally good and very popular high quality cooking using local produce, a good choice of wines by the glass, and four well kept real ales; swift service by friendly young staff. £25.20|£5.85

BAMBURGH NU1835 **Copper Kettle Tea Rooms** *21 Front St (01668) 214315* 18th-c cottage nr castle, with beams, panelling, and copper implements; light lunches, home-made scones and cakes, more substantial suppers, a fine range of teas inc many fruit and herb ones, and a good choice of other drinks; no smoking;

cl winter Mon, Dec to mid-Feb; limited disabled access. £10.50|£3.75

BARNARD CASTLE NZ0516 **Market Place Teashop** *29 Market Pl (01833)* *690110* Long-standing tearoom in 17th-c building with flagstones and an open fire, smart uniformed waitresses, home-made cakes, light lunches, a good choice of teas, and a friendly relaxed atmosphere; cl Sun am, all day winter Sun, Christmas-New Year; disabled access|£3.50

CARTERWAY HEADS NZ0452 **Manor House Inn** *Kiln Pit Hill (01207)* *255268* Popular slate-roofed stone house with fine southerly views over moorland pastures; enticing food from a wide changing menu (served all day now), a partly no smoking restaurant (with a huge collection of jugs), and a friendly atmosphere; comfortable bdrms, nice breakfasts; cl pm 25 Dec. £25|£7.75

CORBRIDGE NY9864 **Valley** *Old Station House, Station Rd (01434)* *633434* Extremely friendly indian restaurant in attractively reworked sandstone station house with wide choice of very good Indian food and kind service; also, a special train service for parties from Tyneside with uniformed escort and free travel, and your order is phoned ahead to be ready on arrival - good fun; cl lunchtimes, cl Sun, 25 Dec, 1 Jan. £25

CRASTER NU2519 **Craster Restaurant** *(01665) 576230* Upstairs restaurant overlooking the harbour with candles on the tables, exceedingly welcoming staff, and huge helpings of fairly priced really fresh fish from the owners' fish depot - they have their own smoking yard, too; cl Sun pm, Mon (except bank hols), Oct-Apr; well behaved younger children lunchtime only, over 12 in evening. £19|£8

DURHAM NZ2643 **Bistro 21** *Aykley Heads House (0191) 384 4354* Light and airy mediterranean-style restaurant in former 17th-c farmhouse, with pine dining chairs on wooden or flagstoned floors, a good choice of very enjoyable interesting modern cooking, a thoughtful wine list, and professional but relaxed service; cl Sun and all public hols; disabled access. £30|£8.50

GREAT WHITTINGTON NZ0071 **Queens Head** *(01434) 672267* Simple but civilised stone inn with two beamed, comfortable and neatly furnished rooms, a wide choice of good interesting food, a no smoking restaurant, log fires, well kept real ales, decent wines, and quite a few malt whiskies; cl Mon exc bank hols; children lunchtime only; disabled access. £25|£6

HAYDON BRIDGE NY8364 **General Havelock** *(01434) 684283* Very civilised old stone terraced house with smart stripped-stone back dining room overlooking the Tyne, good interesting bar lunches and stylish restaurant meals from a monthly changing menu, well kept real ales, good wines by the glass, pleasant service, and a friendly local atmosphere; cl Sun pm, Mon; disabled access. £27|£6

HEDLEY ON THE HILL NZ0759 **Feathers** *(01661) 843607* Little stone local with three neatly kept traditional bars, woodburners, straightforward furnishings, a charming, relaxed and welcoming atmosphere, imaginative meals from a twice-weekly changing menu, and well kept real ales; cl wkdy lunchtimes exc bank hols, 25 Dec; disabled access. £20|£6.95

NEWCASTLE UPON TYNE NZ2563 **Café 21** *19-21 Queen St (0191) 222 0755* Very popular quayside restaurant with a bustling informal atmosphere, helpful staff, especially good modern european cooking attractively presented, and a carefully chosen wine list with good value house wines; no smoking area; cl Christmas and bank hols; £30/£2-course lunch £13

NEWCASTLE UPON TYNE NZ2666 **Fisherman's Lodge** *Jesmond Dene (0191) 281 3281* In a pretty spot down a long leafy lane, this popular restaurant has an attractive bar and elegant dining room, and specialises in delicious fresh seafood - though the local meat and lovely puddings are quite a draw too; professional service and reasonably priced wines; cl Sun and bank hols. £46 dinner/3-course set lunch £19.50

NEWFIELD NZ2033 **Fox & Hounds** *Stonebank Terrace (01388) 662787* Comfortable and gently lit, mainly no smoking, with candles and flowers, big brass platters on dark pink timbered walls, and big windows looking over steeply rolling countryside; good winter fires, appealing attractively priced food (more elaborate in the evening), good house wines, and friendly, thoughtful service; Sat night fully booked well ahead; cl Sun pm, Mon, 2 wks Jan/Feb; no children; disabled access. £23.75|**£4.95**

NEWTON-ON-THE-MOOR NU1705 **Cook & Barker Arms** *(01665) 575234* Beautifully prepared imaginative food in bustling stone pub's unfussy, long beamed bar, with partly panelled walls, paintings by local artists, a coal fire and coal-effect gas one, and a no smoking area; changing real ales, decent whiskies and 12 wines by the glass; bdrms; cl 25 Dec pm; disabled access. £22.40/3-course meal Sun, Mon, Tues pms for two, £30|**£6.95**

RENNINGTON NU2119 **Masons Arms** *(01665) 577275* Friendly and spotlessly kept old coaching inn with good value quickly served bar food inc nice daily specials, a comfortably modernised beamed lounge bar, friendly helpful staff, real ales, and decent breakfasts; comfortable bdrms; no children. £20.45|**£6.95**

SHINCLIFFE NZ2940 **Seven Stars** *High St N (0191) 384 8454* Just ten minutes' or so drive from central Durham, this early 18th-c village inn with its pretty window-boxes and creepers has a civilised but largely unspoilt and welcoming atmosphere; the lounge has a coal fire in a handsome Victorian fireplace, copper kettles hanging from the beams, real ales, enjoyable and imaginative bar food from a changing menu (the candlelit dining room is no smoking), and quite a few malt whiskies; parking can be tricky. £23|**£7.75**

WARENFORD NU1328 **Warenford Lodge** *(01668) 213453* Very individual old (though rather modern-feeling) dining pub with stripped stonework, a big stone fireplace, comfortable extension with woodburner, really good attractively presented imaginative food, and decent wines; children in evening dining room only; cl Mon, Tues-Fri am (all day winter Tues), all Jan; children in restaurant (not bar); limited disabled access. £18|**£6.90**

Special thanks to Brian and Anna Marsden, Michael Doswell, B Sedgwick

NOTTINGHAMSHIRE

**Some good family outings, tracts of appealing countryside,
low prices; Nottingham itself has some nice surprises**

With a diverse range of attractions, an energetic nightlife (including some quirky pubs) and good shops, Nottingham appeals to all sorts of people. We've chosen a trip to the caves of Nottingham as our top Nottinghamshire Family Attraction this year (entertaining tours make it a fascinating experience for every member of the family). Other excellent attractions range from interesting museums (the Galleries of Justice is our favourite) to an unusual science centre.

Enjoyable excursions for younger children include the Making It! Discovery Centre in Littleworth and, for a different kind of fun, the fairytale-themed Sundown Adventureland in Rampton. In Farnsfield, you'll find a busy working farm, and nearby Wonderland has quite a bit for families too. For outdoor adventure, head for Sherwood Forest: the visitor centre in Edwinstowe is a good place begin (there's an enjoyable farm park and a little amusement park there too). There are prehistoric caves at Creswell.

Splendid Newstead Abbey was the home of Lord Byron. By contrast, in Eastwood you can see D. H. Lawrence's much humbler birthplace, with various other Lawrence haunts dotted around; Mr Straw's House in Worksop is a remarkable 1920s time capsule. There's a huge doll collection in Cromwell, and in Upton you'll find antique clocks; Ruddington has a few things worth seeing.

The county has some charming and interesting villages, and one or two attractive old towns such as Southwell (the Workhouse here is thought-provoking) and Newark (with a castle and air museum). The mansions and families which gave the name of the Dukeries to the countryside in the north are long gone, but broad tracts of landscaped wooded parkland remain, such as Clumber.

Where to stay

BLIDWORTH SK5555 **Holly Lodge** *Rickett Lane, Blidworth, Mansfield, Nottinghamshire NG21 0NQ 01623 793853* **£54***; 4 neat, comfortable rms in converted stables. Victorian hunting lodge in 15 acres with fine country views, a woodland walk, and tennis; log fire in sitting room, a relaxed and friendly atmosphere, light suppers if ordered (local restaurants and pubs close by), good breakfasts, and helpful owners; no smoking; children at owner's discretion

LANGAR SK7234 **Langar Hall** *Church Lane, Langar, Nottingham, Nottinghamshire NG13 9HG (01949) 860559* **£130***, plus special breaks; 10 lovely, nicely old-fashioned rms, some in wing and courtyard as well. Fine country house in spacious grounds with family portraits in the hall and up the stairs, a friendly homely drawing room, library, small modern bar, pillared dining hall with paintings for sale, antiques and fresh flowers, a relaxed informal atmosphere, lively, helpful owner and willing young staff, and very good food; disabled access; dogs welcome in bedrooms ☺

NOTTINGHAM SK5739 **Lace Market** *29-31 High Pavement, Nottingham, Nottinghamshire NG1 1HE (0115) 852 3232* **£125**, plus special breaks; 42 modern,

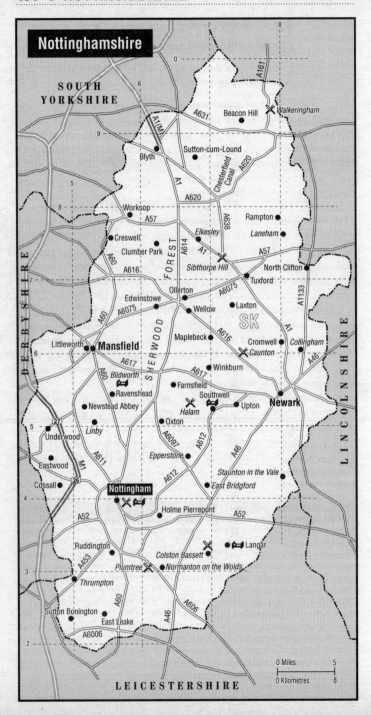

Nottinghamshire

SOUTH YORKSHIRE

DERBYSHIRE

LINCOLNSHIRE

LEICESTERSHIRE

Beacon Hill
Walkeringham
Sutton-cum-Lound
Blyth
Chesterfield Canal
A631
A161
A620
A1(M)
A1
A620
Worksop
A57
Rampton
Creswell
Elkesley
Laneham
Clumber Park
A638
FOREST
A614
A1
A57
A616
A60
Sibthorpe Hill
North Clifton
Tuxford
A1133
Ollerton
A6075
Edwinstowe
A6075
Wellow
Laxton
SK
SHERWOOD
Maplebeck
A616
Cromwell
Collingham
Littleworth
Mansfield
Caunton
A1
A617
Winkburn
A46
A60
A617
Blidworth
Farnsfield
Ravenshead
Southwell
Newark
Newstead Abbey
Halam
Upton
27
Oxton
Underwood
Linby
A6097
A612
Epperstone
A46
Eastwood
M1
A611
A612
Staunton in the Vale
26
East Bridgford
Cossall
Nottingham
Holme Pierrepont
A52
A52
Ruddington
Langar
A453
Colston Bassett
Plumtree
Normanton on the Wolds
Thrumpton
A60
Sutton Bonington
East Leake
A46
A606
A6006

0 Miles 5
0 Kilometres 8

comfortable rms. Next to a lovely church, this Georgian town house has a relaxed atmosphere, friendly young staff, a convivial bar with daily papers, wood-strip floors and strong but subtle colours, good brasserie-style food in contemporary restaurant, and enjoyable breakfasts; cl 25-26 Dec; dogs welcome in bedrooms

SOUTHWELL SK7053 **Old Forge** *Burgage Lane, Southwell, Nottinghamshire NG25 0ER (01636) 812809* **£74***, plus special breaks; 4 rms. 200-year-old former blacksmith's house with welcoming owner, interesting furnishings, super breakfasts in conservatory overlooking the Minster, and pretty terrace; disabled access; dogs welcome in bedrooms

To see and do

Nottinghamshire Family Attraction of the Year

NOTTINGHAM SK5739 **Nottingham's Caves** Not for nothing is this known as the City of Caves; thanks to the soft Sherwood sandstone, hundreds of caves, tunnels and cellars were dug under Nottingham from medieval times, for a variety of purposes. If you enjoy going underground, you can combine two very different cave tours for a fascinating look at how and why they were used. The longest-established is the 50-minute tour run by the Castle Museum - quite strenuous, but with knowledgeable and informative guides. You explore passageways and caverns used by the Duke of Newcastle as a wine cellar, and by Edward III as a prison for David II of Scotland. There are 300 steps down, but it's all very atmospheric, and you learn a lot about the city and its history. Tours leave the castle at 11am, 2pm and 3pm Mon-Sat; they may have more in summer. Tours can be cancelled due to rock-falls or if heavy rain leaves the caves wet and slippery - check first if you're making a special journey, on (0115) 915 3700. Tours are £2 for adults, £1 for children. On Sundays between Apr and Oct similar tours are run by the Nottingham Civic Society rather than castle staff; they usually start on the hour from noon. Children will prefer the more elaborate Caves of Nottingham, now renamed the City of Caves (entry via Upper Level, Broadmarsh Centre), and much improved since the city's excellent attraction the Galleries of Justice became involved. The old audio guide has been replaced by costumed actors entertainingly leading you through man-made caverns that over 750 years have been used as slums, for brewing, as a unique underground tannery, and as an air raid shelter. The situations are brought vividly to life, and younger visitors are really drawn into what's going on. Entry is £4 for adults, and £3 for children, with a family ticket £12.50; they're usually closed only on some Christmas and Easter bank hols, but best to check on (0115) 952 0555 - as we went to press we heard unconfirmed whispers that they might be closed from summer to allow work on the shopping centre above. You can get combined tickets with either the Galleries of Justice, or the Tales of Robin Hood (for details of both, see main listings below).

BEACON HILL SK7490 Above the Chesterfield Canal at Gringley on the Hill, this gives magnificent views in all directions; you can make out the towers of Lincoln Cathedral on a clear day. The Three Horse Shoes in Walkeringham is handy for something to eat.
BLYTH SK6185 An attractive small town, with

interesting wall paintings in the **church**; the cheerful old Angel is useful for lunch. **Hodsock Priory Gardens** (off B6045 S) Especially lovely at snowdrop time, and they've a collection of Victorian beehives; plant sales; open 31 Jan to 7 Mar; (01909) 591204; *£3.50.
CHESTERFIELD CANAL SK7283 This has scope for towpath walks; one attractive stretch is by the Gate Inn at

Clarborough (good value food).

CLUMBER PARK SK6275
One of the great former Dukeries
estates, nearly 4,000 acres of farmland,
parks, lake and woodland and the
longest lime avenue in Europe, almost 2
miles long. Other surviving features
include a Victorian gothic chapel, stable
yard, and ornate entrance lodges. The
superb 19th-c glasshouses incorporate
a palm house, vineries and working bee
colonies, and overlook the walled
kitchen garden. The estate is
outstanding for its walks (120 different
types of tree here offer year-round
colour), enough for a full-day excursion.
You can also hire bikes and electric
wheelchairs. Meals, snacks, shop,
disabled access; cl 25 Dec and concert
days; (01909) 544917; £3.60 per
vehicle; NT.

COSSALL SK4842
Attractive village in D. H. Lawrence
country: he was once engaged to the
girl who lived in Church Cottage
(Church Lane). Head N up Awsworth
Lane as Lawrence must often have
done, past the Gardeners (good value
lunchtime food) to the Gate Inn in
Awsworth, which pleasantly keeps up
the Lawrence mood, and is handy for
strolls in Rushcliffe Country Park.

CRESWELL SK5474
Creswell Crags Visitor Centre
Stone Age man lived in the caves and
rock shelters of this limestone gorge
right by the Derbyshire border (the
village is actually across the border).
Even on days when there aren't cave
tours it's an intriguing prehistoric site
and, in 2003, the first Ice Age art ever to
be found in Britain was discovered here
(not open to the public). There's a good
visitor centre, reconstructions of Ice
Age family life, and other displays and
activities. In summer and school
holidays a tour for children leaves at
11.30am, best to check for other cave
tour dates. You can't go into the caves
wearing sandals or open shoes. Picnic
area, shop, disabled access; cl Nov-Jan
exc Sun; (01909) 720378; site free, cave
tours £2.75. The Mallet & Chisel in
nearby Whitwell has cheap food.

CROMWELL SK7961
Vina Cooke Museum of Dolls 🏠
(Old Rectory) Thousands of toys and
objects related to childhood, in an
imposing 17th-c rectory. Especially
lively on Easter Mon, with morris
dancers, crafts and the like. Shop;
usually cl 12-2 pm, Fri, and Nov-Feb
(exc by appointment), but best to
check; (01636) 821364; £3.

EAST LEAKE SK5525
**Manor Farm Animal Centre and
Donkey Sanctuary** 🏠 You can pet
and feed some of the animals or walk a
goat; an interactive nature trail leads to
a lake where you can try pond dipping,
and there are rides to a play fort. Also
adventure playground, indoor activity
centre, straw maze and pony rides (£1).
Snacks and picnic areas, shop, disabled
access; cl Mon, and 24 Dec-2 Jan;
(01509) 852525; £4. The Star at West
Leake is good value for lunch.

EASTWOOD SK4647
**D. H. Lawrence Birthplace
Museum** (8a Victoria St) The writer
was born in this typical working-class
house in 1885; it's been carefully
restored to how he knew it. Shop
(where you can buy all his works); cl 24
Dec-2 Jan; (01773) 763312; £2, £3.50
with entry to Durban House. Craft
workshops next door (usually cl Sun).
Two rooms in Lawrence's early
boyhood home on Garden Rd are
furnished as he described them in *Sons
and Lovers*; open by appointment with
John Elliott (01773) 712132; donations.
The chatty Foresters Arms
(Newthorpe) is appealing.
Durban House Heritage Centre
Decent centre housing an exhibition on
D. H. Lawrence and his mining
hometown, with original manuscripts
and changing displays such as the copy
of *Lady Chatterley's Lover* used as
evidence in the notorious obscenity
trial; also here, the Rainbow Gallery has
changing art exhibitions. Snacks, shop,
disabled access; cl 24 Dec-2 Jan;
(01773) 717353; £2, £3.50 with D.H.
Lawrence birthplace museum.

EDWINSTOWE SK5865
Sherwood Forest Farm Park (Lamb
Pens Farm, off A6075) Unusual breeds of
traditional farm animals, water buffalo
and wallabies, pets' corner, and colourful
waterfowl on a sizeable lake. Also an owl
garden, adventure playground (with a
separate section for the under-5s), and

picnic area. They usually have some activities in a barn, but it's very much a place for fine weather. Special events may include an Easter treasure hunt. Home-baked teas and snacks, shop, mostly disabled access (can be tricky around the lakes); open daily Easter to mid-Oct; (01623) 823558; £5.
Sherwood Forest Visitor Centre With an exhibition on Robin Hood, the visitor centre is a good springboard for the forest itself, only a fraction of what it once was (it used to cover a fifth of the county) but still miles across, though the heathland that Robin himself would have known has largely been swallowed up either by farmland or by forestry plantation. Good waymarked paths and footpaths, the most popular being to the Major Oak (a huge hollow tree in the heart of the forest). Meals, snacks, shop, disabled access; (01623) 823202; car park £1.50, free in winter. A couple of minutes' walk away **Sherwood Forest Fun Park** has a few fairground rides and attractions; usually open Mar-Nov but may close in very bad weather, best to check; (01623) 823536; free, charges for rides. Nearby too **Sherwood Forest Art and Craft Centre** has 16 craft studios housed in a purpose-built centre; cl Mon and Tues Oct-Mar; (01623) 825786. The best drive is the B6034 N towards Worksop, then the right turn to Carburton and Clumber Park.
FARNSFIELD SK6257
White Post Modern Farm Centre (A614, 1m W) Bustling modern working farm with everything from a mouse town to llamas, quails, snakes and fish, and a goat mountain. In the summer holidays (ring for times) an enjoyable show talks you through a farmer's year, with the help of dogs, sheep and rats. You can buy food for many of the animals, and pet some of them. They're particularly strong on pigs, and may have hatching eggs in their huge incubator. Most displays and animals move indoors if the weather is bad (and there's an indoor play area with a new sledge run). As well as farm trails and pony rides, there's also a bat house and aviary; lots of activities inc reptile handling sessions. Meals, snacks, heated picnic area, shops (inc a pet

shop), disabled access; open daily; (01623) 882977; £6.50. The Plough in the village has decent food.
Wonderland (1m W) Useful for families. As well as a bar for the grown-ups there's lots for children inc junior roller-coaster, train rides, woodland walk, tropical house with free-flying butterflies, a maze, indoor play area, pets and farm animals, crazy golf, and a scented garden. Meals, snacks, shop, disabled access; cl 24-26 Dec and first 3 wks in Jan; (01623) 882773; £5.50 high season, £4.60 low. Combs Farm Shop nearby is a good one.
HOLME PIERREPONT SK6339
Holme Pierrepont Hall Early Tudor manor house with interesting early 15th-c timbers, and an elaborate parterre in the formal courtyard garden. Several rooms inc the ballroom and billiard room have been restored. Teas, shop, disabled access to gardens only; open Thurs Jun, Weds-Thurs July, Tues-Thurs Aug, and Mon pm on Easter, spring and summer bank hols - but best to check; (0115) 933 2371; £4.50, £2 garden only. The Black Lion in Radcliffe on Trent has decent food.
LANGAR SK7234
Naturescape Wildflower Farm You can buy native species of wildflowers and grasses here, and the gardens are pleasant to stroll around (best Jun-July). Visitor centre and tearoom, picnic area, shop, limited disabled access; open daily Apr-end Sept; (01949) 860592; free.
LAXTON SK7267
Unique for having kept the pattern of its **medieval farming**, with different villagers each owning strips of the three great fields. You can walk the grass paths, or sykes, which divide groups of these strips - the visitor centre behind the Dovecote (a good village pub) explains it all. The church has a fine 15th-c screen. In landscaped memorial gardens, at Beth Shalom, there's a centre dedicated to the Holocaust (not recommended for children under 12). Snacks, shop, some disabled access; usually open Wed-Sun Jan-Nov (daily Aug), but phone first; (01623) 836627; £6.
LITTLEWORTH SK5361
Making It! Discovery Centre (Littleworth) In the former Mansfield

Brewery, the centre shows the process of making a new product, from having the initial idea, through testing and producing it, to marketing the finished result. Lots of touch screens, hands-on activities and practical things to do; in the marketing section, you end up on the front page of a newspaper, launching your product. Along the way you'll learn about bar codes, circuits and all sorts of manufacturing processes. The highlight is the final part, where you make something yourself; you can choose between eight different kits (inc in the price) and put together a boat, rocket, or even a clock - which you can take home with you afterwards. Under-12s love it (although it's best suited to those who can read), and there's lots to stimulate older visitors too. Good value Internet café, shop, disabled access; cl two weeks over Christmas; (01623) 473273; *£5.95.

MANSFIELD SK5361

Mansfield Museum and Art Gallery (Leeming St) Very good for local history, with displays of 18th-c porcelain, local watercolours, a natural history gallery, and a thorough look at Mansfield's industrial heritage. Shop, snacks, disabled access; cl Sun and bank hols; (01623) 463088; free. Hidden away behind shop fronts, **White Lion Yard** (Church St) was discovered after a rock fall, and has been re-created through the restoration of two ancient buildings and four adjoining 18th-c man-made caves. Once used as store rooms and workshops (you can still see a bread oven's flue), the caves now house a visitor centre covering the history of the Yard and Mansfield's development, and a restaurant; disabled access; open pm Thurs and Fri, plus Sat all day, or by arrangement; (01623) 463026; free.

MAPLEBECK SK6961

Delightfully rustic village; the Beehive's a classic country tavern, and nearby Woodborough and Lambley are also worth a look.

NEWARK SK7953

Attractive old market town with some interesting buildings in its side streets, a fine church, and walks by the River Trent, with summer boat trips (60-75 mins) from the Castle; (01636) 525246; £5. Useful museums include the

Millgate Folk Museum on Millgate (cl am wknds, bank hols, cl 25-26 Dec; (01636) 655730; free; (lunchtime food at the nearby riverside Navigation Waterfront); and the local history collection at **Newark Museum** on Appletongate (cl 1-2pm, Thurs, bank hol ams, and Sun exc pm Apr-Sept; (01636) 655740; free; decent fresh food in the nearby Fox & Crown.

Newark Air Museum 🔠 (Winthorpe, NE) Over 60 aircraft and cockpit sections from across the history of aviation inc transport, training and reconnaissance aircraft, helicopters, and diverse jet fighters and bombers inc two russian MiGs; half the exhibits are under cover, so fine all year round. Snacks, shop, disabled access; cl 24-26 Dec; (01636) 707170; £4.25.

Newark Castle 🔠 The ruins date from the 12th c, and there's still a fair bit to see; it was partly destroyed during the Civil War, then later had periods as a cattle market and a bowling green. The gardens have been relandscaped as they were in Victorian times, and there's a bandstand, with concerts on summer Sun. Good explanatory displays at the **Castle Story Exhibition** in the grounds; shop, disabled access to gardens only; gardens cl 25-26 Dec, 1 Jan; (01636) 655765; free (castle tour £2, 10am, 12pm, 3pm Weds and Fri-Sat, but less frequently in winter when it's best to phone for times, (07971) 486324).

NEWSTEAD ABBEY SK5454 (off A60) Splendid former home of Lord Byron, in gorgeously romantic grounds; many of his possessions can still be seen. Rooms are decorated in a variety of styles from medieval through to Victorian, and there are substantial remains of the original priory. Adventure playground, and dressing up for children. Meals, snacks, summer shop, limited disabled access; house cl am and Oct-Mar, grounds cl 25 Dec and last Fri in Nov only; (01623) 455900; house and gardens £4, gardens only £2. The Horse & Groom in the attractive nearby village of Linby is a useful stop, as is the Griffins Head at Papplewick (B683/B6011).

NORTH CLIFTON SK8272

Pureland Meditation Centre & Japanese Garden (Trent Lane)

Japanese garden reflecting the harmony of nature and inner peace of man, and a meditation centre (open all year). Snacks, shop, some disabled access; garden cl Mon, and Nov-Mar; (01777) 228567; *£4.50.

NOTTINGHAM SK5739

Although Nottingham is a big city it does have a pleasantly personal feel in its vibrant centre, and with traffic discouraged in the central streets they are nice for a wander, with plenty of trendy clothes and shoe shops and the like. The parts around the parish church (which has some interesting carvings) and the Lace Market (worth peering into, the Piano and Pitcher here is in an impressive converted church) are particularly attractive. In the evenings and wknds there's almost a festival feel, with lots of young people around. Perhaps because of its enormous and growing student population, the town has an amazing number of decent bars and pubs. The Via Fossa (Canal St) and Pit & Pendulum (Victoria St) are fun to look around, and other useful lunch places are Fellows Morton & Clayton (Canal St; brews its own beer), the quaint old Bell (Angel Row), Limelight (attached to the Playhouse) and Lincolnshire Poacher (Mansfield Rd). There's a contemporary art gallery in Angel Row (cl Sun). They're just starting a 6-year project to improve the central shopping centre, and by the time we go to press a new tram system from the train station to Hucknall will be up and running, and five Park and Rides will help reduce the amount of traffic around the city.

Attenborough Nature Reserve

Unusual reserve with good bird-watching down by Beeston at the extensive partly wooded Attenborough lakes; on the far side a path takes you along the spit of land dividing them from the mighty River Trent. The Manor at Toton is a useful nearby dining pub.

Brewhouse Yard Museum 🖼

(Castle Boulevard) Museum of Nottingham life spread over five 17th-c houses with period rooms, schoolroom and reconstruction of a shopping street and caves. Lovely historic roses and plants descended from original Victorian plants in the cottage garden.

Snacks, shop, some disabled access (video of upper floors); cl 25-26 Dec, 1 Jan; (0115) 9153600; £1.50 wknds and bank hols, otherwise free.

Castle Museum and Art Gallery

Up on the summit, this dates from the 17th c, but the gateway is from an earlier 13th-c fortress. It now houses an appealing museum, with a history of the site and the underground passages. Meals, snacks, shop, disabled access; cl 25-26 Dec and 1 Jan; (0115) 915 3700; £2 wknds and bank hols, otherwise free.

Caves of Nottingham See separate family panel on p.459.

Djanogly Art Gallery (University Arts Centre, University Park, SW of centre) Good temporary exhibitions; Meals, snacks, shop, disabled access; cl am Sun, am bank hols, 24-26 Dec, 1 Jan; (0115) 951 3189; free.

Galleries of Justice 🖼 (Shire Hall, High Pavement) The grim realities of a 19th-c trial and prison life are re-enacted with verve at this first-rate centre, set around Victorian courtrooms in use through to 1986. On arrival children are given a criminal identity number and sent for trial in the Criminal Court. 'Prisoners' are then led down to the cells, where dedicated staff acting out their parts as warders, gaolers and a fellow prisoner with real verve prepare them for their fate, lock them in a cell or put them to the treadmill. The other highlight is a police station experience, where you can try your hand at cracking a murder case. Traditional displays about justice through the ages, prisons and legal issues, the world's largest collection of handcuffs and other restraints, and temporary exhibitions about anything from the great train robbery to Judge Dredd. The Centre of which this is a part has recently won the Gulbenkian Prize for its work in educating young offenders in citizenship and justice. Snacks, shop, disabled access; cl Mon (exc school hols), and 24 Dec-2 Jan; (0115) 952 0555; £6.95, joint ticket with caves £9. The News House round the corner in Canal St has enjoyable fresh food.

Green's Mill and Science Centre (Windmill Lane) Once home to the

19th-c mathematical genius and miller George Green, this is Britain's only inner city working windmill: the restored tower mill still produces flour, and you can try grinding corn on part of an old millstone. Among the exhibits at the hands-on Science Centre next door is a weather satellite receiver showing pictures live from space. Shop, limited disabled access; cl Mon (exc bank hols) and Tues - best to phone to check if the mill is working; (0115) 915 6878; free.

National Ice Centre (Lower Parliament St) With two ice rinks (one Olympic size), it covers the full range of related sports from ice-hockey to speed skating; also regular concerts and events, and courses in the school hols. Snacks, shop, disabled access; centre open daily, but best to phone for skating times; (0115) 853 3000; skating from £3.20 (£1.40 extra skate hire).

Nottingham Lace During the industrialisation of the 18th and 19th c, Nottingham developed an international reputation for lace-making, becoming one of the biggest lace-producing cities in the world. A few places still produce lace, and a good place to buy it is the Lace Market Centre (3-5 High Pavement). You can see plenty of examples at the **Lace Centre**, a pretty 15th-c house with lace hanging from almost every beam, much of it for sale (lace-making demonstrations pm summer Thurs). Shop; cl Easter Sun, 25-26 Dec; (0115) 941 3539; free.

Tales of Robin Hood 🖼 (Maid Marian Way) Robin, his men and their tales are brought to life as you travel in cars through the sights, sounds and smells of a re-created medieval Sherwood Forest. A film looks at the truth behind the stories, there's an interactive quiz and you can try brass rubbing; wknd displays such as falconry or historical weaponry, and special events. Meals, snacks, shop, disabled access; cl 25-26 Dec; (0115) 948 3284; £6.95, £8.50 combined with the caves.

Wollaton Hall (Wollaton Park, 3m W) Splendidly ornate Tudor house with the city's natural history collection. The delightful 500-acre grounds have two adventure playgrounds, a sensory garden, and picnic areas. Snacks, shop, disabled access to the ground floor

only; cl 24-26 Dec and 1 Jan; (0115) 915 3900; £2 wknds and bank hols, free at other times, car parking £2 for the day. The **Yard Gallery** has changing exhibitions and sales that explore art and the environment (cl 24-26 Dec and 1 Jan). The adjacent **Industrial Museum** (Courtyard Buildings) looks at lace-making and other local industries, and has working steam-powered machines (beam engine steamings last Sun of month); cl 24-26 Dec and 1 Jan; (0115) 915 3910; £1.50 wknds, £2 joint ticket with Wollaton Hall, also free wkdys.

OLLERTON SK6567

Ollerton Mill (Market Pl) The only working watermill in the county, still working as it did in the early 18th c, in a pleasant setting on the edge of Sherwood Forest. The good tearoom has a viewing panel of the mill race, and river views (open Weds-Sun and bank hols Mar-Nov), shop; mill open Sun Apr-Sept; (01623) 822469; £1.50. The White Hart opposite the church in this pretty market place has good value food.

Rufford Country Park (off A614 S) Pleasant woodland, arboretum, 18th-c lake, park and formal gardens on edge of Sherwood Forest. At the centre are the ruins of a 12th-c Cistercian abbey, with an exhibition on Cistercian life in the vaulted undercroft; also craft centre and gallery, shops and family activities some wknds. Meals, snacks, shop, disabled access; cl 25 Dec; (01623) 822944; free; parking £1.50, free winter wkdys.

OXTON SK6251

Attractive village; the lane up hill N below the power lines leads to an Iron Age hill fort.

RAMPTON SK7978

Sundown Adventureland (Treswell Rd; N of A57) This cheerful leisure park is best for children up to 10. It's full of decent life-size representations and tableaux of stories and fairy-tales, from the Wild West to the Three Little Pigs. There are gentle rides and several themed play areas, one under cover (height restrictions apply in here). Good Christmas displays, when Santa gives every child a present. Snacks (mostly fast food), shop, some disabled access; cl 25 Dec to mid-Feb; (01777) 248274; £6.

RAVENSHEAD SK5753

Longdale Craft Centre 🖼
(Longdale Lane) Very good craft centre, partly set out as a Victorian village street, with rows of period workshops and a small museum. Restaurant, snacks, shop, disabled access; (01623) 794858; cl 25-26 Dec; *£2.

Papplewick Pumping Station 🖼
(Longdale Lane) Working Victorian waterworks in fine building with two beam engines; best to ring for steam days (when they have miniature steam train rides around the landscaped gardens), though open for static displays pm Sun Easter-Oct, maybe other days too. Club members sail model boats, yachts and steam boats on the cooling pond most Suns; as we went to press they were improving disabled access and re-landscaping the grounds; (0115) 963 2938; £1.50 (£3 steam days). The Burnstump in the Country Park is a good value family dining pub.

RUDDINGTON SK5732

Framework Knitters Museum
(Chapel St) Housed in restored 19th-c workshops, cottages, frameshop and a chapel, this museum explores the industry for which Nottinghamshire was once famous. Besides reconstructed cottages you can see the machinery working, inc the bizarre circular sock-knitting machines. Snacks, shop, disabled facilities in chapel, inc lift; open Weds-Sat Easter-Dec and Sun Easter-Sept; (0115) 984 6914; £1.50.

Nottingham Transport Heritage Centre (Loughborough Rd) Steam trains usually leave every hour from here between 11.30am and 4.30pm on Sun and bank hol Mons Apr to mid-Oct, but phone to check; the train now runs as far as Rushcliffe Halt, and the 9-mile round-trip lasts 50 mins. There's also a classic bus collection, and miniature and model railway. Meals, snacks, shop, mostly disabled access; open Sun and bank hol Mon Easter-Oct and Dec, plus Sat summer school hols; (0115) 940 5705; £5.

Village Museum (Church St) Reconstructed Edwardian shops; open pm Thurs and bank hol Mon mid-Apr to Sept, plus pm Weds and Fri in Aug; (0115) 914 6645; £1.

SOUTHWELL SK7053

Southwell Minster Magnificent 12th-c cathedral, a fine sight from miles around (especially at night when it's floodlit), and glorious to walk through. Fine leaf carvings in the chapter house, and lovely choir screen; Evensong is sung daily during term-time, and it's worth catching one of the regular concerts. There's also a smart visitor centre. This attractive old town, small and quiet, is the home of the bramley apple, developed by Henry Merryweather in the 19th c. The original tree survives in a private garden at 75 Church St, and another prospers at his descendant's garden centre on Halam Rd, where there's a small exhibition on the subject. The Bramley Apple just down from the cathedral has decent food.

Workhouse (Upton Rd) The National Trust's only workhouse, and one of the best preserved; it was designed by the Reverend Beecher as an experiment in social improvement. The heavy red-brick exterior is still intimidating, and the interior is chilling - a wonder of utilitarian design; once inside families were efficiently broken up, the deserving poor segregated from the feckless, men from women, adults from children. The rooms are austere but light, kept so by layer after layer of whitewash. The warden looked down on it all from his high central perch. Shop, limited disabled access; open pm daily exc Tues and Weds Apr-Oct; (01636) 817250; £4.40.

SUTTON BONINGTON SK5025
Pleasant village to saunter through; the Star over in West Leake has good value home cooking.

SUTTON-CUM-LOUND SK6985

Wetlands Waterfowl Reserve 🖼
(off Loundlow Rd) Lagoons full of ducks and swans, and many more wild birds inc parrots and emus in the surrounding countryside. Also owls, deer, monkeys, llamas, wallabies, prairie dogs, and a children's farm. Meals, snacks, shop, disabled access; cl 25 Dec; (01777) 818099; £2.50. The canalside Gate at Clarborough has good value food.

TUXFORD SK7371

Walks of Life Heritage Centre
(A6075 Lincoln Rd) Unusual collection

of vehicles - dating back to around 1840 - which rely on human muscle power, from prams and biers, to tradesman's delivery vehicles and fire carts. Open pm Weds, Sun and bank hols Apr-Oct; (01777) 870427; £1.50. The Mussel & Crab (B1164 N) is a pleasant restaurant specialising in fish.

UNDERWOOD SK4851

Felley Priory Garden (A608, just off M1 junction 27) Developed over the last 25 years or so around a romantic old house (not open) dating back over 400 years, these richly planted hillside gardens have several areas nicely broken up by thick hedges, rose and clematis pergolas, and old masonry. They span styles from medieval to high Victorian and later, and are filled with mainly old-fashioned plants, often rare; there's a rose garden with over 90 varieties. Plants sales (all grown here), tearoom, disabled access; open Weds and Sat, am Tues and Fri (plus some Suns), best to phone; (01773) 810230; £2.50. The Red Lion (Church Lane) has good value family food.

UPTON SK7254

British Horological Institute Includes a museum of clocks and timepieces from marine chronometers to the first telephone speaking clock. Some exhibits are over 300 years old, so don't expect them to keep perfect time. Disabled access to ground floor; open wknds Apr-Oct; (01636) 813795; £3.50. The nearby Cross Keys is a useful lunch stop.

WELLOW SK6665

An attractive village, unusual for its permanent maypole - which used to be the trunk of a Sherwood Forest tree, but is now metal. It stands on the only genuine village green in the county, kept that way since the village was founded in the 12th c (all the others were just open spaces used by the villagers and itinerant traders for buying and selling, which have been grassed over since all that stopped). The 16th-c Olde Red

Lion has good value fresh food.

WINKBURN SK7158

Attractive village; unusually, its simple 12th-c village church was formerly a temple of the Knights Hospitaller.

WORKSOP SK5880

Mr Straw's House (7 Blyth Grove) One of the NT's most unusual properties, an ordinary 1920s semi, left untouched by two brothers who inherited it when their parents died. Even the calendar remains unturned. A fascinating time-capsule, it's open for prebooked timed tickets only - by limiting numbers the National Trust ensure that you can get a really good feeling of what it was like to live here; cl Sun, Mon, and Nov-Mar; (01909) 482380; *£4.40. The Mallard at the station (½ mile away) is an apt refreshment stop. The priory church is worth a look for the elaborate scrollwork on its 12th-c yew door.

Other attractive villages with decent pubs include Collingham SK8663, East Bridgford SK6943 (the Reindeer has good fresh fish), Elkesley SK6875, Epperstone SK6548, and, with their more Leicestershire-like character, Colston Bassett SK7033 (the Haby Lane dairy makes good Stilton), Linby SK5351, Normanton on the Wolds SK6232 and Staunton in the Vale SK8043.

The **River Trent** gives a tremendous sense of power even when it's on its best behaviour, sliding swiftly and massively along; its occasional floods are devastating, and most years it claims lives. Villages giving pleasant access to it include Laneham SK8076 and Thrumpton SK5031.

Decent pubs and inns in good riverside spots include the Hazleford Ferry at Bleasby SK7149, Lazy Otter in Wyke Lane, Farndon SK7651, Bromley Arms at Fiskerton SK7351, Unicorn Hotel at Gunthorpe SK6844, Ferry Boat at Stoke Bardolph SK6441, Waterfront at West Stockwith SK7995 and Ferry at Wilford SK5637.

Please let us know what you think of places in the *Guide*. Use the report forms at the back of the book, write us a letter or log on to www.goodguides.co.uk

Where to eat

CAUNTON SK7459 **Caunton Beck** *(01636) 636793* Built in 1820, this civilised, roomy and welcoming place was carefully restored using reclaimed oak and Elizabethan timbers, and has an open fire, daily papers and magazines, and a wide choice of imaginative food, served all day from breakfast onwards; good house wines, real ales, and pleasant staff; disabled access. £25

COLSTON BASSETT SK6933 **Martins Arms** *School Lane (01949) 81361* Civilised, rather smart pub with particularly good imaginative food in bar and no smoking restaurant (lovely puddings), a marvellous choice of up to eight well kept real ales, a fine choice of malt whiskies, quite a few wines by the glass, an open fire, and smart uniformed staff; disabled access. £35|**£8.50**

HALAM SK6754 **Waggon & Horses** *The Turnpike (01636) 813109* Heavily oak-beamed dining pub with friendly, attentive young licensees, an interesting mix of seating, lots of pictures from kittens to Spy cricketer caricatures on walls painted sky blue, terracotta or mustard, and candles throughout the divided rooms; a wide choice of enjoyable and often inventive food, well kept real ales, decent wines, and piped jazz. £25.50|**£7.50**

NOTTINGHAM SK5639 **Harts Restaurant** *Standard Court, Park Row (0115) 911 0666* Lively, popular brasserie with cheerful modern décor, friendly polite staff, dynamic british cooking with mediterranean influences (super fish and interesting vegetarian dishes), delicious puddings, and short, thoughtful wine list; theatres nearby; cl 26 Dec, 1 Jan; disabled access. £35|**£8.95**

NOTTINGHAM SK5740 **Lincolnshire Poacher** *161 Mansfield Rd (0115) 941 1584* Cheerful town pub with a short choice of tasty, good value, home-made food using fresh local produce (inc lots of vegetarian dishes); a dozen interesting real ales, lots of whiskies, decent wines, pleasant service, a big wood-floored bar with breweriana, a lively smaller bar, and chatty back snug; popular with young people in the evening.|**£5.50**

NOTTINGHAM SK5536 **Restaurant Sat Bains** *Hotel Des Clos, Trent Side (0115) 986 6566* (Trent Side, Old Lenton Lane, off A52/A453) Converted Victorian farm buildings close to the River Trent with neat gardens, Hotel Des Clos houses an intimate and fashionable dining room; high-backed brown leather chairs, dark beams and cream walls hung with stylish food photographs, interesting contemporary cooking imaginatively presented, a well chosen if pricy wine list, and proficient service; spacious rustic bdrms; cl Sun, Mon, Sat am, bank hols; children over 8; partial disabled access. £58 for 9 courses/£2-course lunch £17.95

NOTTINGHAM SK5739 **World Service** *Newdigate House, Castle Gate (0115) 847 5587* Fine Georgian house, lavishly decorated, with indonesian masks, panelled walls, polished tables on tiled floors, and staff in Indonesian-style dress; most attractively presented french/pacific rim-influenced food, and a good choice of wines at all prices; no smoking in dining room; cl 1-3 Jan; disabled access. £45/ 2-course lunch £10.50

PLUMTREE SK6132 **Perkins Restaurant and Bar** *Old Railway Station, Station Rd (0115) 937 3695* Delightfully converted old railway station with very popular fresh and delicious modern dishes, excellent friendly service, and good wines; cl Sun pm, Mon; children must be well behaved; partial disabled access. £25/2-course fixed menu £9.75

SIBTHORPE HILL SK7273 **Mussel & Crab** *Sibthorpe Hill (01777) 870491* Friendly, well run dining pub with spacious lounge bar, a mediterranean-style restaurant leading off, most enjoyable food with a strong emphasis on fish, a thoughtful wine list (quite a few inc champagne by the glass) with helpful notes, and two outside terraces; good disabled access. £24.50|**£7**

WALKERINGHAM SK7792 **Three Horse Shoes** *High St (01427) 890959* Warmly welcoming distinctive pub, rather like a French logis, with quite amazing flowers and hanging baskets (using 9,000 plants); a wide choice of often inventive food, and well kept real ales; disabled access. £22|**£6.25**

Special thanks to Michael and Jenny Back, Stuart Paulley

OXFORDSHIRE

Delightful for older visitors, from Oxford's dreaming spires and great museums, through a fine clutch of stately homes, to the antiques shops and markets of charming country towns; some good family places, too

Oxfordshire has lots of rewarding villages and small towns to potter around, with picturesque stone houses (in the NW corner many glow with golden stone), and antiques shops and teashops. The countryside is varied, from the edge of the Cotswolds in the W and sweeping downland in the S to the lush fringes of the Chilterns in the E, with some of the finest Thames scenery. There are very good hotels and places to eat in - at a price.

Oxford is a magnet for visitors, and no wonder: a rich academic history, splendid buildings and unique museums (including England's oldest, the Ashmolean, and that intriguing old-fashioned treasure-house the Pitt Rivers) help make it one of Britain's most enchanting cities - though beware the crowds in summer. Riverside Henley and Abingdon are pleasant for wandering, as is the little Cotswolds town of Burford.

Our Oxfordshire Family Attraction is Wellplace Zoo in Ipsden (refreshingly low-key entertainment that doesn't cost an arm and a leg). Cogges Farm Museum in Witney (Victorian re-creations and animals), and the Cotswold Wildlife Park near Burford (hundreds of creatures, and attractive grounds) are good choices for family excursions; the animal sanctuary at Wigginton Heath is designed with children in mind.

An impressive diversity of houses range from Blenheim Palace in Woodstock (one of England's grandest), to handsome Jacobean Chastleton House (feels like a proper family home), Nuffield Place (1930s furnishings, and a vintage car display), and 18th-c Buscot Park (amazing art collection, fine grounds). Admirers of William Morris find his house at Kelmscott absorbing, and Mapledurham has a 15th-c watermill as well as an Elizabethan mansion; well worth visiting too are the houses and gardens at Broughton, Rousham, Stonor, Milton and Kingston Bagpuize. Dorchester Abbey is striking. There are colourful gardens in Waterperry.

If you're interested in transport, you can choose between the Didcot Railway Centre and the Oxford Bus Museum in Long Hanborough. Banbury has a good local history museum (and a historic dockyard), and the model railway in Long Wittenham has splendid period detail; the brewery tour in Hook Norton is interesting.

Where to stay

BURFORD SP2512 **Burford House** *High St, Burford, Oxfordshire OX18 4QA* (01993) 823151 **£105**, plus winter breaks; 8 cosy individually decorated rms. Attractive partly stone and partly timbered 14th-c building, with plenty of personal touches in the two comfortable lounges (one for residents only), log fires, super breakfasts, and lots of plants in pretty stone courtyard; may cl 2 wks Jan/Feb
BURFORD SP2412 **Lamb** *Sheep St, Burford, Oxfordshire OX18 4LR (01993)*

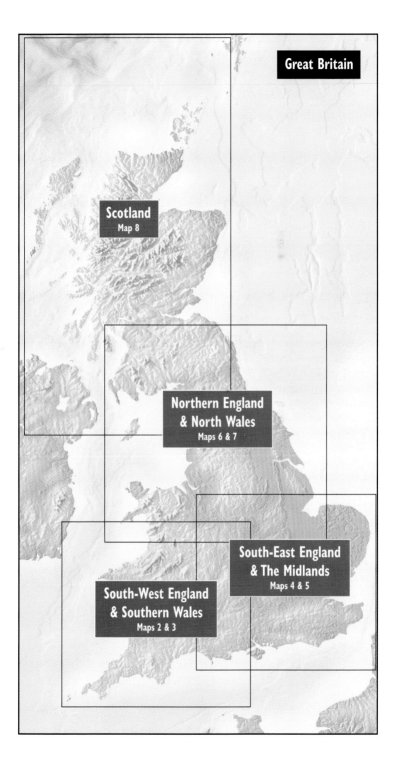

Great Britain

Scotland
Map 8

Northern England
& North Wales
Maps 6 & 7

South-East England
& The Midlands
Maps 4 & 5

South-West England
& Southern Wales
Maps 2 & 3

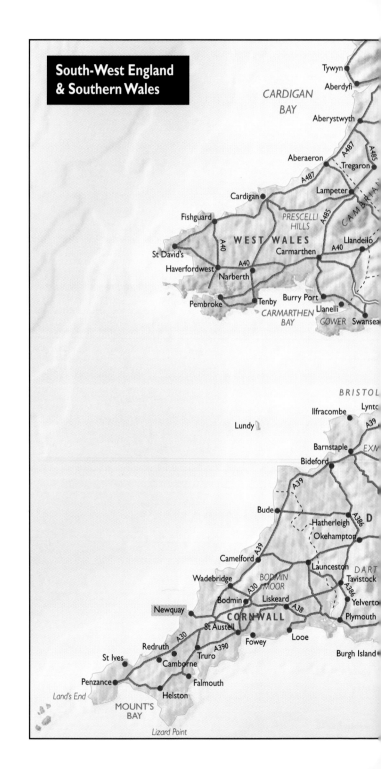

South-West England & Southern Wales

CARDIGAN BAY

Tywyn
Aberdyfi
Aberystwyth
Aberaeron
Tregaron
A487
A485
A487
Cardigan
Lampeter
PRESCELLI HILLS
A485
CAMBRIAN
Fishguard
WEST WALES
Llandeilo
St David's
Carmarthen
A40
A40
Haverfordwest
A40
Narberth
Pembroke
Tenby
Burry Port
Llanelli
CARMARTHEN BAY
GOWER
Swansea

BRISTOL
Ilfracombe
Lyntc
Lundy
A39
Barnstaple
EXN
Bideford
A39
Bude
Hatherleigh
A386
D
Okehampton
Camelford
Launceston
DART
A39
Wadebridge
BODMIN MOOR
Tavistock
A30
A386
Bodmin
Liskeard
Yelverto
Newquay
A38
Plymouth
St Austell
CORNWALL
Redruth
A30
A390
Fowey
Looe
St Ives
Truro
Burgh Island
Camborne
Penzance
Falmouth
Land's End
Helston
MOUNT'S BAY
Lizard Point

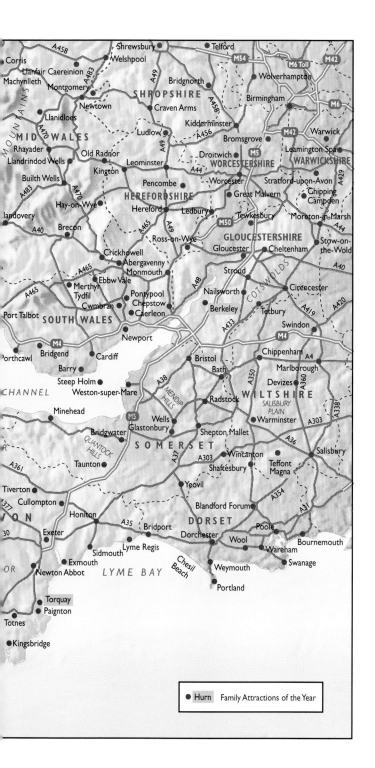

Family Attractions of the Year: ● Hurn

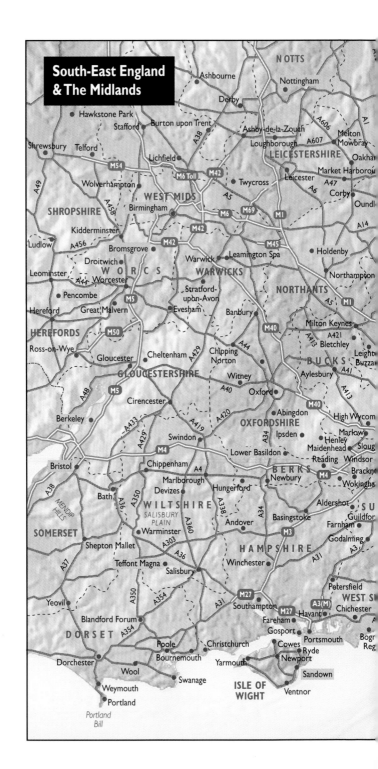

South-East England & The Midlands

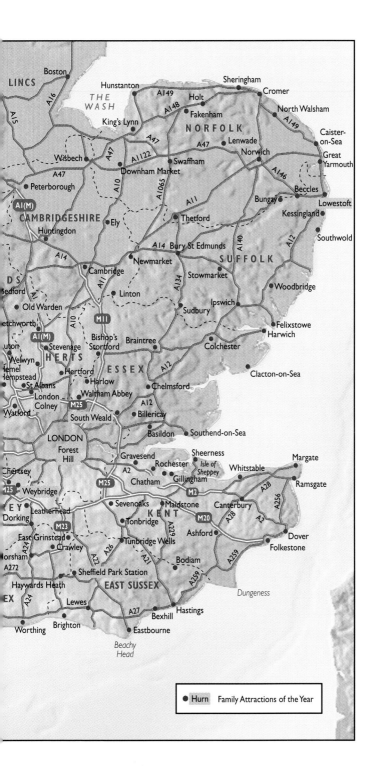

LINCS

Boston

Hunstanton

THE WASH

A149 Holt

Sheringham
Cromer
North Walsham

King's Lynn

A148 Fakenham

NORFOLK

A47 Lenwade
Norwich

Caister-on-Sea

Great Yarmouth

Wisbech

A47

A1122
Downham Market

Swaffham

A146

Beccles

Peterborough

A47

A10

A1065

A11

Bungay

Lowestoft

Thetford

Kessingland

A1(M)

CAMBRIDGESHIRE

Ely

Southwold

Huntingdon

A14 Bury St Edmunds

A14

A11

Newmarket

SUFFOLK

A140

A12

DS
Bedford

Cambridge

A11

Stowmarket

Woodbridge

Old Warden

Linton

A134

Ipswich

Sudbury

etchworth

A10

Felixstowe
Harwich

Luton

A1(M)

Bishop's Stortford

Braintree

Colchester

Welwyn
Hemel Hempstead

Stevenage

HERTS

ESSEX

A12

St Albans

Hertford

Harlow

Clacton-on-Sea

London
Colney

Waltham Abbey

Chelmsford

Watford

M25

A12

South Weald

Billericay

LONDON

Basildon

Southend-on-Sea

Forest Hill

Gravesend

Sheerness

Margate

Chertsey

A2

Rochester
Chatham

Isle of Sheppey

Whitstable

M25

Gillingham

Ramsgate

Weybridge

M2

A28

EY
Dorking

Leatherhead

Sevenoaks

Maidstone

Canterbury

A256

KENT

M20

A28

East Grinstead

M23

Tonbridge

A229

Ashford

A2

Dover

Horsham

Crawley

A22 A26

Tunbridge Wells

A21

Folkestone

A272

A24

Sheffield Park Station

Bodiam

A259

Haywards Heath

EAST SUSSEX

A259

EX

A24

Lewes

A27

Hastings

Dungeness

Worthing

Brighton

Bexhill

Eastbourne

Beachy Head

| ● Hurn | Family Attractions of the Year |

Northern England & North Wales

SCOTLAND

Ayr

A76

A7

A68

A68

CHE

KEILDER FOREST

NORTHUM

A74(M)

Dumfries

A69

Stranraer

A75

Carlisle

SOLWAY FIRTH

A595

A686

CUMBRIA

Cockermouth

Bassenthwaite Lake

Keswick

Penrith

A66

Derwent Water

Ullswater

Whitehaven

CUMBRIAN MTNS

A591

Brough

A595

Windermere

Windermere

Kendal

Sedbergh

ISLE OF MAN

Dalton-in-Furness

Barrow-in-Furness

Morecambe

FOREST OF BOWLAND

A65

Lancaster

LANCS

Fleetwood

Clitheroe

IRISH SEA

Blackpool

A565

Preston

M55

Burn

M55

Blackbur

Rochda

Bury

Wigan

Bolton

Manchester

Liverpool

Birkenhead

Salford

Warrington

M62

Holyhead

Llandudno

Prestatyn

Widnes

M56

ANGLESEY

Beaumaris

A55

Runcorn

Knutsford

Bangor

Conwy

Ellesmere Port

Northwich

Caernarfon

Denbigh

Chester

A54

Llanberis

Capel Curig

CHESHIRE

A49

Crew

SNOWDON

Betws-y-Coed

Wrexham

Nantwich

Blaenau Ffestiniog

Corwen

Llangollen

Whitchurch

Porthmadog

NORTH WALES

Chirk

Market Drayto

Pwllheli

A494

Bala

Ellesmere

Hawkestone Par

Harlech

Oswestry

A5

Barmouth

A458

Welshpool

Shrewsbury

Telfor

Dolgellau

SHROPSHIRE

M5

CARDIGAN BAY

Machynlleth

A483

A49

MID WALES

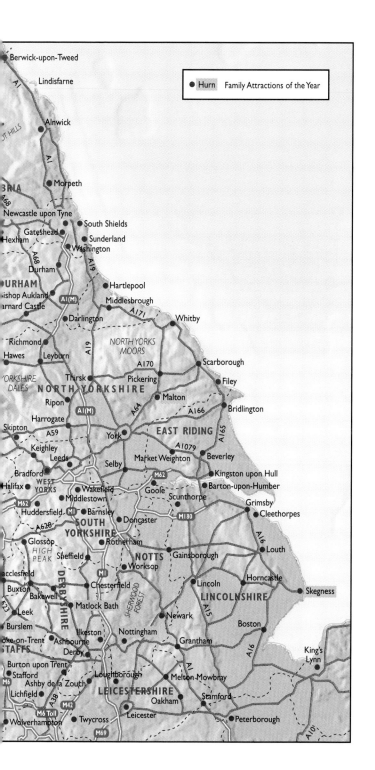

Berwick-upon-Tweed

Lindisfarne

UT HILLS

Alnwick

A1

BRIA

Morpeth

A68

Newcastle upon Tyne

Hexham   Gateshead   South Shields

Sunderland

Washington

A19

Durham

A68

URHAM

ishop Aukland   A1(M)   Hartlepool

arnard Castle   Middlesbrough

Darlington   A171   Whitby

Richmond   NORTH YORKS MOORS

Hawes   Leyburn   A19

YORKSHIRE DALES   Thirsk   Pickering   Scarborough

NORTH YORKSHIRE   A170   Filey

Ripon   Malton

A1(M)   A64

Harrogate   A166   Bridlington

Skipton   A59   York

Keighley   A1079   EAST RIDING   A165

Leeds   Market Weighton   Beverley

Bradford   Selby   M62

Halifax   WEST YORKS   Wakefield   Goole   Kingston upon Hull

Middlestown   Scunthorpe   Barton-upon-Humber

M62   Huddersfield   M1   Barnsley   Doncaster   M180   Grimsby

A628   SOUTH YORKSHIRE   Cleethorpes

Glossop   Rothetham

HIGH PEAK   Sheffield   NOTTS   Gainsborough   A16   Louth

acclesfield   Worksop

Buxton   Chesterfield   Lincoln   Horncastle

Bakewell   DERBYSHIRE   SHERWOOD FOREST   LINCOLNSHIRE   Skegness

23   Leek   Matlock Bath   A15

Burslem   Newark   Boston

oke-on-Trent   Ashbourne   Ilkeston   Nottingham   A16

TAFFS   Derby   Grantham   King's Lynn

Burton upon Trent   A1

Stafford   Loughborough   Melton Mowbray

Ashby de la Zouth   M6

Lichfield   A38   LEICESTERSHIRE   Oakham   Stamford

M42   Peterborough

M6 Toll   Twycross   Leicester   A10

Wolverhampton   M69

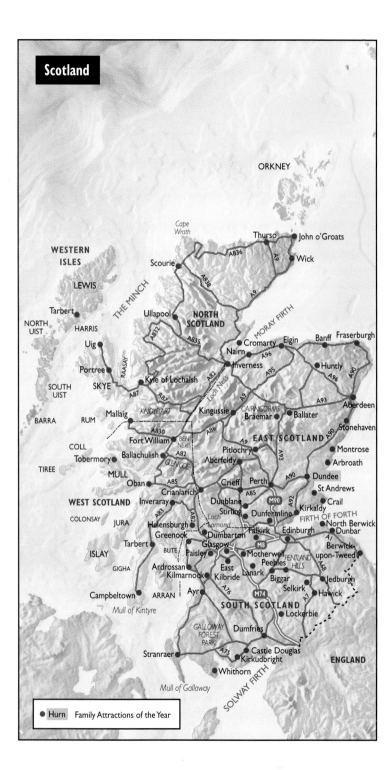

Scotland

ORKNEY

Cape Wrath

Thurso • John o'Groats

WESTERN ISLES

Scourie • A836 • Wick

LEWIS

A838 A9

Tarbert •

NORTH UIST

HARRIS

THE MINCH

Ullapool • **NORTH SCOTLAND**

MORAY FIRTH

Uig •

A835 Cromarty Elgin Banff Fraserburgh

Nairn A96

Portree • Inverness • Huntly

RAASAY A95 A96 A90

SOUTH UIST

SKYE Kyle of Lochalsh Loch Ness A9

A87 A93 Aberdeen

BARRA RUM Mallaig KNOYDART Kingussie CAIRNGORMS Braemar Ballater Stonehaven

A830 A86 Fort William BEN NEVIS A9 **EAST SCOTLAND** A90

COLL A82 Pitlochry Montrose

Tobermory • Ballachulish GLENCOE Aberfeldy A93 Arbroath

TIREE MULL Oban A85 Crieff Perth A90 Dundee

Crianlarich A85 St Andrews

WEST SCOTLAND Inveraray Dunblane A92 Crail

COLONSAY JURA A83 Stirling Dunfermline Kirkaldy

Loch Lomond Falkirk FIRTH OF FORTH

Helensburgh M90 North Berwick

Greenock Dumbarton Edinburgh Dunbar

Tarbert BUTE Paisley Glasgow M8 Berwick-upon-Tweed

ISLAY Motherwell PENTLAND HILLS

GIGHA Ardrossan East Kilbride Peebles A68

Kilmarnock Lanark Biggar Jedburgh

Campbeltown ARRAN Ayr Selkirk Hawick

A76 M74 **SOUTH SCOTLAND** A7

Mull of Kintyre Lockerbie

GALLOWAY FOREST PARK Dumfries

Stranraer A75 Castle Douglas **ENGLAND**

Kirkudbright

Whithorn SOLWAY FIRTH

Mull of Galloway

● Hurn Family Attractions of the Year

823155 **£125**, plus special breaks; 15 newly upgraded rms. Very attractive 500-year-old Cotswold inn with lovely restful atmosphere, spacious beamed, flagstoned and elegantly furnished lounge, classic civilised public bar, bunches of flowers on good oak and elm tables, three winter log fires, antiques, imaginative food in beautifully refurbished restaurant, and pretty little walled garden; disabled access; dogs welcome in bedrooms

CHOLSEY SU6086 **Well Cottage** *Caps Lane, Cholsey, Wallingford, Oxfordshire OX10 9HQ (01491) 651959* **£40**; 2 neatly kept, lemon-yellow rms in garden flat overlooking courtyard. Extended old workman's cottage with pretty rose-filled garden, open fire in sitting room, bird prints and paintings in dining room where breakfast is taken around one big table, and plenty of places nearby for evening meals; horse riding is available as the owners have four horses; disabled access

CLIFTON SP4931 **Duke of Cumberlands Head** *Clifton, Banbury, Oxfordshire OX15 0PE (01869) 338534* **£65**; 6 rms in sympathetic extension. Pretty thatched 17th-c stone inn with a friendly atmosphere, very good food in bar and no smoking back restaurant, enjoyable breakfasts, log fire, well kept beers and wines, and helpful service; tables in garden; dogs welcome

GREAT MILTON SP6202 **Manoir aux Quat' Saisons** *Church St, Great Milton, Oxfordshire OX44 7PD (01844) 278881* **£165**, plus winter breaks; 32 opulent rms. Luxurious Jacobean manor in 27 acres of parkland and lovely gardens with an impeccable kitchen garden; sumptuous lounges with fine furniture, beautiful flowers and open fires, conservatory, exquisitely presented superb food (at a price), and exemplary service; residential cookery courses; disabled access ☺

HENLEY SU7682 **Red Lion** *Hart St, Henley-on-Thames, Oxfordshire RG9 2AR (01491) 572161* **£170**, plus special breaks; 26 rms, some with river views. Handsome family-run 16th-c riverside hotel with comfortable public rooms, very good interesting food in elegant Regency-style restaurant, and particularly helpful warmly friendly staff

HORTON-CUM-STUDLEY SP5912 **Studley Priory** *Horton-cum-Studley, Oxfordshire OX33 1AZ (01865) 351203* **£175***, plus special breaks; 18 rather luxurious rms. Once a Benedictine nunnery, this lovely Elizabethan manor stands in 13 wooded acres; fine panelling, 16th- and 17th-c stained-glass windows, antiques, big log fires, and good sofas and armchairs in the elegant drawing room and cosy bar, smartly uniformed friendly service, and seasonally changing menus in attractive high-beamed restaurant, hung with lots of landscape prints; grass tennis court and croquet; dogs welcome in bedrooms

KINGHAM SP2523 **Mill House** *Station Rd, Kingham, Chipping Norton, Oxfordshire OX7 6UH (01608) 658188* **£120***, plus special breaks; 23 good rms with country views. Carefully renovated 17th-c flour mill in seven acres with trout stream; comfortable spacious lounge, open log fire in lounge bar, original features such as two bread ovens, a cosy popular restaurant, and very good interesting food; disabled access; dogs welcome in bedrooms

KINGSTON BAGPUIZE SU3997 **Fallowfields** *Southmoor, Kingston Bagpuize, Abingdon, Oxfordshire OX13 5BH (01865) 820416* **£120***, plus special breaks; 10 rms. Delightful Gothic-style manor house with elegant, relaxing sitting rooms, open fires, delicious, imaginative food using home-grown produce in attractive conservatory dining room, courteous helpful service, and 12 acres of pretty gardens and paddocks; tennis court; no smoking; lots to see nearby and plenty for children; cl 24-25 Dec; dogs welcome ☺

LONG HANBOROUGH SP4214 **Old Farmhouse** *Station Hill, Long Hanborough, Witney, Oxfordshire OX29 8JZ (01993) 882097* **£50***; 3 rms, 1 with own bthrm. Former farmhouse dating back to 1670, plenty of character inc beams, flagstones and inglenook fireplace; quality breakfasts with home-made preserves, charming cottage garden with conservatory filled with geraniums; Oxford only 10-minute train ride away, and Blenheim Palace and Woodstock are nearby; cl Christmas

MOULSFORD SU5983 **Beetle & Wedge** *Ferry Lane, Moulsford, Wallingford, Oxfordshire OX10 9JF (01491) 651381* **£185**, plus special breaks; 11 pretty rms, most with a lovely river view. Civilised riverside hotel where Jerome K. Jerome wrote *Three Men in a Boat* and where H. G. Wells lived for a time (it was the Potwell in *The History of Mr Polly*); informal old beamed Boathouse Bar and lovely conservatory dining room (both with wonderful food - but must book), a carefully chosen wine list, open fires, fresh flowers, a riverside terrace and waterside lawn with moorings; nice walks; they are kind to families; disabled access; dogs welcome in bedrooms

NORTHMOOR SP4202 **Rectory Farm** *Northmoor, Witney, Oxfordshire OX29 5SX* (01865) 300207 **£55**; 2 light and airy rms with garden views, showers. Ancient farmhouse with a relaxed, informal atmosphere, kind and helpful hosts, stone mullioned windows, comfortable sitting room with Tudor fireplaces and timbered walls, excellent breakfasts, and lovely garden; home-made teas on arrival; cl mid Dec-2nd wk Jan; no children

OXFORD SP5009 **Cotswold House** *363 Banbury Rd, Oxford OX2 7PL* (01865) 310558 **£78***; 7 comfortable rms with showers. Beautifully kept modern no smoking Cotswold stone house with particularly helpful owners, residents' lounge, very good breakfasts, pretty flowers throughout, and neat back garden; children over 6

OXFORD SP5106 **Old Bank Hotel** *92-94 High St, Oxford OX1 4BJ* (01865) 799599 **£178**; 42 distinctive, luxurious rms, with lovely bthrms. Stylish hotel with a Georgian façade masking a partly Elizabethan building; an impressive collection of 20th-c british art, excellent modern food with an italian slant in contemporary Quod restaurant and bar with zinc-topped bar, leather seating and stone floors, a carefully chosen wine list, courteous helpful staff, and seats out on the terrace, overlooking the garden; cl 24-25 Dec; disabled access

OXFORD SP5107 **Old Parsonage** *1 Banbury Rd, Oxford OX2 6NN* (01865) 310210 **£180***; 30 lovely rms. Handsome and civilised 17th-c parsonage, fairly central, with very courteous staff, good breakfasts and excellent light meals in cosy bar/restaurant; small lounge, open fires and fine paintings, and pretty little garden; they provide picnics; cl 23-27 Dec

OXFORD SP5106 **Randolph** *Beaumont St, Oxford OX1 2LN* (01865) 247481 **£190***, plus special breaks; 111 rms. Fine neo-Gothick Victorian hotel facing the Ashmolean Museum; elegant comfortable day rooms, grand foyer, graceful restaurant with lovely plasterwork ceiling, and cellar wine bar; disabled access; dogs welcome

SHILLINGFORD SU5991 **Shillingford Bridge Hotel** *Shillingford Rd, Shillingford, Wallingford, Oxfordshire OX10 8LZ* (01865) 858567 **£135**, plus special breaks; 40 rms. Riverside hotel with own river frontage, fishing and moorings, spacious comfortable bars and attractive airy restaurant (all with fine views), squash, outdoor heated swimming pool, and Sat dinner-dance; disabled access; dogs welcome away from restaurant

SHIPTON-UNDER-WYCHWOOD SP2717 **Shaven Crown** *High St, Shipton-under-Wychwood, Chipping Norton, Oxfordshire OX7 6BA* (01993) 830330 **£95***, plus special breaks; 9 comfortable rms. Densely beamed, ancient stone hospice built around striking medieval courtyard with seating by lily pool and roses; impressive medieval hall with a magnificent lofty ceiling, sweeping stairway and old stone walls, log fire in comfortable bar, intimate candlelit restaurant, well chosen wine list, good friendly service, warm relaxed atmosphere, and bowling green; disabled access; dogs welcome away from restaurant

STONOR SU7488 **Stonor Hotel** *Stonor, Henley-on-Thames, Oxfordshire RG9 6HE* (01491) 638345 **£150***, plus special breaks; 11 individually decorated rms looking over intimate walled garden. Elegantly restored 18th-c coaching inn, with good imaginative food in charming conservatory restaurant and flagstoned Blades Bar; friendly staff; disabled access; dogs welcome in bedrooms

UFFINGTON SU3089 **Craven** *Fernham Rd, Uffington, Faringdon, Oxfordshire SN7 7RD* (01367) 820449 **£80***, plus special breaks; 5 pretty rms, most with own bthrm. Very attractive, 17th-c thatched and cream-walled house with beamed sitting room, log fire in inglenook fireplace, antiques, a friendly relaxed atmosphere, and good food in beamed farmhouse kitchen; Sunday lunches available on request; lots of nearby walks; disabled access

WOODSTOCK SP4416 **Feathers** *Market St, Woodstock, Oxfordshire OX20 1SX* *(01993) 812291* **£145**, plus special breaks; 20 individually decorated rms. Lovely old building with a fine relaxing drawing room and study, open fires, first-class friendly staff, a gentle atmosphere, daily-changing imaginative food inc lovely puddings, and a sunny courtyard with attractive tables and chairs; dogs welcome in bedrooms

To see and do

Oxfordshire Family Attraction of the Year

IPSDEN SU6386 **Wellplace Zoo** Nicely low-key and undeveloped, this cheery little place is excellent value: a family of four will pay only £7 for a visit. Of course you won't get the extensive facilities offered at some other animal attractions, but that rather adds to its charm, and younger children will be just as happy meeting the residents here as they would at places costing far more to get in. When it opened 35 years ago it concentrated on birds (still very much in evidence), but today you'll find rabbits, lemurs, meerkats, guinea-pigs, ponies and otters alongside the macaws, flamingoes, owls and penguins. There are a few unexpected sights too, including a rather large triceratops. It's designed very much with children in mind, so there are opportunities for getting close to the animals, and feeding some of them. They usually have a range of shrubs and plants for sale. There's a very basic play area (good for the very smallest children only) and space for picnics. Coffee shop (wknds and school hols), shop, disabled access; cl wkdays Oct-Mar (exc most school hols); (01491) 680473; £2.50 adults, £1 children. They don't take credit or debit cards.

ABINGDON SU4997
Attractive Thames-side town, until 1974 the county town of Berkshire. Much expanded around its old partly pedestrianised core, which still has a fine old gatehouse, medieval bridge, and several handsome old buildings and almshouses around the impressive 15th/16th-c **church** of St Helen (its steeple is 13th c), unusually wider than it's long, at the junction of East and West St. A good museum in the 17th-c former county hall has changing exhibitions and craft displays; free (you may be able to visit the roof on summer Sat; £1). Remains of the partly Norman Benedictine abbey, once the second most powerful in England, have been restored, with part now housing a local theatre. The riverside Old Anchor is prettily placed for lunch.

ARDINGTON SU4388
Attractive small village, with several craft workshops in the Home Farm buildings, and an upmarket dining pub.

BANBURY SP4540
The busy shopping town was actually without its famous cross for 250 years,

between the Puritans destroying it in 1602 and the construction of its replacement in 1859. In the church graveyard is the tomb from which Jonathan Swift borrowed the name Gulliver for his traveller. The interesting old Reindeer in Parsons St is good for lunch. The B4035 towards Sibford Ferris runs through attractive hilly farmland; the loop N through North Newington, Shutford and Epwell is good too.

Banbury Museum There's quite a bit to keep families happy at this new lottery-funded local and social history museum. As well as interactive displays on the Oxford Canal, there's a costume display (dating back to the 17th-c), and a collection of Victorian toys; temporary exhibitions, and special events throughout the year. Tourist information centre, café, shop, disabled access; cl 25-26 Dec (and maybe Easter Sun); (01295) 259855; free. Also here is **Tooley's Boatyard** (dating from around 1795 it's the oldest working dry dock in Britain); the hour-long guided tours inc demonstration by a blacksmith and a short boat ride. Shop, disabled access; tours 2.30pm Fri and Sat (maybe other days too), phone to book; (01295) 272917; £5.50. You can also have a meal on the restaurant narrowboat *Rosamund the Fair*; phone for details; (01295) 278690.

BENSON SU6292

Benson Veteran Cycle Museum Private collection of over 500 bicycles from between 1818 and 1930; open am (exc Sun) Easter-Aug by appointment with Mr Passey, on (01491) 838414; free. Down by the river at the Cruiser station you can hire boats; (01491) 838304; Apr-Oct; from £25 per hour. The footpath beyond the weir bridge leads to Wallingford. The Home Sweet Home at Roke is a charming dining pub.

BIX BOTTOM SU7285

Oxfordshire Way This long-distance path gives one short easy walk with a palpable sense of peace, from the lane out past Bix Hall to Valley End Farm.

Warburg Reserve Extensive wildflower-rich rough grassland and ancient beechwood, good for wild orchids and butterflies, besides birds and perhaps deer.

BROUGHTON SP4138

Broughton Castle 🏰 (B4035 SW of Banbury) Striking early 14th/16th-c house with proper moat and gatehouse, originally owned by William of Wykeham. Exceptional oak panelling, period furniture, and Civil War relics. Some rooms have bare stone walls under elaborately plastered ceilings, an unusual combination that works rather well. *Shakespeare in Love* was partly filmed here. Snacks, shop, disabled access to ground floor only; open pm Weds, Sun (plus pm Thurs July-Aug) and bank hols Easter to mid-Sept; (01295) 276070; £5.50. The Joiners Arms over in Bloxham has enjoyable food.

BURFORD SP2512

Lovely small Cotswold town with interesting shops and teashops along its pretty main street. The church is particularly intriguing, with a super graveyard, and 17th-c graffiti by some of the 400 Leveller mutineers imprisoned here by Cromwell. The town has an interesting little museum in the Tudor market house; open pm Tues-Fri, Sun and bank hol Mon, plus all day Sat Apr-Oct; (01993) 823196; free. It's full of attractive pubs: the best for food and atmosphere is the Lamb, and the Mermaid serves food all day at wknds. Burford does get very busy indeed with visitors, and it's worth noting that several smaller and altogether quieter nearby villages are, in their way, as pretty: Taynton, the Barringtons (just over the Gloucs border), Fulbrook, Swinbrook and Asthall. All except the first have the additional attraction of a decent pub. There are attractive walks between these, along the River Windrush for much of the way - the back roads along the Windrush Valley give pleasant drives, too.

Cotswold Wildlife Park (Bradwell Grove, A361, 2m S of junction with A40) One of the things that makes this place so enjoyable is the way it's been attractively laid out in the grounds of a Gothick manor house. It's spread over 160 acres of the estate's gardens and parkland, and even parts of the house have been nicely adapted: the former stables and outbuildings are a reptile house and Bat Belfry, and the old dining room is an animal-themed brass-rubbing centre. Hundreds of different animals range from flamingoes and ostriches through zebras and the delightful red panda, to lions, and rhinos, all in spacious re-creations of their natural environments. Everything's well signposted and labelled. Various animal encounters and feeding displays throughout the day. A children's farmyard has the usual petting opportunities, and there's a good adventure playground (with an old-fashioned carousel in summer). A narrow-gauge railway operates Apr-Oct (£1 extra). There's also a tropical house (plenty of interesting plants, and exotic birds), insect and butterfly house, and a 49-metre (160-ft) walk-through aviary. Plenty of space for picnics. Some summer wknds they may have birds of prey displays, and there's a grotto in the run-up to Christmas. Meals and snacks, shops (one specially for children), disabled access; cl 25 Dec; (01993) 823006; £8.

BUSCOT SU2496

Buscot Park (A417) What makes this 18th-c house really special is the amazing collection of art and furnishings amassed by its owners; paintings by Reynolds, Gainsborough, Rembrandt, Murillo and several of the Pre-Raphaelites (inc a splendid series by Burne-Jones), with some more recent pictures too. The attractive grounds have formal water gardens and a walled kitchen garden, and pick-your-own in summer. Teas (when house is open); open pm Weds-Fri and bank hols (plus pm Mon-Tues garden only) and pms every 2nd and 4th wknd in the month Apr-Sept (plus 1st wknd in May), best to check; (01367) 240786; £6.50, £4.50 grounds only; NT. The Thames-side Trout (A417 towards Lechlade) is popular for lunch.

CHALGROVE SU6396
Attractive small village, with notable medieval wall paintings in the 11th-c **church** - which owns the village pub, the good Red Lion.

CHASTLETON SP2429
Chastleton House (off A44 NW of Chipping Norton) This handsome restored Jacobean manor house was little changed by the family who lived in it 1605-1991, really feeling like a well worn-in family house of that period, and not oversmartened despite the lovely plasterwork, beautiful oak and walnut furnishings, embroideries, Jacobite glassware, even the Bible Charles I took to the scaffold. Peaceful Jacobean gardens inc topiary, and the first-ever standard croquet lawn. Car park up hill from house. Open pm Weds-Sat Apr-Oct; (01608) 674355; *£5.80, they advise you to have a prebooked timed ticket; NT. There's pleasant walking in the area between this village, Cornwell and (just over the Gloucs border) Adlestrop. The Red Lion in nearby Little Compton has good food.

CHECKENDON SU6682
Wall painting (Church of St Peter and St Paul) It wasn't until the church organ was taken away to be repaired in 1999 that this almost perfectly preserved fragment was discovered. Covering 18 sq ft and dating from the 1330s, it depicts a gesturing figure and three knights on horseback, and is thought to belong to a much larger series of paintings destroyed in Victorian times. The subject is still unclear, but it may be of 'Christ in the Cornfield'; open all year; donations welcome. The Black Horse here is a classic village local. Other churches with fine wall paintings are those of Shorthampton SP3220, South Leigh SP3908 and South Newington SP4033.

CHINNOR SP7500
Chinnor & Princes Risborough Railway Four-mile train trips up into Buckinghamshire; trains most wknds Apr-Oct and Dec, some steam-hauled ones (usually Suns Apr-Oct); (01844) 353535 for timetable (you may need to book for special events).

CHIPPING NORTON SP3127
Chipping Norton Museum of Local History Local history in the Co-op Hall of this pleasant old stone-built wool town; shop; open 2-4pm Tues-Sat and bank hols Oct-Easter; (01608) 643779; £1. The market place is unusually wide (market Weds, farmers' market fourth Fri of month), there's a pretty church, fine 17th-c almshouses, and a good few antiques and book shops; the Chequers and Blue Boar do nice lunches. The roads to Hook Norton, or B4026/B4022 to Witney, are good Cotswoldy drives.

CLAYDON SP4549
Bygones Museum Sizeable collection of antiques and memorabilia from the 19th and early 20th c, with everything from sewing machines, lawn mowers and a printing press to tractors and steam engines; also ten re-created shop windows, and a picnic area. Meals, snacks, shop, disabled access; cl Mon-Tues, plus Nov-Mar; (01295) 690258; £2.50.

COLESHILL SU2393
This attractive village is owned by the NT; lots of good walks nearby, and the Radnor Arms has decent food.

COWLEAZE WOOD SU7295
Between the M40 and Christmas Common, this has forest art exhibits scattered around as part of a sculpture trail. You may see red kites soaring overhead, and the Fox & Hounds on Christmas Common is a good dining pub.

CROPREDY SP4646
An attractive village, where you may find sheep grazing the raised churchyard. The thatched Red Lion has decent food.

CUXHAM SU6695
Pretty thatched houses by the stream
which runs along beside the road.

DEDDINGTON SP4631
Deddington Castle 12th-c fortress
remains; there are attractive stone
buildings around the village square, inc
several antiques shops, and the
Deddington Arms and Unicorn (useful
for lunch; the Unicorn has a nice garden).

DIDCOT SU5290
Didcot Railway Centre 🚂 The
biggest collection anywhere of Great
Western Railway stock, housed in the
original engine shed, inc 20 steam
locomotives, a diesel railcar and lots of
passenger and freight rolling stock.
Meals, snacks, shop, disabled access;
open wknds all year, daily 31 May-end
Aug, best to ring for steam dates, which
usually include Sun and Weds in
summer hols; (01235) 817200; £4-£8
depending on event. The town itself
more or less sprang up around the
railway. The Fleur de Lys out at East
Hagbourne has good value food.

DORCHESTER SU5894
Dorchester Abbey Impressive and
well preserved abbey, with 12th-c nave
and rare lead font. The tower was rebuilt
in 1605 and has a 14th-c spiral staircase,
as well as a sanctuary with an exceptional
Jesse window from the same period, and
some mosaic-like 12th-c glass in other
windows. They've recently installed
heating and improved facilities in the
abbey to allow for more concerts. The
adjacent former guesthouse now houses
a little museum. In summer they do very
individual ever-so-english teas (pm
Weds-Sun (exc Fri) and bank hols), all
home-made and quite addictive. Shop,
good disabled access; museum cl Mon,
wkdys in Oct and all Nov-Apr; (01865)
340007; free. The Fleur de Lys opposite
does good lunches. The whole village is a
lovely place to explore, with interesting
antiques shops. The River Thames has
pleasant walks starting and finishing here;
you can cross at Day's Lock, and a short
walk brings you to Wittenham Clumps
(alternative access from adjacent car
park), a pair of hillocks which look across
the Chilterns and Berkshire Downs.

EWELME SU6491
One of Oxfordshire's prettiest and
most unspoilt villages; the cheerful

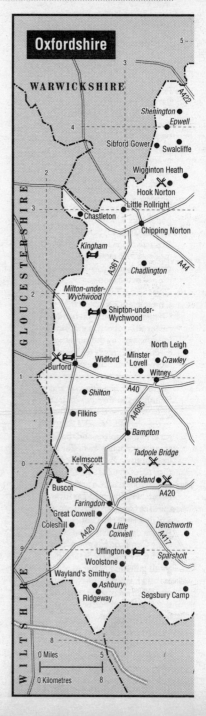

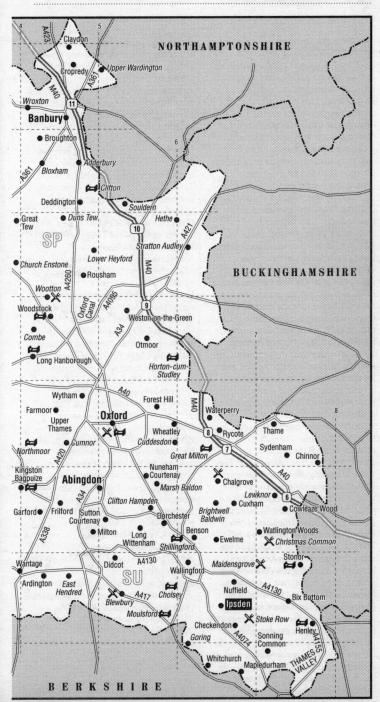

NORTHAMPTONSHIRE

Claydon
A423
Cropredy
A361
Upper Wardington
M40
Wroxton
11
Banbury
Broughton
Adderbury
A361
Bloxham
Clifton
Deddington
Souldern
Great Tew
Duns Tew
Hethe
SP
10
A421
Church Enstone
Lower Heyford
Stratton Audley
Rousham
A4260
M40
BUCKINGHAMSHIRE
Wootton
Oxford Canal
A4095
Woodstock
9
A34
Weston-on-the-Green
Combe
Otmoor
Long Hanborough
Horton-cum-Studley
Wytham
A40
Forest Hill
Waterperry
Farmoor
M40
Upper Thames
Oxford
Wheatley
8
Rycote
Thame
Cuddesdon
7
Sydenham
Chinnor
Northmoor
Cumnor
Great Milton
A420
Nuneham Courtenay
Chalgrove
A40
Kingston Bagpuize
Abingdon
Marsh Baldon
Lewknor
6
A34
Clifton Hampden
Cuxham
Cowleaze Wood
Garford
Frilford
Sutton Courtenay
Dorchester
Brightwell Baldwin
Milton
Benson
Watlington Woods
A338
Long Wittenham
Ewelme
Christmas Common
Shillingford
Wantage
Didcot
A4130
Wallingford
Maidensgrove
Stonor
Ardington
East Hendred
Cholsey
A417
Nuffield
A4130
Bix Bottom
Blewbury
Ipsden
Stoke Row
Moulsford
Checkendon
Henley
Sonning Common
A4074
A4155
Goring
Whitchurch
Mapledurham
THAMES VALLEY

B E R K S H I R E

Shepherds Hut has enjoyable fresh food.

FARMOOR SP4405

Farmoor Reservoir Sailing, bird-watching, and other activities inc trout fishing, though you'll need a permit (from £16 for half a day); (01865) 863033; free.

FILKINS SP2207

Cotswold Woollen Weavers Friendly working woollen mill, with demonstrations of traditional production methods in 18th-c buildings. Snacks, well stocked shop, some disabled access; cl am Sun, 25-31 Dec; (01367) 860491; free. It's a nice village, and the Five Alls has good food and bedrooms.

FOREST HILL SP5807

Above Oxford, this gives several pleasant walks from the White Horse pub.

FRILFORD SU4397

Millets Farm Centre Pick-your-own fruit and veg and a garden centre, animals, walks, picnic and play areas, and an unusually extensive farm shop which takes in a bakery, delicatessen, butcher's and fishmonger. A maize maze is usually open daily throughout the school summer hols (£4.50), and there's go-karting (summer hols). Meals, snacks, disabled access; cl 25 Dec; (01865) 391555; free. In nearby Fyfield, the ancient White Hart, owned by an Oxford college for 400 years, is well worth a visit.

GARFORD SU4394

Venn Mill (A338 N of Wantage) The area's regularly used working water-powered corn mill; you can buy their own wholemeal flour; open 2nd Sun in month; (01235) 868789; £1.50 includes a free bag of flour. The Black Horse in nearby East Hanney has good food.

GREAT COXWELL SU2693

Great Coxwell Barn As noble as a cathedral according to William Morris, a 13th-c stone-built tithe barn 46 by 13 metres (152-ft long, 44-ft wide), with beautifully crafted timbers supporting the roof; 50p. In charming thatched Little Coxwell the Eagle is pleasant for lunch.

GREAT TEW SP3929

The most charming village in the area (some would say in all England). It's an outstanding series of golden stone 17th- and 18th-c cottages, some

thatched and others with stone-slabbed roofs, around an attractive sloping green and among ancient trees, with wooded slopes above. The Falkland Arms (open all day summer wknds) is good.

HENLEY SU7781

Agreeable, well heeled Thames-side town famed for its summer regatta. You can usually see other rowing races or practices on the river throughout the year, or hire your own boat on (01491) 572035; from £8 an hour. The informal Anchor (Friday St) is a good value pub nr the river, and the civilised Three Tuns (Market Pl) is pleasant for lunch; just over the bridge in Remenham, the Little Angel is a good dining pub.

Greys Court (Rotherfield Greys, 3m W) Attractive gabled Tudor house with interesting ruins of its medieval predecessor; the gardens are even more alluring, with white and rose gardens, ancient wisterias, a kitchen garden, wheelhouse, icehouse and brick maze. Teas, bookstall, some disabled access; gardens open pm Weds Mar and Oct, Tues-Sat Apr-Sept; house open Weds-Fri, bank hol Mon, plus 1st Sat in month, Apr-Sept; (01491) 628529; *£5, *£3.50 gardens only; NT. The village **church** is delightful, and the Maltsters Arms dining pub has lovely country views, and good nearby walks. The B480 to Watlington is a pleasant Chilterns drive.

River and Rowing Museum 🖼 (Mill Meadows) In a stunning modern building, this has comprehensive displays on the sport inc the Regatta, and the history and life of the river itself; also special events. Meals, snacks, shop, disabled access; cl 24-26, 31 Dec, 1 Jan; (01491) 415600; £4.95.

HOOK NORTON SP3433

Hook Norton Brewery Visitor centre and little museum charting the history of this charming 150-year-old brewery; tours are 10am Mon-Fri, and occasional evenings Apr-Sept (other times too) phone to book (01608) 730384; £7.50 inc samples and a glass. As well as the 25 horsepower steam engine which has provided nearly all the brewery's power since it first opened, you can also usually see the shire horses at work (they're still used to carry out some local deliveries); cl wknds (exc Sat in Dec) 25-26 Dec, 1 Jan, and over Easter; £2 for museum. The stone-built village is attractive, and the Sun has good food.

IPSDEN SU6386

Wellplace Zoo *See separate family panel on p.471.*

The charming King William IV at Hailey has good food (and great views). Ian Smith can arrange **horse-drawn waggon rides** through these pretty Chilterns fringes; most fine summer days he runs two-horse waggons from Darkwood Farm, Park Corner on a local pub tour; (01491) 641324. Even by car, these are pleasant Chilterns drives - for instance the loop S of Nettlebed through Highmoor Cross, Stoke Row and Nuffield.

KELMSCOTT SU2599

Kelmscott Manor The summer home of William Morris until his death in 1896, now with one of the best assemblages of Morris memorabilia, standing out all the more for its domestic setting. Works by other Pre-Raphaelite artists inc splendid paintings by Rossetti, who initially shared the lease. Meals, snacks, shop, disabled access; open Weds (exc 1-2 pm), and pm 3rd Sat of month Apr-Sept, plus pm 1st and 3rd Sat July-Aug; (01367) 252486; £7. There's a nice Thames-side walk of 1½ miles E to the Swan at Radcot Bridge.

KINGSTON BAGPUIZE SU4098

Kingston House (off A415) Charming 17th-c manor house, remodelled in the early 18th c, with lovely panelling, attractive furnishings and friendly unstuffy feel; peaceful garden with mature flowering shrubs, woodland walks, and Georgian gazebo. Snacks, shop, disabled access to garden; open various Sun and bank hol Mon pms 7 Feb-10 Oct, phone for dates; (01865) 820259; *£4.50, *£2.50 garden only. The Hinds Head has enjoyable food.

LITTLE ROLLRIGHT SP2931

Rollright Stones Dramatic and mysterious Bronze Age stones, chiefly in a circle about 30 metres (100 ft) across, now thought to date from between 1500 and 2000 BC; legend has it that the stones are a king and his men tricked by a witch into falling under her spell, and petrified. It's supposed to be impossible

to count them as you can never tell where you started. The Gate Hangs High nr here is very good for lunch.

LONG HANBOROUGH SP4314

Oxford Bus Museum 🅰 (Old Station Yard) Around 45 vehicles, from Oxford horse trams to rather more modern machines (up to the 1960s), some roadworthy, others being restored. Snacks, shop, disabled access; open wknds, Weds and bank hols Easter-Oct; (01993) 883617; £2.50. The Hand & Shears at Church Hanborough is a good dining pub.

LONG WITTENHAM SU5493

Pendon Museum of Miniature Landscape and Transport

Charming exhibition showing a highly detailed model railway and meticulously researched model 1930s village scenes; you can see modellers working on the exhibits (first Sun of month), and they're always happy to chat. Special events to celebrate their 50th anniversary. Snacks, shop; open pm wknds and bank hols, plus pm Weds July-Aug; (01865) 407365; £4. The Plough (long garden by the Thames) is handy for lunch.

MAPLEDURHAM SU6776

Very attractive little community with lovely beechwoods full of birds; the nicest way to reach it is by boat from the Caversham Promenade at Reading (summer only); (0118) 948 1088.

Mapledurham House Impressive Elizabethan mansion in pretty Thames-side parkland, with paintings and family portraits, great oak staircases, and moulded Elizabethan ceilings. In the grounds is the last **watermill** on the Thames to use wooden machinery; dating from 1423, it still produces flour, bran and semolina. Also riverside walks and island with picnic area. Teas, shop, disabled access to ground floor only; open pm wknds and bank hols Easter-end Sept; (0118) 972 3350; £6 house and watermill, £4 house only, £3 watermill only. You can stay in one of the lovely cottages on the estate (some thatched).

MILTON SU4892

Milton Manor Elegant 17th-c manor house with splendid Strawberry Hill 'gothick' library, interesting chapel, walled garden, and unusual collections of teapots and fine china. Phone for opening times and prices; (01235) 862321. The cherry orchards around Milton Hill are a fine sight when the white blossom is out in spring, and around July roadside stalls sell plump red-black fresh cherries - the Grove Farm Shop (A4130) is especially friendly. The Cherry Tree pub in nearby Steventon is a useful food stop.

MINSTER LOVELL SP3211
One of the prettiest and most unspoilt old villages in the area; there's an attractive 15th-c church, village green, and 15th-c bridge over the River Windrush narrow enough for the welsh drovers to use for counting the sheep in the flocks they brought this way each year. The smart Old Swan does light lunches.

Minster Lovell Hall Imposing and attractively set, this was being used as ramshackle farm buildings until its 'restoration' as neat ruins in the 1930s. Macabre stories about the 15th-c Hall usually involve people being shut up in various places and forgotten about until their skeletons are discovered much later. Open every day, free. There's a well restored medieval dovecot nearby.

NORTH LEIGH SP3813
Roman Villa Occupied between the 2nd and 4th c, when it was a very grand place with several dozen rooms, it's now just a few neat but poignant traces, in a very pleasant wooded setting; free. The medieval village church, with a Saxon tower, is lovely inside, and the Woodman is popular for lunch.

NUFFIELD SU6787
Nuffield Place 🏠 The home of Lord and Lady Nuffield 1933-1963, with the original 30s furnishings. Good gardens with mature trees and shrubs inc rhododendrons, lawns, pond and rockery, as well as Lady Nuffield's own Wolseley and a display of vintage cars (Lord Nuffield was the founder of Morris Motors). Teas, shop, disabled access to ground floor only; open pm 2nd and 4th Suns of month May-Sept, plus last Sun in Apr; (01491) 641224; £3.50. The Crown pub here has decent food.

NUNEHAM COURTENAY SU5599
Harcourt Arboretum (A4074) Part of the Oxford University botanic department, with a good collection of conifers introduced in 1835, a 13-acre bluebell wood, traditional english meadow and lots of rhododendrons. Disabled access; cl wknds Nov-Apr, 22 Dec-3 Jan and Good Fri-Easter Mon; (01865) 343501; free, car park £2.

OTMOOR SP5614
Several square miles of flatland, so poorly drained that in very wet weather its river actually flows backwards, and interesting to walk through (there are several paths). Because serious farming is virtually out of the question, it does have more natural wildlife than most places in the county, and having purchased some of the land from local farmers, the RSPB (backed by local authorities) is working on a long-term project to make it an even more outstanding refuge, and there's now visitor access to the site. The Abingdon Arms at Beckley, with a pretty garden, is one good starting-point; the Nut Tree at Murcott is a good dining pub (not Mon).

OXFORD SP5105
On first impression this can seem quite a frenetic city: the ancient university buildings with their medieval lanes and scholarly corners are surrounded by a bustling largely industrialised town, with a formidable amount of traffic. Some of the major city centre thoroughfares have been pedestrianised in a bid to relieve the nightmarish congestion problems (you can't drive your car through the centre between 7am and 6.30pm). If you don't come by train or coach, it's certainly a good idea to leave your car at one of the five Park and Rides around the ring road; 60p parking, and £1.70 return bus fare. Guided walks around the city and colleges usually leave from the tourist information centre (15/16 Broad St) at 11am and 2pm daily (more often in the summer) exc 25-26 Dec; £6.50. For first-time visitors, hop-on-and-off **tour buses** take in many of the best sites and last about an hour (£9). Many of the city's oldest or most interesting buildings are grouped around the Bodleian Library, the Sheldonian Theatre and the splendid domed Radcliffe Camera (also a library). This partly cobbled central university area is most attractive, but does sometimes overfill with visitors. In the streets and

lanes leading off, the honey-coloured stone makes for a harmony that unites different styles and different centuries. There are a few good shops dotted about; Blackwells is the main bookseller, with several branches around the Broad St area.

Colleges Most allow visitors into at least some of their quads, and do have a wonderful timeless appeal. One of the few they failed to impress was William Cobbett, who wrote in his *Rural Rides* that he 'could not help reflecting on the drones that they contain, and the wasps they send forth'. Newcomers are often surprised to discover that the colleges are all separate bodies, each firmly maintaining its own dons, rules and traditions; the university itself is little more than an administrative umbrella. Several charge admission, notably Christ Church, New, Magdalen, Trinity, Balliol and Brasenose. Access may be more limited in term-time. A few may let you in only with a guide; ideally though, it's worth trying to explore at your own pace away from the crowds - afternoons are best, with more colleges open then. Besides colleges we pick out individually, more are tucked down some of the town's prettiest streets, such as charming Exeter, Jesus and Lincoln down Turl St, and Corpus Christi and Oriel around Merton Lane and Oriel Sq. This last college has a very attractive and unusual entrance to its dining hall. Trinity on Broad St, though not large, is very grand. Around Radcliffe Sq, Brasenose is quaint (and has good views of the surrounding skyline from its quads), and Hertford has its Bridge of Sighs over New College St, in itself worth exploring for some more unusual and less busy views and a good look at the grotesques carved on the backs of some of the buildings. Worcester and St John's have particularly nice gardens, and many of the other colleges' private Fellows' Gardens not usually open to visitors can be seen under the National Gardens Scheme.

Christ Church (St Aldates) The best known college, a magnificently stately place begun by Cardinal Wolsey in the 16th c, but soon taken over by Henry VIII. The main entrance is through Tom Tower, designed by Christopher Wren and named after its famous bell that rings out 101 times at nine o'clock every night - in less liberal times the hour when students were due back in their rooms. The hall is worth a look, with its remarkable hammerbeam roof, paintings of alumni and benefactors by all the most expensive portrait-painters of the period, and the long tables laid out with silver for meals. The elaborate little cathedral is England's smallest, and doubles as the college chapel. It has some excellent stained glass by Burne-Jones, fantastic pendent vaulting in the choir, and some of the original Norman priory work. Entry into the college may be limited on Suns. A hidden treasure unnoticed by most visitors is the college's Picture Gallery (Canterbury Quad), with an important collection of Old Master paintings and drawings, and various temporary exhibitions. Shop; cl 1-2pm, am Sun, and 1 wk at Easter and Christmas, guided tours by arrangement; (01865) 276172; £2.

Keble College (Parks Rd) Brightly Victorian and very red brick, with perhaps the most famous Pre-Raphaelite painting of all, Holman Hunt's *Light of the World*, in its chapel.

Magdalen College (High St) The most beautiful college, its tower a dramatic sight for visitors entering the city from the S. The quads and cloisters are very pleasant to stroll through, but the chief attraction is the deer park, an unexpected haven in the heart of the bustling city. There's a circular path around this meadow (you can't go in) called Addison's Walk; in spring it's a mass of snowdrops and daffodils, then has hundreds of thousands of fritillaries in later spring, and after that the deer. Over a small bridge is the Fellows' Garden with a small ornamental lake - a very peaceful, sheltered spot; usually only cl 25 Dec and 1 Jan; (01865) 276000; £3.

Merton College (Merton St) The most ancient buildings, with the country's oldest library.

New College (Holywell St) Impressive chapel, atmospheric wisteria-covered cloisters, and remains of the city wall. Nearby, the tucked-away Turf Tavern is a splendid ancient place, usually busy with students.

St Edmund Hall (Queens Lane) The only surviving medieval college, complete with Norman crypt.

University College (High St) Harmonious buildings - and an interesting monument to Shelley despite having thrown him out.

Ashmolean Museum (Beaumont St) The country's first museum, and still one of its finest, opened in 1683 and rehoused in this imposing building from 1845. The well arranged galleries include marvellous european paintings from the Renaissance to the 20th c, and antiquities from ancient Egypt, Greece and Rome; they've also a collection of asian art inc a gallery of modern chinese paintings. Meals, snacks, shop, disabled access; cl Mon (exc bank hol pms), 3 days for St Giles Fair (early Sept), and a few days over Christmas and Easter; (01865) 278000; free.

Bate Collection of Musical Instruments (St Aldates) Outstanding continually developing collection of early keyboards, woodwind, brass, percussion and other instruments; the staff are very friendly. Shop, some disabled access; cl am, wknds (exc Sat am during term-time), and a few days at Christmas and Easter, but phone to check; (01865) 276139; free.

Bodleian Library (Broad St) One of the oldest in Europe, its splendidly grand quad dominated by the Tower of the Five Orders. Most of it is closed to the public, but there's a free exhibition and you can visit the beautifully vaulted 15th-c Divinity School; guided tours show some of the library's treasures inc the Chancellor's Court, Convocation House and Duke Humfrey's Library, the oldest reading room. Tours usually leave at 10.30am, 11.30, 2 and 3pm mid-Mar-Oct; 2 and 3pm only wkdys in winter, best to phone first; (01865) 277224; no under-14s, excellent shop, limited disabled access (with notice); cl Sat pm and all Sun; £4. Altogether the library houses over 7 million volumes, going down six storeys under the centre of the city and occupying 180km (110 miles) of shelving.

Carfax Tower Right at the traditional centre of Oxford, all that remains of a 14th-c church; good views from the top, and the bells in the tower are interestingly designed. Shop; cl 25 Dec-1 Jan; (01865) 792653; £1.50.

Castle Mound There isn't much left of the Norman castle, save a tower and crypt of the castle church, and an underground well chamber, but the Mound gives quite good views over the city and its surroundings.

Christchurch Meadow A lovely unspoilt expanse of green astonishingly close to the busy city streets. You can gaze across the fields of grazing longhorn cattle to the spires in the distance, or walk under overhanging trees along the banks of the river to the boathouses; college eights row from here all year, in just about any weather.

Covered market (High St) A maze of stalls with something different at every turn; speciality shops, cafes, delicatessen and old-fashioned butchers and poultry merchants. The Oxford Sandwich Co do excellent take-away sandwiches here, and Ben's Cookies are a favourite with students.

Curioxity (Gloucester Green) The Old Fire Station complex houses a theatre and a nightclub as well as this interactive science gallery, which has enough to keep children captivated for an hour; visitors can experiment with the exhibits, and the staff are helpful. Shop; open wknds, and daily during school hols (phone to check over Christmas and Easter); (01865) 247004; £2.50. This area, interestingly rejuvenated with trendy shops, cafés and bustling markets on Weds and Thurs, was once one of the less desirable parts of town. Not far from here among the fashionable shops and boutiques of Little Clarendon St, George & Davies is a good ice-cream parlour.

Iffley Meadows These are conserved for wildlife, and in late spring are a sea of purple snake's-head fritillaries. The towpath walk by pretty Iffley Lock is pleasant, passing the Isis Tavern, which has food all day and can't be reached by road.

Modern Art Oxford (Pembroke St) This excellent modern art museum has the sort of exhibitions and displays not often found in galleries outside London; special events and tours. Meals, snacks, disabled access; cl Mon, am Sun, and and bank hols, plus 25 Dec and I Jan - worth checking; (01865) 722733; free.

Museum of Oxford (St Aldates) Interesting little local history museum, with re-created rooms, maps, and period music. Shop; cl Mon, Sun am, Good Fri, 24-26 Dec and I Jan; (01865) 252761; £2.

Museum of the History of Science (Broad St) Excellent collection of national importance, in one of the city's nicest old buildings; temporary exhibition gallery, special events and talks. Shop, limited disabled access; cl am, Mon, bank hols, and 25 Dec-I Jan; (01865) 277280; free.

Oxford Story 🏛 (Broad St) One of Europe's longest dark rides, with cars designed as desks taking you through a cheerful and well researched re-creation of university history, complete with sights, sounds and smells. A useful introduction to the city (esp for families), though no substitute for the real thing; special events during most school hols. Good shop (you can just visit here, using the entrance on Ship St), disabled access; cl 25 Dec; (01865) 728822; £6.75.

Oxford University Museum of Natural History (Parks Rd) Victorian Gothic structure specialising in natural history - outstanding if solidly earnest collection, usually enlivened by a working beehive in summer. Shop, disabled access to ground floor; cl am, and a few days over Easter and Christmas; free.

Pitt Rivers Museum (entrance via University Museum, Parks Rd) This fascinating close-packed ethnographic museum is off the tourist track. Beyond the main hall with its natural history and cathedral-like iron and glass roof, is the ethnographic collection - wonderfully eclectic to the point of being quite overwhelming, so it's worth spending £1 on the audio tour or chatting to the knowledgeable attendants to focus on the highlights. A lot of it is very odd indeed - a lucky charm in the form of a 91-year old hot cross bun, a case full of skulls and shrunken heads, severed fingertips and an inuit coat made from seal intestines. It's arranged in themes (don't miss the drawers beneath the main cases - most can be pulled out and

are stashed with yet more exhibits); firmly traditional, with neat handwritten labels, the Victorian atmosphere is part of the charm. Shop; cl am and 24-26 Dec and Easter wknd; (01865) 270927; free.

Port Meadow This is the best outlying area for Oxford walks, an expanse of waterside common land with grazing horses and flocks of geese, which extends N from Jericho and can be reached on the far side of the Oxford canal via Walton Well Rd, crossing the Thames and turning right along the W bank. Just beyond the far end of Port Meadow is the ruin of 12th-c Godstow Nunnery, where Fair Rosamund the mistress of Henry II is buried; nearby, the riverside medieval Trout pub is touristy but very attractive, and there are often peacocks around here. A second well sited riverside pub, the thatched Perch at Binsey, is another popular walking objective in this direction.

Punting and boat trips Good fun in sunny weather; once you've got the knack it's a very nice way of spending a lazy afternoon. You can hire boats from Magdalen Bridge or Folly Bridge; from around £10/£12 an hour - you'll have to put down a big deposit. Salters run steamer trips from Folly Bridge to Abingdon; May-Sept; (01865) 243421; from £5 for a 40-minute trip.

Ruskin walk From the big garden of the Fishes pub at North Hinksey, a footpath towards Oxford partly follows a causeway built originally by John Ruskin to give students experience of healthy outdoor labour.

Sheldonian Theatre (Broad St) A grand classical building, with a lovely painted ceiling. In its time it's been used for parliaments, and nowadays university ceremonies are held here; you may see gowned students heading for these on some wknds, though the theatre is closed to the public then. Nearby, the Kings Arms is a famous university haunt.

St Mary's (High St) Interesting university church with fine views from the tower, and a nice - if busy - café in the Congregation House (the oldest university building); shop; usually cl Sun am, Good Fri and 24-26 Dec; (01865) 279111; £1.60.

St Michael at the North Gate
(Cornmarket St) Oxford's oldest
building, this church with its Saxon
tower has displays of silver, clocks and
bells; great views from the tower. Shop,
disabled access to church; cl Sun am,
and 25 Dec; £1.50.

University Botanic Garden (High
St) Britain's oldest botanic garden,
founded in 1621, with 8,000 species of
plant from all over the world. It's a
lovely place to sit for a while, or wander
through on the way to the river. Shop,
disabled access; cl Good Fri and 25 Dec;
(01865) 286690; £2.50 Apr-Sept,
otherwise free (donations welcome).
They also administer the Harcourt
Arboretum at Nuneham Courtenay.

University Parks There are
countrified walks almost from Oxford's
city centre. The Parks (primarily playing
fields) are the closest place for a good
stroll - and in summer you can watch
first-class cricket matches for free.

Waterside walks The rivers Thames
and Cherwell cut strikingly rural
corridors through the city, though
walks along the Cherwell may be
impeded by closed college gates. They
are most likely to be open in mid-
afternoon.

OXFORD CANAL SP4816
For towpath walks, there's access from
the Boat pub at Thrupp SP4816. The
towpath is shadowed by the railway, so
you can walk by the canal from one
village to another, for example from
Lower Heyford SP4824 to Nethercott
SP4820, and return by train. The
website www.yourowntowpath.com is
handy if you fancy doing part of the 77
mile Oxford Canal Walk or phone
(01788) 890666 for information.

RIDGEWAY SU2885
Near the N crest of the downs, the
Ridgeway tracks right across from
Wiltshire to Berkshire. This broad
grassy trackway was used as a herding
highway for some 2,000 years before
the Romans came, and after the break-
up of the Roman empire came back into
use for the same purpose, well into
medieval times. It's now part of the
long-distance path network, and gives
good walking with fine views. The
particularly atmospheric short stretch
nr Compton Beauchamp takes in the

ancient sites of Waylands Smithy, the
White Horse and Uffington Castle; the
friendly Rose & Crown in the pretty
village of Ashbury makes a good base
for this bit.

ROUSHAM SP4823
Rousham House Nicely unspoilt
17th-c house embellished by court
artists and architects, and remodelled in
the 18th c by William Kent to give the
external appearance of a Gothic Tudor
mansion. It still has Civil War shooting
holes in the door. Excellent 18th-c
classically landscaped garden with
buildings, cascades, statues and vistas in
30 acres of hanging woods above the
River Cherwell, and walled flower and
vegetable gardens. No children under
15. Some disabled access to grounds;
house open pm Weds, Sun and bank
hols Apr-Sept, gardens open daily all
year; (01869) 347110; £3 house, £3
garden. There's a 12th-c church, and
the Bell in a pretty square of thatched
cottages at Lower Heyford has
enjoyable food, and canal walks nearby.

RYCOTE SP6604
Rycote Chapel (off A329) Peaceful
little 15th-c private chapel, later visited
by both Elizabeth I and Charles I. Shop,
disabled access; as we went to press the
site had just been sold, so best to ring
for details; (01844) 339346, or (02392)
581059.

SEGSBURY CAMP SU3883
Extensive Iron Age hill fort, later used
by the Romans, with good views;
reached by the dead-end lane up past
the Sparrow in Letcombe Regis.

**SHIPTON-UNDER-
WYCHWOOD** SP2717
Old houses around a lovely big sloping
green; the Shaven Crown is a fine
ancient inn.

SIBFORD GOWER SP3537
There are pleasant walks in the
countryside around the quiet village of
Sibford Gower, which has a handsome
manor house; the 17th-c Bishop Blaize
pub has lovely views from its splendid
garden.

SONNING COMMON SU7079
Herb Farm (Peppard Rd) Extensive
range of herb plants and products, with
over 200 different species in the display
garden, and a Saxon-design maze
(summer only; £1.50). Refurbished

coffee shop, shop, disabled access; cl
25-26 Dec, and 1 Jan; (0118) 972 4220;
free. The Greyhound (Gallowstree
Common Rd) has good food.

STONOR SU7489
Stonor House Even older than the
stately Tudor façade suggests, with
beautiful furnishings, paintings,
sculptures and tapestries, and
mementoes of Jesuit scholar Edward
Campion, one of the many Catholic
recusants who found refuge here during
the Reformation. There are lovely
gardens, a medieval chapel, and a
wooded deer park. Snacks, shop; open
pm Sun and bank hols Apr-Sept, plus pm
Weds July-Aug; (01491) 638587; £6,
chapel and garden only £3.50. The
smart Stonor Arms is useful for lunch.
The deer park is skirted by an attractive
right of way from the village, and you
can link this with the famous and
unusual Maharajah's Well in the
charming village of Stoke Row; or for a
longer Chilterns walk you can continue
E to Turville in Buckinghamshire.

SUTTON COURTENAY SU5093
An attractive village to stroll through,
with things to look out for - like Asquith
and Orwell, unlikely bedfellows in their
final rest in the graveyard. The smart Fish
restaurant is good, and the 16th-c
George & Dragon does popular bar food.

SWALCLIFFE SP3737
Swalcliffe Barn (B4035) A very well
preserved tithe barn, with much of its
medieval half-cruck timber roof intact;
there's a display of agricultural and
trade vehicles, and a local history
exhibition. Shop, disabled access; open
pm Sun and bank hols Easter-Oct;
(01295) 788278; free. The village is
pretty, and the picturesque thatched
Stags Head has good food.

SYDENHAM SP7301
A charming village, with a lovely church;
the low-beamed Crown's licensees are
doing good value home cooking.

THAME SP7006
Well worth a look for its splendid range
of unspoilt architecture. The very wide
main street has escaped any significant
development this last century, and has
medieval timber-framed buildings next
to stately Georgian houses; the 13th-c
church is attractive. The 15th-c Bird
Cage Inn used to be the town lock-up,

the interesting old Swan has good bar
food, and the thatched and timbered
Old Trout is a pleasant restaurant-with-
rooms.

THAMES VALLEY SU7678
Shared with Berks and Bucks, this has a
classic, very english sort of beauty, with
boating scenes, superb trees and
riverside architecture. Riverside walks
on the Oxfordshire side are possible
only in places, notably between Henley
and Sonning - for instance to Shiplake
Lock from the Plowden Arms at
Shiplake; you can also get down to the
Thames from the Perch & Pike dining
pub at South Stoke SU5983.

UFFINGTON SU3089
Charming village, with decent food at
the Fox & Hounds. Opposite here is
John Betjeman's former home Garrards
Farm; as warden of the magnificent
13th-c St Mary's church, he made sure
even its oil lamps were preserved.
Tom Brown's School Museum
(Broad St) Young Mr Brown's
schooldays were based on those the
author Thomas Hughes passed here;
there's an exhibition on his life and
work. Shop; open pm wknds Easter-
Oct; (01367) 820259; 60p.
Uffington Castle High above the
village, this Iron Age fort covered over
30,000 sq metres (eight acres) but had
only one gateway; great views over the
vale below. On the hillside a 115-metre
(375-ft) **white horse** carved into the
chalk is now thought to be around
3,000 years old; it's a striking design,
very Celtic. If you stand in the centre of
the eye and turn around three times
with your eyes closed, any reasonable
wish will be granted. This is one good
setting-off point for the Ridgeway. The
flat-topped little hill below is said to be
where George killed the dragon. A bit
over a mile E, off the B4507, the turning
off up towards the downs opp the
Kingston Lisle road almost immediately
passes a cottage on the left which has
outside a huge pitted flint rock, locally
known as the blowing stone: if you blow
in the right hole and in the right way you
can produce a splendid deep blast of
sound.

UPPER THAMES SP4001
W of Oxford, the Thames flows
through low-lying country, giving the

sort of walk you enjoy more for the people you're with than the scenery itself. The Maybush dining pub on the A415 at Newbridge is a useful focus for pleasant if undramatic riverside strolls through low-lying country, and the Rose Revived here is worth knowing for its big Thames-side lawn. Other pubs handy for quiet Thames walks which also have decent food are the Ferryman off the B4449 S of Stanton Harcourt at Bablock Hythe SP4304 (it runs a ferry for walkers and cyclists by appointment; (01865) 880028); the Talbot on the B4044 nr the Swinford toll bridge SP4409, and the Trout at Tadpole Bridge SP3300 on the unclassified road between Bampton and Buckland.

WALLINGFORD SU6089
Wallingford Museum (High St) Very good sight-and-sound history of the area, complete with reconstructed Victorian street. Shop; cl am (exc Sat), all Mon (exc bank hols), Sun (exc Jun-Aug) and all Dec-Feb; (01491) 835065; £2.50. The George, an old coaching inn nearby, has decent food. There are the ruins of a Norman castle on a hill.

WANTAGE SU3987
Historic town where King Alfred was reputedly born; recently much expanded, though there's an attractive quiet corner by the 13th/15th-c church with its raised graveyard, and in Newbury St (where the Royal Oak does decent lunches Fri/Sat) 17th-c almshouses have a courtyard cobbled with bones. The downland roads S into Berks have fine views.

Vale and Downland Museum Centre (Church St) Nicely diverse, from well displayed local history to a Formula 1 Williams racing car; a children's gallery has good hands-on activities such as brass rubbing, also films and touch-screen computers. The tourist information centre is here as well. Good home-made lunches and cakes, shop, disabled access; cl Sun am, Good Fri, a few days over Christmas and New Year and some bank hols, phone to check; (01235) 771447; £1.50 (unlimited visits for a year).

WATERPERRY SP6206
Waterperry Gardens (nr Wheatley) Colourful 80-year-old gardens with herbaceous borders, formal rose

garden with new and old roses, medieval knot and alpine gardens, and a pleasant river walk; there's a Saxon church with original windows, a little agricultural museum (cl am, and Mon), and a craft gallery with changing exhibitions (cl Mon). Snacks, garden shop with interesting plants, disabled access; cl 25 Dec-1 Jan, and around 17-20 July for an arts and crafts festival; (01844) 339226; £3.75. The Rising Sun in Wheatley has enjoyable food.

WATLINGTON WOODS SU7093
A mass of bluebells in spring, these give great views over Oxfordshire from this steep edge of the Chiltern Hills. The nearby Carriers Arms (Hill Rd) has cheap generous food - and a kite-feeding table.

WAYLAND'S SMITHY SU2885
Midway along the Ridgeway between the Uffington White Horse and the B4000 above pretty thatched Ashbury (where the Rose & Crown is ideally placed for walkers), this was even in Saxon times reputed to be the forge of a magic blacksmith, who would invisibly shoe your horse overnight if you left it there with a silver coin - and exact horrid penalties if you tried to slip by without paying. It's an impressive place, alone on the downs, an excavated neolithic burial chamber rather over 5,000 years old, made with massive sarsen stones each weighing several tons; free.

WESTON-ON-THE-GREEN SP5318
Godwin's Icecream Farm You can get around 50 different flavours of ice-cream at this developing family-run farm (and from a window in the café you may be able to see them milking the cows). Pleasant farm trails, and a new pets' corner. Meals, snacks, shop, disabled access; cl 25-26 Dec and all Jan; (01869) 351647; free.

WHEATLEY SP5805
A place of bizarre-shaped buildings: the unusual octagonal windmill is open by appointment, and usually pm 2nd Sun May-Oct; (01865) 874610; free; while the village lock-up is shaped like a pyramid. The Sun (Church Rd) has good bar food. Garsington has decidely smart open-air operas.

WHITCHURCH SU6377
An attractive little village, with nice

walks nearby. Just over the toll bridge, the riverside Swan has a good range of food all day. At **Boze Down Vineyard** (B471 N), you can get free tastings; pm wknds; cl Jan-Feb; (0118) 984 4031.

WIDFORD SP2712

Widford church and lost village (just outside Burford) The church is very simple, but notable for three things - its medieval wall paintings, the remains of a Roman pavement at the west end of the chancel, and its surroundings, a former village that save one solitary house has now virtually disappeared.

WIGGINTON HEATH SP3834

Waterfowl Park & Children's Animal Centre Set up especially with children in mind, this pleasantly undeveloped place has plenty of baby animals to cuddle, as well as rare breeds, ostriches, emus, uncommon aviary birds, and 10 well set out waterfowl ponds, awash with ducks; play area and pet shop. Wear wellies in wet weather. Summer snacks, shop, disabled access; cl 25 Dec; (01608) 730252; £4. The little White Swan in Wigginton has decent food.

WITNEY SP3609

Saxon kings used to hold their meetings, or witans, here - hence the name. It was a prosperous town in the Middle Ages, and is still well known for its blankets, made here ever since. Quiet and relaxed, with picturesque stone buildings, market square still with its ancient butter cross and 17th-c clock, and quite a few interesting old buildings such as the 13th-c church and 18th-c blanket hall. Just off Church Green you can see the excavated foundations of a 12th-c palace of the Bishops of Winchester; site open daily all year (interpretation centre open pm wknds Easter-mid-Sept; (01993) 814114; free). The Three Horseshoes (Corn St) has good food.

Cogges Farm Museum (Church Lane) This charming old place gives a vivid illustration of Victorian rural life. Most popular with children are the demonstrations of cooking in the Victorian kitchen, and younger visitors can usually try on period clothes. The striking manor house dates back seven centuries in parts; there are taped tours of the upstairs rooms, and an activity

room with Victorian toys and games. Outside are the sorts of animals you'd have found on the farm 100 years ago: heavy horses, pigs, cows, and chickens, with regular feeding displays, and hand-milking in the old dairy. On some days they have weaving, lace-making or butter-making demonstrations; regular special events at wknds. The grounds are attractive, with walled gardens, a riverside walk and a peaceful orchard. Snacks, shop, some disabled access; cl Mon, am wknds, and Dec-Mar; (01993) 772602; £4.40.

WOODSTOCK SP4416

Civilised and prosperous small town, with good antiques shops and fine stone buildings. The Black Prince (riverside garden) and Star (food all day) are useful stops. The graveyard of nearby Bladon church, where Churchill is buried, gives views over Blenheim Park.

Blenheim Palace (A44) One of England's most impressive stately homes: given to the Duke of Marlborough by Queen Anne as a reward for his victory over the forces of Louis XIV, the house itself covers 14 acres, and the grounds stretch for well over 2,000. It's astonishingly grand: highlights include the sumptuous State Rooms, 56-metre (183-ft) Long Library, and elaborate ceiling in the Great Hall, along with plenty of luxurious furnishings and sculpture. Churchill was born here in 1874, and there's a straightforward exhibition on his life. You can walk around on your own, or half-hour guided tours leave regularly. The extensive parkland was landscaped by Capability Brown; you can picnic just about anywhere. Various monuments and statues are dotted around the grounds, and the formal gardens are magnificent, particularly the water terraces and italian garden. There's also a miniature railway, butterfly house, good maze (its design inspired Grinling Gibbons's carvings in the palace), a model village, and play areas. Meals, snacks, shops and plant centre, some disabled access; house and most attractions open mid-Mar to Oct (phone for information about special events outside these times), park open all year; (01993) 811325; full ticket £12.50, entry to the park £10 for a carload (£3.50 for pedestrians), gardens £3.50 - prices are less off peak. For a brief taste of the estate, a public right of way runs through it, with pleasant walks (for example from the attractive village of Combe).

Oxfordshire County Museum (Fletcher's House) Elegant town house with pleasant gardens and good displays. Snacks, shop, disabled access; cl Sun am, Mon, Good Fri, and 25-26 Dec; (01993) 811456; free.

WOOLSTONE SU2987 An attractive village in the Vale of the White Horse; Thomas Hughes reputedly wrote *Tom Brown's Schooldays* in the bar of the friendly White Horse inn here (good value bedrooms).

WYTHAM SP4708 Charming unspoilt village, all houses owned and preserved by Oxford University. The White Hart has modern food all day.

Other charming small towns and villages, all with decent pubs, include Adderbury SP4635, Ashbury SU2685, Bampton SP3103, Blewbury SU5385, Bloxham SP4235 (splendid church spire), Brightwell Baldwin SU6595, Buckland SU3497, Chadlington SP3222, Church Enstone SP3724, Clifton Hampden SU5495, Combe SP4115, Crawley SP3412, Cuddesdon SP5903, Cumnor SP4603, Denchworth SU3791, Duns Tew SP4528, East Hendred SU4588 (interesting church), Epwell SP3540, Faringdon SU2895, Goring SU6080, Hethe SP5929, Lewknor SU7198, Little Coxwell SU2893, Lower Heyford SP4824, Marsh Baldon SU5699, Milton-under-Wychwood SP2618, Shenington SP3742, Shilton SP2608, Souldern SP5131, Sparsholt SU3487, Stratton Audley SP6026, Upper Wardington SP4945, Wootton SP4320 and Wroxton SP4142.

Where to eat

BLEWBURY SU5285 **Blewbury Inn** *London Rd (01235) 850496* Small downland village inn with a charming mix of stylishly simple furnishings and log fire in the left-hand bar, separate dining room, a warmly friendly atmosphere, good imaginative food cooked by the french landlord/chef, nice house wines, and well kept real ales; monthly themed dinners; bdrms. £30/2-course option £19.50

BUCKLAND SU3498 **Lamb** *(01367) 870484* Rather smart 18th-c stone dining pub in a tiny village, with a civilised little bar, sheep and lamb pictures on the cream-painted walls, newspapers to read, and examples of their own chutneys and jams; delicious imaginative food, no smoking restaurant, a dozen wines by the glass, real ales, and smart helpful service; comfortable bdrms; pleasant, tree-shaded garden, and good walks nearby. £28.90|**£6.95**

BURFORD SP2512 **Jonathan's at the Angel** *14 Witney St (01993) 822714* Pretty 16th-c coaching inn with three brasserie-style rooms, beams, white walls and chunky pine furniture, an informal atmosphere, very good modern european cooking from a short but wide-ranging menu, and helpful service; pretty walled garden for summer dining; attractive bdrms; cl Sun pm, Mon, Tues-Weds am in winter (best to phone), 3 wks Jan/Feb; children over 9. £32

CHALGROVE SU6397 **Red Lion** *High St (01865) 890625* Appealing old traditional pub with a smartly contemporary twist to its décor, a log fire and old woodburner, carefully collected prints and period cartoons, and fresh flowers; well kept ales, decent wines, imaginative well presented food, a helpful landlord, and no smoking back dining room; no food Sun pm; cl 25 Dec; children must be well behaved; disabled access. £24.50|**£9.95**

CHRISTMAS COMMON SU7193 **Fox & Hounds** *(01491) 612599* Extended dining pub with barn restaurant and a couple of bars plus unchanged original rooms with beams, big inglenook fireplace, and wooden tables and chairs; good interesting food (they also sell free range eggs and honey), well kept real ales, and decent wines; lovely Chilterns countryside all round with enjoyable walks - especially during the bluebell season; cl 25 Dec; disabled access. £29|**£6**

HOOK NORTON SP3533 **Sun** *High St (01608) 737570* Facing the church in a pretty village, this bustling, friendly pub has a good mix of drinkers and eaters, a flagstoned front bar with a huge log fire and hop-strung beams, a snug carpeted room with comfortable banquettes, and an attractive partly no smoking green-walled restaurant; a wide choice of imaginative popular food (inc very good filled baguettes), real ales, good value wines, and efficient service; bdrms; good disabled facilities. £24.50|**£7.50**

KELMSCOTT SU2599 **Plough** *(01367) 253543* Pretty little inn near Thames with attractively traditional small bar, ancient flagstones, stripped stone walls, and a relaxed chatty atmosphere; a larger cheerfully carpeted back bar, log fires, enjoyable food with interesting daily specials, and well kept real ales; pretty garden with aunt sally, boat moorings, local fishing, and lots of surrounding walks - on the Oxfordshire cycleway, too. £22.75|**£4.50**

MAIDENSGROVE SU6990 **Five Horseshoes** *(01491) 641282* High in the Chilterns beechwoods, this little 17th-c brick house has fine views from several tables in its no smoking dining conservatory, and from the sheltered back garden; rambling bar with log fire and lots of banknotes from around the world, good imaginative food, a decent wine list, well kept real ales, and separate walkers' bar; cl pm 25 Dec, 26 Dec, 1 Jan; children in top bar; partial disabled access. £28|**£7**

OXFORD SP5007 **Branca** *111 Walton St (01865) 556111* Informal, friendly and very popular modern restaurant with lots of exposed brick and lots of glass, a big bar area, and plenty of dark-wood tables and red-seated chairs; a casual, friendly atmosphere, vibrant Italian-influenced cooking, an all-italian wine list, and cheery and attentive service; disabled access. £25|**£5.10**

OXFORD SP5107 **Gees** *61a Banbury Rd (01865) 553540* Relaxed, airy atmosphere, fresh herbs and spices to enliven interesting vegetarian pastas, wild mushrooms and so forth as well as good meat and fish dishes, good unusual wines; in genuine old conservatory; no smoking (except in bar); cl 25-26 Dec; disabled access. £34|**£8.50**

OXFORD SP5007 **Petit Blanc** *71-72 Walton St (01865) 510999* Very popular, stylish and airy two-room brasserie, open all day for breakfast, lunch, afternoon tea and dinner; from the smarter room you can see into the kitchen and watch the preparation of the extremely good mediterranean food; friendly service and helpful notes against each wine listed; children very welcome; cl 25 Dec; disabled access. £30/2-course set menu £13.50

STOKE ROW SU6884 **Crooked Billet** *Nottwood Lane (01491) 681048* Open-plan beamed dining pub with a relaxed homely atmosphere (rather like a french country restaurant), log fires, a wide choice of good interesting food inc vegetarian menu, decent wines and real ales, and big garden by Chilterns beechwoods; live music evenings; children must be well behaved. £30|**£6.95**

TADPOLE BRIDGE SP3300 **Trout** *(01367) 870383* Popular pub peacefully set by the Thames, with a cheerfully bustling atmosphere and a nice mix of drinkers and diners; L-shaped bar with plenty of seats on flagstones, friendly staff, well kept real ales, home-made sloe gin, cherry plum brandy and elderflower cordial, interesting, enjoyable food from a changing menu, and a lovely summer garden. £24.85|**£6.95**

WOOTTON SP4319 **Kings Head** *Chapel Hill (01993) 811340* Pretty beamed 17th-c Cotswold stone pub with civilised no smoking lounge, a nice mix of furniture, open log fire, very good imaginative food inc lovely puddings, well kept real ales, and decent wines; cl Mon, Christmas; no children. £30|**£10.25**

Special thanks to Derek and Sylvia Stephenson, Rebecca Nicholls

Please let us know what you think of places in the *Guide*. Use the report forms at the back of the book, write us a letter or log on to www.goodguides.co.uk

SHROPSHIRE

Classic unspoilt english countryside and medieval market towns, some charming retreats to stay in; several entertaining family destinations, with plenty of farmyard fun

Shropshire, particularly in its southern parts, has plenty of lovely untouched countryside, and some charming places to stay. Drives and walks pass attractive buildings in stone or black and white timbering, while haunting ruins and a set of uncommonly distinctive hills give sleepy views. The splendid Severn Valley Railway passes through beautiful scenery in the south of the county, as does the Severn Way - a riverside walk from mid-Wales to Bristol. In general Shropshire is good value for holiday-makers.

Being as it is largely rural, this is an especially good county for outdoor and farm attractions: this year's top Family Attraction here is a particularly enjoyable choice for a sunny day - the enchanting Hawkstone Park Follies. Readers recommend too the Secret Hills Discovery Centre at Craven Arms, which has good interactive exhibitions on the history of the countryside. Children like the farm parks at Preston-on-the-Weald (lots going on) and Billingsley (friendly traditional place), and this year we've added one in Farlow too; at Onibury you'll find a colourful collection of rare poultry. Oswestry's Park Hall and Acton Scott Historic Working Farm (unusual in that it's aimed at adults as much as children) both have interesting displays on the history of farming.

For a complete change (and with more than enough for a very full day), the preserved and re-created past at Ironbridge, birthplace of the Industrial Revolution, is a real eye-opener. Elsewhere, grand Attingham Park at Atcham (family room and a playground), the fine medieval manor at Stokesay, Boscobel House (King Charles II connections) and the two gardens at or near Hodnet are worth seeking out. There's also an Elizabethan house near Broseley, a Victorian villa in Wellington, and at Quatt a 17th-c house with pleasant grounds; the ruins at Buildwas and Haughmond Abbey are quite something. Cosford is a must for aviation enthusiasts.

With more than 500 listed buildings and a splendidly craggy castle, Ludlow is beautiful. Bridgnorth and Much Wenlock are good choices for a relaxed afternoon, and Wroxeter is the place to be if you're interested in the Romans. Shrewsbury has quite a bit to offer among its more workaday trappings.

Where to stay

ALL STRETTON SO4595 Jinlye *Castle Hill, All Stretton, Church Stretton, Shropshire SY6 6JP (01694) 723243* **£70***, plus special breaks; 7 spacious comfortable rms with lovely views. Charming 16th-c house in large grounds surrounded by National Trust land; log fires in the comfortable lounges (one has an inglenook fireplace, lots of heavy beams, and a mix of interesting furniture), good home cooking in big no smoking dining room, enjoyable breakfasts, and friendly owners; self-catering also; children over 12; disabled access

BISHOP'S CASTLE SO3288 **Castle Hotel** *Market Sq, Bishop's Castle, Shropshire SY9 5BN (01588) 638403* **£65**; 6 spacious rms with fine views. On the site of the old castle keep, this enjoyable 17th/18th-c hotel has good fires, a relaxed and friendly atmosphere, lovely home-made food, well kept beers, and welcoming owners; crown bowling green at top of garden (available for residents); disabled access

CLUN SO2882 **New House Farm** *Clun, Craven Arms, Shropshire SY7 8NJ (01588) 638314* **£55***; 2 rms. Remote 18th-c farmhouse nr the welsh border with plenty of surrounding hillside walks; no smoking homely rooms, packed lunches, good breakfasts, plenty of books, a country garden and peaceful farmland (which includes an Iron Age hill fort), and helpful friendly owner; cl end Oct-Easter; children over 10; dogs welcome in bedrooms

DIDDLEBURY SO5085 **Delbury Hall** *Diddlebury, Craven Arms, Shropshire SY7 9DH (01584) 841267* **£120**; 4 rms. Beautiful stately Georgian house in 80 acres of landscaped parkland with ornamental duck on the lake, trout fishing, flower-filled gardens, and hard tennis court; large hall with fine oak staircase, spacious drawing room, and sitting room, enjoyable food using their own vegetables and eggs, a good wine list, and hearty breakfasts; cl Christmas; children by arrangement and not in dining room

HANWOOD SJ4409 **White House** *Hanwood, Shrewsbury, Shropshire SY5 8LP (01743) 860414* **£65***, plus special breaks; 6 rms, 3 with own bthrm. Charming 16th-c black and white half-timbered house with two sitting rooms, breakfasts using their own eggs, and two acres of garden; no smoking; children over 12

HOPESAY SO3883 **Old Rectory** *Hopesay, Craven Arms, Shropshire SY7 8HD (01588) 660245* **£90***; 3 comfortable rms, one with own sitting room. 17th-c rectory with lovely two-acre garden overlooking Hopesay Hill (NT); comfortable drawing room with log fire and baby grand piano, attractive recently redecorated dining room with excellent home cooking, and hearty breakfasts with home-baked bread; no smoking; super walks from the house; cl Christmas and New Year; no children

HOPTON WAFERS SO6376 **Crown** *Hopton Wafers, Kidderminster, Worcestershire DY14 0NB (01299) 270372* **£75**, plus special breaks; 7 rms. Attractive creeper-covered stone inn in pleasant countryside, with interestingly furnished bar, inglenook fireplace, enjoyable food, decent house wines, beers and malt whiskies, friendly efficient service, and streamside garden; children over 12; dogs welcome in bedrooms

IRONBRIDGE SJ6603 **Valley Hotel** *20 Buildwas Rd, Ironbridge, Telford, Shropshire TF8 7DW (01952) 432247* **£140***, plus special breaks; 35 rms, some in renovated stables and servants' quarters. Carefully refurbished 18th-c country house in secluded grounds close to the famous iron bridge; friendly, pleasant and helpful staff, good food from a varied menu using top quality ingredients in no smoking restaurant

KNOCKIN SJ3321 **Top Farmhouse** *Knockin, Oswestry, Shropshire SY10 8HN (01691) 682582* **£50**; 3 pretty rms. Most attractive Grade I listed black and white timbered house dating back to the 16th c, with friendly owners, lots of timbers and beams, a log fire in the restful comfortable drawing room, good breakfasts in the large dining room, and an appealing garden; grand piano; children over 12; dogs welcome away from dining room

LLANFAIR WATERDINE SO2476 **Waterdine** *Llanfair Waterdine, Knighton, Shropshire LD7 1TU (01547) 528214* **£80**; 3 pretty rms. 16th-c timbered drovers' inn, now a restaurant-with-rooms in beautiful countryside, with lovely views and gardens overlooking the River Teme; inglenook fireplace, watercolours, and leaded windows in bar/lounge, bright conservatory, imaginative cooking in former taproom with fresh flowers, a heavily beamed ceiling and ancient stone floor - marvellous breakfasts; no smoking; cl Sun, Mon exc bank hols; children over 12

LONGVILLE SO5393 **Longville Arms** *Longville, Much Wenlock, Shropshire TF13 6DT (01694) 771206* **£50***; 5 comfortable rms in converted stables, with showers. Warmly friendly inn with two spacious bars, well kept real ales, a wide range of enjoyable food in the new dining room, superb breakfasts, and a large terrace overlooking the big children's play area; disabled access; dogs welcome

LUDLOW SO5174 **Wheatsheaf** *Lower Broad St, Ludlow, Shropshire SY8 1PQ* (01584) 872980 **£50***, plus special breaks; 5 comfortable oak-beamed rms with showers. Attractively furnished small 17th-c pub built into medieval town gate; traditional atmosphere, two log fires, lots of hops, timbers, and exposed stone walls, wide range of good food in bar and no smoking restaurant (super steaks), and real ales; dogs welcome away from restaurant

MUCH WENLOCK SO6299 **Talbot** *High St, Much Wenlock, Shropshire TF13 6AA* (01952) 727077 **£75***, plus special breaks; 6 rms. Dating from 1360 and once part of Wenlock Abbey, this converted 18th-c malthouse is very civilised, with pretty flowers, log fires, prints, pleasant staff, good food in no smoking restaurant and bar, and well kept real ales; cl 25 Dec

NORTON SJ7200 **Hundred House** *Bridgnorth Rd, Norton, Shifnal, Shropshire TF11 9EE* (01952) 730353 **£99***, plus special breaks; 10 cottagey rms with swing and lavender-scented sheets. Carefully refurbished mainly Georgian inn with quite a sophisticated feel, neatly kept bar with old quarry-tiled floors, beamed ceilings, oak panelling and handsome fireplaces, elaborate evening meals using inn's own herbs, friendly service, good bar food, and excellent breakfasts; delightful garden; dogs in bedrooms (£10)

RHYDYCROESAU SJ2430 **Pen-y-Dyffryn Hall** *Rhydycroesau, Oswestry, Shropshire SY10 7JD* (01691) 653700 **£98***, plus special breaks; 12 rms with really helpful information packs about where to go. Handsome Georgian stone-built rectory in five acres with lovely views of the Shropshire and border hills, and trout fishing, hill-walking and riding (shooting can be arranged); log fires in both comfortable lounges, good food using the best local ingredients, helpful staff, and a relaxed friendly atmosphere; cl 20 Dec-20 Jan; dogs welcome

SHREWSBURY SJ4417 **Fitz Manor** *Fitz, Bowmere Heath, Shrewsbury, Shropshire SY4 3AS* (01743) 850295 **£60***; 3 rms, shared bthrm. Lovely black and white timbered 15th-c manor house with oak panelling and log fire in comfortable sitting room, a big dining room with antiques, paintings and parquet flooring, good evening meals, big breakfasts, and friendly owners; outdoor heated swimming pool

STREFFORD SO4485 **Strefford Hall Farm** *Strefford, Craven Arms, Shropshire SY7 8DE* (01588) 672383 **£52***; 3 rms. No smoking Victorian stone-built farmhouse surrounded by 360 acres of working farm; woodburner in sitting room, good breakfasts, and lots of walks; cl Christmas and New Year; disabled access; dogs welcome in bedrooms

WESTON SJ5828 **Citadel** *Weston, Shrewsbury, Shropshire SY4 5JY* (01630) 685204 **£90***; 3 rms in twin turrets. Fine castellated house overlooking Hawkstone Park, with country-house atmosphere, baby grand piano and unusual strapwork ceiling in the elegant sitting room, full-sized table in snooker room, enjoyable food (bring your own wine) in no smoking dining room, and welcoming owners; cl Christmas and Easter; no children

WORFIELD SO7595 **Old Vicarage** *Hallon, Worfield, Bridgnorth, Shropshire WV15 5JZ* (01746) 716497 **£135**, plus special breaks; 14 pretty rms. Restful and carefully restored Edwardian rectory in two acres; two airy conservatory-style lounges, very good interesting food in no smoking restaurant, a fine wine list, a cosseting atmosphere, and warmly friendly, helpful service; good disabled access; dogs welcome in bedrooms

WREKIN SJ6309 **Buckatree Hall** *Wrekin, Telford, Shropshire TF6 5AL* (01952) 641821 **£86**; 62 rms, several with own balconies and many with lake views. Comfortable former hunting lodge dating from 1820, in large wooded estate at the foot of the Wrekin; extended and modernised with comfortable day rooms, enjoyable food in the Terrace Restaurant, and helpful attentive service; dogs welcome in bedrooms

WROCKWARDINE SJ6212 **Church Farm** *Wrockwardine, Telford, Shropshire TF6 5DG* (01952) 244917 **£48**, plus special breaks; 6 individual well equipped rms, most with own bthrm. Friendly Georgian farmhouse on very ancient site overlooking the attractive garden and church; a relaxed atmosphere, particularly good caring service, beams and log fire in lounge, and good daily changing food in traditionally furnished dining room; children over 10; dogs welcome (not in dining room)

To see and do

Shropshire Family Attraction of the Year

HAWKSTONE PARK SJ5628 **Hawkstone Park Follies** Children love exercising their legs and imagination at this delightful place, made up of around 100 acres of steeply wooded parkland, beautifully restored to its full glory. The joy of it is simply wandering round, past various follies and the ruins of a medieval castle, and through intricate arches and passageways hewn out of the rock. Elaborate stories and myths have been created to explain the numerous oddities, though the reality is a little more prosaic: the grottoes and gardens were constructed by the Hill family in the 18th c. There are spectacular views throughout, not least from the top of the obelisk, which if you can face the 152 steps up the spiral staircase is said on clear days to offer views of 13 counties. There's a fantastic underground grotto with tales told by an eerily-convincing laser-powered animatron, and they have a good range of special events. Readers particularly enjoy their well organised Easter egg hunt, but they also have weekends of Arthurian legend, battle re-enactments, falconry displays and countryside activities; there may be an extra charge for some of these. Events around Hallowe'en and Christmas make good use of the wonderfully atmospheric surroundings. Hawkstone's appeal isn't just to families: it's a relaxing place for anyone to explore, at its best in fine weather, and perhaps at its prettiest around rhododendron time. The full circuit can easily take up to three and a half hours and the path isn't always easy going, so sensible shoes are recommended. You may need a torch for some of the caves and tunnels (some of these are closed in Jan). Dogs on leads are allowed. The BBC's fondly remembered *Chronicles of Narnia* was filmed here. Meals, snacks, shop, limited disabled access (no charge for wheelchairs but you can't go much further than the picnic area); open wknds Jan-Mar, daily except Mon and Tues Apr/May/Sept/Oct, and every day Jun-Aug, plus some dates around Christmas; (01939) 200611; £5.50 adults, £3.50 children. They do a very good value family ticket, £15 for two adults and up to three children. Entry is usually a few pounds cheaper between Jan and Mar.

ACTON BURNELL SJ5301
Acton Burnell Castle Ruined red sandstone manor house built in the 13th c, but almost abandoned by 1420; disabled access; free; EH. The Plume of Feathers at Harley is fairly handy for lunch. The Swan at nearby Frodesley has good interesting food.
ACTON SCOTT SO4589
Acton Scott Historic Working Farm (off A49 S of Little Stretton) Good introduction to traditional rural life, with crops cultivated using old rotation methods; all the work is done by hand or horse power, with period farm machinery. Lots of craft demonstrations, daily butter-making, and a few rare breeds. There's a willow maze for children, but unusually this is a farm aimed just as much at adults. Meals, snacks, shop, disabled access

(can be rough on the fields); cl Mon (exc bank hols), and Nov-Mar; (01694) 781306; £4.25. The nicely updated Station Hotel at Marshbrook (B4370, just over the A49) does enjoyable interesting food.
ASTLEY ABBOTS SO7096
Astley Abbots Lavender Farm ▣ (off B4373 N of Bridgnorth) You can pick your own lavender at this friendly farm; also five acres of gardens, and an intriguing look (through an infra-red viewing screen) at bumblebees busy at work, and honey bees too in observation hives. Tearoom, shop, disabled access; open July-Aug; (01746) 763122; farm free, gardens £2.50. The prettily set Pheasant over at Linley does enjoyable lunches.
ATCHAM SJ5409
Attingham Park ▣ Splendidly grand

late 18th-c house near the site of an old Roman town, with an imposing three-storey colonnaded portico. The extensive picture gallery was designed by Nash, who made imaginative use of early curved cast iron and glass for the ceiling. A family room has interactive activities; attractive grounds, deer park and children's playground in the walled garden. Snacks, shop, disabled access by prior arrangement; grounds open daily (exc 25 Dec), house cl am, Weds, Thurs and Nov-mid Mar; (01743) 708123; house and grounds £5, £2.30 grounds only; NT. The Mytton & Mermaid opposite the entrance is a good food stop.

Home Farm 🎫 Rare breeds and traditional farm machinery; you can watch the milking of the jersey cows (3.30pm), and play with the pets. Interactive activities in the discovery barn. Farmhouse teas, shop, limited disabled access; cl am (till 11 in school hols), all day Thurs and Fri (exc school hols), and Dec-Easter; (01743) 709243; £3.25.

BILLINGSLEY SO7183

Rays Farm Country Matters 🎫 Traditional farm in pleasant countryside, with sheep, horses, cattle and llamas, a good collection of owls, and plenty of red, fallow, axis and sika deer; they also have otters. Pleasant woodland walks, myth and legend sculpture trail, play barn and indoor and outdoor picnic areas. They have seasonal activities in the run-up to Christmas. Snacks, shop, disabled access; cl 24 Dec-Jan and wkdys Feb; (01299) 841255; *£4.50. For longer walks, you can try a section of bridleway starting at the farm, meandering eventually into Wales.

BISHOP'S CASTLE SO3288

Quiet historic market town with some fine Elizabethan and Georgian buildings, art, antiques and new age shops, a little railway and transport museum (usually open pm wknds and bank hols Easter-Oct (01588) 638446; free), and a local history museum housed in the curious House on Crutches (open same times as transport museum; (01588) 630007; free). It's handy for exploring Offa's Dyke; the Castle Hotel at the top of the town is good for lunch, and the Six Bells (Church St) is also popular, brewing its own beers.

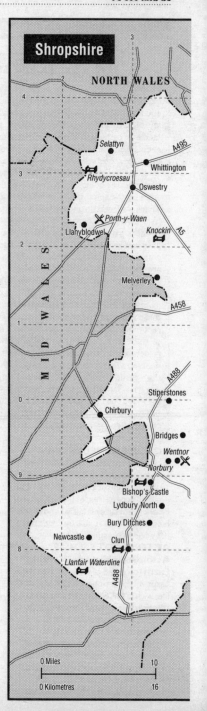

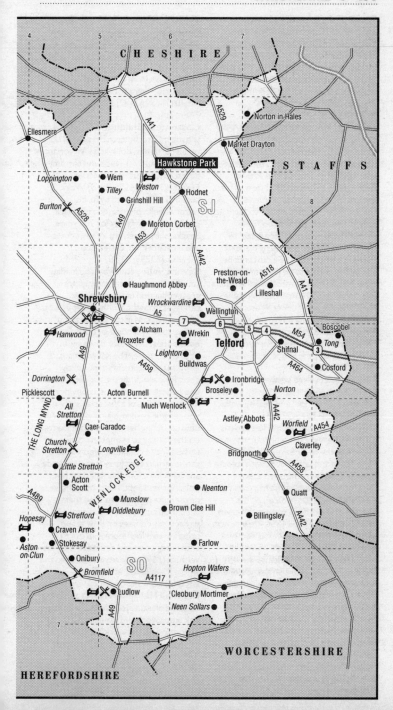

CHESHIRE

4   5   6   7

A41

A529

Ellesmere

Norton in Hales

Market Drayton

STAFFS

Hawkstone Park

Loppington   Wem

Tilley   Weston

Burlton   A528   Grinshill Hill

A49

A53

Hodnet

SJ

Moreton Corbet

8

A442

A518

Preston-on-
the-Weald

Lilleshall

A41

Haughmond Abbey

Shrewsbury

Wrockwardine

Wellington

A5

7

6

5

4

M54

Boscobel

Hanwood

Atcham

Wrekin

Telford

Tong

Wroxeter

Leighton

Buildwas

Shifnal

A464

Cosford

A49

A458

Ironbridge

Broseley

Norton

Dorrington

Picklescott

Acton Burnell

Much Wenlock

Astley Abbots

A442

Worfield

A454

All
Stretton

Caer Caradoc

THE LONG MYND

Church
Stretton

Longville

Claverley

Bridgnorth

A458

WENLOCK EDGE

Little Stretton

Acton
Scott

Neenton

Quatt

A489

Munslow

Diddlebury

Brown Clee Hill

Billingsley

A42

Hopesay

Strefford

Craven Arms

Aston
on Clun

Stokesay

Farlow

Onibury

SO

Bromfield

Hopton Wafers

A4117

A49

Ludlow

Cleobury Mortimer

Neen Sollars

7

WORCESTERSHIRE

HEREFORDSHIRE

Three Tuns Brewery Under new owners, ale is once again being brewed in the four-storey Victorian tower brewhouse across the yard from the friendly pub, and you can arrange a tour of the unusual Grade II listed building, which also houses a little beer museum; (01588) 638797; £1.

BOSCOBEL SJ8308

Boscobel House Interesting old house renowned for sheltering Charles II after the Battle of Worcester, with an unusually well preserved 17th-c garden and cobbled courtyard, and 19th-c décor giving a romanticised view of his escape. Good guided tour. Meals, snacks, shop, disabled access to gardens only; cl Dec-Feb; (01902) 850244; £4.40. The **Royal oak** here is said by some to have been the hiding place of the king, by others to be a descendant, and by still others to be just a fine old tree. The Hartley Arms above the canal over in Wheaton Aston has enjoyable food, and Weston Park at Weston under Lizard (Staffs) is nearby.

White Ladies Priory (just SW) Ruins of Augustinian nunnery destroyed in the Civil War; free; EH.

BRIDGES SO3996

Pleasant quiet village between the Long Mynd and the Stiperstones, with a good pub (the Horseshoe) and nearby walks.

BRIDGNORTH SO7193

On the Severn, this old market town is picturesque without being touristy. It's divided by the River Severn into the High Town and Low Town, with steps between the two - though it's easier (and more fun) to take the hair-raising **Cliff Railway** (70p return). At the bottom of the cliff are some small caves that people lived in till 1856 (they're not open, but labelled). As well as some handsome red brick, High Town has lots of fine timbered buildings, such as the odd town hall built on a sandstone-arched base that straddles the road in the High St. The **castle** up here was largely destroyed in the Civil War, but part of the keep remains, left at a scary tilt by the constant bombardment; the grounds are now a park with good views - the best are from the Castle Walk. The unusual church on nearby East Castle St was designed by Thomas Telford, and near it the Habit is a good

food stop (all day Sun). **North Gate Museum** looks at local history (open Fri-Sun Easter-Oct, bank hols and school hols exc Thurs); the nearby Bear does good lunches. Guided tours usually leave from the tourist information centre at 2.15pm Fri and Sat; (01746) 767147; £2. Some shops cl Thurs pm.

Costume & Childhood Museum (Postern Gate, bottom of High St) Lots of old costumes, dolls, and a Victorian nursery. Usually cl Thurs and Sun am, best to check; (01746) 764636; £1.25.

Daniels Mill (B4555, 1m S) Working cornmill still powered by its big waterwheel; a picturesque old place, run by the same family for 200 years. Snacks, shop; open pm Weds, wknds and bank hol Mon, Easter-Sept; (01746) 762753; £2.50.

Severn Valley Railway The leading standard-gauge steam railway, with a great collection of locomotives, carriages from the 1930s to 1960s. Lots of period details in the stations, and varied scenery along the route; for details see entry under Bewdley, in Worcestershire. The Railwaymans Arms in the station fits in perfectly, good for a snack. At the Kidderminster end (where the station is a convincing modern replica of a Victorian station), you can join regular mainline trains. An unusual outing here is to combine a trip on the railway to Hampton Loade station with a connecting ferry across the Severn; return ferry fare £1, wknds and bank hol Mon, plus daily in school hols, Apr-end Sept. For those who've never quite managed to shed their childhood ambitions, you can take half-day and day courses on driving and firing a steam locomotive - from £145, with more advanced courses inc a 2-day venture (£595) where you get to do the whole 32-mile round trip.

BROSELEY SJ6701

Benthall Hall (just NW) An appealing Elizabethan sandstone house with fine oak woodwork and panelling, decorative plasterwork, interesting garden, and 17th-c church (services 3.15pm 3rd Sun in month). Some disabled access; open pms Tues, Weds, and bank hol Sun and Mon Apr-Sept (plus pm Sun July-Sept); (01952)

882159; £3.75, £2.50 garden only; NT. The Pheasant (Church St) does a good Sun lunch (and evening meals).

Broseley Clay Tobacco Pipe Museum (Duke St) Part of the Ironbridge Gorge Museum (and included in its Passport ticket); see how they made those long clay pipes that are a trademark of olde-worlde pictures. Shop; cl am and Nov-Easter; (01952) 432166; £3.

BROWN CLEE HILL SO5986
Aptly named, at nearly 550 metres (1,800 ft) this is Shropshire's highest point. It has a disappointingly flat top but offers walkers a certain solitary grandeur. The imposing Boyne Arms below its wooded E side at Burwarton has good value food.

BUILDWAS SJ6404
Buildwas Abbey (B4378) Beautiful remains of 12th-c Cistercian abbey - apart from the roof it's practically all still here. Snacks, shop, reasonable disabled access; cl Oct-Mar; £2.20. It's right next to the gigantic cooling towers of a power station, which this close seem to have a geometrical beauty of their own. The Severnside Meadow coming out from Ironbridge has decent food.

BURY DITCHES SO3283
Iron Age ring fort, high on a hill, with superb views of south Shropshire and north Herefordshire.

CAER CARADOC SO4794
(E of Church Stretton) This hill has a pleasingly compact summit, and the pick of the local views. The best start for walks is Hope Bowdler, not far from Shropshire's oldest pub, the Royal Oak at Cardington.

CHIRBURY SO2698
An attractive village, with a famously haunted graveyard.

CLAVERLEY SO7993
An attractive village of black and white timbered houses; the church has impressive medieval wall paintings. The Lion o' Morfe at nearby Upper Farmcote does good food.

CLEOBURY MORTIMER SO6775
Civilised small town, most notable perhaps for its church's crooked spire, though timbered Tudor buildings among its more elegant Georgian ones are picturesque. There's a delightful churchyard at nearby Hopton Wafers,

and good food at the Crown there.

CLUN SO3080
Attractive stone-built village on the edge of the **Clun Forest**, a peaceful pastoral area of rolling partly wooded hills. The ruined Norman **castle** gives fine views from the castle mound; free. Down by the River Clun, the 16th-c stone bridge is very picturesque. The Sun and White Horse are both good for lunch.

COSFORD SJ7805
Royal Air Force Museum (A41) One of the country's best aviation museums, housing a spectacular collection of carefully arranged aircraft inc the Victor and Vulcan bombers, Hastings, York and British Airways airliners inc the last airworthy Britannia, as well as lots of missiles and a display of engines. World War II hangars house an art gallery, hands-on exhibits and a display on the history of military photography. Meals, snacks, shop, disabled access; cl 24-26 Dec, 1 Jan; (01902) 376200; free. The Bell at Tong is a reliable family dining pub.

CRAVEN ARMS SO4282
Secret Hills Discovery Centre 🖪 (A49 just S) Well worth a visit, this grass-roofed structure in 10 hectares (25 acres) of meadows takes a fresh look at the natural and cultural history of the surrounding countryside. Various galleries house interactive exhibitions on topics as diverse as the geology of landscape, and the art and music it has inspired. Readers very much enjoy the simulated balloon ride over the hills, and other attractions include a full-size model of a mammoth skeleton, and craft gallery. Restaurant, shop, good disabled access; cl Mon Oct-Mar, 25-26 Dec and 1 Jan; (01588) 676040; £4.25. In the town's Old Market Hall, the **Land of Lost Content** has three floors of 20th-c british nostalgia. Meals, snacks, shop, disabled access to ground floor only; cl Dec; (01588) 676176; £5.

ELLESMERE WALKS SJ4035
There are several meres or lakes around here - the Mere (with a visitor centre and plenty of geese and ducks) by Ellesmere itself, Blake Mere, and Cole Mere, which has a country park around it. This is close enough to the Shropshire Union Canal to include a

walk along the towpath, with Colemere village a suitable starting place (there's no shop, so it's a good idea to take sandwiches).

FARLOW SO6382

Gobbett Rare Breeds Farm & Nursery Several endangered and minority breeds of cattle, sheep and pigs; also bantams, ducks, geese and turkeys, and normally hatching eggs and day-old chicks. In a remote spot this farm has fine views on clear days; you'll need wellies in wet weather. Tearoom, perennial and conifer nursery; cl Nov-Feb; (01746) 718276; £2.50. The Boyne Arms over at Burwarton has good value food and a good play area.

GRINSHILL HILL SJ5223
(between Grinshill and Clive) This gives walkers much wider views than you'd expect from its modest height, and quite an atmospheric summit, where woods open out by sheer quarried rock-faces. The recently reopened Inn at Grinshill is doing good food.

HAUGHMOND ABBEY SJ5214
(off B5062 E of Shrewsbury) Extensive ruins of Augustinian abbey, inc a fine Norman doorway in the chapter house, some interesting sculpture, and well preserved lodgings and kitchens. Good for picnics. Snacks, shop, some disabled access; cl Oct-Mar; (01743) 709661; £2.20; EH.

HAWKSTONE PARK SJ5628
Hawkstone Park Follies See separate family panel on p.491.
The Caspian Bar of the Hawkstone Park Hotel has good value food.

HODNET SJ6128
Several attractive half-timbered houses here, and some interesting old books in the church. At the **Rocking Horse Workshop** (Drayton Rd) you can watch the production and restoration of traditional rocking horses; cl Sun, Sat pm, and two wks over Christmas, best to phone; (01630) 685888; free.
Hodnet Hall Gardens Twenty-four hectares (60 acres) of lovely landscaped gardens with spacious lawns, lush pools, plants and trees; the astonishingly decorated tearoom is full of big-game trophies. Meals, snacks, shop, disabled access; cl ams, Mon, and Oct-Mar; (01630) 685202; £3.75. The Bear Hotel opposite is good for lunch.

Wollerton Old Hall Garden 🏚
(Wollerton - off A53 N) Full of colour and interest, this lovely three-acre garden with formal and more relaxed room designs has been developed around a 16th-c house (not open). Meals, snacks, disabled access; open pms Fri, Sun and bank hols Easter-Sept; (01630) 685760; £3.80.

IRONBRIDGE SJ6703
This steep town, with intriguing hillside paths and narrow lanes, was the birthplace of the Industrial Revolution: it was Abraham Darby's use here of coke instead of charcoal for smelting which made mass-production of iron possible. Well set among the woods and grassy slopes of the Severn Gorge, it was known as Coalbrookdale until the Darbys built the restored **iron bridge** across the river that today gives the town its name. As their industry took off they produced the world's first iron rails, boats, trains and wheels, and for quite some while the valley, so quiet now, was the biggest iron-making area in the world.

Ironbridge Gorge Museum
Scattered over six miles along the gorge, this amazing collection of museums is based around the sites that give this area its claim to be birthplace of the Industrial Revolution. For most visitors the highlight is the reconstructed Victorian village at Blists Hill; every aspect of 19th-c life is here, from shops, houses, bank, and steam-operated pit, to the school, pub, pig sties and summer fairground. Costumed staff add authenticity, and there are extra activities at wknds and in the hols. A favourite with families is Enginuity, with fun experiments and games to help children learn about engines and power: they can pull a locomotive, and control the flow of water to make electricity. Not all the sites have the same appeal for young children, but several turn up unexpected surprises: the echoes in the remarkable brick kilns at Coalport for example, or the bitumen still oozing from the walls of the Tar Tunnel. The Tile Museum (Jackfield) is due to reopen around Easter, with gaslit galleries and period room settings; tours, demonstrations and hands-on activities, and a specialist tile shop. On

bank hol Sun and Mon the various museums are usually linked by a bus; there are Pay and Display car parks at the Museum of the Gorge and the Iron Bridge itself. Useful leaflets (and the website, www.ironbridge.org.uk) have suggested itineraries. Meals, snacks, shops, disabled access; cl 24-25 Dec, 1 Jan and some parts cl Nov-Mar; (01952) 432166; £12.95 passport (which lasts indefinitely for a single visit to each museum), individual tickets available (Blists Hill £8.25, Enginuity £5.15). The Severnside Robin Hood (Waterloo St) is a popular food pub fairly centrally placed for the ten sites which make up the museum.

Maws Craft Centre (Jackfield) Across a footbridge from the Coalport tile museum, big centre with 20 workshops selling things as diverse as pottery, puzzles and pictures. Snacks, disabled access to ground floor; cl 25 Dec (different workshops have different opening times); (01952) 883030; free. The 18th-c Boat has good food, and summer barbecues in its big garden.

Merrythought Teddy Bear Shop (Buildwas Rd/Dale End) There's a small vintage teddy and toy display in the famous shop that has been making bears here since the 1930s. Disabled access; (01952) 433029; cl 25 Dec and 1 Jan; free. The cheerful nearby Malthouse (the Wharfage) has enjoyable food, and pictures for sale by local artists.

Museum of Steel Sculpture ⊞ (Cherry Tree Hill) Dramatic sculptures inspired by the industrial heritage, in ten attractive acres. Disabled access; cl Mon exc bank hols, and Dec-Feb; (01952) 433152; £2. Just down the hill the Coalbrookdale Inn (Wellington Rd, opposite the Museum of Iron), is a good lunch stop (not Sun).

Severn Gorge This has such fascinating and picturesque (though not always exactly pretty) scenery that its industrial monuments cry out for a tour on foot. Steep lanes and paths connect Ironbridge and Coalbrookdale (inc a pleasant terraced walk between the river and the partly Elizabethan Golden Ball on Wesley Rd, off Madeley Hill, and an old railway track and a path along the base of Benthall Edge Wood assist walking routes along the gorge. A fine

linear walk can be taken from Broseley, descending NW into the gorge via Corbett's Dingle to Coalport. From Coalport, you can even follow the river all the way S to Bridgnorth.

LILLESHALL SJ7314
Lilleshall Abbey Impressive ruins of 12th-c abbey in pleasant setting surrounded by yew trees - it's a nice spot for a picnic, peaceful and undisturbed; open daily Apr-Oct; free; EH.

LLANYBLODWEL SJ2422
This attractive village, with its ancient riverside Horseshoe pub, has an exuberantly decorated church, full of bright colours and Victorian lettering.

LONG MYND SO4294
The partly heather-covered Long Mynd, England's southernmost grouse moor, has great character, with the much smaller but very striking Caer Caradoc facing it across the valley. For walks, it's best reached from Church Stretton. The bracken-and-bilberry-clad massif has a flat plateau-like top, crossed by the Port Way, an ancient track dating from neolithic times. Its sides are cut into by a series of narrow, remote-feeling valleys, of which Cardingmill Valley (NT) is best known because of its relative accessibility. The Green Dragon in Little Stretton and Yew Tree in All Stretton are good food stops.

LUDLOW SO5174
Beautiful 12th-c town, its original grid plan still obvious today. The best road in is via Wigmore and Leinthall Starkes - lovely views as you approach. Dotted around are 500 listed buildings, with particularly good examples down Broad St, a charming mixture of Tudor and Georgian architecture. Book well in advance if you're planning to visit during the cultural festival (end Jun/early July). The most famous building is the lavishly carved and timbered Feathers Hotel on the Bull Ring. The Broadgate, the only one of the town's 13th-c gates to have survived, is interesting. Quite a few antiques shops, and they're proud of their food here, with a Sept food and drink festival (usually 2nd wk - check on (01584) 861586); the Merchant House and Olive Branch (see Where to Eat) are fine restaurants, and the Unicorn (bottom of Corve St) and Church Inn (Buttercross) do nice pub lunches. The

Wheatsheaf (Lower Broad St) is interestingly built into the medieval town wall. The town is overlooked by the rather volcanic-looking Titterstone Clee to the NE.

Castle Lodge 🏠 (Castle Sq) Tucked up by the castle walls, this is reputed to have more wood panelling than any other house in England, and was once home to Elizabeth I's Master of Requests. Still inhabited today, it was originally built in the 13th c, and rebuilt in 1580; the sparsely decorated rooms with lovely doors and fine ceilings are spread over three floors, and have plenty of atmosphere. The persian carpets displayed throughout the house are for sale. Some disabled access; usually open daily; (01584) 878098; £3.

Ludlow Castle Dating from around 1086, this splendid fortress has lots of original parts inc the Norman keep, and the chapel with its unusual circular nave. The towers and battlements on their wooded crag over the River Teme have wonderful views, and a properly 'castle-ish' feel. Shakespeare plays are performed here during the end Jun/beginning July festival, also various events throughout the year. Shop, cl 25 Dec, and wkdys Jan; (01584) 873355; *£3.50.

Ludlow Museum (Castle St) Good local history museum with lots of hands-on activities. Shop; cl 1-2pm, all day Sun exc Jun-Aug and bank hol wknds, and all Nov-Mar; (01584) 875384; free.

St Laurence church (off King St) Ludlow's parish church dominates the town almost as much as the castle, with its magnificent pinnacled tower; it's in an attractive tranquil enclave behind the old buttermarket, and has a wonderful sense of timeless peace inside. Magnificently intricate carvings, especially on the ceiling and the choir stalls; tours available. Shop, disabled access; Oct-Mar it's open 11-4pm only, other times you can visit all day (exc am Sun unless you want to attend the service); (01584) 872073; £1 suggested donation, £1.50 for tower.

LYDBURY NORTH SO3485
Walcot Hall Big walled garden, 30-acre arboretum with rhododendrons, azaleas, specimen trees, and a mile-long lake in front of fine Georgian house (open only pms 25-26 May or by appointment) built for Clive of India; free-standing ballroom, stable yard with matching clock towers. Mostly disabled access; gardens cl ams, also Tues-Thurs and Nov-Apr; (01588) 680570; *£3. You can stay in various wings of the house, and fishing can be arranged.

MARKET DRAYTON SJ6734
The traditional home of gingerbread; the unique local recipe is locked in a bank, but you can still find plenty of toothsome samples in the shops. The Gingerbread Man (Adderley Rd) is a decent family dining pub.

MELVERLEY SJ3316
Craft Centre and church The stables of the Old Rectory have a craft centre (open Fri-Sun Apr-Sept and by appointment; (01691) 682455). The beautiful black and white St Peter's church was rebuilt in 1406 after Owain Glyndwr burned the previous one; it has a fine Jacobean pulpit and chain Bible. The Old Three Pigeons over at Nesscliffe has popular food, with Kynaston Cave and good cliff walks nearby.

MORETON CORBET SJ5623
Moreton Corbet Castle Destroyed by Parliament in 1644, but you can still see a small 13th-c keep and the substantial ruins of the once-grand Elizabethan house; disabled access; free. There are some elaborate tombs and a beautiful chancel in the adjacent **church**; the 18th-c Raven at Tilley up towards Wem is a good dining pub.

MUCH WENLOCK SJ6200
Lovely little medieval market town, with lots of timbered and jettied buildings. The Talbot, George & Dragon, Gaskell Arms and Wheatland Fox all have enjoyable food.

Much Wenlock Museum Local history in the Old Market Hall, with displays on geology, natural history and local doctor William Penny Brookes, founder of the modern Olympic Games - the town still holds its own version of the games every summer. (01952) 727679; cl 1-2pm and Sun (exc Jun-Aug), and all Oct-Mar; free.

Much Wenlock Priory Has its origins in the 7th c, but it's the magnificent remains of the 11th-c building and later additions you can see

today, all set off well by striking clipped topiary. The chapter house has remarkably patterned interlaced arches. Snacks, shop; disabled access; cl Mon-Tues Nov-Mar, 25-26 Dec and 1 Jan; (01952) 727466; £3 (inc audio tour); EH.
Wenlock Edge This very long smooth hill is wooded (and much quarried) along its flanks, but has possibilities for walks. The B4371 along Wenlock Edge has good views, and the Wenlock Edge Inn is a useful stop.

NEWCASTLE SO2482
An attractive village, with good local walks, and a decent pub, the Crown.

NORTON IN HALES SJ7038
Attractive village with a 13th-c church and a mysterious brading stone on its green. The Hinds Head has good food; good nearby walks.

ONIBURY SO4378
Wernlas Collection of Rare Poultry 🏛 (Green Lane, W of A49) Huge collection of large fowl and bantams with some really unusual ones (they've around 220 breeds of rare chicken), plus donkeys; about 15,000 chicks are hatched each year, so usually some for children to handle. This is also a commercial venture and much of the stock is for sale; they can give you advice on keeping chickens. Summer snacks, shop; cl Mon (exc bank hols and mid-July to mid-Sept); (01584) 856318; £3.

OSWESTRY SJ2929
Cambrian Railway Museum (Oswald Rd) Steam engines and railway memorabilia; as we went to press the engines were all in pieces, but they hope to have one in steam by the spring; shop; cl 25 Dec, but phone to check; (01691) 671749; £1. In the bustling town itself, the Butchers Arms (Willow St) has good value food, and out at Candy to the W the Old Mill does some inventive meals.
Old Oswestry (just N) Impressive Iron Age hill fort covering nearly 30 hectares (68 acres). The elaborate western defensive entrance and five ramparts remain; free; EH.
Park Hall (Park Hall, Burma Rd - off A495 NE) Looks at past, present and future farming techniques and countryside activities, in restored Victorian farm buildings (80% is under cover), with vintage farm machinery inc

a working gas engine. A play barn houses a bouncy castle and pedal tractor circuit, and there's a soft play area and computer centre; also a collection of rare cars and bikes. Animals inc shire horses, rare breeds of cattle, pigs, sheep and poultry, and more cuddly creatures in the pets corner. There's also a woodland area with unusual tree carvings and adventure playground, children's driving school (chances to test drive electric vehicles), and quad bikes. With milking demonstrations (by hand or machine) at 1pm, tractor-drawn carriage rides and various activities, it's a good half-day's fun for families with smaller children. Meals, snacks, shop, good disabled access; cl 25-26 Dec and Mon-Thurs in winter term-times; (01691) 671123; *£4.85.

PICKLESCOTT SO4399
Attractive tucked-away village, with good value wknd lunches in the delightfully placed ancient Bottle & Glass, and good walking nearby.

PRESTON-ON-THE-WEALD SJ6814
Hoo Farm Animal Kingdom 🏛 Plenty to do at this enthusiastically run farm. Highlights include a sheep steeplechase Easter-Sept afternoons (exc Fri) at 3pm with a Tiny Tote for bets, an air rifle range and quad biking for children over 6. Play barns house a miniature tractor circuit, an area where children can bottle-feed lambs and collect eggs, a display of creepy-crawlies and reptiles, and plenty of games inc air hockey. Outside are ride-on electric tractors, lots of animals inc llamas and ostriches, as well as a nature trail, a big walk-in beehive with glass window, a craft centre and an evergreen maze, with a trail for toddlers to follow. Quite a few seasonal displays and activities in Dec. Snacks, picnic areas, shop, disabled access; cl Mon Sept-Nov, and 24 Dec-22 Mar; (01952) 677917; £4.25, children get a free return visit. Entry to the site is free in the run-up to Christmas, though there's a charge for the special displays.

QUATT SO7487
Dudmaston (off A442) 17th-c house with the old flower-painting collection of Francis Darby of Coalbrookdale,

modern art, and lakeside and woodland walks in the extensive parkland. Snacks, shop, disabled access; cl all ams, Thurs-Sat and Oct-Mar, house also cl Mon exc bank hols; (01746) 780866; £4.10; garden only £3; NT. Parts of the estate are open for public access all year, and there's a pleasant 1½ mile walk down to the quaint ferry across the Severn to the Severn Valley Railway halt at Hampton Loade (see Bridgnorth).

SHIFNAL SJ7407

Much expanded under the influence of nearby Telford, but still with a villagey heart and attractive buildings, inc an interesting church and some worthwhile food pubs such as the 17th-c White Hart (High St).

SHREWSBURY SJ4912

Though your first impression is of a workaday town of modern shops and offices, the central street layout is still largely medieval, with oddly named streets (Shoplatch, Murivance, Wyle Cop), and plenty of quiet corners tucked away up narrow alleys and courtyards. It's rich in striking architecture, both Tudor timbering and Georgian brick. Around The Square numerous buildings reflect the medieval wool fortunes, inc the old market hall; in the adjacent High St, Owens Mansion and Irelands Mansion are fine half-timbered houses worth looking at from outside. Even McDonalds is in a medieval building. The walk up Castle St is worth while, passing the original Grammar School building and the half-timbered Council House Court. Nearby the church of St Mary has one of the tallest spires in England and is known for its beautiful stained glass, some dating back to the 14th c. The unusual Greek Revival St Chad's church (St Chad's Terrace) caused great controversy when it was built in 1792 because of its round nave (even the pews are circular). Shrewsbury Abbey (Abbey Foregate) is well known through the novels of Ellis Peters. Besides the church (partly 11th-c) very little of the abbey buildings survive. A guided walk of the town leaves the Tourist Information Centre daily at 2.30pm May-Oct exc Sun in Oct and Sat only Nov-Apr (£3), or you can pick up a trail leaflet (95p) which will take you

round some of the more interesting buildings. The original town is almost entirely ringed by a loop of the Severn which has quiet waterside paths and parks, and you can take a river cruise (hourly in summer from Victoria Quay by the Welsh Bridge). The Armoury (Victoria Quay) has good food, the 12th-c St Julian's church (St Alkmunds Sq) has a nice restaurant, and other useful stops are the no smoking Three Fishes (Fish St, just around the corner from the ancient Bear Steps area), and Cromwells (Dogpole).

Scenic drive Heading SW from Shrewsbury, the old coach road through Longden and Pulverbatch is an attractive drive - great views the further you go.

Shrewsbury Castle and Shropshire Regimental Museum 12th-c castle, guarding the narrow neck of land between the river's loop. It was refurbished by Thomas Telford in 1790 when the romantic Laura's Tower was built, though still has parts of the earlier building. It includes the **Shropshire Regimental Museum**, with military displays from the American War of Independence to the present day. Shop, some disabled access; open Weds-Sat mid-Feb to 20 Dec, plus Tues and bank hols in May; (01743) 358516; £2. The attractive grounds (cl Sun Oct-May) are free.

Shrewsbury Museum & Art Gallery (Barker St) Impressive timber-framed building with social and natural history, and some Roman remains; the art gallery has changing exhibitions. Shop; cl Sun/Mon Oct-May; (01743) 361196; free.

Shropshire Wildlife Trust (Abbey Foregate) Wildlife garden with medieval buildings, displays on Shropshire's wildlife, and a tourist information centre; special events some wknds; shop; cl Sun and bank hols; (01743) 284280; free.

STIPERSTONES SO3799

The rather eery Stiperstones are outcrops of harder quartzy rock leaving strange-shaped boulders, tors and crests on the skyline - and strange tales among the people living nearby. The ridge is crowned by dramatic rocks and has a splendid view; a short walk from a nearby car park (you can make an interesting 8½-mile circuit with a stop at the More Arms at Shelve), or you can take the longish walk up from the former lead-mining village of Snailbeach, where the friendly Stiperstones Inn has enjoyable fresh food all day (inc local whinberry pie). An unusual route up is from the Sun at Norbury (good food and a nice place to stay).

STOKESAY SO4381

Stokesay Castle (off A49) One of the finest examples of a medieval manor house, in a notably charming setting. The hall with its cruck-framed roof and Early English windows is just as it was 700 years ago, and there's a timbered Tudor gatehouse. Good views from the top of the tower, and excellent Walkman tour. Summer snacks, shop; cl 1-2pm, Mon-Tues Nov-Mar, 24-26 Dec and 1 Jan; (01588) 672544; £4.50. The Plough up at Wistanstow has good home cooking.

TELFORD SJ7008

Wonderland 🖼 (Telford Town Park) The attractions at this 450-acre park are a useful enough distraction for younger children if you happen to be in the area, with some re-creations of fairy tales and nursery rhymes, a maze, indoor (unlimited rides £2) and outdoor play and picnic areas, road train rides (£1), pedalo boat hire (£3 for 20 mins), and crazy golf (£1). Snacks, shop, disabled access; cl wkdys Oct-Mar and two wks over Christmas; (01952) 591633; £3.

WELLINGTON SJ6510

Sunnycroft Surviving virtually unaltered, this typical late Victorian gentleman's suburban villa still contains much of its original contents; the grounds, like a mini estate, are interesting too. Open pms Sun and Mon 28 Mar-31 Oct; (01952) 242884; *£4.20, *£2.20 garden only. The owner probably knew the well run nearby Cock in its days as a coaching inn.

WEM SJ5128

Mythstories 🖼 (Morgan Library, Aston St) Exploring myths, legends and stories from all around the world, this unusual attraction is rated very highly by us for its ability to catch and hold the interest of children of most ages. Everyone will hear a story, and there are lots of innovative activities; Shop, disabled access; cl am, Fri-Sat and Nov-

Mar exc by appointment; (01939) 235500; £3.50.

WHITTINGTON SJ3131

(off A5) Handsome remains of 13th-c **Whittington Castle**; the Olde Boot alongside does food.

WREKIN SJ6108

(just W of Telford - and towering boldly over it) The Wrekin is no Everest (an easily attained 407 metres, 1,334 ft), but because it's so isolated on the edge of the Shropshire uplands it offers walkers a huge panorama, spanning places over 100 miles apart; just below, the Huntsman in Little Wenlock is handy for refreshment.

WROXETER SJ5608

Roman Vineyard Friendly little place producing several wines; also lavender farm, rare breeds, and some interesting glacial stones - not to mention a Roman wall. Teas, farmshop (with various lavender-based products), disabled access; usually open daily (exc 25 Dec) but there's not much to see in winter; (01743) 761888; free.

Wroxeter Roman City One of the country's most important Roman sites, though most of the remains are buried under fields. The colonnade and municipal bath are well preserved, with useful explanatory boards, and the museum has a good range of finds from the town (then Britain's fourth biggest) and the earlier fortress. Recent theories suggest that King Arthur was a 5th-c warlord ruling from a post-Roman city in the region - possibly this one. Snacks, shop; some disabled access; cl 24-26 Dec, 1 Jan; (01743) 761330; £3.70 inc audio guide; EH. The Horseshoes at Uckington is a decent family dining pub.

Other attractive villages, all with decent pubs or other eating places, include Aston on Clun SO3982, Leighton SJ6105, Little Stretton SO4392, Loppington SJ4729, Lydbury North SO3586, Munslow SO5287, Neen Sollars SO6672, Neenton SO6488, Norbury SO3692 (good walks), Selattyn SJ2633 (unusual church), Tilley SJ5027, Tong SJ7907, Wentnor SO3893 and Worfield SO7595.

Where to eat

BROMFIELD SO4877 **Cookhouse** *(01584)* 856565 Once the home of Clive of India, this handsome brick house looks from the outside like an immaculately maintained Georgian home, but inside is smartly contemporary and brightly modernised: fresh flowers on the sleek space-age bar counter, newspapers to read, and light wooden tables, and a cosier back room with huge brick fireplace, exposed stonework, and soaring beams and rafters; very good well presented food in the café-bar style dining room; some areas are no smoking; seats on secluded terrace outside; cl 25 Dec pm; disabled access. £29.50|**£7.95**

BURLTON SJ4526 **Burlton Inn** *(01939)* 270284 Attractively restored pub with three cottagey connecting rooms, fresh flowers, very attractively presented food from a seasonal menu, well kept real ales, and neatly uniformed helpful staff; bdrms; cl 26 Dec, 1 Jan and bank hol Mon am; disabled access. £28|**£7.50**

CHURCH STRETTON SO4593 **Acorn Wholefood** 26 *Sandford Ave (01694)* 722495 Simple, unpretentious family-run restaurant with friendly service in several no smoking rooms, good filling food (mostly vegetarian) changing daily, delicious puddings and soups, and cream teas with a choice of around 30 teas; cl Weds-Thurs (but open Thurs during school hols); children must be well behaved. £10.75|**£5**

DORRINGTON SJ4702 **Country Friends** *(01743)* 718707 Cosy half-timbered no smoking restaurant with consistently enjoyable interesting food, inc lovely puddings and british cheeses with home-made bread; super breakfasts; bdrms; cl Sun-Tues, two wks mid-July and 1 wk in Oct. £39|**£9**

IRONBRIDGE SJ6603 **Malthouse** *Wharfage (01952)* 433712 Nicely decorated large pub with a laid-back feel, opposite the river; spacious bar with lots of scrubbed wooden tables, candlelight, local artists' work, good interesting food using local produce, real ales, several wines by the glass, and helpful staff; no smoking restaurant; live music Weds-Sun pms; bdrms; cl 25 Dec. £25|**£7.95**

LUDLOW SO5175 **Merchant House** 62 *Lower Corve St (01584)* 875438 Two simply furnished rooms in friendly and relaxed Jacobean house with exceptionally good food from set 3-course menu, good value interesting wines, and competent service; cl Sun, Mon, Tues-Thurs ams, Christmas and 1 wk in spring. £40.50

LUDLOW SO5174 **Olive Branch** 2/4 *Old St (01584)* 874314 Cheery wholefood restaurant in 17th-c former inn, with a changing range of tasty lunchtime meals and snacks inc often inventive vegetarian meals (and meaty ones, too), super puddings, and teas with home-made cakes and scones; cl 25-26 Dec; disabled access. £18|**£6**

PORTH-Y-WAEN SJ2623 **Lime Kiln** *(01691)* 831550 Good inventive blackboard food using lots of local produce in cheerful attractively opened-up pub with stripped pine woodwork and furniture on quarry tiles, warm coal fires, interesting photographs, no smoking corner; friendly helpful staff, well kept real ales, good value wines, and picnic-sets in side garden with boules pitch; cl Mon. £22.20|**£7.95**

SHREWSBURY SJ4912 **Armoury** *Victoria Quay, Victoria Ave (01743)* 340525 Airy smartly converted warehouse with row of big arched windows overlooking river; interesting bistro-style food, eight well kept real ales, 20 wines by the glass, 50 malt whiskies; cl 25 Dec and 1 Jan; no children after 9pm. £25.50|**£6.45**

SHREWSBURY SJ4912 **Sol** 82 *Wyle Cop (01743)* 340560 Welcoming and relaxed split-level restaurant decorated in cheerful mediterranean colours with imaginative enjoyable food (super Cornish fish dishes and attractively presented puddings), a reasonably priced wine list, and helpful service; cl Sun-Mon. £25.25|**£8**

WENTNOR SO3892 **Crown** *(01588)* 650613 16th-c inn in quiet village with beams, standing timbers, good log fire, collection of china and glass, and mix of tables set for eating in the main area; snug end with comfortable sofas, a good choice of enjoyable food, and a cosy beamed restaurant; fve well kept real ales, decent wines, helpful friendly staff, and fine views of the Long Mynd from seats on the neat back lawn; children must be well behaved; bdrms. £22.60|**£6.50**

Special thanks to Michael and Jenny Back, Dave Irving, Paul Kennedy

SOMERSET

Excellent range of attractions for all ages, from first-class city museums to country farms and wildlife centres; also beautiful Bath, charming towns and villages, traditional seaside resorts and some interesting scenery; good value

Elegant Bath is highly rewarding for a break, especially out of season, when you can appreciate the enjoyable museums and gorgeous buildings without the crowds. By tradition, we also include Bristol in this chapter. Though it's not so much a place to wander around, Bristol has got more than enough to make it well worth day visits: plus points for families include the unusual British Empire & Commonwealth Museum (our Somerset Family Attraction), the exceptional zoo, and popular @Bristol.

The American Museum in Britain at Claverton takes an absorbing look at America's past, and 16th-c Montacute House has a fine collection of Tudor and Jacobean paintings. Tyntesfield is a very special stately home, but the National Trust have a huge task in making it suitable for large-volume visiting, so numbers will probably be strictly limited at first. The Fleet Air Arm Museum in Yeovilton has lively displays as well as around 40 aircraft, and Haynes Sparkford Motor Museum is great if you're into classic cars and motorcycles. Glastonbury, Taunton, Chard and Bridgwater all have decent local museums.

Treats for animal-lovers include Horse World at Whitchurch, Cricket St Thomas Park (the walk-through lemur wood is a highlight), Washford's Tropiquaria (amazing indoor jungle), Keynsham's Avon Valley Country Park (falconry displays and a superb playground), Highbridge (you can feed some of the residents), and Banwell (fun even if it's wet).

Among Somerset's many gardens, we pick out the ones at Barrington Court (a fine 16th-c house too), Castle Cary (the town is pretty), Cheddon Fitzpaine, and Cannington College (thousands of different plants) as especially interesting for gardeners. Other lovely gardens include those at East Lambrook, Greenham, Tintinhull and Tolland. Cider drinkers can choose between visits to Dowlish Wake (in the autumn you can even see the cider being made), Bradford-on-Tone's Sheppy's Cider (run by the same family for over 200 years) and the county's only cider distillery at Kingsbury Episcopi.

Pretty Wells (England's smallest city) and Dunster (fine medieval buildings and a castle) are pleasant places for day-trippers. There are good walks on the brooding Mendips, and Glastonbury still captures the imagination. On the coast, Minehead is a pleasant traditional resort, and Weston-Super-Mare has a few things to entice families; Clevedon and Burnham-on-Sea are appealing too. Wookey Hole Caves & Papermill are exciting, and the Showcaves and Gorge big draws for Cheddar; if you want to avoid the crowds, Ebbor Gorge is a handy alternative.

The countryside is dotted with landmark church towers, pinnacled,

504 • SOMERSET

turreted and gargoyled. Many churches, particularly in the W, have intriguingly carved 15th- and 16th-c bench-ends, also fine oak waggon roofs, brass candelabras and carved screens. In the hillier parts, buildings are generally of stone, varying in colour and character from the Cotswold style of the NE, through the pale limestones of the Mendips and the golden warmth of south Somerset's Ham stone, to the rugged and stolid greys of the hamlets tucked into the green folds of the Quantocks.

Over in the W the countryside feels very secluded and self-contained, with each small valley of the Quantocks seeming a private world. The Blackdown Hills are charmingly untouristy, too - classic quiet english countryside with some lovely villages, some with delightfully eccentric names. The Somerset Levels are an interesting contrast - vivid green marshy pastures, rewarding for wildlife and for traditional crafts, notably basket-making. Towards the E, richer more rolling farmland with small valleys and wooded hillsides offers some gentle country drives.

Exmoor (including its Somerset part) is covered as a separate section in the Devon chapter.

Where to stay

BARWICK ST5613 **Little Barwick House** *Barwick, Yeovil, Somerset BA22 9TD* *(01935) 423902* **£108**, plus special breaks; 6 attractive rms. Carefully run listed Georgian dower house in 3½ acres 2m S of Yeovil, and thought of as a restaurant-with-rooms; lovely relaxed atmosphere, log fire in cosy lounge, excellent food using local produce, a thoughtful wine list, super breakfasts, nice afternoon tea, and particularly good service; cl 2 wks Jan; £5 for; dogs welcome in bedrooms

BATH ST7464 **Badminton Villa** *10 Upper Oldfield Park, Bath BA2 3JZ (01225) 426347* **£70***; 5 rms. Big no smoking Victorian house with marvellous city views, comfortable lounge, good breakfasts, and helpful friendly owners; cl 22 Dec-1 Feb; children over 8

BATH ST7565 **Old Boathouse** *Bath Boating Station, Forester Rd, Bath BA2 6QE* *(01225) 466407* **£65***; 4 rms. Edwardian boating station with black and white timbered verandah overlooking river, free launch to Bath centre, punting and rowing boats for hire, sitting room with river views, new conservatory, and separate restaurant; no smoking; children in cottage only; partial disabled access; cl Christmas

BATH ST7464 **Paradise House** *86-88 Holloway, Bath BA2 4PX (01225) 317723* **£89**, plus special breaks; 11 rms (room 5 has a super view). Classically elegant early 18th-c hotel, lovingly restored, with marvellous views over the city; pretty breakfast room, restful drawing room, log fire, and spacious walled gardens; peaceful, though only 7 mins' walk to centre; cl 24-26 Dec

BATH ST7465 **Queensberry** *Russel St, Bath BA1 2QF (01225) 447928* **£119**; 29 lovely rms. Four beautifully decorated Georgian town houses in quiet residential street, with comfortable, restful drawing room, open fire, attractive modern restaurant (Olive Tree: super mediterranean cooking and tempting puddings) and professional service; seats in the courtyard garden; disabled access

BATH ST7465 **Royal Crescent Hotel** *16 Royal Crescent, Bath BA1 2LS (01225) 823333* **£215***, plus special breaks; 45 luxurious rms. Elegant Georgian hotel in glorious curved terrace, with comfortable antique-filled drawing rooms, open fires and lovely flowers; imaginative modern cooking in Pimpernel Restaurant (in summer you can eat in the delightful garden), and impeccable service; health spa, gym and croquet; they are kind to children; disabled access; dogs welcome

BATH ST7565 **Villa Magdala** *Henrietta Rd, Bath BA2 6LX (01225) 466329* **£86***, plus winter breaks; 18 comfortable rms. Overlooking Henrietta Park, this elegant, quietly set Victorian house is only 5 mins' walk to the centre; good breakfasts in attractive dining room, a spacious comfortable lounge, and friendly helpful staff; no smoking; cl Christmas; children over 7

BECKINGTON ST7952 **Pickford House** *Bath Rd, Beckington, Frome, Somerset BA11 6SJ (01373) 830329* **£42**, 5 rms with river view, some with balcony, most with own bthrm. Honey-coloured hilltop stone house, with open fire in sitting room, bar, delicious evening meals (by arrangement) and breakfasts, a relaxed friendly atmosphere, helpful courteous owners and friendly collie; big garden with swimming pool; you can take over the house with a group of friends for a gourmet wknd; cl mid-Nov; disabled access; dogs welcome in bedrooms

BEERCROCOMBE ST3020 **Frog Street Farm** *Hatch Beauchamp, Taunton, Somerset TA3 6AF (01823) 480430* **£54**, plus special breaks; 3 rms. Peaceful 15th-c listed farmhouse deep in the countryside on a big working farm; beams, fine Jacobean panelling, inglenook fireplaces, a warmly friendly owner, delicious food (much produce from the farm, local game and fish; bring your own wine), and traditional breakfasts; no smoking; cl Nov-Mar; children by arrangement

BRISTOL ST5873 **Hotel du Vin & Bistro** *Narrow Lewins Mead, Bristol BS1 2NU (0117) 925 5577* **£145**; 40 loft-style rms with spacious bthrms. Part of a small chain (others in Birmingham, Brighton, Tunbridge Wells and Winchester); attractively converted former Sugar House with big pillars and arched cellars, wine prints, posters and empty bottles, comfortable armchairs on stripped wooden floors, and a bustling but relaxed dining room with white napery; particularly good imaginative mediterranean-style cooking, helpful efficient staff, and an interesting wine list; disabled access

CANNINGTON ST2538 **Blackmore Farm** *Blackmore Lane, Cannington, Bridgwater, Somerset TA5 2NE (01278) 653442* **£52***; 6 rms. Grade I listed manor house dating from 15th c, with garderobes, beams and stone archways, good breakfasts around a huge table in the Great Hall, and log fire in comfortable sitting room; no evening meals; large garden with croquet, and animals to see (this is a working farm); self-catering, too; disabled access

CRICKET MALHERBIE ST3611 **Old Rectory** *Cricket Malherbie, Ilminster, Somerset TA19 0PW (01460) 54364* **£80**; 5 rms. Pretty and beautifully restored mid 16th-c thatched house with unusual windows, Tudor carved beams, deep sofas and thick carpets in sitting room, imaginative evening meals and enjoyable breakfasts in dining room with original Georgian shutters and french windows opening on to the garden, and charming hosts; cl Christmas; no children

GLASTONBURY ST4938 **Number Three Hotel** *3 Magdalene St, Glastonbury, Somerset BA6 9EW (01458) 832129* **£90***; 5 individually furnished pretty rms, 3 in the Garden House. Lovely Georgian house (once home to Winston Churchill's mother) by Glastonbury Abbey, with antiques and fresh flowers, enjoyable breakfasts in attractive dining room, and a fine floodlit walled garden; cl Christmas and New Year

HATCH BEAUCHAMP ST3020 **Farthings** *Hatch Beauchamp, Taunton, Somerset TA3 6SG (01823) 480664* **£105**, plus special breaks; 10 spacious rms (inc a cottage suite) with thoughtful extras. Charming little Georgian house in three acres of gardens with helpful and hard-working long-serving owners, open fires in quiet lounge and convivial bar, and good varied food using fresh local produce; can arrange golf and other activities; children must be well behaved; dogs welcome in suite

HINTON CHARTERHOUSE ST7759 **Homewood Park** *Hinton Charterhouse, Bath BA3 6BB (01225) 723731* **£145**, plus winter breaks; 19 lovely rms. Charming Victorian hotel on the edge of Hinton Priory and in ten acres of gardens and woodlands; flowers, oil paintings and fine furniture in graceful relaxing day rooms, and an elegant restaurant with very good imaginative food (honey from their own bees - you can help them collect it); tennis, croquet, and outdoor swimming pool; disabled access

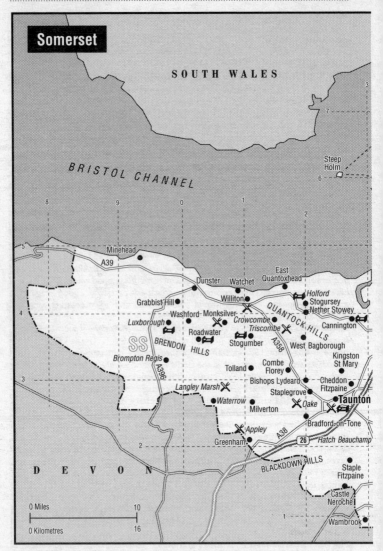

Somerset

SOUTH WALES

BRISTOL CHANNEL

Steep
Holm

Minehead
A39

Dunster Watchet   East
Quantoxhead

Grabbist Hill   Williton   Holford
                           Stogursey
       Washford Monksilver   QUANTOCK Nether Stowey
Luxborough   Crowcombe   HILLS Cannington
          Roadwater Triscombe
   BRENDON HILLS   Stogumber   West Bagborough
                                Kingston
                                St Mary
Brompton Regis   Tolland Combe
                       Florey   Cheddon
                   Bishops Lydeard Fitzpaine
Langley Marsh   Staplegrove   **Taunton**
   Waterrow   Oake
          Milverton
                         Bradford-on-Tone
Appley   A38
Greenham   26 Hatch Beauchamp

D E V O N

BLACKDOWN HILLS   Staple
                          Fitzpaine
                       Castle
                       Neroche

0 Miles   10   Wambrook
0 Kilometres   16

HOLFORD ST1541 **Combe House** *Holford, Bridgwater, Somerset TA5 1RZ* *(01278) 741382* **£86**, plus special breaks; 16 rms. Warmly friendly former tannery (still has waterwheel) in a pretty spot, with comfortable rooms, log fires, good home-made food, and a relaxed atmosphere; heated indoor swimming pool and tennis court; cl 7 Nov–11 Feb (but open Christmas and New Year); dogs welcome in bedrooms

HUNSTRETE ST6461 **Hunstrete House** *Hunstrete, Pensford, Bristol BS39 4NS* *(01761) 490490* **£185***, plus special breaks; 25 individually decorated rms. Classically handsome, mainly 18th-c country-house hotel on the edge of the Mendips, in 92 acres inc lovely Victorian walled garden and deer park; comfortable and elegantly furnished day rooms with antiques, paintings, log fires, fresh garden flowers, a tranquil atmosphere, excellent service, and very good food using home-

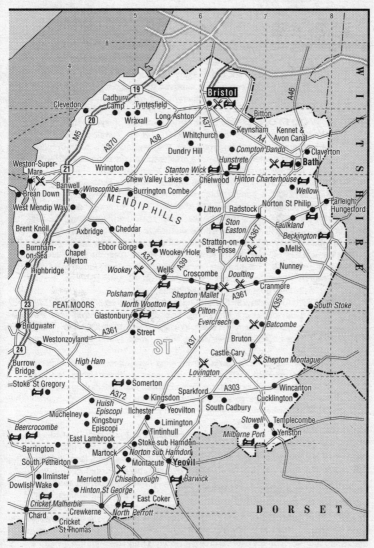

grown produce when possible; croquet lawn, heated outdoor swimming pool, all-weather tennis court, and nearby riding; limited disabled access; cl 4-12 Jan; dogs welcome in bedrooms

LUXBOROUGH SS9738 **Royal Oak** *Luxborough, Watchet, Somerset TA23 0SH* (01984) 640319 **£65**; 12 rms. Unspoilt and interesting old pub in idyllic spot, marvellous for exploring Exmoor; bar rooms with log fires in inglenook fireplaces, beams, flagstones, character furnishings and a thriving feel, four distinctive dining rooms (three no smoking), good food, and well liked breakfasts; dogs welcome in bedrooms

MILBORNE PORT ST6718 **Old Vicarage** *Sherborne Rd, Milborne Port, Sherborne, Dorset DT9 5AT* (01963) 251117 **£82**; 6 rms, some in annexe. Charming Victorian house with an interesting mix of furnishings from East and West, pleasant

guest lounge and conservatory overlooking the gardens, good asian food in no
smoking dining room cooked by Mr Ma at wknds, and enjoyable breakfasts; cl Jan;
children over 5

NORTH PERROTT ST4709 **Manor Arms** *Middle St, North Perrott, Crewkerne,
Somerset TA18 7SG (01460) 72901* **£54***, plus special breaks; 9 rms in restored
coach house inc a fine panelled and beamed one. Comfortable and attractive 16th-c
inn with friendly helpful licensees, beams, exposed stone, and inglenook fireplace,
and good home-made food in small restaurant and bar; garden with play area;
disabled access

NORTH WOOTTON ST5641 **Riverside Grange** *Tanyard Lane, North
Wootton, Wells, Somerset BA4 4AE (01749) 890761* **£49**; 2 well equipped rms.
Quietly set converted tannery on river edge and overlooking a cider orchard;
charming, welcoming owner and enjoyable breakfasts (places in nearby village for
evening meals); no smoking; cl Christmas and New Year; no children

NORTON ST PHILIP ST7755 **George** *High St, Norton St Philip, Bath BA3 6LH
(01373) 834224* **£90***; 8 comfortable rms of real character in galleried wing.
Carefully restored, exceptional building that has been offering hospitality to
travellers for nearly 700 years; individual bars with trusses and timbering, fine old
stone fireplaces, really heavy beams, 18th-c pictures, oak dressers and settles and
so forth, a marvellous restaurant, good food, real ales, decent wines, and organised,
friendly service; a stroll over the meadow behind the pub (past the picnic-sets on
the narrow grass pub garden) leads to an attractive churchyard around the
medieval church whose bells struck Pepys (here on 12 June 1668) as 'mighty
tuneable'; cl 25-26 Dec; dogs welcome in bedrooms

POLSHAM ST5142 **Southway Farm** *Polsham, Wells, Somerset BA5 1RW (01749)
673396* **£48***, plus special breaks; 3 rms. Friendly creeper-covered Georgian
farmhouse on a working farm between Wells and Glastonbury, open fire in
comfortable sitting room, attractive dining room, good breakfasts, and pretty
garden

ROADWATER ST0337 **Wood Advent Farm** *Roadwater, Watchet, Somerset
TA23 0RR (01984) 640920* **£50***, plus special breaks; 5 rms. Relaxed, spacious
farmhouse on 340 acres of working farm within Exmoor National Park, great walks;
log fire in comfortable lounge, good country cooking using their own produce, grass
tennis court, outdoor heated swimming pool, and fishing, clay pigeon and pheasant
shooting; children over 11; dog kennels

SHEPTON MALLET ST6342 **Charlton House and Mulberry Restaurant**
Charlton Rd, Shepton Mallet, Somerset BA4 4PR (01749) 342008 **£155***, plus special
breaks; 17 attractive and stylish rooms with nice extras, and large bthrms.
Substantial Georgian hotel in landscaped grounds; bare-boarded rooms with
oriental rugs, dark red walls with lots of old photographs and posters, and showcasing the owners' Mulberry style of new-but-used look informal furnishings; smart
dining room and 3-bay conservatory with lots of interesting plants and lovely
flowers on the tables, newly restored 18th-c orangery dining room, exceptionally
good modern cooking, beautifully presented, interesting wines, and helpful, efficient
uniformed staff; seats on the back terrace overlooking a big lawn, unusual miniature
moated castle as a water feature on the front lawn, and croquet; new health spa;
they are kind to children; dogs welcome in bedrooms

SOMERTON ST4828 **Lynch Country House** *4 Behind Berry, Somerton, Somerset
TA11 7PD (01458) 272316* **£50***; 8 prettily decorated rms, plus 3 extra in summer
cottage. Carefully restored and homely Georgian house, with books in comfortable
lounge, and good breakfasts (no evening meals) in airy room overlooking tranquil
grounds and lake with black swans and exotic ducks; cl New Year; disabled access;
dogs welcome in bedrooms

STANTON WICK ST6162 **Carpenters Arms** *Stanton Wick, Pensford, Bristol
BS39 4BX (01761) 490202* **£84.50**; 12 rms. Warm and attractively furnished tile-
roofed inn, converted from a row of miners' cottages, in peaceful countryside; big
log fire and woodburner, stripped stone and beams, a wide choice of good food inc

generous breakfasts, well kept beers, and friendly efficient staff; pianist Fri and Sat pms; cl 25-26 Dec

STOGUMBER ST1037 **Hall Farm** *Station Rd, Stogumber, Taunton, Somerset TA4 3TQ (01984) 656321* **£40**; 7 rms. Old-fashioned B&B with optional evening meals (bring your own wine) - wonderfully unpretentious, with warmly friendly staff; cl Christmas and New Year; well behaved dogs welcome; disabled access

STOKE ST GREGORY ST3527 **Rose & Crown** *Woodhill, Stoke St Gregory, Taunton, Somerset TA3 6EW (01823) 490296* **£53**; 6 rms, some with own bthrm, nearby studio and cottage. Very friendly 17th-c cottagey inn with a cosy and pleasantly romanticised stable theme, generous helpings of particularly good value food in no smoking dining room, excellent breakfasts, a decent wine list, and efficient service from hard-working family in charge; seats out on enclosed terrace; self-catering nearby; partial disabled access

STON EASTON ST6254 **Ston Easton Park** *Ston Easton, Bath BA3 4DF (01761) 241631* **£150**; 22 really lovely rms. Majestic Palladian mansion of Bath stone with beautifully landscaped 18th-c gardens and 26 acres of parkland; elegant day rooms with antiques and flowers, an attractive no smoking restaurant with good food (much grown in the kitchen garden), fine afternoon teas, library and billiard room, and extremely helpful, friendly and unstuffy service; children over 7 in dining room

TAUNTON ST2224 **Castle** *Castle Green, Taunton, Somerset TA1 1NF (01823) 272671* **£175***, plus special breaks; 44 lovely rms. Appealingly modernised partly Norman castle, its front almost smothered in wisteria, with fine old oak furniture, tapestries and paintings in comfortably elegant lounges, really excellent modern english cooking, good breakfasts, a range of good value wines from a thoughtful list, and efficient friendly service; pretty garden; disabled access; dogs welcome in bedrooms

WELLS ST5445 **Infield House** *36 Portway, Wells, Somerset BA5 2BN (01749) 670989* **£52***; 3 comfortable rms (best view from back one). Carefully restored no smoking Victorian townhouse with period furnishings and family portraits, elegant lounge (with lots of local guidebooks), good breakfasts in dining room with Adam-style fireplace, evening meals by arrangement, and friendly personal service; cl 1 wk early Dec and 1 wk Jan; children over 12; dogs welcome in bedrooms

WOOKEY HOLE ST5347 **Glencot House** *Glencot Lane, Wookey Hole, Wells, Somerset BA5 1BH (01749) 677160* **£90***; 13 rms, many with four-posters. In 18 acres of pretty gardens and parkland (with own cricket pitch), this Jacobean-style Victorian mansion has some fine panelling, carved ceilings, antiques and flowers in the public rooms and hallways, a friendly atmosphere, and good food in the restaurant; fishing, table tennis, snooker, and small indoor jet stream pool; two friendly dogs and pet pig, lots to do nearby; cl New Year; they are kind to children; dogs welcome in bedrooms ☺

To see and do

Somerset Family Attraction of the Year

BRISTOL ST5972 **British Empire & Commonwealth Museum** (Clock Tower Yard, Temple Meads) Much more fun than you might initially think, this enterprising new museum - in a former railway station designed by Brunel - tells the story of the rise and fall of the British Empire and the emergence of the Commonwealth, from John Cabot's journey from Bristol to the New World in 1497 to the present day. There's masses of information here, but it's been put together with plenty of flair, and a good deal of thought about how to engage children. The subject matter isn't always comfortable, but it's riveting stuff, an extraordinary story, meticulously and objectively told. Rare film, historic photographs and sound recordings provide all the detail you could want, from all points of view, with plenty of interactive displays and exhibits livening things up for younger visitors. As well as computer games and push-button video stations, there's a chance to sample exotic spices and try on costumes, and they have extra family activities in school holidays, when you can have a go at games from around the world. As well as the 16 themed galleries, there are changing large-scale exhibitions: their very popular one on sport and games (again, plenty of interactive features) runs until January 4. Meals and snacks, shop, disabled access; cl 25-26 Dec; (0117) 925 4980; £5.95 adults, £3.95 children. The family ticket is good value: £14 for two adults and two children. There may be extra charges for some special exhibitions. It's worth checking out their website (www.empiremuseum.co.uk) for special offers; as we went to press they had a voucher there for accompanied grandchildren to get in free. They have a free car park at weekends only; it fills up fast, so if you come by car you'll probably need to use one of the public car parks nearby. You're better off coming by train: the museum is right by the station, and you'll get a discount by showing your ticket.

AXBRIDGE ST4354
Pleasant small town with an appealing largely medieval square and narrow winding High St, unusual in this part of the world for its jettied timber-framed buildings. The rambling old Lamb on the corner of the tranquil market square is good for lunch.
King John's Hunting Lodge (The Square) Actually built around 1500 so having no connection with King John (nor in fact with hunting) - but no less attractive for that. It houses a local history museum. Shop, disabled access to grounds; open pm only Apr-Sept; (01934) 732012; free; NT.
BANWELL ST3860
Court Farm (Wolvershill Rd, off A371 N) Much of this lively farm park (the county's biggest) is under cover, so it's good even in the wet. Friendly animals from shire horses to ferrets, with feeding sessions throughout the day, and summer pony rides; also play barns

and an adventure fort, as well as tractor rides, and a themed summer children's maize maze (20p). Snacks and picnic areas, shop, disabled access; cl Mon Nov-Feb, 24-26 Dec and 1 Jan; 01934 822383; £4.95. The 17th-c Woolpack (St Georges, just beyond M5 junction 21) has good reasonably priced food.
BARRINGTON ST3918
Barrington Court In the grounds of a splendid 16th-c house, a magnificent series of gardens influenced by Gertrude Jekyll, inc rose garden and traditional walled kitchen garden (you can buy the produce in the shop). The house shows off the reproduction furniture of Stuart Interiors. Meals, snacks, plant centre, disabled access to garden and ground floor; house and grounds open Thurs-Sun Mar and Oct, plus Mon-Tues Apr-Sept; (01460) 241938; £5.20; NT. The village itself is attractive, and the Royal Oak does good lunches.

BATH ST7564

For many this is England's most rewarding old town, though its throngs of summer visitors tend to mask its charms a bit then. Many places enjoyably recall the days of Beau Nash and the building of Bath as a fashionable resort; other draws go back to the Roman Baths, and come right up to date with the new Bath Spa complex. The Roman Baths and the Museum of Costume offer a joint ticket (£12), and the American Museum on the edge of the city at Claverton is well worth visiting. Parts not to be missed include the great showpieces of 18th-c town planning, Queen Sq, the Circus and the Royal Crescent; the quieter Abbey Green and cobbled Abbey St and Queen St; and the great Pulteney Bridge (there's a fine view of it from the bridge at the end of North Parade, or the riverside Parade Gardens, where brass bands play in summer). The narrow little lanes between the main streets can be fascinating; there are some interesting and unusual shops to browse around. In summer lots of informal eating places have tables outside. Walcot St has a good flea market (Sat), and every Sat a farmers' market by Green Park Station has lots of fresh fruit and vegetables. The beautifully restored historic **Theatre Royal** presents more pre-West End productions than anywhere else in the country. Don't try to drive around the city: Bath's streets were laid out for travel by sedan chair, not car, and a tortuous one-way system seems designed to deter drivers rather than to make traffic flow more easily. It's better to leave your car at one of the city's four park-and-ride sites and take the shuttle bus in. Walking around Bath is a delight; there are flat parts, though to make the most of it you have to be prepared to slog up some of the steeper streets. Readers particularly enjoy the somewhat irreverent **Bizarre Bath** walking tours that leave the Huntsman Inn on North Parade Passage at 8pm daily, Apr-Sept (£5) - more street theatre than a typical tour; or you can go on one of the free daily walking tours which leave from outside the Roman Baths at 10.30am and 2pm (10.30 only

on Sat). The rush of a day trip doesn't do justice to the host of things worth seeing, and it's best to stay, preferably out of season; if you want to visit during Bath's early summer Music Festival, book accommodation well ahead.

Balloon trips Hot-air balloons give a good view of the city as it's shown in the great architectural drawings. They take off, subject to weather, from the Royal Victoria Park; (01225) 466888; from £139.

Bath Abbey & Abbey Heritage Vaults Particularly renowned for its fan vaulting, the current building is the third great church to be built on this site, begun in 1499. The Elizabethans called it the Lantern of the West because of its profusion of stained glass. Most impressive is the great E window, depicting 56 scenes from the life of Christ. On one side of this is a finely carved memorial to Bartholomew Barnes (1608), and on the other beautiful medieval carving of the Prior Birde chantry. Restoration has returned the interior's gradually blackened Bath stone to its more appealing honey colour. Bookshop, disabled access; cl Good Fri, 24-26 Dec, 1 Jan, and during private services (usually Sun); £2.50 suggested donation. The carefully restored 18th-c vaults have a very good exhibition on the abbey's history. Disabled access; cl Sun; (01225) 422462; £2.50.

Bath Postal Museum 🏛 (Broad St) First-class exploration of the development of the postal system since the 16th c, inc a full-scale replica Victorian post office; it was from here that the world's first postage stamp was sent in 1840, and there's a 1930s Post Office and telephone exchange. Snacks, shop, disabled access to ground floor only; cl Sun, 23-28 Dec and 1 wk in Jan; (01225) 460333; *£2.90. Just round the corner the Old Green Tree (Green St) is a good pub with decent food.

Beckford's Tower (Lansdown Rd) Italianate tower with fine views from the top, and a museum commemorating the well travelled collector William Beckford; also art gallery and original furniture from the tower. Shop; open wknds and bank hols Easter-Oct; (01225) 460705; £3.

Boating Cruises leave Pulteney Bridge landing stage at a quarter to and a quarter past the hour (weather permitting, not Oct-Easter). Boats and punts can be hired Apr-Oct from the Boating Station on the River Avon, Forester Rd, Bathwick; meals and snacks; (01225) 312900; £5 for an hour. The revivified **Kennet & Avon Canal** is one of Bath's pleasures, with quiet towpath walks along to Bathampton and beyond; it has quite a few colourful narrow-boats in summer. You can cycle right into the centre along the Avon Cycleway, cycle tracks converted from the old Bath and Bristol railway. A nice waterside family eating place is the Boathouse (Newbridge Rd), on the outskirts nr a marina.

Building of Bath Museum 🏛 (The Vineyard, Paragon) Fascinating displays on how John Wood and others transformed the town and its architecture, with full-scale reconstructions, original tools, and a fabulous model of the entire city, lighting up when you press the buttons. Shop; cl Mon (exc bank hols), and Dec-11 Feb; (01225) 333895; £4. The nearby Star is an appropriately antiquated pub.

Envolve (Green Park Rd) Visitor centre for the exemplary charity which promotes environmental awareness among the local community. Disabled access; cl Sat pm, all Sun and bank hol wknds; (01225) 787910; free.

Georgian Garden (Gravel Walk) Between Royal Crescent and Queen Sq, this like them is a reminder of Bath's heyday, re-creating the original layout and the kind of plants that would have been used in a small town garden in the 1760s. Cl wknds, bank hols and all Nov-Apr; (01225) 477752; free.

Holburne Museum of Art (Gt Pulteney St) Fine old building displaying art and objects collected in the 19th c by Sir Thomas William Holburne, inc Old Master paintings, portrait miniatures and italian bronzes. Meals, snacks, shop, disabled access; cl Sun am, Mon, and mid-Dec to mid-Feb; (01225) 466669; £4.

Jane Austen Centre 🏛 (Gay St) Jane Austen lived in this street 1801-6, and this enjoyable centre takes a comprehensive look at the novelist's life, as well as the ways in which the city influenced her writing. Displays include re-creations of a Georgian shop-front and town garden, exhibitions on places mentioned in her novels, and elegant costumes; also news on Austen-related events and walking tours (£4.50, gives 20% discount on entry to centre). Shop, disabled access; cl 24-26 Dec, 1 Jan; (01225) 443000; £4.45. Just along George St, the Porter does good vegetarian food.

Museum of Bath at Work 🏛 (Julian Rd) The highlight here is the engaging **Mr Bowler's Business**, an elaborate re-creation of a factory first established in 1872, providing various services from plumbing and engineering to gas-fitting and bell-hanging. Everything is just as it was then, inc the antique soda fountain that turned out such intriguingly named drinks as Cherry Ciderette. Snacks, shop; cl wkdys Nov-Mar; (01225) 318348; £3.50.

Museum of Costume & Assembly Rooms (Bennett St) Dazzling - more than 150 figures in original costumes from the late 16th c to the present, one of the most impressive displays of fashion and fashion accessories in the world. It's housed in the Assembly Rooms built in 1771 by John Wood the Younger, where the audio-guide has a particularly entertaining commentary - listen out for the bun fight. Summer snacks, shop, disabled access; cl 25-26 Dec, and Assembly Rooms may be closed other dates for functions; (01225) 477785; £5.50. Along the same street is a small **Museum of East Asian Art**; cl Mon (exc bank hols) and am Sun; disabled access; (01225) 464640; £3.50.

No 1 Royal Crescent The most splendid example of the architecture that sprang up in the town's Georgian heyday. In 1768 it was the first house built in Bath's most regal terrace, two floors (and now the basement kitchen too) restored and beautifully furnished in the style of that time. Shop; cl Mon (exc bank hols), end Nov to mid-Feb, and Good Fri; (01225) 428126; £4. The Crescent is closed to traffic at one end, with the hope of reducing damage inflicted by tour buses.

Prior Park Landscape Garden
(Ralph Allen Drive, off A3062 S) In a
sweeping valley, this striking 18th-c
landscaped garden is being
comprehensively restored by the
National Trust; work on the Palladian
bridge is now complete and a new
circuit walk has been opened (in the
summer they plan to start work on
restoring the wilderness area, with
guided tours of the restoration in
progress). Capability Brown and
Alexander Pope originally helped with
the design, and there are plenty of
unique ornamental features (inc 18th-c
graffiti on the Palladian bridge).
Woodland walks offer views over Bath.
Note you can't drive all the way here:
there's no car parking on site or nearby
(though there are some spaces for
disabled visitors, phone to book). You
can walk from town, but the hill is long
and steep, so best to take the number 2
or 4 bus. Cl Tues Feb-end Nov, Mon-
Thurs Dec-Jan, 25-26 Dec, 1 Jan;
(01225) 833422; £4.10. If you are in a
car, the Hope & Anchor over at
Midford is good for lunch.

Pump Room This stylish 18th-c
mecca for the fashionable was built
directly above the Roman temple
courtyard; you can catch a glimpse of
the baths next door. It now houses a
restaurant serving morning coffee,
lunches and teas to the strains of the
Pump Room Trio. You can sample the
hot spa water, which always comes out
at 46°C (116°F); cl 25-26 Dec; (01225)
444477; 50p a glass.

Roman Baths Founded by AD 75, and
undoubtedly one of Britain's most
remarkable Roman sites. They were
built to service pilgrims visiting a temple
to Sulis Minerva, which had been
constructed around a sacred hot spring.
After this the spring played a dual role -
as both a focus for worship, and a
reservoir supplying the baths with spa
water. The temple and baths were all but
forgotten until the 18th c, when
workmen chanced upon a bust of
Minerva, and it was not until 1878 that
most of what you see today was
uncovered. The main baths are pretty
much intact, though the columns are
19th-c reconstructions. In July and Aug
they're open at night and quite

beautifully floodlit. A **museum** shows
finds made during excavations, inc the
bust of Minerva, a remarkable Gorgon's
Head pediment, and lead tablets
inscribed with messages and thrown into
the spring by pilgrims; also models and an
audio-guide. Meals, snacks, shop, some
disabled access (though not to baths
themselves); cl 25-26 Dec; (01225)
477785; £8.50, inc an audio-guide.

**Sally Lunn's Refreshment House &
Museum** (North Parade Passage)
Reputedly the oldest house in Bath, a
charming partly timbered medieval
structure, still preserving in its cellars
the original kitchen of the legendary
Sally Lunn, who in the 17th c created her
famous brioche bread buns here. Meals
and snacks (inc of course the buns, made
to a secret recipe), shop; cl 24-26 Dec
and 1 Jan; (01225) 461634; 30p.

Thermae Bath Spa At a price, you
should now be able to bathe in the city's
natural thermal spa waters (a luxury
denied since 1978 when the baths were
closed by doubts over the purity of the
source). Just 100 metres from the
famous Roman Baths (see below), this
stunning Millennium Commission
project comprises one purpose-built
and two restored bath houses, with a
visitor centre in a former pump room.
The focal point is the new spa complex
strikingly crafted from Bath stone and
glass (we had hoped for an opening last
February, but various delays culminated
in new granite cobbling, which had to be
ripped up in Aug - as we went to press,
fingers were crossed for an opening in
Dec 2003). The building, crowned with
a roof-top open-air pool, is a 'centre for
well-being', a health-minded pleasure-
seeker's paradise replete with
whirlpools, steam rooms, massage
rooms, and other restorative
treatments; there's also a restaurant.
Open daily exc 25, 31 Dec, and 1 Jan;
bathing prices start at £17 for 2 hrs,
phone for details; (01225) 331234.

Victoria Art Gallery (Bridge St)
European Old Masters and 18th- to
20th-c british paintings and drawings, as
well as decorative arts inc porcelain,
glass and watches. Disabled access to
ground floor only; cl Sun am, all day
Mon, 25-26 Dec; (01225) 477233; free.
Boaters nicely placed just over Pulteney

Bridge has enterprising snacks.

William Herschel Museum & Star Vault (New King St) Interesting Georgian home and workplace of William Herschel, the astronomer (and composer), with period rooms, models of his telescopes, and other scientific equipment. He discovered the planet Uranus from the back garden. Bookshop; cl am (exc wknds), Weds, and Dec-10 Feb; (01225) 311342; *£3.50.

BISHOPS LYDEARD ST1729
Attractive village, interesting church with handsome carving.

BITTON SD6769
Avon Valley Railway (Bitton Station) Friendly little railway extending lines along the old Midland Railway towards Bath and North Somerset (hence its inclusion in this chapter, though Bitton itself is actually just over the Gloucestershire border). A platform linking the railway to Avon Valley Country Park (see Keynsham, below) should be completed by Easter. Snacks, shop, disabled access; open Sun and bank hols May-Sept and Easter, Weds and Thurs in Aug, and wknds in Dec; (0117) 932 7296 for timetable; £4.

BRADFORD-ON-TONE ST1722
Sheppy's Cider 🖾 (Three Bridges) The Sheppy family has been making cider here since the early 19th c, and you can follow the process through a video. Tastings in the shop, and a little museum. Tearoom (Jun-Sept), shop, disabled access to shop and museum; cl Sun Christmas-Easter; (01823) 461233; farm free, museum *£2. The White Horse has enjoyable food.

BREAN DOWN ST2958
Protruding into the Bristol Channel between Weston-Super-Mare and acres of holiday camps, this gives the best coastal walk in east Somerset.

BRENDON HILLS SS9738
These give breezy walks with long views; the Royal Oak at Luxborough is a good base.

BRENT KNOLL ST3450
The attractive village has a church with remarkable carved bench-ends; the Red Cow is a popular dining pub. A path leads up to the prominent summit giving the village its name.

BRIDGWATER ST3036
Once you're through the industrial outskirts, some central bits are worth seeing: Castle St is the finest early 18th-c street in the county. Cross Rifles (Bath Rd) has good value food.

Blake Museum (Blake St) Now the local history museum, this picturesque house was probably Robert Blake's 1598 birthplace, and you can still see some of his personal possessions (inc his sea chest) and a diorama of his great victory over the spaniards at Santa Cruz; also displays on the Monmouth rebellion, and a maritime gallery. Shop; cl Sun, Mon, Good Fri, and 25 Dec-2 Jan; (01278) 456127; free.

BRISTOL
A busy industrial city, with the usual big-city problems, this nevertheless has plenty of attractions to fill an enjoyable day. An excellent initiative here is free entry to five of the city's best museums: City Museum & Art Gallery, Industrial Museum, Georgian House, Red Lodge and Blaise Castle Museum (see separate entries). It's easily reached from Bath or from one of the cosseting nearby country-house hotels we list, and day visits are made easy by good rail connections, and the motorway that plunges right into the city's heart. There are plenty of cafés, pubs and bars, and with two universities, there's a lively nightlife. The city's prosperity is based on trade through its port, though aerospace is now the most important component of a wide manufacturing base; the modern docks are seven miles away at Avonmouth, but the 19th-c Floating Harbour now provides a backdrop for a variety of attractions in the heart of the city. The centre jumbles together the evidence of its long prosperity, with medieval churches, Georgian terraces and Victorian commercial palaces, and a miscellany of modern buildings ranging from the bland to the downright ugly; although much of the centre is pedestrianised, traffic, with its noise, can still be intrusive and isolates some odd and interesting corners (the transport system here has recently been judged the worst in twelve of our biggest cities outside London). A walk from John Wesley's chapel, in the heart of the Broadmead shopping district, up Union St and right along Corn St, then down

to the Harbourside, passes some striking buildings, including the Corn Exchange and the old Council House on Corn St, and the Grand Hotel (1869), the Guild Hall (1843), and an art nouveau façade on Broad St. The Theatre Royal (1766), on King St, is one of the oldest working theatres in the country. An extensive covered market is centred around the Corn Exchange (Corn St); there's a farmer's market on Weds, and a street market Fri and Sat. Besides places mentioned below, the Commercial Rooms (Corn St), Old Fish Market (Broad St) and Horts City Tavern (Broad St) are useful central places for a cheapish lunchtime bite. A 250-mile cycle way runs from here to Padstow in Cornwall, keeping off roads as much as possible.

@Bristol (Harbourside) Explore is the part to head for if your time is limited: full of interactive and hands-on features, it lets you star in your own TV show, play virtual volleyball, or get an idea of how it feels to be in the eye of a tornado. The latest technology gives a new spin to time-honoured activities like generating electricity or making things fly, and there are novelties like the virtual sperm journey and the walk-in womb. Especially good is the Imaginarium, a next-generation planetarium that looks like a metal sphere and takes you into a 3-D virtual universe. There are also workshops. Wildwalk is a well put together walk-through journey around evolution, particularly strong on insects, with lots of videos and multi-media bits; its best part is the re-created tropical rain forest, with free-flying birds and butterflies. These sections, and a huge IMAX cinema with a screen four storeys high, are linked by appealingly landscaped squares and avenues, dotted with trees, sculptures, shops and restaurants. Café, shop, disabled access; cl 25 Dec; (0845) 345 1235; £6.50 IMAX or Wildwalk, £7.50 Explore, the All-Star ticket (everything exc Imaginarium) is £16.50.

Blaise Castle House Museum (Henbury, 4m NW, off B4047) A spacious and locally popular undulating park with some woodland, and adventure play area. The late 18th-c

house contains displays of everyday objects from toys and dolls to Victorian water closets and baths. The castle itself is a Gothic folly built in 1766 within the now scarcely discernible ramparts of an Iron Age hill fort. Shop, disabled access to ground floor only; museum cl Thurs and Fri, and all Nov-Mar, park open daily; (0117) 903 9818; free. Nearby Blaise Hamlet is a NT-owned estate village designed by John Nash.

Bristol Cathedral To the N of the harbour, this was originally an Augustinian abbey and is perhaps the country's most splendid example of a hall church (where the nave, choir and aisles are all the same height). A real mix of architectural styles, highlights include its 14th-c Decorated Chancel 'with its confounding diagonal vistas' (Pevsner), its splendid Chapter House (one of the finest Norman rooms in Britain), and the candlesticks given in thanks by the privateers who rescued Alexander Selkirk (whose adventures inspired Daniel Defoe to write *Robinson Crusoe*). Snacks, shop; (0117) 926 4879; free (donations welcomed).

Bristol Industrial Museum (Princes Wharf) In a converted dockside transit shed, and especially good on transport, with locally built steam locomotives and aircraft (inc a mock-up of Concorde's flight deck), and a good look at the development of the port; there's always something in steam at wknds offering rides; a crane (£1), several different boats (£3), or the train. Shop, disabled access; cl Thurs and Fri, 25-26 Dec and 1 Jan; (0117) 925 1470; free. Steam trains run along the docks between here and the SS *Great Britain* every ¼ hr 12-5pm on selected days Mar-Oct; £1.

Bristol Zoo Gardens (Clifton Downs; easily reached by buses 8, 508 and 509 from the centre) One of the most enjoyable zoos in the country, excellent value, with lots to see. High points include a transparent underwater walkway letting you watch penguins and seals from almost every conceivable angle (look out for the rare albino penguin born here, Snowdrop), a re-created rain forest area, the interactive Twilight World with its nocturnal desert, forest and walk-through bat enclosure, and Bug World, showing off inhabitants as diverse as flat-tailed scorpions and moon jellyfish. The zoo is particularly good for monkeys and gorillas, and there's a big open-air aviary, as well as a reptile house and aquarium. Feeding and talks throughout the day, and a good adventure playground, with separate areas for toddlers; extra activities in the summer hols. The Zoolympics trail is fun, encouraging children to measure their skills against some of the animals. Everything is spread over beautifully laid-out gardens, with spacious lawns and colourful borders; a fair bit is under cover, including some picnic areas. Meals, snacks, shop, good disabled access; cl 25 Dec; (0117) 973 8951; £8.90.

British Empire & Commonwealth Museum See separate family panel on p.510.

Cabot Tower Brandon Hill Park at the end of Great George St is an urban nature reserve; its tower rewards those willing to climb the hundreds of steps with probably the best views of the city. Snacks; cl 25 Dec; free. Nearby **St George's**, built to commemorate the Battle of Waterloo, has good lunchtime concerts on Thurs, usually with seats available on the day, but best to check on (0117) 923 0359.

Christmas Steps At the top of the steps of this famously old-fashioned alley, quaintly lined by steep buildings, is the tiny late 15th-c **Chapel of the Three Kings of Cologne** (the 'three kings' are the three wise men whose shrines are in Cologne Cathedral); the warden of the nearby almshouses can let you in. At the bottom is the lodge of **St Bartholomew's** - all that remains of the 13th-c hospital and almshouse which once stood on this site. The St Michael's area is a good place for specialist shops.

City Museum & Art Gallery (Queens Rd) Good collections of fine and applied art, archaeology, geology, and history - well worth a look. Meals, snacks, shop, mostly disabled access; cl 25-26 Dec; (0117) 922 3571; free. The neo-Gothic Wills Memorial tower next door is a distinctive landmark.

Clifton This elegant suburb is the quiet side of Bristol and a good place for peaceful strolls, with handsome Georgian terraces (it's got more Georgian buildings than Bath), an antiques market (Victorian Arcade, cl Sun, Mon), and a big park right on the spectacular Avon gorge facing the NT woodlands on the crags opposite. The remarkably modern-looking **Clifton Suspension Bridge**, was Brunel's first major civil engineering commission; the foundation stone was laid in 1831, but the bridge wasn't completed till 1864, five years after his death. A **Visitor Centre**, due to reopen in Aug after refurbishments, will tell you more; shop, disabled access; (0117) 974 4664; £1.90. The Hope & Anchor (Jacobs Well Rd) and Alma (Alma Vale Rd) do good cheap food.

Create Centre (Smeaton Rd, Spike Island) Environmental centre with hands-on displays about recycling, and an ecohome with organic garden (pms only) showcasing methods for greener everyday living. Also changing exhibitions of local art. Shop, café, disabled access; cl wknds and 24-29 Dec; (0117) 925 0505; free.

Docks Now largely restored, with distinctive blue and yellow ferries (Apr-Sept) linking several points. The Old City around King St, between the waterfront and the Bristol Old Vic, has quiet cobbled streets of Georgian buildings, pleasant to wander through; the Llandoger Trow, the last timber-framed building here, has reasonably priced food. Elsewhere some of the bigger warehouses (and even the boats) have been pressed into service as museums, café-bars and the like; it's a good place to head for nightlife. The Arnolfini contemporary arts complex (a big former tea warehouse), is currently undergoing major refurbishment and will reopen early 2005.

Historic Boat Trips (from Princes Wharf) The 1860s steam-tug Mayflower, the 1930s fireboat Pyronaut and the tug John King give interesting trips round the dock in the summer - best to check times with the Industrial Museum; (0117) 925 1470; £3. From Apr to Oct the **pleasure steamers** Waverley and Balmoral run fairly frequent day cruises from here, along the Avon and Severn or to Devon, Wales or Lundy; (0141) 221 8152 for timetable. The Balmoral has surprisingly well kept real ale in its bar.

Lord Mayor's Chapel (College Green) Rare civic church dating from the 13th c, with glorious 16th-c stained-glass windows, floor tiles and fan-vaulted ceiling; cl Mon and 12-1pm; tours by appointment only Tues-Sat; (0117) 929 4350; donations.

New Room - John Wesley's Chapel (Horsefair) Incongruously set in a shopping centre, but much as it was when Wesley preached here (from his famous double-decked pulpit, as well as a less-known predecessor, returned here from Anglesey in 1999); the oldest Methodist chapel in the world, built in 1739 and rebuilt in 1748. Guided tours (with costumed guides) by arrangement. Shop, disabled access to ground floor only; cl Sun, Good Fri, and 25-26 Dec; (0117) 926 4740; free (£2.80 tour).

Red Lodge (Park Row) The house was altered in the 18th c, but on its first floor still has the last surviving suite of 16th-c rooms in Bristol, as well as a wonderful carved stone chimney-piece, plasterwork ceilings and fine oak panelling. They occasionally open the reconstructed Tudor-style garden (now overlooked by an ugly car park). Open Sat-Weds and most bank hols Apr-Oct; (0117) 921 1360; free. There are several elegant Georgian streets round here, notably Great George St, where the **Georgian House**, built in 1790 for a wealthy sugar merchant, is a fine illustration of a typical townhouse of the day. Three floors are decorated in period style, inc the below-stairs area with kitchen, laundry and housekeeper's room. Times as for Red Lodge; (0117) 921 1362; free.

SS Great Britain On the dockside, on some summer wknds a small steam railway will whisk you along the old cargo route to and from this ship, designed by Brunel as the first iron, screw-propelled, ocean-going vessel, and a real departure from what had gone before. A £10m restoration project to conserve and interpret the ship and re-create the Victorian dockyard is due for completion in the autumn; you can go behind the scenes to see some of the work being done. A

replica of *Matthew*, John Cabot's ship, lies alongside it. Meals, snacks, shop; cl 24-25 Dec; (0117) 926 0680; *£6.25. This includes entry to the **Maritime Heritage Centre**, with reconstructions and original machinery illustrating the city's long history of ship-building. The nearby diesel-powered firefloat *Pyronaut* (1934) and Fairbairn steam-crane (1876) operate occasional summer wknds. The Cottage, a handsomely converted customs house a walk W along the waterfront, has wholesome food all day, and fine views from its terrace.

St Mary Redcliffe (Redcliffe Hill) Elizabeth I described this as 'the goodliest, fairest and most famous parish church in England' (though now it's moated by a car park and a dual carriageway). Most of the current building was built in the 14th c and enlarged in the 15th. Notable features include a wonderful hexagonal outer porch, the tomb of Admiral Sir William Penn, the father of Pennsylvania's founder, and the Handel Window, where eight passages of the *Messiah* commemorate the great composer's ties with this church. Wkdy meals and snacks, shop, disabled access but no facilities. May be free organ recitals Thurs lunchtimes during term-time; (0117) 929 1487.

St Werburgh's City Farm (Watercress Rd) Half an hour's walk from the centre, this working urban farm is kept going largely by volunteers who look after the animals and tend the various gardens (inc a scented one); also adventure playground and wildlife pond. Meals and snack, farm shop, disabled access; usually open daily; (0117) 942 8241; free.

University Botanic Gardens (Bracken Hill, North Rd, Leigh Woods) Set around students' halls of residence, these attractive gardens with several rock and water features (and a new chinese garden), will be open till around autumn, when they will relocate to the Holnes (Stoke Bishop); so best to phone then. Some disabled access; usually cl wknds and bank hols, guided tours by appointment (£3.50); (0117) 973 3682; free.

BRUTON ST6834
Fascinating little town, with interesting
and individual shops - antiques, books
and prints. Worth looking out for are
the Bartons, narrow alleys leading
down from the High St to the river
(which you can cross either by
footbridge or by using stepping stones).
St Mary's church is on the site of a
medieval Augustinian priory and abbey -
the old abbey wall with its buttresses still
stands in Silver St. The church has a
spectacular altar-piece, and in the chancel
is a fine effigy of Sir Maurice Berkely, a
great survivor who was standard-bearer
to Henry VIII, Edward VI and Elizabeth I.
Thefts have made them lock the church
recently; the church office (just over
Church Bridge; (01749) 812372) may
allow access. Readers enjoy the town
trail, leaflets from tourist information
centre (the delicatessen next door has a
good coffee shop, and a range of local and
french cheeses). The Castle Inn is good
for lunch. The drive up towards Alfred's
Tower gives some open views; the Bull
up there at Hardway is a reliable dining
pub.
Gants Mill & Garden There's been
milling on the site since 1290, and this is
now one of the last working watermills
in the county; in the past it's been a
fulling mill, silk mill and grist mill, and
today it grinds barley. The attractive
colour-themed garden has water
features, sculptures on display, and a
bog garden. Snacks, shop, disabled
access to garden; open pms Sun, Thurs
and bank hols, 15 May-end Sept;
(01749) 8132393; £4.
BURNHAM-ON-SEA ST3050
In summer a bustling inexpensive family
seaside resort, with wide beaches,
sandy dunes, and the usual holiday
facilities. Its plain-looking **church**
surprises with its collection of Grinling
Gibbons carvings from the long-
demolished Palace of Whitehall in
London. Dunstan House (B3140) has a
good food range, and well equipped
play area.
Animal Farm Adventure Park 🖾
(Red Rd, N of Berrow) Good fun for
children, with animals and conservation
trails, trampolines, huge slides and play
areas (inc one for the under-7s and one
under cover). Meals, snacks, shop,

some disabled access; cl 24-27 Dec;
(01278) 751628; £4.70. The nearby
sand dunes include a small **nature
reserve**.
BURRINGTON COMBE ST4858
An easy walk by the B3134 (the best
drive through the Mendips), this great
steeply wooded limestone gorge on the
N flank of the Mendips can be combined
with walks up on to Black Down for
memorable views in all directions, and
over the heather and cranberry tops to
Dolebury Warren, where the site of an
Iron Age hill fort marks a splendid
Mendip viewpoint. Other good starting
points for Mendips walks include the
Crown at Churchill, Swan at
Rowberrow, and Ring o' Bells at
Compton Martin.
BURROW BRIDGE ST3428
Somerset Levels Basket Centre
(Lyng Rd) Sells baskets made from local
materials cut on the surrounding Levels
as well as other crafts. Shop; cl Sun,
Tues, some bank hols, plus 2 wks for
hols - so best to check; (01823) 698688;
free. The Rose & Crown at East Lyng
has good food.
CADBURY CAMP ST4572
This Iron Age hill fort makes a good
destination for a walk from the engaging
Black Horse in Clapton-in-Gordano, by
a lane past the church, which leads to a
footbridge high over the M5. Don't
confuse this with the more famous
Cadbury Castle down towards Yeovil.
CANNINGTON ST2539
**Cannington College Heritage
Gardens** Extensive gardens inc over
10,000 different types of plant, display
and ornamental beds. Meals, snacks,
disabled access; open daily; (01278)
655000; £1. The Malt Shovel at Bradley
Green has decent food, and there's a
nice drive to Nether Stowey via
Combwich and Stogursey.
CASTLE CARY ST6432
Very attractive - basically a medieval
market town, now with a useful range
of traditional family-run shops and
crafts and antiques shops. The 18th-c
Roundhouse is Britain's smallest
prison.
Hadspen Garden 🖾 (off A371 2m
SE) Beautiful two-hectare (five-acre)
gardens surrounding fine 18th-c house;
many old favourite plants, but also lots

of exotics. The unique D-shaped walled garden provides a rare micro-climate and has colour-themed borders of herbaceous plants and old-fashioned roses, and there's a lily pond and flower meadow. Teas and snacks, nursery, some disabled access; open Thurs-Sun and bank hols Mar-Sept; (01749) 813707; £4. The Stags Head in nearby Yarlington relies heavily on local produce for its good meals.

CASTLE NEROCHE ST2715
This isolated ruined Norman fortification, with more the aspect now of a hill fort than a castle, is the central feature of well marked woodland walks down towards the Blackdown Hills S of Taunton; fine views at the top.

CHAPEL ALLERTON ST4150
Ashton Windmill The only complete windmill left in Somerset, built in the 18th c, with splendid views over the Cheddar Gorge and Somerset Levels. Shop; open pm Sun, bank hols Easter-Sept, plus pm Weds July-Aug, phone to check; (01278) 435399; free.

CHARD ST3108
Chard Museum (High St) Good local history displays inc one on John Stringfellow, who flew a powered flying-machine in 1848, local industries such as lace-making, and a collection of early artificial limbs. Shop, disabled access to ground floor only; cl pm Sat, Sun (exc July-Aug), and Nov-Apr; (01460) 65091; £2. The Phoenix (Fore St) has good value food. The local tourist board do good cycle routes. Forde Abbey, just over the border in Dorset, is particularly worth visiting.

CHEDDAR ST4553
In its older part, this extended village has a very fine market cross, with some interesting shops and a tall-towered 14th/15th-c **church**. The Gardeners Arms and thatched Kings Head (both 16th-c, in Silver St) have enjoyable food. Cheddar gets astonishingly busy in summer, when every building seems to be either a tearoom or a shop selling cheese or cider.

Cheddar Gorge The area's big attraction, a magnificent limestone gorge with picturesque cliffs, formed when a cavern roof collapsed. Further up the dramatic B3135 road through the gorge, it rapidly loses its commercialised trappings. When you reach the far end two worthwhile paths leave the road. On the E side is a quiet dale with two nature reserves, Black Rock and Velvet Bottom. On the S side, the West Mendip Way climbs through woods and gives access to another path which skirts the top of the gorge (the views into it are hair-raising). The look-out tower up at the top has views of the Somerset Levels and Glastonbury Tor. You can also get up to this via the 274 steps of Jacob's Ladder from the road at the W entrance to the gorge.

Cheddar Gorge Cheese Co Village (The Cliffs) Shops and traditional crafts based around a factory that thanks to its location claims to make the only genuine cheddar cheese in the world. You can watch each stage of the seven-hour process, and of course taste the matured product. Also fudge-making, scrumpy sampling, and less flavoursome crafts inc lace- and candle-making. Snacks, shops, disabled access; cl 25-26 Dec and 1 Jan; (01934) 742810; now free.

Cheddar Showcaves Well worth a look, this busy spot boasts two quite remarkable showcaves, and it's efficiently organised for families. The highlight for adults is probably Gough's Cave, named after the retired sea captain who stumbled across it in 1890; this series of stunning underground caverns goes on for around a quarter of a mile, each area more dramatic than the last, with spectacular stalactites and stalagmites joining to form columns (they've an audio tour for this part). Nearby Cox's Cave is smaller, and more beautifully coloured; it has several very narrow passageways. Children may prefer the Crystal Quest, a cave entertainingly fitted out with goblins, wizards, and a smoke-filled dragon; a story and challenge lead them through. An exhibition is devoted to Cheddar Man, Britain's oldest complete skeleton, with a re-creation of what his world was like, 9,000 years ago. A new museum is due to open at Easter, with exhibitions on the cave and on cannibalism, complete with a virtual-reality tour. The ticket also includes a Mar-Oct tour bus through some of the narrow roads of the gorge. Meals,

snacks, unusual shops; cl 24-25 Dec;
(01934) 742343; *£9.50. You can
arrange introductory sessions of caving,
climbing and abseiling for children over
11 (you have to book in advance, and
there are height restrictions; *£15).

CHEDDON FITZPAINE ST2428
Hestercombe Gardens 🏡 (N of
village) Raised walks, sunken lawns and
a water garden are all part of the grand
design which Lutyens and Gertrude
Jekyll created for this beautifully
restored garden around what is now
Somerset Fire Brigade HQ; also
intriguing landscaped Georgian garden
with woodland walks and classical
temples, pleasant even on a gloomy day,
and a re-created Victorian shrubbery.
Tearoom, shop (inc plant sales), limited
disabled access; cl 25 Dec; (01823)
413923; £5. As we went to press they
were hoping that their application for
£3.9m from the heritage lottery fund
for further restoration work would be
successful. The Bathpool Inn over on
the A38 is a useful food stop.

CHELWOOD ST6361
Lady Farm (A368 fim E of A37
Chelwood roundabout) Nicely varied
4½-hectare (11-acre) garden, with
formal garden areas, large tracts of
prairie and steppe planting, a spring-fed
watercourse, and two lakes. Snacks;
open Sun July-Sept; (01761) 490770; £4.
The Carpenters Arms at Stanton Wick
has decent food.

CHEW VALLEY LAKES ST5760
The Chew Valley Lake itself and
Blagdon Lake are more popular as
breathing places for people living
nearby than as places for visitors from
afar; both are pleasant large stretches of
water, with managed fishing, and the
B3130 and B3114 have pleasant views.
The Queen Adelaide in Blagdon does
generous meals.

CLAVERTON ST7864
American Museum in Britain
(Claverton Manor, just SE of Bath)
Quite a contrast to the rest of Bath's
attractions, a fascinating illustration of
american history and life, in lovely
gracious surroundings. Eighteen rooms
are fully furnished and decorated to re-
create the style of transatlantic homes
from the 17th to the 19th c, while the
grounds include a replica of part of

George Washington's garden at Mount
Vernon, and an arboretum. Collections
of folk art and patchwork quilts with
sections on Native Americans and
Shakers, and good special events.
Snacks, shop; cl am, all day Mon (exc
bank hols), and mid-Dec to mid-Mar;
(01225) 460503; £6.

CLEVEDON ST4071
Pleasant for a stroll, with a restored
Victorian **pier** (£1), with sailings and
fishing; above the tollhouse, a gallery
sells paintings. Round the corner in
Waterloo House is a **Heritage
Centre** (usually cl Weds Oct-Mar and
25 Dec); donations. Good views from
Church Hill, and in Moor Lane the
Clevedon Craft Centre has 15
varied workshops and a tearoom; most
parts cl am Sun, Mon, and Tues; (01275)
872149. Hill Rd is a Victorian shopping
street with some antiques shops (and
decent food in the Regent). The Moon
& Sixpence and newly renovated Little
Harp are seafront family dining pubs
with views to Wales.
Clevedon Court (B3130 just E) Much
of the original structure of this manor
house, built in 1320, is still intact,
though it has interesting later additions
inc a charming 18th-c garden. Open
pm Sun, Weds, Thurs and bank hol
Mon Apr-Sept; (01275) 872257; £4.70;
NT.

COMBE FLOREY ST1531
Combe Florey church Charming
church with attractive carvings; Evelyn
Waugh lies buried outside.

CRANMORE ST6643
East Somerset Railway Steam trips
along what's known as the Strawberry
Line, as well as engine shed and
workshops, with nine steam
locomotives and rolling stock, and art
gallery with wildlife paintings by David
Shepherd, who founded the railway.
Meals and snacks (on steam days), shop,
disabled access; usually open daily
(exc 25 Dec), though trains don't run
every day - best to ring for timetable;
(01749) 880417; £6, less when no trains
running. The village is quiet and
pleasant.

CREWKERNE ST4409
Thriving town with some decent
antiques shops and a number of
inexpensive tearooms, restaurants and

hotels; we like the White Hart (East St/Market Sq) and for its cheerfully different belgian-influenced approach the Old Stagecoach (Station Rd). The Heritage Centre (Market Sq) is worth popping in to. Shop, disabled access to ground floor; usually open Thurs, plus Weds, Fri and am Sat Easter-Oct (cl 1-2); (01460) 77079; £1. **Lower Severalls Garden** (off A30 NE) will interest gardeners; snacks, nursey; usually cl Thurs, Sun (exc May-Jun), and mid Oct-Feb; (01460) 73234; £2.50.

CRICKET ST THOMAS ST3708
Cricket St Thomas Park 🖼 In the lovely parkland of a great estate (still remembered by fans of *To The Manor Born*), this wildlife centre with a good emphasis on conservation is home to over 600 animals, many endangered in the wild. A highlight is a walk through the lemur woods - you can watch them swinging happily from the trees above. There's plenty more to amuse children inc a pets corner, miniature railway, crazy golf and safari jeep rides. Meals, snacks, shop, disabled access; cl 25 Dec; (01460) 30111; *£6.95.

CROSCOMBE ST5844
Croscombe is an attractive village, with great 17th-c woodwork in its 15th-c church. The George has good home-made food, and the long walk from here to Wells (you'll need a map) gives unforgettable views of the cathedral.

CUCKLINGTON ST7527
Cucklington church 13th-c, with small side chapel dedicated to St Barbara, whose sacred well lies further down in the village.

DOWLISH WAKE ST3712
Perry's Cider Mills They've been making cider here for centuries, and between Oct and Nov you can watch it being produced (phone first to check). The cider mill is in a group of thatched 16th-c buildings around a yard with brightly painted old farm wagons and so forth. Enthusiastically run, with a video on cider-making, liberal tastings and half a dozen different ciders for sale, in old-fashioned earthenware flagons if you want. Shop, disabled access; cl Sun pm, 25-26 Dec, 1 Jan; (01460) 52681; free. To keep up the cheerful mood, get them to tell you the history of Dinnington Docks at the pub of that

name over in Dinnington; good food.
DUNDRY HILL ST5666
Just S of Bristol's suburbs, this gives walkers views over the city, Chew Magna and Blagdon lakes, and the Mendips.

DUNSTER SS9943
Well worth a day of anybody's time, with fine medieval houses along the wide main street below the wooded castle hill, as well as a handsome octagonal former yarn market and market cross, a lovely 15th-c priory **church** with particularly tuneful bells, and a well established **doll museum** in the Memorial Hall (cl Oct-Mar; (01643) 821220; £1). If you plan to visit Exmoor, the National Park Information Centre is a useful first stop. The Dunster Castle Hotel has enjoyable food, and there's a wealth of tearooms.

Dunster Castle Dramatically set in an 11-hectare (28-acre) park rich with exotic flora and even subtropical plants, the castle was largely rebuilt in the 19th c, but has older features inside such as the 17th-c oak staircase and gallery with its brightly painted wall hangings. Excellent views. Shop in 17th-c stables, disabled access (a buggy avoids the steep climb up the hill); castle cl Thurs, Fri, and 2 Nov-20 Mar (gardens open all year); (01643) 821314; *£6.80, £3.50 garden and park only; NT.

Old Dovecote (St Georges St) In summer you can go right up this 12th-c dovecote, special for still having its potence, or revolving ladder, used for harvesting the plump squabs from the nesting boxes.

Watermill 🖼 Well restored 18th-c mill still grinding and selling flour; teas in a pleasant riverside garden. Cl Fri, and all Nov-Mar; (01643) 821759; £2.20.

EAST COKER ST5412
Charming quiet village; T S Eliot's ashes are buried here, and there's information about his ancestors in the church. The Helyar Arms has good food and comfortable bedrooms.

EAST LAMBROOK ST4318
East Lambrook Manor Garden 🖼 Well loved cottage garden around a 15th-c house (not open), developed by Walter and Margery Fish in the 1950s and 60s, and described by Mrs Fish in

her immensely popular book, *We Made A Garden*. They hold a national collection of geraniums, the original plant nursery area has been restored, and art exhibitions and garden courses are held in the converted 17th-c malthouse. Meals, snacks, plant sales, shop, some disabled access; cl Nov-Jan; (01460) 240328; £3.95. The flagstoned Wyndham Arms at Kingsbury Episcopi (between here and Muchelney - see below) does enjoyable lunches.

EAST QUANTOXHEAD ST1343
Delightful village with archetypal duckpond, tiny church with fine oak carvings, and walks to the coast. The Hood Arms at Kilve does good meals.

EBBOR GORGE ST5248
If you like Cheddar Gorge but don't like the souvenir stall, coach parties and all, then Ebbor Gorge is for you. It's the same sort of thing, above Wookey Hole, but altogether quieter and more unspoilt. It has an attractive nature trail, and a good walk runs from Wookey Hole through the gorge to Pen Hill for panoramic views. The Hunters Lodge and New Inn up around Priddy have sensibly priced food.

FARLEIGH HUNGERFORD
ST8057
Farleigh Hungerford Castle
Extensive ruins of 14th-c castle, with monuments in the chapel to the Hungerford family, who once owned the land from here to Salisbury. Snacks and picnic area, shop, limited disabled access; cl 1-2pm and Mon-Tues Nov-Mar, 24-26 Dec and 1 Jan; (01225) 754026; £2.50 inc audio tour; EH. The Hungerford Arms has a family dining room overlooking it.

GLASTONBURY ST4938
Tales of King Arthur can be found all over the country, but are especially prominent here; they like to say that bones reinterred in the abbey in 1191 were those of Arthur and Guinevere. The best approach is by the B3151, showing the town below the famous Tor. The NT recently carried out urgent structural work on St Michael's tower there (the parapet was beginning to move), and it's now open to the public again. You can walk there (it takes about 25 mins) or catch a park-and-ride bus from the abbey car park

(Magdalene St, Easter-Sept; £1), as there is no parking at the Tor. Glastonbury has quite a New Age feel, probably because of all the legends and the famous annual rock festival. The brasserie of the Hawthorns Hotel (Northload St) is good for lunch, and the medieval carved façade of the George & Pilgrims is one of the sights of the town, which the bypass has made much more pleasurable.

Chalice Well (Chilkwell St) Legend has it that the Holy Grail was hidden here; the spring, now set in a colourful 2½-acre garden, has apparently had healing powers ever since. True or not, it's a nice peaceful spot. Shop, disabled access; (01458) 831154; *£2.60.

Glastonbury Abbey These noble ruins are said to mark the location of the birth of Christianity in this country. The story goes that Joseph of Arimathaea struck his staff into Wearyall Hill, where it took root. Offshoots of the tree, the famous Glastonbury Thorn, have flourished to this day, with a fine specimen here. The remains of the church date mainly from 1539, though the Lady Chapel is much older. An interpretation area has a good range of stories connected with the site, and in the summer, a monk actor will tell you more about how the monks used to live. Snacks (July-Aug), shop, disabled access; cl 25 Dec; (01458) 832267; £3.50.

Glastonbury Tribunal (High St) Glastonbury was formerly an island rising from a vast inland lake, and you can almost see this from the top of the Tor, the highest point of the hills and ridges among which the little town nestles, with fantastic views. Excavations here have revealed a prehistoric **lake village** covering three or four acres below it, consisting of nearly a hundred mounds surrounded by a wooden palisade. Lots of items and timbers from the village have been unusually well preserved thanks to the waterlogged state of the site, and some of the finds, giving a fascinating insight into the life of the settlement, are shown in this fine 15th-c merchant's house. The tourist information centre is here too, and there's some notable plasterwork in the lower back room.

Shop, cl 25-26 Dec; (01458) 832954;
£2; EH.

Somerset Rural Life Museum
(Chilkwell St) The Abbey Barn and
outbuildings have displays of traditional
regional skills such as cider-making,
peat-cutting and basket-weaving. Also
orchard, rare breeds, and bee garden
with hives. Summer snacks, shop, some
disabled access; cl Mon exc bank hols,
plus Sun Nov-Mar, am wknds Apr-Oct,
25-26 Dec, 1 Jan, Easter and Good Fri;
(01458) 831197; free.

GRABBIST HILL SS9843
Not as famous as Dunkery Hill (and less
frequented even in summer), but
recommended to walkers in search of
rewarding views; it can be climbed from
nearby Dunster.

GREENHAM ST0821
Cothay Manor and Gardens
Picturesque 7-acre plantsman's garden
surrounding a fine classic medieval
manor. Laid out in the 1920s and
redesigned and replanted over the last
ten years, a series of small formal
gardens (inc colour-themed gardens,
and bog and cottage gardens) lead off a
200-yard yew walk. Teas, plant sales,
disabled access; open pms Weds,
Thurs, Sun and bank hols May-Sept;
(01823) 672283; £4. Go via the Globe
over at Appley, for a good lunch first.

HIGHBRIDGE ST3146
Alstone Wildlife Park 🖼 Unspoilt
family-run animal park with various
animals to feed inc red deer, llamas,
wallabies, and a hand-reared mongolian
camel, also rare breeds and owls,
peacocks and waterfowl; space for
picnics (dogs on leads welcome). Snacks,
disabled access; open Easter-Oct;
(01278) 782405; £3.50. The Crossways
at West Huntspill is a useful food stop.

ILCHESTER ST5222
Charming, with a useful range of well
stocked little shops. Used to be a
Roman town, and one of the houses has
a piece of Roman paving. The whole of
the green fronting the Town Hall is said
to be the burial ground of Plague
victims. The comfortable Ilchester
Arms has good food.

ILMINSTER ST3614
Ilminster church Magnificent 15th-c
tower, all turrets, pinnacles and
gargoyles.

KENNET & AVON CANAL
ST6470
Attractively restored, with a good
footpath alongside, it runs from Bristol
through Hanham (where the Lock &
Weir is a charmingly placed pub),
Keynsham (the Lock-Keeper is another
good pub here), Saltford and Bath to
the spectacular aqueduct at Avoncliff
(and beyond, across Wiltshire and into
Berkshire).

KEYNSHAM ST6768
Avon Valley Country Park (Pixash
Lane, off A4) Lots of animals from rare
breed pigs to wallabies, deer park,
riverside trails (inc plenty of places to
fish), an excellent adventure playground,
and free boating on the pond. There's
also a soft play area, quad bikes, falconry
displays, and land-train rides. Meals,
snacks, shop, disabled access; cl Mon
(exc school hols and bank hols), and
Nov to 2 wks before Easter; (0117) 986
4929; *£5. The waterside Lock-Keeper
(A4175) has enjoyable food, and nearby
Saltford has one of England's most
ancient manor houses.

KINGSBURY EPISCOPI ST4321
Somerset Cider Brandy Co
Somerset's only cider distillery, with
huge copper stills, oak vats and wooden
presses, traditional cider orchards to
stroll through, and tastings of their
cider brandy. Shop; cl Sun, 25 Dec;
(01460) 240782; free. The village green
has an ancient lock-up, and the
Wyndham Arms is attractive for lunch.
Anyone with a serious interest in cider
shouldn't miss the Rose & Crown at
Huish Episcopi N of here (A372 E of
Langport) - a classic old-fashioned
Somerset cider pub.

KINGSDON ST5226
Lytes Cary Manor Most of the
surviving building dates from the 16th c,
though there are interesting earlier
features inc the 14th-c chapel, and the
Tudor Great Hall. The attractive garden
was designed and stocked by Henry
Lyte, a notable Elizabethan
horticulturist; otters have returned to
the river banks. Plant sales, disabled
access to garden only; usually open pm
Mon, Weds, Fri, and Sun Apr-Oct, but
best to check as they're carring out roof
repairs; (01458) 224471; £5; NT. The
Kingsdon Inn does good home cooking.

KINGSTON ST MARY ST2229
Pretty village, with attractive church.

LIMINGTON ST5422
Limington church Interesting for its effigies of the Giverney family, dating back to the 1300s.

LONG ASHTON ST5571
Ashton Court Estate Well over a square mile of historic woods and grassland, with two deer parks, pitch and putt golf, and views across Clifton and Bristol to the hills beyond. The large manor house (not open) is mostly 19th c, although some parts date from medieval times. Part of the stables is now a visitor centre (usually open wknds Apr-Sept, most pm wkdys July-Aug, and Sun in winter; (0117) 963 9174. Snacks, shop, disabled access; park open all year; free. The Angel has imaginative food.

MARTOCK ST4619
The magnificent **church** has a splendid roof; also look out for the old Court House turned into a Grammar School by William Strode in 1661, with the inscription above the door 'Martock neglect not your opportunities' in english, latin, hebrew and greek. The Nags Head (East St) has enjoyable food, not Mon.
Somerset Guild of Craftsmen (B3165 S) A big, multi-roomed display of Guild members' work inc jewellery, paintings and furniture. Good coffee shop, disabled access to ground floor only; cl Sun around Christmas-Easter, and 25-26 Dec and 1 Jan; (01935) 825891; free.

MELLS ST7249
Delightful and venerable stone-built village, with marvellous church and graveyard, charming ancient inn (the Talbot), pleasant walks nearby.

MERRIOTT ST4412
Scotts of Merriott Perhaps the last of the big general retail nurseries to raise and grow most of their own trees and shrubs, on 90 acres - well worth a visit by gardening folk. Shop, mostly disabled access; cl wkdys, 25 Dec, Easter Sun; (01460) 72306; free. In the village **D B Pottery** (Highway Cottage, Church St) make a range of items at good prices using a variety of glazing techniques; (01460) 75655; free. The Haselbury Inn in Haselbury Plucknett does enjoyable

inexpensive lunches.

MILVERTON ST1225
The parish church has some fine carving, and the High St is charming.

MINEHEAD SS9646
There's an easily missed area of sloping streets and thatched cottages around the church, with Church Steps a quaint steep back lane. Around this original fishing village is a spacious resort, its beach and promenade sheltered by the wooded hills to the NE. It has the usual attractions, a lively harbour, a sizeable holiday camp, a modern shopping area, and a lovely cedar-fenced seafront walkway. The Old Ship Aground has good value food and pleasant harbour views. There's an unusual **pottery shop** (cl 1-2pm, Sat pm and all day Sun) on Park St. From the harbour you may be able to catch the *Waverley* (paddle steamer) or *Balmoral*, along the Bristol Channel or to Lundy Island. The clifftop Blue Anchor at the end of the B3191 E has decent food, great views. The South West Coast Path starts here.
West Somerset Railway Steam trains run from the Minehead terminus along the coast to Watchet and then inland to Bishops Lydeard - a splendid long run stopping at several little stations. Snacks, shop, very good disabled access, with a specially adapted coach; station open daily, trains run most days May-Sept, and they have Santa specials, phone for a timetable; (01643) 704996; £11 full return fare.

MONKSILVER ST0737
Combe Sydenham Country Park (B3188) Over 500 acres of Exmoor-edge woodland, with walks and trails, and play areas; the 16th-c house is open only to groups; (01984) 656284; £5 car park. The Notley Arms is good for lunch.

MONTACUTE ST4917
Montacute House Magnificent 16th-c honeyed stone house in beautiful little village, with interesting tapestries, furniture, paintings and ceramics, in rooms with decorated ceilings, ornate fireplaces and fine panelling. A highlight is the collection of Tudor and Jacobean paintings from the National Portrait Gallery, and the formal gardens are impressive. Enjoyable meals and snacks, shop, disabled access to grounds only; cl Tues and Nov-Mar; (01935) 823289;

*£6.90, *£3.70 garden only; NT. The park is open to walkers. In the village, parts worth seeing include the Borough (a quite charming square of two-storey houses), and Abbey Farm and the Monk's House - all that remains of a Norman priory destroyed during the Dissolution. The 16th-c Kings Arms is good for lunch.

MUCHELNEY ST4224
Muchelney Abbey The abbey was founded in the 9th c (perhaps earlier), but the well preserved ruins date from the 15th, inc part of the cloister, and the abbot's lodging with its splendidly carved fireplace. Shop, limited disabled access; cl Nov-Mar; (01458) 250664; £2.50; EH. The tiny 14th-c priest's house opposite is worth a quick look; open Tues-Sat and Sun pm Apr-Oct; (01458) 250664; £2.60. The **John Leach Pottery** has a few items on display in the abbey, with the main showroom a couple of minutes' drive S (cl 1-2, and most Suns).

NETHER STOWEY ST1939
An appealing large village with winding streets, handy for both Exmoor and the Quantocks, with good views over the Levels from the mound of the former Norman castle. The Rose & Crown (open all day) is a useful food stop, and the road up wooded Cockercombe gives a lovely sense of the Quantocks' feeling of peace and timelessness. Follow it down to the pretty village of Crowcombe on the W side, which has a delightful church and archetypal old Quantocks pub, the Carew Arms; it is generally the roads on this W side that give the best views.

Coleridge Cottage (Lime St) The poet moved here in 1796; he lived here with a pig or two, and his friends the Wordsworths resided in considerably more style not far away - to the locals, the two families were the long-haired weirdos of the day. Open pm Thurs-Sun and bank hol Mon Apr-19 Sept; (01278) 732662; £3.20; NT.

NORTON ST PHILIP ST7756
Norwood Rare Breeds Farm (B3110 N; this rd has some steep intricate views) Friendly organic farm on high open land with plenty of traditional and rare breeds, nature trails, and good views. You can go right up to the animals, and watch the pigs being fed. Meals, snacks, good farm shop (year round), disabled access; cl mid-Sept to late Mar; (01373) 834356; £4.50. In the village, the George is a splendid ancient building, and across the meadow behind is an attractively set medieval church with bells which struck Pepys as 'mighty tuneable'.

NUNNEY ST7345
Nunney Castle This 14th-c fort was reduced to ruins in the Civil War, but has one of the deepest moats in the country; it and its feeder stream running through the green of this quaint and quiet village are jostling with ducks. The castle's layout and round towers were supposedly modelled on France's Bastille; free. There's a small covered market place just above the stream, and nearby are 18th-c weavers' cottages. The **church**, as usual in so many Somerset villages, is well worth a look, and the George has decent food.

PEAT MOORS ST4241
Peat Moors Visitor Centre (Shapwick Rd, Westhay) In the heart of the peat-cutting area of the Levels, with an excellent exhibition on the topic, and a reconstructed Iron Age village. Craft demonstrations some summer wknds. Snacks, shop, disabled access; cl Nov-Mar; (01458) 860697; £2.50. The Olde Burtle Inn over past Catcott Burtle has enjoyable food.

QUANTOCK TOPS ST1537
The moorland tops of these hills are quite a different world, where ancient trackways lead past prehistoric cairns and burial mounds; Exmoor, the Bristol Channel, South Wales and the Mendips are in sight. Walkers have easy access to the moor from the tiny road crossing the ridge between Nether Stowey and Crowcombe.

QUANTOCK WALKS ST1540
The Quantock Hills have the most for walkers in W Somerset (short of Exmoor). Their secretive quality is illustrated by the dense broad-leafed woodlands on the N side, where shady combes display splendid spring and autumn colours. The village of Holford is a good starting-point: the paths begin with helpful signposts, though you may soon be bemused by the complexity of the path junctions. Holford Combe is

reasonably easy to find, and a map will get you to the ancient hill fort site capping Dowsborough, from where a moorland track leads gently N to Holford. Another good approach is from Kilve, from where you can take a path to and along the coast, then through East Quantoxhead to the north Quantock slopes for a remarkably varied circuit.

QUANTOCKS - WESTERN SLOPES ST1139
The west slopes of the Quantock Hills, less wooded than the NE side, have some charming valleys enclosed by plunging slopes, with tracks along the bottom: Bicknoller with its fine church (good carvings) is an attractive start for walks, and the Blue Ball at Triscombe is an excellent port of call.

RADSTOCK ST6854
Radstock Museum (Waterloo Rd) Local history museum, with mining displays, a reconstructed Victorian classroom and Co-op shop. Temporary exhibitions throughout the year; snacks, shop, disabled access; cl am, Mon (exc bank hols), and all Dec-Jan; (01761) 437722; £3. The Radstock Hotel has plentiful food.

SOMERTON ST4928
Built in light grey stone, this market town has a 17th-c market cross and fine old Georgian buildings in the quiet main square, where the Globe has good food. **St Michael's church** is stupendous, its roof supposedly created by monks of Muchelney from 7,000 fetter pieces, among which is a beer barrel - apparently a reference to Abbot Bere.

SOUTH CADBURY ST6325
An attractive scatter of golden cottages huddle around the church with its striking gargoyled tower; Waterloo Crescent is a distinctive row of farm workers' cottages built in 1815.
Cadbury Castle Its Arthurian connection is the main draw. The legendary king and his knights are still said to sleep below the turf of this huge hill fort, waking on Christmas Eve to ride down the hill, along what's long been known as King Arthur's Hunting Causeway, and through the village on their pilgrimage to Glastonbury. The castle, covering about 18 acres, is in fact

a massive Iron Age camp: many relics have been found there - especially Roman artefacts. It's quite a steep climb, and can be muddy; stout walking shoes recommended. Compton Pauncefoot just E is pretty.

SOUTH PETHERTON ST4317
The **church** has the second-highest octagonal tower in the country. The Brewers Arms has enjoyable food.

SPARKFORD ST6127
Haynes Sparkford Motor Museum (A359) Huge collection of gleamingly restored vintage and classic cars and motorcycles; you should be able to see some being test-driven outside on their event and family fun days (usually a few days each year); new play bus and activity centre for children. Meals, snacks, shop, disabled access; cl 25 Dec, 1 Jan; (01963) 440804; £6.50. The Sparkford Inn is a nice place for lunch.

STAPLE FITZPAINE ST2618
Pretty village with an attractive pub, the Greyhound; a quiet drive with good views loops along the S edge of Staple Hill then crosses the B3170 to run over Culmhead (where the Holman Clavel is another good stop), along the Blackdown Hills, passing the Merry Harriers (an excellent dining pub), and then the Wellington Monument.

STAPLEGROVE ST2027
Staplecombe Vineyards Friendly little vineyard, with self-guided tours of the fields, then back at the house a cheery couple happy to chat. Shop, disabled access; cl Sun am, but phone first; (01823) 451217; free, inc tastings. The Cross Keys (A358/B3227 roundabout) is a useful food stop.

STEEP HOLM ST2260
A small island a few miles off shore, its 20 hectares (50 acres) a nature reserve teeming with rare plants, wildlife and historic remains. Terrific views from the rugged cliffs. You can get snacks out here, and there's a shop in former Victorian barracks, but it's not really suitable for the disabled. Boat trips to the island run from Knightstone Causeway, Weston, Apr-Oct - Mrs Rendell has dates and times on (01934) 632307 (booking essential); all-day trip £15.

STOGUMBER ST0937
Charming village with cottage gardens,

an unblemished main street, and an interesting **church**; the White Horse has decent food.

STOGURSEY ST2042

Stogursey church Exceptional Norman church with charming carved 15th- and 16th-c pew ends - fascinating figures, faces and grotesques.

STOKE ST GREGORY ST3326

Willow & Wetlands Visitor Centre 🏛 (Meare Green Court, towards N Curry) How the area - the most important wetland region in England - developed from marsh and swamp, showing its wildlife (complete with birdsong), and the rise and decline of its willow-growing and basket-making industries, inc a good video, and a museum of products from bath chairs and prams to hot-air balloon baskets (willow is still really the only thing that will do for these). This is a working willow-weaving firm; tour of willow yards and workshop £3.50. Tearoom, shop, disabled access (exc museum); cl Sun, and 25-26 Dec; (01823) 490249; free. The Rose & Crown at Woodhill is good for lunch.

STOKE SUB HAMDON ST4716

Ham Hill Country Park Nearly 60 hectares (140 acres) of grassland and woodland, full of wildlife and plants. The hill has provided the stone for many of the villages in the area, producing that distinctive warm honey-coloured look. The elevated area of old stone quarries gives walkers splendid views; you can go E from here on paths past St Michael's Hill, topped by an 18th-c pepperpot tower, to Montacute.

Stoke sub Hamdon Priory The former 14th- and 15th-c priory manor house has long since vanished, but its fine thatched barn and the screens, passage and Great Hall of the chantry can still be seen; cl Nov-Mar, free. The village is charming, and the Fleur de Lis is good for lunch. Between here and Montacute is a striking folly, St Michael's Tower; it's one of three, all built by neighbouring friends in the 18th c - whenever one had a flag up it was an invitation for the others to go round for a hearty evening.

STRATTON-ON-THE-FOSSE ST6550

Notable for the spectacular modern

(though not modern-looking) Downside Abbey. The olde-worlde Somerset Wagon over on the B3139 has enjoyable food.

STREET ST4836

Shoe Museum (High St) Examples of footwear from Roman times to the present, along with machinery and advertising material. Shop, disabled access wkdys only; cl 10 days over Christmas; (01458) 842169; free. Behind here **Clarks Village** is an attractively laid out factory outlet shopping centre; some real bargains.

TAUNTON ST2224

Busy and prosperous shopping country town, with a lively Tues cattle market, a general market every Sat, and a farmers' market every Thurs. It's not of great visual distinction; the best bit is Hammet St, a short street of 18th-c red brick terraces leading to the county's biggest **church**, which has an exceptionally ornate roof, lofty Perpendicular chancel and lovely pinnacled tower. The Tudor House on Fore St is attractive. Just behind Riverside Pl at the **Shakespeare Glassworks** visitors can watch glass-blowing in the workshop (01823) 333422; in Bath Pl **Makers** is a decent craft shop selling local hand-made crafts (cl Sun). Besides the good Castle Hotel, the Masons Arms in Magdalene St is good for lunch (not Sun).

Somerset County Museum Fine museum in part of the former castle (whose 13th-c portcullised gate-tower is absorbed into the County Hotel), with a rare Bronze Age shield. The biggest hoard of Roman silver coins ever found in Britain is on show here; thousands of them, dating from the 3rd c. Shop, disabled access to ground floor only; cl Sun, Mon (exc bank hols), Good Fri, 25 Dec-2 Jan; (01823) 320201; free.

Somerset Cricket Museum (Priory Avenue) Old building, thought to have been the gatehouse for the priory that once stood by this cricket ground: bats, balls and blazers, cards, cuttings and caps, and a cricketing reference library too. Some disabled access; open wkdys Apr-Oct; (01823) 275893; £1.

TEMPLECOMBE ST7022

Ancient village with stocks still in place; the name comes from the medieval order of Knights Templar, dedicated to the protection of the Holy Sepulchre and pilgrims to it. The church, supposedly founded by King Alfred's daughter, houses a 13th-c painting of Christ, found by accident in an outhouse; possibly an early copy of the Turin Shroud, which the Knights Templar may have had in their possession for a while.

TINTINHULL ST5020

Tintinhull House Garden Colourful and attractive 1930s formal garden sheltered by walls and hedges, around 17th-c house with Queen Anne façade (not open). Teas; open pm Weds-Sun 24 Mar-Sept; (01935) 822545; *£4.20; NT. The nearby Lamb has bargain lunches.

TOLLAND ST1131

Gaulden Manor Gardens ☒ (B3224) The gardens of this nicely tucked-away medieval manor house are pleasant, with a rose garden and bog garden. Plant sales, mostly disabled access; open pm Sun, Thurs and bank hols Jun-Aug; (01984) 667213; £3.25.

TYNTESFIELD ST5071

This stunning 128-year-old stately home is thought to be the country's finest Gothic Revival house; unlike other properties of this period, which have been divided and stripped of their original features, Tyntesfield has kept its original furnishings and contents. The estate, covering neary a square mile, is also wonderfully unspoilt, containing a sumptuous chapel, home farm, gardens and parkland. As we went to press, the National Trust had not yet decided on opening arrangements for 2004, but access is likely to be by pre-booked guided tour, with a park and ride from Nailsea; phone for details (01985) 843600; or look at their website www.nationaltrust.org.uk.

WAMBROOK ST2908

Attractive village, in quiet countryside suiting both walkers and cyclists; the Cotley Inn here has good inexpensive food.

WASHFORD ST0440

Cleeve Abbey (signed S) Remarkably well preserved 12th-c Cistercian abbey, the gatehouse, dormitory and refectory all in good condition. Fine timbered roof, detailed wall paintings and

traceried windows, and an exhibition on monastic life. Snacks, shop, some disabled access; cl 1-2pm Nov-Mar, 24-26 Dec, 1 Jan; (01984) 640377; £3; EH.

Tropiquaria Animal and Adventure Park ☒ (A39 - easy to spot by tall radio masts) An amazing transformation of a 1930s BBC transmitting station into an indoor jungle with high waterfall, tropical plants, free-flying birds and weird and wonderful animals. You can touch all sorts of creatures: plenty of snakes and lizards, perhaps a tarantula. There's an aquarium beneath the hall, while out in the landscaped gardens are birds, lemurs, chipmunks, guinea-pigs and wallabies, as well as a couple of good play areas inc two pirate adventure ships and an indoor play castle. A delightful puppet theatre has 20-min marionette and shadow puppet shows (worth checking first). Also an intriguing collection of vintage radios and televisions. Meals, snacks, shop, disabled access (not to aquarium); open daily Easter-Oct, then wknds and school hols Nov-Mar; (01984) 640688; £6. The nearby station on the steam line from Minehead has a little **railway museum** devoted to the old Somerset & Dorset Railway; open daily May-Sept, phone for winter opening; (01984) 640869; £1. The Washford Arms is handy for lunch.

WATCHET ST0743

This appealing small working port has a marina (the only one on the S side of the Bristol Channel), a tidal harbour with fishing boats and coasters, and enough industry to keep it from being too touristy. In Harbour Rd a dedicated **Working Boat Museum** has hands-on activities for children inc a boat they can clamber around in, and a trail; usually open pms Tues-Thurs and wknds Easter-end Sept; shop, mostly disabled access; (01984) 634242; free. The friendly little **Market House Museum** in Market St has local history displays; cl 12.30-2.30, and end Oct-Easter; donations welcome. The Bell (Market St) has good value simple food.

WELLS ST5546

With a population of only 9,500 this delightful place wouldn't normally even qualify as a big town, but in fact it's

England's smallest city. The **Vicars Close** is said to be one of the oldest complete medieval streets in Europe; the cathedral's Vicars Choral still live here, passing the 15th-c Chain Gate to the cathedral itself. The Fountain, a good nearby dining pub, is popular with the choir - you may even be served by a Vicar Choral. There are a good few other attractive old buildings, many now used as offices and shops (inc several antiques shops), and several grouped around the Market Pl - where the Crown is a reliable lunch stop. The High St (with the pleasant old City Arms) and Saddler St have recently been made more pedestrian-friendly. The B3139 through Wedmore and side roads off it give a good feel of the dead flatness of the Somerset Levels.

Bishop's Palace Moated and fortified, approached through a 14th-c gatehouse; it's quite dramatic going across the drawbridge. The beautiful series of buildings still has some original 13th-c parts, notably the banqueting hall (though only the shell remains) and undercroft, as well as several state rooms and a long gallery hung with portraits of former bishops. The grounds are the site of the wells that give the city its name, producing on average 150 litres (40 gallons) of water a second. Also lovely gardens, decent arboretum, and a pair of swans trained to ring a little bell under the gatehouse window when they're hungry (so many people feed them in summer that this isn't terribly often). Meals, snacks, shop, disabled access to ground floor; open Mon-Fri, plus bank hols and pm Sun Apr-Oct; (01749) 678691; £3.50, perhaps more for special exhibitions.

Wells Cathedral Stunning structure right in the centre, its three towers stretching up against the Mendip foothills. The spectacular W front is reckoned by many to be the finest cathedral façade in the country; dating from the 13th c, it carries 293 pieces of medieval sculpture. Unmissable oddities inside include the wonderful scissors-shaped inverted arches, the north transept's 14th-c clock where horsemen still joust every ¼ hour, and the fine carvings in the south transept, inc various victims of toothache and

four graphic scenes of an old man stealing fruit and getting what for. The embroidered stallbacks in the choir (1937-1948) are a riot of colour, and the library, with documents dating back to the 10th c, is at 51 metres (168 ft) the longest medieval library building in England. Evensong is at 5.15 wkdys, 3pm Sun. Meals, snacks, shop, disabled access; (01749) 674483; £4.50 suggested donation.

Wells Museum (Cathedral Green) Tudor building with good local history museum inc notable embroidery samplers, and stone figures originally on the W front of the cathedral, but now too fragile to be returned there. Shop, some disabled access; cl Tues Oct-Apr, 25 Dec; (01749) 673477; £2.50.

WEST BAGBOROUGH ST1733 Tiny village well placed below the Quantocks, with an unusual red sandstone church; the Rising Sun, rebuilt after a fire, has generous food and doubles as an art gallery.

WEST MENDIP WAY ST3956 This long-distance footpath, all the way between Wells and Weston-Super-Mare, crosses the Mendip plateau, poor windswept sheep pasture on top, pocked with unseen caverns used by potholers, and more visible Bronze Age funeral barrows; there are some stunning views from the section along Crook Peak, Compton Hill and Wavering Down. A path up from Compton Bishop ST3955 gives good access.

WESTON-SUPER-MARE ST3161 Friendly family seaside resort, its latin epithet added in the 19th c in an attempt to be one up on the fashionable french resorts. An ambitious seafront development comprising an up-to-the-minute leisure complex with an indoor swimming pool, cinema, cafés, and plenty of parking is now under way and due for completion late 2005. The quietest beaches are to the N, around Sand Bay. The Claremont Vaults, with good views from the N end of the seafront, is a low-priced dining pub, the olde-worlde Woolpack out at St Georges has good food, and there are pleasant walks (and a toll road) through the woods around the Iron Age fort above the town.

Helicopter Museum 🖾 (B3146, was

A370) An unexpected find, with over 70 helicopters and autogyros on show. Usually on the second Sun each month (Mar-Oct), they have an open cockpit day, when some helicopters are opened up for visitors to inspect, and others even offer flights. Snacks, shop, disabled access; cl Mon and Tues (exc summer and bank hols), and 25-26 Dec, 1 Jan; (01934) 635227; £4.95.

Heritage Centre (Wadham St) Displays on local history; meals, snacks, shop, disabled access to ground floor only; cl Sun and bank hols; (01934) 412144; £1.

North Somerset Museum (Burlington St) Local history museum focusing mainly on Victorian domestic life, with reconstructed shops and lots of seaside displays; it includes adjacent Clara's Cottage, a typical Westonian home of the 1900s with period kitchen, parlour and bedroom. Snacks, shop, disabled access to ground floor only; cl Sun, 25-26 Dec, 1 Jan; (01934) 621028; *£3.50.

Seaquarium ⊞ (Marine Parade) Right by the beach, with walk-through underwater tunnel, and plenty of sharks, rays and seahorses; talks and feeding sessions throughout the day. Snacks, shop, disabled access; cl 25-26 Dec; (01934) 641603; £4.95 (they stamp your hand so you can come back).

WESTONZOYLAND ST3534
Steam museum ⊞ Pretty village with a **steam pumping station**. Snacks, shop, disabled access; open Sun pm; in steam 1st Sun of month Apr-Oct, plus pm Sun and Mon bank hol wknds; (01823) 257516; £2.50 (£3 steam days). The Sedgemoor Inn (a Royalist base before the Battle of Sedgemoor, with interesting memorabilia) has decent food.

WHITCHURCH ST6167
Horse World ⊞ (Staunton Lane, off A37 S edge of Bristol) Home to over 220 rescued and retired horses, ponies and donkeys; what makes it special is the range of other attractions on offer, with plenty to fill a busy half day. Pleasantly restored farm buildings house an interactive museum examining the origins of the horse and its influence on the human world, a

video theatre, and an extensive collection of tack and harnesses. There's a twice-daily horse presentation, a nature trail around the paddocks, an indoor and outdoor play area, plenty of space for picnics, other animals to meet such as goats, cows, chickens and ducks (you can handle some of the smaller animals), and pony rides. Meals, snacks, shop, disabled access; cl Mon Sept-Easter, 22 Dec-1 Jan; (01275) 540173; £4.50.

WILLITON ST0740
Bakelite Museum (Orchard Mills, off Bridge St) Incongruously but charmingly housed in an 18th-c watermill, this unusual and surprisingly interesting museum is devoted to vintage plastics from the Victorian age to World War II. Exhibits range from jelly moulds and ashtrays to a Bakelite plastic coffin, and replica miniature 1930s 'pod' caravans; other items include early refrigerators, lots of radios, and a horrific-looking hair perming machine. Cream teas, shop, disabled access to ground floor; open Thurs-Sun Easter-Oct, daily in school hols; (01984) 632133; £3.50, free for wheelchair users. The cheerful thatched Masons Arms (B3191 N) does good value lunches.

WINCANTON ST7128
Fine Georgian houses and many of the multitude of inns and hotels survive from the coaching era; lots still have old coach-entry gates. The **church porch** has a medieval relief of St Eligius. The Red Lion (Market Pl) has enjoyable food.

WOOKEY HOLE ST5347
Wookey Hole Caves & Papermill ⊞ Guided tours of half a mile of dramatic subterranean tunnels and caverns, using remote-controlled lighting and special effects to spotlight the geological features and bring to life associated history and myths (young children may find it all a bit scary). Just along the river the papermill demonstrates paper production (visitors can usually have a go too), and also houses a Magical Mirror Maze and Old Penny Arcade. A bustling place, all under cover, so ideal when the sun's not shining. Meals and snacks, shop, disabled access exc to caves; cl 17-25 Dec; (01749) 672243; £8.80. As we went to

press, the site was up for sale, although they hope to keep it open as a visitor attraction, so best to phone. The Burcott Inn nearby is a good choice for lunch.

WRAXALL ST4872
Noah's Ark Zoo Farm (Failand Rd) Busy centre (committed to a creationist as opposed to evolutionary viewpoint) with around 60 different kinds of animals from geckos and parrots to lemurs and yaks. Tractor rides, a nature and archaeology trail, and good indoor and outdoor play areas (inc one for toddlers); also a 4-metre (14ft) model of Noah's ark (a display aims to prove the Flood really happened), and a food and farming exhibition. Meals, snacks, shop, disabled access; cl Sun, Mon, plus Nov to mid-Feb, best to phone first; (01275) 852606; £6. The Black Horse in Clapton-in-Gordano is a charming nearby pub.

WRINGTON ST4862
Barley Wood Walled Gardens 🖫 (Long Lane) This Victorian walled garden has views over Wrington Vale, craft workshops and a good farm shop. Meals, snacks and a picnic area; cl 1st two weeks Jan; (01934) 863713; £2. In the village the Plough (open all day) has good value food.

YENSTON ST7121
Gartell Light Railway The friendly staff who run this 2-ft gauge railway through attractive Blackmore Vale countryside succeed in making it enjoyable, even though the line's under a mile long. The trains leave every 15 mins, along the track of the defunct Somerset & Dorset Railway; there's a little railway museum, a picnic area by a lake, and a visitor centre. Snacks, shop; usually open last Sun in month Jun-Oct, plus bank hol Mon Easter, May and Aug, and for two Santa wknds in Dec - best to phone; (01963) 370752; £4 for a day's unlimited travel.

YEOVIL ST5515
Museum of South Somerset (Hendford) Good range of local history and reconstructed Roman and

Georgian rooms. Shop, disabled access; usually cl Sun, Mon and bank hols, plus Sat Oct-Mar, and around a wk over Christmas and New Year; (01935) 424774; free. There's little else in the town to interest visitors, beyond a partly 14th-c church (and perhaps the dry-ski centre).

YEOVILTON ST5423
Fleet Air Arm Museum 🖫 (Royal Naval Air Station, off A359) Big place concentrating on the story of aviation at sea from 1908, and the history of the Royal Naval Air Service. Lively displays on the WRENS, the Falklands and Gulf Wars, jets and helicopters, as well as around 40 historic aircraft, and lots of models, paintings, weapons and photographs, plus an exhibition on supersonic flight. A highlight is the carrier hall, which leads you through various parts of the aircraft carrier while it is involved in an assignment: lots of flashing lights and dialogue as you follow the tour of the bridge, the operations room, and best (and noisiest) of all the flight deck. Viewing galleries look out over the aircraft using this busy base. Also adventure playground, and hi-tech flight simulator. You could easily spend a good few hours here. Meals, snacks, shop, disabled access; cl 24-26 Dec; (01935) 840565; £8.50. The Kingsdon Inn is the best nearby place for lunch.

Other attractive villages, all with decent pubs, include Batcombe ST6838, Brompton Regis SS9531, Compton Dando ST6464, Crowcombe ST1336, Evercreech ST6438, Faulkland ST7354, Hinton St George ST4212, Huish Episcopi ST4226, Litton ST5954, Luxborough SS9837, North Perrott ST4709, Norton sub Hamdon ST4615, South Stoke ST7641 (picturesque views from the steep nearby lanes), Waterrow ST0425, Wellow ST7458 and Winscombe ST4157. High Ham ST4231, Pilton ST5940 and Stowell ST6822 are also well worth a visit.

Where to eat

APPLEY ST0621 **Globe** *Appley* *(01823) 672327* Cheerfully run and unspoilt 15th-c pub with a relaxed chatty atmosphere, consistently enjoyable food inc adventurous specials and vegetarian meals, and super puddings; no smoking dining room; cl Mon am exc bank hols. £25|**£6.95**

BATCOMBE ST6838 **Three Horseshoes** *(01749) 850359* Honey stone, slate-roofed pub serving good, imaginative food under new licensees in bustling main room decorated with pretty ivy stencils and artificial ivy, fruit and flower decorations, and a few naive farm animal paintings on the lightly ragged dark pink walls; a woodburner and big open fire, attractive stripped stone dining room, well kept real ales, a good choice of wines, and big well equipped play area in garden. £30|**£11.95**

BATH ST7464 **Moody Goose** *7a Kingsmead Sq (01225) 466688* Stylish basement restaurant with large namesake pottery goose, paintings on whitewashed walls, fresh flowers on crisp white tablecloths, deft modern english cooking, and a thoughtful wine list; cl Sun and bank hols; children over 7; disabled access. £40/2 courses £14

BATH ST7464 **Old Green Tree** *12 Green St (01225) 448259* Genuinely unspoilt pub with enjoyable lunchtime food, a bustling cheerful atmosphere in its three oak-panelled little rooms, a no smoking back bar, several well kept real ales, lots of malt whiskies, and a nice little wine list with a dozen by the glass; they do not take bookings; cl 25-26 Dec and 1 Jan; no children.|**£5.50**

BATH ST7564 **Rajpoot** *4 Argyle St (01225) 466833* Exceptionally good carefully cooked indian food in attractively decorated restaurant, particularly good service (you are met at the door by a colourfully uniformed doorman), and used by stars of screen and stage; cl 25-26 Dec. £20|**£6.95**

BRISTOL ST5873 **Brazz** *85 Park St (0117) 925 2000* Bustling, modern place with bright furnishings, a small stylish bar, eye-catching fish tank, and good value, enjoyable food usefully served all day; cl 25 Dec. £21.50|**£6.95**

BRISTOL ST5774 **Fishworks Seafood Café** *128 Whiteladies Rd (0117) 974 4433* Bustling, lively restaurant where you choose your fish or seafood from the absolutely fresh produce that is then simply cooked and presented - though there are some interesting dishes; helpful efficient staff, and a short, good value, mainly white wine list; cl Sun pm and Mon. £35|**£10**

BRISTOL ST5872 **Riverstation** *The Grove (0117) 914 4434* Converted ex-River Police HQ on waterfront with informal downstairs café and deli, airy first-floor restaurant, contemporary furnishings, enjoyable popular modern british cooking with mediterranean slant, and a fine choice of wines by the glass; regular art exhibitions; cl 25-26 Dec, 1 Jan; disabled access downstairs only. £33/2 courses £11.50

CHISELBOROUGH ST4614 **Cat Head** *Cat St (01935) 881231* Relaxing country pub with neatly traditional flagstoned rooms, plenty of flowers and plants, woodburner, light wooden tables and chairs, some high-backed cushioned settles, and curtains around the small mullioned windows; a carpeted area to the right is no smoking; very good interesting bar food, real ales, nice wines, and friendly licensees; very attractive garden with seats, and views over the peaceful village. £25.30|**£8.50**

DOULTING ST6545 **Waggon & Horses** *Beacon (01749) 880302* 18th-c inn with stone-mullioned latticed windows, a rambling bar with interesting pictures for sale, two no smoking rooms, a choice of enjoyable bar food, decent house wines, cocktails, real ales, and a lovely big walled garden with various fancy fowl (they sell the eggs), a goat and horses; big raftered gallery for art shows and classical music; cl 25 Dec; children must be very well behaved; disabled access. £29|**£7.90**

HOLCOMBE ST6649 **Ring o' Roses** *Stratton Rd (01761) 232478* Quietly placed and extensively modernised open-plan country pub, relaxed and comfortably civilised, with consistently good modern cooking using only local suppliers, afternoon teas, decent wines, local ciders and ales, and helpfully efficient service; no smoking restaurant, modern prints, gently lit parlourish area with sofas and cushioned chairs, pleasant panelled lounge, daily papers; peaceful farmland views from picnic-sets on terrace and lawns; bdrms. £27.75|**£4.50**

LANGLEY MARSH ST0729 **Three Horseshoes** *(01984) 623763* Unpretentious red sandstone pub with short changing choice of enjoyable food using some produce from their own garden (no chips or fried food), a wide range of often unusual real ales, farm ciders, no fruit machines or pool tables, skittle alley, tables outside, and sloping back garden with play area and farmland views; good nearby walks; cl Sun pm, Mon and 2 wks early July; children over 8. £18|£5

LOVINGTON ST5931 **Pilgrims Rest** *(01963) 240597* Quietly placed and civilised country bar/bistro with good interesting food cooked by the landlord, using fresh ingredients; chatty and relaxed, with sunny modern prints, settees and easy chair by cosy inner area's big fireplace, snug heavy-beamed eating area and no smoking dining room; nice wines by the glass, well kept ales from the nearby brewery, daily papers, some tables outside; cl Sun pm, Mon and Tues am. £30|£10

MONKSILVER ST0737 **Notley Arms** *(01984) 656217* Immensely well liked, friendly pub with beamed L-shaped bar, candles and fresh flowers, woodburners, reasonably priced very good food (they don't take bookings, so get there early), well kept beers, especially nice licensees, and neatly kept cottagey garden running down to a swift clear stream; pub games, skittle alley, and table tennis; cl 25 Dec and 2 wks late Jan-earlyFeb; disabled access. £17|£3.75

OAKE ST1426 **Royal Oak** *Hillcommon (01823) 400295* Bustling refurbished country pub (much is no smoking) with several separate areas; a big woodburner, lots of fresh flowers and brasses, evening candles, and popular back dining room; particularly interesting daily specials (and good value OAP meals Tues and Thurs), several real ales, and cheerful service; seats in the sheltered garden. £27|£10

SHEPTON MALLET ST6144 **Blostins** *29 Waterloo Rd (01749) 343648* Friendly little candlelit evening bistro with consistently good interesting food inc lovely puddings, and fairly priced wines; cl Sun-Mon, 1 wk Jan, 1 wk Easter and 2 wks Aug. £25

SHEPTON MONTAGUE ST6731 **Montague Inn** *(01749) 813213* Tastefully furnished country pub with friendly licensees, stripped wooden tables, kitchen chairs and a log fire in the attractive inglenook fireplace, a gently upmarket atmosphere, particularly good food using as much organic produce as possible, well kept real ales, fine wines, and elegant candlelit dining rooms (one is no smoking); pretty back garden and terrace with nice views; cl Sun pm and Mon; children in family room and restaurant. £25.30|£6

TAUNTON ST2224 **Brazz** *Castle Bow (01823) 252000* Stylish, lively brasserie with fun décor inc an interesting aquarium, good interesting bistro-type food, and reasonably priced wines (ten by the glass); disabled access. £29.90|£7.95

TRISCOMBE ST1535 **Blue Ball** *(01984) 618242* Enjoyable pub on the first floor of a lovely 15th-c thatched stone-built former coaching stables: three stepped levels with carefully crafted oak partitions, interesting, tasty food, 400 wines (they will open any bottle under £20 for just a glass), well kept real ales and old cognacs; the decking at the top of the terraced garden makes the most of the peaceful views; disabled access. £33|£9

WESTON-SUPER-MARE ST3261 **Reflections** *22 Boulevard (01934) 622457* Informal family-run restaurant, a good café at lunchtimes (exc Sun, when decent set lunch); on Thurs, Fri and Sat evenings serves well presented high quality meals; cl Sun-Weds pms and early Jan for 10 days. £23.95|£5.50

WILLITON ST0741 **White House** *11 Long St (01643) 632306* Charming shuttered Georgian hotel under the same friendly owners for over 30 years, with antiques and more modern furnishings, paintings and ceramics, very good carefully cooked food using the best local produce, and a fine choice of reasonably priced wines; good breakfasts; bdrms; cl Oct-May. £46

WOOKEY ST5245 **Burcott Inn** *Wookey Rd (01749) 673874* Little roadside pub, neatly kept and friendly, with two small front bars, open fire, a roomy attractive back restaurant, nice bar food, well kept real ales, and a sizeable garden; no food Sun-Mon pms; cl 25-26 Dec and 1 Jan; children over 5; disabled access. £17.60|£6

Special thanks to B and K Hypher, M G Hart

STAFFORDSHIRE

An outstanding theme park, other good family draws, interesting Potteries visits, and some lovely countryside with good walking; good value places to stay and eat in

This year our Staffordshire Family Attraction is newcomer Ceramica, with entertaining and informative displays on the history of the Potteries. To find out more about the area's pottery industry, head for the cluster of museums and showrooms around Stoke-on-Trent. Particularly popular are the visitor centres for Royal Doulton and Wedgwood (where they've now extended the factory tours); Spode is the birthplace of fine bone china, and children enjoy having a go at the Gladstone Pottery. For what goes into all those mugs, the Bass Museum and Burton Bridge Brewery take a look at Burton upon Trent's brewing industry from opposite ends of the spectrum.

Alton Towers is the county's major attraction, a thrilling day out, with rides for all ages and levels of bravery. Tamworth has the double draw of Drayton Manor theme park (a little zoo as well as fun rides) and the castle. At Blackbrook Zoological Park in Winkhill you'll find exotic creatures and a children's farm; Eccleshall and Stowe-by-Chartley have enough to fill a relaxed afternoon.

Magnificent Shugborough Hall (working rare breeds farm and puppet collection), and Weston Park (adventure playground, pets corner and miniature railway) are family-friendly great houses. Readers of Samuel Johnson will enjoy visiting his birthplace in attractive Lichfield, and (new to the *Guide* this year) Erasmus Darwin House has interesting displays on its former owner. Izaak Walton's Cottage in Shallowford will interest fly-fishermen. Elsewhere are charming gardens in Biddulph and Willoughbridge, and steam railways in Blythe Bridge and Cheddleton.

The Peak District limestone country (NE of county) is a beautiful area for walking and driving (for Dove Dale see Derbyshire chapter). In the more industrial S of the county, Cannock Chase has miles of fine landscape, and the extensive canal network provides some unexpectedly attractive walks.

Where to stay

BETLEY SJ7847 **Adderley Green Farm** *Heighley Castle Lane, Betley, Crewe, Cheshire CW3 9BA (01270) 820203* **£48***, plus special breaks; 3 rms. Georgian farmhouse on big dairy farm, with good breakfasts in homely dining room, and large garden; cl Christmas and New Year; children over 5; dogs allowed by prior arrangement

CHEADLE SK0044 **Ley Fields Farm** *Leek Rd, Cheadle, Stoke-on-Trent, Staffordshire ST10 2EF (01538) 752875* **£46**; 3 rms. Listed Georgian farmhouse on working dairy farm in lovely countryside with lots of walks; traditional furnishings in lounge and dining room, good home cooking, and friendly welcome; cl Christmas and New Year

CHEDDLETON SJ9651 **Choir Cottage** *Ostlers Lane, Cheddleton, Leek, Staffordshire ST13 7HS (01538) 360561* **£59***; 3 pretty rms with four-posters in 17th-c cottage next to owners' home, with private entrance. No smoking, with

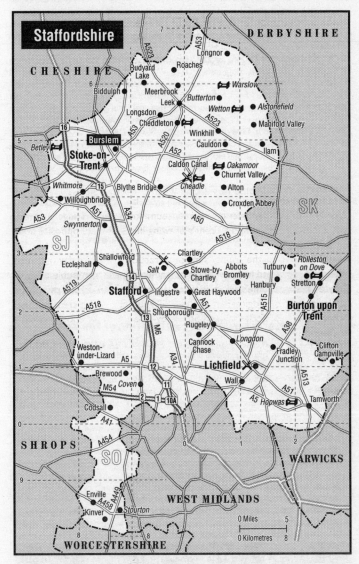

Staffordshire

comfortable lounges, attractive dining room with country views, and good breakfasts
HOPWAS SK1704 **Oak Tree Farm** *Hints Rd, Hopwas, Tamworth, Staffordshire B78 3AA (01827) 56807* **£100**; 8 comfortable, spacious and pretty rms. Carefully restored no smoking farmhouse with elegant little lounge, fresh flowers, an attractive breakfast room, a friendly atmosphere, enjoyable breakfasts, gardens overlooking the River Tame, indoor swimming pool and steam room; cl Christmas-New Year; no children; dogs welcome in bedrooms
OAKAMOOR SK0544 **Bank House** *Farley Lane, Oakamoor, Stoke-on-Trent, Staffordshire ST10 3BD (01538) 702810* **£65**, plus special breaks; 3 lovely big rms. Carefully restored no smoking country home in neat gardens on the edge of the Peak National Park, with lovely views; log fire in comfortable drawing room, library,

piano in the inner hall, and most enjoyable food (by prior arrangement using home-grown and local produce) - super home-made breads, brioches, pastries and jams and marmalade at marvellous breakfast; friendly dog and cats; lots to do nearby; cl Christmas; dogs welcome in bedrooms

ROLLESTON ON DOVE SK2327 **Brookhouse Hotel** *Station Rd, Rolleston on Dove, Burton Upon Trent, Staffordshire DE13 9AA* (01283) 814188 **£99***, plus wknd breaks; 19 comfortable rms with Victorian brass or four-poster beds. Handsome ivy-covered William & Mary brick building in five acres of lovely gardens with comfortable antiques-filled rooms, and good food using seasonal local produce in elegant little dining room; children over 12; disabled access; dogs welcome in bedrooms

WARSLOW SK0858 **Greyhound** *Warslow, Buxton, Derbyshire SK17 0JN* (01298) 84249 **£41.12**; 4 clean and comfortable rms with shared bthrm. Warm, welcoming atmosphere in comfortably refurbished slated stone inn handy for Peak District, with generous helpings of home-made food inc hearty breakfasts; live Sat evening entertainment

WETTON SK1055 **Olde Royal Oak** *Wetton, Ashbourne, Staffordshire DE6 2AF* (01335) 310287 **£50**; 4 rms. Shuttered old stone village inn in lovely NT walking country, with a warmly cheerful welcome; an attractive older part leads into a more modern-feeling area, with open fires, country furniture, a sun lounge overlooking a small garden, decent food, and nice breakfasts; cl Weds and last wk Nov

To see and do

Staffordshire Family Attraction of the Year

BURSLEM SJ8649 **Ceramica** (Market Pl) Burslem's stately town hall has been ingeniously transformed to house this well conceived Millennium project, focusing not just on the history and development of the ceramic industry, but also on how it's shaped and affected the area and its people. So while for most families Alton Towers will always be the county's must-see destination, this is well worth a pause en route to get a good flavour of what the Potteries are all about. The main exhibitions are on the upper floor, set around a striking glass tower, with displays and videos covering all the main local manufacturers, memories of local people, and a section on author Arnold Bennett, whose *Anna of the Five Towns* was based on the area. But much more satisfying is the children's section on the ground floor, which manages to pull off the not inconsiderable feat of making pottery fun for younger visitors. A good range of interactive displays make clear how clay is transformed into ceramics, and you can 'leg' a narrowboat through a tunnel, and take a flying carpet ride over the Potteries. 2003 was their first season, and in the summer holidays they had extra children's activities which it's hoped they'll repeat this coming year, including the chance to make your own egyptian or art deco pot. Snacks, shop, disabled access; cl Tues (except summer hols); (01782) 8320012; £3.50 adults, £2.50 children. A family ticket - two adults and two children - is £9. To park you'll need to use the Pay and Display areas nearby.

ABBOTS BROMLEY SK0824
Half-timbered houses and red brick Georgian buildings, as well as a 17th-c butter cross, in a village famed for its ancient Horn Dance which is held annually in early Sept; (01283) 840224; pleasant countryside around. The nicely placed Goats Head has good food.

ALTON SK0743
Alton Towers (off B5032) 200-acre giant theme park with lots of features, state-of-the-art rides and a very broad appeal (height limits on some attractions). You need a full day to fit everything in, and can book timed rides in advance on two attractions, saving a

couple of pounds on the admission price. The latest new family ride is the Spin Ball Whizzer, a roller-coaster based on a pin ball machine, where you're the ball. Other famous rides include Oblivion (a vertical drop ride) and Nemesis (whisks you through unfeasible angles at a greater G-force than experienced by astronauts in a rocket launch). Several areas are geared for younger children, inc an indoor play area. Dozens of other attractions include log flumes and lovely extensive gardens. Staying at their splendidly zany hotel gets you into the park half an hour before the main gates open; and now a second hotel called Splash Landings incorporates the Cariba Creek Waterpark (only for Alton Towers hotel guests). This is by no means a cheap day out, many features have queues (the average wait is 10 mins, but can be longer), and litter can occasionally annoy. But it's a firm recommendation, with first-class presentation and facilities. Meals, snacks, shop, disabled access (on most rides too); open mid-Mar to early Nov, phone first; (08705) 204060; full price entry is £26 for adults, and £21 children aged 4-12; parking £3 (wkdy off-peak tickets £5 cheaper). You can usually buy a good value second day's entry from any of the information points around the park.

BIDDULPH SJ8858
Biddulph Grange Garden (Grange Rd) Notable and really quite charming high Victorian garden, originally divided into smaller themed gardens to house specimens from all over the world, and now extensively restored (inc most recently the ice house); you can prebook a guided tour (£6.60). Snacks, shop; cl am, all day Mon (exc bank hols), Tues, Good Fri and Nov-Mar (exc wknds mid-Nov to mid-Dec, when it's free); (01782) 517999; £4.60; NT. You can get a voucher for a reduced ticket for Little Moreton Hall in Cheshire, 7 miles away, past the prettily placed Egerton Arms in Astbury (good value lunches).

BLYTHE BRIDGE SJ9441
Foxfield Steam Railway 🖼 Five-mile return trip through scenic countryside: ticket gives unlimited travel for the whole day (not during special events). Staff are particularly friendly, and there's a museum (Weds

and Sun in season) and a collection of locomotives and rolling stock. Steam trains run Sun and bank hols end Mar-end Oct (and wknds in Dec for Santa specials) but best to check; (01782) 396210; £4.50. The Red Lion at Dilhorne, overlooking the wooded Cheadle Hills with plenty of country walks, has good value food.

BREWOOD SJ8808
Charming small town, with many attractive Georgian and older buildings: the Admiral Rodney (Dean St) and Bridge Inn (High Green) have good value food.

BURSLEM SJ8649
Ceramica *See separate family panel on p.536.*

BURTON UPON TRENT SK2523
The town is dominated by its connections with what used to be the british brewing industry (now largely foreign-owned), and the **Bass Museum** (Horninglow St) with a virtual historic tour and audio-guide explores this topic in some detail - with an emphasis on Bass and the company's famous shire horses. You can tour the brewery (no under-13s); also indoor and outdoor play areas, and special events. Meals, snacks, shop, disabled access; cl 25-26 Dec, 1 Jan; (0845) 600 0598; £7.95 brewery tour and museum, £5.50 museum only.

Burton Bridge Brewery A complete contrast to the giant breweries that dominate the town, this shows brewing at the very opposite end of the scale; viewings Weds pm by appointment only; (01283) 510573. The attached pub has lunchtime snacks.

CALDON CANAL SK0348
The towpath gives many miles of good interesting walks. There's usually something happening at the Froghall Wharf canal terminus (inc narrow-boat trips Sun and Thurs mid-May to Aug; (01538) 266486; from £8.50, inc snacks or meals), with an interesting walk along the canal to remote Consallforge, where the traditional Black Lion has enjoyable food. The nearby Nature Park continues this strange lost-valley scenery. There's also good access to this, the most attractive of Staffordshire's canals, from the good Boat pub at Cheddleton, and from

Denford nr Leek.
CANNOCK CHASE SK0215
Lovely woodland and rolling heath,
threaded with quiet side roads - the
breathing space for the more industrial
part of Staffordshire, and appreciated all
the more if you read up on the area's
industrial heritage. Dotted around its
26 square miles are Iron Age hill forts,
nature trails, streams, pools and
springs, and lovely spots for picnics or
dramatic views; fallow deer are often
seen. There's a good museum just
outside Hednesford (usually cl wknds
Oct-Easter; free), and an information
centre at Marquis Drive; decent
campsites. The canalside Moat House at
Acton Trussell is popular for food.
Castle Ring This large hill fort has fine
views over the forests of Cannock
Chase to the Trent Valley. The nearby
Park Gate pub has a good food choice.
CAULDON SK0749
Notable for its pub, the **Yew Tree**; a
very unpretentious place packed with an
extraordinary and delightfully higgledy-
piggledy collection of remarkable
bygones, esp mechanical music.
CHARTLEY SK0228
Chartley Castle (just over 6 miles W
of Uttoxeter) A fine old ruin, with good
views.
CHEDDLETON SJ9752
Cheddleton Flint Mill (Cheadle Rd)
Fully preserved 17th- and 18th-c water
mills, with a little museum. Shop; cl am,
and Nov-Mar; (01782) 502907; free.
The Boat does decent lunches, with
pleasant canal walks from it.
Churnet Valley Railway 🚂 (Station
Rd) Small steam locomotive museum in
Victorian station building, complete with
signal box and engine sheds. Steam and
diesel trains run the 10½m scenic round
trip between Cheddleton and Froghall.
Meals, snacks, shop; open Sun and bank
hols mid-Mar to Oct, Weds July-Aug,
and other times for special events,
phone for a timetable; (01538) 360522;
train trip £7, donations for museum only.
CHURNET VALLEY SK0545
Very pretty walks from Alton or
Oakamoor; the best goes through
Hawksmoor and Greendale to pass the
broad fishponds in wooded Dimmings
Dale and comes back down to the river
past an old smelting mill - and a good

café called the Ramblers Retreat.
Hawksmoor Wood is itself an attractive
nature reserve, and the Talbot by Alton
Bridge is useful for lunch.
CLIFTON CAMPVILLE SK2510
Clifton Campville church One of
those rare country churches that seems
practically perfect in every way.
CODSALL SJ8604
Notable in summer for its profusion of
lupins; the listed Codsall Station
buildings have been interestingly
redeveloped as a pub.
CROXDEN ABBEY SK0639
Ruins in quiet surroundings, with some
towering arches surviving; EH. The
Raddle at Hollington is a handy family
country pub.
ECCLESHALL SJ8329
Fletchers Garden Centre (Bridge
Farm, Stone Rd) Plenty to amuse
children, inc adventure playground, a
miniature railway (wknds, bank hols and
school hols Easter-Oct), crazy golf
(£1.50) and about 20 enclosures in a
little wildlife centre (£2.50). Restaurant,
shop; cl 25-26 Dec, 1 Jan; (01785)
851057. The George (Castle St) does
food all day wknds, and on the other
side of town the Star out at Copmere
End is prettily set overlooking the lake,
with pleasant walks.
ENVILLE SO8287
Staffordshire Way This way-marked
footpath offers scope for walking; the
17th-c Cat, with generous food, is a
useful place to join it.
FRADLEY JUNCTION SK1513
Trent & Mersey Canal Generally
less opportunity for towpath walks than
with other Staffordshire canals, but this
junction, with a waterside pub and lots
happening on the water, is an attractive
place for a stroll.
GREAT HAYWOOD SJ9923
There are interesting **canal walks**
from here, and the longest **packhorse
bridge** in the country is nearby.
HANBURY SK1728
The Cock pub on Hanbury Hill is a start
for several attractive walks, inc a
poignant one to the vast crater left by
the 1944 Fauld bomb dump explosion, a
tragedy understandably not much
publicised at the time.
ILAM SK1350
Attractive estate village in the Manifold

Valley (nr its junction with Dove Dale), surrounded by a NT-owned country park which runs on both banks of the River Manifold and was formerly the parkland for 19th-c Gothic Ilam Hall; free access to the park but pay and display parking; NT tearoom, shop and information centre.

INGESTRE SJ9824

Ingestre church Designed by or under Christopher Wren, and reckoned by some to be the finest small 17th-c church outside London.

KINVER SO8582

(the one right over in the W) Interesting village, with some of Britain's only rock houses nearby, still lived in around 50 years ago; phone the warden for information on visits; (01384) 872418. The canalside Vine (Dunsley Rd) has good value italian and other food, and the Fox (A458 Stourton—Enville) is a good dining pub well placed for the nearby country park - which gives good views from an Iron Age hill fort.

LEEK SJ9756

Brindley Mill (Mill St) Well restored water mill with an informative exhibition, and good demonstrations. Open pm wknds and bank hol Mon Easter-Sept, and pm Mon-Weds in Aug; (01538) 381446; £2.

Coombe Valley Bird Reserve This nearby RSPB reserve has a shop, and disabled access; cl 25 Dec; (01538) 384017; free. The A53 high moorland road N has good views, and E of here the B5053 gives an excellent impression of the dales country (the Jervis Arms at Onecote is a useful family stop).

LICHFIELD SK1109

The attractive centre is largely pedestrianised, with many 18th-c and older buildings among the more modern shops (and antiques shops). The **cathedral**, with its three graceful spires and close with lovely half-timbered buildings around it, is magnificent inside, and its W front is memorable, esp at dusk or in the dark when shadows seem to bring the profusion of statues to life. Wonderful illuminated 8th-c gospels in the chapter house; cl during services and concerts; (01543) 306240; suggested donation £3. On Sat May-Sept you can see two bleak 16th-c cells under the Guildhall

(Bore St); (01543) 264972; 40p. The Queens Head (Queen St) and appealingly traditional Scales (Market St) do good value food.

Erasmus Darwin House (Beacon St) Museum dedicated to the life and work of Erasmus Darwin (Charles Darwin's grandfather), a leading doctor, scientist, botanist, inventor and poet. They've re-created his surgery, and computers (and models) help demonstrate some of his theories; introductory video and audio-guide. Re-created 18th-c herb garden, temporary exhibitions, special events and guided tours. Shop, disabled access; cl Mon-Weds, am Sun and bank hol Mon, Good Fri, and a few days over Christmas and New Year; (01543) 306260; £2.50.

Heritage Exhibition and Treasury (Market Sq) Worth a look, in a sympathetically restored church; now also home to the Staffordshire millennium tapestry, depicting the county's history; cl 25-26 Dec and 1 Jan; £3.50. Sometimes (not for under-12s) you can go up to the viewing platform in the spire, which has splendid views of the surrounding area; phone to check; £2.

Samuel Johnson Birthplace Museum (Breadmarket St) Dr Johnson was born here in 1709; the house is now furnished in period, with many mementoes of him. Shop; cl ams Oct-Mar, 25-26 Dec, 1 Jan; (01543) 264972; *£2.20 - and a nice celebratory gesture, free entry on Sat nearest to Dr Johnson's birthday, 18 Sept.

LONGNOR SK0865

Pleasantly villagey former market town with cobbled market place, a good craft centre and coffee shop, and good food in the interesting 14th-c Olde Cheshire Cheese; nice setting in rolling limestone country.

LONGSDON SJ9655

Deep Hayes Country Park (Sutherland Rd; village off A53, 2m SW of Leek) Pleasant mixture of two freshwater pools, stepping stones, waterfalls, woods and meadows redeveloped from a reservoir built in the mid-19th c by the Potteries Waterworks. A wknd visitor centre has details of ranger-led and self-guided walks, as well as a shop and disabled facilities - one path is suitable for wheelchairs; (01538) 387655; free (inc parking). Readers recommend a walk around the park then through farmland, stopping for a snack in the Holly Bush nr Denford, and returning along the canal.

MANIFOLD VALLEY SK1350

The surfaced Manifold Track takes in the best section of this limestone dale, from the B5054 (W of Hartington) S to the A523 nr Waterhouses. This has fewer of the sensational rock features that abound in Dove Dale, but plenty of charm - more or less steep riverside pastures, ancient woodland in the narrower steeper gorges, waterside caves; there's good access to the hills above it, such as Wetton Hill, which have attractive views. The best viewpoint of all, not to be missed, is Thor's Cave, high above the dale. The branch off up Hamps Dale is extremely pretty. There are good pubs nearby at Warslow, Wetton and Hulme End.

MEERBROOK SJ9959

Tittesworth reservoir Large reservoir with visitor centre and restaurant, nature trails and bird hides, adventure playground and a sensory garden for the partially sighted. Restaurant, shop; cl 25 Dec; (01538) 300400; £1.50 all-day parking. The Three Horseshoes on nearby Blackshaw Moor is a reliable food stop.

ROACHES SJ9963

These form an impressive western barrier at the edge of the Dark Peak; this is perhaps the most exhilarating of several moorland walks from the side roads off the A53 N of Leek. A walk here can be combined with the path through the unspoilt Dane Valley to Danebridge on the Cheshire border, with its good 16th-c pub, the Ship; hidden in the woods above the Dane is Lud's Church - not a church, but a miniature chasm reputed to have been a hiding place for religious dissenters.

RUDYARD LAKE SJ9459

Though man-made it's perhaps one of Staffordshire's prettiest sights (Kipling owed his given name to his father's delight in it); you can hire a boat (£5 an hour), and the muddy marshland provides a haven for wading birds. The meadows and forested slopes above are pleasant for walks and picnics; alternatively, the Knott Inn up the road at Rushton Spencer has good food, and is on the Staffordshire Way long-distance path.

RUGELEY SK0418

Quite a few attractive old buildings, inc a beautiful 12th-c **church**.

SHALLOWFORD SJ8729

Izaak Walton Cottage (Worston Lane) Thatched home of the author of *The Compleat Angler*, with displays on the development of angling, period herb garden and picnic orchard. Snacks, shop, disabled access to ground floor only; cl ams, Mon-Tues (exc bank hols), and Nov-Mar; (01785) 760278; free. The Worston Mill at Little Bridgeford is attractive for lunch.

SHUGBOROUGH SJ9921

Shugborough Hall & County Museum (A513) Imposing ancestral home of the Earls of Lichfield, begun in the late 17th c and enlarged in the 18th; magnificent state rooms, restored working kitchens, interesting puppet collection, and exhibition of the present Earl's photography. The park has a variety of unusual neo-classical monuments, working rare-breeds farm (£2), and restored corn mill. Meals, snacks, shop, disabled access; grounds cl 23 Dec-Mar, everything else cl Mon and Oct-Feb (exc Sun in Oct and special events); (01889) 881388; house and museum £6, NT (£2 charge to enter estate, for NT members as well). The canalside Wolseley Arms towards Rugeley is a handy food stop.

STAFFORD SJ9223

Greengate St has what's said to be the biggest timber-framed house in the country, built with local oak in 1595 and designed in the shape of the letter E to honour Queen Elizabeth; period room settings, and military displays. Cl Sun and Mon; (01785) 619130; free. The Picture House (Bridge St/Lichfield St) has decent food all day.

Shire Hall Gallery (Market Sq) Handsome former county hall and crown court used until 1991; you can look round one courtroom. Also art, craft and photography exhibitions, and good craft shop. Snacks, shop, limited disabled access; cl Sun, during exhibition changes, and bank hols, best to phone; (01785) 278345; free.

Stafford Castle (A518 SW) Norman

remains, rebuilt in Gothic Revival style in the early 19th c, then allowed to fall into disrepair. Interactive displays in good visitor centre, and a medieval herb garden. Snacks, shop, disabled access to visitor centre; grounds open all year, visitor centre and castle cl Mon (exc bank hols), 25 Dec-Mar; (01785) 257698; free.

STOKE-ON-TRENT SJ8745
The Potteries The five linked towns within the Stoke-on-Trent conurbation still produce some of the finest china and pottery in the country; it's a strange, disjointed urban landscape, nothing like as grimy as it once was. You can tour several of the factories, and most have museums or a visitor centre. Three of the best sights are close to rail stations: Etruria Industrial Museum (Etruria station), Spode (Stoke) and Gladstone Pottery Museum (Longton).

Etruria Industrial Museum 🖼 (Lower Bedford St, Etruria) This well restored and enjoyable museum sandwiched between two canals and based around the only surviving steam-powered potter's mill in the country (grinding flint for the ceramics industry right up to 1972; the modern factory that succeeded it is adjacent) has an exhibition hall inside. Museum cl am, Thurs-Fri, plus wknds Jan-Mar, engine in steam one wknd each month May-Nov, best to check; snacks, shop; (01782) 233144; £2.35. The friendly Plough (off A53 opposite Festival site in Etruria) has good value food.

Ford Green Hall 🖼 (Smallthorne) An interesting little 17th-c house and garden with special events. Snacks, shop, disabled access to ground floor, cl am wkdys, Fri and Sat and 25 Dec-1 Jan; snacks, shop, disabled access to ground floor; (01782) 233195; £1.75.

Gladstone Pottery Museum 🖼 (Uttoxeter Rd, Longton) Particularly engrossing, a complete Victorian pottery very appealing to families with lively demonstrations and interpretation, the story of the loo, historic tile gallery and 19th-c doctor's surgery. The museum's very much hands-on, and even hands-in - they're quite keen to get your fingers round the clay, and children love throwing pots (though it can work out expensive as

there are additional charges for activities). It's quite possible to spend up to half a day here. Meals, snacks, shop, mostly disabled access; cl Christmas week; (01782) 319232; *£4.95.

Penkhull Despite the development of the Potteries on the slopes below and all around, this hilltop enclave somehow preserves an undisturbed village feel. The Greyhound up here has good value snacks.

Potteries Museum & Art Gallery (Bethesda St, Hanley) With around 5,000 ceramic items on show, this is the best place to see the full range of ceramics produced locally over the centuries. There are also displays on the history of the Potteries, and even a Spitfire, produced by local son R J Mitchell. Meals, snacks, shop, disabled access; cl Sun am and 25 Dec-1 Jan; (01782) 232323; free.

Royal Doulton Visitor Centre (Nile St, Burslem) Potted history of the famous fine china company, with craft demonstrations, and a well displayed collection of Royal Doulton. Factory tours wkdys (exc factory hols) at 10.30am and 2pm (1.30 Fri), booking recommended; no under-10s on factory tour. Meals, snacks, good shop, disabled access to visitor centre only; cl over Christmas and New Year, best to phone then; (01782) 292434; visitor centre £3, visitor centre and tour £6.50.

Spode (Church St) The birthplace of fine bone china, this is the oldest manufacturing ceramics factory in the Potteries, and still the most atmospheric. A museum has rare and precious pieces, esp in the beautifully laid-out Blue Room, and you can watch craft demonstrations (on the tour), and have a go at painting a piece yourself. Meals, snacks, mixed outlet factory shop, disabled access; no tours wknds though shop and visitor centre open daily, cl 25-26 Dec, 1 Jan; tours by appointment; (01782) 744011; visitor centre and museum free; factory tour £4.50, 2½-hour connoisseur's tour £7.50.

Wedgwood Story Visitor Centre (Barlaston) Tells the story of this famous pottery, through a range of interactive and audio-visual displays. A self-guided audio tour leads you round various exhibitions on the history of the pottery, and the factory itself - where you can see traditional skills inc enamelling and hand-painting. Now on wkdys an extended tour lets you see more of the factory (with the latest technology from robots to laser-guided vehicles); you can also choose to take in the Coalport factory, where they manufacture the famous figurines. A demonstration area lets you throw your own pot and paint your own plate. Restaurant and bistro (food is served on Wedgwood china), good shop, full disabled access; cl over Christmas, best to ring then; (01782) 204218; £8.95 inc tour of Coalport factory, £7.95 wkdys, £7.25 wknds.

STOWE-BY-CHARTLEY SJ9927
Amerton Farm Well liked by readers, with a farm shop, garden centre, craft workshops, pottery, wildlife rescue centre (£1.50), and little steam railway (Sun and bank hols Apr-Oct, diesel summer Sat; £1.40). Meals, snacks, shop (try their delicious home-made ice-cream), good disabled access; cl 25-26 Dec and 1 Jan; (01889) 270294; free. The Plough opposite is handy for lunch.

STRETTON SK2624
Claymills Pumping Station Well preserved pumping station with Victorian steam-driven workshop, blacksmith's forge, and Britain's oldest working electricity generator. Two of the four beam engines are working, as is one of their five Lancashire boilers. Snacks, shop, disabled access; open Thurs and Sat, phone for dates of their eight steaming wknds; (01283) 509929; donations (£3 on steam days). The Spread Eagle over in the nice village of Rolleston on Dove does good value food all day.

TAMWORTH SK2003
A worthwhile town trail links a number of historic buildings; **St Editha's church** has windows by William Morris. The Market Vaults (Market St) and Moat House (Lichfield St) have decent bar food.
Drayton Manor Family Theme Park (off A4091 S) Popular theme park, with more than enough to keep a family happy for the day; rides for the brave inc Europe's only stand-up roller-coaster, and the fastest water ride in Britain; they've recently added Excalibur, a family boat ride through the legends of King Arthur. There are tamer rides for small children, mini golf, circus, a little zoo (with a discovery centre), nature trail and a new miniature train. Meals, snacks, shop, disabled access; cl Mon-Tues in Oct and all Nov-Mar, other days too so phone first; (01827) 287979; £17.50.
Snowdome (River Drive) Try your luck at skiing, snowboarding, tobogganing, sledging and tubing on real snow at this indoor centre. Competent skiers can take to the pistes as they wish, but novices need a lesson first (must book in advance); regular events. Bar and restaurant overlooking the slope, mountain sports shop, disabled access (and lessons); cl 25 Dec; (08705) 000011; hourly ski or snowboard sessions start from £15 (inc ski/board hire), tobogganing £6.50 for 30 mins.
Tamworth Castle (off Market St) Glorious mixture of architectural styles, from the Norman motte and bailey walls through the furnished Elizabethan hall to the Jacobean state apartments. Perhaps more museum than historic home, with a fair amount to please children, inc interactive gallery and high-tech talking heads. Snacks, shop; cl am, Mon, and wkdys Nov-Feb half-term, and Christmas bank hols, best to check; snacks, shop; (01827) 709629, £4.50.

TUTBURY SK2129
Pleasant village where cut glass has been manufactured for many years; you can still see glass-cutting and -blowing and buy glass at Georgian Crystal (01283) 814534, and Tutbury Crystal (01283) 813281. An attractive ruined **castle** has good views, a Great Hall dressed as a 1570s State Room, a Tudor garden, and birds of prey; snacks; cl Mon-Tues and mid-Sept to Easter Sun; (01283) 812129; £3.50. The Norman church has elaborate carvings.

WALL SK0806
Wall Roman Site (just off A5) An important military base from around AD50; excavations began in the 19th c and revealed one of the most complete Roman bathhouses in the country, also the remains of a substantial *mansio* (Roman hotel). Good audio tour, and finds from the area. Snacks, shop; cl Nov-Mar; (01543) 480768; £2.60; EH.

The Boat (A461, just SW of A5 roundabout) is a good lunch stop.

WESTON-UNDER-LIZARD SJ8010

Weston Park 🏛 (A5) Each of the richly decorated rooms at this striking 17th-c house has its own guide, as good with the family gossip as they are with the facts about the furnishings and art. Highlights are the very elegant dining room (with its excellent collection of works by Van Dyck), the library, home to over 3,000 books, and notable paintings, including works by Rubens, Gainsborough and Constable. The family silver is also on display, and there's a small toy museum, and letters and mementoes of Disraeli, who was a frequent 19th-c visitor. Landscaped by Capability Brown, the grounds are huge, with a deer park, restored 18th-c terrace garden, brightly planted broderie garden, and interesting trees and shrubs; in the last century it took 37 gardeners to look after it all. Good adventure playground, pets corner, and miniature railway (extra charge); regular events. Meals, snacks, shop, disabled access; usually open wknds Easter-early Sept, daily in July-Aug (but as they may cl for special events inc the music festival V2004, it's best to check); (01952) 852100; house and gardens £4.75, gardens only £2.50.

WILLOUGHBRIDGE SJ7539

Dorothy Clive Garden (A51) Woodland gardens created by the late Col Harry Clive in memory of his wife; at their best perhaps in spring and early summer, but lovely all year. Rhododendrons, azaleas, old roses, water garden, rock garden and stunning view. Tearoom with good home-made cakes, disabled access; cl Nov-Mar; (01630) 647237; *£3.80. The Falcon in Woore does good lunches.

WINKHILL SK0551

Blackbrook Zoological Park Unusual species and aviaries, as well as waterfowl, insects and reptiles, under-5s' playroom and children's farm - all much enjoyed by readers. Tearooms, shop, good disabled access; cl 25-26 Dec; (01538) 308293; £6.25. At pretty Waterhouses nearby you can hire bikes from the Old Station Car Park, (01538) 308609; around £8 for 3 hrs. The attractively set Cross there has decent food - or treat yourself at the Old Beams.

Other attractive villages, with decent pubs, include Alstonefield SK1355, Butterton SK0756, Coven SJ9006, Longdon SK0714, Rolleston on Dove SK2427, Salt SJ9527, Stourton SO8585, Swynnerton SJ8535 and Whitmore SJ8141.

There's good **canal access** from the **pleasant pubs** at Acton Trussell SJ9318, Amington SK2304 (the Gate), Armitage SK0816, Gnosall SJ8220, Hardings Wood SJ8354, High Offley (Anchor, in Peggs Lane) SJ7725, Norbury Junction SJ7922, Filiance Bridge in Penkridge SJ9214, Forton SJ7521, Shebden SJ7626 (great echoes under the aqueduct) and Wheaton Aston SJ8412.

Where to eat

CHEADLE SK0342 **Queens at Freehay** Counslow Rd (01538) 722383 Thriving atmosphere in well run pub with an attractively decorated lounge bar that opens through an arch into a light and airy dining area; carefully cooked good food with interesting daily specials, well kept real ales, and quick attentive service; cl 25-26 Dec and 31 Dec-1 Jan pms; disabled access. £25|£7.95

LICHFIELD SK0705 **Boat** Walsall Rd, Summerhill (01543) 361692 (A461 SW) Well run modern pub with café furniture, cheerfully light area, dominated by big floor-to-ceiling food blackboards, opening on to the kitchen doing good choice of well prepared food; real ales; dogs welcome in bar. £25.45|£6.50

SALT SJ9627 **Holly Bush** (01889) 508234 Thatched house dating in part from 14th c, with pretty hanging baskets and a big back lawn, some ancient beams in several cosy areas, a more modern back extension, coal fires, popular food (the daily specials are the thing to go for), Sun roasts, and well kept ales; children in eating area if eating; bar food all day Sat-Sun; disabled access. £21.95|£7.95

Special thanks to Michael and Jenny Back, M Wright

SUFFOLK

Good for quiet breaks, with appealing and picturesque small towns and villages, lonely beaches, some charming countryside, and rewarding country houses; a few good family outings

Clare, Lavenham and Long Melford are the best of a bunch of delightfully strollable villages and little towns with colour-washed timbered buildings, glorious churches, attractively restored windmills - and lots of antiques shops. Bury St Edmunds has quite a bit to offer, and Newmarket is intriguing for anyone with even a passing interest in horseracing.

For a pleasant seaside break in quiet surroundings, Southwold, Walberswick, Aldeburgh and Orford are all fine choices. Even at the height of summer you can walk for miles along empty beaches and coastal bird land. The attractive drowning village of Dunwich and the Shotley peninsula are rewarding for walkers too.

Hardly changed since it inspired some unforgettable paintings, Constable country (around East Bergholt by the border with Essex) is still exceptionally pretty. If you're interested in british painting, you can combine trips to Flatford Mill (*The Haywain*), with the excellent collection of paintings at Christchurch Mansion in Ipswich, and Gainsborough's House in Sudbury.

Lowestoft is home to our Suffolk Family Attraction (the Pleasurewood Hills Theme Park), as well as a good transport museum and sandy beaches. The Suffolk Wildlife Park in Kessingland makes a great day trip for families. Children can get really close to the animals at Easton Farm Park, readers like the farm at Baylham, and Giffords Hall in Hartest has a vineyard as well as animals. There's an owl sanctuary at Stonham Aspal, and a bustling equestrian centre in Wickham Market.

Stately homes that make a special effort to appeal to the whole family are the beautiful Kentwell Hall in Long Melford (rare breeds farm and lively re-creations), and Ickworth House at Horringer (play area and special events, along with fine collections of art and Georgian silver). Other great houses include Euston Hall (superb art collection and interesting grounds), unusual Somerleyton Hall (there's a maze), the turreted Tudor hall in Long Melford, and the surprisingly venerable house in Wingfield.

In Stowmarket, the Museum of East Anglian Life has plenty for a family outing. Going further back in time, the archaeological site at Sutton Hoo is a must if the Anglo-Saxons hold any interest for you, and at West Stow you can see a reconstructed Anglo-Saxon village. Enthusiasts will want to visit the air museum at Flixton, there's a good collection of instruments in Cotton, and at South Elmham you can go on brewery tours.

There's much to appeal to cyclists here, with quiet back roads, lots of villages, gentle gradients, and a very low accident rate; for an especially safe route, try the one at Alton Water near Stutton. There are lovely gardens at Helmingham, Stanton and Coddenham. Bird-watchers will enjoy Minsmere Reserve near Westleton.

Suffolk is great for relaxing, and eating out here is a real treat (fresh local fish is a speciality). Prices are quite appealing, for both things to do and places to stay.

Where to stay

BEYTON TL9363 **Manorhouse** *The Green, Beyton, Bury St Edmunds, Suffolk IP30 9AF* (01359) 270960 **£52**, plus special breaks; 4 pretty rms, 2 in house, 2 in barn conversion. Overlooking the village green, this charming no smoking 15th-c longhouse has lots of beams in the sitting/dining room, fresh flowers, antiques and paintings by the friendly owner's mother, super breakfasts, enjoyable dinners (by arrangement), and large garden; cl Christmas; no children

BILDESTON TL9949 **Crown** *High St, Bildeston, Ipswich, Suffolk IP7 7EB* (01449) 740510 **£65**; 13 individually furnished rms. Lovely timber-framed Tudor inn with a comfortable well furnished beamed lounge, open fires, good food in popular restaurant, welcoming courteous service, an attractive two-acre informal garden - and resident ghost; self-catering apartment; disabled access; dogs welcome

BURSTALL TM0944 **Mulberry Hall** *Burstall, Ipswich, Suffolk IP8 3DP* (01473) 652348 **£50**; 2 comfortable rms. Once owned by Cardinal Wolsey, this lovely old farmhouse has a fine garden, an inglenook fireplace in the big beamed sitting room, excellent food (ordered in advance) in pretty dining room, very good breakfasts with home-baked bread and preserves, and helpful friendly owners; tennis and croquet; cl Christmas-New Year

BURY ST EDMUNDS TL8564 **Angel** *3 Angel Hill, Bury St Edmunds, Suffolk IP33 1LT* (01284) 714000 **£119**; 65 individually decorated rms. Thriving creeper-clad 15th-c country-town hotel with particularly friendly staff, comfortable lounge and relaxed bar, log fires and fresh flowers, and good food in elegant restaurant and downstairs medieval vaulted room (Mr Pickwick enjoyed a roast dinner here); disabled access; dogs welcome in bedrooms

CAMPSEY ASH TM3255 **Old Rectory** *Station Rd, Campsey Ash, Woodbridge, Suffolk IP13 0PU* (01728) 746524 **£75**; 7 comfortable, pretty rms. Very relaxed and welcoming no smoking Georgian house by church, with charming owner and staff, log fire in comfortable and restful drawing room, quite a few Victorian prints, first class food from a set menu in summer conservatory or two other dining rooms with more log fires, a good honesty bar, a sensational wine list with very modest mark-ups on its finest wines, and sizeable homely gardens; cl Christmas; small well-behaved dogs welcome

HADLEIGH TM0242 **Edgehall** *2 High St, Hadleigh, Ipswich, Suffolk IP7 5AP* (01473) 822458 **£70***, plus special breaks; 8 pretty rms. Friendly family-run Tudor house with Georgian façade, comfortable carefully restored rooms, personal service, traditional english cooking using home-grown produce in no smoking dining room, and attractive walled garden with croquet; self-catering also; dogs welcome in bedrooms

HIGHAM TM0335 **Old Vicarage** *Higham Rd, Higham, Colchester, Essex CO7 6JY* (01206) 337248 **£58***, plus special breaks; 3 rms, 2 with own bthrm. Charming Tudor house nr quiet village with very friendly owners, pretty sitting room with fresh flowers, log fire and antiques, and enjoyable breakfasts in attractive breakfast room; play room with toys for children, grounds and fine gardens with river views (they have boats), tennis court, trampoline, and heated swimming pool; dogs welcome ☺

HINTLESHAM TM0743 **College Farm** *Hintlesham, Ipswich, Suffolk IP8 3NT* (01473) 652253 **£52***; 4 spacious rms, 2 with own bthrm and 1 self-contained rm in converted stable. Late 15th-c farmhouse on 600-acre farm with neat garden, guests' lounge with TV and inglenook fireplace, hearty Aga-cooked breakfasts in separate dining room, and friendly owners; walks around the farm, and riding and golf nearby; no smoking; cl Christmas and New Year; children over 10

HINTLESHAM TM0843 **Hintlesham Hall** *Hintlesham, Ipswich, Suffolk IP8 3NS* (01473) 652334 **£110**, plus special breaks; 33 lovely rms. Magnificent mansion,

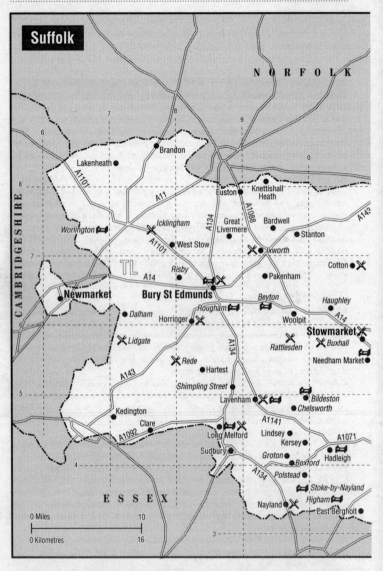

mainly Georgian but dating from Elizabethan times, in 175 acres with big walled gardens, 18-hole golf course, outdoor heated swimming pool, croquet, and tennis; restful and comfortable day rooms with books, antiques and open fires, fine modern cooking in several restaurants, a marvellous wine list, and exemplary service; snooker, sauna, steam room, gym, and beauty salon; well behaved children over 10 in evening restaurant; dogs welcome in bedrooms

LAVENHAM TL9149 **Angel** *Market Pl, Lavenham, Sudbury, Suffolk CO10 9QZ (01787) 247388* **£75***, plus special breaks; 8 comfortable rms. 15th-c inn with original cellar and pargeted ceiling in attractive residents' lounge, several Tudor features such as a rare shuttered shop window front, civilised atmosphere, good food in bar and restaurant, lots of decent wines, several malt whiskies, well kept real

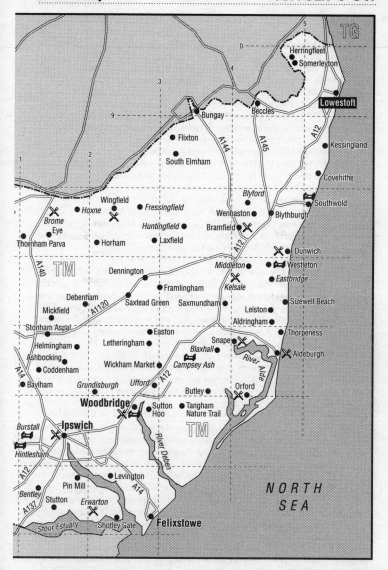

ales, thoughtful friendly service, and maybe live classical piano Fri pm; cl 25-26 Dec;
disabled access; dogs welcome in bedrooms

LAVENHAM TL9149 **Lavenham Priory** *Water St, Lavenham, Sudbury, Suffolk
CO10 9RW (01787) 247404* **£90**; 5 big rms and 1 suite with sloping beamed ceilings,
antiques, fresh flowers, and pretty bthrms. Dating back to the 13th c, this is a lovely
Grade I listed house once owned by Benedictine monks: Elizabethan wall paintings,
beams and oak floors, a huge flagstoned Great Hall, inglenook fireplaces, and all
lavishly restored; lovely civilised breakfasts, evening meals by arrangement, and
helpful, friendly owners; a charming garden with herb beds, kitchen garden and
some fine trees; cl Christmas-New Year; children over 10

LAVENHAM TL9149 **Swan** *High St, Lavenham, Sudbury, Suffolk CO10 9QA*

(01787) 247477 **£120**; 51 smart rms. Handsome and comfortable Elizabethan hotel that incorporates several fine half-timbered buildings inc an Elizabethan house and the former wool hall; lots of cosy seating areas, interesting historic prints and alcoves with beams, timbers, armchairs and settees, good food in lavishly timbered no smoking restaurant with a minstrels' gallery (actually built only in 1965), afternoon teas, intriguing little bar, and friendly helpful staff; dogs welcome (£10)

LONG MELFORD TL8645 **Bull** *Hall St, Long Melford, Sudbury, Suffolk CO10 9JG (01787) 378494* **£110**, plus special breaks; 25 rms, ancient or comfortably modern. An inn since 1580, this fine black and white hotel was originally a medieval manorial hall, and has handsome and interesting carved woodwork and timbering, and an old weavers' gallery overlooking the courtyard; a large log fire, old-fashioned and antique furnishings, enjoyable food, and friendly service; dogs by prior arrangement

NEEDHAM MARKET TM1053 **Pipps Ford** *Norwich Rd, Needham Market, Ipswich, Suffolk IP6 8LJ (01449) 760208* **£71**, plus winter breaks; 8 pretty rms with antiques and fine old beds, 4 in converted Stables Cottage. Lovely 16th-c farmhouse in quiet garden surrounded by farmland alongside attractive river; log fires in big inglenook fireplaces, good imaginative food using home-baked bread, locally produced meats, honey, eggs, and preserves, and organic local veg and herbs, and conservatory with subtropical plants (some meals can be communal); cl 2 wks over Christmas; children over 5; disabled access; dogs in Stables Cottage

ROUGHAM TL9063 **Ravenwood Hall** *Rougham, Bury St Edmunds, Suffolk IP30 9JA (01359) 270345* **£96**, plus special breaks; 14 comfortable rms with antiques, some rms in mews. Tranquil Tudor country house in seven acres of carefully tended gardens and woodland; log fire in comfortable lounge, cosy bar, good food in timbered restaurant with big inglenook fireplace (home-preserved fruits and veg, home-smoked meats and fish), a good wine list, and helpful service; croquet and heated swimming pool; they are kind to children and have themed occasions for them and lots of animals; disabled access; dogs welcome away from restaurant ☺

SOUTHWOLD TM5076 **Crown** *High St, Southwold, Suffolk IP18 6DP (01502) 722275* **£110***; 14 rms, 11 with own bthrm. Outstanding old inn with excellent imaginative food in no smoking restaurant and smart but relaxed main bar, inventive breakfasts, lots of interesting properly kept and fairly priced wines by the glass, well kept real ales and friendly helpful staff

SOUTHWOLD TM5076 **Swan** *Market Pl, Southwold, Suffolk IP18 6EG (01502) 722186* **£130**, plus winter breaks; 42 well equipped rms with newspapers, and some overlooking the market square. 17th-c hotel with comfortable and restful drawing room, upstairs reading room, a convivial bar, interesting enjoyable food in elegant no smoking dining room, fine wines, well kept real ales (the hotel backs on to Adnams Brewery), and polite helpful staff; children must be over 5 in evening dining room

STOKE-BY-NAYLAND TL9836 **Angel** *Polstead St, Stoke-by-Nayland, Colchester, Essex CO6 4SA (01206) 263245* **£69.50**; 6 comfortable rms. Civilised and elegant dining pub in Stour Valley with Tudor beams in cosy bar, stripped brickwork and timbers, fine furniture, huge log fire and woodburner, decent wines, and particularly good, imaginative and reasonably priced bar food; cl 25-26 Dec and 1 Jan

WESTLETON TM4469 **Crown** *The Street, Westleton, Saxmundham, Suffolk IP17 3AD (01728) 648777* **£77**; 19 quiet, comfortable rms. Smart, extended country inn in lovely setting with good nearby walks; comfortable bar, no smoking dining conservatory, more formal restaurant, a wide range of enjoyable attractively presented food (nice breakfasts, too), log fires, several well kept real ales, decent wines, and a pretty garden with outside heaters; cl 25-26 Dec; disabled access; dogs welcome (not in restaurant)

WOODBRIDGE TM2548 **Seckford Hall** *Seckford Hall Rd, Great Bealings, Woodbridge, Suffolk IP13 6NU (01394) 385678* **£120***, plus special breaks; 32 comfortable rms. Handsome red brick Tudor mansion in 34 acres of gardens and parkland with carp-filled lake, putting, and leisure club with indoor heated pool, beauty salon, and gym in lovely tithe barn; fine linenfold panelling, huge fireplaces, heavy beams, plush furnishings and antiques in comfortable day rooms, good food (inc lovely teas with home-made cakes), and helpful service; cl 25 Dec; dogs welcome in bedrooms

WORLINGTON TL6973 **Worlington Hall** *Mildenhall Rd, Worlington, Bury St Edmunds, Suffolk IP28 8RX (01638) 712237* **£75**; 9 comfortable rms with decanter of sherry and fruit. 16th-c former manor house in five acres with a 9-hole pitch and putt course, comfortable panelled lounge bar with log fire, good food in relaxed candlelit bistro, and friendly staff; dogs welcome

To see and do

Suffolk Family Attraction of the Year

LOWESTOFT TM5495 **Pleasurewood Hills Theme Park** 🔲 (off A12) There's not too much at this theme park you won't have seen in some form elsewhere, but they've efficiently brought together all the rides and features you'd want or expect, so although it's not cheap, it's a reliable bet for a full day's entertainment. There's a good mix for most ages, with watercoasters, log flumes, spinning cups, dodgems and quite a few rollercoasters and thrill rides. The most recent addition is the swinging, spinning Frisbee, but the most popular remains the Magic Mouse, a stomach-churning cross between a waltzer and a traditional coaster; it gets busy, so to avoid a wait best to head here first. There's an indoor soft play area (with an area for very young children), and quite a few live shows, including circus performers and displays of parrots and sealions. A miniature railway or chairlift can take you round the park, and there's space by the lake for picnics (along with some model dinosaurs). The go-karts have an extra charge. Meals, snacks, shop, disabled access; open wknds and holidays from Easter-Sept, and daily from May half-tem to early Sept, plus Oct half-term for Halloween; (01502) 508200; £13.50 adults and children over 1.3 metres tall, £11.50 children between 1 metre and 1.3 metres, and free for children under a metre (but they can't go on rides with height restrictions). A family ticket for four people is £46. Entry includes a voucher for a discounted return visit.

ALDEBURGH TM4656
Fishing village, once an important port, with quaint little streets running down to the shingle beach where the fishermen still haul in and sell their catch, and a much loved boating pond; touristy, but in a quiet way. Benjamin Britten, founder of the town's annual music festival, and his companion the singer Peter Pears are now buried side by side in the churchyard. The Avocet Gallery (High St) has tin toys and automata to play with; usually cl Sun pm, and pms and wknds in winter; (01728) 452928. The bustling beach-side Cross Keys does enjoyable bar lunches, as does the Mill (summer cream teas too). There's an RSPB reserve just N at North Warren, and the Landmark Trust offer self-catering accommodation (at a price) in the Martello Tower, the largest and most northerly of the east coast's defences.
Moot Hall Museum 16th-c brick and timber, with outside staircase; scene of the trial in Britten's *Peter Grimes*. It has displays on maritime history and coastal erosion, and finds from the Anglo-Saxon ship burial at Snape. Shop; usually open pm wknds Apr-May, Sept-Oct, plus daily pm Jun, and all day July-Aug (exc lunchtimes) though best to check; (01728) 454666; £1.
ALDRINGHAM TM4461
Aldringham Craft Market Three extensively stocked galleries of crafts and art. Snacks, disabled access; cl 25-28 Dec, 1-2 Jan; (01728) 830397; free. The Parrot & Punchbowl has good wines and decent food.
ASHBOCKING TM1855
James White/Big Tom Company (Helmingham Rd) Spicy tomato- and apple-juice making and tasting. Farm

shop, snacks; phone to book a tour wkdys Sept-Mar; (01473) 890202; free. The Moon & Mushroom over at Swilland has good food.

BARDWELL TL9473

Bardwell windmill Carefully restored and now an attractive sight; usually open daily; (01359) 251331; donations. The village green, with ancient church opposite 16th-c pub, is attractive, too.

BAYLHAM TM1152

Baylham House Rare Breeds Farm ⊞ (Mill Lane) Recommended by readers, this friendly working farm has rare breeds of cattle, sheep, pigs (which may come when called), goats and poultry, and a riverside walk and picnic area; a visitor centre has information about the Roman site underlying the farm. Snacks (inc cream teas), shop, disabled access; cl 25-26 Dec; (01473) 830264; £3.50. The Highwayman at Creeting St Mary does good value lunches.

BECCLES TM4290

Beccles and District Museum (Ballygate) Decent local history museum housed in a 17th-c school. Shop, disabled access, open pm Tues-Sun and bank hols Apr-Oct; (01502) 715722; free.

William Clowes Print Museum (Newgate) Interesting look at the development of printing from 1800 onwards, with wide range of machinery, woodcuts and books. Open wkdys (until 2pm) Apr-Sept, or by appointment; (01502) 712884; free.

BLYTHBURGH TM4575

Blythburgh church Magnificent building in a lovely setting above the marshes; the White Hart is a good family dining pub.

BRAMFIELD TM4073

Bramfield church Interesting building, with an unusual detached round tower. The Queens Head has good food.

BRANDON TL7884

Brandon Country Park Largely pine woods, and pleasant to stroll around; for a car-borne impression of Thetford Heath, the best road is the B1106.

Brandon Heritage Centre (George St) Brandon used to be the centre of the Stone Age flint industry, so among

the local history here is a reconstructed flint-knappers' workshop; also displays on the fur industry and Thetford Forest. Shop, disabled access; open Sun pm, Sat, and bank hols Apr-Oct; (01842) 814955; 50p.

BUNGAY TM3389

Right in the centre of this historic little market town are the ruins of its Norman **castle**, with twin towers and massive flint walls; there's a visitor centre; cl 25-26 Dec; (01986) 896156; £1. Bungay straddles the county border.

BURY ST EDMUNDS TL8464

This busy shopping town has a good deal of character, with quite a few attractive Georgian and earlier houses, and several antiques shops. The **cathedral** gained that status only in 1913; parts are 15th-c, but the hammer-beamed ceiling is 19th-c, and work on building the tower should be completed by the summer. The nearby Queens Head (Churchgate St) has good food. Another fine old church, **St Mary's** (Crown St), contains the tomb of Mary Tudor. Walking tours usually leave the tourist information centre at 2.30pm every day mid-May to end-Sept; (01284) 764667; £2.50. The Linden Tree (Out Northgate St), Old Cannon (Cannon St) and Cupola House (Traverse) are other useful food places.

Art Gallery (Market Cross) A fine Robert Adam building with changing exhibitions and a decent recently refurbished craft shop. Disabled access; cl Sun, Mon, between exhibitions, and over Christmas; (01284) 762081; £1. The intriguing nearby Nutshell (The Traverse) is the tiniest pub imaginable.

Greene King Brewery Visitor Centre (Westgate St) You can go on an hour's tour of this highly successful brewery, where Greene King has made beer for over 200 years (usually 11am and 7pm Mon-Fri, 11am and 2pm Sat, phone to book (01284) 714382; £6, evening £7); lots of samples, which after all the stairs (wear comfortable shoes) you'll probably feel you deserve. A museum follows the history of brewing, and the fortunes of families Greene and King. Shop, disabled access to museum only; usually cl am wkdys, all Sun; £2.

Manor House Museum ⊞ (Honey

Hill) Georgian mansion with a marvellous collection of watches, clocks and other timepieces, as well as period costumes, quite a few hands-on displays, and children's quizzes, inc a mouse hunt. Meals, snacks, shop, disabled access; cl Mon, Tues, Good Fri, 25-26 Dec and 1 Jan; (01284) 757076; £2.50, free for locals.

Moyses Hall Museum 🎫 (Cornhill) As well as a good range of redisplayed Suffolk history (inc gruesome relics of the 'Murder in the Red Barn' - the murderer's account of his trial is bound in his own skin), there's a gallery on the Suffolk Regiment, and an interactive gallery; it's all housed in an 800-yr-old building. Shop, disabled access; cl Good Fri, 25-26 Dec and 1 Jan; (01284) 706183; £2.50, free for locals.

Theatre Royal (Westgate St) Britain's third-oldest working theatre, and very handsome - built in 1819 by William Wilkins, the designer of London's National Gallery. It's owned by the NT, and you can look round or go behind the wings on a guided tour (11.30am and 2.30pm Mon and Weds and 11.30am Sat Jun-Aug); open Mon, Weds and Sat (exc 1-2pm) Apr-Sept, cl for rehearsals, best to phone and check; (01284) 769505; free entry (guided tour £2.50).

BUTLEY TM3751
Butley Pottery (Butley Barns, Mill Lane) Working pottery, with café, restaurant and disabled access; cl Mon-Weds (exc Jun-Aug when open daily, and Apr-Jun when open Weds-Sun), and Jan to mid-Feb; (01394) 450785; free. The Oyster pub is good for lunch. The B1084 Woodbridge—Orford is a quietly attractive drive, and the even quieter back road S to Capel St Andrew passes the remains of a medieval abbey gatehouse.

CLARE TL7645
One of the area's very special timber-and-plaster villages, with a huge and beautiful **church**, the sketchy ruins of a **castle** on an Iron Age earthwork above the River Stour, some remains of a 13th-c Augustinian priory, and little modern intrusion; nature trails around the castle. There's a three-storey antiques warehouse (Maltings Lane), and the Bell and the Swan (which does not allow children) have decent food. The A1092

to Long Melford, with a back road on to Lavenham, links this trio of lovely villages, and passes Cavendish, also pretty, with an attractive medieval church, and good value food at the 16th-c Bull. The back roads N of here are also pleasant drives, with plenty of colour-washed old houses.

Clare Ancient House Museum (High St) Local history in an attractive listed 15th-c building. Shop; open pm Thurs-Fri and Sun, and all day Sat and bank hols May-Sept, and over Easter; (01787) 277662; £1.

CODDENHAM TM1252
Shrubland Hall Gardens 🎫 Stunning Victorian gardens inc formal terrace and a wild woodland garden; there's a magnificent conservatory (not open) and enchanting follies inc a swiss chalet. Limited disabled access; open pm Sun and bank hol Mon Apr-Sept; (01473) 830221; £3. The 17th-c Sorrel Horse at Barham has good value food.

COTTON TM0667
Mechanical Music Museum & Bygones 🎫 Large collection of instruments and musical items taking in not just the expected organs, street pianos, polyphons and gramophones, but dolls, fruit bowls and even a musical chair. Their pride and joy is the Wurlitzer theatre pipe organ in the reconstructed cinema. Snacks, shop, disabled access; open Sun pm Jun-Sept, plus first Sun in Oct (a fair organ enthusiasts' day); (01449) 613876; *£4. The Trowel & Hammer is good for lunch.

COVEHITHE TM5281
Covehithe church Attractive building; just down the lane this stretch of coast is good for nature walks, especially out of season. The Five Bells at South Cove has good value food.

DEBENHAM TM1763
This attractive village has a fine partly Saxon **church**; the pottery in Low Rd specialises in unusual teapots; snacks, shop; cl 25-26 Dec; (01728) 860475; free.

DENNINGTON TM2866
Dennington church Interesting and attractive church - with excellent sermons - in pleasant surroundings. The Queens Head next door is good.

DUNWICH TM4770
Once quite a sizeable town, but it's

slipping slowly under the sea - most is now submerged. Some say that on quiet nights, when there's a swell running after a storm, they can hear the bells of a submerged church tolling. **Dunwich Museum** (St James St) has interesting exhibitions on the village's erosion; shop, disabled access; cl Nov-Feb; (01728) 648796; free. There are some fragmentary ruins of a friary up on the cliffs. Excellent coastal walks along the cliffs, beaches and heathland of Dunwich Heath, which has a NT tearoom.

EAST BERGHOLT TM0733
Bridge Cottage, Flatford 17th-c cottage near the mill immortalised by Constable, with a good interpretative centre for his paintings. Good teas, shop, disabled access; cl Mon and Tues (exc May-Sept), wkdys Jan-Feb, and Christmas-New Year, limited opening times in winter so best to phone; (01206) 298260; free; NT. Guided walks through areas that inspired his work leave here several times a day May-Sept (£2). You can hire rowing boats for trips along the River Stour. The mill itself and its famous partner **Willy Lott's Cottage** are both owned by the NT and leased by them to the Field Studies Council. You can see inside only by taking part in one of their many courses, such as art and photography, or popular wildlife watching wknds; (01206) 298283. The church with its uncompleted tower has a unique 16th-c timber-framed bell cage, and the Kings Head (with a haywain out in front) has good value food. From the village the walk along the water-meadows by the Stour is East Anglia's most famous walk - picturesque views immortalised by Constable, and well worth while. This ties in with the more elevated Essex Way to make a very worthwhile circular walk, from Dedham to Lawford church, then via Manningtree Station (extraordinarily good station buffet) to join the Stour itself.

EASTON TM2758
Easton Farm Park Delightful small working farm in 14 hectares (35 acres) of attractive countryside, with plenty of opportunities for children to get close to the animals. As well as poultry, suffolk punch horses, pigs and goats,

there are usually some young animals. Daily pony rides (no extra charge), animal handling and egg-collecting sessions. There are indoor and outdoor play areas (inc a new area for the under-3s), as well as token-operated battery-powered tractors, and a full-size one to scramble over. Other attractions include a working blacksmith, face-painting, environmental trail and vintage farm machinery. Snacks, picnic areas, shop, mostly disabled access (they're very helpful); cl end Sept to mid-Mar exc Feb and Oct half-terms; (01728) 746475; £5.25. The quaint White Horse has decent food, and the Wickham Market—Debenham road through here via Brandeston and Cretingham has some attractive views.

EUSTON TL8978
Euston Hall (A1088) Elegant house built by Charles II's Secretary of State Lord Arlington. The highlight is probably the excellent art collection, with several portraits of the king, his family and court, inc works by Lely and Van Dyck; the staff are friendly. The grounds were laid out by John Evelyn, William Kent and Capability Brown, so reflect centuries of development, with stately terraced lawns, fine trees, a lake, river walks and newly restored watermill, lovely rose garden and classical temple. Teas in former kitchen, shop, disabled access to grounds and tearoom; open Thurs pm 17 Jun-16 Sept, plus Sun pm 27 Jun, 18 July, and 5 Sept; (01842) 766366; *£4.

EYE TM1473
Eye church Beautiful stonework and rood screen.

FELIXSTOWE TM2832
Quite a busy port, with a ferry (passengers, not cars) across to Harwich, and further afield to Zeebrugge. Thanks to its beaches and relatively dry climate it's developed into a popular low-price family resort. The White Horse (Church Rd) has inexpensive food and a play area. Along the coast N, past a Martello Tower, golf course and quiet sand dunes, is the gently attractive and altogether quieter little settlement of Felixstowe Ferry, with another foot-ferry across the estuary of the River Deben (going to Bawdsey), and good value food inc local

seafood in the Ferry Boat and Victoria, both very family-friendly.

Landguard Fort 18th-c, and well worth a look; open daily Apr-Nov; (01394) 277767; £3. Displays on local history in adjacent museum; usually open pm Sun and bank hol Mon Apr-end Oct, plus pm Weds Jun-Sept; £1.

FLIXTON TM3288

Norfolk & Suffolk Aviation Museum 🅰 (Homersfield Rd) Aircraft and related items from the Wright Brothers to the present day, with aeroplanes displayed outside and in the hangars. Snacks, shop, disabled access; cl Fri and Sat (plus Thurs and Mon Nov-Mar), and all mid-Dec to mid-Jan; (01986) 896644; donations. The Buck nearby has good food (inc a Sun carvery).

FRAMLINGHAM TM2863

The sloping market square is attractive, and the **church** has an excellent hammer-beam roof. The Station Hotel (B1116 S) has interesting food, and the B1116 N to Fressingfield is quite a pleasant drive.

Framlingham Castle (B1116) 12th c, where Mary I heard that she had become queen. Unusually the entire curtain wall has survived (you can walk all the way along it), and there are 13 towers, some 17th-c almshouses, and an array of Tudor chimneys. Good views, interesting local history museum. Snacks, shop, disabled access to ground floor only; cl 24-26 Dec, and 1 Jan; (01728) 724189; £4; EH.

GREAT LIVERMERE TL8871

There's a charming shortish walk from the church here, past the Ampton Water lake, to Ampton church. A longer path leads through farmland from Great Livermere to Ixworth.

HADLEIGH TM0242

Old market town with some striking buildings (inc the church, famously painted by Gainsborough); there's a nearby woodland RSPB reserve. The Ram has bargain food.

HARTEST TL8352

The village green is attractive; at the end by the church, the Crown (under new licensees) has good food.

Giffords Hall (Shimpling, just SE) 33 acres with vineyard and winery, wildflower meadows, rare breeds of sheep, cattle, pigs, goats, wallabies, and domestic fowl, and a rose garden. It's perhaps best known among gardeners for its sweet peas, and they have a rose and sweet pea festival the last two wks in Jun. Meals, snacks, shop, disabled access; cl Oct-Easter; (01284) 830464; £3.50. They do B&B.

HELMINGHAM TM1857

Helmingham Hall Gardens (B1077) Beautiful gardens pretty much as they were in Tudor times. The grand battlemented house they stand around (not open) is ringed by a moat, over which the drawbridge is still raised each night. Extensive deer park with hundreds of red and fallow deer, as well as highland cattle and soay sheep, and magnificent old oak trees. Constable painted several views of the woodlands. Snacks, shop (inc Helmingham produce), disabled access; open Sun pm 2 May-12 Sept; (01473) 890363; £4. The welcoming Dobermann at Framsden has good food.

HERRINGFLEET TM4797

Herringfleet windmill An attractive sight above the river (open occasionally when it's working, usually summer Suns; (01473) 583352).

HORHAM TM2172

St Mary's churchyard The churchyard here has for generations been conserved as natural grassland around its older graves, cut only after the flowers have seeded; so from spring onwards it's a mass of wild flowers, with plenty of butterflies (and beehives). The White Hart in the quiet village of Stradbroke has decent simple food.

HORRINGER TL8261

A serenely attractive village with well spaced colour-washed buildings, and a good dining pub (the Beehive).

Ickworth House, Park and Gardens Very untypical stately home, an oval rotunda 30 metres (98 ft) high, with two curved corridors filled with a fascinating art collection inc pictures by Gainsborough, and an exceptional array of Georgian silver. They try hard to make sure children enjoy their visit, with quizzes, trails, handling boxes and a free touch tour, introduced primarily for partially sighted visitors. Outside are formal italianate gardens, and 1,800 acres of attractive parkland with woodland walks and cycle routes.

There's a decent-sized play area, special events and activities for children, and themed events in the run-up to Christmas. Meals, snacks, shop, plant centre, good disabled access; house cl am, also Weds-Thurs, and Nov-18 Mar; garden cl 22 Dec-1 Jan, park open all year (exc 25 Dec); (01284) 735270; £6.10 house, park and garden; £2.80 park and gardens only; NT.

IPSWICH TM1644

After King John granted a charter in the 13th c, this flourished as a port sending cloth to the continent; the port is still quite active. The busy town has quite a few things to look at on day visits, and a pedestrianised centre (traffic schemes make getting in and out by car rather slow). Cardinal Wolsey set up a college here, but all that remains is the 16th-c gatehouse in College St. The Ancient House in the Butter Market (now a kitchenware shop) has some 15th-c carvings, exceptionally neat pargeting (decoratively patterned external plasterwork) and even a priest's hiding hole - if it's not too busy, ask the staff to show you. Dotted about the town are several attractive **medieval churches**, nicely floodlit at night. The finest is the 15th-c St Margaret's (Soane St); St Mary at the Elms (Elm Rd) has the town's oldest cottages behind it. The Golden Lion (Cornhill), County (opposite County Hall) and Old Rep (Tower St) have decent food.

Christchurch Mansion (Soane St) Perhaps the town's highlight; the original 16th-c house was altered in the following century after a fire, but since then it's escaped any further redevelopment. The rooms are furnished in period style, with a Victorian wing inc servants' quarters, and the Suffolk Artists' Gallery has the best collection of works by Constable and Gainsborough outside London. Snacks, shop, disabled access to ground floor only; cl am Sun, Mon (exc most bank hols), 24-26 Dec, 1 Jan, Good Fri, but best to check; (01473) 433554; free. The **Wolsey Art Gallery** next door has frequently changing exhibitions, and the surrounding park has play areas and a bird reserve.

Ipswich Museum (High St) The natural history section has been painstakingly restored to how it was in its Victorian heyday, and includes the first gorillas brought to Europe in the mid-19th c. Other parts have quite an emphasis on Roman Suffolk. Snacks, shop, disabled access to ground floor only; cl Mon, Good Fri, 25 Dec, 1 Jan; (01473) 433550; free.

Transport Museum (Lupin Rd) In an old trolley-bus depot, a developing collection of around 100 ancient commercial and engineering vehicles built or used in the area, from fire engines to buses and milk floats. Snacks, shop, disabled access; open Sun and bank hols Apr-end Nov, and pm wkdys during school hols; (01473) 715666; £3.

KEDINGTON TL7046

Kedington church One of Suffolk's many attractive churches, this is unusual for its Saxon crucifix.

KERSEY TM0044

A very pretty one-street village, full of timbering and attractive and colourful plasterwork. It runs from the fine 14th-c church down to a ford with ducks, and up the other side; several craft and antiques shops. The quaint old Bell has popular food.

KESSINGLAND TM5286

Suffolk Wildlife Park (A12) Attractively set in almost 40 hectares (100 acres) of coastal parkland, this very committed place looks after mainly animals from Africa, many of which you won't be able to see anywhere else in the country. Some of the residents are from critically endangered species, and they're proud of their breeding successes. Everything children most like to see is here: from lions, cheetah and giraffes, to snakes, flamingoes and meerkats, and they've very rare white rhinos (shown off to great effect in their spectacular rhino house). There are plenty of feeding displays and talks spread throughout the day; also play areas inc a separate section for under-5s, and perhaps extra activities in the summer hols. A train makes it easier to get round the site. Meals, snacks, shop, disabled access; cl 25-26 Dec; (01502) 740291; £6.50-£7.95.

KNETTISHALL HEATH TL9480

This country park has some pleasant strolls - and if you're overflowing with energy (and several days' supplies), you may even be tempted northwards on the Peddars Way, waymarked from here all the way to Norfolk's N coast. For more sedentary souls, the Mill (B1111, over towards Market Weston) has good food.

LAKENHEATH TL7182
Lakenheath church One of Suffolk's elegant and charming churches, though now a bit hidden away among the sprawl edging the nearby huge air base.

LAVENHAM TL9149
One of the finest surviving examples of a small medieval town, this lovely place has delightfully rickety-looking 14th- and 15th-c timbered buildings wherever you look; many now house tearooms or antiques shops. The old wool hall has been incorporated into the ancient timbered Swan Hotel, well worth a look despite its prices. The Angel opposite the Guildhall is good for lunch. Self-guided audio tours of the town are available from the pharmacy, 98 High St (01787) 247284; £3. The A1141 through Monks Eleigh and then the B1115 to Hitcham, through Chelsworth (where the prettily set Peacock has enjoyable food), is a pretty drive.
Guildhall (Market Pl) Picturesque 16th-c timbered building, at various stages in its life a town hall, prison, workhouse and wool store; its beamed interior has interesting local history displays. Disabled access to tearoom (cl Mon) and shop; cl Nov-Feb, wkdys Mar and Nov, and Mon-Tues Apr; (01787) 247646; *£3.25; NT.
Little Hall 🔲 (Market Pl) Delightful 14th-c house, attractively presented, showcasing the Gayer-Anderson collection of books, pictures and antiques, with a pleasant enclosed garden. Open Weds, Thurs, wknds and bank hols Easter-Sept; (01787) 247179; *£2. There's a good wildlife art gallery nearby.

LAXFIELD TM2972
Laxfield church Well worth a visit, in tucked-away quiet surroundings; nearby is a charmingly preserved very old-fashioned pub, and a small museum (open pm wknds and bank hols mid-May to Sept; (01986) 798460; free).

LEISTON TM4462
Long Shop Steam Museum 🔲 (Main St) Big industrial museum in

preserved buildings of Garrett Engineering Co, with steam engines, steam rollers, traction engines, and memorabilia from the nearby World War II air base. Picnic garden, shop, limited disabled access; cl Nov-Apr; (01728) 832189; *£3.50. The Engineers Arms opposite has so much memorabilia it seems almost an extension. The sizeable shopping town has the fragmentary remains of a 14th-c abbey off the B1122 just N.

LETHERINGHAM TM2858
Letheringham watermill Pretty, and surrounded by nice gardens; occasional open days in summer.

LEVINGTON TM2338
A pleasant spot, with ancient almshouses, a marina below, and the Ship, which has good food and estuary views (no children inside).

LINDSEY TL9744
St James's chapel A charming little thatched flint and stone chapel, built during the 13th c but inc some earlier work too.

LONG MELFORD TL8645
A very nice old place to stroll around: the fine green and exceptionally long main Hall St are lined with buildings from various eras, many with lovely timbering. Lots are now antiques shops (not cheap, but interesting). The **church** of Holy Trinity is glorious, with ornate carvings and dozens of spectacular windows; very attractive when floodlit at night. The Black Lion on the green and handsome medieval Bull are good food stops.
Kentwell Hall Beautiful Tudor mansion with genuinely friendly lived-in feel, best during their enthusiastic re-creations of Tudor and 1940s life (several wknds Apr-Sept), when everything is done as closely as possible to the way it would have been done then - even the speech. It's surrounded by a broad carp-filled moat, and there's a rare breeds farm in the grounds. Meals, snacks and picnic area, shop, disabled access; house usually cl am, Sat (exc Aug and bank hol wknds) plus Oct to mid-July (exc Sun Apr-Oct and Easter wk), best to check; (01787) 310207; most re-creations cost around £9, though the Great Annual one is £12. On non-event days entry is £6.50, or

£4.75 garden and farm only.

Melford Hall Turreted Tudor house mostly unchanged externally since Elizabeth I with hundreds of servants and courtiers stayed here in 1578; it also still has the original panelled banqueting hall. Fine collection of chinese porcelain and Beatrix Potter memorabilia; the gardens have a Tudor banqueting house. Some disabled access; cl am, Mon (exc bank hols), Tues, and wkdys Apr and Oct, all Nov-Mar; (01787) 880286; £4.50; NT.

LOWESTOFT TM5492

Britain's most easterly town, this is the area's main fishing port, so the harbour always has lots to see. It's developed as a resort thanks to its beaches (South Beach has the best bathing water) and proximity to the Broads. Cobbled streets of old buildings survive in the part known as The Scores, and the early medieval **parish church** is imposing and attractive. The last surviving steam drifter, the *Lydia Eva*, in dry dock here, is being restored and is expected to open to the public early 2005. The seaview Jolly Sailors near the quaint Pakefield church is good value for lunch, and has an all-day Sun carvery. The building of the world's tallest wind turbine, just N at Ness Point, has now been approved and work is expected to begin in the next two years.

East Anglia Transport Museum (Carlton Colville; B1384 SW of Lowestoft) Lots of lovingly restored vehicles around three acres of woodland. The best part is the reconstructed 1930s street scene used as a setting for working trams, trains and trolley-buses. Snacks, shop, some disabled access; open Easter, then Sun May-Sept, plus usually pms Sat and Weds Jun-Sept, and wkdy pms in summer hols and half-terms, phone to check; (01502) 518459; £4.50. The nearby Crown (A146) does good cheap lunches.

Maritime Museum (Whapload Rd) Housed under the lighthouse on Whapload Rd; shop, disabled access; cl Oct-Easter; (01502) 561963; 75p. There's a small **Royal Naval Museum** nearby; usually cl 12-2pm, Tues, Sat, and mid-Oct to Easter; (01502) 564344; free.

Mayhem Adventure Play (East Point Pavilion, Royal Plain) Lively children's play area themed as an underwater world. Meals, snacks, shop, disabled access; cl 25-26 Dec and 1 Jan; adults free, children from £2.50 an hour (£2.95 in school hols); (01502) 533600. It shares the rather grand old pavilion with the tourist information centre and good local history displays.

Pleasurewood Hills Theme Park *See separate family panel on p.549.*

MICKFIELD TM1461

Mickfield Water Garden Centre Two acres of ornamental water gardens and working nursery, with displays of freshwater fish, secret garden and lily pond. Garden centre, snacks, disabled access; cl 25 Dec; (01449) 711336; free.

NAYLAND TL9734

Well rewards a stroll - its fine **church** has an altar painting by Constable; the old White Hart is now a smart restaurant.

NEEDHAM MARKET TM0854

Needham Market church The marvellous hammer-beam roof has been described as 'a whole church seemingly in the air'.

NEWMARKET TL6463

Newmarket has been the centre of horseracing since 1605, when James I used to slope off here, and in the early morning people driving through are quite likely to have to give way to a string of racehorses. The tourist information centre (occasional exhibitions, when you can go upstairs) is housed in the remains of Charles II's 17th-c palace; cl Sat pm, Sun and 25 Dec; (01638) 667200; free. The Rutland Arms (High St) and Bedford Lodge Hotel (Bury Rd) are useful for lunch.

National Horseracing Museum 🔲 (High St) The stories and scandals of the sport's development through the centuries, with trophies, videos of classic races, a display on the history of betting, and racing relics from saddles to skeletons. You don't have to be interested in racing to get something out of it. Meals, snacks, shop, disabled access; cl Mon (exc bank hols and July-Aug), and Nov-Easter; (01638) 667333; £4.50. They also organise informative tours of the local breeding and racing scene, with a look at horses at work on the gallops, and visits to a training yard, stud and the equine swimming pool; booking essential on (01638) 560622; prices start at around £17.

National Stud (A1304 W) Tours of this mecca of horse breeding by arrangement; (01638) 663464. Snacks, shop, disabled access; guided tours are at 11.15am and 2.30pm Mon-Sat (2.30pm only Sun), cl Oct-Feb (exc race days); £5. The Kings Head at Dullingham is a good nearby lunch spot.

ORFORD TM4249

Dunwich Underwater Exhibition 🖾 (Front St) The process of coastal erosion is well illustrated; Meals, snacks, shop; cl 25-26 Dec; 60p.

Havergate Island Bird-watchers can arrange whole-day trips to this marshy RSPB reserve by calling the Minsmere visitor centre (01728) 64828; permits usually available every Thurs and 1st and 3rd Sats of month Apr-Aug, then first Sat of the month Sept-Mar; around £5 inc boat trip from Orford quay. A sea wall walk S from the quay gives close-up views across to the island.

Orford Castle 🖾 When Henry II commissioned this castle it was right on the shore, but since then the river has silted so much that it's now slightly inland. It has an amazing 18-sided keep rising to 27 metres (90 ft), supported by three extra towers. Good views from the top (as usual, at the end of a spiral staircase). Snacks, shop; cl Mon-Tues Nov-Mar, 24-26 Dec, 1 Jan; (01394) 450472; £4; EH. The **church** has the ruined chancel arches of a Norman predecessor in the graveyard. There's a long lane down to the shore with its quay and old smugglers' inn, the good Jolly Sailor. The road through Iken Heath to Snape is a pleasant drive through quiet pinewoods.

Orford Ness After years of belonging to the Ministry of Defence (who barred access to anyone who wasn't in uniform), this magnificently desolate spit just opposite the quay is now owned by the NT and open to the public, though it's more for serious wildlife fans than day trippers. Ferries leave the quay roughly every 15 mins 10am-2pm Tues-Sat July-Sept and Sat only mid-Apr to Jun and Oct - phone to check; (01394) 450057; £5.70. There are also longer boat trips from the quay.

PAKENHAM TL9369

Pakenham watermill 🖾 (Mill Rd) 18th-c watermill by a pretty millpond, restored to working order by preservation society; they hope to restore the Tudor mill house too. There's a picnic area and a pleasant riverside walk. Snacks, shop (selling their own flour); open pm Weds, wknds and bank hols (and often am Thurs) Easter-Sept; (01359) 270570; £2.50.

Pakenham windmill (Thurston Rd) Carefully restored and now an attractive sight; cl 1-2pm and Sun; (01359) 230277; donations.

PIN MILL TM2037

A nice spot below the wooded slopes by the River Orwell, with Thames barges on tidal moorings, and much favoured by artists; the Butt & Oyster here is attractively placed for a bite to eat.

RIVER DEBEN TM3041

Broad winding river close to the coast, with good walks best reached from side roads off B1083 S of Shottisham, where the thatched Sorrel Horse is a useful stop. On the opposite bank, the Maybush at Waldringfield has enjoyable food and lots of tables out by the water; river cruises run from the quay (May-Sept).

SAXMUNDHAM TM3863

This pleasant bypassed village has yet another fine **church**. Nearby Yoxford has good value food at the Griffin.

SAXTEAD GREEN TM2564

Saxtead Green Post Mill (A1120) Traditional Suffolk windmill dating from 1796, meticulously brought back into perfect working order, but it's a steep climb up the staircase. Audio tour, shop, cl 1-2pm, Sun, and all Nov-Mar; (01728) 685789; £2.50; EH. Attractive surroundings; the Old Mill House over the green has good home-made food.

SHOTLEY GATE TM2434

At the meeting of the Stour and Orwell estuaries, this is at the hub of a rewarding walk with good views across to Harwich and its shipping. Start inland at Shotley and cross the fields either N to the Orwell or S to the Stour, then follow the waterside. The Bristol Arms, with great estuary views, has good fresh fish (and various things for sale at Christmas and in the summer), and up the hill, the colossal mast of HMS *Ganges* (now a police training centre) is a dizzying sight.

SIZEWELL BEACH TL4761
Generally virtually deserted out of season, and pleasurable walking ground despite the rather graceless Sizewell nuclear power plant in the distance. Agate and other semi-precious stones are common among the pebbles, even sometimes amber after stormy E winds; heathland, an old railway track walk and The Meare (Thorpeness's lake) justify detours inland.

SNAPE MALTINGS TM3957
The converted and expanded 19th-c **maltings** are home of the Aldeburgh Music Festival begun by Benjamin Britten, with other concerts throughout the year. The centre is pleasant to wander around, with unusual shops and galleries. The Plough & Sail just outside is good for lunch; up in the village, the Crown (with a bar re-created in Britten's *Peter Grimes*) and Golden Key are both good, too.

SOMERLEYTON TM4997
Somerleyton Hall (B1074) This interesting Jacobean house was rebuilt in the anglo-italian style in the 1840s, and today is still very much lived-in, with period furnishings and paintings. The lovely gardens have a maze, and there is occasional live music. Snacks, shop, disabled access; open pm Sun, Thurs and bank hols Easter-Oct, plus pm Tues and Weds July-Aug and perhaps other times, best to check; (01502) 730224; £5.80. The Plough at Blundeston, home of Barkis ('is willing') in *David Copperfield*, is useful for lunch. A couple of miles N of here, wooded **Fritton Lake** attracts numerous wildfowl, particularly in autumn and winter.

SOUTH ELMHAM TM3385
St Peter's Brewery 🖼 Medieval St Peter's Hall, in a pretty spot by a moat with black swans, has in its outhouses this more modern small brewery, whose excellent bitters, porters and fruit beers are made with water from their own source. Good tours take in the whole brewing process, as well as parts of the hall. Meals and snacks, shop, some disabled access; open Fri-Sun and bank hols plus Thurs July-Aug, tours every hour 12-4pm; (01986) 782322;

free entry to site, £3.50 tour.
SOUTHWOLD TM5076
Once an important fishing port, now a quite enchanting and civilised little resort, with its restored pier joining the distinctive lighthouse as a second landmark. The pier has a fantastical water clock, striking every half-hour with all sorts of entertaining action - a modern-day rival to Southwold Jack in the nave of the interesting **church** (worth a look too). Contact the tourist information centre for information about tours of the lighthouse (no children under 1m); (01502) 724729; £2. The Denes is the best beach. Across the golf course or along the breezy sea wall you come to the harbour, a tidal inlet, with its cheerful mix of beached fishing boats, multitudes of sailing boats, and tall black fishing shacks (only four or five are now still in use); the Harbour Inn here is full of character. There's no end of other good pubs and inns supplied by the local Adnams brewery (their wholesale wine shop has interesting stock). For food, the Crown is outstanding, and the smart Swan Hotel is good; the Kings Head is popular with families, and the Lord Nelson has the most atmosphere. The rowing-boat ferry (in the same family for around 80 years; cl end Oct-Easter) goes over to **Walberswick** on the other side of the water - an attractively decorous seaside village, popular with artists ever since Wilson Steer's days there in the 1890s. The Bell here is a striking old inn, and the 15th-c church, parts now destroyed and other bits looking shaky, is attractive. The circular walk from Southwold, along the sea wall and over the river by ferry to Walberswick, returning along the course of the former railway line over the footbridge into Southwold, makes a very pleasant stroll and allows exploration of both. The drive round by car between Southwold and Walberswick is several miles.
Amber shop and museum (Market Pl) The longest-standing retailer of amber in Britain, with an impressive collection of related ornaments from 19th-c chinese scent bottles to fossilised insects. Shop, disabled access; cl 25-26 Dec; (01502) 723394; free.

River Blyth Broad river winding close to the coast, with delightful waterside paths, and marshy and heathy expanses to explore around its mouth.

Southwold Museum (Bartholomew Green) Decent local history collection, in a 17th-c dutch-gabled cottage. Shop, disabled access (but no facilities); usually open pms Easter-Oct; free.

STANTON TL9671

Wyken Hall Gardens Formal herb, knot and woodland gardens, walled old-fashioned rose garden, copper beech maze, pond, woodland walks, and vineyard. A very nice unspoilt estate, just right for exploring. Good restaurant and snacks in medieval barn (open all year), unusual country shop, disabled access; cl am, all Sat, and Oct-Mar; (01359) 250262; £3.

STONHAM ASPAL TM1459

Suffolk Owl Sanctuary 🖭 (Stonham Barns, A1120) Flying displays Apr-Oct, and every species of british owl plus hawks, falcons, vultures and eagle; also woodland trails with red squirrel enclosure, pond-dipping and songbird viewing hide. Meals, snacks, shop, disabled access; usually cl 23 Dec-3 Jan; (01449) 711425; £4.75. Around 30 small businesses share the site, inc various craft workshops, crazy golf and garden centre. You can get something to eat here, or the Ten Bells does bargain home-made food.

STOUR ESTUARY WALKS TM1534

Stutton gives access to a fine stretch of the broad Stour estuary just S, with good bird-spotting opportunities. The Kings Head does bargain lunches.

STOWMARKET TM0458

Museum of East Anglian Life 🖭 (Iliffe Way, opp Asda) Excellent 70-acre open-air museum. Children look at the reconstructed buildings with a genuine sense of astonishment, and even the 1950s domestic room settings seem prehistoric to fresher eyes. Most of the buildings have been removed from their original settings and rebuilt here; the oldest is a splendid 13th-c timber barn, now housing a collection of horse-drawn vehicles. Among the rest are an old schoolroom, a smithy, chapel, windpump, and a very pretty watermill. They're quite spread out, so a fair bit of walking is involved. Also wandering around are various traditional farm animals, and on some Suns they have demonstrations of local crafts and skills like wood-turning and basket-making; their occasional event days are usually around the spring and summer bank hols. There's a decent rustic-style adventure play area, and it's great for a picnic. Meals, snacks, shop, disabled access; cl Nov-Mar; (01449) 612229; *£6.50.

STUTTON TM1534

Alton Water Reservoir Attractive man-made lake circumscribed by a cycle track which takes in some interesting features on the way, inc the Tattingstone Wonder, a folly built for a local squire with pious pretensions who wanted to look across the valley and see a church - the ecclesiastic façade hides a row of almshouses (not open to public); cycle hire is £5.80 for 3hrs; (01473) 328873. Also bird reserve (several hides), fishing (permits available from visitor centre), and watersports; (01473) 328408. Café, some disabled access (though gravel paths might prove tricky for wheelchairs); reservoir open all year, facilities cl wkdys Nov-Easter; (01473) 328268; parking £1 a day, £2 Sun. In the village itself, the Kings Head has good value food.

SUDBURY TL8741

Gainsborough's House 🖭 (Gainsborough St) The painter was born here in 1727, and the house has an excellent collection of his work. Plenty of period furniture and china too, and contemporary arts and crafts. Shop, disabled access to ground floor only; cl ams Sun and bank hols, Good Fri, and between Christmas and New Year; (01787) 372958; £3.50. This market town is pleasant, with stalls on Thurs and Sat; the nearby Waggon & Horses (Acton Sq) has enjoyable fresh food.

SUTTON HOO TM2849

One of the most famous archaeological sites in the country, where in 1939 the discovery of an Anglo-Saxon ship burial and burial ground of an early 7th-c ruler made historians completely reinterpret the Dark Ages. A modern-looking reinterpretation of an Anglo-Saxon Hall houses a permanent exhibition on the site's history, inc a full-size reconstruction of the royal burial within the ship (complete with everything the king would want in the afterlife, including a game and a lyre). Another houses changing exhibitions (which run from Mar-Oct), with finds from various Anglo-Saxon sites (inc Sutton Hoo itself) on loan from the British Museum; also restaurant, visitor centre and shop. Guided tours (12.30, 1.30, 2.30pm) at wknds, allow access to the burial mounds (extra charge), phone to check. Excellent disabled access; facilities cl wkdys Nov-Feb, and Mon-Tues Mar-May and Oct; (01394) 389700; £4; NT. The site is open every day throughout the year; £2.50 car parking when facilities are closed. A turn off the B1083 S takes you to the Ramsholt Arms at Ramsholt for lunch among waterside pinewoods, with quiet walks along the Deben estuary.

TANGHAM NATURE TRAIL TM3548

A short walk among the plantations off the B1084 towards Woodbridge specially designed for disabled people; there are also longer walks through the pinewoods here, where red squirrels often show themselves.

THORNHAM PARVA TM1073
St Mary's church Britain's largest surviving medieval altar-piece 3½ metres (12 ft) long has recently been returned to this handsome little thatched Norman church after an eight-year restoration; 14th-c wall paintings too. There are good walks around here, and the nearby village of Thornham Magna has a restored Victorian walled garden; the thatched Four Horseshoes there is useful for something to eat.

THORPENESS TM4759
At the S end of Sizewell beach, this curious place was built as a holiday village in a deliberately fanciful olde-worlde style, with quite a few attractive mock-Tudor houses (one even masking a water-tower), a sizeable picturesque boating lake, and a windmill (brought over from Aldringham). The Dolphin has enjoyable food.
North Warren Miles of RSPB nature reserves stretching along the coast between Thorpeness and Aldeburgh; nature trails, many different birds (esp good for wildfowl in winter), butterflies and dragonflies; (01728)

688481; free.
WENHASTON TM4275
Wenhaston church Attractive building, with a 15th-c wall painting (in excellent condition) full of lovely devils; it's a nice peaceful village, too.

WEST STOW TL7971
West Stow Country Park 🏕
Attractive, with 50 hectares (125 acres) of heath and woodlands bordered by the River Lark. There's a nature trail, bird hides and bird-feeding, but the most interesting feature is the reconstructed **Anglo-Saxon Village**, its buildings erected using the same methods and tools as in the 5th c. A visitor centre houses original finds from the Anglo-Saxon site; occasional costumed days, and special events. Snacks, shop, disabled access; cl 25-26 Dec; (01284) 728718; park free, village £5 (£6 special events). The Red Lion at Icklingham has good food.

WESTLETON TM4369
A pleasant village with an attractive green; the Crown is useful for lunch.
Minsmere Reserve Big RSPB reserve with over 200 species of bird recorded every year among the heath, woods, marshes and lagoons - good observation hides, and enjoyable walks at any time of year. The heathlands around here are also home to red deer, and are spectacularly carpeted with heather in summer. Snacks, well stocked shop, disabled access (can be difficult in places - readers recommend getting in touch with the warden for details); cl Tues, and 25-26 Dec; (01728) 648281; £5 for non-RSPB members. The reserve is skirted by public paths, and one hide is available free for public use, but you need an entry sticker for the rest of the reserve. Approach points are Dunwich and the pretty village of Eastbridge. Mount Pleasant Farm at Dunwich, which borders the reserve, is now owned by the RSPB and NT, who intend to turn it back into heathland to link the existing Minsmere and Dunwich heathlands.

WICKHAM MARKET TM2956
Valley Farm Riding & Driving Centre (f[m W on B1078) Family-run equestrian centre offering a wide range of activities from all-day pony treks to carriage driving, and even stunt riding.

They also have a collection of animals inc suffolk punch horses, a donkey, goats, a mule, and a breeding herd of camargue horses. Snacks, shop, disabled access; cl 25-26 Dec (site cl to visitors Nov-Mar); (01728) 746916; site free, riding lessons start from £20 for 30 mins. The comfortable Three Tuns at Pettistree has civilised food (and bedrooms now).

WINGFIELD TM2276
Wingfield College and Gardens
Quite a surprise to find a splendid medieval timber-framed building behind the Georgian façade. One of its 18th-c owners constructed the Palladian exterior to make his home more fashionable, using false ceilings, floors and windows so skilfully that for 200 years the house's early origins were forgotten. Striking great hall and period interiors, topiary, walled gardens, and garden sculptures; art displays in visitor centre. Snacks, shop, disabled access; open pm Weds, Fri, wknds and bank hols Apr-Sept; (01379) 384888; £3.90. It's also the home of Wingfield Arts, a varied programme of events across the region; phone for a programme. The De La Pole Arms has good food.

WOODBRIDGE TM2749
Quietly attractive and rather dignified market town, with many fine buildings and interesting book and antiques shops, and a **church** of great style and interest. The Anchor (Quay St), Bull and Kings Head (Market Hill) and Old Mariner and Olde Bell & Steelyard (New St) all do decent bar lunches. The B1079 and then B1077 up to Eye is a pleasant drive on an old coach road.
Buttrums Mill (Burkitt Rd) Six-storey tower mill, fully restored, with displays of its history. Shop; open pm Sun and bank hols Easter-Sept, plus pm Sat May-Aug; £1.50.
Tide Mill Restored 18th-c mill on busy quayside, its wheel usually working when tides allow. Shop, disabled access

to ground floor only; cl Oct-Apr exc wknds Oct and Apr; (01473) 626618; £1.50. The Wilford Bridge Hotel nearby at Melton is a good lunch stop, and well placed for river walks.
Woodbridge Museum (Market Hill) Tells the story of Woodbridge from its Anglo-Saxon roots to the present. Shop, disabled access (but no facilities); usually cl Sun am, all day Mon and Tues (exc bank and school hols), Weds, and Nov-Easter, best to check; (01394) 380502; £1.

WOOLPIT TL9762
The **church** here has a hammer-beam roof, and a translation of the village tale that in the 12th c two slightly strange-looking green-skinned children were found by a pit that was suddenly blasted in the earth one night; the boy soon died, but the girl lived, and grew up to marry a local lad and have children. She never said more about her origins than that she'd come from a land far far away. The drive to Buxhall (where the Crown is a good pub) is pretty.
Woolpit & District Museum (The Institute) Small but interesting, with annually changing local history displays (and more on the 12th-c children). Shop, disabled access; open wknds and pm bank hols mid-Apr to Sept; (01359) 240822; donations.
Other attractive villages, all with decent pubs, include Bentley TM1138, Bildeston TL9949, Blaxhall TM3657, Blyford TM4277 (and nearby Holton windmill is pretty), Boxford TL9640, Chelsworth TL9848, Dalham TL7261, Eastbridge TM4566, Fressingfield TM2677, Groton TL9541, Grundisburgh TM2250, Haughley TM0262 (Jacobean manor house in lovely grounds), Hoxne TM1777, Huntingfield TM3374, Ixworth TL9370, Middleton TM4367, Polstead TL9938, Risby TL8066 (with a decent antiques centre), Ufford TM2953 and Shimpling Street TL8752.

Where to eat

ALDEBURGH TM4656 **Regatta** *171-173 High St (01728) 452011* Bustling seaside restaurant decorated with pennants and seaside murals, and specialising in fresh local seafood - though they also offer interesting meat dishes and fine puddings; a relaxed atmosphere, friendly service, and no smoking area; cl winter Sun pm and winter Mon-Tues; disabled access. £21|£7

BRAMFIELD TM3974 **Queens Head** *The Street (01986) 784214* Popular pub with pleasantly relaxed high-raftered lounge bar, a good log fire in impressive fireplace, no smoking side bar, family room, and wide choice of very good interesting food inc organic dishes (super puddings also); well kept real ales, good wines, and maybe home-made elderflower cordial; cl 26 Dec. £27|**£7.95**

BROME TM1376 **Cornwallis** *Rectory Rd (01379) 870326* Very civilised largely 19th-c country hotel grandly approached down a tree-lined drive through its 20-acre grounds, with imaginative choice of excellent food in elegant restaurant, nicely planted Victorian-style side conservatory, and beamed and timbered 16th-c bar - stylish and comfortable, with a good mix of old and antique tables, oak settles and cushioned library chairs, and a handsome woodburner; well kept real ales, an extensive, carefully chosen wine list with 20 by the glass, and warm friendly service from attentive young staff; comfortable bdrms. £29.75|**£5.95**

BURY ST EDMUNDS TL8564 **Maison Bleue** *31 Churchgate St (01284) 760623* Airy french seafood restaurant with big seaside mural, super fish dishes (and some meaty ones too), a thoughtful wine list, and helpful friendly staff; cl Sun, Mon, Jan. £27.45|**£7.95**

BUXHALL TL9957 **Crown** *Mill Rd (01449) 736521* Welcoming 17th-c timbered country pub with carefully cooked individually prepared enjoyable food emphasising fresh seasonal ingredients, well kept real ales, decent wines, and quick friendly service; intimate little candlelit bar, open fire in big inglenook, low hop-hung beams and standing timbers, a further light and airy room; seats on heated terrace and in pretty garden; cl Sun pm. £25|**£10.95**

COTTON TM0667 **Trowel & Hammer** *Mill Rd (01449) 781234* Civilised wisteria-covered pub with a spreading series of quiet rooms, fresh flowers, lots of beamery and timber baulks, a big log fire, good interesting food, and a large pretty back garden with swimming pool; cl 25 Dec. £21.50|**£7.95**

DUNWICH TM4770 **Flora Tearooms** *Fore St (01728) 648433* Extended former fisherman's hut right on the beach, with great views of the sea and fishing boats, famous for very good fish and chips but also other snacks, teas and home-made cakes; cl Dec-Feb; disabled access.|**£6.75**

DUNWICH TM4770 **Ship** *St James's St (01728) 648219* Pleasant old pub by the sea, with a bustling atmosphere, helpful staff who cope cheerfully with the crowds, fresh fish off the boats on the beach, traditionally furnished bar, conservatory, sunny back terrace, and well kept garden; bdrms; the RSPB reserve at Minsmere is close; cl 25 Dec pm; children welcome away from bar. £23.45|**£6.25**

ERWARTON TM2134 **Queens Head** *The Street (01473) 787550* Remote and unspoilt little pub with lovely views, a welcoming unpretentious atmosphere, a cosy coal fire in beamed bar, good well priced bar food inc fresh fish and game in season and decent value Sun lunch, well kept real ales, and friendly service; cl 25 Dec; disabled access. £23.95|**£5.50**

HORRINGER TL8261 **Beehive** *The Street (01284) 735260* Particularly well run and pretty ivy-covered pub with extremely helpful service, friendly atmosphere, excellent imaginative food with lots of daily specials and a puddings board, attractively furnished little rambling rooms, woodburner, well kept real ales and decent wines; no food Sun pm. £25|**£7.95**

ICKLINGHAM TL7872 **Red Lion** *The Street (01638) 717802* Civilised and rather smart thatched pub with a nice mix of wooden chairs, candlelit tables, fresh flowers, inglenook fireplace and heavy beams, very good food inc lots of fresh fish dishes and seasonal game choices, well kept real ales, and country wines; disabled access. £30|**£8.95**

IPSWICH TM1644 **Mortimers Seafood Restaurant** *1 Duke St (01473) 230225* This is the place for really fresh daily changing fish and shellfish, simply cooked; a thoughtful french wine list and relaxed atmosphere; cl Sun, 2 wks Christmas; disabled access. £25|**£4.95**

IXWORTH TL9370 **Theobalds** *68 High St (01359) 231707* Consistently good imaginative food in 17th-c restaurant with log fires, beams and standing timbers in cosy rooms, very good wine list, and kind service; cl Sat am, Sun pm, Mon, 10 days in summer; children in evening over 8 only. £34|**£9**

KELSALE TM3866 **Harrisons** *Main Rd (01728) 604444* White-painted 16th-c thatched cottage housing a pretty, two-storey timbered dining room offering modern and traditional cooking using the best local produce; a short well priced wine list, and friendly efficient service; cl Sun, Mon, from 24 Dec pm for 2 wks. £29.15/2-course lunch Tues-Fri £11.50

LAVENHAM TL9149 **Great House** *Market Place (01787) 247431* Restaurant-with-rooms in ancient house behind a handsome Georgian façade; bare boards, antiques, open fires (inc an inglenook in the restaurant itself), very good french cooking plus lighter lunches and a super french cheeseboard, friendly staff, mainly french wines, and attractive flower-filled courtyard for outside eating; charming beamed bdrms; cl Sun pm, Mon, Jan. £27.90|**£8.50**

LIDGATE TL7257 **Star** *The Street (01638) 500275* Quaint old place with interesting charming and friendly spanish landlady, small bar, big log fire, handsomely moulded heavy beams and polished oak and pine tables, big helpings of enjoyable food (plenty of mediterranean influences), good wines and ales, a cosy simple dining room, and tables in front and in the little rustic back garden; cl Sun pm. £30|**£7.50**

LONG MELFORD TL8646 **Black Lion** *Church Walk (01787) 312356* Comfortable, well run and civilised hotel with a mellow bar, an oak serving counter, deeply cushioned sofas, leather wing armchairs and antique fireside settles, and an eating area with leather dining chairs around handsome tables set for the good, stylish, daily-changing bar food; no smoking restaurant, large portraits, of racehorses and of people, and helpful efficient service by neatly uniformed staff; real ales, a fine range of wines by the glass (inc champagne), and good generous cafetière coffee; appealing Victorian walled garden; good bdrms. £24.75|**£8.50**

LONG MELFORD TL8645 **Chimneys** *Hall St (01787) 379806* Lovely beamed 16th-c building with very good carefully prepared interesting food, a thoughtful wine list, and helpful staff; paintings for sale; cl Sun, bank hols (exc Easter); partial disabled access. £44.65/2 courses £12

NAYLAND TL9734 **Anchor** *1 Court St (01206) 262313* Recently carefully refurbished, with a light and sunny bare-boards front bar, interesting old photographs of pipe-smoking customers and village characters on pale yellow walls, farmhouse chairs around a mix of tables, and coal and log fires; a similarly furnished carpeted room leads to a small sun room; enjoyable, enterprising food (they also have their own back smokehouse), real ales, a nice choice of wines by the glass inc local ones, and perky young service; separate no smoking restaurant up steep stairs, and picnic-sets out by the peaceful River Stour. £25|**£7.50**

NAYLAND TL9734 **White Hart** *High St (01206) 263382* Smart 15th-c restaurant-with-rooms in lovely countryside, with tiny bar, rather formal dining room, particularly good french-influenced cooking, a wide choice of wines, and polite willing service; cl Mon (apart from bank hols), 26 Dec-9 Jan; disabled access. £35|**£6.95**

ORFORD TM4249 **Butley Orford Oysterage** *(01394) 450277* Simple restaurant with its own oyster beds, fishing boat and smokehouse; very popular locally and with yachtsmen for its wonderfully fresh fish, decent wines, and brisk friendly service; disabled access; cl pm Sun-Thurs mid Sept-May. £25|**£6.80**

RATTLESDEN TL9758 **Brewers Arms** *Lower Rd (01449) 736377* 16th-c village pub with pleasantly simple beamed lounge and small lively public bar, very welcoming friendly service, imaginative food, decent wines, well kept ales, and magnificent old bread oven in main eating area; children must be well behaved; cl Mon; disabled access. £25.40|**£5.95**

REDE TL8055 **Plough** *The Green (01284) 789208* Welcoming partly thatched cottage in lovely spot, with particularly helpful owners, lots of well presented fresh fish and game in season, imaginative daily specials, good evening restaurant, decent wine, and lovely sheltered cottagey garden; cl Sun pm; children over 3; disabled access. £27.45|**£10.50**

SNAPE TM3958 **Crown** *Bridge Rd (01728) 688324* Unspoilt smugglers' inn with a relaxed and warmly friendly atmosphere, old brick floors, beams, big brick inglenook and nice old furnishings; particularly good interesting well presented food served by smiling staff, pre- and post-concert suppers, a thoughtful wine list (16 by the glass inc champagne), well kept real ales, and tables in pretty garden; bdrms; cl 25 Dec, 26 Dec pm; no children; partial disabled access. £27.65|£8.75

STOWMARKET TM0360 **Tot Hill House** *Tot Hill* (01449) 673375 Although beside a busy road, once inside this friendly and charming family restaurant, the atmosphere is welcoming and peaceful; comfortable furnishings, smart, helpful staff, highly enjoyable and interesting modern cooking, and a varied wine list; no smoking in dining room; cl Mon, Tues, Sat am, Sun pm, 2 wks Jan, 2 wks July; disabled access. £38.50

WINGFIELD TM2276 **De La Pole Arms** *Church Rd* (01379) 384545 Beautifully restored village inn, tucked away in lovely countryside; deliberately simple yet elegant décor, interesting bric-a-brac, comfortable traditional seating, a pleasantly civilised feel, courteous friendly staff, and very good popular bar food; no smoking restaurant and well kept real ales; disabled access. £27.50|£7.95

WOODBRIDGE TM2748 **Captain's Table** *3 Quay St* (01394) 383145 16th-c cottage with three interlinked beamed rooms, cheerful décor, enjoyable interesting food inc plenty of fresh fish, helpful service, and a thoughtful wine list; cl Sun pm, Mon (except bank hols), 1st 2 wks Jan; disabled access. £24|£6.95

Special thanks to Michael and Jenny Back

SURREY

Some top-notch family outings, and the big surprise is Surrey's quiet side - special gardens, great estates, peaceful commons, heaths, miles of woodland, and perfect walking territory

The theme parks at Thorpe Park (Chertsey) and Chessington are terrific for an action-packed day out, and Brooklands Museum in Weybridge (motor-racing displays and a hands-on science gallery for children) is our Surrey Family Attraction. Farnham's bustling Birdworld & Underwater World has plenty to do even on wet days (colourful birds too at pretty Busbridge Lakes in Godalming), and families can choose from several enjoyable farm parks.

The National Trust Surrey Hills Explorer is a useful bus service if you want to visit the attractions near Dorking. From Dorking station it connects with the town centre, Ranmore, Denbies Wine Estate (absorbing even if you're not a wine buff), Polesden Lacey at Great Bookham (once the centre of Edwardian high society), and Box Hill (a good place for walks); phone for a timetable (01372) 453401; £3.

Some superb gardens include England's oldest landscaped garden in Esher, the mix of styles at Wisley (lots of ideas for gardeners), and Painshill Park at Cobham (full of surprises); the arboretum at Hascombe is especially pretty in spring and autumn. Elsewhere, there's a vineyard in Godstone, and the Hogs Back Brewery at Tongham does tours. Horseracing fans have a choice of racecourses besides popular Epsom.

Great houses to visit are Loseley Park near Guildford (an Elizabethan mansion with lovely gardens), grand Clandon Park (West Clandon), and nearby Hatchlands (East Clandon). The Rural Life Centre at Tilford is interesting. Two little-known treats for art lovers are Watts Picture Gallery at Compton, and the Hannah Peschar Sculpture Garden in Ockley. For something quite different, try the intriguing tour through the network of tunnels underneath Reigate.

Despite its commuter-belt image, Surrey is England's most wooded county, and away from the urban corridors much of the countryside is beautifully preserved, and quite hilly. The National Trust owns vast tracts of the finest scenery, and walkers have an excellent choice, with relatively free access. Leith Hill is a favourite with walkers, and the Chatley Heath Semaphore Tower at Ockham Common is a good starting place for exploring the surrounding woodland. This county has some lovely villages too, and Outwood has Britain's oldest working windmill. A boat trip along the River Wey & Godalming Navigation (see Guildford) or a cycle ride along the Downs Link Path are other fine-weather suggestions.

Where to stay

BAGSHOT SU9062 **Pennyhill Park** *College Ride, Bagshot, Surrey GU19 5ET* *(01276) 471774* **£246.50**, plus special breaks; 123 individually designed luxury rms and suites. Impressive Victorian country house in 120 acres of well kept gardens and parkland inc a 9-hole golf course, tennis courts, outdoor heated swimming pool, clay pigeon shooting, archery, fishing, and an international rugby pitch; friendly courteous staff, wood-panelled bar with resident pianist, comfortable two-level lounge and reading room, very good imaginative food in two restaurants, jazz Sun lunchtime, and terraces overlooking the golf course; disabled access; dogs welcome (£75 supplement)

CHERTSEY TQ0467 **Crown** *7 London St, Chertsey, Surrey KT16 8AP (01932) 564657* **£65**, plus special breaks; 30 comfortable modern rms. Bustling, friendly place with some original features and open fire in large bar, conservatory extension, good food, attractive restaurant, and lovely big garden; disabled access; dogs welcome

EWHURST TQ0840 **High Edser** *Shere Rd, Ewhurst, Cranleigh, Surrey GU6 7PQ (01483) 278214* **£55***; 3 charming rms, shared bthrm. 16th-c timber-framed farmhouse in lovely countryside, with comfortable residents' lounge, friendly owners, open fire in breakfast room; tennis court in grounds; cl Christmas and Easter

FARNHAM SU8145 **Farnham House** *Alton Rd, Farnham, Surrey GU10 5ER (01252) 716908* **£110**, plus special breaks; 25 comfortable rms. Attractive Victorian Gothick manor house with oak panelling and open fires in comfortable public rooms, restaurant, and tennis court and outdoor heated swimming pool in five-acre gardens; cl 25-26 Dec; disabled access

HASLEMERE SU9228 **Deerfell** *Blackdown, Haslemere, Surrey GU27 3LA (01428) 653409* **£48***; 3 comfortable rms, 1 with shared bthrm. Comfortable no smoking stone coach house with wonderful views and good nearby walks; generous meals in handsome dining room (ordered in advance), open fire in sitting room, pictures, antiques and old rugs, a sun room, good breakfasts, and friendly owners; cl Christmas/New Year; children over 6; dogs by prior arrangement

HASLEMERE SU9232 **Lythe Hill Hotel & Spa** *Petworth Rd, Haslemere, Surrey GU27 3BQ (01428) 651251* **£125***, plus weekend breaks; 41 individually styled rms, a few in the original house. Lovely partly 15th-c building in 20 acres of parkland and bluebell woods (adjoining the NT hillside) with floodlit tennis court, croquet lawn, and jogging track; plush, comfortable and elegant lounges, a relaxed bar, two no smoking restaurants (one with french cooking, the other with traditional english), and good attentive service; new spa with swimming pool, sauna, steam and beauty rooms and gym; disabled access; dogs welcome

HOLMBURY ST MARY TQ1144 **Bulmer Farm** *Holmbury St Mary, Dorking, Surrey RH5 6LG (01306) 730210* **£54***; 8 big comfortable rms, 5 in no smoking barn conversion with own showers. Attractive and welcoming 17th-c farmhouse on 30-acre beef farm in lovely countryside, with oak beams and inglenook fireplace in attractive sitting room, breakfasts with home-made preserves in neatly kept dining room, and large garden; self-catering also; children over 12; dogs in self-catering unit

HORLEY TQ2943 **Langshott Manor** *Langshott, Horley, Surrey RH6 9LN (01293) 786680* **£185***, plus special breaks; 15 individually furnished rms. Elizabethan house in fine three-acre garden with roses and lakes; beams, oak panelling, fresh flowers and open fires in elegant rms, and enjoyable traditional cooking in no smoking restaurant; disabled access

NUTFIELD TQ2950 **Nutfield Priory** *Nutfield, Redhill, Surrey RH1 4EL (01737) 824400* **£140***, plus special breaks; 60 rms. Impressive Victorian Gothick hotel in 40 acres of parkland with lovely elaborate carvings, stained-glass windows, gracious day rooms, a fine panelled library, cloistered restaurant, and even an organ in the galleried grand hall; extensive leisure club with indoor heated swimming pool; dogs welcome in bedrooms

To see and do

Surrey Family Attraction of the Year

WEYBRIDGE TQ0862 **Brooklands Museum** 🎫 (B374) In its 1920s and 30s heyday this enjoyable place was almost as fashionable as Ascot, and its history is littered with records and important events. It was the world's first purpose-built motor-racing circuit, the site of the first British Grand Prix, the backdrop to the first 100 mph motor ride, and the setting of the first flight in a british-built aircraft. Those glory days are exhaustively re-created in a comprehensive series of displays, with a growing collection of racing cars, motorbikes and bicycles displayed in the restored clubhouse, and plenty of restored planes (including a Wellington bomber and a good few vintage Vickers and Hawker planes) in hangars around the sizeable site. Anyone interested in motoring or aviation history will be enthralled, and others may be surprised at how much they get out of it - just walking round the original banked concrete racetrack is surprisingly enjoyable. A trail leads you round all the exhibits (there's a good one on the history of the Grand Prix in a converted motoring shed), and there are often special events at weekends. Best of all is the annual Brooklands at Home in August, when they show off the fact that most of the exhibits here are still working, sometimes quite spectacularly. Their useful website - www.brooklandsmuseum.com - has all the upcoming dates; admission is generally the same as on non-event days. The museum's general appeal has been considerably widened with the addition of a hands-on science gallery - not as hi-tech as some, but children hugely enjoy it. You can build your own suspension bridge, power a train by hand, and send messages across the room using pulses of light. Meals, snacks, shop, good disabled access; cl Mon (exc bank hols), Good Fri, Christmas wk; (01932) 857381; £7 adults, £5 children 6-16. The family ticket is excellent value: two adults and up to three children are £18.

ABINGER COMMON TQ1245
Charmingly set village with pretty church, ancient pub (the Abinger Hatch) and duckpond surrounded by woodland - popular for walks.

ALBURY TQ0547
Attractive village with pleasant walks nearby, and glimpses of the Victorian mansion Albury Park - or at least its famous chimneys. The Drummond Arms is a civilised place for lunch.
St Peter and St Paul church (Albury Park) This pleasantly set disused Saxon church to the SE of the village has some interesting monuments; the nearby William IV (Little London) is an attractive walkers' pub.

BANSTEAD WOOD TQ2657
Popular strolling-ground, surprisingly peaceful despite the proximity of Surrey's northern suburbia and heavily used trunk roads. The prettily set Well House on Chipstead Lane has decent food.

BETCHWORTH TQ2149
Attractive village, pleasant for strolls along an annotated trail from a church where *Four Weddings and a Funeral* was filmed. The Dolphin is a decent pub, the Red Lion more of a dining place, and there's a nice drive via Brockham and Newdigate to Rusper in Sussex.

BOX HILL TQ1751
Surrey's most popular viewpoint, with a summit car park and walks on its steep juniper and boxwood slopes: wild orchids and butterflies in early summer, perhaps field mushrooms in early autumn; the Running Horses down on the B2209 has good food.

CHALDON TQ3155
Attractive church, particularly worth a visit for its unique wall painting of the *Ladder of Salvation*.

CHERTSEY TQ0467
A good few Georgian buildings in its main streets, and pleasant walks by the Thames - for instance from the

Kingfisher dining pub (Chertsey Bridge Rd).

Chertsey Abbey Medieval remains standing in Abbeyfields Park.

Chertsey Museum (the Cedars) Recently reopened in its original Georgian building (and now with more space for displays), this interesting museum has galleries devoted to changing fashions and attitudes towards children, accessories and local history. There's also a hands-on discovery zone, special events and temporary exhibitions. Improved shop, snacks, full disabled access; cl am wkdys, all day Sun, Mon, Easter bank hols and 25-26 Dec, 1 Jan; (01932) 565764; free.

Great Cockcrow Railway 🅰 (Hardwick Lane, Lyne, slightly NW) A notable miniature steam railway, with a unique signalling system. Snacks, disabled access; open Sun pm Apr-Oct; (01932) 255500; £2.50. The Golden Grove on St Ann's Hill out towards here is a nice spot for lunch.

Thorpe Park (A320 N) There's a tremendous amount to do here, with plenty of rides for thrill-seekers, and gentler activities for younger children. High points include a ten-looping roller-coaster, fun spinning water rapids ride, Detonator (which winches you up to 30 metres and fires you back down to the ground at nearly 50mph), and Vortex, where you're spun round at high speeds and then swung backwards and forwards; a recent addition is Nemesis: Inferno, a roller-coaster themed around a volcano, and another thrill ride Samurai is due to open in Apr. You'll still find old favourites like Loggers Leap (the highest log flume in the country), and there are plenty of less frantic rides for younger children, particularly in the Octopus's garden area; also several play areas, and lots of water-based activities around Neptune's Kingdom, and a man-made beach and pools (worth bringing swimming costumes). Across the lake (reached by either a train or waterbus) is a decent-sized traditional working farm, with animals and craft centre. Readers highly recommend their special events, and the staff are friendly. Although it's very well organised (and maintained), expect crowds and queues on busy summer days. Meals, snacks,

shop, disabled access; open end Mar-Oct, though usually cl some wkdys at either end of the season, best to phone first; (0870) 444 4466; from £19-£26 (you can save money by booking in advance).

CHESSINGTON TQ1762

Chessington World of Adventures (A243) This is the place to head for unadulterated fun. The big thrill ride is Rameses' Revenge, which spins you round 360 degrees at speeds of up to 60 mph, while plummeting towards a rock-lined water-blast pit. Though the more traditional-seeming Rattlesnake looks a little gentler it still packs quite a punch (all have height restrictions); Dragon's Fury is the new roller-coaster for families. There's plenty to amuse younger children, from the Dragon River log flume and Action Man Training HQ to the simpler rides around Toytown, and under-8s have a new park area. Also, there's the once-famous zoo from which everything else developed, with sea lion and penguin displays at set times throughout the day, and a good reptile and insect house. A monorail gives bird's-eye views of the lions, tigers and meerkats, and from an african-style game lodge you can watch their large family of gorillas. Meals, snacks, shop, some disabled access; open Apr-Nov, and 19 Dec-4 Jan (exc 25-26 Dec and 1 Jan), best to check Sept-Nov as they close some days for maintenance; (0870) 4447777; from £19-£25 depending on the season. The Star down towards the M25 is a good value food stop.

CHIDDINGFOLD SU9635

Exceptional village in fine countryside, with one window of its church made up from locally excavated fragments of 13th-c glass made here.

Ramster 🅰 (A283 S) Splendid Edwardian woodland garden, bog garden and millennium garden. Teas, plant sales, disabled access; open 24 Apr-27 Jun; (01428) 654167; £4. The nearby Rams Nest does good value lunches, in appealing surroundings.

COBHAM TQ1159

Quite a busy shopping town, with some fine older buildings around the church and in Church St; just SW, Downside Common is a classic cricket green, with

cottages scattered around it, and an attractive pub - the Cricketers.
Cobham mill (Mill Rd) Prettily set working watermill, authentically restored by enthusiastic locals. Shop, limited disabled access; open pm 2nd Sun of month Apr-Oct; (01932) 867387; free, donations welcome.
Painshill Park (A425 slightly W) These beautiful 18th-c landscaped gardens are a continual surprise, with a lake with seemingly endless bays and inlets, a chinese bridge, waterwheel, grotto, Gothic temple, even a turkish tent, and other follies at every turn (some are being restored as part of ongoing renovation work). Lots of unusual trees and shrubs too. Meals, snacks and picnic area, shop, disabled access (best to ring); cl Mon (exc bank hols), plus Tues Nov-Feb, and 25 Dec; (01932) 868113; £6.
COMPTON SU9547
Watts Picture Gallery (Down Lane) Tranquil rural setting for memorial gallery to Victorian Symbolist painter and sculptor G F Watts (in his time one of the most celebrated artists in the world), with over 250 of his works. Shop, disabled access to main gallery; cl Thurs, and am Mon, Tues, Fri and Sun, plus 24-25 Dec and Good Fri; (01483) 810235; free. Just down the road the unique circular Watts Chapel in the village cemetery is covered in Celtic and art nouveau decoration, and was designed and built by his wife Mary Watts and villagers. The village church is attractive, and the tearoom nearby serves over 25 different teas.
DEVIL'S PUNCHBOWL SU8936
A spectacular fold of the downs, with nature trails through mixed woodlands, quiet valleys and sandy heaths with scattered ponds. The area is quite developed but the woods and intricacy of the landscape give it a wholesome country feel, and the footpath network is dense. **Gibbet Hill** above the A3 gets a view over most of it.
DORKING TQ1649
Pleasant market town with lots of antiques shops, and a local museum in West St (open pms Weds and Thurs and all day Sat; (01306) 743821; donations). The roads S of the A25 W of here are the county's most pleasant

drives, and the steep road up Box Hill N opens a great panorama. The 16th-c Kings Arms in West St has decent food.
Denbies Wine Estate 🔟 (A24 just N) Britain's biggest vineyard, and at 107 hectares (265 acres) bigger than most in Europe. The tour is unique and you don't have to be a wine buff to enjoy it. Beginning with a 20-minute film in their unusual 360-degree cinema, you are then taken through the winery on a road train to the cellars where you can try out some of their produce. An outdoor train tour takes you round the vineyard (Apr-Oct, £4). Meals and snacks (in conservatory restaurant) and B&B, big shop, good disabled access; cl 25-26 Dec, 1 Jan; (01306) 876616; £7.25, combined ticket for outdoor and indoor tours £10.25. Fine views and walks nearby, and the Stepping Stones at Westhumble has enjoyable food.
DOWNS LINK PATH TQ0735
Follows a disused railway track through pleasant countryside - popular for walks and family cycling. The Thurlow Arms at the former Baynards Station nr Cox Green is handy for access.
EAST CLANDON TQ0651
Hatchlands (A246) Handsome 18th-c brick house with more floors than are visible from the outside, thanks to an ingenious use of false windows. The grand rooms are especially notable for their ceilings and fireplaces, early examples of the work of Robert Adam. A fine collection of historic keyboard instruments includes a piano once owned by Marie Antoinette. The formal garden was designed by Gertrude Jekyll. Meals, snacks, shop, disabled access; cl Nov-Mar, house and garden also cl am plus Mon, Fri (exc Aug) and Sat exc bank hols; park walks daily from 11; (01483) 222482; £6, £2.50 park walk; NT. A visit here is easily combined with Clandon Park at West Clandon (joint ticket £9). The Wishing Well is a good value dining pub.
EPSOM TQ2158
The Derby held here, and first run in 1780, is one of the oldest flat races in the world - and a grand social event; (01372) 726311 for dates. The nearby Derby Arms is a reliable food pub. Other famous racecourses in this area include Sandown Park (01372) 463072;

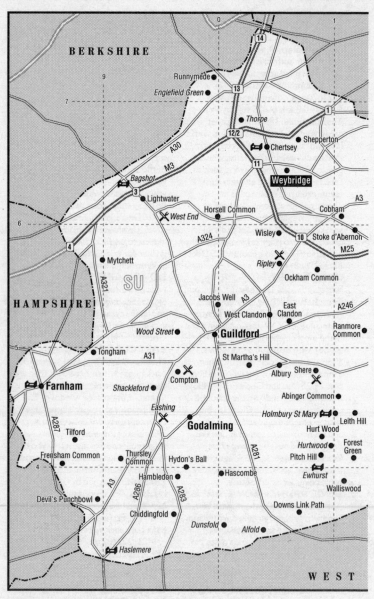

Kempton Park (01932) 782292; and
Lingfield (01342) 834800.
Horton Park Children's Farm
(B280 W) Plenty of animals to feed and
cuddle, tractor rides (50p), an
adventure playground and indoor play
area. Meals, snacks and picnic area,
shop, disabled access; cl 25-26 Dec;

(01372) 743984; £4.30.
ESHER TQ1464
Claremont Landscape Garden (off
A307) The oldest surviving landscaped
garden in the country, laid out by
Vanbrugh and Bridgeman before 1715
and extended and naturalised by
William Kent; 20 enchanting hectares

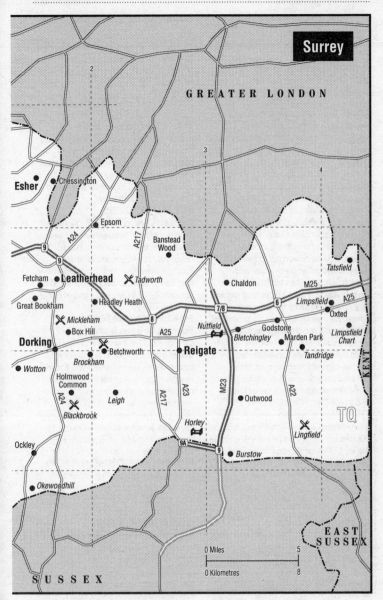

Surrey

GREATER LONDON

Esher ● Chessington

● Epsom

Banstead Wood

Tatsfield

Fetcham ● **Leatherhead** ✕ Tadworth

Great Bookham ● Headley Heath

● Chaldon

M25 A25

● Limpsfield

Oxted

✕ Mickleham

● Box Hill

Nutfield

Godstone

● Bletchingley   Marden Park

Limpsfield Chart

Dorking ✕ Betchworth ● **Reigate**

Wotton Brockham

Tandridge

Holmwood Common

● Leigh

● Outwood

A22

✕ Blackbrook

Horley

✕ Lingfield

Ockley

● Burstow

● Okewoodhill

EAST SUSSEX

0 Miles   5

0 Kilometres   8

SUSSEX

KENT

TQ

(49 acres) with lakes, turf amphitheatre, grotto, island, guided walks in summer, children's trail and braille guide. Meals, snacks, shop, disabled access; cl Mon Nov-Mar, 25 Dec; (01372) 467806; *£4; NT. On the other side of town Marneys in a pretty spot on Weston Green (Alma Rd) has good interesting food.

FARNHAM SU8346
Handsome town that owed its Georgian heyday to the importance of local corn and hops. Many elegant buildings from this period remain, and there are some even older ones such as the early 17th-c Spinning Wheel. The area around Castle St is especially nice

to stroll round, and on the outskirts there's enjoyable food at the Spotted Cow in Lower Bourne and Bat & Ball in Wrecclesham.

Birdworld & Underwater World 🅰️ (Holt Pound, off A325 3m SW - actually just over the Hampshire border) This popular place has masses of birds from tiny tanagers to rheas, emus and ostriches, spread over 10 hectares (26 acres) of thoughtfully laid out gardens and parkland. Children can go right up to some of the birds, and to the animals in the farmyard (some of which they can feed), and there's always a section with baby birds. They have a good programme of shows, feeding sessions and displays, and school hol children's activities. Other highlights include the parrots flying around their aviary, and the decent aquarium with tropical and other freshwater and marine fish, and a few alligators in a jungly swamp. There are several decent play areas, and many features are under cover. Interesting talks on their birds of prey, though the feeding of these is not for the squeamish. The woodland trail leads round to a very good, extensive garden centre. Meals, snacks, shop, disabled access; usually cl wkdys Nov to mid-Feb (exc Christmas school hols), and 25-26 Dec; (01420) 22140; £9.75. The Halfway House down the A325 at Bucks Horn Oak has good fresh food.

Castle For 800 years a residence of the Bishops of Winchester. Most of the buildings have been adapted to suit the briefing organisation based here, but the major rooms, inc the great hall, can be seen on a guided tour Weds 2-4 pm. Snacks, shop; cl 25 Dec-1 Jan; (01252) 721194; £2.50.

Castle Keep Administered separately; includes the massive foundations and entrance of a Norman tower. Shop; usually open Easter-Oct, but phone to check; (01252) 713393; £2.50, inc Walkman tour; EH.

Foyer and James Hockey Galleries 🅰️ (Surrey Institute of Art & Design, Falkner Rd) Balanced programmes of exhibitions inc art, craft, design and multi-media, housed in two galleries, one a swish extension. Disabled access; cl Sun and bank hols; (01252) 892668; free.

Maltings Gallery (Bridge Sq) Diverse arts and crafts. Meals, snacks, limited disabled access; cl wknds (exc special events), 1 wk over Christmas, and Easter wknd; (01252) 726234; free, may be a small charge for national exhibitions.

Museum of Farnham (West St) Excellent local history museum; some William Cobbett memorabilia (his picturesque birthplace in Bridge Sq is now a pub named after him), and a pleasant walled garden. Shop, disabled access to ground floor; cl Sun and Mon, around a wk at Christmas, and Good Fri; (01252) 715094; free.

FETCHAM TQ1555

Bocketts Farm Park 🅰️ Working farm in a pretty, historic setting, with traditional and rare breeds, tractor rides, play areas, goat milking, pig racing, a huge four-lane slide and a new play barn. Meals, snacks, shop, disabled access; cl 25-26 Dec and 1 Jan; (01372) 363764; £4.75.

FOREST GREEN TQ1241

Forge & Dragon Gallery (B2127 Ockley Rd) Picturesque working forge dating from the 16th c, and prettily set by the village green (where the Parrot has good food). A gallery shows the resourceful work of resident artist/ironworker James Davies - usually on hand to discuss any personal requests. Some disabled access; cl 1-2pm, Sun, and 24 Dec-2 Jan; (01306) 621022; free.

FRENSHAM COMMON SU8540 Popular for walks, with heather and woodland around a lake formed in the 13th c for fish breeding. The Holly Bush does good value food.

GODALMING SU9643 Attractive town with a good few interesting buildings and, because of its narrow streets (part cobbled and pedestrianised), a more old-fashioned feel than most in Surrey. The 18th-c Kings Arms & Royal (High St) is a nice place for a bar lunch, and its Tsar's Lounge is worth seeing.

Busbridge Lakes 🅰️ (Hambledon Rd, off B2130 S) Very pretty spot with three lakes in fine parkland - exotic waterfowl, peacocks, ornamental pheasants and many other kinds of bird, as well as follies and grottoes throughout the grounds. Snacks, shop; only open 9-18 Apr, 2-3 and 30-31 May, and 21-30 Aug; (01483) 421955; £4. Down in Hambledon the Merry Harriers has reasonably priced simple food, with good walks nearby.

Godalming Museum (High St) 15th-c house with local history, interactive displays, Gertrude Jekyll gallery and Jekyll-style walled garden. Snacks, shop, some disabled access; cl Mon, Sun and around Christmas-New Year; (01483) 426510; free. The town hall opposite is known affectionately by the locals as the Pepper Pot.

GODSTONE TQ3551
Attractive despite its main roads, spread around a broad green with a duck pond, and a pretty group of houses around the imposing **church**, 14th/15th c with a Norman tower. The White Hart is a sound beamed and timbered dining pub.

Godstone Farm (Tilburstow Hill) Friendly small 16-hectare (40-acre) working farm; children are encouraged to touch the animals, and even climb in with some of them; good play areas. Meals, snacks, shop, disabled access; cl 25-26 Dec; (01883) 742546; £4.30 per child (accompanied adults free).

Godstone Vineyard (Quarry Rd, just off A22 N) Looking up to the downs, this friendly vineyard produces a range of ciders and apple juice as well as its wines; free tastings. Meals, snacks, shop, disabled access; cl 24-26 Dec, and 1 Jan; (01883) 744590. Quarry Rd winds on down into Flower Lane, where the same people own Flower Farm, with pick-your-own produce; cl Oct-Apr; (01883) 743636; free.

GREAT BOOKHAM TQ1352
Polesden Lacey (off A246 S)
Attractive Regency house once at the centre of Edwardian high society, now with photographs of some of the notable guests, as well as splendid tapestries, porcelain, Old Masters and other art. The spacious grounds have a walled rose garden, and open-air theatre. In Mar they're unveiling the latest phase in their 2-year garden restoration project: the potting shed, Edwardian coldframes and nursery will be open to the public. Meals, snacks, shop, disabled access; house cl Mon exc

bank hols, Tues, and all Nov-Mar, grounds open all year; (01372) 458203; *£3 house only, *£5 grounds only; NT. On the other side of the extended commuter village, the Bookham Commons, with a mixture of thorny scrub (full of birds), small lakes, marshy bits and oak woods, are well wooded and attractive. In Effingham nearby, the Plough has honest home cooking.

GUILDFORD SU9949
The area's biggest town (despite having a cathedral it's not a city), Guildford is older than you might at first think; although many of the buildings are Georgian-fronted, what's behind often dates back much further. The sloping High St has attractive parts as well as its briskly modern shops, with interesting buildings inc the **Abbots Hospital** and the **Grammar School**. Tunsgate Arch is the start for free guided walks of the town - 2.30pm every Sun and Weds, also 11.30am Mon May-Sept, also 7.30 Thurs till end Aug.

Grange Air Champagne Balloon Flights (Bannisters Field) If you're brave enough (and you don't get the champagne till afterwards), hot-air balloons give a good view of the area, flights most days (exc winter), weather permitting; phone for information (01420) 520717; £139.

Guildford Boat House (Millbrook) Old-established boat house where you can hire narrow and rowing boats for the Wey Navigation (see below); cl Oct-Mar (exc narrow boats, available all year) phone for information; (01483) 504494. Nearby the Weyside does enjoyable up-to-date food in a lovely riverside setting.

Guildford Castle The hill of the ruined 12th-c **castle** has fine views of the town, and a garden in the former castle ditch. Restoration work on the castle has revealed evidence of an earlier reception chamber, and as we went to press the council had just agreed extra funding for a new visitor centre to view the chamber; they hope to reopen in spring, but best to phone; (01483) 444333.

Guildford Cathedral The cathedral which was begun in 1936 (and completed in 1961) is one of only two entirely 20th-c Anglican cathedrals in the country; it's quite austere, but has a cool elegance inside. Meals, snacks, shop, disabled access; (01483) 565287; donations.

Guildford Museum (Quarry St) Local history from prehistoric man to the Victorians, with a display on Lewis Carroll, who died here in 1898. Shop; cl Sun, Good Fri, 25-26 Dec and some bank hols; (01483) 444751; free. Carroll is buried in the cemetery on the Mount, the continuation of the High St.

Guildhall (High St) Mainly Tudor, with one of the few surviving sets of Elizabethan standard measures. Disabled access to ground floor only; usually open only for guided tours at 2 and 3pm Tues and Thurs, cl last 2 wks Aug, and 23 Dec-2 Jan, phone to check; (01483) 444035; free.

Loseley Park (off B3000, 3 miles SW) Most people are familiar with the name from the yoghurts and ice-cream produced here. The Elizabethan mansion was built in 1562, and has fine panelling, paintings and tapestries; it's been home to the More-Molyneux family for almost 450 years. The walled gardens include an amazing rose garden with over 1,000 bushes, and a fountain garden. Meals, snacks, shop and plant sales, limited disabled access; cl Mon exc bank hols, Tues, house open pm 2 Jun-29 Aug, gardens open May-Sept; (01483) 304440; £6 house and gardens, £3 gardens only. Within a pleasant walk, the Withies at Compton is a good civilised dining pub.

River Wey & Godalming Navigation This 17th-c canal, passing through some fine scenery, by 1763 linked Godalming (where the wharf has some handsome Georgian buildings) with the Thames. A visitor centre at **Dapdune Wharf** here has interactive exhibitions on the waterway and the people who lived and worked on it, housed in a restored Wey barge. A former gunpowder store now houses a hands-on activity area; they also have children's trails, guided nature walks and various special events, and you can take a 40-min boat trip from here (£2.50, best to phone for dates). Snacks and picnic areas, shop, disabled access; cl Tues, Weds and Nov-Mar; (01483) 561389; £3. The locks and towpath

have been restored by the NT, and you can walk all the way from Godalming to Weybridge, some 20 miles, or hire boats from Farncombe Boat House; Mar-Nov; (01483) 421306.

HAMBLEDON SU9639
You can climb inside what's said to be a witch's tree in front of the church here; walk round the tree three times and the witch may well appear. Restore your poise in the Merry Harriers; pleasant walks nearby. Open by appointment, 16th-c timber-framed **Oakhurst Cottage** (Cricket Green) has been restored and furnished as a simple labourer's dwelling; (01428) 684090; cl am, plus Fri, Mon, Tues, and all Nov-Mar; £3; NT.

HASCOMBE SU9940
Lovely village with an interesting **church**; the White Horse is popular for lunch (with a great garden), and the B2130 S and then the Dunsfold—Chiddingfold back road is a pleasant drive.

Winkworth Arboretum (B2130 just NW) Nearly 40 hectares (100 acres) of lovely hillside woodland, with fine views over the North Downs - esp nice in spring, and with unusual flaring colours in the autumn; dogs welcome on leads. Snacks, shop spring-autumn, limited disabled access; (01483) 208477; *£4; NT.

HEADLEY HEATH TQ2053
Sandy walks and rides through heather, birch woods - and as summer wears on rather too much bracken.

HOLMWOOD COMMON TQ1845
Popular for walks, with undulating oak and birch woods and lots of good paths; the Plough at Blackbrook is good for lunch.

HORSELL COMMON TQ0060
A touch of interest for walkers in the sandpits which inspired and saw the start of H G Wells's *War of the Worlds*; the Cricketers by the green at Horsell Birch has decent food (all day Sun and bank hols).

HURT WOOD TQ0943
Large areas of private broadleafed forest around here are open to walkers; relatively unfrequented, so it's a good place to spot birds and wild animals.

HYDON'S BALL SU9739
There's unspoilt walking terrain off the road between Loxhill and Hydestile S of

Godalming, with Hydon's Ball a fine viewpoint, though rather hard to find.
JACOBS WELL TQ0053
Burpham Court Farm Park 🐄 The bit children like best is the help-the-farmer session (around 3pm in winter, 4pm in summer), where they get the chance to join in activities such as feeding the pigs, collecting eggs or bringing in the goats. They've llamas and an aviary as well as rare breeds; play and picnic areas, seasonal activities (inc lambing Feb-Apr and shearing May-Jun), and you can buy a day ticket to fish here. Snacks, shop, some disabled access (but no facilities); cl 25-26 Dec; (01483) 576089; £3.95; voucher entitles you to a free bag of animal feed.
LEATHERHEAD TQ1658
Fire & Iron Gallery (Oxshott Rd, A244 N) Unusual exhibitions of ornamental metalwork. Shop; limited disabled access; cl Sun, and bank hols; (01372) 386453; free.
Museum of Local History (Church St) In a pretty timber-framed 17th-c building, and well worth a visit. Shop, disabled access to ground floor; open Sat and pm Thurs-Fri Apr-Christmas; (01372) 386348; free. The Dukes Head in the pedestrianised High St is pleasant for lunch, and there are riverside walks nearby.
LEITH HILL TQ1343
Perhaps the best stretch of country for walkers in Surrey, with heather, sandy walks, steep pine woods and tremendous views. An 18th-c tower on top of the hill, the highest point in SE England, is the best viewpoint of all, with a new telescope at the top, and an unexpected view of S London - which feels 100 miles away. Snacks; open wknds and bank hols, plus Weds mid-Apr to Sept; (01306) 711777; £1.50. Friday Street, with a lake, is one starting point for switchback routes S through a series of brackeny summits to the tower. Leith Hill can also be approached through attractive farmland from the S, from Ockley, or from the Parrot (good mealtime food, open all day) at Forest Green.
LIGHTWATER SU9262
Lightwater Country Park Visitor centre with heathland exhibition and plenty of nature trails. Snacks, shop,

disabled access; park open all year, visitor centre usually open Sun plus pm Tues-Fri in school hols, cl Jan-Mar; (01276) 479582; free. The Inn at West End is handy for a good lunch.
MARDEN PARK TQ3653
A peaceful spot for strolls - surprising, as it's so near suburbia and even the M25.
MYTCHETT SU8955
Basingstoke Canal Now fully rehabilitated; in its Surrey section it does not pass through such fine scenery as the Wey Navigation, but its towpath has been well restored. The **Canal Visitor Centre** (Mytchett Place Rd) has displays on the canal, and good access to its towpath, with boat trips (usually wknds and bank hols Apr-Sept, and daily in school hols Easter-Oct). Snacks, shop, disabled access; cl Mon (exc bank hols and school summer hols), wknds Oct-Easter; (01252) 370073; free.
OCKHAM COMMON TQ0858
Chatley Heath Semaphore Tower (Old Lane, off A3 to Effingham) Unique tower rather like a lighthouse, the only surviving member of a chain that sent messages by visible signals between the Admiralty in London and Portsmouth, long before telephones or telegraph; excellent views from the top of the 88 steps. Surrounding it is over a square mile of heath and woodland, with a nature trail and good walks (inc the 20-minute trek from the car park to the tower). Shop; open pm wknds and bank hols Apr-Sept, plus Weds in school hols, 1st Sun of month only during winter; (01372) 458822; £2. The extraordinary 'gothick' Hautboy (Ockham Lane) has good food.
OCKLEY TQ1439
Some attractive old houses along the Roman road here, with the Inn on the Green, Kings Arms and Old School House all doing good value food.
Hannah Peschar Sculpture Garden (Black and White Cottage, Standon Lane) Lush garden filled with contemporary sculpture: the water garden is now more like a tropical rainforest than the cottage garden it started as, and the sculptures and ceramics blend perfectly with its unusual design. Mostly disabled access but no facilities; open Fri-Sat, and pm Sun and bank hols (Tues-Thurs by

appointment) May-Oct; (01306) 627269; £8.

OUTWOOD TQ3245

Spread around an attractive common, with an antiques shop, and adjacent NT woodlands which are ideal for a picnic.

Outwood post mill Very well preserved, Britain's oldest working windmill, built in 1665. It's a lovely spot, 120 metres (400 ft) up, with ducks and geese wandering freely in the grounds. The adjacent woods look lovely in Apr when the bluebells are out. Shop, disabled access to ground floor only; open pm Sun and bank hols Easter to mid-Oct; (01342) 843644; £2.

OXTED TQ4055

Titsey Place and Gardens Below the North Downs in parkland that's peaceful despite the nearby M25, this is one of Surrey's largest surviving great estates. Although parts date back to the 16th c, most of the rooms inside are 19th-c (one bedroom is early Georgian). The grounds include four hectares (ten acres) of formal gardens with a walled kitchen garden. The picturesque hamlet has an ancient yew tree reputed to be 1,000 years old. Shop; open pm Weds and Sun mid-May to Sept; (01273) 407056; £4.50 house and gardens, £2 gardens only. On the B269 the Botley Hill Farmhouse is a popular dining pub, and over in Tatsfield the Old Ship prettily set opposite the duckpond on Westmore Green has enjoyable food.

PITCH HILL TQ0842

Though largely wooded, this is good country for walkers, with pleasant views on the relatively open approach from Ewhurst; above the village, the Windmill pub has glorious views from its garden.

RANMORE COMMON TQ1551

Chalk downland with sheep, wild orchids and dense woodlands, within close range of Polesden Lacey. You can walk on the well marked North Downs Way, which emerges on to unspoilt downland on Denbies Hillside (car park nearby), a rich site for butterflies; here you look over Dorking and the Weald. The main landmark hereabouts is St Barnabas church by Gilbert Scott, the so-called 'Church on the North Downs' of 1859, hinting at the grandeur of his

other projects such as the Albert Memorial. The Stepping Stones at Westhumble has good value food.

REIGATE TQ2548

Barons Cave tours Below the peaceful castle grounds is a network of old tunnels, prime among them this splendid cavernous passageway with all sorts of myths and stories attached. The tours are enthusiastic and entertaining; for an appointment ring Malcolm Tadd of the Wealden Cave and Mine Society on (01737) 823456; cl Oct-Apr; £3.50. Among the few surviving original buildings in this mainly modern town are one or two timber-framed houses around the High St, where the beamed Red Cross has decent food.

Windmill church (off A25 W) The 250-year-old former windmill on Reigate Heath was converted into a church in 1880. They still have services on the 3rd Sun each month in summer and perhaps at Christmas. Disabled access; open all year - if closed, key at golf clubhouse. There are pleasant walks out here, and the Skimmington Castle is a classic country pub.

RUNNYMEDE TQ0071

(A328) A field by a main road; not worth visiting unless you are fascinated by Magna Carta, though up the hill beyond the trees, the nearby memorials to John F Kennedy and the named aircrew who died during World War II are dignified and touching. The Barley Mow at Englefield Green has good value food.

SHEPPERTON TQ0766

One of the best places to watch the comings and goings on the **River Thames**, with the **Wey Navigation** joining the river here; the big Thames Court (Ferry Lane), with a good waterside terrace, has decent food all day, and there's a quiet and attractive 18th-c village square with a pleasant church.

SHERE TQ0747

Very picturesque village, with 17th-c timber-framed cottages, a grassy-banked stream with ducks and ford, and lots of interesting corners. In the partly Norman **church** a quatrefoil blocked hole in the chancel wall marks the spot where a 14th-c anchorite had herself walled in, being fed through another hole outside. The Malt House is a decent local history museum, and the ancient White Horse is a good place for lunch. The village is within reach of both the North Downs around Ranmore Common and the greensand hills to the S; the view from the Ewhurst road is particularly memorable.

ST MARTHA'S HILL TQ0348 (E of Guildford) The church on its summit can be reached only on foot, and by starting from the attractive village of Chilworth, you can see the long-abandoned gunpowder mills by the Tilling Bourne.

STOKE D'ABERNON TQ1259 **Stoke d'Abernon church** Notable for the earliest surviving memorial brass in Britain, dating from the 13th c; set in the floor of the chancel, it's very well preserved.

THURSLEY COMMON SU9040 Mainly pleasant sandy walking country, with heather and quite often unusual birds, also boggy patches with shallow ponds where dragonflies breed.

TILFORD SU8543 **Rural Life Centre** 🖼 (The Reeds, just W) Carefully displayed collection of historic farm machinery, tools and crafts, spread over four hectares (ten acres) of field and woodland, with an arboretum, playground, narrow gauge railway on Sun, and 19th-c cricket pavilion, chapel and village hall. Meals, snacks, shop, disabled access; cl Mon (exc bank hols), Tues, and mid-Oct to Mar exc Weds; (01252) 795571; £5. The village has a massive oak tree, thought to be 800 years old; the Barley Mow between the river and the attractive cricket green is a pleasant spot for lunch, there are nice walks in the area, and it's not far from here to the remains of Waverley Abbey.

TONGHAM SU8848 **Hogs Back Brewery** 🖼 (Manor Farm, The Street) Tours of friendly little brewery, using traditional methods to produce its nine distinctive regular ales, and sometimes seasonal ones too. The shop has over 500 different british, belgian and german beers (as well as their own), alongside english wines and farm ciders. Tours 6.30pm Weds, Thurs and Fri, 11am and 2.30pm Sat, 2.30 Sun, other times by

arrangement; shop open daily (exc 25-26 Dec and 1 Jan); mostly disabled access; (01252) 783000; tour £6.50 (inc tastings and commemorative glass). You can also try their beer with an enjoyable lunch at the nearby Shepherd & Flock (Moor Park Lane, off A31/A325 roundabout).

WALLISWOOD TQ1138 Attractive village, with delightful woodland walk from the old-fashioned Scarlett Arms to the 13th-c church.

WEST CLANDON TQ0451 **Clandon Park** (A247) Grand 18th-c house with unusual collection of porcelain birds, Meissen figurines, and fine furnishings and paintings. Regular concerts in the grand two-storeyed Marble Hall. Also the Queen's Royal Surrey regimental museum. The gardens have a Maori house brought over from New Zealand in 1892, a grotto and a sunken dutch garden. Meals, snacks, shop, disabled access to ground floor; cl Fri, Sat and Mon exc bank hols, and all Nov-Mar (exc Sun-Thurs 1-23 Dec) ; (01483) 222482; £6, joint ticket with Hatchlands £9; NT. The 16th-c Bulls Head does good value lunches.

WEYBRIDGE TQ0862 **Brooklands Museum** See *separate family panel on p.567.* In the town the waterside Old Crown (Thames St), Badgers Rest (Oatlands Chase) and Prince of Wales (Cross Rd) do good value food.

WISLEY TQ0658 **Wisley Garden** (A3) These 240-acre gardens have come a long way since they were developed in 1904 as experimental gardens for the Royal Horticultural Society; it's a mix of grand landscaped gardens with all sorts of model and trial gardens, orchard, woodland and alpine meadow. There are exemplary glasshouses; look out for herons. The gardens get very busy (esp at wknds) but are big enough to cope; special events and demonstrations. Good meals and snacks, shop and garden centre, disabled access; cl 25 Dec; (01483) 224234; £6.

Other attractive villages, all with decent pubs, include Alfold TQ0334, Bletchingley TQ3250 (Norman church), Brockham TQ1949 (lovely green and church), Dunsfold TQ0036 (ditto), Englefield Green SU9970 (handy for Savill Garden in Berkshire), Holmbury St Mary TQ1144, Hurtwood TQ0845, Leigh TQ2246, Limpsfield TQ4053 (church where Delius is buried), Limpsfield Chart TQ4251 (good walks), Ripley TQ0556, Shackleford SU9345, Thorpe TQ0268 and Wood Street SU9550.

Beside those mentioned, other **churches** worth a look include Burstow TQ3140, Okewoodhill TQ1337, Tandridge TQ3750, Tatsfield TQ4156 and Wotton TQ1247. You'll usually have to get the key from a local keyholder.

Popular starts or finishes for **walks** include the William IV at Little London TQ0646, Sportsman at Mogador TQ2452, Donkey at Charleshill

SU8944, Plough high on its hill at Coldharbour TQ1543 and Surrey Oaks at Newdigate TQ1942.

Besides places already mentioned for the **River Thames**, the Swan in Staines TQ0471 (The Hythe), the Magpie in Sunbury TQ1068 (Thames St), the Swan (Manor Rd) and Weir (Sunbury Lane) in Walton-on-Thames TQ0966 and the Fox on the River (Queens Rd) in Thames Ditton TQ1561 all have good views and access to the river. The county council has guided walks all year, exploring historical or more usually natural history themes; a typical Sun might have eight or more to choose from. For the current programme ring (08456) 009009.

Where to eat

BETCHWORTH TQ2149 **Dolphin** *The Street* (01737) 842288 Bustling, genuinely friendly village local with homely front room, panelled back bar, three open fires and some 400-year-old flagstones, real ales and 18 wines by the glass, popular good value food, and seats on the front courtyard and on lawn; no children inside. £19.85|£6.95

BLACKBROOK TQ1846 **Plough** (01306) 886603 Popular pub with award-winning hanging baskets and window-boxes, a no smoking red saloon bar and public bar with a formidable collection of ties, old saws on the ceiling, and flat irons and bottles, and generous helpings of good imaginative food inc popular curry evenings; very friendly service from smart staff, 16 wines by the glass, and well kept real ales; pretty cottagey garden with Swiss play house for children; cl Sun pm, 25-26 Dec, 1 Jan; limited disabled access. £30.50|£7.95

COMPTON SU9547 **Tea Shop** *Down Lane* (01483) 811030 Well liked cottagey teashop doing morning coffee, light lunches and afternoon tea, home-made cakes, scones and jams, free range eggs, a wide range of drinks inc interesting juices, seltzers, and fruity mineral waters, lots of indian, chinese, herbal and fruit teas, and different coffees; cl 24 Dec-6 Jan; partial disabled access.|£3.50

EASHING SU9443 **Stag** (01483) 421568 (Lower Eashing, just off A3) Partly 15th-c pub tucked away by converted mill buildings, charming old-fashioned bar on the right, cosy room beyond with dark-wallpapered walls, stag's head and big stag print, cookery books on shelves by the log fire, and an extensive, rambling, similarly furnished area on the left with a big woodburner in a huge fireplace; enjoyable food from big blackboard lists, well kept real ales, 15 wines by the glass, attentive and chatty neatly dressed staff, and a table of daily papers; tables out among mature trees; bdrms. £24|£8.25

LINGFIELD TQ3844 **Hare & Hounds** *Lingfield Common Rd* (01342) 832351 Homely country local with a light, airy open-plan bar (soft lighting and nightlights in the evening), bare boards and flagstones, an informal variety of scatter-cushioned dining chairs and other seats, black and white pictures of jazz musicians, and piped jazz; wide range of good imaginative food using local produce in quieter dining area with big abstract-expressionist paintings, well kept real ales, decent wines, and quick friendly service; tables out in a pleasant split-level garden, some on decking, and nice surrounding walks; no food Sun pm; dogs in bar. £30|£7.95

MICKLEHAM TQ1753 **King William IV** *Byttom Hill* (01372) 372590 Relaxed and unpretentious pub cut into the hillside with fine views from the snug front bar, a spacious back bar with log fires and fresh flowers, wide range of interesting daily specials inc good vegetarian choice, well kept ales, lovely terraced garden, and nice walks; cl 25 Dec, 26 Dec pm and 31 Dec; children over 12. £24|**£6.50**

MICKLEHAM TQ1753 **Running Horses** *Old London Rd (01372)* 372279 Attractive white-painted substantial inn with big sash windows and lovely flowering tubs and hanging baskets; two neatly kept relaxed bar rooms with fresh flowers, a big inglenook, lots of race tickets hanging from a beam, some good racing cartoons and hunting pictures; smart side restaurant with linen-covered tables, enjoyable, ambitious food (you can eat the restaurant food in the bar but not vice versa), well kept real ales, and good if pricy wines by the glass, from a serious list; professional bow-tied staff; plenty of seats out facing the church. £30|**£7.95**

RIPLEY TQ0556 **Michels** *The Clock House (01483)* 224777 Charming Georgian house with carefully cooked seasonal food (inc some unusual dishes), a good range of wines, and courteous, helpful service; cl Sun pm, Mon, part of Jan and Aug. £32/ 3-course lunch £15

SHERE TQ0747 **Kinghams** *Gomshall Lane (01483)* 202168 Beamed 17th-c cottage with a relaxed atmosphere, unpretentious surroundings, cheerful service, good sound cooking from a shortish menu inc daily fish dishes and vegetarian choices, and nice puddings; cl Mon and 25 Dec-3 Jan; disabled access. £35|**£10.95**

TADWORTH TQ2356 **Gemini** *28 Station Approach Rd (01737)* 812179 Bustling local restaurant with very good modern cooking using influences from all over the world, super puddings, a mainly french wine list, and courteous service; cl Sat am, Sun pm, Mon and 2 wks from Christmas; children over 12; disabled access. £37.95|**£10.50**

WEST END SU9460 **Inn at West End** *42 Guildford Rd (01276)* 858652 (A322) Open-plan roadside dining pub with constantly changing, consistently good food inc lots of fresh fish, and friendly efficient service; smart line of dining tables, crisp linen, attractive modern prints on canary yellow walls, also chatty bar area with plenty of pale woodwork and woodburner, tiled garden room and pleasant garden; good drinks inc espresso machine and good value champagne by the glass (landlord is a wine merchant, and can also supply by the case), daily papers; children over 5. £30|**£7.50**

Special thanks to Paul Kennedy, Nathalie Soanes, Michael and Jenny Back

SUSSEX

Lots to please everyone, from lively Brighton and action-packed family days out to interesting small towns and villages, stunning gardens, noble houses and castles, and attractively varied scenery

Of all the coastal resorts in Sussex, Brighton is the one with the most wide-ranging appeal. With a buzzing atmosphere, absorbing museums (two of the best have been recently revamped), and unusual shops and cafés, there's a whole host of things to keep all sorts of people busy. Though more restrained, Eastbourne in summer is another good choice for families. Picturesque Rye is ideal for a civilised afternoon, and nearby Camber Sands is one of the area's best beaches; Bognor Regis has clean water for swimming, Littlehampton has a lively new visitor centre, and Worthing is pleasant. Hastings has a few things to tempt the day-tripper, and Chichester has some handsome buildings.

Out of a crop of castles the most impressive are Bodiam and Arundel, and at Pevensey there are remarkable ruins; in the grounds of Herstmonceux Castle, there's a science centre. Newhaven Fort is perfect for exploring. Historic houses with more of a grown-up appeal are beautiful Glynde Place, Goodwood House (especially worthwhile if you're into riding), Elizabethan Parham House in Pulborough, and the more intimate St Mary's House in Bramber. You can visit Kipling's handsome home in Burwash, and fans of the Bloomsbury set will get much out of a visit to Charleston Farmhouse in Firle and Rodmell's Monks House. Standen (East Grinstead) is a fine example of the Arts and Crafts movement, and there's a restored 17th-c house in South Harting. Fishbourne Roman Palace and the Roman Villa and Museum in Bignor are unmissable for anyone fascinated by Roman Britain, and for more recent history, head to pretty Battle.

There's a great deal in Sussex to appeal to families. The Weald & Downland Open-Air Museum in Singleton has enough to occupy a whole day (there's an open-air museum in Amberley as well). Good bets for children include Drusillas Park zoo in gorgeous Alfriston, and the friendly Seven Sisters Sheep Centre in East Dean, and there are farm parks too at Wisborough Green, Coombes and Whitesmith.

Bentley Wildfowl & Motor Museum in Halland, Earnley Gardens, Knockhatch Adventure Park in Hailsham, and Paradise Park in Newhaven all have an entertaining medley of attractions for family excursions. Heaven Farm in Danehill and Stonywish country park at Ditchling are relaxing on a sunny day. Bird-lovers enjoy Wildfowl & Wetlands Trust in Arundel, and the falconry centre in aptly named Birdham.

Sussex is blessed with some of the county's very best gardens. Especially worth highlighting are Wakehurst Place at Ardingly (administered by the Royal Botanic Gardens, with something to see all year round), massive Leonardslee at Lower Beeding (another favourite, with its wallaby, deer, and a collection of Victorian motorcars), romantic Nymans at Handcross, Borde Hill near Haywards Heath (charming woodland walks), Pashley Manor Gardens near Ticehurst (wonderfully relaxing), Great Dixter at Northiam (you can look round the 15th-c house too), and Sheffield Park (autumn is a particularly nice time to visit). Also in Sheffield Park is the beautiful Bluebell line, the earliest preserved steam railway in Britain, and this year's top Sussex Family Attraction.

The Sussex countryside has very varied yet characteristic scenery: the South Downs, with handsome flint buildings and expansive views, culminating in Beachy Head and its nearby cliffs; the fascinating yew forests of Kingley Vale (fun for family walks); the sparsely wooded high sandy heathland of the Ashdown Forest; and the intricate landscapes of The Weald. Much of the coast is developed, but the great sea inlet of Chichester Harbour has some very attractive places along its shore.

Sussex has a good network of country walks; trails along the Saxon Shore and a 1066 Country Walk are noted in a free brochure, *Walk South East England*, available from most tourist information centres here (and also in Kent and Surrey). A 90-mile High Weald Landscape Trail, running from Horsham to Rye and crossing four counties, includes both trailside accommodation and transport links for day-walkers. A booklet (£8) is available from bookshops and tourist information centres, or phone (01622) 221526.

Quite a few of the places we recommend to stay in here are fine buildings in their own right.

Where to stay

ALFRISTON TQ5203 **George** *High St, Alfriston, Polegate, East Sussex BN26 5SY* (01323) 870319 **£60**; 7 rms. 14th-c timbered inn opposite the intriguing façade of the Red Lion, with massive low beams hung with hops, appropriately soft lighting, a log fire (or summer flower arrangement) in a huge stone inglenook, lots of copper and brass, plenty of sturdy stripped tables, and a thriving atmosphere; popular home-made food, a cosy candlelit restaurant, nice breakfasts, well kept real ales, and a jovial landlord; seats out in the charming flint-walled garden behind; cl 24-27 Dec; dogs welcome

AMBERLEY TQ0213 **Amberley Castle** *Church St, Amberley, Arundel, West Sussex BN18 9ND* (01798) 831992 **£188**; 19 very well equipped charming rms. Magnificent 900-year-old castle with suits of armour and weapons in the day rooms - as well as antiques, roaring fires and panelling; friendly service, imaginative food in no smoking 13th-c dining room, and exceptionally pretty gardens; children over 12

ARLINGTON TQ5507 **Bates Green** *Tye Hill Rd, Arlington, Polegate, East Sussex BN26 6SH* (01323) 482039 **£70***; 3 rms. Originally an 18th-c gamekeeper's cottage, now a no smoking farmhouse on a 123-acre sheep farm; beams and log fire in oak-panelled sitting room, tea and home-made cake on arrival, and big breakfasts with home-made preserves; sizeable plantsman's garden (open under the National Gardens Scheme), and a fine wood with lovely May bluebells and plenty of wildlife; cl Christmas; children over 10

BATTLE TQ7714 **Little Hemingfold Hotel** *189 Hastings Rd, Battle, East Sussex TN33 0TT* (01424) 774338 **£90***, plus special breaks; 12 rms. Partly 17th-c, partly early Victorian farmhouse in 40 acres of woodland, with trout lake, tennis, gardens, and lots of walks (the two labradors may come with you); comfortable sitting rooms, open fires, restful atmosphere and very good food using home-grown produce at own candlelit table; tennis court; children over 7; cl 2 Jan-12 Feb; dogs welcome in bedrooms

BATTLE TQ7414 **Powder Mills** *Powdermill Lane, Battle, East Sussex TN33 0SP* *(01424) 775511* **£110**, plus special breaks; 40 rms, some in annexe. Attractive 18th-c creeper-clad manor house in 150 acres of park and woodland with four lakes and outdoor swimming pool, and next to the 1066 Battlefield; country-house atmosphere, log fires and antiques in elegant day rooms, attentive service, and good modern cooking in Orangery restaurant; children over 10 in evening restaurant; disabled access; dogs welcome

BOSHAM SU8004 **Millstream** *Bosham Lane, Bosham, Chichester, West Sussex PO18 8HL (01243) 573234* **£129***, plus special breaks; 35 rms. Warmly friendly hotel in charming waterside village, with attractive bar and sitting room, open fire and fresh flowers, very good food using fresh local produce, good wine list, streamside garden; disabled access; dogs welcome in bedrooms

BRAMBER TQ1810 **Old Tollgate** *The Street, Bramber, Steyning, West Sussex BN44 3WE (01903) 879494* **£90.90**, plus special breaks; 31 smart and spacious rms. In a quiet village at the foot of the South Downs, this neatly kept hotel has comfortable public rooms, a popular carvery-style restaurant, tasty breakfasts, and helpful staff; disabled access

BRIGHTON TQ3004 **Grand** *97-99 Kings Rd, Brighton, East Sussex BN1 2FW (01273) 224300* **£240**, plus special breaks; 200 handsome rms, many with sea view. Famous Victorian hotel with marble columns and floors and fine moulded plasterwork in the luxurious and elegant day rooms; good service, very good food and fine wines, popular afternoon tea in sunny conservatory, a bustling nightclub, and health spa with indoor swimming pool; disabled access; dogs welcome in bedrooms ☺

BRIGHTON TQ3004 **Hotel du Vin & Bistro** *2-6 Ship St, Brighton, East Sussex BN1 1AD (01273) 718580* **£142**; 37 rms and 3 loft suites. Close to the seafront and set in the popular Lanes area, this hotel is housed in an unusual collection of part Gothic-styled buildings; lots of wood, brick, glass, and a feeling of space, a bustling bar, billiards gallery, good bistro food using the freshest of local ingredients, a fine wine list, and helpful young staff

BRIGHTON TQ3004 **Topps** *16-17 Regency Sq, Brighton, East Sussex BN1 2FG (01273) 729334* **£84**; 15 lovely comfortable rms, 11 with gas-effect coal fires and many with sea view. Carefully furnished and immaculately kept Regency town house nr seafront with thoughtful, attentive service, good breakfasts in attractive basement room, and a library/reception room

CHARLTON SU8812 **Woodstock House** *Charlton, Chichester, East Sussex PO18 0HU (01243) 811666* **£72**, plus special breaks; 12 rms. 18th-c country house close to Goodwood with a friendly, relaxed atmosphere, log fire in homely sitting room, cocktail bar, imaginative food in attractive dining room (also open to non-residents), and sun-trap inner courtyard garden; lots to see nearby and plenty of downland walks; dogs welcome in bedrooms

CHICHESTER SU8604 **Suffolk House** *East Row, Chichester, West Sussex PO19 1PD (01243) 778899* **£95**; 11 rms, some overlooking garden. Friendly Georgian house in centre and close to the cathedral, with homely comfortable lounge, little bar, traditional cooking in no smoking restaurant, good breakfasts, and small walled garden; disabled access; dogs by arrangement

CLIMPING TQ0000 **Bailiffscourt** *Climping St, Climping, Littlehampton, East Sussex BN17 5RW (01903) 723511* **£210**, plus special breaks; 39 rms, many with four-poster beds, winter log fires and super views. Mock 13th-c manor built only 60 years ago but with tremendous character - fine old iron-studded doors, huge fireplaces, heavy beams and so forth - in 30 acres of coastal pastures and walled gardens: elegant furnishings, enjoyable modern english and french food, fine wines, a relaxed atmosphere, and spa with indoor swimming pool, outdoor swimming pool, tennis and croquet; children over 7 in restaurant; disabled access; dogs welcome away from restaurant

CUCKFIELD TQ3024 **Ockenden Manor** *Ockenden Lane, Cuckfield, Haywards Heath, West Sussex RH17 5LD (01444) 416111* **£150**, plus special breaks; 22 individually decorated, pretty rms. Dating from 1520, this carefully extended manor house has antiques, fresh flowers and an open fire in the comfortable sitting room, good modern cooking in fine panelled restaurant, cosy bar, and super views of the South Downs from the neatly kept garden (in 9 acres)

EAST GRINSTEAD TQ3634 **Gravetye Manor** *Vowels Lane, East Grinstead, West Sussex RH19 4LJ (01342) 810567* **£202**; 18 lovely rms. Elizabethan manor house in magnificent grounds and gardens and run for four decades by the Herbert family; antiques, fine paintings, and lovely flower arrangements in spacious panelled public rooms, an excellent restaurant offering superb food using home-grown produce (inc spring water and free-range eggs) and their own home-smoked fish and meats, an exceptional wine list, exemplary service, and a relaxed, almost old-fashioned atmosphere; children over 7 (but babies welcome); restaurant cl 25 Dec pm to non-residents

EAST HOATHLY TQ5116 **Old Whyly** *Halland Rd, East Hoathly, Lewes, East Sussex BN8 6EL (01825) 840216* **£100**; 3 rms. Handsome 17th-c manor house in lovely garden with tennis court and swimming pool, fine antiques and paintings, delicious food, and super breakfasts with their own honey and eggs; plenty of walks nearby and very close to Glyndebourne (hampers can be provided); children must be well behaved; dogs welcome in bedrooms

EASTBOURNE TV6198 **Grand** *King Edward's Parade, Eastbourne, East Sussex BN21 4EQ (01323) 412345* **£165**, plus special breaks; 152 rms, many with sea views. Gracious and very well run Victorian hotel, with spacious, comfortable lounges, lots of fine original features, lovely flower arrangements, imaginative food in elegant restaurants, and courteous helpful service; leisure club and outdoor pool and terraces; disabled access; dogs (small) by arrangement ☺

ETCHINGHAM TQ6828 **King John's Lodge** *Sheepstreet Lane, Etchingham, East Sussex TN19 7AZ (01580) 819232* **£70***; 4 rms. Jacobean house in lovely 4-acre gardens - wonderful views, romantic and secret gardens, a wild garden with rose walk, white garden, and lily pond - plants and statuary for sale; guests' private sitting room, stone-mullioned windows, heavy beams and inglenook fireplaces, breakfasts served in Elizabethan dining room (on terrace in fine weather), and evening meals by arrangement; swimming pool, tennis court and croquet; cl Christmas and New Year; children over 7

FAIRLIGHT TQ8611 **Fairlight Cottage** *Warren Rd, Fairlight, Hastings, East Sussex TN35 4AG (01424) 812545* **£60***, plus winter breaks; 3 rms, one with four-poster. Comfortable and very friendly no smoking house in fine countryside with views over Rye Bay and plenty of rural and clifftop walks; big comfortable lounge (nice views), good breakfasts in elegant dining room or on new balcony; children over 10; dogs welcome

FITTLEWORTH TQ0118 **Swan** *Lower St, Fittleworth, Pulborough, West Sussex RH20 1EL (01798) 856429* **£65***; 15 rms. Attractive 14th-c inn with big inglenook log fire in comfortable lounge, friendly service, enjoyable food in beamed restaurant, attractive panelled side room, and sheltered back lawn; good nearby walks

FRANT TQ5935 **Old Parsonage** *Church Lane, Frant, Tunbridge Wells, Kent TN3 9DX (01892) 750773* **£87***, plus special breaks; 4 very pretty rms, 2 with four-posters. Just two miles from Tunbridge Wells, this carefully restored imposing former Georgian rectory has antiques, watercolours and plants in elegant sitting rooms, a spacious Victorian conservatory, good food in candlelit dining room, and balustraded terrace overlooking quiet 3-acre garden; several nearby walks; children over 7; dogs welcome in bedrooms

HARTFIELD TQ4837 **Bolebroke Mill** *Perry Hill, Edenbridge Rd, Hartfield, East Sussex TN7 4JP (01892) 770425* **£68**, plus special breaks; 5 rms, some in the mill and some in adjoining Elizabethan miller's barn. A working mill until 1948, this ancient place was mentioned in Domesday Book and is surrounded by mill streams and woodland. The internal machinery has been kept intact and steep narrow stairs lead

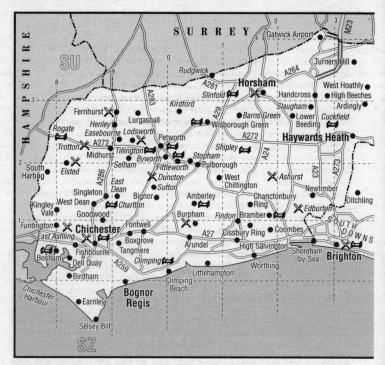

to bedrooms that were once big corn bins. Both this and the barn have their own sitting room; breakfasts are marvellous (good nearby pubs and restaurants for other meals), and the owners very friendly; no smoking; cl 1 wk before Christmas to 12 Feb; children over 8

LEWES TQ4109 **Shelleys** *High St, Lewes, East Sussex BN7 1XS (01273) 472361* **£150**, plus special breaks; 19 pretty rms. Once owned by relatives of the poet, this stylish and spacious 17th-c town house is warm and friendly, with good food, nice breakfasts and bar lunches in elegant dining room, and seats in the quiet back garden; limited disabled access

MAYFIELD TQ5826 **Middle House** *High St, Mayfield, East Sussex TN20 6AB (01435) 872146* **£75**; 5 spacious rms, some with four-posters. Old-world Elizabethan hotel nr church, with lovely panelled restaurant, red leather chesterfields and armchairs by cosy log fire, chatty locals' bar with big open fire, wide choice of bar food, attractive back garden and pleasant views

PEASMARSH TQ8823 **Flackley Ash** *Peasmarsh, Rye, East Sussex TN31 6YH (01797) 230651* **£124**; 45 rooms. Attractive and extended Georgian house in 5 acres of landscaped gardens with croquet and putting; good, nicely presented food using local produce in the conservatory or dining room, log fire in lounge bar, and indoor heated pool and leisure centre; dogs welcome in bedrooms

PETWORTH SU9721 **Old Railway Station** *Station Rd, Petworth, West Sussex GU28 0JF (01798) 342346* **£114***, plus special breaks; 8 rms, some in Pullman railway cars. Petworth's former railway station, carefully restored, with large lounge and dining area (the former waiting room with original ticket office windows), fine breakfasts, friendly owners, terrace and garden; disabled access

ROGATE SU8022 **Mizzards** *Rogate, Petersfield, Hampshire GU31 5HS (01730) 821656* **£64**; 3 rms. 16th-c house in quiet country setting with a comfortable and elegant sitting room, enjoyable breakfasts in vaulted dining room, outside swimming

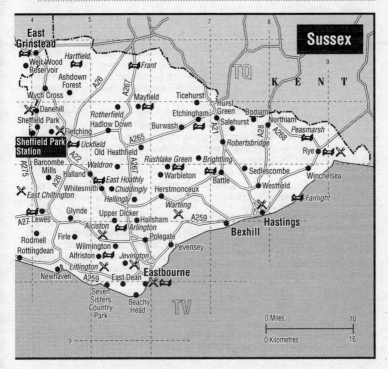

pool, attractive landscaped gardens and lake, and fine farmland views; no evening meals; no smoking; cl Christmas; children over 9

RUSHLAKE GREEN TQ6218 **Stone House** *Rushlake Green, Heathfield, East Sussex TN21 9QJ (01435) 830553* **£150**; 7 rms, some with four-posters. In a thousand acres of pretty countryside (with plenty of walks and country sports) and surrounded by an 18th-c walled garden, this lovely house was built at the end of the 15th c and extended in Georgian times; there are open log fires, antiques and family heirlooms in the drawing room, a quiet library, an antique full-sized table in the mahogany-panelled billiard room, wonderful food in the panelled dining room, fine breakfasts, and a cosseting atmosphere; cl 24 Dec-2 Jan; children over 9; dogs welcome in bedrooms

RYE TQ9120 **Jeakes House** *Mermaid St, Rye, East Sussex TN31 7ET (01797) 222828* **£88**; 11 rms (two with four-posters) overlooking the rooftops of this medieval town or across the marsh to the sea, 10 with own bthrm. Fine 16th-c building, well run and friendly, with good breakfasts, lots of books, comfortable furnishings, swagged curtains, linen and lace, a warm fire, and lovely peaceful atmosphere; children over 11; dogs welcome in bedrooms

RYE TQ9220 **Little Orchard House** *West St, Rye, East Sussex TN31 7ES (01797) 223831* **£76**; 2 four-poster rms. Beautifully furnished fine old house with antiques and personal prints and paintings, Georgian panelling, big open fireplace in study, good generous breakfasts (the friendly owners will make evening reservations at any of the many nearby restaurants), and an unexpectedly wonderful secluded garden; children over 12

RYE TQ9220 **Old Vicarage** *66 Church Sq, Rye, East Sussex TN31 7HF (01797) 222119* **£90**, plus special breaks; 4 pretty rms with newspaper and glass of sherry, and 2 rms carefully redecorated. Charming quietly placed mainly 18th-c house with helpful friendly owners, oak floors, comfortable sitting room or small library, log fire in elegant dining room, and marvellous breakfasts with freshly baked breads, free-range eggs, and home-made jams, bread, muesli and ketchups; no smoking; cl Christmas; children over 8

SHIPLEY TQ1523 **Goffsland Farm** *Shipley Rd, Southwater, Horsham, West Sussex RH13 7BQ (01403) 730434* **£42**; 2 rms inc 1 family rm with own access. 17th-c Wealden farmhouse on 260-acre family farm with good breakfasts, afternoon tea and evening meals by arrangement, and a friendly welcome; horse-riding and plenty of surrounding walks; dogs welcome

SLINFOLD TQ1131 **Random Hall** *Stane St, Slinfold, Horsham, West Sussex RH13 7QX (01403) 790558* **£90**; 13 comfortable rms. Restored 16th-c farmhouse with lots of beams and dark furnishings, flagstones, copper, brass in lounge, a friendly relaxed atmosphere, good breakfasts, and cocktail bar; cl last wk Dec-1st wk Jan

TILLINGTON SU9622 **Horse Guards** *Tillington, Petworth, West Sussex GU28 9AF (01798) 342332* **£65**; 2 spacious clean rms and little self catering cottage. Prettily set 18th-c dining pub in lovely village setting with neatly kept and cosy beamed front bar, imaginative restaurant-style food, 10 wines by the glass, and real ales; dogs welcome in the cottage

UCKFIELD TQ4718 **Horsted Place** *Little Horsted, Uckfield, East Sussex TN22 5TS (01825) 750581* **£155**, plus special breaks; 20 fulsomely decorated spacious rms. Stately Victorian country house on extensive estate, with antiques, flowers and log fires in luxurious drawing rooms, delicious food and good wine list in no smoking dining room, and croquet and tennis; reduced green fees at East Sussex National Golf Club; cl first wk Jan; children over 7; disabled access

WISBOROUGH GREEN TQ0625 **Old Wharf** *Wharf Farm, Wisborough Green, Billingshurst, West Sussex RH14 0JG (01403) 784096* **£70**; 3 rms with views over farmland and canal. Carefully restored no smoking canal warehouse with fine old hoist wheel, comfortable sitting room with log fire, breakfasts using free-range eggs, walled canalside garden, and friendly atmosphere; cl Christmas and New Year; children over 12

To see and do

Sussex Family Attraction of the Year

SHEFFIELD PARK STATION TQ4023 **Bluebell Railway** (A275) The golden age of steam lives on at this lovingly maintained standard gauge railway, the first to be preserved in this way, and still one of the best. Whenever you see a period railway on television or in films, it's more than likely to be this one: everything here has a wonderfully genuine feel of the past, from the period carriages to the splendid stations decked out with nostalgic advertisements. You don't have to be a train buff to enjoy it, and you can plan a very enjoyable day out around the full return journey, stopping off at various stages along the way (the full ticket allows unlimited travel on the railway for that day). The nine-mile trip runs from Sheffield Park via Horsted Keynes to Kingscote (an extension from here to East Grinstead should be completed within five years; until then there are weekend bus connections). The journey passes woodlands that are a mass of bluebells in late spring (usually at their best in mid-May), hence the name of the line. You can buy tickets for shorter stages of the trip, but it does make sense to start at Sheffield Park, not least because the Victorian station has the most facilities and attractions, including a collection of some 30 locomotives, and a model railway. It's much harder to start at the Kingscote end: there's no parking, so you're limited to the days when the East Grinstead bus is running. At Horsted Keynes you can watch restoration work on some of the carriages, and there's a big field for a picnic or to let off steam. They're proud of the fact that you'll never see a diesel train anywhere along the line - even the shunting is done with steam. On some days they use some of the oldest locomotives still working in this country; their extraordinarily detailed website at www.bluebell-railway.co.uk has full details of the timetable, and of special events like their Santa specials, Pullman dining specials, and visits by Thomas the Tank Engine (his creator, the Revd W Awdry, based his Fat Controller on the man who organised the railway's restoration in the late 1950s). Dogs are welcome. You can get combined tickets covering entry to either of the two National Trust properties nearby, the gardens at Sheffield Park, or Standen near East Grinstead. Shop, café, disabled access (with notice); trains wknds all year, daily May-Sept and school hols; (01825) 720800; a full return ticket is £8.50 for adults, and £4.20 for children 3-16. The family ticket can be good value, covering two adults and up to three children for £23.

ALFRISTON TQ5102
In a sheltered spot below the downs, and with inviting paths along the Cuckmere River, this is one of the south-east's most appealing villages - at quieter times of year (in high summer the ice-cream eaters, teashops and curio shops somewhat blunt its appeal). It has thatched, tiled and timbered houses, and a fine **church** built on a Saxon funeral barrow, by a large green just off the single main street. One of the most engaging buildings in the village is the Star Inn, with its Old Bill, a bright red figurehead lion on one corner taken as a trophy from a 17th-c dutch ship, and some intricate painted 15th-c carvings among its handsome timbering. The George and Market Cross are good for lunch. All alone just E of the village is **Lullington church**, a tiny fragment of a building with scarcely enough space for a congregation of 15. Just over a mile S of Alfriston, the road gives good views of the famous Cuckmere meanders.

Clergy House (The Tye) This thatched, half-timbered 14th-c cottage was in 1896 the first building to be taken over by the National Trust. Carefully restored, it now tells a story of medieval life and building methods; charming cottage garden. Shop; cl Tues, also Fri (Mon instead 3 Nov-19 Dec), wkdys till 27 Mar, and all 20 Dec-Feb; (01323) 870001; *£3; NT.

Drusillas Park (up towards A27) They keep only animals that they can provide with everything they'd have in the wild, so no lions, tigers or elephants, but plenty of smaller and arguably more entertaining creatures. You watch the meerkats through a little dome, there's a walk-through fruit bat enclosure, and Penguin Bay has underwater viewpoints. Elsewhere is everything from snakes and other creepy-crawlies to a splendid range of monkeys. There's a farmyard area, and Pet World gives younger visitors a chance to get close to rabbits, chinchillas and perhaps even snakes. The play areas are good, and they've recently added the interactive Mokomo's Jungle Rock experience (animatronic animals explain the food chain); a jolly little railway chuffs its way around the park, and there's a paddling pool and sand play area. Some of the extras have an additional charge: an activity centre open at wknds and in school holidays costs from £1.50 an activity; also £2.50 for face-painting, £1 for miniature golf, £1.50 to pan for gold, and 60p for the bouncy castle. Good meals and snacks, picnic areas, shops, excellent disabled access (there's also a sensory trail); cl 24-26 Dec; (01323) 874100; £9.49.

English Wine Centre (up by A27) Good cross-section of wines made in this country, as well as regional foods and crafts. Shop, disabled access; cl 23 Dec-2 Jan; (01323) 870164; free, tours (of vineyard and beyond) and tastings from *£6.95.

AMBERLEY TQ0212
Tucked beneath the South Downs, an enchantingly peaceful thatched village, facing the **Wild Brooks**, a large expanse of watermeadows which form an important habitat for wetland plants and birds. Its imposing castle is now a good hotel, not that easy to see, though you can peer into it from the churchyard. There's enjoyable food in the unspoilt Black Horse, and the Sportsman (lovely downs views).

Amberley Working Museum (by Amberley Stn) A carefully thought-out open-air museum covering 36 acres of former chalk quarry and limeworks, with plenty of traditional crafts and re-created workshops; they've added a new exhibition hall for the narrow-gauge railway collection. Lots going on, from pottery and cobbling to a working village telephone exchange. Meals and snacks in new restaurant, shop, disabled access; cl Mon and Tues (exc school or bank hols), and Nov-Mar; (01798) 831370; £6.75. The riverside Bridge Inn at nearby Houghton Bridge is great in summer; the B2139 is a pleasant drive.

ARDINGLY TQ3431
Wakehurst Place Garden (B2028 towards Turners Hill) The 'Kew in the Country', administered by the Royal Botanic Gardens and the most visited National Trust site, with a tremendous variety of interesting trees and shrubs inc many tender rarities. Lakes and water gardens, steep Himalayan glade, woodland walks and fine rhododendron species. Plenty to see throughout the year, and all very peaceful; a new visitor centre, with a shop and plant centre, should be completed by spring. The building of the Millennium Seed Bank houses one of the largest international conservation projects ever undertaken, to safeguard over 24,000 plant species from around the world against extinction, and to secure the future of Britain's flowering plants; an interactive exhibition tells you more about the scheme. Meals, snacks, plant and book sales, disabled access; cl 25 Dec, 1 Jan; (01444) 894004; £7 (free to NT members). Guided walks usually start in front of the mansion at 11.30am and 2.30pm (2pm in winter) most days, phone to check (£1 extra). The Gardeners Arms (children in garden only), Oak and Ardingly Inn do good lunches. Nearby **Ardingly Reservoir** offers pleasant strolls by its shores, or you can seek out the restored **Ouse Valley Viaduct**, an astonishing railway-age span carrying the London to Brighton line, best appreciated from below (access by path nr road SE of Balcombe).

ARUNDEL TQ0107
Decidedly french-looking from a distance, with its spikily Gothic revival Roman Catholic **cathedral** and vast

castle dominating the hilltop town. A fine range of historic buildings line the steep High St and side streets, with antiques shops to browse around, and a local history museum (High St; usually cl Sun am, and Oct-Mar; £1). The Swan has decent food. There's scope for walking straight out of town into some choice countryside within a few minutes - along the canalised River Arun, or past the lakes in Arundel Park and up on to the South Downs. Or you can take a boat trip from Buller's boatyard with Arundel Cruises; (01903) 882609.

Arundel Castle Seat and home of the Dukes of Norfolk and their ancestors for nearly a thousand years - a magnificent sight, a great spread of well kept towers and battlements soaring above the town and the trees around it. The keep and the curtain wall are the oldest parts; the rest dates mainly from the 19th c, and seven restored Victorian bedrooms are now on view (£1 extra). Excellent art collection, inc portraits by Van Dyck, Gainsborough and Canaletto, as well as 16th-c furniture, and personal possessions of Mary, Queen of Scots; the library is a highlight, and there are Victorian flower and vegetable gardens. Meals, snacks, shop, limited disabled access; cl am, Sat, Good Fri and all Nov-Mar; (01903) 883136; £9.

Wildfowl & Wetlands Trust (Mill Rd) Over 60 acres of well landscaped pens, lake, and paddocks, home to over a thousand ducks, geese and swans from all over the world inc rare species; hides overlook the various habitats. They've recently added a children's discovery trail, reed bed boardwalk, and a wildlife art gallery; children's activities in school hols and as we went to press they were building a new environmentally friendly education centre, due for completion in August; they also hope to offer boat trips around the reserve this summer. Meals, snacks, shop, disabled access; cl 25 Dec; (01903) 883355; £5.50. The lane past the Trust ends at a little cluster of houses by an isolated church and former watermill. On the way to the Trust, the Black Rabbit has a superb location and does food.

ASHDOWN FOREST TQ4832
A surprisingly wild place for Sussex: partly wooded, but predominantly hilly, rolling heathland punctuated by clumps of Scots pines - instantly familiar from the E H Sheppard drawings for A A Milne's *Winnie the Pooh* stories. Five Hundred Acre Wood is the Hundred Acre Wood of Pooh's world, and with a little searching you can find, SW of Hartfield, the reconstructed Poohsticks Bridge made from locally grown oak and, by the B2026, Gills Lap (the 'enchanted place' at the top of the forest, near Piglet's house), where a memorial to Milne has been placed near the triangulation point. There's free access for walkers to all the paths (far more exist than are shown on OS maps); the useful 1:30,000 scale walkers' map issued by the Ashdown Forest Centre shows all the paths and rides as well as naming the car parks - extremely helpful given the forest's lack of other landmarks, though for longer walks you may need a compass. Handy pubs for forest walks include the Foresters Arms at Fairwarp and Hatch at Colemans Hatch. To the N, the attractive village of **Hartfield** has Pooh Corner (a shop with the world's widest range of Pooh-related items), an unusual station conversion (now the village play group) and a good food pub, the Anchor. On the W side of the Forest, **Nutley windmill** was saved by enthusiastic locals; open pm last Sun of month Mar-Sept, 2nd wknd in May (also most Weds); (01435) 873367; donations.

BARCOMBE MILLS TQ4316
One of Sussex's secrets, with lazy riverside walks (or rowing boat hire) from the tucked-away Anchor pub here.

BATTLE TQ7515
Takes its name from certainly the most celebrated and perhaps the most disorganised skirmish in english history, thrashed out here in 1066. The main street (carrying a fair bit of traffic, so not exactly peaceful) has a lot of attractive old buildings, several housing antiques shops and cafés; beyond them the town extends into spreading new estates. The **church** of St Mary has some 13th-c wall paintings, and the Squirrel (A269) has generous cheap home cooking and a big family garden.

Battle Abbey The **battlefield** has a mile-long walk around it with a good audio tour explaining what happened. Four years after the bloodshed William built an abbey on the site as penance, the altar reputedly on the very spot where Harold fell. Not much is left of the original building, but later remains include the monks' dormitory and common room, and the great 14th-c gatehouse which looms over the small market square. Snacks, shop, mostly disabled access; cl 24-26 Dec, 1 Jan; (01424) 773792; £5; EH.

Battle Museum of Local History (High St) Good local history museum in an ancient Almonry; you can see the only battle axe found from the Battle of Hastings, and a reproduction of the Bayeux Tapestry. Meals, snacks, shop, disabled access; cl Sun am and Nov-Mar; (01424) 775955; £1. The little garden here is pretty.

Weald views The B2096 Heathfield road gives views S to Beachy Head from its highest points, near Netherfield and just before Dallington. Off this road any of the narrow side roads N into the countryside between Burwash and Dallington take you into the most unspoilt part of the steep Wealden woods and pastures.

Yesterday's World 📷 (High St) Carefully reconstructed period shops, railway station and the like; lots of hands-on activities, and mini golf. Snacks inc home-made fudge (summer only), shop; cl 25-26 Dec; (01424) 774269; £4.95.

BEACHY HEAD TV5997
Part of the county's best coastline, stretching W to the Seven Sisters and Cuckmere Haven. There are dizzying views from this towering, crumbly 163-metre (534-ft) sheer chalk cliff (the highest in the country) that constitutes the end of the South Downs, with the lighthouse dwarfed far below; it's a sadly popular suicide spot. It's easily reached from Eastbourne, and the eponymous hotel, open all day, has decent food.

BEXHILL TQ7407
A low-key seaside town with a pebble beach interrupted by cumbersome groins - an unlikely setting for a gem of Bauhaus architecture, the shoreside De La Warr Pavilion designed by Mendelsohn and Chermayeff. It's now an arts and social centre with changing exhibitions, events in the main hall, theatre, restaurant and pleasant sea-view café-bar upstairs. Usually open daily (free) though parts may be closed for refurbishments, which are due to finish in the autumn. The italian-run café opposite is good value, and the town's junk shops are always worth a browse.

Bexhill Museum of Costume In the delightful grounds of the Old Manor House up towards the tiny 'Old Town', a good look at 18th- to 20th-c fashions, with accessories and other domestic items as well as the clothes. Shop, disabled access; cl am wknds, Weds Apr-May and Sept-Oct, and all Nov-Mar; (01424) 210045; £2.

BIGNOR SU9814
Roman Villa & Museum One of the largest villas discovered so far, with marvellous mosaics housed in quaint thatched buildings erected by the farmer on whose land the site was found in 1811. One mosaic, 25 metres (82 ft) long and still in its original position, is the longest in Britain. Snacks, shop, some disabled access, and largely under cover; cl Mon Mar-Apr (exc bank hols), and all Nov-Feb; (01798) 869259; £3.80. The White Horse at nearby Sutton has good food (and good value bedrooms), and the top of Bignor Hill (just S of the Villa; not signed) is excellent for picnics and views. Here you can follow Stane St, a highly evocative Roman road (now a path with some of the original ditch and surface in evidence), taking a strikingly straight course SW through attractive landscapes.

BIRDHAM SU8401
Sussex Falconry Centre (Lockacre Aquatic Nursery, Wophams Lane) Originally set up as a breeding and rescue centre, then opened to the public with birds such as falcons, hawks, vultures, eagles and owls flown throughout the day in summer at 11.30am, 1.30 and 3.30pm. Snacks, pet shop, disabled access; cl Mon (exc bank hols), and 2 wks over Christmas and New Year; (01243) 512472; £4.75 (£2 Oct-Mar). This area S of Chichester is flat country, full of nurseries and huge glasshouses; the Lamb towards West

Wittering is a popular dining pub.

BODIAM TQ7825

Bodiam Castle With its exterior still virtually complete, this is a proper picture-book castle; a classic example of 14th-c fortification, with massive walls rising sheer from the romantic moat, and round drum towers steadfastly guarding each corner. Built to withstand attack from the French, it was only ever besieged by other Englishmen, and on both occasions was rather weedily handed over without a fight. The interior was destroyed around the time of the Civil War, and wasn't repaired until Lord Curzon bought it in 1916. There are a couple of short films on medieval castle life. Splendid views from the battlements, and lots of space for picnics; quiz sheets for children, enjoyable special events, and extra activities in the summer hols (but it can get busy then). Meals, snacks, shop, limited disabled access; cl wkdys Nov to mid-Feb; (01580) 830436; *£4.20, *£2 car park charge. The Curlew (B2244 just W) does good meals. In summer you can put together a very enjoyable full day out by taking the 45-minute boat trip to the castle through peaceful countryside from Newenden (they don't run in bad weather); (01797) 280363 for times. And the Kent & East Sussex Railway (see Tenterden entry in our Kent chapter) runs steam trains to Bodiam's restored station.

BOGNOR REGIS SZ9398

An old-fashioned seaside family resort, popular above all for its award-winning beach (clean water for swimming, and seafront showers). Its pier, one of the oldest, was originally 305 metres (1,000 ft) long, but has been shrinking - the pavilion end sank in 1965, and a 20-metre mid-section was swept away in a 1999 storm. Two museums share the same building on the High St: one contains local history inc some hands-on displays, and re-created street shops, and the other has a wireless display of 40 years of valve radio. Shop, disabled access; both cl Mon (exc bank hols), and Nov to wk before Easter; (01243) 865636; free. The Styne has some interesting buildings; the Alex (London Rd) does good value food.

BOSHAM SU8004

(pronounced 'Bozom') The Saxon **church** here figures in the Bayeux Tapestry, and the village is a lovely cluster of old cottages around it, the green, and a broad, almost landlocked, inlet of Chichester harbour, busy with boating in the summer. Don't be tempted to park on the shore - the incoming tide is well known for its trick of lapping around parked cars. Very pleasant to stroll around, with good antique shops and craft galleries, esp on Bosham Lane. The White Swan up by the A259 roundabout has enjoyable food.

BOXGROVE SU9007

Boxgrove Priory Now the parish church, this 12th-c building is one of the most outstanding Early English churches in the region, with a surprising 16th-c painted ceiling, free-standing chantry chapel, and the haunting remains of various monastic buildings outside. The Anglesey Arms at Halnaker has decent food.

BRAMBER TQ1810

St Mary's House 🏛 Striking medieval house, with fine panelling, and an unusual Elizabethan painted room; there's a pretty garden with topiary. Concerts in spring and autumn. Teas, shop; open pm Sun, Thurs, and bank hols Easter-Sept; (01903) 816205; *£5. The Castle Hotel, named after the nearby castle ruin (free access, EH), has reasonably priced food and a charming back garden. Adjacent Steyning has some of the best village streetscapes in Sussex, with particularly choice timber-framed and Georgian buildings, a museum, a pleasant Tudor pub (the Chequer), and a grand Norman church.

BRIGHTON TQ3104

A thriving resort as well as a big shopping town, Brighton owes some of its lively feel to two vigorous nearby universities and several language schools for foreign students; on hot days the seafront between the two piers becomes one huge open-air bar, thick with rollerbladers, drummers, beach volleyball players and hair-braiders. There's also a booming gay scene, and things really liven up during the massive three-week Brighton Festival in May. The city still has plenty of glistening white Regency buildings dating from its fashionable days in the 18th c, when the idea that sea-bathing was good for you sent London's finest scurrying to the coast. The oldest part is the (mostly pedestrianised) Lanes - 17th-c fishermen's cottages squeezed together in narrow twisting byways, now crammed with jewellery and antiques shops, restaurants and bars. English's here is entertaining for lunch. The North Laine area (SE of the station) is slightly more trendy, with good buskers, funky shops and cool cafés. Lots of money has been invested in regeneration projects, and the Brighton Dome concert hall, and the Theatre Royal have now been restored. Throughout, there's no shortage of simple places to eat (notably in the Lanes, Preston St near the West Pier, and St James's St), inc the Cricketers (Black Lion St), Greys (Southover St, Kemp Town), and Basketmakers Arms (E end of Gloucester Rd). The George (Trafalgar St) is popular for its all-day organic vegetarian and vegan food, and the trendy Freemasons (Western Rd, Hove) has good contemporary food upstairs. The council are keen to improve access to the South Downs, and a bus service runs to Devil's Dyke and Ditchling Beacon; phone for information (01273) 292480.

Barlow Collection (University of Sussex, Falmer; off A27 N) One of Europe's finest collections of chinese ceramics, it's usually open 11.30-2.30 Tues and Thurs (exc Dec-Jan, Apr and Aug), but phone to check first, as we were unable to make contact with them before we went to press; (01273) 606755; free.

Booth Museum of Natural History (Dyke Rd) Wide-ranging collection of animal skeletons (inc some dinosaur bones), as well as the Victorian collection of birds the museum was first built to house. Shop, disabled access; cl Thurs, am Sun, 25-26 Dec, 1 Jan and Good Fri; (01273) 292777; free.

Brighton Fishing Museum (Kings Rd) The seafront Arches across from the Old Ship Hotel used to be occupied by local fishermen. Though a couple still are, the rest are now given over to little craftshops and artists. One houses this collection of local boats, nets, models

and pictures. Shellfish stall and fish smokery, shop, disabled access; cl 25-26 Dec, and any day Nov-Apr when the weather is poor; (01273) 723064; free.

Brighton Marina (E of centre) This modern place is lively in summer, with tables out by the water, boat rides and so forth. A waterfront entertainment centre includes a factory shopping outlet, bars and restaurants, a celebrity walk of fame, and a casino. An electric train usually runs (from Apr to mid-Sept) along the beach from the pier.

Brighton market On Sun mornings there's a good market in the station car park; do get there well before breakfast for the bargains, as it's become a major source of supply for the countless Brighton antiques dealers. Near here **St Bartholomew's church** (Anne St) is a strange Grade I listed building, like a huge brick barn, but supremely impressive inside. Film buffs will be well satisfied with the Duke of York's cinema at nearby Preston Circus, which shows the kind of movies not always found outside London.

Brighton Museum and Art Gallery (Church St) Reopened in 2003, after being reorganised inside and out. You now enter from the Pavilion gardens, rather than the street, and it's organised into a number of themed rooms exploring very different subjects. Downstairs the main hall still has splendid art nouveau furniture, plus some avant garde pieces (an armchair made of wire; another resembling a baseball mitt), and there's an ethnography gallery, with exotic masks, spears etc. Excellent galleries on Brighton's social history, inc the town's role as a place for dirty weekends - and models of Brighton in the early 19th c, plus taped recollections of residents to listen to; Mr Willett's Popular Pottery is an eye-catching collection of ceramics from centuries past (fascinating even for non pottery-buffs) that show aspects of political, culutural and social history - some pieces for example have a political propaganda message, others are sporting, others merely frivolous. Upstairs are temporary exhibitions, fashion and paintings. Café, shop, disabled access; cl Mon (exc bank hols), am Sun, 24-26 Dec, and 1 Jan; (01273) 290900; free.

Brighton Pier The hub of the seafront, Brighton Pier is packed with the usual amusements, but also sports palmists' booths and the like; it looks magnificent at night. The older West Pier, Britain's only Grade I listed pier, is looking very doomed following a storm and a series of arson attacks in 2003, but restoration is still promised and may even begin late this year.

Brighton Toy and Model Museum (Trafalgar St) Over 10,000 objects, from Victorian dolls to Meccano. Shop, disabled access; cl Sun, Mon, and bank hols, phone for opening times over Christmas; (01273) 749494; £3.50.

British Engineerium (Nevill Rd, Hove) All sorts of road, locomotive and marine steam engines, as well as tools and models in a restored Victorian water-pumping station. Shop, limited disabled access; cl wk before Christmas-27 Dec, engines in steam first Sun in month; (01273) 559583; £4.

Foredown Tower (Foredown Rd, Portslade) Very well done, with a **camera obscura** (best on bright days, shown on the hour) as well as astronomy displays, and splendid views. They can arrange visits to Portslade Old Manor, a ruined medieval house a short stroll away. Snacks, shop; cl Mon-Weds; (01273) 292092; £2.50.

Hove Museum and Art Gallery (New Church Rd) Revamped in 2003 to a very high standard and a good freebie, the permanent exhibition is in three parts. One gallery concentrates on Hove's history, plus there's some art (mostly early 20th-c british). Another has all manner of childhood objects as if stashed away in a dark attic - inc drawers you can pull out and discover eerie dolls' heads, a tin bath full of model soldiers, and a suitcase full of toy animals - almost entirely visual in scope, it also features a messy bedroom, and a display of toys through the ages. The story of the Hove Pioneers focuses on cinema and moving images in the pre-Hollywood era, and although it's only a small room, there's masses to look at; the hub of the collection are the films of G A Smith and James Williamson, who made movies in Hove in 1897-1905 (you can watch samples of their output), also displays of early film equipment and the development of moving pictures from 'flick books' onwards. Downstairs are temporary exhibitions, and an excellent tearoom. Snacks, shop, disabled access; cl Mon (inc bank hols), am Sun, 25-26 Dec and 1 Jan; (01273) 290200; free.

Museum of Penny Slot Machines (250C Kings Rd Arches) Nostalgic collection of over 50 vintage seaside amusements from penny slot-machines to strength-testers and fortune-tellers. Shop, disabled access; usually open wknd and school hol pms Easter-Sept, plus fine weather Sun pm in winter; free (charge for individual games - they change your money into old coins).

Preston Manor 🏛 (A23) Entertaining and vivid illustration of life in Edwardian times, with fully furnished period rooms; restored walled gardens with fish pond and a pets' cemetery. Shop; cl am Sun-Mon, Good Fri, 25-26 Dec; (01273) 290900; £3.70, joint ticket with entry to Royal Pavilion £8.20.

Regency Town House 🏛 Hove, the quieter half of the resort, is just W of Brighton proper. On the way you may be able to visit this Regency house in Brunswick Square - being restored as a Heritage Centre, but they have regular open days and wknd tours - see their website www.rth.org.uk or phone for dates (01273) 206306; £2.50, £3 tours.

Royal Pavilion Nash's flamboyant indian-style confection should be top of anyone's itinerary: the most eccentric of all Royal palaces, a riot of chinoiserie inside. Queen Victoria was the last monarch to own it, but was hardly its greatest fan; if the town council hadn't bought it from her she might well have demolished it. The interior has been restored to its full overblown glory, and the gardens have been returned to their original Regency layout. The whole building is beautifully floodlit at night. It's less busy after 3 o'clock - and better still out of season, when you may find more going on. Delightful upstairs tearoom overlooking garden, shop, disabled access to ground floor only; cl 25-26 Dec; (01273) 290900; £5.80, joint ticket with Preston Manor £8.20.

Sea Life Centre (Marine Parade) Lively displays of british and tropical creatures inc rays, eels, seahorses, and even turtles; there's an exhibition devoted to creatures with claws, and in Jan they hope to add 'Lair of the Octopus', complete with a giant pacific octopus; also touch pools and a soft play area. Meals, snacks, shop, disabled access; cl 25 Dec; (01273) 604234; £7.95.

West Blatchington windmill 🏚 (Holmes Ave, Hove) With local history and milling displays; shop, disabled access, open pm Sun and bank hols May-Sept; (01273) 776017; £1.

BURPHAM TQ0309

Great views from this attractive hill village (which sometimes surprises with the sight of a herd of buffalo - they produce mozzarella), with pleasant walks from here along the river or through hilly Arundel Park into Arundel. The George & Dragon has good food.

BURWASH TQ6724

The single main street of this ridge village has many attractively restored tile-hung cottages, with lime trees along its brick pavement. The graveyard of the Norman-towered church gives fine views over the Dudwell Valley, and the flower-decked Bell is useful for lunch. Around here the intricate landscapes of the Sussex Weald show steep slopes and valleys, ancient woods and hedgerows punctuated by great oaks, pretty villages, tile-hung or weatherboarded oast houses and wood-and-tile barns with their long cats'-slide roofs.

Batemans (off A265) Handsome early 17th-c stone-built ironmaster's house, home to Rudyard Kipling 1902-1936. His study is kept much as it was then, as is the hefty pipework he installed for a pioneer hydro-electric lighting plant. The attractive gardens have a quaint operating watermill, grinding flour every Sat at 2pm. Dog crèche, snacks, shop, disabled access to ground floor only; cl Thurs, Fri (exc Good Fri), and Oct-Mar; (01435) 882302; *£5.50; NT. Good little-used walks up the wholly unspoilt valley from here, where you can look for Kipling landmarks such as Pook's Hill and Willingford Bridge (aka Weland's Ford).

CHANCTONBURY RING TQ1312

One of the great South Downs landmarks, a Romano-British temple site within an Iron Age earthwork, now a prominent hilltop clump of trees: a bracing walk, best reached from Steyning (the Tudor Chequer has generous food) or Washington, or from Cissbury Ring.

CHICHESTER SU8504

Partly pedestrianised and easy to get around, this handsome former Roman city is one of the country's finest examples of Georgian town planning and architecture. The **South Downs Planetarium** (signposted from Kingsham Rd) has regular shows based around themes such as the northern lights. Snacks, shop, disabled access; phone for times; (01243) 774400; £6. Useful central pubs for food are the Fountain (Southgate), Nags (St Pancras), Dolphin & Anchor (West St), and lively Toad (redundant church, West St).

Centurion Way This short stretch of disused railway track has been converted to an easy route for cyclists (and walkers) W of Chichester to Mid Lavant, where the Earl of March Arms has cheap generous food.

Chichester Cathedral Mostly Norman, and unusual for rising straight out of the town's streets rather than a secluded close. The spire collapsed in 1861 (the latest in a long line of structural problems), and was rebuilt, but even now the scaffolding always seems to be up as restoration work continues. Highlights include the 14th-c choir stalls, John Piper's Aubusson tapestry, and the window by Chagall. Guided tours (not Sun) at 11.15am and 2.30pm Easter-end Oct. Meals, snacks, shop in the medieval bell tower, disabled access; cl only for special services and events; (01243) 782595; £2 suggested donation. The Bishops Palace gardens are very pleasant.

Chichester District Museum (Little London) Enthusiastic local history museum in an 18th-c corn store, with some hands-on activities for children, changing exhibitions and regular events; cl Sun, Mon and bank hols; free. The **Guildhall** (Priory Park) began life as a 13th-c Greyfriars church, and later the poet William Blake was brought to trial here (1804); it now houses more local history items. Open

pm Sat Jun-Sept; (01243) 784683; free.
The Park Tavern opposite has decent
food.

**Mechanical Music & Doll
Collection** (Church Rd, Portfield) A
multitude of barrel, fair and dutch
street organs, music boxes and
phonographs - all restored and ready to
play. Shop, disabled access; open pm
Weds Jun-Sept; (01243) 372646; £2.50.

Pagham Harbour (off B2145 S)
Peaceful nature reserve, largely silted
marshy tidal flats, full of wading birds
and wildfowl, particularly in spring and
autumn. Depending which side you
approach from, the Lamb at Pagham and
Crab & Lobster at Paglesham are both
handy lunch stops.

Pallant House Gallery (North
Pallant) Due to reopen in the spring
with nine new galleries and complete
disabled access; they hope to show
major travelling exhibitions in the
future, alongside an already substantial
collection of modern art. The old wing,
an interesting Queen Anne town house
with Edwardian kitchen and fine
furnishings, has fine Bow porcelain, and
an excellent range of carefully chosen
20th-c art - Freud, Sutherland, Piper,
Nicholson and the like. Meals, snacks,
shop; cl Sun am, all day Mon (exc bank
hols), 25-26 Dec; (01243) 774557; £4,
children free.

St Mary's Hospital (St Martin's Sq)
13th-c hospital with a splendid tiled
roof, unique misericords in its chapel,
and a pretty walled garden. Disabled
access; open wkdys by appointment;
(01243) 783377; donations.

CHICHESTER HARBOUR SU7702
The most attractive views for walkers
are from the shoreside path which
skirts the quiet unspoilt peninsulas of
Thorney Island and Chidham.

Boat trips Peter Adams runs these
around Chichester Harbour, full of
yachts and dinghies in summer; he also
runs bird-watching boat trips in winter.
They leave from Itchenor (where the
Ship has good food) and are best at high
tide; (01243) 786418; £5. There's also a
passenger ferry between here and the
landing at the end of the lane S from
Bosham (usually daily Jun-Aug, wknds
only Apr, May and Sept).

East Head A NT-owned promontory

on the E entrance of Chichester
Harbour, a sandy spit with dunes
overlooking the marshes and mudflats
of the estuary.

CISSBURY RING TQ1308
Another of the great downland
landmarks, a huge ramparted Iron Age
hill peppered with much earlier flint
mines, and good views over to the Isle
of Wight (looking surprisingly near). It's
quite close to Findon, where the Gun is
good for lunch. The walk from here to
Chanctonbury Ring is pleasant.

CLIMPING BEACH TQ0000
This allows an attractive few miles'
walk; this bit of coast between
Middleton-on-Sea and Littlehampton is
the only appreciable undeveloped
seaside stretch in W Sussex, apart from
Chichester Harbour.

COOMBES TQ1908
Church Farm 🖭 Trailer rides over
farmland and through conservation
areas - you have to book, but it's great
fun, especially in the lambing season.
Snacks, shop, and they've recently
improved disabled access; usually open
daily Mar to mid-Apr, and Tues, Thurs
and Sun at 2.30pm in Aug, but best to
check; (01273) 452028; *£4. They also
have a coarse fishing lake.

DANEHILL TQ4026
Heaven Farm (Furners Green, A275
S) A handy place for a relaxing easy-on-
the-pocket afternoon, with an
interesting 1½-mile nature trail (look
out for the wallabies), and a farming
museum spread over various 19th-c
farm buildings. There's also an aviary,
and lots of free-roaming poultry and
game, plenty of space for picnics, and a
caravan and camping site; fine views.
Snacks, craft shop; cl Dec-Feb, plus
museum cl am, all Mon, Fri and Sat;
(01825) 790226; £2.50 nature trail, £1
museum. The Coach & Horses in
Danehill has good food.

DELL QUAY SU8303
Attractive waterside hamlet with
remains of a Roman quay.

DITCHLING TQ3313
Ditchling Beacon Right by the road,
with superb views all around, especially
out over the villages and towns to the
N; a nice walking area of preserved
sheep-cropped unimproved downland,
with chalk hill blue butterflies in

summer. The village below is pleasant, with a tearoom, the 14th-c Bull, and a decent **museum** - inc displays on artist/typographer Eric Gill and other local craftsmen (shop, disabled access; cl Mon (exc bank hols) and mid-Dec to mid-Feb; £3.50). Developing **Stonywish Nature Reserve** (East End Lane) has farm animals, woodland walks, and a good play area. Tearoom, shop, disabled access; cl 25-26 Dec; (01273) 843498; £3.50. The B2116 to Offham has views of the South Downs, and off it the Jolly Sportsman at East Chiltington has very good food.

EARNLEY SZ8297

Earnley Gardens 🎫 (Almodington Lane) This five-acre site is quite a busy day out; as well as the 17 long-established themed gardens, exotic birds and free-flying butterflies, there's a shipwreck display, small animal farm, and a refreshingly informal nostalgia museum, Rejectamenta. This takes in thousands of everyday objects from the last 100 years, collected over 30 years by a former art student who says she just can't stop. Meals, snacks, shop, disabled access; open mid Mar-Oct; (01243) 512637; around £7 everything, £4.50 just gardens and butterflies or just nostalgia museum, £1.50 crazy golf.

EAST DEAN TV5597

Seven Sisters Sheep Centre 🎫 (Gilberts Drive) A particularly enjoyable and genuine place to visit, with 47 different types of sheep, some tame enough to touch and feed. There's a good commentary when the sheep are milked, demonstrations of yoghurt- and cheese-making, and daily shearing and wool handling displays. Other animals include pigs, horses, goats, chickens and ducks, with a barn where children can fuss rabbits, chinchillas and so on; a tractor/trailer ride across the farm is 50p extra. The best time of all is the Mar-May lambing season, when children can bottle feed the lambs. Snacks, shop (with products made from ewe's milk), good disabled access; usually open wkdy pms and all day wknds Mar to mid-May, then July to mid-Sept (all day in school hols), best to check; (01323) 423302; *£3.50. The village itself is prettily set around a sloping green, with an attractive pub,

the Tiger. A lane past the farm continues to the **Birling Gap**, a cleft in the coastal cliffs famous since smuggling days, with walks up to Belle Tout, a former coastguard station and lighthouse moved back 17 metres (55 ft) in 1999 to save it from coastal erosion, and on to Beachy Head.

EAST GRINSTEAD TQ3835

Standen (off B2110 W) A fine example of the many talents of the 19th-c Arts and Crafts Movement. Designed by Philip Webb (even down to the unusual light fittings), a friend of William Morris, and little changed since, the inside is decorated with several different William Morris wallpapers, and many of the furnishings are of the period. Meals, snacks, shop, limited disabled access; cl Mon (exc bank hols), Tues and Nov-Mar; (01342) 323029; *£6, *£3.30 garden only; NT.

EASTBOURNE TV6198

The Duke of Devonshire still owns much of this civilised seaside resort; as he prohibits seaside tat the place has a more dignified and solid feel than many of its livelier rivals - appealing to people who appreciate old-fashioned virtues. It's perfect for seafront strolling with its terraces of stucco-fronted hotels overlooking the long shingle-beach, and stripy deckchairs set for bandstand concerts: the Dotto Train (a land train rather than a real train) covers the whole seafront from Sovereign Park near the smart marina (where there are boat tours, shops and eateries) to the Holywell Tea Chalet (May-Sept). The latter is just beneath Beachy Head, the towering cliff at the end of the South Downs; you can walk up from here, or during May-Sept take a cruise from Sovereign Harbour (daytime and evening; (01323) 470821). Along the pier, the restored 1901 Camera Obscura, with its 360 degree view of Eastbourne, is usually open pm daily. Plenty of the usual seaside attractions too, inc mini golf, boating lake (in Princes Park), go-karts and the recently renovated Treasure Island Adventure Park (both in Royal Parade) has sandpits and paddling pools. Close to the railway station are some of the town's most rewarding shops for browsers, inc the Enterprise Shopping Centre (with 50 stalls), and the area of 'Little Chelsea' (Grove Rd and South St), with antiques, art, crafts, second-hand books and cafés; Camilla's Bookshop in Grove Rd is densely stashed with second-hand tomes across two floors. The **Lifeboat Museum** (King Edwards Parade) makes up in enthusiasm what it lacks in size; (01323) 730717; shop, disabled access, cl Jan-Easter; free.

Heritage Centre (Carlisle Rd) A survey of the development and future of the seaside resort, with photographs, postcards, models and a new video show; they plan to add an exhibition on the Devonshire family's connection with the town; (01323) 721825; £1.

How We Lived Then 💷 (Cornfield Terr) A real labour of love and one of the most comprehensive museum of shops we've come across, more than 100,000 items collected by the couple who run the museum and live in a flat above it; this nostalgia fest started as a private collection which grew and grew, and friends suggested they turn it into a museum. It's packed within four floors of tiny 'rooms' and imaginatively displayed. Shop, disabled access to ground floor only; cl 24-26 Dec; (01323) 737143; £3.50.

Miniature Steam Railway Park Eighth-scale miniature steam and diesel-hauled passenger trains run almost a mile around a lake (you can buy a ticket to fish here; £6). Also model railways, play and picnic areas, willow maze, and nature trail. Meals, snacks, shop, disabled access; open Easter-end Sept; (01323) 520229; £3.95.

Redoubt Fortress (Royal Parade) A perfectly preserved early 19th-c circular fort, housing a more interesting than average military collection, featuring medals, weapons, Churchill's telescope, regimental uniforms and a model of the fort showing what it was like when in use (shop; cl early Nov-Easter; (01323) 410300; £3). Open-air 1812 Night concerts (every Weds and Fri late Jun-early Sept) always end in a firework display.

Towner Art Gallery & Museum (High St, Old Town) Elegant 18th-c building in the old town, with mainly 19th- and 20th-c british art, local history and archaeology; also changing exhibitions inc contemporary art and local history displays. Shop, limited disabled access; cl am, and all day Mon (exc some bank hols), 25-27 Dec, 1 Jan and Good Fri; (01323) 417961; free entry, charges for some exhibitions. The church just over the road is lavish; next to it the Lamb is a nice old pub.

Wish Tower (King Edward's Parade) One of the 103 Martello Towers built in case of french invasion during the Napoleonic Wars; contains a fascinating collection of puppets, dating back three centuries and including asian shadow puppets and Punch and Judy characters. Shop; usually open wknds Easter-Oct, plus wkdys mid-July to Aug; (01323) 411620; £1.80. A few steps away is the tiny Lifeboat Museum; shop, disabled access, cl Jan-Easter; free.

ETCHINGHAM TQ7126
Etchingham church Lovely sturdy ancient semi-fortified building in honey-coloured stone - quaintly, the station is built to match.

FERNHURST SU8928
Nicely varied surrounding countryside for walkers; much is densely wooded, but there are some chances to get out on to the open hillsides - as on Woolbeding Common and the S tip of Black Down. The prettily tucked-away Red Lion has good value food.

FIRLE TQ4707
A classic example of a living estate village (belongs to Firle Place), in a hidden corner off the A27, with a decent pub (the Ram). Firle Beacon, a South Downs landmark, is a lovely walk above the village (car park nearby, at top of hill), or you can walk along an easy track at the foot of the downs.

Berwick church 1940s murals by the Bloomsbury Group; the Cricketers Arms here is a good lunch place.

Charleston Farmhouse (A27 Firle—Selmeston) Delightful 17th/18th-c house which was the home of Duncan Grant and Clive and Vanessa Bell; decorated by them, it and its magical garden still evoke the atmosphere of those Bloomsbury days. Tours last around an hour (there's limited seating in rooms), and you really need an interest in the house's inhabitants to properly enjoy it. Snacks, shop, disabled access; cl am (exc July-Aug), Mon (exc bank hols), Tues, and Nov-Mar; entry on Weds-Sat is by tour only, best to check; (01323) 811265; £6. Nr here at Alciston, the Rose Cottage has very good home cooking.

Firle Place 🏛 (off A27) Beautiful house, essentially Tudor but remodelled in the 18th c, with some real treasures of european and english painting, and wonderful furnishings. Meals, snacks, shop, disabled access to ground floor; open pm Weds and Thurs Jun-Sept; (01273) 858335; £5.

Middle Farm (A27 E) You can sample ciders straight from the barrel before buying (they call this the national collection of cider and perry); also farmhouse cheeses, english wines, good sausages, organic meats, and other produce. A children's farmyard has sheep, goats and other small animals (daily milking demonstrations), and there's a play area; lots going on at apple harvest time. Restaurant, bakery, plant and crafts shops, disabled access; cl 25-26 Dec; (01323) 811411; site free, £2 for farmyard.

FISHBOURNE SU8304
Roman Palace (Salthill Rd) This magnificent villa with its 100 or so rooms was occupied from the 1st to the 3rd c, and is the largest known residence from the period in Britain. Some archaeologists now think the Romans first landed here (and not in Kent as was originally supposed), to reinstate the recently evicted king. They probably built his successor this place. You can see 25 mosaic floors (some are quite remarkable, and it's a bigger collection than anywhere else in Britain), and a garden has been laid out according to its 1st-c plan. Much of the palace is buried beneath nearby housing. Snacks, shop, disabled access; cl wkdys mid-Dec to Jan; (01243) 785859; *£5.20. The Bulls Head has good food.

FLETCHING TQ4223
Attractive village - often Sussex's Best-Kept Village; and it has a charming waymarked Millennium Walk; the Griffin is a very good food pub.

FONTWELL SU9406
Denmans Garden (off A27) Colourful series of vistas over 3½ acres, inc exuberantly oriental-feeling areas with a gravel stream, ornamental

grasses, bamboos and flowering cherries, as well as a beautiful richly planted walled garden. Meals, snacks, plant sales, disabled access; cl Nov-Feb; (01243) 542808; £2.95. In the pretty nearby village of Eartham there is a small but charming church; the George there, open all day summer wknds, is an enjoyable dining pub.

GATWICK AIRPORT TQ2740
Skyview (S Terminal) Visitor gallery, with a multi-media show demonstrating a typical airport day, a good explanation of cockpit controls, and splendid runway views. Shop, disabled access; cl 25 Dec; (01293) 502244; £1.50.

GLYNDE TQ4509
Glynde Place Elizabethan manor house in beautiful setting, extensively remodelled inside in the 18th c, but outside left pretty much unchanged. Portraits and mementoes give a good grounding in the family history, while outside are pleasantly wild parklands and lawns. Snacks, shop; open pm Weds, Sun and bank hols Jun-Sept, best to phone; (01273) 858224; £5. There's a neat neo-Palladian **church** nearby, and the Trevor Arms has decent food. The Glyndebourne Festival, with its decidedly smart operas and marvellous auditorium designed by Sir Michael Hopkins, takes place May-Aug; tickets are very scarce, but it's always worth ringing on the day for returns, and you have a better chance of getting into the Touring Opera during the shorter (and cheaper) October season; (01273) 813813.

GOODWOOD SU8808
Goodwood House 🏛 Unusual-looking flint house in beautiful downland countryside, especially renowned for its paintings, inc works by Canaletto and Stubbs. There's quite a riding feel - it was acquired by the first Duke of Richmond in 1697 so that he could ride with the local hunt, and the stables added during 18th-c alterations seem grander even than the house. The restored drawing room contains 18th-c french furniture. Snacks, shop, disabled access; open pms Sun and Mon mid-Mar to end Oct (plus Tues-Thurs in Aug); (01243) 755040; £7. The adjacent **racecourse** is the setting for Glorious Goodwood, and around 19 race days a

year; also monthly antiques markets; (01243) 755022 for dates. The Royal Oak at East Lavant is a good nearby dining pub.

Sculpture at Goodwood (Hat Hill Copse, towards East Dean) Excellent changing exhibitions of sculpture in 20 acres of beautiful wooded parkland; it's established an excellent reputation in the few years it's been open, so it's a shame the high admission price limits it to people with more than just a passing interest in the subject. Shop, some disabled access; cl Sun-Weds (exc bank hol) and Nov-Mar; (01243) 538449; *£10. This is a good area for a country drive; the Anglesey Arms at Halnaker has enjoyable food.

HADLOW DOWN TQ5424

Wilderness Wood (A272) 62 acres of working woodland, good for learning about forests and their wildlife, or for a pleasant stroll. Several picnic areas and play area, occasional demonstrations of heavy horses and other traditional woodland working methods, and a discovery trail for children; their bluebell walk during end Apr-May is popular. Teas and snacks, shop (they make chestnut furniture and other goods), disabled access; cl 25-26 Dec; (01825) 830509; £2.50. Nearby Buxted has enjoyable food in the White Hart.

HAILSHAM TQ5709

Knockhatch Adventure Park 🔢 (A22, W of Hailsham) Plenty to do in this 80-acre park which has a children's farm and birds of prey centre, adventure playgrounds, and more unusual attractions such as a laser adventure game (£3.25), and karting (£3.50). Also crazy golf, boating lake, woodland trail, picnic area, and a ski centre (phone first). Snacks, shop, disabled access; cl term-time wkdys, and all Nov-Easter, but best to check (ski slope only cl 24-25 and 31 Dec and 1 Jan); (01323) 442051; £6.75.

HALLAND TQ4815

Bentley Wildfowl & Motor Museum Busy estate centred around Tudor farmhouse converted into Palladian mansion, filled with fine furnishings and paintings, inc watercolours by local artist Phillip Rickman. The motor museum has gleaming veteran, Edwardian and

vintage vehicles, while the lakes and ponds that surround it are home to countless varieties of rare, endangered and exotic wildfowl. There are also woodland trails, a little adventure playground, on-site craftsmen and artists, and miniature trains that steam through the grounds (wknds Easter-Oct plus Weds in Aug). Special events (may be a charge) run from veteran and vintage car and other transport rallies to fire brigade and birds of prey displays. Snacks, shop, disabled access; cl Nov-Mar, house also cl am (but rest open wknds in Nov and Feb-Mar, daily from mid-Mar); (01825) 840573; £5.50, less in winter. The Black Lion (A22/B2192) has decent food.

HANDCROSS TQ2629

Nymans Garden (B2114) Perhaps the most romantic of all Wealden gardens, rewarding at any time. Rare trees inc magnificent southern beeches and eucryphias, as well as fine camellias, rhododendrons and magnolias, countless other interesting flowering shrubs, a secluded sunken garden, and an extensive artfully composed wilderness. Meals, snacks, plant sales, shop, disabled access; cl Mon (exc bank hols), Tues, and wkdys Nov-Feb; (01444) 400321; *£6.50; NT. The Wheatsheaf (B2110 W) has good food.

HASTINGS TQ8209

The seaside town has a really dramatic setting in the cliffs, unique in the south-east, with the aptly named Old Town huddled below the ruins of the castle. The labyrinth of alleys and stepped paths threading through its former fishermen's quarter make for highly enjoyable wandering, and it's refreshingly not over-tidy. Down below, the fishermen still haul their boats up on to the beach and sell excellent fresh fish by the unusual tall black wooden net huts. At each end of the cliffs is a steep funicular railway down to sea level (90p). The First In Last Out in the Old Town has interesting food and brews its own beer. The rest of the town is a busy shopping town, rather run-down in parts, with 19th-c resort buildings nearer the seafront, seaside hotels and B&Bs, a good prom (with miles of cycle path), and shingle beach.

Clambers Play Centre (White Rock Gdns) Well kept indoor and outdoor activities for under-12s inc climbing frames, ball ponds, huge sand pit, paddling pool, play houses, and a separate play area for younger children - handy for a rainy day. Meals, snacks (baby food available), and picnic tables, cl 25-26 Dec, and 1 Jan; (01424) 423778; £4.75 for around 2 hrs for children, adults free. For those with energy still left, Hastings Adventure Golf next door is open daily in summer; *£4.

Fairlight Cove A good destination for walks from Hastings Old Town, by a path climbing on to the sandstone cliffs for a rugged couple of miles; the tumbled appearance of the coast here bears witness to the occasional cliff-falls. The Cove Continental does enjoyable lunches.

Fishermen's Museum (Rock-a-Nore Rd) Interestingly housed in a former fishermen's church, and crammed full of stuff; the centrepiece is a 29-ft sailing lugger, there's an audio-visual presentation, and a huge stuffed albatross. Shop, disabled access, cl 25 Dec; (01424) 461446; donations.

Hastings Castle Bracingly set above crumbling cliffs and the tracked lift, the evocative Norman ruins (which encompass, unusually, a collegiate church) are close to the site of William the Conqueror's first english motte and bailey castle. There's a lively audio-visual exhibition on the Battle of Hastings. Shop, some disabled access; cl 24-26 Dec; (01424) 781112; £3.20.

Hastings Museum and Art Gallery (Johns Pl, Bohemia Rd) A little out of the centre, but worth a look for its native american displays; children may prefer the dinosaur gallery. Shop, limited disabled access; cl 25-26 Dec and Good Fri; (01424) 781155; free.

Shipwreck Heritage Centre (Rock-a-Nore Rd) Find out more about local wrecks, with lots of items brought up from the sea bed from wine bottles and muskets to a cabin boy's leg bones, the remains of a Roman ship as well as a Victorian river barge; also an audio-visual show, a few hands-on activities, and you can see radar and live satellite weather pictures. Shop, disabled access; cl a few days over Christmas; (01424) 437452; donations.

Smugglers Adventure (Cobourg Pl) A labyrinth of deep caverns and passages, with models, museum and well done life-size tableaux illustrating life for an 18th-c smuggler; spooky lighting and sound effects in places. Shop; cl 24-26 Dec; (01424) 422964; £5.75.

Underwater World (Rock-a-Nore Rd) With walk-through underwater tunnel and a tropical marine section with coral. Snacks, shop, mostly disabled access; cl 24-26 Dec; (01424) 718776; £5.75.

HAYWARDS HEATH TQ3226

Borde Hill Garden (Balcombe Rd, N) Lovely 40-acre gardens most noted for their rare trees and shrubs introduced a century ago from the Himalayas and Andes; woodland, lakeside and parkland walks, and a mix of informal and more formal areas - gorgeous rhododendrons and magnolias, flaming autumn maples, roses, herbaceous borders, italian garden, restored Victorian greenhouses. Meals, snacks, plant sales, disabled access; (01444) 450326; *£6. The White Harte in Cuckfield does bargain lunches.

HERSTMONCEUX TQ6410

Herstmonceux Castle (SE of village) This handsome 15th-c moated castle is surrounded by extensive Elizabethan gardens; there's a visitor centre, play area, nature trail, and they do guided tours of the castle Sun-Fri (extra charge). Tearoom, shop, disabled access; cl Nov-Easter; (01323) 833816; grounds and gardens £4.50. The site also includes (run separately) a hands-on science centre, and astronomy displays in six former Greenwich Royal Observatory buildings; four of the domes are now completely restored with working telescopes, following a lengthy restoration project. Observation evenings and special events; phone for details. Snacks, shop, disabled access; cl wkdys Nov-Feb (plus last wknd Dec and 1st wknd Jan); (01323) 832731; £5.40, joint ticket with castle £8.90. The Ash Tree over at Brownbread Street has good old-fashioned home cooking.

HIGH BEECHES TQ2730

High Beeches Gardens (B2110, Handcross) Well worth a visit, 20 acres of landscaped woodland and water gardens, lots of rare plants, and wildflower meadows. Meals and snacks; cl am, Weds (plus Sat Jul-Aug), Nov-Mar; (01444) 400589; £5.

HIGH SALVINGTON TQ1206
High Salvington windmill An 18th-c post mill; open pm 1st and 3rd Sun of month Apr-Sept; (01903) 262443; £1.

HORSHAM TQ1730
Horsham Museum (The Causeway) Timber-framed medieval house with well organised local history (subjects range from gardening and cooking to crime and punishment), and an extraordinary collection of early bicycles. The small but pretty garden has some unusual wild cyclamen. Shop, some disabled access; cl Sun and bank hols; (01403) 254959; free. The town's much developed, but this quiet corner by the church is particularly attractive. The Black Jug (North St) has good food.

HURST GREEN TQ7328
Merriments Garden 🖻 (Hawkhurst Rd) Varied four-acre demonstration garden with lots of planting ideas, some unusual plants, and comprehensive nursery inc rare hardy plants. Tearoom, disabled access; garden open beginning Apr to mid-Oct, nursery all year; (01580) 860666; £3.50.

KINGLEY VALE SU8210
An interesting walk though needing some stamina, whether you approach via the nature trail on the S side or from Stoughton to the N. This nature reserve is one of Europe's finest yew forests, a magical place where the trees create some eerie pools of darkness on the S slopes of the downs; a fun place for family walks, with the low branches so good for climbing or hiding in. Above, you can look over Chichester Harbour from a pair of prehistoric burial mounds.

LEWES TQ4110
The administrative capital of East Sussex, this is a pleasantly unrushed country town below the quarried white edge of the South Downs. It has attractive old buildings, mainly with Georgian façades (often covering older structures) though with a few stone-built or timber-framed specimens, particularly along its steep High St and in the little narrow alleys and other streets alongside. This is where you'll

see Sussex tile-hanging at its best; there's also quite a lot of 'mathematical tiling' - sham bricks over timbered buildings to make them look more progressive. There are several decent antiques shops, a good regional auction house (Gorringes; (01273) 472503 for viewing days), and an attractive complex of **craft shops** in a former candlemaker's factory in Market Lane; café, cl Sun; (01273) 472322. The Brewers Arms (High St), Gardeners Arms and John Harvey (both Cliffe High St), interesting Lewes Arms (Mount Pl) and Snowdrop (South St) are all useful for lunch. Bill's by the river bridge in Cliffe High St is a greengrocer's with an in-house café, where you can eat things from the shop. From Bell Lane on the SW edge you can follow the old Juggs Road track, used by the Brighton fishwives, up past Kingston and the downland nature reserve by Newmarket Hill to the outskirts of Brighton itself. There are more public paths than the OS map suggests; from the town centre you can walk up Chapel Hill, through the golf course and on via an unspoilt dry valley to **Mount Caburn**, rather grandiosely named for its size but capped by an Iron Age fort and with views towards the coast; it's also popular with paragliders.

Anne of Cleves House (Southover High St) Henry VIII's fourth wife got this fine 16th-c house as part of her divorce settlement. She probably never came here, but its rooms give a good idea of regional life over the following two centuries. Shop; cl Sun and Mon Nov-Feb; (01273) 474610; £2.80, combined ticket with castle £5.80. Guided tours of the ruined Norman **priory** leave here in summer; phone David Edy (01323) 894199 for details.

Lewes Castle Unusual for being built on not one but two artificial mounds, more recently thought to be part of a prehistoric complex of mounds (Lincoln is the only other such place we know of). The roof of the keep gives the best view of the town, and there's a good museum of local history. Shop; cl Mon in Jan, and 24-26 Dec; (01273) 486290; £4.30.

Southover Grange Gardens (Southover Rd) Diarist John Evelyn's handsome boyhood home is now the District Registry Office, but you can visit the attractive gardens; teas May-Sept weather permitting; cl 25 Dec; free.

LITTLEHAMPTON TQ0202
Little sign here of its age (it was an important port up to the 1500s), but its long sandy beaches make it a popular simple family resort. Towards the W, beyond the River Arun, there's quite an extensive area of unspoilt dunes between beach and golf course. The 18th-c Arun View right on the river does good lunches.

Littlehampton Museum (Church St) This early 19th-c manor house has displays on local history and archaeology - and more than 200 model ships. Shop, disabled access; cl Sun and Mon, and 25 Dec-1 Jan; (01903) 738100; free.

Look and Sea New visitor centre, right by the water, covering the geography, geology and history of the area (subjects range from the 500,000 year old Boxgrove Man to Ian Fleming - creator of James Bond). Plenty for children inc computer games, fossil rubbing, and you can even have a go at playing the Roman board game Tabula. Great views from the 25-metre (80-ft) glass viewing tower. Tourist information centre, coffee shop, shop, mostly disabled access (best to phone); cl a few days over Christmas; (01903) 718984; £4.50.

LOWER BEEDING TQ2225
Leonardslee Enormous Grade I listed garden loved by our readers, in a 240-acre valley with seven beautiful lakes; marvellous rhododendrons, magnolias, oaks and unusual conifers, delightful rock garden, extensive alpine house, bonsai exhibition, Victorian motorcar collection, Behind the Doll's House (an interesting model of an early 20th-c country estate), and wallabies and deer. The gardens are on the edge of the ancient St Leonard's Forest. Meals, snacks, plant sales, some disabled access (ring to check); cl Nov-Mar; (01403) 891212; May £7 (£8 May wknds and bank hols), other times £6.

LURGASHALL SU9327
Attractive small village, with an unusual loggia outside the largely Saxon **church**

where parishioners walking in from a distance could eat their sandwiches. The Noahs Ark here is prettily placed for an enjoyable lunch. Lurgashall Winery (Windfallwood) produces a wide range of traditional country wines, meads and liqueurs; snacks and free tastings.

MAYFIELD TQ5826
One of Sussex's prettiest villages, with interesting shops, and pleasant hilly terrain around it. A reasonable network of paths includes a short waymarked circular walk. The Middle House is a handsome and civilised 16th-c half-timbered inn.

MIDHURST SU8821
Little market town with some attractive half-timbered buildings, and several antiques shops; H G Wells went to school here. The Angel (North St) is a civilised place for lunch, the Bricklayers Arms and Wheatsheaf (Wool Lane) are good value too, and the tourist information centre is very helpful. On the outskirts lie the ruins of Cowdray House (the estate is known for its July polo competition, and for the bright 'Cowdray yellow' paintwork on all estate buildings).

NEWHAVEN TQ4500
Genuine fishing harbour (with fish for sale), outside the compact town centre, not really a tourist place; a long harbour wall attracts anglers, and there's a popular shingle beach on the W side. Ferries and Sea Cat service to Dieppe in France from here. The harbourside Hope has decent food.

Newhaven Fort (Fort Rd) Built 120 years ago in case of french attack, this is a big place to explore, with underground installations, period reconstructions and exhibits of life during the World Wars, tunnels burrowing into the cliffs, super views from its ramparts, and an assault course for children. Snacks, shop, disabled access to exhibitions only; cl wkdys in Nov, and all Dec-Mar; (01273) 517622; £4.90.

Paradise Park (Avis Rd) Garden centre with exhibition on the last few million years of evolution, complete with earthquake experience and life-size moving dinosaurs. Themed gardens inc an indoor oriental garden, caribbean and seaside gardens, and there's also a model village with miniaturised Sussex landmarks, history trail, crazy golf and a miniature railway. Meals, snacks, shops, disabled access, cl 25-26 Dec; (01273) 512123; £5.99, garden centre free.

NEWTIMBER TQ2614
Southdown Llama Trekking You don't actually ride on these friendly creatures - they carry your lunch; (01273) 383807; shop; cl Nov-Mar; £50 per person (or £75 if you share a llama) for a 5-mile trek.

NORTHIAM TQ8225
Great Dixter (turn off A28 at Post Office) Timbered 15th-c house, carefully restored and added to by Lutyens in the early part of last century. He designed the attractive gardens too; originally arranged as a series of distinct areas, they have since been stocked more informally with interesting plants by the gardening writer Christopher Lloyd who lives here. Snacks, plant sales; cl am, all day Mon (exc bank hols), and end Oct-Mar; (01797) 252878; *£6.50, *£5 gardens only. The White Hart at Newenden has decent food.

OLD HEATHFIELD TQ5920
Charming peaceful hamlet, with good food in the ancient Star by the interesting church; a different world from the sprawly small town of Heathfield nearby, which sprang up around a defunct railway (it now functions as the Cuckoo Trail for walkers and cyclists - see Polegate). The town does surprise with a growing cluster of good value bric-a-brac shops, an excellent delicatessen specialising in unusual cheeses, and first-rate farmer/butcher - Pomfrets.

PETWORTH SU9721
Petworth Cottage Museum 🔁 (High St) Convincing reconstruction of an estate worker's cottage in 1910. Cl am, and Mon (exc bank hols), Tues and Nov-Mar; (01798) 342100; £2.50.
Petworth House Splendid, its magnificent rooms filled with one of the most impressive art collections in the country, inc dutch Old Masters and 20 pictures by Turner, a frequent visitor. Other highlights include the 13th-c chapel, grand staircase with frescoes, and the carved room, elegantly decorated by Grinling Gibbons. You can see extra rooms Mon-Weds. Meals, snacks, shop, disabled access; cl Thurs,

Fri and Dec-Feb; (01798) 342207; *£7; NT. The deer park, with stately trees and prospects still recognisable as those glorified by Turner, is open all year; free. The town (cruelly carved up by busy traffic) is now an antiques honeypot, with dozens of antiques shops in its narrow streets of attractive old houses. The Angel Hotel fits in well, and has a good wknd carvery; the Well Diggers (A283 E - almost a museum of the rural 1920s) and stylish Badgers (A285 S) have good food too.

PEVENSEY TQ6505
Pevensey Castle Formidable castle based around huge 4th-c Roman fort, with massive bastions and walls of Roman masonry still up to 9 metres (30 ft) high in places. The Norman keep was built by William the Conqueror, and you can see interesting interior details inc fireplaces, dungeons and an oubliette. Shop, some disabled access; cl Mon and Tues Nov-Mar, 24-25 Dec, 1 Jan; (01323) 762604; £3; EH. The Castle Cottage restaurant does decent food, inc light summer lunches in the castle garden.

POLEGATE TQ5804
Cuckoo Trail Surfaced track following the route of a former railway to Heathfield, with links into Eastbourne; good for traffic-free walking or family cycling - the mileposts, crafted by local artists, each have a cuckoo hidden in their design.
Filching Manor Motor Museum (Jevington Rd, Wannock) Gleamingly restored vintage cars, shown to great effect in the grounds of a striking manor house. Unique panelling in the minstrels' gallery, and Donald/Sir Malcolm Campbell connections. They also have a go-kart track (Weds-Sun and bank hols; £15 for 15 mins). Snacks, disabled access; museum entry only by guided tour; 2.30pm wknds and bank hols, but phone before to check; cl Oct-Easter; (01323) 487838; £5. The Eight Bells in Jevington is a good value food stop, with plenty of walks nearby.

PULBOROUGH TQ0518
The town has some attractive buildings down towards the river; the Waters Edge, with lake views, has a good choice of food. There's an RSPB Reserve just S, and the Citrus Centre (off A283 E, just

past White Horse pub; cl Mon/Tues) has all sorts of orange, lemon and related trees.

Nutbourne Vineyards (Nutbourne Manor) 8-acre vineyard with tours and tastings, visitor centre in a former windmill, and a family of llamas. Shop; no tours wkdy ams (exc bank hols) and Oct-Apr, best to check; (01798) 815196; free. The Elephant & Castle in West Chiltington has good value food.

Parham House Charming Elizabethan house, still a family home, its panelled rooms full of notable portraits, furniture, oriental carpets and rare needlework. The surrounding grounds are really very special; a four-acre walled garden has a greenhouse, herbaceous borders, vegetable garden and an apple orchard, and the 18th-c pleasure grounds include a maze designed for children. Snacks in 15th-c kitchen, shop, plant sales, some disabled access; open pm Weds, Thurs, Sun and bank hol Mon Easter-Sept, plus pm Tues and Fri in Aug; (01903) 744888; £6, £4 garden only.

RODMELL TQ4206

Monks House Just a quiet lived-in house, in a pleasant village, but a beautifully kept place of pilgrimage for followers of the Bloomsbury Group, as Leonard and Virginia Woolf lived here from 1919; Virginia drowned herself in the river nearby in 1941, and Leonard died in 1969. Open Weds and Sat pm Apr-Oct; (01892) 890651; *£2.80; NT.

ROTTINGDEAN TQ3602

Grange Museum and Kipling Gardens A pretty place, where enthusiastic local volunteers look after both the handsome Georgian grange, now a **museum** (usually cl Weds, Sun am and over Christmas and New Year, best to phone; (01273) 301004; free), and the pleasant two-acre **Kipling Gardens**, well restored Victorian gardens named after the author who lived here for five years from 1897. Burne-Jones was a resident for a while too, designing the windows made by William Morris for the Early English **church**.

RYE TQ9321

Enchanting, and still relatively unspoilt despite its many charms. Before the wind and sea currents did their work, the little town was virtually surrounded by sea, and as one of the Cinque Ports played an important part in providing men and ships for coastal defence. It's built on a hill crowned by the partly Norman **St Mary's church** (with a notable churchyard, and very early turret-clock, two quarter-jacks by it striking the quarter-hours); up here the largely cobbled streets still follow a 12th/13th-c narrow layout, with most of the houses lining them dating from the 16th c. The town is full of antiques shops, book shops, craft shops and a good kitchenware shop; Rye Art Gallery (107 High St) is a non-profit trust with several floors selling the best of local art and craft. The views are lovely, and steep Mermaid St with its handsome old Mermaid Inn is famously photogenic.

Camber Castle This massive Tudor fort had the sea lapping up to it when it was built, but is now stranded a mile or so inshore by the encroaching shingle (open wknd pms July-Sept; (01797) 223862; £2; EH). Beyond it the Ship on Winchelsea Beach is a welcoming refuge. **Camber Sands** on the other side of the river is the finest sandy beach in the SE, with plenty of room for walking (though it is massively popular in summer, when roads can be gridlocked; try taking a bike on the train and using the cycle path from Rye for a less congested journey).

Heritage Centre (Strand Quay) A useful introduction, with a sound-and-light show based around an intricate town model, and a self-guided Walkman tour (£2.50). Shop, disabled access; cl Christmas wk; (01797) 226696; £2.50.

Lamb House (West St) Built in 1723 for former mayor James Lamb, and chiefly devoted to mementoes of the author Henry James, who lived here 1898-1916; after his death E F Benson, who also became mayor, moved here. Open pm Weds and Sat Apr-Oct; (01892) 890651; *£2.75; NT.

Rye Castle Museum (just below Church Sq) Lively local history museum now split between two sites: the main gallery is in East St, while other displays are housed in the striking 13th-c Ypres Tower (as in Wipers) - good views of the harbour from here too, and the

Ypres Castle pub just below has good food. Shop, disabled access to East St museum; Ypres Tower cl 1-2pm, Tues, Weds Apr-Oct, and wkdys Nov-Mar, East St cl am wkdys, Tues, Weds and all Nov-Mar; (01797) 226728; £1.90 per site or £2.90 joint ticket.

Rye Harbour Because of the build-up of shingle along this coast, it's now a mile or two from the town, though yachts and fishing boats do still come right up the river to the pretty quay. The Inkerman Arms has good fresh fish. Tony Easton will take you **sea fishing** for the day, phone for details; (01797) 252104. The expanse of shingle stretching around the river mouth is now preserved as a **nature reserve**, with hides to watch the shore birds.

SALEHURST TQ7424
Attractive tucked-away village with 14th-c church and good pub, the Salehurst Halt.

SEDLESCOMBE TQ7719
Attractive village, with an unusual organic vineyard; shop, limited disabled access; cl wkdys Jan-Easter; (0800) 980 2884; tours £3.50.

SELSEY BILL SZ8592
One of the nicest and cleanest **beaches** along the S coast. The Lifeboat (Albion Rd) has good value food inc local crab.

SEVEN SISTERS COUNTRY PARK TV5199
(A259, Exceat) Part of a magnificent and quite unspoilt sweep of coastline, with the River Cuckmere meandering its way through sheep-grazed meadows to a vast shingle bank at Cuckmere Haven, the only undeveloped estuary in Sussex (no car access to sea; about a mile's walk - good level path). From here you can walk up on to the Seven Sisters (open access), a series of vertical chalk headlands forming the spectacular finale of the South Downs Way (leading on to Beachy Head above Eastbourne). Opposite the car parks is an exhibition (cl wkdys Nov-Mar) on the surrounding area (the heritage coast); you can hire bikes from the Cuckmere Cycle Co at adjacent Granary Barn; (01323) 870310, and eat at the Exceat Farmhouse. For an interesting circular walk you can head inland by Friston Forest, West Dean and East Dean. The roomy Golden Galleon

just W does good food and brews its own beer.

SHEFFIELD PARK TQ4124
Sheffield Park Garden 🖽
Wonderful 120-acre garden partly landscaped by Capability Brown, since then imaginatively planted with many varieties of tree unknown to him, especially chosen for their autumn colours. Also marvellous rhododendrons, azaleas and water-lilies on the lakes. Snacks, shop, disabled access; cl Mon (exc bank hols), all wkdys Jan-Feb and 21 Dec-4 Jan; (01825) 790231; *£5.20; NT. The Griffin at Fletching nearby is very good for lunch.

SHEFFIELD PARK STATION TQ4023
Bluebell Railway See separate family panel on p.587.

SHOREHAM-BY-SEA TQ2106
Though not one of England's more famous ports, this is quite a busy one, with several attractive old buildings around the harbour. Inland, in Old Shoreham, the early Norman **church** is accompanied by some handsome old houses (among them the good 16th-c Red Lion). The recently restored and extended Norman/14th-c building called **Marlipins** contains an absorbing local and maritime museum; cl Sun-Mon (01273) 462994; £1.50. The next-door pub of the same name does tasty bar lunches. Cross the footbridge over the estuary and turn right for a wonderful array of house boats, some converted from very ancient-looking craft with all manner of subsequent home improvements. Just W is striking **Lancing College Chapel**, begun in 1868, with a soaringly handsome nave, and elaborate stained-glass window.

SINGLETON SU8713
Weald & Downland Open-air Museum (A286) Fascinating collection of over 45 historic buildings rescued from all over the south-east, dismantled and re-erected here. They're arranged to form an authentic-looking village, with outlying farm and agricultural buildings, medieval farmstead and shops, blacksmith's forge, tollhouse and Victorian schoolroom. You can buy flour from the working watermill, and watch craftsmen preparing timber frames in the timber-built but

impressively futuristic gridshell building. At Winkhurst Farm you can try Tudor food authentically prepared in the working kitchen (phone to book their Tudor dinners). Well organised children's activities might include brick-laying or basket-making. Snacks, shop, some disabled access, but the site is rather steep; cl Nov-Feb (exc wknds and Christmas wk, best to check then); (01243) 811348; £7. The 16th-c Fox & Hounds nearby is a good stop.

SOUTH DOWNS TQ2609

Open rolling downland, becoming more appealing to walkers (it's very popular at wknds), with increasing incentives for farming here to turn away from arable crops and intensive livestock production. A public enquiry is about to begin to investigate the possibility of setting up a South Downs National Park. The steep N slopes are the most impressive. **Devil's Dyke** above Brighton is one tremendous viewpoint within visible Iron Age ramparts, usually busy with kite-fliers. Although it's a bit crowded around the car park and modern pub there, things get better close by - head along the South Downs Way in either direction. The Dyke itself is a magnificent dry valley cutting deep into the downs, making a lovely route down to Poynings. The Shepherd & Dog at nearby Fulking has a pretty, informal garden huddled beneath the downs, and makes a good focal point for round walks. Other high points are Wolstonbury Hill, and the Jack and Jill windmills nr Clayton.

SOUTH HARTING SU7819

A pretty downland village, with good value food in the nicely set 17th-c Ship. The chalk Harting Downs involve no more than a level stroll from the road above the village; with more good food, the Coach & Horses in the pleasant nearby village of Compton is another good base for walks in this area.

Downland drive The roads around here give attractive drives - the B2141 and B2146 S of South Harting, the Walderton—East Mardon back road between them, and the downs-foot road E through East Harting, Elsted, Treyford and Cocking.

Uppark ⊞ (B2146 S) Splendid 17th-c

house, extensively restored after a disastrous fire in 1989. Incredibly, most of the house's public treasures were rescued, even the wallpaper. The grounds, designed by Humphrey Repton, have a woodland walk and fine views towards The Solent. Meals, snacks, shop, disabled access; cl Fri, Sat and Nov-Mar, house also cl am; (01730) 825415; *£5.50; NT. The Ship and White Hart are handy for pub lunches.

TANGMERE SU9106

Military Aviation Museum (off A27) Good collection of flying memorabilia based around the former RAF station where H E Bates finished writing *Fair Stood the Wind for France*. Displays include a DeHavilland Sea Vixen and an english Electric Lightning fighter. Snacks, shop, disabled access; cl Dec-Jan; (01243) 775223; £4. The nearby Bader Arms has more memorabilia; and the 16th-c thatched Gribble at Oving is an attractive place for lunch.

TICEHURST TQ7029

Pashley Manor Gardens (B2099) Now one of the most charming gardens in the south-east, eight acres of beautifully restored mainly Victorian formal gardens around a handsome house once owned by the Boleyn family. Magnificent old trees, delightfully placed moat and walled garden, views, folly, fine shrubs, roses, herbaceous beds, and clever focal points; very relaxed and peaceful. Tulip festival in early May, and a summer flower festival in Jun, also sculpture and botanical art exhibition every summer. Snacks, plant sales, shop, limited disabled access; cl Sun, Mon (exc bank hols) and Fri, and all Nov-Mar; (01580) 200888; £6. The village is attractive; up a side road at Three Legged Cross, Maynards has good pick-your-own.

TURNERS HILL TQ3335

Tulleys Farm Huge range of pick-your-own soft fruit and vegetables (Jun-Oct), as well as a tearoom, and a good farm shop; special events around Hallowe'en and Easter; cl 25-26 Dec; (01342) 718472. There's an annual crop labyrinth (don't worry if you get stuck, from a watchtower an eagle-eyed guide will lead you to the centre) with other activities for younger children inc tractor rides, straw mountain and mini mazes; mid-July to mid-Sept; £5. The Crown is a spacious and enjoyable dining pub.

UPPER DICKER TQ5509

Michelham Priory Part of a 13th-c Augustinian priory, with 14th-c gatehouse by the moat (which has plenty of waterfowl). Interesting furniture, tapestries and local ironwork, as well as crafts, working watermill, and rope museum. Meals, snacks, shop, disabled access to gardens and ground floor only; cl Mon (exc bank hols and Aug), and all Nov-Feb; (01323) 844224; £5, 50% discount for EH members.

WARBLETON TQ6018

Right off the beaten track and as a result very unspoilt - the village has more pre-1750 Sussex barns than anywhere else in the county. The Warbil in Tun is a friendly dining pub.

WEIR WOOD RESERVOIR TQ3935

A pleasant waterside walk traces along its N shore, with paths leading up to Standen House.

WEST CHILTINGTON TQ0918

West Chiltington church Beautiful building in lovely downland countryside - this is windmill country, too. The village is pretty, and the Elephant & Castle has good value food and a good family garden.

WEST DEAN SU8612

West Dean Gardens Old roses, very long 1911 pergola, wild garden, walled kitchen garden with all sorts of espaliered fruit trees and impressive 19th-c glasshouses, and interesting collection of stately mature conifers in park and arboretum; a splendid downland setting, notably peaceful and relaxed. Meals, snacks in the visitor centre, shop and plant sales, limited disabled access; cl Nov-Feb; (01243) 818210; *£5.50. The Fox Goes Free at Charlton is good for lunch.

WEST HOATHLY TQ3632

Attractive village tucked quietly away from the road, with tremendous views from the lane down past the ancient Cat dining pub. On a clear day you can see the whole sweep of the South Downs between Chanctonbury Ring and the Long Man of Wilmington.

Priest House Near the 13th-c church, 15th-c timbered house, now a folk museum with a little cottage garden

containing over 150 herbs. Shop, some disabled access; cl Mon, Sun am, and Nov-Feb; (01342) 810479; £2.70. They can arrange guided tours of the village.

WESTFIELD TQ8115

Carr Taylor Vineyard One of England's most successful commercial vineyards, producing sparkling wine as well as still. Snacks, shop, disabled access (but no facilities); cl 25 Dec-1 Jan; (01424) 752501; free, wine trail £1.50.

WHITESMITH TQ5213

Blackberry Farm Aimed mostly at children under seven, lots of the attractions at this friendly working farm are under cover, so there's quite a bit to do even when the weather isn't great. Activities from pat a pet sessions to pony grooming and egg collecting; also tractor rides, an adventure playground, and you can camp here. Meals, snacks, shop, disabled access; cl Tues, and wkdys Jan-Feb, best to check; (01825) 872912; £4.

WILMINGTON TQ5403

Long Man of Wilmington Gigantic chalk-cut figure so far impossible to date - guesses hover anywhere between the early 18th c and the Bronze Age. You can take paths up to the top of the South Downs and carry on S over glorious downland towards **Lullington Heath** National Nature Reserve, which gives some idea of how the downs looked before large-scale agriculture; botanically unusual for its mixture of chalkland and heathland flora. The Giants Rest in Wilmington has good home cooking.

WINCHELSEA TQ9017

A rare example of a planned medieval town (now decidedly village-like in character), ranged around a grid of peaceful streets, and an interesting contrast in style to nearby Rye. Storms, french raids and the Black Death put paid to Winchelsea's commercial importance. Most of the buildings are post-medieval: there are fine 17th-c and 18th-c houses with much older vaulted cellars in their basements, while the tranquil church of St Thomas is elaborately decorated, with some fine old stained glass and medieval tombs. The New Inn is popular for lunch. There are three town gates: one of them, the New Gate, is in a field some way S, and in view from the well waymarked 1066 Country Walk, which gives some wide views over Romney Marsh and the sea; it's worth taking this path to the Queens Head at Icklesham, which has good food. The Royal Military Canal, from here to Hythe in Kent, was a never-used Napoleonic defence meant as a sort of glorified coastal moat - now a peaceful spot for coarse fishing.

WISBOROUGH GREEN TQ0526
Fishers Farm Park (Newpound Lane) Friendly farm, well equipped for children up to 10, with animal show and petting areas, good indoor and outdoor play areas, quad bikes and mini tractor rides; they've recently added a climbing wall and bumper boats. Meals, snacks, shop, disabled access; cl 25-26 Dec; (01403) 700063; £8, less in winter. The Three Crowns (A272) has good value food.

WORTHING TQ1402
Restrained but rather charming town, with a pleasant seafront; in the same mould as Brighton but altogether quieter. The formerly separate village of West Tarring has enjoyable food in two welcoming old pubs, the Vine and George & Dragon. At nearby Goring-on-Sea, the English Martyrs' Church (Compton Ave) has a unique nearly full-sized reproduction of the Sistine Chapel ceiling.

Worthing Museum and Art Gallery (Chapel Rd) Highlights are a rich archaeological collection, costume galleries, a Victorian nursery, and a sculpture garden; temporary exhibitions. Shop, disabled access; cl Sun and some bank hols; (01903) 239999; free.

WYCH CROSS TQ4235
Ashdown Llama Park Working farm with breeding herds of llamas and alpacas; they've a little museum, farm trail, and adventure playground. Snacks and picnic area, shop, disabled access; cl 25-26 Dec; (01825) 712040; £3.50. The Sussex Country Information Centre is based here too (01825) 713812, and Barnsgate Manor Vineyard (a few miles down the road at Herons Ghyll) has great views from its attractive restaurant.

Other attractive villages, all with civilised pubs doing decent food, include Barns Green TQ1227, Brightling TQ6921 (the pub is at nearby Oxleys Green), Byworth SU9820, Chiddingly TQ5414, Easebourne SU8922, the other East Dean SU9013, Elsted SU8119, Findon TQ1208, Fittleworth TQ0118, Funtington SU7908, Hellingly TQ5812, Henley SU8925, Jevington TQ5601, Kirdford TQ0126, Lodsworth SU9223, Robertsbridge TQ7323, Rotherfield TQ5529, Rudgwick TQ0833, Rushlake Green TQ6218, woodland Selham SU9320 (partly pre-Norman church), Slaugham TQ2528, Stopham TQ0218, Sutton SU9715, Waldron TQ5419 and West Chiltington TQ0918 (both have ancient churches).

Where to eat

ALCISTON TQ5005 **Rose Cottage** *(01323) 870377* In the same family for over 30 years, this charming little wisteria-covered cottage is full of harnesses, traps, ironware and bric-a-brac; Jasper is the talking parrot (mornings only); very good promptly served food (esp the simply cooked fresh fish) using organic vegetables and their own eggs, well kept real ales, decent wines and a good range of other drinks like kir and Pimms, a small no smoking evening restaurant, and seats outside; cl 25-26 Dec; children over 10. £26.85|**£7.25**

ASHURST TQ1816 **Fountain** *(01403) 710219* Welcoming 16th-c country pub with a carefully restored main dining room, charmingly rustic bar with flagstones, heavy beams and inglenook log fire, well kept real ales, freshly squeezed apple juice from their own press in Sept (proceeds to a children's charity), and decent wines; popular imaginative food using local produce, pleasant attentive service, a prettily planted garden (inc raised herb beds for the kitchen), and plenty of tables on the wooden decking; no credit cards, cold food only Sun, Mon pms, cl 25, 26 Dec pms, no children inside. £26|**£6.95**

BRIGHTON TQ3105 **Black Chapati** *12 Circus Parade (01273) 699011* Particularly good eastern cooking with anglo-indian influences in starkly furnished restaurant with white walls and black tables and chairs, and breton cider - wine does not always suit the style of food; cl ams, Sun-Tues pms; disabled access. £29

BRIGHTON TQ3004 **Browns** *3-4 Duke St (01273) 323501* Relaxed and chatty restaurant with an airy spacious feel, bentwood chairs around wooden tables, lots of greenery, ceiling fans, and enjoyable reasonably priced english food with european influences; welcoming for families; cl 25-26 Dec; disabled access. £25.80|£7.50☺

BRIGHTON TQ3203 **One Paston Place** *(01273) 606933* Just off the seafront, this airy enjoyable restaurant has a big mural, very good modern british food inc super fish and game dishes, nice puddings, decent house wines, and a friendly atmosphere; cl Sun, Mon, 3 wks in winter, 2 wks; no children in the evening. £51.50

BRIGHTON TQ3103 **Terre à Terre** *71 East St (01273) 729051* Very popular and lively vegetarian restaurant with stripped floors, subtle lighting and honey-coloured walls, a very relaxed, informal and friendly atmosphere, innovative and extremely good meat-free food, and plenty of organic wines and beers; cl Mon am, 24-26 Dec; disabled access. £27|£8.50

BURPHAM TQ0308 **George & Dragon** *(01903) 883131* Smartly comfortable dining pub with splendid views down to Arundel Castle and river; good promptly served food with unusual specials inc good vegetarian dishes, elegant restaurant - worth booking; no food Sun pm; cl Sun pm during winter; children over 8; disabled access. £28.85|£6.95

CHICHESTER SU8606 **Comme Ça** *67 Broyle Rd (01243) 788724* Busy little restaurant close to Festival Theatre with good classic french cooking, popular Sun lunches and children's menu; cl Sun pm, Mon, 2 wks Christmas and New Year; partial disabled access. £35|£11.95

CHICHESTER SU8604 **St Martin's Tea Room** *3 St Martin's St (01243) 786715* Handsome brick Georgian-fronted house with pretty garden for summer eating, good lunchtime snacks and meals (mainly vegetarian but with some fish dishes) and afternoon teas using organic produce; cl Sun and bank hols; disabled access. £20|£5.95

DANEHILL TQ4128 **Coach & Horses** *(01825) 740369* Cottagey pub in attractive countryside with a really relaxed chatty atmosphere, well kept real ales, a lower part leading to dining area with flowers, candles, woodburner and hops on beams, enjoyable interesting bar food (the specials are well worth checking out), and good wines; big back garden with plenty of seats, with more out in front; no food Sun pm (exc bank hol wknds); cl 25 Dec pm, 26 Dec, 1 Jan pm; seated children welcome; disabled access. £28|£4.95

DUNCTON SU9517 **Cricketers** *(01798) 342473* Pretty little white pub with enjoyable popular food from light bites to more elaborate meals, a friendly, chatty and relaxed mix of diners and drinkers, inglenook log fire and country chairs around scrubbed wooden tables; well kept real ales and decent wines; charming garden with plenty of seats and proper barbecue area. £26|£8.95

EAST ASHLING SU8207 **Horse & Groom** *(01243) 575339* (B2178) Charming country pub with nice scrubbed trestle tables on old pale flagstones and woodburner in big inglenook in the proper front bar, big blackboard listing the changing choice of good food, and extensive back dining area (entirely no smoking); well kept real ales, a fine choice of wines by the glass, efficient but friendly and informal service, french windows to garden with picnic-sets; comfortable bdrms in adjoining barn conversion. £25.50|£8.80

EAST CHILTINGTON TQ3615 **Jolly Sportsman** *Chapel Lane (01273) 890400* Tucked-away dining pub with stripped wooden floors, contemporary light wood furniture and modern landscapes on pale yellow-painted brick walls in the informally civilised restaurant, chatty little bar, imaginative cooking from a changing menu, remarkably good wine list and well kept real ales; rustic tables and benches under gnarled trees in a pretty cottagey front garden; cl Sun pm, Mon, 4 days at Christmas; disabled access. £32.50/2 courses £11.50

EASTBOURNE TV6099 **Downland** *37 Lewes Rd (01323) 732689* Pretty candlelit evening restaurant in well run small hotel, with carefully prepared innovative food, good vegetables and lovely puddings, a relaxed atmosphere, and friendly service; bdrms; cl am; children over 10. £21

EASTBOURNE TV6199 **Pavilion Tea Rooms** *Royal Parade (01323) 410374*
Bustling tearoom by the prom with neatly uniformed friendly staff, attractive
bamboo furniture, and morning coffee, enjoyable light lunches, and afternoon teas;
cl 25 Dec. £25|£6

EDBURTON TQ2111 **Tottington Manor** *Edburton Rd (01903) 815757* Set in
its own grounds with lovely views, this country house has particularly good food
using fresh seasonal produce in bar and no smoking restaurant, winter log fire,
friendly service and a relaxed atmosphere; bdrms; cl Sun pm, Mon, 1st 2 wks Jan;
children over 5; disabled access. £42/2 course lunch £14.50

ELSTED SU8119 **Three Horseshoes** *(01730) 825746* Cosy Tudor pub in lovely
setting with fine views of South Downs from the garden (and good nearby walks);
snug rustic rooms with huge log fires, ancient beams and venerable furnishings, very
good english country cooking inc lovely puddings, well kept real ales, decent wines
by the glass; well behaved children. £27.50|£8

FERNHURST SU8926 **Kings Arms** *Midhurst Rd (01428) 652005* (A286 S)
17th-c dining pub, relaxed and civilised, with very low heavy black beams, big log fire
under a long low mantelbeam, smaller no smoking room with often intriguing bottle
openers and quite a few wine-orientated pictures, fresh flowers, a table of local
newspapers, and welcoming service; good interesting food inc popular daily specials
and plenty of fresh fish, well kept changing real ales, carefully chosen wines, and
seats in the fair-sized garden. £28|£8.50

FLETCHING TQ4223 **Griffin** *(01825) 722890* Civilised and chatty old country
inn with blazing log fires in quaintly panelled rooms, old photographs and hunting
prints, very good innovative food, well kept beers, a good wine list with lots (inc
champagne) by the glass, relaxed friendly atmosphere, and lovely garden; bdrms; cl
25 Dec; disabled access. £32|£8

HASTINGS TQ8209 **Harris** *58 High St (01424) 437221* Relaxed, informal and
chatty, reasonably priced mainly spanish food (enjoyable tapas), friendly staff in long
white aprons, and decent wine; cl Sun- Mon (exc bank hols). £22|£6.50

HORSHAM TQ1730 **Black Jug** *31 North St (01403) 253526* Most attractively
refurbished Edwardian town pub with a relaxed atmosphere, a big airy bar around
central servery, lots of old prints and photographs, a plant-filled conservatory, very
popular interesting bar food, chilled flavoured vodkas, well kept real ales, 14 wines
by the glass, and small back terrace. £30|£8.95

JEVINGTON TQ5601 **Hungry Monk** *(01323) 482178* Long-standing popular
candlelit evening restaurant (also Sun lunch) with three beamed sitting rooms, bar, little
dining room, open fires, a friendly dinner-partyish atmosphere, and good interesting
food; cl Mon-Sat am, bank hols (exc Good Fri), 24-26 Dec; children over 5. £38.50

LITLINGTON TQ5201 **Litlington Tea Gardens** *(01323) 870222* Established
150 years ago, these tearooms still keep their quaint Victorian elegance, with
seating outside on an attractive sheltered lawn under a copper beech and ginkgo, in
renovated beach huts with open fronts, or indoors; colourful hanging baskets and
flowering tubs, quick efficient service; morning coffee, light lunches, and cream teas;
handy for Alfriston; cl Mon (exc bank hols) and last Sun in Oct-1 wk before Easter;
disabled access.|£5.50

LODSWORTH SU9321 **Halfway Bridge** *Midhurst Rd (01798) 861281* Civilised
family-run pub with big helpings of inventive home cooking in no smoking restaurant
or attractively decorated comfortable bar rooms, log fires, well kept real
ales, ciders and wines; bdrms; cl Sun pm in winter; children welcome over 10;
disabled access. £27.90|£7.95

RYE TQ9220 **Flushing Inn** *4 Market St (01797) 223292* Attractive old timber-
framed building with particularly good local fish and seafood (local meat dishes,
too), various gastronomic events; note the fine 16th-c wall painting; bdrms; cl Mon
pm, Tues, first 2 wks Jan, 1st 2 wks Jun. £38|£9

RYE TQ9220 **Landgate Bistro** *5-6 Landgate (01797) 222829* Simply furnished
beamed bistro (evenings only) with good accomplished english cooking, nice

puddings, relaxed service, and a carefully chosen little wine list; cl ams, Sun-Mon, 2 wks summer and 2 wk Christmas. £29

TROTTON SU8322 **Keepers Arms** *(01730) 813724* 18th-c beamed and timbered pub, sofas by big log fire, some unusual pictures and artefacts, interesting medley of old or antique furniture, pretty candelabra, and bowls of fruit and chillies; particularly good interesting food inc yummy puddings, friendly service, relaxed atmosphere, well kept real ales and decent wines; country views from the latticed windows, and tables out on a terrace in front; cl Sun pm, Mon, 1 wk over Christmas; children must be well behaved; disabled access. £22|£5

WARTLING TQ6509 **Lamb** *(01323) 832116* Attractive little country pub, chatty and bustling (particularly in the evening), tiny entrance bar, no smoking snug with beams, timbering and church candles on the tables, and a dining room (no smoking until 9.30pm) with a mix of homely sofas around low tables by the fireplace, lots of big candles and fresh flowers; well liked food from an interesting menu, local ales, and good wines (inc champagne) by the glass; seats on the flower-filled back terrace. £25|£7.95

Special thanks to Ben Dyson, J A Snell, Gemma Warren, E G Parish

WARWICKSHIRE
(with Birmingham and the
West Midlands)

**Excellent family days out, and a lively mix of other places to visit,
including some outstanding museums and art galleries**

Birmingham has a fantastic range of family attractions, and new
developments in the city centre are making it a more appealing place to
visit. This year, the National Sea Life Centre there is the top
Warwickshire Family Attraction, and other high points for families are
headed by Thinktank (an excellent discovery centre), and Cadbury World
(unmissable for chocolate-lovers). A bonus is that quite a few of the very
good museums and art galleries here are free, as are those in nearby
Walsall - its New Art Gallery is a real eye-opener.

Warwick, with its lively castle and some worthwhile museums, has
plenty of character - a good place for a short stay. Stratford-upon-Avon is a
magnet for theatre-goers and Shakespeare devotees (there's a money-
saving all-in ticket for most Bard-related sites), and has a few things to
tempt besides. Coventry has quite a bit to attract the day-tripper (including
some first-class transport museums). Leamington Spa still has some of its
heyday elegance. In and around Wolverhampton striking Wightwick
Manor, Bantock House and Moseley Old Hall are unexpected treasures.

The excellent re-creation of a Black Country village in Dudley has
something to keep all ages engrossed (there's a zoo nearby, too). Children
like the farm parks at Middleton, Bodymoor Heath and Tanworth-in-
Arden. A big plus for the county are the outstanding transport museums:
we recommend particularly the one at Gaydon (a real pleasure if you like
classic cars). Elsewhere, there are dazzling displays at the glass museum in
Kingswinford, and innovative organic gardens at Ryton-on-Dunsmore.

Rewarding historic houses include the grand Palladian Ragley Hall in
Alcester (adventure playground, maze and woodland walks), Coughton
Court (in the same family for around 600 years), Farnborough Hall (plenty
inside to catch the eye). The fine houses at Baddesley Clinton and
Packwood do a joint ticket; Charlecote Park and Kenilworth Castle are
good choices when it's sunny. Upton House has an exceptional range of
paintings, and the 18th-c mansion in Compton Verney now houses an
interesting art collection too.

The countryside (which edges into the Cotswolds in the S) is quietly
attractive, laced with canals and dotted with charming villages and
appealing places to stay (some of them notable value).

Please let us know what you think of places in the *Guide*. Use the report forms
at the back of the book, write us a letter or log on to www.goodguides.co.uk

Where to stay

AVON DASSETT SP4150 **Crandon House** *Avon Dassett, Leamington Spa, Warwickshire CV33 0AA (01295) 770652* **£46***, plus winter breaks; 5 no smoking rms, 2 in converted dairy. Welcoming farmhouse on small working farm with rare breeds livestock, fine views, big garden, comfortable sitting rooms (one with woodburner), and extensive breakfast menu with home-made marmalade and preserves and free-range eggs; cl Christmas; children over 8

BIRMINGHAM SP0687 **Hotel du Vin & Bistro** *25 Church St, Birmingham, Warwickshire B3 2NR (0121) 200 0600* **£147**; 66 stylish rms, named after wine producers. In the converted Birmingham eye hospital, this early Victorian building is right in the old city centre; basement bar with leather sofas, Bubbly Bar with a choice of 50 champagnes, imaginative modern cooking in wooden-floored bistro, an excellent wine list, super breakfasts, lovely flower arrangements, and friendly, professional staff

BISHOP'S TACHBROOK SP3262 **Mallory Court** *Harbury Lane, Bishop's Tachbrook, Leamington Spa, Warwickshire CV33 9QB (01926) 330214* **£195***, plus special breaks; 18 comfortable rms. Fine ancient-looking house - actually built around 1910 - with elegant antiques and flower-filled day rooms, attentive staff, and excellent food using home-grown produce in oak panelled restaurant; ten acres of lovely gardens with outdoor swimming pool, tennis, and croquet; children over 9; disabled access; dogs welcome in bedrooms

BLACKWELL SP2343 **Blackwell Grange** *Blackwell, Shipston-on-Stour, Warwickshire CV36 4PF (01608) 682357* **£65***; 3 pretty rms. 17th-c Cotswold farmhouse with log fire in comfortable beamed sitting room, large inglenook fireplace in flagstoned dining room, good home cooking using own free-range eggs (evening meal by arrangement; bring your own wine), pretty garden, and nice country views; cl 24-25 Dec; children over 12, but parents with younger children stay in annexe; good disabled access; dogs by arrangement

HOCKLEY HEATH SP1571 **Nuthurst Grange** *Nuthurst Grange Rd, Hockley Heath, Solihull, West Midlands B94 5NL (01564) 783972* **£165**; 15 comfortable, spacious rms with lots of extras. Red brick, creeper-clad Edwardian house in landscaped gardens, with light, airy and prettily decorated public rooms, lovely fresh flowers, enjoyable modern british cooking using home-grown produce, good breakfasts, and pleasant helpful staff; cl Christmas; disabled access; dogs welcome in bedrooms

ILMINGTON SP2143 **Howard Arms** *Ilmington, Shipston-on-Stour, Warwickshire CV36 4LT (01608) 682226* **£98***, plus special breaks; 3 stylishly comfortable rms. Neatly kept golden stone 17th/18th-c inn opposite village green with pleasant sheltered garden and terrace; beamed and flagstoned dining bar with antiques and country furniture, open fires, friendly service, very good food, and decent wines; cl 25 Dec; children over 8

LITTLE COMPTON SP2630 **Red Lion** *Little Compton, Moreton-in-Marsh, Gloucestershire GL56 0RT (01608) 674397* **£40**; 3 rms, shared bthrm. Attractive 16th-c stone inn with low beams, log fires, separate dining area, extensive menu with tasty food, no smoking area, real ales, long wine list, and seats in the sizeable attractive garden; children over 8

LOXLEY SP2755 **Loxley Farm** *Stratford Rd, Loxley, Warwick, Warwickshire CV35 9JN (01789) 840265* **£70***; 2 suites with their own sitting rooms in attractive barn conversion. Not far from Stratford, this tucked-away, thatched and half-timbered partly 14th-c house has low beams, wonky walls and floors, antiques and dried flowers, open fire, helpful friendly owners, and good Aga-cooked breakfasts; peaceful garden, and fine old village church; cl Christmas and New Year; dogs welcome in bedrooms

PILLERTON HERSEY SP3048 **Dockers Barn Farm** *Oxhill Bridle Rd, Pillerton Hersey, Warwick, Warwickshire CV35 0QB (01926) 640475* **£48**; 3 cosy, beamed rms decorated with stencils. Quietly set and carefully converted 18th-c threshing barn surrounded by fields of sheep and ponies; friendly owners, flagstoned dining room, lots of family portraits, nice old furniture, and an interesting garden; cl Christmas;

children over 8; dogs welcome in bedrooms

SHERBOURNE SP2562 **Old Rectory** *Vicarage Lane, Sherbourne, Warwick, Warwickshire CV35 8AB (01926) 624562* **£75**; 7 rms with hand-carved four-posters and brass beds. Charming 17th-c country house (new owners this year) with cosy sitting room, big log fire in inglenook fireplace, beams, flagstones and elm floors, and enjoyable breakfasts; cl Christmas and New Year; no children

STRATFORD-UPON-AVON SP1954 **Carlton** *22 Evesham Pl, Stratford-upon-Avon, Warwickshire CV37 6HT (01789) 293548* **£40***; 8 homely rms, some with own bthrm. Neatly kept and very welcoming no smoking Victorian house, close to theatre and restaurants, with helpful owners, very good breakfasts in airy dining room, and little garden; no children; disabled access to one room

STRATFORD-UPON-AVON SP1954 **Caterham House** *58-59 Rother St, Stratford-upon-Avon, Warwickshire CV37 6LT (01789) 267309* **£80**, 10 individually decorated rms with antiques and fresh flowers. Popular Georgian house a few mins from Royal Shakespeare Theatre; interestingly furnished sitting room opening on to pretty terrace, french country-style furniture, and excellent breakfasts (plenty of restaurants nearby for evening meals); dogs welcome in bedrooms

STRATFORD-UPON-AVON SP2054 **Melita** *37 Shipston Rd, Stratford-upon-Avon, Warwickshire CV37 7LN (01789) 292432* **£72***, plus special breaks; 12 well equipped, no smoking rms. Friendly family-run Victorian hotel with pretty, carefully laid-out garden, comfortable lounge with open fire, extensive breakfasts; close to town centre and theatre; cl Christmas and New Year; dogs welcome in bedrooms

STRATFORD-UPON-AVON SP2054 **Shakespeare** *Chapel St, Stratford-upon-Avon, Warwickshire CV37 6ER (0870) 400 8182* **£110**, plus wknd breaks; 74 comfortable well equipped rms. Smart hotel based on handsome lavishly modernised Tudor merchants' houses, with comfortable bar, good food, quick friendly service, and civilised tea or coffee in peaceful chintzy armchairs by blazing log fires; seats out in back courtyard; three mins' walk from theatre; disabled access; dogs welcome in bedrooms

STRATFORD-UPON-AVON SP2056 **Welcombe Hotel** *Warwick Rd, Stratford-upon-Avon, Warwickshire CV37 0NR (01789) 295252* **£185**, plus special breaks; 64 rms with antiques and luxurious bthrms. Jacobean-style mansion in parkland estate with 18-hole golf course, and two all-weather floodlit tennis courts; deeply comfortable day rooms inc fine panelled lounge, open fires and fresh flowers, elegant restaurant (children over 13 in evening), and good service; disabled access

SUTTON COLDFIELD SP1394 **New Hall** *New Hall Drive, Sutton Coldfield, West Midlands B76 1QX (0121) 378 2442* **£154**w, plus special breaks; 60 lovely rms (the ones in the manor house are the best). England's oldest moated manor house, in 26 beautiful acres, with luxurious day rooms, a graceful panelled restaurant with carefully cooked imaginative food using the freshest (often home-grown) produce, and excellent service; they can hold wedding ceremonies, and have a leisure club; partial disabled access

WALCOTE SP1258 **Walcote Farm** *Walcote, Alcester, Warwickshire B49 6LY (01789) 488264* **£44**; 3 rms with fine views, 1 with a late 16th-c window. Attractive 16th-c farmhouse in pretty hamlet with plenty of surrounding walks; a warm welcome from friendly owners, log fires in inglenook fireplaces, beams and flagstones, good breakfasts (several local pubs for evening meals), and pretty garden; no smoking; cl Christmas-New Year; children over 5

WARWICK SP2864 **Forth House** *44 High St, Warwick, Warwickshire CV34 4AX (01926) 401512* **£74***, plus special breaks; 2 appealing and spacious suites - 1 almost a garden flat with its own kitchen. Prettily decorated no smoking house with a lovely, surprisingly big garden, and good breakfasts; disabled access; self-catering flat also

WILMCOTE SP1658 **Pear Tree Cottage** *7 Church Rd, Wilmcote, Stratford-upon-Avon, Warwickshire CV37 9UX (01789) 205889* **£56***; 5 rms. Charming half-timbered Elizabethan house owned by the same family for three generations, with beams, flagstones, country antiques, a cosy atmosphere, good breakfasts, and sizeable shady garden; self-catering also; cl 24 Dec-2 Jan; children over 3

To see and do

Warwickshire Family Attraction of the Year

BIRMINGHAM SP0686 **National Sea Life Centre** 🔲 (Waters Edge, Brindley Pl) This excellent little chain has centres in several seaside resorts around the country (and indeed some abroad), but this one, miles from any natural beach or coast, is easily the best. They're very committed to their cause, and keep only creatures that will flourish in the environment they've created, but though there's a serious side they're not at all po-faced - a visit is great fun as well as instructive. And while plenty of aquariums have walk-through tunnels, the showpiece here goes one better: you go through a totally clear tube in a one million litre tropical ocean tank, with creatures above, below and all around you. It's been designed to show off their two giant green turtles, who arrived at the centre in 2003. Altogether there are around 60 displays housing 3,000 british marine and freshwater creatures shown off in careful re-creations of their natural habitats: the sharks are always a highlight, but look out too for the otters, the seahorses, and the huge spider crabs. Touchpools let you get close to crabs and starfish, and there are plenty of friendly, helpful staff on hand to answer questions. There's a very good programme of talks and displays throughout the day, and a themed soft play area for younger visitors. Everything's undercover, and it will easily keep most age groups happy for a couple of hours. The only downside is that it can get very busy; come early or late to avoid the crowds. Norman Foster designed the building. Meals, snacks, shop, disabled access; cl 25 Dec; (0121) 643 4700; £8.95 adults, £6.50 children; a family ticket (two adults, two children) is £29.95. They'll stamp your hand so you can go in and out all day.

ALCESTER SP0755
Ragley Hall (off A46/A435 S) Privately owned family home of the Marquess and Marchioness of Hertford, this perfectly symmetrical Palladian house stands in nearly a mile of parkland and formal gardens; excellent baroque plasterwork in Great Hall, fine paintings (inc some modern art) and a mural by Graham Rust; adventure playground, maze and woodland walks in the grounds, many special events inc good outdoor concerts. Meals, snacks, shop, disabled access; cl Mon-Weds, all Oct-Mar; (01789) 762090; £6, grounds also open every day during main school hols. The nearby village of Arrow is attractive and interesting to stroll around, despite some development. Fruit farming around here is much rarer than it used to be, but you can still find delicious fresh dessert plums for sale in Sept. The county's best drive (partly in Worcs) circles this area, via Wixford (the Three Horseshoes has good food), Radford, Inkberrow, Holberrow Green, New End, Kings Coughton,

Walcote, Aston Cantlow, Wilmcote and Temple Grafton.
ANSLEY SP2792
Hoar Park Craft Centre & Granary Antiques (B4114, nr Ansley) Children's farm (£1.50), antiques and garden centres, and tearoom, as well as various craft shops housed in 18th-c farm buildings. Some parts cl Mon (exc bank hols), all parts cl 25-26 Dec; (024) 7639 4433; free.
ARBURY SP3388
Arbury Hall (off B4102 just S of Nuneaton) Splendid-looking mansion, the original Elizabethan house elaborately spruced up in the 19th c to make it one of the best examples of the Gothic Revival style. The writer George Eliot was born on the estate, and her *Mr Gilfil's Love Story* describes some of the rooms - not unreasonably comparing the dining room to a cathedral. Some work by Wren in the stables, and the gardens are a pleasure. Snacks, shop, limited disabled access; open pm Sun and Mon of bank hol wknds Easter-Sept; (024) 7638 2804;

£6.50, £4.50 gardens only.

ARMSCOTE SP2444

Picturesque Cotswold stone village; good imaginative food in the Fox & Goose.

ASHBY CANAL SP3688

Canal towpaths offer some of Warwickshire's nicest walks, and this canal has perhaps the prettiest of them, heading off into the Leics countryside from its junction with the Coventry Canal at Marston Junction on the edge of Bedworth.

AUSTREY SK2906

Attractive village with black and white timbered houses and cottages, some thatch. The Bird in Hand has decent food.

BADDESLEY CLINTON SP2072

Baddesley Clinton House Romantic 15th-c moated manor house, mostly unchanged since the 17th c. Interesting portraits, priests' holes, chapel and garden with pretty walks. The family history is intriguing. Meals, snacks, shop, some disabled access; cl am, and Mon (exc bank hols), Tues and mid-Dec to Feb (house also cl early Nov-Dec; shop and restaurant open till Christmas); (01564) 783294; *£6.20 (timed ticket system), *£3.20 garden only, *£9 joint ticket with Packwood, *£4.50 gardens only joint ticket; NT. The nearby **church** has a lovely E window, and the canalside Navigation at Lapworth and prettily set Cock Horse at Rowington do decent food.

BIRMINGHAM SP0786

The city has a long heritage despite its mainly modern centre, and a rich and varied industrial history taking in everything from guns to chocolate buttons. The centre is far from beautiful but has had a major facelift in the past few years, and the revamped canals and main attractions make a rewarding day out: among the 1960s brutalist architecture there are some fine examples of 19th-c civic pride, notably around Victoria Square with the italianate domed Council House and grecian-style Town Hall (no longer used as such). Recent developments have brought a lively new focus of restaurants, bars, hotels and offices to the Gas St/Brindley Pl area around the canals (there are more miles of canals here than in Venice, and they provide some attractive walks, such as from the centre to the Jewellery Quarter), with plenty of crafts and entertainments too - including the acoustically wonderful Symphony Hall. The redeveloped central Bullring, opened in Sept 2003, is much more pedestrian-friendly, with 150 front-line shops inc two department stores (the new metal-faced Selfridges is dazzling); it gives the centre a more optimistic feel. The stunning **Millennium Point** with its excellent interactive discovery centre is another recent addition, and great efforts are being made to continue to enhance the city's look, with a monster new library and City Park in the pipeline. In recent years the city has become much more fun for nightlife, and there are enough pubs to keep visitors happy: the Old Joint Stock (Temple Row W), Metro (Cornwall St), Bennetts (Bennetts Hill) and Tap & Spile (Brindley Wharf) are our current recommendations. Birmingham is well known for its balti houses, and one of the best places to head for a good curry is the Sparkford area.

Aston Hall (Aston, 2m NE of centre) Strikingly grand Jacobean mansion with panelled long gallery, balustraded staircase and magnificent plaster friezes and ceilings. In an incongruously urban setting, this is what gives the nearby football club Aston Villa its name. Snacks, shop, disabled access to ground floor; cl am, all Mon, and Nov-Good Fri; (0121) 327 0062; free (and more satisfying than a good many houses you'd have to pay for). A few minutes' walk away on Witton Lane, a **transport museum** in a former tram depot is open wknds and bank hols; shop, disabled access; (0121) 322 2298; £1.

Barber Institute of Fine Arts (Birmingham University, E gate) A relaxed and well-displayed gallery, enjoyable without being overwhelming; the art is eclectic, with a little of just about everything. Quite a lot of Impressionist works as well as european masters. Snacks, shop, disabled access; cl Sun am, 25-26 Dec, 1 Jan, Good Fri; (0121) 472 0962; free. The university (marked out by its huge clock tower) is on the outer fringes of Edgbaston, a couple of miles S of the

city centre (if you don't fancy the drive, it's an easy 7-min train ride to the university from Birmingham New Street). This area developed as a smart residential part of town, where industry and commerce gave way to parks and greenery, much of which still remains. **Birmingham Museum and Art Gallery** (Chamberlain Sq) Perhaps the best collection of Pre-Raphaelite paintings anywhere, plenty still looking as brilliantly, almost shockingly, fresh and detailed as when they were first painted (Millais's *Blind Girl* and Ford's *The Last of England* are among the instantly familiar canvases). Other notable paintings too, and lots of coins and archaeology. The Water Hall expansion houses the museum's modern and contemporary art collection. Meals, snacks, shop, disabled access; usually cl Suns am, 24-26 Dec, and 1 Jan; (0121) 525 2193; free (exc special exhibitions). Local boy Burne-Jones, a leading light in the Pre-Raphaelite movement, was responsible for four stunning windows in **St Philip's church** on Colmore Row nearby, since 1905 the city's cathedral. The Old Contemptibles (Edmund St) is a useful nearby Edwardian pub, quite striking in its own right.
Birmingham Nature Centre (A441 Pershore Rd) British and european animals in indoor and outdoor enclosures designed to resemble natural habitats. Meals and snacks, shop, disabled access; cl wkdys Nov-1st wknd in Apr; (0121) 472 7775; £1.60.
Blakesley Hall 🏠 (Blakesley Rd, Yardley, 6m E of centre) This timber-framed 16th/17th-c farmer's house, furnished according to an inventory of 1684, now has a visitor centre (with a café and exhibitions), and a replanted 17th-c herb garden. Shop, disabled access to ground floor and garden; cl am, all Mon and Nov-Mar; (0121) 464 2193; free.
Botanical Gardens 🏠 (Westbourne Rd, Edgbaston) A 6-hectare (15-acre) hillside respite from the virtually treeless city centre, with a historic garden (Roman, medieval and Tudor garden styles), 19th-c cottage garden, lots of rhododendrons and azaleas, tropical house (with lily pool, bananas

and cocoa), subtropical house, mediterranean house, national bonsai collection, and an arid house. Bands play on summer Suns and bank hol pms. Meals, snacks, shop, disabled access; cl 25 Dec; (0121) 454 1860; £5.50, £6 summer Suns and bank hols, voucher valid for one child per adult.
Cadbury World Not a factory tour, but a specially built centre with all you could feasibly want to know about how Cadbury's chocolates are made and marketed. The history of chocolate is given something of a corporate bias, but the exhibitions have been put together with a real sense of fun. Many of the major parts have been specially designed with younger visitors in mind (and the centre is probably most enjoyable for them) with highlights such as the alternative view of chocolate-making offered in the Fantasy Factory, and Cadabra - a nicely silly ride through an imaginative themed world. What really sticks in the memory is the chance to sample fresh liquid chocolate, straight from the vat; you can have a go at dipping it into moulds. Older visitors may prefer the nostalgic Cadbury's TV adverts from the last 40 years, and there's a collection of period wrappers shown in a 1930s-style sweet shop. The outdoor play area is good, and there are plenty of picnic-sets next to it. Meals, snacks, good shop (you get a goodie bag when you enter, so don't visit till the end), mostly disabled access; cl most days Nov-Feb - booking essential, entry by timed ticket only; (0121) 451 4159; £8.75.
Court 15 As we go to press, the city's last surviving complete courtyard of early 19th-c back-to-back houses is about to be handed over to the National Trust. Four of the houses will be re-created to show different periods in their history (based around actual families who've lived there), and you'll be taken round by guided tour. It's due to open the end of July, so best to phone first to check. Shop, limited disabled access (virtual tour of upstairs); usually cl only 25-26 Dec, 1 Jan; entrance by pre-booked timed ticket only; (0121) 753 7757; £3.80; NT.
Ikon Gallery (Oozells Sq) Vibrant contemporary art in stunningly converted school building. Café (with

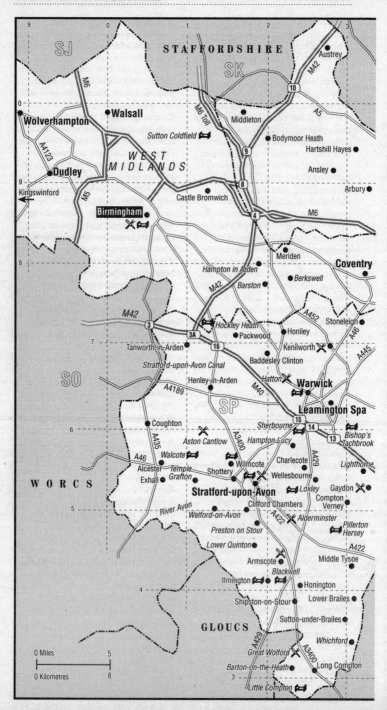

SJ

STAFFORDSHIRE

SK

M6

9

10

Austrey

M42

Middleton

A5

9

Bodymoor Heath

Sutton Coldfield

Hartshill Hayes

Wolverhampton

Walsall

WEST

Ansley

A4123

MIDLANDS

8

Dudley

Arbury

Kingswinford

M5

Castle Bromwich

M6

Birmingham

4

Meriden

Coventry

Hampton in Arden

Berkswell

M42

Barston

A452

Stoneleigh

M42

3

Hockley Heath

Honiley

A46

3A

Packwood

A445

Tanworth-in-Arden

16

Kenilworth

SO

Stratford-upon-Avon Canal

Baddesley Clinton

Henley-in-Arden

Hatton

Warwick

A4189

M40

SP

Leamington Spa

Coughton

15

Sherbourne

14

A435

Aston Cantlow

Hampton Lucy

Bishop's

6

13

Tachbrook

A46

Walcote

Charlecote

A429

Lighthorne

Alcester

Temple

Shottery

Wilmcote

Exhall

Grafton

Wellesbourne

WORCS

Stratford-upon-Avon

Loxley

Gaydon

Clifford Chambers

Compton

Verney

River Avon

Welford-on-Avon

A422

Alderminster

Pillerton

Preston on Stour

Hersey

Lower Quinton

A422

Armscote

Middle Tysoe

Blackwell

Ilmington

Honington

GLOUCS

Shipston-on-Stour

Lower Brailes

Sutton-under-Brailes

A429

Whichford

Great Wolford

A3400

Long Compton

Barton-on-the-Heath

Little Compton

0 Miles 5

0 Kilometres 8

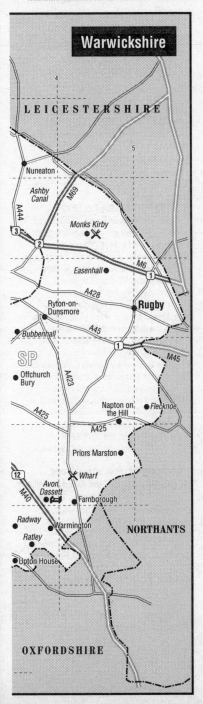

tapas), shop, disabled access; cl Mon
(exc bank hols), 24 Dec-2 Jan, and
during installation of exhibitions so best
to phone; (0121) 248 0708; free. The
next-door Petit Blanc complements it
well on the food side.

Museum of the Jewellery Quarter
(Vyse St) The Jewellery Quarter is the
grid of Victorian streets north of the
city centre that's home to some 400
specialist costume jewellery
workshops, plus scores of jewellery
shops (a more recent arrival); a useful
area for browsing or repairs. This
fascinating museum is in the former
premises of the Smith & Pepper
company, whose antiquated gaslit
workshops changed little from the early
20th c until closure in 1981; there's a
good exhibition about the industry, plus
a lively tour of the workshops with
demonstrations and entertaining
stories given by the guides. Snacks,
shop, disabled access; cl Mon (exc bank
hols), and Nov-Mar; (0121) 554 3598;
free. The Rosevilla has decent food.

National Sea Life Centre *See
separate family panel on p.615.*

Pen Room (Argent Centre, 60
Frederick St) Cheerfully run little
museum in a handsome building,
focusing on the city's past importance
to the pen trade; you can try out lots of
different pens, and there's even the
chance to make your own nib. Shop,
disabled access; cl am Sun, and 25-26
Dec; (0121) 236 9834; free.

Sarehole Mill (Hall Green, 3m SE of
centre) Working 18th-c watermill, with
displays explaining the milling process,
and on Victorian farming; Tolkien often
came here as a child. Cl am, Mon (exc
bank hols) and Nov-Apr; (0121) 777
6612; free. Other local sites that
influenced Tolkien are listed on a leaflet
available at tourist information centres,
and a Tolkien Trail, following where the
writer lived as a child, went to school,
and might have dreamed up various
characters, has been devised to catch
interest generated by *The Lord of the
Rings* films.

Selly Manor Museum (Maple Rd,
A441 4m S) When the Cadbury family
moved their factory out of the city
centre in 1879, part of their plans for this
new garden suburb involved uprooting

timber-framed manor houses from elsewhere and re-erecting them here; two survive as this museum, with herb garden, crafts and various exhibitions. Shop, disabled access to ground floor only; cl Mon and am wknds Apr-Sept, plus pm wknds in winter, and 2 wks at Christmas; (0121) 472 0199; £2.

Soho House (Soho Avenue, off A41 NW of centre) Elegant former home of Matthew Boulton, famous for his development of the steam engine with James Watt, and possibly the first centrally heated house in England since Roman times. Headquarters in the 18th c of the Lunar Society, this was where the scientific brains of the day would meet, close to Boulton's long-vanished 'manufactory', the world's first mass-producing factory. The house is furnished in 18th-c style with Boulton-related displays. Snacks, shop, disabled access; cl Mon (exc bank hols), and Nov-Easter; (0121) 554 5929; free.

Thinktank (Millennium Point, Curzon St, Digbeth) Massive museum of science and discovery, the ten comprehensive galleries squeeze in dozens of interactives, and well put together displays on everything from local industry and inventions to life in the future and how the body works. Children of all ages have lots to keep them entertained; while younger ones have fun pushing buttons on the hands-on digestive system, older siblings are challenged by activities based around medical ethics. Most fun for under-7s is Kids in the City, full of games designed to show the range of jobs people do, and elsewhere, visitors can find out how everyday objects work, explore Birmingham in the past, and discover how animals communicate with each other. Adults aren't left out, as it's hard not to be stimulated by the wealth of information. One gallery has a good collection of steam engines (including the oldest active one in the world). There may be extra activities in the holidays (when it can seem a bit noisy and crowded). There's also a huge IMAX cinema. Meals, snacks, shop, disabled access; cl 24-26 Dec; (0121) 202 2222; £6.95, £6 for the IMAX, £10.50 joint ticket. Millennium Point is the biggest millennium project outside London, costing a whopping £114 million; looking at the amazing museum building it's easy to see where at least some of that went.

Tyseley Locomotive Works (Warwick Rd, Tyseley; A41 3m SE) Working railway museum with fully equipped workshop, steam locomotives, and several historic carriages and wagons. Shop, limited disabled access; open wknds and bank hol Mon; (0121) 707 4696; £2.50. On summer Suns the **Shakespeare Express** runs steam trips from Birmingham Snow Hill to Stratford-upon-Avon (£15 return; same phone number).

BODYMOOR HEATH SP2095
Kingsbury Water Park 30 lakes and pools, created by gravel excavations, in 620 landscaped acres. Waterside and woodland walks, nature trails (maps and leaflets at the visitor centre), and two play areas. You can fish (from £1.90, under-16s fish for free at Mitchell's Pool), and there's jet bike hire. Meals, snacks, shop, good disabled access (mobility scooters available free); cl 25 Dec; (01827) 872660; free, £2.20 for parking. The park also contains **Broomey Croft Children's Farm**; all the usual farm animals for children to feed, plus tractor rides (wknds and school hols), and play and picnic areas. Snacks, shop, disabled access; cl Sept-Easter exc wknds and usually half-terms; (01827) 873844; *£3.50. The canalside Dog & Doublet has decent food.

CASTLE BROMWICH SP1489
Castle Bromwich Hall Gardens 🏛 (Chester Rd) Restored 18th-c formal gardens, with authentic collection of period plants, inc historic vegetables and herbs, plus a holly maze. Snacks, plant sales, disabled access; cl am, Mon (exc bank hols) and Fri, and Nov-Mar; (0121) 749 4100; £3.50.

CHARLECOTE SP2656
Charlecote Park 100 hectares (250 acres) of parkland where Shakespeare is said to have poached, with deer, and the descendants of reputedly the country's first flock of Jacob sheep. Well furnished Great Hall and Victorian kitchen, an impressive Tudor gatehouse, and a garden designed by Sir Edmund Fairfax Lucy; there's a

playground too. Meals, snacks, shop, disabled access; cl Weds (exc July-Aug and after bank hols), Thurs, and Nov-early Mar (exc garden open wknds Nov-Dec), house also cl am; (01789) 470277; *£6.40, *£3 gardens only; NT. By the park is a charming little 19th-c estate village of timbered cottages, and a show Victorian church. In nearby pretty Hampton Lucy, which has a lovely church, the Boars Head has good value food.

CLIFFORD CHAMBERS SP1952
Pretty black and white timbered houses and cottages, and a Tudor former rectory which some have claimed to be Shakespeare's true birthplace.

COMPTON VERNEY SP3152
Designed by Robert Adam (in 40-acres of Capability Brown parkland), this 18th-c mansion has recently been transformed into an art gallery. As well as southern and northern european art, there's a british collection (focusing on portraits from the 1500s and 1600s), an east asian collection (inc chinese bronzes and ceramics dating from 1500 BC), and a rare collection of british folk art; regular temporary exhibitions. Meals, snacks, shop, disabled access; due to open at Easter, so phone for opening times and prices; (01926) 645500.

COUGHTON SP0860
Coughton Court (A435) Several priests' holes are hidden in this mainly Elizabethan house, renowned for its imposing gatehouse and beautiful courtyard; the Throckmortons have lived here since 1409. Notable furniture and porcelain, and an exhibition on the Gunpowder Plot; the grounds have a lake, two churches, pleasant walks, formal gardens, and a play area. Meals, snacks, shop, plant sales, disabled access to ground floor; usually cl Mon (exc bank hols), and Tues Sept-Jun, and all Oct-Mar (exc wknds Oct and late Mar); (01789) 400777; *£8.25 house and gardens, *£5.50 grounds only, *£2.50 walled garden only; NT. The Green Dragon on the fine old green at Sambourne and interesting Old Washford Mill at Studley are good for lunch.

COVENTRY SP3379
More a place to dip into than to fix on as your base for a short holiday, but there's certainly enough here for a very full day out. The area around the cathedral has just enough remaining of pre-war Coventry to hint at what the city was like before being virtually rased in 1940; here and there you find older buildings (some seamlessly repaired), some set starkly against postwar developments (the audio tour from the tourist office takes you round the best bits; £1.75). Among the most eye-catching of the half-timbered survivors are in Spon St (several buildings moved here from other parts of the city), and the beautiful almshouses of Ford's Hospital (Greyfriars Lane) and Bond's Hopsital (Hill St). Much of the postwar centre was developed with 1940s and 50s pedestrian precincts (Britain's first), now (somewhat controversially) given the status of listed buildings. The new grand plan is to link up the historic centre from the cathedral steps to the Transport Museum (near the surviving city gateway, and by a stretch of the old town wall), with new squares at either end. One of the town's most famous inhabitants was 11th-c Lady Godiva, commemorated best by the Coventry Clock - where she pops out in the pink every hour (and the statue in Broadgate). The picturesque Old Windmill (Spon St), Browns (food all day, Earl St), medieval Whitefriars (Gosford St), Royal Court Hotel (Tamworth Rd, Keresley End), Flying Standard (Trinity St - food all day), Greyhound out at Sutton Stop (Aldermans Green/Hawkesbury - a canal arts trail runs out to here) and Prince William Henry and William IV (both Foleshill Rd - authentic indian) are all popular for lunch.

Car Factory Tours Fascinating insight into one of the most complicated production processes: you can visit Jaguar and Peugeot, both by appointment only. It's well worth doing both, as the experience is so contrasting: Jaguar (Browns Lane) prides itself on the hand-crafted approach to its building of luxury limousines and sports cars (the leather interiors derive from special cattle herds in Argentina), and has a museum as well as an interactive Formula One gallery, while Peugeot is robotic in the extreme with extraordinary machines that seem to take on an animate life of their own. Prebooking through the tourist centre (024) 7622 7264; both tours free (small charge for Formula One gallery).

Coombe Country Park Pleasant 450-acre park, with woodland and lakeside walks, arboretum, formal gardens and a heronry (around Jan to end July); there's a children's playground, and a good visitor centre has interactive displays, a video, and special events throughout the year. Meals, snacks, shop, disabled access; visitor centre cl 25-26 Dec; (024) 7645 3720; free, £2 car parking.

Coventry Cathedral (Priory Row) The two cathedrals stand side by side as a memorial to the wartime destruction of what had been one of Britain's finest half-timbered cities: the roofless old cathedral with its intact 14th-c tower has been preserved as a poignant ruin alongside the highly unorthodox new cathedral (voted in a recent poll as Britain's favourite 20th-c building, though it certainly doesn't appeal to all tastes). Beyond the etched glass façade the immediate impression is of austerity, enlivened by Sutherland's tapestry from the end of the nave the view back reveals the full extent of Piper's luscious stained glass. Meals, snacks, shop, disabled access; cl 15-19 Nov for degree ceremonies, and occasional other days; (024) 7622 7597; £3 suggested donation. The new Priory Square should be completed in May. Nearby, spacious **Holy Trinity** church hit the news in 2003 with the restoration of its remarkably well-preserved 15th-c Day of Judgement wall painting (one of the finest such murals yet discovered in Britain), hidden under black varnish for well over a century.

Coventry Transport Museum (St Agnes Lane) The largest collection of british road transport in the world, focusing mainly on what's been produced over the years in Coventry, the birthplace of the british motor industry. It's arranged as a walk through time, with street scenes, a World War II blitz experience, and visions of the future, with a look at the evolution of the bicycle, and some 500 machines

from antique Daimlers to futuristic prototypes; the introductory gallery (opening at Easter as part of a wholesale refurbishment, which will see new space for temporary exhibitions and a café, plus better disabled access) explains the social history too. There is also a celebration of Coventry's role in manufacturing Thrust SSC, the supersonic machine that broke the land speed record: a simulator helps you experience its blast across the american desert. Snacks, shop, disabled access; cl 24-26 Dec; (024) 7683 2425; free.

Herbert Art Gallery and Museum (Jordan Well) Subject of a major upgrade (hoping to re-open in full around May, but possible further expansion after then), with temporary exhibitions, performance spaces and Godiva City, a lively interactive history of Coventry throught the ages; pictures by Graham Sutherland and some immortal images of Lady Godiva. Meals, snacks, shop, disabled access; cl am Sun, and a few days over Christmas; (024) 7683 2381; free.

Lunt Roman Fort (Coventry Rd, Baginton) Fun reconstruction of 1st-c Roman fort giving a rare opportunity to see such a site in all its glory. Good interpretative displays. Shop, picnic area, some disabled access; cl Weds, other wkdys Oct-Jun (exc bank hols, 31 May-4 Jun and 17 July-30 Aug), and all Nov-Mar, best to check; (024) 7683 2381; £2. The Old Mill is a well run pub.

Midland Air Museum (Coventry Airport) Displays of civil and military aircraft spanning more than 70 years. Snacks, shop, disabled access; cl 25-26 Dec; (024) 7630 1033; £4. The Old Mill is a smart nearby dining pub.

Priory Gardens Visitor Centre The TV archaeology programme *Time Team* helped identify long-lost parts of Coventry's first cathedral (which was abandoned at the Dissolution and disappeared soon after), and the visitor centre is the result of a two-year dig. You can see the foundations and many sculpted stones, along with an exceptional fragment of wall painting, and some stained glass depicting a female head that may be Godiva herself: touch-screen computers re-create how the building looked, and from Mar there will be free tours (twice daily) of the undercroft, where the most remarkable finds were made. Shop, disabled access, cl Sun am, 25-26 Dec, 1 Jan; (024) 7655 2242; free.

St Mary's Guildhall (Bayley Lane) In a cobbled street beside the cathedral, one of Britain's finest medieval guildhalls, and miraculous survival of the bomb carnage, complete with minstrels' gallery and flemish tapestries; Shakespeare was thought to have performed here, and Mary Queen of Scots spent time as a prisoner in the tower. Open Easter Sun-Sept (exc Fri and Sat), provided there aren't any civic functions, best to check; (024) 7683 2381; free.

Toy Museum (Much Park St) Toys from 1740 to 1990, in a 14th-c monastery gatehouse. Cl am (exc pre-booked visits); (024) 7622 7560; *£1.50.

DUDLEY SO9591

Black Country Living Museum (Tipton Rd, 1m N of town centre) Good value, well thought out, open-air museum (with much under cover), giving a good feel of how things used to be in the Black Country, the heavily industrialised and proudly individual areas in the W part of the Birmingham conurbation. It's an authentically reconstructed turn-of-the-century village, complete with cottages, chapel, chemist, baker, pub, and trips into limestone caverns (summer only) or even down a mine, as well as black and white comedies from Laurel and Hardy or Harold Lloyd in the old cinema, school lessons in the school room, and an old-fashioned working fairground just outside the village (extra charges for rides). Staff in period costumes illustrate traditional crafts and test-drive old vehicles, and there are plenty of extra activities for children during school holidays. Meals and snacks (and space for picnics), shop, mostly disabled access; cl Mon and Tues Nov-Feb, and several days over Christmas, best to phone; (0121) 557 9643; £9.60.

Dudley Museum and Art Gallery (St James's Rd) Some fine paintings, well displayed geology, and appealing temporary exhibitions. Shop, disabled access to ground floor but no facilities; cl Sun and bank hols (plus the Tues following a bank hol Mon); (01384)

815575; free.

Dudley Zoo 🅰 (Broadway) Based around an impressive **ruined castle** - a rather special place for a zoo. Meals, snacks, shop, disabled access (although site is hilly); cl 25 Dec; (01384) 215313; £7.95.

Tunnel boat trips The Dudley Canal Trust do boat trips along part of a unique network of canal tunnels and limestone mines. Trips Mar-Nov, and some days in Dec, phone for times; (01384) 236275; £3.50.

EXHALL SP1055

Pretty black and white timbering, and some pleasant gently hilly walks nearby; very quiet, as no through road. The attractively set riverside Fish at Wixford has good food.

FARNBOROUGH SP4349

Farnborough Hall Palladian villa filled with splendid sculptures, paintings and fine rococo plasterwork; the staircase, hall and two main rooms are on show. The 18th-c landscaped gardens have a couple of ornamental temples, and views from the terrace walk - less impressive than they were thanks to the arrival of the M40. Disabled access to ground floor only; open pm Weds and Sat Apr-Sept and first May bank hol, terrace also open pm Thurs and Fri by arrangement only; (01295) 690002; *£3.80, *£1.90 terrace walk only; NT. The Inn at Farnborough has good imaginative food.

GAYDON SP3354

Heritage Motor Centre 🅰 (Banbury Rd) Busy centre with the world's biggest collection of classic british cars - 200 in all, and around 150 are on display, starting with an 1895 Wolseley. Also hundreds of drawings, photographs, trophies and models, hi-tech displays and video shows. There's a 4-wheel-drive demo circuit, go-kart track (for the over 8s), and a nature reserve. The design of the building is incredible, especially inside. Meals, snacks (lunchtimes only), shop, disabled access; cl 24-26 Dec; (01926) 641188; £8. The Malt Shovel has good value food (see *Where to eat*).

HARTSHILL HAYES SP3194

Country park with mixed woodland, opening out at the top for broad views towards the Peak District. The

Coventry Canal below allows more extended rambles.

HENLEY-IN-ARDEN SP1565
More small town than village, but a pretty conservation area, with good churches, and a heritage centre in the High St. The Bird in Hand (A34) has good value food.

HONILEY SP2472
The village has virtually gone now, and there are only vestiges of the big house, but you can still sense the vanished settlement around the surviving 18th-c church.

HONINGTON SP2642
Attractive village, its church prettily set on the edge of the lawn of Honington Hall, a charming little manor house built in the early 1680s, and re-modelled in the 1740s, with some fine plasterwork, and 15 acres of grounds. Open pm Weds and bank hol Mon Jun-Aug, entry by guided tour only; (01608) 661434; *£4. The Cherington Arms over at Cherington does good lunches, with pleasant nearby walks.

ILMINGTON SP2143
Quietly attractive village with peaceful path to partly Norman church, lovely inside; pleasant walks on hills above. The Howard Arms is good for lunch.

KENILWORTH SP2772
Kenilworth Castle ⬛ Dramatic castle (England's largest castle ruin) transformed in turns by John of Gaunt and Robert Dudley, Earl of Leicester and favourite of Elizabeth I - who was royally entertained here in 1575 with no expense spared. The keep is the oldest part; from the Elizabethan garden (replanted in 1970) you can see the thickness of the walls, as one side was destroyed in the Civil War. Adjacent are the kitchens, with subterranean buttery, and the Great Hall, one of the finest ever built and with some tracery still intact, while Leicester's apartments (where Elizabeth stayed) rises a full four storeys. Various re-enactments and Shakespeare plays, operas plus children's activities summer hol wknds. Meals, snacks, shop, disabled access (but no facilities); cl 24-26 Dec, 1 Jan; (01926) 852078; £4.50 inc audio tour; EH. The old part of town has an attractive main street, with mostly red-brick Georgian and some thatch, and just below the

churchyard in the Abbey Fields (free access) are the former abbey gateway, abbey barn and the abbey fish pond.

KINGSWINFORD SO8888
Broadfield House Glass Museum (Barnett Lane) Excellent collection of glass from nearby Stourbridge, displayed to dazzling effect. Clever use of lighting shows off the exhibits quite spectacularly, and even the audio-visual shows create a sense of excitement. One of the area's least expected treasures. Shop, disabled access to ground floor; cl Mon (exc bank hols), phone for Christmas and Easter opening; (01384) 812745; free.

LEAMINGTON SPA SP2864
Elegant spa resort popularised by the rich who came to take the waters in the 18th and 19th c. Still many fine Regency buildings, though today the town is better seen as a civilised shopping centre, and perhaps as a base for sallies into the surrounding countryside - or into Warwick, across the River Avon. Beautifully laid out, **Jephson Gardens** (The Parade) are well worth strolling around, with a nectar garden for butterflies, and boating on the lake. The Benjamin Satchwell (The Parade) and Hogshead (Warwick St) have decent food.

Art Gallery & Museum (Royal Pump Rooms, The Parade) Restored Regency bath house originally built in 1814 but later extended and remodelled to suit changing fashions. It's now home to the town's decent museum and art gallery, as well as its library and tourist information centre. Meals, snacks, shop, good disabled access; cl Thurs am, all Mon, and 25-26 Dec; (01926) 742700; free.

LONG COMPTON SP2932
This pleasant Cotswoldy village of thatched stone houses has some antiques shops, and a pretty garden with a sundial; the Red Lion has good value food.

LOWER BRAILES SP3139
Attractive Cotswold-edge village with lovely slender-spired church, pretty stone houses, good views, nice old inn - the George.

MERIDEN SP2482
A cross on the green marks what the village feels is the centre of England -

one of the streams rising in the village pond ends up in the Severn and the other over in the Humber. The Bulls Head (good value food all day) used to be the manor house.

MIDDLE TYSOE SP3344
Charming village; the Norman Knight by Whichford's attractive village green does good value lunches (not Tues; nearby pottery).
Interesting walk The walk S from Upper Tysoe over Windmill Hill (which does have a windmill) takes you to the church on the edge of Compton Wynyates park, giving views of the attractive Tudor manor - a refreshing bit of brick building, in this Cotswold-edge stone country.

MIDDLETON SP1797
Ash End House Farm (off A4091) Friendly farm set up specifically for children; animals from a shire horse to baby chicks and fluffy ducklings, as well as rare breeds of goats, pigs and sheep. A pony ride is included in the price, and there's plenty under cover for wet days. Snacks, shop, disabled access; cl 25 Dec-2 Jan, and wkdys Jan; (0121) 329 3240; £4.50 children, adults half-price.
Middleton Hall (A4091) Varied architecture in the house, also nature reserve, walled gardens, and a play area. There's a good craft centre in the stables. Meals, snacks, shop, some disabled access; house open Sun and bank hol pms Easter to mid-Sept (£2.50, £4 bank hols - when there are special events on); craft centre usually open Weds-Sun all year; free (01827) 283095. The Green Man is a decent family dining pub.

NAPTON ON THE HILL SP4661
Attractive village on a rounded hill above a curve in the Oxford Canal - perhaps the prettiest canal in this part of the world, with pleasant towpath walks, and enjoyable food from the Folly. Great views of seven counties from the hill.

NUNEATON SP3691
Nuneaton Museum & Art Gallery (Coton Rd) Nicely set in colourful Riversley Park, with display on George Eliot. Meals, snacks, shop, disabled access; cl Sun am, all day Mon (exc bank hols), and 25 Dec; (024) 7635 0720; free. The central Felix Holt has decent food all day.

OFFCHURCH BURY SP3565
Attractive riverside parkland, with a pleasant walk winding through from the thatched Stags Head (good value food).

PACKWOOD SP1772
Packwood House (off A34) Friendly old house with origins as a 16th-c farmhouse, carefully restored and not at all commercialised; interesting panelling, furniture and needlework, and in the garden unusual yew trees clipped to represent the Sermon on the Mount; look out for the 18th-c bee boles built into the S face of the garden terrace wall. Snacks, shop, some disabled access; cl Mon (exc bank hols), Tues and Nov-Mar; (01564) 782024; *£5.60, garden only *£2.80; joint tickets with Baddesley Clinton *£9, *£4.50 gardens only; NT. The Boot at Lapworth (B4439) is a fairly handy canalside dining pub.

PRIORS MARSTON SP4857
Attractive old houses around the village green, and unusual blue brick paths; the ancient Holly Bush has good food. You can walk up Marston Hill behind, and quite a good network of paths around nearby Priors Hardwick takes you down to the Oxford Canal. The old drovers' Welsh Road through here via Southam to Cubbington is a pleasant drive; just before Offchurch it crosses the remarkable Fosse Way, a quiet Roman road running dead straight from Brinklow through Stretton-on-Dunsmore and Princethorpe down to Halford.

RIVER AVON SP0950
There is a pleasant riverside walk from the Cottage of Content at Barton.

RUGBY SP5075
Rugby Art Gallery & Museum (Little Elborow St) Impressive centre housed in an attractive modern building, with a fine collection of modern and contemporary art inc works by L S Lowry and Freud (you can make an appointment to see paintings not on show) and changing exhibitions, as well as a display of Roman artefacts and a decent look at local social history; the building also houses the town's library. Shop, disabled access; cl Sun and bank hol ams, all day Mon, and 25-26 Dec, 1 Jan; (01788) 533201; free.

Rugby Museum (St Matthew's St) The game the school invented is commemorated at this shop that's been making the standard rugby ball since 1842. You can watch them do it, and there are related displays (inc a film) and collections. Shop, some disabled access; cl Sun and bank hols; (01788) 567777; free. The friendly Three Horseshoes Hotel not far off in Sheep St has interesting food.

Rugby School Founded in 1567, moving to its current site in the mid-18th c. A museum on Little Church St looks at its history and former pupils, such as Rupert Brooke and Lewis Carroll. Shop, disabled access; cl 12.30-1.30pm, Sun am and 2 wks at Christmas; (01788) 556274; £1.50. Guided tours of the school buildings leave here at 2.30pm most days but ring to check; £4 (inc museum entry).

RYTON-ON-DUNSMORE SP3874
Ryton Gardens 🔾 (Wolston rd, off A45) Even readers who describe themselves as dedicated gardeners learn a lot from this interesting place, home of the Henry Doubleday Research Association, the organic gardening and farming organisation, which also champions tasty but endangered varieties of veg. It's landscaped with thousands of organically grown plants and trees; herb garden, rose garden, garden for the blind, and shrub borders among the displays, as well as a cooks' garden where all the plants are edible, the Paradise Garden dedicated to the late Geoff Hamilton, and a vegetable garden specially for children. An absorbing new £2 million visitor centre is dedicated to vegetables. Designed to look like a fantasy garden, the roof is planted with sedums, and there are interactive displays, and demonstrations from gardeners and cooks. Very good meals and snacks in organic restaurant, shop, disabled access; cl 25 Dec-1 Jan; (02476) 303517; £3.95.

SHIPSTON-ON-STOUR SP2540
Small town with quite a busy shopping centre, but also rewarding to stroll through, with a good church and quite a few handsome old stone buildings, antiques shops among them. The White Bear (High St) and thatched Black Horse (Station Rd) are good for lunch.

SHOTTERY SP2055
Anne Hathaway's Cottage A substantial thatched Tudor farmhouse, the home of Anne Hathaway until her marriage to William Shakespeare. Displays of domestic life during the period, and colourful cottage garden. Snacks, shop; cl 23-26 Dec; (01789) 292100; £5. The Bell is handy for something to eat away from the tourists.

STONELEIGH SP3271
Though primarily known as the showground for the Royal Show, with an increasing number of permanent displays, the village itself has an attractive sandstone Norman church, and timber-framed houses.

Stoneleigh Abbey, shows off architectural styles spanning 900-years; highlights inc the magnificent staterooms in the 18th-c baroque west wing, a medieval gatehouse, and the Gothic Revival style Regency stables. It's been home to the Leigh family for over 350 years (famous visitors inc Jane Austen and Charles I); 690 acres of parkland and gardens. Tearoom; open Sun, Tues-Thurs and bank hols Good Fri-Oct, tours leave at 11am, 1pm and 3pm, best to check; (01926) 858585; £5.

STRATFORD-UPON-AVON SP2055
Visitors who look at the town just as a town can be disappointed, but if you have a grounding in Shakespeare's plays the interesting buildings seem that bit more interesting - and not so outnumbered by the workaday ones, the high-priced antiques shops and the gift shops. The gardens by the River Avon make a memorable setting for the Royal Shakespeare Theatre. If you're looking forward to a good production at the theatre that evening, or, better still, able to run through much of the verse in your head, then you'll love Stratford. But if you've always thought Shakespeare overrated, then you'll think the same about Stratford, too. The pub with the most thespian connections is the Mucky Duck (Southern Way); the Arden Hotel has the closest bar to the Memorial Theatre, with good snacks. Useful places for lunch include the quaint old Garrick (High St), Brasserie (Henley St), Vintner Wine Bar (Sheep St) and Slug &

Lettuce (Guild St/Union St). Tea in the smart Shakespeare Hotel (Chapel St) is relaxing, and the White Swan Hotel (Rother St) has a pre-Shakespeare mural of Tobias, the angel and the fish. There's a little art gallery/gift shop housed in a narrow boat in the Canal Basin (Bancroft Gardens).

Butterfly Farm (Swans Nest Lane, off A3400 S side of bridge) Cascading waterfalls and tropical blossoms, with up to 1,500 exotic butterflies flying free in a rainforest habitat; also an incredible collection of spiders and insects. Snacks, shop, disabled access; cl 25 Dec; (01789) 299288; £4.25.

Falstaffs Experience (Sheep St) In the 17th-c barn adjoining splendid Shrieves House, this gives a brief but theatrical look at the town's history, with re-creations (inc a slum, Civil War tavern, and a plague-ridden cottage), an old penny arcade, and a statue garden. Shop; cl 25 Dec, but best to ring in winter as their opening times vary then; (01789) 298070; £3.75.

Hall's Croft (Old Town) Lovely gabled Tudor home of Dr John Hall, who married Shakespeare's daughter; good displays on the medicine of the time, Elizabethan and Jacobean furniture, and a walled garden. Meals, snacks, shop, disabled access to ground floor; cl 23-26 Dec; (01789) 292107; £3.50.

Harvard House (High St) Late 16th-c home of the mother of the man who founded Harvard University - no direct connection with Shakespeare, but a striking example of houses of his day with possibly the most ornately carved and timbered frontage in the town, and home to the Museum of British Pewter. Shop; cl Tues and Weds, plus Mon-Thurs Sept-Jun (exc bank hols), plus all Nov-Apr; (01789) 204507; £1.50.

Holy Trinity church (Waterside) 15th-c, where Shakespeare was baptised and buried; cl Sun am and for other services; £1 to enter the chancel where the grave is.

New Place/Nash's House (Chapel St) Shakespeare died here in 1616; the house was destroyed in the 18th c, but the Elizabethan knot garden remains, and the adjacent house, former home of the writer's granddaughter, has a good collection of furniture and local history.

Disabled access to ground floor and gardens only; cl 23-26 Dec; (01789) 292325; £3.50.

Ragdoll Shop (Chapel St) Ragdoll make lots of children's TV programmes inc *Teletubbies* and *Boohbah*. The shop has plenty to amuse small children inc play areas and a replica of Teletubbies' Home Hill, and they can talk to their favourite characters on the phone. Shop, disabled access; cl 25-26 Dec, 1 Jan; (01789) 404111; free.

Royal Shakespeare Theatre (Waterside) Shakespeare's plays are of course still performed here by the Royal Shakespeare Company. You can book guided tours of the Royal Shakespeare Theatre and their other theatre, the Swan (usually at 1.30pm, 5.30pm, and after evening performances; best to phone as they quickly get booked up); the gallery has temporary exhibitions. Meals, snacks, shop, disabled access for plays but not tours; phone for opening times as they depend on performances; (01789) 403405; £2 for gallery, theatre tours £4. The RSC productions themselves are performed in repertory, so if you're in the area for a few days it's quite possible to see several. Advance booking is recommended - (01789) 403403 - though some tickets are kept back for each performance and sold on the day from 9.30am; don't leave it much later, they go pretty fast. A two-hour guided walk around Shakespeare's Stratford leaves the RSC 10.30am Sat and every day during the Easter hol, Thurs Apr-Sept, plus Sun July-Sept; (01789) 403405; £6.

Shakespeare's Birthplace (Henley St) Though there's no guarantee the playwright really was born here, there are interesting period features, and good interpretative displays. Shop, disabled access to ground floor; cl 23-26 Dec; (01789) 204016; £6.50. If you want to see all the Shakespearian houses it makes sense to buy a joint ticket; this costs £13, and covers this, New Place, Hall's Croft, and the Shottery and Wilmcote sites. You can also buy tickets covering just the three in-town sites for £9. A tour bus with commentary links the sites but costs £11 (it offers discount to sites); (01789) 294466.

Teddy Bear Museum ▣ (Greenhill St) Delightfully displayed, furry friends of all shapes and sizes - mechanical and musical ones, ones that belonged to famous people, and some that are famous themselves; children's quiz. Shop; cl 25-26 Dec; (01789) 293160; *£2.50.

STRATFORD-UPON-AVON CANAL SP1867
This gives some pleasant towpath walks; the Fleur de Lys at Lowsonford is a good start.

SUTTON-UNDER-BRAILES SP3037
Attractive stone-built village, with some pleasing Cotswold countryside around it - good walks.

TANWORTH-IN-ARDEN SP1270
Umberslade Children's Farm
Family-run farm with animals to stroke and feed, and play areas for letting off steam. Also nature trails and walks, and a goat-milking area. Snacks, shop, disabled access; dates were unconfirmed as we went to press, but usually cl Nov and Jan to mid-Feb; (01564) 742251; £4.

UPTON HOUSE SP3645
▣ (A422 nr Ratley) The exceptional art collection is the main draw here, an enormous range of paintings inc works by Bosch, El Greco, Bruegel (Pieter the elder and Jan) and Hogarth, and an exhibition of posters commissioned by Shell all sensibly arranged and displayed. Also Brussels tapestries and Sèvres porcelain. The fine garden has terraces, herbaceous borders, a kitchen garden, 1930s bog garden and ornamental pools, as well as a national collection of asters. Meals, snacks, shop, some disabled access; open pm Sat-Weds and Good Fri Apr-Oct; (01295) 670266; *£6.50 house and garden, garden only *£3.50; NT. There's a timed ticket system on bank hols. Ratley itself is a pretty village, with a lovely church and good home cooking in the Rose & Crown; and the Castle on Edge Hill is a very interesting place for lunch, with terrific views.

WALSALL SP0198
Jerome K Jerome Birthplace Museum (Bradford St) Dedicated to the life and work of the author of *Three Men in a Boat*, with a reconstructed

1850s parlour. Open Sat 12-2pm, or by appointment; (01922) 653116; free. The good value Green Dragon (High St, a short walk away) fits in well with the period.

New Art Gallery (Gallery Sq) This imaginative building has collections of european art inc great paintings by Rembrandt, Goya, Constable, Manet, Degas and Freud. Lots has been done to make the gallery appeal to all ages and tastes, and there's an interactive children's gallery, plenty of seating, and sensibly low hanging heights so that you don't have to strain. Everything's very accessible. The centrepiece is the Garman Ryan collection - over 300 works donated to the local people by Kathleen Garman, Jacob Epstein's widow, in 1973, and shown in a sort of two-storey house within the building itself - this cleverly gives the feeling of looking at somebody's private collection. Also changing exhibitions, activity and conference rooms, library and a rooftop terrace. Meals, snacks, shop, disabled access; cl Mon exc bank hols, phone over Christmas; (01922) 654400; free. The light and airy next-door Wharf Bar 10 has good value tasty snacks.

Walsall Leather Museum (Littleton St West) Well restored Victorian leather goods factory with tours of aromatic workshops and leather-making demonstrations (not Sun); also displays about the history of the local leather trade and a trail of the town's historic leather quarter. Meals, snacks, shop (lots of local leather goods), disabled access; usually cl Sun am, Mon (exc some bank hols), Good Fri and a few days over Christmas; (01922) 721153; free.

WARMINGTON SP4047
National Herb Centre (Banbury Rd) Wide range of herbs in display gardens in an attractive valley; also walks, nature trails and a children's activity area. Bistro, herb and plant centre, disabled access; cl 25 Dec-1 Jan; (01295) 690999; free. In the charming sleepy village, the Plough has decent food.

WARWICK SP2864
Though many older buildings survived a major fire in 1694, today's centre is dominated by elegant Queen Anne rebuilding. Some of the oldest structures

are to be found around Mill St, which is very attractive to stroll along; there are a good few antiques and other interesting shops. There's a farmers' market on the 3rd Fri of each month. The Tilted Wig (Market Pl - neat bedrooms too) and Zetland Arms (Church St) do good lunches; the Saxon Mill (Guy's Cliffe) is a prettily placed waterside family dining pub, and the Warwick Arms Hotel does good value teas.

Doll Museum (Castle St) Half-timbered Elizabethan house with comprehensive collection of antique dolls and toys. A fun video shows the exhibits come to life. Shop; cl Nov-Mar exc Sat; (01926) 495546; £1.

Lord Leycester Hospital (High St) Delightfully wonky half-timbered building built in 1383, still used as a home of rest for retired servicemen. Fine old guildhall, candlelit chapel, gatehouse and courtyard, and garden with Norman arch and a 2,000-year-old urn from the Nile. Meals, snacks, shop, disabled access to ground floor only; cl Mon, Good Fri, 25 Dec; (01926) 491422; *£3.40.

Mill Garden Delightful series of plantings in a super setting on the river beside the castle - very nice to stroll through, with plenty of old things to look at along the way; some disabled access; open Easter-Oct; (01926) 492877; £1.

St John's House (St John's) 17th-c house with exhibits from the county museum, a changing collection of costumes, several room reconstructions, and an under-5s discovery room. The Royal Warwickshire Regiment museum is also here, and there's a garden with a picnic area. Shop, disabled access to ground floor only; cl Mon (exc bank hols), and Sun am, plus pm Sun end Sept-Apr, 25-26 Dec and 1 Jan; (01926) 412132; free.

St Mary's church (Old Sq) Splendid medieval church on the town's highest point, with Norman crypt, chapter house and magnificent 15th-c Beauchamp chapel. In good weather you can sometimes go up the tower (£1.50), for excellent views.

Warwick Castle (Castle Hill) Well liked by readers, this lively place is one of the country's most splendid castles, with plenty for all ages, especially in summer; although it's not cheap, you can spend up to a whole day exploring every corner, though half a day is probably enough for most families. The influence of the Tussauds group, who own the site, shows in the flair for presentation, and of course the castle's waxwork inhabitants, done in careful and convincing life-size detail. Live castle-dwellers add to the fun: perhaps the jocular wandering rat-catcher, or an instructive bowman. The rooms are excellently preserved, and their fine furnishings and art well worth braving the crowds for; the armoury really kindles interest. The marvellous grounds were designed by Capability Brown and, as well as the delightful gardens (look out for peacocks), have pleasant strolls along the banks of the River Avon; the views from the parklands are dramatic. They've restored the Mill and Engine House, which in Victorian times provided the castle with electricity. Good café, shop, disabled access to grounds only; cl 25 Dec; (0870) 4422000; from £13.50 to £11.25, depending on the season.

Warwickshire County Museum (Market Pl) In the 17th-c Market Hall, with lots of fossils, a Sheldon tapestry map of the county, and live bees; temporary exhibitons. Shop, disabled access to ground floor; cl Sun exc May-Sept, Mon all year (exc bank hols), and 25-26 Dec; (01926) 412501; free.

WELLESBOURNE SP2653

Wartime Museum Partly housed in the underground HQ of a former RAF base, a collection of aeronautical archaeology, wartime memorabilia and several aircraft. Shop, some disabled access (not underground); open Sun and bank hol Mon (exc 25-26 Dec); (01608) 622480; £1.50. In the village by the church, the Kings Head is a well run food pub.

Wellesbourne watermill (B4086) Historic watermill still producing flour in secluded rural setting, with striking wooden wheel. Helpful staff, nature trails and traditional crafts. Meals and snacks (with home-made flour), shop; usually cl Mon-Weds (exc bank hols and Tues-Weds school summer hols) and Oct-Easter, but phone to check;

(01789) 470237; £3.50.

WILMCOTE SP1658

Mary Arden's House & Shakespeare Countryside Museum Research has shown that picturesque Palmer's Farm, for the last 70 years treated as the home of Shakespeare's mother, wasn't even built until five years after she'd left the village. Her real home was the neighbouring early Tudor Glebe Farm, which you can also look around (it's furnished in Victorian style). The farm barns now re-create Elizabethan farm life, and there are country crafts, rare breeds and daily falconry displays; children's play area. Snacks, shop, disabled access to ground floor only; cl 23-26 Dec; (01789) 293455; £5.50. The Masons Arms has good generous home cooking.

WOLVERHAMPTON SJ9400

Continuing redevelopment and improvements are making the town more appealing to visitors. It has some points of interest, such as medieval St Peter's church, a reminder of the city's pre-industrial wool prosperity; it was also once the heartland of lock- and clock-making. The interesting art gallery in Lichfield St has a good collection of contemporary and pop art, and a sculpture gallery; snacks, shop, disabled access; cl Sun and all bank hols, plus 24 Dec; (01902) 552055; free. The quaint Combermere Arms (Chapel Ash) is the nicest pub for lunch here. Wightwick Manor and Moseley Old Hall (see below) right out on the outskirts are splendid.

Bantock House and Park (1m SW of centre, off A454) The ground floor of this Edwardian family home has been restored, and upstairs are displays on the city's history inc some interactive ones; they have a decent collection of decorative art. In 17 hectares (43 acres) of parkland, with re-created formal gardens and a dutch garden, also a nature trail and play area; special events. Meals, snacks, shop, disabled access; cl Mon, and Nov-Mar (exc pms Fri-Sun); (01902) 552195; free.

Moseley Old Hall (Featherstone, off A460/A449 4m N, just over Staffs border) Tudor house famed as a hiding place for Charles II after the Battle of Worcester. The façade has altered since, but the furnishings and atmosphere in its panelled rooms don't seem to have changed much, and there's a 17th-c knot garden. Readers particularly enjoy the guided tours. Teas, shop, limited disabled access; cl am, also Mon (exc bank hols), Tues, Thurs-Fri, and all Nov-late Mar (exc tours on Sun Nov to mid-Dec), best to check; (01902) 782808; *£4.60; NT.

Wightwick Manor (just off A454, 3m W) Only a century old, but beautifully and unusually designed by followers of William Morris, and a fine testimonial to the enduring qualities of his design principles. Flamboyant tiles, fittings, furnishings and glass, and lots of Pre-Raphaelite art. Also period garden with yew hedges and topiary. Snacks, shop, some disabled access; open pm Thurs, Sat and bank hol wknds Mar-Dec, garden also open Weds (plus house open pm Weds in Aug); (01902) 761400; *£6, *£3 garden only; NT. The Fieldhouse Inn is a useful food pub just below the car park.

Other attractive villages, almost all with decent pubs, include Avon Dassett SP4049, Barston SP2078, Barton-on-the-Heath SP2532 (no pub), Berkswell SP2479 (pretty Norman church), Bubbenhall SP3672, Easenhall SP4679, Flecknoe SP5164, Hampton in Arden SP2081, Hampton Lucy SP2557, upmarket Lighthorne SP3355, Lower Quinton SP1847, Monks Kirby SP4683 (huge church), Preston on Stour SP2049, Radway SP3748 (we've had no pub recommendation here yet), Ratley SP3847 (lovely church), Temple Grafton SP1255 (Shakespeare's 'Hungry Grafton'), Warmington SP4147, Welford-on-Avon SP1452 and Whichford SP3134.

Canals give some of the county's best walking opportunities. Besides places already mentioned, useful canalside pubs include the Rose & Castle at Ansty SP3983, Kings Head at Atherstone SP3097, Waterman at Hatton SP2467 (by a flight of locks), Black Boy and Herons Nest at Knowle SP1876, Navigation and Boot at Lapworth SP1670, Anchor at Leek Wootton SP2868, Two Boats at Long Itchington SP4164, Manor Arms at Rushall SK03001 (handy too for Park Lime Pits nature reserve), Boat at Stockton SP4365 (the flight of locks usually has plenty going on), Wharf Inn SP4352 (A423 Banbury-Southam), and Bulls Head at Wootton Wawen SP1563.

Where to eat

ALDERMINSTER SP2348 **Bell** *(01789) 450414* Popular and rather civilised dining pub nr Stratford, with excellent imaginative food using fresh local produce (and they hold regular food and music evenings), several neatly kept communicating areas with flagstones and wooden floors, fresh flowers, good wines, real ales, obliging service, and no smoking restaurant; conservatory and terrace overlooking garden; disabled access. £29|**£8.95**

ARMSCOTE SP2444 **Fox & Goose** *(01608) 682293* Attractive pub with contemporary décor, bright velvet cushions on wooden pews and stools, warm red and cream walls, big mirrors, lots of stylish black and white animal pictures, polished floorboards, flagstones and log fire; friendly service, imaginative enjoyable food, well kept real ales, good wines, and lots of soft drinks; tables on elegant deck overlooking big lawn with fruit trees; bdrms; cl 25-26 Dec, 1 Jan. £25|**£7.50**

ASTON CANTLOW SP1461 **Kings Head** *21 Bearley Rd (01789) 488242* Carefully restored and beautifully timbered Tudor pub with a massive inglenook fireplace and flagstones in comfortable village bar, an old-fashioned snug, a gently upmarket atmosphere, inventive food from a creative menu in the carpeted main room, cheerful service, well kept ales, and decent wines; disabled access. £30|**£9.95**

BIRMINGHAM SP0686 **Bank** *4 Brindley Pl, (0121) 633 4466* Branch of the fashionable London restaurant, this busy place is bright and modern with lots of efficient staff, kitchen views through glass wall, huge varied choice of french-style dishes inc some fine fish and attractively presented puddings, and a good range of wines; next door to the National Sea Life Centre; cl 1 Jan, 1st bank hol in May; disabled access. £40|**£12**

BIRMINGHAM SP0586 **Petit Blanc** *9 Brindley Pl, 2-3 Oozells Sq (0121) 633 7333* Part of Raymond Blanc's small brasserie chain, this stylish and spacious restaurant is relaxed and friendly, with helpful staff, good modern cooking with a french bias, plenty of choice, lovely puddings, and a short, well chosen wine list; cl 25 Dec; they are kind to children; disabled access. £38.50|**£12**

GAYDON SP3654 **Malt Shovel** *Church Rd (01926) 641221* Popular bar with a good relaxed atmosphere, log fire, milk churns and earthenware containers in a loft above the bar, steps up to a snug area with comfortable sofas, and busy dining room with a mix of pubby and dining tables; enjoyable unpretentious food cooked by the chef-landlord, real ales, and friendly efficient staff. £21.75|**£7.35**

GREAT WOLFORD SP2434 **Fox & Hounds** *(01608) 674220* Inviting 16th-c stone inn with a good mix of locals and visitors in the cosy low-beamed old-fashioned bar; candlelit tables, flagstones and a roaring log fire, really enjoyable imaginative daily specials, and a little tap room with several changing real ales; bdrms; cl Mon; disabled access. £25|**£5.25**

HATTON SP2367 **Falcon** *Birmingham Rd (01926) 484737* Well reworked old pub with five calm, relaxing open-plan rooms working their way around a central island bar; lots of stripped brickwork, low beams, tiled and oak-planked floors, big Turkey rugs and a nice mix of stripped and waxed country tables; a big barn-style back dining area is no smoking; wide choice of interesting food, well kept real ales, and decent wines; seats out on lawns. £24|**£6.95**

KENILWORTH SP2872 **Clarendon House** *6 High St (01926) 857668* Comfortable hotel that started life in 1430 and billeted Roundhead troops in the Civil War; stylish and relaxed partly no smoking modern bar/brasserie with comfortable sofas and black-framed cane chairs, contemporary prints on mainly orange or yellow walls, and a 'complaints department' which is a deep stone well imprisoning a mock skeleton; a wide choice of snacks and up-to-date light dishes, nicely served with linen napkins, real ales and good wines, and efficient continental staff. £24|**£4.95**

MONKS KIRBY SP4682 **Bell** *Bell Lane (01788) 832352* Busy pub with warmly chatty spanish landlord, timbered and flagstoned rambling rooms, cheerful locals, good tapas and plenty of Spanish dishes as well as more usual bar food, an extensive wine list, well kept real ales, and quite a few whiskies; cl Mon am, 26 Dec, 1 Jan; disabled access. £30.50|£6.75

STRATFORD-UPON-AVON SP2055 **Benson's** *4 Bards Walk (01789) 261116* Close to Shakespeare's birthplace, this light and airy tearoom has lots of plants and flowers, neatly dressed staff, papers and magazines to read, a wonderful patisserie, a marvellous choice of teas and coffees (plus Pimms, buck's fizz and kir), and breakfasts, morning coffee, lunches, and afternoon tea; no smoking; cl Sun in winter; disabled access. £18.50|£5

STRATFORD-UPON-AVON SP2054 **Garrick** *25 High St (01789) 292186* Attractive ancient pub with small, heavily timbered irregularly shaped rooms, some walls stripped back to bare stone and others heavily plastered, theatrical posters, and long upholstered settles and stools made from barrels on bare boards; small air-conditioned back dining room with an open fire, well kept real ales, enjoyable bar food (sandwiches served all day), and very friendly staff. £22|£5.95

STRATFORD-UPON-AVON SP2054 **Opposition** *13 Sheep St (01789) 269980* Small bustling restaurant with friendly atmosphere, generous helpings of enjoyable food, and a good choice of drinks - handy for theatres and open for after-show meals; cl 25 Dec; disabled access. £28|£7.95

STRATFORD-UPON-AVON SP2054 **Russons** *8 Church St (01789) 268822* Cheerful and popular bistro in 17th-c malthouse with very good imaginative food (plenty of fresh fish) and good value simple wine list; pre-theatre meals, too; cl Sun-Mon, wk between Christmas and New Year, 1 wk Easter, 2 wks end Aug; children over 8. £28|£7.95

STRATFORD-UPON-AVON SP2054 **Thai Boathouse** *Swans Nest Lane (01789) 297733* Above a working boatyard right on the river, this popular restaurant has simple wooden tables on bare boards, lots of rope fancywork, and views of the RSC theatre; good interesting modern bistro dishes using influences from all over the world (enjoyable fish dishes), a short reasonably priced wine list, and friendly helpful service; cl 25 Dec. £28|£7.50

WHARF SP4353 **Wharf Inn** *Wharf Rd (01295) 770332* (just off A423) Open-plan pub by Bridge 136 of the South Oxford Canal with a smart tall-windowed dining area: plain solid tables and high-backed chairs on mainly wood strip or tiled floors, a big oriental rug, walls in canary yellow, eau de nil or purple, modern artwork, and end windows so close to the water that you feel right by it; enjoyable food (inc full english breakfast), real ales, good coffee, and efficient, friendly service; canal shop, playhouse on stilts, and waterside garden. £21|£5.50

Special thanks to Brian and Anna Marsden, Mike Paley, Peter Gondris, B and K Hypher, Mrs J Piercey, Mrs J M Preston

Please let us know what you think of places in the *Guide*. Use the report forms at the back of the book, write us a letter or log on to www.goodguides.co.uk

WILTSHIRE

**Sedately charming towns, villages and countryside, great estates,
stone age survivals, and a few super family outings**

Wiltshire's claim to world-wide fame is its profusion of prehistoric sites.
The household name is, of course, Stonehenge, and it's well worth a visit,
but Avebury too has a great deal to offer (the Alexander Keiller Museum is
a good place to find out more about the area's marvels).

The most appealing countryside is along the valleys of the southern
chalk streams - intimate scenery with stone or flint houses and sparkling
rivers. The northern parts have some quietly attractive drives and walks,
especially around Marlborough. Running across the county, the restored
Kennet & Avon canal has lots of scope for enjoyable boat trips or relaxing
towpath walks. Wiltshire is also dissected by several cycleways; many
tourist information centres have routes and maps, and you can get advice
on cycling and walking here by phoning (01980) 623255.

The beautiful small city of Salisbury, with its lovely cathedral precinct, is
a good place for a short quiet break. Several attractive little towns
elsewhere in the county include handsome Bradford-on-Avon
(Westwood Manor and Iford Manor Garden are worth stopping for),
Devizes (lots of grand buildings), Malmesbury (tranquil abbey) and
Marlborough. Castle Combe and Lacock (lovely abbey, photography
museum and country park) are exceptionally pretty villages.

Longleat is brimful of attractions, even aside from the famous safari
park. With a completely different sort of appeal, Steam in Swindon is good
fun even if railways aren't something you're usually keen on. Our pick for
Wiltshire's top Family Attraction this year is Farmer Giles Farmstead in
Teffont Magna (a fun taste of life on a dairy farm). Children enjoy too
bustling Roves Farm in Sevenhampton, and Cholderton Rare Breeds Farm;
at West Knoyle you can even visit a working bison farm.

Corsham Court (outstanding art collection), Wilton House (with an
interesting carpet museum nearby) and Lydiard Park (excellent value) all
richly repay a visit. Bowood at Calne and Stourhead at Stourton offer
stunning landscaped gardens, and interesting houses. You'll find other
memorable gardens at Holt (with a medieval manor nearby), Tollard Royal
and Middle Woodford. Steam fanatics will relish the chance to see the
oldest beam engine in the world at work in Crofton.

Where to stay

BRADFORD-ON-AVON ST8261 **Bradford Old Windmill** *4 Masons Lane,
Bradford-on-Avon, Wiltshire BA15 1QN* (01225) 866842 **£79***; 3 rms and one suite;
one rm with waterbed, another with round bed, and the third with a Gothic iron
bed. Interesting and carefully converted windmill with log fire in attractive circular
lounge (former grain store), lots of books, a friendly atmosphere; good vegetarian
evening meals with dishes from Thailand, Nepal, Mexico and so forth (Mon, Thurs

and Sat only), and fine breakfasts eaten around communal refectory table; pretty cottagey garden; no smoking; cl Jan-Feb, Christmas; children over 6

BRADFORD-ON-AVON ST8359 **Widbrook Grange** *Trowbridge Rd, Widbrook, Bradford-on-Avon, Wiltshire BA15 1UH (01225) 864750* **£110**; 20 pretty rms, many in carefully converted courtyard cottages. Handsome stone former farmhouse in 11 acres, with comfortable drawing rooms, good food in elegant dining room, a sunny conservatory, and indoor swimming pool and gym; cl 24 Dec-31 Dec; disabled access

BRADFORD-ON-AVON ST8361 **Woolley Grange** *Woolley Green, Bradford-on-Avon, Wiltshire BA15 1TX (01225) 864705* **£140**, plus winter breaks; 23 rms, with fruit and home-made biscuits. Civilised Jacobean manor house with a relaxed informal atmosphere, lovely flowers, log fires and antiques in comfortable and beautifully decorated day rooms, and pretty conservatory; delicious food using local (or home-grown) produce, often organic, inc home-baked breads and muffins and home-made jams and marmalades for breakfast, marvellous staff, and swimming pool, tennis, badminton, and croquet; particularly well organised for families, with nannies and plenty of entertainment; disabled access; dogs welcome in bedrooms ☺

CALNE ST9871 **Chilvester Hill House** *Chilvester Hill, Calne, Wiltshire SN11 0LP (01249) 813981* **£80***; 3 charming spacious rms. Big Victorian house freshly decorated in William Morris style, with neat gardens and grounds, particularly helpful friendly owners, comfortable sitting rooms with antiques, good breakfasts and honest no-choice dinners around large table in separate dining room (using home-grown or local), and plenty of local sights; cl 1 wk spring and/or autumn; children over 12 (babies allowed)

CASTLE COMBE ST8477 **Manor House** *Castle Combe, Chippenham, Wiltshire SN14 7HR (01249) 782206* **£177**, plus special breaks; 47 lovely rms, some in mews cottages just 50 yds from the house. 14th-c manor house in 360 acres of countryside inc an italian garden and parkland; gracious day rooms with panelling, antiques, log fires and fresh flowers, a warm friendly atmosphere, and very good innovative food; 18-hole golf course with full range of practice facilities, croquet, boules, and all-weather tennis court, and heated outdoor swimming pool

CHICKSGROVE ST9730 **Compasses** *Lower Chicksgrove, Tisbury, Salisbury, Wiltshire SP3 6NB (01722) 714318* **£65** plus special breaks; 4 rms. Lovely thatched house in delightful hamlet with old bottles and jugs hanging from the beams, good freshly cooked food, well kept real ales, and peaceful farm courtyard, garden and play area; cl 25-26 Dec; disabled access; dogs welcome in bedrooms

COLERNE ST8272 **Lucknam Park** *Colerne, Chippenham, Wiltshire SN14 8AZ (01225) 742777* **£251**, plus special breaks; 41 luxurious rms. Noble Georgian house reached by a long beech-lined drive through extensive grounds, with elegant carefully furnished day rooms, panelled library, lovely flowers, antiques and paintings, and excellent food and extremely good service in charming restaurant; snooker, hairdresser, leisure spa with indoor swimming pool, gym and beauty salon, and floodlit tennis courts; croquet; an all-weather equestrian centre; children over 8 in evening restaurant; disabled access

CROCKERTON ST8642 **Springfield House** *23 Crockerton, Warminster, Wiltshire BA12 8AU (01985) 213696* **£64***, 3 rms with garden views. Charming, welcoming 17th-c house on the edge of Longleat Estate, with a comfortable sitting room, breakfast room and terrace, lawn tennis, and an acre of south-facing garden; lots to do nearby; cl Christmas; children over 6

CRUDWELL ST9592 **Old Rectory Country House Hotel** *Crudwell, Malmesbury, Wiltshire SN16 9EP (01666) 577194* **£98**, plus special breaks; 12 big homely rms. Elegant, welcoming country-house hotel, formerly the rectory to the Saxon church next door; three acres of lovely landscaped Victorian gardens, an airy drawing room, interesting and enjoyable food in panelled no smoking restaurant, a relaxed atmosphere, and unpretentious service; dogs welcome in bedrooms

DEVIZES SU0061 **Bear** *Market Pl, Devizes, Wiltshire SN10 1HS (01380) 722444* **£75**; 25 rms. Very much at the town's heart, this beamed 16th-c inn has an old-fashioned feel, a wide choice of food from snacks to more elaborate meals in the oak-panelled Lawrence Room and formal restaurant; cl 25-26 Dec

EBBESBOURNE WAKE ST9924 **Horseshoe** *Ebbesbourne Wake, Salisbury, Wiltshire SP5 5JG* (01722) 780474 **£60***; 2 rms. Particularly welcoming pub with beautifully kept little bar, open fire, fresh flowers and interesting bric-a-brac on beams, popular home-made food in bar or no smoking restaurant, big breakfasts and nice Sunday lunches, well kept real ales, pretty little garden, play area, and pets' corner in paddock; cl 25 Dec

FORD ST8476 **White Hart** *Ford, Chippenham, Wiltshire SN14 8RP* (01249) 782213 **£79***; 11 spacious, well equipped rms. Very well run, popular and attractive ivy-covered inn in lovely spot by trout stream; an old-fashioned atmosphere, heavy black beams, big woodburner in ancient fireplace, particularly good imaginative food, well kept real ales, malt whiskies and fine wines and attentive cheerful service; disabled access

GASTARD ST8867 **Boyds Farm** *Chapel Knapp, Gastard, Corsham, Wiltshire SN13 9PT* (01249) 713146 **£46***, plus special breaks; 3 rms. Friendly and handsome 16th-c house on family-run working farm with pedigree Herefords; homely lounge, patterned carpets, woodburner, traditional breakfasts; no evening meals (local pubs nearby); cl Christmas-New Year

GRITTLETON ST8680 **Church House** *Grittleton, Chippenham, Wiltshire SN14 6AP* (01249) 782562 **£68***, plus special breaks; 4 big comfortable rms. Large Georgian rectory on the edge of a lovely village, in 11 acres of gardens and pasture with a heated indoor swimming pool and croquet; relaxed and friendly house-party atmosphere, open fire, antiques and paintings in the drawing room, very good imaginative food using organic home-grown vegetables and fruit (advance notice needed), and breakfasts with their own eggs; children under 2 and over 12

HEYTESBURY ST9242 **Angel** *High St, Heytesbury, Warminster, Wiltshire BA12 0ED* (01985) 840330 **£65***; 8 comfortable light rms. 16th-c coaching inn with armchairs, sofas, and a good fire in cosy homely lounge, a long chatty beamed bar, and good service from friendly staff; wide choice of consistently good food in charming back dining room that opens on to secluded garden; disabled access; dogs welcome in bedrooms

LACOCK ST9168 **At the Sign of the Angel** *Church St, Lacock, Chippenham, Wiltshire SN15 2LB* (01249) 730230 **£99**, plus special breaks; 10 charmingly old rooms with antiques This fine 15th-c house in a lovely NT village is full of character, with heavy oak furniture, beams and big fireplaces, a restful oak-panelled lounge, and good english cooking in three candlelit restaurants; cl Christmas; disabled access; dogs welcome in bedrooms

LITTLE LANGFORD SU0436 **Little Langford Farmhouse** *Little Langford, Salisbury, Wiltshire SP3 4NR* (01722) 790205 **£60***; 3 spacious rms with period furniture. Victorian gothick farmhouse with turreted entrance hall and plenty of original features, sitting room with open fire, friendly owners, a baby grand, billiards room, light suppers if arranged beforehand, and big garden; can observe the working farm (dairy and arable), and there are plenty of downland walks; no smoking; cl Nov-Feb; children over 12

MALMESBURY ST9387 **Old Bell** *Abbey Row, Malmesbury, Wiltshire SN16 0BW* (01666) 822344 **£120**, plus special breaks; 31 attractive rms. With some claim to being one of England's oldest hotels and standing in the shadow of the Norman abbey, this fine wisteria-clad building has traditionally furnished rooms with Edwardian pictures, an early 13th-c hooded stone fireplace, two good fires and plenty of comfortable sofas, magazines and newspapers; cheerful helpful service, very good food, and attractively old-fashioned garden; particularly well organised with facilities and entertainments for children; disabled access; dogs welcome in bedrooms ☺

MILDENHALL SU2169 **Fisherman's House** *Mildenhall, Marlborough, Wiltshire SN8 2LZ* (01672) 515390 **£65***; 3 lovely rms, most with own bthrm. Extremely pretty house with lawns running down to the River Kennet, fresh flowers and stylish furniture, friendly owners, and good breakfasts in airy conservatory; cl 25-26 Dec; children over 12

NETTLETON ST8378 **Fosse Farmhouse Hotel** *Nettleton, Chippenham, Wiltshire SN14 7NJ (01249)* 782286 **£125***, plus special breaks (inc some interesting craft wknds); 3 rms. 18th-c Cotswold stone house extensively restored with decorative french antique furniture and pretty english chintzes; morning coffee, lunch and cream teas served on the lawns or in very attractive dining room; antiques shop with dried flowers and decorative items in former dairy behind the house; dogs welcome in bedrooms

PURTON SU0987 **Pear Tree** *Church End, Purton, Swindon, Wiltshire SN5 4ED (01793)* 772100 **£120***, plus special breaks; 17 very comfortable, pretty rms. Impeccably run former vicarage with elegant comfortable day rooms, fresh flowers, fine conservatory restaurant with good modern english cooking using home-grown herbs, helpful caring staff, and 7½ acres inc a traditional Victorian garden; cl 26-30 Dec; disabled access; dogs welcome

SALISBURY SU1430 **Farthings** *9 Swaynes Close, Salisbury, Wiltshire SP1 3AE (01722)* 330749 **£50**, plus special breaks; 4 rms, most with own bthrm. Spotlessly kept no smoking house with friendly owners, good breakfasts, and pretty garden; nr cathedral; no children

SALISBURY SU1428 **Rose & Crown** *Harnham Rd, Harnham, Salisbury, Wiltshire SP2 8JQ (01722)* 399955 **£95***; 28 rms in the original building or smart modern extension. It's almost worth a visit just for the view - well nigh identical to that in the most famous Constable painting of Salisbury Cathedral; elegantly restored inn with friendly beamed and timbered bar, log fire, good bar and restaurant food, and charming Avonside garden; disabled access; dogs welcome

SALISBURY SU1431 **Stratford Lodge** *4 Park Lane, Salisbury, Wiltshire SP1 3NP (01722)* 325177 **£75***, plus special breaks; 8 rms. Warmly friendly and relaxed Victorian house with antique furnishings, fresh flowers, generous helpings of very good carefully prepared evening food, super breakfasts in conservatory, and quiet garden; children over 5

WARMINSTER ST8944 **Bishopstrow House** *Bishopstrow, Warminster, Wiltshire BA12 9HH (01985)* 212312 **£160***, plus special breaks; 32 sumptuous rms, some with jacuzzi. Charming ivy-clad Georgian house in 27 acres with heated indoor and outdoor swimming pools, indoor and outdoor tennis courts, fitness centre and beauty treatment rooms, and own fishing on River Wylye; very relaxed friendly atmosphere, log fires, lovely fresh flowers, antiques and fine paintings in boldly decorated day rooms, and really impressive food; disabled access; dogs welcome ☺

WARMINSTER ST8745 **Old Bell** *42 Market Pl, Warminster, Wiltshire BA12 9AN (01985)* 216611 **£55***, plus special breaks; 15 comfortable rms. 14th-c country-town hotel with traditional bar food, bistro and restaurant, good choice of wines, pretty central courtyard, and friendly service; cl Christmas; lots to do nearby

WINSLEY ST7960 **Burghope Manor** *Winsley, Bradford-on-Avon, Wiltshire BA15 2LA (01225)* 723557 **£90**; 8 rms. Lovely 13th-c family home in attractive countryside, with carefully preserved old rooms and an interesting fireplace engraved with Elizabethan writing, antiques in big drawing room, welcoming caring owners, nice breakfasts, and evening meals by arrangement; self-catering in Dower House in grounds; cl Christmas and New Year; children over 10

WOOTTON BASSETT SU0783 **Marsh Farm Hotel** *Wootton Bassett, Swindon, Wiltshire SN4 8ER (01793)* 848044 **£92**, plus special breaks; 50 rms. Handsome Victorian farmhouse in landscaped grounds with particularly warm and friendly atmosphere, comfortable lounge, convivial bar, and enjoyable food in conservatory restaurant; cl 25-31 Dec; disabled access

To see and do

Wiltshire Family Attraction of the Year

TEFFONT MAGNA ST9832 **Farmer Giles Farmstead** Quite a big site, with lots to see, this friendly working dairy farm is particularly good value for money - and as lots is under cover, it's a farm that won't disappoint if the weather's poor. Children can stroke or feed some of the animals, or perhaps even hand-milk a cow or groom the donkey. All the animals you'd expect are here, with lots of smaller furry ones in the pets corner, and several in nicely accessible open paddocks. They've diversified into wine-making (you can try their wines in the restaurant) and you can stroll round the vineyards while exploring the rest of the site. Every couple of hours they have 20-minute tractor and trailer rides, and there are decent play areas inside and out, as well as some obsolete tractors to clamber over. An exhibition of old farm equipment is more interesting than you'd expect: look out for the sack lifting device, which lifted bags weighing up to eleven stone on to a man's back. Meals, snacks, shop, picnic area, disabled access; cl weekdays Nov to mid-Mar; (01722) 716338; £3.95 adults, £2.95 children. A family ticket is £13.

ALTON BARNES SU1061
Kennet & Avon Canal Here the canal lies close enough to Pewsey Down nature reserve for an afternoon's walk to incorporate both features; the spine of the downs here is followed by the Wansdyke, an ancient earthwork which runs across the downs for miles from Morgans Hill, near Calne. nearly as far as the Savernake Forest. The canalside Barge at Honeystreet is a good lunch stop.

ANSTY ST9526
Pleasant village, notable for England's tallest maypole.

AVEBURY SU1070
Avebury Stone Circle This spectacular 4,500-year-old henge monument encompasses the pretty village - where Stones does good vegetarian food. It's the largest stone circle in Europe, the 200 surviving stones enclosed in a massive earthen rampart nearly a mile in circumference. Originally, there were two smaller internal stone circles, too. The site was excavated in the 1920s and 1930s, in the most unusual way. A marmalade magnate bought the entire village, and had the stones re-erected - many had become buried or dilapidated (recent research suggests that one important stone may have been re-erected upside down, after he refused to accept the work of a rival archaeological expert). Work was recently carried out to straighten the stones, which had developed a list over the last few decades. The **Alexander Keiller Museum** named after him gives a succinct introduction to the archaeological wonders of the area, inc a new interactive barn gallery exhibition. Meals, snacks, shop, disabled access; cl 24-26 Dec; (01672) 539250; *£4.20; NT.

Avebury Manor (behind church) Much altered house, formerly a monastery. The present buildings date from the early 16th c, with Queen Anne alterations and then Edwardian renovations. The attractive topiary and flower gardens contain medieval walls and some ancient evergreens. Disabled access to most of garden (but not to house); cl am, Weds-Sat (exc gardens, also open Fri and Sat) and Nov-Mar; (01672) 539250; *£3.80, gardens only *£2.90; NT.

Fyfield Down SU1470 Primeval-feeling and unkempt, scattered with outcrops known as sarsen stones, the raw material of Avebury Stone Circle and of part of Stonehenge.

Silbury Hill SU1068 This towering prehistoric mound, purpose unknown, is the largest man-made mound in Europe - it would have taken a thousand men about ten years to build. There's a parking and viewing area, or you can walk the short distance from Avebury car park; there's no access to the top of

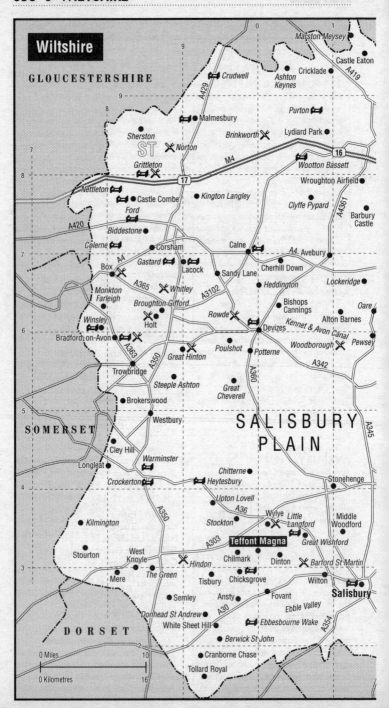

Wiltshire

GLOUCESTERSHIRE

Marston Meysey
Castle Eaton
Crudwell
Cricklade
Ashton Keynes
Malmesbury
Purton
Sherston
Brinkworth
Lydiard Park
ST
Norton
Wootton Bassett
Grittleton
Wroughton Airfield
Nettleton
Castle Combe
Kington Langley
Clyffe Pypard
Ford
Barbury Castle
Biddestone
Colerne
Corsham
Calne
Avebury
Box
Gastard
Cherhill Down
Lacock
Sandy Lane
Monkton Farleigh
Whitley
Heddington
Lockeridge
Oare
Broughton Gifford
Bishops Cannings
Winsley
Holt
Rowde
Alton Barnes
Bradford-on-Avon
Devizes
Kennet & Avon Canal
Pewsey
Great Hinton
Poulshot
Potterne
Woodborough
Trowbridge
Steeple Ashton
Great Cheverell
SOMERSET
Brokerswood
SALISBURY
Westbury
PLAIN
Cley Hill
Warminster
Longleat
Chitterne
Stonehenge
Crockerton
Heytesbury
Upton Lovell
Kilmington
Wylye
Stockton
Little Langford
Middle Woodford
Stourton
Teffont Magna
Great Wishford
West Knoyle
Hindon
Chilmark
Dinton
Barford St Martin
Mere
The Green
Tisbury
Chicksgrove
Wilton
Salisbury
Semley
Ansty
Fovant
Donhead St Andrew
Ebble Valley
White Sheet Hill
Ebbesbourne Wake
DORSET
Berwick St John
Cranborne Chase
Tollard Royal

0 Miles 10
0 Kilometres 16

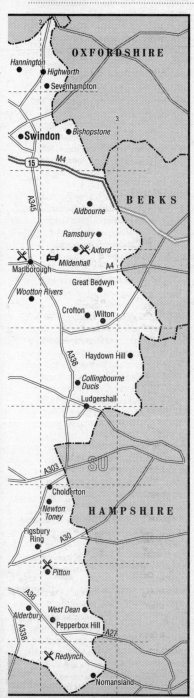

the hill (where a huge shaft, perhaps a relic of 1776 treasure-hunters, suddenly opened up a few years ago).

West Kennett Avenue Leading away from the circle is this 1½-mile avenue of stones, virtually destroyed by ploughing and mostly replaced by modern concrete posts. It leads to the site of the Sanctuary, a stone circle (on the site of an earlier wooden temple) that was similarly razed, then marked out with posts in modern times.

West Kennett Long Barrow The prehistoric remains of a 5,000-year-old chambered tomb and barrow (one of the largest in the country), where several dozen people were buried. Take a torch if you want to venture in behind the massive entrance stone: the chamber with two side chapels runs some 9 metres (30 ft) or more into the barrow. You have to park in either the car park next to Silbury Hill or the layby at the bottom of the field next to the A4, and then walk about half a mile up the track. The Waggon & Horses at Beckhampton (of *Pickwick Papers* fame) is quite handy.

Windmill Hill Reached by footpath NW, this, the earliest monument in the area, is a neolithic enclosure dating back some 5,000 years. There's not a great deal to see apart from mild lumps, but the site is quite evocative.

BARBURY CASTLE SU1476 One of Wiltshire's 4,500 recorded ancient sites. Many are scarcely a lump in the ground, but this Iron Age camp at the northernmost point of the Marlborough Downs, splendidly remote and on the long-distance Ridgeway Path, still has formidable ramparts. There is a car park nearby, but you can also walk up to it from Ogbourne St George (where the Old Crown has enjoyable food) along Smeathe's Ridge, a preserved stretch of downland, gorse and all.

BISHOPS CANNINGS SU0364 Attractive village, with an outstanding **church**. The Crown has good value food, and the Kennet & Avon Canal is a walk away.

BOX ST8268 An attractive up-and-down village, its interesting parts hidden down the steep valley below the A4, with cottages and

houses using the same stone that's been quarried nearby since Roman times. There's a story that on 9 Apr, Brunel's birthday, the rising sun shines right through the great railway tunnel he quarried through the hill above here (you can see the restored grand entrance from the A4). The Quarrymans Arms up above has good food.
Hazelbury Manor (off B3109 just E) Richly varied landscaped gardens, with a medieval archery alley, stone and yew circles, fountain, waterfall, pond, large rockery, formal areas and laburnum walk, all laid out as a sort of giant maze. Open by appointment; (01225) 812952; £3. In Chapel Plaister on the way, look out for the 15th-c chapel for Glastonbury pilgrims on the little hilltop green.

BRADFORD-ON-AVON ST8260
Attractive hillside town given a distinguished air by the same sort of golden stone as was used in Bath; it's very steep, and has some handsome buildings reflecting its past wealth as a wool town - and quite a few serious antiques shops. Nr the Norman parish church is a tall narrow late **Saxon church**, unusual for having virtually no later additions. The Dandy Lion (Market St) is good for lunch. From here you can cycle around 11m E to Devizes or 10m W to Bath along the towpath of the Kennet & Avon Canal. Cycle hire from TF Cycles, at the Lock Inn (Frome Rd); £6 for 1st hour, then £1 an hour after that; canoe (£14 for half a day) and boat hire too; (01225) 867187.
Avoncliff A short walk along the canal, this quite steep gorge is shared by canal, river and railway, the canal disdainfully stepping over the river by way of a restored aqueduct. The Cross Guns has remarkable views over it.
Barton Farm Country Park (Pound Lane) Between the river and canal, a short walk from the town centre. Lovely walks, bird-watching, riverside picnic area, also rowing, canoeing and fishing. The medieval **tithe barn** (its massive stone-slab roof supported by an impressive network of great beams and rafters) was built to store Shaftesbury Abbey's share of the farm's output. Some other medieval farm buildings have been converted into craft

shops, workshops, galleries, and a tearoom.
Iford Manor Garden (just past Westwood) Well worth the trek down narrow lanes, this charming garden is notable for its stylish Edwardian italianate riverside terraced garden, with romantic cloisters, colonnade and statues; architect Peto fully takes advantage of the hillside setting, and the views are lovely. Good cream teas wknds and bank hols May-Aug; cl am, Mon, Fri (exc bank hols), and Oct-Apr (exc Sun Apr and Oct and Apr bank hols); (01225) 863146; *£4.
Westwood Manor (above Avoncliff, just SW) Fully furnished 15th-c stone manor house with its original Gothic and Jacobean windows, fine 17th-c plasterwork, and modern topiary garden. No facilities; cl am, Sun-Mon, Thurs-Fri and 30 Sept-4 Apr; (01225) 863374; *£4.40; NT. The church in Westwood village has some interesting late medieval stained glass.

BROKERSWOOD ST8352
Country Park & Woodland Railway 80 acres of ancient woodland, with carp lake, adventure playground, play trail, picnic and barbecue areas, and a little woodland railway (wknds and school hols Easter-Oct). Meals, snacks, shop, limited disabled access; (01373) 822238; cl 24-26 Dec, 1 Jan; £3. The Poplars over at Wingfield does good lunches.

CALNE SU0069
Atwell-Wilson Motor Museum About 90 vehicles, mostly vintage cars but also lorries, mopeds and classic motorbikes, plus lots of motoring memorabilia; there's a little play area and a 17th-c water meadow walk. Shop, disabled access; usually cl Fri-Sat (exc Good Fri), best to check; (01249) 813319; £2.50.
Bowood 🖾 (off A4) The extensive Capability Brown parkland and colourful pleasure gardens are the glory of Bowood, with their temples, cascades and hermit's cave shielded from the outside world by further miles of partly wooded grounds; a woodland garden is open for rhododendron walks during flowering season (late Apr-May, phone to check). Much of the main building was demolished in 1955, but

there's plenty left, inc the impressive library designed by Robert Adam. Joseph Priestley discovered oxygen here in 1772 and it's home to an excellent collection of watercolours. There's an outstanding adventure playground and soft play area. Meals, snacks, shop, limited disabled access; cl Nov-Mar; (01249) 812102; £6.25. The Lansdowne Arms at Derry Hill, near the house, is nice for lunch.

CASTLE COMBE ST8477
For many the prettiest village in Britain, this has a classic group of stone-tiled Cotswoldy cottages by the turreted church, at the bottom of a tree-clad hill running down to a trout stream and its ancient stone bridge. Preservation of the village is taken so seriously that you won't even see television aerials on the houses; several villagers occasionally open their beautifully kept gardens for charity. Best of all during the week out of season; at other times it does get a great many visitors, even though the car park is some way up the hill. The charming old Castle Inn has good food. The village has surroundings that are equally appealing, and attractive paths along deep peaceful valleys.

CASTLE EATON SU1495
Attractive village, by a quiet stretch of the upper Thames, pleasant for strolling. The Red Lion, with a roomy conservatory, has decent food.

CHERHILL DOWN SU0469
This large NT area of ancient downland has free access for walkers. A range of man-made features of various periods adorn its slopes, inc an Iron Age hill fort (Oldbury Castle), an assortment of long barrows, tumuli and ancient field systems, a figure of a white horse, and the mid-19th-c Lansdowne Monument; the site is rich in chalkland flora such as orchids, and associated butterfly and bird life.

CHICKSGROVE ST9730
Charming tucked-away hamlet; peaceful walk to Sutton Mandeville church, and back by the Nadder Valley, and good imaginative food at the Compasses.

CHILMARK ST9732
Attractive village, with a partly 13th-c church. The Black Dog, with links to early Massachusetts settlers, has good food these days.

CHOLDERTON SU2042
Cholderton Rare Breeds Farm 🏠
(Amesbury Rd, just off A338) Fun, friendly and well laid out, good for families with young children. There are plenty of opportunities to get close to the animals, inc the youngest of the 50 or so breeds of rabbit they keep. Other friendly residents include Coco the donkey, and some pygmy goats. Visitors really enjoy their National Grunt pig racing (twice a day at wknds and in school hols, usually around 12.30 and 3.30pm); also tractor and trailer rides, a couple of play areas inc one for under-7s, and trampolines. Nature trails lace through orchards and woodland, and there are tranquil water gardens in the attractive grounds. Meals, snacks (good cream teas), shop, disabled access; cl Nov to mid-Mar; (01980) 629438; £5.50. The Malet Arms at Newton Toney does good lunches.

CLEY HILL ST8344
This steep-sided hill just W of Warminster involves a short, puffy stroll to the Iron Age hill fort at its summit, looking across Longleat Park.

CORSHAM ST8770
Corsham Court Fine house and park begun in 1582 but later added to and developed by those busy masters Capability Brown, John Nash, Robert Adam and Humphry Repton. The paintings are among the best in any stately home in Britain, inc works by Lippi, Reynolds, and Van Dyck. The extensive lawns and a Georgian bath house are patrolled by peacocks. Cl am, Mon (exc bank hols), Fri, wkdys Oct to mid-Mar, and all Dec (01249) 701610; £5, £2 garden only. Nearby are some attractive former weavers' cottages; the church, on the edge of the park, is largely 12th c, partly Saxon. The Methuen Arms is good for lunch.

CRANBORNE CHASE ST9319
Some of the finest walking in the S of Wiltshire is to be found here close to the Dorset border, where the county's abundant chalk downland shows at its best. A good example is Ashcombe Bottom N of Tollard Royal, a deep remote valley which plunges into the heart of the Chase. The Grove Arms at Ludwell has good food.

CRICKLADE SU1093
Small town quietly separated from the busy A419, with some attractive buildings and a glorious tower crowning the fine parish church. At the end of the High St, just N of the Thames, a path on the left off the slip road heading back towards the A419 leads to a broad riverside meadow kept unimproved for decades, and mown only in July after the numerous wild flowers have seeded. The Vale has up-to-date food.

CROFTON SU2662
Crofton Beam Engines Still pumping water into the Kennet & Avon Canal, the oldest working beam engines in the world, an 1812 Boulton & Watt, and an 1845 Harveys of Hayle. Snacks, shop; cl Oct- Easter, engines usually static, but in steam bank hol wknds and last wknds of Jun, July and Sept, best to check; (01672) 870300; static *£3, steam wknds *£4.50.

DEVIZES SU0061
Lots of grand old buildings in this interesting and friendly town, and a good town trail takes most of them in. There's still an active market square (with a statue of Ruth Pierce, who fell dead on the spot after telling a porky and calling God to witness it as true).The 29 locks of the Kennet & Avon Canal coming up Caen Hill from the W form one of the longest flights of locks in the country. The HQ of the Canal Trust on the Wharf has a museum; cl 25 Dec-Feb; (01380) 729489; £1.50. The handsome Bear (Market Pl) and Moonraker (A342) are good for lunch.

Broadleas (Potterne Rd) Rare plants in secluded dell among rhododendrons, magnolias and other fine flowering shrubs, unusual trees, particularly good in spring with sheets of bulbs under flowering trees. Snacks, unusual plant sales; open pms Sun, Weds and Thurs, Apr-Oct; (01380) 722035; *£4.

Wiltshire Heritage Museum (Long St) First-class local history, particularly good on finds from the area's ancient sites (the Bronze Age gallery is especially interesting); art gallery with John Piper window. Shop, some disabled access; usually open daily (exc most bank hols); (01380) 727369; £3 (maybe less), free on Mon and pm Sun.

DINTON SU0031
Philipps House and Dinton Park
Fine early 19th-c mansion with interesting Portland stone staircase and underfloor heating system. The surrounding parkland offers plenty of scope for a stroll. Some disabled access; house usually open Sat 10am-1pm and Mon 2-5pm Apr-Oct, park open all year; (01985) 843600; house *£3, park free.

EBBLE VALLEY SU0024
The valley of the Ebble chalk stream winds prettily through a sleepy stream of villages from Odstock to Alvediston - a delightful drive.

FIGSBURY RING SU1833
(off A30 E of Salisbury) Iron Age hill fort with good views over Salisbury.

FOVANT SU0128
Regimental Badges Huge chalk carvings on the escarpment, clearly seen from the road, cut by troops stationed here in World War I - a sight to rival England's various white horses. The Pembroke Arms, with touching memorabilia of the time, has good value food.

GREAT BEDWYN SU2764
Bedwyn Stone Museum Fascinating little open-air museum demonstrating the ancient art of stonemasonry (the nearby church has fine examples of the finished product). Disabled access but a bit bumpy in places; cl 25 Dec; (01672) 870234; free. The Three Tuns has good value food.

HAYDOWN HILL SU3156
Reached from the E by a walk up from pretty thatched Vernham Dean in Hampshire (where the George has good food), this has the ramparts of a hill fort bounded by steep gradients on its S side; the three counties of Berkshire, Hampshire and Wiltshire meet close by at SU3559.

HOLT ST8663
Great Chalfield Manor (N of Holt) Beautiful medieval moated manor house, restored in 1905 and still with its original Great Hall. Large gardens. Guided tours only, at 12.15, 2.15, 3, 3.45 and 4.30pm; cl Fri-Mon and Nov-Mar; (01225) 782239 to book; *£4.40; NT. Next door is a small 13th-c parish church.

The Courts Garden (B3107)
Weavers used to come here to settle

their disputes; the 15th-c house isn't open, but the extensive formal gardens are lovely and full of yew hedges, pools and borders. Grounds beyond are given over to wild flowers among interesting trees, with an orchard and herb and vegetable gardens. Snacks, some disabled access; cl Weds, and mid-Oct to Mar; (01225) 782340; £4.20; NT. The Toll Gate (Ham Green) does good interesting food.

KENNET & AVON CANAL
ST8559

This restored canal runs right across the county, and there are pleasant boat trips from several places, among them Bradford-on-Avon and Devizes, or you can hire a boat for the day in Hilperton (01225) 769847 or Semington (01380) 870654. In the canal's restoration, a great deal of attention has been paid to the natural environment, so it's attractive for walks alongside; in winter you may even see a kingfisher flashing along it. For a more sedentary view, try the Barge Inn at Seend Cleeve ST9361, French Horn at Pewsey Wharf SU1560, Barge at Honeystreet SU1061 or Bridge Inn at Horton SU0563. The Golden Swan at Wilcot SU1461, Crown at Bishops Cannings SU0363, Somerset Arms at Semington ST3960 and Hop Pole at Limpley Stoke ST7861 are also within a walk.

LACOCK ST9168

A favourite village of both visitors and film-makers (see for instance the first Harry Potter film), its grid of quiet and narrow streets a delightful harmony of mellow brickwork, lichened stone and timber-and-plaster. The church is 15th-c, and nothing in the village looks more recent than 18th c. It's remained so remarkably unspoilt because most of its buildings were owned for centuries by the Talbot family, until they left them to the NT in 1944. It gets very busy in summer, but the Trust has preserved it against a surfeit of antiques shops (you'll find all you want in the nearby old market town of Melksham). The village does on the other hand have a splendid collection of pubs - the George is the best.

Lackham Country Park 🏛 Plenty of family activities, inc rural life museum, walled garden and glasshouses, animal farm, pleasant woodland walk. The 500-acre estate is the home of the Wiltshire College Lackham, and the old roses are worth catching from May to July. Snacks, shop, plant sales, disabled access; open Sun and bank hols (plus Tues-Thurs in Aug) Easter-Aug; (01249) 466847; £2.

Lacock Abbey Tranquil spread of mellow stone buildings around a central timber-gabled courtyard, based on the little-altered 13th-c abbey. Tudor additions include a romantic octagonal tower, and there was a successful 18th-c gothicisation. Surrounded by meadows and trees, this was the setting for Fox Talbot's experiments which in 1835 led to the creation of the world's first photographic negative - a picture of part of the abbey itself. There's an interesting museum devoted to this in a 16th-c barn at the gates, and the gardens are evidence of Fox Talbot's skills in other fields. Limited disabled access (not to abbey); cl Good Fri, Tues and 31 Oct-1 Mar, Abbey also cl ams and 31 Oct-27 Mar; (01249) 730227; *£7, museum, grounds and cloisters only *£4.40; NT. The photography museum is also open winter wknds (exc Christmas-New Year).

LONGLEAT ST8043

(off A362 4m W of Warminster) Few places can boast such a range of activities for families, and the Passport ticket allows you to spread the attractions over more than one visit. Children will probably get most excited about the safari park, which as well as the famous lions has rhinos, camels, and a rare white tiger. If you haven't got a car you can go by bus (it gets booked up very quickly, so go early in the day). A boat trip goes round Gorilla Island, where two gorillas live in a miniature stately home. Also displays of parrots and butterflies, a narrow-gauge railway, simulator ride, pets' corner, and an elaborate play area in a full-size mock castle. Older visitors may prefer the collection of dolls' houses or the peaceful formal gardens laid out by Capability Brown, and of course there's the handsome 16th-c house itself, much restored inside, but with impressively grand formal rooms, and the individual murals of the colourful current Marquess of Bath. He has had several mazes and labyrinths built around the grounds: the yew hedge maze is the world's longest. Changing exhibitions, lots of extra events, and you can get coarse fishing permits. Meals, snacks, shop, disabled access; largely cl Nov-early Apr, house also cl Oct (exc arranged tours), phone to check; (01985) 844400. You can get individual tickets for the attractions, but it works out much cheaper to buy the all-in Passport Ticket, £16 adults.

LUDGERSHALL SU2651
Ludgershall Castle The ruins of a Royal castle and hunting palace, still with some of the original large Norman earthworks, as well as the later flint walling; free; EH. The church is also Norman; the Queens Head has cheap food. The nearby area is very pretty and unspoilt, the little villages of the Chutes, Tangley and Vernham Dean straddling the Hampshire border all worth a look (with the pubs over that way worth exploring too).

LYDIARD PARK SU1084
🖼 (nr M4 junction 16, or A3102) Painstakingly restored grand Georgian house, with interesting early wallpaper, rare painted glass window, and elegant furnishings much as they would have been when first installed. Extensive lawns, lakes and well wooded parkland, with nature walks and adventure playgrounds. Snacks, shop, disabled access; cl Sun am, 24-26 Dec, 1 Jan, and pm second Sat in May; (01793) 770401; house £1.50 - quite a bargain. The adjacent parish **church** has interesting monuments to the St John family, who lived in the house for 500 years, and the Sun at Lydiard Millicent has enjoyable food and a pretty garden.

MALMESBURY ST9387
Yet another charming old town, especially around the green facing its serene Norman abbey, from the tower of which a medieval monk called Elmer made one of the earliest semi-successful attempts at flight - he covered a couple of hundred yards, but did break both legs when he crash-landed. The picturesque Old Bell is almost as old as the abbey beside it, and the Kings Arms and Smoking Dog (both High St) are popular for lunch. The B roads radiating from here are all quite pleasant drives.

MARLBOROUGH SU1868
One of the area's most attractive towns; its very pleasing wide High St has a market each Weds and Sat. The annual autumn Mop Fair (as in most market towns, formerly for the hiring of servants) has been revived here as a general celebration. Even the more modern additions don't look obtrusively out of place among the harmonious mix of Georgian and Tudor buildings. You can see renovations in progress and sometimes craftsmen in action at the 17th-c Merchants House (High St) which has some completed and period furnished rooms; cl Mon-Thurs and all Oct-Easter; (01672) 511491; £3. The Bear and Castle & Ball are useful for lunch. The Broad Hinton road N gives a good feel of the downs' great open spaces, as does the Manton—Alton Priors road to the SW, passing one of the area's several white horses cut into the chalk, and leading into a pleasant valley drive through Allington and Horton to Devizes. To the E, the quiet road along the Kennet Valley has some attractive views, with pleasant walks and a good food stop at the Red Lion in Axford; there are also walks through the surviving miles of Savernake Forest woodland.

MERE ST8132
Attractive village, dominated by its 30-metre (100-ft) church tower, and with good views from Castle Hill. New people in the George (where Charles II stayed after the Battle of Worcester) are doing good food.
White Sheet Hill Easily reached from Mere (via a road bridge over the busy A303) or Stourton, this lofty chalk downland is studded with antiquities - among them a Neolithic causewayed camp and Bronze Age barrows. It's a good site for cowslips, orchids and such butterflies as Adonis and Chalkhill Blues.

MIDDLE WOODFORD SU1236
Heale Gardens & Plant Centre 🖼 Eight acres of lovely formal gardens beside the Avon chalk stream, with lots of varied plants; the water garden is especially nice in spring and autumn. Snacks, shop, specialist plant sales (with an emphasis on old-fashioned roses and cottage garden plants), disabled access; gardens cl Mon (exc bank hols), and 25-

26 Dec; (01722) 782504; £3.75. The Bridge Inn in nearby Upper Woodford has good food and a nice riverside garden, and this Salisbury road along the Avon's quieter bank is a pretty drive (as is the continuation N of Amesbury, through Fittleworth and East Chisenbury).

NOMANSLAND SU2517
Forest-edge walks There are some pleasant walks in countryside that's unusual for Wiltshire, around the good value Lamb down on the edge of the New Forest.

PEPPERBOX HILL SU2125 (off A36 5m SE of Salisbury) Named after the hexagonal 17th-c tower (built as a folly) on its summit. You can't get into the tower, but the site commands fine views over Salisbury itself, and S as far as Southampton.

Bentley Wood Beyond East Grimstead N of here, a nature reserve with good walks.

SALISBURY SU1429
A beautiful and gently relaxed city, with a good many fine old buildings, particularly around the lovely cathedral close. The most extensive close in the country, it's always been a distinct area of town, and the gates to it are still locked each night. The buildings cover a variety of architectural styles from the 13th c to the present, and while of course its great glory is the elegant cathedral itself, you can't help being struck by how impeccably mown the lawns are. Outside the close, there are some interesting antiques and other little independent shops, and the broad Market Sq still has a traditional market each Tues and Sat; parking in town can be tricky then, so it's a good idea to take advantage of the Park and Ride system (they plan others) parking at Old Sarum to the N on the A345. A pleasant way to see the town is by horse-drawn omnibus, and short tours start and finish at the Guildhall; usually Mon-Sat Easter-Oct (not in bad weather), plus market days until Christmas; £2.50; (0771) 8046814. The Haunch of Venison (Minster St) is an interesting old town tavern. Besides places we describe individually below, the close also includes striking St Anne's Gate, a regimental museum (cl Mon Jan-Mar and Nov, and all Dec-3 Jan; (01722) 414536; £2.75).

Medieval Hall (West Walk, The Close) The regular 40-min sound and picture shows in this 13th-c hall give a colourful introduction to the city and its environs. Teas during the show, disabled access (but not facilities); cl Oct-Mar and for occasional special events; (01722) 324731; *£2.25.

Mompesson House (The Close) Exquisite Queen Anne building, probably the most interesting in the close, with period furnishings, china and paintings, remarkable collection of 18th-c drinking glasses, and interestingly carved oak staircase. Tearoom with good home-made cakes, disabled access to ground floor; cl Mon, Thurs-Fri and Nov-9 Apr; (01722) 335659; *£4, 80p gardens only; NT. The NT shop is a couple of minutes' walk away on the High St.

St Thomas's church (St Thomas's Sq) Originally built for cathedral workers and mainly rebuilt in the 15th c; has a well preserved medieval Doom painting; (01722) 322537.

Old Sarum (off A345 2m N) This substantial and easily defended Iron Age hill fort continued as a town right through the Roman occupation and Dark Ages into Norman times. In the early 13th c there was a general move to the much more fertile site of the present city, and the fort gradually fell into decline, becoming a quarry for the new centre; consequently there's not much left, but the views are splendid, and the foundations give interesting clues to ancient architecture and styles. Snacks, shop; cl 24-26 Dec, 1 Jan; (01722) 335398; £2.50; EH.

Salisbury & South Wiltshire Museum (Kings House, The Close) Local history and archaeology in lovely building, with excellent up-to-date Stonehenge gallery, collections of Wedgwood china, costume, lace and embroidery, and some beautiful local watercolours by Turner. One of its more obscure but intriguing exhibits is an aestel, an Anglo-Saxon jewel with links to King Alfred, found by a metal-detector enthusiast in a Wiltshire field. Meals, snacks, shop, disabled access; cl Sun (exc pm July-Aug), 25-26 Dec;

(01722) 332151; £3.50.

Salisbury Cathedral Begun in 1220 and completed in only 38 years - giving a rare uniformity of style. The magnificent spire (added in 1315 along with the tower) is at 123 metres (404 ft) the tallest in the country, and many would say the finest in the world. 332 winding spiral steps take you to the top of the tower, giving spectacular views of the city and surrounding countryside - and you can peer up into the spire, with its internal medieval scaffolding. Also notable are a fascinating floor-mounted 14th-c clock (the oldest working mechanical clock in Europe), and the tomb of the first Earl of Salisbury, who gave the church one of only four surviving editions of the Magna Carta; it's still on show in the Chapter House, alongside remarkable early silver. The cloisters stand out too. Meals and snacks (with good views of the spire), shop, disabled access; (01722) 555120; £3.80 suggested donation, tower tour £3. The guides are entertaining and knowledgeable. There's a classic view of the cathedral from across the water meadows, where the Old Mill has decent food.

SALISBURY PLAIN ST9648
Despite the army presence, there is free public access for walkers to the eastern part of the ranges (though do stick to the paths): the landscape here is really remote, unblemished by development or modern agriculture, and harbouring some of the richest archaeology in Europe. One of the most rewarding areas is S of Everleigh and W of North Tidworth, taking in Sidbury Hill and Haxton Down. The A360 gives drivers a taste of the emptiness of this almost unbroken expanse of rolling high ground, perhaps sighting an occasional tank rumbling along. The Angel at Upton Scudamore is a good dining pub.

SANDY LANE ST9668
Attractive village; the road from here through Bowden Hill is the prettiest approach to Lacock.

SEMLEY ST8926
Attractive village, with an interesting church; the Benett Arms is good.

SEVENHAMPTON SU2188
Roves Farm 🔲 The eight-week spring lambing season is one of the best times to come to this friendly farm, but it's lively at any time, with pig, sheep and goat racing, lots more animal action such as summer shearing, and a clever two-acre living willow maze. Also huge barns with craft sessions and play areas indoors as well as out, bouncy castle, and long tractor trailer rides. Good café, shop, disabled access; cl Mon-Tues in term time and Nov-Feb; (01793) 763939; £5. The Saracens Head in Highworth has good value food.

STONEHENGE SU1142
(off A344) One of the most famous prehistoric monuments in the world; everyone knows what it looks like, and how they got the stones here has been pretty much sorted out (the larger ones local, the smaller ones all the way from South Wales), but nobody's really sure exactly what Stonehenge (with its careful astronomical alignments) was for. In the interests of conservation, you can't normally go right up to the stones (see below), but you can get pretty close, and the fact that people are kept back means that your photos won't be cluttered by the crowds. The best views are very early in the morning from the track from Larkhill, and on the other side of the A344 and from byways 11 and 12 on the other side of the A303 towards Normanton Down burial mounds; or on a cold clear winter evening looking W past the monument towards the sunset; the ancient stones look very impressive silhouetted against the sky. Even in the crowded light of day the place never quite loses its power to inspire awe. The car park area and busy main roads nearby detract a little, but great improvements here and to the visitor centre are in the pipeline, and may be completed by 2006. Snacks inc home-made cakes, shop, disabled access (and a Braille guide); (01980) 624715 - but beware, it's a very long-winded answering machine; cl 24-26 Dec, 1 Jan; £5 (inc very good audio tour); EH. Private access outside normal hours (not Oct-Nov) can be booked in advance, phone (01980) 626267 (£10 for an hour visit); or Astral Travels (0870) 902 0908 organise day trips from London (£52). Good walks from here around associated ancient monuments (leaflet

available in the car park).

Woodhenge The scant traces of another prehistoric monument further E which consisted of six rings of timber posts in a ditch; the positions are now marked by concrete posts, and a cairn marks the central spot where the tomb of a little girl ceremoniously axed to death was found.

STOURTON ST7835

Stourhead (off B3092) Marvellous 18th-c landscape garden, laid out in italian style by the banker Henry Hoare II following his return from the grand tour; a beautifully harmonious landscape of temples, lakes, bridges and splendid trees and other plants. Remarkable views into Somerset from King Alfred's Tower, the tall 18th-c folly at the far end, though there are 221 steps (cl am and Nov-Mar; £1.85). The early Georgian Palladian house has some good Chippendale furniture, and the church in the grounds is in a lovely hillside setting. Meals, snacks, shop, art gallery, disabled access; garden open all year, house cl Weds-Thurs and Nov-19 Mar; (01747) 841152; *£9.40 for gardens and house, *£5.40 for one or the other (£1.30 less for gardens Nov-Feb) - if you can do only one, make it the gardens; NT. The Spread Eagle at the entrance is good for lunch and does cold food all day.

SWINDON SU1484

Much older than you might think, this bustling market town and business centre was caught up with a vengeance in the railway age, and in the Railway Village had one of the earliest examples of a planned workers' estate. The Savoy (Regent Circus) has decent food in an interestingly converted cinema.

National Monuments Record Centre (Great Western Village, off Kemble Drive) The public archive of English Heritage, full of information on England's architecture and archaeology. Lots of photographs (inc some from the mid-19th c, and aerial shots of all of England), plus maps, plans and data about historical buildings and ancient sites. There may be guided tours of the building (the former General Office of the Great Western Railway) usually on the third Sat in the month - phone to check on (01793) 414797. Meals,

snacks, disabled access; cl Sat-Mon, and Christmas-New Year and bank hols; (01793) 414700; free. Steam is in the same former railway complex.

Steam (Kemble Drive, next to the well signed Great Western Designer Outlet Centre) In the former works of the Great Western Railway, this brings to life the sights and sounds of the railway age, when 12,000 people used to work here to produce everything needed to keep it running. It has good reconstructions and up-to-date display techniques to get you really involved - as well, of course, as several of the locomotives built here. Particularly good fun is a simulator that re-creates the experience of riding on a steam train footplate. There's as much emphasis on the people who worked and travelled on the railways as there is on the trains, and children have plenty to keep them amused, from the various touch-screen games and hands-on activities to a track layout where younger visitors have fun shunting the trucks. Other displays focus on Isambard Kingdom Brunel and the GWR's days as the 'holiday line'. Good programme of special events. Snacks, shop, disabled access; cl 25-26 Dec, 1 Jan; (01793) 466646; £5.95. There are lots of bargains at the outlet shopping centre next door, and decent food in the Old Pattern Shop.

Swindon & Cricklade Railway £ (Blunsdon, off B4553 N) One of the only live steam projects in the area, gradually being restored, with trips through the countryside, and small museum. Snacks, shop, disabled access; open Sun and bank hols (exc 25-26 Dec and 1 Jan); (01793) 771615; £3 (more on special event days).

Swindon Museum & Art Gallery (Bath Rd) Includes works by 20th-c artists such as Moore and Lowry, as well as local history displays. Shop, disabled access to ground floor only; cl Sun am, bank hols; (01793) 466556; free. Round the corner in Victoria Rd the Victoria serves good value organic food.

TEFFONT MAGNA ST9831

Very attractive village of charming stone-built cottages, with neatly banked stone-walled gardens; the Black Horse is a pleasant lunch stop.

Farmer Giles Farmstead *See separate family panel on p.637*

TISBURY ST9429

Charming small town, left behind by the main roads so largely unspoilt, with some fine old buildings, riverside church, and just outside to the E an immensely long medieval tithe barn. The lovely old Crown and ancient Boot both do decent food.

Old Wardour Castle (a couple of miles S) Remains of a substantial 14th-c lakeside castle. Though badly damaged in the Civil War, its walls still stand to their original 18 metres (60 ft), and you can walk almost to the top (signs and the audio guide indicate what life was like when the castle was still lived in). It's a lovely peaceful setting, landscaped in the 18th c, with country walks of varying lengths from the car park. Shop, disabled access to grounds only; cl 1-2 and Mon-Tues Nov-Mar, and 24-26 Dec, 1 Jan; (01747) 870487; £2.60; EH.

TOLLARD ROYAL ST9517

Larmer Tree Gardens (off A354) Attractive Victorian pleasure gardens in the heart of Cranborne Chase. Laid out by General Pitt Rivers, they were the first privately owned gardens open to the public but then closed for almost a century. Pheasants, macaws and peacocks may strut their stuff, you can play croquet (by arrangement), and the temples and grottoes are an appealing backdrop to the band concerts they have summer Suns; also adventure playground and special events. Teas, some disabled access; cl Fri, Sat, all July and Nov-Easter; (01725) 516228; £3.75.

TROWBRIDGE ST8557

Trowbridge Museum (Court St) Interestingly incorporated into a modern shopping centre, this former woollen mill now houses a local history museum. Displays of working textile machinery (they operate a loom on Sat), reconstructions of a weaver's cottage and draper's shop, interactive exhibits and regular temporary exhibitions. Shop, disabled access; cl Sun-Mon, 24-26, 31 Dec and 1 Jan; (1225) 751339; free. The Sir Isaac Pitman nearby in Castle St is a useful food stop.

WEST KNOYLE ST8531

Bush Farm Bison Centre A trail takes you round this peaceful working farm and, as well as bison, you can see red deer, elk, pigs and sheep, and there are woodland and lakeside walks; also a native american and wildlife gallery, and a shop selling elk and bison meat. Mostly disabled access (need a strong pusher); farm cl Mon-Tues, and Oct-Mar (though shop and gallery open Thurs and Fri in winter), phone to check; (01747) 830263; £4.50 farm, gallery free. The prettily set Fox & Hounds at East Knoyle has fairly priced fresh food.

WESTBURY ST8951

To the E you can see the huge Westbury white horse cut into the chalk of the downs; late 18th-c, it was an 'improvement' on an altogether older one which may have been Saxon, and which faced in the opposite direction. Above the white horse is an extensive Iron Age hill fort, with good views right down to the Mendips in Somerset.

WHITE SHEET HILL ST9424

The Harepath here is a high track giving sweeping views; you can branch off into a forest plantation. Below is the pretty thatched village of Berwick St John, the Talbot has decent food. Note that Wiltshire has a second hill with the same name, above Mere.

WILTON SU0931

Wilton Carpet Factory 🖼 (King St) Surprisingly interesting demonstrations of how they make Wilton and Axminster carpets, as well as a museum and carpet-making exhibition. Tours usually four times a day between 11am and 5pm, best to book on (01722) 744919. Meals, snacks, shop, disabled access; cl wknds and 10 days over Christmas and New Year; *£4. There is a shopping village next door.

Wilton House Particularly satisfying to visit; the original house was damaged by a fire in 1647, and superbly redesigned by John Webb and Inigo Jones, the latter responsible for the magnificent Double Cube room, considered by many to be one of the country's finest surviving rooms from this period; it's full of splendid works by Van Dyck. The Tudor kitchen and

Victorian laundry have both been well restored to give a good impression of their original use. The furnishings and art are exquisite, and a doll's house re-creates some parts of the house in miniature. The 21-acre grounds inc an adventure playground, water and rose gardens, restful cloister garden, a striking Palladian bridge, and woodland walks; plenty of space for picnics. Meals, snacks, shop, disabled access; cl Nov-Mar; (01722) 746720; £9.75, £4.50 grounds only. The ornately italianate 19th-c **church** incorporates all sorts of treasures, esp its magnificent medieval continental stained glass and 2,000-year-old marble pillars. Wiltons (Market Pl) is good for lunch, and the charming Victoria & Albert in nearby Netherhampton is nicely off the tourist track, with a pleasant riverside walk into Salisbury.

WILTON SU2661

Wilton windmill (off A338 E of Burbage) Wessex's only working windmill, built in 1821 after the construction of the Kennet & Avon Canal had diverted the water previously used to power mills. Now restored, it's beautifully floodlit most evenings, and they hope to open a new display area in the spring. Snacks, shop (sells flour milled on site); open pm Sun and bank hols Easter-Sept; (01672) 870266; £2. This little village of Wilton (not to be confused with the larger town near Salisbury) is attractive; the Swan has good if not cheap food.

WROUGHTON AIRFIELD SU1379

Science Museum A storage facility for lots of the larger items from the National Museum of Science and Industry with national collections of aircraft, rockets, hovercraft, and road transport vehicles, and one of the best displays of tractors in the world. Not really aimed at entertaining the general public, it's open all Aug wkdys, Oct half term, and if you book for their tours on the first and third Weds of the month; plus usually open for special events around eight times a year. Snacks, shop, disabled access; (01793) 846200; now free (it used to be £5).

WYLYE SU0037

Charming village in delightful valley, amazingly peaceful given the closeness of the A303; one lane is called Teapot St, and the 14th-c Bell is a good dining pub.

Other attractive villages, all with decent pubs, include Aldbourne ST2675, Alderbury SU1827, waterside Ashton Keynes SU0494, Axford SU2370, Berwick St John ST9323 (steep walks nearby), Biddestone ST8773, Bishopstone SU2483, Broughton Gifford ST8763, Chitterne ST9843 (good walks), Collingbourne Ducis SU2453, thatched Clyffe Pypard SU0777, Donhead St Andrew ST9124, Great Cheverell ST9754, Great Hinton ST9059, Great Wishford SU0735, Hannington SU1793, Heddington ST9966, Highworth SU2092, Kilmington ST7736, Kington Langley ST9277, Lockeridge SU1467 (good walks), Marston Meysey SU1297, Monkton Farleigh ST8065, Newton Tony SU2140, Oare SU1563, Pewsey SU1560, Pitton SU2131 (wood and downland walks), Potterne ST9958, Poulshot ST9559, Ramsbury ST2771, Sherston ST8585, Steeple Ashton ST9056, Stockton ST9738, The Green ST8731 (nr East Knoyle), Upton Lovell ST9440, West Dean SU2527, Winsley ST7961 and Wootton Rivers SU1963.

Where to eat

AXFORD SU2370 **Red Lion** *(01672) 520271* Welcoming brick and flint pub with fine views over valley from sheltered garden or bustling beamed and pine-panelled bar, good popular food in bar and no smoking restaurant (enjoyable daily specials and fresh fish and game), decent wines, and well kept real ales; cl 25-26 Dec; disabled access. £32|£7

BARFORD ST MARTIN SU0531 **Barford** *Grovely Rd (01722) 742242* Pleasantly old-fashioned 16th-c coaching inn with some interesting squared oak panelling and a big winter log fire in the front bar, other chatty interlinked rooms, good service from friendly staff and the welcoming israeli landlord; tasty, reasonably priced food inc popular Fri evening barbecue (Mar-Oct) and bargain three-course meal (Mon), lots of israeli wines, and well kept ales; seats on terrace with more in back garden. £22.90|**£7.50**

BOX ST8369 **Quarrymans Arms** *Box Hill (01225) 743569* Unspoilt tucked-away hillside pub with fine views, two small interesting knocked-together rooms with quarrying memorabilia, a wide choice of enjoyable and popular home-cooked food, well kept real ales, and very friendly staff; bdrms. £24|**£7.95**

BRADFORD-ON-AVON ST8261 **Dandy Lion** *35 Market St (01225) 863433* Particularly relaxed and friendly, with an interesting mix of people, big windows on either side of the door with a table and chairs in each, high-backed farmhouse chairs and old-fashioned dining chairs on the stripped wood floor, newspapers to read, nostalgic pop, and a snug little back room; very well liked and reasonably priced food, real ales, good coffee, and candlelit upstairs restaurant; £27.50|**£5.50**

BRINKWORTH SU0184 **Three Crowns** *The Street (01666) 510366* Friendly atmosphere in villagey pub with imaginative food from a changing menu that covers an entire wall, ten wines by the glass, well kept real ales, elegant no smoking conservatory, and garden looking out towards church and rolling country; get there early as it is very busy; cl 25-26 Dec; disabled access. £36|**£6**

GREAT HINTON ST9059 **Linnet** *(01380) 870354* Attractive old brick pub with pretty summer-flowering tubs and window-boxes; little right-hand bar with lots of interest on the green walls, comfortable wall banquettes, a biggish rather smart dining room with pink ragged walls, bric-a-brac, plenty of dining chairs and tables, reliably good food in enjoyable bar snacks and imaginative daily specials and evening choices, real ales, quite a few malts, and nice summer Pimms. £32|**£7.75**

GRITTLETON ST8680 **Neeld Arms** *The Street (01249) 782470* 17th-c black-beamed pub, largely open-plan, with some stripped stone, log fire in big inglenook, flowers on tables, and a friendly mix of seating from Windsor chairs through scatter-cushioned window seats to some nice arts and crafts chairs and a traditional settle; parquet-floored back dining area with an inglenook woodburner; good food from changing blackboard (nice breakfasts, too), well kept ales, a fine choice of good value wines by the glass, and a welcoming, companiable atmosphere created by the cheerful outgoing landlord; bdrms. £22.75|**£7.50**

HINDON ST9033 **Angel** *High St (01747) 820696* Attractively refurbished 18th-c coaching inn with Victorian prints and artefacts in the pubby red-painted traditional bar, flagstones, a lovely log fire, and candlelight, a civilised no smoking lounge, a smartened up long dining room with a huge window giving you a view of the busy kitchen, enjoyable popular food inc imaginative daily specials, well kept ales, a dozen wines by the glass, and daily papers; seats in flower-filled back courtyard; good bdrms; cl Sun pm, Dec 26, Jan 2. £27|**£7**

HOLT ST8561 **Toll Gate** *Ham Green (01225) 782326* Popular dining pub furnished and decorated with flair - part with cosy settees and a log fire, the rest more adapted to eating; hunting prints on pinkish walls, black panelling, charming high-raftered restaurant (formerly a chapel for weavers working here) with attractive bric-a-brac; beautifully presented imaginative food inc good value set lunch, kind helpful service, eight or so wines by the glass, good coffee, farm cider, half a dozen well kept changing beers; cl Sun pm. £25|**£6.50**

MARLBOROUGH SU1969 **Munchies** *8 The Parade (01672) 512649* Marvellous range of really interesting and delicious take-away sandwiches with daily changing home-made fillings using the freshest ingredients; cl Sat-Sun; disabled access|**£2.50**

MARLBOROUGH SU1869 **Polly Tea Rooms** *26 High St (01672) 512146* In centre of pretty High St, well known for very good cream teas, with home-made bread, scones, jams and cakes; also light lunches and cooked breakfasts; cl evenings, and 25-26 Dec, 1 Jan|**£8.50**

NORTON ST8884 **Vine Tree** *(01666) 837654* Civilised dining pub with a lively atmosphere in its three smallish rooms, sporting prints, lots of stripped pine, candles in bottles on the tables, and some old settles; a wide range of enjoyable food from a seasonally changing menu, well kept real ales, ten wines by the glass, and a no smoking dining area; picnic-sets in a two-acre garden, a good play area, and three boules pitches. £30|£6.95

PITTON SU2131 **Silver Plough** *White Hill (01722) 712266* Stylish village inn with lots to look at in comfortable beamed front bar, good bar snacks and more elaborate meals with emphasis on fresh fish and seafood, well kept real ales, country wines, and efficient service; bdrms; cl pms 25-26 Dec. £26|£7.95

REDLYNCH SU2120 **Langley Wood** *(01794) 390348* Very good innovative food and a carefully chosen wine list in homely and warmly friendly creeper-covered restaurant-with-rooms, in its own grounds; cl Mon-Tues; disabled access. £30|£9.75

ROWDE ST9762 **George & Dragon** *High St (01380) 723053* Interesting old pub with log fire, a fine collection of brass keys, and plenty of dark wood, a simple no smoking dining room, exceptional imaginative food (esp delicious fresh fish and lovely puddings), a relaxed atmosphere, and well kept real ales; cl Sun, Mon, 25 Dec, 1 Jan; children must be well behaved. £20|£7

WHITLEY ST8866 **Pear Tree** *Top Lane (01225) 709131* Attractive honey-coloured stone farmhouse with a civilised, friendly and chatty atmosphere, front bar with cushioned window seats, some stripped shutters, a mix of dining chairs around good solid tables, a variety of country pictures, and a little fireplace on the left, with a lovely old stripped stone one on the right; popular big back restaurant, enticing and delicious food beautifully presented and served by first-class staff, well kept real ales, a good wine list with ten by the glass, and seats on the terrace; bdrms; cl 25-26 Dec; disabled access. £32|£8.75

WOODBOROUGH SU1159 **Seven Stars** *Bottlesford (01672) 851325* Civilised pub in seven riverside acres, with attractively moulded panelling in the main bar, a hot coal fire in a range at one end and a big log fire at the other, a pleasant mix of seats and tables, cosy nooks, and retired wine bottles on delft shelves; attractive back dining area, good daily changing anglo-french cooking (inc marvellous veg, winter game and summer seafood), exemplary wine list with a dozen by the glass, and very friendly owners; cl Sun pm, Mon; children must be well behaved. £27|£7.95

WYLYE SU0037 **Bell** *High St (01985) 248338* Cosy and civilised little 14th-c country pub, three log fires, neatly kept black-beamed and timbered rustic front bar, and comfortably carpeted no smoking restaurant with pristine white linen and a more sophisticated feel; very well cooked bar food using fresh ingredients with interesting daily specials, four well kept real ales, seven wines by the glass, quite a few country wines, daily papers, and seats out on pleasant walled terrace and in back garden; no children; fine downland walks nearby; disabled access. £32.80|£7.95

Special thanks to B and K Hypher, Mrs Y Champion

WORCESTERSHIRE

Memorable landscapes, classic black and white timbered villages, and some entertaining outings

The Avoncroft Museum of Historic Buildings in Bromsgrove is this year's winner of the title Worcestershire Family Attraction: an enjoyably relaxed place, it's especially pleasant if the weather's fine - like many of the county's attractions. Also good for families, the attractive little town of Bewdley is home to the West Midlands Safari Park (exotic animals and fairground rides), and splendid Severn Valley Railway steam trips leave from here too. Busy Worcester has some handsome medieval buildings, and a couple of interesting places to visit (the Commandery is a hit with children, and there's an unusual porcelain museum). Cotswolds-edge Broadway is picturesque (with a fine country park).

Guided tours make the most of Hagley Hall, and at Hartlebury Castle you can visit some of the state rooms (Victorian folk displays too); Hanbury Hall has outstanding painted ceilings. The awesome ruin of the italianate palace in Great Witley is thought-provoking - with the unusual surroundings, this makes quite a special outing. At Elgar's birthplace in Lower Broadheath a museum celebrates his life and work (the Elgar trail starts here too).

Children like feeding the animals at the Wildlife Sanctuary and Fishery at Shatterford, and bird-lovers enjoy the friendly Domestic Fowl Trust at Honeybourne, and the Falconry Centre in West Hagley. There are gardens at Burford and Croome Park (Severn Stoke), and this year we've added an arboretum near Wolverley, and a vineyard just outside Upton-upon-Severn.

The Malvern Hills which dominate the county provide one of England's great ridge walks. On their flanks the elegant spa town, Great Malvern, is good to explore around and gives easy access to this wonderful hill scenery. The orchards make blossom time (usually April through early May) and harvest time (September) appealing seasons to visit Worcestershire: local tourist board trails make it easy to see the best of this, especially in the Vale of Evesham. Prices are generally low, making the area good value for short breaks.

Where to stay

ABBERLEY SO7367 **Elms** *Stockton Rd, Abberley, Worcestershire WR6 6AT* (01299) 896666 **£140**, plus gourmet breaks; 21 comfortable rms. Lovely Queen Anne mansion with fine views from the well kept grounds, elegant restful drawing room with antiques, log fires and flowers, other reception rooms with original ornate plasterwork and finely carved fireplaces, very good food and wines in airy restaurant, and friendly efficient staff

BROADWAY SP0937 **Broadway Hotel** *The Green, Broadway, Worcestershire WR12 7AA* (01386) 852401 **£125**; 20 well kept rms. Lovely 15th-c building, once a monastic guest house, with galleried and timbered lounge, cosy beamed bar, attractively presented food served by attentive staff in airy comfortable restaurant, and seats outside on terrace; dogs welcome in bedrooms

BROADWAY SP0937 **Lygon Arms** *High St, Broadway, Worcestershire WR12 7DU (01386) 852255* **£245**, plus special breaks; 69 lovely period rms (some more modern, too). Handsome hotel where Oliver Cromwell and King Charles I once stayed; interesting beamed rooms, oak panelling, antiques, log fires, fine traditional food in the Great Hall with minstrels' gallery and heraldic frieze, excellent service, and charming garden; health spa; disabled access; dogs welcome in bedrooms

CHADDESLEY CORBETT SO8873 **Brockencote Hall** *Brockencote, Chaddesley Corbett, Kidderminster, Worcestershire DY10 4PY (01562) 777876* **£145***, plus special breaks; 17 individually decorated rms. Grand country-house hotel in 70 acres with half-timbered dovecot and lake, and plenty of wildlife; large, airy and attractively furnished rooms, conservatory lounge with garden views, elegantly refurbished restaurant with enjoyable modern french and english cooking, and very good service; disabled access

EVESHAM SP0443 **Evesham Hotel** *Coopers Lane, off Waterside, Evesham, Worcestershire WR11 1DA (01386) 765566* **£119***, plus special breaks; 40 spacious rms with games and jigsaws. Comfortably modernised and cheerful family-run hotel with a warmly friendly, relaxed and jokey atmosphere, popular restaurant with very good food (esp lunchtime buffet), huge wine and spirits list, and sitting room with games and toys; indoor swimming pool surrounded by table tennis and table football, and grounds with croquet, trampoline, swings and putting; particularly well organised for families (but they do not get overrun by children); cl 25-26 Dec; dogs welcome in bedrooms ☺

HANLEY CASTLE SO8342 **Old Parsonage Farmhouse** *Hanley Castle, Worcester, Worcestershire WR8 0BU (01684) 310124* **£55**, plus special breaks; 3 neatly kept rms. Very comfortable and friendly 18th-c house close to some fine walking country and with views over the big garden to the Malvern Hills; two sitting rooms (one no smoking), open fire, pot plants and dried flowers, lovely food in bright yellow dining room, an extensive wine list (Mr Addison keeps over 100 wines), and fine breakfasts inc home-made marmalade; cl mid-Dec to mid-Jan; children over 12

HIMBLETON SO9459 **Phepson Farm** *Phepson, Droitwich, Worcestershire WR9 7JZ (01905) 391205* **£52***, plus winter breaks; 6 rms, 4 in renovated farm buildings. Relaxed and friendly 17th-c farmhouse on small sheep farm with a fishing lake; a comfortable guests' lounge, good breakfasts in separate dining room; self-catering apartment; cl Christmas and New Year; dogs welcome in bedrooms

KEMERTON SO9437 **Upper Court** *Kemerton, Tewkesbury, Gloucestershire GL20 7HY (01386) 725351* **£120**; 6 rms, plus several cottages. Lovely Georgian Cotswold manor with Domesday watermill, a lake (lots of wildfowl and free fly-fishing in season), and dovecote in 15 acres of fine gardens, outdoor heated swimming pool, tennis court, croquet, and boating; relaxed atmosphere and many antiques (the owners run an antiques business and there is always something for sale) in elegant rooms, very good food using home-grown produce (by prior arrangement) around candlelit communal table, and nice breakfasts; Manor cl Christmas; children in cottages only; good disabled access

MALVERN SO7647 **Cowleigh Park Farm** *Cowleigh Park, Cradley, Malvern, Worcestershire WR13 5HJ (01684) 566750* **£60***; 3 rms. Carefully restored and furnished black and white timbered 17th-c farmhouse in own grounds, surrounded by lovely countryside, with good breakfasts and light suppers or full evening meals (prior booking); self-catering also; cl Christmas; children over 7; dogs welcome in bedrooms

MALVERN WELLS SO7742 **Cottage in the Wood** *Holywell Rd, Malvern, Worcestershire WR14 4LG (01684) 575859* **£99***, plus special breaks; 31 compact but pretty rms, some in separate nearby cottages. Family-run Georgian dower house with quite splendid views across the Severn Valley and marvellous walks from the grounds; antiques, log fires, comfortable seats and magazines in public rooms, and modern english cooking and an extensive wine list in attractive no smoking restaurant; disabled access; dogs welcome in bedrooms

WICKHAMFORD SP0642 **Wickhamford Manor** *Manor Rd, Wickhamford, Evesham, Worcestershire WR11 6SA (01386) 830296* **£75***; 3 rms. Striking 16th-c timbered manor, once owned by Queen Elizabeth I and first mentioned in the Domesday Book; set in 20 acres of woodland and pasture with a 12th-c dovecote and lake (created by monks when the abbot lived in a grange here); big log fire in beamed drawing room, good breakfasts in the flagstoned kitchen, and a really warm welcome from the friendly owners; tennis and coarse fishing; cl Easter, Christmas and New Year; children over 12

To see and do

Worcestershire Family Attraction of the Year

BROMSGROVE SO9468 **Avoncroft Museum of Historic Buildings** 🏛 (2m S at Stoke Prior, by A38 bypass and B4091) A recent reader's note neatly sums up the appeal of this enjoyable place: 'Relaxing, peaceful, informative, friendly - and good cakes'. Around 25 buildings from the last seven centuries have been saved from demolition and rebuilt here; they began by rescuing timber-framed houses (there's a magnificent timber-framed merchant's house), but soon started salvaging other threatened buildings too. There's a Victorian church, a gaol, even a 1946 prefab. A lovely working windmill is particularly popular with children, and, more incongruously, there's a unique collection of telephone kiosks, from Tardis-style police boxes to unlovely modern hutches, with everything in between. Several of the buildings are furnished inside, but it's very much a place to visit on a dry day, when children can make the most of the open spaces. It's a very atmospheric spot: donkeys and chickens wander about, and there's an almost palpable feel of the past. The staff are particularly helpful and enthusiastic, and children get far more out of it than you might expect; the play area is very sympathetically designed, and on some bank holiday weekends they have a miniature railway. Most weekends they have some sort of extra event, usually designed to appeal to families, and often featuring some sort of period reconstruction or re-enactment; their website, www.avoncroft.org.uk, has the full schedule. An activity centre has a few hands-on and computer displays. Meals, snacks, picnic area, shop, disabled access; open Mar-Oct, though usually closed Mon except in summer, and Fri at either end of the season; (01527) 831363; £5.50 adults, £2.75 children over 5. The family ticket is good value: two adults and three childen for £14.50.

ABBERLEY SO7567
Notable for its picturesque, steeply hump-backed packhorse bridge, looking more like a part of Devon or Derbyshire; ironically, cars have to use a more ancient crossing, the shallow ford beside it. The village was once owned by John of Gaunt, and the Manor Arms has good food.

ABBERLEY HILLS SO7567
(nr Stourport) Little visited by walkers but rewarding for them: partly wooded, with good views and close to the extraordinary ruins of Witley Court.

ABBOTS MORTON SP0255
Charming village, with a lovely church. In nearby Inkberrow you can eat in the Old Bull, the photogenic model for the Ambridge pub in *The Archers*.

ASHTON UNDER HILL SO9938
Charming black and white timbered houses and a good Norman church; made all the more attractive by the brooding backdrop of Bredon Hill.

BEWDLEY SO7874
Attractive small town, with riverside walks and interesting side streets; the Little Pack Horse (old High St) is full of

character, and the smart old George (Load St) has an enjoyable restaurant. **Bewdley Museum** (Load St) An 18th-c row of butchers' shops houses this local history museum, which has daily craft demonstrations. Shop, some disabled access; cl Nov-beginning Apr; (01299) 403573; free.

Severn Valley Railway Britain's leading standard-gauge steam railway, with 16 miles of track from Kidderminster at this end to Bridgnorth in Shropshire. The route largely follows the Severn and as there aren't many roads in the valley this is the only way of seeing some parts of this delightful countryside. You'll cross a particularly dramatic single-span 60-metre (200-ft) bridge. A return journey takes around 2½ hours, but it's fun to base a day around it, getting off at stations on the way, and strolling around villages and surrounding countryside (there are plenty of well marked footpaths and riverside walks). Most trains have refreshment cars, and there are cafés in the stations at Bewdley, Kidderminster and Bridgnorth (which also has a notable collection of locomotives). You can usually watch work on some of the fine old carriages in the yard at Bewdley, which also has a good model railway, and the showpiece station here has been splendidly restored. Various special events inc Santa Specials in the run-up to Christmas; you may find different fares and trains then. Trains run wknds all year, and daily May-Sept and in local school hols; (01299) 403816. A full return fare allows unlimited travel that day, getting on or off as you please; £10.50.

West Midlands Safari Park (Spring Grove, just E on A456) Enjoyable drive-through safari, where you can even feed some of the animals through the car window (feed available from the ticket office). It's good for children because as well as the animals there's an adjacent leisure park, with around 30 rides. The animal reserves are home to over 40 rare and exotic species, so lions, tigers, elephants, camels, giraffes and wolves have the run of the park while you sit in your car. There's also an entertaining sea lion show, a seal aquarium with well positioned viewing platforms, hippo feeding displays, insect and reptile house, and Animal Encounter sessions. It costs extra to go into the leisure park; with a good mix of children's rides from gentle carousels and dodgems to a log flume and a couple of decent roller-coasters. Meals, snacks, shop, mostly disabled access; cl Nov to two wks before Easter; (01299) 402114; £6.75 inc a free return visit any time during the rest of the season (exc bank hols). You can buy individual tickets for rides in the leisure park, but it's better value to buy an all-day wristband: £8 for anyone 1.2 metres and over, otherwise £6.50.

BREDON SO9236
Attractive village above River Avon with a magnificent medieval tithe barn. The two stone figures sitting astride the rectory roof are supposedly Charles II and Oliver Cromwell. The Fox & Hounds is a good food pub.

Bredon Hill The Vale of Evesham's one notable feature for walkers is an outlier of the Cotswolds, distinctively rounded and on cloudy days rather ominous. It's dotted with Bronze Age barrows, three Iron Age hill forts, a Norman castle, a folly and a holy well. Although easily reached from Overbury, the best walk over it is from Bredon's Norton to Elmley Castle.

BRETFORTON SP0944
One of the prettiest black and white thatched villages, with an interesting church and a splendid medieval pub, the Fleece, left to the National Trust after being in the same family for several centuries; a proper pub, it's kept just as it was as a farmhouse pub, with a magnificent collection of Jacobean oak furniture and pewter.

BROADWAY SP0937
Exceptionally harmonious stone-built Cotswold village, with the golden stone and uneven stone-tiled roofs perfectly blending the grand houses and the humbler cottages together, in a long, grass-lined main st. It's decidedly on the coach-tour trail, and gets very busy indeed in summer. Fine things for sale in expensive antiques shops, and a very grand old inn, the Lygon Arms, with a useful side brasserie. The Broadway Hotel also does good bar lunches, the stately Lygon Arms has a good adjoining brasserie, the Crown & Trumpet in

Church St is an archetypal Cotswold pub,
and the Buckland Manor does good teas.
Broadway Tower (off A44 SE) Above
the village, this late 18th-c folly has
marvellous views that on a clear day -
with the help of the telescope - are said
to stretch over 13 counties. There are
exhibitions on the history of the tower
and regular visitor William Morris,
while the country park around it has
nature trails, and maybe farm animals
(as we went to press, the owner of the
animal park was looking for a new
manager). Meals, snacks (and picnic
area), shops, some disabled access;
cl wkdys Nov-Mar; (01386) 852390; £3,
animal park also £3.
Magic Experience 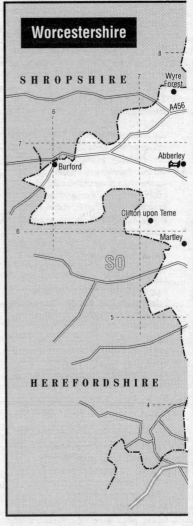 Museum with
decent collection of old teddy bears,
toys and magical animated scenes. Shop;
cl Mon, 25-26 Dec and Jan; (01386)
858323; £2.50.
Vale of Evesham farm shops Good
for all manner of local produce inc eggs,
jams, pickles and trout as well as fruit
and veg, but the highlights of the year
are asparagus in May and apples and
particularly plums in Sept. The A44 W
almost always has good fare.
BROMSGROVE SO9468
**Avoncroft Museum of Historic
Buildings** See separate family panel on
p.654.
The nearby Navigation (B4091), nr the
Worcester & Birmingham Canal, does
good lunches.
BURFORD SO5968
Burford House Gardens (off A456,
W of Tenbury Wells) Delightfully set by
the River Teme, these tranquil gardens
are the home of a national collection of
clematis. Lots of other colourful plants
too, a wild flower garden, and on the
ground floor of the Georgian house a
contemporary art gallery (mid-Jun to
Sept). Meals, snacks, plant sales,
disabled access; cl 25-26 Dec and 1 Jan;
(01584) 810777; £3.95. The Ship in
Tenbury has good imaginative food.
CHADDESLEY CORBETT
SO8973
Despite the trunk road, this is an attractive
village, with a fine partly Norman **church**.
The Talbot offers a good choice of food.
CHILDSWICKHAM SP0738
This streamside village has some
delightful timbered stone cottages, and

good food in the Childswickham Inn.
CLENT SO9380
Clent Hills Country Park A fine high
hillscape for walkers, open and
exhilarating, with waymarked routes.
The Fountain at Clent is a good dining
pub (food all afternoon, Sun).
CLIFTON UPON TEME SO7161
A pleasant village, with lots of quiet
strolls above the orchards.
DROITWICH SO8963
Droitwich Spa Brine Baths (St
Andrews Rd) Just the thing after an

exhausting morning's sightseeing - you don't drink the water of this famous spa town, but float in it. Meals, snacks, disabled access; cl Easter Sun, 25-26 Dec and 1 Jan. The baths open from 11.30am; (01905) 794894; £7.25 (inc sauna). Interesting buildings in the town include the timbered houses around the High St, and the Sacred Heart church (Worcester Rd) with its fine stained-glass mosaics. The Old Cock (Friar St) is an enjoyable food stop.

Heritage Centre (Victoria Sq)

Exhibition on broadcasting inc items from the BBC Home Service radio station which was once based at nearby Wychbold, also brass rubbing and a look at Droitwich's past as a prehistoric salt settlement. Shop, disabled access; cl Sun and bank hols; (01905) 774312; free.

ELMLEY CASTLE SO9841
Very old-fashioned village below Bredon Hill, with attractive houses strung out between its lovely church and the millpond, where the Old Mill has good value food and comfortable

bedrooms, and the quaint ancient
Queen Elizabeth tavern gives a
delightful glimpse of Worcestershire
several decades ago.

EVESHAM SP0343
The pedestrianised market square has
some fine buildings around it, inc a 12th-c
abbey gateway; the church's striking
16th-c bell tower is well preserved, and
some altogether more ruined remnants
in the town park beyond lead to riverside
meadows. The tourist information
centre is in another attractive abbey
building, the Almonry, a Tudor timbered
house with a museum and nice gardens
(cl Sun pm Nov-Feb, and two wks over
Christmas and New Year; £2.50). The
Green Dragon (Oat St), visibly brewing
its own ales, has inexpensive food. In Apr
or early May the orchard drive through
Harvington, the Lenches, Badgers Hill,
Fladbury Cross, Wood Norton and
Chadbury is pretty.

FECKENHAM SP0061
Attractive green and some fine
Georgian red brick; the Lygon Arms has
nice fresh food.

FLADBURY SO9946
This appealing village offers walks by the
River Avon, a 9th-c Saxon cross, and a
handsome Georgian village green. The
Chequers, dating from the 14th c, has
good generous food.

GREAT MALVERN SO7745
Elegant hillside spa town with easy
access to inspiring hill scenery; the
B4232 to Wynds Point from Upper
Colwall has some of the best high views
and plenty of fine walks, while the
B4218 on the E side gives several good
views of the hills themselves. A good
few galleries and craft workshops inc
Hibernian Violins (Players Ave); cl
wknds. The Nags Head (Bank St) is a
charming place, with interesting food.
Barnard's Green House On the E
side of the Malvern Hills, this has an
attractive garden with a wide range of
plants and gardening ideas around a
gracious 17th-c house (not open). The
owner is an authority on dried flowers.
Teas, plant sales, disabled access; open
Thurs pm (and some Sun pms, phone to
check) Apr-Sept; (01684) 574446;
*£2.50. The nearby Bluebell is useful for
lunch.
Malvern Hills Forming a grand

backdrop to the Vale of Evesham, these
offer good walking. From a distance they
look a formidable mountain range, but
seem to get milder and more welcoming
as you approach. The gentle up-and-
down path along their spine makes one
of England's great ridge walks, with the
Cotswolds and Midland plain on one
side and wilder Wales on the other. The
Herefordshire Beacon, capped by
ramparts of an Iron Age hill fort, is easily
reached from the car park on the A449
near Little Malvern. Great Malvern is
well placed for the Worcestershire
Beacon, the highest point of the range
(425 metres, 1,395 ft), and for long
circular walks. The Chase Inn at Upper
Colwall, Malvern Hills Hotel by the
British Camp car park on Wynds Point,
and Brewers Arms at West Malvern are
also useful start or finish points. On
their Herefordshire side, Ledbury and
Eastnor are good bases for rambles into
the attractive western slopes.
Malvern Museum (Abbey Rd) This
splendid former gatehouse of a
Benedictine monastery houses a
museum with displays on local history,
Malvern spring water, Morgan cars,
radar, and Elgar's life; there's a new
audio guide. Shop; cl Weds in term
time, all Nov-Easter; (01684) 567811;
£1. Nearby and within a churchyard full
of exotic trees brought back from the
Empire, the beautifully proportioned,
cathedral-like **Priory Church** has rare
mural tiles and some wonderful
misericords (inc one depicting a
mooner).
Picton Garden 🖾 (Old Court
Nurseries, Walwyn Rd, Colwall) On
the W side of the Malvern Hills, this has
a nicely laid out cottagey collection of
hardy plants and shrubs, and a rock
garden. Best late Sept-early Oct when
the national collection of asters are at
their best. Plant sales, disabled access;
open Weds-Sun Aug, daily Sept to mid-
Oct and by appointment to end Oct;
(01684) 540416; £2.50. The nearby
Crown has good food.

GREAT WITLEY SO7765
Witley Court Astonishing ruined
shell of Jacobean house transformed
into an italianate palace by the Earl of
Dudley, and partly destroyed by fire in
1937. It's an elaborate place, with an

enormous Perseus fountain, evocative balustraded garden (very special to wander through), a sculpture trail in the new contemporary heritage garden, and woodland walks. Overlooking the lake beside it, a gloriously baroque church is no less dramatic, and one of the county's great finds; it has splendid paintings and stained glass around the largely papier mâché interior. Snacks, visitor centre, shop, some disabled access; cl Mon-Tues Oct-Mar, 24-26 Dec, 1 Jan; (01299) 896636; £4.65 inc audio tour; EH. The Hundred House (a former court) is handy for lunch.

HAGLEY SO9180
Hagley Hall Completed in 1760, this was the last of the great Palladian houses; guided tours take in the fine rococo plasterwork, 18th-c furniture and family portraits inc works by Reynolds and Van Dyck, and then you can stroll around the picturesque deer park. Snacks; open pm wkdys Jan and Feb, plus some bank hol wknds, best to phone; (01562) 882408; £4. The Fountain over at Clent is a good dining pub.

HANBURY SO9463
Hanbury Hall 18th-c country house with outstanding painted ceilings and staircase, fine porcelain, exhibition on the Vernon family, ice-house, a working mushroom house, and an orangery in the grounds; the formal gardens include a reconstructed 18th-c bowling green. You can book rooms in the N and S wings, or the lodge on the edge of the estate. Snacks, shop, some disabled access; cl am, Thurs, Fri, and Nov-Feb; (01527) 821214; *£5.40; NT. The church, high on a hill, has superb views over the countryside. The Gate Hangs Well (Woodgate) is a good value dining pub.
Jinney Ring Craft Centre (B4091 Droitwich Rd) Twelve craft workshops in beautiful timbered barns and pretty gardens, from pottery to violin-making; craft gallery and some wknd courses. Meals, snacks, shop, some disabled access; cl Mon and a few days at Christmas; (01527) 821272; free.

HANLEY CASTLE SO8342
Well worth a stop, a rustic little place around a great cedar tree, with an unusually unspoilt pub, the Three Kings.
HANLEY SWAN SO8142
An attractive village, with a good value

traditional pub, the Swan, by the village green and large duck pond.
HARTLEBURY SO8371
Hartlebury Castle 🖾 Mainly 18th-c, this is the official residence of the Bishop of Worcester, and (Tues-Thurs only) you can visit some of the elegant state rooms. It also houses the **County Museum**, inc Victorian folk life and costumes, room displays, and gypsy caravans. Snacks, shop; cl am Fri and Sun, all day Sat, Good Fri, and all Dec-Jan; (01299) 250416; £2.50. The White Hart has good value food.

HARVINGTON SP0549
One of the area's oldest villages, brilliantly black and white. The Golden Cross has nice food.
Harvington Hall 🖾 Moated Elizabethan manor house with secret chapels, the largest number of priest hides in England, and original wall paintings; also herb garden and picnic area. Snacks, shop, disabled access to ground floor; cl Mon, Tues, wkdys Mar and Oct, and all Nov-Feb; (01562) 777846; *£4.20.

HONEYBOURNE SP1147
Domestic Fowl Trust (Station Rd) Friendly place with rare breeds of sheep, hens, ducks, geese and turkeys (good signs on enclosures), plus young chicks for children to handle, adventure playground and an indoor play area. You'll need wellies on wet days. Summer snacks, shop, limited disabled access; cl 25 Dec; (01386) 833083; £3. The Kings Arms over at Cleeve Prior has good food.

KIDDERMINSTER SO8376
Not an alluring place to visit, but a terminus of the excellent Severn Valley steam railway (see Bewdley), with a cheerful and very good value replica of Edwardian station refreshment rooms.
Kingsford Forest Park (Blakeshall, 2m N) 80-hectare (200-acre) park with pine woods, birch groves and plenty of walks and trails. Very nice unspoilt feel - even the signposts and picnic-sets are made at the saw mill here. The canalside Vine in Kinver (Dunsley Rd) has good value italian food.

LICKEY HILLS COUNTRY PARK SO9975
(B4096 NE of Bromsgrove) A good example of the interesting topography

W of Birmingham: high (rising to over 300 metres, 1,000 ft), and densely wooded, a fragment of primeval forest, with the views suddenly opening out over the sprawling city; waymarking makes the maze of paths and tracks less confusing. There's a sculpture trail, wheelchair pathway and viewing platform, visitor centre with leaflets and information on guided walks, tearoom, and large adventure playground; (0121) 447 7106. The Peacock at Forhill has good value food.

LOWER BROADHEATH SO8157
Elgar Birthplace Museum (Crown East Lane) Modest cottage where the composer was born in 1857; now, as he wanted, a museum of his life and work. Downstairs are displays of photographs and letters, the desk where he did his writing and the piano from the music shop where he worked, while upstairs is devoted to his hobbies - from cycling and golf to puzzles and amateur scientific experiments; the gardens are recreated from an old painting of the cottage. A modern visitor centre concentrates on his music and inspirations, with audio and visual displays, manuscripts, portraits of friends, and memorabilia. Shop, disabled access to centre, gardens, and ground floor of cottage; cl 23 Dec-Jan; (01905) 333224; £4.50 (audio tour £1). You can pick up routes and information here about the Elgar Trail around the area. The Bear & Ragged Staff over at Bransford is a good dining pub.

MARTLEY SO7559
Martley church Notable for its 13th-c wall paintings. The Admiral Rodney (Berrow Green) has good food.

OFFENHAM SP0546
Still has its original gaily striped maypole in its wide black and white main street; a nice village.

OMBERSLEY SO8463
Attractive mix of handsome black and white timbered houses with elegant Georgian brick; the Crown & Sandys and Kings Arms are popular for restaurant food.

OVERBURY SO9537
Immaculate stone-built estate village, with older buildings and fine church. In the pleasant adjacent village of Kemerton the Crown has good value food, and scope for Bredon Hill walks.

PERSHORE SO9445
Very much a working town, this 'capital' of the fruit- and vegetable-growing area around it stages an annual plum festival (Aug bank hol Mon). It's a pleasant place, largely Georgian, with an impressive abbey, and River Avon walks. The Brandy Cask (Bridge St) has a nice riverside garden, good value food and brews its own beer. Heading out along the A4104 SW, when you've passed the Oak in Defford keep your eyes skinned for a group of cottages on your right; the last, surrounded by farm animals and without an inn sign, is the Monkey House, a uniquely old-fashioned cider tavern. In the opposite direction, Charlton is a pretty thatched village.

REDDITCH SP0468
Forge Mill Needle Museum and Bordesley Abbey 🏛 Redditch was the centre of the needle-making industry, and this working 18th-c scouring mill (used to clean the needles before they were sold) shows how they were made; extraordinary variety of needles on show, temporary needlework exhibitions, special events throughout the year. The visitor centre explains the excavation of the 12th-c Cistercian abbey alongside, with its medieval watermill (thought to be one of the oldest in Britain), and there are some hands-on activities for children, and a new audio guide. Snacks, shop, some disabled access; cl am wknds Easter-Sept, plus all Fri and pm Sat Feb-Easter and Oct-Nov, all Dec-Jan; (01527) 62509; £3.50. The surroundings are pretty, and there are picnic-sets. It's not far from here to the **Arrow Valley Countryside Centre**. With wildlife displays and exhibitions, a children's play area and an enjoyable lakeside walk (good for wheelchairs and buggies), this provides a useful introduction to the 900-acre landscaped park. Meals, snacks, shop, some disabled access; (01527) 464004; free (charges for watersports).

RIPPLE SO8737
Appealing village, with finely carved choir seats in its largely 13th-c church. The Fleet at Twyning on the other side of the M50 junction is an interesting Severnside pub with a big garden.

SEVERN STOKE SO8745
Croome Park 🅐 Gradually being restored, this was Capability Brown's first complete landscape, helping make his reputation and establish a new style of parkland design; the elegant park buildings and other structures are mostly by Robert Adam and James Wyatt. Snacks, some disabled access; cl Tues and Weds, mid-Dec to Mar; (01905) 371006; *£3; NT. The Rose & Crown (A38) has good value food.

SHATTERFORD SO7980
Wildlife Sanctuary and Fishery 🅐 Animals here include roaming goats and sika deer, also red deer, llamas, sheep, pigs, ponies, wallabies and rhea in enclosures: you can feed them all; fishing permits available too. Snacks, picnic area, shop, disabled access; cl 25 Dec; (01299) 861597; *£3.50. The smart Bellmans Cross does good lunches. Nearby, pretty Upper Arley has one of Britain's oldest arboretums; snacks, disabled access; open Wed-Fri and Sun Apr-Oct; (01299) 861368; £3.

SHRAWLEY SO7964
Eastgrove Cottage Garden (Sankyns Green, off A443 E of Great Witley) Cottage garden with abundance of plants and arboretum around half-timbered 17th-c farmhouse (not open). Home-made ice-cream, good plants for sale, disabled access; cl am, also Mon (exc bank hols), Tues, Weds (Sun too Sept/Oct), and all Aug and mid-Oct to Apr; (01299) 896389; *£3.

SPETCHLEY SO8953
Spetchley Park Gardens (A422) Thirty acres of gardens, with sweeping lawns and herbaceous borders, rose lawn, and interesting trees and shrubs. The adjacent park has both red and fallow deer. Snacks, disabled access (but no facilities); cl Sun am, all day Sat, Mon (exc bank hols), and Oct-Mar; (01905) 345213; £4. The Berkeley Knot is handy for lunch.

STONE SO8675
Stone House Gardens 🅐 Unusual walled garden with colourful plants, especially climbers and tender flowering shrubs; interesting plant sales. Cl Sun-Tues and Oct-Feb; (01562) 69902; £2.50. The Hare & Hounds at Shenstone does good value lunches.

UPTON-UPON-SEVERN SO8340
Tiltridge Vineyard (Upper Hook Rd, W) You can wander round the vineyard, and taste some of the wines. Shop, disabled access; usually only cl am Sun, but best to check in winter; (01684) 592906; free. The Anchor over at Welland is an appealing place for lunch.

WEST HAGLEY SO8979
Falconry Centre 🅐 (Hurrans Garden Centre, Kidderminster Rd S) Daily flying displays of hawks, owls and falcons; day falconry courses (£80). Snacks, shop, limited disabled access; cl 25-26 Dec, and Easter Sun; (01562) 700014; £3. The Fountain at Clent is the best nearby place for lunch.

WICHENFORD SO7759
Wichenford dovecote Unusually constructed timber-framed wattle-and-daub 17th-c dovecote with nearly 600 nesting boxes. Open daily Apr-Oct and in winter by appointment, cl Good Fri; (01743) 708100; £1; NT.

WICK SO9645
This riverside village has attractive houses and a good church.

WOLVERLEY SO8279
Steeply gabled cottages below a brick-built hilltop church, and the decent cliffside Lock Inn by the quaint Staffs & Worcs Canal.

Bodenham Arboretum & Earth Centre (Hobro, a mile N of B4189) Peaceful place giving plenty of scope for pleasant walks, with around 2,600 different varieties of tree in 63 hectares (156 acres), lakes and pools, and an innovative visitor centre, built into the hillside; it's all set within a working farm. Meals and snacks (not winter), shop, limited disabled access (there's about a mile of disabled pathway); open daily; (01562) 852444; £4. The Bellmans Cross at Shatterford has a good restaurant.

WORCESTER SO8554
Though it's a busy commercial centre and a bit knocked about by 20th-c planners (the dual carriageway really goes too close to the historic core), the city has some splendid medieval buildings dotted about, with lots of half-timbered houses, particularly around Friar St, where the Lemon Tree has good food, and New St (the King Charles here is a good restaurant). College Green forms the gracious

cathedral close, entered by an archway from the Georgian houses of Edgar St, and containing the Gothic sandstone building of the King's School. Kleve Walk is an attractive riverside walk below the cathedral, with a view of the Malverns. Plenty of shops, inc some nice specialist ones, and cafés in Hopmarket Yard, a former coaching inn. The tourist information centre is in the handsome Georgian Guildhall (usually cl Sun).

City Museum and Art Gallery (Foregate St) Local and natural history, contemporary art exhibitions, and children's activities. Meals, snacks, shop, disabled access; cl Sun, 25-26 Dec, 1 Jan, Good Fri and Easter Mon; (01905) 25371; free. The cheerful nearby Dragon (Upper Tything) has good value food.

Commandery (Sidbury) Lively museum wholly devoted to the Civil War, in striking timber-framed 15th-c building (originally a monastic hospital) by a lock on the canal, with a superb Great Hall sporting a hammerbeam roof, while upstairs remarkably well-preserved wall-paintings depict saints (including the extremely nasty martydom of St Erasmus, who suffered death by disembowelling and became patron saint of stomach pains). During the Civil War it became the headquarters of Charles II at the Battle of Worcester; displays cover the battles seen through the eyes of a soldier and of a king, the Civil War in general and the architecture of the building. Lots to read, and an informative video, though relatively few artefacts. Unusual special events and historic military displays. Snacks, shop; cl am Sun, 25-26 Dec, 1 Jan; (01905) 361821; £3.95.

Greyfriars (Friar St) Beautiful and carefully restored medieval timber-framed town house, with delightful walled garden. Cl am, Sun-Tues and Nov-Mar; (01905) 23571; *£3.20; NT.

Museum of Worcester Porcelain (Severn St) Home of Royal Worcester, the country's oldest continuous producer of porcelain, and one of the few museums in the country to be in 250 years' continuous use. The museum is in three areas - 18th, 19th and 20th c - inc a dinner service made for Nelson and some preposterously flamboyant Victorian items. The wkdy factory tours (no under-11s) take in all the stages of production, inc assembly of figurines and painting by hand, and the finished article as well as factory seconds are on sale. Meals, snacks, shop, disabled access to museum only; cl 25-26 Dec and Easter Sun; (01905) 746000; factory tour £5.50 (plus also longer connoisseurs' tours), tour of the museum and visitor centre £5, museum £3.50. Opposite, the comfortable Salmon Leap and the Potters Wheel have decent food.

Worcester Cathedral Founded on the site of a Saxon monastery, in a calm and peaceful setting overlooking the river. It took from 1084 to 1375 to build, and has an attractive 14th-c tower (excellent views; usually open Sat and summer school hols), Norman crypt, and the tombs of Prince Arthur and King John, the latter topped by the oldest Royal effigy in the country. Lots of Victorian stained glass, and some monastic buildings. They do guided tours (book on (01905) 28854). Meals, snacks, shop, some disabled access; open daily; £3 suggested donation.

Worcester Woods Country Park (just E off A442) Ancient woodland and wildflower meadows with waymarked circular walks, trails and map-reading games, information displays in countryside centre, and play, picnic and barbecue areas. Meals, snacks, shop, some disabled access; park open daily, centre cl 25-26 Dec, 1 Jan; (01905) 766493; free. The Swan at nearby Whittington has good value food.

WYCHBOLD SO9165

Webbs Garden Centre (A38 towards Bromsgrove) One of the best in the country, attractively laid out with terrace gardens and riverside displays, a massive choice of things to buy, and events throughout the year. Meals, snacks, disabled access; cl 25-26 Dec and Easter Sun; (01527) 860000; free.

WYRE FOREST SO7574

This major broadleaved woodland, on the Shropshire border, has numerous ready-made Forestry Authority trails (leaflets available from the visitor centre), also cycle hire (01299) 402776. The Royal Forester nearby, if open, is useful for lunch.

Where to eat

BRANSFORD SO8052 **Bear & Ragged Staff** *Station Rd (01886) 833399* Stylish dining pub with proper tablecloths, linen napkins, and fresh flowers, very good imaginative food inc super fresh fish dishes, fine views over rolling country from the relaxed and cheerful interconnecting rooms, open fire, no smoking restaurant, well kept beers, a fine choice of wines, lots of malt whiskies, and willing helpful service; children until 9pm; disabled access. £27.75|**£7.50**

BREDON SO9236 **Fox & Hounds** *Church St (01684) 772377* Pretty, thatched pub in an attractive setting next to a church down a lane leading to a river and bedecked with brightly coloured hanging baskets; comfortably modernised bar with a welcoming atmosphere, stripped timbers and dressed stone pillars, a central wood-burning stove, and dried grasses and flowers, a smaller side bar with an open fire at each end, and a no smoking restaurant; attractively presented bar food served by friendly, efficient staff, well kept real ales, and wines by the glass. £29|**£7.95**

CROWLE SO9256 **Old Chequers** *Crowle Green (01905) 381275* Handy for the motorway, this smoothly run much-modernised dining pub rambles extensively around an island bar, with pubby furniture, lots of pictures for sale at the back, and a coal-effect gas fire at one end; there's a big square extension on the right with more tables; popular generous food (all home-made) includes good value imaginative light lunches plus more substantial dishes, prompt, friendly service, well kept real ales, and picnic-sets on the grass behind; cl Sun pm, 25-26 Dec, 1 Jan; no children; disabled access. £20|**£6**

KEMPSEY SO8548 **Walter de Cantelupe** *34 Main Rd (01905) 820572* Popular roadside pub with friendly relaxed bar, quite a mix of furniture, flowers and candles on tables, a good big fireplace, interesting food, well kept real ales, a good choice of wines by the glass, and hard-working landlord; bdrms; cl Mon exc bank hols, no food Sun pm and second half of Jan; no children after 8.15pm. £22.30|**£7.25**

WELLAND SO8039 **Anchor** *Drake St (01684) 592317* Pretty, fairy-lit Tudor cottage with a welcoming L-shaped bar, a spreading comfortably furnished dining area, nicely set with candles and pink tablecloths and napkins, attentive staff, an extensive choice of enjoyable, changing bar food, and well kept real ales; picnic-sets on lawn, and field for camping with tents or caravans; bdrms; handy for the Three Counties Showground; cl Sun pm exc bank hols; children in restaurant if booked. £28|**£5.25**

WORCESTER SO8454 **Browns** *24 Quay St (01905) 26263* Most attractive and spacious warehouse conversion with big windows overlooking river, excellent modern cooking inc fish and vegetarian dishes, and good wines; cl Sat am, Sun pm, Mon, Christmas-New Year; well behaved children over 8; disabled access. £38/ 2 courses £21

WORCESTER SO8554 **King Charles House** *29 New St (01905) 22449* From where King Charles I made his escape through the back door, closely pursued by Cromwell's forces, and now a relaxed restaurant ; enjoyable food, open fires, and a relaxed atmosphere in downstairs restaurant and upstairs bar; cl Sun, bank hols, 25-26 Dec. £27.50|**£7.50**

WYRE PIDDLE SO9647 **Anchor** *Main Rd (01386) 552799* Relaxing 17th-c pub with lovely views over lawn, river and on over the Vale of Evesham; friendly, neatly kept little lounge with log fire in attractively restored inglenook, comfortable bar, and generous reasonably priced popular food; cl 26 Dec; disabled access. £25|**£6.95**

Special thanks to Nathalie Soanes, Mrs Y Champion, Peter Gondris, Paul Kennedy, Rebecca Nicholls, Ben Dyson

YORKSHIRE

The mass of things to see and do, with nice places to stay and sensible prices, make friendly Yorkshire excellent for holidays. The city of York is ideal for a short break (we've given it a chapter to itself), and we have separate sections on the other three main areas. With the Dales, first-class walking country, we include Ripon, Harrogate, and their surroundings (virtually all North Yorkshire W of the A19). The Moors and East Yorkshire (North Yorkshire E of the A19 along with the administrative county of East Yorkshire) also include memorable walks and drives, with plenty to keep children amused on the coast. West and South Yorkshire (particularly West Yorkshire) have an outstanding range of unusual visitor attractions (often free), with lively towns.

York

**Great for a short break, full of life and atmosphere,
with lots to see and do**

York's centre, ringed by medieval city walls, has twisting alleys filled with lovely ancient buildings, interesting shops, and lively cafés, pubs and bars - and all this is virtually traffic-free, so wonderful for carefree strolling. It has plenty of remarkably varied things well worth visiting - good for all ages. The magnificent Minster is one of Britain's great sights, the Castle Museum and National Railway Museum are first-class, and Jorvik Viking City is among the country's most popular heritage centres (though over rather quickly for the price). This is undeniably a tourist city, with crowds at the main attractions. You can do the circuit of the 13th-c city walls and their many towers in a couple of hours or so, mostly on top. One of the best stretches, with good views of the Minster, is between the Monk Bar and Bootham Bar. There's a good fun guided ghost walk at 7.30pm (exc 24-31 Dec) beginning at the Shambles; (01904) 608700; £3. Shaped like a bike wheel, the Millennium Bridge over the Ouse is part of a 23-mile walkway which takes in villages and choice countryside around the city. York's racecourse is a good one, with monthly meetings; the Ebor Festival in August is the biggest event in the northern racing calendar. The York Pass is worth considering if you plan to visit lots of sites in one go (£21 for a day, it covers more than 30 of the city's attractions), and there are Nov-Mar special offers on many of the major attractions, restaurants, and places to stay - phone the tourist information (01904) 621756 or take a look at their website www.visityork.org for more information.

Where to stay

YORK SE5952 **Arnot House** *17 Grosvenor Terrace, York YO30 7AG* (01904) 641966 **£58***; 4 recently refurbished rms named after North Yorkshire abbeys. Friendly, very well run no smoking Victorian terraced house with lots of original features, antiques and paintings, substantial breakfasts, and a pleasant relaxed atmosphere; cl Jan; no children

YORK SE5849 **Curzon Lodge** *23 Tadcaster Rd, Dringhouses, York YO24 1QG* (01904) 703157 **£67**, plus winter breaks; 10 rms, some in former old coach house and stables. Charming early 17th-c house in marvellous spot just S of city centre overlooking Knavesmire racecourse, with an attractive and comfortable drawing room, a sunny farmhouse dining room (enjoyable breakfasts), and parking in grounds; no smoking throughout; cl Christmas; children over 7

YORK SE6050 **Dairy Guesthouse** *3 Scarcroft Rd, York YO23 1ND* (01904) 639367 **£60***; 5 attractive rms, most with own bthrm. Carefully restored and recently refurbished no smoking Victorian house with lots of original features and attention to detail, enjoyable breakfasts with vegetarian and vegan dishes, warmly hospitable atmosphere, and charming little flower-filled courtyard; cl Jan; disabled access; dogs welcome in bedrooms

YORK SE6052 **Dean Court** *Duncombe Pl, York YO1 7EF* (01904) 625082 **£140***, plus special breaks; 39 attractive, quiet rms. Next to the Minster, this comfortable hotel has a country-house atmosphere and fresh flowers in restful lounge areas, very helpful efficient staff, enjoyable food in the elegant restaurant, and tearoom/conservatory serving late breakfasts, light lunches and so forth; good for families, with thoughtful extras; children over 6 in evening restaurant; partial disabled access ☺

YORK SE5952 **Grange Hotel** *1 Clifton, York YO30 6AA* (01904) 644744 **£140**, plus special breaks; 30 individually decorated rms with antiques and chintz. Close to the Minster, this Regency town house has elegant public rooms, an open fire, newspapers, good breakfasts, excellent restaurant food (there's also a brasserie), and warmly friendly staff; car park; disabled access; dogs welcome in bedrooms

YORK SE6052 **Hazelwood** *24-25 Portland St, York YO31 7EH* (01904) 626548 **£90**, plus winter breaks; 14 individually styled rms. Just 4 mins walks from the Minster, this no smoking, neatly kept Victorian house has quite a few original features, a cosy neatly kept lounge, attractive dining room, helpful owners, and a pretty little garden; off-street parking; children over 8; limited disabled access

YORK SE5951 **Holmwood House** *112-114 Holgate Rd, York YO24 4BB* (01904) 626183 **£85***, plus special breaks; 14 pretty rms (2 attractively refurbished this year), some with four-posters or spa baths, and 1 garden suite. Built as two 19th-c houses, this no smoking hotel is 7 mins from the city walls, with open fire in comfortable sitting room, and very good breakfasts; children over 8

YORK SE5947 **Middlethorpe Hall** *Bishopthorpe Rd, Middlethorpe, York YO23 2GB* (01904) 641241 **£190**, plus special breaks; 30 elegant rms, most in the adjoining courtyard. Lovely, immaculately restored William III country house just S of the city, with fine gardens and parkland, antiques, paintings and fresh flowers in comfortable, quiet day rooms, and excellent food and service; indoor swimming pool and health and fitness spa; children over 8

Please let us know what you think of places in the *Guide*. Use the report forms at the back of the book, write us a letter or log on to www.goodguides.co.uk

To see and do

ARC (St Saviourgate) This refreshingly accessible archaeology centre aims to get you involved personally in a hands-on encounter with the past. With archaeologists on hand for advice, you're encouraged to probe the city's Viking history by yourself, using genuine period relics inc bones, tiles and pottery to piece together a personal impression of Viking-age York. Very much on the school-trips circuit, it's usually open to individuals only in school hols, so best to check out of term-time. It's in a beautifully restored medieval church, with a sensory garden. Snacks, shop, disabled access; cl wknds during term-time, Sun only during school hols, and around 20 Dec-4 Jan; (01904) 543402; £4.50. The Tudor Black Swan (Peaseholme Green) is handy for something to eat.

Barley Hall (Swinegate) The Archaeological Trust that runs the ARC (and the Jorvik Centre) restored this medieval family home, complete with audio tour. Shop, disabled access to ground floor only; cl Mon (exc bank hols), ams Nov-Feb, and 25 Dec-2 Jan; (01904) 610275; *£3.50. The nearby Punch Bowl has good food.

Castle Museum (Tower St) In 18th-c prison buildings on the site of the former castle (part of the outer wall still stands), this is one of the best social history museums in the country, with a huge range of everyday objects from the past four centuries shown in convincingly reconstructed real-life settings, from Edwardian streets to prison cells and more contemporary living rooms. There's even a watermill, by the river outside. They have one of only three Anglo-Saxon helmets in the world. Again, best out of term-time. Shop, disabled access ground floor only; cl 25-26 Dec, 1 Jan; (01904) 687687; £6.

Churches Besides the Minster, the city has a good few other fine medieval churches, though many are no longer used for services. Most were built during the prosperous 15th and 16th c, and among the finest are Holy Trinity (Goodramgate, which also contains in Our Lady's Row the oldest houses in the city) and St Helen's (St Helen's Sq).

All Saints (North St) has some fascinating windows illustrating the last 15 days of the world.

City Art Gallery (Exhibition Sq) Well displayed collections running from Old Masters to the lusciously romantic nudes of William Etty, with some very handsome stoneware pottery. Shop, disabled access; cl 25-26 Dec and 1 Jan; (01904) 687687; now free. The nearby York Arms (High Petergate) has good value food.

Clifford's Tower (Tower St) This former castle keep is perhaps York's most interesting building after the Minster. You can walk around the top of the walls (children especially like this bit, and climbing the grassy slopes), and there are good views of the city. It gets its name from Roger Clifford, who was hanged from the tower in chains. There's an unusual Lowry painting of the tower in the City Art Gallery (see entry above). Shop, Braille guide; cl 24-26 Dec, 1 Jan; (01904) 646940; £2.50. EH. The Kings Arms down on King's Staith by the river is a handy stop.

Fairfax House 🏛 (Castlegate) Magnificently restored mid-18th-c town house, probably one of the finest in England, its richly decorated rooms fully furnished in period style. Much of the impressive collection of paintings, pottery, clocks and Georgian furniture was donated by the great-grandson of the confectionery baron Joseph Terry, and there's a re-created mid-18th-c meal; changing exhibitions. Shop, some disabled access by arrangement (steps at front); cl Fri (exc guided tours, 11am and 2pm), am Sun, 25 Dec, and 6 Jan-14 Feb; (01904) 655543; £4.50.

Guildhall (St Helen's Sq) Exact replica of the original 1446 building, destroyed in a 1940 air raid. The stone walls of the earlier building form the framework of the new one. Disabled access; usually cl wknds Nov-Apr, am Sun in summer, and bank hols; (01904) 613161; free. Harkers nearby, rather smart, has decent food (and part of a Roman gateway in its basement).

Jorvik (below Coppergate Shopping Centre) Well researched re-creation of Viking life: a time capsule carries you back to the year 975, then a viewing car floats you over a muddy road, past street scenes with workshops and alleys, and even up through a two-storey house, all enhanced (if that's the word) with smells from the polluted River Foss, a cess-pit, and the reek of newly tanned leather. A darkened futuristic gallery brings seemingly mounted artefacts slowly to life (using illuminations and mirrors) as they would have appeared in contemporary Jorvik. You're unlikely to spend as much as an hour here, so you have to reckon on the realism rather than the time you spend here making this worth while. It's best to book ahead, to cut the queue (which can be phenomenal). Snacks, shop, disabled access; cl 25 Dec; (01904) 643211; £7.20.

Maize Maze (Grimston Bar Park & Ride, off A1079 E) This maze covered a whopping great 12 hectares (30 acres) in 2003, with 1½ million plants, and they hope the one in 2004 will be as big (though as we went to press they'd not yet finalised the design). Picnic and play areas, snacks (inc good ice-cream), shop, disabled access, dogs allowed on leads; usually open late July-end Sept, phone to check; (01904) 415 364; £3.50. And see Murton Park below.

Merchant Adventurers' Hall (Piccadilly) The largest timber-framed building in the city, and one of the finest in Europe. Built for the powerful Merchant Adventurers' Company in the mid-14th-c and hung with banners of medieval guilds, it has a chapel and undercroft as well as the great hall itself. Shop, disabled access; cl Sun 26 Sept-21 Dec, and all 22 Dec-4 Jan; (01904) 654818; £2.

Micklegate Bar Museum Another of York's medieval gateways, now housing social history displays. Cl wkdys Nov-Jan, 25-26 Dec, 1 Jan, and possibly other times depending on the weather (also closed when the city walls are shut), so best to check; (01904) 634436; £2.

Murton Park (Murton, off A166 just E of A64) Busy four-hectare (ten-acre) park, excellent for children and best known for its Museum of Farming, with exhibitions of agricultural equipment, some animals and a Land Army display. Also here, the Derwent Valley Light Railway (Sun and bank hols) has trips along what was once known as the Blackberry Line, and there's a reconstructed Dark Age settlement and Roman fort (aimed mostly at children). Café and picnic area, shop, disabled access; cl 24 Dec-4 Jan; (01904) 489966; *£4.50. The Maize Maze (see above) is in this area, and further out this way, the Agar Arms at Warthill has good value food in pretty surroundings.

National Railway Museum (Leeman Rd) Somewhere to spend a whole day, celebrating the great railway age with lots of panache; the background sounds and smells of a steam-era station add to the atmosphere. The centrepiece is the spectacular great hall, in which tracks radiate from a central turntable with a display of two dozen great locomotives from the museum's huge collection; their latest acquisition is the Japanese Bullet Train, completely opened up for visitors to walk through and sit in (a videos tells you more about it). Children get the most out of the Interactive Learning Centre, where plenty of hands-on exhibits and activities vividly explain how trains and railways work, though they're also bound to relish the chance to build their own model train in the excellent Works wing, where you can also watch the engineers and craftsmen as they carry out conservation work. The Working Railway looks at the technology behind Britain's rail network, with a live link to York station's signal box. A miniature railway operates most wknds and school holidays, with steam train rides during school hols. You can usually get a road train from York Minster to the museum in summer. Meals, snacks (and picnic areas), shop, disabled access; cl 24-26 Dec; (01904) 621261; free. Their all-day car park costs £4.50.

Richard III Museum (Monk Bar, Goodramgate) The most striking and best preserved of York's four turreted medieval gateways houses this museum dedicated to the much-maligned monarch (or, depending on your point of view, evil hunchbacked murderer). Displays are themed as if he were on trial - you put your verdict in the appropriate Guilty or Innocent book on the way out. Shop; cl 25-26 Dec; (01904) 634191; *£2. The nearby Royal Oak has good value food.

Treasurer's House (Chapter House St; next to the Minster) There's been a house here since Roman times - this one dates from the 17th c, and the basement has an exhibition on its history. The timbered hall is very fine, as is the period furniture and kitchen. Good meals and snacks; cl Fri, all Nov-Mar; (01904) 624247; *£4.50; NT.

York Brewery [🖼] (Toft Green) Tours and tastings daily pm Mon-Sat (not 25-26 Dec or 1 Jan). Shop; (01904) 621162; £4.25 - inc a pint of their beer. Just along the road from here, the Bar Convent has a museum looking at early Christianity (and decent accommodation); museum tours usually Mon-Fri (not bank hols, late-Dec-Jan, and Thurs-Tues Easter wknd - best to check) 10.30am and 2.30pm; (01904) 643238; £3 (inc tour).

York Dungeon (Clifford St) Carefully researched exploration of 2,000 years of superstition, torture and various forms of death, full of gore (definitely not for the faint-hearted). There's an extensive Guy Fawkes Experience and Dick Turpin Story, an exhibition on the Plague, and Gorvik gives the low-down on the bloodthirsty Vikings. Snacks, shop, some disabled access; cl 25 Dec; (01904) 632599; £8.95.

York Minster A glorious example of Gothic architecture, in soft-coloured York stone, this is Britain's largest medieval building, begun in 1220 and taking a staggering 250 years to build. The recent decision to charge for admission has caused concern among many connected with the cathedral, but if the decision is rescinded (as we hope it may be), you would anyway most likely want to leave a generous donation for the delight of looking around this building, so very costly to maintain. The richly detailed interior contains more original medieval glass than any other church in England - and indeed is reckoned to house half of all that's known in the country. Look out for the great E window which shows Genesis and Revelations in 27 panels, the splendid five sisters window in the

N transept, and the beautiful ceilings of the central tower and chapter house. The choir screen has 15 niches containing statues of the kings of England from William the Conqueror to Henry VI. There's a display on the church's turbulent history in the Undercroft, Treasury and crypt. Meals, snacks, shop, disabled access and facilities (touch and hearing centre, braille guides, guide dogs welcome); cl Sun am, and occasionally for major services; (01904) 557216; £4.50; Undercroft museum, Treasury and crypt £2.50 (combined with entry, £6). You can climb the tower for good views of the city (£2.50). Largely traffic free, the Close outside is fairly quiet, but not enclosed, and without the tranquil serenity of say Exeter, Salisbury or Winchester.

York Minster Conference & Banqueting Centre (College St, opposite Minster) 15th-c St William's College, with three finely timbered rooms - and a good restaurant. Shop; cl 25-26 Dec, Good Fri, and if they have conferences, so best to phone and check; (01904) 557233; £1.

York Model Railway [🖼] (York Railway Station) Lovingly re-created miniature town and country landscape, running as many as 25 trains at a time, also a Thomas the Tank Engine working display, with lots of buttons for children to press; a third model shows a typical germanic town in day and night. Good shop, disabled access (phone to check); cl 25-26 Dec; (01904) 630169; *£3.40, discount voucher for one child per adult.

Yorkshire Museum (Museum Gardens) A real treasure-trove, crammed with myriad archaeological finds and riches from Roman, Anglo-Saxon, Viking and medieval times, inc the fabulous medieval Middleham Jewel. All set out very sensibly, with the displays effectively put into context. Shop, snacks (summer only), disabled access; cl 25-26 Dec, 1 Jan; (01904) 687687; £4, less for York residents. Outside are four hectares (ten acres) of botanical gardens by the wall: a big space for this city site, peaceful and attractive, around a shapely group of ruins inc the Benedictine St Mary's

abbey and the Multangular Tower (medieval, on a Roman base), as well as a working observatory.
A picturesque riverside walk takes you
to the pleasant village of Bishopthorpe (handy for the racecourse), where the Marcia does good value lunches.

Where to eat

YORK SE6051 **Betty's** *6-8 St Helen's Sq (01904) 659142* Famous tearooms opened in 1937 with fine teas and coffees (they import their own), good sandwiches, salads and hot specialities, delicious scones, tea breads and pastries, home-made milk shakes, Alsace wines, and evening pianist; cl 25, 26 Dec, 1 Jan; disabled access. £30|£6.50

YORK SE6050 **Meltons** *7 Scarcroft Rd (01904) 634341* Smart and friendly little restaurant with banquettes under the murals, lots of wood and mirrors, very good imaginative modern cooking using tip-top ingredients (plenty of vegetarian choice), lovely puddings, fairly priced wines, and a relaxed friendly atmosphere; no smoking on ground floor; they've opened another restaurant, Meltons Too at 25 Walmgate; cl Sun, Mon am, 24 Dec-14 Jan, 1 wk Aug; disabled access. £40

YORK SE6052 **St William's College Restaurant** *3 College St (01904) 634830* Lovely 15th-c buildings with enclosed courtyard for outside summer eating next to York Minster, with varied food, and candlelight in evening; cl Sun and Mon pms in winter; disabled access. £25|£6.95

YORK SE6052 **Treasurer's House Tearoom** *Minster Yard (01904) 646757* Lovely National Trust property, once home to the medieval treasures of York Minster, with a tearoom in the converted cellars: traditional and herbal teas, good coffee, fruit wines, home-baked cakes and scones, savoury dishes and good puddings, all served by friendly staff; no smoking; cl Fri, cl Nov-end Mar.|£2.30

The Yorkshire Dales, Harrogate & Ripon

Dramatic scenery, great for walkers - family outings too, and castles, stately homes, and abbey ruins

The magnificent landscape is the special attraction here, with some of Britain's most invigorating scenery. The Dales' steep stone-walled pastures, majestic moors, wind-carved limestone crags and rushing streams give drivers and especially walkers a succession of captivating quickly varying views. Each of the main dales or valleys has its own distinct character, and there are plenty of appealing villages and colourful market towns. The visitor centres at Malham (near particularly striking Dales scenery) and Aysgarth (by a romantic series of waterfalls) are good places to begin.

Civilised Harrogate is in easy reach of both Dales and Moors, and a comfortable base to explore from (Harlow Carr gardens here are very special). Ripon (increasingly appealing, with three law and order museums, and a new interpretation centre) and Richmond are appealing, and Hawes too has quite a bit to offer day-trippers.

You'll find well preserved castles at Skipton (still an incredible amount to see at this romantic place), Ripley (beautiful, with splendid gardens), and

Castle Bolton (great views); poetic Fountains Abbey is the largest monastic ruin in the country. Venerable houses include stately Beningbrough Hall (fine paintings, and good special events), Newby Hall (children like the grounds best), and Edwardian Sion Hill Hall at Kirby Wiske (lots of antiques). There are fine terraced gardens near Leyburn, and rare trees and shrubs (and a falconry centre) in the arboretum just outside Bedale.

The theme park at North Stainley (with a new birds of prey centre nearby), has plenty to thrill, while the enchanting Forbidden Corner at Coverham is an unusual find. There's a friendly farm in Aiskew (we've added another open farm this year, near Reeth), a birds of prey centre at Giggleswick, and you can fish at Kilnsey. Other rewarding pastimes include the scenic train journey over the Pennines from Settle to Carlisle, and a trip on the steam railway from Embsay to tranquil Bolton Abbey. There are caves to explore in Clapham, and Masham offers a choice of brewery tours.

Where to stay

ALDBOROUGH SE4066 **Ship** *Low Rd, Aldborough, Boroughbridge, North Yorkshire YO51 9ER (01423) 322749* **£49***; 3 rms. Friendly and neatly kept 14th-c pub nr ancient church and Roman town, with coal fire in stone inglenook and old-fashioned seats in heavily beamed bar, ample food, separate restaurant, good breakfasts, well kept real ales, and seats on spacious lawn; cl 24-26 Dec

BAINBRIDGE SD9390 **Rose & Crown** *Bainbridge, Leyburn, North Yorkshire DL8 3EE (01969) 650225* **£74**, plus special breaks; 12 comfortable rms. 15th-c coaching inn overlooking lovely green, with antique settles and other old furniture in beamed and panelled front bar, open log fires, cosy residents' lounge, big wine list, and home-made traditional food in bar and restaurant; pets welcome by prior arrangement; disabled access; dogs welcome

BOLTON ABBEY SE0753 **Devonshire Arms** *Bolton Abbey, Skipton, North Yorkshire BD23 6AJ (01756) 710441* **£210**, plus special breaks; 41 individually furnished rms with thoughtful extras. Close to the priory itself and in lovely countryside, this civilised former coaching inn owned by the Duke of Devonshire, has been carefully furnished with fine antiques and paintings from Chatsworth; log fires, impeccable service, beautifully presented imaginative food in elegant Burlington restaurant and more informal brasserie and bar, and super breakfasts; health centre; children over 12 in restaurant; disabled access; dogs welcome away from restaurants

BRAFFERTON SE4370 **Laurel Manor Farm** *Brafferton, North Yorkshire YO61 2NZ (01423) 360436* **£60**; 3 big beamed rms. Tall Georgian house with lovely views, surrounded by 28 acres of farmland: rare breeds, horses, fishing in the River Swale, 1,500 trees, carefully planted landscaped gardens, and croquet and tennis; open fire in comfortable sitting room, antiques and family photographs, aircraft models and pictures, good breakfasts and enjoyable candlelit family dinners using home-grown produce (by arrangement), and friendly, attentive owners; horses and other pets welcome in stable room; dogs welcome in bedrooms

CRAY SD9479 **White Lion** *Cray, Skipton, North Yorkshire BD23 5JB (01756) 760262* **£60**, plus special breaks; 8 comfortable, newly furnished rms all with showers. Welcoming little pub spectacularly isolated 335 metres (1,100 ft) up with super views, lots of walks, traditional feel with flagstones, beams and log fires, good bar food, and decent wines; residents only 25 Dec; partial disabled access; dogs welcome

FEIZOR SD7967 **Scar Close Farm** *Feizor, Austwick, Lancaster, Lancashire LA2 8DF* *(01729) 823496* **£52***, plus special breaks; 4 clean well appointed rms. Friendly converted barn on working farm with big guest lounge, books, magazines and TV, and big breakfasts and homely evening meals - packed lunches, too; lovely quiet countryside; disabled access

HARROGATE SE2955 **Alexa House** *26 Ripon Rd, Harrogate, North Yorkshire HG1 2JJ (01423) 501988* **£70***, plus winter breaks; 13 rms, some in former stable block. Attractive Georgian house with friendly staff, comfortable lounge, good home cooking in no smoking dining room, and marvellous breakfasts; good disabled access; dogs welcome in bedrooms

KNARESBOROUGH SE3457 **Dower House** *Bond End, Knaresborough, North Yorkshire HG5 9AL (01423) 863302* **£94**, plus special breaks; 31 clean, comfortable rms. Creeper-clad 15th-c former dower house with attractively furnished public rooms of some character, good food in Terrace Restaurant, super breakfasts, helpful service, and leisure and health club; partial disabled access; dogs welcome in bedrooms

LONG PRESTON SD8355 **Maypole** *Main St, Long Preston, Skipton, North Yorkshire BD23 4PH (01729) 840219* **£49**, plus winter breaks; 6 comfortable rms. Neatly kept 17th-c pub with generous helpings of enjoyable traditional food (and nice breakfasts) in spacious beamed dining room, open fire in lounge bar, real ales, and helpful service; dogs welcome

MALHAMDALE SD8962 **Miresfield Farm** *Malham, Skipton, North Yorkshire BD23 4DA (01729) 830414* **£50***; 10 rms. Spacious old farmhouse with good freshly prepared food in beamed dining room, pleasant conservatory and two lounges (one with open log fire), and lovely garden by stream and village green; partial disabled access; dogs welcome in bedrooms

MARKINGTON SE2764 **Hob Green** *Markington, Harrogate, North Yorkshire HG3 3PJ (01423) 770031* **£110***, plus winter breaks; 12 well equipped pretty rms. Lovely gardens and over 800 acres of rolling countryside surround this charming 18th-c stone hotel; comfortable and pretty lounge and garden room, log fires, antique furniture, fresh flowers, relaxed atmosphere, good interesting food, decent choice of wines, and friendly service; dogs welcome in bedrooms

NEWTON-LE-WILLOWS SE2189 **Hall** *Newton-le-Willows, Bedale, North Yorkshire DL8 1SW (01677) 450210* **£90***; 3 spacious rms. Handsome Georgian house with quiet gardens and acres of paddocks; lots of fine antiques, paintings and wall hangings, tranquil drawing room with an open fire and french windows into the garden, cosy homely snug with another fire, honesty bar, good breakfasts in light breakfast room (home-made fruitcake, tea and coffee always available), enjoyable food in elegant dining room (by prior arrangement), and a helpful and hospitable owner; cl Christmas and New Year; children over 13 (or by arrangement); dogs welcome in the stable block by arrangement

RAMSGILL SE1171 **Yorke Arms** *Ramsgill, Harrogate, North Yorkshire HG3 5RL (01423) 755243* **£210*** inc dinner, plus special breaks; 14 attractive rms inc a cottage on the village green. Enjoyable small former shooting lodge (a restaurant-with-rooms) with antique furnishings, log fires, exceptionally good imaginative cooking in comfortable dining rooms and Beckside room, fine wines, real ales, courteous service, and lovely surrounding walks; children over 12 in dining room; dogs in cottage suite

RICHMOND NZ1700 **Millgate House** *Millgate, Richmond, North Yorkshire DL10 4JN (01748) 823571* **£70***; 3 rms, 2 overlooking the garden. Georgian town house with lots of interesting antiques and lovely plants, a peaceful drawing room, warm friendly owners offering meticulous attention to detail, and good breakfasts in charming dining room which also overlooks the garden; it is this award-winning small garden with views over the River Swale and the Cleveland Hills beyond that is so special, filled with wonderful roses, ferns, clematis and hostas - they have a booklet listing the plants; children over 10; dogs welcome in bedrooms

RICHMOND NZ1404 **Whashton Springs Farm** *Whashton, Richmond, North*

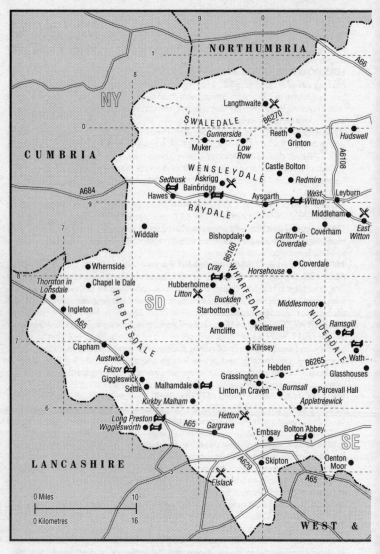

Yorkshire DL11 7JS (01748) 822884 **£52***; 8 comfortable rms (2 refurbished this year). Attractive stone-built Georgian farmhouse on 600-acre working mixed farm; log fire in comfortable sitting room, good country breakfasts in attractive dining room (no evening meals) and lovely surrounding countryside; cl Christmas and New Year; self-catering coach house also; children over 5 for B&B; partial disabled access

RIPLEY SE2860 **Boars Head** Ripley, Harrogate, North Yorkshire HG3 3AY (01423) 771888 **£120***, plus special breaks; 25 charmingly decorated rms. In a delightful estate village, this fine old coaching inn has a relaxed, welcoming atmosphere, with comfortable sofas in attractively decorated lounges, long flagstoned bar, notable wines by the glass, fine food in bar and restful dining room, and unobtrusive service;

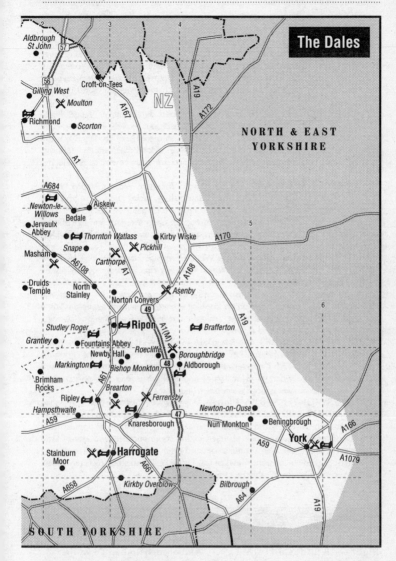

The Dales

Aldbrough St John
Gilling West
Croft-on-Tees
Moulton
Richmond
Scorton
NZ
A167
A19
A172
NORTH & EAST YORKSHIRE
A1
A684
Newton-le-Willows
Aiskew
Bedale
Jervaulx Abbey
Thornton Watlass
Kirby Wiske
A170
Snape
Pickhill
Masham
Carthorpe
A6108
A1
A168
Druids Temple
North Stainley
Asenby
Norton Conyers
Studley Roger
Ripon
Brafferton
A1(M)
A19
Grantley
Fountains Abbey
Roecliffe
Newby Hall
Boroughbridge
Markington
Bishop Monkton
Aldborough
Brimham Rocks
Brearton
A61
Ripley
Ferrensby
Newton-on-Ouse
Hampsthwaite
A59
Knaresborough
Nun Monkton
Beningbrough
York
A166
Stainburn Moor
Harrogate
A661
A59
A1079
A658
Kirkby Overblow
Bilbrough
A64
A19
SOUTH YORKSHIRE

games, videos and special menus for children; disabled access; dogs welcome in bedrooms

RIPON SE3171 **Ripon Spa** *Park St, Ripon, North Yorkshire HG4 2BU (01765) 667172* **£99**, plus special breaks; 40 individually furnished rms, many overlooking the grounds. Neatly kept friendly and comfortable Edwardian hotel with seven acres of charming gardens, yet only a short walk from the centre; attractive public rooms, winter log fires, and good food in bar and restaurant; disabled access; dogs welcome away from eating areas

SEDBUSK SD8790 **Stone House** *Hawes, North Yorkshire DL8 3PT (01969) 667571* **£84**, plus special breaks; 22 rms (many bthrms refurbished this year), 5 with own conservatories. Small, warmly friendly Edwardian hotel in a stunning setting with magnificent views; country-house feel and appropriate furnishings, attractive oak-panelled drawing room, billiard room, log fires, and exemplary service offering good local information; pleasant extended dining room (newly redecorated) with excellent wholesome food (special needs catered for) inc super breakfasts, and reasonable choice of wines; wonderful walks; P G Wodehouse stayed here as a guest of the original owner who employed a butler called Jeeves - it was on him that Wodehouse based his famous character; cl Jan; good disabled access; dogs welcome in bedrooms

STUDLEY ROGER SE2970 **Lawrence House** *Studley Roger, Ripon, North Yorkshire HG4 3AY (01765) 600947* **£96***; 2 spacious, lovely rms. Attractive Georgian house with two acres of lovely garden on the edge of Studley Royal and Fountains Abbey; fine antiques and pictures, log fires, good breakfasts, and delicious evening meals; cl Christmas and New Year; children by arrangement; dogs welcome in bedrooms

THORNTON WATLASS SE2385 **Buck** *Thornton Watlass, Ripon, North Yorkshire HG4 4AH (01677) 422461* **£65***, plus fishing, racing and special breaks; 7 rms, most with own bthrm. Cheerful country pub overlooking cricket green in very attractive village, with interesting beamed rooms, open fire, jazz Sun lunchtimes, enjoyable food in no smoking dining room, and lots of nearby walks; cl pm 25 Dec; dogs welcome in bedrooms

WATH SE1467 **Sportsmans Arms** *Wath, Harrogate, North Yorkshire HG3 5PP (01423) 711306* **£90***, plus special breaks; 13 lovely rms. Friendly, quietly placed 17th-c restaurant-with-rooms, with lovely views, an elegant bar, delicious food using the best local produce (fish from Whitby, game from the moors, and Nidderdale lamb, pork and beef) in no smoking evening restaurant, super lunchtime bar food, a carefully chosen wine list, and attentive service from the long-standing owner and his genuine staff; cl 25 Dec

WEST WITTON SE0688 **Wensleydale Heifer** *West Witton, Leyburn, North Yorkshire DL8 4LS (01969) 622322* **£80***, plus special breaks; 9 rms. Friendly, recently refurbished 17th-c coaching inn with comfortable furnishings, log fires and oak beams, and a cosy bar; good local game and fresh seafood in bistro or spacious restaurant; children over 5; dogs welcome in bedrooms

WIGGLESWORTH SD8056 **Plough** *Wigglesworth, Skipton, North Yorkshire BD23 4RJ (01729) 840243* **£79**, plus special breaks; 12 well equipped rms, some in newer extension. Friendly and well run early 18th-c country inn with popular food in conservatory restaurant, oak panelled dining room and bar, and lots of little rooms surrounding bar area - some smart and plush, others cosy and friendly; big breakfasts, packed lunches, and views of the Three Peaks; no smoking family room; seats in secluded garden; disabled access

To see and do

AISKEW SE2787
Big Sheep & Little Cow Farm Small-scale dairy farm, with friendly sheep and dexter cows (Britain's smallest), pigs and chicks, and an under-cover animal display - the family in charge love talking to visitors; there's also a new play barn, quad bikes (£3), and pony rides. Snacks, shop selling ewe's milk and ice-cream made here from it, some disabled access; open from Easter, they hope to open all year now (exc 25-26 Dec); (01677) 422125; £4.

ALDBOROUGH SE4066
Aldborough Roman Town The northernmost civilian Roman town was here, its houses, courts, forum and temple surrounded by a massive 6-metre (20-ft) wall. All that's left is a couple of pavements, the position of the wall and, in the museum, some finds from the site. Shop; open Easter-Oct (sometimes cl 1-2pm); (01423) 322768; £2; EH. It's a pleasant village with an impressive church (check out the sundial); the Ship opposite is good for lunch.

ARNCLIFFE SD9371
Appealing tucked-away Dales village,
well placed for walks. The road up
Littondale is pretty, and that to
Langcliffe in Ribblesdale runs through
dramatic scenery. The Falcon is an
archetypal Dales inn.

ASKRIGG SD9491
Elegant stone houses around neat
streamside greens, walks to nearby
waterfalls, fine 15th-c church, and two
decent pubs.

AYSGARTH SE0188
Aysgarth Falls The Lower Fall is the
most spectacular of this famously
romantic series of waterfalls, via a path
over the road from the car park. The
falls are the National Park's chief visitor
honeypot and do get crowded,
particularly through Aug (when even
parking can be a problem here). They're
better in late spring or early autumn,
when there tends to be more water in
the river and therefore a better show.
In severely cold weather they can be
stunning, with wonderful ice sculptures
building up. There's generally a small
charge to see the Upper Fall (it's on
private land), but you can see it almost
as well, without paying, from the bridge
on the road. The main car park (£2 for
the day) has a **National Park Centre**,
with displays on the Dales, and useful
walks, maps, and guides. Café, shop,
disabled facilities; cl Mon-Thurs Nov-
Mar, best to check over Christmas;
(01969) 663424; free. The nearby
Palmer Flatt does decent lunches.
Walking routes hereabouts don't join
up that neatly, but you can follow paths
to West Burton, an idyllic village, with
good value food at the Fox & Hounds
on its long green.
Yorkshire Carriage Museum (Yore
Mill) A collection of Victorian coaches
and carriages housed in a 150-year old
mill; they hope to open a rare breed pig
centre by the school summer hols.
Meals, snacks, large charity shop (free
entry); usually only cl 25 Dec, but also
some wkdys, best to check; (01969)
663399; £1. The George & Dragon is a
good place for lunch.

BAINBRIDGE SD9390
Delightful, its broad sloping green still
with the village stocks. The ancient
Rose & Crown, open all day, has

enjoyable food. **Low Mill**, a restored
18th-c corn mill, has a collection of fully
furnished hand-made doll's houses, all
produced on the premises; open by
appointment; (01969) 650416; £1.

BEDALE SE2685
Thorp Perrow Arboretum (off
B6268 S) Well laid-out 85-acre
landscaped lakeside collection of rare
trees and shrubs among some splendid
mature specimens that have been
growing here for over 400 years.
Particularly strong on oaks, ornamental
cherries, willows and hazels, and lovely
for spring walks when the bulbs are out;
also a falconry centre and tearoom
(usually cl wkdys mid-Nov to mid-Feb).
Shop, disabled access; (01677) 425323;
*£5.75. In the pretty streamside village
of Snape nearby, the friendly Castle
Arms has good food (and there is
indeed a castle).

BENINGBROUGH SE5358
Beningbrough Hall Stately early
18th-c baroque mansion, with a good
collection from the National Portrait
Gallery, also marvellous staircase with
balusters carved in imitation of wrought
iron, fine carvings, and a big restored
Victorian dairy. Regular events for
families, and lovely formal gardens.
Meals, snacks, shop, disabled access to
ground floor only; cl Thurs, and Fri (exc
July-Aug, Good Fri), and all Nov-27
Mar, house also closed am; (01904)
470666; *£6, garden only *£5; NT. The
riverside Dawnay Arms at Newton-on-
Ouse does decent bar lunches

BISHOPDALE SD9885
One of Wensleydale's tributary dales,
broader than the others but still quite
dramatic for walkers.

BOLTON ABBEY SE0754
Beautiful spot in lovely rolling wooded
parkland on a knoll above the River
Wharfe. Most of the priory buildings,
dating from the 12th to the 16th c, are
in ruins, but the central core of the main
church is still used for Sunday services.
19th-c additions such as stained glass
(some by Pugin) and murals oddly don't
strike a false note. The car park (£4)
gets rather full in summer. The
Devonshire Arms is very fine for lunch.
Attractive walks lead off in most
directions: the landscape has a lowland
beauty, with the ruined abbey, the turf

banks of the Wharfe and the oaks of the Strid Wood. A steep ascent from Howgill is rewarded by views from Simon's Seat, perched on the edge of moors.

BRIMHAM ROCKS SE2065
(off B6265) Spectacular and extraordinarily weathered gritstone pinnacles, tors and boulders facing the winds at a height of 290 metres (950 ft), conjuring up people, animal heads and other strange figures - a Victorian guidebook declared that they were 'grim and hideous forms defying all description and definition'. Children like them a lot - Henry Moore said that when he was a boy they strongly moulded his imagination. Exhibition room, shop and snacks; site open all year, centre usually cl wkdys (exc Jun-Sept and bank hols), all Nov-Feb (exc Sun Nov-Dec, and school hols in Oct and Feb), and perhaps in bad weather; (01423) 780688; parking £2.50; NT. The Royal Oak down at Dacre Banks is a friendly food stop.

CASTLE BOLTON SE0095
Apedale Head This spectacular viewpoint is reached by a 3-mile plod up tracks NW; on fine days it feels like the top of the world, with views encompassing both Wensleydale and Swaledale.

Bolton Castle (off A684) A massive 14th-c structure towering over the tiny single-street village built for it. Considering it was partly dismantled in 1645 and has been empty ever since, it's still in fine shape; great views from the 30-metre (100-ft) towers, dungeons and restored medieval gardens. Snacks, shop; cl a wk over Christmas; (01969) 623981; £4. The Kings Arms at Redmire has good food.

CHAPEL LE DALE SD7477
Nr the Hill Inn on the Ingleton—Ribblehead road, a tiny church in a pretty wooded setting has a memorial made from fossilised marble to the 100 or so men, women and children who died during the building of the Settle—Carlisle line; their bodies are buried in unmarked graves, and the railway's engineer is also buried here, separately.

CLAPHAM SD7469
Attractive village that has turned walking and caving into something of an industry. The riverside New Inn has

good honest food (a good place for walkers to stay in).

Ingleborough Cave One of the most easily visited of the vast network of caverns plunging into the limestone hills around here - and we think the only one that wheelchairs can go all the way through. It's in the grounds of the outdoors centre at Ingleborough Hall - formerly the family home of the great plantsman Reginald Farrer, who in his short life introduced and eulogised many notable plants from the Himalayas and China. The **Reginald Farrer nature trail** leads past Farrer's woods and small lake to the cave (40p); unusually, it's a place that looks better in wet weather. Snacks, shop, some disabled access; cl wkdys (unless by appointment) end Oct-Easter, and 25-26 Dec; (01524) 251242; £4.50.

COVERDALE SE0481
Wensleydale's major tributary valley, relatively very quiet; fairly gentle in its lower reaches (where the Foresters Arms in pretty Carlton is a useful lunch stop - not Mon or Tues), climbing high into a wild and untamed-feeling world of lonely sheep farms.

COVERHAM SE0986
Forbidden Corner (Tupgill Park Estate) Enchantingly different, and really memorable: a labyrinth of tunnels, chambers, follies and surprises imaginatively laid out in an attractive 1½ hectare (four-acre) walled garden. A clue-guide leads you over stepping stones, down dead ends, and through water walls to the centrepiece, a story-book underground grotto. Other features include a huge glass pyramid, a 6-metre (19-ft) giant, optical illusions (a normal-looking corridor shrinks to a mere burrow), and statues that range from picnicking bears to griffins (watch out for the ones that squirt water). You can buy food to feed the mirror carp, and there are panoramic Coverdale views. Snacks, shop; open pm daily Apr-Oct (all day Sun), plus Sun Nov-24 Dec, phone to book; (01969) 640638; £6.

CROFT-ON-TEES NZ2809
Right on the border with Co Durham is a pleasant church where Lewis Carroll's father was parson; there's a plaque in memory of the writer, complete with an enamelled White Rabbit, and an

unusual family pew reached by a staircase. If the church is closed, the key is kept at the Croft Spa Hotel across the road. Nice river views.

DENTON MOOR SE1450
Above the pleasantly wood-flanked reservoirs at Fewston (where the 18th-c Sun has decent food inc summer afternoon teas), this offers scope for fairly stretching walks, though nothing to compare with the Dales themselves.

DRUIDS TEMPLE SE1879
Nr the hamlet of Ilton a no-through road leads up to woodlands where you can walk to this scaled-down Stonehenge, built by a landowner in the 1820s as work for local unemployed people.

EMBSAY SE0053
Embsay & Bolton Abbey Steam Railway ⊞ Steam trips along a track prettily set beneath limestone crags, through to Bolton Abbey. Collection of old locomotives and carriages; the quaint cabman's shelter was brought over from Ilkley. Snacks, two shops (remarkable range of books), disabled access; usually open Sun all year, daily last two wks July and all Aug, plus other days - phone for a timetable; (01756) 710614; *£6, discount voucher not valid for special events. The Elm Tree has good hearty food (and comfortable bedrooms).

FOUNTAINS ABBEY SE2769
Fountains Abbey & Studley Royal Water Garden (off B6265) The largest monastic ruin in the country, this romantic place was founded in 1132 by Cistercian monks, in a delightful riverside setting. Most of the remains are 12th-c, but the proud main tower is 15th-c. Opposite are the lovely landscaped gardens begun by William Aislabie in the 1760s, which include ornamental temples and follies, formal water gardens, lakes aflutter with waterfowl, and 400 acres of deer park. The most beautiful approach is through the extraordinarily ornate Victorian church at the far end (may be restoration in progress, best to phone for opening), and this 'back-door' entrance is the most tranquil too; you can also explore three floors of the 12th-c watermill that produced flour for the monks. A helpful modern visitor

centre blends in and doesn't spoil the view. Free guided tours of abbey 11am, 2.30pm, 3.30pm Apr-Oct (no tour 3.30pm Oct), and tours of water garden 2pm Apr-Oct, phone to check. Meals, snacks, shop, good disabled access; cl Fri Nov-Jan, and 24-25 Dec; (01765) 608888; *£5.50, deer park - an excellent strolling ground - free; NT. The very civilised Sawley Arms in Sawley just W does good food.

GIGGLESWICK SD7867
Falconry & Conservation Centre (top of Crows Nest, off A65 N of Settle) Well organised, with lots of vultures, eagles, hawks, falcons and owls, and regular flying displays (from noon). Meals, snacks, shop, disabled access; usually cl wkdys Oct-Nov and all Dec, but as we went to press the centre was up for sale so best to check; (01729) 825164; £4.95. The village down by the Ribble below is peaceful and pretty, with good food in the 17th-c Black Horse near the church.

GLASSHOUSES SE1764
Yorkshire Country Wines (The Mill) Traditional country wines produced in 19th-c flax mill, with free tastings, antiques, and tearoom overlooking the River Nidd; limited disabled access. Cl Mon, Tues, and wkdys Nov-Easter, winery tours (£2.50) are on Fri and Sat at 11.45am; (01423) 711947.

GRASSINGTON SE0063
At the heart of Wharfedale, a pleasant small town or large village around a sloping cobbled square, depending a lot on walkers and other visitors, with some attractive shops and a few interesting old buildings; there's a National Park information centre. The Devonshire on the square and Black Horse just off are good for lunch. The B6160 gives lovely Wharfedale views, and the B6265 to Pateley Bridge also has memorable views (and passes the colourfully lit underground Stump Cross Caverns, well worth a look if you're passing).

GRINTON SE0498
Attractive Wensleydale village with a charming church known as the Cathedral of the Dales, and pleasant walks nearby. The riverside Bridge Inn (open all day) has decent food.

HARROGATE SE3054

This elegant and self-confident inland resort has kept its Victorian spa-town atmosphere (and from summer, you'll once again be able to visit the handsome Turkish Baths) despite now filling many of its handsome hotels with up-to-date conferences and so forth. The layout of the town is very gracious, and you couldn't ask for better shops (interesting antiques and some top-notch specialist shops). Almost every available space is filled with colourful plant displays, as if to shake off the gloom of the dark stone buildings. The first thing a visitor notices is the great sweep of The Stray, open parkland which runs right along and through the S side of the centre. The first sulphur well was discovered in the 16th c and named the Tewit Well, after the local word for the lapwings which led a local sporting gent to ride into what was then a smelly bog. It's up on The Stray, grandly encased in what looks like an italianate mausoleum. The elegant buildings of the compact central area run down from here to the pleasantly laid-out Valley Gardens, very Victorian, with a curlicued central tea house. The relaxed tempo of the place, and the clean bracing climate (it's quite high on the moors), have made it a popular retirement area. Besides the places mentioned in *Where to eat*, the Drum & Monkey (fish restaurant/wine bar, Montpellier gardens) and Hedleys (wine bar, Montpellier Parade) are good for lunch or a snack; the café of the Theatre Royal is also pleasant, as is the Lascelles Arms out in Follifoot.

Harlow Carr (Crag Lane, off B6162 W) Now one of the Royal Horticultural Society's gardens, 24 hectares (nearly 60 acres) of lawns, streams, pools, rockeries, rhododendrons, woodland, spring bulbs and many other interesting plants. This year, six new areas represent gardening styles in 1804, the 1850s, the 1890s, the 1920s, 1951, and the 1970s (to be the subject of a six-part TV series, *Gardens Through Time*). Also a museum of gardening, model village and scented garden, and courses and workshops. The finest strolling ground near Harrogate and getting quite busy these days, though still a place of real peace and fresh moorland air out of season, when the excellent collection of heathers comes into its own. Good meals and snacks, plant centre, disabled access; (01423) 565418; *£5. The New Inn on the B6162, and the adjacent Harrogate Arms, also have good value food.

Mercer Art Gallery (Swan Rd) An early spa building, with an excellent fine art collection, and temporary exhibitions and events. Shop, disabled access; cl Mon (exc bank hols), Sun am, 24-26 Dec and 1 Jan; (01423) 556188; free.

Royal Pump Room Museum (Crown Place) The central sulphur wells are housed here, enclosed by glass to contain the reek; you can still sample a glass of the water at the original spa counter, now the ticket counter for the museum. The Victorian pump room building contains displays on the town's spa history, and changing exhibitions. Shop, disabled access; cl Sun am, 24-26 Dec and 1 Jan; (01423) 556188; £2.50.

Turkish Baths & Health Spa Due to reopen at the beginning of June, following extensive work to restore it to how it would have looked at the end of the 19th-c; as well as sauna and steam rooms, there'll be a whole range of beauty and relaxation treatments. Café, shop, good disabled access; phone for more information; (01423) 556746; from £10.50 for a turkish bath.

HAWES SD8789

Busy in summer with hikers and coach-parties exploring Wensleydale, but picturesque, and a proper market town, its Tues mart full of livestock in late summer; some good antiques shops too. The bustling White Hart has good value food, and occasional craft fairs upstairs.

Dales Countryside Museum (Station Yard) Interesting displays of local crafts and domestic and industrial life as well as hands-on exhibits, re-creations, a static steam locomotive and displays on transport; also changing exhibitions, demonstrations and special events. Shop, disabled access; cl a few days over Christmas and New Year; (01969) 667450; £3.

Hardraw Force (just N at Hardraw) England's tallest waterfall cascading over a 30-metre (100-ft) lip; it's best after rain (though the paths can be muddy then), and at dry times you may see barely a trickle; £1 charged at Green Dragon pub. A longer excursion follows the Pennine Way from Hawes and over the River Ure. The valley above the falls is attractive, and this can be a start for the long day's walk to Great Shunner Fell.

High-level drives The B6255 S to Ribblehead gives fine upland views, and the Buttertubs Pass northwards through High Shaw over into Swaledale is a spectacular drive (the Buttertubs are deep ferny holes near the summit where carriers used to cool their butter in hot weather).

Outhwaites Ropemakers (A684, Town Foot) They've been making rope for 200 years - see how it's done. Shop (not just great hawsers, useful things too like dog-leads), disabled access; cl wknds (exc Sat July-Oct), 10 days at Christmas, and Good Fri; (01969) 667487; free.

Wensleydale Creamery (Gayle Lane) You can watch the cheese being made by the traditional method, all by hand, and there's a fascinating visitor centre, with a well set out dairying/cheese museum; readers enjoy coming here. The shop (busy in summer) has samples of their variously flavoured cheeses - our favourite was the one with blueberries. Very good café, disabled facilities; cl 25 Dec; (01969) 667664; £2.

HEBDEN SE0263

Hebden lead mines The walk up Hebden Beck is rewarding, with its legacy of old lead-mine workings; you can go on to take in Grassington and the path along the River Wharfe.

HUBBERHOLME SD9377
Beautifully placed riverside Dales hamlet at the meeting of Wharfedale and Langstrothdale with a good 13th-c church, built on an ancient burial site, with Norman tower, unusual rood loft and pews by Thompson of Kilburn - with their little carved mouse trademark. The charmingly set George, J B Priestley's favourite pub, has good food and bedrooms. A walk not to be missed is up to Scar House and along a level turfy terrace, which commands

magnificent views down Wharfedale, to Cray (the White Lion's a good pub there). The walk can be expanded to include Buckden (then return to Hubberholme along the river) - in fact there are rewarding walks between all the Wharfedale/Littondale places flagged on our map, with pub food available in each of them.

INGLETON SD6973
Steep and pretty village, full of walkers. The Wheatsheaf, with hawks in its garden, has good value fresh food. On the edge, **Ingleton Glen** is a lovely wooded gorge walk up the River Twiss, not too strenuous, past a series of picturesque waterfalls; most people take it about a mile, as far as Thornton Force, a textbook example of geological faulting; £6 for car (inc passengers), £3 adult on foot. It takes 2-4 hours to do a full circuit, over the moor and back past more falls on the River Doe. The Country Harvest (half a mile W, on the A65), has a good range of foods (inc an incredible selection of cheeses), an enjoyable café, and a play area; readers tell us it's well worth stopping at. The B6255/B6479 is a very scenic long way round to Settle.

White Scar Cave (B6255 towards Hawes) The country's longest show cave and one of the most spectacular, with underground waterfalls and streams, and an Ice Age cavern. Wrap up well - the guided tour takes about 80 mins so gets chilly. Snacks, shop, some disabled access by arrangement; cl 25-26 Dec (and sometimes after heavy rain); (01524) 241244; £6.75.

JERVAULX ABBEY SE1785
Less imposing than Fountains, Rievaulx and Bolton, but in some ways even more appealing - perhaps because the rough-cropped grass and wild flowers around the shattered walls emphasise the slightly melancholy atmosphere of a place of great worldly wealth and power that's come to nothing. Tearoom (cl end Oct-mid-Mar), shop, disabled access; abbey open all year; (01677) 460391; £2. The Blue Lion at East Witton nearby has superb food.

KETTLEWELL SD9672
Popular Wharfedale village for walkers, with three decent pubs; there are exhilarating views from the back roads

from here up into Coverdale, and to Hawes via Hubberholme.

KILNSEY SD9767

Kilnsey Park & Trout Farm 🔲 (B6160) Two lakes for fly-fishing, plus a fun-fishing area for children, adventure playground, and good shop with fish, oven-ready game and other local produce. There's an aquarium, and nature trails in a wildflower reserve with a good number of orchids; look out for red squirrels - this is a conservation area for them. Good meals and snacks (inc tasty trout from their smokery, and local cheeses), disabled access; cl 25 Dec; (01756) 752150; £2.50, £3.85 for children's fishery (50p for spectators), and fly fishing from around £16 per day. The Tennants Arms has decent food, and views of memorably bulging Kilnsey Crag.

KIRBY WISKE SE3684

Sion Hill Hall Splendid Edwardian mansion, one of the last great country houses to be built, with period furnishings and an enormous collection of antiques. Shop (inc bric-a-brac), disabled access to ground floor only; open pms Easter Sun and bank hol Mon, plus pm Weds Jun-Sept (guided tours May-Oct by arrangement), best to check; (01845) 587206; £4.50, £1.50 grounds only. The Nags Head at Pickhill does good lunches.

KNARESBOROUGH SE3557

The little town above the steeply picturesque river gorge, with its spectacular railway viaduct, is pleasant and colourful (esp on Weds market day), with some attractive buildings. The chemist's shop on the square is said to be the oldest in the country; established in 1720, it still has all its original fittings. You can hire **rowing boats** down on the river (£3 well spent), and there are pleasant riverside paths and walks: from Abbey Rd for example you should be able to see the intriguing **House in the Rock**, and a 15-min walk down here brings you to St Robert's Cave, the riverside home of a 12th-c hermit. The Mother Shipton has good value food.

Knaresborough Castle All that remains are the 14th-c keep, secret medieval sally port, and a 16th-c

courthouse (now a museum) but it's easy to imagine what an imposing sight it must have made, glowering over the gorge of the River Nidd - a suitable spot to hide Thomas à Becket's murderers. Shop, limited disabled access; cl Oct-Easter; (01423) 556188; £2.50 inc a guided tour.

Mother Shipton's Cave and Well In the 19th c quite a little tourist industry was concocted for the toffs from Harrogate around the alleged 16th-c prophecies of Mother Shipton. The cave she lived in is pleasantly set in riverside parkland, along with this limestone spring, which quickly coats teddy-bears and other unlikely objects in rock; there are guided tours, and a local history museum. Snacks, shop; cl wkdys Nov-Feb, and 25 Dec; (01423) 864600; *£4.95.

LANGTHWAITE NZ0002

Idyllic Dales hamlet, with good circular walks from the nice Red Lion - and this Arkengarthdale road up to the remote but very popular Tan Hill Inn is a very fine drive.

LEYBURN SE1190

Bustling little agricultural town with a proper country atmosphere and lively market (Fri): the Sandpiper's the nicest pub, and Tennants (Harmby Rd) is Europe's largest auction room for house clearances and antiques. At the **Teapottery** (Leyburn Business Park, A684) you can see craftsmen at work on these imaginative teapots (wkdys only). Snacks, good shop, disabled access; cl 25-26 Dec and 1 Jan; (01969) 623839; free. In 2002 a new local railway company reopened a train service - the first for 50 years - from Northallerton on the main East Coast line (change at Leeming Bar, but plans for through trains); should be a big boost for the whole Wensleydale area. Off the A684 W are fine drives: up Coverdale to Kettlewell; up Bishopdale on the B6160 and on down past Cray into Wharfedale; up into the Eden Valley's Cumbrian headwaters on the B6269; and the Carperby—Castle Bolton—Reeth road.

Constable Burton Gardens 🔲 (A684 E) A series of fine terraced gardens around a handsome Georgian house (not open); the cyclamen at the end of the short lime avenue flower beautifully at the end of summer, and it's worth trying to catch their tulip festival (around May). Disabled access but no facilities; open mid-Mar to mid-Oct; (01677) 450428; £2.50. The nearby Wyvill Arms is good.

LINTON IN CRAVEN SD9962
A gem of a Dales village, with lovely stone buildings, set off by lawns running down to a duck-filled stream crossed by a delightful packhorse bridge. The busy Fountaine has enjoyable food all day.

MALHAMDALE SD9062
Perhaps the most remarkable and certainly the most visited of all Dales landscapes, cut tortuously and deeply out of the limestone by the River Aire and its steep tributaries, leaving spectacular cliffs, extensive upland stretches of bare fissured rock (so-called limestone pavements), craggy bowls carved out of the overhanging hillsides, and sparkling waterfalls. The dale is compact enough to be explored on foot, with well beaten paths linking the natural sites. Just above the village, **Malham Cove** is a great craggy cliff; the Pennine Way climbs to a famous tract of limestone pavement on its top. You can keep on through a landscape of limestone scars, disappearing streams and green turf to the lake of **Malham Tarn**. E of Malham, a level path leads along the stream to **Janet's Foss** waterfall, and to the romantic severity of dramatic **Gordale Scar**, Malhamdale's most memorable natural feature, where a stream makes a spectacular leap from the rocks.
Malham Justifiably touristy village on the Pennine Way, with a good National Park information centre and a couple of useful pubs.

MASHAM SE2280
(pronounced Mazzum) Civilised small market town, with an interesting church, and dignified Georgian houses around its broad market square - which comes to life on Weds and Sat. The Kings Head does enjoyable food.
Black Sheep Brewery (Wellgarth) Set up by a breakaway member of the Theakston family a few years back, its beers since proving very popular. The tours are fun and imaginative: best to book (no tours 25-26 Dec); (01765)

689227 - evening tours are best, with more time to enjoy samples at the end; disabled access (not on tour); £4.50. Good place for refreshments, too.
Theakston Brewery & Visitor Centre Next to the big Scottish & Newcastle brewery, this explains the brewing process behind Theakstons beer, inc their Old Peculier. Shop; cl Nov-Mar (exc tours Weds and wknds Nov and Dec), best to phone first; (01765) 684333; visitor centre £1, enthusiastic tours of the brewery £4.50.
Uredale Glass (Market Pl) Hand-made glassware, with glass-blowing demonstrations (Mon-Fri). Shop; cl 25-26 Dec and 1 Jan, best to phone for opening times in Jan; (01765) 689780; free.

MIDDLEHAM SE1287
Attractive and civilised stone-built village, largely Georgian, still with the style that came from its days as the country's top racehorse-training centre in the 18th and early 19th c. Even now there are times when it seems to have more horses than people: pick up breeding and gallops gossip in the White Swan and Black Swan, both good, on the sloping square. This is a great area for self-catering accommodation - and fine walking country.
Middleham Castle This 12th-c structure dwarfs the village. For a time it was the home of young King Richard III. Only the huge keep and some later buildings remain, but there are marvellous views from the top, and an informative exhibition centre. Snacks, shop, disabled access; cl 1-2pm and Mon and Tues Jan-Mar, 24-26 Dec, 1 Jan; (01969) 623899; £3; EH.

MUKER SD9197
Attractive Swaledale hamlet, with very good woollens shop, well liked tearooms, and decent food in the friendly Farmers Arms. Between here and Keld, the River Swale cuts through a deep valley and tumbles over waterfalls; there are paths on both sides of the river, or you can take a more upland route over neighbouring Kisdon.

NEWBY HALL SE3467
(off B6265 E of Ripon) In beautiful

formal gardens covering 10 hectares (25 acres), this late 17th-c mansion has Robert Adam interiors, an important collection of classical sculpture and Gobelins tapestries, a good range of Chippendale furniture, and masses of antique chamber pots. In the grounds are a miniature railway, children's adventure garden, paddling pool, woodland discovery walk and sculpture park. Meals, snacks, shop, some disabled access; house cl Mon (exc bank hols), and end Sept-Mar; (01423) 322583; £7.20, £5.70 garden only.

NIDDERDALE SE1073

This quiet yet beautiful valley has an impressive solitary grandeur. Just outside the National Park, it and the hills above are less liberally laced with footpaths and open-access moorland than the other dales here, and attract far fewer visitors - but there are plenty of relatively unfrequented walks, often on good paved but untarred tracks. The Nidderdale Way allows a fine fairly gentle walk of a couple of hours or so, up on to the high pastures (see lambs being born in spring) and moorland at Glasshouses and back, with spectacular views almost all the way. It's well signed; start from the good Royal Oak in Dacre Banks and take the lane a couple of hundred yards past the church. The stretch between the attractive small town of Pateley Bridge and the little village of Lofthouse is dominated by the sheltered two-mile waters of Gouthwaite Reservoir, serenely set below the hills with some tall trees alongside. From Lofthouse a path runs beside the River Nidd, with picturesque tracks among small woods and ruined farmhouses, to Scar House Reservoir, quite exposed at the valley head; high, exposed routes line the N side of the dale up here.

How Stean Gorge To the W of Lofthouse, this is a spectacular ravine pocked with pot-holes and caverns; a footpath snakes between miniature cliffs, with bridges giving views into the gorge; there's also a visitor centre and children's play area; (01423) 755666.

NORTH STAINLEY SE2876

Lightwater Valley Theme Park 🏞

Family fun from the nostalgic pleasure of a steam train to the white-knuckle, green-faced thrills of one of the world's biggest roller-coasters; another roller-coaster is entirely underground. Meals, snacks, shop, disabled access; usually open wknds and school hols (not Christmas) Easter-Oct, and daily Jun-early Sept, phone to check; (0870) 458 0040; £13.50. There's an adjacent factory shopping village (open all year), and a new **birds of prey centre**; disabled access; open with the theme park, plus wknds throughout the year, best to phone; (01765) 635010; £3.25. The Staveley Arms does decent food.

NORTON CONYERS SE3076

(3½ miles N of Ripon) The same family have lived in this late medieval house for around 380 years, and the furniture and pictures reflect the fact that it's still very much a family home. Charlotte Brontë used the building as one of her models for Thornfield Hall. Look out for the hoofprint on the stairs. Attractively planted 18th-c walled garden. Seasonal pick-your-own fruit, shop (with unusual hardy plants), limited disabled access; house open pm bank hols Sun and Mon Easter-29 Aug, pm daily 28 Jun-3 July, garden also open Thurs all year, phone to check; (01765) 640333; house £4, garden free. The Bull and Bruce Arms in West Tanfield are useful for lunch.

NUN MONKTON SE5057

This attractive village is in appearance almost more like France than Yorkshire, with its broad avenue, and the stately meeting of the rivers Nidd and Ouse.

PARCEVALL HALL SE0660

Parcevall Hall Gardens 🏞

Surrounding an Elizabethan house, 6 hectares (16 acres) of woodland gardens charmingly set on a hillside E of the main Wharfedale Valley. Superb views from the cliff walk; tearoom (usually open when garden open exc Mon, perhaps Tues too in Sept), picnic area, plant sales; cl Nov-Easter exc by appointment; (01756) 720311; £3.

RAYDALE SD9187

(nr Bainbridge) The most interesting of Wensleydale's subsidiary valleys for walkers. Its lower neck is quite narrow, but it broadens out into quite a broad sheltered bowl of valley, with Semer Water, a sizeable glacial lake which legend has it was conjured up by a wandering beggar to drown a village that had spurned him. It's Yorkshire's third-largest natural lake, and has a path along its half-mile-long S side, but to make up circular routes you have to do some road walking. The walled track (a Roman road) just N has wide-ranging views as it descends to Bainbridge.

REETH SE0399

Attractive Swaledale village with a high, wide, sloping green (the local brass band plays out here on some summer wknds); the Buck and Kings Arms are popular for lunch. The village is a centre for rambles ranging from pottering along the meadows by the Swale to walks over moors into adjacent Arkengarthdale (where the ascent on to Fremington Edge is memorable).

Hazel Brow Farm The friendly staff are what make tours of this family-run organic farm so enjoyable, and there are various sociable pets and farm animals for children to meet, as well as pedal tractors, quizzes, and different trails; cows are milked at 5pm, and Apr is the month for lambing. Snacks, shop, craft displays, disabled access (exc nature trail); cl Fri, Mon, and Oct-Mar; (01748) 886224; £4.

RIBBLESDALE SD7776

Climbing above Settle into severe and grand mountain scenery, this is craggy and remote, a strange landscape riddled with pot-holes, which you can see from some paths - inc some gaping chasms of sensational size. A friendly refuge is the Hill Inn at Chapel le Dale (good food). A major magnet for walkers is the **Three Peaks Walk**, 24 miles taking in the summits of Ingleborough, Pen-y-Ghent and Whernside. This is a tough undertaking in its entirety, but each of the peaks on its own is a manageable half-day excursion: choose a clear day - not just for the magnificent views but for your own safety. Below Settle, the valley is less interesting for walkers, and marred by some quarrying.

Ingleborough Best approached from Clapham, along the Reginald Farrer Trail, via Ingleborough Cave (see Clapham) and Gaping Gill, a vast pot-hole; from the peak (721 metres - 2,365 ft) the panorama extends far across Lancashire and into Cumbria.

Pen-y-ghent Reached from Horton in Ribblesdale, where the Crown is good value; its satisfyingly compact summit (694 metres - 2,277 ft) is the craggiest feature on the Pennine Way, which near here passes some pot-holes inc Hull Pot.

RICHMOND NZ1600

One of Britain's most satisfying small towns, on a spectacular hillside high above the Swale, with steep and pretty streets of old stone buildings, and a splendid broad sloping market square (still cobbled, and perhaps the biggest in the country; market day is Sat). Scollards Hall, built in 1080, is possibly the oldest domestic building in Britain. The very friendly **Richmondshire Museum** is worth a look, with some detailed re-creations inc the vet's surgery from the TV series *All Creatures Great and Small*. Shop, disabled access; cl Nov-Good Fri; (01748) 825611; £1.50. An attractive riverside walk beneath the towering bulk of its castle heads W through Hudswell Woods, with an extension to Whitcliffe Scar, a cliff above the Swale with an exciting path along its top. The army connection with the town is still strong; nearby Catterick Camp is the biggest in the north. The Black Lion in Finkle St is good value, as is the Coffee Bean Café (Market Pl).

Easby Abbey Extensive remains of a 12th-c Premonstratensian abbey, a pretty riverside walk SE; free; EH.

Green Howards Museum (Market Sq) In a converted 12th-c church, this includes among duller regimental history the blood-stained pistol holsters of the Grand Old Duke of York. Shop, mostly disabled access; usually cl wknds in Feb-Mar and Nov, Sun am late-May to Sept, all day Sun in Apr and Oct, and all Dec-Jan, best to check; (01748) 822133; £2.50.

Richmond Castle These austere and intricate ruins dominate the town, and overlook the River Swale from a high rocky outcrop; they've recently opened a heritage garden designed to reflect the castle's history. Shop, some disabled access; cl 24-26 Dec and 1 Jan, and perhaps in bad weather; (01748) 822493; £2.90; EH.

Theatre Royal (Victoria Rd) Recently

reopened after extensive restoration work, this is the country's oldest and most authentic working theatre still in its original form, and complete with gallery, boxes and pit. Built in 1788, it doesn't look much from the outside, but the immaculate interior is really special. New café, shop, museum and guided tours (£2.50, on the hour); cl Sun, best to phone for bank hol opening times; (01748) 823710.

RIPLEY SE2860

Ripley Castle (off A61) Beautifully picturesque, in the same family for 26 generations. Most of the current building dates from the 16th c, inc the tower housing a collection of Royalist armour. For some the main attraction is the splendid gardens, the setting for a national collection of hyacinths and (under glass) a fine tropical plant collection; also lakeside walk. Very good meals and snacks, shops inc a superb delicatessen, some disabled access; cl Sept-May (exc Tues, Thurs and wknds), and 25-26 Dec and 1 Jan; (01423) 770152; *£6, *£3.50 gardens only. The attractive village was rebuilt around a french theme in the 1820s, and consequently has a rather continental feel; the Boars Head Hotel is a fine old place for lunch.

RIPON SE3171

On Thurs colourful stalls fill the attractive and ancient market sq; it's largely unspoilt, lined with specialist shops and old inns and hotels. At 9pm each night the Wakeman, a red-coated bugler, blows a buffalo horn here, as one has done for centuries (the Wakeman's House, a 16th-c timber-framed building, stands on the corner of the square). Going from here down one of the town's engagingly narrow old streets, you're rewarded by a magnificent view of the elegant Early English W front of the cathedral. By the spectacularly tiled Victorian swimming baths, the Spa Gardens are a peaceful little retreat, with floral displays, putting, crazy golf and an ornate bandstand. A leaflet from the tourist office takes in Ripon on foot (five themed trails inc Law and Order Trail and Lewis Carroll's Ripon) and there are pleasant waterside walks along the river Skell, and from the canal basin to

the marina, where there's a short circular walk and a bird hide overlooking a flooded gravel pit. The Golden Lion just off the market sq has good value food, while Appletons on the square has legendary pork pies, haslet and home-made brawn; there are several options along Kirkgate. Fountains Abbey is within a walk from here, and Newby Hall and Norton Conyers are also quite close.

Markenfield Hall (off A61 S) This enchanting moated and fortified manor house, built in 1310 by Edward II's treasurer, is one of the oldest continuously lived in houses in England. Open around 1st fortnight in May and 2nd fortnight in Jun, phone to check; (01765) 603411; £3.

Ripon Cathedral Spectacularly floodlit at night, this is one of the largest half-dozen in the country, and has plenty to see, inc very fine carving indeed in both stone and wood, and a 7th-c crypt - probably the oldest surviving crypt outside Italy. Lewis Carroll (real name Charles Dodgson), son of a Ripon canon, wove features from the cathedral crypt and figures depicted on the misericords (inc inspirations for the Queen of Hearts and the Cheshire Cat) into *Alice in Wonderland*, *Through the Looking-Glass* and *The Hunting of the Snark*. Shop, disabled access; (01765) 603462; £3 suggested donation.

Thorpe Prebend House Walk down the steps out of the S side of the cathedral yard and you'll find this newly restored medieval canon's house that has been successively added to over the centuries. Opening officially at Easter (it had a brief trial period in Sept 2003), it houses an interpretation centre for the town and its surroundings, from the days of St Wilfrid to the house's royal connections to the war poet Wilfred Owen; it will also have Jacobean herb and knot gardens, and there are plans to build a restaurant. A human-sized White Rabbit and other figures pay homage to Lewis Carroll. Plenty of interactive displays. Shop, disabled access; best to phone for opening details; (01765) 603462; around £3.

Yorkshire Law and Order Museums A charitable trust runs the

Ripon's three law and order museums dotted around town, all within easy walking distance of each other. The largest, the **Prison and Police Museum** (St Marygate) occupies a former house of correction that was later used as a police station, and has all sorts of reminders of how things were carried out: you can turn the crank (a deliberately useless punitive exercise), experience solitary confinement in a dimly lit cell, feel the weight of a manacle, try on prison and police uniforms, see a birching stool and learn about the Sinkler brothers who had the unique distinction of being transported to Australia twice from the Courthouse in Ripon. Built in 1830, the **Courthouse Museum** (Minster Rd) itself has a tiny jurors' room plus the main court itself (where courtroom scenes in the TV series *Heartbeat* have been filmed) which was in use up to 1998; a video re-creates trials that happened here. The **Workhouse Museum** (Allhallowgate) is within what was the vagrants' wing of the workhouse (the 'deserving poor' being housed in the main part of the workhouse, now council offices), and displays evoke life taken to the lowest common denominator, inc re-creations of the meagre rations. Yet this wasn't as bleak as many other workhouses, and children at least had the benefit of some education - records show one orphan becoming a bank manager, and another a surgeon. Shops, disabled access; open Apr-Oct, pm, plus am July-Aug; between £1 and £3.50 per museum, *£5 combined tickets for all three, valid for 1 week; (01765) 690799.

SETTLE SD8163
The town has wound down a bit in recent years, with many of the old shops gone, but market day (Tues) around the Shambles is still fun; look out to the right of here for the Folly, an extraordinary 17th-c townhouse. Mary Milnthorpe & Daughter is a good antique jewellery and silver shop, Poppies tearoom provides welcome relief from shopping, and the Golden Lion has good food.
Riverside walk There's a pleasant and gentle Ribblesdale walk from Langcliffe (just N) to Stainforth Force. A short

walk W of Stainforth, a packhorse bridge crosses the river at Knight Stainforth, a particularly lovely stretch of the Ribble.
Settle—Carlisle Railway A magnificent 72-mile route carved up through Ribblesdale across the wild moors between here and Cumbria, and then dropping down through the lovely Eden Valley; (08457) 484950 for times and fares (cl 25-26 Dec), £16.40 for a day return; the most scenic stretch is from Settle to Appleby. Throughout the year on wknds and occasional Weds a programme of walks connects with the moorland stops; they start quite early, and dates and times are listed on the timetable, or take a look at their website www.settle-carlisle.org. Aside from the setting, it's an ordinary railway line. The B6479 is not quite comparable to the train, but a good drive.
SKIPTON SD9851
On Sat the High St has a colourful market (at least some stalls most other days too, exc Sun, Tues and Thurs); the bustling Red Lion here cooks with lots of local produce, and in Sheep St the 17th-c Woolly Sheep is good value. The 14th-c church has a 16th-c rood screen and interesting stained glass. A canal runs through the town.
Skipton Castle 12th-c, and properly romantic, with sturdy round towers, broad stone steps, and a lovely central flagstoned and cobbled courtyard with a seat around its 350-year-old focal yew tree. One of the best-preserved medieval castles in Europe, it really is remarkable how much is left, interior and all - very few other castles have kept their roofs and stayed habitable. The medieval arched gateway still stands - the word 'Desormais' meaning 'Henceforth' carved above it is the motto of the family who lived here 1310-1676. Meals, snacks, shop; cl Sun am, 25 Dec; (01756) 792442; £4.80. The Black Horse opposite is popular for lunch.
STAINBURN MOOR SE2452
The area E of the Dales really has nothing to compare with the Dales themselves for serious walking, but this moorland W of Harrogate has some possibilities for fairly stretching walks, for instance from the car park by the

woods along the side road W from Beckwithshaw; it gets more scenic to the W around the reservoirs of the Washburn Valley.

STARBOTTON SD9574

Tiny but delightful Wharfedale village; a good base for walks, for example along the river to Kettlewell, then back up over the high land; or follow less obvious paths W to Arncliffe in Littondale - which is very similar to the Wharfedale parent valley, though with a flatter, damper valley floor.

SWALEDALE SE0098

The northernmost of all the dales, and one of the least visited - giving more chance of getting away from it all at even peak times. Its bold hills, abundant stone barns and extreme tranquillity make it a walkers' favourite. It's grandly austere for the most part, though quite heavily wooded as it drops down towards Richmond. The steeper parts have some fine waterfalls. The upper slopes, especially towards the Durham and Cumbrian borders, are wild and empty, except for the scattered flocks of hardy clean-limbed swaledale sheep with their dark faces, grey muzzles, thick fleeces, and curly-horned rams. The meadowland down in the valleys of this dale and its broad tributary **Arkengarthdale** is largely unimproved, with slow-growing natural grasses and lots of wild flowers. Many of the area's 1,200 traditional stone hay barns which are such a distinctive feature here have been rehabilitated, with generous National Parks grant aid. **Gunnerside** still has around it many of the 'rushes' where lead-miners dammed streams to form torrents that could break up the lead-bearing rock strata below; this whole area was an important lead centre until Victorian times, and other visible mementoes are ruined mill buildings, tunnel entrances and spoil heaps.

WATH SE1467

Attractive Dales hamlet spreading up the valley, with pleasant walks along past the reservoir to Ramsgill - beyond there is a splendid moorland drive over to Masham. The Sportsmans Arms has good food.

WENSLEYDALE SD9889

More expansive in character and not quite as dramatic as Swaledale, but richly picturesque; its unspoilt villages and numerous waterfalls make for pleasurable walking. It used to be one of the richest dales, its broad pastures and countless sheep supporting the wealthy abbeys and castles whose ruins now add so much interest to its scenery. Wensleydale sheep are very distinctive, with long fleecy dreadlock curls. Upper Wensleydale (around and W of Hawes) is steep and wild; E of here the valley starts broadening out, with richer lower pastures, and more regular farmland below Middleham.

WHARFEDALE SD9769

With its tributary valley Littondale and its headwaters up in the steep conifer plantations at the top of Langstrothdale, this is one of England's most popular areas for walkers, and very beautiful indeed in parts. The Dales Way follows the River Wharfe for the length of the dale, except between Kettlewell and Grassington. Upper Wharfedale above Grassington has a level floor of sheltered well drained pastures with the river winding through, a few grey stone barns, and steep sides laced with dry-stone walls, gnarled woodland and occasional austere crags, climbing up to high fairly level tops some 365 metres (1,200 ft) above the valley floor. The smaller villages are delightfully private and unspoilt, their grey or whitewashed stonework blending perfectly with the long scars of the limestone terraces above them. Away from the valley floor, stone-walled grassy tracks are the easiest ways of gaining height.

Below Grassington is an extremely pretty stretch where the valley winds more sinuously past Burnsall, Appletreewick, and Bolton Abbey, below hills which though less grand are more varied in shape, with rather sensitively laid-out conifer plantations adding a slightly subalpine feel to some of the views.

WHERNSIDE SD7381

(736 metres - 2,415 ft) Sometimes criticised by keen walkers as the boring one of the Three Peaks, this is Yorkshire's highest point, and has an exhilarating ridge section. Start from the magnificent **Ribblehead Viaduct** which carries the Settle—Carlisle railway over the head of the dale (the Station Hotel here is a comfortable

halt). Reaching a height of 165-ft above its foundations, the viaduct crosses Batty Moss (during its construction the site of a shanty town housing over 2,000 railway workers).

WIDDALE SD8287

This steep-sided and dramatic tributary of Wensleydale has extensive conifer plantations above.

Other attragctive villages and small towns here, all with decent pubs or inns, include Aldbrough St John NZ2011, Appletreewick SE0560, Austwick SD7768, Bilbrough SE5346, Bishop Monkton SE3366, Boroughbridge SE3967, Brearton SE3261, Buckden SD9477, Burnsall SE0361, Carlton-in-Coverdale SE0684, Cray SD9379, East Witton SE1586 (ancient houses, long wide green), Gargrave SD9354 (on the Pennine Way), Gilling West NZ1804, Grantley SE2369, Gunnerside SD9598, Hampsthwaite SE2659, Horsehouse SE0481, Hudswell NZ1400, Kirkby Malham SD8961, Kirkby Overblow SE3249, Low Row SD9897 (popular with potholers), Middlesmoor SE0874, Newton-on-Ouse SE5160, Ogden SE0730, Ramsgill SE1271, Redmire SE0591, Roecliffe SE3765, Scorton NZ2500, Snape SE2784, Thornton in Lonsdale SD6873 (Conan Doyle was married in the charming church), Thornton Watlass SE2486 and Wigglesworth SD8157.

Where to eat

ASENBY SE3975 **Crab & Lobster** *Dishforth Rd (01845) 577286* Thatched dining pub with nautical-theme dining pavilion, heavily beamed L-shaped bar with lots of bric-a-brac, a relaxed, informal but civilised atmosphere, delicious highly enjoyable food, a fine wine list with plenty by the glass, well kept real ales, and an interesting garden; opulent bdrms. £33.25|£11

ASKRIGG SD9491 **Rowan Tree** *(01969) 650536* Cosy little candlelit stone barn run by irish husband and german wife, just a few tables so booking advisable, good imaginative evening meals and reasonably priced wine list; cl Mon and Tues, cl Jan-Feb; children over 12. £26

BOROUGHBRIDGE SE3966 **Black Bull** *6 St James Sq (01432) 322413* Attractive 13th-c inn with big stone fireplace and brown leather seats in main bar area (served through an old-fashioned hatch), a cosy, traditional snug, well liked interesting bar food, well kept real ales, enjoyable wines (with nine by the glass), and afternoon teas; friendly and attentive service; bdrms; disabled access. £23|**£5.95**

BREARTON SE3261 **Malt Shovel** *(01423) 862929* Popular village pub with friendly, helpful licensees, heavily beamed rooms with open fires and lively hunting prints, enjoyable bar food, well kept real ales, and a fine choice of malt whiskies and wines; no food Sun pm, cl Mon. £16|**£6.50**

CARTHORPE SE3083 **Fox & Hounds** *(01845) 567433* Pretty little extended village house with two log fires and some evocative Victorian photographs of Whitby, an attractive high-raftered, no smoking restaurant with lots of farm and smithy tools, enjoyable interesting food (fine daily specials and puddings inc yummy home-made ice-creams), decent wines, and helpful, friendly service; cl Mon, first wk Jan; disabled access. £20/2-course mid-week menu £11.95

EAST WITTON SE1486 **Blue Lion** *(01969) 624273* Stylish and civilised dining pub with log fire, daily papers, bric-a-brac and rugs on flagstones in the distinctive old rooms, exceptionally good imaginative food, nice breakfasts, a carefully chosen wine list, real ales, and pretty garden; bdrms; disabled access. £32.65|**£8.50**

ELSLACK SD9249 **Tempest Arms** *Elslack (01282) 842450* 18th-c stone pub with a lively, welcoming atmosphere and good mix of customers, especially at wknds; a series of quietly decorated areas have comfortable armchairs, cushioned built-in wall seats, and stools, and lots of tables; quite a bit of stripped stonework, nice prints on cream walls, three log fires (one in a dividing fireplace); part of the bar and all of the restaurant are no smoking; very good food from a menu used in both bar and restaurant, well kept real ales and several wines by the big or small glass. £24|**£8.25**

FERRENSBY SE3660 **General Tarleton** *Boroughbridge Rd (01423) 340284*

Smart, bustling 18th-c dining pub with beams and open fires, relaxed atmosphere, interesting food inc super puddings in bar/brasserie and more formal dining room, polite service, and plenty of wines by the glass from a good list; bdrms; cl 25 Dec; disabled access. £29.20|**£7.50**

HARROGATE SE3055 **Betty's** *1 Parliament St* (01423) 502746 Famous cake shop with special blends of teas and coffees, alsace wines, wonderful light home-cooked meals, traditional afternoon tea, over 75 different delicious cakes and pastries; they also have two tearooms in York, one in Ilkley and one in Northallerton - same details apply to each; cl 25-26 Dec, 1 Jan. £15|**£5.65**

HARROGATE SE2954 **William & Victoria** *6 Cold Bath Rd* (01423) 521510 Busy wine bar with upstairs evening restaurant and hearty helpings of decent country cooking; cl Sat am, Sun; first 3 wks Jan; disabled access. £26|**£6.95**

HETTON SD9658 **Angel** *(01756) 730263* Extremely popular and particularly well run dining pub with old-fashioned rambling rooms, consistently excellent imaginative food, very good service from hard-working friendly staff, well kept real ales, and over 300 wines; cl 2 wks Jan; children must be well behaved; disabled access. £34|**£8.50**

LANGTHWAITE NZ0002 **Charles Bathurst** *Arkengarthdale* (01748) 884567 In a lovely - if bleak - spot, with wonderful views and lots of surrounding walks, this solid-looking converted cottage has light pine tables, country chairs and benches on the stripped floors, a roaring fire, a no smoking dining room, popular, imaginative food using local ingredients, a short but interesting wine list, and well kept real ales; cl Mon-Thurs am Nov-beg Feb; pretty bdrms. £21|**£7.25**

LITTON SD9074 **Queens Arms** *(01756) 770208* Welcoming, quietly placed 17th-c inn with good popular food, big collection of cigarette lighters in main bar, another room with more of a family atmosphere, and two coal fires; cl Mon exc bank hols, Jan; pretty bdrms; disabled access. £22|**£7.95**

MASHAM SE2280 **Floodlite** *7 Silver St* (01765) 689000 Bustling little candlelit restaurant with lots of bric-a-brac, particularly good sound cooking using top local ingredients with emphasis on fish and game, lovely puddings, and a sizeable fairly priced wine list; cl Mon, am Tues-Thurs. £23/2-course lunch £12.50

MOULTON NZ2303 **Black Bull** *(01325) 377289* Decidedly civilised, well run pub with old-fashioned style and standards of service, memorable bar snacks (excellent smoked salmon), imaginative meals in conservatory restaurant or in the Brighton Belle Pullman dining car, and good wines; cl Sun, 24-26 Dec; children over 7; disabled access. £30|**£5.95**

PICKHILL SE3483 **Nags Head** *(01845) 567391* Deservedly popular old inn run for 30 years by two brothers, with a nice mix of customers, busy tap room, smarter lounge, no smoking restaurant, particularly good food inc interesting daily specials and lovely puddings, friendly efficient staff, a fine wine list and well kept real ales; bdrms; disabled access. £25|**£7.95**

North York Moors & East Yorkshire

Plenty of nicely varied outings, plus wild open countryside and interesting coastline

The North York Moors National Park is less visited than the Dales, but gives walkers (and drivers) broad and inspiring landscapes. Its valleys have rich pastures, with red-tiled stone farmhouses, twisting rivers, quiet roads, and few villages. The higher moorland is generally very grand and empty, mile after mile of heather scoured by breath-snatching winds, where the few walkers have for company scatterings of hardy sheep and the occasional harsh cry of a grouse. The North Yorkshire Moors Railway passes through wonderful countryside.

Genteel Scarborough has plenty for families in summer, and the cliffy coast N has lots of character, with some delightful little fishing villages. The traditional seaside town of Bridlington is attractive, and there are excellent bird-watching opportunities at Bempton Cliffs and Flamborough Head, just N. Steep Whitby, with its dramatic abbey, is a working fishing port with plenty of interest, and the shoreline of picturesque Robin Hood's Bay is great for fossil hunting. Hull, increasingly worth a visit, has some fascinating free museums, as well as an excellent marine centre, The Deep. Inland, Helmsley and Beverley are attractive little towns. Middlesbrough, nicely cleaned up these days, has quite a lot to interest all ages in and around it; like other places in this northern part, it makes the most of its Captain Cook connections.

Awesome Castle Howard, the charming Elizabethan houses at Burton Agnes and Sproatley, and Sledmere House are treats if you appreciate magnificent houses, and Nunnington Hall has an unusual collection of miniature rooms. On a more modest scale, in Coxwold you can see Laurence Sterne's Shandy Hall (nearby Newburgh Priory is worth stopping at too). Duncombe Park in Helmsley and Sutton Park in Sutton-on-the-Forest have lovely grounds. The area is also spread with haunting ruins - Rievaulx Abbey is the most dramatic.

The re-created World War II scenes at Eden Camp just outside Malton are superb for parents and their children - it's the top Yorkshire Family Attraction this year. Fort Paull (fun to explore) has a good range of special events, and for more military history head for Beverley and Elvington. Cruckley Farm in Foston on the Wolds, Staintondale's Shire Horse Farm and the developing centre at East Ayton are worth bearing in mind for uncomplicated family afternoons. Elsewhere, there's a mining museum at Skinningrove, and an engaging folk museum at Hutton-le-Hole.

Where to stay

AMPLEFORTH SE5678 **Carr House Farm** *West End, Ampleforth, North Yorksire YO62 4ED* (01347) 868526 **£45***; 3 rms. In peaceful undulating farmland and with an acre of garden, this no smoking 16th-c stone farmhouse has beams and oak panelling, a flagstoned dining room with an inglenook, and separate lounge; good breakfasts using home-made preserves, local bacon, and fresh farm eggs; aromatherapy, beauty treatments, and massage available; children over 7

BLAKEY RIDGE SE6799 **Lion** *High Blakey, Kirkbymoorside, North Yorkshire YO62 7LQ* (01751) 417320 **£58***, plus winter breaks; 10 good rms, most with own bthrm. The fourth-highest inn in England, this has spectacular moorland views, rambling beamed stripped stone bars, blazing fires, generous helpings of decent food served all day, good breakfasts, candlelit restaurant, quite a few real ales, and genuinely friendly licensees and staff; monthly live music nights; fine walking country; disabled access; dogs welcome in bedrooms

EGTON BRIDGE NZ8004 **Horse Shoe** *Egton Bridge, Whitby, North Yorkshire YO21 1XE* (01947) 895245 **£55***, plus special breaks; 6 simple rms, 3 with own bthrm. Beautifully placed inn by River Esk (stepping stones big enough for children to sit on), with lots of friendly wild birds and a pleasant sheltered lawn; open fires, attractive traditionally furnished bars, well cooked food inc excellent breakfasts in cottagey dining room, and decent wines; no accommodation 25 Dec; dogs in bar only

FLAMBOROUGH TA2270 **Manor House** *Tower St, Flamborough, Bridlington, East Yorkshire YO15 1PD* (01262) 850943 **£70***; 2 rms, the more expensive one has a 17th-c four-poster. Beautifully restored Georgian house with log fire and books in the sitting room, lots of antiques (Mrs Berry is a dealer), good breakfasts, and a friendly atmosphere; the old stable block has antiques and intricate local hand-knitted fishermen's sweaters called ganseys for sale; cl Christmas; children over 8

HAROME SE6481 **Pheasant** *Mill St, Harome, Helmsley, North Yorkshire YO62 5JG* (01439) 771241 **£94***, plus special breaks; 12 rms. Family-run hotel with a relaxed homely lounge, and traditional bar with beams, inglenook fireplace and flagstones, good very popular food using their own eggs, vegetables and fruit, efficient service, and indoor heated swimming pool; cl Dec-Feb; children over 7; disabled access; dogs welcome in bedrooms

HAWNBY SE5690 **Laskill Grange** *Easterside, Helmsley, York YO62 5NB* (01439) 798268 **£62***, plus special breaks; 6 rms, some in beamy converted outside building. Attractive and welcoming creeper-covered stone house on big sheep and cattle farm near Rievaulx Abbey; open fire, antiques and books in comfortable lounge, conservatory overlooking the garden, good food using home-grown produce, and own natural spring water; self-catering also, with a play area; cl 25 Dec; partial disabled access; dogs welcome

HELMSLEY SE6183 **Black Swan** *Market Pl, Helmsley, North Yorkshire YO62 5BJ* (01439) 770466 **£134**, plus special breaks; 45 well equipped and comfortable rms. Striking Georgian house and adjoining Tudor rectory with beamed and panelled hotel bar, attractive carved oak settles and Windsor armchairs, cosy and comfortable lounges with lots of character, and a charming sheltered garden; dogs welcome in bedrooms

KILBURN SE5179 **Forresters Arms** *Kilburn, North Yorkshire YO61 4AH* (01347) 868386 **£64***, plus special breaks; 10 clean, bright rms. Friendly old coaching inn opposite the pretty village gardens; sturdy but elegant furnishings made next door at Thompson mouse furniture workshop, big log fire in cosy lower bar, interesting Henry Dee bar in what was a stable with manger and stalls still visible, and enjoyable food in restaurant and beamed bar; cl 25 Dec; disabled access; dogs welcome away from dining room

MIDDLETON SE7887 **Cottage Leas Country Hotel** *Nova Lane, Middleton, Pickering, North Yorkshire YO18 8PN* (01751) 472129 **£83***, plus special breaks; 12 comfortable rms. Delightful, peaceful 18th-c farmhouse with extensive gardens, informal rooms, beamed ceilings, open log fire in cosy lounge, a well stocked bar, and enjoyable creative food; partial disabled access; dogs welcome

SCARBOROUGH TA0091 **Wrea Head Hotel** *Scalby, Scarborough, North Yorkshire YO13 0PB* (01723) 378211 **£120***, plus special breaks; 20 individually decorated rms inc 2 luxury four-poster rms. Victorian country house in 14 acres of parkland and gardens; friendly staff, minstrels' gallery in oak-panelled hall and lounge, open fires, a bow-windowed library, pretty flowers, and good food in airy restaurant

THORNTON LE DALE SE8783 **Allerston Manor House** *Thornton le Dale, North Yorkshire YO18 7PF* (01723) 850112 *(off A170 E)* **£90***, plus special breaks; 3 well equipped rms. Built around a 14th-c Knights Templar Hall, this Queen Anne house overlooks Allerston church and is on the edge of the National Park; comfortable and spacious drawing room, enjoyable dinners using local produce eaten around one big table (bring your own wine), and good breakfasts using eggs from their own hens; children over 12

WASS SE5579 **Wombwell Arms** *Wass, North Yorkshire YO61 4BE* (01347) 868280 **£62***, plus winter breaks; 3 individually furnished rms. Attractive, warmly welcoming small inn with a spotless central bar, three low-beamed comfortable dining areas (one restaurant is no smoking), good imaginative food, enjoyable breakfasts, well kept real ales, and decent wines; cl Mon and Sun pm during Jan-Mar;

dogs welcome in bedrooms

WILLERBY TA0230 **Willerby Manor** *Well Lane, Willerby, Hull, East Yorkshire HU10 6ER (01482) 652616* **£74**w; 51 individually decorated rms. Originally the home of an Edwardian shipping merchant, this carefully extended hotel is surrounded by three acres of gardens; airy and attractive conservatory, dining bar and more formal restaurant, good food, helpful service, and health club with swimming pool

To see and do

Yorkshire Family Attraction of the Year

MALTON SE7973 **Eden Camp** (A64/A169 N) Hugely informative, great value, and good fun too, this popular place brings wartime Britain vividly to life. It's been created around a former prisoner of war camp, with each of the huts taking a different theme, from the rise of the Nazis, to the Blitz, and the role of women in wartime. Though there are some traditional displays, the emphasis is very much on re-creating a more tangible impression of life during World War II, with sights, sounds and smells: there's a bombed-out street, reconstructed period shops, and Bomber Command ops rooms. It's been very well put together, and though some parts work better than others, the overall effect is excellent - you can't help absorbing masses of fascinating detail, particularly about the everyday activities of the time, from what was on the radio to what you'd eat or buy in the shops. It's surprisingly engaging for children, for whom the highlight is usually the inspired Music Hall: a 20-minute show includes most of the well known wartime songs, but there's a twist - all the performers are puppets. There's an assault course too, with a section for younger children. It takes at least three hours to take it all in, and much longer if you're especially interested in the subject; one hut has all the front pages of the war, while six others take a chronological overview of its politics and events. There's a look at other wars too, including a re-created trench from World War I, and displays on conflicts since 1945. Outside are quite a few wartime and military vehicles, but most displays are under cover, so it's ideal in any weather. During the week in term-time you'll find it's very much on the school trips circuit; if that bothers you, most have usually gone by mid-afternoon. Dogs are welcome on a lead (except in café). Meals and snacks in NAAFI, picnic areas, shop, disabled access; cl 24 Dec to mid-Jan; (01653) 697777; £4 adults, £3 children. No credit or debit cards.

BECK HOLE NZ8202
Charming tucked-away village; Birch Hall here is a unique cross between country tavern and village store. The most rewarding way to get here is walking along the historic rail trail along the abandoned line that preceded the current North Yorkshire Moors Railway route, between Grosmont and Goathland.

BEMPTON TA1973
Bempton Cliffs The RSPB bird reserve here has the biggest colony of seabirds in the country, with up to a quarter of a million of them nesting in the cliffs. Best views of puffins Jun-July, but plenty of skuas and shearwaters later in summer, with wknd boat trips from Flamborough (North Landing) or Bridlington, though what you'll see depends on the weather. Snacks, shop, some disabled access; visitor centre cl all Jan, wkdys Dec and Feb; (01262) 851179 - book well ahead for the boats; £3 car parking charge, RSPB members free.

BEVERLEY TA0339
Attractive country town, in a way like a small-scale York, with much the same sort of appeal. It's partly pedestrianised, with many fine Georgian buildings, several antiques shops and the like, but

unlike York is still very much an honest market town rather than a tourist place. There's a market on Sat (and a little one on Weds), and the racecourse is central to local life. The Corner House (Norwood) has good food. The B1248 N gives rolling Wolds views.

Art Gallery & Museum (Champney Rd) Includes lots of pieces by Fred Elwell the woodcarver, famous for his paintings of the town and its characters. Cl 12.30-1.30pm wknds, all Mon and Tues, and a wk over Christmas; (01482) 392780; free.

Beverley Minster Wonderful 13th/14th-c building, considered by some to be one of the most architecturally interesting in Europe, with elegant buttressing and elaborately pinnacled towers. The W front is richly carved yet extraordinarily harmonious. Inside are several delights, inc the intricately carved Percy tomb canopy, the unusual Saxon *fridstol* (one of only two such seats in the country), and the biggest collection of misericords in Britain. Shop, disabled access; open daily exc 25 Dec and during weddings and funerals, guided tours in summer and by appointment in winter; (01482) 868540; £2 suggested donation.

Museum of Army Transport (Flemingate) Huge hangar with all sorts of military vehicles inc Blackburn Beverley aircraft, tanks and cars, many displayed in realistic settings from World War II farm-building camouflage to desert scenes; there's also a junior assault course. Snacks, shop, disabled access; cl 24 Dec-2 Jan; (01482) 860445; £4.50.

St Mary's church (Hengate) The former wealth of the town can be guessed at from the magnificence of another subsidiary church not far from the Minster (and originally intended to be a chapel for that marvellous building); the weather-vane on the SW turret is said to have been the last design by Pugin, who sketched it on the back of an envelope. Opposite is the White Horse, a quaint old gaslit bare-boarded tavern.

BLACKTOFT SE8424
Attractive Humber-side village; its pub the Hope & Anchor, with tables out by the waterside, is great for bird-watchers,

right by the RSPB marsh reserve.

BOLTON PERCY SE5341
Behind its medieval gatehouse the 15th-c church has perhaps the most unusual **churchyard** in the country: local lecturer Roger Brook has transformed it into a splendidly colourful garden, with more than a thousand different types of plant creeping around and over the head-stones. Rather like a semi-wild cottage garden, it houses part of the national collection of dicentras and is open all the time. The Crown has generous simple food (not Mon or Tues).

BRIDLINGTON TA1767
Famous for its bracing image in the heyday of the traditional seaside resort, and the way the scenery rolls down to the long sands of the shore still gives that feeling. The centre is a quay and small harbour, with the usual summer attractions, but the original core of the town is half a mile in from the sea, with some charming old houses among the more modern ones around the heavily restored priory church. A 14th-c gateway (the Baylegate) gives some idea of how imposing the priory must have been before the Dissolution. The cheerfully nautical Hook & Parrot (Esplanade) has decent lunchtime food. The coast to the S is generally much flatter.

Bondville Model Village (Riviera Dr, Sewerby) Readers enjoy this; snacks, shop, disabled access; cl Oct-Easter; (01262) 401736; £2.50. A walk along the low cliff from here towards Flamborough Head soon brings you to a strip of woodland by a stream; if you follow the lane up from here past the car park and along the wood, you come to Iron Age earthworks which cut right across the head - making it a pretty impressive defensive position.

John Bull's World of Rock (Carnaby Industrial Estate, off A614 SW) See how they squeeze the words into the candy, and perhaps even personalise your own stick of the seaside favourite. Open Easter-Sept; (01262) 678525; £1.50 factory and exhibition.

Park Rose Pottery (Carnaby Covert Lane, off A614 SW) Factory visits and a seconds shop, as well as 12 acres of strollable parkland with play areas; an owl and bird of prey sanctuary and bee exhibition is usually open Easter-Oct (best to check; (01262) 606800; £1.75). Meals, snacks, shop, disabled access; cl 25-26 Dec; (01262) 602823; site entry free.

Sewerby Hall (NE edge) In spacious parkland right on the coast, with a miniature zoo and aviary (good for children), and a charming garden. The elegant early 18th-c house includes some Amy Johnson memorabilia - the pioneer aviator lived nearby. A little land train links the gardens with central Bridlington in summer. Snacks, shop, disabled access (but not to the hall); grounds open daily all year, house usually cl Oct-Easter; (01262) 673769; £3.10 (free when house closed).

BUGTHORPE SE7757
Attractive village, especially in spring, with an interesting church; the Fleece at nearby Bishop Wilton is a good value dining pub.

BURTON AGNES TA1063
Richly decorated Elizabethan house, with fantastically carved Great Hall, 16th-c antiques, and some splendid Impressionist paintings. A fine walled garden has colourful borders, there's a pets corner and topiary bushes. Meals, snacks, shop, disabled access to gardens and ground floor only; cl Nov-end Mar; (01262) 490324; £5.20. The earlier Norman manor house stands between here and the church. The attractive church at nearby Kilham has a Norman door; the 18th-c Bell in Driffield is pleasant for lunch.

BYLAND ABBEY SE5478
The jagged ruins of this abbey, built by the Cistercians, date from the 12th c. Enough detail survives to show how fine it must have been: look out for the well preserved floor tiles and carved stone. Good for picnics. Shop, disabled access; cl Tues-Weds (exc July-Aug), and all Nov-Mar; (01347) 868614; £2; EH. The nearby Abbey Inn is most enjoyable for lunch. The drive past here from Bagby (SE of Thirsk), Kilburn and Coxwold, and on via Wass and Ampleforth to Oswaldkirk, is very attractive.

CASTLE HOWARD SE7170
(off A64 W of Malton) Magnificent 18th-c palace designed by Sir John Vanbrugh, who up to then had no architectural experience whatsoever, but went on to create Blenheim Palace. The striking 90-metre (300-ft) long façade is topped with a marvellous painted and gilded dome, an unforgettable sight beyond the lake as you approach from the N. Splendid apartments, sculpture gallery and long gallery (58 metres, 192 ft, long to be exact), magnificent chapel with stained glass by Burne-Jones, and beautiful paintings inc a Holbein portrait of Henry VIII. The grounds are impressive but inviting, inc the domed Temple of the Four Winds by Vanbrugh, a beautiful rose garden with over 2,000 roses, a notable woodland garden, and the family mausoleum designed by Hawksmoor. There's a good unobtrusive adventure playground. Meals, snacks, shop, disabled access; cl Nov to mid-Feb; (01653) 648333; £9. A grand public road runs through the grounds, from Slingsby on the B1257; the vast estate is also threaded by a few public footpaths which gain glimpses of the great house and the landscaped parts of its grounds. The Bay Horse at nearby Terrington has good food.

CLEVELAND WAY NZ8215
One of the best ways of encountering the North York Moors is by this well marked long-distance path, which takes a 110-mile horseshoe course from Helmsley to Filey Brigg around the moorland escarpments of the Hambledon and Cleveland hills, before a coastal finale along the highest cliffs on the eastern seaboard. Highlights include Sutton Bank, Roseberry Topping and the coast around Staithes, Robin Hood's Bay, Ravenscar and Hayburn Wyke; a particularly fine section can be reached off the B1257 N of Chop Gate NZ5703 (where the Buck does good food). The path westwards on the N slopes of the moors takes in rock outcrops. The frequent bus service between Scarborough and Whitby is useful for getting you back if you're walking shorter coastal sections; phone for bus times; (01947) 602146.

COXWOLD SE5377
Neat and very appealing little stone-built village, very harmonious; the attractive pub is open all day in summer. **Newburgh Priory** (just S) Charming

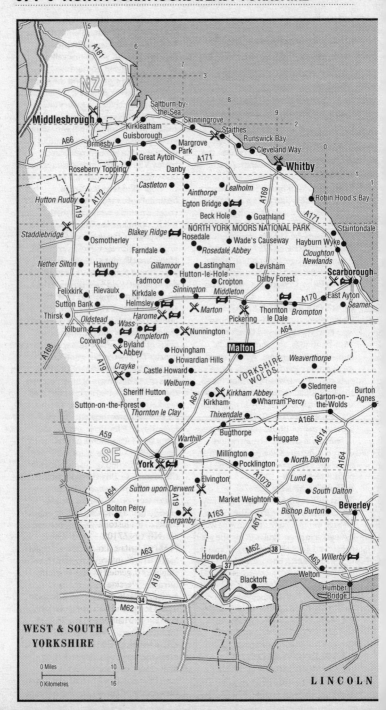

NZ

A181

5

6

7

3

Saltburn-by-
the-Sea

8

9

2

0

1

1

Middlesbrough

Kirkleatham

Skinningrove

Staithes

Runswick Bay

Guisborough

Ormesby

A66

Margrove
Park

Cleveland Way

Great Ayton

A171

Whitby

Roseberry Topping

Danby

Robin Hood's Bay

A169

A171

Castleton

Lealholm

Hutton Rudby

A172

Ainthorpe

Egton Bridge

Staintondale

A19

Beck Hole

Goathland

Staddlebridge

Blakey Ridge

Rosedale

NORTH YORK MOORS NATIONAL PARK

Wade's Causeway

Hayburn Wyke

Osmotherley

Rosedale Abbey

Cloughton
Newlands

Nether Silton

Farndale

Hawnby

Gillamoor

Lastingham

Levisham

Scarborough

Fadmoor

Hutton-le-Hole

Dalby Forest

Felixkirk

Rievaulx

Kirkdale

Cropton

Middleton

A170

East Ayton

Sutton Bank

Helmsley

Sinnington

Seamer

Thirsk

Harome

Marton

Thornton
le Dale

Brompton

Oldstead

Wass

Pickering

Kilburn

A168

Coxwold

Byland
Abbey

Ampleforth

Nunnington

A64

A19

Hovingham

Crayke

Howardian Hills

YORKSHIRE
WOLDS

Weaverthorpe

Castle Howard

Welburn

Sheriff Hutton

A64

Kirkham Abbey

Sledmere

Burton
Agnes

Sutton-on-the-Forest

Kirkham

Garton-on-
the-Wolds

Thornton le Clay

Wharram Percy

Thixendale

A166

A59

Bugthorpe

Huggate

A614

Warthill

Millington

A164

SE

York

Pocklington

North Dalton

Elvington

Lund

A1079

Sutton upon Derwent

South Dalton

Bolton Percy

Market Weighton

Beverley

Thorganby

A163

Bishop Burton

A63

A614

M62

38

A63

Willerby

Howden

37

Welton

A19

Blacktoft

Humber
Bridge

34

M62

**WEST & SOUTH
YORKSHIRE**

0 Miles   10

0 Kilometres   16

LINCOLN

Malton

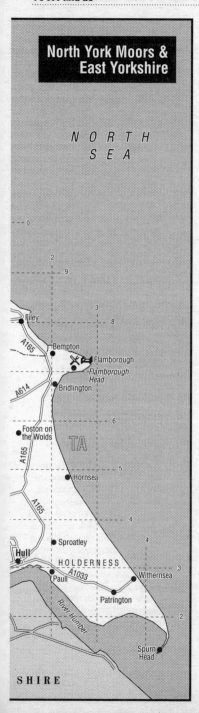

North York Moors & East Yorkshire

NORTH SEA

Filey

Bempton

Flamborough

Flamborough Head

Bridlington

Foston on the Wolds

TA

Hornsea

Sproatley

Hull

HOLDERNESS

Paull

Withernsea

Patrington

River Humber

Spurn Head

SHIRE

old house, partly Norman with Tudor and Georgian additions. One of the family married Oliver Cromwell's daughter, who is supposed to have rescued her father's headless corpse and had it reburied here; the room with the tomb is on the tour. The 40-acres of grounds inc a lake, water gardens and walled gardens. Snacks; open pms Weds and Sun Apr-Jun and perhaps bank hols, best to check; (01347) 868435; *£5 inc guided tour, *£2.50 grounds only.

Shandy Hall Laurence Sterne's quaint house has been well restored, the little study much as it must have been when he wrote the closing parts of *Tristram Shandy* here. This, his second living, was given to him by a local landowner after publication of the first two volumes. Outside is a lovely walled garden. Shop with unusual plant sales; open May-Sept, house pm Weds and Sun, gardens daily exc Sat; (01347) 868465; £4.50, £2.50 garden only. Close by is the attractive 15th-c church of which Sterne was parson - it still has the box pews it had in his day.

CROPTON SE7588

Cropton Brewery The small family-run brewery has guided tours (best to phone for times), and samples of their robustly flavoured beers, and the adjacent New Inn is good; shop; (01751) 417330; £2.95.

DALBY FOREST SE8789

The E part of the North York Moors National Park has large forest plantations; this area has colour-coded trails. Varied walking is to be had by taking in the moorland to the W (extending to the car park on A170 S of Saltergate Inn) and the mushroom-like rocks of Bridestones nature reserve.

DANBY NZ7108

Moors Centre (Lodge Lane) Helpful National Park information centre, with exhibitions, guided walks and events; terraced riverside and woodland grounds. Meals, snacks, shop, disabled access to ground floor only; cl wkdys Jan-Feb (exc Feb half-term), and 25 Dec (reduced hours in winter); (01439) 772737; free, £1.50 charge for car park. This area has decent **horse riding centres**, good for experts and beginners alike; the Moors Centre has the full list, and can also provide numbers for the various cycle hire firms dotted about the region. The Fox & Hounds at Ainthorpe has good fresh food.

EAST AYTON SE9985

Betton Farm and Visitor Centre
Exhaustive exhibition on bees and honey-making, with sales of wax and honey-based products; also craft shops, play area. Tearoom, bakery, farm shop, some disabled access; cl 25-26 Dec; (01723) 865198; £2.95. There`s also a children's farm on the same site (usually open same times as Betton Farm; (01723) 863143; £1), as well as a birds of prey centre (usually open daily Easter-Sept; (01723) 865116; £3). The Cayley Arms in the pretty village of Brompton has good food, and the Forge Valley drive to Hackness runs through ancient woodlands.

EGTON BRIDGE NZ8005
Charming Eskdale village, pleasantly eccentric, with lovely Esk views; the riverside Horse Shoe is good.

ELVINGTON SE6748

Yorkshire Air Museum Part of a World War II airfield and base preserved as it was then, with fine aircraft, a restored control tower and plenty of other memorabilia inc engines, models, photographs; there's also an air gunners museum, and replicas of the Wright Flyer and Cayley Gliders; special events. Meals, snacks, shop, disabled access; cl 25-26 Dec; (01904) 608595; £5. The St Vincent Arms at Sutton upon Derwent is good for lunch.

FADMOOR SE6789
Attractive village on charming drive from Kirkbymoorside, on over Rudland Slack and past Cockayne to Helmsley. The Plough has good food.

FARNDALE SE6697
The largest dale in the National Park, with characteristic North York Moors scenery - lush green fields and red-roofed yellow-stone houses beneath the brooding moorland plateau. It's famous for its miles of wild daffodils in Apr, introduced and naturalised here many centuries ago; worries that they may be declining have prompted an ambitious new research and conservation partnership between local farmers and the National Park's ecology department. They're at their best around Low Mill, and any walk to enjoy them gives the chance of coming back down the ancient green lane of Rudland Rigg, for spectacular views. The friendly Feversham Arms at Church Houses, right next to the daffodil reserve, does good value food.

FELIXKIRK SE4684
Attractive village, with prettily floodlit church and good drive to Kepwith and Nether Silton; the Carpenters Arms is a good dining pub.

FILEY TA1180
Much quieter resort than Scarborough, its neighbour up the coast, with the main road dropping down a steep little valley between the church and the old town (and under a footbridge linking the two) to the beach, where fishermen still beach their boats. A park-and-ride operates in the summer. Filey Brigg, the rocky headland N of the town beyond the sands, marks the end of the Cleveland Way; to the S are holiday camps, and the seafront Coble Landing Bar has decent food and great views.

Filey Museum 🖼 (Queen St) Small and attractively homely local museum in former medieval fishermen's cottages. Shop, disabled access to ground floor and garden (video of the upper floor), and good facilities for the blind; cl am Sat, and all Nov-Mar; (01723) 515013; £2.

FLAMBOROUGH TA2270
A blowy place high on the headland, with some old houses in the core around the 15th-c church, and interesting for the nearby cliff scenery. Down below past the holiday camp the natural rock harbour is well sheltered, with a lifeboat station, and there are fine views of coast and sea from the point of the headland, by the lighthouse. You may be able to buy a local version of guernseys, weatherproof 'ganseys', hand-knitted in the round. The Seabirds is good for lunch, and the B1259 and B1229 are the most interesting coast roads. There is some quite exciting walking, particularly around the N side of Flamborough Head, with the cacophony of thousands of kittiwakes sounding within the inlets; puffins can sometimes be seen on rock ledges. A level mile and a half from the lighthouse along clifftops leads to North Landing (café and car park). A longer walk

making the Head the midway point starts from the village, skirting fields to join the coast path; to avoid anticlimax, walk the southern cliffs first and keep the real drama for later on. To the N the path follows the coast closely nearly all the way, and hilly country coming right to the coast adds interest.

FOSTON ON THE WOLDS TA0855

Cruckley Farm Friendly working farm, with lots of animals to fuss over - inc some very strange-looking rare breeds. Daily milking displays (usually around 10.45am). Snacks, shop, some disabled access; cl Oct to mid-Apr; (01262) 488337; £3.50. The Trout at Wansford has decent food.

GARTON-ON-THE-WOLDS SE9859

12th-c **church**, very High Church inside, with 19th-c mosaics and frescoes.

GOATHLAND NZ8301

In the heart of the moors, this is the picturesque setting for TV's *Heartbeat* (beware coachloads of fans). There are interesting walks from here, inc the short one from opposite the church to **Mallyan Spout**, a lovely waterfall which tumbles into the side of a fine wooded smooth-rocked gorge. The rambling Inn on the Moor (Mill Green Way) does good meals.

GREAT AYTON NZ5610

Captain Cook Schoolroom Museum 🏛 (High St) In two rooms of the Postgate School (built in 1704) where James Cook got his early education, it features a reconstruction of an early 18th-c school, and interactive displays about the explorer's early life and later achievements. Shop, disabled access; cl am (exc July-Aug), and all Nov-Mar exc by appointment; (01642) 722208; £2. The Royal Oak overlooking the elegant village green has good food.

GUISBOROUGH NZ6116

Gisborough Priory 12th-c ruined priory, one huge window rising dramatically from the rest of the more or less foundation-level ruins. The gatehouse is fairly well preserved, and it's a charming spot for a picnic. Shop; cl Mon (plus Tues Oct-Mar), phone for opening times over Christmas; (01287) 633801; £1.15; EH. The Fox nearby has

decent food, and the market town is attractive.

HAWNBY SE5489

Attractive village, on the very scenic Rievaulx Abbey—Osmotherley rd; the Hawnby Hotel is well set for walkers.

HAYBURN WYKE TA0096

From the Hayburn Wyke Hotel (a lively pub with popular food) steep Victorian woodland paths wind down to the cliff-sheltered cove; a clifftop path to the S gives fine views.

HELMSLEY SE6184

Lanes run straight up on to the moors from this attractive neatly kept small market town (the B1257 is one of the best moorland roads). There's a large cobbled square (busy Fri market), and enough antiques and craft shops (craft fair most wknds) to please a visitor without seeming too touristy. A lively and bustling place, with a lot of class. The Royal Oak (open all day) does substantial food. A rewarding and very varied drive is past Rievaulx Abbey, Old Byland and Cold Kirby to Sutton Bank, left along the A170 then next right turn to Kilburn, Coxwold, Byland Abbey and back via Ampleforth and Oswaldkirk.

Duncombe Park 🏛 Beautifully restored early 18th-c house, rebuilt after a fire a hundred years ago. The landscaped gardens, with grand terracing, are magnificent, covering around a tenth of the 300 acres of memorable parkland. Meals, snacks, shop, some disabled access; cl Fri-Sat, and end Oct to Easter; (01439) 770213; £6, £3 gardens only. You can wander through the estate, run as a nature reserve, for £2.

Helmsley Castle This 12th-c pile, ruined in 1644, stands within enormous earthworks and dominates the town; good for picnics. Shop; cl 1-2 pm, Mon and Tues Oct-Mar, 24-26 Dec; (01439) 770442; £2.60; EH.

Helmsley Walled Garden 🏛 With a good variety of clematis and roses and a restored Victorian orchid house, this friendly place is continuing restoration started 10-years ago. Dating from 1756, it has an excellent choice of plants for sale, and a good café. Disabled access; cl Nov-Mar; (01439) 771427; £3.

HOLDERNESS TA3029

The area between Wolds, Humber and

coast is flat: rich farming country with huge fields and not many buildings, though the fine village churches often with soaring towers or spires reflect the wealth that this fertile land has put into them in the past. The long southern stretch of fast-eroding coast is flat country too, without a great deal of appeal for walkers - except for long lonely off-season walks above the crumbling cliffs.

HORNSEA TA2145
Sizeable resort; behind the town, Hornsea Mere, 2 miles long, is the biggest natural lake in this region, with herons and other birds.
Hornsea Freeport (Rolston Rd) One of the area's most visited attractions, a leisure centre based around a factory shopping village. Lots of well known brands and stores (some good bargains), and family features such as butterflies (£1), model village (£1), crazy golf (£1), and indoor and outdoor adventure playgrounds (from £1). Meals, snacks, shop, disabled access; attractions cl Nov-Easter, shops cl 25-26 Dec; (01964) 534211; site free.
Hornsea Museum (Newbegin) Enthusiastic folk museum with re-created period rooms, craft demonstrations and large gardens. Shop, mostly disabled access; cl Mon (exc bank hols), Sun am, and Oct-Easter; (01964) 533443; £2.

HOVINGHAM SE6675
Attractive estate village, with wonderfully conserved buildings, pretty gardens, and a pleasant drive S to Sheriff Hutton and Flaxton. The Malt Shovel has good value food.

HOWARDIAN HILLS SE6575
These gentle generously wooded hills have a path followed by the Ebor Way along their N flanks, giving intermittent views across the plain to the North York Moors.

HOWDEN SE7428
Unpretentiously attractive, with cobbled alleys, a fine market hall, a majestic **minster** with a tall tower, the ruins of a charming medieval chapter house, and a small marshland country park down the lane opposite the minster, with ponds and raised walkways. The White Horse is useful for lunch.

HUGGATE SE8855
Attractive Wolds village, with easy walks nearby; the Wolds Inn, with nice bedrooms, has good food.

HULL TA1028
Kingston-upon-Hull is the full name of this big port, surprisingly pleasant for visitors now that the former docks have been so well tidied up. In the centre there's little sign of the decay and serious local government problems which afflicted it in recent years, though parts have a strange but oddly intriguing mix of estuary views, abandoned warehouses awaiting trendification, spaces which seem to have been empty since World War II bombing, and cobbled streets partly inlaid with fragmentary tramlines. On the waterfront a developing esplanade lets you walk for miles along the Humber, though much is still rather desolate: one attractive enclave is the landing stage for the former Humber ferry, with some solid well restored Georgian buildings, an amazing Victorian public lavatory, and Humber views from the waterfront Minerva (which brews its own beer). Nearby, the original dock has become a vast and thriving yacht marina, with cheerfully buoyant modern buildings around it. Princes Quay is now a smart shopping centre (with good value food in the Mission, a converted seamen's mission over in Posterngate). Trunk roads to the modern container and ferry port separate this waterfront from the old town. In Ferensway, in the centre, a £10m building project is now under way to redevelop the bus and train stations, and a big new retail and leisure centre is due for completion around the end of 2005. A core of ancient buildings has survived in the narrow streets around the old town's High St (where the good free museums are concentrated), notably around Holy Trinity church, cobbled Prince St, colourful Victorian Trinity Market and the adjoining arcade which leads to Silver St. A delightful old building nearby is the Olde Whyte Harte; it was in its heavily panelled upper room that the decision was made to lock the town's gate against King Charles in 1642, depriving him of the arsenal that might otherwise have

swung the Civil War in his favour. Old warehouses and shops are turning into trendy new bars, restaurants and loft-style flats, and there's a growing clubbing scene. A free copy of the city's ale trail (a self-guided tour around the best pubs) is available from the tourist information centre in Paragon St, and there's a fish trail for children (40p), with witty pavement brass rubbings and a certificate at the end.

Ferens Art Gallery Enterprisingly run general collection, with lots of maritime paintings, dutch Old Masters, and a good 20th-c british section (inc works by Stanley Spencer and Wyndham Lewis). There's also an interactive children's gallery. Snacks, shop, disabled access; cl Sun am, 24-26, 31 Dec and 1 Jan; (01482) 613902; free.

Hands-on History (South Church Side) In Hull's oldest secular building, originally a school dating from 1583, this has an expanding social history collection; also displays on the Victorians and the Egyptians. Shop, disabled access; cl am Sun, 24-26 Dec and 31 Dec-1 Jan; (01482) 613902; free.

Hull & East Riding Museum (High St) Displays trace the geology, archaeology and natural history of the region up to the medieval period; highlights include the prehistoric Hadholme boat, and a walk-through Roman gallery has a re-creation of late 3rd-c Brough, a little local town. Shop, disabled access; cl Sun am, 24-26 and 31 Dec and 1 Jan; (01482) 613902; free.

Hull Maritime Museum (Queen Victoria Sq) This massive yet solidly stylish three-domed Victorian building has good (and pleasantly old-fashioned) displays on Hull's maritime history. There's a long-established section on whales and whaling (the huge skeletons on display are mentioned in *Moby Dick*), also models of trawlers, figureheads and paintings. Shop, disabled access; cl am Sun, Good Fri, 24-26 and 31 Dec, and 1 Jan; (01482) 613902; free.

Maister House (High St) Only the staircase and entrance hall are open in this mid-18th-c building (the rest is still used as offices), but the Palladian staircase is splendid, and the doors ornate and finely carved. Cl wknds, all bank hols, and 24 Dec-2 Jan; (01482)

324114; 80p inc a guidebook; NT.

Spurn Lightship (Princes Dock, Marina) Operating from the 1920s to the 1970s - interesting to go below decks and imagine being confined to this for weeks at a time, not going anywhere, tossed about in storms or blanketed in fog. Shop, cl Sun am and Oct-Mar; (01482) 613902; free.

Streetlife Museum (High St) This good collection is devoted mainly to local public transport and bicycles, some weird and wonderful. Improvements include a new motor car gallery, a major extension of the carriage gallery (you can now go on a re-created mail coach ride - you may have to queue), a larger street-scene with several new shops, and a hands-on interactive exhibition area. Shop, disabled access; cl am Sun, Good Fri, 24-26 and 31 Dec, plus 1 Jan; (01482) 613902; free. From behind there's a great view of the old warehouses along the River Hull where it meets the Humber - the most evocative part of the waterfront.

The Deep (Tower St, Sammy's Point) This hi-tech exhibition on the sea offers far more than your average aquarium. It's an astonishing building; all the walls are at an angle, and the main bit juts out 30 metres (100 ft) above the Humber estuary. The focus is on the world's oceans: how they were formed, how marine life has developed, and how they're affected by outer space, the equator, and by man; lots of interactives, and the latest lighting and effects bring it all to life. The Polar Galley has a pair of real ice walls, and they have around 500 species of fish from around the planet, some of which take their chances alongside the sharks in their gigantic showpiece aquarium. A futuristic centre has activities and experiments, inc the chance to pilot a submarine or work out a crew's diet. Meals, snacks, shop, disabled access; cl 24-25 Dec; (01482) 381000; £6.50 adults.

Wilberforce House (High St) William Wilberforce was born in this 17th-c house (the introductory video on this remarkable politician is interesting), and its Jacobean and Georgian rooms have a good exploration of the horrors of the slave trade and the struggle for its abolition. Shop, disabled access to ground floor; cl Sun am, Good Fri, Christmas week and 1 Jan; (01482) 613921; free. The Olde Black Boy nearby was the site of slave auctions. On Wilberforce Quay you can see a restored 1960s fishing vessel; tours of the **Arctic Corsair** last about an hour - wear sensible shoes; open Weds, Sat and pm Sun Apr-end Oct; (01482) 658838; £2.

HUMBER BRIDGE TA0225
Humber Bridge Country Park At the N end of the second longest single-span suspension bridge in the world, nearly a mile between the towers, and a very impressive sweep of engineering (there's a footway across as well as the road). Plenty of woodland and clifftop walks, and an old windmill. There's a tourist information centre and café at the bridge amenity area.

HUTTON-LE-HOLE SE7089
£ Neat and pretty streamside village at the mouth of Farndale; sheep wander the streets - though they won't be alone in the summer months. Its excellent **Ryedale Folk Museum** is practically a village itself, made up of various old buildings from the area re-erected in the 3-acre grounds, inc an Elizabethan manor house, gipsy caravan, and an Edwardian photographic studio; craft demonstrations on Mon, and some other days, best to check. Shop, disabled access; cl Nov to mid-Mar; (01751) 417367; £3.50. The friendly Crown does generous food. There's a pleasant walk (an hour or so) over to Lastingham, and the Blakey Ridge road to Castleton is a great drive with classic moorland views.

KILBURN SE5179
Robert Thompson Furniture Workshop The quiet village is almost a place of pilgrimage to this workshop, famous for the unobtrusive little mouse carved as a trademark that you'll see all over North Yorkshire, on church pews and in the better inns and pubs. They make lovely, simple furniture - though not cheap; the oak they use can be seen all around. There's a workshop viewing gallery, and their refurbished visitor centre and museum is due to open at Easter; charge for entry. Cl 2 wks at

Christmas, disabled access. Near the church (with a memorial to Thompson carved by his own craftsmen) the Singing Bird does refreshments, as does the Forresters Arms - full of Thompson work. Up above the village on Roulston Scar is a white horse cut in the turf in 1857 and unique in this part of the country.

KIRKDALE SE6686
Kirkdale church Saxon, with a unique original sundial, and 7th-c Celtic crosses and carved stones.

KIRKHAM SE7365
Kirkham Priory Remains of Augustinian priory in an attractive quiet spot by the River Derwent; finely sculpted lavatorium, graceful arcaded cloister, and handsome 13th-c gatehouse with some finely carved sculptures and shields. Snacks, shop, disabled access; cl wkdys Nov-Mar, 25-26 Dec and 1 Jan; (01653) 618768; £2. The Stone Trough overlooking the ruins has good food (not Mon exc bank hols), and a pleasant path meanders S by a placid stretch of the River Derwent, to Howsham Bridge and beyond.

KIRKLEATHAM NZ5921
Kirkleatham Owl Centre (In the grounds of Old Hall) Birds of prey centre with an emphasis on owls - they've one of the largest collections in the country; around 100 birds on show, inc falcons, buzzards, vultures and kites. They have daily flying displays in school hols (Easter-end Oct, depending on weather); around midday in the early summer, there's usually the chance to meet baby owls and vultures. Snacks, shop, disabled access; cl Mon (exc bank hols), limited opening hours in winter; (01642) 480512; £3. The early 18th-c former school, **Old Hall**, houses a local history museum. Snacks, shop, disabled access; cl Mon (exc bank hols), Good Fri and 25 Dec-2 Jan; (01642) 479500; free.

LASTINGHAM SE7290
Particularly attractive village, its church on a former abbey site, once one of the area's most sacred spots of pilgrimage, with an outstanding 11th-c crypt; the friendly 17th-c Blacksmiths Arms has enjoyable food. The hillside just S gives a classic North York Moors view.

LEVISHAM SE8390

A good spot for walkers, with open scenery around it, a track across the blustery moors, and an attractive valley giving separate routes to and from the Hole of Horcum, just below the A169. The Horseshoe has enjoyable food.

MALTON SE7871

Comfortable market town with some interesting side streets, in prosperous farming and racehorse-training country. Sat is their general market day, and there are cattle markets on Tues and Fri. The Crown, brewing its own beer, welcomes children in its conservatory courtyard. A scenic road towards York is the old coach road parallel to the A64, from Norton to Buttercrambe and Gate Helmsley.

Eden Camp *See separate family panel on p.691.*

MARGROVE PARK NZ6515

South Cleveland Heritage Centre
Right on the edge of the moors, with archaeology, history and wildlife exhibitions, and can organise walks, nature trails and activities. Snacks, shop, disabled access; cl Mon, Tues, and all Oct-Mar; (01287) 610368; free.

MARKET WEIGHTON SE8741

Neat and pleasant old market town with one or two useful antiques shops; the Londesborough Arms has a good restaurant. Here the well signposted Wolds Way long-distance path briefly divides in two, allowing walkers a circuit taking in the old railway line, now the Hudson Way, and the villages of Goodmanham and Londesborough with its fine parkland.

MIDDLESBROUGH NZ5116

Captain Cook Birthplace Museum
⊞ (Stewart Park, Marton, 3m S) Lots that will appeal to children at this interesting museum, which looks at the life and voyages of Captain Cook with hands-on displays, computer inter-actives and films; also discover what it was like to be an ordinary sailor in the 18th c. The landscaped grounds are impressive too. Snacks, shop, disabled access; cl Mon (exc bank hols), 25-26 Dec, 1 Jan; (01642) 311211; £2.40. The stylish nearby Apple Tree has good food.

Dorman Museum (Linthorpe Rd) Recently re-opened after major refurbishments, the eight themed galleries (five are new) house an extensive display of the town's social history; also a discovery centre for children with audio visual displays and hands-on activities, and interesting changing exhibitions. In summer, they run a programme of children's activities. New café, disabled access; cl Mon, 25-26 Dec and 1 Jan; (01642) 358101; free.

Eston Nab (off A174 SE) Outside the North York Moors National Park, this gives walkers a massive view over industrial Teesside.

Nature's World ⊞ (Sandy Flatts Lane/Ladgate Lane - B1380) Thriving environmental demonstration centre, developing all the time, with organic gardens, nature trails, and a number of re-created natural habitats inc a model of the River Tees quarter of a mile long. An innovative earth-sheltered 'eco-structure' houses displays on the latest in environmental technology (solar and geothermal power and so forth), as well as a futuristic hydroponicum. They've also built up a seed bank for locally endangered wildflowers. Splendid home-cooked meals and snacks, shop, good disabled access; cl 24 Dec-2 Jan; (01642) 594895; £4.

Newham Grange Leisure Farm ⊞ (Coulby Newham, off A174) Rare breeds and other animals (with a petting area for children), an agricultural museum with craft displays, reconstructed vet's surgery, and play and picnic areas. Snacks, shop, disabled access; cl wkdys Oct-Mar, 25-26 Dec and 1 Jan; (01642) 515729; £2.10.

Transporter Bridge (A178) Unusual, with the central section serving as a ferry, every 15 mins shuttling cars and pedestrians across the Tees. A visitor centre uses interactive displays to tell the story of the town's industrial heritage, as well as the history of the bridge itself. As we went to press the centre was being refurbished and they were planning guided tours and new exhibitions; centre usually open pm wknds (plus pm Thurs-Fri during school hols) and bank hol Mon; (01642) 246566; 50p, maybe more once refurbished. Bridge cl Sun am, 25-26 Dec, 1 Jan, and maybe in bad weather; crossing 80p cars, 30p pedestrians.

MILLINGTON SE8351

Wolds Way The village is a good base

for round walks based on this well signed way, with the landscape here rolling most attractively.

NORTH YORK MOORS NATIONAL PARK SE6889

Classic views The graveyard of Gillamoor church makes a picturesque foreground for the interlocking moor and valley landscapes which surround it; in this pretty village the Royal Oak has good food. The lane at SE6188 a bit more than a mile N of Carlton, itself N of Helmsley, gives another fine moors view.

NUNNINGTON SE6679

Nunnington Hall Big 16th/17th-c house nicely set on the banks of the River Rye, with fine panelling and a magnificent staircase. A family home for nearly 400 years, with the intriguing Carlisle Collection of miniature rooms, each of them ⅛ life-size. Tearooms, shop, limited disabled access; cl am, all day Mon (exc bank hols) and Tues (exc Jun-Aug), and all Nov-22 Mar; (01439) 748283; *£5, garden only *£2.50; NT. In the attractive village the Royal Oak is a good dining pub, and the church has a fine effigy of a knight said to have rid the district of a Loathly Worm.

ORMESBY NZ5317

Ormesby Hall Elegant 18th-c house with elaborate plasterwork, Victorian laundry and kitchen, model railway, and pleasant gardens and grounds. Snacks, shop, disabled access to ground floor only; cl am, all day Mon (exc bank hols), Fri, Sat, and Nov-Mar; (01642) 324188; *£3.90, garden and railway only *£2.70; NT.

OSMOTHERLEY SE4597

Perhaps more small town than village, but quietly attractive; the Golden Lion, welcoming to walkers, is good for a meal, and the smart Three Tuns is a popular bistro. A lonely stretch of the Cleveland Way well signed long-distance path runs up over the Hambleton Hills from here, with some road access along the way; and the 44-mile Wyke Way path starts here. The **North York Moors Adventure Centre** (Ingleby Cross) can organise climbing, caving, abseiling, orienteering, raft building, mountain biking and canoeing; shop; (01609) 882571.

Mount Grace Priory 🏠 (A19 NW) Carthusian monks not only took a vow of silence but rarely emerged from their own individual cells. One of those cells at this ruined 14th-c priory has been fully restored, giving a good illustration of how the monks must have worked and lived. The ruins are better preserved than those of any other Carthusian establishment in England; in spring an impressive display of daffodils makes it especially attractive, and there are plenty of nice picnic spots in the surrounding woodland. An adjacent 17th-c manor house has an exhibition, and interesting Arts and Crafts connections. Snacks, shop; sometimes cl 1-2pm, plus always cl Mon-Tues Nov-Mar, 24-26 Dec, 1 Jan; £3.20; EH.

PATRINGTON TA3122

Patrington church Glorious, with lovely carving inside - its graceful spire beckoning you from a long way off.

PAULL TA1625

Fort Paull 🏠 Based around the only Napoleonic fort left in Yorkshire, and best in summer, with frequent special events from classic car rallies and battle reconstructions to falconry days. Underground labyrinths contain re-creations from key moments in the fort's development, from a coastal defence originally built by Henry VIII in the mid-16th c to an anti-aircraft station during World War II. Also period military vehicles and guns (children can clamber over some of them), and you can have a go on a rifle range and archery field (each £1, ask a member of staff on wkdys). There's a children's assault course, nature trails and craft shops; good views over the Humber estuary. Meals, snacks, shop, limited disabled access; cl 25-26 Dec, 1 Jan; (01482) 882655; £4.50.

PICKERING SE7984

Another attractive small town, usually very quiet (busier Mon market day), with vividly restored medieval murals in the splendid tall-spired church. The White Swan has good food; the A169 N has sweeping moorland views (up there the Saltergate Inn is a useful stop).

Beck Isle Museum Charmingly set 17th-c riverside house with a wonderful collection of local bygones and period shops. Shop, good disabled access; cl Nov-Mar; (01751) 473653; £3.

North Yorkshire Moors Railway

(Pickering Station) Steam trips through some lovely countryside and nostalgically restored stations, a distance of 18 miles; the line was originally built by George Stephenson. You can stop off at Goathland, and the Grosmont end has various locomotives and antique carriages (and nearby, there's a friendly interactive science centre; usually open same times as the station; £1.75). Meals, snacks, shop, disabled access; cl Nov to mid-Mar (exc Nov and Dec wknds, and over New Year); (01751) 472508 for timetable; *£12 full return journey. The nearby Station Hotel has decent food.

Pickering Castle Tall ruins of 12th-c keep and later curtain walls and towers, with fine views from its imposing castle mound above the town; an exhibition in the chapel focuses on the history of the castle and forest. Snacks, shop, some disabled access; cl 1-2pm, Mon and Tues Nov-Mar, 25-26 Dec and 1 Jan; (01751) 474989; £2.60; EH.

POCKLINGTON SE8048
An open-faced market town below the Wolds, with a good few handsome buildings; the Feathers is popular for lunch (and has decent bedrooms). The B1246 Driffield road runs through some quite picturesque hills.

Burnby Hall (B1247 S) Famous for their water-lilies, with dozens of varieties in two lakes; also lots of koi carp, and an intriguing collection of all sorts of ethnic material and sporting trophies from across the world. Snacks, shop, disabled access; cl Oct-Mar; (01759) 302068; £2.70. From out here it's not far to the Plough at Allerthorpe (good for lunch).

RIEVAULX SE5785
Rievaulx Abbey Elegant and evocative ruins of magnificent and once highly prosperous abbey, among the wooded hills of Rye Dale (the most dramatic views are gained by walking down the dale from the N). The nave, dating from 1135, is one of the earliest built in England. Also among the spectacular three-tiered remains is a fine 13th-c choir; there's a visitor centre, and interesting museum with hands-on displays about the site's history. The graceful colonnades, arches and lancet windows are especially impressive without the crowds, early or late on a wkdy out of season. Snacks, shop, some disabled access; cl 24-26 Dec, 1 Jan; (01439) 798228; £3.80; EH. Besides the many places in Helmsley not far off, the Hare over in Scawton (a pleasant drive) is good for lunch.

Rievaulx Terrace & Temples This half-mile grass-covered 18th-c terrace overlooks the abbey, with dramatic views. Each end is adorned with a classical temple; one a small tuscan rotunda built to while away the hours in peaceful contemplation, the other, an elaborate ionic creation, for hunting parties. An ideal spot for a picnic, with good frescoes and an exhibition on landscape design. Snacks, shop; cl Nov to mid-Mar; (01439) 798340; £3.30; NT.

ROBIN HOOD'S BAY NZ9505
Picturesque fishing village, once popular with smugglers and still largely unspoilt (though there are quite a few shops and cafés for visitors now), its cottages clustered steeply above the rocky shore - a rich hunting-ground for fossil hunters at low tide, when a surprising expanse of sand is exposed beyond the fascinating rock pools. You can walk along a fine section of cliffs to Ravenscar, where a geological trail takes in old alum quarries; an abandoned railway provides an easy walkway back. The Laurel down in the village is a charming fishermen's pub; the Victoria Hotel up on the cliff has a good choice of food. The village car park is also up at the top - quite a climb.

Old Coastguard Station Visitor Centre In the old coastguard lookout, with displays about the forces that shaped the bay. Shop, disabled access; cl wkdys Oct-May (exc Oct and Feb half-term) and a wk over Christmas and New Year; (01947) 885900; free.

ROSEBERRY TOPPING NZ5712
A memorable viewpoint on the extreme N edge of the moors, reached by a moorland walk from Gribdale Gate car park E of Great Ayton; a popular circuit goes by way of Airy Home Farm, the childhood home of Captain Cook. The Kings Head (Newton, A173) is a popular dining pub.

ROSEDALE SE7296
With its lush fields and red-roofed

yellow-stone houses sheltering warmly below the gaunt moorland, this now seems to typify the quiet pastoral countryside of the area. But until the early 20th-c it was a busy iron-working site: the old railway track that once served the quarries loops around the moor above, and makes an easily followed stroll. The Milburn Arms has good food. The hillside at the top of the dreadfully steep Rosedale Chimney road heading S over Spaunton Moor gives motorists too a classic view.

RUNSWICK BAY NZ8016
Very pretty harbourless fishing village, with fresh fish and great views from the Royal; an attractive stretch of the well signed Cleveland Way long-distance path runs from here to Staithes (or you can begin closer from tiny Port Mulgrave).

SALTBURN-BY-THE-SEA NZ6621
Originally a superior Victorian seaside resort, with traces of those days still in the italianate valley garden and the water-balanced cliff lift by the pier. The Ship Inn, a good pub right by the boats pulled up on the beach, is probably the most ancient building. The beach is sheltered by the great headland of Warsett Hill to the S, and a grand section of the well signed Cleveland Way long-distance path takes walkers over this and beyond.

Saltburn Smugglers Heritage Centre ⊞ (Whitby Rd) Vivid interactive exhibition on the town's smuggling heritage, housed in old seaside cottages. Shop; cl Oct-Apr; (01287) 625252; £1.95.

SCARBOROUGH TA0488
All the usual seaside attractions in a place of some style, its two great curves of firm sandy beach separated by the small harbour below a high narrow headland. Between castle and cliff are the remains of a Roman signal station, one of five such structures built in the 4th c to warn of approaching raiders. To the S is the older part of the resort, with antique tracked cliff lifts between prom and the pleasant streets of the upper town; a house associated with Richard III here is now a restaurant. The train station has one of the longest benches in the world - 139 metres (456

ft) long, it can seat 228 people; the Steven Joseph theatre opposite is run by Alan Ayckbourn. Interesting churches include medieval St Mary's, where Anne Brontë is buried, and 19th-c St Martin's with elaborate work by William Morris, Burne-Jones and other Pre-Raphaelites. One entertainingly quaint tradition is the summer staging of miniaturised sea battles with all sorts of special effects among the ducks on the lake of Peasholm Park in the less seasidey N part of town; phone the tourist information for dates and times; (01723) 373333. Good views of the bay from the top of Oliver's Mount (and harbour views from the Golden Ball on the front); good value food all day in the very grand Lord Rosebery (Westborough), and the stylish Raffels (Falsgrave Rd/Belgrave Cres), a former gentleman's club, has a plush restaurant.

Cleveland Way S of Scarborough to Filey is an agreeable few hours' walk along the well signed Cleveland Way, though of less scenic significance than the cliffs further N. Oddly, the Way stops just short of Filey, at the headland of Filey Brigg, although there is nothing to prevent you from walking on into town.

Rotunda Museum (Vernon Rd) Georgian local history museum, with a Bronze Age skeleton, displays on the resort's Victorian heyday and seaside activities. Shop; cl Mon and Weds-Fri Apr-May (exc Easter), Mon Jun-Sept, all Oct-Mar; (01723) 374839; £2.50 joint ticket valid for a year with Wood End Museum and Art Gallery.

Scarborough Art Gallery (The Crescent) Striking italianate villa with good temporary exhibitions, and the chance for children to dress up as a character from a painting. Snacks, shop; cl Mon, also Sun-Weds Oct-May and a wk over Christmas and New Year; (01723) 374753; £2.50 joint ticket with Rotunda and Wood End Museum.

Scarborough Castle Looking down over the town from the headland, this stands on the site of british and Roman encampments. It was a Royal palace of some importance until the reign of James I. Remains include the 13th-c barbican, medieval chapels and house, and the shell of the original 12th-c keep; audio tour, and great coastal views from the walls. Snacks and picnic area, shop, disabled access; cl 24-26 Dec, 1 Jan; (01723) 372451; £3; EH.

Sea Life & Marine Sanctuary ▣ (Scalby Mills) Busy marine sanctuary with seal pups, otters (they have a rear and release programme), turtles, seahorses, and an impressive new penguin area, plus thousands of other sea creatures; feeding sessions and talks throughout the day, a touch-pool, and a soft play area for younger children. Meals, snacks, shop, disabled access; cl 25 Dec; (01723) 376125; £7.50.

Terror Tower ▣ (Martin Marine, Foreshore Rd) A diversion for children on wet days, with ghoulish reconstructions of horror film sets, and actors adding to the tension. Shop; cl Oct-Apr exc pm wknds; (01723) 501016; £2.95.

Wood End Museum (The Crescent) The Sitwells lived here for 60 years from 1870 (Edith was born here), and there are displays of their work and associated memorabilia. Also lots of fossils, and Victorian conservatory with tropical plants - though not the free-flying birds that once mingled with party-goers. Shop; cl Mon, and Oct-May exc Weds and wknds; (01723) 367326; £2.50 joint ticket with Rotunda and Scarborough Art Gallery.

SHERIFF HUTTON SE6566 Attractive village, with a ruined castle and a 12th-c church with an effigy of a child, said to be Richard III's only son, Prince Edward; there are some interesting motte and bailey earthworks behind the church. The Highwayman has enjoyable food.

SKINNINGROVE NZ7119 **Tom Leonard Mining Museum** ▣ Good mining museum well demonstrating the reality of work underground. You can see how the stone is drilled, charged with explosives and fired. Shop, disabled access; cl ams, Sun (exc July-Aug) and Nov-Mar; (01287) 642877; *£3.50. The village is industrial, with a steel-rolling mill - far from picturesque, but it has strong local colour, with its odd shanty town of pigeon-fanciers' sheds spreading over the cliff. Walkers can join the well signed Cleveland Way southwards to

ascend monumental Boulby Cliff, the highest point on the E coast, before re-entering the National Park.

SLEDMERE SE9365 **Sledmere House** Grand 18th-c mansion decorated and furnished in the style of the period, with one showpiece room done in turkish tiling and a library bigger than many public ones. There's an 18th-c walled garden, and the extensive park was landscaped by Capability Brown. They usually play their pipe organ pm Weds, Fri and Sun. Meals, snacks, shop, disabled access. Cl before 11.30am, all day Mon and Sat (exc bank hols) and 3rd Sun Sept to Easter; (01377) 236637; £5, garden only £3. The Triton nearby is a handy food stop.

SPROATLEY TA1836 **Burton Constable Hall** ▣ The wonderful exterior gives away this delightful house's Elizabethan origins, but the inside was extraordinarily remodelled in the 18th c. Around 30 beautifully preserved rooms to see, with a sweeping long gallery and some intriguing collections. Capability Brown landscaped the 200 acres here, and there's a riding centre in the stables. Snacks, shop, mostly disabled access; cl am, all day Fri, and Nov-Easter Sat; (01964) 562400; £5. Camping, caravanning and seasonal fishing are available, and the Old Blue Bell in Old Ellerby is a cheerful refreshment stop.

SPURN HEAD TA4010 This spit which curls like a claw round the mouth of the Humber estuary has a rough track open to cars almost to its end: a bleak place to some but a paradise for bird-watchers, who often wait here in spring and autumn for glimpses of rare migrant species. Thanks to the vagaries of nature the peninsula is gradually becoming an island, so best to check tide times carefully. The estuary itself is usually grey, solemn and grim. The Crown & Anchor at Kilnsea, open all day, has good value food.

STAINTONDALE SE9998 **Llama trekking** Bruce and Ruth Wright organise this, across the moors or along the coast; the llamas hump your bags while you walk beside them. They can do specialist treks with guides, covering subjects such as the moors,

dinosaurs and smuggling. All treks inc home-made food; cl 25 Dec, treks by advanced booking only; (01723) 871234; from £40 for four hours.
Shire Horse Farm (Staintondale) Friendly little farm with good demonstrations (some in their new outdoor all-weather arena) and talks; nature trails, and bracing clifftop walks along part of the Cleveland Way. Snacks, shop, limited disabled access; cl Mon exc bank hols, Thurs, Sat and mid-Sept to Apr; (01723) 870458; *£3.50. The Falcon (just off A171) has good value food.

STAITHES NZ7818
Steep fishing village, unspoilt down by the shore, where little cottages and the storm-battered Cod & Lobster pose fetchingly against the staggering background of a great red sandstone headland, a striking colour picture as the sun comes up.
Captain Cook & Staithes Heritage Centre (High St) This converted Methodist chapel in the village where the great explorer worked as a young man, in 1745, now houses a decent heritage centre, with a reconstructed street scene showing village life at the time; lots of Cook-related artefacts inc a collection of Webber's superb engravings from the voyages. Also displays looking at the importance of local industries such as fishing, mining and smuggling. Shop, disabled access to ground floor only; cl 25-26 Dec, and wkdys Jan; (01947) 841454; £2.50.

SUTTON BANK SE5182
This steep escarpment gives an enthralling view, particularly from the very popular section of the Cleveland Way that runs S from the A170 along the level clifftop to the white horse cut into the hill. Immediately N of the A170 you can combine the path along the top of the slope with a venture down the nature trail into Garbutt Wood, a nature reserve abutting Gormire Lake, the only natural lake in the National Park. The Black Swan at Oldstead does decent meals.

SUTTON-ON-THE-FOREST SE5864
Sutton Park The friendly 1730s manor house itself is open pms only Weds and Sun, bank hol Mons and Easter Fri, but the delightful grounds are open daily 4 Apr-26 Sept, with terraced gardens (inc a new wildflower meadow), a Georgian ice house, lily pond, pleasant woodland walks, nature trails and an adventure playground. Meals, snacks; (01347) 810249; *£5.50, *£3 gardens only. The village is pretty, and the smart Rose & Crown has good food.

THIRSK SE4281
World of James Herriot 🔠 (23 Kirkgate) A lively look at the country's favourite vet as well as his profession, set in the Skeldale House of his novels; period rooms and hands-on exhibits. Shop, disabled access; cl 24-26 Dec; (01845) 524234; £4.70. The George in the handsome adjoining village of Sowerby has good food.

THORNTON LE DALE SE8383
Despite the main road, one of the most delightful villages in this part of Yorkshire - with an attractive forest toll road running NW to Langdale End. The New Inn has good food and nice bedrooms.

WADE'S CAUSEWAY SE8097
Also known as Wheeldale Roman road, this mile-long stretch of broad paved Roman road up over the moors is well restored and maintained. It's open to walkers only, but reached easily by the narrow moorland lane S from Egton Bridge (or a longish walk S from Goathland).

WELTON SE9627
Wolds Way Good area for round walks based on the well signed Wolds Way, with fine views over the Humber in places. The Half Moon in Elloughton has enjoyable food.

WHARRAM PERCY SE8564
The most famous of the medieval abandoned villages of the Wolds, with lots of grassy humps and an evocative ruined church; EH, free access. From Thixendale (where the Cross Keys has sensibly priced food) a stretch of the well signed Wolds Way gives walkers a view of the village, and takes in a stretch of classic dry valley.

WHITBY NZ8911
Famous as the port at which Count Dracula came ashore; Bram Stoker got the idea for the book in the fishermen's graveyard of the partly Norman church, 199 steps up from the harbour, with

lovely woodwork. You can go on ghost walks at 8pm, leaving from the Whale Bones, West Cliff (phone to book in winter; (01947) 821734; £4). Not too far from the abbey on Church St is a small but interesting workshop where you can watch the famous jet being crafted into jewellery. Away from the bright waterfront the town is steep and quite attractive, with picturesque old buildings (now often rather smart shops and cafés) and some quaint cobbled alleys in its original core E of the busy harbour, where excellent fresh fish is sold straight from the catch in the early morning. Fans of the TV series will enjoy visiting the *Heartbeat Story* in the Shambles (cl wkdys Nov-Mar; (01947) 825067; £3). Besides excellent fish and chips from the Magpie Café, the Duke of York (Church St, at the bottom of the *199 steps) does decent* food all day. In the two wks around the summer solstice the sun both rises and sets above the sea. A replica of Captain Cook's ship will be visiting Whitby, provisionally 13 May-14 Jun, phone the tourist information centre to check; (01947) 602674.

Captain Cook Memorial Museum (Grape Lane) In the house where the great explorer lived as an apprentice in the shipping trade from 1746; rooms are furnished in period style with models, letters and drawings from Cook's later voyages. It's recently been extended into the old cottage next door, and there's a new entrance and four new rooms for displaying their expanding collection. Shop, disabled access; cl Nov-Feb; (01947) 601900; £3.

Dracula Experience (Marine Parade) Children probably won't be satisfied until they've visited this vividly spooky re-creation of scenes from the classic tale. Shop; cl wkdys Nov-Mar; (01947) 601923; *£1.95.

Whitby Abbey 🔳 Impressive set of 13th-c ruins dramatically overlooking the harbour from their windswept clifftop setting. You can see the skeletal remains of the magnificent three-tiered choir and the N transept, and it's an evocative spot for a picnic. An earlier building had been the site of the Synod of Whitby, where the dating of Easter was thrashed out in 664. Also here are a

Celtic Christian cemetery, and a restored 17th-c stone garden made by descendants of the family who bought the abbey after Henry VIII's dissolution of the monasteries. An innovative visitor centre, housed in the roofless shell of a 17th-c house, has well thought out displays of archaeological artefacts with plenty of interactive features, videos and an activity centre, and there's a good audio tour. Snacks, shop, disabled access; cl 24-26 Dec, 1 Jan; (01947) 603568; £3.80; EH.

Whitby Museum (Pannett Park) Delightfully old-fashioned and crowded, with the only surviving part of Captain Cook's original journal, Queen Victoria's nightdress, some spectacular fossils and the hand of a murderer used as a candle-holder by superstitious burglars. Shop, disabled access; cl Sun am all year, plus Mon (exc some bank hols) and pm Tues Oct-Apr, plus 2 wks over Christmas and New Year; (01947) 602908; £2.50.

WITHERNSEA TA3327

Withernsea Lighthouse Towering above the houses of this little resort, with fantastic views for those keen enough to climb the 144 steps. Exhibits on local history, coastguard lifesaving and the RNLI. Teas, shop, disabled access to ground floor only; usually open pm wknds and bank hols (exc Good Fri) end Mar-Oct, plus pm wkdys mid-Jun to mid-Sept; (01964) 614834; £2. The Commercial Hotel has cheap food.

YORKSHIRE WOLDS SE8461 Quiet agricultural chalk country dissected by dry valleys, with extensive views over huge corn fields. The bulk of the off-road walking is found on the well signposted 79-mile Wolds Way from Hessle Haven down on the Humber to Filey Brigg on the coast, where it meets the Cleveland Way. Some of the lesser roads are a delight to walk on, with wide verges, good views and virtually no traffic.

Other attractive villages here, all with decent pubs, include Ainthorpe NZ7008, Ampleforth SE5879 (with its famous school and partly wooded moors), Bishop Burton SE9939, Brompton SE9582, Castleton NZ6908 high above the Esk Valley, Cloughton Newlands TA0196, Crayke SE5670,

Fadmoor SE6789, Gillamoor SE6890, Great Ayton NZ5611, Hovingham SE6775, Hutton Rudby NZ4706, Lealholm NZ7608, Lund SE9748, Nether Silton SE4692, North Dalton SE9352, Oldstead SE5380, Rosedale Abbey SE7395, Seamer TA0284, Sinnington SE7485, South Dalton SE9645, Thixendale SE8461, Thorganby SE6942, Thornton le Clay SE6865, Warthill SE6755, Weaverthorpe SE9771 and Welburn SE7268.

Where to eat

BYLAND ABBEY SE5478 **Abbey Inn** *(01347) 868204* Beautifully placed dining pub opposite haunting abbey ruins, with an interesting series of rambling old rooms, big fireplaces, polished floorboards, and flagstones; very good varied food, decent wines and well kept beers, and big garden; charming bdrms; cl Sun pm, Mon am (exc bank hols); limited disabled access. £26|£7.95

CRAYKE SE5670 **Durham Ox** *West Way (01347) 821506* This is said to be the hill up which the Grand Old Duke of York marched his men; bustling, popular inn with venerable tables and antique seats and settles, flagstones, interestingly carved panelling, enormous inglenook fireplace with winter log fires (flowers in summer), bottom bar with illustrated local history (some of it gruesome) going back to the 12th c, good food inc imaginative daily specials, well kept real ales, seats outside and bdrms in converted farm buildings; cl 25 Dec; no children in restaurant; disabled access. £28|£7.95

FLAMBOROUGH TA2270 **Seabirds** *Tower St (01262) 850242* Friendly old pub full of shipping memorabilia and a few stuffed birds, with enjoyable food (some fresh fish dishes, too), quite a few wines, and cheerful hard-working staff; cl Mon pm in winter; children must be well behaved; partial disabled access. £20|£6.95

HAROME SE6482 **Star** *High St (01439) 770397* Pretty, thatched, 14th-c inn with a charming interior, plenty of bric-a-brac and interesting furniture, two big log fires, daily papers and magazines, and a no smoking dining room; excellent inventive food using the best local produce, well kept real ales, freshly squeezed juices, and quite a few wines by the glass from a fairly extensive wine list; seats and tables on a sheltered front terrace with more in the garden behind; lovely bdrms; cl Mon, 3 wks winter/spring; disabled access. £30

KIRKHAM ABBEY SE7366 **Stone Trough** *(01653) 618713* Quaint beamed inn with small, cosy and interesting bars, log fires, enjoyable inventive food in bar and no smoking farmhouse-style restaurant, and seats outside with valley views; cl Mon (exc bank hols), 25 Dec; children must be well behaved. £26.50|£7.95

MARTON SE7383 **Appletree** *(01751) 431457* Stylish and spotlessly kept dining pub with carefully co-ordinated colour schemes and lighting, a relaxed beamed lounge with comfortable settees and open fire, terracotta-walled dining room with well spaced farmhouse tables, fresh flowers, and masses of evening candles, delicious food using top-quality local produce (free bottle of mineral water and warmly fragrant savoury breads), a good choice of a dozen changing wines by the glass, well kept real ales, and friendly service; they sell their own chutneys, preserves and so forth; seats on a sheltered flagstoned terrace. £23.40|£7.90

MIDDLESBROUGH NZ4920 **Purple Onion** *72-80 Corporation Rd (01642) 222250* Bustling Victorian building filled with bric-a-brac, ornate mirrors, and house plants, an informal atmosphere, downstairs cellar bar with live music, particularly good interesting food, friendly staff, and decent wine list; cl Sun, Mon; disabled access. £28.45|£6.75

NUNNINGTON SE6679 **Royal Oak** *Church St (01439) 748271* Attractive little dining pub nr Nunnington Hall with log fires, beams hung with copper jugs, antique keys and earthenware flagons, carefully chosen furniture, and enjoyable generous home-made bar food - super daily specials; cl Mon. £21|£5

PICKERING SE7984 **White Swan** *Market Pl (01751) 472288* Former coaching inn with very comfortable recently reworked bedrooms, a charming country atmosphere, panelling, and log fire in small and civilised front bar, another log fire in no smoking snug, an attractive no smoking dining room, and busy but comfortable family room; particularly good imaginative food using carefully sourced local produce (lunchtime dishes are simpler and breakfasts are enjoyable), well kept real ales, and an impressive wine list. £32|£6.95

SCARBOROUGH TA0488 **Golden Grid Fish Restaurant** *4 Sandside (01723) 360922* Very long-standing and famous fish restaurant (candlelit at night) overlooking the harbour, serving snacks, lunches (super daily-fresh fish), vegetarian dishes, and afternoon teas; disabled access. £15|£4.95

STADDLEBRIDGE SE4499 **McCoys Bistro** *Cleveland Tontine (01609) 882671* A rather special place with a friendly bustling atmosphere in ground-floor bistro, some eccentric furnishings, old-fashioned music, particularly good modern food, a thoughtful wine list, a quieter dining room open only Fri and Sat evenings, and good breakfasts; bdrms; cl 25-26 Dec, 1 Jan. £35.95|£8.95

STAITHES NZ7818 **Endeavour** *1 High St (01947) 840825* Popular little quayside restaurant (lunch by prior booking only) at the bottom of a steep hill, with lovely fresh local fish (delicious meat and game, and vegetarian dishes, too), super puddings, decent good value wine list, and friendly service; bdrms; cl Sun, Mon (open bank hols); well behaved children only. £30

SUTTON UPON DERWENT SE7047 **St Vincent Arms** *Main St (01904) 608349* Family-run pub with a relaxed atmosphere in traditional panelled front parlour, a huge fire in the big stone fireplace, high-backed old settles, collections of plates and whisky jugs, very popular and enjoyable home-made food in spacious dining room, friendly staff, up to nine well kept beers, and good choice of wines; big garden. £20|£6

THORGANBY SE6841 **Jefferson Arms** *Main St (01904) 448316* Handsome old village inn with a bistro feel in the stylish and spacious main bar; delightful little beamed lounge with leather sofas and armchairs, open fire and fresh flowers, and narrow conservatory; quite a choice of interesting food, real ales, and a decent wine list; quiet bdrms; cl Mon, Tues am; children must be well behaved. £25|£7.95

WHITBY NZ9011 **Duke of York** *124 Church St (01947) 600324* Bustling, welcoming pub with fine outlook over harbour entrance and western cliff from the comfortable beamed bar (lots of fishing memorabilia), a wide choice of good value fresh local fish as well as other things, well kept real ales, decent wines, and quick, pleasant service; bdrms; disabled access. £15.50|£5.95

WHITBY NZ8911 **Magpie Café** *14 Pier Rd (01947) 602058* Overlooks the town and river, with lots of wonderfully evocative sepia photographs of old Whitby, and much liked for its delicious fresh haddock served by cheerful staff; cl 5 Jan to 6 Feb. £20|£5.45

West & South Yorkshire

**Full of interesting family outings and first-class museums (many free) -
great possibilities for unorthodox but really enjoyable short breaks**

An unexpected boon for this area is the profusion of 'stately museums' (fine houses, filled with absorbing exhibits, often free): Bagshaw Museum in Batley (charmingly eclectic collection), unusual Brodsworth Hall, and Cusworth Hall Museum are especially worth a mention. Oakwell Hall (good value, with a children's discovery centre), magnificent Harewood House & Bird Garden (almost too much to see, inside and out), sumptuous Nostell Priory (outstanding collection of Chippendale furniture), and huge Conisbrough Castle richly repay a visit too. In interesting Saltaire a huge collection of contemporary art is housed in a Victorian textile mill.

Vibrant Leeds easily keeps all kinds of people happy, with a plethora of good museums (favourites for children are the top-notch Royal Armouries Museum, the Thackray Medical Museum and Abbey House), and other attractions from art galleries to a steam railway, as well as a lively nightlife. The area's other cities are worth considering for a visit, too. Halifax is rewarding, with Eureka! (captivating for younger children), and the engrossing Shibden Hall & Folk Museum. Sheffield, with a much fresher face these days, has an increasing appeal for visitors, including children. Bradford (despite its bad press) has some great places to visit too: the National Museum of Photography, Film and Television and the lively Industrial Museum alone are worth stopping for. Magna puts the less-visited town of Rotherham on the tourist map.

The Tropical Butterfly House in North Anston (animals and birds as well as butterflies), Cannon Hall Open Farm at Cawthorne (the nearby museum is worth popping into), and newcomer St Leonard's Farm Park in Esholt are enjoyable for children. In Middlestown, you can gain a memorable insight into life as a coal miner. There are interesting heritage centres in Elsecar and Golcar; at Denaby Main there's an ambitiously forward-looking environmental centre. Brontë fans should head for Gomersal and Thornton, as well as Haworth (where there's a classic steam railway too).

In the W is a real Yorkshire mix of steep stone cottage terraces, remarkable mill buildings and some dramatic moorland coming right up to the towns, with plenty of exhilarating walking. Ilkley on the edge of the moors is attractive, and Hebden Bridge is also worth a trip, with the Hardcastle Crags above ideal for a peaceful picnic.

With the present counties of West and South Yorkshire, this chapter includes the bottom corner of North Yorkshire, below York itself and the A64.

Where to stay

BRADFORD SE1632 **Victoria Hotel** *Bridge St, Bradford, West Yorkshire BD1 1JX* (01274) 728706 **£75**w, plus special breaks; 60 well equipped rms with CD and video. Carefully renovated Victorian station hotel with many original features and lots of stylish character, bustling bar, popular and informal brasserie serving good modern food, and marvellous breakfasts, small private gym and sauna; disabled access; dogs welcome in bedrooms

HALIFAX SE0829 **Holdsworth House** *Holmfield, Halifax, West Yorkshire HX2 9TG (01422)* 240024 **£114**, plus wknd breaks; 40 traditional, individually decorated, quiet rms. Lovely, immaculately kept 17th-c house a few miles outside Halifax, with antiques, fresh flowers and fires in comfortable lounges, lots of sitting areas in the two bar rooms, friendly, particularly helpful staff, three carefully furnished dining rooms (one oak panelled) with enjoyable food and very good wine list, and garden; cl 1 wk Christmas; dogs welcome in bedrooms

HAWORTH SE0237 **Old White Lion** *6-10 West Lane, Haworth, Keighley, West Yorkshire BD22 8DU (01535) 642313* **£65***, plus special breaks; 14 rms, many with lovely views. Friendly, warm and comfortable 300-year-old inn with three bars, cosy restaurant with enjoyable food, and oak-panelled residents' lounge; nr Brontë museum and church, and Keighley & Worth Valley steam railway; disabled access

LEEDS SE3033 **42 The Calls** *Leeds, West Yorkshire LS2 7EW (0113) 244 0099* **£157.50**w, inc bottle of champagne, plus special breaks; 41 attractive rms using original features, with lots of extras, CD stereo with disc library, satellite TV and good views. Stylish modern hotel in converted riverside grain mill in peaceful spot overlooking the River Aire, with genuinely friendly staff, marvellous food in restaurant and next-door chic but informal Brasserie Forty-Four, and fine breakfasts; cl 4 days over Christmas; disabled access; dogs welcome in bedrooms

LEEDS SE3033 **Malmaison** *Sovereign Quay, Leeds, West Yorkshire LS1 1DQ (0113) 398 1000* **£148.50**, plus wknd breaks; 100 spacious rms with CDs and air conditioning. Stylish new hotel by the River Aire, with bold, modern furnishings, stylish bar and brasserie, contemporary french-style food and decent breakfasts, and helpful friendly service; disabled access

LINTON SE3646 **Wood Hall** *Trip Lane, Linton, Wetherby, West Yorkshire LS22 4JA (01937) 587271* **£160***, plus racing breaks; 44 spacious well furnished rms. Grand Georgian mansion in over a hundred acres of parkland by the River Wharfe; comfortable reception rooms, log fire, antiques and fresh flowers, and imaginative cooking in the no smoking restaurant; indoor swimming pool and health centre; disabled access; dogs welcome in bedrooms

MONK FRYSTON SE5029 **Monk Fryston Hall** *Main St, Monk Fryston, Leeds, West Yorkshire LS25 5DU (01977) 682369* **£108**, plus wknd and special breaks; 29 comfortable rms. Benedictine manor house in 30 acres of secluded gardens with lake and woodland, an oak-panelled lounge and bar with log fires, antiques, paintings and fresh flowers, good honest food, and friendly helpful staff; disabled access; dogs welcome in bedrooms

OTLEY SE2143 **Chevin Lodge** *Yorkgate, Otley, West Yorkshire LS21 3NU (01943) 467818* **£116**, plus special breaks; 50 rms, some in log lodges deep in the woods. Built of finnish logs with walks through 50 acres of birchwood (lots of wildlife), this comfortable hotel has its own leisure club, good food in lakeside restaurant, and friendly service; tennis and fishing; disabled access; dogs welcome in bedrooms

ROYDHOUSE SE2112 **Three Acres** *37-41 Roydhouse, Shelley, Huddersfield, West Yorkshire HD8 8LR (01484) 602606* **£80***; 20 pretty rms. In lovely countryside, this civilised former coaching inn has a welcoming atmosphere in its traditional bars, an exceptional choice of wines, well kept real ales, marvellous imaginative food in two restaurants, and particularly good breakfasts; specialist delicatessen next door; cl 25 Dec, 31 Dec-1 Jan

SCISSETT SE2408 **Bagden Hall** *Wakefield Rd, Scissett, Huddersfield, West Yorkshire HD8 9LE (01484) 865330* **£80**; 17 rms. Handsome hotel in 40 acres of parkland with its own 9-hole par 3 golf course, comfortable airy public rooms inc a bright conservatory bar, well prepared french and english food, and quietly efficient service; no accommodation 24-25 Dec; limited disabled access

SHEFFIELD SK3485 **Charnwood Hotel** *10 Sharrow Lane, Sheffield, South Yorkshire S11 8AA (0114) 258 9411* **£83**w, plus special breaks; 22 comfortable well equipped rms. Friendly extended Georgian house with peaceful lounges, conservatory, and freshly cooked, interesting food in the Brasserie; cl Christmas; disabled access

---

Please let us know what you think of places in the *Guide*. Use the report forms at the back of the book, write us a letter or log on to www.goodguides.co.uk

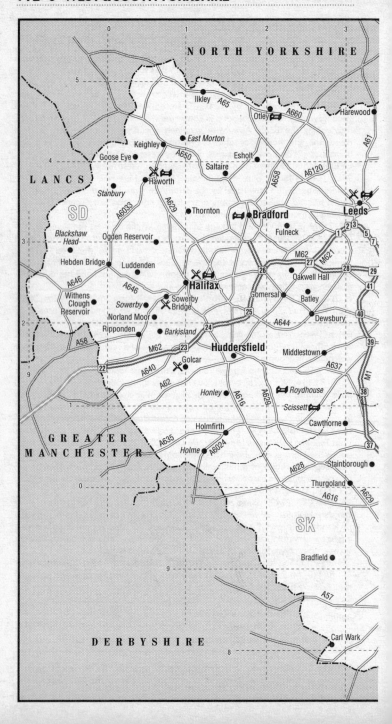

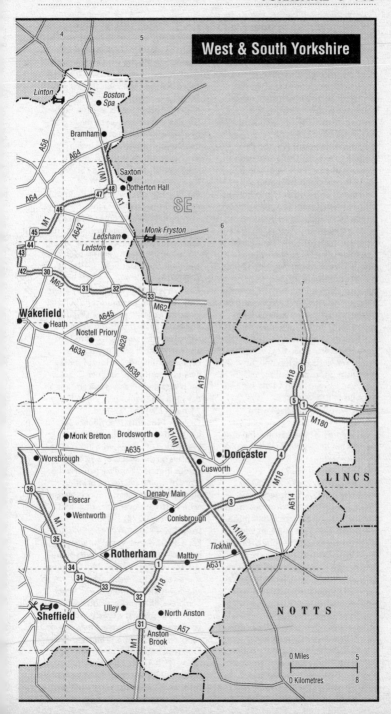

West & South Yorkshire

Linton
Boston Spa
Bramham
Saxton
Lotherton Hall
SE
Monk Fryston
Ledsham
Ledston
Wakefield
Heath
Nostell Priory
Monk Bretton
Brodsworth
Worsbrough
Elsecar
Wentworth
Denaby Main
Conisbrough
Doncaster
Cusworth
LINCS
Rotherham
Maltby
Tickhill
Ulley
North Anston
NOTTS
Sheffield
Anston Brook

A1
A58
A64
A64
A1(M)
M1
A642
M62
A645
A628
A638
A638
A19
M18
M180
A1(M)
A635
M1
A631
A57
M18
A614

0 Miles 5
0 Kilometres 8

To see and do

ANSTON BROOK SK5184
Reached on foot from South Anston, this flows through a wooded valley that interrupts the monotony of the flat farmlands SE of Rotherham. It can be combined with a walk along the towpath of the Chesterfield Canal.

BATLEY SE2325
Bagshaw Museum (Wilton Park) Beautiful Victorian Gothic mansion in pleasant lakeside park, with one of those excellent miscellaneous collections based on the curio-hunting of an individual enthusiast; local history displays too. Shop, some disabled access; cl wknd ams, Good Fri, 25-26 Dec, and 1 Jan; (01924) 326155; free. The Old Hall at Heckmondwike (B6117), once Joseph Priestley's home, is interesting for lunch.

Skopos Motor Museum (Alexandra Mills, just off A652) It's worth the trek off the beaten path to visit this good varied collection of cars, in a pleasant airy building. Vehicles on display range from Edwardian Rolls-Royces to the tiny BMW Isetta, and the only surviving Bramham. Shop, disabled access; 25-26 Dec, and 1 Jan; (01924) 444423; £2.50.

BRADFIELD SK2692
Attractive two-part village, with interesting church and good walks in great scenery. The old Strines Inn up in the hills has decent food (all day wknds and summer).

BRADFORD SE1632
Though horribly knocked about by heavy-handed civic designers in the 1960s and 1970s (and notorious for the riots of 2001), Bradford can still make you gasp at the stone buildings which survive from its zenith as one of Britain's finest Victorian cities. These are a staggering monument to the days when its wools, woollens and worsteds ruled the world: gigantic Renaissance-style woollen and velvet mills, the imposing Wool Exchange (now full of trendy coffee shops), the opulent city-centre cliffs of heavily ornate merchants' warehouses in Little Germany behind the mostly 15th-c cathedral, and the florid exuberance of the municipal buildings such as the Gothic city hall, the neo-classical St George's concert hall, even the great Undercliffe cemetery with its sumptuous Victorian memorials and sweeping Pennine views - it's been called the most spectacular graveyard in Britain. For visitors, the vivid dash of diversity brought by its asian immigrants is a plus, and for a meal you might prefer one of the multitude of pakistani or bangladeshi restaurants to useful pub lunch places such as the Fountain (Heaton Rd), Office (off City St) and Rams Revenge (Kirkgate Pl).

Bolling Hall Museum (off Brompton Ave, S) Classic mainly 17th-c Yorkshire manor house, now home to the city's collection of local furniture. Shop, disabled access to ground floor; usually cl Sun am, Mon (exc summer bank hols) and Tues, but best to check; (01274) 723057; free.

Cartwright Hall Art Gallery (Lister Park) Dramatic baroque-style building in attractive floral park, housing the *Brown Boy* by Reynolds and a good representative selection of late 19th- and early 20th-c paintings; it's their centenary this year, so lots of special events in spring and summer. Snacks, shop, disabled access; cl Sun am, and all day Mon (exc bank hols), 24-26 Dec and 1 Jan; (01274) 751212; free.

Colour Museum (Providence St) Imaginative study of the use and perception of colour, with interactive displays on the effects of light and colour in general, and particularly the story of dyeing and textile printing. Shop, disabled access; cl Sun, Mon, and around 10 days over Christmas and New Year; (01274) 390955; £2.

Industrial Museum (Moorside Rd, Eccleshill) Former Victorian spinning mill well illustrating the growth of the worsted textile industry. Horse-drawn trams (exc in bad weather) carry you up and down the Victorian street, which is complete with workers' cottages, mill owner's house and working Victorian stables with shire horses. Meals, snacks, shop, disabled access; cl Sun am, all day Mon (exc bank hols), 25-26 Dec, 1 Jan, Good Fri; (01274) 435900; free.

National Museum of Photography, Film and Television (Princes View) Eight interactive galleries take in everything from John Logie Baird to the toys from *Play School*. Among the three million items kept here are the world's first negative, very early television footage, and what's generally considered the first example of moving pictures - Louis Le Prince's 1888 film of Leeds Bridge. Wallace and Gromit and Morph explain the secrets of animation, and you can try your hand at operating a camera or reading the news. Favourite parts include the intriguing photography gallery, which shows the cameras used to create the Cottingley fairies, and a stunning gallery showcasing the latest digital technology, where you can experiment with virtual reality; also the cameras used on Ealing comedies and James Bond films. A new exhibition has highlights from the Royal Photographic Society's collection (recently acquired with the help of lottery funding). The five storeys high IMAX screen regularly shows 3D and other films, and more conventionally sized cinemas offer films from around the world; they do guided tours. Meals, snacks, excellent shop, disabled access; cl Mon (exc bank hols and school summer hols), 25 Dec; (0870) 701 0200; free, IMAX cinema £5.95.

BRAMHAM SE4041

Bramham Park 🏛 The garden here is really quite beautiful, very much in the grand style - Versailles comes to Yorkshire. Long prospects of ornamental lakes, cascades, temples, statuary, grand hedges and stately trees and avenues surround a classical Queen Anne house of great distinction. Some disabled access to gardens; house open by written appointment only, gardens open daily Apr-Sept exc during horse trials (7-14 Jun) and Leeds festival (16 Aug-4 Sept), but best to check; (01937) 846000; grounds and gardens £4. The Red Lion has enjoyable food.

BRODSWORTH SE5007

Brodsworth Hall and Gardens Grand house vividly illustrating life in Victorian times; the family that lived here closed off parts of the house as their fortunes waned, inadvertently preserving the contents and décor exactly as they were (right down to the billiard score-book). Richly furnished

rooms, lots of marble statues, and busily cluttered servants' wing; a new exhibition covers the use of chintz in english country houses. The family commissioned some of the largest and fastest yachts of the Victorian era, and an exhibition charts the history of these splendid vessels. The marvellous formal gardens and parkland are gradually being restored. Meals, snacks, shop, disabled access; cl am, Mon (exc bank hols), and all Nov-Mar (exc gardens open wknds); (01302) 722598; £6; EH.

CARL WARK SK2581

On the edge of the Peak District, this hill fort is set handsomely in a great bowl fringed by gritstone outcrops, and offers a more interesting walk than most in South Yorkshire. The Fox House nearby (A6187/A625) has good value food.

CAWTHORNE SE2708

Cannon Hall Open Farm Unusual animals such as wallabies and llamas among the residents at this busy working farm; also baby animals throughout the year, with piglets born regularly. Good play areas, and mostly concreted so doesn't get muddy. Meals, snacks, shop, disabled access; cl 25 Dec; (01226) 790427; £2.75. Cannon Hall itself is now a museum with paintings (mostly Old Masters) and fine furniture, glassware and pottery, in a series of period rooms and galleries; also a military collection, and special events. Snacks (wknds and school hols), shop; open Weds-Fri and pm wknds Apr-Oct, pm Sun only Nov-Dec and Mar; (01226) 790270; free. The grounds are an attractive country park (£1.50 parking). The village is pleasant, and the Cherry Tree overlooking the park from High Hoyland has a small popular restaurant.

CONISBROUGH SK5198

Conisbrough Castle 🏛 Mightily impressive 12th-c castle with uniquely designed 27-metre (90-ft) keep - circular, with six buttresses and a curtain wall with solid round towers. An added roof and floors re-create something of the original feel, and there's a good audio-visual show; special events in summer. Meals, snacks, shop; cl 24-26 Dec, 1 Jan; (01709) 863329; *£3.75; EH. Sir Walter Scott set much of *Ivanhoe* here, writing the novel while staying at the Boat at Sprotbrough nearby; then a riverside farm, it's now a good dining pub.

CUSWORTH SE5403
Cusworth Hall Museum (Cusworth Lane, just W of Doncaster) Excellent museum of South Yorkshire life, in an elegant 18th-c house. Displays on mining, transport, costume and entertainment, and especially popular gallery of toys and childhood. Meals, snacks, shop, disabled access to ground floor only; cl Sun am, 25-26 Dec, 1 Jan and Good Fri; (01302) 782342; free.

DENABY MAIN SK4999
Earth Centre Perhaps the most ambitious of all the country's environmental centres, this Millennium Commission project is sited in a great tract of former coal-mining land, being rehabilitated over the last decade or so. Overlooked by mighty Conisbrough Castle and rarely busy, the centre aims to promote environmental issues in an enjoyable way through a range of attractions taking in an interactive nature trail (with pond-dipping, eco-friendly games and an area designed to stimulate all your senses along the way), galleries looking at the history and future of the planet's development, and specially themed gardens dotted with often bizarre-looking constructions. There's also a rainforest-themed adventure playground, a new play area (Bluebeard's Galleon), and adventure golf. Meals, snacks, shop, disabled access; cl 25 Dec and 1 Jan; (01709) 512000; £5, £10 for one day's unlimited use of all activities. You can stay here too. The nearby Cadeby Inn is a good restaurant pub.

DEWSBURY SE2522
Dewsbury Museum (Crow Nest Park, Heckmondwike Rd) Cheerful place, with a collection of toys dating back to the 1900s, a new interactive exhibition on the role of toys in our lives, a children's trail, and a re-created 1940s classroom; temporary exhibitions and events too. Snacks, shop, some disabled access; cl am wknds, 25-26 Dec and Good Fri; (01924) 325100; free. The station buffet in the town is famously good.

DONCASTER SE5802
Not a great deal to attract visitors apart from its race meetings, but there is some fine architecture, especially around the High St and Market Pl, and a junk market on Weds.

Doncaster Museum and Art Gallery (Chequer Rd) Archaeology displays, local history and a good deal of natural history; parts may be shut till the refurbishment is finished (they hope this summer). Shop, good disabled access; cl Sun am, 25-26 Dec, 1 Jan and Good Fri; (01302) 734287; free.

ELSECAR SK3899
Elsecar Heritage Centre (Wath Rd) Developing centre in restored industrial workshops, with a history centre (cl Mon; £1.50) where you can dress up and star in a Victorian melodrama, and a beam engine, bottle museum, craft workshops and new antiques centre. On Sun Mar-Oct a diesel or steam loco runs to the Hemingfield Basin (£2.50). Meals, snacks, shop, disabled access; cl 25 Dec and 1 Jan; (01226) 740203; free. The Milton Arms (Armroyd Lane) is a welcoming pub where the landlady does the cooking.

ESHOLT SE1840
St Leonard's Farm Park (Chapel Lane) You can handle and feed some of animals at this working dairy farm, with play areas (inc a popular straw barn), nature trails and mini tractors; pony and tractor rides some days (£1 extra). New tearoom, shop, disabled access; cl Mon (exc bank and school summer hols), wkdys mid-Sept to mid-Oct, and Mar to mid-Apr, all mid-Oct to Feb, phone to check; (01274) 598795; £2.75. The TV series *Emmerdale* used to be filmed in the picturesque village.

FULNECK SE2232
Built by the Moravians in the mid-18th-c (even today most of the inhabitants are Moravian), this unique place has fine Georgian buildings, inc the appealingly simple church; there's also a craft centre (cl Sun-Tues). A little museum has displays on the history of the Moravians and the village; re-created Victorian parlour, lace and embroidery, even inuit carvings, and one of the the country's oldest fire engines. Shop; open pm Weds and Sat Easter-Oct; (0113) 2564147; £1.

GOLCAR SE0915
Colne Valley Museum 🄴 (Cliffe

Ash) Enthusiastic museum spread over three weavers' cottages, with hand weaving, spinning and clog-making in gas-lit surroundings, and a re-created 1850s living room; occasional craft festivals. Snacks, shop, limited disabled access; open pm wknds and some bank hols; (01484) 659762; *£1.40. There's a good year-round walk along the Huddersfield Canal's restored towpath between here and Marsden in *Last of the Summer Wine* country. Up on Slades Rd, Bolster Moor, the Golcar Lily has good food.

GOMERSAL SE2026
Red House Museum (Oxford Rd) Former cloth merchant's home which vividly re-creates the 1830s in its nine carefully furnished period rooms. Charlotte Brontë often stayed at the house, and it featured as Briarmains in her novel *Shirley*. The gardens have been restored in 1830s style, and the restored barn and cartsheds have exhibitions on the Brontës and local history. Snacks, shop, disabled access to ground floor; cl am wknds, Good Fri, 25-26 Dec and 1 Jan; (01274) 335100; free.

GOOSE EYE SE0240
Interesting preserved village; good drives around here. The Turkey has decent food and brews its own beer.

HALIFAX SE0925
Another town with an impressive show of former textiles wealth, interesting to drive through when it's quiet on a summer evening or a Sunday, and surrounded by a splendid ring of moorland. The centre's been cleaned up and partly pedestrianised, which makes it pleasant to potter through, and there are several first-class attractions, with the town now going through something of an artistic renaissance. The medieval church has an extremely grand spire and fine carving: look out for Old Tristram, the life-size painted carving of a beggar which was used to collect alms. The 17th-c waterside Shibden Mill (Shibden - off A58 via Kell Lane) is a lovely place for a meal.
Bankfield Museum (Ackroyd Park, Boothtown Rd) Collection of textiles, costume and contemporary crafts, as well as a regimental museum and display of toys. Snacks, shop, disabled access to ground floor only; cl Sun am, Mon (exc

bank hols), and 24 Dec-3 Jan; (01422) 354823; free.
Dean Clough Enormous carpet mill, faced with demolition when it closed down some years ago, but now well restored and home to a thriving complex of galleries and small businesses; best are the Crossley Gallery and Henry Moore Studio, the latter a great showcase for contemporary sculpture; (01422) 250250; cl 25-26 Dec, 1 Jan; free.
Eureka! (Discovery Rd) Remarkable hands-on museum designed exclusively for children; few places are as likely to spellbind anyone between around 3 and 12. Each of the four main galleries ostensibly explores one subject, but in fact covers a multitude of topics and ideas. Particular highlights are the broad-based Things Gallery, full of bright colours and images, the communications gallery (you can put your picture on a front page, save a yacht in distress, or read the TV news), and Living and Working Together, where children try their hand at grown-up activities like filling a car with petrol at the garage, working in a shop or bank, or making a meal in the kitchen. They've recently been awarded £3.8m for a 3-year project to boost the way they are breathing life into science, technology, engineering and maths; a new interactive gallery focusing on music and creativity through science is planned. Snacks, shop, disabled access; cl 24-26 Dec; (01422) 330069; £5.95.
Piece Hall (centre) This magnificent Renaissance-looking galleried and arcaded building, opened in 1776, was built by the merchants of Halifax as a market for their cloth. It houses many specialist shops selling books, antiques and bric-a-brac, and there's an art gallery (cl Mon exc bank hols) and other exhibitions. Meals, snacks, shop, disabled access; cl 25-26 Dec and 1 Jan; (01422) 358087; free. There are market stalls in the italianate courtyard on Sat, Thurs (second-hand), a few on Fri and Sun.
Shibden Hall & Folk Museum (Godley Lane, off A58 just E) Excellently refurbished 15th-c house, each room illustrating a different period from its history. In the barn a folk museum has an interesting collection of horse-

drawn vehicles, while outside are reconstructed 19th-c workshops, a cottage and even a pub. Boating lake, miniature railway, play area and woodland walks in the 36-hectare (90-acre) park. For many this is a real Halifax highlight. Snacks, shop, limited disabled access; cl Sun am, and 24 Dec-2 Jan; (01422) 352246; £3.50.

Wainhouse Tower This 75-metre (250-ft) folly offers good views if you can manage all those steps. Shop; usually open bank hols (not Christmas), Easter, Father's Day, last Sun in July, and the 2nd Sun in Sept, but best to check (01422) 393213; £1.55.

HAREWOOD SE3245

Harewood House & Bird Garden 🖼 (A61) The area's most magnificent stately home, inside and out. The 18th-c exterior is splendidly palatial, and inside is some glorious restored Robert Adam plasterwork. Fine Chippendale furnishings, exquisite Sèvres and chinese porcelain, and paintings by Turner, El Greco, Bellini, Titian and Gainsborough. Capability Brown designed the grounds which stretch for well over a mile, with very pleasing lakeside and woodland walks, a spectacular formal cascade, an outstanding collection of rhododendron species and other more recently introduced himalayan and chinese plants, and the famous landscaped bird garden (you could spend half a day in just this part). Charles Barry's Terrace has an excellent gallery with contemporary art and crafts. Try to visit the 15th-c **church**, with a splendid array of tombs, and a curious tunnel under the wall of the churchyard, so that servants could arrive unseen by sensitive souls. The adventure playground is first-class. Meals, snacks, shop, disabled access; cl Nov-Mar (exc wknds Nov-Dec); (0113) 218 1010; £9.50 everything, £6.75 bird garden and grounds only (please quote reference 434 with discount voucher, which excludes Sun and bank hols). The Harewood Arms opposite has good food, and just N Wharfedale Grange has **pick-your-own** fruit.

HAWORTH SE0237

A touristy village with plenty of craft shops, antiques shops and tea shops catering for all the people drawn here by the Brontës (spelt Brunty before father Patrick went posh). A visit out of season catches it at its best, though at any time the steep cobbled main street has quieter more appealing side alleys. Most of the family are buried in the churchyard, except Anne, interred in Scarborough. For the most evocative views and atmosphere go up to the moors above town, very grand and not much different from when the Brontës knew them - despite the japanese footpath signs. The Old White Lion (West Lane) and the 17th-c Old Hall (Sun St) are good value for lunch. The A6033 is an interesting drive to Hebden Bridge, and there's a fine old moors road via Stanbury (with its nice Old Silent pub) over to the Colne Valley in Lancashire.

Brontë walks The Pennine moors around here are a favourite stamping-ground for walkers, with a good walk W through Penistone Hill Country Park to the much-visited **Brontë Waterfalls**, and on through a remote valley to Withins, the original Wuthering Heights. There are plenty of paths, though finding the way across fields frequently entails searching for unprominent stone stiles over the dry-stone walls.

Keighley & Worth Valley Railway Actually begins just N at Keighley (where you can connect with mainline trains) but is based here. Run by enthusiastic volunteers, the line was built to serve the valley's mills, and passes through the heart of Brontë country. The prettiest station is Oakworth (familiar to many from the film *The Railway Children*). Snacks, shop (open daily exc 25 Dec), some disabled access; steam trains (good buffet car) run wknds all year, Tues-Thurs last 2 wks Jun, daily July-early Sept, and Easter school hols, best to check; (01535) 645214 for timetable; £7 return, £10 unlimited travel for one day.

Museum of Rail Travel (Ingrow Railway Centre, A629) Collection of historic railway carriages and a steam locomotive; unusually displays focus on what rail travel was like for passengers, and you can sometimes watch restoration work taking place. Snacks, shop, disabled access; cl 25 Dec;

(01535) 680425; £1.50.

Parsonage Museum The Brontës' former home has some 80,000 visitors a year (it was something of a tourist attraction even while Charlotte still lived here). The house is very carefully preserved, with period furnishings, very good changing exhibitions, and displays of the siblings' books, manuscripts and possessions inc the sisters' writing table. In autumn 2003 they won a 10-year landmark case against Customs & Excise, enabling them to claim back around £596,000 in VAT payments - they now hope to improve disabled access to the ground floor, and add a virtual tour of upstairs. Shop; cl 24-27 Dec, 2-31 Jan; (01535) 642323; £4.80.

HEATH SE3519
Extraordinarily old-fashioned common with gipsy ponies alongside 18th-c mansions (and contrasting views over Wakefield); the gaslit Kings Arms here is good.

HEBDEN BRIDGE SD9927
Engaging small town deep in a valley below the moors, and stepped very steeply up the hillsides. The White Lion (Bridge Gate) has good value food all day. In summer there are horse-drawn barge trips along the canal basin; (01422) 845557. The hold of one barge in the marina has been converted into a **visitor centre** with a traditional boatman's cabin (cl Nov-Easter; free). From Hebden Bridge, you can gain access to the Mary Towneley Loop, a circular 47-mile route (the first part of the Pennine Bridleway National Trail, which will eventually stretch almost 350 miles from Derbyshire to Northumbria), good for walkers, horse-riders and cyclists; you can hire bikes at Blazing Saddles in Hebden Bridge; (01422) 844435. Phone for a map (0161) 2371061.

Hardcastle Crags A beauty spot above the wooded river valley, ideal for walks or a picnic. The Nutclough House on the way up also has decent food.

Heptonstall An interesting and ancient village, a crippling climb up a fearsomely steep cobbled lane above Hebden Bridge; Sylvia Plath is buried in the churchyard. The adjacent early 17th-c Cross Inn has good value hearty food. There's a rewarding scenic path along Heptonstall Crags (the cliffs above the wooded valley of Colden Water). An exhilarating old high road leads out to Widdop and beyond (for fine views and walks), and another runs via Colden and Blackshaw Head.

HOLMFIRTH SE1408
Instantly recognisable as the setting for TV's *Last of the Summer Wine*, with evocative little alleys, several good pubs, and a handsome Georgian church. **Compo's World** 🏛 (Huddersfield Rd) An exhibition on *Last of the Summer Wine*, the longest-running comedy series in the world. Meals, snacks, shop; cl 25 Dec; (01484) 681408; *£1.50. The Rose & Crown (Victoria Sq) nicely fits the mood.

HUDDERSFIELD SE1416
There's a great sense of style in many of its buildings, especially around the station and central square, and much of the centre is now closed to traffic; it well repays an afternoon visit. The A640 W is a good moorland drive.

Huddersfield Narrow Canal
Running between here and Ashton-under-Lyne in Lancashire, the whole canal is now navigable. The highest in Britain, it rises 134 metres (440 ft) through 42 locks to Marsden, where the Standedge Tunnel is Britain's longest (over three miles), and deepest - the Tunnel End pub there has decent food. The **Standedge Visitor Centre** will tell you more about the canal's history, with interactive exhibitions; there's a play area, and you can go on a short guided boat trip. Cl Mon and Tues Nov-Mar, and 24 Dec-2 Jan; (01484) 844298; £4.50 inc boat trip.

Jubilee Tower (Almondbury) Castle Hill is 275 metres (900 ft) high, overlooking the surrounding moors; the restored tower with its 165 steps gives unrivalled views, even over the Pennines and Peak District. Shop; open pm wknds and bank hols Easter-mid-Sept; £1.20. The Bowl nearby is a good food pub.

Tolson Museum (Ravensknowle Park) The myths and legends asssociated with Castle Hill are outlined in this former wool baron's mansion, which also has a look at the textile industry; there's a collection of horse-drawn vehicles, and a puzzle trail for the under-5s. Snacks, shop, disabled access; cl am wknds and 24 Dec-2 Jan; (01484) 223830; free.

ILKLEY SE1147

Owes its Victorian and Edwardian spaciousness and style to the mid-19th-c and later craze for hydropathic 'cures', which produced quite a rash of luxurious hydros using the town's pure moorland spring water. Their forerunner was the simple little bath-house built in the mid-18th c around the ice-cold spring up on the moor just S at White Wells - you can still follow the paths the infirm took by donkey. The group of quaintly shaped rocks known as the Cow & Calf up here also makes a pleasant short walk above the town. The church has three lovely Saxon crosses, and just beside it are traces of a Roman fort. There are a good few prehistoric remains around the town, the best known of which is the Bronze Age Swastika Stone, a symbol of eternity carved on a flat rock by a moorland path SE of the town, above wooded Hebers Ghyll; the stone is marked on the Ordnance Survey 1:50,000 map, at SE095469. Hebers Ghyll itself is a picturesque ravine with steep Victorian walkways, and the town with its attractive gardens and interest-ing shops makes a nice stop. Ilkley Moor S of the town has potential for satisfying high-level walks. Reliable lunch places are the Bar t'at (Cunliffe Rd), Cow & Calf (moors road SE towards Hawksworth) and Wheatley (Ben Rhydding).

Manor House Gallery & Museum (Castle Yard) One of the few buildings in town to predate the 19th c, an Elizabethan manor house built on the site of a Roman fort, with local history displays. Shop; cl Sun am, all day Mon (exc bank hols) and Tues, 25-26 Dec and Good Fri; (01943) 600066; free.

KEIGHLEY SE0542

(pronounced Keithly) A busy working town with a pleasant centre. The Grinning Rat near the 16th-c church is popular for lunch, and the newish Dalesway (Bradford Rd, Sandbeds) is a useful family dining pub.

Cliffe Castle Museum and Gallery (Spring Gardens Lane) This 19th-c mansion is now a museum with local natural history, and displays of minerals

and fossils; also temporary exhibitions, and some furnished rooms. Though quite close to the centre, it's in a park well above the main road, with aviaries and greenhouses. Shop, disabled access to ground floor only; cl Sun am, all day Mon (exc bank hols), 25-26 Dec, Good Fri; (01535) 618231; free.

East Riddlesden Hall 🏠 (Bradford Rd, just NE) Interesting early 17th-c oak-panelled stone manor house with attractive plasterwork, period textiles and furniture. There's a medieval monastic pond, an orchard garden and herbaceous border (plants for sale), huge tithe barn, and children's quiz and play area. Snacks, shop, some disabled access; cl am, and Mon (exc July-Aug), Thurs, Fri, and all Nov-Mar; (01535) 607075; *£3.80; NT.

LEEDS SE2934

Leeds alone among big UK cities is not suffering a serious population drain; people like living there, and want to stay. It's prosperous again these days (flourishing financial services industry), with bright young evening crowds around the bars and clubs of its compact and largely traffic-free centre, which has a virtually 24-hour café culture. For visitors, it's now really rewarding to visit, with something for all ages: its Royal Armouries Museum is an outstanding family day out, Tropical World is popular with children, and there's plenty more to fill a short stay. With the exception of the Royal Armouries and City Art Gallery, the museums and attractions are widely spread and too far to reach on foot; there's a hop-on hop-off tourist bus during the school summer hols, and this year the council hopes to extend it to the whole summer season. By day the city centre is ideal for shopping and exploring on foot, with all sorts of interesting and engaging Victorian architectural details to spot: the highlights are the splendid covered arcades (Victorian, Edwardian and modern), the Town Hall, the huge and exuberantly glass-roofed market (Europe's biggest; where Marks of Marks & Spencer fame set up his first penny bazaar in 1884), the former Dysons jewellers (Briggate; now part of Marriotts Hotel, and used for wedding receptions, but you can peer through the window into the wonderfully preserved brass and mahogany interior), and the handsome oval Corn Exchange, now full of small shops. Park Square is a handsome Georgian creation overlooked by an extraordinary Victorian building bristling with minarets. The City Varieties Hall still has authentic old-style music hall programmes (this was the home of the *Good Old Days*), while the West Yorkshire Playhouse is a useful meeting place with fine city views from its good café/bar, and the sumptuous Grand is home of Opera North. Whitelocks (Turks Head Yard, off Briggate) is a marvellous old city tavern, very much a Leeds institution. The Waterfront area has been partly restored and partly redeveloped; you can walk along the river in places, although building work around Clarence Dock and the Royal Armouries Museum has made parts inaccessible. The so-called Dark Arches, beneath Leeds City station, are reached by a rather grotty approach through Neville St: as you walk along a subterranean street towards Granary Wharf there's an extraordinary view where you cross an underground river gushing from the dark, bricky gloom.

Abbey House 🏛 (opposite Kirkstall Abbey) You can wander freely through re-created Victorian streets at this enjoyable museum, and right through some of the shops, inc their ironic conjunction of tavern, smoker's pipe maker and undertaker. There's an interactive gallery on childhood (some good games and interesting facts here), and another gallery shows what life would have been like as a medieval monk. Outside are gardens, a play area, and picnic tables. Meals, snacks, shop, disabled access; cl all Mon, am Sat, 25-26 Dec, and 1 Jan; (0113) 230 5492; *£3.

Armley Mills Industrial Museum 🏛 (Canal Rd) Once the largest woollen mill in the world, now a huge museum, its floors given over to a massive display of textile machinery. Also a printing gallery, reconstructions of a small 1930s clothing factory, a 1920s-style cinema, and demonstrations of railway locomotives (bank and summer hols,

phone to check). Snacks and picnic area, shop, disabled access; cl Sun am, Mon (exc bank hols), 25-26 Dec, 1 Jan; (0113) 263 7861; *£2.

Corn Exchange (Call Lane) This impressive 1860s building is now filled with neat little specialist and trendy clothes shops, and has places for tea, coffee, and so forth.

Henry Moore Institute (The Headrow) Effectively an annexe of the Leeds City Art Gallery, this delightful place has temporary exhibitions of sculpture from Roman times to the present (they don't actually show anything by Henry Moore); guided tours by arrangement. Shop, disabled access; cl bank hols, plus 24 and 31 Dec, and 2 Jan; (0113) 246 7467; free. It stays open late on Weds.

Kirkstall Abbey (off A65, 2m NW of centre) Built in the 12th c and in attractive grounds, this is one of Britain's best-preserved Cistercian monasteries; (0113) 230 5492; free.

Leeds City Art Gallery (The Headrow) Excellent collection of 19th and 20th-c british art, inc good watercolours and sculpture gallery with carefully chosen works by Henry Moore, also Pre-Raphaelites and Stanley Spencer. Meals, snacks, shop, limited disabled access; cl Sun am and bank hols; (0113) 247 8248; free. It stays open late on Weds.

Leeds City Museum Resource Centre (Moorfield Rd, out at Yeadon) Offering access to the excellent stored collections of the closed Leeds City Museum; the highlight is Natsef Amun (Keeper of the Bulls), an important egyptian mummy which has been in the city for almost 200 years; also displays of local wildlife, minerals and fossils, and exhibits from ancient Greece and Rome. Shop, some disabled access (notice preferred); open by appointment only Mon-Fri; (0113) 214 6526; free.

Meanwood Valley Urban Farm (Meanwood) Small working organic farm on regenerated waste land N of centre, with rare breeds, organic market garden, environment centre and a new play area. Meals, snacks, shop selling organic farm produce, good disabled access; café cl Mon; (0113) 262 9759; *£1.

Middleton Railway Running from Tunstall Rd to Middleton Park, this is the oldest running railway in the world and was the first to be authorised by Parliament in 1758. Later it was the first to succeed with steam locomotives, and in 1960 became the first standard-gauge line to be operated by volunteers. With a picnic area, fishing, nature trail and playgrounds as well as the shed with a large collection of industrial steam and diesel engines on display, there's plenty for families here. Snacks, shop, disabled access; diesel or steam trains most wknds and bank hols Apr-Christmas; (0113) 271 0320 or www.middletonrailway.org.uk for timetable; £2.50.

Roundhay Park (off A58) A mile or more of rolling parkland, well known for concerts and events. On Princes Avenue here the Canal Gardens are a very pleasant and peaceful corner of the city, with several national flower collections (inc dahlias and violas), lots of roses, and ornamental wildfowl; free. The Roundhay dining pub has very cheap food.

Royal Armouries Museum (Clarence Dock, Waterfront) The city's top indoor attraction is a stunning modern building overlooking the river and the Leeds & Liverpool Canal, with its own purpose-built tilting yard, staging jousting, fencing, duelling, and hunting dogs and birds of prey. The five galleries inside are so all-embracing and imaginatively laid out that there's something to interest almost everyone, delving into such subjects as hunting, oriental warfare, self-defence and tournaments. Among some of the stranger exhibits is an astonishing suit of armour made for an elephant, a bespectacled and horned helmet made for Henry VIII which is supposed to look frightening but just looks comical, and a special pistol for bicyclists to shoot fierce dogs with. Touch-screen interactives let you try your skills as a general in the Zulu Wars or in dressing Henry VIII in armour, and for £2 you can try the shooting galleries (crossbows and a police-style shooting range). Events each half-hour include story-telling, martial arts, and actors recounting battles past. Outside you can chat to skilled craftsmen making armour, leather and other items, and see the falcons in their mews. Meals, snacks, shop, good disabled access; cl 24-25 Dec; (0113) 2201999; free.

St John's Church (New Briggate) Exceptional 17th-c church, with an unusual double-aisled nave and plaster ceilings you'd expect in a country house rather than an ecclesiastical building. Overall, the quality and completeness of the original dark wood furnishings is really striking, with the pews, pulpit and ornate screen. Open daily, free, but future access to visitors is in question.

Temple Newsam House (5m E, S of A63) Capability Brown designed the wonderful two square miles of landscaped parkland and gardens in which this house stands, an extraordinary asset for any city. Recently reopened after extensive restoration and damp-proofing, the house itself dates from Tudor and Jacobean times, and contains the city's very good collections of decorative and fine art, as well as an exceptional assemblage of Chippendale furniture; they do free tours on Tues. Rare breeds and a working organic farm in the grounds, picnic and play areas. Shop, disabled access (with a lift now); grounds open daily (free, £1.50 car park), house cl Mon, 25-26 Dec; (0113) 264 7321; £4.

Thackray Medical Museum 📷 (St James's Hospital, Beckett St) A surprising favourite not only for readers but also their children, this dynamic museum puts the emphasis more on social history than on science. But there are interactive displays on how the body works, and good reconstructions showing the progress of medical care in Britain, inc some deliciously gruesome parts on surgery before the development of anaesthetics. Children particularly like the part where they pick a character, then discover their fate as they work their way around the museum. Meals, snacks, shop, disabled access; cl 24-26, 31 Dec, 1 Jan; (0113) 244 4343; £4.90.

Thwaite Mills Watermill (Stourton, 2m S) This water-powered mill was the focus of a tiny island community perched between the River Aire - which drives the mill wheels - and the

Aire & Calder Navigation. The restored Georgian mill-owner's house has displays on the site's history; guided mill tours every hour. Snacks, shop, disabled access; cl wkdys during school term-times, Mon (exc bank hols), am wknds, 24-26 Dec, 1 Jan; (0113) 249 6453; £2.

Town Hall (Headrow) One of the grandest of all the northern town halls, this is a potent symbol of the city's commercial might in Victorian times, a classical design of 1853 by Charles Brodick. You can usually get a free pass from the reception desk and look into the splendid Victoria Hall (Mon-Fri, providing it is not in use), with its immense pipe organ, and there are free tours of the whole building by arrangement; (0113) 247 7989. The ornate Victoria behind is a landmark Leeds pub.

Tropical World (Roundhay Park) Huge conservatory with the biggest collection of tropical plants outside Kew, along with all sorts of exotic trees, reptiles, fish, birds and butterflies, in careful re-creations of their natural settings. Meals, snacks, shop, disabled access; cl 25-26 Dec; (0113) 266 1850; £3.

LOTHERTON HALL SE4436 (B1217 Garforth—Tadcaster) Edwardian house with displays ranging from oriental art to british fashion, as well as paintings, silver and ceramics, and some lovely furnishings. The restored grounds are good for strolling, with a bird garden, an interesting bronze statue in the front rose garden, and a 12th-c chapel. Snacks and picnic area, shop, disabled access to grounds and café only; cl Mon (exc bank hols), am Sun, 24-26 Dec, and Jan-Feb; (0113) 281 3259; £2 house, grounds free, £2 car park. The Swan in nearby Aberford is popular for lunch.

LUDDENDEN SE0426 Interesting village with Brontë connections; the enormous Oats Royd Mill in the valley is a remarkable sight. Luddenden Dean valley gives lovely walks, and up near the top the Cat i' th' Well (off Castle Carr Rd, Wainstalls) has above-average food.

MALTBY SK5489 **Roche Abbey** 🏛 (off A634 SE) A fine gatehouse to the NW and the still-standing walls of the S and N transepts are all that's left of this 12th-c Cistercian abbey, but they make an impressive sight. Some disabled access; cl Nov-Mar; (01709) 812739; £2; EH.

MIDDLESTOWN SE2416 **National Coal Mining Museum** (Caphouse Colliery, New Rd) A fascinating glimpse of life as a miner, inc an excellent underground tour which takes you 140 metres (450 ft) down, exploring miners' work from the 1800s to the present. The hour-long tour is led by former miners, with lots of exciting tales to keep children enthralled. You'll be issued with a hard hat and belt; wear sensible shoes, and warm clothing even in summer. Arrive well before noon at wknds or school hols to get on a tour (places are limited, for safety). There are quite a few things to see on the surface as well, inc many of the original pit buildings, and plenty of the old machinery and equipment. Well organised interactive displays give an intriguing insight into the miners' home lives, and there are several happily retired pit ponies. A good indoor play area for under-5s (they're not allowed to go underground). Meals, snacks, shop, disabled access (even underground, though helpful to arrange it in advance); cl 24-26 Dec, 1 Jan; (01924) 848806; free.

MONK BRETTON SE3706 **Monk Bretton Priory** The red sandstone remains of an important 12th-c priory, with 14th-c gatehouse (restored), church and other buildings, as well as some unusually well preserved drains; EH; free. The ancient Mill of the Black Monks is pleasant at lunchtime (live music for young people most nights).

NORLAND MOOR SE0521 S of Sowerby Bridge, this gives walkers views from the Calderdale Way into adjacent Calderdale, with the Rochdale Canal along its foot.

NORTH ANSTON SK5284 **Tropical Butterfly House** (Woodsetts Rd) Friendly place with insects, reptiles, snakes, birds of prey and farm animals, besides the butterflies; they positively encourage you to touch as well as look. Also tractor trailer rides (exc winter) and interactive display boards. Meals (in season and wknds), snacks, shop, disabled access; cl 24-26 Dec and 1 Jan; (01909) 569416; £4.80. The Duke of Leeds over in Wales (Church St) does good value lunches, not Mon-Tues.

NOSTELL PRIORY SE4017

🖼 (off A638) This sumptuous Palladian mansion, with an additional wing built by Adam in 1766, has perhaps the best collection of Chippendale furniture anywhere, all designed for this house. Other highlights include the tapestry room, charming saloon, servants' hall and great kitchen, and a remarkably intricate 18th-c dolls' house. The most attractive grounds have woodland walks and a lovely rose garden, with coarse fishing on the lakes; special events. Near the entrance is an interesting **medieval church**. Meals, snacks, shop, disabled access; cl am, plus Mon, Tues, and Nov to mid-Mar (exc wknds till mid-Dec), grounds also open from 11am and first 2 wknds in Mar, best to check; (01924) 863892; house and gardens £5, grounds only £2.50; NT. The Spread Eagle has good value food.

OAKWELL HALL SE2127

(signed off A651/A652 S of Birkenshaw) Moated Elizabethan manor house, altered in the 17th c and still furnished to give something of the atmosphere then; look out for the unusual dog gates at the foot of the staircase. Also period formal gardens, extensive country park with adventure playground, visitor centre and, for children, the Discovery Gallery - a hands-on exploration of the four 'elements', earth, air, fire and water. Snacks, shop, disabled access to ground floor only; Discovery Gallery and visitor centre cl am wknds, Good Fri, best to phone over Christmas and New Year; (01924) 326240; £1.40 house (free Nov-Feb), visitor centre and Discovery Gallery free. The ancient Black Bull opposite the partly Saxon church in nearby Birstall has good cheap food.

OGDEN RESERVOIR SE0630

N of Halifax, this is well served with paths for walkers (inc a stretch of Roman road). The Moorlands (A629) is popular for lunch.

OTLEY SE2045

Archetypal Yorkshire market town on the River Wharfe with a most attractive atmosphere; Fri and Sat (plus Tues in summer) are market days. The Rose & Crown (Bondgate) is good value for lunch.

The Chevin Behind the town, this is not a high hill, but gives walkers a grand view of Wharfedale; Chevin Forest Park offers plenty of scope for enjoyable walks.

RIPPONDEN SE0318

Rather austerely attractive, with medieval packhorse bridge; the B6113 and B6114 above here are interesting moors roads. The 14th-c Old Bridge has good food.

ROTHERHAM SK4091

Magna (off A6178, SW of centre; Templeborough) In an awesomely converted former steel works, this centre puts a colourful spin on the story of the steel industry. It has four themed pavilions based around the main elements used in steel-making: Earth, housed in the basement, re-creates the drama of working in a quarry; Air is an inflated structure, designed to look like an airship hovering over the main factory floor; Water gives children plenty of excuses to soak their parents; and Fire, set around a giant live flame, uses audio-visual displays to illustrate how man has controlled fire for his benefit, as well as its explosive (and destructive) possibilities. Plenty of emphasis on hands-on activities and interactive experiences. Meals, snacks, shop, disabled access; cl 24-25 Dec; (01709) 720002; £8.

SALTAIRE SE1337

The pioneering industrial village Titus Salt developed in Shipley in the 1850s, now a World Heritage Site. Salt's beautifully thought out classically designed village was so successful that even now it's a favoured place to live. It's well worth looking around, and you might want to try the antique **cable railway** (60p return). There's a splendid flight of locks on the Leeds—Liverpool Canal.

1853 Gallery (Victoria Rd) Named from the year when the magnificent mill it's housed in was built, with one of the largest collections of contemporary art in the country, inc around 300 works by David Hockney, especially some of his intriguing experiments with photography. Huge bookshop, disabled access; (01274) 531163; cl 25-26 Dec, 1 Jan; free. Some good smart shops, and a restaurant in the building too.

Victorian Reed Organ Museum (Victoria Hall, Victoria Rd) Unique, with some eye-opening exhibits, inc one organ no bigger than a family Bible. If you're an organ-player you may get the chance to try some of those on display. Shop, limited disabled access (with notice); cl Fri, Sat, and Dec-Jan; (01274) 585601; £2.50.

SAXTON SE4736
Attractive village with decent pub; don't miss the magnificent church, where Lord Dacre is buried sitting on his war horse - the 1461 Battle of Towton site is just N. The Greyhound by the church is a charming unspoilt pub.

SHEFFIELD SK3281
A vast industrial city that spreads out to the edges of the Pennines, with the Peak District on its back doorstep - even from the centre there are surprising vistas of the hills. Although much of the city centre is uninspiring, having been redeveloped extensively in post-war years, parts are benefitting from a major facelift, notably around the Town Hall (itself worth a peek in for its flamboyantly Victorian entrance hall; Tudor Square, Winter Garden and the new Peace Gardens are just beyond it) and the cheerful new waterfront development called Victoria Quays. Near the cathedral is the compact pre-Victorian centre, including Paradise Square and one or two Georgian streets leading into it; the Moon Café (St James's St) is a good value vegan café in one handsome building. Sheffield has also reinvented itself as a city of sport; attractions include Ice Sheffield (Coleridge Rd; (0114) 223 3900), an Olympic-sized skating facility, and Sheffield Ski Village (Vale Rd; (0114) 276 9459), with the largest dry ski slope in Europe (plus a virtual snow half pipe for snowboarders, and a toboggan run for under-16s). Getting about needs a street map and quite a bit of journeying, but there's an efficient modern tram; this runs out to the giant indoor

shopping mall at Meadowhall. Besides Smith's of Sheffield, good value food can be found at the Bankers Draft (all day; Market Pl).

Abbeydale Industrial Hamlet Museum (Abbeydale Road S - A621 SW) Atmospheric evocation of the early industrial age, this 18th-c steel-making community by the River Sheaf (which supplied the power) features crucible steel furnaces, workshops and workers' cottages. An audio tour guides you round the works and explains the processes; living history events some Suns. Meals, snacks, shop; cl Fri and Sat; (0114) 236 7731; £3. Along Abbeydale Rd is a concentration of antiques and bric-a-brac shops, inc several antiques centres. 5 mins' drive away by the B6375 and A625 the Dore Moor Inn is a well run family dining pub.

Bishop's House (Meersbrook Park, off A61 S) Striking 15th- and 16th-c yeoman's house, now a good museum of social history. Limited disabled access; cl wkdys exc by appointment; (0114) 278 2600; free.

Fire Police Museum The history of fire-fighting in a Victorian fire/police station, with themed areas inc a reconstructed fireman's bedroom and a car crash scene, fire appliances from an 18th-c manual pump cart to a 1974 Angus Jaguar, and hands-on exhibits; also model railway, play area and Fireman Sam video. Snacks, shop; open Sun (exc 26 Dec), and bank hol Mon; (0114) 249 1999; *£3. The Fat Cat nearby in Alma St has good cheap food.

Graves Art Gallery (Surrey St) Well worth a visit; above the public library and just across the street from the Millennium Galleries; 19th- and 20th-c art, inc works by Cézanne and Picasso, plus changing contemporary exhibitions. Cl Sun; (0114) 278 2600; free. The Red Lion in nearby Charles St has good simple food.

Kelham Island Industrial Museum (around Alma St, signed from centre) Lively exploration of Sheffield's industrial development in an area of small factories that's quite atmospheric for strolling around (from the tram stop at Shalesmoor you walk past the imposing archway of the Green Lane works, and the river bridge close by reveals a view). The museum was totally revamped for 2003, and the displays delve into steel and cutlery making in particular, with Tom Parkin's cutlery workshop (discovered in 1973 and preserved exactly as it was), the mighty River Don engine, in use up to 1978 and still in steam (12, 2 and 4pm Sun, 11am and 2pm Mon–Thurs); plus some zany exhibits such as a 365-blade 'year knife' and the world's heaviest bomb. You can also watch craftsmen at work. Snacks, shop, disabled access; cl Fri–Sat, and 24 Dec–1 Jan; (0114) 272 2106; £3.50. The Fat Cat here has really good cheap food.

Millennium Galleries and Winter Gardens (Arundel Gate) This elegant complex is the focal point of the city centre's redevelopment, with four exhibition spaces and several pleasant minimalist-style cafés. Adjoining and effectively within the same building is the Winter Garden, a gloriously roofed wood and glass modern glasshouse enclosing palms and other exotica, which makes an enticing, tranquil refuge from the city bustle. The Millennium Galleries include a metalwork gallery on the city's heritage, the Ruskin collection (previously at Norfolk St), and collections from London's Victoria & Albert Museum (which has been closely involved in the development); also changing craft and design exhibitions. Cafés, shop, disabled access; cl 24–26 Dec and 1 Jan; (0114) 278 2600; free, £4 for special shows; Winter Garden open daily, free. Several theatres and cinemas nearby, inc the Crucible Theatre in Tudor Sq.

Sheffield Bus Museum (Tinsley) Diverse collection of buses with related memorabilia and a big model railway. Snacks, shop; open pm wknds Easter–Christmas for restoration work, with special open days every couple of months when the displays are more lively; (0114) 255 3010; £1.50.

SOWERBY BRIDGE SE0623
Worth a stop if you're passing; turn down to the canal basin, a busy place since the 2003 completion of the £25m restoration of the trans-Pennine Rochdale Canal, which ends here. Running 32 miles from Manchester, the canal was hailed as a miracle of engineering ('the Everest of Canals') when it opened in 1804. The multi-level Moorings overlooking it has enjoyable food.

STAINBOROUGH SE3103
Wentworth Castle Gardens A heritage lottery grant of around £9 million is being used to restore these Grade I gardens and the surrounding Stainborough Park. Mostly laid out in the 18th c with Victorian and Edwardian additions, the 16-hectare (40-acre) gardens have national collections of rhododendrons, magnolias and camellias. Some disabled access (steep slopes); guided tours probably pm Tues and Thurs mid-Apr to end Aug, and some Sun pms (perhaps other times too), but phone to check; (01226) 731269; £2.50.

THORNTON SE1032
Brontë Birthplace 🏠 (72 Market St) Born here rather than in Haworth, the Brontë siblings lived here till 1820. Re-created in Regency style and still lived in; the knowledgeable owner (a writer herself) is happy to show you around. Shop; usually open pm Sun, Tues and bank hol Mon Apr–Sept, though best to check as the property is up for sale (01274) 830849; £4. The Ring o' Bells (Hill Top Rd, off B6145) is a good dining pub with great views.

THURGOLAND SE2900
Wortley Top Forge Built in 1640, this is one of the very few water-powered iron forges left anywhere in the world; there's a collection of steam and other engines, and a miniature railway usually runs when the forge is open; guided tours and a picnic site. Shop, phone for disabled access; open pm Sun and banks hols early Feb–late Nov; (0114) 288 7576; £2.

ULLEY SK4687
Pleasant walks around a reservoir, also good for fishing and watersports; the Royal Oak, in a lovely setting by the church, is a popularly priced dining pub.

WAKEFIELD SE3221
A number of handsome buildings include its cathedral, much restored in Victorian times but with some fine 15th-c masonry and carvings (and a marvellous spire - the tallest in Yorkshire), its rare 14th-c bridge chapel over the River Calder, some

Georgian and Regency houses most notably around Wood St and St John's Sq, and its imposing civic buildings. **Wakefield Art Gallery** (Wentworth Terrace) Good collection of 20th-c painting and sculpture, internationally famous for its galleries devoted to two famous local sculptors - Barbara Hepworth and Henry Moore. Shop; cl Sun am, all Mon, and 25 Dec; (01924) 305796; free.

Wakefield Museum (Wood St) Along with the unique collection of preserved animals and exotic birds gathered by local explorer Charles Waterton, and an exhibition on sports and games, this has plenty of opportunities for hands-on activities. Shop, good disabled access; cl Sun am, 25 Dec, 1 Jan; (01924) 305351; free.

Yorkshire Sculpture Park (West Bretton; A637 SE) Major contemporary and modern sculpture carefully and imaginatively displayed in nearly a square mile of fine 18th-c landscaped parkland. There are 16 works by Henry Moore in the adjacent country park, often surrounded by grazing sheep, and there's a visitor centre. Meals, snacks, shop, disabled access; cl 24-25 and 31 Dec; (01924) 830302; free (though £1.50 car parking charge).

WENTWORTH SK3898 Reckoned by some readers to be the prettiest village they've ever seen. The George & Dragon, with a craft and antiques shop nearby, has enjoyable food.

WITHENS CLOUGH RESERVOIR SD9822 S of Hebden Bridge, this has a path for walkers - and the more energetic can climb up to the prominent monument on Stoodley Pike, for the views. The nearby Hinchcliffe Arms has enjoyable food (not Mon).

WORSBROUGH SE3503 **Worsbrough Country Park** (A61) Hard to believe this was once a busy industrial area; the only sign of those days is the working corn mill, now the **Worsbrough Mill Museum** but still producing stoneground flour. Snacks, shop, some disabled access; usually cl Mon (exc bank hols), Tues, Mon-Sat Nov, Dec and Mar and all Jan-Feb; (01226) 774527; £1 museum, £1 car

park. About a mile away, **Wigfield Farm** is a hit with children, with traditional and rare breeds. Café and picnic area, shop, disabled access; cl 2 wks Christmas-New Year; (01226) 733702; £2. The peaceful 80 hectares (200 acres) also include nature trails, and you can hire bikes (07811) 804991.

Other attractive or attractively placed villages with decent pubs include Barkisland SE0420, Blackshaw Head SD9527, Boston Spa SE4345, East Morton SE1042, Esholt SE1840, Holme SE1006, Honley SE1312, Ledsham SE4529 and nearby Ledston SE4328, Sowerby SE0423, Stanbury SE0037, and Tickhill SK5993 (esp church and semi-ruined castle).

Other useful pubs in fine positions or with good views include Dick Hudsons on the Otley rd at High Eldwick above Bingley SE1240, the Castle overlooking the reservoirs nr Bolsterstone SK2796, Brown Cow by open-access woods at Ireland Bridge (B6429) nearer Bingley, Strines nr Strines Reservoir above Bradfield SK2692, Stanhope Arms on Windle Edge Lane nr Winscar Reservoir by Dunford Bridge SE1502, New Inn at Eccup SE2842, Malt Shovel at Harden SE0838, Robin Hood at Pecket Well outside Hebden Bridge SD9928, Cherry Tree on Bank End Lane at High Hoyland SE2710, Fleece at Holme SE1006, Buckstones on the A640 towards Denshaw high above Huddersfield SE1416, Blacksmiths Arms on Heaton Moor Rd at Kirkheaton SE1818, Shepherds Rest and Top Brink on Mankinholes Rd at Lumbutts SD9523 (bracing walks to Stoodley Pike monument), Hinchcliffe Arms at Cragg Vale, Mytholmroyd SE0126 (the B6188 S is a good moors road), Hobbit up Hob Lane, Norland SE0723, Grouse on Harehills Lane, Oldfield, nr Oakworth SE0038, Causeway Foot on the Keighley Rd by Ogden Reservoir SE0631, Waggon & Horses (A6033) and Dog & Gun (off B6141 towards Denholme), both nr Oxenhope SE0335, Pineberry on the A644 Keighley rd out of Queensbury SE1030, Brown Cow (A672) dramatically overlooking Scammonden Reservoir SE0215, Clothiers Arms in Station Rd, Stocksmoor, nr Shepley

SE1810, White House on the B6107 or Rose & Crown up Cop Hill at Slaithwaite SE0813, Blue Ball nr Soyland SE0120, Sportsmans Arms at Hawks Stones, Kebcote on Stansfield Moor SD9227, Ring o' Bells on Hill Top Rd at Thornton SE0933, Freemasons Arms on Hopton Hall Lane at Upper Hopton SE1918, Cross Keys overlooking the restored Rochdale Canal at Walsden SD9322, Delvers on Cold Edge Rd and Withens on Warley Moor Rd at Wainstalls SE0428, and Pack Horse at Widdop SD9333.

Where to eat

GOLCAR SE1015 **Weavers Shed** *86 Knowl Rd (01484) 654284* Warmly friendly restaurant-with-rooms in a converted cloth-finishing mill, with beams and flagstones, particularly good modern british cooking using home-grown fruit and vegetables and good local meat and fish, enjoyable breakfasts; cl Sun, Mon, Sat am, 25 Dec-1 Jan; spacious attractive bdrms. £30/2-course menu £9.95

HALIFAX SE0726 **Design House** *(01422) 383242* Stylish modern restaurant in thriving carefully restored carpet mill complex, with enjoyable modern cooking to match; relaxed and friendly atmosphere, good service, and thoughtful wine list; cl Sun, Mon pm, Sat am, 25-26 Dec; no children in evening; disabled access. £30|**£7.95**

HAWORTH SE0237 **Weavers** *15 West Lane (01535) 643822* Charming evening restaurant made up of weavers' cottages, with lots of bric-a-brac, photographs, and spinning mementoes, delicious food, cheerful service, and a good loyal following; bdrms; cl Sun pm, Mon, Tues and Sat am, 2 wks after Christmas. £26/2-course set menu £12.50|**£26**

LEEDS SE3033 **Brasserie Forty-Four** *42-44 The Calls (0113) 234 3232* Originally a grain mill (below 42 The Calls, see *Where to stay*), this riverside restaurant is simply furnished with modern designs, and serves enjoyable british and mediterranean food (very good value early evening set menu and wine list); cl Sat am, Sun, bank hols; partial disabled access. £40/2-course lunch £11.50

LEEDS SE3033 **Pool Court at 42** *42-44 The Calls (0113) 244 4242* Cleverly converted quayside grain mill (also incorporating Brasserie Forty-Four and the stylish hotel, 42 The Calls), this smart modern restaurant has a calm atmosphere, very enjoyable food with french leanings, lovely puddings, and an interesting wine list; cl Sat am, Sun, bank hols; children over 3; disabled access. £61.50

LEEDS SE2736 **Salvos** *115 Otley Rd, Headingley (0113) 275 5017* Welcoming Italian restaurant run by the same family for over 30 years, with good modern food (popular and interesting daily specials) and cheerful service; cl Sun; disabled access. £22/2-course rapido menu £5

LEEDS SE2933 **Sous le Nez en Ville** *The Basement, Quebec House, Quebec St (0113) 244 0108* Imaginative popular food in fashionable panelled restaurant with tiled floors and exposed brickwork, a very good wine list, and efficient service; cl Sun, bank hols (but open Good Fri), 25 Dec, 1 Jan. £18.95|**£9**

SHEFFIELD SK3187 **Thyme** *34 Sandygate Rd (0114) 266 6096* Popular restaurant with a relaxed chatty atmosphere, pale wooden dining chairs on the stripped wooden floor, bright artwork on white walls, stylish modern cooking using influences from all over the world, and a good wine list; cl Sun pm; disabled access. £32/2-course lunch £20

SOWERBY BRIDGE SE0321 **Millbank** *(01422) 825588* (Mill Bank Rd, off A58) Stylish gastropub in quiet rural spot with glorious views from terrace; bar and pubby area with real ales, flagstones, benches, and open fire; dining room with modern local paintings, photographs and sculpture, very good food from a short but accomplished menu, a good local cheeseboard, thoughtful small wine list, and pleasant professional service; live (free) jazz Sun pm; cl Mon. £28.70

Special thanks to M L Rayner, Lesley Lewis, T D Surgenor, J Chilver, Margaret Dickinson, Michael and Jenny Back

LONDON

Masses to see and do - and many of the best bits are free

The fact that so many of the top places are free here - and that just walking around can be such a pleasure, now that the weekday congestion charge has made the central traffic so much less unpleasant - is a valuable counterweight to the undeniable fact that otherwise London prices are very high. Many restaurants simply price themselves out of reach (as a result, they have been going out of business at a phenomenal rate recently), and London's hotels are notoriously expensive. But with numbers of big-spending foreign visitors down, you'll find most hotels keen to offer a very special price 'on the night'; and of course we have been particularly keen to look out for good value.

Our top choice of places to visit include the Horniman, Natural History and Science Museums, the Tower of London, a trip to Greenwich with all its attractions, the London Aquarium (all great for families), the Imperial War Museum, the London Eye, the British Museum, the National Gallery, Somerset House, and the Museum of London. Most of these are free. And of course there are those costly crowd-pullers the London Dungeon and Madame Tussaud's. The Victoria & Albert museum is going from strength to strength these days, and the Tate Modern has a very different sort of appeal.

Then there are the 'must-sees': the Houses of Parliament, Buckingham Palace, Westminster Abbey, St Paul's, Trafalgar Square, the parks, the street markets, the riverside, and the essential walk from Piccadilly Circus through Leicester Square to Covent Garden. And to see if there's a special event you really shouldn't miss, check www.visitlondon.com.

As well as all those obvious draws, a host of lesser-known places delight the people who discover them. Prime examples, again mostly free, are the Sir John Soane's Museum, the National Army Museum, the Geffrye Museum, Firepower, 18 Folgate St, the Wallace Collection, the Museum of Childhood and the new Museum in Docklands. And there are the special places further out, such as Kew Gardens and Richmond. The currently fashionable Victorian aesthetic of the newly opened Red House could tempt you out to Bexleyheath.

London is surprisingly easy to explore on foot. Quite a number of people lead guided walks. Original London Walks are consistently good and have a choice of more than ten a day. Usually starting from a tube station, walks last about two hours. You don't need to book, and they cost about £5; (020) 7624 3978 or www.walks.com.

Travelcards are good value tickets for the day, weekend or longer, valid on buses, tube and rail trains (not the morning rush hour). Increasingly, you have to buy your bus ticket before you get on (machines at stops). London's tube is a straightforward though often unpleasantly crowded and in summer unbelievably hot way of getting around. Pocket tube and bus route maps are free from ticket offices. In the text, we have grouped things to see and do under the heading of the most convenient tube station, using the ⊖ symbol - or the ⇌ symbol if it's surface rail instead.

Where to stay

Hotel prices in London change from day to day, depending on availability and timing. The prices given below can be used as a guideline but may well be quite different by the time this book is published. It is always worth asking for special deals.

22 Jermyn Street Hotel *22 Jermyn St SW1Y 6HP (020) 7734 2353* **£246.75**; 5 rms and 13 suites - spacious with deeply comfortable seats and sofas, flowers, plants, and antiques. Stylish little hotel owned by the same family for over 80 years and much loved by customers; no public rooms but wonderful 24-hr service, helpful notes and suggestions from the friendly owners, in-room light meals, and a warm welcome for children (with their own fact sheet listing shops, restaurants, and sights geared towards them, free video library, old-fashioned and electronic games, and own bathrobes); disabled access; dogs welcome ☺

Basil Street Hotel *8 Basil St SW3 1AH (020) 7581 3311* **£240.88**, plus special breaks; 80 pretty, decent-sized rms. Handy for Harrods and Hyde Park, this very civilised, privately owned Edwardian hotel has a relaxed atmosphere, antiques, fine carpets and paintings in the public rooms, a panelled restaurant with reliably enjoyable food, afternoon teas in lounge, and ladies' club (named after a parrot who had to go when his language became inappropriate); helpful courteous service - many of the staff have been here for years; disabled access; dogs welcome in bedrooms

Capital *22-24 Basil St SW3 1AT (020) 7589 5171* **£337.88**; 48 luxury rms with lovely fabrics, fine paintings, marble bthrms, and tempting extras. Exclusive little hotel nr Harrods with a warm welcome and log fire in reception, intimate panelled bar with good nibbles, a small lounge, exemplary service, and exceptional french-inspired food in chandelier-lit restaurant; disabled access; dogs welcome in bedrooms

Chesterfield *35 Charles St W1X 8LX (020) 7491 2622* **£307**, plus special breaks; 110 well equipped, pretty rms. Charming hotel just off Berkeley Sq, with particularly courteous helpful staff, afternoon tea in panelled library, a relaxed club-style bar with resident pianist, and fine food in attractive restaurant or light and airy conservatory; dogs welcome in bedrooms

Claridge's *Brook St W1A 2JQ (020) 7629 8860* **£350**, plus luxury breaks; 203 excellent rms. Grand hotel long used by royalty and heads of state, with liveried footmen, lift attendants and valets, elegant and comfortable day rooms, and civilised colonnaded foyer where the Hungarian Quartet plays; lovely formal restaurant (now Gordon Ramsay at Claridge's) with fantastic food and wine and exemplary service; free tennis at Vanderbilt Racquet Club; disabled access

Claverley *13-14 Beaufort Gardens SW3 1PS (020) 7589 8541* **£140**, plus special breaks; 33 individually decorated rms, most with own bthrm. Friendly privately owned Edwardian house with comfortable lounge, panelled reading room, and good breakfasts in cheerful dining room

Conrad London *Chelsea Harbour SW10 0XG (020) 7823 3000* **£185**; 160 luxury suites, meticulously refurbished this year, with a light and spacious living room area (many have sofa-beds so two small children could stay with parents at no extra cost). London's first 'suite hotel', tucked away in the quiet modern enclave of the Chelsea Harbour development and overlooking its small marina; enjoyable mediterranean and asian-influenced dishes in newly redecorated Aquasia restaurant and bar, friendly service, and health club; disabled access; dogs welcome (if small)

Covent Garden Hotel *10 Monmouth St WC2H 9HB (020) 7806 1000* **£287.88**, plus special breaks; 58 big individual bdrms with smart bthrms. Stylish luxury hotel nr theatres, with wrought-iron staircase from foyer to panelled upstairs drawing room and library, richly coloured interesting furniture, and popular ground-floor brasserie; state-of-the-art screening room for film companies, and a film club for hotel guests; they are kind to children; limited disabled access

Durrants 26-32 George St W1H 6BJ (020) 7935 8131 **£192**; 92 well equipped rms, with own bthrms; the quietest are at the back. Managed by the same family for over 70 years, this surprisingly quiet central hotel, behind a delightful Georgian façade, has fine paintings and antiques, a clubby bar, and relaxing lounges; cosy panelled restaurant with essentially english cooking, attractive breakfast room, and helpful pleasant staff; disabled access

Goring 15 Beeston Pl SW1W 0JW (020) 7396 9000 **£276**w, plus special breaks; 74 individually decorated rms, some with balconies overlooking pretty garden. Built in 1910 by the grandfather of the present Mr Goring, this family-run, impeccably kept and very english hotel has a particularly welcoming atmosphere (many staff have been there for years), very good cooking in the elegant restaurant, a super wine list, comfortable lounge for afternoon tea, airy cocktail bar, and staunchly loyal customers; disabled access

Halkin 5 Halkin St SW1X 7DJ (020) 7333 1000 **£280**w, plus special breaks; 41 stylish well equipped rms, with wonderful marble bthrms. Despite its Georgian exterior, the décor and furnishings here are ultra-modern but enjoyable, and there's a particularly good thai restaurant overlooking the garden; fine breakfasts, and really charming staff; much liked by businessmen, too; disabled access; dogs if very well trained and by prior arrangement

Hazlitts 6 Frith St W1V 5TZ (020) 7434 1771 **£229.13**, plus special breaks; 23 rms with 18th- or 19th-c beds and free-standing Victorian baths with early brass shower mixer units. Behind a typically Soho façade of listed early Georgian houses, this is a well kept and comfortably laid-out little hotel that's very handy for the West End; good continental breakfasts served in your bedroom, snacks in the sitting room, lots of restaurants all around; kind, helpful service; dogs welcome if small and well-behaved

Knightsbridge Green Hotel 159 Knightsbridge SW1X 7PD (020) 7584 6274 **£166***, plus special breaks; 28 no smoking suites with sitting room. Friendly family-owned hotel, carefully refurbished and neatly kept, with very good in-room breakfasts (no restaurant), bar service, free coffee and tea in lounge, and helpful efficient staff; disabled access

L'Hotel 28 Basil St SW3 1AS (020) 7589 6286 **£145**; 12 well equipped rms. Small family-owned french-style city hotel, nr Harrods, and set above the neatly kept well run Metro wine bar where continental breakfasts are served - as well as good modern french café food; friendly staff; disabled access; dogs by prior arrangement

Leonard 15 Seymour St W1H 5AA (020) 7935 2010 **£258.50**; 44 rms inc 21 luxury suites - with fine paintings, antiques, lovely fabrics, fresh flowers, videos, satellite TV, and hi-fi system; smart 18th-c town house with marvellous staff, light modern meals 24 hours a day in café bar, and compact exercise room; roof terrace; disabled access ☺

Meridien Piccadilly 21 Piccadilly W1V 0BH (020) 7734 8000 **£190**w, plus special breaks; 266 luxurious rms. In the heart of the capital and close to theatres and shops; attractive quiet public rooms, professional and friendly service, popular afternoon tea, marvellous food in the Oak Room restaurant, and free membership of the largest health club in a London hotel; one child under 12 free in parents' room; partial disabled access

Number Sixteen 16 Sumner Pl SW7 3EG (020) 7589 5232 **£193.88**; 41 individually styled rms, some with views of the garden. Four carefully refurbished town houses with a relaxed, friendly atmosphere, lots of pictures, antiques, and bowls of fresh flowers in two lovely drawing rooms, an airy conservatory overlooking the garden, and enjoyable breakfasts

One Aldwych 1 Aldwych WC2B 4BZ (020) 7300 1000 **£273.50**w, plus special breaks; 105 luxury bdrms and suites with fresh fruit and flowers delivered daily. Close to theatres and Covent Garden, this fine Edwardian hotel has an impressive foyer with a giant statue of an oarsman in his boat, huge flower arrangements and contemporary paintings throughout, two bars, three restaurants, and helpful friendly staff; health facilities inc indoor swimming pool with underwater music; disabled access

Pelham Hotel *15 Cromwell Pl SW7 2LA (020) 7589 8288* **£235**, 50 rms and suites, individually designed combining antique furniture and modern decor. Luxurious Victorian town house near South Kensington tube station and the museums, with a country house-type atmosphere, huge bowls of flowers, opulent décor and an open fire in drawing room, a cosy dark-panelled library, and good modern british cooking in cheerfully decorated restaurant and wine bar

Rubens *39-41 Buckingham Palace Rd SW1W 0PS (020) 7834 6600* **£194**, plus special breaks; 172 well equipped, individually furnished rms inc luxurious suites in the Royal Wing. Opposite Buckingham Palace and nr Victoria Station, this attractive hotel has comfortable day rooms inc lounge with views of the Royal Mews, open fire in bar, and library restaurant with fine international food; dogs welcome in bedrooms

Swiss House *171 Old Brompton Rd SW5 0AN (020) 7373 2769* **£89**; 15 rms. Festooned with ivy and flower boxes, this is a warmly friendly and good value family-run hotel, relaxed and tidy inside, with very good buffet continental breakfasts - english breakfast available, too; dogs welcome in bedrooms

Tophams Belgravia *24-32 Ebury St SW1W 0LU (020) 7730 8147* **£140**; 39 cosy rms, 34 with own bthrm. Small, charmingly old-fashioned hotel made up of several town houses with a friendly country-house atmosphere, downstairs bar, attractive lounges, good modern cooking in the elegant restaurant, and decent wines; cl Christmas and New Year; partial disabled access

Trafalgar *25 Cockspur St SW1Y 5BN (020) 7870 2900* **£155.90**w, plus special breaks; 129 rms, many looking down over Trafalgar Sq (these are the ones that make this notable). Handsome Cunard building rebuilt internally as stylish new hotel (a Hilton, but not recognisable as such), minimalist but comfortable modern décor and furnishings, big cool bar, friendly and informal but punctilious young staff

The West End

Famous for its shopping and window-shopping, from the daunting bustle of Oxford St, through the bookshops around Charing Cross Rd, the specialist food and cookery shops of Soho, and the elegant stores of Regent St and Piccadilly, to the ultra-smart clothes shops of South Molton St and Bond St. There are great opportunities for window-shopping in the auction houses and fine art galleries. The West End is synonymous with theatre; it's worth knowing that on Leicester Sq an official half-price ticket booth, Tkts, sells off surplus tickets for that day's performances: a queue usually builds up, so get there early (open Mon-Sat 10am-7pm and Sun 12-3.30pm). Highlights here include the National Gallery and Trafalgar Sq, Piccadilly with the Royal Academy, the sumptuous Wallace Collection (in an elegant remodelled 18th-c house), and colourful Covent Garden (the London Transport Museum and Theatre Museum here are good fun for families). Chinatown is a vivid enclave, Neal St is a focus for vegetarian restaurants and rather alternative shops, and there are staunchly old-fashioned institutions of englishness and english cooking like Rules or Simpsons - among an extraordinarily eclectic crowd of other places to eat.

To see and do

BOND STREET ⊖

Handel's House 🏛 This was Handel's home for 36 years until his death in 1759; he composed the *Messiah* here, and there's a display on his life and work. The rooms have been authentically refurbished and fitted out as described in Handel's will, with period instruments on show. Shop, disabled access; cl Sun am, all Mon, 24-26 and 31 Dec, 1 Jan; (020) 7495 1685; *£4.50. Note the neighbouring blue plaque showing where Jimi Hendrix lived.

Mayfair W of Regent St and N of Piccadilly (and only the shortest of strolls from them; Bond St and Green Park tube stns are handy). This is mostly a quietly discreet area of elegant town houses, smart well established hotels, and richly unobtrusive offices. Grosvenor Sq is gloomily forbidding these days with its heavy anti-terrorist presence, and equally famous Berkeley Sq doesn't have any special appeal for visitors, though there are plans to brighten it up with lights in the trees, band concerts and public art displays, and to encourage fashion boutiques to nearby Bruton St (birthplace of Queen Elizabeth II). Bond St with its continuation New Bond St is the area's main street for shopping, though unless you want to spend a great deal of money on top-notch designer clothes and shoes, jewellery, glass or oriental rugs this is likely to be confined to the window. Plenty of art and antiques galleries, and a good indoor antiques market (124 New Bond St). Aspreys is a remarkable place, famous for its opulent luxury goods and glittering with an awesome tonnage of gems and precious metals. Nearby is a charming life-size sculpture of Churchill chatting to Roosevelt on a bench - you can sit with them. Sothebys auction rooms are fascinating to wander around. Other small and prestigious art galleries are dotted throughout Mayfair, particularly in nearby Dover St and (mainly contemporary) Cork St; Grays antiques market off 58 Davies St has hundreds of indoor stalls. South Audley St has Hobbs of Mayfair, a smart delicatessen, and Goode's, a magnificent glass and china shop. Higgins in Duke St is the Queen's coffee-man. The best Mayfair pub is the Red Lion in Waverton St; the grander Audley (Mount St) is also good. W of Regent St and N of Piccadilly (and only the shortest of strolls from them; Bond St and Green Park tube stations are handy).

Wallace Collection (Hertford House, Manchester Sq) Excellent art collection beautifully displayed in an elegant 18th-c house, improved and remodelled by the american architect Rick Mather, 100 years after it was first opened as a museum. It's visually very seductive, with probably the best collection of 18th-c french paintings in the world, inc luscious offerings from Watteau, Boucher and Fragonard. Also great Canalettos, fine works by Rembrandt, Rubens and Van Dyck, works by british painters, furniture (mostly 18th-c french), notable assemblage of Sèvres porcelain, and an amazing array of arms and armour, oriental as well as european. In places feels more like a historic home than a museum. There's a public library in the basement, and a licensed café in the glass-covered sculpture garden. Meals, snacks, shop, disabled access (phone for parking); cl Sun am, 24-26 Dec, 1 Jan, Good Fri, May Day bank hol; (020) 7563 9500; free. The O'Connor Don (Marylebone Lane) is a civilised nearby place for a snack lunch.

CHARING CROSS ⊖ ⇌

Trafalgar Square Many people think of this as the heart of central London (distances to and from central London used to be measured from the Cross on the Strand). For a long time it's certainly seemed at the heart of London's traffic, but that's all changed with the highly successful new scheme to confine the traffic to the S and E edges, making the square a gloriously open pedestrianised space in front of the National Gallery. Named for the naval victory of 1805, it was designed by Nash and completed in 1841; the fountains were added a century later. Recently there's been an enjoyable series of changing sculptures on the fourth plinth; the final design is to be decided by the end of the year (you can see the six short-listed models in the National Gallery). The centrepiece, **Nelson's Column**, stretches up 56 metres (185 ft), its base guarded by four huge identical lions. Although many people still associate Trafalgar Square with innumerable pigeons, Mayor Ken Livingston's reduced feeding programme seems to be working - you can certainly walk across these days without being plagued by feathered kamikazes.

National Gallery This magnificent building right on Trafalgar Sq houses the national collection of western european painting, with around 2,300 pictures dating from 1250 to 1900. You'll enjoy it most if you're firm and restrict yourself to just a few of the galleries, rather than trying to see everything. It's hard to pick out highlights (the whole collection is worth studying), but don't miss the Sainsbury Wing, which gives perfect lighting and viewing conditions for its treasure-trove of early Renaissance works. The East Wing is currently being extended and restored, but should re-open around July with better disabled access, improved visitor facilities and a new courtyard. It gets very busy, especially on a Sat, or at any time around the Impressionist works. From Oct, you'll be able to see first british exhibition of Raphael's paintings and drawings (admission charge; and other promising shows this year include Bosch and Brueghel (24 Jan-4 Apr), and El Greco (admission charge; 11 Feb-23 May). There's a hi-tech audio tour (by donation), with a commentary on every single picture in the main gallery. Meals, snacks, shop, disabled access; open until 9pm every Weds, cl 24-26 Dec, 1 Jan and Good Fri; (020) 7747 2885; free, charges for some exhibitions.

National Portrait Gallery (St Martin's Pl, just round the corner) Grandly illustrates british history, with paintings of kings, queens and other notable characters arranged in chronological order from the top floor (medieval) to the present. The immensely stylish Ondaatje Wing includes Tudor and 20th-c galleries where Shakespeare rubs shoulders with the Rolling Stones, and a rooftop restaurant gives views across Trafalgar Sq and Whitehall. Meals, snacks, shop (where computer technology allows them to print you a poster of any painting in the gallery), disabled access; cl 24-26 Dec, 1 Jan and Good Fri; (020) 7306 0055; free, £6 for some special exhibitions.

St Martin-in-the-Fields This elegant church has frequent lunchtime and evening concerts; (020) 7839 8362 for programme. Unmistakable for its blue clock-dial - the only clock in this part of London that seems always to keep the right time - the church has a busy and very well liked coffee and snack bar in its crypt, with frequent art exhibitions; also brass-rubbing centre, shop (inc all the Academy of St Martin-in-the-Fields CDs), and a daily market; disabled access to church, but not crypt; all proceeds support the mission of the church, particularly the homeless - you're likely to see plenty of bodies huddled in shop doorways in the surrounding streets, a sadly common sight all over London, but especially obvious around here.

Theatres Theatres abound off Trafalgar Sq, with a group based around this end of Charing Cross Rd, and another up along the Strand. Marked out by the globe on top of the building, the Coliseum (St Martin's Lane) is the home of the English National Opera. You can usually get decently priced seats on the day, from 10am, if you do want to hear operas translated into English instead of the original; (020) 7632 8300; it's due to reopen in Feb after a £41m refurbishment to return it to its 1904 glory. Almost next to the Coliseum, the Chandos is a good pub with food all day, down past the Post Office the underground Tappit Hen is an atmospheric wine bar, and there's no end of smart little coffee shops and cafés near by - Gabys (30 Charing Cross Rd) does perfect hot salt beef sandwiches.

COVENT GARDEN ⊖

Partly pedestrianised, the former vegetable, fruit and flower market with its elegant buildings is now made over to smart café-bars, boutiques and stalls, such as those in the covered piazza, selling good but expensive handmade clothes and craft items. There's a bustling cosmopolitan atmosphere, and good street entertainers. The Jubilee Market specialises in different wares on different days. The many bars and restaurants are always lively at night, but again they're not cheap. One of the delights of this area is its range of unusual or specialist **shops**. In the streets around the Piazza, Knutz (Russell St) has everything for the practical joker, and Penhaligon's (Wellington St) sell lovely old-fashioned toiletries. On the other side of the market, N of the tube station, interesting shops are set in a labyrinthine network of attractively rejuvenated alleys and streets; you will get lost, but wandering around is great fun, and they all lead back to roughly the same area. Neal St is rewarding for its small craft and specialist shops, and Neal's Yard is full of healthy living - delightful in summer with its fresh paint and tubs of flowers; a multi-storey mini-mall here has a good airy atrium-effect basement coffee bar. Floral St has elegant and expensive clothes and shoe shops. The Africa Centre on King St may have exhibitions of african art and culture. No shortage of places to eat around here, but useful pubs for lunch or refreshment include the idiosyncratic modern Porterhouse on Maiden Lane (food all day), and the Lamb & Flag on Rose St, an attractive 300-year-old pub with good value snacks, its back room still much as Dickens described it.

London Transport Museum (The Piazza) On the site of the former Flower Market, this is a surprisingly fun attraction. You can race a tram and a bus, delve into feely boxes, design your own bus, and see why a steam train doesn't suit the Underground. The main show is quite traditional, but they don't mind if you climb aboard some of the buses, trams and tube trains, and there are good touch screens throughout. Costumed actors tell nostalgic transport tales, and there might be story-telling, face-painting or craft workshops in school hols. Work is now underway on a £17.5m extension to the museum set to open in 2006. Snacks, interesting shop, disabled access; cl 24-26 Dec; (020) 7836 8557; £5.95.

Royal Opera House Beautifully restored and extended, you can now look around the foyer areas and various exhibitions. Readers greatly enjoy the backstage guided tours, led by enthusiastic guides - interesting even if you're not an opera or ballet buff. Tours vary depending on what is happening on the day, and usually start at 10.30am, 12.30 and 2.30pm Mon-Sat (exc last 2 wks Aug), phone first; (020) 7212 9389; £8. A limited number of tickets for performances are available on the day, from 10am; (020) 7304 4000. There are lovely views across Covent Garden from the good (but not cheap) Amphitheatre restaurant.

St Paul's church The actors' church, full of interesting memorials to performers. Pepys watched the first-ever Punch and Judy show here in 1662. Outside its back gate, facing the covered market, the theatrical tradition continues, with jugglers, clowns, mountebanks and unusual musicians performing on the cobbles.

Theatre Museum (Russell St) Exhaustive look at events and personalities on the stage over the last few hundred years. Posters, puppets and props are among the permanent collection, which although astonishingly comprehensive is arranged a little confusingly; it's easy to find yourself going round backwards. The very good temporary displays leave the deepest impression: there are always free stage make-up demonstrations, and you can dress up in the costume workshops. Shop, disabled access; cl Mon, 24-26 Dec and 1 Jan; (020) 7943 4700; free.

Theatre Royal (Drury Lane) The oldest working theatre in the world, first opened in 1663 (Nell Gwynn was one of its earliest performers), but rebuilt several times over the next few centuries. Tours show backstage features inc the intriguing hydraulic lift beneath the stage, still in use. Meals, snacks, shop, disabled access to theatre but not tour; tours 2.15pm and 4.45pm (exc Weds and Sat when tours are

10.15am and 12noon), best to check as there are no tours in between shows; (020) 7850 8793; £8.50.

LEICESTER SQUARE ⊖

All central London's attractions are within easy walking distance of here, with several of the more interesting theatres little more than five mins' stroll. The tube station's various exits are a favourite with Londoners stuck for a place to meet; hordes of them mill around anxiously looking for the friends they finally discover they've been standing next to for half an hour. Around the bustling edges of the pedestrian square, attractively cleaned up in recent years and usually with living statues and other free entertainment, are several huge cinemas, pricy but with excellent sound; you can see films more cheaply at the Prince Charles in Leicester Pl, leading off (where Notre Dame de France has an impressive Jean Cocteau mural). Marked out by its dramatic ornamental gate, **Chinatown** has developed its own character; the inviting supermarkets and shops along pedestrianised Gerrard St and in neighbouring streets are fascinating, with their weird and wonderful vegetables, strange squidgy things in little cellophane packets, and odd-smelling dried meats and fish; plenty of authentic chinese restaurants. Back by the tube station, this stretch of Charing Cross Rd is justifiably famous for its **bookshops**, specialist and general, new and second-hand, as are the side alleys between here and St Martin's Lane; Cecil Court is perhaps the best of these alleys. The Salisbury on St Martin's Lane is a sumptuously Victorian pub, all red velvet and cut glass. Not far away towards Covent Garden is Stanfords (Long Acre), the best map and guidebook shop in Britain; on the way, the upstairs Photographers Gallery (Gt Newport St) is always worth a look. Leicester Sq is very handy for Soho, described below under Tottenham Court Rd.

MARBLE ARCH ⊖

Striking in itself, it was originally a grand entrance for Buckingham Palace, moved here decades ago. Over the road **Speakers Corner** on the edge of Hyde Park is where every Sun morning you can still hear impassioned diatribes on all sorts of causes. Also on Sun you can see what's probably the longest free open-air art exhibition in the world, with the work of 300 artists and craftsmen laid out along the park railings on Bayswater Rd; the Swan opposite gives a pleasant break. The tube station - with so many exits it's a real initiative test finding your way out - is also handy for Oxford St.

Hyde Park Riding Stables (Bathurst Mews) Can organise horse-riding in the park; cl Mon and 24 Dec-3 Jan; (020) 7723 2813; from £40 an hour.

OXFORD CIRCUS ⊖

The heart of the city's busiest shopping areas, crowded and noisy Oxford St to the left and right, and altogether nicer Regent St to the S. **Oxford St** doesn't have a lot of character, but is full of good stores such as Selfridges, John Lewis (the self-service restaurant is good for lunch), Marks & Spencer, the giant music shops HMV and Virgin Megastore, and the usual High Street chains. South Molton St and St Christopher's Pl on either side of Oxford St are full of designer clothes shops and smart cafés. **Regent St** is one of the grandest streets in the whole area, with a splendid curve as it reaches Piccadilly Circus. A harmonious street of considerable character, with the fine shops definitely enhancing its appeal, even if all you want to do is browse. Liberty's is a splendid art nouveau timbered building full of gorgeous soft furnishings and clothes, oriental and leather goods, jewellery and a good gift department. Other high points include Mappin & Webb for fine china, glass, and jewellery; Hamleys, a marvellous toy shop (not cheap, though); and Aquascutum, great for expensive classic english clothes. The Old Coffee House in Beak St around the corner from here, and Red Lion in Kingly St, are useful for lunch. Carnaby St, tucked away behind, has some rather florid men's shops and good street-fashion houses, but is mainly full of small boutiques with trendy accessories, leather goods and tacky souvenirs.

PICCADILLY CIRCUS ⊖

Another lively hub of London life, with famous streets radiating off in every

direction, each quite different in
character; handsome Piccadilly roughly
to the W, the theatres of bustling
Shaftesbury Avenue to the E, with
smarter ones on Haymarket to the S,
Regent St (£500 million is being invested
in reinvigorating it over the next ten
years) coolly curving N towards Oxford
Circus, and of course the famous statue
of Eros, where all the foreign students
sit to be photographed. The streets
around here are excellent for shopping.
On opposite sides of the traffic islands in
Piccadilly Circus are Tower Records,
three floors of pop, classical and jazz
(open till midnight), and Lillywhites, the
long-established sports clothes and
equipment store. On Piccadilly,
Waterstones is the biggest bookshop in
Europe, while friendly Hatchards
further down is a nicely old-fashioned
bookshop where the staff can still
sometimes turn vague requests into
actual books. Almost next door,
Fortnum's (Fortnum & Mason) has
superior if expensive clothes, as well as
the foods for which they're world-
famous. Nearby, the Burlington Arcade
is an elegant Regency covered arcade of
expensive but good shops (excellent
cashmere, for instance), with a delightful
set of rules, still enforced, that stop
people whistling, singing or running in its
confines. The Ritz is gorgeously
flamboyant inside: well worth the high
price of having a frogged and liveried
waiter bring you a cup of tea. Behind
Piccadilly's S side is Jermyn St, where
among other splendid but top-of-the-
range shops you can buy fine cheeses at
Paxton & Whitfield's, briar pipes at
Astleys, hand-made shoes at Tricker's,
hand-made shirts from Turnbull &
Asser, flat hats at Bates, old-fashioned
toiletries at Floris, and a haircut or shave
at Trumper's; the ground floor museum
of deco watches and bijouterie at
Dunhill's is well worth a look. The Red
Lion in Duke of York St just off here is a
little gem of a pub, with decent snacks
(but very busy on wkdy lunchtimes).
Funland A surprise to find in the
centre of London, and quite
unexpected behind the preserved
façade of the vast Trocadero building;
filled with state-of-the-art rides and
games (as well as a cinema and 10-pin
bowling alley). The myriad flashing and
bleeping attractions all have individual
charges; cl 25 Dec.
Royal Academy of Arts (Burlington
House, Piccadilly) Splendid building
with excellent changing exhibitions for
most of the year, then from early Jun to
mid-Aug its famous (often notorious)
Summer Exhibition. They've recently
restored five rooms of Burlington
House to their 18th-c splendour, and
on display to the public for the first time
are items from the Academy's
collection, mainly british art from the
18th-c right up to the present (free).
Meals, snacks, shop, disabled access; cl
24-25 Dec; (020) 7300 8000; admission
charge to exhibitions varies - usually
between £7 and £10. The £3 million
transformation of the grand courtyard
has made it an attractive setting for
exhibitions of contemporary sculpture.
TOTTENHAM COURT ROAD ⊖
Soho Often heady mix of the tawdry
and the fashionable, its coffee bars and
cafés swarming with colourful young
people in the evenings. Many of Soho's
Georgian terraces are rather run-
down, with peepshows and naughty
video shops stuffed into basements and
ground floors. But there are parts that
have had much of their original quiet
charm restored, like Soho Sq and
Meard St, and it's still good for
restaurants, and for shops connected
with food or cooking. Old Compton St,
central London's gayest street, has a
good few interesting shops, the
Algerian Coffee Stores which also sells
lots of fruit teas, and two cheap but
good wines and spirits shops. Milroys in
Greek St has a wonderful collection of
hundreds of different malt whiskies.
The little Dog & Duck in Frith St and
Coach & Horses in Poland St (the
Private Eye pub) are two of the nicest
Soho locals; in Romilly St another
Coach & Horses is also on the well
known Soho characters circuit, and
Kettners, now part of the Pizza Express
chain, is a very entertaining old building.
The area as a whole forms a sort of
square, with the tube stations at
Leicester Sq, Piccadilly Circus,
Tottenham Court Rd and even Oxford
Circus all just as handy.

Westminster

This centre of court and government is pleasant to walk around, much of it with only light traffic, and with few shops to add extra people to the wide pavements. Westminster Abbey and Buckingham Palace are divided by St James's Park - a fine stroll between the two. A tour of the Houses of Parliament during the summer recess is most rewarding. Tate Britain and Westminster Cathedral are other highlights here.

To see and do

GREEN PARK ⊖
The park itself is the smallest of the parks in Central London. It's not a formal garden but, watered by the Tyburn stream which runs below the park, stays genuinely green even in hot summers when London's other grassy spaces are dry and dusty. It's a short stroll to **Shepherd Market**, a colourful place where Mayfair lets its hair down, no longer a market but busy with cafés, good wine bars and a nice pub (the Grapes), and little lanes to wander down.

Clarence House (St James's/The Mall) This early 19th-c town house, designed by John Nash, is now Prince Charles's official London residence (and feels much more like a lived-in house than Buckingham Palace). Occupied for over 50 years by the late Queen Mother, it still has much of her private art collection (mostly 20th-c), and fine examples of english porcelain and silver, and Fabergé, as well as family photographs and paintings of favourite racehorses. Guided tours (summer only) take in five of the ground-floor rooms, used for official engagements. Shop, disabled access; phone well in advance to book (020) 7766 7303; £5.

Clubland The area around St James's St and Pall Mall seems to have more gentlemen's clubs than anything else, but there is a good number of interesting upmarket **shops** too: hand-made shoes at Lobb's, hats at Locks, fishing equipment at Hardy's, several cigar shops, and fine wines at Berry Bros & Rudd. This last is the only shop in London still to look both inside and out just as it did in the early 19th c (though they now have two more modern side rooms), and they are very helpful even if you want just one humble bottle. On Pall Mall Farlows' has recently opened a new country sports and expeditions outfitting megastore. Christie's auction galleries are on King St (the friendly Red Lion off here in Crown Passage is useful for a snack), and there are quite a few other top-of-the-market antiques and book shops nearby, especially up Duke St.

Spencer House (St James's Pl) Overlooking Green Park, this gleaming town house was built for the first Earl Spencer in the mid-18th c. Its sumptuous rooms, restored to their full glory, were among the first neo-classical interiors in Europe. The garden, replanted with flowers and shrubs appropriate to the late 18th and early 19th c, is open on certain days in spring and summer (phone for details). Disabled access; house open for guided tours Sun (exc Jan and Aug); (020) 7499 8620; *£6, no children under 10.

St James's Palace Though comparatively domestic-looking, this is exceptionally harmonious and carries a real feel of Old London. It's not open to the public (its apartments are used by members of the Royal Family and their officials) but is well worth strolling past. If you stand on the Friary Court, Marlborough Road side of the palace you can see the guardsmen leaving here at 11.05am to go to Buckingham Palace, and coming back at around 11.40pm.

PIMLICO ⊖
Tate Britain (Millbank and Atterbury

St) Designed in classical style to house the collection of Sir Henry Tate, this building still widely and fondly known as just the Tate Gallery has the world's greatest collection of british art, marking its rise and fall from the Tudors to the Turner Prize, by way of Constable, Rossetti and Epstein to name but a few. Galleries are organised chronologically, and rooms are devoted to artists such as Gainsborough, Hogarth, Sickert and Hockney, while more are given over to the art collected for the nation by the Tate in the late 20th c. The gallery recently recovered two stolen Turners after an eight-year hunt across Europe (and managed to make £15m profit on the insurance). Good changing exhibitions, and a interesting hi-tech audio guide; the gardens have been redesigned to include sculpture courts. Two shops, restaurant, disabled access through the Manton entrance in Atterbury St; cl 24-26 Dec; (020) 7887 8000; free (exc for special exhibitions). A new boat service allows you to hop down the river to Tate Modern (stopping off at the London Eye on the way). Though the Tate Gallery restaurant is particularly good (with a witty mural by Rex Whistler), you might find the Morpeth Arms nearby useful, with its views of the glossy MI6 ziggurat across the river.

ST JAMES'S PARK ⊖

This is the best approach to the palace (you can get there more quickly, though less attractively, from Victoria). The oldest of London's Royal Parks, it was drained and converted into a deer park for Henry VIII, and redesigned in the style of Versailles by order of Charles II. It was then reworked by Nash for George IV, and this is the park which we see today, its relaxing lakeside environment particularly enjoyed by lunch-breaking office workers (and by hundreds of more or less exotic waterfowl, inc the pelicans which are fed daily at 3pm). The park is beautifully floodlit at night. **The Mall** Running all the way along the top of the park, this ceremonial route was laid out from 1660 for Charles II, between the palace and the magnificent Admiralty Arch. Along it, as well as various grand buildings and government departments,

are a couple of good contemporary art galleries, with various changing exhibitions at the **Mall Galleries** ((020) 7930 6844 for exhibition info; free to around £2.50), and a wonderfully informal little restaurant and bar at the **ICA** which, with exhibitions and cinemas too, is an excellent place to spend several hours (cl am; (020) 7930 0493; £1.50 day membership, £2.50 at the wknd).

Buckingham Palace A marvellous position, surrounded by Royal Parks and looking commandingly along the stately Mall towards Admiralty Arch. At the grand front palace gates the guards still keep their unflinchingly solemn positions: you can watch the **changing of the guard** every other day at 11.30am; the ceremony may be late or even cancelled in exceptionally wet weather, and sometimes it's held at St James's Palace; phone (020) 7414 2279 to check.

Buckingham Palace tour Now firmly established as one of London's most visited attractions, usually drawing around 400,000 visitors in the eight weeks it's open. The main appeal is that this is where the Queen actually lives - her official London residence, and where she meets other Heads of State; the Royal Standard flies above it when she's home. But beyond that, while perhaps not the most satisfying of the Royal palaces, it does pile a magnificent series of opulent sights into your walk through the state rooms. Highlights include the beautiful Picture Gallery, 46 metres (150 ft) long and filled with paintings from the Royal Collection, the spectacular Grand Staircase, and the throne room with its predominant impression of gold, red and splendour. Tours are unguided, and there aren't many clues to help you, so it's definitely worth buying the guide book. Theoretically you see everything at your own pace, but in practice you're likely to be carried along in the stream of other people, and you won't get much of a chance to linger. You leave the palace with a short walk through a section of the 17-hectare (42-acre) gardens, with a good view of the Garden Front of the palace and the 19th-c lake. Tickets are sold from an office opposite the palace by the entrance to Green Park, though it's advisable to book a day or two in advance, on (020) 7766 7300. Shop, disabled access (with notice); open early Aug to end Sept; £12.

Guards Museum 🖻 (Wellington Barracks, Birdcage Walk) Military ephemera spanning 350 years of Grenadier, Coldstream, Scots, Irish, and Welsh Guards regimental history. Shop with large collection of antique and modern toy soldiers, disabled access by prior arrangement; cl 19 Dec-Jan; (020) 7414 3271; £2.

Queen's Gallery (Buckingham Palace Rd) This former palace chapel is dedicated to changing exhibitions of items from the Royal Collection: until 7 Mar the Royal Fabergé collection is on display (over 300 pieces inc eggs made for the russian Czar's family), along with an exhibition on his work, and from 26 Mar there will be an exhibition of King George III's and Queen Charlotte's possessions (they were the first occupants and decorators of Buckingham Palace), inc some unusual clocks, barometers and watches commissioned by the king. Disabled access (booking advised); cl 25-26 Dec; (020) 7766 7301; £6.50.

Royal Mews (Buckingham Palace Rd) Contains the State Coaches, private driving carriages and even sleighs of the Royal Family, as well as the immaculately turned out carriage horses. The longest painting in the Royal collection is here too, a 36-metre (120-ft) canvas depicting William IV's Coronation procession. Shop, disabled access; cl Oct-Mar, plus some days in Jun, best to check; (020) 7321 2233; £5.

VICTORIA ⊖ ⇄

RHS Lindley Library (80 Vincent Sq) The finest horticultural library in the world, as well as around 50,000 books (ranging from a 1514 edition of Pliny the Elder's *Historia Naturalis* to contemporary gardening manuals), it also provides a home for 22,000 paintings and drawings of plants, 1,500 periodicals, and a computer archive; also drawings and exhibition room, darkroom, and good disabled access. Cl wknds and bank hols; (020) 7821 3050; free. The RHS hold regular flower

shows filled with beautifully arranged displays by specialist nurserymen; (020) 7649 1885 for information; admission charge.

Westminster Cathedral (just off Victoria St) Completed in 1903, this red-brick Roman Catholic building is an astonishing structure, very un-english, with handsome mosaics and marble work in its richly ornamental interior. At night its black ceiling seems almost to disappear in the darkness. Its Byzantine splendour is welcome relief from the glassy governmental cliffs of Victoria St, and its tall tower gives great views over central London, and across to the London Eye (lift; £3). Snacks, shop, disabled access (not to tower); (020) 7798 9055; donations.

WESTMINSTER ⊖

Banqueting House (Whitehall) The only surviving part of the Palace of Whitehall, designed by Inigo Jones and built in 1619; it was a Royal residence until late that century. Charles I was executed here, and it was also the site of his son's restoration. The severely classical hall is pretty much all there is to see, but an entertaining audio tour and good audio-visual exhibition keep your interest for quite some time. The highlight is the wonderful ceiling painted by Rubens, commissioned by Charles I to glorify the Stuart monarchy. They've put mirrored tables underneath, so you can study the detail without straining your neck; don't lean on these though - they're on wheels and liable to speed off like errant supermarket trolleys. Shop; cl Sun, 23 Dec-2 Jan; (020) 7839 7569; *£4. The partly 13th-c Silver Cross is an interesting old pub, the huge and very ornate Lord Moon of the Mall another useful refuge.

Cabinet War Rooms (King Charles St, just off Whitehall) An intriguing series of more than 20 rooms built to provide Sir Winston Churchill, the War Cabinet and his Chiefs of Staff with a safe place from which to plan their strategies during World War II; they've recently opened the private chambers of Churchill and his wife, inc their kitchen and Mrs Churchill's bedroom. These rooms, as well as the Cabinet Room and Map Room, were preserved intact from the end of the war, and the other rooms have been authentically restored since. Quite basic, they're very evocative, with sound-effects adding to the atmosphere. A museum dedicated to Churchill's life will open here in 2005. Shop, disabled access; cl 24-26 Dec; (020) 7930 6961; £7, children free.

Cenotaph (Whitehall) Designed by Lutyens, this is a sombre reminder of last century's two World Wars, standing indomitably in the centre of the road. Initially it was planned as a temporary symbol, but strong public feeling led to the original wooden structure being replaced by the permanent stone version you see today.

Downing St Famous as the residence of the Prime Minister at No 10 and the Chancellor of the Exchequer at No 11 (the current incumbents have swapped to give Mr Blair and family more space). For long those were the street's only numbers, but a No 12 has recently emerged, housing more ministers. You can't get past the gates, but you can at least have a passing look at its surprisingly modest buildings.

Houses of Parliament Across the road from St Margaret's church, these buildings are now of course the main seat of government, but until Henry VIII moved to Whitehall Palace in 1529, the site was the main residence of the monarch - when they answer the phone today they still call it the Palace of Westminster, and there are still tennis balls stuck in the rafters of the palace from 16th-c courtly tennis matches. The present 19th-c building was designed by Charles Barry, though the gothick detail which has given so much life to what would otherwise be rather a tiresomely deadpan classical façade is by Pugin. One end of the extraordinary 286-metre (940-ft) structure finishes in a lofty Victorian tower (which flies the Union Jack when Parliament is in session), and the other in the clock tower which contains **Big Ben**, the 3½-ton bell whose sonorous hourly rings are one of the best-known sounds in the world. Inside, over two miles of passages link the central hall and two chambers - the Houses of Lords and Commons to the N and S of the building

respectively. The Commons sits from 2.30pm Mon-Weds, all day from 11.30am-7.30pm Thurs, and 9.30am-2pm some Fri; to watch the antics from the Strangers' Galleries, you'll need to queue by St Stephen's Gate (on the left for the Commons, right for the Lords - rather appropriate in a way) - or arrange it first with your MP. A letter from your MP can also give access to what's called the Line of Route, going through both Houses and the Members' Lobby and Divisions Lobby, to Westminster Hall, from 1224 to 1882 the chief law court of the country. It witnessed such trials as those of Sir Thomas More and Charles I, and organising admission is worth the trouble even just to admire the magnificent hammer-beam roof, the earliest surviving example of its kind; alternatively you can book yourself in for a good (if rather hurried) guided tour during the summer recess, early Aug to late Sept, phone to check; (0870) 906 3773; £7. The Westminster Arms in Storeys Gate across the square is a good pub, and you're likely to see politicians in the imposing Albert up Victoria St.

Jewel Tower (Parliament Sq) Opposite the statue of Oliver Cromwell (whose attitude towards Parliaments when he was Lord Protector was not unlike that of Charles I - they were more trouble than they were worth), this 14th-c building has an exhibition on Parliament's history. It was originally a huge treasure chest for Edward III. Shop, cl 24-26 Dec, 1 Jan; (020) 7222 2219; £2; EH.

Mounting the Guard (Whitehall) A survival of the kind of Royal pageantry which once filled this area can be seen in this daily ceremony at Horse Guards Parade, 11am Mon-Sat and 10am Sun.

St Margaret's church (Parliament Sq) The official church of the House of Commons, worth a look particularly for its exceptional 16th-c dutch stained glass; Sir Walter Raleigh is buried here.

Westminster Abbey Surely one of the most impressive pieces of architecture to survive from the Middle Ages: Edward the Confessor transformed it into the crowning place of english kings, and his body now lies in the great shrine of the present building, erected in the 13th c on the site of his original. Pretty much every king and queen up to George II was crowned here; Henry VII's chapel is particularly impressive, and there are splendid tombs erected by James I for his mother Mary Queen of Scots, and his predecessor Elizabeth I, under whose orders Mary had been executed. Perhaps it's in revenge for this that Elizabeth was lumped in with her sister Mary I, with whom she never got on. The loosely named Poets' Corner takes in a wide range of cultural figures. If you like history the **museum** in the Norman undercroft shouldn't be missed - it has effigies of many ancestors of the Royal Family made from their death masks, and often wearing their own clothes. There's a small medieval garden in the charming tranquil cloisters. Snacks, shop, limited disabled access; cl 25 Dec and Good Fri, and Sun (exc for services); (020) 7654 4900; £6 inc entry to museum, Chapter House and Pyx Chamber; audio tour £2.

Westminster Central Hall This Edwardian building functions as a Methodist church and is also one of London's premier meeting places (the first United Nations Assembly was held here in 1946). The impressive Great Hall has a magnificent organ (free recital afternoons on the first Sun of each month in summer), and the views from the Dome roof are terrific. Just turn up at the Visitor Services reception desk for a free guided tour; (020) 7222 8010.

Knightsbridge, Chelsea & Kensington

The three great South Kensington museums, all free, between them have something for everyone: the gorgeous collections of the Victoria & Albert; and the lively Natural History and Science Museums, both favourites for children. There's grandeur in Kensington Palace, the less-visited but free Leighton House, and across Hyde Park the excellent Apsley House. Harrods seems irresistible to most visitors. Down towards the Thames, the Chelsea Physic Garden and the nearby free National Army Museum are both rather special. A placid grid of clean-cut, subdued Georgian terraced houses contrasts with the ostentatious bustle of the King's Rd in the S and the hubbub of the Portobello Rd market (Sat is the day for collectables) in the N.

To see and do

FULHAM BROADWAY ⊖
The best tube station for the clutch of good value **antiques shops** towards the bottom end of Fulham Rd. You can quickly cut through to the interesting series of more specialised shops on the New Kings Rd, some of which yield unexpected treasures: lovely old clocks, imposing model ships, garden furniture, and ornaments going back to the 16th c. In the opposite direction is the unfrequented, rather melancholy tranquillity of the somewhat overgrown **Brompton Cemetery**.
Chelsea Harbour (Lots Rd) This modern development includes a striking modern covered mall (mainly luxurious soft furnishings specialists), with popular Deals Restaurant, the stylish Canteen, the smart but relaxed Matts café, and an adjacent marina. Children like the glass-sided lifts which

swoop up into the big dome, and on Sun pms they often have jazz by the marina.

Chelsea World of Sport (Fulham Rd) Best if you're in a group, and especially absorbing for young boys; sports enthusiasts will enjoy testing their skills on the 30 different challenges at this attraction, and there's also a display on Chelsea Football Club. Meals, snacks, shop, disabled access; cl Mon, 25 Dec; (020) 7915 2222; £10 if you book in advance.

HIGH ST KENSINGTON ⊖

Albert Memorial (Kensington Gardens) A gleaming golden monument to Queen Victoria's beloved husband: intricate mosaics, classic high Victoriana, marvellously grand.

Holland Park One of London's lesser-known open spaces, a wooded park with peacocks, summer open-air theatre and airy restaurant.

Kensington Gardens Surrounding the palace, and well worth a wander, though less lush than neighbouring Hyde Park, with tree-lined formal avenues. There's a toy boats lake, a good, safe playground, a fetching statue of Peter Pan, and a tree trunk carved with all sorts of little fairies and animals. On a sunny day you could be forgiven for thinking you'd stumbled on a beach club, as the grass is covered with prone bodies soaking up the sun.

Kensington Palace State Apartments (Kensington Gardens) Once-humble town house remodelled by Sir Christopher Wren and then enlarged by William Kent, the birthplace of Queen Victoria, and principal private Royal residence until the death of George II. Princess Margaret and Princess Diana lived here, and it's still the home of Prince and Princess Michael of Kent; as we went to press, they were hoping to open Princess Margaret's apartments to the public by the autumn. The state rooms are quite magnificent, with elaborate furnishings and décor, while other rooms are interesting for their comparatively restrained understatement and personal history. Make sure you look up at the ceilings: some are exquisitely painted, inc an effective trompe-l'oeil dome (a couple of the patterns transfer very nicely to stationery in the gift shop). There are pictures and furniture from the Royal collection, and this is home to the Royal Ceremonial Dress Collection, with items of Royal, ceremonial and court dress dating from the 18th c to today, inc a display of the Queen's dresses and Diana's evening gowns. There's a small formal sunken garden. Café in imposing Orangery, shop, disabled access to the dress collection only; cl 24-26 Dec; (020) 7937 9561; £10.50.

Kensington shops This is a good area for shopping, especially if you consider yourself young and fashionable. An unusual haven from the crowds is the **Roof Gardens** above BHS on the High St; these extraordinary gardens are often closed for private functions, so you'll need to check first on (020) 7937 7994; free. Their restaurant (open Thurs and Sat evenings) does very good food. Good food pubs in this area include the Windsor Castle (Campden Hill Rd; excellent courtyard garden) and (a walk up Kensington Church St, which has some interesting antique shops) the Churchill Arms - surprisingly good thai food.

Leighton House (12 Holland Park Rd) This splendid 19th-c house is a uniquely opulent monument to High Victorian Art, its lavish décor and collections created by Lord Leighton, former President of the Royal Academy. The centrepiece Arab Hall has a fountain and an almost dazzling assemblage of islamic tiles, and there's a fine collection of paintings by Millais, Burne-Jones, and Leighton himself. Shop; tours Weds-Thurs at 2.30pm; cl Tues, 25-26 Dec and 1 Jan; (020) 7602 3316; £3.

Linley Sambourne House (18 Stafford Terrace) Recently re-opened after more than two years of restoration, this is the home of the celebrated *Punch* cartoonist, with a fine collection of his work - it's a fascinating example of a Victorian town house in its original state. Open wknds by guided tours only; 10, 11.15am and 1, 2.15 and 3.30pm; open dates over Easter and summer bank hols undecided as we went to press, best to book; (020) 7602 3316 ext 305; £6.

Serpentine Gallery (Kensington Gardens) Often has some of London's most interesting exhibitions, concentrating on challenging modern and contemporary art, and younger artists. Bookshop; cl 25 Dec and 1 Jan; phone for a programme (020) 7402 6075; free. Each year they invite top architects to design a summer pavilion which is erected next door, and sold for charity in Sept; last year's by the brazilian architect Niemeyer was a stunner.

HYDE PARK CORNER ⊖

Apsley House The Duke of Wellington's elegant former home, designed by Robert Adam. It was known as Number One London, as it was the first house past a toll gate into London at the top of Knightsbridge. The magnificent building has been painstakingly restored; everything gleams and looks as good as new, and works by Correggio, Rubens and Velazquez, as well as outstanding silver and porcelain amassed by Wellington as gifts from grateful kings and emperors, are back in their original positions (not always to their best advantage). Sumptuous furnishings, décor and sculpture - inc a statue of Napoleon by Canova that has him looking quite different from the usual image. Shop, limited disabled access; cl Mon (exc bank hols), 24-26 Dec, 1 Jan, Good Fri, May Day bank hol; (020) 7499 5676; £4.50 inc audio guide.

Hyde Park These 340 acres used to be a Royal hunting park, and in 1851 were the site of the Great Exhibition, and following massive riots the right of public assembly was established in 1872, creating Speakers' Corner. Now it's very much a city park, complete with cycle lanes, roller-bladers, and summer sun-bathing. You can hire boats on the Serpentine Lake, or even swim at the Lido. A water-feature memorial to Diana Princess of Wales should be completed in the summer. At the park's bottom corner is the relentless torrent of traffic around Hyde Park Corner; the subway can bring you up near the entertaining neo-baroque gates erected in honour of the late Queen Mother.

Wellington Arch Last occupied some 30 years ago as a police station, Decimus Burton's magnificent triumphal arch, somewhat stranded in the whirl of traffic around Hyde Park Corner, has been lavishly restored by English Heritage. You can walk through three floors of galleries (displays on the arch and other statues and monuments cared for by English Heritage) to the roof, for unusual views of Green Park and Hyde Park, or even to watch the mounted horse guards who pass through its columns daily at 10.30 and 11.30am (10.30 only on Sun). They kindly provide umbrellas if it's raining. Shop, disabled access; cl Mon (exc bank hols), Tues, 24-26 Dec, 1 Jan; (020) 7930 2726; £2.50.

KNIGHTSBRIDGE ⊖

Harrods (87-135 Brompton Rd) A wonderful place to browse, and has most things anyone could want - there's even a personal shopper available to help you choose. But it's the food halls that visitors to London really enjoy; they're divided into fruit and vegetables, an interesting delicatessen, grocery, meat, poultry, fish (the display of fresh fish at the end of the room is legendary), bread and cakes, flowers, and wines - and the downstairs pantry is not as expensive as you might think.

Sloane St Headed by Harvey Nichols, a long-standing fashion store now split into numerous famous-brand boutiques; its 5th-floor food store is superb, alongside a very good bar/restaurant. The street stretching down from here has had something of a renaissance recently, with international designers jostling to open very expensive new stores. In the handsome terraces beyond Sloane St can be found the charming Grenadier (Wilton Row; no food in the bar, but a snug little restaurant) and the surprisingly countryish Nags Head (Kinnerton St).

NOTTING HILL GATE ⊖

Portobello Rd Famous for its market - fruit and veg during the week, antiques and everything else on Sat from 5.30am, with most dealers there by 8am; with well over a thousand dealers you can still pick up a bargain. The quality and prices are higher at the Notting Hill end; it's more bric-a-brac as you get towards Ladbroke Grove. Portobello Gold (no 95) has good interesting food all day, and the Sausage & Mash café (no 268) is very popular.

SLOANE SQUARE ⊖

The heart of Chelsea, with Peter Jones, the mecca of the Sloanes, on the square itself (a sister department store of John Lewis, it's good value for money), and stylish kitchenware at David Mellor nearby. Just around the corner, the Antelope in Eaton Terrace is a useful lunch stop. King's Rd leading off the square used to be the height of trendiness in the 60s and 70s, but is now really just another shopping street. The bottom end of Sloane St has two interesting though expensive shops: Partridges, a fancy food shop, and the General Trading Company, with a fine collection of oddities, besides good-looking houseware, soft furnishings, antiques, glass and so forth.

Carlyle's House (Cheyne Row) The home of the writer from 1834 till his death, with lots of letters and personal possessions (look out for the mahogany sideboard, brought back to the house after 70 years), and an early piano played by Chopin. There's a charming little Victorian walled garden. Cl am, also Mon (exc bank hols), Tues, Good Fri and Nov-Mar; (020) 7352 7087; *£3.80; NT. The nearby Kings Head & Eight Bells, across a green and a busy road from the Thames, is almost villagey, with elegant Chelsea Old Church at the far end of the green. The grandiose 'Tudor' mansion facing the river here is in fact largely brand new.

Chelsea Physic Garden (Royal Hospital Rd) A real haven of peace, this was started in 1673 to study the plants used in medicine by the Worshipful Society of Apothecaries. It's still used for botanical and medicinal research (there's a unique garden of medicinal plants), but is also full of lovely and unusual plants which thrive here in Thames-side London's warm micro-climate. Snacks, shop (inc rare plants grown here), disabled access; open pm Weds and Sun Apr-Oct, for the Chelsea Flower Show, and occasional other days; (020) 7352 5646; £5. The Coopers Arms in nearby Flood St has good food.

National Army Museum (Royal Hospital Rd) Surprisingly little visited but well and honestly presented - the history of the men of the british, indian and colonial armies from the Battle of Agincourt to the present day, told with photographs, models, uniforms, prints and other mementoes inc the skeleton of Napoleon's horse and a lamp used by Florence Nightingale. Interactive exhibits test your map reading and rank recognition, there's an astonishingly detailed 70,000-man model of the Battle of Waterloo, and an interesting exhibition about the Army of today. Portraits by Gainsborough and Reynolds, and the collections of the former Museum of the Women's Royal Army Corps. Snacks, shop, disabled access; cl 24-26 Dec, 1 Jan, Good Fri, May Day; (020) 7730 0717; free.

Pimlico Rd An interesting collection of antiques and other small shops (and Peter's Restaurant, a very good value all-day italian-run café which has been a taxi-drivers' haunt for well over 30 years).

Royal Hospital (Royal Hospital Rd) Christopher Wren's most glorious secular building, which still houses over 350 Chelsea Pensioners. Shop, limited disabled access; cl noon-2 pm, Sun am (though you can go to the service in the Chapel at 11am on Sun); (020) 7881 5204; free. The adjacent spacious Ranelagh Gardens are the site of the Chelsea Flower Show in May.

SOUTH KENSINGTON ⊖

Brompton Oratory (Brompton Rd) Roman Catholic, and heavily magnificent - sombre despite the pallor of its marble. The Swag & Tails round the corner in Fairholt St has good sensibly priced food.

Holy Trinity Brompton London's most fashionable church, at the forefront of evangelical Anglicanism. Its gardens lead you into a very peaceful corner of residential London, with a decent pub in Ennismore Mews (the Ennismore Arms, which does Sun lunches).

Natural History Museum (Cromwell Rd) One of the most appealing places for families in the capital, constantly updating or adding attractions, and with displays that could keep most visitors enthralled for a week. Picking out highlights of this wonderful place isn't easy. There's an entire gallery devoted to dinosaurs, with lots of touch-screen activities and information and the popular life-like replica robotic *Tyrannosaurus rex*; until May there's a big, and very popular, T-rex exhibition (£3.50) helping visitors to decide whether the dinosaur was a killer or a scavenger. More gently evocative are the complete skeletons in the museum's main hall, a grand and noble sight below the intricately painted ceilings of the remarkable Romanesque building. The creepy-crawlies are another good bet, and the Earth Galleries are worth putting near the top of your list; there's an earthquake simulator, and you can see where real earthquakes have occurred in the last few days. An extensive new wing, the Darwin Centre, offers an interactive look at the museum's collection; there are tours every half hour to the labs where scientists work, and to see the bigger specimens; there's also a public viewing gallery on the ground floor displaying zoological exhibits (some packed away for over 100 years) from such famous expeditions as those of the *Beagle* and *Endeavour*, and from contemporary expeditions. Scientists give presentations to centre visitors daily, and you may be treated to live video link-ups to laboratories round the world. Remember to pick up one of the maps and guides as you go in, as it's a vast place, covering four acres. Meals, snacks, shops, disabled access; cl 25-26 Dec; 020 7942 5000; free.

Royal Albert Hall (Kensington Gore) The home of the summer Promenade Concerts and many other concerts throughout the year; completed in 1871, this huge oval arena was built in honour of Prince Albert. Below its massive metal and glass dome a terracotta frieze shows Man's progress in arts and sciences down the ages. Before modern technology (in the form of giant suspended mushrooms) got to grips with its acoustics, the hall used to be famous for its echo - it was said that this was the only hall where you could hear the works of modern composers twice. An eight-year £66.3m development programme has just been completed; improvements include restoration of the building inside and outside, relandscaping of the gardens, creation of a new South Porch, and better pedestrian and disabled access.

Science Museum (Exhibition Rd) Amazing museum, with its splendid Wellcome Wing devoted entirely to contemporary science, medicine and technology. Other galleries look at subjects such as genetics, the internet and the future role of science, and *Grossology* gives children a graphic exploration of all the yucky bodily functions they seem to enjoy; there's also an IMAX cinema (£7.10). The area has been designed to hold fast-changing, interactive exhibitions with plenty of hands-on displays, workshops and demonstrations, and a multi-sensory activity area aimed at under-8s (but parents seem to love it too). Elsewhere in the museum, exhibits range from Stephenson's *Rocket* to the Apollo 10 space capsule, and there are newly landscaped gardens outside. They hold various special events, such as all-night camp-ins which enthral children 8-11 (£30 per child (£25 adult) inc science shows, treasure hunts, workshops and breakfast - bring a snack and a sleeping bag). Meals, snacks, shop, disabled access; cl 24-26 Dec; (0870) 870 4868; free (visitor numbers have nearly doubled since they dropped the admission charge).

Victoria & Albert Museum (Cromwell Rd) Britain's national museum of applied and decorative arts has one of the finest collections in the world; it was founded in 1852 by Prince Albert, and houses all manner of decorative arts, from all ages and countries. The galleries run to over seven miles, inc a spectacular glass gallery (with touch-screen computer displays), a dazzling silver gallery, and the world's greatest collection of Constables. The magnificent British Galleries display art and design from the Tudor age to the Victorian era, featuring designers from Chippendale and Adams to Morris and Mackintosh. The galleries combine modern displays, five restored period rooms and interactive technology. Highlights include James II's wedding suit, Canova's *Three Graces*, and the 5-metre (17-ft) high Melville Bed. The first retrospective of the work of designer Vivienne Westwood takes place 1 Apr-11 July. Meals, snacks, shop, disabled access; cl 24-26 Dec, late-night opening Weds and last Fri of the month; (020) 7942 2000; free, charge for some exhibitions.

The City & East End

The City, with traffic cut to a minimum these days, is much more pleasant to walk through than it used to be. Its most typical financial buildings are mainly Victorian and Edwardian, and its landmark churches are mostly elegant classical designs, but the ground-plan follows the narrow twisting streets and alleys of medieval times - though because of the Great Fire of 1666 only a handful of buildings are medieval or Tudor. Very few people actually live here: for each one that does, another 60 or 70 flood in each day to work here, then flood out again at night - when the area becomes virtually deserted, as it is at wknds. Originally, particular streets came to be associated with particular crafts and trades, and this is reflected in the street names - Carter Lane, Hosier Lane, Cloth Fair, Ropemaker St, Milk St, Silk St, Coopers Lane and so forth. The great City Livery Companies representing the various trades have effectively run local government in the City for 800 years or more, and it's only now that the franchise is being widened to allow more modern financial institutions a share in local government here. Many guilds have only a tenuous connection with the original crafts involved in their trades. But in Billingsgate Market, still controlled by the ancient Fishmongers Company, you can still see the fish trade being carried on in much the same way as ever (West India Dock Rd, early morning Tues-Sat). Though the halls of the City Livery Companies may have been rebuilt since they were first established in the Middle Ages, they still house some remarkable treasures. Some are open to visit, but only by prior arrangement: book in January for one of the limited tickets, through the City of London Information Centre, St Paul's Churchyard, EC4; (020) 7332 1456. Around St Paul's and the Tower of London (a hit with children), the layout is more open, and far less affected by the City's human tides. Besides the Tower, St Paul's and the host of glorious churches, highlights here include some rewarding free museums: the excellent Museum of London, the Geffrye Museum, the Museum of Childhood, and the Ragged School Museum are all well worth visiting. The new Museum in Docklands is impressive, and 18 Folgate St makes for a most unusual guided tour. Two of the river's most striking monuments, Tower Bridge and much further downstream the Thames Flood Barrier, have enjoyable visitor centres. The liveliest glimpse of East End life nowadays is to be had on Sun mornings around Brick Lane and Petticoat Lane markets. A boat leaves the pier by Embankment tube station hourly and stops in several useful places on the way to Canary Wharf; (020) 7977 6892; £5 return. A distinctive new skyline landmark is the elegant Norman Foster Swiss Re building, or 'erotic gherkin' as it's commonly become known.

Please let us know what you think of places in the *Guide*. Use the report forms at the back of the book, write us a letter or log on to www.goodguides.co.uk

To see and do

ALDGATE EAST ⊖

19 Princelet St Well worth catching on one of its few open days, this early 18th-c Huguenot master silk weavers' home and Victorian synagogue has a fascinatingly history; an evocative place (partly because it's not restored), it gives a good idea of the East End's mixed cultural history. Phone for openings or check their website www.19princeletstreet.org.uk; (020) 7247 5352; donations welcome.

Brick Lane The community here is now largely asian, and Brick Lane is lined with lively curry houses; waiters outside try to entice you in with offers of free drinks, 20% off your bill and so forth, and it can be quite a struggle to decide which one to settle for (readers like Sweet & Spicy, cheap and authentic). The bagel bakery along here is popular too; you can watch them being made, and it's open 24 hrs. Brick Lane is also home to a lively street market (Sun 8am-2pm), a riot of colour, smells and sound, inc some very entertaining market patter; some of the food and other wares are quite exotic. There are plenty of bargains for early risers (and things to avoid - we've even seen someone specialising in second-hand felt-tip pens). Also on Sun, nearby Petticoat Lane Market (Middlesex St/Wentworth St) is the biggest street market in London, with plenty of clothes and other goods. Once the haunt of Jack the Ripper, the area of Whitechapel, around here, is still one of London's poorest. Elegant Whitechapel Art Gallery (Whitechapel High St) has an interesting programme of mostly contemporary art shows (cl Mon; most are free). The Good Samaritan (Turner St, behind Royal London Hospital) has good value pub food.

Spitalfields Market (Commercial Street) Organic fruits, vegetables, and other specialist foods, as well as crafts, antiques, bric-a-brac and clothes stalls; lots of good (and inexpensive) food stalls to choose from - we're fond of the Square Pie Company. It's open Mon-Fri (11am-3pm) and all day Sun - when it's especially bustling. The Ten Bells pub just opposite is well known for its Jack

the Ripper connections.

BANK ⊖

Some of the City's finest buildings are around here, though with most you'll have to content yourself with looking at just the outside. Besides the Bank of England itself, handsome or interesting buildings include the neo-classical Custom House on Lower Thames St, Lloyds of London on Lime St, and the Renaissance-style Royal Exchange on Cornhill, with several proud columns in front.

Bank of England Museum (Bartholomew Lane) This neo-classical fortress does still contain oodles of gold - and you can handle a real gold bar in the small but interesting museum, which shows how computerised currency speculators work, and lets you try your hand at being a dealer. Shop, disabled access; cl wknds and bank hols; (020) 7601 5491; free.

Leadenhall market (Whittington Ave, off Gracechurch St) Victorian iron- and glass-covered market, vibrant with Cockney humour yet quite smart, and filled with seafood, game, fruit and veg; cl around 4pm and wknds. The Lamb's top-floor dining bar gives good views of the market activity.

BARBICAN ⊖

Could be called the north bank's equivalent to the South Bank Centre - certainly its aesthetic equal. This complex includes theatres, exhibition halls, galleries, and what some would say is the city's most comfortable cinema; there's often free entertainment in the foyers. Work is now under way to make the labyrinthine foyers and entrances easier to navigate, though the £12¼m project won't be finished till 2006.

Museum of London (London Wall; Barbican tube station) No other city museum in the world is quite as comprehensive as this; anyone with just a passing interest in history will find it compelling. London's development is told through chronological reconstructions and period clothes, music and various remains, from a medieval hen's egg to an early (and quite different) tube map - ever heard of the station called Post Office? The 18th-, 19th- and 20th-c sections have almost too much to take in. Excellent redeveloped galleries cover Roman London (the building adjoins a stretch of original Roman wall - there's a new entrance here, and they've recently added a model of the lifting machine that provided Roman London with water), remarkable research on a 14th-c Black Death cemetery near the Tower of London, the rich historical clues that have emerged from a Tudor rubbish dump, and a World City gallery - London's history through the French Revolution through a reconstructed Victorian street to the outbreak of World War I. London before London takes you back to the days of Iron Age settlements and locally roaming elephants. Meals, snacks, shop, disabled access; cl Sun am, 24-26 Dec, 1 Jan; (020) 7600 0807; free.

BETHNAL GREEN ⊖
Columbia Road Flower Market Entirely devoted to flowers, and garden and house plants, with bargains as it closes around 2pm on Sun.
Museum of Childhood (Cambridge Heath Rd) This very special little museum houses the V&A's collection of toys, dolls, doll's houses, games, puppets and children's costumes. Excellent programme of events and children's activities (most wknds and school hols) - most completely free. Meals, snacks, shop, good disabled access; cl Fri, 24-26 Dec, 1 Jan; (020) 8980 2415; free. The Approach Tavern (Approach Rd) is an enjoyable unpretentious food pub.

DOCKLANDS ⊖
Once the heartland of Britain's trade-based Empire, these 8½ square miles have become the biggest redevelopment site in Europe, the old warehouses imaginatively converted into smart apartments and office blocks. Britain's tallest building, the 244-metre (800-ft) **Canary Wharf** is the great landmark; most of its floors are filled with offices, but there's now a busy and constantly expanding covered shopping mall at ground level. A growing cluster of modern but contrasting towers around the central skyscraper is carefully set off by

beautifully designed small public gardens, and the Thames-side walkways here have been enlivened by a swelling number of good café-bars and restaurants. Most parts of Docklands are reached and seen best by the **Docklands Light Railway**, which generally stays open even when the Underground closes; the best bit is between West India Quay and Island Gardens, where you can get off and walk through the foot tunnel under the Thames to Greenwich. The Jubilee Line tube extension has brought with it some architecturally spectacular stations, the most eye-catching of which are Canary Wharf (designed by Sir Norman Foster) where you descend by escalator from the eyelid-like glass roof entrance to a vast naturally lit hall, and North Greenwich, with its roof cleverly complementing the adjacent Millennium Dome - now rather a pathetic landmark, as it stands abandoned, awaiting future redevelopment. Some docks have been brightly reworked and appeal to visitors: St Katharine's Dock (Tower Hill tube station is quite handy), which has a lively marina, a quite cheerful pastiche of a Victorian pub in the Dickens Inn, and lots going on, and Tobacco Dock, with an american-style factory shopping centre. Further E down the river is the gigantic closeable **Thames Flood Barrier**, built to protect the city from freak tides; a Visitor Centre on Unity Way, Woolwich SE18, has an exhibition on the construction of the barrier, a working scale model and a children's play area. Cafe, shop, disabled access; cl 24 Dec-2 Jan; (020) 8305 4188; £1.
Museum in Docklands (West India Quay, Hertsmere Rd) In a converted Georgian warehouse which once used to hold the West India Company's sugar, coffee and rum), this new museum traces the story of the area from Roman settlement, to hub of the colonial empire, and more recently to the closure of wharfs and dock systems between 1967-81, right up to its current regeneration. The 12 galleries contain artefacts (ranging from massive whale bones to World War II gas masks) from the Museum of London and the Port of

London Authority collections; highlights include the reconstruction of Wapping waterfront in its 19th-c heyday, and a lively interactive gallery for children. Temporary exhibitions and regular special events. Restaurant, coffee shop, shop, disabled access; cl 25-26 and 31 Dec, 1 Jan; (020) 7001 9800; £5.

FARRINGDON ⊖

Museum of the Order of St John (St John's Lane) Housed in a 16th-c gatehouse and 12th-c crypt, silver, paintings and furniture belonging to the medieval Order, and an interactive gallery covering its more modern offshoot, the St John Ambulance. Shop, disabled access to ground floor; cl Sun, bank hol wknds; (020) 7324 4000; free, £5 donation requested for guided tours of the gatehouse and priory church on Tues, Fri and Sat at 11am and 2.30pm. The Eagle in Farringdon Rd/Bakers Row has outstanding food.

St Bartholomew the Great church (W Smithfield) Mainly Norman, with a 16th-c gateway into the market precincts. Shop, disabled access; cl Mon, pm Sat, 1-2.30pm Sun; (020) 7606 5171; £3 donation. The nearby Bishops Finger is a pleasant retreat, and on wkdys you can get breakfast from 7.30am in the Butchers Hook & Cleaver - the name a reminder that Smithfield is London's streamlined and updated wholesale meat market.

LIVERPOOL ST ⊖ ⇌

18 Folgate St Guided tours of a quite remarkable house, now named after the late Dennis Severs who made it such fun to visit - but be warned, this is no ordinary guided tour, and one far more suited to adults than children. It doesn't do the place justice to say that it's been furnished and decorated in period style - to all intents and purposes you are back in the 18th c, with candles and firelight flickering away, food and drink laid out on the table, even urine in the chamber-pots. Open 2-5pm first and third Sun of month (£8) and 12 noon-2pm on the Mon following the first and third Sun (£5), phone to check; (020) 7247 4013. Elaborate candlelit tours Mon evening (booking required); £12. Dirty Dicks (Bishopsgate) re-creates a traditional City cellar tavern, also fun for visitors.

MILE END ⊖

Ragged School Museum (Copperfield Rd) This canalside warehouse was one of the many 'ragged' (or free) schools set up by Dr Barnardo in Tower Hamlets in the late 19th c. Displays concentrate on the school's history (there's a re-created Victorian classroom), life in the East End in the 1890s, and the work of the great philanthropist himself. An exhibition takes a detailed look at the area's social history over the last 200 years or so, through the eyes of local people inc a former waiter, and an usherette from the People's Palace theatre. Snacks, shop, disabled access to ground floor only; open Weds, Thurs, and pm first Sun of month (exc at Christmas, cl for two weeks); (020) 8980 6405; free.

MONUMENT ⊖

(Monument St) A fluted Doric column designed by Wren and Hooke at an exact height of 202 ft (62 metres) to mark the spot where the Great Fire of London began in 1666 - in Pudding Lane 62 meters from its base. The city views from the top are tremendous, though there are 311 spiral steps up. The viewpoint was designed as a cage to prevent people jumping off. Cl 24-26 Dec; (020) 7626 2717; £2.

OLD STREET ⊖

Geffrye Museum (Kingsland Rd; Liverpool St/Old St tube station) One of London's most friendly museums, yet least-known; 18th-c almshouses converted to show the changing style of the english domestic interior. Displays go from lovely 17th-c oak panelling and furniture through elegant Georgian reconstructions and Victorian parlours to the latest in interior design inc a contemporary loft-style dwelling. They've given the gardens similar treatment, showing trends in domestic horticulture through the ages, inc a notable herb garden. Excellent programme of exhibitions, special events, talks and activities. Meals, snacks, shop, disabled access; cl Sun am, all day Mon (exc pm bank hols), 24-26 Dec, 1 Jan, Good Fri; (020) 7739 9893; free.

John Wesley's House & Chapel (49 City Rd) The father of Methodism had his house and chapel built here in 1778, and they're still much as they were then, with plenty of his personal possessions. You can see Wesley's tomb in the chapel, and the crypt has a museum on the history of Methodism. Shop, disabled access to museum only; cl bank hols, Thurs 12.45-1.15pm, and 24 Dec-1 Jan, also limited opening Sun (when services); (020) 7253 2262; donations. The nearby Fox (Paul St) has good interesting food.

ST PAUL'S ⊖

Guildhall (off Gresham St) 15th-c, where the Court of Common Council, over which the Lord Mayor presides, administers the City of London. The Lord Mayor's Banquet is held in the great hall, hung with the banners and shields of the City's 102 livery companies. Underneath is the largest 15th-c crypt in the City; there's also a clock museum, library with unrivalled collection of City-related manuscripts and books. Disabled access; cl Sun, and for civic occasions, phone to check (020) 7606 3030; book for guided tours on (020) 7332 1460; free. The striking **Guildhall Art Gallery** on the east side of Guildhall Yard displays about 250 works of art ranging from Royal portraits through period views of historic London to contemporary works, and temporary exhibitions. In 1988, Museum of London archaeologists unearthed London's only **Roman Amphitheatre**, under Guildhall Yard (a black line across the yard marks its shape). Through a complex process the remains have now been integrated with the structure of the new art gallery, and you can now enter the amphitheatre by the route taken by gladiators and wild animals. Light displays complete missing sections of the structure - quite a convincing jump back 2,000 years. Shop; cl Sun am, 25-26 Dec, 1 Jan; £2.50, free Fri and after 3.30pm (last entry 4.30pm). The nearby Red Herring has good lunchtime food.

St Anne & St Agnes church (Gresham St) Particularly worth knowing for the Bach cantatas that grace its Lutheran services (every Sun); (020) 7606 4986 for programme.

St Mary le Bow church (Cheapside)

The one with the famous Bow Bells; often Thurs lunchtime concerts, and possibly interesting Tues dialogues (the rector in conversation with a distinguished guest). Meals and snacks; cl wknds, the wk following Good Fri, and 25 Dec-1 Jan; (020) 7248 5139. Williamsons nearby (off Bow Lane), well rebuilt in Jacobean style after World War II bomb damage, has food all day (and ornate wrought iron gates supposedly presented by William and Mary when the Lord Mayor lodged here).

St Paul's Cathedral 🏛 Despite the attempts of brasher, taller modern buildings to take over, and the controversial new Paternoster Square development just NE, this masterpiece still asserts itself proudly as the area's real landmark, its unmistakable shape repeatedly looming out above the streets. Its huge dome is a pleasing shape after the stolid self-satisfaction of the Victorian and Edwardian masonry which dominates this area. Originally the cathedral was Gothic in style, with a towering 150-metre (500-ft) spire. It fell into disrepair and Wren was assigned to work on its renovation. He didn't relish the job, and no doubt was delighted when the Great Fire of London swept the old church away, allowing him to construct something entirely new. His mainly classical design is unlike any other cathedral in Britain, and took just 35 years to build. The setting for various State occasions, it's full of interesting monuments - the one to John Donne was the only complete figure to be salvaged from the Great Fire. Look out for the wonderful carving on the exterior - some of which is by Grinling Gibbons, who also did the choir stalls. Other highlights include the dizzying Whispering Gallery, the panoramic views from the top, and the crypt, full of tombs and memorials to notable figures from british history. Meals, snacks, shop, disabled access; cl Sun, Good Fri, 25 Dec and for occasional services; (020) 7236 4128; £6. The City Pipe by the tube station is an enjoyable wkdy wine bar, and the heavy-beamed Olde Watling (Watling St) was knocked up by Wren as a commissariat for his site workers.

TOWER HILL ⊖

Tower Bridge Experience Inside the landmark bridge, with wonderful views from its glass-covered walkways, 43 metres (142 ft) above the Thames, displays explore the Bridge's historic links with the Tower. Lively multi-media shows are designed to leave you feeling proud to be british. The bridge is unusual not just for its design, but because it's still fully operational, raising the roadway from each side drawbridge-style to allow ships to pass; you can see some of the Victorian machinery that used to power this. Snacks, shop, disabled access; cl 24-25 Dec and 1 Jan; (020) 7940 3985; *£4.50. The Anchor Tap (Horselydown Lane, almost directly below the bridge) has simple low-priced food.

Tower of London Picturesque classic castle, the most notable building to survive the Great Fire of London. A lot of fun to look at even superficially, it dates back to the late 11th c, though the site had been used as a defensive position by the Romans much earlier. It's witnessed all sorts of gruesome goings-on, with not even the highest or mightiest safe from imprisonment or even execution: Walter Ralegh, Lady Jane Grey and two of Henry VIII's wives spent their last days in the Tower. There's a mass of things to see, inc enough medieval weaponry and armour to equip an army, and not forgetting the Beefeaters and the ravens - you need a fair bit of time to see everything properly. To satisfy an apparently insatiable public demand for gore, they've recently introduced an exhibition on torture, with replicas of torture instruments (inc a rack), and interactive displays; this is being extended to include exhibitions on prisoners held in the tower, and from Easter to end Sept there will be various trails around the tower, and special events to highlight the lives of various of its prisoners. The Jewel House shows off the Crown Jewels to dazzling effect; on the busiest days those tempted to linger are gently drawn along by moving floorways. Two towers that were part of Edward I's medieval palace are furnished in period style; one room in this part has been left untouched to show what a difficult job the restoration was. A reorganisation of the oldest part, the White Tower, has revealed that the inside of the fortress when built was much less imposing than was suggested by the formidable exterior - they were clearly just trying to intimidate the locals. You can also walk along the elevated battlements. Meals, snacks, shop, some disabled access; cl 24-26 Dec, 1 Jan; (020) 7709 0765; £13.50. Nearby All Hallows, the oldest church in the City of London, has a brass rubbing centre, and part of a Roman pavement; headless prisoners were often buried here.

Bloomsbury, Holborn & Regent's Park

Some little-known treasures are to be found in Bloomsbury and Holborn, a civilised if slightly faded area of Georgian squares, gardens and courts between the City and Westminster - legal and academic London. Strolling through the courtyards of the Inns of Court, particularly the Middle Temple (Temple) and Gray's Inn and Lincoln's Inn (Holborn), takes you back to a calmer century, and in Lincoln's Inn the unusual Sir John Soane's Museum is not to be missed. Somerset House (Temple) with its fountain-filled courtyard certainly makes a dramatic impact, but not everyone knows about the three different collections of fabulous art treasures inside. The British Museum (Russell Square) with its splendid courtyard is vastly satisfying and this part of London's must-see; the British Library at King's Cross has some intriguing exhibits, too, and the London Canal Museum combines nicely with a boat trip up the Regent's Canal to Camden. Bloomsbury merges into a smarter area to the West, over towards Marylebone (inc Madame Tussaud's), with Regent's Park (and the Zoo) on its north border; away from the shopping streets of Marylebone High St and Baker St this is largely residential, and the capital of private medicine and dentistry - a very rich little enclave. Bloomsbury does have a large number of hotels, especially for the more budget-conscious visitor, though many are on the tawdry side. Ones which can be recommended include the Academy (17 Gower St WC1E 6HG (020) 7631 4115), the Morgan (24 Bloomsbury St WC1B 3QJ (020) 7636 3735) - both handy for the British Museum - and the George (60 Cartwright Gardens WC1H 9EL (020) 7387 6789).

To see and do

BAKER STREET ⊖
London Planetarium (Marylebone Rd) This shows off one of the most advanced star projectors in the world, and surround-sound gives their enjoyable presentations an added sense of realism. Make sure you get to each show on time - stragglers barely have a moment to find a seat before the lights are dimmed. Interactive displays too - you can even see how much you'd weigh on another planet. Meals, snacks, shop, disabled access, cl 25 Dec; (0870) 400 3000; £2.50, joint ticket with Madame Tussaud's available. Opposite, the café of St Marylebone church has good value simple vegetarian meals.
Madame Tussaud's (Marylebone Rd) Almost half of overseas visitors place this famous waxworks museum at the top of their list of things to do in London, which explains why the queues can be so long and slow-moving (it definitely makes sense to phone in advance for queue-avoiding timed tickets), and perhaps why german TV presenters and japanese sumo wrestlers crop up among more familiar simulacrums. Some of the models are uncannily realistic (some talk, breathe, and in the case of J-Lo, even blush), others rather less so; the Blush exhibition allows visitors to get up close to models such as Kylie, Brad Pitt and Madonna, and you can have your picture taken in the paparazzi enclosure

on the World Stage. Highlights are the famous Chamber of Horrors, Chamber Live! (over 12s only) - a face-to-face meeting with serial killers, and the entertaining Spirit of London finale - you sit in a black cab and are whisked through a cheery interpretation of the city's history. This part is excellently put together, and in places rather witty, but is over a little quickly - like the waxworks as a whole. As you can be in and out of the museum in little over an hour, you're paying more per minute here than practically anywhere else in Britain. Meals, snacks, shop, disabled access; cl 25 Dec; (0870) 400 3000; ticket prices vary according to times and seasons so best to phone, joint ticket available with the Planetarium.
Sherlock Holmes Museum 🏛
(221b Baker St) To many people the world over, Baker St calls to mind only one thing - Conan Doyle's great detective. This famous address has various Holmes paraphernalia (avid readers enjoy recognising objects mentioned in the stories), and something of the atmosphere of the books re-created in the apartment the characters occupied in the books; also waxwork models of characters from the stories, and you can look through period newspapers. Shop; cl 25 Dec; (020) 7935 8866; £6. There's a giant bronze statue of the super-sleuth outside Baker St station.

GOODGE STREET ⊖

Pollock's Toy Museum 🔁 (1 Scala St) Housed in a rather charming setting, a wide range of playthings from all over the world and from all periods, almost as if lots of enthusiastic children had just left them scattered through these little rooms. Mechanical and optical toys, teddy bears, furniture, board games and theatres, and a proper toy shop downstairs. Shop; cl Sun and bank hols; (020) 7636 3452; £3.

HOLBORN ⊖

Legal London A perfect example of the tranquil architecture of this area, Lincoln's Inn Fields is a large open space with trees and lawns surrounded by handsome houses, also tennis courts and summer band concerts; it's a pleasant place to spend a summer afternoon. Nearby, the Gothic **Royal Courts of Justice** are impressive, and you can also stroll through the gardens of **Gray's Inn**, said to have been laid out by Francis Bacon around 1600. This area really is legal London, and you'll usually find a good number of lawyers in the splendid Cittie of Yorke (22 High Holborn), an enormous and very atmospheric basement pub with little private booths down one side. Another fine pub in this area is the classic Lamb in Lamb's Conduit St.

Sir John Soane's Museum (13 Lincoln's Inn Fields) One of London's hidden highlights, built by the architect for his splendid collection of pictures, books and antiquities. It's most eccentric, full of architectural tricks and mirrors, which form a complex natural-lighting system for the antiquities covering most of the walls. There's a lovely picture by Turner and an egyptian sarcophagus, but the highlights are Hogarth's acid series on *The Rake's Progress* and *The Election*. When you've seen them the guide swings open the hinged 'walls' and further treasures emerge inc choice Piranesi drawings and a scale model of the Bank of England. At the back of the Picture Room is a monument to his dog ('Alas, poor Fanny!'); you ring the bell to get in, and sign a visitors' book. The guides are very friendly and helpful, and the guidebook worthwhile. Work to extend the musuem should be finished in 2005, and will inc a large exhibition on Robert Adam, and Soane's models. Shop, limited disabled access; cl Sun, Mon, bank hols and 24-26 Dec; open first Tues evening of every month; (020) 7405 2107; free (donations welcome). The breakfast room of Soane's first house, no 12 next door, can also be visited.

KING'S CROSS ⊖ ≠

British Library (Euston Rd) This vast modern library has good exhibition space for its national treasures (which range from the Magna Carta to Beatles manuscripts, and Jane Austen's writing desk), and changes its displays frequently, as well as mounting special exhibitions (till Mar they've one based on chinese printmaking); also guided tours, and a good programme of events. The entrance courtyard has a gigantic bronze of a crouching seated Sir Isaac Newton, by Paolozzi after William Blake, and impressive entrance gates. Meals, snacks, shop, disabled access; usually only cl 24-26 Dec, and 1 Jan; (020) 7412 7332; free. The Euston Flyer over the road has decent food.

London Canal Museum (12-13 New Wharf Rd) The history of London's canal network is told in this former ice warehouse, with displays about the people who strove to make a meagre livelihood by living and working on them, the horses which pulled their boats, and the cargoes they carried. You can peer down into a huge ice well, where winter ice was once stored into summer; temporary exhibitions. Book and gift shop, disabled access to ground floor; cl Mon (exc bank hols), plus a few days over Christmas and New Year; (020) 7713 0836; £2.50. The Waterside on the Battlebridge Basin (York Way) has food all day.

REGENT'S PARK ⊖

(Gt Portland St or Regent's Park tube station) Covering over 400 acres, this is the culmination of a glorious swathe of Regency terraces designed by John Nash, which can be seen almost all around it; the buildings of Park Crescent are among the finest. The park was originally intended to be the setting for a palace for the Prince Regent, after whom it was named: now, besides plenty of paths to stroll along, it includes the lovely Queen Mary's Rose

Garden, the spectacular Avenue Garden (restored to its 1864 glory), a boating lake, bandstand concerts on summer Sun, and an open-air theatre where Shakespeare and other plays are performed in the summer (phone to book; (020) 7486 2431).

London Zoo (Regent's Park or Camden Town tube station) There are lions, giraffes and so forth, and the monkeys and sloth bears which use the famous Mappin Terraces as a sort of animal playground, but it's with smaller creatures that the zoo currently excels. Highlights include the Web of Life, a live animal exhibition housed in a glass building with a ventilation system inspired by termites' nests. This shows how animals adapt to different environments, and how new species evolve; animals chosen to illustrate this include sea-horses, a swarm of locusts, and organisms not normally visible to the naked eye, viewed in a micrarium. At the irresistible children's zoo, you can get right up to the animals (and help feed the pigs), and they've the biggest reptile house of any UK zoo; at the spellbinding Moonlight World day and night are reversed so you can watch nocturnal creatures such as vampire bats. The 1930s architecture of the penguin pool remains quite something (there are regular penguin feeding times too). Meals, snacks, shop, disabled access; cl 25 Dec; (020) 7722 3333; *£13.50.

Primrose Hill Once part of the same hunting park as Regent's Park, now popular strolling ground for this wealthy residential area. The modest rounded summit gives eye-opening views of the city. Nearby Chalk Farm has a good choice of eating places (look out for celebrities).

Regent's Canal The canal offers an excellent walk from Little Venice to Camden Lock, passing by Regent's Park and Primrose Hill; boat cruises also operate along here - one-way tickets available. Jason's is one of several companies who now run along the stretch of Regent's Canal between Little Venice and Camden Lock; (020) 7286 3428; £6.95 return. Another, the London Waterbus Company, make a stop for passengers who want to get off at the zoo; (020) 7482 2660 for timetable.

RUSSELL SQUARE ⊖
British Museum (Great Russell St) Monumental 19th-c building housing spectacular collections of priceless man-made objects from all over the world, some of them over 300,000 years old. The range is staggering; some of the many highlights are the Elgin Marbles (or Parthenon Sculptures as some now call them), the wonderful and intriguing egyptian galleries, the comprehensive galleries of greek vases, the oriental antiquities, the Amaravati sculpture, and fascinating collections of non-western art and culture. Don't try to take it in all at once - decide what interests you most and stick to that, or your head will start reeling with the extent of this treasure-house before you've got even a tenth of the way through. Try to arrive early as it can get very busy. Readers are full of praise for the Foster-designed Great Court, the largest covered public square in Europe; an uplifting place, it's home to monumental sculpture from around the world, as well as cafés, restaurants and lecture theatres. The famous Reading Room now has a public reference library giving visitors access to exhibits not on show. Meals, snacks, shop, disabled access; cl 24-26 Dec, 1 Jan, and Good Fri; (020) 7323 8000; free exc for special exhibitions, museum tours £8. Just up Gower St, Waterstone's is a first-class bookshop, and in Museum St the Coffee Gallery is good for a light lunch or patisserie.

Charles Dickens Museum 🏛 (48 Doughty St) Dickens lived here during his 20s, and in that period wrote the *Pickwick Papers*, *Oliver Twist* and *Nicholas Nickleby*. The drawing room has been reconstructed to appear as it was then, and there are pictures, personal possessions and original manuscripts and first editions. His wife's sister died here in 1837, an event which the writer later used as the model for the death of Little Nell in *The Old Curiosity Shop*; special exhibitions too. Shop; cl 25-26 Dec, and 1 Jan; (020) 7405 2127; £4. Round the corner in Roger St the Duke of York has good interesting modern food.

TEMPLE ⊖
Dr Johnson's House (17 Gough Sq) A perfect example of early 18th-c

architecture, just as Dr Johnson himself was a perfect example of 18th-c barbed slightly flawed gentility. Between 1749 and 1755 he wrote his great *English Dictionary* here, and there are various memorabilia from his learned life on show. Shop; cl Sun and bank hols; (020) 7353 3745; £4. The passages and walkways around here are a good reminder of how London's streets used to be laid out; the 17th-c Olde Cheshire Cheese nearby is a splendid old tavern.

Middle Temple Hall Of all the Inns of Court, this is perhaps the most impressive, and it boasts many famous literary figures among its former members. Most of the buildings date from after the reign of Elizabeth I or the Great Fire, but the name points to an older history: the land was owned by the Knights Templar from about 1160. The hall is a fine example of Tudor architecture, with a double hammer-beam roof and beautiful stained glass. There is a table made from timber from Sir Francis Drake's *Golden Hind* - he was a member of the Middle Temple - while a single oak tree from Windsor Forest supplied the wood for the 9-metre (29-ft) long High Table. Open 10-11.30am and 3-4pm wkdys (exc bank hols, Easter week, Whitsun week, Aug and 2 wks at Christmas); shop, disabled access; (020) 7427 4800; free. The Temple has an unusual round church. Up on Fleet St the Old Bank of England is a spectacular pub conversion.

Somerset House (Strand; on Sun when Temple Station is cl, Charing Cross is not far) Built as government offices in the later years of the 18th c (on the site of an earlier spectacular Royal palace; archaeological finds inc an early 17th-c silver river god mask are now on show), and for years the HQ of the Inland Revenue, this grand building designed by Sir William Chambers is now a great place to visit. It houses three major art collections, spread throughout several buildings surrounding a central paved courtyard with a stunning series of waterspouts. It's long been the home of the **Courtauld Institute Gallery** (North Wing), an outstanding collection of

Impressionist and Post-Impressionist paintings inc works by Monet, Renoir, Degas and Cézanne, also Michelangelo, Rubens, Goya and other masters; (020) 7848 2526; £5. Opened more recently, the **Gilbert Collection** (South Building) is a spectacular assortment of objets d'art (mostly gold and silver) made for the rich and famous over the past 500 years, from six jewel-encrusted gold snuffboxes owned by Frederick the Great of Prussia (valued at over £1m each) to a massive wine cistern weighing nearly 36kg (80lb), and even a pair of silver chamber-pots; (020) 7420 9400; £5. The **Hermitage Rooms**, on the ground floor of the South Building, house rotating exhibitions from the famous State Hermitage Museum (formerly known as the Winter Palace) in St Petersburg, and furnishings attempt to re-create something of that museum's Imperial Russian splendour; (020) 7845 4630; £6. The River Terrace - open as a public promenade for the first time in 100 years - has an open-air café, restaurant and shop; all the galleries have full disabled access; Somerset House cl 25 Dec (free), all collections cl 24-26 Dec; (020) 7845 4600. In winter, the courtyard holds an ice rink, and in summer it's filled by quite an army of fountains - also outdoor plays and concerts then.

St Bride's church (Fleet St) A Wren masterpiece, its splendid steeple the influence for today's traditional three-tiered wedding cake; good Sun choir and frequent short lunchtime recitals; (020) 7427 0133 for programme. There's an interesting **museum** in the partly Roman crypt (cl bank hols, no disabled access; free). Caxton set up his first printing press alongside, and ever since St Bride's has been the parish church for anyone involved in the press. This was useful in the days when adjoining Fleet St was the hub of newspaperland; today it's really just a passage between the law courts and the City - but look out for relics of the newspaper kingdoms such as the black-glass former Daily Express Building. The nearby Old Bell is a nice old tavern.

South of the River

The south side of the Thames has perked up enormously in the last two or three years, with the elegant London Eye its centrepiece. Tate Modern on Bankside draws vast numbers of happy visitors, and the London Aquarium, an interesting Dali gallery, and the big highly contemporary new Saatchi gallery are all in the grandiose building that used to house London's bureaucrats. The riverside walkway has a growing number of bars and cafés, and the South Bank arts centre has a more lively and welcoming feel these days, with pleasant bars and so forth. Children seem to find the expensive London Dungeon irresistible, and older ones enjoy the marvellous Imperial War Museum, and HMS *Belfast*. Britain at War is a strong draw, and followers of fashion won't want to miss Zandra Rhodes' Fashion and Textile Museum. Some of the gruesome surgical instruments at the Old Operating Theatre make a visit to the dentist seem an appealing alternative. Bankside's rich theatrical heritage has been well exploited over the last few years, with the magnificent reconstruction of Shakespeare's Globe Theatre (excellent summer productions and an enjoyable permanent exhibition). The best views of the Houses of Parliament are from the quiet riverside walk between Westminster Bridge and the ancient palace of the Archbishop of Canterbury by Lambeth Bridge. For an alternative way of seeing the sights, the unusual London Duck Tours make quite a splash. Though the South Bank and its attractions are well signposted from Waterloo, if you have time to spare the walk is more pleasant over the new pedestrian bridge from Embankment, or from Westminster.

To see and do

BOROUGH ⊖
London Fire Brigade Museum 🔳
This less well known museum looks at the history of firefighting since 1666. As well as an extensive collection of old fire appliances and memorabilia, you can find out about the personalities of various fire brigade chiefs. The building too is interesting - it was the home of the first chief officer of the Metropolitan Fire Brigade, and you might see recruits training at an adjacent centre; guided tours by appointment. Shop; cl wknds and bank hols; (020) 7587 2894; *£3.

ELEPHANT & CASTLE ⊖
Bermondsey market (Bermondsey St/Long Lane) Get up very early on Fri for the bargains: when the antiques dealers start arriving around 5am, other dealers literally pounce on the choice items while they're being set out, and by 8 or 9am things are more ordinary. It's probably the biggest primary source of antiques and bric-a-brac in London, and can be the most exciting.

LAMBETH NORTH ⊖
Florence Nightingale Museum (St Thomas Hospital, Lambeth Palace Rd) On the site of the first School of Nursing, a re-created Crimean War hospital ward, and various artefacts and possessions of the Lady with the Lamp. Shop, disabled access; cl 24 Dec-2 Jan, Good Fri and Easter Sun; (020) 7620 0374; £4.80.

Imperial War Museum (Lambeth Rd; not far to walk from Waterloo or even Westminster) There's an extraordinary amount of things to see at this incredible place, with more than enough to fill a day. As you go in you're met by dozens of tanks, guns, searchlights and rockets, dramatically displayed in a huge hall with planes hanging from the ceiling, and touch screens launching videos and archive films to put it all in context. Most of the permanent exhibitions are downstairs, very much the heart of the museum, with comprehensive galleries on the First and Second World Wars, and on the conflicts since. Big cases show off everything from uniforms and weapons to posters, pictures and letters, with old newsreels and period music wherever you go; there's lots to look at, but plenty for children to press, pick up or even try on. A highlight is the very well put together Trench Experience, which vividly re-creates the conditions faced by british troops in World War I, and other displays look at the work of the Secret Services and the Merchant Navy; there's an excellent (and often harrowing) art gallery. Get there when it opens to avoid the crowds. Meals, snacks, shops (inc a special shop for children), disabled access; cl 24-26 Dec; (020) 7416 5000; free. The museum - hard to miss with its big naval guns outside - is housed in the former lunatic asylum known as Bedlam, the name a corruption of Bethlehem; the site was originally a hostel set up in the 13th c by the bishop of that town. The adjacent gardens have plenty of space for picnics. **Lambeth Palace** (S end of Lambeth Bridge) The official residence of the Archbishop of Canterbury, with a charming late 15th-c red-brick exterior. The adjacent **Church of St Mary** has the tombs of several archbishops, and Captain Bligh of the *Bounty* is buried here too. Just by the S gateway is a little **Museum of Garden History** founded as a memorial to the Tradescants, father and son, gardeners to Charles I and Henrietta Maria, with a small area planted with plants grown in their time. Snacks, shop, some disabled access; cl mid-Dec to early Feb; (020) 7401 8865; £3 suggested donation. **LONDON BRIDGE** ⊖ ⇌ **Bankside and the Pool of London**

This area is very much on the up, with quite a bit of redevelopment going on in the old buildings, and plenty more to come. Strictly speaking London Bridge divides Bankside from the Pool of London, but for visitors they really run into one another, united by the river and the good riverside walkway with its fine Thames and City views - Wren is said to have watched the building of St Paul's from here, and Pepys certainly did watch London burning down in the Great Fire, from near the interesting old Anchor tavern. One of the best cross-river views of St Paul's is from the modern Founders Arms pub. For centuries this area was London's entertainment centre, full of theatres, bars and licensed brothels. In Clink St are the medieval remains of the Bishop of Winchester's palace, once said to be the biggest building in Europe but now reduced to a single wall and wistful rose window. Nearby, fun children's activities take place on board a full-size replica of Francis Drake's *Golden Hind*; cl 26 Dec, but phone to check as it occasionally closes for functions; (0870) 0118 700; £2.50. The latest landmark is the remarkable staggered circular glass palace near Tower Bridge, for the Mayor and Greater London Assembly. A ramp leads to a glazed viewing gallery and function room at the top, where there are good views over London (or if you prefer of the assembly at work - phone for days; (020) 7983 4100); the ground floor has an exhibition area and coffee shop, and the elegantly paved new plaza is prettily lit at night. **Borough Market** (8 Southwark Street) This has a terrific selection of wholesale fruit and vegetables, with good specialist stalls inc cheeses, meat and fish from producers and farmers across the country (we recommend the popular, tasty chorizo sandwiches); Fri and Sat. The Market Porter has sensibly priced food and a great beer range. **Bramah Tea and Coffee Museum** 🔳 (40 Southwark St, Bankside) Founded by tea trader Edward Bramah, this is almost scholarly but surprisingly interesting, meticulously charting the history of these two favourite commodities inc smuggling, tea auctions, opium trading, the Boston tea party and ceramics. Leaf teas and ground coffee, snacks, shop, disabled access; cl 25-26 Dec; (020) 7403 5650; *£4.

Britain at War 🖼 (Tooley St) A splendidly put together re-creation of Blitz-hit London, from reconstructed streets and air-raid shelters to a BBC radio station and GI club. The special effects are suitably dramatic, with lots of smoke, smells and noise. Also authentic period newsreels and front pages, wartime shop windows and a bombed-out pub, and lots of fascinating little details. Shop, disabled access; cl 24-26 Dec; (020) 7403 3171; £7.50.

Clink Prison Museum 15th-c prison, possibly the oldest in Britain, which gave its name, the Clink, to all the others. Now a museum, with some cell reconstructions, and hands-on displays, also a selection of the usual gory restraining and torturing devices. Shop; usually only cl 25 Dec and 1 Jan; (020) 7403 6515; £4.

Design Museum (Butlers Wharf, by Tower Bridge) Intriguing museum dedicated to 20th- and 21st-c design, fashion, creative technology and architecture, with a permanent collection of design classics, and good changing exhibitions; as this isn't cheap, it's a good idea to check you're interested in the temporary exhibitions before you go. Snacks, interesting shop selling expensive designer items, disabled access; cl 25-26 Dec; (020) 7940 8790; £6.

Fashion and Textile Museum Founded by Zandra Rhodes, this brightly coloured new museum showcases the work of local and international fashion and textile designers, with rotating displays of vintage and contemporary designs. Cl Mon, and a few days over Christmas and New Year; (020) 7403 0222; £6.

Globe Theatre 🖼 The most famous of Southwark's 1600s theatres, Shakespeare's Globe has been reconstructed close to its original site, where it was open from 1599 to 1642 (when the Puritans closed it down). It couldn't be more different from the West End: shaped like an O, the three-tiered open-topped theatre is 30 metres (100 ft) in diameter, seating audiences of 800 with a further 600

promenaders; it's the first building in London to be built with a thatched roof since the Great Fire. Shakespeare's works are performed almost the way they were in the early 1600s - no spotlights, canned music or elaborate sets. Anyone who tells you the seats are uncomfortable has rather missed the point (and you can hire cushions); standing is much cheaper. There are entertaining tours during the day; an exhibition under the building looks at the life and works of Shakespeare and has displays on the Globes old and new - a good substitute if you can't make a performance. Very good café and restaurant with river views, shop, disabled access; tours daily, although there are no tours summer pms, there are tours of the nearby Rose Theatre site; cl 24-25 Dec (020) 7902 1500; £8. The 17th-c galleried George in Borough High St, back past London Bridge station, gives another idea of how the area's buildings used to look back then; NT.

Hays Galleria (off Tooley St) An old dock attractively converted into a shopping arcade, with several places to eat inc a good river-view pub, and a fascinating whimsical pirate-ship working sculpture by David Kemp.

HMS *Belfast* (E side of Southwark Bridge) Docked permanently in the pool of London, this is the only surviving example of the big-gun armoured warships built for the Royal Navy in the first half of the 20th c. This floating museum has sound and light displays re-creating life at sea, and there's masses to see among its nine decks, from the ship's gun decks to its sick bay. Snacks, shop, limited disabled access; cl 24-26 Dec; (020) 7940 6300; £6, children free.

London Dungeon (Tooley St) A sensationalised look at London's seamy underside, so only for unsqueamish children, with witchcraft, torture, black magic and death (inc a grisly Jack the Ripper section), all presented in ghoulishly life-like waxwork scenes. The Great Fire of London takes you back to the fury of that urban inferno, and the Judgement Day water ride treats you to a trip on an executioner's barge. The whole place is very atmospheric and well laid out, though parents may find the scariest thing about it is the price. Snacks, meals, shop, disabled access; cl 25 Dec (open later in the evenings mid-July to early Sept); (020) 7403 7221; £12.50.

Old Operating Theatre 🖼 (St Thomas St) The 300-year-old church of St Thomas has a unique restored 19th-c operating theatre in its roof (originally this space was deemed far enough from the rest of the hospital for patients' screams to be out of earshot), and a museum looking at the history of surgery and herbal medicine, with some particularly gruesome bits of surgical equipment on show; special events. Shop; cl 15 Dec-5 Jan; (020) 7955 4791; £4.

Southwark Cathedral 🖼 Off the busy main road and quite a contrast to the buildings cluttered all around it, this is well worth a look, with parts over 600 years older than the present late 19th-c nave. There are interesting memorials to William Shakespeare (whose brother is buried here) and the poet John Gower, and a chapel is dedicated to John Harvard, founder of the american university named after him, who was baptised here in 1607. An exhibition in the visitor centre uses touch-screen computers to show finds from recent excavations at the cathedral, while interactive tower-top cameras give views of London (you can contrast these with various views recorded from the 16th c onwards from the same viewpoint), and a mini-theatre has a film on the cathedral's history. Meals, snacks, shop, disabled access; usually cl 25 Dec, Easter Sun and Good Fri and occasionally during services; (020) 7367 6700; £4 suggested donation, £2.50 for audio guide, £3 exhibition (discount voucher valid for this).

Vinopolis (Bank End, Bankside) Cavernous vaulted arches housing a celebration of all things Bacchic. A self-guided audio tour takes you around displays on the world's wine-growing regions, their culture and history, and afterwards you can sample five wines or champagnes from a choice of 200 (all of which feature in the exhibition). Restaurant, two shops, disabled access; cl 24-26 Dec, 1 Jan; (0870) 241 4040; £12.50.

SOUTHWARK ⊖
Tate Modern (Bankside) Standing proudly robust on the bank of the Thames opposite St Paul's Cathedral, this masterfully gentrified former power station is a salient landmark amid the cluster of exciting developments in this part of the city. Designed by Sir Charles Gilbert Scott in 1947 (the architect of Liverpool's Anglican Cathedral, Waterloo Bridge, and designer of the red telephone box), it stood derelict for nearly 15 years, until the Tate Gallery acquired it in 1994. Today, its cathedral-like windows give splendid views over central London, and a series of stunning top-lit galleries provide perfect lighting for artworks. The collection covers every modern movement from Pop Art to Surrealism, with works by all the great modern artists inc Dali, Picasso, Matisse, and Duchamp. An insistence on themed displays does rather jumble things up so that the real gems can seem hidden among lesser stuff, and there tends to be too much emphasis on the merely trendy, but this is a great place. There are around three major loan exhibitions a year, as well as an education centre, auditorium, café with outdoor terrace and a restaurant with river views. Very good disabled access, but phone first; (020) 7401 5120; cl 24-26 Dec; free (exc special exhibitions). The stunning Millennium footbridge makes access from the north bank of the Thames easier, and gives great views - worth a visit in its own right for the unique sense it gives you of floating over the Thames, as it seems so very much less substantial than any other bridge.

WATERLOO ⊖ ⇌
BFI London IMAX (Waterloo Rd/York Rd roundabout) Britain's largest screen (the height of five double-decker buses), in an eye-catching cylindrical glass building; you can see 2D and 3D films (quite a surprise if it's your first time). Café, disabled access; daytime and evening screenings; cl 25 Dec, 1 Jan, phone (020) 7902 1234 for details; £7.50.

Gabriel's Wharf (Upper Ground) One of quite a few projects to have sprouted along the river in recent years: a relaxed place, with a number of cheery designer and craft workshops, along with cafés, restaurants, and events. Studio Six has a good menu with lots of fish, and opposite is a tricycle rickshaw base.

Oxo Tower Wharf Offers great views over the city from the top of the lavishly restored art deco tower, with its landmark logo, cafés, bars and restaurants, designer shops and galleries with temporary exhibitions; cl 25 Dec and 1 Jan, design shops also cl Mon; (020) 7401 2255; free.

South Bank Centre This stretch of the riverside, home to a string of externally unlovely but world-class theatres, concert halls, cinemas and galleries (not for nothing do they boast that it's the biggest arts complex), is to undergo a radical redevelopment over the next few years. Part of the project - funded in part by the Arts Council and Heritage Lottery Fund - aims to cheer up the surroundings by extending Jubilee Gardens, and adding an open-air performance space and a new area for skateboarders. Other parts of the scheme include the renovation of the Royal Festival Hall (due to be completed in 2006), and the incorporation of shops and bars whose takings will contribute to the overall reconstruction. For the time being, annual open-air festivals, and the stalls of books going down to the river, bring quite a buzz on a sunny day. Inside there are frequent free performances and interesting small exhibitions in the foyers of the various halls. The National Theatre, as well as the excellent productions in its three different-sized auditoriums, has interesting artistic exhibitions, and guided tours behind the scenes; (020) 7452 3400 to book a tour (£5; cl Sun). The National Film Theatre has good themed screenings and events as well as a riverside café. The Hayward Gallery, which specialises in world-class art exhibitions, has recently been refurbished; to celebrate this they've launched a big exhibition called 'Saved!', displaying masterpieces rescued by the National Art Fund over the last century. There are good places to eat - often accompanied by live music in the foyer of the Royal Festival Hall, which is London's premier concert hall;

its river-view People's Palace is a good modern restaurant and bar. It's a short walk from here to the London Eye and other attractions in and around County Hall (a rather longer one to the Imperial War Museum); and now the shiny new Golden Jubilee Bridge twin footway sweeps elegantly across the Thames from over on the Embankment.

WESTMINSTER ⊖

Dali Universe 🖼 (County Hall) Devoted entirely to the great spanish Surrealist, this is part of the exciting tourist development around County Hall. Most of the 500 works on display have never been exhibited in Britain before, and among them is the spectacular oil painting created for the set of Hitchcock's 1945 film *Spellbound*, and the infamous *Mae West Lips* sofa. Snacks, shop, disabled access; cl 25 Dec; (020) 7620 2720; £8.50. Outside, a series of fantastical Dali sculptures have certainly brought some artistic panache to the riverside walkway.

London Aquarium (County Hall, a pleasant walk across Westminster Bridge from Westminster tube stn) One of Europe's biggest collections of underwater life; the main Atlantic and Pacific tanks are spectacular in their sheer size, giving great views of the sharks, stingrays and conger eels swimming round the Easter-Island style giant heads. The creatures (and divers - daily at 12pm, often more entertaining than the fish) have plenty of room to swim about. The rest of the displays - arranged in different themed areas representing rivers, coral reefs and rainforests - are a more conventional size, so you may have to wait a couple of minutes to get right up to them. Some areas are fairly imaginative, making good use of sound and light effects, and of course the fish and sea life are quite spectacular, with breath-taking colours and patterns. Well sized touch tanks let you stroke a ray or gingerly handle a crab. To avoid the crowds at wknds and school holidays, try to come early or late in the day. Shop, disabled access; cl 25 Dec; (020) 7967 8000; £8.75. Great London views from outside.

London Duck Tours First-time visitors to the capital won't find a better introduction than this quirky tour.

What makes it so different is that after an hour or so of travelling past the best-known sights by road, you suddenly veer down a slipway near Vauxhall Bridge, and the distinctive vehicle takes to the water, rounding off the tour with a half-hour or so trip down the Thames. In their original form, the amphibious vehicles played a role in the D-Day landings. You'll probably need to book in advance, they run from 10am until dusk; cl 25 Dec and perhaps some days in Jan, best to check; (020) 7928 3132 to book; £16.50 adults. Tours leave from Chicheley St, opposite the London Eye queueing area.

London Eye (County Hall) This gigantic steel wheel is the most successful and popular of the country's Millennium attractions. It stands nearly 140 metres (450 ft) above the Thames - the fourth-tallest structure in London, three times the height of Tower Bridge. On a clear day, passengers can see up to 25 miles in each direction from its 32 glass capsules, although pre-booked tickets (the way to avoid queues) mean you can't guarantee perfect viewing conditions. Each rotation (or flight, as the operators British Airways insist on calling them) takes 30 mins, and tickets must be collected from County Hall 15-30 mins in advance - it's all very well organised. There's a coffee shop by the ticket office, and capsules are fully accessible by wheelchair; cl 25 Dec, Jan; (0870) 5000 600; £11, children (must be accompanied by adults) £5.50, the 'flight' can be combined with a 45-min river cruise; £20.

Saatchi Gallery Focusing on large-scale shows by contemporary british artists (with much talked-about pieces such as Tracey Emin's *My Bed*, Marcus Harvey's *Myra* and Damien Hirst's pickled shark on permanent display). Galleries are devoted to up and coming artists, as well as changing exhibitions (one on the Chapman Brothers runs till Mar). Shop, disabled access; usually open daily, but best to check; (020) 7823 2363; £8.50.

Further Afield

Here we include places which, despite being away from the centre, appeal so much at least to some people that, for them, even a short stay in London would be incomplete without them. A classic example is the entertaining Horniman Museum (Forest Hill), our top Family Attraction for London this year. A trip down the Thames from Westminster is a fun way to begin a full day out at Greenwich, now an enjoyable destination for families, with wonderful alternative views over the city from the park, children's displays at the *Cutty Sark*, and its star attractions, the National Maritime Museum and the Royal Observatory. Kew is also very appealing, with its glorious glasshouses and memorable vistas, as is the earlier grandeur of the Great Conservatory at Syon House, Brentford. Firepower over in Woolwich takes a lively look at the history of the artillery, and for bird-lovers the Wetland Centre at Barnes is outstanding (full wheelchair access, too). Hampton Court Palace is a rewarding outing (the famous gardens are worth a visit in themselves), and Kenwood in Hampstead provides an idyllic setting for a summer evening concert.

To see and do

London Family Attraction of the Year

FOREST HILL ⇌ Horniman Museum (London Rd) Few museums can have as remarkable a range of collections as this extraordinary place, founded by tea trader Frederick Horniman in 1901 to house the splendidly varied oddities and artefacts he'd picked up from every continent. There's a little of everything here, and you never quite know what you'll come across next: beside a stuffed fruit bat is a 19th-c german Apostle clock, while just round the corner from a handful of mummy cases is a gruesome-looking torture device. Children love it, and on any visit you'll see dozens of wide-eyed faces as captivated by traditionally displayed cases as by the latest touch-screen displays. A stunning new £13 million extension has radically changed the look of the place: you now come in by an entrance in the delightful six-hectare (16-acre) grounds, and there are plenty of new galleries and exhibits. The layout is excellent, with plenty of space, and real thought put into the design and lighting. Standing out among the new areas is the wonderful Music Gallery, showing off an enormous collection of virtually everything that's ever been used to make any sort of noise; the exhibits are all behind glass, but touch screen displays let you hear the sound of every single one - and there's a side room for younger visitors to try some hands-on musical experiments. More established favourites remain, notably the excellent Natural History gallery, with hundreds of stuffed and preserved animals, including several examples of species now extinct. Also in here are some bizarre living toads, which as they hop around reveal some unlikely patterns and colours. There's plenty to inspire the imagination: look out for the unfeasibly large masks worn only after months of exhaustive neck exercises, or the intriguing Voodoo altars packed with gaudy symbolism. Elsewhere are a small aquarium, a comprehensive african gallery, and a hands-on room (open at weekends) where you can handle exhibits from the collections. They may have extra activities in summer holidays. For some the architecture itself is a highlight, from the art nouveau main building to the modern extensions and a splendid Victorian conservatory. Outside the colourful gardens have plenty of benches (and picnic tables), a small, slightly scruffy, collection of unusual birds and farm animals, and free summer Sunday concerts in the bandstand. The grounds cover one of London's biggest hills, so there are great views over the capital (and plenty of sledging locals when it snows). Meals, snacks, shop, disabled access; cl 24-6 Dec; (020) 8699 1872; free (though may be charge for the big temporary exhibitions). The streets behind have plenty of unmetered parking.

BARNES ⇌
Wetland Centre 4 miles from the heart of the city, this Wildfowl and Wetlands Trust reserve is an incredible feat of environmental transformation. A hundred acres of reservoir have been broken up and resculpted to create over 30 lakes, linked by 27 bridges. With 30,000 trees and countless aquatic plants, the centre is starting to attract wildlife from kingfishers through grebes, teal, plovers and herons to even bitterns now - not to mention newts. There are seven hides, and a three-storey viewing tower, but for those who like bird-spotting in comfort, a glass-walled observatory with views across the reserve relays live pictures via CCTV from the hides. A fun-looking discovery centre has lots of hands-on activities for children, with re-created wetland habitats. A visitor centre has touch-screen displays on the wildlife seen at the reserve, along with a café and shop. It's all been designed to accommodate wheelchair access, and there's even a lift in the observation tower. At peak times, the centre

provides a bus service from Hammersmith, Barnes, and perhaps other stations, to prevent traffic from disturbing the wildlife. Meals, snacks, shop, disabled access; cl 25 Dec; (020) 8409 4400; £6.75. The Bulls Head (Lonsdale Rd) is quite handy for cheap refreshment.

BRENTFORD ⇌

Syon Park The London home of the Duke of Northumberland, this was built on the site of a medieval abbey and remodelled from its Tudor original by Robert Adam - it's widely considered to be one of his finest works. The ceiling by Cipriani and the magnificent Scagliola floor are particular highlights, but a visit here can keep the whole family entertained, with 16 hectares (40 acres) landscaped by Capability Brown, Thames-side watermeadows, and a giant indoor adventure playground. Snacks, shop, disabled access to café and gardens only; house open Weds, Thurs, Sun and bank hol Mon (and all Easter wknd) mid-Mar to Oct, gardens open daily exc 25-26 Dec; (020) 8560 0882; house and gardens £6.95, gardens only £3.50. Also in the grounds is the **London Butterfly House** (shop, disabled access; cl 25-26 Dec; (020) 8560 0378; £4.95) and, with a range of endangered species, the **Aquatic Experience** (shop, disabled access; cl 24-26 Dec, 1 Jan; (020) 8847 4730; £4).

CAMDEN TOWN ⊖

A bohemian's idyll, with a very wide variety of unusual shops from radical bookshops to fashion workshops, and comic shops. Lots of restaurants and cafés too, and good delis serving the area's italian and greek communities. The area's biggest draw is its wknd series of lively **markets**, particularly the interesting craft, handmade fashion and other stalls around the attractively converted former warehouses of Camden Lock. There's also a covered market on Camden High St, the Inverness St market for fruit and veg, and the Stables, where the best food stalls are to be found. Go and browse, but be warned about the huge crowds - the markets here draw 200,000 people every wknd.

Jewish Museum 🖼 (129 Albert St) Excellent look at jewish life, history and religion, with a particularly fine collection of ceremonial art, portraits and antiques, and various audio-visual displays. Shop, disabled access; cl Fri-Sat, all bank and jewish hols; (020) 7284 1997; *£3.50. Another branch on East End Rd, Finchley - (020) 8349 1143 - traces the history of jewish immigration and has a moving exhibition on the Holocaust. The Princess of Wales up towards Primrose Hill (Chalcot Rd/Regents Park Rd) does good bistro food.

CHISWICK ⇌

Chiswick House (Burlington Lane - A316) Surrounded by beautiful classical gardens (the first true example of english naturalistic landscaping), this fine Palladian villa was designed by Lord Burlington in 1728. Sumptuously decorated, with the lavish blue velvet room as a particular highlight; there's an exhibition and video on the house and gardens. Snacks, shop, phone for disabled access; cl Mon (exc bank hols), Tues, pm Sat, and all Nov-Mar; (020) 8995 0508; £3.50 inc audio tour. Chiswick Mall is an 18th-c Thames-side village, well worth a stroll.

ELTHAM ⇌

Eltham Palace (Court Yard) In attractive grounds on the site of an early 14th-c Royal palace, this splendid 1930s mansion was built around part of a medieval hall erected for Edward IV. Re-created by English Heritage, the art deco interior reflects the glamour of its age; on wet days they give you blue overshoes to wear to protect the floors. Teas, shop, disabled access; cl Mon (exc bank hols), Tues, Sat, and around 21 Dec-Jan; (020) 8294 2548; house and grounds £6.50, grounds only £4; EH.

FOREST HILL ⇌

Horniman Museum See *separate family panel on p.763.*

GREENWICH ⇌

A World Heritage Site, this is the sort of place that's worth coming back to again and again. Once a favoured residence of the Royal Family, Greenwich has a long and illustrious maritime heritage, still reflected in the museums, boats and grand old ships you can visit. On wknds, the covered market has arts and crafts, while outdoor markets on High Rd and Stockwell St have antiques, junk and second-hand books. You should be able to get boat trips from the pier up to Westminster (around £7.80 return). The Cutty Sark (Lassell St) and Trafalgar (Park Row) are good river-view dining pubs. Three of the most enjoyable places, the Queen's House, National Maritime Museum and Royal Observatory, are all free, and the Ranger's House now holds a fabulous art collection. We've heard good things from readers about the new 90-min guided tours which leave from the helpful visitor centre (ground floor of Royal Naval College), usually 2pm daily (£4); (020) 8269 4747; there are also 90-min guided walks from the tourist information centre (Cutty Sark Gardens) at 12.15 and 2.15pm (£4); phone to check; (0870) 608 2000. If you prefer to go under your own steam, a route booklet (£2) lets you follow one of five Millennium Heritage Trails.

Cutty Sark In dry dock not far from Greenwich Pier, this clipper built in 1869 was the fastest of her time - she once sailed 363 nautical miles in a single day. On board, you can visit the crew's and officers' cabins; there's an impressive collection of ships' figureheads, and children's display panels and activities. The clipper is in danger of being sold abroad if £8m is not found for her preservation; designed to last only 30 years, she was built from a rare combination of wrought iron clad in timber. Shop, disabled access access to entry level only; usually only cl 24-26 Dec, but phone to check; (020) 8858 3445; £4.25.

Fan Museum (12 Crooms Hill) Unique changing collection of around 3,000 fans and related items from all over the world. They even do fan-making classes. Shop, disabled access; cl Sun am, all day Mon, and a few days over Christmas and New Year, but best to check; (020) 8305 1441; £3.50.

Greenwich Park The oldest enclosed Royal Park, with wonderful views from its landscaped slopes, which run from Blackheath down towards the river; it's a great place for a picnic. A herd of deer graze in a smallish area of woodland and wild flowers known as the Wilderness, and there's a big children's playground.

National Maritime Museum (Romney Rd) Enclosed by a spectacular glass canopy roof, this is now one of the country's most impressive and enjoyable museums. The 20 galleries have displays on topics as diverse as passengers, piracy, deep-sea diving, sea power, and oceans and the environment. Hundreds of exhibits range from contemporary art and great battle-scene masterpieces, to Nelson's bloodstained coat and Prince Frederick's gilded Royal barge; you can see some of the thousands of exhibits not on display on computers, and there are plenty of hands-on activities. It's all great fun and combines nicely with a visit to the Royal Observatory and Queen's House. Meals, snacks, shop, disabled access; cl 25-26 Dec, am 1 Jan; (020) 8312 6565; free, may be charges for special events.

Queen's House (Romney Rd) On the site of the original magnificent Royal palace, this early 17th-c house was the first Palladian-style villa in the country, designed by Inigo Jones for Anne of Denmark. Once the setting for balls and banquets, it's now used to show more of the National Maritime Museum's excellent maritime art collection; the first-floor galleries host changing art exhibitions, while the ground floor has a display on the house's architecture and the famous people associated with it. Meals, snacks, shop, disabled access; cl 24-26 Dec, am 1 Jan, and sometimes it closes early, so best to phone; (020) 8858 4422; free.

Ranger's House (Chesterfield Walk, Blackheath) This lovely stately home was the 19th-c official residence of the Greenwich Park ranger. Now on display here is the impressive life-time collection of Julius Wernher who built a fabulous fortune mining diamonds; treasures include italian and dutch Old Master paintings, 18th-c english paintings by Reynolds and Romney, byzantine and medieval ivories, wonderful Renaissance bronzes, jewellery and majolica pottery, Sèvres porcelain and Limoges enamels. Shop, disabled access; cl Mon, Tues, and around 24 Dec-Feb; (020) 8853 0035;

£4.50 inc audio-guide. Blackheath and Greenwich Park opposite are civilised places, good for a pleasant stroll.

Royal Naval College This glorious group of buildings was designed initially by Wren in the 17th c, and then completed by Hawksmoor and Ripley - it's a magnificently preserved part of old London. Visitors can see an interesting chapel and a notable painted hall. You can find out more about the college at the visitor centre (handily, next to the good tourist information centre). Meals, snacks, shop; chapel cl Sun am, 24-26 Dec; (020) 8269 4747; free. The view from across the river (there's a pedestrian tunnel under the Thames here) looks like an 18th-c print come to life.

Royal Observatory Greenwich (Greenwich Park) The original home of Greenwich Mean Time - standing as it does on the Prime Meridian of longitude zero. The brass line marking the meridian is still there set in the ground: standing over it with one foot in the western hemisphere and one in the east is irresistible. The Wren-built observatory was founded by Charles II in 1675, and now houses a comprehensive collection of historic instruments for time-keeping, navigation and astronomy. Good views from the top. The Time Ball is rather confusing - it can go down and up so fast you barely notice it. Shop, some disabled access; cl 24-26 Dec; (020) 8312 6565; free.

HAMPSTEAD ⊖
Prides itself on its villagey atmosphere, and off the main streets its maze of twisting lanes is very picturesque and seductively charming. It's home to artistes of all kinds, and well heeled bohemians in general; in some streets a commemorative blue plaque on the front of the house is almost compulsory. Particularly attractive parts include early Georgian Church Row, and Squires Mount (where the Regency-looking house at the end on the left, in fact built in the 1950s, belonged to Richard Burton and Elizabeth Taylor). The gaslit Holly Bush, prettily tucked away up Holly Mount, is a good pub, as is the Flask in Flask Walk (a long-standing favourite of local actors).

2 Willow Road The first Modern Movement house acquired by the National Trust. Designed and built by the architect Erno Goldfinger, it has a good range of work by the artists and intellectuals who lived around Hampstead in the 1930s - as well as the only working TV on show in any NT property. Guided tours from 12.15pm Sat only Mar and Nov, Thurs-Sat Apr-Oct; (020) 7435 6166; *£4.60, joint ticket with Fenton House £6.40; NT.

Fenton House (Hampstead Grove) Fine William and Mary merchant's house in a walled garden, with oriental, english and european china and an exceptional collection of early keyboard instruments; they've recently restored one of the bedrooms. Their period-music concerts on some summer evenings are well worth catching. Shop, disabled access to ground floor and garden; cl am, also Mon, Tues, and Nov-Mar exc Mar wknds; (020) 435 3471; *£4.60; NT.

Hampstead Heath North London's best open space, with lakes, hilly prospects, and some wonderful views of the city skyline - Parliament Hill has a direction-finder pointing out various landmarks. On one edge is the ancient Spaniards Inn, still as popular as when Dickens made it famous in the *Pickwick Papers*.

Kenwood House (Hampstead Lane) Achieved its present splendid proportions in the 18th c at the hands of Robert Adam. The refurbished rooms show off well the splendid collection of paintings, inc works by Rembrandt, Vermeer and Turner. The grounds are lovely, and summer concerts are idyllic when it's fine, with the music drifting across the lake, and sometimes a fireworks finale. Meals, snacks, shop, disabled access to ground floor only; cl 24-26 Dec, 1 Jan; (020) 8348 1286; free; EH.

Sigmund Freud's House (20 Maresfield Gdns) Extraordinary collection of antiquities from various ancient cultures, as well as Freud's library, papers and indeed his desk and couch. Shop, some disabled access; open pm Weds-Sun (exc 25-26 Dec and Good Fri); (020) 7435 2002; £5. A monumental seated statue of Freud by

Oscar Nemon can be seen outside the Tavistock Clinic on nearby Belsize Lane.

HAMPTON COURT ⇌

Bushy Park Another Royal Park, formerly reserved for hunting. Wren laid out its famous double chestnut avenue, which runs from Teddington Gate to the great house.

Hampton Court Gardens Elaborately landscaped, fine mix of formal and informal (esp the Wilderness, full of spring flowers), bounded by deer park with golf course. William III's quiet Privy Garden has been restored to its intricate 1702 design, with fountains, stonework, topiary and elaborate sand patterns cut into lawn. The famous maze swallows up 300,000 people a year, and the annual flower show here is one of the world's biggest. Open as palace; Privy Garden and maze £3.50 each (unless you are also visiting the palace, see below), gardens free, cl 25 Dec. The Kings Arms (Lion Gate) is a decent food stop.

Hampton Court Palace An amazing place, just as a Royal palace should be. Begun by Cardinal Wolsey in the early 16th c, the house's splendour soon so pricked Henry VIII's jealousy that Wolsey felt compelled to present it to his king in an attempt to appease him. Successive monarchs have left their architectural marks: the hammer-beamed hall and kitchens were Henry's addition, the Fountain Court was designed by Wren for William and Mary, and much comes from the work of the Victorians (the chimneys mostly date from then). The rooms have managed to keep their distinctive styles, from the starkly imposing Tudor kitchens (themselves taking up 50 rooms) to the elaborate grandeur of the Georgian chambers. The King's Staircase is wonderfully over the top, and the Picture Gallery has the finest Renaissance works from the Royal collection, inc Pieter Bruegel the Elder's fascinating *Massacre of the Innocents*. Look out too for the carvings by Grinling Gibbons and the cartoons by Mantegna in the Lower Orangery. There are several excellent audio guides you can pick up and listen to as you go along, with no extra charge.

Meals, snacks, shops, disabled access; cl 24-26 Dec; (0870) 752 7777; £11.50 inc entry to Privy Garden and maze.

River Thames There are pleasant Thames-side walks around Hampton Court, and summer cruise boats from here back down to Westminster; (020) 7930 4721; £12.

HIGHGATE ⊖

An easy walk across the Heath from Hampstead, this dates largely from the Victorian period and still keeps a villagey atmosphere, centred as it is around the High St. The village is dominated by Highgate School (which Betjeman attended and where T S Eliot taught). There are lots of pubs in this area, and some smart little cafés. The Grove, a row of very elegant Victorian houses, has been home to such diverse musicians as Lord Menuhin and Sting.

Highgate Cemetery (Swains Lane) The most impressive of a series of landscaped and formal cemeteries started in the early decades of Victoria's reign on the then outskirts of the city, very well restored over the last 20 years, and still in use. The cemetery has the tombs of many household names (inc Karl Marx), though the best thing is the sheer atmosphere of the jumbled trees, shrubs and crumbling ivy-covered monuments. The E cemetery is open all year (exc 25-26 Dec and during funerals; £2), the W by guided tour only (not wkdys Dec-Feb; £3), phone before visiting; (020) 8340 1834.

KEW ⊖ ⇌

Kew Bridge Steam Museum (Green Dragon Lane) Over the bridge from the gardens, by the train station, this splendid old pumping station houses five Cornish beam engines - one of which you can walk through while it's working. Also a narrow gauge railway (Sun), and surprisingly interesting exhibition on the development of London's water supply: there are peepholes into the sewers. It won't engross you unless you've at least some interest in the subject - in which case you'll find the engines prime examples of their type. Wknd meals and snacks, shop, some disabled access; cl Christmas wk, Good Fri; (020) 8568 4757; £4.60 wknds and bank hols (when engines in steam), £3.60 wkdys.

Kew Gardens Started in 1759 by George III's mother as three or four hectares (nine acres) landscaped by Capability Brown, by 1904 they had grown to cover 120 hectares (300 acres), with the foundations of the present wonderful collection firmly laid. The glasshouses include the magnificent modern Princess of Wales range and the remarkable restored Victorian Palm House, as well as an Evolution House with plants from up to 400 million years ago. The gardens near the entrance are largely formally arranged, and drift into attractively landscaped woodland, glades and tree collections further out. As well as a museum, there's a gallery; they hold an excellent programme of special events (designed to appeal to everyone, not just gardeners) inc jazz concerts some evenings in July. A wonderful place you can come back to time and time again - always discovering something new. Meals, snacks, shop (great for unusual plant books), disabled access; cl 25 Dec, 1 Jan; (020) 8332 5655; £7.50. The Coach & Horses on the green has decent food. In summer you can come to Kew by cruise boat from Westminster - see the numbers we give for Hampton Court and Richmond.

Queen Charlotte's Cottage (Kew Gardens) This rusticated summer-house, built for the Royal Family in the 18th c, is open occasional wknds July-Aug, phone to check; (0870) 752 7777; free with admission to the gardens.

OSTERLEY ⊖

Osterley Park House One of the most complete examples of Robert Adam's work, this elegant neo-classical villa was built on the foundations of a Tudor mansion. It's set in an estate that runs to over half a square mile, with pleasure grounds and 16th-c stables (still in use); changing art exhibitions in the Jersey Gallery. Meals, snacks, shop, disabled access; cl am, also Mon, Tues and Nov-Mar exc Mar wknds; (020) 8232 5050; £4.50.

RICHMOND ⊖ ⇌

Agreeable if much extended Thames village, Britain's most affluent corner, with lots of fine 18th-c houses esp around the Green and up Richmond Hill (a 1902 Act of Parliament protects the river and meadow view immortalised by Turner - the cows are now owned by a local preservation trust). There's a little local history museum in the Old Town Hall; shop, disabled access; usually cl Mon, pm Sun (all day Sun Oct-Apr), and bank hols, best to check over Christmas; (020) 8332 1141; free. The riverside White Cross has decent food. The river here is really attractive for strolls, and there are summer cruise boats from here back down to Westminster, stopping at Kew (more fine riverside walks) on the way; (020) 7930 2062.

Ham House (Petersham) A pleasant two-mile walk W along the river from Richmond to this outstanding Stuart mansion (once at the centre of Restoration court life) with 17th-c formal gardens, in a charming little old-world hamlet; there's a new exhibition on the development of the garden, and a video on the house. Snacks, shop, disabled access; cl am, also Sun-Tues and all Nov-Mar; (020) 8940 1950; *£7, *£3 garden only; NT. If you happen to be in Twickenham you can get a ferry across; usually Feb-Oct; (020) 8892 9620; 60p. The New Inn on Ham Common has good home-made food.

National Archives (Ruskin Ave/Middleton St) The national archive of records great and small, with anything from your great grandfather's marriage licence to cabinet papers once they've been released; efficient search mechanisms and helpful staff. The little museum showcases some of the most famous documents of the past 1,000 years; displayed according to themes, changing exhibits have included Shakespeare's will, Guy Fawkes's confession, a letter from Jack the Ripper, the Dam Busters' log book, and the deed poll showing Elton John's name change. They have special events, and the grounds have little lakes with ducks and fish. Meals, snacks, shop, disabled access; cl Sun, bank hol Sat and Mon, 1-6, 24-27 Dec, and 1 Jan, best to check; (020) 8876 3444; free, you need to bring ID (UK driver's licence, credit or bank card or passport).

Richmond Park The most country-like of all London's parks (and the largest walled urban park in Europe), with great rolling spaces and wildlife (inc herds of deer and birds of prey), and english oaks over 500 years old. There's a good formal garden and café at Pembroke Lodge, and the Isabella Plantation's rhododendrons and azaleas are a must-see in season.

Strawberry Hill House It's hard to believe that this fanciful place, created by Horace Walpole, was once just a coachman's cottage. An outstanding and very influential example of an 18th-c Gothic Revival building, the exterior has hardly changed since additions by the Waldegrave family in the mid-19th c. Unfortunately the whole fabric of the place has become seriously weakened over the years, especially the interiors, and pressure is growing for urgent restoration. Meals and snacks during term-time, shop; 90-minute tours (the rooms are just shells) leave at 2, 2.45 and 3.30pm Sun May-Sept; (020) 8240 4224; £5.

STAMFORD BROOK ⊖
Fullers Brewery Tours The oldest brewery in London, with a comprehensive tour looking at its history, and demonstrations showing its mix of traditional methods and the latest technology; there's a pub on site. Tours (no under-14s) Mon, Weds-Fri, phone to book; (020) 8996 2063; £5.

WHITE CITY ⊖
BBC Backstage Tours (Wood Lane) As it's a working studio, what you see depends on what is being produced on

the day, but among other things you're likely to go to the BBC's News Centre, look into studios, and visit a dressing room; tours (no children under 10) last around 1½ hours and involve a fair bit of walking. Snacks, shop, disabled access; cl Sun, and a few days over Christmas; phone to book at least a day in advance; (0870) 603 0304; £7.95.

WOOLWICH ⇌
Firepower (Royal Arsenal West, Warren Lane) In restored former Ministry of Defence research buildings, and part of the overall redevelopment of the Royal Arsenal, this museum brings to life the history of artillery since Roman times: plenty of big guns and military vehicles, alongside uniforms, photographs, books and manuscripts. Lots to appeal to families, with interactive displays and so forth, and an audio-visual show gives an idea of what it felt like to be in the middle of a battle. Some of the displays have a more personal side to them, with recorded recollections of former servicemen and women, and a poignant show of medals. Meals, snacks, shop, disabled access; cl Mon (exc bank hols), Tues Apr-Sept and Mon-Thurs Oct-Mar; (020) 8855 7755; £6.50. A new Heritage Centre (Artillery Sq), combining the Borough Museum from Plumstead and the local history library from Blackheath, has just opened; disabled access; cl Sun, Mon and all bank hols; (020) 8854 2452; free.

More Specialised Expeditions

To see and do

ANGEL ⊖
Camden Passage This and the surrounding streets have a great collection of **antiques shops**, well worth the expedition if that interests you; Sat and Weds there's an antiques market (books Thurs), and on Sun (10-2pm) there's a popular farmer's market - we recommend the burgers. The Duke of Cambridge (St Peter's St) has

good food, if you can't choose among the swathe of other cafés and restaurants around here.

BEXLEYHEATH ⇌
Red House Commissioned by William Morris for his wife, and designed by Phillip Webb, this gorgeous Arts and Crafts house first opened to the public in summer 2003. You can still see some of the original features and fixed items

of furniture designed by Morris and Webb, as well as wall paintings and stained glass by Burne-Jones. They plan to restore the garden, which is said to have inspired Morris's early designs of wallpaper and fabric. Teas (in the carriage house), shop, disabled access to ground floor only; open by pre-booked guided tour Weds-Sun, cl 25-26 Dec and 1 Jan; (01494) 755588; *£5; NT. Parking is at Danson Park, around a 15-min walk away.

CHISLEHURST ⇌
Chislehurst Caves ⊞ (entrance off Caveside Close nr the Olde Stationmaster, B264; nr Chislehurst railway station) 45-min lamplit tours of labyrinthine tunnels and passageways first carved out of the rock over 8,000 years. They've been used by flint knappers, druids, and as an air-raid shelter during the war. Meals, snacks, shop; cl Mon and Tues (exc school hols), around a wk over Christmas; (020) 8467 3264; £4. The Sydney Arms (Old Perry St, off A422 E) has good value food.

COLINDALE ⊖
RAF Museum Hendon (Grahame Park Way) The story of flight from early times, with over 70 full-size aeroplanes (inc a recently donated P51 Mustang), a lively Battle of Britain Experience, and an interesting examination of the impact of flight on history and politics. A highlight is the Fun 'n' Flight gallery, which has good hands-on exhibits (you can have a go at the controls of a modern jet trainer), and dramatic simulator rides include one which lets you imagine you're piloting a Red Arrow. Excellent for enthusiasts and flying-minded children, and warmly recommended by several of our contributors; special events throughout the year. A new exhibition hall traces the history of aviation from the earliest gliders and kites to the Eurofighter, and alongside the hall a restored 1917 hangar has examples of early aircraft. Meals and snacks (you can sit right among the exhibits), good shop, disabled access; cl 24-26 Dec, 1 Jan; (020) 8205 2266; free.

HIGHBURY & ISLINGTON ⊖
Estorick Collection of Italian Art (39A Canonbury Sq) This outstanding collection of modern italian art includes fine futurist works by artists inc Balla and Boccioni, as well as later figurative works by Modigliani and Sironi; also temporary exhibitions. Meals, snacks, shop, disabled access; cl Mon, Tues, am Sun and 24 Dec-4 Jan; (020) 7704 9522; £3.50. The appealingly villagey little Compton Arms (Compton Ave) has good value food.

HOMERTON ⇌
Sutton House ⊞ (Hackney Central is the nearest station) Built in 1535 by Henry VIII's Principal Secretary of State, it was then home to successive merchants, silk-weavers, Victorian schoolmistresses and Edwardian clergy. Although altered over the years, it remains essentially Tudor, and the oak-panelled rooms and carved fireplaces survive intact. An exhibition will tell you more about the house and its inhabitants, and there's an art gallery with changing exhibitions, and special events. Café/bar, shop, disabled access to ground floor; all cl am, Mon-Tues and 19 Dec-21 Jan, house also cl Thurs and Jan, best to check; (020) 8986 2264; *£2.20, free family days last Sun in month Mar-Nov; NT.

KNOCKHOLT ⇌
South London walks The SE fringes of London give way to surprisingly rural North Downs countryside, still within the London borough of Bromley, around Knockholt, High Elms and Downe; paths are plentiful and well maintained. Only the view over South London from behind Knockholt church shows how close you are to the capital. The nearby Three Horseshoes has good value food.

PADDINGTON ⊖ ⇌
Alexander Fleming Laboratory Museum ⊞ (St Mary's Hospital, Praed St) The laboratory in which Alexander Fleming discovered penicillin by chance in 1928 has been reconstructed, and an accompanying display and video tell the story of the bacteriologist and the life-saving antibiotic. Shop; cl pms, all Fri-Sun, bank hols, and 25 Dec-3 Jan; (020) 7886 6528; £2.

ST JOHN'S WOOD ⊖
Lord's Tour ⊞ (St John's Wood Rd) Tours of the famous club and grounds, inc the space-age media centre (if not in

use), the players' dressing room, and the excellent MCC Museum, with an exhaustive collection of cricket memorabilia, such as the Ashes urn and 18th-c paintings of the game. Meals, snacks, shop, disabled access to most of the ground; tours usually daily at 12 and 2pm (and at 10am Apr-Sept) exc winter bank hols, and during major matches and preparation days, phone to check; (020) 7616 8595; £7.

TWICKENHAM ⇌
Marble Hill House In 27 hectares (66 acres) of parkland overlooking the Thames, this Palladian villa was built for Henrietta Howard, mistress of George II; audio tours take you around the lavishly gilded rooms. Snacks, shop, disabled access to ground floor; cl Mon (exc bank hols), Tues and all Nov-Mar; (020) 8892 5115; £3.50. The riverside White Swan is pleasant for lunch.
Museum of Rugby (Rugby Rd) Combines tours of the 75,000-seat home of rugby union with an excellent museum of related memorabilia under the East Stand; interactive displays and period reconstructions illustrate the game's history, and there's plenty of footage from classic matches. Meals, snacks, shop, disabled access; cl Mon (exc bank hols), 24-26 Dec, Good Fri, and a day after match days; four tours a day (only two on Sun), best to book on (020) 8892 8877; £8, £3 for just museum (match days only, when there are no tours). The Turks Head (Winchester Rd) has decent food.

WALTHAMSTOW CENTRAL ⊖
William Morris Gallery (Lloyd Park, Forest Rd) William Morris lived here 1846-1858, and the house has an excellent collection of his work: fabrics, furnishings and wallpaper, much of it still fashionable today. Pre-Raphaelite works upstairs include pictures by Burne-Jones and Rossetti. The attractive grounds are ideal for picnics. Shop, disabled access to ground floor only (this is where the main exhibition is); cl 1-2pm, all day Mon, Sun (exc first Sun in month) 25-26 Dec and 1 Jan; (020) 8527 3782; free.

WANDSWORTH TOWN ⇌
Young's Brewery Tours Working museum of english brewing through the ages. Tours are usually Tues, Weds,

Thurs and Sat (12 and 2pm), and last about 1½ hours, phone to book; (020) 8875 7005; shop; £5.50.

WARWICK AVENUE ⊖
Puppet Theatre Barge (Little Venice) This wonderful floating puppet theatre is moored here Nov-Jun, touring the Thames in the summer. Performances for children on wknds and during the school hols, and on Sat evenings in summer there are productions for older children and adults. Snacks; they can accommodate up to three wheelchairs; phone in advance, box office (020) 7249 6876; £7.

WEST DULWICH ⇌
Dulwich The village still is villagey, with imposing 18th-c houses, duckpond, good pub (Crown & Greyhound), and an almost rural feel (there's even a toll road). There are good walks, in Dulwich Park (best in rhododendron time), and through Dulwich Wood to adjacent Sydenham Hill Wood - the largest fragment of ancient woodland in inner London, and a most surprising place (just big enough to lose your way in), with woodpeckers among the oak and hornbeam trees. The best of the wood is a nature reserve fiercely guarded against developers by the London Wildlife Trust; a trail starts from the Crescent Wood Rd entrance on the Sydenham side. The nearby Dulwich Wood House (Sydenham Hill) is popular for food.
Dulwich Picture Gallery (between College Rd and Gallery Rd) This rather austere brick building, designed by Sir John Soane in 1811, was England's first public gallery when it opened six years later. It's home to an impressive collection of 17th- and 18th-c works by artists inc Rembrandt, Van Dyck and Canaletto, as well as changing exhibitions. Café, shop, disabled access; cl Mon (exc bank hols) and 24-26 Dec, 1 Jan and Good Fri; (020) 8693 5254; £4.

WIMBLEDON ⊖ ⇌
Southside House (Woodhayes Rd) Still lived by the descendants of Robert Pennington, who built it in 1687; famous visitors inc Anne Boleyn, Charles I, Nelson, and Marie Antoninette, and you can still see the bed where the Prince of Wales slept in 1750. Open

Weds and wknds Easter Sat-Sept, entry by guided tour only at 2, 3, and 4pm, best to check; (020) 8946 7643; £5. The olde-worlde Crooked Billet by the nearby Common is popular for generous food.

Wimbledon Lawn Tennis Museum (Church Rd; also quickly reached from Southfields tube) Trophies, pictures and other tennis memorabilia trace the development of the game through the last century. Also highlights of past Wimbledon Championships, and an interesting display on the changes in tennis fashions. You can see the famous Centre Court outside, and they do behind-the-scenes guided tours (phone for details). Café, shop, disabled access;

cl 24-26 Dec, 1 Jan and every day during the Championship fortnight (unless you've gone to watch the tennis); (020) 8946 6131; *£6. If you're in London during Wimbledon fortnight it's always worth popping along to the club in the early evening around 5.30 or 6 - lots of people leave then and their seats are resold cheaply.

Wimbledon Windmill Museum 🏛️ Around the common is an attractive old core, and a striking **windmill** on Windmill Rd (open Sat pm, Sun and bank hols Apr-Oct; (020) 8947 2825; £1).The common, with its ponds and windmill, is one of the best strolling grounds provided by South London's numerous commons and parks.

Where to eat

Bank *1 Kingsway WC2* (020) 7234 3344 Large, modern brasserie between the city and Theatreland with interesting décor (the slanted glass decorations hanging from the ceiling are quite a sight), an open kitchen, and reliably good brasserie-type food from a very varied menu (as well as lunch and dinner, they also serve breakfasts, from 7am, pre-theatre meals, and wknd brunches inc a children's menu); there's another branch in Westminster and one in Birmingham; cl bank hols; no children in bar after 5pm; disabled access. £40/2-course set meal £12.50

Bibendum *Michelin House, 81 Fulham Rd SW3* (020) 7581 5817 Magnificent art deco Michelin building housing a light and spacious restaurant with exceptionally good european-style cooking (more elaborate in the evening), marvellous wine list, and courteous well trained staff; the unpretentious downstairs oyster bar is a fine place for a lighter (and cheaper) meal; cl 24-26 Dec; disabled access. £55 dinner, £25 weekday lunch

Bishop's Finger *9-10 West Smithfield EC1* (020) 7248 2341 Swish little bar-cum-restaurant with fresh flowers on elegant tables set on polished bare boards, comfortably cushioned chairs under a wall lined with prints, distinctive food from an open kitchen, well kept real ales, a wide choice of wines, and friendly service; upstairs evening bar; cl Sat, Sun, bank hols; disabled access. £17|£6.75

Blue Elephant *4-6 Fulham Broadway SW6* (020) 7385 6595 Luxurious thai food among waterfalls and exotic jungle greenery, with produce flown in weekly from Thailand; the set meals are better value; cl Sat am, 24-26 Dec; disabled access. £50|£15

Bombay Brasserie *Courtfield Cl SW7* (020) 7370 4040 Grand colonial-style furnishings in big restaurant and conservatory, with good authentic indian food using recipes from all over India (lots of vegetarian dishes), and courteous helpful staff; cheaper at lunchtime when there's a buffet; cl 25 and 26 Dec; children over 10; disabled access. £35/£18.95 buffet lunch

Browns *82-84 St Martin's Lane WC2* (020) 7497 5050 Spacious bar and restaurant in what was once the City of Westminster's County Courts; big mirrors and potted plants, bentwood seats, wooden tables, and panelling, helpful service, and enjoyable good value food; other branches in Bath, Brighton, Cambridge, Edinburgh and Oxford; disabled access. £30.55/2-course lunch £10.95 ☺

Café in the Crypt *St Martin-in-the-Fields Church WC2* (020) 7930 0089 Popular place under the lovely arches of the church with a relaxed atmosphere, good freshly prepared daily changing food; shop, free lunchtime concerts, candlelit evening concerts, brass rubbing; cl 25 Dec, pm Maundy Thurs, Good Fri am. £16.50|£7

Christopher's *18 Wellington St WC2 (020) 7240 4222* Fashionable place with high ceilings and rococo décor spread over three floors, enjoyable modern american cooking (good value pre- and post-theatre meals), cheery speedy service, and lots of american wines; there's also a branch in the Thistle Victoria Hotel at 101 Buckingham Palace Road; cl Sun pm. £28/pre-theatre 3-course meal £16.50

Chutney Mary *The Plaza, 535 King's Rd SW10 (020) 7351 3113* Very good interesting indian food (with some anglo touches) in light conservatory and two dining rooms, plus a verandah bar, opulent décor, a good choice of drinks, and knowledgeable staff; only set lunch available on Sun; cl pm 25 Dec; some disabled access. £35/3-course set lunch £16.50

Clarkes *122-124 Kensington Church St W8 (020) 7221 9225* Long established restaurant, with consistently good and very popular food from a deceptively simple no choice menu using the best ingredients, friendly staff, and an interesting choice of wines; cl Sun, 10 days over Christmas; disabled access. £48|**£8.50**

Cork & Bottle *44-46 Cranbourn St WC2 (020) 7734 7807* Basement wine bar we've liked for over 30 years, nr West End theatres - good food inc interesting salads, cold buffet and unusual hot dishes, excellent wines, and cheerful service; children at manager's discretion; cl 25 and 26 Dec, 1 Jan. £22.50|**£6.95**

Cross Keys *1 Lawrence St SW3 (020) 7349 9111* Bustling Victorian pub, attractive outside with foliage and flowers, with an appealing and roomy high-ceilinged flagstoned bar around island servery, roaring fire, all sorts of brassware hanging from the rafters, lots of atmosphere, and a good mix of customers; also, a light and airy conservatory-style back restaurant; well kept real ales, a good choice of wines by the glass, enjoyable, interesting bar food, and attentive staff. £28|**£9**

Duke of Cambridge *30 St. Peter's St N1 (020) 7359 3066* Well furnished cornerhouse and London's first completely organic pub, with a big, busy main room, simply decorated and furnished, lots of chunky wooden tables, pews and benches on bareboards, a couple of big metal vases with colourful flowers, daily papers, good lighting, a warmly inviting atmosphere, and a steady stream of varied customers; a couple of smaller candlelit rooms for eating, a changing choice of well presented imaginative food, four organic real ales on handpump, organic lagers, and organic wines, many by the glass; cl Mon am, 25-26 Dec; disabled access. £35|**£8**

E&O *14 Blenheim Crescent W11 (020) 7229 5454* Fashionable restaurant with slick décor - small benches and low-slung chairs on a dark wood floor and bare white walls - chic, pan-asian adventurous cooking, and a wide-reaching wine list. £36

Eagle *159 Farringdon Rd EC1 (020) 7837 1353* Particularly good mediterranean-style food in popular stylish pub where open kitchen forms part of the bar, well kept real ales, lots of wine by the glass, properly made cocktails, a lively and chatty atmosphere (lots of young media folk), and simple furnishings; daily specials run out early, so get there early. £23|**£7.50**

Ebury Wine Bar *139 Ebury St SW1 (020) 7730 8206* Said to be London's first wine bar (established 1959) with a loyal following, an excellent list of wines by the glass, and enjoyable modern cooking; they have another bar restaurant called Carriages opposite the Royal Mews in Buckingham Palace Rd, and Joe's Brasserie at 130 Wandsworth Bridge Rd; cl Sun am 1 May-31 Aug, 24 Dec-2 Jan. £34|**£7.50**

Fino *33 Charlotte St W1 (020) 7436 9781* Down a grand staircase to a light, blond, big basement dining room and bar with clean modern furnishings, red-seated chairs and lots of high-seated bar stools on beige flooring tiles, helpful staff, plenty of spanish wines, finos, and manzanillas, and especially good, nicely presented, imaginative tapas dishes|**£25**

Fire Station *150 Waterloo Rd SE1 (020) 7401 3267* Remarkable conversion of a former fire station with two chatty front rooms, plenty of wooden pews, chairs and long tables, some brightly red-painted doors, modern art on the walls, newspapers to read, very good imaginative food, a decent choice of wines, and well kept real ales. £27/2-course early-bird meals £10.95|**£9.95**

Food For Thought *31 Neal St WC2 (020) 7836 9072* Long-established and consistently good unlicensed vegetarian restaurant in former banana ripening warehouse, with take-away service upstairs and communal eating at long tables downstairs - you can also eat at tables outside; no corkage (Oddbins is round the corner); cl Sun pm, Christmas and New Year, Easter Sun. £9.75|**£4.20**

Fortnum & Mason *181 Piccadilly W1 (020) 7734 8040* Famous store with elegant 4th-floor St James's Restaurant (must book), Fountain Restaurant (ground floor), Patio Restaurant, and Salmon and Champagne bar (mezzanine) doing good breakfasts, morning coffee, lunches, fine afternoon tea and pre-theatre meals; cl Sun, bank hols; disabled access. £20|**£10.50**

Gavroche *43 Upper Brook St W1 (020) 7408 0881* London was put on the eating map when this quietly decorated club-like restaurant was opened by the Roux brothers 30 years ago; exemplary classic french cooking with modern touches (lovely puddings and perfect cheeses, too), attentive service from french staff, and a classy but expensive wine list (some reach four figures); the set lunch is real value; cl Sat am, Sun, bank hols, Christmas and New Year. £80/set lunch £47.25

Gay Hussar *2 Greek St W1 (020) 7437 0973* Very long-standing hungarian restaurant with bags of atmosphere (downstairs has the most), good generous authentic food (especially enjoyable on a cold winter's day), and friendly service; cl Sun, bank hols. £30|**£10**

Greenhouse *27a Hays Mews W1 (020) 7499 3331* In a mews hidden away in Mayfair, this upmarket restaurant is a mixture of traditional and modern décor, a larger bar, and a water feature in the garden; enjoyable modern english food (lovely puddings), and thoughtful wine list; cl Sat am, bank hols, Christmas; disabled access. £50/2-course lunch £20

Livebait's Café Fish *36-40 Rupert St W1 (020) 7287 8989* Bustling restaurant on two floors with lots of fish prints, closely set tables on wooden floors, swift service, particularly fresh fish including platters of shellfish, a good atmosphere, and plenty of customers; mostly white wines; disabled access. £25|**£12**

Locanda Locatelli *8 Seymour St W1 (020) 7935 9088* Sophisticated, stylishly appointed restaurant with warm and friendly staff, a relaxed and intimate atmosphere, accomplished italian cooking including marvellous bread and italian cheeses, and italian-only wines; cl Sun, Christmas, Easter and bank hols; disabled access. £25|**£9.50**

Mon Plaisir *19-21 Monmouth St WC2 (020) 7836 7243* Rambling french bistro with super bustling atmosphere, good value well prepared food, decent wines, and friendly staff; good value pre-theatre menus; cl Sat am, Sun, bank hols, Christmas, New Year. £32/3-course set lunch £15.95

Moro *34-36 Exmouth Market EC1 (020) 7833 8336* Simply decorated restaurant with smart bentwood chairs on bare boards, cream and green walls, side bar with high stools, open-plan kitchen, and thriving atmosphere; interesting modern cooking with spanish, north african and middle eastern influences, a short, thoughtful wine list, and informal but punctilious service; cl Sat am, Sun, bank hols, Christmas, Easter, bank hols; disabled access. £37|**£16**

Nobu *Metropolitan, 19 Old Park Lane W1 (020) 7447 4747* Chic and very fashionable first-floor restaurant overlooking Hyde Park, with innovative beautifully presented japanese food touched with south american influences, helpful friendly staff, lots of sakis and good choice of wines; prices can quickly add up; cl Sat and Sun am, 25-26 Dec; children over 10; disabled access. £70/set lunch £25

Oxo Tower Restaurant & Brasserie *Oxo Tower Wharf SE1 (020) 7803 3888* Briskly modern brasserie and restaurant on 8th floor of South Bank redevelopment, light and airy, with busy open kitchen, lots of functional tables and chairs, and promptly served modern english food; panoramic view over the Thames and City - best in summer from tables on the outside terrace; cl 25-26 Dec; disabled access. £60/2-course brasserie weekday lunch £18.50

Painted Heron *112 Cheyne Walk SW10 (020) 7351 5232* Two-storied, simply furnished restaurant overlooking the Thames with contemporary british artwork on the walls, and exceptionally good, imaginative Indian food; walled terrace for outside summer meals; cl Sat am; disabled access. £35

Poons *27 Lisle St WC2 (020) 7437 4549* Atmospheric unlicensed and unmodernised chinese restaurant with extremely good value tasty barbecued and wind-dried food; cl Good Fri, 24-26 Dec; open Sun till 5.15pm. £17|**£5.75**

Porte des Indes *32 Bryanston St W1 (020) 7224 0055* Grand and exotic indian restaurant with wonderful flower arrangements, a huge marble waterfall, palm trees and potted plants, and jungle murals; good interesting dishes from 7 regions of India and some unique recipes from the resident french creole communities of Pondicherry; cl Sat am, 24-27 Dec; disabled access. £50/lunchtime buffet £19.90

Quaglino's *16 Bury St SW1 (020) 7930 6767* Fashionable restaurant with big stone staircase to antipasti bar overlooking huge dining room with flamboyantly painted pillars, fine flowers, highly modern attractive furnishings, and buoyant buzzing atmosphere; modern cooking and a good wine list; cl 25 Dec, am 26 Dec, 1 Jan; no children in bar in evening; disabled access. £47/2-course lunch £16.50

Racine *239 Brompton Rd SW3 (020) 7584 4477* Unpretentious brasserie with dark leather banquettes, wooden floors and lots of mirrors, a bustling atmosphere, welcoming staff, reasonably priced and very good regional french cooking, and mainly french wines; cl 24-25 Dec; disabled access. £35|**£10.50**

Rebato's *169 South Lambeth Rd SW8 (020) 7735 6388* Busy high-ceilinged bar with friendly barman and waiters, good choice of tapas, paella and suckling pig, and spanish wines; also spanish restaurant; cl Sat am, Sun, 25 Dec. £24|**£3.95**

Roussillon *16 St Barnabas St SW1 (020) 7730 5550* Bright and spacious dining room in a quiet and smart residential street, with elegant furnishings and fresh flowers on all tables; delicious seasonal food using the best ingredients, friendly and attentive service, and an extensive wine list; cl Sun, ams Sat-Tues, 1 wk Christmas, 2 wks Aug; children over 8. £55/2-courses £18

Rules *35 Maiden Lane WC2 (020) 7836 5314* One of London's oldest restaurants (1798), smart and very british (a firm local favourite, as well as loved by tourists), with good english food including fine seasonal furred and feathered game and oysters; an interesting history; cl 4 days over Christmas. £44|**£15.95**

Sardo *45 Grafton Way W1 (020) 7387 2521* Welcoming italian restaurant with simple décor, wooden dining chairs around burgundy and white-clothed tables, wooden framed picture frames filled with flowers in little test tubes, particularly good food with plenty of sardinian overtones, italian wines, and efficient, friendly service; cl Sat am, Sun, bank hols; disabled access. £38|**£12**

Simpsons in the Strand *100 Strand WC2 (020) 7836 9112* There are two restaurants here: Simply Simpsons upstairs has light pink Adam-style décor, serves contemporary british food, and has a smart casual dress code; cl Sun pm, 25-26 Dec. £35/2-course meal £22. Downstairs is Grand Divan which is much more formal (jacket and tie), with heavy wooden panelling and ornate plasterwork, a club-like atmosphere, and traditional english cooking inc nursery puddings, roasts carved as you want them at your table on silver-domed trolleys, and full english breakfast; cl Sat am, 25-26 Dec; disabled access. £50/2-course set lunch £20

Souk *Litchfield St WC2 (020) 7240 1796* Basement restaurant with moroccan décor - low vaulted ceilings, drapes, ceramic tiles and mirrors, banquettes with colourful cushions, pouffes, low wooden or brass patterned tables, and dim lighting and candlelight; generous and enjoyable moroccan food, mint tea, and occasional belly-dancing; cl 25-26 Dec. £20|**£5.95**

Wagamama *4 Streatham St WC1 (020) 7580 9365* You will have to queue to get into this trendy, simply furnished japanese basement restaurant with its long tables and benches for communal eating; very friendly cheerful service, noisy informal atmosphere, good healthy food - raw salads, ramens (huge bowls of noodles with meat, vegetables and japanese additions), rice dishes, sake, grape and plum wines, beer, and free green tea; good value; no smoking; disabled access. £30|**£7**

Special thanks to Philip Black, Roy and Lindsey Fentiman, Paul Kennedy, B and K Hypher, Mrs D E Reynolds, Nathalie Soanes, Duncan Cloud, Roger and Jenny Huggins, Michael and Jenny Back

SCOTLAND

Scotland gives rewarding scope for all sorts of different breaks and holidays. We have been unashamedly selective, in creaming off only the best of what this beautiful country has to offer visitors - including over a hundred really nice places to stay in, often at most attractive prices, as well as dozens of eating places that do justice to Scotland's first-class raw materials. And there's no shortage of excellent outings for all ages; many of the hundreds of memorable places to visit are free.

We have divided the country into four areas.

South Scotland includes Edinburgh (excellent for a city break), Glasgow, and many of Scotland's most interesting places to visit, as well as some charming and very peaceful countryside. It's the best part to go to if you've never been to Scotland before.

East Scotland also has plenty of interesting places to visit, plus a marvellous variety of scenery from Highland grandeur to placid lochs and rich valleys, from intimate fishing villages and sandy beaches to rugged cliffs. For a grand tour, the fastest roads run up this side.

West Scotland is less populated, with a glorious and intricate series of mountain and coastal landscapes. It has far fewer family outings, though we have tracked down some rewarding days out. We've defined this area as N of the Clyde and S of the Great Glen, with Loch Lomond marking its E edge.

North Scotland, everything N of the Great Glen, has fewer places to visit (and fewer visitors - part of its charm for many). There is magnificent scenery on the W coast and on Skye, a quieter sandy E coast, and some wild and desolate places in the N.

Outside Edinburgh, Glasgow and areas within easy reach, many places close over winter - and others change to shorter winter opening hours in Sept, rather than Oct (the usual month for a change in England). For the scenery, the best time to visit is May and Jun, when the days are very long, the great gardens are at their best, and the sun is often more likely to shine than later. In high summer, the roads (often narrow and twisting in the West and Highlands) can get clogged by summer crowds, and in the north the midges can be real spoil-sports then.

A three-hour drive will get anyone living N of Manchester or York well into South Scotland. Beyond that, you really need a longer stay to make the driving worth while. Rail and air, of course, bring Scotland much closer. The fastest trains, when they run on time, do the London—Edinburgh trip in around 4 hrs. Direct flights connect London and some regional airports with Edinburgh, Glasgow, Inverness and Aberdeen, with some local connections from there.

Visit Scotland have special offers (especially in autumn) on transport, accommodation and attractions; phone (0131) 332 2433 or take a look at their website www.visitscotland.com. Historic Scotland looks after most of the castles and abbeys we list. A good value Explorer ticket admits you to all their properties; £15 for 3 days out of 5, £20 for 7 days out of 10, or £23 for 10 days out of 21. You can get them from all HS properties, most tourist information centres, or in advance on (0131) 668 8800.

South Scotland

All sorts of places to visit, from spectacular castles, mansions and gardens to lively discovery centres, bustling coastal towns, and lovely islands; and Edinburgh is a wonderful holiday city

Unbeatable for a break, the beautiful city of Edinburgh has a tremendous amount to offer everyone, from great galleries, museums and historic buildings, to plenty of entertaining family treats. Glasgow also has lots to fill a visit, from excellent museums and galleries to its lively and eye-catching Science Centre.

Outside these two cities, there's a host of places with appeal for families. New Lanark is perhaps the pick of several absorbing excursions into the living past, with the Scottish Mining Museum in Newtongrange another real eye-opener. Budding young inventors will love a trip to the Big Idea in Irvine, and Motherwell has Scotland's biggest theme park. Galloway Forest Park is ideal when the weather is fine. Perky Largs (Vikingar! here is appealingly lively), and over on the E coast, Dunbar and Eyemouth make good seaside trips. The islands of Bute and Arran both tempt with enjoyable expeditions for a day or longer.

This part of Scotland has an abundance of ancient castles, romantic ruined abbeys, and some glorious gardens and grand houses to explore. Culzean is a great favourite, the opulent furnishings at Manderston near Duns have to be seen to be believed, and Newhailes House near Musselburgh is interesting for being left 'as found'. Many other stately homes are more appealing to children than you might expect: ancient Traquair, Paxton House, Bowhill House near Selkirk, and Drumlanrig Castle by Thornhill are especially enjoyable for all ages.

The Borders hills are grand and relatively little-visited - peaceful get-away-from-it-all walking. A Freedom of the Fairways pass covers a round on the finest Borders golf courses. The gentler SW corner is one of Britain's friendliest areas, and a great place for utter relaxation.

Where to stay

AAUCHENCAIRN NX8149 **Balcary Bay** *Auchencairn, Castle Douglas, Kirkcudbrightshire DG7 1QZ (01556) 640217* **£116***, plus special breaks; 20 rms with fine views. Once a smugglers' haunt, this charming and much liked hotel has wonderful views over the bay, neat grounds running down to the water, comfortable public rooms (one with log fire), a relaxed friendly atmosphere, good enjoyable food inc super breakfasts, and lots of walks; cl 1 Dec-mid-Feb; disabled access; dogs welcome in bedrooms

BEATTOCK NT0603 **Auchen Castle** *Beattock, Moffat, Dumfriesshire DG10 9SH (01683) 300407* **£95**; 25 pleasantly decorated rms, some in Lodge. Smart but

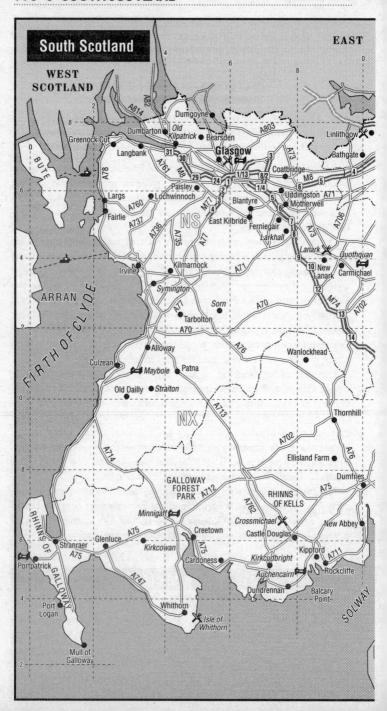

South Scotland

WEST SCOTLAND

EAST

BUTE

ARRAN

FIRTH OF CLYDE

RHINNS OF GALLOWAY

SOLWAY

NS

NX

GALLOWAY FOREST PARK

RHINNS OF KELLS

Dumgoyne
Dumbarton
Old Kilpatrick
Bearsden
Greenock Cut
Langbank
Glasgow
Linlithgow
Bathgate
Coatbridge
Paisley
Uddingston   A71
Motherwell
Largs
Lochwinnoch
Blantyre
Fairlie
East Kilbride
Ferniegair
Larkhall
Lanark
Quothquan
Carmichael
Kilmarnock
New Lanark
Irvine
Symington
Sorn
Tarbolton
Wanlockhead
Alloway
Culzean
Maybole
Patna
Old Dailly
Straiton
Thornhill
Ellisland Farm
Dumfries
Minnigaff
Crossmichael
New Abbey
Creetown
Castle Douglas
Stranraer
Glenluce
Kirkcowan
Kippford
Portpatrick
Cardoness
Kirkcudbright
Rockcliffe
Auchencairn
Port Logan
Dundrennan
Balcary Point
Whithorn
Isle of Whithorn
Mull of Galloway

A82
A814
A78
A761
A760
A737
A796
A735
A77
A70
A76
A713
A714
A747
A75
A762
A711
A712
A803
A73
M8
A71
A706
A702
M74

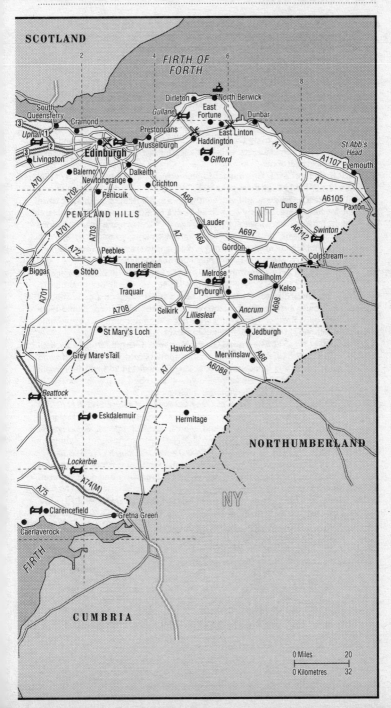

SCOTLAND

FIRTH OF
FORTH

South
Queensferry
Uphall
Livingston
Cramond
Prestonpans
Edinburgh
Musselburgh
Dirleton
Gullane
East
Fortune
North Berwick
Dunbar
East Linton
Haddington
Gifford
St Abb's
Head
Eyemouth
A1
A1107
A1
Balerno
Dalkeith
Newtongrange
Crichton
A70
A702
A701
Penicuik
PENTLAND HILLS
A703
A68
Lauder
A697
NT
Duns
A6105
Paxton
A6112
Swinton
A72
A701
Peebles
Innerleithen
Gordon
Coldstream
Biggar
Stobo
A7
A68
Melrose
Smailholm
Nenthorn
Kelso
Traquair
Dryburgh
A708
Selkirk
Lilliesleaf
Ancrum
A698
St Mary's Loch
Jedburgh
Grey Mare's Tail
Hawick
Mervinslaw
A68
A7
A6088
Beattock
Eskdalemuir
Hermitage
NORTHUMBERLAND
Lockerbie
A74(M)
NY
A75
Clarencefield
Gretna Green
Caerlaverock
FIRTH
CUMBRIA

0 Miles   20
0 Kilometres   32

friendly country-house hotel in lovely quiet spot with a trout loch and spectacular hill views, good food, and peaceful comfortable bar; dogs welcome in bedrooms

CLARENCEFIELD NY0669 **Comlongon Castle** *Clarencefield, Dumfrieshire DG1 4NA (01387) 870283* **£130***; 14 rms. Magnificent 15th-c castle keep with 18th-c mansion house adjoining - suits of armour and a huge fireplace in oak-panelled great hall, good food in Jacobean dining room, and a relaxing drawing room; dungeons, battlements, archers' quarters and haunted long gallery; cl first 2 wks Jan

EDINBURGH NT2573 **Balmoral Hotel** *1 Princes St, Edinburgh EH2 2EQ (0131) 556 2414* **£230***, plus special breaks; 188 luxurious rms. In city centre and handy for visitor attractions. Splendid Victorian hotel with wonderfully opulent entrance hall, elegant day rooms, lovely flowers, particularly friendly helpful staff, and very good food in several restaurants; excellent leisure facilities; good disabled access; dogs welcome in bedrooms

EDINBURGH NT2473 **Bonham** *35 Drumsheugh Gdns, Edinburgh EH3 7RN (0131) 623 6060* **£195**, plus special breaks; 48 stylish, individually designed rms with all the latest technology, and some with views to the Firth of Forth. Chic town house in a quiet square, cleverly converted from a former maternity hospital (and then a university residence), with plenty of original Victorian features among more contemporary designs, lovely fresh flower arrangements, paintings by scottish artists throughout, good modern cooking in oak-panelled restaurant (open to non-residents, too), and professional but friendly staff; disabled access

EDINBURGH NT2374 **Channings** *12-16 South Learmonth Gdns, Edinburgh EH4 1EZ (0131) 332 3232* **£225**, plus special breaks; 46 individually designed bdrms. Originally five Edwardian town houses and now a stylish hotel on a quiet cobbled street overlooking private gardens; relaxed club-like atmosphere, comfortable lounges with open fires, contemporary wine bar and conservatory, and enjoyable modern french food in restful downstairs restaurant

EDINBURGH NT2572 **Ellesmere Guest House** *11 Glengyle Terrace, Edinburgh EH3 9LN (0131) 229 4823* **£30**; 6 comfortable, spotless rms. Warmly friendly and homely guest house in a quiet spot overlooking Bruntsfield Links and short walk from city centre, with friendly helpful owners and good hearty breakfasts in combined no smoking dining room/lounge; children over 12

EDINBURGH NT2572 **Elmview** *15 Glengyle Terrace, Edinburgh EH3 9LN (0131) 228 1973* **£75***; 3 large rms. Quietly placed in fine Victorian terrace overlooking a park 15 mins' walk from the castle and centre; carefully maintained, elegantly furnished, good breakfast and welcome; no children

EDINBURGH NT2674 **Greenside** *9 Royal Terrace, Edinburgh EH7 5AB (0131) 557 0022* **£100***; 16 individually decorated rms. Family-run hotel in Georgian terrace with friendly atmosphere, big lounge, hearty breakfasts, and quiet terraced garden; disabled access

EDINBURGH NT2574 **Howard** *34 Great King St, Edinburgh EH3 6QH (0131) 557 3500* **£275**, plus special breaks; 18 luxurious rms inc 5 suites. Discreet hotel in three Georgian town houses, with comfortable, elegant public rooms, and courteous friendly service; separate breakfast room and dining room though dinner can be served in your room by your butler. There are restaurants in their sister hotels, Channings and the Bonham; cl Christmas

EDINBURGH NT2776 **Malmaison** *1 Tower Pl, Leith, Edinburgh EH6 7DB (0131) 555 6868* **£148.50**, plus special breaks; 100 stylish rms with CD players and satellite TV. Converted baronial-style seamen's mission in the fashionable docks area of Leith with very good food in the downstairs french brasserie, cheerful café bar, gym, and friendly service; free parking; disabled access; dogs welcome in bedrooms

EDINBURGH NT2474 **Seven Danube Street** *7 Danube St, Edinburgh EH4 1NN (0131) 332 2755* **£120***, 5 fine rms with plenty of extras. Quietly placed Georgian house with charming helpful owners, comfortable lounge, a relaxed homely atmosphere, marvellous breakfasts served at one big table, and small garden; no smoking; cl Christmas; dogs by arrangement

ESKDALEMUIR NY2595 **Hart Manor** *Eskdalemuir, Langholm, Dumfriesshire DG13 0QQ (01387) 373217* **£83***, plus special breaks; 7 recently refurbished rms. 19th-c shooting lodge with lovely views and fine hill-walking country all around; a warm, relaxed atmosphere in lounge and library, particularly good individual totally home-made country cooking, a thoughtful wine list and choice of malt whiskies, and superb breakfasts; no smoking; cl Christmas; children over 12

GIFFORD NT5367 **Tweeddale Arms** *Gifford, Haddington, East Lothian EH41 4QU (01620) 810240* **£70**, plus special breaks; 15 rms. Civilised late 17th-c inn in quiet village, with comfortable sofas and chairs in tranquil lounge, gracious dining room, wide choice of good daily-changing food, and charming service; cl 1 Jan; disabled access; dogs welcome in bedrooms

GLASGOW NS5965 **Babbity Bowster** *16-18 Blackfriars St, Glasgow G1 1PE (0141) 552 5055* **£59.50**; 6 clean simple rms, showers. Warmly welcoming rather continental place with decent breakfasts (served till late), attractively decorated airy bar, and a cheery first-floor restaurant which hosts a gallery as well as a programme of musical and theatrical events; cl 25 Dec, 1 Jan

GLASGOW NS5865 **Malmaison** *278 West George St, Glasgow G2 4LL (0141) 572 1000* **£153.50**; 72 smartly quirky very comfortable rms. Stylishly converted Scottish Episcopal church with greek façade, striking central wrought-iron staircase, a relaxed contemporary atmosphere, friendly staff, enjoyable french food in attractive brasserie/bar; gym; disabled access

GLASGOW NS5567 **One Devonshire Gardens** *Glasgow G12 0UX (0141) 339 2001* **£215**; 38 opulent rms. Elegant cosseting hotel a little way out from the centre, with luxurious Victorian furnishings, fresh flowers, exemplary staff, and fine modern cooking in the stylish restaurant; dogs welcome in bedrooms

GULLANE NT4983 **Greywalls** *Duncar Rd, Gullane, East Lothian EH31 2EG (01620) 842144* **£240**, plus special breaks; 23 individually decorated rms. Overlooking Muirfield golf course, this beautiful family-run Lutyens house has antiques, open fires and flowers in its comfortable lounges and panelled library, very good food and fine wines in the restaurant, impeccable service, and lovely Gertrude Jekyll garden, all of a piece with the perfect design of the house; cl Nov-Mar; disabled access; dogs welcome in bedrooms

INNERLEITHEN NT3336 **Traquair Arms** *Innerleithen, Peeblesshire EH44 6PD (01896) 830229* **£70**, plus special breaks; 15 comfortable rms. Very friendly hotel with interesting choice of good food in attractive dining room, cosy lounge bar, friendly service, superb local Traquair ale, and nice breakfasts; cl 25-26 Dec, 1 Jan; disabled access; dogs welcome away from restaurant

LOCKERBIE NY1283 **Dryfesdale Hotel** *Dryfebridge, Lockerbie, Dumfriesshire DG11 2SF (01576) 202427* **£95***, plus wknd breaks; 16 rms, 6 on ground floor. Relaxed and comfortable former manse in five acres, open fire in homely lounge, good food in pleasant restaurant, garden and lovely surrounding countryside, putting and croquet; cl 26 Dec; good disabled access; dogs welcome in bedrooms

MAYBOLE NS3103 **Ladyburn** *Kilkerran, Maybole, Ayrshire KA19 7SG (01655) 740585* **£120**, plus special breaks; 5 rms. Quietly set family home dating from the 1600s and set on the edge of the magnificent estate of Kilkerran; antiques, books and open fires in comfortable drawing room and library, good traditional scottish/french cooking, and friendly staff; shooting and fishing can be arranged; newly refurbished self-catering flat also (children allowed here but not in main house); cl 2 wks Nov, 4 wks Jan-Mar

MELROSE NT5433 **Burts** *Market Sq, Melrose, Roxburghshire TD6 9PN (01896) 822285* **£96***, plus special breaks; 20 rms. Welcoming 18th-c family-run hotel close to abbey ruins in delightfully quiet village; coal fire in bustling bar, residents' lounge, consistently popular imaginative food, exceptional breakfasts; cl 26 Dec; dogs welcome in bedrooms

MINNIGAFF NX4165 **Creebridge House** *Creebridge, Newton Stewart, Wigtownshire DG8 6NP (01671) 402121* **£108**, plus special breaks; 19 rms inc 2 with four posters. Attractive country-house hotel in three acres of gardens with relaxed friendly atmosphere, open fire in comfortable drawing room, cheerful bar, and big choice of delicious food inc fine local fish and seafood in garden restaurant; dogs welcome in bedrooms

NENTHORN NT6938 **Whitehill Farm** *Nenthorn, Kelso, Roxburghshire TD5 7RZ (01573) 470203* **£48***; 4 rms, 3 with shared bthrm. Comfortable farmhouse on mixed farm with fine views, big garden, log fire in sitting room, and good home cooking; no babies; cl Christmas and New Year; dogs welcome

PEEBLES NT2344 **Cringletie House** *Cringletie, Peebles EH45 8PL (01721) 730233* **£115**; 14 pretty rms. Surrounded by 28 acres of garden and woodland and with fine views, very welcoming quiet turreted baronial mansion, delicious food using home-grown vegetables, extensive scottish breakfasts, and excellent service; children over 8; dogs welcome in bedrooms

PORTPATRICK NX9954 **Crown** *Portpatrick, Stranraer, Wigtownshire DG9 8SX (01776) 810261* **£72**, plus special breaks; 12 attractive rms. Atmospheric harbourside inn with rambling and interestingly furnished old-fashioned bar, airy art deco dining room, good food with an emphasis on local seafood, super breakfasts, and carefully chosen wines; dogs welcome in bedrooms

PORTPATRICK NX0252 **Knockinaam Lodge** *Portpatrick, Stranraer, Wigtownshire DG9 9AD (01776) 810471* **£195** inc dinner; 10 individual rms. Lovely very neatly kept little hotel with comfortable pretty rooms, open fires, wonderful food, and friendly caring service; dramatic surroundings, with lots of fine cliff walks; children over 12 in evening restaurant (high tea at 6pm); dogs welcome in bedrooms

QUOTHQUAN NT0140 **Shieldhill** *Quothquan, Biggar, Lanarkshire ML12 6NA (01899) 220035* **£118**, plus special breaks; 16 pretty rms. Partly 12th-c castle in fine setting with comfortable oak-panelled lounge, open fires, library, particularly good food in no smoking restaurant, and warm friendly service; disabled access

SWINTON NT8347 **Wheatsheaf** *Main St, Swinton, Duns, Berwickshire TD11 3JJ (01890) 860257* **£90**; 7 rms with baths or showers. Warmly friendly inn with exceptionally good food, a pleasantly decorated and relaxed main lounge plus small pubby area, new reception lounge, and no smoking front conservatory; garden play area for children; cl Mon, 25 Dec, 1 Jan; dogs welcome in bedrooms

UPHALL NT0571 **Houstoun House** *Uphall, Broxburn, West Lothian EH52 6JS (01506) 853831* **£180**, plus wknd breaks; 71 comfortable rms, quite a few in extension. 17th-c house divided into three distinct buildings: fine food in three panelled dining rooms, vaulted bars (one with a fire nearly all year), quiet lounge, lovely grounds, and leisure complex with swimming pool, sauna, gym, tennis courts and italian bistro; disabled access; lap dogs welcome

We welcome reports from readers

This *Guide* depends on readers' reports. Do help us if you can – in return, we offer a discount on the next edition to people who've helped us with reports for it. Tell us what you think about places already in it, and anything extra you think we should say about them. And send us your ideas for inclusion in the next edition: places to visit, eat at or stay in, attractive drives or walks, maybe even unusual shops you know of. Use the card in the middle, the report forms at the end, or just write – no stamp needed: *The Good Britain Guide*, FREEPOST TN1569, Wadhurst, E Sussex TN5 7BR. Or log on to www.goodguides.co.uk

To see and do

ALLOWAY NS3318
Burns National Heritage Park A key stop on the Burns Trail: the poet was born here in 1759. The associated local sites are grouped together under the above name. The introductory visitor centre the **Tam O'Shanter Experience** (Murdochs Lone) is a multi-media show bringing Burns's famous poem vividly to life. Up the road you can explore the tiny rooms of the poet's birthplace, thatched Burns Cottage, and an adjacent museum of his life has a good collection of manuscripts and letters. In the other direction, S of the centre, the **Burns Monument** was built in 1823 to a fine design by Thomas Hamilton Jr, and is adorned with characters from Burns's poems sculpted by James Thom. Meals, snacks, shop, disabled access; cl 25-26 Dec, 1-2 Jan; (01292) 443700; £5. The **Head of Ayr Farm Park** (Dunure Rd) is useful for restless children; snacks, shop, disabled access; cl mid-Oct to Mar; (01292) 441210; £4.75.

ARRAN NS0037
This rewarding island is just under an hour by ferry from Ardrossan, a popular public-transport day trip from Glasgow, with summer ferries from Claonaig on Kintyre too; (01475) 650100 for ferry enquiries. It has a marvellous variety of scenery from subtropical gardens to mountain deer forest, and has beautifully set and highly regarded golf courses. Brodick the main settlement has several places to hire bikes. The Kingsley on Brodick esplanade has decent home cooking, and the Brodick Bar (Alma Rd) is simple good value. On the opposite side of the island near Machrie are several intriguing Bronze Age stone circles. Arran has a good circular walk up and down Goatfell, prominent for miles around, and you can follow the shore right around the N tip, the Cock of Arran. Up near here the waterside Catacol Hotel has decent food. There's a good walk on the W coast, from Blackwaterfoot to the King's Cave, which supposedly sheltered Robert the Bruce.

Arran Brewery The island's first modern brewery, with rewarding views over Brodick Bay and Goatfell Mountain. A viewing gallery in the visitor centre looks over the microbrewery itself, and you can sample some of the beers you've watched being made. Shop, reasonable disabled access; cl winter Tues and Sun; (01770) 302353; £1.
Brodick Castle and Garden Fine old castle, in lovely surroundings between the sea, hills and majestic mountain of Goatfell. Partly 13th-c, and extended in 1652 and 1844, it's very fierce-looking from the outside, but comfortably grand inside - even a little homely in places. There are almost a hundred antlered heads on the walls of the main staircase. It's surrounded by magnificent formal gardens, with the highlight the woodland garden started in 1923 by the Duchess of Montrose, inc many lovely rare and tender rhododendrons. Adventure playground, plants for sale, meals, snacks, shop, limited disabled access; castle cl Nov-Mar, garden and country park open all year; (01770) 302202; £7; NTS.

BALCARY POINT NX8149
On the W side of sandy Auchencairn Bay, this makes for a good peaceful walk from the pretty village of Auchencairn. The Balcary Bay Hotel has good bar food, and lovely views from its terraces.

BALERNO NT1666
Malleny House Garden 🏠 (off A70 E) Charming gardens that are home to a national collection of 19th-c shrub roses (best in late Jun), as well as four ancient clipped yew trees - the survivors of a dozen planted four centuries ago, already old when the present house was built in the 18th c. Limited disabled access; (0131) 449 2283; £2; NTS. The handsome Johnsburn House Hotel does good lunches.

BATHGATE NS9970
Cairnpapple Hill (just E of Torpichen, off B792) One of the most important prehistoric sites in the country, a stone circle and series of successive burial

cairns that seems to have been used for around 3,000 years from neolithic times to the 1st c BC, and especially during the second millennium BC. Extraordinary views from this raw and atmospheric hilltop site, known locally as 'windy ways'; HS.

BEARSDEN NS5472

Roman Bath House (Roman Rd) Probably the best surviving visible Roman building in Scotland, built in the 2nd c for the garrison at Bearsden Fort, part of the short-lived Antonine Wall defences; free. The appropriately named 55BC (Drymen Rd) has decent food.

BIGGAR NT0437

Several good museums here.

Gasworks (Gasworks Rd) This striking old building is now a museum on the coal-gas industry; disabled access, open pm Jun-Sept; (01899) 221050; £1.

Gladstone Court Museum ⬚£ (North Back Rd) Houses an entire reconstructed village street; cl Sun lunchtime and mid-Oct to Easter; (01899) 221050; *£2.

Greenhill Covenanters House ⬚£ (Burn Braes, Biggar) 17th-c farmhouse originally at Wiston but moved piece by piece and reassembled here; meals and snacks; cl Mon-Fri, am wknds and mid-Oct to Easter; £2.

Moat Park Heritage Centre ⬚£ Good local history collections, and the centrepiece of the town's several worthwhile museums. Shop, meals and snacks, disabled access; cl Sun lunchtime and mid-Oct to Easter; (01899) 221050; £2.

Puppet Theatre (just off A702) Magical and different, with really big puppets that glow in the dark. You can book a tour of backstage and the museum (minimum groups of four). Teas, shop, disabled access (phone first); cl 25 Dec, 1 Jan, and some winter Suns and Mons; (01899) 220631; shows £6, tours £2.50.

BLANTYRE NS6958

David Livingstone Centre (Station Rd, off A724) The birthplace of the famous explorer, with a museum on his life and work inc personal belongings. Adventure playground in the landscaped grounds. Meals, snacks, shop, disabled access; cl Sun am, Jan-

Mar; (01698) 823140; £3.50. The Cricklewood at Bothwell (B7071) is a good dining pub.

BUTE NS0864

This popular Glasgow holiday island is a ½-hr ferry trip from Wemyss Bay/Skelmorlie; it has a mix of fresh air and ebullient summer entertainments. Rothesay, the island's main resort, stretches picturesquely around its bay, the pleasantly faded grandeur of its Victorian heyday nicely setting off the striking ironwork of the 1920s Winter Garden near the pier; the seafront Black Bull has good food. There's lovely open country in the N, its southern tip is rewarding too, and the West Island Way allows walks with great vistas all along the island's W side - you may see seals on the shore, and there's a bird hide suitable for wheelchairs at Kirk Dam NS0863. The beachside Port Royal at Port Bannatyne has all-day food with a russian flavour.

Bute Museum (Stuart St, Rothesay) Decent museum, worth a visit (shop, disabled access; cl winter Sun and Mon, Christmas and New Year; £1.50). The gents' at the harbour, built in 1899, has ornate wall tiles and fine ceramic mosaic floors. (01700) 505067; £1.50.

Monastery of St Blane NS0953 Ruined Norman chapel in a delightful spot, a short way uphill from the road - just sheep and the occasional walker.

Mount Stuart (off A844, just E of Upper Scoulag) In this bracingly bleak landscape, the spectacular Victorian Gothic mansion is almost a shock; the elaborate rooms (scene of Stella McCartney's 2003 wedding party) are splendidly over the top too. The 120 hectares (300 acres) of landscaped grounds and woodland include several pretty gardens, as well as a pinetum of mature conifers and a nicely isolated stretch of sandy beach, reached via a lime avenue. Meals, snacks, shop, disabled access; cl Tues, Thurs, and Sept-Apr; (01700) 503877; £7, garden only £3.50.

Rothesay Castle Moated massive-walled 13th-c fortress, a favourite home of King Robert II, and fought over for centuries; shop; in Oct-Mar cl Thurs pm, Fri and Sun am; £2.20; HS.

Victorian Fern House and Gardens (Ascog Hall, S of Rothesay)

The only one of its kind in Britain, a turreted mansion's 1870s glazed grotto restored and replanted with one of the most impressive collections of ferns to be found outside a botanic garden, inc many species from the southern hemisphere - one is thought to be over 1,000 years old. Cl Mon, Tues and Nov-Easter; (01700) 504555; £2.50.

CAERLAVEROCK NY0265
Caerlaverock Castle 13th-c, protected not just by its moat but by the wild swampy marshes around it - spruce plantations are being felled to bring the landscape back to its former look. It has an unusual triangular inner courtyard, and elaborate projecting tops for dropping missiles on assailants. Snacks, shop, some disabled access; cl Sun ams Oct-Mar and 25-26 Dec and 1-2 Jan; (01387) 770244; £3; HS.
Wildfowl & Wetlands Trust The Caerlaverock salt marshes are a reserve with outstanding hide facilities and observation towers. Countless wildfowl flock here, especially barnacle geese; between Oct and Apr there are generally around 13,000 of them, very dramatic when they're all in flight. Snacks, shop, some disabled access; cl 25 Dec; (01387) 770200; £4. The Nith at Glencaple has good food and a picture-window dining room.

CARDONESS NX5955
Cardoness Castle (A75) Well preserved 15th-c four-storey tower house, overlooking the Water of Fleet; interesting fireplaces. Shop; cl Sun am, cl wkdys Nov-Mar; (01557) 814427; £2.20; HS. The Murray Arms and Masonic Arms in Gatehouse of Fleet have good value food.

CARMICHAEL NS9338
Discover Carmichael Visitor Centre 🖭 (A73 N of Biggar) Among the eclectic attractions here are a collection of waxwork models of Scotland's heroes and heroines, various period re-creations inc a Victorian wash-house, a baby animal farm, free horse and cart rides, and an exhibition on wind energy, all within the attractive grounds of the Carmichael Estate. Also outdoor adventure play areas, buggy racing and a deer park walk. Meals, snacks, farm shop specialising in home-reared meat, disabled access; cl Jan-Feb;

(01899) 308169; *£3.25.
CASTLE DOUGLAS NX7462
Threave Castle (off minor road Bridge of Dee—Townhead) The Black Douglas, Archibald the Grim, built this in the 14th c; four storeys high, it stands on an islet in the River Dee, so you have to get a ferry across (ring the bell and the custodian will come to get you). Shop; cl Oct-Mar; (0131) 668 8800; £2.20 inc ferry; HS. In the town the Douglas Arms has enjoyable local food.
Threave Garden (1m W off A75) The National Trust for Scotland's horticulture school, with plenty to see through the year in its walled garden, glasshouses and waymarked nature trails (the estate is 1,500 acres). If you're there in spring, don't miss the massed display of over 200 varieties of daffodil. 19th-c scottish baronial Threave House is now also open to the public, showing the main rooms and a museum of country life. Meals, snacks, shop, some disabled access; house cl Nov-Feb and Mon-Tues and Sat; (01556) 502575; *£5, £9 inc house; NTS.

CLARENCEFIELD NY0669
Comlongon Castle (B725) 15th-c, unusually well preserved, with interesting original features inc dungeons, kitchen, great hall and even privies. Pre-booking essential; (01387) 870283; £2 - and see *Where to stay*.

COATBRIDGE NS7265
Summerlee Heritage Park (off W Canal St) Ambitious centre looking at the local iron, steel and engineering industries. Lots going on, spread over 10 hectares (25 acres) of a former iron works; the working machinery creates a real feeling of authenticity. The site has Scotland's only working electric tramway. Snacks, shop, disabled access (but not to mine); cl 25-26 Dec, 1-2 Jan; (01236) 431261; free (tram 75p).
Time Capsule (Buchanan St) Fun - swimming pools and leisure centre with a loose historic theme: water chutes whizz you through the origins of man, and a woolly mammoth holds court in the centre of the ice rink. Cl 25 Dec, 1 Jan; (01236) 449572. *£4.35 waterworld, *£5.05 ice age inc skate hire.

COLDSTREAM NT8240
Hirsel Country Park Pretty lakeside and woodland walks (best May-Jun)

through the huge Hirsel Estate (nearly 5 square miles), with Douglas highland cattle and various waterfowl (there's a hide by the lake); also a craft centre and gallery, and a little museum has displays on the estate. Tearoom and picnic area, shop, disabled access; *£2 per car.

CRAMOND NT1877
Charming preserved former fishing village, the once-humble cottages now snapped up by Edinburgh's professionals. The Cramond Inn has good value food.

Lauriston Castle Interesting, with mostly Edwardian décor and antiques, and garden inc a japanese friendship garden. Disabled access to grounds only; open for guided tours only (not Fri), phone for times; (0131) 336 2060; £4.50.

River Almond walk W of Edinburgh, from the Cramond Brig Hotel on the A90, you can walk along the wooded valley to Cramond, cross the Almond by ferry, then go along the shore past Dalmeny House, and finish below the Forth Bridge at South Queensferry. There are frequent buses back to the start, and to Edinburgh.

CREETOWN NX4759
Gem Rock Museum 🔖 (Chain Rd) Enormous private collection of gem stones and minerals, some displayed in an atmospheric crystal cave. Also a fossilised dinosaur egg and dung, and meteorites. Meals, snacks, shop, disabled access; cl wkdys 23 Dec-31 Jan but open by appointment wkdys in Dec and Feb; (01671) 820357; £3.25

CRICHTON NT3861
Crichton Castle (2½m SW of Pathhead) Not far from Edinburgh, but really remote-feeling, as it's reached only by a half-mile walk from the car park by Crichton church; medieval tower house, with grim external defences for an elegant late 16th-c italianate interior courtyard. Cl Nov-Mar and Thurs and Sun pm and Fri in Oct; (01875) 320017; £2.20; HS.

CULZEAN NS2310
Culzean Castle (pronounced 'Cullane') A day here is one of the most popular outings in the region. The 18th-c mansion has great presence and brilliance, and the grounds (nearly a square mile) are among the finest in

Britain, lushly planted and richly ornamental, with woods, lake, an abundance of paths, bracing clifftop and shoreline walks, and an 18th-c walled garden. The house was splendidly refashioned by Robert Adam, and has been well restored to show off his work to full effect. Meals, snacks, shop, disabled access; house cl Nov-Apr, park open all year; (01655) 884455; £9; NTS. You can stay in rather smart self-contained apartments on the top floor.

DALKEITH NT3167
Edinburgh Butterfly & Insect World 🔖 (Dobbies Nursery, off A720 at Gilmerton jnctn) Gloriously coloured exotic butterflies, as well as scorpions and tarantulas, bee garden, and rainforest frogs. Handling sessions mean you can get even closer to some of the animals. Meals, snacks, shop, disabled access; cl 25-26 Dec, 1 Jan; (0131) 663 4932; £4.35. The Sun (Lothianbridge - A7 S) has good value food.

DIRLETON NT5184
Dirleton Castle (A198) Grandly rebuilt after a siege in 1298, only to be destroyed again in 1650 - though you can still see plenty of the original squared 13th-c masonry. It has a charming garden planted in the 16th c, with ancient yews and hedges around a bowling green, and what is thought to be the longest herbaceous border in the world. Cl Sun am Oct-Mar; (01620) 850330; £3; HS. The Castle Hotel and Open Arms in this pleasant golfing village are both good for lunch.

DRYBURGH NT5932
Dryburgh Abbey Remarkably complete ruins in a lovely setting among old cedars by the River Tweed - its graceful cloisters are very peaceful. Walter Scott is buried here (and on the B6356 N the signposted Scott's View is idyllic). Shop, some disabled access; cl Sun am in winter, Dec, 1-2 Jan; (01835) 822381; *£3; HS. The Buccleuch Arms at St Boswells is a civilised place for something to eat.

DUMBARTON NS4074
Dumbarton Castle (A82) Perched on a rock 73 metres (240 ft) above the River Clyde, with dramatic views of the surrounding countryside. Most of what can be seen dates from the 18th and 19th c, though there are some earlier

remains. Snacks, shop; cl Sun am, Thurs pm and Fri Oct-Mar; (01389) 732167; £2.20; HS. The Ettrick in the picturesque Clydeside village of Old Kilpatrick has good value food.

DUMFRIES NX9775

A pleasant red sandstone town, the biggest in the SW, with close Burns connections. The Globe Tavern (off High St) has two rooms still very much as they were when this was his regular haunt (Anna Park, a barmaid, bore his child).

Burns Mausoleum (St Michael's churchyard) The tomb of Robert Burns, his on-and-off wife Jean Armour, and their five sons; you can usually make an appointment to visit at the Burns House; free.

Museum and Camera Obscura 🏛 (Church St) In the tower of an 18th-c windmill, this has a camera obscura and local history. Shop, limited disabled access; cl 1-2pm, Sun, and Mon Oct-Mar; (01387) 253374; museum free, camera obscura £1.50.

Robert Burns Centre 🏛 (Mill Rd) Exhibition and audio-visual display in handsome stone-built watermill, as well as an interesting scale model of the town at the time he wrote. Meals, snacks, shop, disabled access; cl Sun am, and 1-2 pm and Sun Oct-Mar; (01387) 264808; free; £1.50 for audio-visual exhibition.

Robert Burns House (Burns St) Where he lived for the three years before his death; has original letters and manuscripts along with the chair in which he wrote his last poems and songs, and an upstairs window has his signature scratched in the glass. Shop; cl Sun am, and 1-2 pm and Sun Oct-Mar; (01387) 255297; free.

DUMGOYNE NS5282

Glengoyne Distillery You can go on a 50-min guided tour of this prettily set 150-year-old distillery. Cl am Sun, best to phone over Christmas; shop, some disabled access; (01360) 550254; £3.95 inc a taster.

DUNBAR NT6779

The harbour here is pretty, with some picturesquely jagged fragments of the medieval castle in the John Muir Country Park, and good walks nearby, along the cliffs and by the marshy inlets of Belhaven Bay; the harbourside

Starfish has good seafood. Quite a few good clean beaches near here, notably Belhaven, nearby Whitesands Bay, and the one at Thorntonloch a few miles down the coast.

DUNDRENNAN NX7547

Dundrennan Abbey (A711) 12th-c Cistercian abbey famous as the place where Mary Queen of Scots is thought to have spent her last night in Scotland, now ruined columns and arches soaring from neat lawns. Cl Thurs pm, Fri, and Sun am in Oct, also 8-9, 15 Oct; wkdays and Sun am Nov-Mar; (01557) 500262; £1.80; HS.

DUNS NT8054

Edin's Hall Broch Off the A6112 from Duns, this is one of very few such Iron Age strongholds in the Lowlands.

Manderston 🏛 (2m E, off A6105) Splendidly lavish house built for the plutocrat racecourse owner Sir James Miller; he told the architect to spare no expense, so ended up with the world's only silver staircase. Other gloriously extravagant parts are the painted ceilings, and a ballroom decorated in Miller's racing colours. Also fine formal gardens, and an unusual biscuit-tin museum. Teas, shop, limited disabled access; open Thurs pm and Sun am mid-May-Sept; (01361) 883450; £6.50, £3.50 grounds only. The Wheatsheaf at Swinton isn't far, for a very good meal.

EAST FORTUNE NT5578

Museum of Flight (East Fortune Airfield, B1347) Scotland's National Museum of Aviation, with over 40 aeroplanes from a Spitfire to a Vulcan bomber, also Britain's oldest surviving aircraft (1896), and displays on famous flyers and air traffic control. Café, shop, disabled access; cl wkdays Nov to mid-Mar; (01620) 880308; £3.

EAST KILBRIDE NS6055

Museum of Scottish Country Life (Philipshill Rd, off A726 W) In 70 hectares (170 acres), this is home to the rural life collection of the National Museums of Scotland, with galleries on the environment, rural technology, and people; there's also a picture gallery and film room, and they hold special events in the arena. A working farm owned by the same family for 400 years shows farming methods from the 1950s, when horses were still being used alongside machines. Meals, snacks, shop, disabled access; (01355) 224181; £3.

EAST LINTON NT5875

Hailes Castle (minor rd SW) 13th/14th-c, another brief stopping point for Mary Queen of Scots; now in ruins, but lovely in spring, with wild flowers along the stream; free.

Preston Mill (B1407) One of the oldest working water-driven oatmeal mills left. It's a pretty spot with geese and ducks, and an old dovecote nearby. Shop, limited disabled access; cl am, also Tues, Weds and end Oct-Mar; (01620) 860426; £3.50; NTS. The Drovers Inn has good food.

EDINBURGH NT2573

Edinburgh is one of Britain's most rewarding cities for visitors. It always looks good, and there are lots of interesting places within a pleasant walk of each other. It's dominated by the ancient silhouettes of Edinburgh Castle on its castle cliff and of the long erratic line of tall, thin Old Town buildings stretched along beside it. Up here narrow streets and alleys with steep steps between them and courtyard closes leading off the **Royal Mile** have a real flavour of the distant past, with a good many interesting ancient buildings (and a lot of the city's antiquarian bookshops and other interesting specialist shops). When the authorities decided to redevelop the city in the 18th c, they did it not by knocking down the medieval buildings, but instead by creating an entirely new part of the city, working from scratch. The resulting New Town is a masterpiece of spacious Georgian town planning, stretching out handsomely below the steep crag of Castle Rock and its medieval skyline. Walking tours in the evenings are often led by students, and the literary pub tour is particularly good fun; (0131) 226 6665; £7. New Town highlights are Charlotte Sq, Moray Pl, Ainslie Pl and Randolph Crescent. The regular bus services have good value daily and weekly passes, and it is worth getting used to the public transport (the city council has plans, unpopular with residents, for a car toll). The hop-on hop-off tour bus ticket gives discounts to some of the places to visit. The August Festival has great music and

dance, and a fun Fringe which in 2003 had its most popular season so far. The city's at its best then; if you do visit the festival, make sure you've got accommodation sorted out well in advance. Edinburgh's pubs and bars are a special delight, chatty places often of great character. Among the best for atmosphere are the Bow Bar (Victoria St), Bannermans Bar (Cowgate), Bennets Bar (Leven St), Café Royal and Guildford Arms (both West Register St), Cumberland (Cumberland St), Athletic Arms (Angle Park Terrace/Kilmarnock Rd) and Kays Bar (Jamaica St West); for food, we recommend the Abbotsford, Kenilworth and Milnes (all Rose St), Dome (George St), Braidwoods (West Port), and down by the Forth the Starbank (Laverockbank Rd), Old Chain Pier (Trinity Crescent) and Fishers and Ship on the Shore (The Shore, Leith). The corner lobby bar of the Balmoral Hotel is a relaxing spot at the hub of the town. For a fuller meal, the city has a remarkable number of good value bistro-style restaurants (as well as the places we mention in the *Where to eat* section). Lots of good shops are dotted around town, especially on or near Princes St - its tall, mainly Georgian buildings lining just the one side, giving an expansive view across the sunken gardens to the castle. Parallel George St has some superior shops, while Rose St, an alley between the two, has plenty of pubs and cafés. More bars around the Grassmarket and Lawnmarket, a lively area of the Old Town; Victoria St has interesting shops. Iain Mellis (Bruntisfield Pl) specialises in farm cheeses, and Valvona & Crolla (Elm Row) is a dazzling delicatessen, with an excellent italian bistro at the back.

Arthur's Seat Out beyond Holyrood in Holyrood Park is this saddle-back mountain, a great volcanic mass giving a wonderful panorama over the city, and a pleasant place for wandering, with a hill fort on top and the largely unspoilt Duddingston village below it (the Sheep Heid here is a good pub).

Blackford Hill Virtually a mountain within the city, giving walkers great views of Edinburgh.

Calton Hill Dominating the E end of Princes St, with magnificent views over the city. An unusual sight up here is a romantic Doric colonnade, intended to be a full replica of the Parthenon (until the money ran out).

Clan Tartan Centre 🏛 (Leith Mills, Bangor Rd) Displays of various clans and their costume, computers that let you trace your own scottish heritage, and a factory shop with good value Pringle knitwear and tweeds. Meals, snacks, shop, disabled access; cl 25 Dec, 1 Jan; (0131) 553 5161; free.

Craigmillar Castle (A68) On the city's SE outskirts, this is a seemingly impregnable 14th-c tower house (it did in fact fall to the English in 1544), within an impressive double curtain wall; lots to see, and a proper castle feel. Snacks, shop; cl Fri, Thurs pm and Sun am in Oct-Mar, 25-26 Dec, 1 Jan; £2.20; HS.

Dynamic Earth (Holyrood Rd) This exemplary exhibition shows the story of the planet using hi-tech effects and state-of-the-art displays. It vividly relates the story of evolution using giant screens, dramatic sounds and commentary, and evocative smells, spread over eleven hugely different and often quite spectacular display areas. You can see a volcano erupt, experience an earthquake, watch animals swinging through trees in the rainforest, and take a helicopter flight over the glaciers of Scandinavia. The finale is a colourful film taking in images of storms, hurricanes, and sunsets, with a serious environmental message of course - but hearing it has rarely been so much fun; play area for younger children. Meals, snacks, shop, disabled access; cl Mon-Tues Nov-Mar, and 24-26 Dec; (0131) 550 7800; £8.95.

Edinburgh Castle Perched on its hill above the city, this is a place of great magnetism; it's been a fortress since at least the 7th c, and excavations show there's been a settlement here for 4,000 years. The oldest building today is the beautiful St Margaret's Chapel, thought to have been built in the 12th c and little changed since. Other highlights include the apartments of Mary, Queen of Scots, Mons Meg (the 15th-c belgian cannon with which James II cowed the Black Douglases), the scottish crown jewels (centuries older than the english ones), and for

romantics the Stone of Destiny or scottish coronation stone; the polished natural rock protruding into the building also stays in the memory. This spring a new exhibition prompted by graffiti in the castle's prison vaults explores its links - through men imprisoned there - with the revolutions in France and America. Glorious views from the battlements, over the Firth of Forth to Fife beyond. You can wander around on your own, but the official guides are a great bonus - they leave from the drawbridge, several times a day. Meals, snacks, shop, mostly disabled access; cl 25-26 Dec; (0131) 225 9846; £8.50 (inc audio tour); HS. If you're around at lunchtime, look (and listen) for the firing of the One o' Clock Gun from the parapet.

Edinburgh Dungeon 🏛 (Market St) All too realistic scenes recalling the darker moments in scottish history, from the body-snatching of Burke and Hare through a witch-finding boat raid to the Glencoe Massacre during the clan wars. Snacks, shop, cl 25 Dec; (0131) 240 1000; £8.50.

Edinburgh Zoo (Corstorphine Rd; A8 W) Best known for its Penguin Parade most afternoons at 2.15 (Apr-Oct); there are plenty of other rare and odd-looking animals around the attractive grounds. Children enjoy the yew-hedge maze loosely themed around Darwin's theory of evolution; it has several fountains along the way that periodically shoot out jets of water (summer only). Extra events and activities in summer hols. Meals, snacks, shops, disabled access (though a little hilly); open every day (inc 25 Dec); (0131) 334 9171; £8.

Georgian House (Charlotte Sq) Archetypal New Town period house, part of Robert Adam's magnificent terrace along the N side, refurbished in the style of 1800. Shop; cl 25 Dec-Feb; (0131) 226 3318; £5; NTS. Close by, nr Queen St, beyond a further strip of gardens, is another Georgian area with some interesting shops.

Greyfriars Kirkyard (off Candlemakers Row) Interesting little 17th-c church and graveyard (famous residents inc Greyfriars Bobby, the dog which never left its dead master's side, and Sir Walter Scott's father); look out for mort safes, cage-like devices designed to protect corpses from grave-robbers; open daylight hours; free.

National Gallery of Scotland (The Mound) Fine neo-classical building with particularly good examples of most european schools and periods inc a £20 million Botticelli *Madonna and Child*, barely seen for over a century. Plenty of scottish paintings too, with many great works by Ramsay, Raeburn, Wilkie and McTaggart. Few would dispute that it's one of Britain's best galleries. Look out for the rather incongruous portrait of one of the donor's dogs - it has to be hung here as a condition of the donation of other pictures. Shop, disabled access; cl 25-26 Dec; (0131) 624 6200; free (exc major exhibitions).

Nelson Monument (Calton Hill) Best of all for the views of Edinburgh - if you can face the 31-metre (102-ft) climb to the top. Every day at 1pm (exc Sun) the time ball drops as the gun at the castle goes off. Shop; cl Mon am, Sun, 25-26 Dec, 1-2 Jan; (0131) 556 2716; £2.

Palace of Holyroodhouse (Canongate) Imposing yet human-scale palace with its origins in the Abbey of Holyrood, founded by David I. Later the court of Mary Queen of Scots, it was used by Bonnie Prince Charlie during his occupation of Edinburgh, and is still a Royal residence for part of the year. The oldest surviving part is James IV's tower, with Queen Mary's rooms on the second floor, where a plaque on the floor marks where her secretary Rizzio was murdered in front of her. The throne room and state rooms have period furniture, tapestries and paintings from the Royal collection and are much more inviting than many english palaces. The new Queens Gallery at the entrance to the Palace has changing exhibitions from the Royal Collection (separate charge). In summer a path takes you back to the forecourt via the palace gardens. Shop, meals and snacks, limited disabled access by prior arrangement; cl Good Fri, 25-26 Dec and occasional other dates (if the Queen is in residence, for example) - best to check on (0131) 556 5100; £7.50. As we go to press, the hope is that the nearby new scottish

parliament building will be completed this July (but don't hold your breath - that's already a couple of years late, and costs seem likely to overrun the current estimate of £369m, against the £40m originally agreed).

Royal Botanic Garden (Inverleith Row) A magnet for plant-lovers, founded as a physic garden in 1670 at Holyrood, then transplanted here (just N of the centre) in the early 19th c. Covering nearly 30 hectares (72 acres), it has various splendid themed areas, with a woodland garden, peat garden, arboretum, the biggest collection of chinese plant species anywhere (even China), and the glasshouses which include palm houses, fern house and aquatic house. Meals, snacks, shop, disabled access; cl 25 Dec, 1 Jan; (0131) 552 7171; free.

Royal Mile Between castle and palace at the heart of the Old Town (for most people Edinburgh's two must-sees) is this a largely medieval street, around which you'll find all sorts of interesting or historic houses and features, and quaint lanes leading off in all directions. The following places (down to the Museum of Edinburgh) are listed in order, as you go down the Mile towards Holyrood. Usefully, it's punctuated with cafés and bars in which to stop and work out your next move, starting with the old-world Ensign Ewart on the left as you leave the castle.

Scotch Whisky Heritage Centre (Castlehill) Entertainingly illustrates the story of the national drink, starting off with a shortish journey in a barrel-shaped car through well put together sets and tableaux. The full tour is a useful introduction to the distilling process; if you haven't been to a real distillery it's a good substitute, and there's a decent sample and well stocked shop at the end. Meals, snacks, disabled access; cl 25 Dec; (0131) 220 0441; £7.50.

Camera Obscura 🖼 (Castlehill) These 19th-c revolving lenses and mirrors create unique panoramas of the city as soon as the lights go down, with a good commentary (best on a sunny day); also kaleidoscopes, trick mirrors and holograms. Shop; cl 25 Dec; (0131) 226 3709; £5.75.

Gladstone's Land (Lawnmarket) Six-storeyed early 17th-c building, still with its arcaded front, and refurnished in period style. The walls and ceilings have remarkable tempera paintings. Shop; cl Sun am, and Nov-Mar; (0131) 226 5856; £3.50; NTS.

Writers Museum (Lady Stair's Close, off Lawnmarket) Named after its 18th-c occupant, this partly 1622 building houses a collection of manuscripts and objects associated with Robert Burns, Walter Scott and R L Stevenson. Shop; cl Sun exc during Festival, 25-26 Dec, 1-2 Jan; (0131) 529 4901; free.

Real Mary King's Close (Warristons Close, High St) Tour the warren of underground streets and closes (many of which have been hidden for centuries) below today's city. Costumed characters inc Foul Clinger and the daughter of Mary King help bring those plague-ridden days all to life. Cl 25 Dec; (08702) 430160; £7.

St Giles Cathedral (High St) The Royal Mile widens out briefly around Scotland's High Kirk, the city's most impressive ecclesiastical building, mainly 15th-c but dating from around 1120. Topped with an ornate crown-like tower, it has monuments to famous Scots from Knox (minister here until his death) to R L Stevenson. Shop, snacks; cl Sun am, 25-26 Dec, 1-2 Jan; free guided tours; (0131) 225 9442; free.

Parliament House (Parliament Sq) Just behind the cathedral, this was the seat of scottish government until the Union of 1707, and now houses the supreme law courts of Scotland. Don't miss the fine hammerbeam roof in the hall. Some disabled access; cl wknds and public holidays; (0131) 225 2595; free.

Museum of Childhood (High St) The first of its type and still one of the best, a charming collection of games, toys and dolls from all over the globe. Shop, some disabled access; cl Sun (exc pm during Festival and July-Aug); (0131) 529 4142; free.

Canongate Tolbooth (Canongate) This elaborate building houses an excellent social history exhibition, the People's Story, with reconstructions built very much around first-hand accounts of Edinburgh life. Shop, disabled access; cl Sun (exc pm during Festival), 25-26 Dec, 1 Jan; (0131) 529 4057; free.

Museum of Edinburgh (Canongate) 16th-c, with well refurbished galleries on glass, pottery and trade; other collections include scottish pottery, Edinburgh silver, local history, and even Greyfriars Bobby's collar and bowl. The exhibits are thoughtfully - even artistically - arranged; also temporary exhibitions. Shop; cl Sun (exc pm during Festival), cl 25-26 Dec, 1-2 Jan; (0131) 529 4143; free. The Canons Gait nearby is a smart bar, and Cadenheads (no 172) sell many unusual whiskies .

Royal Museum/Museum of Scotland (Chambers St) A tremendous variety of collections, covering virtually anything you might care to poke around in, now shared between a gloriously light and spacious Victorian building, and its grand new counterpart next door. Children particularly enjoy the intricate working scale models of early engines, but it has something for everyone. Meals, snacks, shop, disabled access; cl Sun am and 25 Dec; (0131) 225 7534; free.

Royal Yacht Britannia 🖼 Displays about the yacht and its Royal past in an onshore visitor centre, and a chance to explore five decks of the ship in which the Queen and Prince Philip cruised the world. Shop, disabled access; cl 25 Dec, 1 Jan; (0131) 555 5566; £8.

Scott Memorial (Princes St) After the castle, probably Edinburgh's most memorable building: remarkably ornate, with its handsome if mucky exterior (they've kept the dirt, as cleaning seemed more damaging). The crypt of the very handsome Gothic-Revival St John's episcopal church on Princes St has interesting vegetarian and vegan food.

Scottish National Gallery of Modern Art (Belford Rd) Breathtaking collection inc great works by Picasso, Barbara Hepworth and Lichtenstein. Meals, snacks, shop, disabled access; cl 25-26 Dec; (0131) 624 6200; free (may be charges for temporary exhibitions). Across the road the **Dean Gallery** houses extensive collections of Dada and Surrealist art; Sir Eduardo Paolozzi's collection of prints, drawings, and the contents of his studio are here too, with changing modern art exhibitions. Cl 25-26 Dec; snacks, shop, disabled access; free. A little off-centre over the Water of Leith, but worth the walk.

Scottish National Portrait Gallery (Queen St) The history of Scotland through a huge and varied collection of portraits in a variety of media. Meals, snacks, shop, disabled access; 25-26 Dec; (0131) 624 6200; free.

Water of Leith Walkway W of the centre, and following the often very picturesque and ravine-like 12 mile course of the river from Balerno to Leith. Quaint little Dean Village is surprisingly close to the heart of the city, yet unaffected by all the New Town building above it; further N you can leave the river and head into the Royal Botanic Garden. The Visitor Centre halfway along the river at Slateford includes an interactive exhibition on the river's heritage and wildlife (shop, snacks, disabled access; cl Mon, Tues Oct-Mar; (0131) 455 7367; £1.90). The river eventually winds down to Leith itself (a once prosperous and separate dockland area now swallowed up by the city, its waterfront reviving again with trendy bars and restaurants). The Scottish Malt Whisky Society (Giles St), dedicated to cask-strength top-quality malt whiskies, has a downstairs bar/restaurant; (0131) 554 3451.

ELLISLAND FARM NX9283
£ (off A76) Robert Burns lived here from 1788 to 1791, trying unsuccessfully to introduce new farming methods. There are displays of material associated with the poet (who wrote *Tam o' Shanter* and *Auld Lang Syne* while living here), and cattle and sheep wander around much as they must have done then. Lovely riverside walk. Shop, some disabled access; cl Sun am, and Sun-Mon Oct-Mar; (01387) 740426; *£2.50.

ESKDALEMUIR NY2597
Beautifully set mountain village, famous for its cruel winter weather; it also has an unexpected tibetan Buddhist temple and monastery.

Southern Upland Way The longest of only three official long-distance paths in Scotland, this route makes a 212-mile coast-to-coast journey over the hills from Portpatrick to Cockburnspath. It's a good basis for day walks, for instance from this village, though large distances between places often make it hard to find focal points.

EYEMOUTH NT9464
Understated family holiday seaside town around busy but pretty fishing harbour, with a decent beach. The Ship overlooking the harbour has reasonable food, and the Anchor at Coldingham is strong on local fish.

Eyemouth Museum (Market Pl) Good local history museum in former church, with magnificent tapestry commemorating the terrible gale of 14 Oct 1881 which drowned 189 fishermen (139 from Eyemouth). (01890) 750678, cl Sun Oct and Nov-Easter; £2.

St Abb's Head The best of the E coast scenery for walkers; walk from Eyemouth or St Abbs, with a good path along the cliffs - noisily crowded with breeding seabirds in late spring, with high breezy walks, and a lighthouse.

St Abbs A steep and pretty little seaside village nearby, with a sandy beach and old fishing harbour.

FAIRLIE NS2156
Kelburn Castle & Country Centre Castle with walled garden, adventure course, children's secret forest, woodland walks; Shop, house cl Nov-Easter; £5.

FERNIEGAIR NS7453
Chatelherault Country Park (Carlisle Rd) Originally built by William Adam as a hunting lodge and summer house for the Dukes of Hamilton; a grand avenue of trees once linked this restored hilltop building with Hamilton Palace (now demolished). The former kennels house a visitor centre with displays on the history of the house, the local area and its wildlife. The Banqueting Room and Duke's private apartments can still be seen, and the grounds include restored Georgian gardens, woodland trails, rare white park cattle (much closer to wild ancestors than today's breeds), and a children's adventure playground. Ranger-led walks. Snacks, shop, disabled access; house cl Fri; cl 25-26 Dec, and 1-2 Jan; (01698) 426213; free.

GALLOWAY FOREST PARK
NX3672
Attractive and easily accessible, taking in around 100 lochs, 300 miles of river, great views, and many miles of forest, mountain and moorland. Many trees are fairly recent replantings, the original woodland having fallen victim from the 15th c onwards rapidly to the demand for timber. Many of the lochs are ringed by waymarked walks and trails, and there are plenty of scenic drives and cycle routes. Visitor centres (Apr-Oct only) at Kirroughtree, Glen Trool and Clatteringshaws all have exhibitions and information to help you make the most of the forests, inc details of where you can fish, and the best places to spot wildlife. Stones mark 14th-c battles between Scotland and England, and the 1680s Killing Time, when scottish covenanters were hunted down and killed in the government's attempts to impose bishops on the scottish church.
Loch Trool NX4180 Particularly attractive trails around the loch, a good informative summer visitor centre nearby, and a memorial stone commemorating a 1307 battle between Robert the Bruce and the armies of Edward I.
Merrick NX4285 The highest point in SW Scotland, a worthwhile but long and strenuous walk up from Glen Trool.
Wood of Cree NX3771 One of the best surviving stretches of ancient forest, with an RSPB reserve among its trees and marshes.

GLASGOW NS5865
There's a real zing and vitality about this proud city (Scotland's biggest), which is making great strides in its efforts to shake off its rather rough image, including embarking on a 10-year massive redevelopment of the waterfront - through 2004, new shopping areas, cafés and restaurants and perhaps a new transport museum should be opening here. Already a waterbus is helpful for visitors. Glasgow has excellent art galleries and interesting museums (while the Kelvingrove gallery is being refurbished, some works are being shown at the McLellan Galleries); it also houses the Royal Scottish National Orchestra, with a fine-sounding concert hall, the Scottish Opera and the Scottish Ballet. Though there are many places to see and visit, a snag for visitors is that they are scattered around this sprawling city, and often poorly signposted: the Burrell Collection, one of the most interesting places of all, is tucked away in the suburbs. Families will find it worth investing in a Day Tripper ticket, which allows virtually unlimited train and underground travel (£14 for two adults and up to four children). This also makes it easy to get out to the really attractive parks fringing the city (we list these after the other attractions here, starting with Greenbank Garden). Besides the restaurants and bars mentioned in *Where to eat*, Glasgow is full of places to eat out in, formal and informal; interesting and undaunting pubs and bars include the Auctioneers (St Vincent Pl), Blackfriars (Bell St), Bon Accord (North St), and Horseshoe (Drury St). Shoppers will find much here to keep them occupied: Glasgow has more shops than anywhere in Britain outside London.
Botanic Gardens (Great Western Rd) Sloping gently down to the River Kelvin, these are famous for their fantastic glasshouses, particularly the huge Kibble Palace, with its soaring tree ferns interspersed with Victorian sculpture (they are doing a major restoration and the palace will be closed for at least a year). You can see plays here in the summer. Snacks, disabled access; (0141) 334 2422; cl 25-26 Dec; free.
Burrell Collection (Pollok Country Park, SW Glasgow) A couple of miles out in the suburbs, but not to be missed - and rarely too crowded. Splendidly and imaginatively housed in a modern building created to show its different parts to perfection, the huge collection - far too much to see at one go - includes egyptian alabaster, chinese jade, oriental rugs, remarkable tapestries, medieval metalwork and stained glass, even medieval doorways and windows set into the walls, as well as paintings by Degas, Manet and Rembrandt among others. Good meals and snacks, shop, disabled access; cl 25-26 Dec, 1-2 Jan; (0141) 287 2550; free

(parking £1.50). See entries for Pollok Country Park and House below.

Pollok Country Park (SW) One of the best of the several parks and gardens you'll find around Glasgow, with waterside and woodland trails, rose garden, clydesdale horses and highland cattle. Shop, snacks, disabled access; (0141) 632 9299; free.

Pollok House 🖼 (Pollok Country Park) Treasures here include silver, ceramics and porcelain, but it's the paintings (for which the house was largely redesigned 100 years ago) that stand out, with a collection of spanish masters such as Goya and El Greco cannily acquired in the mid-19th c when they were greatly undervalued. Meals, snacks, shop; disabled access; cl 25-26 Dec, 1-2 Jan; (0141) 616 6410; £5.

Charles Rennie Mackintosh tours 🖼 Sauchiehall St, a link between the museum/university quarter and the centre, is an ordinary shopping street, but well worth the walk for the ground-breaking designer and architect's most famous building, the Glasgow School of Art (Renfrew St, just off; the tours are highly recommended, (0141) 353 4526), and the decoratively mirrored Willow Tea Room (open till 5pm), furnished to his designs, too. Shop, some disabled access; cl Sun Oct-Jun, 25 Dec, 1 Jan; *£5.

Clyde walks A walkway tracks along the cleaned-up Clyde waterfront, and building work has begun on the £500 million 10-year regeneration of one central stretch, with a landmark new conference centre. The world's last ocean-going paddle steamer, the handsomely restored 1940s *Waverley*, makes summer runs from Anderston Quay; (0141) 221 8152 for times. Some Clydeside pubs well outside Glasgow with decent food and good sea views include the Cardwell at Cardwell Bay in Gourock and the Spinnaker there, and the Lookout down in Troon Marina.

Clydebuilt (Braehead Shopping Centre, off M8 junctions 25a and 26) This interesting extension of Irvine's Scottish Maritime Museum enjoyably tells the story of Glasgow and the Clyde from the tobacco lords of the 17th c, through the city's days as a global centre for shipbuilding, right up to the present. Interactive exhibits let you steer your own ship, make a fortune as an ocean trader, and for a taste of the real thing you can take control of a real steam engine and go aboard the oldest Clyde-built vessel still afloat. Shop, disabled access; cl Fri, 25 Dec and 1 Jan; (0141) 886 1013; *£3.50. On Clyde Waterbus route; (07711) 250969.

Gallery of Modern Art (Royal Exchange Sq, Queen St) Big gallery concentrating on living british artists - not just scottish. Lively café-bar (open some evenings too), shop, good disabled access; cl 25-26 Dec, 1-2 Jan; (0141) 229 1996; free.

Glasgow Cathedral 12th-c, dedicated to St Mungo, the founder of the city. It's very well preserved, though most fittings date from the 19th c; best parts are the crypt, a gracefully vaulted affair built in the mid-13th c, and the Blackadder aisle. Summer shop; cl Sun am, 25-26 Dec, 1-2 Jan; (0141) 552 6891; free. The area around here, the oldest part of Glasgow, has been largely obliterated by the adjacent early 20th-c hospital and extensive 1960s redevelopment, but the spectacular Necropolis graveyard survives - interesting to wander around, with a fine overview from the cathedral.

Glasgow Science Centre (Pacific Quay) Incorporating three main attractions, the four-storey Science Mall, the 100-metre (328-ft) Glasgow Tower (closed as this *Guide* went to press because of design problems but due to reopen early 2004), and IMAX theatre. The Mall and theatre are strikingly clad in shimmering titanium, while the tower is the only one in the world capable of revolving 360 degrees from the ground up. The Science Mall has hundreds of interactive and hands-on displays, a planetarium, and the Virtual Science Theatre. The Tower has multimedia displays and presentations on past and future developments in Glasgow, as well as splendid views from the top. Meals, snacks, shop, disabled access; cl 24-25 Dec, 1 Jan; (0141) 420 5000. Science Mall £6.95, Tower or the IMAX £5.95, double ticket £9.95.

House for an Art Lover (Bellahouston Park, by M8 junctions 23/24) Built to 1901 designs by Charles

Rennie Mackintosh, with an exhibition of decorative rooms, and contemporary art exhibitions. Meals, snacks, shop, disabled access; cl Thurs-Sun pms, opening times Mon-Thurs in Oct-Mar vary so best to ring, but always cl Fri-Sun pms (0141) 353 4770; £3.50. The Empire Exhibition of 1938 was held in this spreading park, which includes a Victorian walled garden and sweeping lawns.

Hunterian Art Gallery (Hillhead St) Dr Hunter bequeathed the core of fine paintings which form the basis of this beautifully hung collection. A grand range of works by Whistler, interesting and well chosen contemporary british art and sculpture, and an amazing re-creation of the home of Charles Rennie Mackintosh (cl 12.30-1.30pm), the designer/architect whose exuberant yet very disciplined and clean-lined art nouveau buildings stand out among the more traditional solidity of much of Glasgow. Shop, disabled access with prior notice; cl Sun; (0141) 330 5431; free.

Hunterian Museum (Gilbert Scott building, University Ave) Scotland's first public museum, housing the university collections of ethnographic, palaeontological and anthropological material, along with lots of archaeology, and a coin display. Shop, disabled access; cl Sun, public hols and 24 Dec-2 Jan; (0141) 330 4221; free. The exhibitions were also founded by Dr William Hunter, the 18th-c physician (see above).

Lighthouse (11 Mitchell Lane) One of the largest temporary exhibition spaces for architecture and design in Europe, with four exhibition floors, and a permanent Mackintosh Interpretation Centre with interactive displays and models - good views over the city from the Mackintosh Tower. Restaurants, cafés, shops, disabled access; cl Sun am, 25-26 Dec, 1-2 Jan; free, £3 for Mackintosh Centre and tower. The interesting Horseshoe (round the corner in Drury St) has cheap food upstairs.

McLellan Galleries (Sauchiehall St) Spacious and well lit, these are giving a temporary home to some of the Glasgow Art Gallery's great collection (particularly strong in Impressionists and Post-Impressionists, as well as scottish artists), while that is closed for renovation. Snacks, shop, disabled access; cl Mon, 25-26 Dec, 1-2 Jan; (0141) 332 7521; free.

Merchant City The area around George Sq and Buchanan St was built on a grid plan in the 19th c, and visually has something in common with New York City - Americans say they feel at home here. With its proud Victorian buildings cleaned back to their warm sandstone, this smart shopping quarter is the city's most comfortable area to stroll around. The City Chambers here is a spectacular monument to 1880s civic pride, marble everywhere; free tours. The Counting House is a splendid pub in an opulent converted bank nearby. There are café-bars and bistros off Princes Sq, and antiques stalls in Victorian Village (W Regent St). On the SE edge of this area, between Gallowgate and London Rd past the Tolbooth, the Barras (barrows) is an entertaining wknd flea-market. With around 800 stalls it's one of the biggest covered markets in the world, great for bargains or just passing time; try the plump fresh clappie doos (mussels).

Museum of Transport (Kelvin Hall, Bunhouse Rd) Plenty of vehicles for the enthusiast, from trams to ships; a walk-through car showroom is arranged as if some were for sale, with original prices displayed on the windscreens. Meals, snacks, shop, disabled access; cl 25-26, 31 Dec, 1-2 Jan; (0141) 287 2720; free.

Museum quarter NW of the centre, the West End, Kelvingrove and the University quarter have some elegant streets, the main concentration of museums, and the botanic gardens.

People's Palace (Glasgow Green) Very enjoyable social history museum looking at Glaswegians over the centuries, in a park just SE of centre. Shop; disabled access; cl 25-26 Dec, 1-2 Jan; (0141) 5540 223; free. The museum's café is in the adjacent Winter Gardens, a massive conservatory with huge tropical plants.

Provan's Lordship (Castle St) Glasgow's oldest house, used by the Prebend of Provan - a canon of the cathedral. Dating from 1471, this sole survivor of the 32 prebendal houses which used to stand around the cathedral has been carefully restored and furnished according to several period styles. Cl 25-26 Dec, 1-2 Jan; (0141) 552 8819; free.

Scotland Street School Museum Designed by Mackintosh, this spectacular building originally had a capacity of 1,250 pupils in 21 classrooms, and now houses a lively museum with displays on the history of education in Scotland from 1872, and reconstructed classrooms: Victorian, World War II, and 1950s-60s, also an Edwardian cookery room. Displays also show the architectural history of the school and Mackintosh's designs, and the history of the school and local area inc interactive displays and a photographic database. Audio-visual, activity programme and temporary exhibitions. Cl 25-26, 31 Dec, 1-2 Jan; (0141) 287 0500; free.

Scottish Football Museum 🖾 (Hampden Park) This enjoyably covers such themes as football's origins, women's football, fans, other games influenced by football, even some social history too. Lots of memorabilia (inc the world's oldest football ticket), audio-visual and hands-on displays, and they've reconstructed the 1903 changing room and press box from the original stadium. Best to book for the 45-min guided tours. Snacks, shop, disabled access; cl match days and for special events, and a few days over Christmas, phone to check; (0141) 616 6100; £5, stadium tour £5, combined ticket £7.50. For more of not quite the same, you can also tour the clubs: Celtic (0141) 551430; or Rangers (0870) 600 1972.

St Mungo Museum of Religious Life (Cathedral Precinct) Unique collection of art from all the world's major religions - and some rather obscure ones too. Everything from an egyptian mummy mask to Dali's *Christ of St John of the Cross*, and in the grounds Britain's only permanent Zen garden. Meals, snacks, shop, disabled access; cl 25-26 Dec, 1-2 Jan; (0141) 553 2557; free.

Tall Ship 🖾 (Glasgow Harbour, Stobcross Rd) Late 19th-c sailing ship, *Glenlee*, one of only five Clyde-built

sailing ships still afloat; an interactive exhibition tells her story. The adjacent pumphouse houses a gallery, shop and café. Disabled access; cl 25-26 Dec, 1-2 Jan; (0141) 222 2513; £4.50.

Tenement House (145 Buccleuch St) One-floor late 19th-c flat well worth a visit for its vivid impression of life for many Glaswegians a century ago. The same woman lived here from 1911 to 1965 and in that time scarcely changed a thing; its time-capsule quality was preserved by a subsequent owner, and then the flat, still with its original furnishings and fittings, was left to the National Trust for Scotland. Cl Nov-Mar and ams; (0141) 333 0183; £3.50; NTS.

University of Glasgow Visitor Centre (University Ave) Interactive displays on the history and life of the university (founded in 1451), with tours around some of its grander features, such as the Lion and Unicorn Staircase, Bute and Randolph Halls and Memorial Chapel. Snacks, shop, disabled access; (0141) 330 5511; cl Christmas-New Year and Sun.

Greenbank Garden (Flenders Rd, Clarkston, off A726) Aims to encourage and help owners of small gardens, so has lots of different shrubs and flowers to spark ideas, and horticultural advice. Also garden and greenhouse designed to meet the needs of disabled gardeners. Summer teas, shop, disabled access; cl 25-26 Dec, 1-2 Jan; (0141) 616 5126; *£3.50; NTS.

Linn Park (Cathcart/Castlemilk) Lots to do - riverside walks, nature trails, golf course, as well as a ruined 14th-c castle, an adventure playground for the disabled (prior arrangement preferred), and an equestrian centre; (0141) 637 3096. Visitor centre open most wknd pms; (0141) 637 1147; free.

Mugdock Country Park (N Glasgow) Good strolling ground, with two castle ruins, a view over Glasgow, and an attractive loch.

Rouken Glen Park (Thornliebank) A place of great tranquil beauty, with a walled garden, gorgeous lawns, and woodland walks to a waterfall at the head of the glen.

Victoria Park (Victoria Park Drive N) Tree-lined park where the remains in the Fossil Grove, some of them 330 million years old, were discovered by workmen digging a path in the late 19th c.

West Highland Way Level walks from Milngavie can take in the early stages of the West Highland Way, which starts here (the appropriately named West Highland Gate is a busy dining pub). The determined can press on along glen routes all the way up to Fort William - the scenery getting better all the way.

GLENLUCE NX1858

Glenluce Abbey Ruined Cistercian abbey founded in the late 12th c, in beautiful surroundings. Limited disabled access; cl winter Sun am, cl winter wkdys; (01581) 300541; £1.80; HS.

GORDON NT6439

Mellerstain House (just W, off A6089) William and Robert Adam both worked on this striking Georgian house, which has impressive plasterwork and furnishings, and paintings by Van Dyck and Gainsborough. Every great house in Scotland seems to have something that belonged to Bonnie Prince Charlie - this one has his bagpipes. Very pleasant terraced gardens and parkland, with fine views towards the distant hills. Snacks, shop, disabled access to ground floor only; cl ams, Tues, Sat and Nov-Mar; (01573) 410225; £5.50.

GREENOCK CUT NS2472

Part of an elaborate abandoned water scheme for Greenock below, this allows a level walk meandering around a hillside terrace giving views into the Highlands.

GRETNA GREEN NY3167

Old Blacksmith's Shop It's now tourists rather than runaway couples that flock to the 19th-c Old Blacksmith's Shop in this little Borders village. More people come here than to any other scottish attraction outside Edinburgh, despite the fact that there's really very little to see. An exhibition centre looks at the once thriving marriage business. Cl 25-26 Dec, 1 Jan; (01461) 338224; £2.

GREY MARE'S TAIL NT1814

Spectacular waterfalls, a pretty walk from the A708 car park NE of Moffat, up a narrow glen. You can continue beyond them along Tail Burn to Loch Skeen.

HADDINGTON NT5173

A pretty market town, with an impressive late medieval parish church; the comfortable George and Maitlandfield House hotels, and the aptly named Waterside Inn (over a pedestrianised 16th-c bridge), all have above-average food.

Lennoxlove 🏛 (B6369 S) With a 15th-c core and additions in every century since, this was bequeathed its unusual name by the Duchess of Lennox (La Belle Stewart), in memory of her husband. Among reminders of other members of her family are the casket and death mask of Mary Queen of Scots. In the grounds the Cadzow herd of white park cattle are said to be descended from the sacrificial cattle of the Druids. Meals, snacks, disabled access; cl ams, Mon-Tues, Fri-Sat and Nov-Easter; (01620) 823720; £4.25.

HAWICK NT5014

Drumlanrig's Tower (Towerknowe) Fearsome-looking 16th-c tower with state-of-the-art displays of Borders history, some quite gripping. Shop, disabled access; cl Sun am and Oct-Mar; (01450) 377615; £2.50.

Hawick Museum and Scott Art Gallery (Wilton Lodge Park) Museum boosted by its appealing setting in a park with riverside walks and gardens, also newish craft and archaeology exhibitions. Shop, disabled access to ground floor; cl 12-1pm, am wkdys and Sun and all day Sat Oct-Mar, 8-9 Jun, 25 Dec-3 Jan; (01450) 373457; free.

HERMITAGE NY4995

Hermitage Castle Almost perfect from the outside, the well restored but very forbidding remains of a 14th-c Borders stronghold reeking of dire deeds. Shop, limited disabled access; cl Sun am, Thurs pm and Fri in Oct, and Nov-Apr; (01387) 376222; £2; HS.

INNERLEITHEN NT3336

Robert Smail's Printing Works (High St) Fully restored Victorian printer's shop, with water-powered press; you can try your hand at metal typesetting and hand-print your own bookmark. Shop, limited disabled access; cl Tues-Weds; (01896) 830206; £3.50; NTS. The Traquair Arms is the place to eat.

IRVINE NS2740

Big Idea 🏛 (Harbour St) In a huge sand-dune-shaped building on the tip of the Ardeer Peninsula, this giant inventors' workshop celebrates a century of Nobel Laureates as well as previous creations and innovations. A pedestrian drawbridge leads you to a vast array of inventions from life-saving machines to utterly ridiculous contraptions, and hundreds of exhibits with which you can interact thanks to a specially designed electronic key. You're actively encouraged to come up with your own inventions, and best of all, after testing them out, you get to take the end product home. Meals, snacks, shop, disabled access; cl Mon-Tues in winter; (08708) 404030; £7.95.

Scottish Maritime Museum 🎨 (Gottries Rd) Down by the harbour, very much a working museum, with lots of restoration work on the good range of historic vessels. Snacks, shop, some disabled access (not to boats); (01294) 278283; £2.50. The nearby Keys has decent food (all day wknds).

Vennel Gallery 🎨 (Glasgow Vennel, off Townhead) Art gallery and museum, and behind, a reconstruction of the Heckling Shop where, as a young man, an unwilling Burns tried to learn the filthy trade of flax dressing. Happily for him, during a New Year's Eve party his aunt knocked over a candle and burnt the building to ashes. Shop, disabled access; cl 1-2pm and Mon-Thurs; (01294) 275059; free.

JEDBURGH NT6420

Castle Jail and Museum (Castlegate) Local history museum. Shop, snacks, disabled access; cl Oct-Mar; (01835) 863254; £2.

Jedburgh Abbey The most complete of the ruined 12th-c Borders monasteries founded by David I, and an impressive sight despite its town setting. Imposing 26-metre (86-ft) tower, splendid W door, and audio-visual show in visitor centre. Snacks, shops, disabled access; cl Sun am Oct-Mar, 25-26 Dec, 1-2 Jan; (01835) 863925; £3.50; HS. The Pheasant has good food (and makes a point of having good value pheasant in season). Just off the A68 S of town are the mainly 16th-c ruins of Ferniehurst Castle.

Mary Queen of Scots House (Queen St) Charming 16th-c fortified dwelling where Mary had to prolong her 1566 stay because of a near-mortal fever (she was later to say she wished she'd died here). There's a good interpretation of her life. Shop; cl Dec to mid-Mar; (01835) 863331; £3.

KELSO NT7035

Floors Castle 🎨 (1m NW) Magnificent building designed by William Adam in 1721, and much embellished in the next century. It's reputed to be Scotland's biggest inhabited house, with a window for every day of the year. Splendid collection of tapestries and french furniture, and wonderful walled garden (best July-Sept). Shop, good home-made meals and snacks, disabled access; cl end Oct-Mar; (01573) 223333; £5.75.

Kelso Abbey The greatest and wealthiest of the four famous Borders abbeys, though today not much of the building remains. Cobbles (Beaumont St) and the Queens Head (Bridge St) have good value food.

KILMARNOCK NS4339

Dean Castle (off Glasgow Rd) A magnificent collection of restored buildings dating from the 1350s. For 400 years it was the stronghold of the Boyds of Kilmarnock, and today it shows off important collections of arms and armour, musical instruments, tapestries and Burns's manuscripts. It's surrounded by 80 hectares (200 acres) of woodland, with nature trails, deer park, riding and other activities. Snacks, shop; admission by guided tour (pms) only; (01563) 522702; free. The 18th-c Wheatsheaf in the pretty village of Symington on the other side of town has good original food.

KIPPFORD NX8355

Charming yachting place, usually plenty to watch in summer. The Anchor here is good.

LANGBANK NS3673

Finlaystone (A8, 1m W) Some say the garden here is the finest in Scotland - formal and walled, with woodland walks, adventure playgrounds, and picnic areas. The house has connections with Robert Burns and John Knox (unlikely partners), and there's a visitor centre (cl mid-week in winter) with displays on the Clan Macmillan and Celtic art. Tearoom, shop; gardens open all year; (01475) 540505; £3. The modern Langbank Lodge nearby has sensibly priced food (inc afternoon tea and scones) and incredible Clyde views.

LARGS NS2059

The pick of the traditional Clydeside resorts, with boats across the narrow strip of water to the island of Great Cumbrae. The pleasure steamer *Waverley* calls here in summer, and Nardinis (Esplanade) is a vintage tearoom - or rather tea palace, with acres of immaculate tables and smartly aproned motherly waitresses.

Vikingar! (Barrfields Centre, Greenock Rd) Lively look at the Vikings in Scotland, from their arrival to their defeat at the Battle of Largs. Very much an 'experience', with lots of interactive displays, and a multi-media show as the centrepiece. There's an adjacent swimming pool, play area, theatre and cinema. Meals, snacks, shop, disabled access; cl Dec-Jan and wkdys Nov and Feb; (01475) 689777; £4.

LAUDER NT5347

Thirlestane Castle (off A68 and A697) Stately yet charming castle with restored assemblage of pictures, interesting collection of old toys (some of which children can touch), some outstanding plasterwork in the 17th-c state rooms, woodland walk and picnic areas. There's an adventure playground and dungeon display. Meals, snacks, shop; cl Sat and Nov-Easter; (01578) 722430; £5.50. The Eagle and Lauderdale Hotel are useful for lunch.

LINLITHGOW NT0580

Blackness Castle Built in the 1440s, massively strengthened in the 16th-c as an artillery fortress (walls up to 5.5 metres, 18 ft, thick), ship-shaped waterside Blackness served as an ammunition depot in the 1870s. You can walk along the top of some of the walls, and climb up to the roof of the central tower. Cl Thurs pm, all day Fri and Sun am Nov-Mar; £2.20; (01506) 834807; HS.

House of the Binns (3m E, off A904) The battlemented home of the Dalyell family since 1621, with some splendid plaster ceilings and a fine collection of furniture and porcelain. Limited disabled access (some of the best parts are upstairs); cl pms, Fri and Oct-May; (01506) 834255; £5; NTS.

Linlithgow Palace The birthplace of Mary Queen of Scots, a magnificently sombre lochside ruin. You can still see the chapel, great hall and a quadrangle with an impressive fountain. Shop, limited disabled access, cl 25-26 Dec and 1-2 Jan; (01506) 842896; £3; HS. In the town a pleasant old tavern, the Four Marys, is named for her maids-in-waiting Mary Carmichael, Mary Hamilton, Mary Beaton and Mary Seaton, with relevant memorabilia.

Linlithgow Story (High St) Local history museum. Shop; cl Sun am, Nov-Easter; (01506) 670677; £1.

LIVINGSTON NT0366

Almond Valley Heritage Centre 🆓 (off A705) Excellent and innovative museum packed full of things to prod, sniff, shake and discover (it has a laboratory area specially for children), plus working farm and watermill, play areas, narrow-gauge railway and trailer rides. Meals, snacks and picnic area, shop, disabled access; cl 25-26 Dec, 1-2 Jan; (01506) 414957; *£3.

LOCHWINNOCH NS3558

Castle Semple Nature Reserve 🆓 (A760) RSPB nature reserve in beautiful countryside, with fine views, good woodland and marsh nature trails, wildlife garden, a viewing area with telescopes and binoculars, and three observation hides. Snacks, shop, disabled access; cl 24-25 Dec, 1-2 Jan; (01505) 842663; *£2. The Brown Bull does wholesome bar lunches.

MELROSE NT5034

Abbotsford House (B6360 3m W) Set grandly on the River Tweed, this was the home of Sir Walter Scott until his death in 1832. You can still see his mammoth 9,000-volume library, and several of the historical oddities he liked to collect, like Rob Roy's sporran. Snacks, shop, disabled access; cl Nov to mid-Mar; (01896) 752043; £4.

Eildon Hills Above the town, these are splendidly compact, giving a very pleasing ridge walk along the top.

Melrose Abbey The ruins are among the finest in the country - best in moonlight, as Scott says (though he admitted he never saw them thus himself). Look out for the wonderful stonework on the 14th-c nave (and the pig playing the bagpipes).

Archaeological investigations now leave little doubt that this was the burial place of Robert the Bruce's heart. Shop; limited disabled access; cl Sun am Oct-Mar, 25-26 Dec, 1-2 Jan; (01896) 822562; £3.50; HS. Just opposite are good views of the abbey and Eildon Hills from Harmony Garden (St Mary St), a tranquil walled garden around an early 19th-c house.

Priorwood Garden 🚹 (Abbey St) Specialises in flowers suitable for drying, with a herb garden, woodland area and orchard with apples through the ages. Snacks, shop, disabled access; cl Sun am and Jan to mid-Apr; (01896) 822493; *£2.50; NTS.

MERVINSLAW NT6713

Jedforest Deer & Farm Park (A68) Working farm with different breeds of deer as well as other animals inc hawks, owls and rare breeds. Good for children, and peaceful trails nearby. Also ranger-led activities and walks. Snacks, shop, disabled access; cl Nov-mid-Apr; (01835) 840364; £4.

MOTHERWELL NS7456

M & D's Theme Park In over two square miles of parkland, this is Scotland's biggest theme park, with more than 40 rides and attractions, and a large indoor entertainment complex (cl 25 Dec, 1 Jan), a bowling alley (£3.50), play area and arcade games. Meals, snacks, shop, disabled access; cl Nov-Mar; (01698) 333777; £12.50 for a day's wristband with unlimited rides.

MULL OF GALLOWAY NX1530 Beautifully unspoilt, Scotland's SW toe; good coastal walking.

MUSSELBURGH NT3272

Newhailes House 🚹 (A6095 W) Once home to the influential Dalrymple family, this 17th-c house with its impressive rococo interiors and fine furnishings has recently been carefully conserved 'as found' rather than restored, leaving textiles faded and paint chipped - it's the cultural equivalent of wearing white socks to ask why the £12 million five-year project hasn't left everything pristine. Once the largest in Scotland, the library drew praise from Dr Johnson (the books, currently in storage at the National Library, should be returned

after further conservation work). The 32-hectare (80-acre) grounds are being restored too, and an old stable block has a visitor centre (free). Snacks, shop, disabled access; cl ams, Tues-Weds and Nov-Mar; (0131) 653 5599; pre-booked guided tours £7; NTS.

NEW ABBEY NX9562

Criffel This summit gives walkers an astonishing view of the english Lake District over the Solway Firth.

New Abbey Corn Mill Restored 18th-c corn mill; shop; cl 1-2pm all year, plus Thurs pm, Fri and Sun am Oct-Mar, 25-26 Dec, 1-2 Jan; (01387) 850260; £2.80; HS.

Shambellie House of Costume (A710 just N) Dazzling displays of costume, thoughtfully arranged in appropriately furnished rooms of mid-19th-c scottish baronial house. Snacks, shop; cl Nov-Mar; (01387) 850375; £2.50.

Sweetheart Abbey (A710) One of the area's most romantic ruins, with a lofty arched nave open to the sky, and a touching story attached. Shop; cl Thurs pm and Sun Oct-Mar, 25-26 Dec, 1-2 Jan; (01387) 850397; £1.80; HS. The village around it is appealing, and the Abbey Arms has a good lunchtime menu.

NEW LANARK NS8842 (off A73) Now a UNESCO World Heritage site, this has enough to keep families amused for a good chunk of the day. Dramatically located and Scotland's best example of an industrial village, it was founded in 1785 by mill owner and social pioneer Robert Owen. Many of the old millworkers' buildings (showing living conditions of the 1820s and 1930s) have been interestingly converted to modern accommodation, and there's a hotel in a renovated 18th-c cotton mill (01555) 667200, so the place has the feel of a living village rather than a museum. Re-created interiors include a village store, Robert Owen's house, a millworker's house, and Robert Owen's school, where a theatre show tells the story of millgirl Annie McLeod. The visitor centre has a time travel ride. The village can be busy at wknds. Meals, snacks, shop, disabled access; cl 25 Dec, 1 Jan; £5.95. In Lanark itself the Crown (Hope

St) has a decent restaurant.

Falls of Clyde The countryside here is spectacular, with a short walk snaking around river cliffs through a verdant gorge to these falls that used to power the mill. A visitor centre here has lots of information on badgers; (01555) 665262; cl before 11am (midday in winter), and 25 Dec. The falls are dramatic when the hydro-electric station upriver opens the sluices.

NEWTONGRANGE NT3363

Scottish Mining Museum 🏛 (Lady Victoria Colliery, A7, Newtongrange) Easy to spend an interesting half-day here, exploring the highs and lows of the scottish coal industry on two floors of displays, interactives and magic helmets, plus audio tour of the old mine workings interspersed with short films, and a coal face mock-up explained by an ex-miner; play area. Good value meals and home-baked snacks, good shop, disabled access; cl 25 Dec, 1 Jan; (0131) 663 7519; *£4.

NORTH BERWICK NT5585

Prettily sited resort on the sands of the Firth of Forth, a holiday destination for nearly 200 years. Excellent shoreside walks along the sands between here and Aberlady, with stop-off possibilities at Dirleton and Gullane; seaside walks are helped by the good bus service connecting all the shoreside villages between here and Edinburgh, though the hinterland is dull. The arch topping volcanic Berwick Law is a whale's jaw.

Boat Trips Readers enjoy the boat trips from the harbour, for instance to see the puffins on Craigleith, go round the 105-metre (345-ft) gannet-whitened cliffs of the Bass Rock, or perhaps land on Fidra.

Scottish Seabird Centre (North Berwick Harbour) Each year over 150,000 seabirds (inc the largest colony of gannets in the world) return to the islands off this town, and remote cameras in the centre let you see the birds and wildlife up close in comfort; telescope deck, auditorium. Shop, café with wonderful views across the islands of Forth, disabled access; cl 25 Dec; (01620) 890202; £4.95.

Tantallon Castle (off A198 3m E) Formidable coastal stronghold of the Douglases, mentioned by Scott in his poem *Marmion*. From the clifftop the red-walled ruins look across the Firth of Forth to the Bass Rock, making it one of the most majestically sited castles in Scotland; cl Thurs pm and Fri in winter, 25-26 Dec, 1-2 Jan; (01620) 892727; £3; HS.

OLD DAILLY NS2401

Bargany Gardens (Old Dailly) Fine ornamental trees, woodland walks, rock garden and a lily pond enveloped by azaleas and rhododendrons; plants for sale. Mostly disabled access; open May only; (01465) 871249; *£2. The Kings Arms over at Barr (a pretty drive) has enjoyable food.

PAISLEY NS4863

Coats Observatory (High St) Displays on astronomy, meteorology and space flight. Shop, cl 1-2pm, and Mon (exc bank hols), best to check for Christmas opening; (0141) 889 2013; free.

Paisley Museum and Art Gallery (High St) Paisley is not just a place but a pattern, so as well as a very wide range of 19th-c art, the appealing museum has a marvellous collection of antique and more modern paisley shawls, along with the looms on which they were made. Shop, some disabled access; cl Sun am and all Mon (exc bank hols), 25-26 Dec, 1-2 Jan; (0141) 889 3151; free. The Anchor (Glasgow Rd) does decent lunches.

Sma' Shot Cottages You can see two distinct periods in the town's weaving history at this unusual museum. Guides take you around a fully restored and furnished mid-18th-c weaver's cottage, and then across the yard to a row of three cottages, showing what life was like in the 1940s. They've a working loom (occasional demonstrations), and a local history display. Tearoom, shop selling locally produced crafts, limited disabled access; cl Oct-Mar, Sun-Tues and Fri and ams ; (0141) 889 1708; free.

PATNA NS4308

Dunaskin Heritage Centre 🏛 (Dalmellington Rd) Well preserved Victorian ironworks (employing up to 1,400 people at its 19th-c peak) in attractive rolling countryside, with a period cottage, reconstructed manager's office, industrial machinery, an audio-visual show about Ayrshire life in the 19th and early 20th c, fun play area based around the principles of an iron furnace, and nature trails around the site. Meals, snacks, shop, disabled access; cl Nov-Mar; (01292) 531144; £4.50.

PAXTON NT9352

Paxton House (B6461) Built in 1758 by the love-struck Patrick Billie, who hoped to marry an aristocrat at the court of Frederick the Great; the marriage never took place, but the result was a splendid neo-Palladian mansion, designed and later embellished by the Adam family, and furnished by the Chippendales; 18th-c german/prussian costume display. Also woodland and riverside walks, highland cattle, and adventure playground designed by the Territorial Army. Meals, snacks, shop, disabled access; house cl Nov-Mar but grounds open all year; (01289) 386291; £6, £3 gardens only. Cantys Brig towards Berwick has good food.

PEEBLES NT2540

Attractive if sedate Borders town, with quite a lot for visitors; the Tontine Hotel (High St) and Park Hotel (Innerleithen Rd) do good bar lunches.

Kailzie (B7062, 2m SE) Extensive grounds with lovely old trees flanked by azaleas and rhododendrons, formal rose garden, walled garden, trout pond and small art gallery; also children's play area. Meals, snacks, shop, some disabled access; restaurant and gallery cl Nov-mid-Mar; (01721) 720007; £2.50 (£2 Oct-Apr).

Neidpath Castle (off A72 just W) Spectacularly set, converted from the original 14th-c tower in the late 16th and early 17th c. There's a rock-hewn well, small museum (children like the mummified rat), period kitchen, and a pit prison - not much chance of escape, as some of the walls are 3½ metres (11 ft) thick. Super views from the parapets. Shop; cl am Sun and all mid-Sept to Easter; (01721) 720333; £3.

PENICUIK NT2360

Edinburgh Crystal Visitor Centre (Eastfield) Demonstrations of glass-blowing, cutting and engraving, with an exhibition on the crystal's history. Meals, snacks, shop, disabled access;

tours daily, cl 25-26 Dec, 1-2 Jan; (01968) 675128; £3.50. The Horseshoe out on the Peebles road is a civilised dining pub.

PENTLAND HILLS NT1558

Within easy reach of Edinburgh, genuine uplands with some good high-level walks and attractive reservoirs.

PORT LOGAN NX0942

Logan Botanic Garden 🏛 (off B7065) A specialist garden of the Royal Botanic Garden of Edinburgh, with a wide range of plants from the warm temperate regions of the southern hemisphere. Meals, snacks, shop, plant sales; cl Nov-Feb; (01776) 860231; *£3.50. The village itself has a natural sea pool where fat fish will eat from your fingers; the Inn does good food. Great sunsets here.

PORTPATRICK NX9954

Attractive harbour town, usually with something going on down by the water, and good food in the waterside Crown.

PRESTONPANS NT3874

Industrial Heritage Museum (B1348 Prestongrange Rd) Based around the oldest documented coal mining site in Britain. Steam and diesel locomotives, a Cornish beam engine, and displays on other local industries, from brick and pipe making to brewing and weaving. Lots going on, esp at wknds, and family workshops during the summer. Snacks, shop, some disabled access; cl late Oct-Mar (may be open Christmas week); (0131) 653 2904; free.

RHINNS OF GALLOWAY NX0650

This hammerhead of land in the extreme W of the area is largely empty even in high summer, a very peaceful place, with cliffs (especially on the S point), rocks and small coves.

RHINNS OF KELLS NX7274

This ridge has energetic hill walking from Forrest Lodge NW of New Galloway.

ROCKCLIFFE NX8453

Attractive yachting village, with a good peaceful walk to Castle Hill Point headland, and beyond by vast stretches of tidal sands. The Clonyard House at Colvend has good value food.

SELKIRK NT4227

Bowhill House (off A708, 3m W)

Outstanding collection of paintings, inc works by Canaletto, Van Dyck, Gainsborough and Claude, as well as impressive furnishings and porcelain, and memorabilia relating to Scott and Queen Victoria. Also restored Victorian kitchen, adventure playground, very active little theatre, and surrounding country park. Snacks, shop, disabled access; grounds cl am, all Fri (exc in July), and all Sept-late Apr; house open daily July only; (01750) 22204; *£6.

Selkirk Glass (off A7 just N) Demonstrations of paperweight-making. Meals, snacks, factory shop, disabled access; cl 25-26 Dec, 1-2 Jan and the day of the Selkirk Common Ridings; (01750) 20954; free.

Sir Walter Scott's Courtroom (Market Pl) Low-key exhibition on Sir Walter Scott in the former courtroom where, as sheriff, he dispensed justice to the people of Selkirk. Shop, limited disabled access; cl Sun am Oct and Sun Sept-Apr; (01750) 20761; free. The decorous town is good for bargain-hunting for the tweeds, woollens and cashmeres which are woven and knitted here; the Queens Head has freshly cooked food.

SMAILHOLM NT6334

Smailholm Tower (just S, signed off the B6404 NE of St Boswells) Classic 15th-c Borders tower house, very well preserved - all 17 metres (57 ft) of it. Display based on Scott's book *Minstrels of the Borders*, and an exhibition of dolls. Shop, limited disabled access; cl wkdays in winter; (01573) 460365; £2.20; HS.

SOUTH QUEENSFERRY NT1378 Notable for its views of the two great Forth bridges on either side, with piers to potter on; the Hawes Inn, famous from *Kidnapped*, is still going strong, and the Two Bridges has a pleasant conservatory restaurant looking up to the bridges. A well signposted cycle track links North Queensferry (over the bridge) to Edinburgh.

Dalmeny House (B924, 3m E) Despite its Tudor Gothic appearance, this splendidly placed house dates only from the 19th c - it has a superb hammer-beamed roof, as well as fine furnishings, porcelain and portraits.

Good walks in the grounds and on the shore. Snacks; open Sun-Tues pms in May and July-Aug; (0131) 331 1888; £4. In Dalmeny Norman St Cuthbert's church is well preserved and interesting.

Hopetoun House (off B904, 2m W) This huge place is probably Scotland's best and certainly most palatial example of the work of William and Robert Adam. The magnificent reception rooms have a remarkable art collection with works by Canaletto and Gainsborough, while the superb grounds include a deer park and a flock of rare sheep. The rooftop gives wonderful views. Meals, snacks, shop, some disabled access; cl Oct-Mar; (0131) 331 2451; £6, £3.50 grounds only.

Inchcolm Abbey Much-raided medieval ruins on a memorable island site in the Firth, reached by a 30-min ferry trip from South Queensferry; also from North Queensferry, weather permitting; cl Nov-Mar; (0131) 331 4857; £11 inc ferry; HS.

ST MARY'S LOCH NT2320 A pretty spot for walks, tracked by the Southern Upland Way along its E shore; the Tibbie Shiels Inn is a handy stop.

STOBO NT1534

Dawyck Botanic Garden (B712) Another specialist garden of the Royal Botanic Garden, particularly noted for its arboretum rich in mature conifers (inc a larch believed to have been planted in 1725), with notable asiatic silver firs and many rarities. Snacks, shop; cl 18 Nov-13 Feb; (01721) 760254; *£3.

STRANRAER NX0760

Castle Kennedy Gardens (A75, 4m E) Prettily set between two lochs (with lots of good walks around), these gardens were first laid out in the early 18th c, then after years of neglect were restored and developed in the 19th. They're particularly admired for their walled garden, rhododendron collection and flowering shrubs. Snacks, shop, limited disabled access; cl Oct-Mar; (01776) 702024; £3.

TARBOLTON NS4327

Bachelor's Club (off A77 S of Kilmarnock, and off A76, 7½m NE of Ayr) 17th-c thatched house where Burns and his friends formed a debating club in 1780. Shop; cl ams, Wed-Thurs and Oct-Mar; (01292) 541940; £2.50; NTS. The Wheatsheaf over at Symington has good food.

THORNHILL NX8599
Drumlanrig Castle (off A76)
Spectacular almost theatrical pink sandstone mansion built in the late 17th c, with a glory of fine panelling and furnishings (mainly Louis XIV), and splendid paintings by Holbein, Rembrandt and Murillo - in August 2003 thieves walked out with one possibly by Leonardo da Vinci; you can see what's said to be Bonnie Prince Charlie's campaign kettle. Also craft workshops, adventure playground, peacocks wandering over the lawn, working forge, and extensive woodland walks. Meals, snacks, shop, disabled access; castle cl Sun am, and Sept-Apr, grounds cl Oct-Apr; (01848) 330248; £6. In Thornhill the comfortable Buccleuch & Queensberry has good value food.

TRAQUAIR NT3336
Traquair House (B709) The oldest inhabited house in Scotland and possibly the whole UK; no fewer than 27 english and scottish kings have stayed here, starting with Alexander I in 1107. The Bear Gates have remained closed since 1745 when Bonnie Prince Charlie passed through them for the last time - they won't open again unless the Stewarts regain their place on the throne. It's an enticing pile, and particularly popular with our contributors, with plenty to see. As well as the house and gardens, there's an 18th-c brewery (still producing tasty beers), brewery museum (and shop), antiques and craft shops, and also a maze and substantial adventure playground. Meals, snacks, shop, some disabled access; cl Jan-Mar and Nov-Dec (exc for pre-booked parties); (01896) 830323; £5.60, grounds only £2.50.

UDDINGSTON NS6960
Bothwell Castle Picturesquely set and extensive 14th-c ruin by the river, once the finest stone castle in the country and virtually impregnable; shop; cl Thurs pm, all day Fri and Sun am Oct-Mar; (01698) 816894; £2.20; HS.

WANLOCKHEAD NS8713
Museum of Lead Mining (B797) Guided tours of an 18th-c lead mine, heritage trail and miners' cottages furnished in the styles of 1740 and 1890. You can have a go at panning for gold. Meals, snacks, shop, limited disabled access; cl Nov-1 April; (01659) 74387; £4.95. This remote village is Scotland's highest.

WHITHORN NX4736
Isle of Whithorn Picturesque harbour with boat trips and lots of yachtsmen: the Steam Packet has good local fish.
Whithorn Dig Scotland's first-recorded Christian settlement was established here by St Ninian 1,500 years ago. Archaeologists have been hard at work investigating the several churches which preceded the ruined 13th-c priory you can see today: the excellent visitor centre and museum have plenty of the finds, with some fine Celtic crosses. Shop, disabled access; museum and visitor centre cl Nov-Easter (though you can still wander round the priory ruins then); (01988) 500508; £2.70; HS.
Other attractive places with decent pubs include Ancrum NT6325, Gifford NT5368, Kirkcowan NX3260, Kirkcudbright NX6851 (particularly enjoyable), Lilliesleaf NT5325, Larkhall NS7651, Old Kilpatrick NS4673, Sorn NS5526, Straiton NS3804 and Symington NS3831.
Some **Clydeside pubs** with decent food and good sea views include the Cardwell at Cardwell Bay in Gourock NS2477 and the Spinnaker there, and the Lookout in Troon Marina NS3230.
Others with a decent bite to eat and particularly well placed for walkers, drivers or just strollers in these parts include the Murray Arms, Masons Arms and Angel at Gatehouse of Fleet NX5956, Golf Hotel and Old Clubhouse at Gullane NT4882, Breadalbane Hotel at Kildonan NS0231, Swan at Kingholm Quay NX9773, Border at Kirk Yetholm NT8328, Gordon Arms at Mountbenger NT3125 and Buccleuch Arms at St Boswells NT5931.

Where to eat

CROSSMICHAEL NX7366 **Plumed Horse** *Main St (01556) 670333* In an unremarkable building, this simply but attractively decorated restaurant offers perfectly timed and presented modern cooking with quite an emphasis on absolutely fresh fish; especially good value set lunch, charming service, and a short wine list; cl Mon, Sat am, Sun pm; well behaved children welcome, disabled access. £41

EAST LINTON NT5977 **Drovers** *5 Bridge St (01620) 860298* Comfortable 18th-c inn with prints and pictures for sale, cosy armchairs, a basket of logs by the woodburner, hops around the bar, very good interesting food (more elaborate in the evening), a good range of real ales, and partly no smoking upstairs restaurant. £22|£7

EDINBURGH NT2473 **Atrium** *10 Cambridge St (0131) 228 8882* Next to Usher Hall and Traverse Theatre, unusually modern restaurant with wire sculptures, railway sleepers, dim lighting from glass torches, cheerful friendly staff, interesting wine list, and very good imaginative modern scottish food - lunchtime two-course set menu, too; cl Sat am, Sun (except during Festival), Christmas and New Year; disabled access. £45|£9

EDINBURGH NT2776 **Fishers** *1 Shore (0131) 554 5666* Bustling, lively bistro overlooking the Leith waterfront, with an informal, friendly atmosphere, a dark bar with a few tables and bar counter, and light airy dining room; exceptionally good imaginative fish dishes, enjoyable straightforwardish puddings, a well chosen fairly priced wine list, and genuinely helpful, quick, cheerful service; cl 25-26 Dec, 1 Jan. £32|£12

EDINBURGH NT2672 **Kalpna Indian Restaurant** *2-3 St Patrick Sq (0131) 667 9890* Extremely good indian restaurant with carefully cooked, very fresh and interesting vegetarian food, and polite efficient service; cl Sun am, Christmas and New Year, disabled access. £20|£5.50

EDINBURGH NT2676 **Restaurant Martin Wishart** *54 The Shore (0131) 553 3557* Tiny, simply furnished restaurant on the fashionable Leith dockside waterfront, with colourful modern paintings on plain white walls, stone floors, modern french-accented food - super fish dishes and lovely puddings - from a sensibly short menu, and a well balanced wine list; cl Sat lunchtime, Sun/Mon; disabled access. £59/3-course lunch menu £18.50|£18.50

EDINBURGH NT2676 **Vintners Rooms** *The Vaults, 87 Giles St, Leith (0131) 554 6767* Bustling restaurant - a former fine old sale room, above ancient wine vaults; most enjoyable french provincial cooking plus more modern dishes, super puddings, and a good wine list; you can also choose to eat in the more informal bar; cl Sun and 2 wks from Christmas. £45|£10

GLASGOW NS5567 **Amaryllis** *1 Devonshire Gdns (0141) 337 3434* Gordon Ramsay has brought a trusted protégé from London to cook in this fine hotel's restaurant (it's an independent operation); simple furnishings and décor, delicious modern european cooking, and a marvellous, if not cheap, wine list; cl Mon, Tues and 1-2 Jan, disabled access (there are steps to the entrance). £35/£18 for 2 courses

GLASGOW NS5965 **Café Gandolfi** *64 Albion St (0141) 552 6813* Named after the famous brothers who produced early cameras, this Merchant City favourite has the brothers' photographs of italian restaurants and cafés in the Glasgow district during that period, interesting furniture and stained glass, imaginative and enjoyable modern scottish cooking with international flavours using consistently high quality local produce, often organic, a thoughtful wine list, a relaxed informal atmosphere, and helpful friendly service; cl 25-26 Dec and 1-2 Jan; children welcome until 8.30 pm; £20|£6

GLASGOW NS5965 **Rogano** *11 Exchange Pl (0141) 248 4055* Long-standing restaurant in splendid 1930s deco woodwork and chromium, with quite an emphasis on fish - vegetarian and meaty dishes, too; Café Rogano (downstairs) is open all day for lighter meals; cl 25 Dec, 31 Dec and 1-2 Jan. £45.50|£16.50

GLASGOW NS5667 **Ubiquitous Chip** *12 Ashton Lane (0141) 334 5007* Friendly and informal restaurant (no chips, hence the name) in Victorian coach house with interesting modern scottish cooking, outstanding wines (at fair prices); disabled access; cl 25 Dec and 1 Jan. Upstairs is cheaper. £45|**£12**

HADDINGTON NT5173 **Waterside** *1-5 Waterside* (01620) 825674 A really lovely spot on a sunny day with a fine view across the water, this long two-storey white house has very good bistro-style food, a good range of wines and real ales in two plush rooms with a woodburner, and a more formal stripped-stone conservatory; disabled access to bistro. £35|**£6.95**

ISLE OF WHITHORN NX4736 **Steam Packet** *Harbour Row* (01988) 500334 Well run inn with big picture windows over the picturesque working harbour (several bedrooms have good views too); comfortable low-ceilinged bar with plush button-back banquettes and green leatherette stools, boat pictures, stripped stone and a woodburner; lower-beamed dining room with good wildlife photographs, rugs on its wooden floor, and a solid fuel stove, and small eating area off the lounge bar; good well prepared meals with some imaginative touches, a carefully chosen wine list, real ales, 24 malt whiskies, and friendly helpful staff; garden seats. £22.50|**£6.50**

LANARK NS8843 **Vigna** *40 Wellgate* (01555) 664320 Imaginative italian menu with good basics, more imaginative dishes, and lots of fresh fish; cl Sun am and 1st or 2nd wk in Jan. £29|**£5.95**

LINLITHGOW NT0378 **Champany Inn** *Champany* (01506) 834532 Wonderful aberdeen angus beef as well as lovely fresh fish (they also have their own smoke-house), home-made ice-creams, and good wines; cheaper bistro-style meals in their Chop and Ale House next door; bdrms; main restaurant cl Sun (bistro open all week), 25-26 Dec and 1-2 Jan; disabled access; children over 8 in restaurant. £40.50|**£15.95**

East Scotland

Plenty for all ages, from spectacular castles to lively family outings; richly varied scenery, and appealing seaside towns and villages

Some of this area's castles are breath-taking: favourites include those at Turriff, Crathes, Ballindalloch, Blair Atholl and Craigievar. Grand Haddo House in Tarves makes a busy outing, in Falkland there's a Renaissance palace, and Fort George holds good special events in summer. The Royal connection adds a special dash to Balmoral Castle's lovely grounds, and Leith Hall in Kennethmont has stunning grounds as well as elegantly furnished rooms (garden lovers should make a beeline for Kildrummy, Kemnay and Muthill too). There are lively museums in Oyne, Kingussie and Falkirk (the Falkirk Wheel is another interesting new draw here), and Kirkcaldy has a good art gallery.

Discovery Point in Dundee, centred on Scott's Antarctic expedition ship, is an excellent family outing (our Scottish Family Attraction of the year), and so is Sensation there. Elsewhere Aviemore and nearby Glenmore have a good and growing choice of outdoor and animal-orientated attractions - two unusual places we've added there this year are the Loch Garten Osprey Centre, and a sled dog centre among the mountains. Other family winners here include Blair Drummond's Safari and Adventure Park, the Highland Wildlife Park at Kincraig (also here, Working Sheepdogs is quite an eye-opener), and the Auchingarrich Wildlife Centre in Comrie. The friendly deer centre near Cupar and the sheepdog school at Aberfoyle are fun; the aquarium at North Queensferry is one of the best in the country. The Landmark Forest Theme Park in Carrbridge is useful for keeping energetic children occupied, and there are acres of free fresh-air fun in Mintlaw and Bo'ness (good steam railway here too).

Picturesque Stirling has quite a bit to offer families (its castle is great fun), and civilised St Andrews has a quiet charm. Riverside Inverness and Perth are attractive without being too touristy. The thriving city of Aberdeen has lots for visitors.

The best scenery here is in the N: both Highland, and the valleys - the well known Spey, Dee and Don, and lesser-known places such as the Angus glens of Glen Clova, Glen Esk and Glen Isla. The huge new Cairngorms National Park has hardly got off the ground yet, but will focus more attention on this northern part. Further S, the very pretty Trossachs are also part of a National Park. The coast has appealing fishing villages in Fife's East Neuk (the East Neuk being the local name for the E part of the Fife coast) and a little-known but charming stretch from Nairn to Aberdeen, with good sands, quaint little coves and awesome crags.

Where to stay

ABERDEEN NJ9305 **Ferryhill House** *169 Bon Accord St, Aberdeen AB11 6UA (01224) 590867* **£50**w; 9 rms. Well run small hotel with comfortable communicating spacious bar areas, well over 100 malt whiskies, real ales, friendly staff, a wide choice of food in bar and restaurant and lots of tables on neat well sheltered lawns

ARDEONAIG NN6634 **Ardeonaig Hotel** *Ardeonaig, Killin, Perthshire FK21 8SY (01567) 820400* **£90**, plus special breaks; 16rms. Extended 17th-c farmhouse on S shore of Loch Tay with log fire in snug and lounge, library with fine views, bistro or formal dining using fresh local produce; salmon fishing rights on the loch; a drying and rod room, and boats and outboards; shooting, stalking and pony trekking can be arranged, lots of walks; cl 3-13 Jan; dogs welcome in bedrooms

AUCHTERARDER NN9211 **Gleneagles Hotel** *Auchterarder, Perthshire PH3 1NF (01764) 662231* **£320**, plus special breaks; 275 individually decorated rms. Grand hotel in lovely surroundings with attractive gardens and outstanding leisure facilities: three championship golf courses inc the PGA Centenary Course, shooting, riding, fishing, health spa, tennis, squash, croquet and even falconry, lots of children's activities inc playroom with arts and crafts; comfortable, elegant high-ceilinged day rooms, a fine bar, exceptional service, pianists, enjoyable food using local produce (much is home-grown) in four restaurants, famous afternoon teas; disabled access; dogs welcome in bedrooms ☺

AVIEMORE NH8810 **Lynwilg House** *Aviemore, Inverness-shire PH22 1PZ (01479) 811685* **£60**; 3 rms. Attractive, quietly set 1930s-style house in four acres of landscaped gardens with open fire in spacious lounge, lovely breakfasts with their own free-range eggs and home-baked bread, super dinners using home-grown produce, and charming owners; plenty to do nearby; cl Nov-Dec, Jan; dogs welcome

BALLATER NO3696 **Auld Kirk** *31 Braemar Rd, Ballater, Aberdeenshire AB35 5RQ (01339) 755762* **£70***, plus special breaks; 7 attractive rms, inc 2 family rms. 19th-c church converted to a hotel in 1990, still with bell tower, stained glass and exposed rafters; original pillared pine ceiling in refurbished restaurant, other public rooms with homely décor; cl 25-27 Dec, 1-4 Jan; disabled access; dogs welcome in bedrooms

BALLATER NO3695 **Balgonie Country House** *Braemar Pl, Ballater, Aberdeenshire AB35 5NQ (01339) 755482* **£125***, plus special breaks. 9 pretty rms. Quietly set and spotless Edwardian house with fine views from four acres of mature gardens, particularly helpful owners, fresh flowers, games and books in lounges, and most enjoyable food using the best local produce; cl 6 Jan-10 Feb

BLAIRGOWRIE NO1244 **Kinloch House** *Blairgowrie, Perthshire PH10 6SG* (01250) 884237 **£190*** plus special breaks; 18 individually decorated rms. Creeper-covered 19th-c country house in 25 acres of parkland with highland cattle and fine views; relaxed lounges, comfortable bar, pretty conservatory with lots of plants, and fine choice of carefully prepared food in an elegant dining room; popular sportsmen's room with own entrance, drying facilities, gun cupboard; fitness suite and swimming pool; cl 18-30 Dec; dogs by arrangement

BRIDGE OF CALLY NO1551 **Bridge of Cally Hotel** *Bridge of Cally, Blairgowrie, Perthshire PH10 7JJ* (01250) 886231 **£70**, plus winter breaks; 18 rms. In an acre of grounds along the River Ardle, this former drovers' inn is a friendly family-run place with good value home-made food using seasonal game in restaurant and comfortable bar; dogs welcome

CALLANDER NN6208 **Poppies** *Leny Rd, Callander, Perthshire FK17 8AL* (01877) 330329 **£60***, plus special breaks; 9 rms. Small private hotel with excellent food in popular and attractive candlelit dining room, comfortable lounge, helpful friendly owners, and seats in the garden; children over 12; cl Jan; dogs welcome in bedrooms

DALCROSS NH7451 **Easter Dalziel Farm** *Dalcross, Inverness IV2 7JL* (01667) 462213 **£46***; 3 rms with shared bthrm. Early Victorian farmhouse on 210 acres of family-run mixed farm (beef cattle and grain) with friendly helpful owners, log fire in lounge, good scottish breakfasts in big dining room and - when farm commitments allow - evening meal using own beef, lamb and veg; self-catering cottages, too; cl Christmas and New Year; welcome by arrangement

DUNBLANE NN7606 **Cromlix House** *Cromlix, Dunblane, Perthshire FK15 9JT* (01786) 822125 **£275***, plus special breaks; 14 rms inc 8 spacious suites. Walking, loch and river fishing or shooting on 2,000 acres around this rather gracious country house; relaxing day rooms with fine antiques and family portraits, an informal atmosphere, very good food using local produce in two dining rooms, and courteous service; cl 2-26 Jan; dogs welcome in bedrooms

DUNKELD NN9849 **Kinnaird House** *Kinnaird Estate, Dunkeld, Perthshire PH8 0LB* (01796) 482440 **£375** inc dinner; 9 spacious individually decorated rms. 18th-c country-house hotel on 9,000-acre estate with very restful civilised atmosphere in deeply comfortable antiques-filled rooms with lovely flowers, family mementoes and pictures, log fires, good creative food in no smoking dining room with early 19th-c frescoes, and a fine wine list; excellent fishing on River Tay and three hill lochs, and shooting; children over 12; disabled access

EAST HAUGH NN9656 **East Haugh House** *East Haugh, Pitlochry, Tayside PH16 5TE* (01796) 473121 **£138** inc dinner, plus special breaks; 12 rms, 5 in converted bothy, some with four-posters and one with open fire. Turreted stone house with lots of character, delightful conservatory bar in cream and navy with a fishing theme, house-party atmosphere and particularly good food inc local seafood, game in season cooked by chef/proprietor, and home-grown vegetables; excellent shooting, stalking and salmon and trout fishing on surrounding local estates; cl 20-27 Dec; disabled access to one room; dogs welcome in bedrooms

ELGIN NJ2163 **Mansion House** *The Haugh, Elgin, Morayshire IV30 1AW* (01343) 548811 **£135**; 23 rms. Relaxed and friendly scottish baronial mansion in private woodland with extensive lawns, pretty public rooms, fresh flowers, lovely food inc fine breakfasts, and good wine list; leisure club facilities inc swimming pool

FINTRY NS6287 **Culcreuch Castle** *Fintry, Glasgow G63 0LW* (01360) 860555 **£124***; 15 individually decorated rms (inc 4 family rms) with lovely views. Central Scotland's oldest inhabited castle, nearly 700 years old, in beautiful 1,600-acre parkland and surrounding hills and moors, with log fires and antiques in the public rooms, good freshly prepared food in candlelit panelled dining room, and a friendly relaxed atmosphere, play area; 8 modern scandinavian holiday lodges, too; disabled access; dogs by arrangement ☺

GLENDEVON NN9705 **Tormaukin** *Glendevon, Dollar, Clackmannanshire FK14 7JY* (01257) 781252 **£90**; 12 comfortable rms, some in converted stable block. Neatly kept 18th-c inn in good walking country, with loch and river fishing, lots of golf courses in reach, beamed dining room and softly lit bar, very good food using fresh local produce (soup and coffee all day), and fine breakfasts, also a self-catering chalet; disabled access; dogs welcome in bedrooms

GLENROTHES NO2802 **Balbirnie House** *Markinch, Glenrothes, Fife KY7 6NE (01592) 610066* **£190**, plus special breaks; 30 rms. Fine Georgian country house in 400-acre park landscaped in Capability Brown style, with fresh flowers, open fires and antiques in gracious public rooms, extremely good inventive food, and a big wine list; disabled access; dogs welcome in bedrooms

GRANTOWN ON SPEY NJ0227 **Culdearn House** *Woodlands Terrace, Grantown on Spey, Morayshire PH26 3JU (01479) 872106* **£110**, plus special breaks; 7 rms. Carefully run Victorian granite stone house with homely décor, friendly atmosphere, and enjoyable scottish food; packed lunches on request; cl 1 Dec-mid Feb; children over 10; partial disabled access

INVERNESS NH6245 **Bunchrew House** *Bunchrew, Inverness IV3 8TA (01463) 234917* **£160***, plus special breaks; 14 individually decorated rms. Friendly 17th-c mansion W of town by Beauly Firth with fine views and landscaped gardens, log fire in the elegant panelled drawing room, and traditional cooking using local produce and local game and venison; cl 22-26 Dec; dogs welcome in bedrooms

INVERNESS NH6343 **Dunain Park** *Inverness IV3 8JN (01463) 230512* **£178***; 13 rms inc 6 suites with own lounge. 18th-c italianate mansion in six acres of well tended gardens and woodland, overlooking the River Ness and Caledonian Canal; charming owners, traditional homely décor with family photographs and china ornaments, log fires and fresh flowers, wonderful food using home-grown produce and local game, fish and aberdeen angus meat, generous breakfasts, and 200 whiskies; small warm swimming pool, sauna, lots of walks and golf courses nearby; disabled access; cl 7-23 Jan; dogs welcome in bedrooms

KINCLAVEN BY STANLEY NO1437 **Ballathie House** *Stanley, Perth PH1 4QN (01250) 883268* **£170**, plus special breaks; 42 pretty rms, some luxurious and some in new building with river views from balconies. On a vast estate with fine salmon fishing on the River Tay (lodges and facilities for fishermen) and plenty of sporting opportunities, this turreted mansion has a comfortable and relaxed drawing room, separate lounge and bar, good enjoyable modern scottish cooking, croquet and putting; disabled access; dogs welcome in bedrooms

KINNESSWOOD NO1703 **Lomond Country Inn** *Main St, Kinnesswood, Kinross KY13 9HN (01592) 840253* **£70***, plus special breaks; 10 comfortable rms, 8 in an extension. Attractive little inn in village centre with views across Loch Leven, open fires, informal bustling bar, well kept real ales, and good reasonably priced bar and restaurant food; cl 25 Dec; dogs welcome in bedrooms

KIRKTON OF GLENISLA NO2160 **Glenisla Hotel** *Glenisla, Blairgowrie, Perthshire PH11 8PH (01575) 582223* **£50**; 8 rms. Attractively placed peaceful 17th-c coaching inn, prettily restored with natural unpainted wood throughout, happily unmatched furniture, bar with open fire and two real ales, good food, cheerful warm atmosphere; nice garden; cl 25-26 Dec; dogs welcome in bedrooms

PEAT INN NO4509 *Peat Inn, Cupar, Fife KY15 5LH (01344) 840206* **£155***, plus special breaks; 8 luxurious suites. Famous restaurant with rooms: beams and white plaster walls, log fires and comfortable sofas, friendly service, fine interesting food using the best local produce inc plenty of game and seafood, and an excellent wine list; cl Sun and Mon, 25 Dec, 1 Jan; disabled access; dogs welcome in bedrooms

PITLOCHRY NN9162 **Killiecrankie House Hotel** *Killiecrankie, Pitlochry, Perthshire PH16 5LG (01796) 473220* **£130***, plus special breaks; 10 spotless rms. Comfortable country hotel in spacious grounds with splendid mountain views; mahogany-panelled bar, cosy sitting room with books and games, a relaxed atmosphere, and excellent locally sourced food and good wine list in elegant restaurant; cl Jan-early Feb; disabled access; dogs welcome in bedrooms

SCONE NO1526 **Murrayshall House** *Perth PH2 7PH (01738) 551171* **£130**, plus special breaks; 41 rms inc 14 suites, plus lodge which sleeps 6. Handsome mansion in 300-acre park, very popular with golfers (it has two of its own courses);

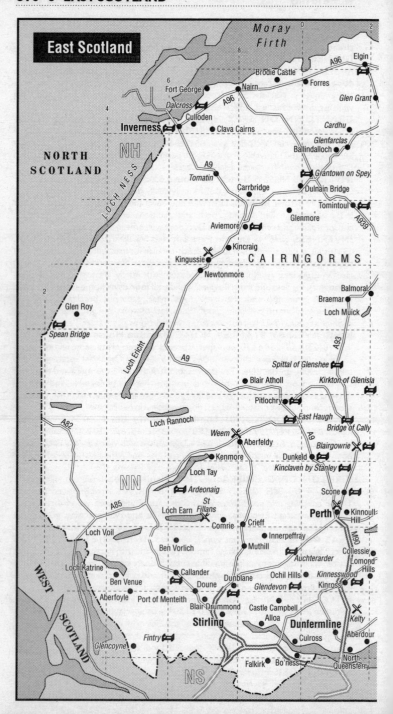

East Scotland

Moray Firth

Elgin

Brodie Castle
Forres

A96

Fort George
Nairn
Glen Grant

Dalcross
A96

Culloden
Cardhu

Inverness
Clava Cairns
Glenfarclas
Ballindalloch

NORTH SCOTLAND
NH
Grantown on Spey

A9
Dulnain Bridge

Tomatin
Carrbridge
Tomintoul

Glenmore
A939

Aviemore

Kincraig
C A I R N G O R M S

Kingussie

Newtonmore
Balmoral

Braemar
Loch Muick

Glen Roy

Spean Bridge

Loch Ericht
A93

A9
Spittal of Glenshee

Blair Atholl
Kirkton of Glenisla

Pitlochry

Loch Rannoch
East Haugh

Weem
Bridge of Cally

Aberfeldy
Blairgowrie

A82
Kenmore
Dunkeld

Loch Tay
Kinclaven by Stanley

Ardeonaig
Scone

St Fillans
Perth

A85
Loch Earn
Kinnoull Hill

Loch Voil
Comrie
Crieff

Ben Vorlich
Innerpeffray

Muthill
Collessie

Loch Katrine
Auchterarder
Lomond Hills

Ben Venue
Callander
Ochil Hills
Kinnesswood

WEST SCOTLAND
Aberfoyle
Doune
Dunblane
Kinross

Port of Menteith
Glendevon

Blair Drummond
Castle Campbell
Kelty

Stirling
Alloa
Dunfermline
Aberdour

Fintry
Culross

Glencoyne
North Queensferry

Falkirk
Bo'ness

NS

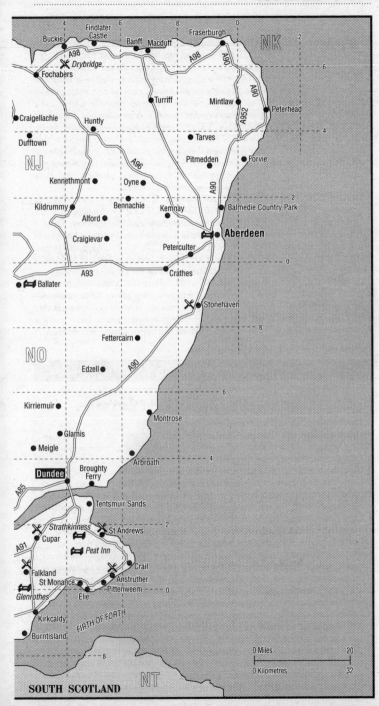

NK

Findlater
Castle
Buckie
Banff Macduff
Fraserburgh
A98
Drybridge
A98
Fochabers
A90
Turriff
Mintlaw
A952
Peterhead
Craigellachie
Huntly
Dufftown
NJ
Tarves
Kennethmont
Oyne
Pitmedden
Forvie
A96
A90
Kildrummy
Bennachie
Kemnay
Balmedie Country Park
Alford
Craigievar
Aberdeen
Peterculter
Ballater
A93
Crathes
Stonehaven
NO
Fettercairn
Edzell
A90
Kirriemuir
Montrose
Glamis
Meigle
Arbroath
Dundee
Broughty
Ferry
A85
Tentsmuir Sands
Strathkinness
St Andrews
A91
Cupar
Peat Inn
Crail
Falkland
Anstruther
St Monance
Pittenweem
Glenrothes
Elie
Kirkcaldy
FIRTH OF FORTH
Burntisland
NT

0 Miles 20
0 Kilometres 32

SOUTH SCOTLAND

comfortable elegant public rooms, warm friendly staff, relaxed atmosphere, imaginative food, and good wines; disabled access; dogs welcome

SPEAN BRIDGE NN2891 **Letterfinlay Lodge** *Letterfinlay, Spean Bridge, Inverness-shire PH34 4DZ (01397) 712622* **£80***, plus special breaks; 13 rms, most with own bthrm. Secluded and genteel family-run country house right on the edge of our East Scotland area and well placed for the west too, with picture window in extensive modern bar overlooking loch; elegantly panelled small cocktail bar, good popular food, friendly attentive service; grounds run down through rhododendrons to the jetty and Loch Lochy; fishing can be arranged; cl Nov-Apr; dogs welcome in bedrooms

SPITTAL OF GLENSHEE NO0672 **Dalmunzie House** *Glenshee, Blairgowrie, Perthshire PH10 7QG (01250) 885224* **£100**, plus special breaks; 16 rms with own bthrm. Old-fashioned former Victorian shooting lodge, off A93, peacefully set in huge estate among spectacular mountains, plenty of walks within it, and own golf course; family-run atmosphere, enjoyable food using local produce, and tasty breakfasts; disabled access; cl Dec; dogs welcome in bedrooms

STRATHKINNESS NO4516 **Fossil House & Cottage** *12-14 Main St, Strathkinness, St Andrews, Fife KY16 9RU (01334) 850639* **£52**; 4 well equipped pretty rms (inc family suite) with fresh flowers - particularly good family room. Once a smallholding, the two stone buildings here have a comfortable little guest lounge and sunny conservatory (no children in these two rooms), plenty of books, board games, videos, and lots of ornaments and fighter aircraft pictures, especially helpful friendly owners, really super breakfasts, and barbecue facilities in the garden; no smoking

TOMINTOUL NJ1718 **Argyle House** *7 Main St, Tomintoul, Ballindalloch, Banffshire AB37 9EX (01807) 580766* **£32***; 5 rms, most with own bthrm. Small family run guesthouse, originally a temperance hotel, and recently carefully renovated; library with books for guests to borrow, good breakfasts in dining room, and a genuine welcome from the friendly owners; lots to do nearby; dogs welcome in bedrooms

To see and do

Scotland Family Attraction of the Year

DUNDEE NO3929 **Discovery Point** (Docks) Splendidly upgraded over the last couple of years, this first-rate visitor centre is based around the Royal Research Ship *Discovery*, the ship that first made famous Scott of the Antarctic. Built in Dundee, the three-masted vessel has been carefully restored, and it's interesting exploring its narrow passageways and cramped rooms; you can hardly imagine this was home to 37 men for almost three years. But it's the well conceived displays around the quayside and particularly in the visitor centre itself that make this such an appealing place to visit, especially for families; there are plenty of interactive exhibits and hands-on activities, bringing to life not just the journey of the *Discovery* but also the realities of life on board. Best is an area full of experiments illustrating conditions in the Antarctic, and there are lots of touch screens and things to try spread around the other galleries too. You'll also find a good few artefacts belonging to Scott and his crew, and intriguing detail of almost every aspect of the voyage, right down to how much cocoa and custard powder was taken on board. Colourful tableaux illustrate how the *Discovery* was commissioned and built, there's a dramatic film on its two-year imprisonment in the ice and subsequent rescue, and new displays explore what happened to the men involved after they'd returned home, including Scott's tragic race to the South Pole several years later. The presentation throughout is excellent; real thought has been put into making what could have been a fairly ordinary exhibition something far more engaging. Snacks, shop, disabled access; cl 25-26 Dec, 1-2 Jan; (01382) 201245; £6.25 adults, £3.85 children. A family ticket for two adults and two children is £17. You can get a combined ticket with Verdant Works, a restored working jute mill nearby.

ABERDEEN NJ9305
Scotland's third-largest city, with a large active harbour, well worth pottering around, both in the main centre - built in orderly, almost grandiose fashion and virtually all granite (not unlike Edinburgh's New Town in places) - and in the more intimate Old Aberdeen N of the centre (around King's College, St Machar's Cathedral and Seaton Park). There's a popular farmers' market (Belmont St, last Sat in month).The Old Blackfriars (Castle St - lots of character), Ferryhill House Hotel (Bon Accord St) and Royal Hotel (Bath St) are all useful for lunch.
Aberdeen Art Gallery (Schoolhill) First-class collection of british painting since the 16th c, especially strong on contemporary works. Meals, snacks, shop, disabled access; cl Sun am, 25-26 Dec, 1 Jan; (01224) 523700; free.
Aberdeen Maritime Museum (Provost Ross's House, Shiprow) In the third-oldest building here (very striking), with very good displays on the city's nautical heritage. Meals, snacks, shop, disabled access; cl Sun am, 25-26, 31 Dec, 1-2 Jan; (01224) 337700; free.
Marischal Museum (Broad St) In the splendid 19th-c neo-Gothic building of Marischal College, the 16th-c rival to King's College (the two were joined to form Aberdeen University in 1860); innovative displays of material from north-east Scotland, and from many parts of the world, strong on anthropology and archaeology. Cl Sun am, all day Sat, 24 Dec-2 Jan, 7-11 July; (01224) 274301; free.
Old Aberdeen King's Chapel, founded in 1495, is very Oxbridge-like and crowned by a great lantern tower; the chapel is one of the most complete examples of a medieval collegiate church in Britain, and has notable wood-carving inc misericords and canopied stalls. It dominates the pedestrianised villagey High St of the Old Town (N of the centre, really too far to walk), and feels quite separate from the main centre. The extensions N and S of High St have some particularly charming corners in College Bounds and Chanonry. The 4½ hectares (11 acres) of **Cruickshank Botanic Garden** (St Machar Drive)

were first planted in the 19th c, and are divided into various smaller gardens - rock, water, rose and herbaceous - as well as trees and shrubs and a small terrace garden. Disabled access to most areas, cl am wknds May-Sept, cl wknds in winter; (01224) 272704; free. In Chanonry itself is **St Machar's Cathedral**, an austere mainly 15th-c church (the only granite cathedral in the world), notable for its painted wooden heraldic ceiling; disabled access; £2 suggested donation. Close by, leafy Seaton Park is famous for its 14th-c Brig (or bridge) o' Balgownie.
Provost Skene's House (Guestrow) Named after its most famous resident, a stately well restored 16th-c house with refurbished period rooms, remarkable painted ceilings and displays on archaeology and costumes. Snacks, shop; cl am Sun, 25-26, 31 Dec, 1-2 Jan; (01224) 641086; free. The Illicit Still nearby has food all day.
Satrosphere (Constitution St) Lively science and technology centre with over 100 hands-on exhibits, shows, workshops and special events. Gift shop, café with home baking and light lunches, disabled access; cl 25-26 Dec, 1-2 Jan; (01224) 640340; £5.
ABERDOUR NT1985
Aberdour Castle 12th-c castle extended and modified over 500 years; the first-floor gallery gives an idea of how it was furnished in 1650, and the interesting 17th-c walled gardens are being restored around an ancient sundial centrepiece. Snacks, shop, disabled access; cl Thurs and Fri pm in winter; (01383) 860519; £2.20; HS.
ABERFELDY NN8549
This quiet and pleasant small Highland shopping town has a fine 18th-c stone bridge designed by William Adam. Just S of town the delightful verdant 1½ m walk along to the oak-lined Den and Falls of Moness inspired Burns's song *The Birks of Aberfeldy*. Close by in Weem, you can get a good lunch at the Ailean Chraggan. Also in Weem, **Castle Menzies** is a good example of a 16th-c fortified tower house; this was the stronghold and home of Chiefs of Clan Menzies for over 400 years, and has a small clan museum. Shop, disabled access; cl am Sun, and mid-Oct to

Easter (or 1 Apr); (01887) 820982; £3.50.

Dewar's World of Whisky This makes an entertaining stop even if you don't like whisky (or aren't old enough to drink it). An audio guide takes you round the various displays (some interactive) in a 19th-c malting barn; also films, a couple of re-creations, and old adverts. Admission includes a guided distillery tour (not wknds, no disabled access) and a sample. Outside is a restored 1939 steam locomotive and a nature trail. Snacks, shop, disabled access; cl Sun Nov-Mar, 2 wks Christmas-New Year; (01887) 822010; £5.

Highland Adventure Safaris (Dull, off B846 W) Land Rover safari looking for rare wildlife - grouse, elusive mountain hares, red deer, and golden eagles - in spectacular countryside at heights of 900 metres (nearly 3,000ft); highland hospitality by kilted guides inc a local dram; open all year. £30, child £10.

ABERFOYLE NN5200

Lots of woollen shops, and in the heart of Queen Elizabeth Forest Park (the forest visitor centre is good, with helpful walk suggestions), so lovely scenery around. You can hire bikes; (01877) 382614. The Inverard has decent food.

Scottish Wool Centre The scottish sheepdog school show, told by their shepherd in the amphitheatre (cl Nov-Mar; the centre itself is open all year). They have spinning demonstrations, and sheepdogs herd ducks around an intricate course. Meals, snacks, good shop, disabled access; cl 25 Dec; (01877) 382850; £4.

ALFORD NJ5815

Alford Valley Railway (A944) Narrow-gauge passenger railway with one-mile trips, and a good static display at the station. Shop, disabled access; cl Oct-Mar; trains wknds only Apr, May, Sept; open all day Jun-Aug; (019755) 62326; *£2, children £1.

Grampian Transport Museum (A944) Big collection of vintage vehicles, from horse-drawn carriages to sleek sports cars, inc the unique Craigevar Steam Express Tricycle; exciting events all summer; children's playground. Snacks, shop, disabled access; cl Nov-Mar; (01975) 562292;

£4.50 The village's life-size bronze statue of an aberdeen angus bull marks its long association with the breed. The Forbes Arms at Bridge of Alford has good food.

ALLOA NS8892

Alloa Tower (A907, 6m E of Stirling) This beautifully restored 13th-c tower is all that remains of the ancestral home of the Earls of Mar. Although it was splendidly remodelled by the sixth earl before his exile after the 1715 Jacobite uprising, the tower, its walls well over 3 metres (11 ft) thick, retains some rare medieval features inc groin vaulting, a complete timber roof, interior well and underground dungeon. Also some attractive furniture and fine paintings inc works by Raeburn and Kneller. Shop, disabled access to ground floor only; cl am, and 1 Nov-Mar; (01259) 211701; £3.50; NTS.

ANSTRUTHER NO5603

Pretty East Neuk fishing village; May-Sept (weather permitting) you can get boat trips out to the nature reserve of the Isle of May, summer home to countless puffins and seals; (01333) 310103. The 16th-c Dreel does good bar meals.

Scottish Fisheries Museum The many facets of fishermen's life, inc the dangers they face at sea, are shown in this quadrangle of converted old harbourside buildings. There's an excellent collection of models of old fishing boats, with 16 full-sized vessels displayed in a former boatyard and in the adjacent harbour. Cl Christmas and New Year; (01333) 310628; £3.50.

ARBROATH NO6441

Arbroath Abbey Substantial remains of 12th-c abbey, connected with Thomas à Becket and Robert the Bruce. Shop, disabled access to ground floor only; cl 25-26 Dec, 1-2 Jan; (01241) 878756; £3; HS.

AVIEMORE NH8912

Uncompromisingly modern ski-resort village. There are plenty of places to get something to eat in this sizeable tourist development (the Olde Bridge is our current recommendation).

Cairngorms The Cairngorms National Park, Scotland's second and the UK's largest, was established in Sept 2003, centred on these mountains and covering much of their surroundings but oddly cutting off the Perthshire parts; it is intended to improve conservation and access, though there are concerns that with responsibility spread through four local authorities instead of being focused in a single administration the Park will be less than ideally effective. A funicular railway, the highest in Britain, takes you up to the Ptarmigan Station just below the summit of Cairngorm. If you can tear yourself away from the view, an exhibition covers the history and ecology of the mountain. Meals, snacks, shop, disabled access; cl in bad weather, best to check; (01479) 861261; £8.

Loch an Eilein A beautiful draw for walkers, nestling beneath the Cairngorms; a forest track encircles this delightful little loch, with its castle romantically placed on an isle - great echoes here.

Loch Garten Osprey Centre (SW of Nethy Bridge) Just the walk from the car park to the visitor centre can give glimpses of red squirrels and crossbills in this rare surviving caledonian pine forest, but most of all this centre is famous for the ospreys which nest in summer (though in the last couple of years the female has seemed more interested in finding ever-younger mates than in serious family life); CCTV relays it all back to the visitor centre, where staff are on hand to explain. Snacks, shop, disabled access; cl mid-Sept-Mar (01479) 831591; £2.50.

Strathspey Steam Railway 10 miles of great scenery between here and Broomhill. Snacks (not Sat), shop, limited disabled access; usually open daily Jun-Sept, plus other dates and wknds - best to ring for timetable; (01479) 810725; *£9.

BALLATER NO4198
Cambus o' May Walks (A93 E) Extensively quarried until the early 20th c, this pleasantly wooded area is dissected by several walks inc one around a small loch (with picnic area), designed to accommodate wheelchairs. If you're lucky, you might catch a glimpse of red deer and capercaillie among the mix of evergreens.

Old Royal Station (Station Sq) This Victorian railway station has been fully restored to how it would have been in the days when Queen Victoria used it on the way to nearby Balmoral. Displays tell the history of its Royal connections, and lifelike figures inhabit the Royal Waiting Room. Restaurant, Tourist Information Centre, disabled access; cl Christmas and New Year (013397) 55306; free.

BALLINDALLOCH NJ1736
Ballindalloch Castle Romantic castle in a lovely spot in the heart of Speyside whisky country, grandly enlarged around 1845, and still lived in by the Macpherson-Grants whose ancestors settled here in mid-16th c. Furnishings inside are cheerfully light, and there's a fine collection of 17th-c spanish paintings. The Rivers Spey and Avon run through the grounds, which also include a large rock garden, and the oldest herd of aberdeen angus cattle in the world. Enjoyable afternoon teas, well stocked gift shop, disabled access to tearoom and ground floor of castle only; cl Sat, and Oct-Maundy Thurs exc by appointment; (01807) 500206; £5.

Glenlivet Distillery The first Highland malt whisky distillery to be licensed, and thought by many to produce the best; cl Sun am and Nov-Mar; (01340) 821720; free.

BALMEDIE COUNTRY PARK NJ9820
Along a constantly shifting stretch of coast, this is splendidly bleak-feeling despite the closeness of Aberdeen. Visitor centre usually cl winter wknds, though best to check; (01358) 742396. The beaches are clean and safe; the Udny Arms, a pleasant small hotel along at Newburgh, does good bar lunches.

BALMORAL NO2693
Balmoral Castle (off A93) The Royal Family's Highland residence. Prince Albert bought the property four years after he and Queen Victoria had first rented it in 1848, and had a new castle built here by 1855. You can't go inside, but you can explore the wonderful gardens and woodlands, and there are various exhibitions in the ballroom. Also pony trekking and pony cart rides. Snacks, meals, shop, disabled access; cl Aug to end Mar; (013397) 42534; £5. The Inver (A93 E) has good value food.

BANFF NJ6963

Duff House 🏛 This magnificent example of 18th-c baroque architecture has served as a ducal residence, hotel, sanitarium and prisoner-of-war camp in its time. It now houses a splendid collection of paintings and tapestries from the National Galleries of Scotland, hung in sumptuously furnished rooms inc Chippendale furniture designed by Robert Adam. The extensive grounds laid out alongside the River Deveron are pleasant for strolling in, and include a mausoleum and, rather quaintly, the 19th-c headstones of various dogs. Tearoom with very good home-made food, shop, good disabled access including lifts to gallery, cl Mon-Weds Nov-Mar, 25-26 Dec, and 1-2 Jan; (01261) 818181; £4.50; HS.

BEN VENUE NN4706

Allows some good mountain walks comparable in difficulty to some of the fells of the english Lake District. Approach from the roads W of Loch Achray; the Byre on the A821 nr Brig o' Turk has good food.

BEN VORLICH NN6218

Good walking, for those used to pretty hearty fell walking.

BENNACHIE NJ6623

On the E edge of the Grampians near Inverurie, this is not that high but gives walkers tremendous views over lowland Grampian; the gently rolling moorland top has several colour-coded Forestry Authority trails (the lower slopes are forested).

BLAIR ATHOLL NN8665

Atholl Country Life Museum Turn in at the White Horse for this friendly little **folk museum**, with some unusual exhibits inc the largest known trophy in Britain (awarded for shooting). Meals, snacks, shop, disabled access; open pm late May-end Sept, plus wkdy ams July-Aug; (01796) 481232; £3.

Blair Castle (off A9) Nestling among forests and heather-clad hills, this is Scotland's most-visited privately owned house, dating back to the 13th c, though largely renovated in the 18th. You can see 30 rooms, and there's an 18th-c walled garden. A display charts the history of the Atholl Highlanders - the Duke of Atholl's unique private army

that turns out here for its annual parade in May. A piper outside most days in summer adds to the atmosphere. Meals, snacks, shop, disabled access to ground floor only; cl Nov-Mar (winter tours by arrangement); (01796) 481207; *£6.70, £2 for grounds only. The Atholl Arms has good value food all day.

House of Bruar (A9) Country shopping complex with fine specialist foods and clothing; readers like it a lot.

BLAIR DRUMMOND NS7498

Safari and Adventure Park (A84) Wild animals in natural surroundings, with plenty of other activities included in the price, from gentle rides for younger children to the exhilarating Flying Fox slide over the lake. You can explore part of the water in pedal-boats, and boat trips circle Chimpanzee Island leaving the chimps to enjoy their natural habitat undisturbed; one of them made the news recently by stealing a keeper's mobile phone and making anonymous calls with it. Feeding times of lions, sea lions, and penguins are posted in the park. Meals, snacks, shop, disabled access; cl end Sept-Mar; (01786) 841456; £9 (£5 children 3-14) - not bad value if you bring a barbie and make a half-day of it. The Lion & Unicorn at Thornhill does good family lunches.

BO'NESS NS9981

Bo'ness & Kinneil Railway 🏛 Re-creation of the days of steam complete with relocated railway buildings and Scotland's largest collection of locomotives and rolling stock. The 7-mile round trip takes you to the woodlands of the Avon Gorge at Birkhill, for tours of an old fireclay mine. Meals, snacks, shop, disabled access to railway only; trains usually run wknds Apr to mid-Oct, daily (exc Mon) July and Aug, and for special events in Dec, though you can see the locomotives all year; cl Jan, Feb, Mar, Nov; (01506) 822298; £7.50 mine and train, £4.50 train only. (Discount voucher not valid on special event days.)

Kinneil Estate (off Provost Rd, W outskirts) Includes the interesting if not extensive remains of a Roman fortlet, as well as a few later ruins and remains. The converted stables of adjacent Kinneil House (an interesting largely

16th-c building) have a museum on the site's history, with lots of local pottery. You can still see the workshop where James Watt developed the steam engine, and there are pleasant woodland walks and an adventure playground. Shop, limited disabled access; cl winter am and all day Sun and bank hols; (01506) 778530; free.

BRAEMAR NO1491

One of the most beautifully set Highland villages; the Fife Arms (very much on the coach routes) is useful for lunch. A steep path up Morrone takes the most determined walkers along a route used for a race in Braemar's famous Highland Gathering.

Braemar Castle (A93 NE) Highly unusual and charming interior. Shop; cl Fri (exc July-Aug), and all Nov-end Mar; (013397) 41219; *£4.

Highland Heritage Centre (Mar Rd) Good, showing useful film on the area's history and scenery (inc an interesting look at the building of Balmoral Castle), and on the Gathering. Shops, disabled access; cl 25-26 Dec, 1-2 Jan, cl winter lunchtimes; (01339) 741944; free.

Linn of Dee Four or five miles along the Dee rd W (a pretty drive), giving long glen walks into the Cairngorms along Glen Dee and the Lairig Ghru.

BRODIE CASTLE NH9757

£ (off A96) Handsome gabled castle with extensive art collection featuring 17th-c paintings of the dutch school, english watercolours and french Impressionists. Before the National Trust for Scotland took it over in 1980 it had been the seat of the same family since 1160. Outside are woodland walks and wildlife observation hides, and beautiful daffodils in spring. Snacks, shop, limited disabled access; open daily 1-30 Apr and 1 July-31 Aug; open Sun-Thurs May-30 June and 1-30 Sept; grounds open all year; (01309) 641371; £5; NTS. Their occasional evenings of traditional scottish music are good fun. The nearest good place for a meal is the Clifton Hotel in Nairn.

BROUGHTY FERRY NO4630

Broughty Castle Museum (off A930 4m E of Dundee) 15th-c fort rebuilt in the 19th c to defend the estuary, now a local and natural history museum. Plenty of harpoons and whaling exhibits

- whaling used to be one of Dundee's major industries. Snacks, shop; cl Mon Oct-Mar, Sun am, 25-26 Dec, 1-3 Jan; (01382) 436916; free. The Fishermans Tavern and Ship (fantastic view upstairs) are good.

BUCKIE NJ4366

Buckie Drifter Interesting fishing museum with a re-created 1920s quayside, and an interactive exhibition on the life of the herring, and the fishermen who depended on it; you can climb aboard a lifeboat, and there's a collection of marine paintings by Peter Anson. Restaurant with views of the harbour and the Moray Firth, shop, disabled access; cl Sun am and beginning Nov-end Mar; (01542) 834646; £2.75.

BURNTISLAND NT2385

Once famous for shipbuilding (and shipbreaking), now a popular little resort, with an unusual octagonal church where the decision was made to produce the Authorised Version of the Bible in 1601.

CALLANDER NN6207

Quite a busy tourist town, popular in Victorian times thanks to the works of Walter Scott, and still remembered for its appearances in the original *Dr Finlay's Casebook*. The **Hamilton Toy Collection** (Main St) is worth a look if you're passing; usually cl Mon (exc bank hols and during Aug), am Sun, and end Oct-Easter; (01877) 330 004; £2.

Kilmahog Woollen Mill £ (just N) Restored flax mill with 250-year-old working wheel, selling tweeds, tartans and other woollen gifts; also whisky tasting. Meals, snacks, shop; cl 25 Dec; (01877) 330268; free. The Lade Inn out here has good food.

Rob Roy & Trossachs Visitor Centre (Ancaster Sq) The story of Scotland's most whitewashed rascal (or brave supporter of the downtrodden, depending on your point of view), well told with hi-tech displays. Also information on the beautiful surrounding countryside. Shop, disabled access; cl 25-26 Dec and 1-2 Jan; (01877) 330342; £3.25.

The Trossachs The Highlands in microcosm, beloved by coach tours for their dense conifer forests, steep glens and beautifully framed lochs, and now part of Scotland's first National Park.

Perhaps surprisingly, not brilliant for low-level walks unless you like forests; the route on to Callander Crags from Callander is one of the best. The Byre at Brig o' Turk is a good food stop.

CARRBRIDGE NH9022

Landmark Forest Theme Park (B9153) Good family day out, with exhibition on the microscopic world, well signposted forest trails (one through the tree-tops), a covered, elaborate adventure playground (children 5-14), water-coaster, and Forestry Heritage Park with fully operational steam-powered sawmill (Apr-Oct). You can sometimes have a go at log-cutting, and Lex the giant clydesdale horse may be hauling logs to the mill. Great views from the top of the viewing tower. Meals, snacks, shop, disabled access; cl 25 Dec; (01479) 841614; *£8.25. The beautifully placed Dalrachney Lodge Hotel (nr junction A9/A95) does good lunches.

CASTLE CAMPBELL NS9699

Once known as Castle Gloom, this late 15th-c castle was burned by Cromwell's enemies in the 1650s, but still has its courtyard, great hall and barrel roof, as well as splendid views from the tower. Snacks, shop; cl every Sun am, Thurs pm and all day Fri in winter, 25-26 Dec, 1-2 Jan; (01259) 742408; £3; HS. The Kings Seat in Dollar has good home-made food.

Dollar Glen An amazing short track takes you up through these spectacular 24 hectares (60 acres) of Arthur Rackham-esque woodland - catwalks, rock overhangs, jungle-thick vegetation, and a swirling stream below. Take care, some paths are steep and narrow, and can be dangerous after rain. But this is a gripping approach to Castle Campbell.

CLAVA CAIRNS NH7544

A group of circular burial cairns from around 1600 BC surrounded by three concentric rings of great stones, on the banks of the River Nairn.

COLLESSIE NO2712

Fife Animal Park (B937) Unique collection of ostriches, emus and rheas - they have birds of all ages, play areas, and animals such as lambs, pigs and wallabies. Meals, snacks, shop, good disabled access, only open Fri-Sun; may cl Oct-Apr; (01337) 831830; free. The

Albert over in Freuchie has good value food.

COMRIE NN7919

Auchingarrich Wildlife Centre (off B827 S) You can spend a whole day at this 40-hectare (100-acre) park and, as much is under cover, it's enjoyable even if it's wet. As well as rabbits, pigs, sheep and highland cattle, they've animals such as raccoons (see them being fed at 2pm, otters feed an hour later), llamas, arctic foxes and emus; you can watch chicks being born in the hatchery, and a falconry centre has regular summer flying displays (50p). Lots of well thought-out play areas, and space for picnics and barbecues. Summer snacks, shop, disabled access; open daily Easter-Oct, best to phone in winter when parts are shut, and there's an honesty box; (01764) 679469; £4.75.

Deil's Cauldron Beauty spot reached by a signposted circular walk through Glen Lednock from Comrie (the Earthquake House at Comrie records tremors).

Drummond Trout Farm and Fishery ⬆ (off A85 W) Very friendly, especially good for first-time fishermen (if it's not too busy - they're happy to give you some tips); also see how a fishery works, and you can feed the fish. Summer snacks, picnic area (you can bring your own barbecue), shop, disabled access; cl 25 Dec, 1 Jan; open till 10 in summer; (01764) 670500; £2.

CRAIGELLACHIE NJ2944

Speyside Cooperage Visitor Centre (Dufftown Rd) Working cooperage and visitor centre, with viewing area to watch the barrel-makers, and a tasting area. Shop (wide range of wood goods), picnic area, disabled access to exhibition only; cl wknds, and Christmas/New Year; (01340) 871108; £3.10. The fine Telford-built bridge here opened in 1814, and carried traffic until 1973. The little Fiddichside Inn (Keith Rd) is a charmingly old-fashioned fishing pub.

CRAIGIEVAR NJ5609

Craigievar Castle (A980) Perhaps the most fairytale-romantic of the area's castles, this picturesque early 17th-c multiple tower dotted with erratically shaped windows soars to a mushrooming of corbels, turrets and crow-stepped gables. Inside, a warren of narrow staircases climbs through a rich series of ornately beamed and plastered rooms. The National Trust for Scotland are worried that too many people come here, so if you do decide to visit (and it is worth while), try to avoid busy times - it's not a place to absorb coach parties comfortably. Castle open pm only Apr-Sept, cl Weds-Thurs, grounds open all year; (013398) 83635; £9; NTS. The Muggarthaugh at Tough just N has good value generous food.

CRAIL NO6107
One of the prettiest of the East Neuk fishing villages.
Secret Bunker (B940 4m W) Beneath an innocuous-looking farmhouse is a network of underground rooms and corridors from where the government would have run Scotland in a nuclear attack. Meals, snacks, shop, disabled access; cl end Oct-end Mar; (01333) 310301; £7.20.

CRATHES NO7596
Crathes Castle (A93) Beautiful 16th-c tower house with wonderful interiors - esp its ceiling paintings, filled with wise old sayings in a mixture of Scots and English. Best of all are the surrounding gardens, inc a huge walled garden with a remarkable series of carefully toned colour borders. Meals, snacks, shop, some disabled access; cl Nov-Mar; (01330) 844525; £9, £7 garden or castle (£2 car park); NTS. Scott Skinners towards Banchory is good for reasonably priced bar lunches.

CRIEFF NN8621
A pleasant airy town, perched on the edge of the Highlands. A modern visitor centre has a pottery, plant centre, wildlife sculptures, and an exhibition on cattle droving; (01764) 654014; there's a Stuart Crystal factory shop on Muthill Rd. The Knock of Crieff, a wooded hill just above, gives walkers a good viewpoint, and burnside Macrosty Park is enjoyable for a stroll or a picnic, with summer brass band concerts.
The Famous Grouse Experience ⊞ (off A85 NW) Scotland's oldest distillery, dating from 1775 and using the pure water of the Turret Burn; includes the Famous Grouse Experience, a lively look at the history

and production of that well known whisky. There's a statue of the distillery cat Towser, who died in 1987 but is still in the *Guinness Book of Records* as World Mousing Champion - challengers have 28,899 to beat. Meals and snacks, shop, some disabled access; cl 25-26 Dec; (01764) 656565; guided tours £5.95.

CULLODEN NH7445
Culloden Battlefield (B9006) The bleak site of the gruesome massacre in which the 25-year-old Duke of Cumberland destroyed the Highland army of Bonnie Prince Charlie. On the moor a cairn marks this last bloody battle fought on mainland Britain. You can see the Graves of the Clans and the Well of the Dead, as well as the Old Leanach Cottage around which the battle was fought, refurbished in period style. Meals, snacks, shop, disabled access; visitor centre cl 24-26 Dec, all Jan; (01463) 790607; £5; NTS. The Snow Goose over on the A96 is a good place for an informal meal.

CULROSS NS9885
(off A985) Fascinating steeply sloping small town on the Forth, parts virtually unchanged since the 16th and 17th c. Until the 1930s this was because no one could afford any improvements, and since then its red pantiled-roofed houses have been carefully restored and preserved by the National Trust for Scotland (they are still lived in). There are the remains of a 13th-c abbey.
Culross Palace ⊞ Renaissance merchant's house built in 1597 and former home of Sir George Bruce; the first building the newly formed National Trust for Scotland purchased in 1932; fully furnished in 17th and 18th-c style, and at the back is a lovely medieval working garden, the only one of its kind in Scotland. Guides are good at pointing out those small but fascinating details that make the difference between just another building and a real experience. Tearoom and shop open Good Fri-30 Sept and wknds Oct-end Dec; garden open all year; (01383) 880359; *£5; NTS. The price includes admission to the Trust's two other main properties here, the Town House (good visitor centre), and the Study.

CUPAR NO3711
Hill of Tarvit Mansionhouse (off

A916 S) Rebuilt in 1905-7 with a richly Edwardian take on earlier scottish styles, french, Chippendale-style and vernacular furniture, dutch paintings and pictures by Raeburn and Ramsay, flemish tapestries and chinese porcelain and bronzes. Tearoom; cl am (exc July-Aug) and end Oct-Mar; (01334) 653127; house and period grounds *£5, grounds only £2; NTS.

Scottish Deer Centre ⓔ (Bow of Fife; A91 just W) You can stroke the deer and feed the young fawns at this friendly place, which also has nature and heritage trails, daily falconry displays, aerial walkways and observation platforms, and an adventure playground. Snacks, shop, disabled access; cl 25 Dec, 1 Jan; (01337) 810391; *£4.75. There's an adjacent holiday shopping courtyard.

DOUNE NN6901

Doune Castle (A84) 14th-c stronghold with two fine restored towers on the banks of the River Teith. Strong associations with Bonnie Prince Charlie and Walter Scott, and the Knights of Ni - the castle was used in the filming of *Monty Python and the Holy Grail*. Shop; from Nov-Mar cl Thurs-Fri, 25-26 Dec, 1-2 Jan; (01786) 841742; £2.80; HS. The village's bridge is said to have been built out of spite by James IV's tailor when the ferryman refused him passage. The Lion & Unicorn over in Thornhill is good for lunch.

DUFFTOWN NJ3240

Glenfiddich Distillery (A491, just N) The only Highland distillery where you can follow the entire whisky production process from barley to bottle - most other distilleries bottle elsewhere. Enjoyable tours and generous tastings, shop, disabled access; cl Sun am, winter wknds, 2 wks over Christmas; (01340) 820373; free. Dufftown has a useful museum.

DULNAIN BRIDGE NH9823

Speyside Heather Centre ⓔ (Skye of Curr, off A95) Over 300 different types of heather in landscaped garden, along with an exhibition on its various uses, and gift shop inc wide range of heather-based goods. Home-made meals and snacks, garden centre, antique shop and gallery, disabled access; cl 25 Dec, reduced opening

hours Jan-Feb; (01479) 851359; 50p exhibition.

DUNBLANE NN7801

Dunblane Museum This small town is of ancient origin, with plenty of old buildings in its narrow streets, esp around the square of its elegant 13th-c cathedral. This incorporates a much older tower, and has a beautiful oval window that you can see only from outside. The nearby museum, which celebrates its Diamond Jubilee this year, explains the interesting background; cl all day Sun, and Oct-early May; free. The Stirling Arms has good food.

DUNDEE NO3929

Beneath the straightforward modern wrappings of this bustling city, you can uncover signs of its distinguished heritage in a number of museums. The Royal Oak (Brook St - indian), Chequers (South Tay St), Mercantile (Commercial St) and Number 1 (Constitution Rd) are all useful for a decent meal.

Camperdown Country Park (off A90) 160 hectares (400 acres) of fine parkland with golf course, nature trails, woodland footpaths, and wildlife centre with indigenous animals from wolves and bears to wildcats. Also adventure play area themed around the defeat of the Dutch at the 1797 Battle of Camperdown. Snacks, shop, disabled access; cl Christmas and New Year; (01382) 432689; free, £2.40 wildlife centre.

Contemporary Arts Centre (152 Nethergate) £9m centre for contemporary art and film, with two galleries showing changing exhibitions, plus an arts cinema, print studio and activity room for workshops. The trendy Jute Café Bar here has good food; shop, disabled access; centre cl 25-26 Dec, 1-2 Jan, galleries cl Mon; (01382) 909900; free.

Discovery Point *See separate family panel on p.812.*

Frigate Unicorn ⓔ (Victoria Dock) This 1824 vessel is the oldest british-built warship still afloat, now with an audio-visual show and a museum of naval life in her days in commission. Snacks, shop; cl Mon-Tues Nov-Mar, and 2 wks at Christmas/New Year; (01382) 200900; £3.50.

McManus Museum and Art Galleries (Albert Sq) Important works by 19th-c scottish and english artists, and a splendid hall with vaulted ceiling and stained glass. Cl Sun am, 25-26 Dec, 1-2 Jan; (01382) 432084; free.

Mills Observatory (Balgay Park) Exhibits on space research and astronomy, as well as a small planetarium (by prior arrangement, or last Fri in month during winter), and splendid 10-inch refracting telescope. Shop; open Tues-Fri and pm wknds Apr-Sept; open Mon-Fri 4-10pm and wknd pms in winter (exc 25-26 Dec, 1-2 Jan); (01382) 435846; free but £1 for planetarium shows.

Sensation (Greenmarket) This splendid Millennium science centre focuses on the senses, with dozens of fun exhibits and interactive displays. It's designed very much with younger visitors in mind: climbing round a giant head, for example (and sliding out through the nose), or discovering why a strange lump of goo goes hard and then breaks when it's squeezed, or seeing what the world looks like to a dog. Touch-screen games vividly explain everything from germination, with individual seeds clamouring for attention while you decide what they'll need to make them grow, to body temperature, with the chance to see yourself as a thermal image to discover how hot or cold your various parts are. Extra activities in school hols, good temporary exhibitions, and an enjoyable soft play area. Older children like the technosphere, with its computers and multimedia equipment. Meals, snacks, shop, disabled access; cl 25-26 Dec, 1 Jan; (01382) 228800; £5.50 adults, £3.99 children 4-15.

Verdant Works 🏛 (Discovery Point, Riverside Drive) (West Hendersons Wynd) Award-winning look at the jute industry, once an important part of the local economy, with films and interactive displays. Shop, disabled access; cl 25-26 Dec, 1-2 Jan, cl Mon-Tues Nov-Apr; (01382) 225282; *£5.95.

DUNFERMLINE NT0987
Quite a prosperous light-industry town with a distinguished distant past - it was once Scotland's capital.

Abbot House (Maygate) Exhibitions

and relics inc the shrine of St Margaret, and a replica sword that would have been used in the Battle of Bannockburn. Tours using audio-visual technology lead you through the labyrinth of corridors and the twists and turns of Scotland's turbulent past. Meals, snacks, shop; cl 25 Dec, 1 Jan; (01383) 733266; *£3. The cave that St Margaret used to pray in is 84 steps below the Glen Bridge car park (cl Oct-Easter; free).

Andrew Carnegie Museum (Moodie St) Focuses on the man who from humble origins in this house made a fortune in Pittsburgh steel, then gave away over $350 million - all the while claiming he didn't believe in charity. Handloom weaving demonstrations the first Fri of each month, May-Oct. Shop, disabled access; cl am Sun, and Nov-Mar; *£2.

Dunfermline Abbey The remains of a Benedictine abbey and later church buildings are pleasantly set in quiet precincts away from the busy centre. The foundations of the original 11th-c church underlie the more elaborate Norman nave, and the grave of King Robert the Bruce is marked by a modern brass in the choir stalls. The Palace is the birthplace of Charles I. Snacks, shop; cl Sun am in Oct, plus Thurs pm and all Fri Nov-Mar, 25-26 Dec, 1-2 Jan; (01383) 739026; £2.20; HS.

Dunfermline Museum (Viewfield Terrace) Looks at the local manufacture of damask linen (open by appointment only but cl wknds, 25-26 Dec, 1-2 Jan; (01383) 313838; free).

Pittencrieff House Museum (Pittencrieff Park) Fine 17th-c mansion in gently rugged glen, with displays and paintings (cl 25-26 Dec, 1-2 Jan; free).

DUNKELD NO0242
Charming small town by the River Tay. The cathedral has the tomb of the notorious Wolf of Badenoch, Alexander Stewart (the illegitimate son of english King Richard II). There are pretty preserved cottages (NTS), and riverside forest walks through National Trust land around the waterfalls near the Hermitage, an 18th-c folly, and so-called Ossian's Cave. The Atholl Arms is a useful stop.

Beatrix Potter Garden & Exhibition A small garden next to the

Birnam Institute re-creates the house of Mrs Tiggywinkle and Peter Rabbit's burrow (free); Beatrix Potter spent holidays here. The institute houses a café, and various exhibitions inc one on the author herself; (01350) 727674. Birnam is a tiny township, a 15-min walk from Dunkeld across the River Tay. Birnam Wood (of *Macbeth* fame) has a venerable oak, and there's plenty of stirring walking country around.

EDZELL NO5969

Edzell Castle (B966) Some unique features at this pretty old place - the walled garden planted here in 1604, and the charming series of heraldic and mythical sculptures that decorate the walls around it; these alternate with recesses for flowers and nests for birds. They claim to have captured on camera the castle's rather active ghost. Shop, snack, limited disabled access; in winter cl Thurs pm, all day Fri and Sun am, 25-26 Dec, 1-2 Jan; (01356) 648631; £3; HS. The Ramsay Arms in Fettercairn has decent food, and just N there's a lovely drive up Glen Esk, passing a wayside folk museum (tearoom, giftshop; (01356) 670254).

ELGIN NJ2263

Shopping town of some poise, with some handsome ancient buildings and handy for the coast; Thunderton House has decent food.

Elgin Cathedral Founded in 1224, and known as the Lantern of the North and the Glory of the Kingdom because of its extraordinary beauty and fine-traceried windows. There's still quite a lot to see of the ruins: the 15th-c nave has some ancient Celtic cross slabs with Pictish symbols, and you can go inside the spires. A viewing platform in one of the towers gives unrestricted views. Shop, some disabled access; cl winter Thurs pm and all Fri, Sun am, 25-26 Dec, 1-2 Jan; (01343) 547171; £3; HS.

Elgin Museum (High St) Refurbished thanks to a Lottery grant, with a world-famous fossil collection, Pictish stones and changing exhibitions; cl am Sun, end Oct-end Mar; *£2.

Moray Motor Museum (Bridge St) Well worth a look, in a converted mill. Shop, disabled access. Cl late Oct-Mar; (01343) 544933; £3.

Pluscarden Abbey (nr Barnhill, 5m

SW) Fascinating; built in the 13th c, it gradually fell to ruin, but was rebuilt this century by monks from Prinknash Abbey down in Gloucestershire - they now sing a rediscovered chant which may well have been sung by St Columba himself. Shop (with delicious honey); (01343) 890257; open from 4.45am; free.

Spynie Palace (A941 2m N) Former residence of the bishops of Moray, the biggest tower house in Scotland, with good views over Spynie Loch. Shop, disabled access; cl wkdys Nov-Apr; 12.30-1.30pm; (01343) 546358; £2.20; HS.

ELIE NT4999

Attractive fishing village set around a broad bay - the beach is notably clean and safe (and has a good pub, the Ship, virtually on it).

FALKIRK NS8979

Callendar Park (A803 just E) This huge park, with woodland walks and lots of summer activities, includes Callendar House, a striking partly medieval and much extended mansion used briefly as HQ by Oliver Cromwell. Remodelled in the 19th c to look like a french chateau, it was reopened a few years ago as a museum, with costumed guides interpreting its history. Part of the Antonine Wall, the Roman Empire's farthest frontier, bounds the park. Meals, snacks, shop, disabled access; house cl Sun Oct-Mar, 25-26 Dec, 1-2 Jan; (01324) 503770; house £3, park (open all year) free.

Millennium Link This brings nearly 70 miles of canal from Glasgow to Edinburgh back to life, rebuilding a link that was severed over 60 years ago when a flight of 19th-c locks was closed. The project (partly funded by Lottery money) has seen the removal of obstacles inc filled-in stretches and low bridges, and the refurbishment of locks. High point is the spectacular **Falkirk Wheel** (Lime Rd, Tamfour Hill), a rotating boat lift as high as a nine-storey block of flats, to winch vessels weighing up to 600 tonnes up a 24-metre (80-ft) rise; boat trips on the wheel £8. A free visitor centre (£2 car parking) has information about the canal's restoration and the construction of the wheel; (01324) 619888.

Rough Castle (N of B816 E of High

Bonnybridge) One of the best-preserved sections of the Antonine Wall; not too much is left of the Roman fort that once stood here, but you can still see the ramparts, ditches and defensive pits, and make out where the gates were; free.

FALKLAND NO2507
Falkland Palace & Garden Lovely Renaissance palace of the Stuart kings and queens, set below the Lomond Hills. Not all is as old as it looks, but it doesn't really matter - accurate restoration work has created a comfortably cosy and genuinely lived-in feel. Pleasant gardens and grounds, with the 1539 tennis courts said to be the oldest in the country. Shop; cl Sun am, and end Oct-Mar; (01337) 857397; £7, £3.50 garden only; NTS. Parts of the village are delightful and were Scotland's first conservation area. Kind Kyttock's Kitchen (Cross Wynd) is good for light lunches and afternoon teas, and the 17th-c Stag (Mill Wynd), opposite a charming green and round the corner from the medieval village square, has enjoyable food.

FETTERCAIRN NO6573
The square has a magnificent archway erected to commemorate a visit by Queen Victoria, and the Ramsay Arms has decent food. The drive along the twisting and climbing B974 to Banchory is good, with spectacular views from Cairn o' Mount at the top - and when the water's high enough, salmon jumping near the Dee bridge as you enter Banchory.
Fettercairn Distillery (Distillery Rd) One of Scotland's oldest licensed distilleries, with tours, tastings, and good audio-visual show. Shop, disabled access to visitor centre only; cl Sun am, and Oct-Apr; (01561) 340205; free.

FINDLATER CASTLE NJ5467
This windswept cliff-edge ruin makes a good destination for a walk; walkers can enjoy other stretches of this coast around Banff, with the bus service along the main road a useful method of return. The Cullen Bay Hotel has good value food.

FOCHABERS NJ3359
Baxters Highland Village (A96 just W) Explores how the grocery shop set up by George and Margaret Baxter

grew into a company whose food is now sold all over the world. New children's play area, plus landscaped gardens and woodland walk. Meals, snacks, good shops, some disabled access; cl wknds and 25-26 and 31 Dec, 1-2 Jan; (01343) 820393; free.
Folk Museum (High St) Very good; cl Oct-Mar, free. The Gordon Arms is a reliable food stop in this pleasant small town.

FORRES NJ0356
Dallas Dhu Distillery (2m S) Perfectly preserved Victorian distillery, which you can wander around on your own. Animatronic models explain what's happening, and there's an audio tour. Shop (nearly 200 different types of whisky), picnic area, disabled access; cl winter Thurs pm, Fri, Sun am, 25-26 Dec, 1-2 Jan; (01309) 676548; £3.30; HS.
Falconer Museum (Tolbooth St) Good fossil collection; cl Sun, Fri-Sun Nov-Mar, bank hols and public hols; (01309) 673701; free.
Sueno's Stone (E end of town) Mysterious 9th- or 10th-c stone that may have been erected to commemorate a forgotten battle. It's 6 metres (20 ft) high, carved with a cross on one side and groups of warriors on the other. In summer you can usually climb the Nelson Tower in Grant Park for good views of the Moray Firth; free.

FORT GEORGE NH7656
One of the finest examples of an 18th-c artillery building, one of three fortresses built after 1745, when the Hanoverians were taking no risks in keeping this area firmly under their thumb. Very big, with quite a bit to see and special events all year. A highlight is the Seafield Collection of arms and military equipment. Snacks, shop, disabled access; cl Sun am in winter, 25 Dec; (01667) 462777; £5.50; HS. Just off from the fort in the Moray Firth you may be lucky enough to see one of the few inshore schools of dolphins around the UK coast.

FORVIE NK0029
Forvie National Nature Reserve The fifth-largest sand dune system in Britain - and the one least disturbed by people, so lots of wildlife inc Britain's biggest colony of eider ducks. You have to stick to the footpaths and keep dogs on leads so as not to disturb the birds

and other wildlife. Disabled access; visitor centre cl winter wknds; (01358) 751330; free.

FRASERBURGH NJ9967

Museum of Scottish Lighthouses (Quarry Rd) Based around a lighthouse working up to 1991 and dating from 1787; guided tours take you to the top and demonstrate how everything works. Snacks, shop, limited disabled access; cl 25-26 Dec and 1-2 Jan; (01346) 511022; *£5.

GLAMIS NO3847

Glamis Castle (A94) The family home of the Earls of Strathmore, and the childhood home of the late Queen Mother; a splendid creation, utterly suitable as the setting for Shakespeare's murder of Duncan in *Macbeth*. Notable features include the chapel with its painted panels and ceiling, and of course there are those stories about what's locked away in one of the towers. Meals, snacks, shop, limited disabled access; cl Nov-Mar; (01307) 840393; £6.70. The Strathmore Arms is good for lunch.

GLEN ROY NN3088

The glen and its curious Parallel Roads (not actually roads but the tubmarks of a former glacier) can be seen from an easily walked track along its bottom, a spectacular 4-mile route from Brae Roy Lodge (return the same way).

GLENMORE NH9809

Cairngorm Reindeer Centre 🖼 (off B970) Mingle with free-ranging reindeer in a pretty stretch of the Cairngorms; you can feed and stroke them. Guided walks leave the visitor centre every day, weather permitting, at 11am (plus 2.30pm May-Sept). Shop, disabled access to visitor centre only (reindeer here Easter-New Year); cl New Year-Feb half-term; (01479) 861228; £6.

Sled Dog Adventure Centre (off B970 E of Aviemore) Sled dog museum, kennel tour and rides; tour £7.50, sled dog trips £45 for two hours; (07767) 270526; open all year, weather permitting.

HUNTLY NJ5240

Huntly Castle The original medieval castle here was destroyed and rebuilt several times, once by Mary Queen of Scots. Rebuilt for the last time in 1602,

the ruins are worth a look for their ornate heraldic decorations. Shop, disabled access; in winter cl Thurs pm, all day Fri and Sun am, 25-26 Dec, 1-2 Jan; (01466) 793191; £3; HS. In the square is a little local history museum, and a ski centre can teach you how to cross-country ski through the nearby forest. On the outskirts (Depot Rd, not far from Somerfields supermarket), Deans Shortbread has a good factory shop.

North East Falconry Centre 🖼 (Cairnie, off A96 N) Four flying displays a day in a richly meadowed glade, as well as a herd of red deer. Snacks, shop, disabled access; cl Nov-Feb; (01466) 760328; £4.75.

INNERPEFFRAY NN9018

Innerpeffray Library 🖼 Founded in 1680, this is Scotland's oldest free lending library; many rare and interesting books inc a particularly fine collection of Bibles. Snacks; cl 12.45-2pm, all day Thurs (by appointment only Nov-Feb), but always best to check; (01764) 652819; £2.50.

INVERNESS NH6645

The biggest town up here, the main shopping town for the whole of the N of Scotland. It has an attractive riverside setting, and is a handy centre without being too touristy (it has masses of B&B accommodation). There's a little local museum and art gallery on Castle Wynd; cl Sun; snacks, shop; free. James Thins is a good book shop. Nicky Tams (Ness Bank Rd) has decent food, and the Blackfriars (Academy St) is good for local colour. From here the train across to Kyle of Lochalsh gives good Highland views - 2½ hours, the last minutes of which are much the best. There are even early-start day trips to the Orkneys; (01955) 611353. Or keep your feet on the ground with good walks by a flight of locks on the Caledonian Canal from the Clachnaharry Inn just NW.

KEMNAY NJ7212

Castle Fraser (off A944) Once one of the grandest castles of Mar, the z-shaped building incorporates the remains of an earlier one, and there are excellent formal gardens. Snacks, shop; cl Weds and Thurs (exc July-Aug), a couple of wknds in Oct, and Nov-

Easter, grounds open all year; (01330) 833463; castle £7, car park £2; NTS.

KENMORE NN7644

Scottish Crannog Centre Interesting reconstruction of a prehistoric loch dwelling. Shop, disabled access; cl Nov-Mar (exc for groups of 10 or more); (01887) 830583; £4.25. The attractive estate village is pleasant for a stroll, with a poem pencilled by Burns himself on a wall in the welcoming Kenmore Hotel.

KENNETHMONT NJ5430

Leith Hall & Garden 🖾 In nearly half a square mile of interesting grounds, this mansion was home to the Leith family for over 300 years (their estate then ran to about 20 square miles), and the elegantly furnished rooms reflect their lives and tastes; an exhibition examines their long tradition of military service. The gardens are breathtakingly beautiful in June, and dotted elsewhere around the estate are ponds, nature trails, a bird hide, unusual semi-circular stables, and an ice-house. Staff are very friendly; snacks, shop; house cl am, Weds-Thurs, Oct-Apr, grounds open daily; (01464) 831216; £7; NTS. Readers have enjoyed staying in the west lodge, and there's a flat in the mansion.

KILDRUMMY NJ4516

Kildrummy Castle Now in ruins, though still with its original 13th-c round towers, hall and chapel, as well as some later remains. Cl Sun am, Thurs pm and all day Fri Oct-Nov and all Dec-Mar; (01975) 571331; £2.20; HS.

Kildrummy Gardens (A97) Very beautiful indeed and of some botanical interest. There's an alpine garden in an old quarry, a water garden, walks in the woods, a video showing the changes through the seasons, and a small museum. Shop, snacks, disabled access; cl end Oct-Mar; (01975) 571203 and 571277; £2.50. The ruins provide a spectacular backdrop.

KINCRAIG NH8305

Highland Wildlife Park 🖾 (B9152) Owned by the same charity as Edinburgh Zoo, this 73-hectare (180-acre) wildlife park manages to seem a bit wilder than most animal attractions; perhaps it's because they specialise in species once native to the area, so you really get a feeling that the animals could

have wandered out of the surrounding woods and mountains. You drive through the main reserve, which has red deer, wild horses, and enormous bison. The most exciting feature is the wolf territory, where a walkway takes you to a safe vantage point right in the heart of the enclosure. Plenty of rare breeds, inc the wild przewalski's horses, one of the world's rarest mammals, and you may see red squirrels feeding in the forest; daily talks and wknd summer face-painting. Snacks and shop in visitor centre, disabled access; cl in bad weather, so best to check; (01540) 651270; £7.50.

Working Sheepdogs You'll be amazed at how skilfully the sheepdogs work, in teams of up to eight, to manoeuvre sheep and even ducks at these 45-min demonstrations. Shop, disabled access; cl 12-2pm, Sat, and Nov-Apr, phone to check; (01540) 651310; £4.

KINGUSSIE NH7500

Highland Folk Museum (Duke St) Return to the living conditions of the past in a reconstructed Isle of Lewis black house, mill and smokehouse; major exhibits provide an insight into the social history of the people of the Highlands. Shop, disabled access; cl Sun, wknds Oct-Mar, Christmas and New Year (open for guided tours only in winter); (01540) 661307; £2.50. The Scot House (Newtonmore Rd) has good bar food; the town's pronounced Kinoossie.

Highland Folk Park (A86 E) On 34 hectares (85 acres), this reconstructed 18th-c settlement is the Folk Museum's younger but bigger out-of-town offshoot: you can see a water-powered Victorian sawmill, curling hut, pre-war school (with many original fittings) and clock-maker's workshop. Costumed guides help bring history to life, and vintage buses transport you round the site. Snacks, shop, audio-visual centre, disabled access, play area. Cl wknds Oct and all Nov-Mar; (01540) 673551; £5.

KINNOULL HILL NO1423 Just outside Perth, this offers walkers forest tracks and paths, and two folly 'castles' above the River Tay.

KINROSS NO1202

Kinross House Gardens 🖾 Rather fine and formal, with yew hedges, topiary, roses and herbaceous borders and fine views to Castle Island where Mary Queen of Scots was imprisoned. Disabled access; cl Oct-Mar; (01577) 863497; *£2. The Muirs has good value food, as does the Lomond Hotel at Kinnesswood with its quiet views over Loch Leven.

Loch Leven Castle Reached by ferry, the islet fortress where Mary Queen of Scots was imprisoned for a while; she was rowed to freedom by a page boy, but only after she had been persuaded to abdicate in favour of her infant son. Shop; limited disabled access; cl Tues and Fri in Oct, cl Nov-Mar; (0131) 668 8800; £3.50 (inc ferry).

Loch Leven National Nature Reserve RSPB Vane Farm Visitor Centre is part of this reserve, and lies at the S end of the loch, with good facilities for watching the birds; in the winter the evening flights and sounds of the thousands of ducks and geese are very moving. Snacks, shop, disabled access; cl 25-26 Dec, 1-2 Jan; (01577) 862355; *£3. The loch itself is serene rather than dramatic.

KIRKCALDY NT3093
This busy resort and shopping town (birthplace of the economist Adam Smith and the architect Robert Adam) is not too interesting to visitors, but it has a decent museum and art gallery (see below), and there are some charming old wynds and houses in the eastern suburb of Dysart, which has its own picturesque little harbour. On a rocky promontory between here and the main town is ruined 15th-c Ravenscraig Castle, perhaps most notable for its twin towers (where seagulls nest); great views over the Firth of Forth. Snacks, limited disabled access; free.

Kirkcaldy Museum and Art Gallery In the town's attractive War Memorial Gardens, this houses a superb collection of 18th- to 20th-c scottish paintings inc perhaps the largest gathering of works by William McTaggart and the scottish colourist S J Peploe outside the National Galleries of Scotland; also a local heritage museum, and changing exhibitions of art and crafts, photography and natural history. Snacks, shop, disabled access; cl Sun am,

25-27 Dec, 1-3 Jan, 5 May, 21 July; (01592) 412860; free.

KIRRIEMUIR NO3854
Barrie's Birthplace (Brechin Rd) The birthplace in 1860 of the writer of *Peter Pan*: the upper floors are furnished in the style of the period, and next door are displays relating to his work, both literary and theatrical. Teas, shop, disabled access; cl Weds-Thurs Apr-Jun and Sept, cl Oct-Mar exc Oct wknds; (01575) 572646; £3.50, combined with Camera Obscura close by, £5; NTS.

Gateway to the Glens Museum (High St) This 17th-c town house has displays on the town and the West Glens of Angus inc hands-on activities, touch-screen computers, a wildlife diorama and town model. Shop, disabled access to ground floor only; cl Thurs am, all Sun Sept-Jun, 25-26 Dec, and 1-2 Jan; (01575) 575479; free. The Drovers in Memus is an appealing place for traditional food.

LOCH EARN NN5924
With a trunk road alongside, not one of Scotland's quieter lochs - and largely given over to water-skiing and that sort of thing; now included in the Loch Lomand and Trossachs National Park. The Four Seasons at St Fillans has good imaginative food and great views. Lochearnhead offers a round walk from along a nature trail into Glen Ogle and back via the trackbed of an abandoned railway.

LOCH ERICHT NN6284
Very peaceful but does involve foot-slogging to make the most of it. The road from Dalwhinnie on the A9 at the N end runs along the foot of a steep forested slope; the S end of the loch has more varied scenery, but no road once you reach the end of the little road off the B846 at Bridge of Ericht. Beware if you go on via the A889 - the UK's most dangerous road.

LOCH KATRINE NN4009
A lovely stretch of water that inspired Scott's *Lady of the Lake*, with a Victorian steamer, named after the author, which runs trips three times a day (twice on Weds) in summer; cl 26 Oct-week before Easter; (01877) 376316; £6.80 am, £5.80 pm. The main approach to the E end through the Trossachs does

bring a fair bit of summer traffic, but the central part of the loch is served by just a narrow back road, so is fairly peaceful even then.

LOCH MUICK NO2984

Nestling below the dark summit of Lochnagar, which Byron called 'the most sublime and picturesque of the Caledonian Alps', this has paths around its shores, with a car park at the end of the Glen Muick road from Ballater. It was a favourite spot of Queen Victoria's.

LOCH RANNOCH NN6257

Among the quieter and more beautiful lochs, wooded for much of its length. There are peaceful walks from the back road along the S shore.

LOCH TAY NN7745

Remarkably long, with the view seeming to change moment by moment as the clouds flit across the sky. It has a quiet road along its S side. There are easy walks at the E end of the loch, from Kenmore (see above), along the banks of the River Tay, or into the adjacent forest to a viewpoint over the loch.

Ben Lawers This towering bulk, well over 1,200 metres (nearly 4,000 ft), dominates Loch Tay, and is an interesting spot, with alpine wild flowers not found elsewhere in Britain and a quite different feel from other Highland mountains; a steep road leads up the side; the NTS visitor centre is worth a visit.

LOCH VOIL NN5220

Served by just a narrow back road, so fairly peaceful even in summer; it's famous for having Rob Roy's grave at Balquhidder. It's worth keeping on the road beyond the far end of the loch; there's some striking scenery around the picnic site at its end.

LOMOND HILLS NO2206

A level walk from the car park by the road above Falkland gives some pleasant rambles - not to be confused with Loch Lomond, this upland gives views over most of SE Scotland.

MACDUFF NJ7064

Macduff Marine Aquarium 🏛 (High Shore) Huge central tank holding nearly half a million litres, open to the sky - a unique design. Emphasis on fish native to the Moray Firth, with touch pools, audio-visual presentation and dive and feeding shows throughout the week.

Snacks, shop, disabled access, cl 25-26 and 31 Dec, 1-2 Jan; (01261) 833369; £4.20. The Knowes Hotel nearby has enjoyable food and great Firth views.

MEIGLE NO2844

Meigle Museum Outstanding collection of Pictish sculptured stones, all found in or around the churchyard, the largest well over 2 metres (8 ft) tall, and formerly reputed to mark the grave of Arthur's Guinevere. Shop, disabled access; cl 12.30-1.30pm, and Nov-Mar; (01828) 640612; £2; HS.

MINTLAW NJ9847

Aberdeenshire Farming Museum In over 80 hectares (200 acres) of lovely woodland and farmland, criss-crossed with nature trails and with plenty of wildlife, this illustrates two centuries of farming history, with seasonal open-air demonstrations and tours. Meals, snacks, shop, disabled access; park open all year, museum cl wkdys Sept, open all day Oct half-term, cl Nov-Easter; open daily May-Sept, best to phone for times outside these dates; (01771) 622906; free.

MONTROSE NO6856

Montrose Basin Wildlife Centre 🏛 (A934) The enclosed estuary is a rich feeding ground for thousands of native and migrant birds, inc oystercatchers, curlews, pink-footed geese, and eider ducks. This centre has great views, interactive displays and high-powered telescopes. Snacks, shop, disabled access; cl 25-26 Dec, Jan-Mar; (01674) 676336; *£2.50.

MUTHILL NN8616

Drummond Castle Gardens (A822) Majestic formal gardens originally laid out in 1630 by the second Earl of Perth. Lovely views from the upper terrace, splendid early Victorian parterre, and centrepiece sundial designed and built by the master mason of King Charles I. Cl am and Nov-Apr (exc Easter wknd); (01764) 681257; £3.50. Muthill is a conservation village, and the Village Inn has enjoyable food.

NAIRN NH8856

A quiet, relaxed and rather discreet old-fashioned resort, with good clean sheltered beaches.

NEWTONMORE NN7199

Waltzing Waters (Main St) Wacky water, light and music show - a bit like liquid fireworks, with jets of coloured water and lights performing in time to music. Snacks, shop, disabled access; cl for 2 wks in Jan, limited show over Christmas, so best to check; (01540) 673752; £4.

NORTH QUEENSFERRY NT1380
Deep-Sea World ☒ This elaborate aquarium has a spectacular underwater safari, with moving walkways along a transparent viewing tunnel as long as a football pitch, surrounded by all kinds of underwater creatures in a million gallons of water; divers hand-feed the fish and even answer questions, using waterproof communication systems. The sea-horses are popular, and you can stroke some of the creatures kept in the big rock pools, pilot an underwater camera, and try their new tornado boats. Also one of Europe's largest collections of sand tiger sharks - you can watch a spectacular diver feeds, and see pirhana and other dangerous species in the Amazon Experience. The programme of talks, activities and feeding displays is good, and the free behind-the-scenes tours give a good insight into the demands of looking after so many creatures, and an introduction to their successful breeding and conservation programmes. They also have a good collection of amphibians, taking in the world's most poisonous frog, and some snakes. Meals, snacks, shop, disabled access; cl 25 Dec, 1 Jan; (01383) 411880; £7.50 (inc face-painting); they also offer 'shark dives' to over-16s for £100; (01383) 411880.

OCHIL HILLS NS9099
A range of green mountains which rise without preamble from the lowland plain - a striking textbook example of the Highland Fault. A path from Tillicoultry up Mill Glen takes you to Ben Cleuch, the highest point of the range.

OYNE NJ6725
Archaeolink ☒ This lively centre is a fun exploration of the past. A remarkable turf-roofed building houses an audio-visual presentation, there's an exhibition on myths and legends, and you can try out ancient crafts such as weaving, grinding and arrow-making. Outside are the remains of an Iron Age hill fort, a reconstructed Iron Age farm, a Roman marching camp and a sandpit

play area, where younger members of the family can dig for the past. Meals, snacks, shop, disabled access; restricted winter hours, cl Weds-Sat; (01464) 851500; £4.25.

PERTH NO1223
Spaciously laid out along the broad River Tay; with an excellent specialist rhododendron nursery at Glendoick Gardens (A90). There are a couple of decent museums and galleries (the one in George St is well worth a visit; shop, disabled access; cl Sun, Christmas-New Year; free). Handsome St John's Kirk is where John Knox preached the 1559 sermon against idolatry that started the sacking of the scottish monasteries. Greyfriars (South St) is good value for lunch - ironic, as the overfed Grey Friars monks were the first losers to Knox's followers.

Bells Cherrybank Centre National Heather Collection with 900 varieties, plus Pride of Perth exhibition describing the history of the town and its association with Bells whisky; a 50-acre site is under development as an inspirational and educational garden. Cl Oct-Apr but open Easter wknd; (01738) 472800; £3.

Branklyn Garden (Dundee Rd) Barely a hectare (about 2 acres) but seems much bigger, thanks to a remarkable planting of interesting rhododendrons, small trees, asiatic primulas, meconopsis, lilies, himalayan poppies and the like. Snacks, shop, partial disabled access; cl Oct-end Mar; (01738) 625535; £5; NTS.

Caithness Glass (Inveralmond Industrial Estate, N edge) Displays of paperweight-making, with audio-visual theatre, collectors' museum and factory shop. Meals, snacks, shop, disabled access; cl 25-26 Dec, 1-2 Jan; (01738) 492320; free.

Huntingtower Castle (just W) The main thing to see is its interesting painted ceiling; in winter cl Thurs pm, Sun am and Fri, 25-26 Dec, 1-2 Jan; (01738) 627 231; £2.20; HS. The nearby Huntingtower House Hotel has a good restaurant, and a streamside garden.

PETERCULTER NJ7900
Drum Castle (off A93) Still looks out over what's left of the medieval forest granted to the Irvine family by Robert

the Bruce. Mainly a much-altered Jacobean mansion, the house is based around a 13th-c keep, one of the three oldest tower houses in Scotland. There's a historic rose garden. Snacks, shop, limited disabled access; cl am (exc Jun-Aug), and all Nov-Easter, grounds open all year; (01330) 811204; £7; NTS. The Lairhillock Inn at Netherley a few miles S is good for lunch.

PETERHEAD NK1246
One of Europe's busiest fishing ports, with a bustling market and rejuvenated marina. There's a good local history **museum** on St Peter St (cl Weds pm, Sun, 25-26 Dec, 1 Jan; free) and a **heritage centre** (South Rd) with interactive displays on the fishing industry. Shop, meals, snacks, disabled access; open only Jun-Sept; (01779) 473000; £2.80.

Ugie Fish House (Golf Rd) Ancient place selling a good range of wild salmon and trout, caught from the adjacent river in season; cl Sat pm, all day Sun; (01779) 476209; free.

PITLOCHRY NN9458
An inland resort town for a good long time, beautifully set in fine countryside; a happy sort of place, with a comfortable feel, and lots of craft and speciality shops. There's lovely woodland on the banks of man-made Loch Faskally, with walks and nature trails. The Moulin Inn (which brews its own beer) and Old Mill have enjoyable food.

Edradour Distillery (A924 E) Scotland's smallest distillery, founded in 1825 and virtually unchanged since Victorian times. Guided tours (exc Jan-Feb), tastings, shop, some disabled access; Cl 25-26 Dec, 1-2 Jan; (01796) 472095; free. There's another distillery on Atholl Rd.

Killiecrankie Visitor Centre (B8079 NW) Queen Victoria was just one of the people to have found this romantic spot beguiling, but it wasn't always so serene. In 1689 it was the site of a fierce battle when the Highlanders routed the troops of William IV, and a visitor centre tells the tale. Snacks, shop, disabled access; cl end Oct-Mar; (01796) 473233; £2 for parking; NTS. The attractively placed nearby Killiecrankie Hotel does good lunches.

Pitlochry Power Station (Dunkeld Rd) The visitor centre shows how the hydro-electric scheme works, and you may see salmon swimming up the fish ladder. Shop, partial disabled access to shop; cl Nov-Mar, cl wknds except July, Aug and bank hols; (01796) 473152; £2.50.

Scottish Plant Collectors' Garden With a mix of traditional and modern, these extensive gardens aim to celebrate 300 years of pioneer plant collecting. There have been more scottish pioneer plant collectors than any other nationality, and information and stories about various collectors are shown on boards throughout the garden. They have permanent and touring sculptures on show, and outdoor performance areas; free, donation welcome.

PITMEDDEN NJ8828
Pitmedden Garden (A920) Originally planted in the 17th c and pretty much unchanged since, with sundials, fountains and pavilions in elaborate formal gardens. Snacks, shop, limited disabled access; cl end Sept to 1 May; (01651) 842352; £5; NTS. The Redgarth Hotel over at Oldmeldrum has good food.

PITTENWEEM NO5402
Attractive East Neuk fishing town, with some attractive crow-gabled houses (gables in steps, which seagulls rather than crows sit on here), a picturesque harbour, and quite an artists' colony now; the Aug arts festival is a growing draw, with 70 or more display areas, often using private houses, studios and gardens - giving a relaxed and informal feel. The Anchor does enjoyable food.

Kellie Castle & Gardens (B9171 NW) Fine example of 16th- and 17th-c domestic architecture, though parts date from the 15th or possibly 14th c, with good plasterwork, panelling and collections of furniture. Also fairly extensive gardens inc an appealing Victorian walled garden. Snacks, shop, disabled access to ground floor and gardens; cl am, Tues, Weds end Mar-end Sept, and all Nov-Apr, grounds open all year; (01333) 720271; £5, garden only £2; NTS.

PORT OF MENTEITH NN5700
Inchmahome Priory Famous as the refuge of the infant Mary Queen of

Scots in 1543, this charming water's-edge ruined Augustinian priory was founded in 1238 on an island in the Lake of Menteith, and in spring and summer you can get a boat across. Robert the Bruce prayed here before the Battle of Bannockburn. Snacks, shop; cl Oct-Mar; (01877) 385294; £3.50 inc ferry; HS.

SCONE NO1126

Scone Palace (off A93) The seat of government in Scotland from Pictish times, though the current building is largely 16th-c behind an 18th-c castellated façade. It was the site of the Stone of Destiny - the famous coronation stone - until it was seized by the English in 1296 (it's now back in Scotland, at Edinburgh Castle). Good displays of porcelain, furniture, clocks and needlework, and the grounds are pleasant with formal gardens, pinetum, a maze and children's play area. Meals, snacks, shop, some disabled access; cl end Oct-Mar; (01738) 552300; £6.35. Pronounced 'Scoon', by the way.

ST ANDREWS NO5116

This civilised university town doubles as rather a dignified seaside resort, with clean, safe beaches. It's outstanding for golfers, though to play on the hallowed greens of the Old Course you'll need to ring the St Andrews Links Trust on (01334) 466666 before 2pm the day before you want to go, to enter a daily ballot; after that you'll have to tee up £105. There are a few interesting museums on the city's history, some quite lively, and a number of fine buildings belonging to Scotland's oldest university - esp St Leonard's (now a school) and St Mary's colleges. South St is worth strolling along: attractive riggs or small courts and alleys off, the ancient West Port gateway at the end, and Holy Trinity church where John Knox preached his first sermon in 1547. The Saltire, stylish modern West Port and (a mile S) Grange are all good eating places.

Craigtoun Country Park has a boating pond, children's play areas, activities such as crazy golf, a countryside centre and a mini railway; cl wkdys Sept, cl all Nov-Feb; (01334) 473666; £3 (free Mar and Oct when there's less to do).

British Golf Museum ⬚ (Bruce Embankment) Fascinates anyone keen on the game, with up-to-date interactive and audio-visual displays going right through its 500-year history. Assorted memorabilia include lots of glamorous golfing gear. Shop, disabled access; cl Tues and Weds Oct-Easter, 25 Dec-1 Jan (limited winter opening hours); (01334) 460046; £4.

St Andrews Aquarium ⬚ (The Scores) Up-to-date surroundings for displays of tropical fish, sea-horses and resident seals. Meals, snacks, shop, limited disabled access; phone for winter opening, cl 25 Dec, 1 Jan; (01334) 474786; *£5.50.

St Andrews Botanic Garden (just off Canongate) Seven pleasantly landscaped hectares (around 18 acres), with a good range of trees and shrubs, and several glasshouses. Disabled access; (01334) 477178; £2.

St Andrews Castle 13th-c, the scene of Cardinal Beaton's murder during a wave of anti-Catholic feeling in 1546. It was largely demolished in the 17th c, but some substantial ruins remain. The visitor centre has rare examples of medieval siege techniques, and a grim little dungeon hollowed out of solid rock. Shop, disabled access; cl 25-26 Dec, 1-2 Jan; (01334) 477196; £3; joint ticket with the cathedral £4; HS.

St Andrews Cathedral Impressive twin-towered Norman remains; till fervent locals sacked it in the 16th c this was the largest cathedral in Scotland. Shop; cl 12.30-1.30pm Oct-Mar, 25-26 Dec, 1-2 Jan; (01334) 472563; £2.50, joint ticket with the castle £4; HS. Beside it the extraordinary 11th-c St Rule's church is basically just a soaring slender tower built to guide pilgrims to the small shrine below which housed relics of St Andrew; if you can face over 150 steps it gives wonderful views from the top.

ST MONANCE NO5201

At heart an attractive East Neuk fishing village (though this heart is surrounded by modern housing), with an unusual fisherman's church and a restored 18th-c windmill. The Seafood Restaurant has good seafood and sea views.

STIRLING NS7994

Strategically placed on the Firth of Forth, this has just been granted city status: a very unstuffy place, with the university students putting quite a bit of buzz into the atmosphere. Dropping down the steep hill on which the castle stands is an attractive and interesting network of old streets, with a lot of character in their old-to-ancient buildings; the grand late medieval Church of Holy Rude is where Mary Queen of Scots and James VI were crowned as babies.

Argyll's Lodging Built by Sir William Alexander, founder of Nova Scotia, and then passed on to the Earls of Argyll, this is the finest surviving example of a 17th-c nobleman's town house in Scotland. Used as an army barracks and hospital, then a Youth Hostel, the main rooms have now been re-created to look as they would have done in around 1680. Shop; cl 25-26 Dec, phone for opening times over New Year; (0131) 668 8800; £3.30, £7.50 joint ticket with Stirling Castle.

Bannockburn Heritage Centre (A872 S) Plenty of information on Robert the Bruce's finest hour, inc an audio-visual show on the battle itself. Café, shop, disabled access; cl 23 Dec-20 Jan; (01786) 812664; £3.50.

Old Town Jail (St John St) In season, actor-led tours take you through the preserved cells of this 19th-c jail (self-guided audio tour at other times), and an exhibition goes into prison life today. Shop, disabled access; cl 25-26 Dec, 1-2 Jan; (01786) 450050; £5.

Smith Art Gallery & Museum (Dumbarton Rd) Good changing exhibitions; cl Sun am, all day Mon, 25-26 Dec, 1-2 Jan; (01786) 471917; free.

Stirling Castle Provides magnificent views from its lofty hilltop site. It became very popular with the Royal Family in the 15th and 16th c, and most of the buildings date from that period. It's great fun to visit, from the flame-lit medieval kitchen to the splendid Chapel Royal built by James VI (and I of England), and the Great Hall of James V's Renaissance palace. A huge new hammerbeam roof has been crafted here from 350 oak trees, and the restoration of the castle's lavish early 16th-c furnishings continues with on-site tapestry weaving. Snacks, shop; cl 25-26 Dec; (01786) 450000; £7.50 inc Argyll's lodging, parking £2; HS. There's a good visitor centre in a restored building next door, and Whistlebinkies

(St Mary's Wynd), formerly part of the ancient castle stables, has decent food.

Wallace Monument (top of Abbey Craig, just NE) 67-metre (220-ft) Victorian tower with dramatic views from the open windy top of its 246 spiralling steps. Each floor has audio-visual displays, one on Sir William Wallace, another examining other scottish heroes. There is a statue of Wallace as portrayed by Mel Gibson in *Braveheart* in the car park. Snacks, shop; cl 25-26 Dec, 1-2 Jan; (01786) 472140; £5.

STONEHAVEN NO8783

Dunnottar Castle (just S) On a precipitous sea-girt crag stands this the bleak and battered but still extensive and well preserved 14th-c ruin, used for the filming of Mel Gibson's *Hamlet*. It sheltered the scottish crown jewels during the Civil War, but has seen much darker episodes in its time. Cl Sun am in summer, Tues-Thurs in winter, 25-26 Dec, 1 Jan; (01569) 762173; *£3.50.

Swimming Pool This cheerful art deco open-air swimming pool is the only one of its kind in the country; olympic-sized, and filled with salt water, it's heated to 29 deg C (84 deg F). They have floodlit night-time swims most Weds in the summer (10pm-12). Meals, snacks, shop, disabled access; cl Sept-May; (01569) 762134; £3.

Tolbooth Museum (Old Pier) Good local history museum in ancient tolbooth; cl am, Tues, Nov-Apr, partial disabled access; (01771) 622906; free. This old fishing town has more seasidey but discreet Victorian streets in its upper part; the harbourside Marine Hotel has good reasonably priced food.

TARVES NJ8634

Haddo House (off B999) Wonderfully grand yet still very much a family home; designed by William Adam, and refurbished in the 1880s in the Adam Revival style, with fine furniture and art throughout. The chapel (regular services) has stained glass by Burne-Jones; both the house and adjacent hall host concerts and events throughout the year. House open Jun-Aug only, shop cl Nov-Mar; (01651) 851440; £7; NTS. Charming terrace garden leads into 80-hectare (200-acre) country park with waymarked trails, wildlife hides, visitor centre and events;

(011651) 851489; free (car park 20p an hour). Tearooms serving light lunches and snacks; two shops with estate produce, crafts, gifts and souvenirs; children's play areas. Interesting medieval tomb in Tarves churchyard and stunning views from nearby outlook tower called the Prop of Ythsie. The Redgarth down in Oldmeldrum has decent food and gorgeous views to Bennachie.

Tolquhon Castle (off B999 S) Impressive remains of a 15th-c castle; cl wkdys Oct-Apr, 12.30-1.30pm; (01651) 851286; *£2.20.

Tolquhon Gallery Decidedly unstuffy, with exhibitions of contemporary scottish art and crafts. Cl all day Thurs, and wkdys Jan and Feb; (01651) 842343; free.

TENTSMUIR SANDS NO5024 Five miles of shore walking from Kinshaldy car park on the Fife coast; you may see common and grey seals on the sandbanks, and there are good clean beaches - shorter routes back through the forest.

TOMINTOUL NJ1618 Charming Highland village in attractive scenery, real whisky country; the welcoming Glenavon Hotel has decent food.

TURRIFF NJ7550 **Delgatie Castle** 🏰 Dating from 1050 - but like most scottish castles rebuilt in the 16th c when the invention of siege guns demanded greater fortification - some walls are up to 4 metres or more (14 ft) thick. There are fine 16th-c painted ceilings, an unusual turnpike stair built into a wall, and a bedchamber where Mary Queen of Scots spent three nights; displays on the Clan Hay. Excellent tearoom, shop; cl 25 Oct-14 Nov, Christmas-New Year, 18 Mar- 2 Apr; cl Fri-Mon during the winter months they are open; (01888) 563479; *£4. You can stay here too.

Fyvie Castle (off A947) Each of the five towers of this magnificent castle was built in a different century by the family that lived here throughout; the oldest parts date back to the 13th c, and the whole building is one of the most fantastic examples of scottish baronial architecture. Collections of armour and tapestry, and paintings by Raeburn,

Romney and Gainsborough. Snacks, shop; cl am and Weds-Thurs mid-season, cl Nov-Easter; (01651) 891266; £7; NTS. The Towie Tavern does good food.

WHISKY DISTILLERIES

Cardhu NJ1943 (B9102 nr Knockando) Working malt whisky distillery open for tours and tastings; cl wknds Oct-Easter, Sat Easter-Jun; £4.

Glen Grant NJ2749 (Rothes) Founded in 1840 by the brothers Grant, whose malt whisky was one of the first to be bottled and sold as a single malt. Guided tours, tastings, shop, some disabled access; cl Sun am, Nov-Mar; (01340) 832118; free

Glencoyne NS5086 (A81 nr Killearn) Working malt whisky distillery open for tours and tastings; (01360) 550229.

Glenfarclas NJ2138 (Marypark) Producing one of the top malt whiskies, open for tours and tastings; cl Sun and possibly Sat all year, Christmas and New Year; £3.50.

Tomatin NH7929 Tours and tastings; cl wknds exc summer Sats, best to phone; (01808) 511444; free.

Worthwhile inns in good spots for walkers, drivers or just strollers (besides those we've mentioned as places to eat at or stay in) include the lochside Achray at St Fillans NN6924, Bridge of Cally Hotel at Bridge of Cally NO1451, seaview Creel at Catterline NO8778, Loch Ericht Hotel at Dalwhinnie NN6384, Dores Hotel at Dores by Loch Ness NH5930, Clachan overlooking pretty Drymen's green square NS4788, Anchor at Dunipace NS8083, Old Smiddy in the pleasant village of Errol NO2523, Hungry Monk at Gartocharn NS4286, Clova Hotel in Glen Clova NO3373, Guard Bridge Hotel at Guard Bridge NO4518, Old Mill at Killearn NS5285, Cross Keys at Kippen NS6594 (pretty village), Trossachs Hotel nr Loch Achray NN5106, Corriegour Lodge nr Altrua on Loch Lochy NN2390, Loch Tummel Hotel above Loch Tummel NN8460, Meikleour Inn at Meikleour NO1539 (handy for the 30-metre, 100-ft high beech hedge planted in 1746), Pennan Inn in the pretty seaside *Local Hero* village of Pennan NJ8465, Potarch Hotel at Potarch NO6097 and Tomdoun Hotel at Tomdoun NH1501.

Where to eat

ANSTRUTHER NO5603 **Cellar** *24 East Green* (01333) 310378 Off a little courtyard nr the harbour, with beams, stone walls, and peat fires - and wonderful fresh fish, good wines; cl Mon, Tues ams. £47.50|**£15.50**

BLAIRGOWRIE NO1845 **Cargill's** *Lower Mill St* (01250) 876735 Busy bistro, part of a complex with a crafts gallery and coffee shop, antiques warehouse and upholstery business; good varied food inc nice puddings, and several teas and coffees; bright helpful staff; cl Tues and 2 wks Jan; disabled access. £25|**£5**

CUPAR NO3714 **Ostlers Close** *25 Bonnygate* (01334) 655574 Cosy unpretentious much-liked restaurant with lovely food using the best local fresh produce, game and fish, and home-grown herbs, a reasonably priced wine list, and friendly owners; children over 6 but no children in the evenings; cl Sun-Mon, cl Tues-Thurs ams, two wks Oct, Dec 25-26, Jan 1-2. £38|**£10**

DRYBRIDGE NJ4562 **Old Monastery** (01542) 832660 Lovely views from former monastery - as well as very good fish, game and aberdeen angus beef, reasonably priced wines and friendly service; cl Sun pm and Mon-Tues. £30|**£7.95**

FALKLAND NO2507 **Kind Kyttock's Kitchen** *Cross Wynd* (01337) 857477 Popular well known tearoom nr village centre, with enjoyable light home-made meals and super afternoon teas; friendly staff; cl Mon and 24 Dec-5 Jan. £20|**£5**

KELTY NT1393 **Butterchurn** *Cocklaw Mains Farm* (01383) 830169 In the courtyard of a farm, this popular restaurant has fine views over Loch Leven, and serves morning coffee, lunch, afternoon teas, snacks, and traditional high teas using fresh local ingredients; they also sell their own products to take away and have a craft and gift centre, farmyard pets for children, and walks and cycle trails; cl Sun-Thurs pms, 25-26 Dec and 1-2 Jan; disabled access. £27|**£6.95**

KINGUSSIE NH7501 **Cross** *Tweed Mill Brae, Ardbroilach Rd* (01540) 661166 Converted 19th-c stone tweed mill by stream, now a no smoking restaurant-with-rooms, with a relaxed friendly atmosphere, extremely good eclectic scottish cooking (evenings only) using the best local produce, excellent wine list, marvellous cheeses, and super breakfasts; bdrms; cl Sun-Mon pms and Christmas-Jan; disabled access. £40

PERTH NO1123 **Let's Eat** *77 Kinnoull St* (01738) 643377 Very popular restaurant in what was the Theatre Royal; relaxed friendly atmosphere, enjoyable modern cooking inc proper old-fashioned puddings, and short selective wine list; cl Sun-Mon, 2 wks Jan, 2 wks July; disabled access. £25|**£9**

ST ANDREWS NO5016 **Vine Leaf** *131 South St* (01334) 477497 Warmly welcoming and attractively laid out dining room overlooking walled herb garden, super food (inc seafood, game and vegetarian dishes), unobtrusive service and decent wines; cl ams, Sun-Mon and Jan; disabled access. £30

ST FILLANS NN6924 **Four Seasons** (01764) 685333 Long white family-run hotel with wonderful Loch Earn views, generous helpings of very good scottish food inc super fish and game dishes; lunchtime snacks, too; can eat in Tarken Bar, on terrace or in smarter restaurant; comfortable bdrms and chalets; cl Jan-Feb; £38|**£10**

STONEHAVEN NO8595 **Lairhillock** (01569) 730001 Relaxed and friendly extended 18th-c country pub with wide choice of good, popular and imaginative food, well kept real ales, lots of malt whiskies and wines, nice views from cheerfully atmospheric beamed bar, central fire in spacious lounge, and airy conservatory; cl 25-26 Dec, 1-2 Jan, restaurant also cl Tues; disabled access. £30|**£7.95**

WEEM NN8449 **Ailean Chraggan** (01887) 820346 Small friendly inn with lovely views, very good food inc plenty of fresh fish and enjoyable puddings - you can eat in the bar or restaurant - and a very good wine list; comfortable bdrms; cl 25-26 Dec, 1-2 Jan. £22.50|**£9.45**

West Scotland

The pick of mainland Scotland's scenery; few highlights for children

The best place to begin exploring Scotland's first National Park (which covers Loch Lomond and the Trossachs) is the impressive new visitor centre in Balloch, while roads winding slowly along the intricate coast make driving there a succession of glorious sea-and-mountain views.

Aside from coastal Oban (a pleasantly bustling town) and Inveraray (some interesting family attractions), places to visit are mostly low-key, suiting the relaxed pace of life. Families enjoy the good underwater centre at Barcaldine, Hill House in Helensburgh is a fine example of the work of Charles Rennie Mackintosh, and you can get a good sense of the past at the Auchindrain Township Museum. The cluster of ancient sites around Kilmartin is quite thought-provoking, and Mull (and nearby Iona) is well worth the journey - young children will recognise Tobermory as TV's Ballymory. The great west coast gardens (children love the one at Arduaine) are at their peak in May and June.

Where to stay

ARDUAINE NM7910 **Loch Melfort Hotel** *Arduaine, Oban, Argyll PA34 4XG* (01852) 200233 **£120**, plus special breaks; 26 rms, gorgeous sea views. Comfortable hotel popular in summer with passing yachtsmen (hotel's own moorings), nautical charts and marine glasses in airy modern bar, own lobster pots and nets so emphasis on seafood, pleasant foreshore walks, outstanding springtime woodland gardens; disabled access; dogs welcome in bedrooms

BALLACHULISH NN0559 **Ballachulish House** *Ballachulish, Argyll PA39 4JX* (01855) 811266 **£100***, plus special breaks; 8 rms with views. Remote 17th-c house with a friendly atmosphere, elegant rooms, log fires, honesty bar, hearty helpings of good food using local fish and beef, and walled garden, croquet lawn, adjacent golf course; children over 10

CRINAN NR7894 **Crinan Hotel** *Crinan, Lochgilphead, Argyll PA31 8SR* (01546) 830261 **£260** inc dinner, plus special breaks; 20 rms. Rather smart hotel by start of canal to Lochgilphead, marvellous views from stylish formal top-floor restaurant and bedrooms, nautical decorations in lounge bar, lots of local fish and large wine list; cl Christmas and New Year; disabled access; dogs welcome in bedrooms

DERVAIG NM4749 **Druimard Country House** *Dervaig, Tobermory, Isle of Mull PA75 6QW* (01688) 400345 **£130** inc dinner, plus special breaks; 7 rms. Peaceful Victorian country house with wonderful views across the glen and River Bellart, friendly helpful owners, comfortable lounge and conservatory, lots of pictures, books and magazines, good breakfasts, excellent food using the best local produce; the Mull Little Theatre is in the grounds; disabled access; dogs welcome in bedrooms

ELLANBEICH NM7417 **Inshaig Park** *Easdale, Oban, Argyll PA34 4RF* (01852) 300256 **£54**, plus special breaks; 6 rms. Solid family-run stone building on Seil island (bridge to mainland), a hotel since Victorian times, with stunning sea views, good food inc fresh local seafood, friendly bar and warm welcome; dogs welcome in bedrooms

ERISKA NM9041 **Isle of Eriska Hotel** *Ledaig, Oban, Argyll PA37 1SD* (01631) 720371 **£240**; 19 rms. In a wonderful position on small island linked by bridge to mainland, impressive baronial hotel with very relaxed country house atmosphere, log fires and pretty drawing room, excellent food, exemplary service, and comprehensive wine list; leisure complex with indoor swimming pool, sauna, gym and so forth, lovely surrounding walks, and 9-hole golf course, clay pigeon shooting and golf - and plenty of wildlife inc tame badgers who come nightly to the library door for their bread and milk; cl Jan; children over 5 in pool and evening restaurant (high tea provided); disabled access; dogs welcome in bedrooms

FORT WILLIAM NN0973 **Grange** *Grange Rd, Fort William, Inverness-shire PH33 6JF (01397) 705516* **£80** plus special breaks*; 4 rms with loch views. Charming Victorian house in quiet landscaped gardens with log fire in comfortable lounge, fine breakfasts in dining room overlooking Loch Linnhe, and helpful hard-working owners; cl Nov-Mar; children over 12

GIGHA NR6551 **Gigha Hotel** *Isle of Gigha PA41 7AA (01583) 505254* **£79**, plus special breaks; 13 rms, most with own bthrm. Traditional family-run hotel, small and attractive with lots of charm, bustling bar (popular with yachtsmen and locals), neatly kept comfortable residents' lounge, and local seafood in restaurant; self-contained cottages too; cl 25, 26 Dec; dogs welcome in bedrooms

KILBERRY NR7267 **Kilberry Inn** *Kilberry, Tarbert, Argyll PA29 6YD (01880) 770223* **£79**, plus special breaks; 3 ground-floor no smoking rms. Homely and warmly welcoming inn on W coast of Knapdale with fine sea views, old-fashioned character, very good traditional home cooking relying on fresh local ingredients; cl Nov-Mar; disabled access

KILCHRENAN NN0422 **Taychreggan Hotel** *Kilchrenan, Taynuilt, Argyll PA35 1HQ (01866) 833211* **£130***, plus special breaks; 19 rms. Civilised and extensively refurbished hotel with fine garden running down to Loch Awe, comfortable airy bar, attractively served lunchtime bar food, polite efficient staff, good freshly prepared food in no smoking dining room, careful wine list, dozens of malt whiskies, and pretty inner courtyard; cl Christmas; no children; dogs welcome in bedrooms

KILFINAN NR9279 **Kilfinan Hotel** *Kilfinan, Tighnabruaich, Argyll PA21 2EP (01700) 821201* **£84***; 11 rms. Friendly former coaching inn, popular locally, in fine scenery with sporting activities such as shooting and stalking; very good traditional restaurant food often using own game and salmon, decent bar food, and log fires; cl parts of Feb; children over 12

KILNINVER NM8727 **Knipoch** *Knipoch, Oban, Argyll PA34 4QT (01852) 316251* **£150**, plus winter breaks; 20 rms. Elegant very well kept Georgian hotel in lovely countryside overlooking Loch Feochan; fine family portraits, log fires, fresh flowers and polished furniture in comfortable lounges and bars, carefully chosen wines and malt whiskies, and marvellous food inc their own smoked salmon; dogs welcome in bedrooms

ONICH NN0461 **Allt-Nan-Ros** *Onich, Fort William, Inverness-shire PH33 6RY (01855) 821210* **£153** inc dinner*, plus special breaks; 20 rms, many with views over the gardens to the water. Victorian shooting lodge with fine scottish food, friendly atmosphere, bright airy rooms, and magnificent views across Loch Linnhe and the gardens; disabled access; dogs away from eating areas

PORT APPIN NM9045 **Airds Hotel** *Port Appin, Appin, Argyll PA38 4DF (01631) 730236* **£280** inc dinner, plus special breaks; 12 lovely rms. Instantly relaxing 18th-c inn with lovely views of Loch Linnhe and the island of Lismore, blissfully comfortable day rooms, professional courteous staff, and charming owners; the food is exceptional (as is the wine list), there are lots of surrounding walks, with more on Lismore (small boat every hour), clay pigeon shooting and riding; cl 5-22 Jan; dogs welcome in bedrooms

TARBERT NR8768 **Columba Hotel** *East Pier Rd, Tarbert, Argyll PA29 6UF (01880) 820808* **£75.90**, plus special breaks; 10 rms. In a peaceful position on Loch Fyne with views of the surrounding hills, this family-run hotel has log fires in the friendly bar and lounge, an informal and relaxed atmosphere, very enjoyable food using fresh local produce, and quite a few malt whiskies; cl Christmas; dogs welcome in bedrooms

TARBERT NR8571 **Stonefield Castle** *Stonefield, Tarbert, Argyll PA29 6YJ (01880) 820836* **£170** inc dinner, plus special breaks; 33 rms. With wonderful views and surrounding wooded grounds, this scottish baronial mansion has comfortable public rooms and decent restaurant food; snooker room; dogs welcome in bedrooms

To see and do

ARDUAINE NM7910
Arduaine Gardens 🏛 (A816) The 8-hectare (20-acre) seaside gardens here shelter behind extensive windbreaks, though the high viewpoint gives a superb view of coast and islands; almost subtropical, with many rare and tender plants besides the rhododendrons, azaleas, camellias and magnolias which flourish so in this part of the world, the impressive collection of perennials carries the display on into the autumn. Children too love this place. Disabled access, open all year; (01852) 200366; £3.50; NTS. The comfortable Loch Melfort Hotel, with great sea views, does good bar lunches.

AUCHINDRAIN NN0102
Auchindrain Township Museum (A83) The only communal tenancy township to have remained on its ancient site much in its original form. All the little stone buildings have been excellently restored and simply furnished in period style, so you get a real feeling of stepping back into the early 1800s. Shop; cl Oct-Mar; (01499) 500235; £3.80.

BALMAHA NS3881
For a good, strenuous walk, readers recommend following the West Highland Way up to Conic Hill (superb views, popular with kite fliers); you can retrace your steps or make it into a circular mile walk by returning via the road.

BARCALDINE NM9240
Scottish Sea Life Sanctuary (A828) Lively underwater centre, with hi-tech face-to-fish-face displays of native marine life from sea-horses and jellyfish to sharks, also north american river otters with deep-dive pools, streams and underwater views into their holt (home). Conservation exhibits show local loch creatures, and a rescue centre has dozens of playful abandoned seal pups; nature trails, and woodland adventure playground. Meals, snacks, shop, mostly disabled access; cl wkdys Dec-Feb exc school hols; (01631) 720386; £7.50. The Lochnell Arms and Falls of Lora down at Connel are reliable lunch stops.

BEN NEVIS NN1671
Though Britain's highest mountain, this is one of the more easily managed summits, with a long, safe path up: expect big crowds in season. Munro-baggers say it's far from being the best viewpoint mountain, though; a 'munro' is any 3,000-ft peak (914 metres), named for Sir Hugh Munro, who first tabulated them. The mountain is owned by a conservation charity. Just N on Aonach Mor, Britain's only mountain gondola carries visitors up 650 metres (2,150 ft) to Scotland's highest restaurant, and gift shops - the views are spectacular; cl for around 6 wks early Nov-late Dec, and in bad weather; (01397) 705825; *£7.50.

BENMORE NS1391
Botanic Garden (A815) An outstation of Edinburgh's Royal Botanic Garden, with attractive woodland and glorious rhododendrons. Some enormously tall and magnificent conifers here, and a good many rarities. Nice views too. Meals, snacks, shop, disabled access; cl Nov-Feb; (01369) 706261; £3.50. The reopened Coylet Inn (A815 N) has good local food.

CAIRNDOW NN1710
Ardkinglas Woodland Garden (off A83) On a hillside overlooking Loch Fyne, the pinetum here includes one of Britain's tallest trees, a grand fir well over 61 metres (200 ft) and still shooting upwards, as well as the mightiest conifer in all Europe - a silver fir with a girth of over 9 metres (30 ft). Also rhododendrons, azaleas and other exotic plants, and daffodils and bluebells in spring. Open all year; disabled access; *£3. The same people run the Tree Shop (about 2m N at the top of the loch), which specialises in specimen trees, indigenous Highland trees, and shrubs. Also lots of well crafted woodware (inc some lovely toys and puzzles); meals, snacks, shop; (01499) 600261. Next door the Loch Fyne Oyster Bar is renowned for its fresh shellfish, which you can eat in the restaurant or buy in the shop; the Cairndow Hotel with a waterside garden is also good.

COLINTRAIVE NS0374
This attractive village spreads along the shore of the sea loch, with gorgeous

views (for example from the well run Colintraive Hotel) across the narrow Kyles of Bute. There's a short ferry crossing to Rhubodach on Bute.

CORPACH NN1177

Caledonian Canal From Corpach straightforward towpath walks lead NE up a flight of locks known as Neptune's Staircase, with mountain backdrops. There's good access to the locks from the Moorings Hotel (good value basement wine bar) at Banavie.

Treasures of the Earth (Mallaig Rd) Good collection of gemstones, crystals and minerals, imaginatively displayed in carefully lit rock cavities. Shop, disabled access; cl Jan-Feb; (01397) 772283; £3.50.

CRINAN CANAL NR7894

Cut through the nine miles at the top of the Kintyre peninsula at the end of the 18th c, to save coastal sailors many miles of dangerous waters; the end at Crinan is attractive, usually with one or two yachts or even a rare fishing boat waiting to enter the first lock, and the Crinan Hotel is a comfortable lunch stop. The canal towpath allows gentle strolls.

DUNOON NS1878

Brought in easy reach of Glasgow by frequent ferries from Gourock, this fading late Victorian resort has pleasant views from its fine long promenade; very busy in Aug. The local history museum (Castle Gardens) has recreated Victorian rooms. Shop, disabled access; cl Sun am and mid-Oct to Easter; £1.50; (01369) 701422. The waterside Holy Loch Inn (Sandbank, A815 N) has decent food.

FORT WILLIAM NN1174

A largely Victorian town, partly pedestrianised, that manages to combine its role as a regional centre with its other life as a holiday base, particularly for solid Ben Nevis which rises above it, and for the Caledonian Canal which leads on up into the Great Glen and eventually across to the North Sea. The Alexandra and Nevis Bank hotels are useful for food, as is the Ben Nevis Bar; the Nevisport is the place for walking and climbing chat. In summer you can take the Jacobite Express steam train on the **West Highland Line** from here - it goes right up into the Highlands and the views are quite superb; (01463)

239026; cl Oct to mid-Jun.

Inverlochy Castle (NE edge) Partly 13th-c ruins (usually under scaffolding), site of the 1645 battle between Montrose and the Campbells; free.

West Highland Museum (Cameron Sq) Great on Jacobite relics: a secret portrait of Prince Charlie needs a curved mirror to decode it. Shop, limited disabled access; cl Sun (exc in July-Aug); (01397) 702169; £2.

GIGHA NR6549

3 miles offshore, linked by frequent ferries from Tayinloan on the A83 down the W coast of Kintyre; the island (recently bought by the islanders) is a perfect place for really getting away from it all. Apart from the small Gigha Hotel, there are rooms at the Post Office and other places, and you can hire bicycles to explore it properly. The tall leaning Druids Stone by the road N of Tarbert Farm and other carved stones around the ruined medieval chapel are supposed to have mysterious powers. Phone (01880) 730253 for ferry times.

Achamore Gardens Created by Sir James Horlick, who bought the island in 1944; a garden of woodlands filled with rhododendrons and azaleas, many plants brought from his home in Berkshire in laundry baskets. Lots of subtropical plants - the climate and soil are perfect for them. Snacks, shop, limited disabled access; £2.

GLEN NEVIS NN1468

(nr Fort William) Probably the best-known Highland valley, with splendid gorge scenery for an easy long mile's walk to Steall Falls. The Pap of Glencoe and the succession of peaks in the largely unwooded Mamore Forest (access from the Glen) are interesting viewpoint summits; they don't need rock-climbing expertise, just reasonable fitness and plenty of time.

GLENCOE NN1557

The scenery around here is some of Scotland's most beautiful and wild. It's understandably popular with walkers and climbers, who share it with deer, wildcats and golden eagles. The Clachaig and Kings House do food, and restored heather-thatched buildings house a summer local history museum; (01855) 811664; cl Sun; £2. A forest walk runs from the hospital by Glencoe

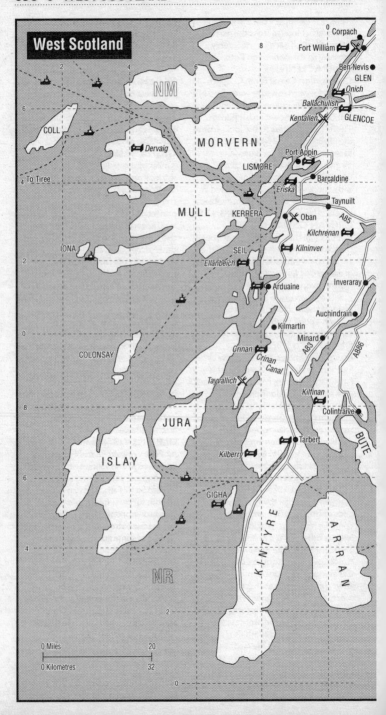

village past a lochan (small loch) above Loch Leven.

Altnafeadh Good start for walks from the top of the glen. The West Highland Way takes a zigzag route N up the Devil's Staircase and through the mountains to Kinlochleven; another hill walk from Altnafeadh heads E up Beinn a' Chrulaiste, one of Glencoe's more manageable peaks.

Glen Etive Reached from Glencoe by a squelchy walk along glens (or a long track from the A82 E of Glencoe), with close-ups of mighty peaks for reward.

Glencoe Visitor Centre 🅰 (A82; 1 mile out of village) Good visitor centre with interactive displays, telling the story of the massacre of 1692, when billeted troops tried to murder all their MacDonald hosts, as well as useful local information and facts about the mountainside and local conservation. Meals, snacks, shop, disabled access; cl Tues-Thurs Nov-Feb; (01855) 811307; £3.50; NTS.

Lost Valley This secret Glencoe pasture-ground was used by the MacDonalds for stolen cattle in times of clan warfare; the walk involves an ascent from the Meeting of the Three Waters.

HELENSBURGH NS2983

Hill House (Upper Colquhoun St) In an area short of many great houses, this austerely scottish landmark is a wonderful example of the work of Charles Rennie Mackintosh; there's an exhibition on his life, and the gardens have been restored to reflect features common to the architect's designs. Teas, shop; cl am, and all day Nov-Mar; (01436) 673900; £7; NTS - it's one of their busier properties. The dignified resort town, attractively placed on the Clyde, has some good views from its broad streets.

INVERARAY NN0908

Beautifully placed and rather self-consciously elegant, this was built as an estate village in the 18th c, and is now a magnet for visitors. The Loch Fyne Hotel is pleasant for lunch, with stunning views; the George is popular too.

Argyll Wildlife Park (Dalchenna; A83 SW) A collection of local or once-local animals (deer, foxes and wildcats) plus chipmunks, wallabies, racoons and so forth - with some eminently tame wild creatures wandering around. Snacks, shop, disabled access; cl Nov-Mar though possibly open wknds; (01499) 302264; £4.

Inveraray Castle Built in 1745, and still the home of the Duke and Duchess of Argyll, it has particularly impressive state rooms, and a striking hall. Snacks, shop, ground floor disabled access; cl Fri and 1-2pm in Apr-May and Oct, Sun am, and Nov-Mar; (01499) 302203; £5.50. Nearby woodland trails include a view over Loch Fyne from Dun na Cuaiche Tower.

Inveraray Jail 🔁 Excellent prison museum, with costumed guides and Katie the governor's cow really bringing the place to life. You can sit and listen to trials, try your hand at hard labour, and even experience being locked up in the airing yards. Watch out for the animated surprises. Shop; (01499) 302381; £5.75.

KILMARTIN NR8395

Dunadd Fort (3m S) This craggy prehistoric hill fort became a 7-9th-c fortress of Dalriada, from which the Celtic kingdom of Scotland was formed. Look out for the carvings nearby of a boar (shielded by glassfibre) and a footprint, which probably mark the spot where early kings were invested with royal power.

Kilmartin church Plain and Victorian, but it has a stunning 10th-c cross; the graveyard has interesting carved medieval tombstones. The simple Kilmartin Hotel is useful for lunch. A short walk away, tracks link the well signed North, Mid and South Cairns (impressive prehistoric burial mounds - you can climb into the North one via trapdoor and ladder, to see sup-and-ring carvings), and the Templewood stone circles.

Kilmartin House Museum Explains the rich and intriguing archaeology of the area. Snacks, shop, disabled access; cl 25 Dec, 1 Jan; (01546) 510278; *£4.50.

KILMUN NS1781

Kilmun forest walks Rare conifers, an arboretum of great beauty, and some striking gum-trees.

LOCH LOMOND NS3884

Loch Lomond, with the Trossachs, have recently been designated a National Park. Straddling the Highland-Lowland divide, the park covers 580 square miles, and in spite of being so close to Glasgow and on every coach company's hit list, the loch (Britain's largest freshwater lake) does have a serene beauty that seems unspoilt by the visitors. Wee birdies sing and wild flowers spring - and the water is often calm enough to reflect the mountains. The best views are from the narrower N end. Surprisingly, there aren't many paths: the shoreline track, partly metalled, on the quieter E side, comes closest to the water; the Oak Tree at Balmaha round here serves enterprising food. Cruises round the lake leave from Balloch, as well as from the pretty village of Luss, a good place to hire a boat for pottering about on the water (there's a visitor centre here too).

Lomond Shores Visitor Centre (Luss Rd, Balloch) This new £60 million visitor centre marks the southern gateway to the new National Park, and is a good place to start. As well as lots of displays (inc interactive ones) and information on the area, there are craft shops, restaurants serving scottish food, and a film, *The Legend of Loch Lomond*, on a screen the size of a tennis court. Disabled access; cl 25 Dec; (01389) 721500; £4.95, £2 for just the viewing gallery at the top of the visitor centre. You can also eat on the Maid of the Loch paddle steamer moored nearby, and the Balloch Hotel has decent food all day.

Balloch Castle Country Park This includes a visitor centre, woodland and meadow trails, walled garden, and fine views. Snacks, shop, limited disabled access; cl Nov-Apr exc Tues and Thurs in Apr; (01389) 758216 (ranger service events (01389) 722600); free.

Ben Lomond The southernmost munro (or peak over 3,000 ft, 914 metres), and the first of 21 in the National Park, with a good walk up from Rowardennan on the E shore. On a really clear day the views are remarkable, to Ben Nevis and the Highland mountains in the N, to the irish coast in the W, and to the hills above Edinburgh in the E - with Loch Lomond itself laid out in special beauty below.

Conic Hill Less than half Ben Lomond's height but more accessible, a straightforward but rewarding climb from Balmaha at Loch Lomond's SE corner.

MINARD NR9799

Crarae Gardens (A83) Lovely gardens noted for their rare ornamental shrubs and rhododendrons, azaleas and conifers, in a beautiful gorge overlooking Loch Fyne. Snacks, shop, and interesting plant sales (summer only), limited disabled access; open all year; (01546) 886614; £3.50; NTS.

MULL NM5055

For most people this island takes a bit of getting to, but if you are within reach its unspoilt coasts are certainly a dramatic lure. A good ferry service goes from Oban and Lochaline (and in summer from Kilchoan). A couple of castellated mansions, one going back to the 13th c and another, 19th-c Torosay Castle, with attractive gardens (tearoom, shop, limited disabled access; open daily Easter-end Oct; £5). You can do trips on Mull's unique little railway; (01680) 812421 for details. The interior is less interesting than the coast, with brackeny moors and conifer plantations over much of it, though there is some mountainous hill walking in the S (as usual, not many defined paths).

Iona (off Mull) Lovely, filled with a sense of spirituality as well as its beautiful restored medieval abbey and touching remains of other ancient shrines; Scotland's first kings were buried here (as is former Labour leader John Smith).

St Columba Visitor Centre (Fionnphort) Visitor centre dedicated to the saint. The little coastal settlement overlooks Iona, and the boats go from here. The Keel Row has decent food.

Tobermory Pretty little waterside town that has shot to fame as 'Ballymory' in a popular toddler's TV programme, and is now full of young families with enraptured little girls cheerfully knocking on doors in search of their favourite characters - considerably lowering the age range of visitors that the island has been used to.

OBAN NM8530

This bustling coastal town is a busy ferry port and a popular place for holidaymakers, with a good cheerful atmosphere; the Oban Inn is fun, the Lorne has enjoyable fresh food, and the Ee-usk has great local fish. Besides the main ferries, there are boats to Lismore, which has shoreside walks and several castle ruins and antiquities, and (just a hop really) Kerrera, for more shoreside walks and a romantic 16th-c ruined castle on its S cliff. A little way S at Cologin, the countrified Barn is useful for lunch, and often has evening folk music.

Dunstaffnage Castle (off A485 4m N) Beautifully set, this was once the prison of Flora MacDonald. It's now in ruins, but you can still see its gatehouse, round towers and massively thick walls. Shop, disabled access to visitor centre only; cl Thurs and Fri Nov-Mar; (01631) 562465; £2.20; HS.

Oban Rare Breeds Farm (A816 Oban—Kilmore) In lovely countryside; you can meet, touch and feed the very visitor-friendly animals (inc llama and alpaca). Teas, shop, pets corner, play and picnic areas, woodland walk, some disabled access; cl Jan to mid-Mar; (01631) 770608; £6.

PORT APPIN NM9045

An attractive little settlement, very peaceful, where you can pick wild blueberries by the roadside, catch a boat across to Lismore (see Oban, above), or just sit by the water keeping your eyes open for the seals that are so common around here. The Pier House has great seafood, and comfortable bedrooms. This is *Kidnapped* country, with the scene of the Appin Murder not far off, and a monument marking where James of the Glens was wrongly hanged at Ballachulish to the N (the Ballachulish Hotel has decent food and wide views).

RIVER LEVEN NN1861

The glen gives a fine walk through semi-wooded terrain, from Kinlochleven to the dam of the gigantic Blackwater Reservoir - with an awesomely bleak view ahead of empty hills.

SEIL NM7819

This little island is linked to the mainland by a short and extremely beautiful 18th-c bridge that people call the Bridge over the Atlantic. There's an attractive walk over to the anchorage on the far side which looks out to Jura; the Tigh an Truish overlooking the water has home-made food.

TARBERT NR8465
Pleasant and quite picturesque small harbourside town, with the shattered ruins of a castle (too shaky to explore); the Tarbert Hotel, with comfortable bedrooms overlooking the harbour, does good local seafood.

TAYNUILT NN0031
Bonawe Iron Furnace (off A85) The most complete remaining charcoal-fired ironworks in Britain, worked until 1876. Iron produced here was used for the cannonballs for Nelson's ships. Shop; cl Thurs pm, Fri and Sun am in Oct, cl Nov–Mar; (01866) 822432; £2.80; HS. The lochside Polfearn Hotel does good food.

Inns with decent food, in good places for drivers, walkers or strollers, include the Loch Shiel Hotel at Acharacle NM6867, Ardentinny Hotel by Loch Long at Ardentinny NS1887, Village Inn at Arrochar NN2903, Galley of Lorne at Ardfern NM8004, Bridge of Orchy Hotel at Bridge of Orchy NN2939, Four Seasons at Inchree NN0263 nr Onich, Kilchrenan Inn at Kilchrenan by Loch Awe NN0222, Portsonachan Hotel on the opposite side of that loch NN1227, Coylet on Loch Eck NS1493, Loch Gair Hotel on Loch Gair NR9190 and Oystercatcher at Otter Ferry NR9384.

Where to eat

CAIRNDOW NN1812 **Loch Fyne Oyster Bar** *Clachan Farm (01499) 600236* Relaxed restaurant in converted farm buildings by Loch Fyne, serving good seafood and smoked fish (they have their own smokehouse); reasonably priced wine list and a warm welcome; cl 25–26 Dec and 1–2 Jan; disabled access. £20|**£8.95**

FORT WILLIAM NN1074 **Alexandra** *The Parade (01397) 702241* Popular hotel in town square with meals and snacks in the Great Food Stop (open all day) and evening restaurant; disabled access. £21.95|**£6.95**

KENTALLEN NN0259 **Holly Tree** *(01631) 740292* Super food in carefully converted railway station, cosy public rooms, lovely shoreside setting (best to book in winter); bdrms; cl ams and Nov–Jan; disabled access. £31

OBAN NM8530 **Ee-usk** *104 George St (01631) 565666* Stylish restaurant with blue and yellow décor, modern artwork, blond wooden tables and blue banquettes, fantastic, absolutely fresh fish and shellfish dishes simply prepared, a short, well chosen wine list, cheerful service, and a relaxed atmosphere. Cl 25–26 Dec, 1 Jan; disabled access. £25.15|**£7.95**

TAYVALLICH NR7487 **Tayvallich Inn** *Kintallen (01546) 870282* Simply refurbished pub overlooking yacht anchorage with super local seafood (other decent dishes too), dining conservatory (no smoking), and friendly service; cl Mon Nov–Mar, 25 Dec and 2 Jan. £18|**£6**

North Scotland

Glorious scenery on the west coast and Skye, miles of beaches on the east coast, a few fine castles and gardens, and some lovely good value places to stay

The W coast has glorious vistas of sea, mountains and islands, while long empty sandy beaches (and good golf courses) make the E coast just right for a quiet summer holiday. Skye is idyllic in good weather. The magnificent mountain scenery of Torridon is perhaps the best place to spot local wildlife, and a dolphin or whale-watching trip from Cromarty can be memorable. The N coast, largely wild and empty, is addictive to some people, harsh and inhospitable to others.

You'll find splendid castles at Golspie (fine collections of furnishings and art), Dornie (in a beautiful position), and on Skye Armadale Castle (lovely walks) and Dunvegan Castle (in the same family for 800 years). There are interesting ruins in Drumnadrochit (children enjoy the monster stuff at Loch Ness 2000 nearby).

Interesting gardens, perhaps unexpected up here, include Attadale at Strathcarron, Inverewe at Poolewe, the little oasis at Kylesku (you get there by boat), and the futuristic Hydroponicum at Achiltibuie. Craig Highland Farm is nice for children.

The Highlands offer ultra-tough mountain walking, but relatively few easier routes on defined paths; shorter circular walks are few and far between. Compared to the uplands of England and Wales there are few obvious walking routes (OS maps show hardly any), and the scale of the scenery is often so vast that you need to walk for hours before the views change. The high peaks are mostly for the dedicated (and fit) enthusiast. There is an informal tradition of allowing general access to the mountains, but there are few rights of way, and areas are often closed for at least part of the grouse-shooting season (12 Aug-10 Dec), particularly its first few weeks, or the deer-stalking season (1 July-20 Oct for stags, 21 Oct-15 Feb for hinds).

Where to stay

ACHILTIBUIE NC0208 **Summer Isles Hotel** *Achiltibuie, Ullapool, Ross-shire IV26 2YQ (01854) 622282* **£114***; 13 comfortable rms. Beautifully placed above the sea towards the end of a very long and lonely road; warm, friendly, well furnished hotel with delicious set menus using fresh ingredients (in which is largely self-sufficient), a choice of superb puddings and excellent array of uncommon cheeses; pretty watercolours and flowers; cl mid-Oct-Easter; children over 8; dogs welcome in bedrooms

APPLECROSS NG7144 **Applecross Inn** *Shore St, Applecross, Strathcarron, Ross-shire IV54 8LR (01520) 744262* **£60**; 7 rms, all with breathtaking sea views over Sound of Raasay, some with shared bthrms. Gloriously placed informal inn with tables out by shore, simple comfortable and friendly bar, log or peat fire in lounge, small restaurant with excellent fresh fish and seafood; cl 25 Dec and 5 Jan; dogs welcome

AULTIVULLIN NC8267 **Catalina** *Aultivullin, Strathy, Thurso, Caithness KW14 7RY (01641) 541395* **£46***, plus special breaks; 1 suite with small fridge. Extended former croft on wild headland just a short walk from the sea; residents have own wing with private lounge and dining room but owners offer a friendly welcome, good breakfasts, and enjoyable 3-course meals - bring your own wine and they will serve you at whatever time you wish to eat; disabled access, no children, no smoking

COLBOST NG2050 **Three Chimneys** *Colbost, Dunvegan, Isle of Skye IV55 8ZT (01470) 511258* **£190***, plus special breaks; 6 chic but comfortable rms in simple but very stylish no smoking crofter's cottage on the edge of a loch, with two cosy stone-walled dining rooms, open fires, warmly friendly helpful owners, exceptionally good imaginative food with a strong emphasis on local fish (though plenty of game and vegetarian, too), super breakfasts, and a carefully chosen wine list; disabled access; cl 6-30 Jan; restaurant cl Sun am and all ams Nov-March

CROMARTY NH7867 **Royal** *Marine Terrace, Cromarty, Ross-shire IV11 8YN (01381) 600217* **£59.80***, plus special breaks; 10 rms. Traditional waterfront hotel (maybe dolphins) with friendly owners and staff, attractive lounges, bars and sun lounge, garden and scottish dishes in dining room; gets very busy in summer; dogs welcome in bedrooms

DRUMNADROCHIT NH4731 **Polmaily House** *Drumnadrochit, Inverness IV63 6XT (01456) 450343* **£126***, plus special breaks; 11 light, pretty rms. Very relaxing and homely hotel in 18 acres, with comfortable drawing room and library, open fires, and excellent food in the no smoking restaurant (wonderful packed lunches too); a happy place for families with well equipped indoor play area with lots of supervised activities, baby sitting and listening, hundreds of children's videos, plenty of ponies and pets, evening children's club, swimming pool, tennis, croquet, fishing, and boating; cl 4 days at Christmas; disabled access; dogs welcome in bedrooms ☺

GARVE NH3874 **Inchbae Lodge** *Garve, Ross-shire IV23 2PH (01997) 455269* **£70**, plus special breaks; 16 rms, some in chalet. Former hunting lodge in lovely Highland setting with comfortable homely lounges, winter log fires, small bar (liked by locals), and good fixed-price evening meals using fresh local produce; lots of wildlife, marvellous walks; cl Christmas; disabled access; dogs welcome

GLENELG NG8119 **Glenelg Inn** *Kirkton, Glenelg, Kyle, Ross-shire IV40 8JR (01599) 522273* **£120**, plus special breaks; 7 individually decorated and comfortable rms, all with fine views. Overlooking Skye across its own beach, carefully renovated old stables with relaxed bar, comfortable sofas and blazing fires, friendly staff and locals, good food using local venison, local hill-bred lamb and lots of wonderfully fresh fish and seafood, and quite a few whiskies; the drive to the inn involves spectacular views from the steep road (and the pretty drive to Glen Beag broch is nice); cl Christmas; disabled access; dogs welcome away from dining room

ISLE ORNSAY NG7012 **Eilean Iarmain** *Isle Ornsay, Isle of Skye IV43 8QR (01471) 833332* **£120**, plus winter breaks; 16 individual rms inc 4 suites (those in main hotel best), all with fine views. Sparkling white hotel with gaelic-speaking staff and locals, big cheerfully busy bar, two pretty dining rooms with lovely sea views, and very good food; disabled access; well behaved dogs welcome

ISLE ORNSAY NG7315 **Kinloch Lodge** *Isle Ornsay, Isle of Skye IV43 8QY (01471) 833214* **£130***, plus winter breaks; 14 rms. Surrounded by rugged mountain scenery at the head of Loch Na Dal, this charming white stone hotel has a relaxed atmosphere in its comfortable and attractive drawing rooms, antiques, portraits, flowers, log fires, and good imaginative food; cookery demonstrations; children by arrangement; cl 22-27 Dec; dogs welcome in bedrooms

LAIDE NG8990 **Old Smiddy** *Laide, Achnasheen, Ross-shire IV22 2NB (01445) 731425* **£70***; 3 pretty rms with thoughtful extras. Really welcoming charming no smoking cottage in lovely spot by sea and mountains, with blazing fire in comfortable homely lounge, and dining room with super breakfasts and delicious evening meals (using local and home-grown produce; bring your own wine); lots of outside pursuits; cl Dec; children over 12; dogs welcome

LYBSTER ND2436 **Portland Arms** *Lybster, Caithness KW3 6BS (01593) 721721* **£75***, plus special breaks; 22 comfortable rms. Big hotel with really friendly staff, log fire in small cosy lounge bar, bistro and informal locals' bar, generous helpings of good fresh food and fine breakfasts; shooting/fishing can be arranged; cl 31 Dec-2 Jan; disabled access to ground floor

MELVICH NC8864 **Melvich Hotel** *Melvich, Thurso, Caithness KW14 7YJ (01641) 531206* **£56***; 14 rms with showers (also have 4 bthrms). Small traditional hotel in lovely spot with homely furniture and peat fires in the civilised lounge, cosy bar, very relaxing atmosphere, friendly owners and staff, good food (esp local seafood and wild salmon), and fine bay views; cl Christmas and New Year

PLOCKTON NG8033 **Plockton Hotel** *41 Harbour St, Plockton, Ross-shire IV52 8TN (01599) 544274* **£90***, plus special breaks; 11 rms, most with own bthrm, plus 4 in cottage annexe. Small notably friendly hotel (not to be confused with Plockton Inn around the corner), in a row of elegant houses by a shore lined with palm trees and flowering shrubs, looking over the sheltered anchorage to rugged mountains, with comfortably furnished lively lounge bar, separate public bar, enjoyable award-winning food in no smoking restaurant, good breakfasts, a good choice of whiskies, and attentive owners; good disabled access; cl 1 Jan

POOLEWE NG8580 **Pool House** *Poolewe, Achnasheen, Ross-shire IV22 2LE*

(01445) 781272 **£260**; 5 beautifully themed suites with remarkable Edwardian and Victorian baths 2½ metres (over 8 ft) tall inc canopied showers. On the shore by the River Ewe, this early 18th-c hotel, remodelled in the 19th by the founder of Inverewe Gardens and recently refurbished, has original panelling, fine doors and friezes uncovered; restful drawing room with open fire, fine antiques and sea views, delicious food with an emphasis on local seafood; plenty of walks and wildlife; cl Jan-14 Feb; children over 12

PORTREE NG4843 **Rosedale** *Quay Brae, Portree, Isle of Skye IV51 9DB (01478) 613131* **£84**, plus special breaks; 23 rms, many with harbour views. Built from three fishermen's cottages with lots of passages and stairs, this family run waterfront hotel has two traditional lounges, small first-floor restaurant with freshly cooked popular food, lots of whiskies in the cocktail bar, helpful staff, marvellous views; cl Nov-Mar; dogs welcome in bedrooms

RAASAY NG5537 **Isle of Raasay Hotel** *Isle of Raasay, Kyle, Ross-shire IV40 8PB (01478) 660222* **£60***, plus special breaks; 12 rms. Victorian hotel with marvellous views over the Sound of Raasay to Skye, popular with walkers and bird-watchers, home-made food with an emphasis on fresh fish; no petrol on the island; disabled access; dogs welcome in bedrooms

SCARISTA NG0192 **Scarista House** *Scarista, Harris, Isle of Harris HS3 3HX (01859) 550238* **£134**, plus special breaks; 5 rms, some in annexe. Marvellously wild countryside and empty beaches surround this isolated small hotel with its antiques-furnished rooms, open fires, warm friendly atmosphere, plenty of books and records (no radio or TV), an impressive wine list, and good food in candlelit dining room using organic home-grown vegetables and herbs, hand-made cheeses, their own eggs, home-made bread, cakes, biscuits, yoghurt and marmalade, and lots of fish and shellfish; excellent for wildlife, walks and fishing; disabled access; cl Christmas and occasionally in winter; dogs welcome in bedrooms

SCOURIE NC1641 **Eddrachilles** *Badcall, Scourie, Lairg, Sutherland IV27 4TH (01971) 502080* **£89.50***, plus special breaks; 11 comfortable rms. Well run hotel in its own 320 acres overlooking Badcall Bay, with wonderful island views; popular with nature-lovers - bird sanctuary nearby, seals, fishing and walking; cl mid-Oct to mid-Mar; children over 3; disabled access

SCOURIE NC1544 **Scourie Hotel** *Scourie, Lairg, Sutherland IV27 4SX (01971) 502396* **£80**; 20 rms with views to Scourie Bay. A haven for anglers, with 36 exclusive beats on 25,000-acre estate; snug bar, two comfortable lounges and good food using plenty of local game and fish in smart no smoking dining room; cl 8 Oct-1 Apr; dogs welcome in bedrooms

SHIEL BRIDGE NG9419 **Kintail Lodge** *Glenshiel, Kyle, Ross-shire IV40 8HL (01599) 511275* **£80**; 12 good value big rms. Pleasantly informal and fairly simple former shooting lodge on Loch Duich, with magnificent views, four acres of walled gardens, residents' lounge bar and comfortable sitting room, good well prepared food inc wild salmon, and fine collection of malt whiskies; dogs welcome in bedrooms

SHIELDAIG NG8153 **Tigh an Eilean** *Shieldaig, Strathcarron, Ross-shire IV54 8XN (01520) 755251* **£115**, plus special breaks; 11 rms. Attractive hotel in outstanding position with lovely view of pine-covered island and sea, kayaks, private fishing and sea fishing arranged, within easy reach of NTS Torridon Estate, Beinn Eighe nature reserve and Applecross peninsula; pretty woodburner in one of two comfortable residents' lounges with well stocked honesty bar, library, modern dining room with delicious food inc home-baked bread; warmly friendly owners conduct occasional astronomical viewings; adjacent pub; cl end Oct-Mar; dogs welcome in bedrooms

SKEABOST NG4048 **Skeabost Country House** *Skeabost Bridge, Portree, Isle of Skye IV51 9NR (01470) 532202* **£95**, plus special breaks; 24 rms, 4 in annexe in Garden House. Smart and friendly little hotel in 29 acres of landscaped grounds on the shores of Loch Snizort; 9-hole 18-tee golf course and 8 miles of salmon and trout fishing; log fires, comfortable day rooms, friendly, helpful staff, and good, enjoyable food; cl mid-Jan to Feb; disabled access; dogs by arrangement

STRONTIAN NM7961 **Kilcamb Lodge Hotel** *Strontian, Acharacle, Argyll PH36*

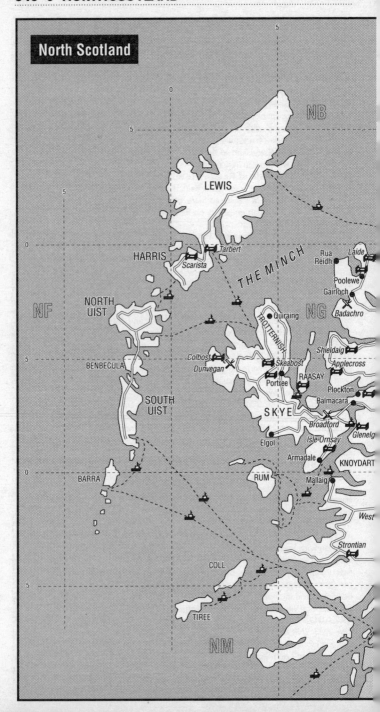

North Scotland

NB

LEWIS

HARRIS

Tarbert

Scarista

THE MINCH

Rua
Reidh

Laide

Poolewe

Gairloch

Badachro

NF

NORTH
UIST

NG

BENBECULA

Quiraing

TROTTERNISH

Shieldaig

Applecross

Colbost

Dunvegan

Skeabost

RAASAY

Plockton

Portree

Balmacara

SOUTH
UIST

SKYE

Broadford

Isle-Ornsay

Glenelg

Elgol

Armadale

KNOYDART

BARRA

RUM

Mallaig

West

Strontian

COLL

NM

TIRE

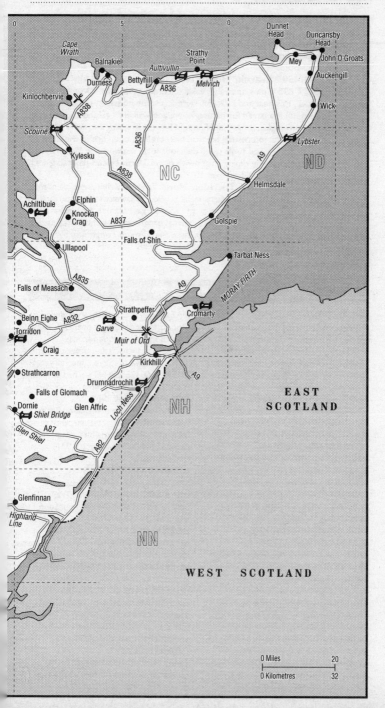

4HY (01967) 402257 **£95***, plus winter breaks; 11 rms. Warm friendly little hotel in 28 acres by Loch Sunart, with log fires in two lounges, carefully cooked food using fresh ingredients from organic kitchen garden, fine choice of malt whiskies in small bar, and a relaxed atmosphere; beach, fishing boat, four moorings and jetty; dogs welcome in bedrooms

TARBERT NB1301 **Leachin House** *Leachin, Harris, Isle of Harris HS3 3AH* (01859) 502157 **£90***, plus special breaks; 2 comfortable rms. Meaning 'house among the rocks', this neat and peaceful Victorian stone house on the loch shores (wonderful sunsets) is a haven for nature-lovers and walkers - guided trips to look for seals, otters and eagles, fishing, and fine wild flowers in spring and early summer; friendly helpful owners, interesting nautical memorabilia, open fire in the drawing room, and particularly good food using delicious local seafood and lamb, served around a communal table in dining room with original 19th-c hand-painted french wallpaper; cl 1 Dec-1 Feb; children over 10

TORRIDON NG8854 **Loch Torridon Hotel** *Torridon, Achnasheen, Ross-shire IV22 2EY* (01445) 791242 **£145**, plus special breaks; 19 comfortable rms. Built in 1887 as a shooting lodge in 58 acres at the foot of Ben Damph by Upper Loch Torridon, this turreted stone house has unusual ornate ceilings and panelling, log fires and innovative cooking; they also run the Ben Damph Lodge nearby; cl Jan; children over 10 in dining room; disabled access

To see and do

ACHILTIBUIE NC0208
Hydroponicum 🖾 Bizarre indoor garden of the future - without any soil. Fascinating guided tours show how plants such as figs, lemons and bananas grow quite happily using the nutrients from the soil, but not the soil itself. Good home-made meals and snacks, shop; disabled access; hourly tours Easter-Sept and twice daily wkdys in Oct (cl Nov-Easter); (01854) 622202; £4.75.
AUCKENGILL ND3664
Northlands Viking Centre (Old School) Interesting displays on how the Norsemen came from Scandinavia to Shetland, Orkney and Caithness, with a model of a Viking longship and other relics. Shop, disabled access; cl Oct-May; (01847) 805515; £1.80.
BALMACARA NG8028
(A67) Huge crofting estate surrounding the Kyle of Lochalsh, with challenging walks through breathtaking scenery; you can still see traditional crofting at Drumbuie and Duirnish, and the NTS have a charming cottage to stay in. The landscape is interspersed with lochs and impressive landmarks like the Five Sisters of Kintail (a fine target for hardened walkers) and Beinn Fhada. The Seagreen Restaurant (Plockton Rd, Kyle) is good.
Lochalsh Woodland Garden (A87

3m E of Kyle of Lochalsh) Wonderful woodland gardens, with peaceful walks, collections of rhododendrons, hydrangeas, fuchsias and other plants, and views towards Skye. Open all year; (01599) 566325; £2; NTS. The Lochalsh Hotel has enjoyable simple bar food.
BALNAKIEL NC3967
The most NW part of mainland Britain, wild, remote and spectacular, with a little craft village (some bits cl Sun, and limited opening in winter; (01971) 511277; free).
BEINN EIGHE NG9963
One of the easier mountain ascents, with a well marked Mountain Trail making a circular route above beautiful island-studded Loch Maree.
BETTYHILL NC7062
Strathnaver Museum Good informative memorial to the notorious Highlands Clearances. Limited disabled access; cl lunchtime, Sun, and Nov-Mar; (01641) 521418; £1.90. The churchyard has a finely carved 9th-c Celtic stone. The Bettyhill Hotel does decent food. Just S is a wonderful **nature reserve**, and the beach nearby is attractive.
CRAIG NG8233
Craig Highland Farm 🖾 This conservation centre for rare breeds of domestic animals and fowl (some you

can feed) is picturesquely set on the shores of Loch Carron; you might catch a glimpse of some wilder creatures too like seals, otters and pine martens, and at low tide you can walk across a coral beach to a heron sanctuary. Snacks, disabled access; cl Oct- Easter; (01599) 544205; *£2.

CROMARTY NH7867

Dolphin Ecosse (Bank House) Boat trips to see the local bottlenose dolphins: they can't guarantee sightings, but nine out of ten of their trips do come across dolphins or porpoise, perhaps even minke whales, and they point out various seabirds and local landmarks along the way. Very friendly and informal, and rated very highly by readers. Best to book on (01381) 600323; shop, snacks, disabled access; *£20. Cromarty itself is a delightfully sleepy place with lots of unspoilt buildings in its well restored core. Hugh Miller's Cottage (Church St) is a surprisingly good little museum about the life of the stonemason turned geologist. Miller House next door will open in 2004 with exhibitions of geology; open Easter-Oct; (01381) 600245; £2.50. The Royal Hotel is a useful food stop, with lovely views.

DORNIE NG8826

Eilean Donan Castle (off A87) Connected to the mainland by a causeway, and unforgettably beautiful. First built in 1220, destroyed in 1719, and then restored at the beginning of the last century, it's perfectly positioned at the meeting point of Lochs Long, Duich and Alsh. Visitor centre with teas and shop, disabled access. The castle cl late Nov to mid-Mar, but the shop stays open; (01599) 555202; *£4.50. The Dornie Hotel has good reasonably priced food inc local seafood.

DRUMNADROCHIT NH5130

Loch Ness 2000 🏢 (Drumnadrochit Hotel) Walk-through multi-media experience tracing the legend from its beginnings in Highland folklore to the scientific investigations of recent years, using the latest technology, laser animations and special effects. There's a kilt-maker on site, and various themed shops inc a whisky shop, keeper's cottage and Nessie shop, a garden with fountain and waterfall, and (from

Easter) boat trips. Meals, snacks, shop, disabled access; cl 25 Dec; (01456) 450573; *£5.95.

Urquhart Castle (just SE) A stronghold since the Iron Age: the present 14th-c remains were once the biggest castle in Scotland, and there's still plenty to see. A piper plays here every day Jun-Aug. The £5 million visitor centre tells the story of the castle and the people who lived here, with a display of artefacts, and a short film about the castle. Café, shop, disabled access to visitors centre inc buggies, but partial to the castle; cl 25-26 Dec; (01456) 450551; £5.50; HS. In the village the Fiddlers Elbow has enjoyable food.

DUNCANSBY HEAD ND4073

A grand spot on a fine day, with an absorbing cliff walk S for a good view of the spectacular Stacks of Duncansby, 60-metre (200-ft) offshore rock pinnacles.

DUNNET HEAD ND2074

Mainland Britain's furthest point N, with views to Orkney. Lovely on a clear early summer's day, with spring flowers in the close turf, and puffins pottering around - but wild and unforgiving when the weather changes.

DURNESS NC4067

Attractively placed near the beautiful sea loch Loch Eriboll, and also has atmospheric boat tours of the Smoo Cave and its underground waterfall. Cl Oct-Apr; (01971) 511704; £3.

Cape Wrath In summer you can make an adventurous expedition to this stormy tip of coast, guarded by a lonely lighthouse, by boat across the Kyle of Durness and then along a very long rough track to the lighthouse itself; for details phone Mrs Mackay; (01971) 511343.

ELPHIN NC2110

Highland & Rare Breeds Farm (A835) Traditional scottish farm animals close up, on a family-worked croft in attractive setting. They sell fleeces and hand-spun wool. Snacks, shop, some disabled access; cl Sept-Jun; (01854) 666204; £3.75.

FALLS OF GLOMACH NH0125

Tremendous waterfall, Scotland's highest, eventually tumbling to a pool 230 metres (750 ft) below the crest of the ravine - a fine wilderness destination for walkers on Kintail, though not at its best in dry seasons.

FALLS OF MEASACH NH1978
With a mighty drop of 60 metres (200 ft), these are the highlight of the mile-long, sheer-sided Corrieshalloch Gorge, owned by the National Trust for Scotland and equipped with a little viewing platform. The swaying suspension bridge high over the gorge is not for the faint-hearted, but gives spectacular views.

FALLS OF SHIN NH5799
(B864 S) A good chance of seeing salmon leaping here in June or early July, esp if there's been a dry spell followed by rain so that the river is in spate.

GAIRLOCH NG8076
Gairloch Heritage Museum
Enthusiastically run, perhaps the most enjoyable of the several heritage museums in the Highlands, with a hands-on exhibition. Shop, disabled access; cl Sun, pm Oct, Nov-Mar exc by arrangement; (01445) 712287; £3. The Old Inn here is a good stop; Gairloch has a beach, and is a good base for hikers; the easy walk up Flowerdale Glen is interesting.

GLEN AFFRIC NH2124
One of the most majestic inland glens, with a walking route along its floor, and one of the largest surviving native pinewoods in Britain.

GLENFINNAN NM9080
Jacobite Monument (A830) Built in 1815 to commemorate the Highlanders who fought and died for Bonnie Prince Charlie, in a commanding position at the head of Loch Shiel. A visitor centre has exhibitions on the prince. Good snacks, shop, disabled access to most areas; visitor centre cl Nov-Mar; (01397) 722250; £2; NTS.

GOLSPIE NC8500
Dunrobin Castle ⊞ (A9) Splendid castle - a gleaming elegantly turreted structure with views out to sea, and gardens modelled on those at Versailles. The family home of the Earls and Dukes of Sutherland for longer than anyone can remember, the site was named after Earl Robin in the 13th c; he was responsible for the original square keep. Drastically renovated and enlarged to cope with a hugely bigger

family in the 19th c, it has fine collections of furnishings and art, and a unique collection of Pictish stones; falconry. Snacks, meals, shop; cl 16 Oct-31 Mar, gardens open all year; (01408) 633177; £6.50. The Ben Bhraggie has good value food in a pleasant conservatory (on Weds you may find the pipe band practising outside).

HELMSDALE ND0315
Timespan ⊞ (Dunrobin St) Visitor centre with reconstructions of scenes from Highland history (with sound effects), art exhibitions and interesting herb garden. Riverside café, shop, disabled access; cl Sun am, Nov-Mar; (01431) 821327;* £4.

JOHN O' GROATS ND3773
Gets its share of visitors under the mistaken impression that it's the most northerly point on mainland Britain. Increasingly developed for tourists, but still a pleasant spot. The hotel on the harbour looking across to the Orkneys has decent food. A 90-min cruise spots seals, puffins and colonies of breeding guillemots, end Jun-Aug 2.30pm; (01955) 611353, *£14; and longer boat trips go from here to the Orkney Islands; (01955) 677535.

KINLOCHBERVIE NC2156
Friendly village with decent beaches, mountains and scenery around; it's most lively around 6pm on Mon-Thurs (2pm Fri), when the fishing boats return to the pier and auction their catch. You can take boat trips round the harbour.

KIRKHILL NH5543
Moniack Castle ⊞ (A862) Former fortress of the Lovat chiefs, now producing traditional country wines and liqueurs, and interesting meat and game preserves, sauces and coulis, and breakfast preserves. There are tastings and tours, and an amusing video. Shop; cl Sun, 25 Dec, 1 Jan; (01463) 831283; *£2.

KNOCKAN CRAG NC2010
(13 miles N of Ullapool on A835)
Open-sided visitor point with turf-roofed room looking over surrounding rocky landscape and hands-on interactivities, graphics, cartoons, sculptures, games, and poetry, all to do with rocks and the landscape and how they tell of volcanoes, ice sheets, oceans and deserts; various routes and trails through Inverpolly national nature

reserve; open all year; free.

KNOYDART NG8100

A real Highland wilderness on the W coast, glorious roadless country that's irresistible to hardened walkers - given good weather, full equipment and strong legs. A thrice-weekly ferry runs from Mallaig to Inverie, where the Old Forge is very hospitable (and open all day).

KYLESKU NC2333

Kerrachar Boat trips to this one-hectare garden, developed since 1995 on the site of a disused croft, take 30 mins and leave from the Old Ferry Pier 1pm Tues, Thurs and Sun mid-May to mid-Sept; phone to book; (01571) 833288; £12.50 inc an hour's visit to the garden and the ferry, children free; snacks, plant sales. The simple Kylesku Hotel has good fresh seafood.

LOCH NESS NH5330

Drumnadrochit (see above) is the best place to begin exploring this striking 24-mile loch with the largest volume of fresh water of any lake in the British Isles; up to 215 metres (700 ft) deep in places, so it's not hard to see why stories sprang up of what was hidden in its waters. You can generally take boat trips on the lake, some of them equipped with sonar for monster-spotting.

MALLAIG NM6797

Bustling fishing port, good for shellfish and prawns; from this most westerly mainland harbour you can take a ferry to the Isle of Skye, the Small Isles or Knoydart. The **Mallaig Heritage Centre** next to the station is worth a look. It tells the story of Mallaig and the surrounding area through photographs, models and films; shop, disabled access; cl Mon/Tues Nov-Mar; £1.80, and at **Mallaig Marine World** you can touch some of the fish; shop, disabled access; usually cl Sun Nov-Easter, a few days over Christmas, and 2 wks in Feb, best to check; (01687) 462292; £2.75. The seaview Marine Hotel does good bar lunches.

MEY ND2872

Castle of Mey The late Queen Mother's beloved northern home, opened to the public after her death on her specific instructions. Surprisingly homely inside, with a lovely traditional walled garden, this 16th-c Z-plan tower house is the most northerly castle in mainland Britain. Shop, limited disabled access (phone first); open daily (exc Mon, and am Sun) 24 May-30 July and 12 Aug-30 Sept; (01847) 851473; £5. The Castle Arms has decent food.

PLOCKTON NG8033

Idyllic waterside village, with palm trees along the village street; the TV series *Hamish Macbeth* was filmed here. The Plockton Hotel has good generous food, and Off the Rails is an enjoyable restaurant in a restored 19th-c railway station.

POOLEWE NG8681

Inverewe Gardens (A832) Unmissable beautiful gardens full of rare and subtropical plants, with a magnificent background of mountain scenery. The Atlantic Drift is responsible for the special microclimate which lets these unusual plants flourish even though this is further N than Moscow. Guided walks wkdys at 1.30pm, mid-Apr to mid-Sept. Meals, snacks, shop, limited disabled access; visitor centre, well stocked cheerful shop and enjoyable restaurant (cl Nov to Apr); (01445) 781200; £7; NTS.

RUA REIDH NG7391

Rua Reidh Lighthouse Remote outpost several miles along a track N of Melvaig; they organise enjoyable walking holidays in the splendidly wild countryside around; shop, tearoom open Tues and Thurs; cl Jan after New Year; B&B or hostel-style rooms - don't worry about the colour of the water, it's just peaty; (01445) 771263.

SKYE NG4829

After Lewis, the biggest of Scotland's islands, now linked to the mainland by a bridge, though the easier access doesn't seem to have spoilt its special air of romance. The coasts have plenty of opportunities for gentle pottering, and for finding quiet coves and bays, particularly on the W coast, where for instance Tarskavaig, or the good Stein Inn in the N, are lovely spots to watch the sun go down. The jagged teeth of the Cuillins mountain range to the SE of the centre are unforgettable. The Skye Riding Centre offers treks around the area; open all year round; 1 hr £14, 3 hrs £36, also disabled riding; (01470) 582419. Besides places mentioned in *Where to stay* and *Where to eat*, the

Misty Isle at Dunvegan, Sligachan Inn (A850/A863 in the middle of the island), Flodigarry Hotel nr Staffin (stunning views from this turreted mansion with Flora MacDonald connections), Ardvasar Hotel, Struan Grill at Struan, Pier Inn at Uig and the waterside Old Inn at Carbost (handy for the Talisker distillery, which can be visited; cl Sun, 25-26 Dec, 1 Jan; *£4; (01478) 614308) all do decent food.

Armadale Castle, Gardens & Museum of the Isles 🖼 The castle was built for Lord Macdonald in 1815, and the surrounding 16 hectares (40 acres) offer beautiful walks among gardens and woodlands. Sleat, this southern peninsula, is known as the Garden of Skye. There's a museum which helps to unravel the complexities of the area's history, and a gallery too. Very good restaurant, shops, disabled access; cl Nov-Mar; (01471) 844305; *£4.60.

Dunvegan Castle Dramatically set on the sea loch of Dunvegan, this has been the home of the Chiefs of Macleod for 800 years; no other scottish castle has been inhabited by the same family for so long. Among its relics is a lock of Bonnie Prince Charlie's hair. Staying here inspired Walter Scott's *Lord of the Isles*. Good meals and snacks, shops; open daily; cl 25-26 Dec, 1-2 Jan; (01470) 521206; £6.50, £4.50 gardens only. There are several good self-catering cottages in the attractive grounds, and summer boat trips go from the jetty to a nearby colony of brown and great grey seals, £4.

Elgol NG5113 A peaceful spot for gorgeous sunset views. Summer boat trips take you to the lonely and dramatic inlet of Loch Coruisk, and one of the island's most lovely shoreside walks runs to Loch na Creitheach at the heart of the formidable Cuillins, a mecca for rock-climbers. The drive up to Torrin, around the head of the loch and past a ruined church and graveyard, is picturesque.

Museum of Island Life (Kilmuir) NG2547 Worth a look; shop, disabled access; cl Sun, and end Oct-Easter; (01470) 552206; £2.

Portree NG4843 Skye's busiest harbour, attractive and quite picturesque, though in summer it tends to swarm with visitors; the harbourside Pier Hotel is right in the thick of the

action, the quieter Cuillin Hills on the outskirts has good value food in its conservatory. The Aros Experience (A87 just S) is worth a look for its displays on island life (and the restaurant does tasty chicken broth).

Quiraing NG4569 A fascinating tumbled rock mass, with a surprisingly manageable path through it.

Raasay (off Skye) Very peaceful island, an ideal place for gentle pottering without lots of competition from other visitors - and for some quite stiff hill walks if that's what you prefer.

Trotternish peninsula NG5163 Quite extraordinary rock scenery and formations like the Old Man of Storr; the Glenview Hotel at Culnaknock up here has good food, and in season the Flodigarry Hotel serves food all day.

STRATHCARRON NG9338

Attadale Gardens 🖼 (A890 S) Attractive gardens with excellent water gardens and winding woodland paths, sheltered by the surrounding hills and steep cliffs. Started in the 1890s, they include rhododendrons, azaleas, bamboo, himalayan poppies and primulas. There is a new japanese garden and also fernery in a geodesic dome. The old sunken garden has been restored, and there is a kitchen garden and conservatory; nursery specialising in unusual plants for sale. Partial disabled access; cl Sun, and 1 Nov-1 Apr; (01520) 722603; *£3. Round the head of the loch, the Rockvilla has a good choice of food.

STRATHPEFFER NH4858 Originally a fashionable 19th-c spa resort (you can look round the beautifully restored Pump Room, by appointment; (01997) 420124), this has quite a different feel from the rest of the area, with its rather continental appearance of dignified hotels and villas stepped up among its wooded slopes; some call it the Harrogate of the North. Up the A835 Rogie Falls are worth the short walk from the car park.

Highland Museum of Childhood 🖼 In restored Victorian railway station, telling the history of childhood in the Highlands among crofters and townsfolk, recorded by oral testimony, displays, photographs and video; fascinating doll and toy collections.

Snacks, shop; disabled access; cl Sun am, and Nov-Mar; (01997) 421031; *£2.

STRATHY POINT NC8269

(W of Thurso) With a lighthouse at the end of a narrow peninsula, a pleasant stroll along the road from its car park.

TARBAT NESS NH9487

Jutting from the S side of Dornoch Firth, this is rather isolated, but worth the journey for the walk around the peninsula, from Portmahomack, past the lighthouse, and then along the S coast past a ruined castle to reach Rockfield.

TORRIDON NG9055

Torridon Countryside Centre

(junction A896 and Diabaig rd) Gateway to a huge area of nature reserve in stunning mountain scenery - some say the best in Scotland. It has displays on the scenery and wildlife, as well as a deer park and deer museum. Visitor centre cl Oct-Easter; £2; (01445) 791221; NTS. Nearby at the Mains are herds of red deer and highland cattle. Torridon is wonderful for challenging walks, and there are a few outstanding easier ones, based for example on Loch Torridon's shores. The Kinlochewe Hotel (A896 E) has decent food; to reach anywhere N of here by car from the S, incidentally, it's much quicker to go by Inverness than to make your way all the way up the W coast.

ULLAPOOL NH1294

A good centre, with quite a busy harbour, a lot going on for a small place - and good eating (besides the places we've picked out, the fish and chip restaurant is very good, with surprisingly presentable white wines, and the Ferry Boat is nice). The Museum and Visitor Centre on West Argyle St has local history displays; cl Sun, limited opening hours Nov-Feb; (01854) 612987; *£3. You can get a ferry out to the Summer Isles.

WEST HIGHLAND LINE NM9080

A good way of seeing Highlands scenery between Fort William and Mallaig:

steam trains in summer, year-round normal trains. The views are terrific.

WICK ND3650

This small harbourside town has attractive houses and a good early 19th-c church.

Caithness Glass Factory (Wick Airport Industrial Estate) Glass-making demonstrations (not wknds), and factory seconds. Meals, snacks, shop, disabled access; cl Sun Jan-Mar; (01955) 602286; free.

Castle of Old Wick (just SE) Ruined four-storey square tower in dramatic clifftop setting, probably dating from the 12th/13th c.

Wick Heritage Centre In eight buildings by the harbour, this very good centre presents the history of the town; cl Sun, and all Oct-Apr; (01955) 605393; *£2.

This is a part of the world where **inns doing a decent bite to eat** are very much at a premium, and a welcome sight indeed after miles of empty road. Besides those listed elsewhere, ones we can recommend for their positions include the Aultbea Inn at Aultbea NG8689, Aultguish Hotel NH3570 on the A835 nr Loch Glascarnoch, Badachro Inn at Badachro NG7773, Northern Sands at Dunnet ND2170, Lock at Fort Augustus NH3709, Cluanie by the loch (walks and maybe eagles) in Glen Shiel NH0711, Garvault Inn extraordinarily isolated on the B871 N of Kinbrace NC8732, Kylesku Hotel at Kylesku NC2234 (the boatman here has taken readers for fascinating 4-hr boat tours), Lewiston Arms at Lewiston NH5029, Loch Carron Hotel on Loch Carron NG9039, Inver Lodge Hotel overlooking Lochinver harbour NC0923, Scrabster Inn at Scrabster ND0970, Ben View at Strontian NM8161, Loch Maree Hotel at Talladale NG8970 and Ben Loyal Hotel at Tongue NC5957. Almost all have bedrooms.

BADACHRO NG7773 **Badachro Inn** *(01445) 741255* Tiny delightfully remote village, pub by a very sheltered beach with two moorings (free for visitors), terrace virtually overhanging the water, also attractively planted lochside lawn; dining conservatory overlooking bay, bar with charming local atmosphere, quiet dining area with big log fire, some interesting photographs and collages, daily papers, delicious fresh local fish, a couple of real ales, a changing wine list and around 50 malt whiskies. £27|£7.95

BROADFORD NG6423 **Fig Tree** *(01471) 822616* Enjoyable home-made food inc fresh fish and vegetarian choices in friendly little place; cl Sun and Oct-Feb; disabled access. £15|£5

DUNVEGAN NG2351 **Macleod's Table** *The Castle (01470) 521206* Decorated with pine throughout, popular family restaurant with very reasonably priced generous morning coffee, snacks and full meals, and afternoon teas; friendly helpful staff; loch cruises, seal colony, castle gardens and craft shops; cl Dec to mid-Mar; disabled access. £13.15|£6.50

KINLOCHBERVIE NC2256 **Old School House** *Inshegra (01971) 521383* Very good food in old school building with school-related items like photographs, maps, notebooks on tables; home-grown vegetables, local fish and venison, enjoyable puddings, and very good service; bdrms in newish building; cl 25 Dec and 1 Jan. £16.50|£2.25

MUIR OF ORD NH5251 **Dower House** *(01463) 870090* Very good modern cooking in attractive hotel restaurant, with fine wines, and friendly service; bdrms and lovely gardens; cl Christmas and 2 wks in Nov. £43

Special thanks to Brian and Anna Marsden, Mrs Edna M Jones, D and M T Ayres-Regan, Susan and John Douglas, Stuart Paulley, Margaret Dickinson, Paul Kennedy, Roger and Jenny Huggins

---

WALES

Wales has a lot to offer families. Enjoyable days out run from animal parks to Celtic myths come alive, from lively and engrossing historic and industrial re-creations to some splendid boat trips, from dramatic show caves to grand houses and gardens which have child-appeal too (Erddig in North Wales actually tops our survey of welsh family attractions this year). There are spectacular private railways, and no end of impressive medieval castles. Prices of places to stay in and to visit are generally attractive, making Wales good holiday value.

North Wales is the most obvious holiday choice, with some good summer holiday resorts and all sorts of family outings. There are some nice towns to wander around, lots of highly dramatic mountain scenery, and stretches of attractive coast.

West Wales has a beautiful coast, with a great coast path in the Pembrokeshire National Park. Even in bad weather, when upland areas are more or less a write-off, the coast preserves a gloomy magnificence. It is a good family holiday area, especially for people who like to keep things simple, and has some interesting and unusual outings.

North Wales

Plenty of good family outings, attractive seaside, and memorable landscapes

There are some really picturesque railways here, many of which seem to extend their tracks a bit each year. Two that stand out are the unique Snowdon Mountain Railway in Llanberis, and the Ffestiniog from Porthmadog to Blaenau Ffestiniog. Near both Llanberis and Blaenau Ffestiniog are particularly enjoyable and engrossing tours of slate workings. You can head for even more underground entertainment, in the copper mine in Beddgelert, or the slate caverns in Harlech (there's a children's farm here too). At the Welsh Mountain Zoo in Colwyn Bay the exotic animals come with the bonus of tremendous views; other attractions for families who like animals include the friendly farms in Bodorgan and Brynsiencyn on Anglesey. For marine life, there's the Anglesey Sea Zoo (near Brynsiencyn) and the Sea Life Aquarium in Rhyl; the seabird centres at South Stack are eye-opening. The Greenwood Centre in Y Felinheli has more than enough to keep active children occupied.

The castles at Caernarfon, Conwy and Harlech are mightily impressive: Bodelwyddan Castle and Plas Newydd at Llanfairpwllgwyngyll are charming. At unusual Penrhyn near Bangor and beautiful Erddig just outside Wrexham (this year's Wales Family Attraction), you get a glimpse of life downstairs as well as upstairs. The rescued buildings at Holywell are well worth a look. Ancient Chirk Castle has lovely gardens, and glorious Bodnant at Tal-y-Cafn is one of Britain's greatest. Bodrhyddan Hall in

Rhuddlan, and Plas yn Rhiw, also have appealing grounds.

Cheerful Conwy (plenty for families), pretty Beaumaris, and the fairytale holiday village of Portmeirion make pleasantly relaxed excursions. There are good long beaches and attractive traditional family resorts (Llandudno's our pick), yet it's easy to get away from the crowds even in high summer - particularly on the shores of the very welsh Lleyn Peninsula.

For many, North Wales's trump card is its magnificent scenery, so richly varied, from Snowdonia's majestic mountain expanses (excellent for a walking holiday) to the intricate and rather intimate scenery of Clwyd, the luscious Vale of Conwy, and the peace of Anglesey. The much less visited Berwyn Hills give memorable scenic drives.

There is a splendid range of places to stay, and many are in superb countryside.

Where to stay

ABERSOCH SH3226 **Porth Tocyn Hotel** *Bwlch Tocyn, Pwllheli, Gwynedd LL53 7BU (01758) 713303* **£106**, plus special breaks; 17 attractive rms, most with sea views. On a headland overlooking Cardigan Bay, a lovely place to stay - with a refreshingly sensible and helpful approach to families (though not solely a family hotel) - and with a new conservatory this year; very friendly hard-working owners and staff, several cosy interconnecting sitting rooms with antiques and fresh flowers, most enjoyable traditional cooking in the restaurant (lots of options such as light lunches, high teas for children as they must be over 7 for dinner in the restaurant, and imaginative Sun lunches), and a happy atmosphere; lots of space in the pretty garden, heated swimming pool in summer, hard tennis court; cl mid-Nov to mid-Mar; disabled access; dogs welcome in bedrooms ☺

BEAUMARIS SH6076 **Olde Bulls Head** *Castle St, Beaumaris, Gwynedd LL58 8AP (01248) 810329* **£95***, plus special breaks; 13 rms with antiques and brass bedsteads. Partly 15th-c pub nr castle, with snug alcoves, low beams and open fire in quaint rambling bar, interesting decorations, popular brasserie, very good restaurant food (esp fish), fine wines, and cheery service; entrance to pretty courtyard closed by biggest single-hinged door in Britain; cl 25-26 Dec, 1 Jan; children over 7 in restaurant in evening

BEDDGELERT SH5948 **Sygun Fawr Country House** *Beddgelert, Caernarfon, Gwynedd LL55 4NE (01766) 890258* **£65**, plus special breaks; 9 rms. Spectacular scenery surrounds this secluded 17th-c hotel, with lots of surrounding walks; beams, stripped stone walls, inglenooks, and a restful atmosphere, a varied imaginative menu, antiques and an informal atmosphere in the restaurant, and 20 acres of mountainside and gardens; cl Jan; disabled access; dogs welcome away from restaurant

BETWS-Y-COED SH7955 **Ty Gwyn** *Betwys-y-Coed, Gwynedd LL24 0SG (01690) 710383* **£60**, plus special breaks; 13 pretty rms, most with own bthrm. Welcoming and well run 17th-c coaching inn with interesting old prints, furniture and bric-a-brac, good food and friendly service; pleasant setting overlooking river and a very good base for the area; children free if sharing parents' room; cl Mon-Weds in Jan; disabled access; dogs welcome in bedrooms

BLAENAU FFESTINIOG SH7045 **Queen's Hotel** *1 High St, Blaenau Ffestiniog, Gwynedd LL41 3ES (01766) 830055* **£65**, plus special breaks; 12 individually decorated rms named after locomotives. By the famous narrow-gauge railway and surrounded by Snowdonia National Park, this most attractively refurbished Victorian hotel has real ales in convivial lounge bar, good all-day food in bistro (converts to more formal evening restaurant with imaginative dishes), and swift friendly service; lots to do nearby; cl 25 Dec

CAERNARFON SH5163 **Seiont Manor** Llanrug, Caernarfon, Gwynedd LL55 2AQ (01286) 673366 **£140**, plus special breaks; 28 luxurious rms. Fine hotel built from the original farmstead of a Georgian manor house, in 156 acres of mature parkland; open fires and comfortable sofas in lounge, restful atmosphere in library and drawing room, imaginative food in restaurant's four interconnecting areas, and leisure suite with swimming pool, gym, and sauna; dogs welcome in bedrooms

CAPEL GARMON SH8156 **Tan-y-Foel Country House** Capel Garmon, Llanrwst, Gwynedd LL26 0RE (01690) 710507 **£120***, plus special breaks; 6 comfortable rms. Charming partly 16th-c stone country house N of village, vibrant modern décor in lounge and breakfast room, warmly friendly relaxing atmosphere, very good robustly flavoured modern food in restaurant using the freshest produce inc local lamb, organic vegetables and home-made bread, interesting wine list; no smoking throughout; mature gardens and marvellous surrounding countryside; limited opening Dec and Jan; children over 7

CAPEL GARMON SH8155 **White Horse** Capel Garmon, Llanrwst, Gwynedd LL26 0RW (01690) 710271 **£58***, plus midweek off-season breaks; 6 simple rms (those in newer part are quietest). Comfortable, homely, low-beamed inn with friendly atmosphere, winter log fires, very good home-made food in bar and cosy no smoking restaurant (some traditional welsh meals), magnificent views, delightful surrounding countryside; cl 24-25 Dec; children over 12

CONWY SH7577 **Sychnant Pass House** Sychnant Pass Rd, Conwy, Gwynedd LL32 8BJ (01492) 596868 **£70***; 10 rms. Victorian house in two acres among the foothills of the Snowdonia National Park; big comfortable sitting rooms, log fires, a relaxing, friendly atmosphere, and enjoyable food (the restaurant is open to non-residents, too); cl Christmas; partial disabled access; dogs welcome away from restaurant

DOLGELLAU SH7015 **Tyddynmawr Farmhouse** Islawrdref, Dolgellau, Gwynedd LL40 1TL (01341) 422331 **£54***; 3 lovely spacious rms. Award-winning 18th-c farmhouse at the foot of Cadair Idris, with wonderful scenery, oak beams, log fires, and welsh oak furniture, marvellous breakfasts with home-made bread, preserves and muesli, and warmly welcoming owners; cl Dec-Jan; no children

GELLILYDAN SH6939 **Tyddyn Du Farm** Gellilydan, Blaenau Ffestiniog, Gwynedd LL41 4RB (01766) 590281 **£58***, plus special breaks; 4 ground floor, private stable and long barn suites with jacuzzi baths, fridges and microwaves, one with airbath. 400-year-old farmhouse on working farm in the heart of Snowdonia, with beams and exposed stonework, and big inglenook fireplaces in lounge; children can help bottle feed the lambs, and look at goats, ducks, sheep and shetland ponies; fine walks, inc short one to their own Roman site; partial disabled access; dogs welcome away from dining room ☺

LLANABER SH5919 **Llwyndu Farmhouse** Llanaber, Barmouth, Gwynedd LL42 1RR (01341) 280144 **£70***, plus special breaks; 7 charming rms, most with own bthrm, some in a nicely converted 18th-c barn. Most attractive 16th-c farmhouse just above Cardigan Bay, with a warm welcome from friendly owners, big inglenook fireplaces, oak beams, mullioned windows, relaxing lounge, enjoyable breakfasts, and good imaginative food in candlelit dining room; cl 25-26 Dec; dogs welcome in bedrooms

LLANARMON D C SJ1532 **West Arms** Llanarmon Dyffryn Ceiriog, Llangollen, Clwyd LL20 7LD (01691) 600665 **£108.90***, plus special midweek breaks; 15 rms. Charming and civilised 16th-c inn with heavy beams and timbers, log fires in inglenook fireplaces, lounge bar interestingly furnished with antique settles, sofas in the old-fashioned entrance hall, comfortable locals' lounge bar, good food, and friendly quiet atmosphere; the lawn runs down to the River Ceiriog (fishing for residents); disabled access; dogs welcome away from restaurant

LLANDRILLO SJ0337 **Tyddyn Llan** Llandrillo, Corwen, Clwyd LL21 0ST (01490) 440264 **£130**; 12 pretty rms. Elegant and relaxed Georgian house with three acres of lovely gardens and surrounded by the Berwyn mountains; fresh flowers in comfortable public rooms, enjoyable food using the best ingredients, and an impressive wine list; fine forest walks (guides available), and watersports, fishing and

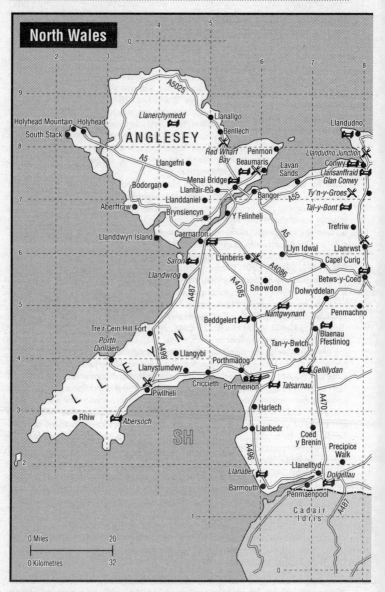

horse riding can be arranged; cl 2 wks Jan; disabled access; dogs welcome in bedrooms

LLANDUDNO SH7882 **St Tudno** *15 North Parade, Llandudno, Gwynedd LL30 2LP (01492) 874411* **£150**, plus special breaks; 18 individually decorated rms, some with sea view. Opposite the pier, this well run, smart Victorian seaside hotel has genuinely helpful and friendly staff, Victorian-style décor in restful no smoking sitting room, a convivial bar lounge, relaxed coffee lounge for light lunches, and attractive no smoking garden-style restaurant with imaginative modern food; good wine list; small indoor pool

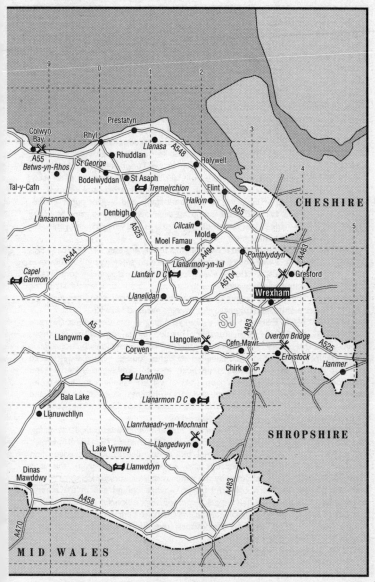

LLANERCHYMEDD SH4284 **Llwydiarth Fawr Farm** *Llanerchymedd, Gwynedd LL71 8DF (01248) 470321* **£60***, plus special breaks; 4 rms in main house, 2 cottage suites in grounds. Handsome Georgian farmhouse on 850-acre cattle and sheep farm, with a particularly warm homely atmosphere and welcome, comfortable lounge with antiques, log fire, books and lovely views, and very good home-made food using farm and other fresh local produce; terrace, lake for private fishing, nature walks, bird-watching; no smoking; cl Christmas

LLANFAIR D C SJ1355 **Eyarth Station** *Llanfair Dyffryn Clwyd, Ruthin, Clwyd LL15 2EE (01824) 703643* **£52***, plus special breaks; 6 pretty rms. Carefully converted old railway station with quiet gardens and wonderful views, a friendly relaxed atmosphere, log fire in airy and comfortable beamed lounge, good breakfasts and enjoyable suppers in dining room (more lovely views), sun terrace and heated swimming pool, and lots of walks; cl Jan-Feb; disabled access; dogs welcome in bedrooms

LLANSANFFRAID GLAN CONWY SH8075 **Old Rectory Country House** *Llanrwst Rd, Glan Conwy, Colwyn Bay, Clwyd LL28 5LF (01492) 580611* **£169** inc dinner, plus special breaks; 6 deeply comfortable rms. Georgian house in pleasant gardens with fine views over Conwy estuary, Conwy Castle and Snowdonia; delightful public rms with flowers, antiques and family photos, delicious food of the highest restaurant standards, and marvellous wines; good breakfasts, warmly friendly staff; cl Dec-Jan; children under 9 months or over 5; dogs in coach house only

LLANWDDYN SJ0219 **Lake Vyrnwy Hotel** *Llanwddyn, Oswestry, Powys SY10 0LY (01691) 870692* **£115**, plus special breaks; 35 rms, the ones overlooking the lake are the nicest - and quietest. Large impressive Tudor-style mansion - much refurbished this year - overlooking lake from hillside in 40 square miles of forestry, with lots of sporting activities (esp fishing); new conservatory looking over the water, log fires and sporting prints in the comfortable and elegant public rooms, relaxed atmosphere, bar, and good food using their own lamb and game from the estate, and home-made preserves, chutneys, mustards and vinegars; enjoyable teas too; dogs welcome in bedrooms

MENAI BRIDGE SH5474 **Wern Farm** *Menai Bridge, Anglesey, Gwynedd LL59 5RR 01248 712421* **£54**; 3 well equipped rms. Attractive no smoking old farmhouse in 100 hectares (250 acres) with lovely views; log fire and board games in comfortable sitting room, antique three-quarter-size billiard table, traditional breakfasts in the conservatory, and friendly helpful owners; tennis court, boules and croquet, and plenty of walks; plenty of places nearby for evening meals; cl Nov-Jan

NANTGWYNANT SH6555 **Pen-y-Gwryd** *Nantgwynant, Caernarfon, Gwynedd LL55 4NT (01286) 870211* **£66***, plus special breaks; 16 rms, some with own bthrm. In two acres, this cheery hotel is by the Llanberis Pass in Snowdonia National Park; warm log fire in simply furnished panelled residents' lounge, rugged slate-floored bar that doubles as mountain rescue post; lots of climbing mementoes and equipment, friendly, chatty games room (lots of walkers, climbers and fishermen), hearty enjoyable food, big breakfasts, and packed lunches; sauna in the trees and outdoor swimming pool, table tennis; private chapel; cl Nov-Dec and midweek Jan-Feb; disabled access; dogs welcome in bedrooms

PORTMEIRION SH5837 **Portmeirion Hotel** *Penrhyndeudraeth, Porthmadog, Gwynedd LL48 6ER (01766) 770000* **£147** in village (26 rms), **£172** in hotel (14 rms), and **£192** in Deudraeth Castle (11 rms), plus winter breaks. On the edge of an estuary and surrounded by beaches and woods (and traffic-free), this is a remarkable place; the hotel down by the water is quite luxurious - elegant rooms with marble, gilt, and rich colourful fabrics - while behind and in the steeply landscaped grounds above it is a well dispersed very colourful italianate village, luscious to look at, inc all sorts of individualistic cottage bedrooms tucked into the hillside; very romantic when the day visitors have left, and lots to do; disabled access. See *To see and do*, below ☺

SARON SH4557 **Pengwern** *Saron, Caernarfon, Gwynedd LL54 5UH (01286) 831500* **£56***, plus special breaks; 3 rms. In 130 acres running down to Foryd Bay, this spacious no smoking farmhouse has marvellous views of Snowdonia, and delicious food using local fresh produce; cl Dec-Jan

TAL-Y-BONT SH7669 **Lodge** *Tal-y-bont, Conwy, Gwynedd LL32 8YX (01492) 660766* **£70**, plus special breaks; 14 rms. Friendly little modern hotel in over three acres on the edge of Snowdonia, with open fire, books and magazines in comfortable lounge, generous helpings of popular food using lots of home-grown produce in no smoking restaurant, and good service; lots of walks; well behaved pets welcome; good disabled access; dogs welcome in bedrooms

TALSARNAU SH6135 **Maes-y-Neuadd** *Talsarnau, Gwynedd LL47 6YA (01766) 780200* **£165** inc 4-course dinner, plus special breaks; 16 luxurious, newly refitted rms. Looking out across Snowdonia, this attractive extended 14th-c mansion (much refurbished this year) stands in ten acres of landscaped hillside; flowers, plants, antiques and open fires, peaceful atmosphere, very good food (herbs and vegetables from their own garden), friendly cats, and charming staff; disabled access; dogs welcome in bedrooms ☺

TREMEIRCHION SJ0771 **Bach-y-Graig** *Tremeirchion, St Asaph, Clwyd LL17 0UH (01745) 730627* **£54***; 3 rms, 2 with brass beds. Wales's first brick-built house with a date-stone of 1567, in 200-acre dairy farm at the foot of the Clwydian Hills; inglenook fireplace in big lounge, home cooking using home-produced beef and lamb and own free-range eggs, and warm welcome; woodland trail, fishing; cl Christmas and New Year

To see and do

Wales Family Attraction of the Year

WREXHAM SJ3247 **Erddig** (well signed S) This very special old house was recently the surprise runner-up (after Chatsworth) in a survey to find Britain's favourite stately home. It stands out for its unique atmosphere, which quickly wins over children too: it doesn't feel at all like a stuffy old house. The Yorke family who lived here were rather frowned upon by their peers for being too soft on their servants, and it's perhaps the unusual closeness they had with their staff that makes it seem such a warm, welcoming place. You can still see the rather touching pictures and poems about the staff on the walls, in much the same way that other families might laud their ancestors. The belowstairs areas such as the laundry, bakehouse and kitchens are perhaps the most unusual feature, but you can explore the grander 'upstairs' rooms just as thoroughly, with their fine collection of 18th-c furniture, and an intriguing assortment of collected ephemera: the Yorkes never really threw anything away. The rooms have no electric light, so if you want to study things closely, avoid visiting on a dull day. On the ground floor is an appealing model of the house. Outside, the big walled 18th-c formal garden is impressive, restored to its original design and reckoned to be one of the best from the period; there are also plenty of ivies, rare fruit trees, and very attractive woodland walks. Look out for some vintage cars and bicycles in the stable yard. The family appeal is broadened on their fairly regular event days, ranging from archery demonstrations and family fun days to their popular annual apple festival in October; all have extra activities for children - check the National Trust's website www.nationaltrust.org.uk for more details. Meals, snacks, shop, some disabled access; open Mon–Weds and wknds Apr–Oct, house cl am; (01978) 355314; house and garden £6.60 adults, £3.30 children, £16.50 families, garden and outbuildings only £3.40 adults, £1.70 children, £8.50 families. National Trust members free.

ABERFFRAW SH3270 **Barclodiad y Gawres** Some 5,000 years old, this 6-metre (20-ft) underground passage tomb at the top of the cliff has the finest british example of tomb carvings, which appear by the entrance and in the side chambers, shown up by a good torch; it's sealed, but you can ask for a key at the Countryside Centre, Aberffraw; (01407) 840845. Hard to believe now, but Aberffraw was once the capital of the North Wales kingdom of Gwynedd. There are some lovely unspoilt coves and beaches nearby; the beach up the road at Rhosneigr is particularly good (and clean).

BANGOR SH5872 Quiet university town with a pedestrianised High St and a restored pier and yacht harbour that adds a lively touch in summer. The Bangor Museum and Art Gallery has exhibitions on local history and archaeology, and collections of welsh furniture (open Tues-Sat; (01248) 353368; free). The Union has decent food. Well signposted from the A55 just before Bangor are the Aber Falls at Abergwynggregyn, the highest falls in Wales at just under 100 feet (30m).

Bangor Cathedral Founded 70 years before the one at Canterbury; the present building is restored 13th- to 15th-c, and has an interesting 16th-c carving of Christ bound and seated on a rock, as well as some fine Victorian stained glass; also, unique 14th-c flemish statues. It is currently undergoing further restoration. Shop, disabled access; cl Sat pm, wk after Christmas; free, £2 suggested donation.

Bangor Museum and Art Gallery (Ffordd Gwynedd) Local history and archaeology, welsh furniture, changing art exhibitions; shop; cl ams, Mon, Sun, 10 days at Christmas, and bank hols; (01248) 353368; free.

Penrhyn Castle (1m E) Splendid 19th-c neo-Norman fantasy built by a slate and sugar magnate: the interior is in suitably grand style, with quite remarkable - and often bizarre - panelling, decoration and furnishings. The 14 rooms that made up the kitchens and service rooms have recently been restored to look as they would have when the Prince of Wales stayed here in 1894. The cathedral-like great hall is heated by the Roman method of hot air under the floor, and one of the beds, made for Queen Victoria, weighs over a ton - carved from slate. An unexpectedly rich collection of paintings includes works by Rembrandt, Gainsborough and Canaletto. They have recently restored the servants' quarters, and in the stableyard is a museum of early locomotives, and a superb doll collection. Surrounded by parkland and woodland, there's also a walled garden and adventure playground. Snacks, shop, disabled access; cl am (exc July and Aug), all day Tues, and Nov-Mar; (01248) 353084;* £7, garden only £4; NT.

BARMOUTH SH6115
Traditional seaside resort with a huge clean beach, a landtrain that runs the length of the promenade, and donkey rides; the Lifeboat Institute on the quay

has some nice old memorabilia and is free. A 7-mile walk, good for bird-watchers, crosses the Barmouth bridge to Morfa Mawddach station, then follows the former railway track all the way along the river bank to Penmaenpool (see below); you can return across the toll bridge to Tai Cynhaiaf for the bus to Barmouth.

BEAUMARIS SH6076
Anglesey's most historic and attractive town faces across to the mainland. Apart from the obvious castle there are several characterful buildings, as well as a yachty waterfront, though the shingle beach is not suitable for swimming. The 15th-c church of St Mary and St Nicholas - easy to spot by its robust square tower - houses the stone coffin of Joan, daughter of King John and wife of the welsh leader Llewelyn the Great. The Olde Bulls Head (dating partly from 1472) and Sailors Return are good for lunch.

Beaumaris Castle One of the most impressive and complete of those built by Edward I, despite the struggle over it with Owain Glyndwr in the early 1400s, and the plundering of its lead, timber and stone in later ages. Beautifully symmetrical, it took from 1295 to 1312 to build (though the money ran out before it could be finished). Shop, good disabled access; cl 24-26 Dec, 1 Jan; (01248) 810361; £3; Cadw.

Beaumaris Gaol Paints a vivid picture of the harshness of the 19th-c prison system, particularly in the dark, poky cells. Shop, very limited disabled access; cl end Sept-Easter exc by appointment, (01248) 810921; £2.75, £3.50 joint ticket with Courthouse.

Courthouse Remarkable survival, dating back to 1614 and still occasionally in use. You can stand in the dock and imagine you're just about to be sentenced. Shop, very limited disabled access; open as gaol (joint ticket £3.50); (01248) 811691; £1.50.

BEDDGELERT SH5948
Pleasant village base for the Snowdon area, with walks along the old railway track through the Aberglaslyn Pass, and W up to the summit of Moel Hebog (one of the easier peaks hereabouts); or easier still, follow Cwm Bychan NE up to a lowish pass, then down to Sygun

Copper Mine for the quiet lane back. The comfortable Tanronen does good value food, and there's good Snowdonia walking around the Aberglaslyn Pass (A498 S).

Sygun Copper Mine 🔲 (A498 NE) Interesting tours through often spectacular underground mine workings, with magnificent stalactites and stalagmites, and traces of gold and silver in the copper ore veins. You're greeted by a wonderful view of the mountains when you come up at the end. Snacks, shop; cl Nov-Jan; (01766) 510101; £5.25.

BENLLECH SH5282 Beautiful clean beach, good even for toddlers - and at low tide you can walk round into Red Wharf Bay; several beach-side cafés and so forth.

BETWS-Y-COED SH7956 Touristy 19th-c inland resort village in a beautiful wooded gorge at the head of the Vale of Conwy. Surrounded by picturesque woodland walks, the village has over a century of catering to visitors behind it, though at peak times the crowds can dilute its appeal. One of the best strolls is along the old riverside railway track by the Afon Llugwy W: the raging Swallow Falls and Fairy Glen just W of the village itself are deservedly regarded as two of the area's finest beauty spots. Longer walks well worth taking in are SW through the woods to Llyn Elsi Reservoir, where mountain views open up and you can return via the Miners Bridge; and further afield NW in the mini lake district around Llyn Crafnant. W of the village, the bizarre Ugly House looks like a series of boulders thrown haphazardly together. The cottagey Ty Gwyn has good food, and the Pont y Pair and Waterloo Hotel are useful too.

BLAENAU FFESTINIOG SH6946 This straggle of village is dwarfed by the vast spoil slopes from the slate mines all around it - once the slate capital of Wales, now with the passing of the industry like a living museum. The Queens Hotel has decent food in its bar and dining room.

Ffestiniog Pumped Storage Power Station 🔲 Guided tours of the first hydro-electric pumped storage scheme in the country, with dramatic views

towards the peaks of Snowdonia. Meals, snacks, shop, a shortened tour is available for the disabled; cl Sat, and end Oct-Easter; (01766) 830310; *£3.95. From the information centre there's an attractive (if slightly hairy) drive into the mountains to Stwlan Dam, which also gives super views.

Llechwedd Slate Caverns (A470) The same company has been mining and quarrying slate here for over 150 years, and their well organised tours of the huge caverns bring the history of the site vividly to life; it's well worth doing both the underground rides. In Deep Mine, Britain's steepest passenger railway takes you 137 metres (450 ft) below the summit of the mountain. Next is a hard-hat walk through ten stunning subterranean chambers, each with a sound and light show illustrating the world of a Victorian miner. You need to be relatively agile (61 steps going down, but 10 more on the way up if we counted right), and bring warm clothing even in summer. The highlight is an eerie underground lake, nicely lit to create atmospheric shadows on the water and the steep, craggy walls. The other tour (the Miners Tramway) explains more about the mining process: battery-powered trains take you around the Victorian workings, through splendid man-made caverns, some of which have tableaux or demonstrations of ancient mining skills. You get off at various points along the way, and the guides give useful talks. Outside you can explore the old buildings of Llechwedd village; the last residents left in the 1970s, but there's a Victorian pub (wholesome inexpensive food), and several shops stocking Victorian-themed goods which you can buy using period money; you can exchange your coins at the former bank, now a museum. Meals, snacks, shops, some disabled access with prior warning; cl 25-26 Dec, 1 Jan; (01766) 830306; both tours costs £11.95, just one is £7.75. The surface attractions are free.

BODELWYDDAN SH9974 **Bodelwyddan Castle** (off A55) The walled gardens around this showy white limestone castle include a glorious mix of woodland walks, flowering plants, aviary and water features. The house (older than its 19th-c exterior suggests) has been very well restored as a Victorian mansion, with furniture from the Victoria & Albert, and paintings and photographs from the National Portrait Gallery. Plenty for children, inc a woodland adventure playground, nature trails, and entertaining exhibitions of puzzles, Victorian games, dressing-up and optical illusions. Snacks, shop, disabled access; cl Mon and Fri, plus Oct-Apr, Christmas week; (01745) 584060; £4.50, grounds only £2. The Kinmel Arms at St George has good interesting food.

Bodelwyddan marble church 19th-c, built of locally quarried stone: an unusual and quite splendid sight.

BODORGAN SH4272

Henblas Park 📠 (Junction 6, A55 - follow the clear signs) Good varied family outing, with sheep-shearing, dog-and-duck displays, tractor rides, different breeds of sheep and other farm animals, also an indoor adventure playground, bouncy castle and ball pool - even a neolithic burial chamber. Meals, snacks, shop, disabled access; cl Sat (exc bank hols) and Nov-Easter; (01407) 840440; *£4.25.

BRYNSIENCYN SH4765

This Anglesey farming village stands close to some impressive prehistoric monuments. On the back road NW to Llangaffo are Caer Leb, with ramparts of a 3rd-century settlement, and Bodowyr chambered tomb. To the W by the A4080 there are more historic humps at Castell-Bryn Gwyn, dating from neolithic times.

Anglesey Sea Zoo (A4080 just S) Excellent collection of local marine life, in tanks specially designed to provide as unrestricted and natural an environment as possible. Also walk-through shipwreck, lobster hatchery, touch pools (school hols only), adventure playground; they sell home-made fudge and ice-cream, and their own good sea salt. Meals, snacks, shop, disabled access; cl beginning Nov to mid-Feb; (01248) 430411; £5.95.

Foel Farm Park Friendly working farm with daily calf feeding, tractor rides, and home-made chocolate (on wkdys you can often see them making it). Restaurant, tearoom and ice-cream parlour, shop,

disabled access; cl late Oct-Mar (exc wknds); (01248) 430646; *£4.25.

Pick-your-own (Gwydryn Hir farm) Pick fruit and veg (open Jun-Sept) while taking in the view of Snowdonia; also farm shop and butchery (open all year) specialising in home-grown produce and home-made soups, jams and cakes; (01248) 430322.

Prehistoric burial chamber A couple of miles NW by the back road towards Llangaffo is what looks like a Stone Age hut, but is actually a burial chamber from which the covering earth has been eroded over the millennia.

CAERNARFON SH4763

Surviving lengths of its 13th-c town walls still crowd in its quaintly narrow streets (quaint, that is, unless you're trying to drive through them). The town harbour is busy with yachts in summer. Besides all the attractions mentioned below, the Welsh Highland Railway (a sister operation of the Ffestiniog Railway - see Porthmadog) runs up to Rhyd Ddu, where the good value Cwellyn Arms has specacular Snowdon views. Down here in the town, the Hole in the Wall and Palace Vaults also have good value food.

Air World (Caernarfon Airparc, off A499 nr Llandwrog - where the Harp has good value food) They encourage you to climb aboard some of the helicopters and aeroplanes here; also a great many model aeroplanes, and pleasure flights. Meals, snacks, shop, disabled access; cl end Nov-beginning Mar (exc by appointment); (01286) 830800; *£4.50.

Caernarfon Castle With its nine polygonal towers and walls of colour-banded stone, this was planned by Edward I as a Royal residence and seat of government for North Wales. Edward's son was born here and presented to the people, setting the precedent for future Princes of Wales. Exhibitions include the regimental museum of the Royal Welch Fusiliers, and an impressive audio-visual display. Shop; usually cl 24-26 Dec, 1 Jan; (01286) 677617; £4.50; Cadw. The square outside, around the statue of former PM David Lloyd George, has a busy Sat market.

Inigo Jones Slateworks 📠 (Groeslon, A487 S) You can go on an audio tour of this working slateworks, established in 1861 primarily to make school writing slates. A showroom displays slate and stone products, with exhibitions on calligraphy and the development of the slate industry, and there's a quiz for children. Snacks, shop, disabled access; cl 25-26 Dec, 1 Jan; (01286) 830242; *£3.80.

Segontium Roman Fort & Museum (A4085) Roman fort dating from AD78; excavations have exposed various rebuildings during its three centuries of importance, and a museum shows some of the finds. There's a tradition that Constantine the Great was born here (and the walls of the nearby castle used to be thought to be modelled partly on the walls of Constantinople). Shop; cl Sun am, 24-26 Dec, 1 Jan; (01286) 675625; free; Cadw.

CAPEL CURIG SH7258
Centrally located amid the Snowdonia highlands, but a bit dominated by the two main roads that cut through the village. This makes a useful starting point for walks up Moel Siabod and to the attractively landscaped reservoirs to the N. Cobdens has reasonably priced food, and Bryn Tyrch (A5 W) is strong on vegetarian and vegan dishes.

CEFN MAWR SJ2841
Ty Mawr Country Park Country park with picnic area, small animal walk, riverside and woodland walks as well as a walk to Thomas Telford's aqueduct, and organic farm with rare breeds; playing field and play area; dogs welcome, park open all year, visitor centre open daily Apr-Sept, cl wkdys Oct-Mar; (01978) 822780; free.

CHIRK SJ2938
The quiet little town, important as a staging post on the former road to Ireland, has something of a bypassed-by-time feel now; the Hand and (B5070 S) Bridge are quite useful for lunch.
Chirk Castle (just W) One of the lucky few of Edward I's castles to survive as an occupied home rather than fall to ruin. The exterior is still much as it was when built 700 years ago, with its high walls and drum towers, though there have been lots of alterations inside: most of the medieval-looking decorations were by Pugin in the 19th c, the elegant stone staircase

dates from the 18th c, and the Long Gallery is 17th-c. The wrought-iron entrance gates are particularly fine, and the formal gardens are magnificent. Meals, snacks, shop, some disabled access; cl am, Mon, Tues (ec bank hols) Nov-Mar; (01691) 777701; *£6, garden only *£3.80; NT. It's right by a well preserved stretch of the earthworks of Offa's Dyke.

COED Y BRENIN SH7226
Forest Park & Visitor Centre (Maesgwn) Excellent introduction to what translates as King's Forest, so called to commemorate the Silver Jubilee of King George V. Some beautifully varied sights and landscapes, as well as wildlife observation hides, and over 50 miles of walks. Snacks, shop, disabled access; cl wkdys Nov-Mar; (01341) 440666; free, £3 all-day parking (there's a threat this may shoot up to an over-hefty £10).

COLWYN BAY SH8480
Made popular in the 19th c by wealthy Lancashire industrialists who retired here (though now rather run down in parts), this busy summer seaside resort has all that's wanted for a family beach holiday, though it's rather eclipsed by Llandudno just along the coast. The quieter end at Rhos-on-Sea has a puppet theatre; mainly open just school hols; (01492) 548166 for programme. The Rhos Fynach opposite the small harbour at this end, once Capt Morgan's home, does decent food, and the Pen-y-Bryn (B5113 S) is a good civilised place for a meal.
Welsh Mountain Zoo 🖼 (Flagstaff Gardens, Old Highway) Lots of exotic animals in natural-looking habitats, but what really distinguishes this 15-hectare (37-acre) zoo from any other is the quite magnificent view over the bay. Also penguin parade and falconry displays. Meals, snacks, shop, mostly disabled access; cl 25 Dec; (01492) 532938; £6.95. In summer a free minibus service runs here from the town station.

CONWY SH7877
Cheerful old town dominated by its castle, the key part of the town's elaborate defensive system - 21 (originally 22) towers linked by walls some 9 metres (30 ft) high, still the

most complete town wall in Wales, with craggy old town gates. You can walk along some parts, looking down over the narrow little streets that still follow their medieval layout. You can go on summer **boat trips**, and the aquarium by the quay has reopened and features sharks, octopus, conger eels, lobsters and crayfish. The friendly Bridge Hotel does good value food.

Aberconwy House 🏠 (Castle St) The only house in the town which survives from the 14th c, once the home of a prosperous merchant. Rooms are furnished in period style, and there's an interesting audio-visual show. Shop; cl Tues, and Nov-end Mar; (01492) 592246; *£2.20; NT.

Butterfly Jungle 🏠 (Bodlondeb Park) Tropical butterflies and birds in free flight in a re-created jungle environment, also exotic plants with rainforest surround-sound; picnic area. Shop, snacks, disabled access; cl Nov-Mar; (01492) 593149; £3.50.

Conwy Castle One of the best-known in Wales, and one of the most important examples of military architecture in the whole of Europe. Built for Edward I in 1283-9, it's very well preserved, still looking exactly as a medieval fortress should - despite the ravages of the Civil War and beyond. There's an exhibition on Edward and the other castles he built. The top of the turrets offer fine panoramic views; the most dramatic views of the castle itself are from the other side of the estuary. Shop; cl 24-26 Dec, 1 Jan; (01492) 592358; £3.50, joint ticket with Plas Mawr £6.50; Cadw.

Conwy Mountain Just W of the town, pleasant walking; not a real mountain but with views of Anglesey worthy of mountain status.

Conwy Suspension Bridge 🏠 Built by Telford in 1826, and restored by the National Trust, who have also opened up its toll house, with the rooms furnished as they would have been in the 19th c. Shop, disabled access; cl Nov-end Mar; (01492) 573282; *£1.10. The other, tubular bridge was built by Stephenson in 1848.

Plas Mawr (High St) Elaborate Tudor mansion, carefully restored, its splendid plasterwork, flagstone floors and huge

fireplaces all looking as good as new. Small shop; disabled access ground floor only; cl Mon (exc bank hols) and 27 Oct-27 Mar; (01492) 580167; £4.50 (no extra charge for audio tour), joint ticket with Conwy Castle £6.50.

Smallest House 🏠 Nicely placed on the quayside is Britain's smallest house, barely 2 metres (6 ft) wide and its front wall only 3 metres (10 ft) high. Squeezed into the two rooms (one up, one down) are all the comforts of home, or at least most - there's no lavatory. Shop, limited disabled access; cl Nov-Mar, Good Fri; (01492) 593484; *75p.

Teapot World 🏠 (Castle St) Splendidly zany collection of unusually shaped teapots from the last 300 years - everything from wigwams to cauliflowers. Shop; cl Nov-Easter; (01492) 596533; *£1.50.

CORWEN SJ0750

Derwen church (off A494 a few miles N) Interesting medieval building with an elaborately carved rood screen and loft, some old wall paintings, and an excellent Celtic cross in the churchyard. The nearby medieval Ty Mawr at Gwyddelwern has tasty food.

Llangar old parish church (B4401 S) Built in the 13th c, with remarkable paintings of the seven deadly sins; it's visited from Rug chapel (and covered by the same ticket). The Crown in Corwen has good value food.

Rug chapel (1m N) 17th-c, not inspiring from the outside, but inside is a riot of colour, almost every available piece of woodwork covered with cheery patterns and paintwork. Shop, disabled access. Cl Mon (exc bank hol wknds), Tues, Oct-Apr; nearby Llangar church is open 2-3pm on the same days; (01490) 412025; £2.40; Cadw.

CRICCIETH SH4937

Restrained resort with a good sheltered sandy beach. The Poachers Restaurant (High St) is good, and the Prince of Wales (The Square) is a reliable food pub.

Criccieth Castle 13th-c remains on a rocky, mounded peninsula above the little town, giving superb views over Tremadog Bay. Parts of the inner walls are well preserved, and there's an impressive gatehouse. A cartoon video looks at Gerald of Wales and other welsh princes. Shop, disabled access; visitor centre cl late Sept-Mar; (01766) 522227; visitor centre £2.50; castle free; Cadw.

DENBIGH SJ0566

Built as a defensive town in the 13th c, with large chunks of the town wall still surviving, as well as some fine arcaded buildings - unusual for Wales. A museum on the High St has interesting finds from nearby Bronze Age sites; (01745) 816313. The beautifully set riverside Brookhouse Mill (just off A525) is nice for lunch.

Denbigh Castle Largely ruined, but still impressive, with a trio of towers and superb archway in the 13th-c gatehouse; the figure on the summit is thought to represent Edward I. Among other remains are what's left of an ambitious church built by the Earl of Leicester, favourite of Elizabeth I. Museum and exhibition in castle and exhibition in Burgess Gate entrance. Snacks, shop, limited disabled access; cl Oct-Apr; castle open all year; (01745) 813385; £2.50; Cadw.

DINAS MAWDDWY SH8513

Meirion Mill Nestling among riverside woods below the mountains on the S fringes of Snowdonia is this charmingly set woollen mill, in the grounds of the old Mawddwy railway station. Meals, snacks, shop (a huge range of country and outdoor clothing, sheepskin and woollen goods, crafts, and gifts), children's playground, disabled access; cl 25-26 Dec; (01650) 531311; free. Nearby is a picturesque packhorse bridge, and there's a scenic walk to so-called King Arthur's Stone at Camlan.

DOLWYDDELAN SH7352

Dolwyddelan Castle Picturesquely set on a lightly wooded crag, these old ruins were reputedly the birthplace of Llewelyn the Great. You can still see a restored keep from around 1200, and a 13th-c curtain wall. Shop; cl 24-26 Dec, 1 Jan; (01690) 750366; £2; Cadw. The village church is attractive, and the Gwydr has cheap food.

FLINT SJ2473

Flint Castle Another fine 13th-c castle, the first built by Edward I to subdue the natives. Parts of the walls and corner towers survive, but the most impressive bit is the great tower

or donjon, which is separated by the moat. Overlooking the River Dee, it has a role in Shakespeare's *Richard II*; usually open daily; free. The Britannia in nearby Halkyn is good for lunch, with fine Dee estuary views from its conservatory.

GRESFORD SJ3454

Gresford church Has some wonderful medieval stained glass, and its bells are often described as one of the Seven Wonders of Wales. A yew tree outside is reputed to be 1,400 years old. The Pant-yr-Ochain has very good food.

HARLECH SH5831

Harlech Castle Splendid-looking structure built in 1283-1289 by Edward I, its rugged glory the massive twin-towered gatehouse. It was starved into capitulation by Owain Glyndwr in 1404, and later dogged defence inspired the song 'Men of Harlech'. Before the sea retreated there was a sheer drop into the water on one side, but it now stands above dunes, with wonderful views of Snowdonia from the battlements. Shop; cl 24-26 Dec, 1 Jan; (01766) 780552; £3; Cadw. The village around it has all that the crowds of summer visitors to the castle and the good beach could want. The riverside Victoria at Llanbedr does decent food. Some of the most sensationally remote scenery in Wales stretches inland E of Harlech, where a few tortuous roads wind past hill farms towards the splendidly isolated lake of **Llyn Cwm Bychan** SH6431. From the car park at the end of the road you can walk along a few miles of the **Roman Steps** (not Roman at all, but an old packhorse route paved with large stone slabs) that heads through some of the most challenging rock-strewn wilderness in the country (the Rhinogs); the summits need advanced scrambling skills, but the secluded little mountain lake of Llyn Du makes a nicely manageable objective instead (turn right off the main path at the top of the path). **Slate Caverns and Children's Farm Park** (Llanfair, A496 S) Two separate attractions - self-guided tours of slate caverns, and a farm where they encourage children to help handle and feed the goats, lambs, pigs etc. They also have birds of prey, and a nature walk has spectacular views. Café, craft shop, disabled access to farm only; farm cl mid-

Sept to early May £3.10, caverns cl mid-Oct to Easter, £3.50; (01766) 780247.

HOLYHEAD SH2482

Long-established fishing town on little Holy Island, now an unassuming resort with some burial chambers and ancient sites not far away. The Victorian breakwater protecting the harbour is Britain's longest. Across the old Four Mile Bridge at Valley the Bull has good value food.

HOLYHEAD MOUNTAIN SH2183

A dramatic hill giving good walks at the W tip of Holy Island, with an Iron Age fort and Roman watchtower site.

HOLYWELL SJ1977

Greenfield Valley Heritage Centre (A548) Farm museum, and an increasing number of buildings rescued from their original sites and rebuilt here. These include a 17th-c cottage, Victorian farmhouse, and a school, all furnished in period style. Also the remains of a Cistercian abbey and a good few relics of the Industrial Revolution. Snacks, shop, disabled access; cl 1 Nov-31 Mar; (01352) 714172; £2.75. The partly 15th-c Llyn y Mawn at Brynford has good generous food (all day Sat).

St Winefride's Well Source of the holy spring that turned the spot into a centre of pilgrimage - it's supposed to have healing powers. There are pleasant walks from here through the valley to the coast.

LAKE VYRNWY SJ0119

This massive reservoir, created at the end of the 19th c, supplies Liverpool with 57 million gallons of water a day. It's an attractive spot (you can drive right round), with a visitor centre and exciting 3D exhibition, a network of waymarked paths, cycle and canoe hire, bird hides (remarkable number of birds), a sculpture trail and picnic areas. Good RSPB shop (wknds only Nov-Mar), cafés, limited disabled access; (0121) 722 4563; free. The friendly Tavern Inn behind the hotel does enjoyable light meals, and has great views from its terrace.

LAVAN SANDS SH6473

(nr Aber) Much of the North Wales coast is built on or ribboned by roads, but this is a notable exception: walks by a vast stretch of tidal sands, with flocks of wading birds.

LLANALLGO SH4986

Din Llugwy ancient village Remains of a 4th-c village: a pentagonal stone wall surrounds two circular and seven rectangular buildings; free. The Pilot Boat (A5025 N) is a good food stop.

LLANBEDR SH5526

Shell Island (Llanbedr) A causeway leads over the sands to this near-island, appropriately named - after winter storms and high tides it's excellent for beachcombing; there are also wild birds and flowers, and you can fish here. Snacks, shop; (01341) 241453; £5 per car.

LLANBERIS SH5760

Plenty of B&Bs, small hotels, shops and cafés for the summer visitors here for Snowdonia, and quite a few craft shops are dotted along the High St. It's a popular area for film-makers (parts of *Tomb Raider 2* were filmed nearby). Sherpa Buses run a good service up the mountain (you can get it from several of the North Wales resorts). Three miles out on the A4809 is a modern working pottery; cl 2 wks at Christmas; (01286) 871931; free.

Dolbadarn Castle (A4086, at the foot of Llanberis Pass) Built in the early 13th c by Llywelyn the Great - it has a round towered keep still standing up to 15 metres (50 ft); free; Cadw.

Electric Mountain Various changing exhibitions, then a coach whisks you off for a tour of the spectacular Dinorwig pumped storage station (one of Europe's biggest), deep in the mountain. Best to book; (01286) 870636. Snacks, shop, disabled access (with notice); cl Mon and Tues Nov-Feb exc some occasions in winter - best to phone; *£6.

Llanberis Lake Railway 🚂 (Padarn Country Park, off A4086) Steam locomotives dating from 1889 to 1948 chug 5 miles along the shore of Llyn Padarn, with a new extension into Llanberis village: ideal for those who want the steam-train experience but don't want to spend too long getting it. Snacks, shop, disabled access; cl Sat (exc July-Aug), and all Nov-Feb; (01286) 870549 for timetable; £5. The station is in a super lakeside park with walks through ancient woodland.

Pen-y-Gwryd Hotel (Nantgwynant, A4086/A498 SE) A great spot for

Snowdon walks, and a base for generations of mountaineers; also a good place for lunch.

Snowdon Mountain Railway (A4086) A masterpiece of Victorian engineering, one of the most spectacular railway journeys you could hope to go on. It's Britain's only public rack-and-pinion railway, its vintage swiss steam or modern diesel locomotives taking you steeply up 4½ miles almost to the summit. The journey lasts an hour, and the views along the way can be magnificent, in clear weather stretching over to the Isle of Man and the Wicklow mountains in Ireland. The summit can be swathed in clouds, and sometimes trains have to terminate at an earlier stop because of ice or strong winds, so ring ahead to check on the day - also, bear in mind that even then conditions can change quickly. And wrap up well - it's chilly up at the summit. Don't let that put you off: this really is a great adventure. Make sure you bring your postcards: mail collected from the top postbox is franked specially. Trains generally leave when there are enough people on board, so are more frequent in the summer hols (usually every half-hour), but can sell out on busy days, so best to book or get there early. You go back on the same train, with a half-hour turn-round. The station at Llanberis has a small exhibition. Special events include their Teddy Bears picnic, when up to two children travel free provided they've brought their teddy. Café and shop at both ends, disabled access (helpful to ring in advance); trains run at least part of the way from mid-Mar to the start of Nov, but usually go to the summit only from May - as we say, best to ring first to be sure; (0870) 4580033; a return trip is £18 for adults, £13 for children under 15 (you can get singles). Early birds can travel for half price on the 9am train (exc July and Aug).

Welsh Slate Museum (Padarn Country Park, off A4086) This intriguing place, stepped steeply into the mountain, and once one of the biggest quarries in the country, is home to a working incline, and a row of reconstructed quarrymen's houses decked out in period furniture from the 1860s, 1900s and 1969. An exhibition on the story of slate is introduced by a 3D show and demonstrated by craftsmen; also children's activity centre. The quarry workshop has been preserved largely in its original state - complete with working craftsmen and machinery. Its water wheel is one of the largest in the world. Snacks, shop with locally designed slate items, disabled access; cl Sat during Nov-Easter; (01286) 870630; free.

LLANDDANIEL SH5069
Bryn Celli Ddu (Llanddaniel Fab) Particularly well preserved Bronze Age burial chamber, with stone slabs at the entrance leading inside the mound to a chamber with upright stones, inc a replica of an incised stone; locked, but key at nearby farmhouse; free. Take a torch.

LLANDDWYN ISLAND SH3863
Really a peninsula, cut off only by the highest of tides, grazed by soay sheep, and with a tiny, remote settlement consisting of a ruined church, some sailors' cottages, a cannon and a lighthouse. Reached by a satisfying walk along a huge beach fringed by dunes and the pine forest of Newborough Warren from a car park in the forest (take Llanddwyn road from Newborough village).

LLANDUDNO SH7882
The main holiday town in the area, and though it does have a long well sheltered curve of good pebbly beach, a prom and a range of resort entertainments, it doesn't feel at all brash. There are charming little shops and boutiques, a well restored pier (from which you can fish), and cable-cars as well as the famously steep quaint tramway up the massive Great Orme headland which protects the main beach - there's a quieter but more exposed beach on the far side. You can walk right up, too; a café on the way has views to justify stopping. At the top is a 12th-c church, a visitor centre with local geology, and more good walking. On the way down a dry ski slope also has a toboggan run. The Kings Head by the tram station is a nice stop, and the Queens Head at Glanwydden, off the Colwyn Bay road, does very good food.
Alice in Wonderland Centre ▣ (Trinity Sq) Jolly exhibition devoted to

Alice in Wonderland, with life-size animated tableaux; the real Alice holidayed in Llandudno as a child. Shop, disabled access; cl winter Sun, 1st 2 wks Nov, 25-26 Dec, 1 Jan; (01492) 860082; *£2.95.

Conwy Valley Railway Railtrack line from Llandudno to Blaenau Ffestiniog, through magnificent scenery, with several useful stops en route.

Great Orme Mines 4,000-year-old copper mine near the summit of Great Orme, the biggest such site so far discovered. It's also the only prehistoric metal mine open to the public, with displays of finds, and underground walks through the cavernous workings themselves; weather permitting, you can sometimes see digs in progress. Teas, shop; cl end Oct-1 Feb; (01492) 870447; £4.50.

LLANELLTYD SH7219

Cymer Abbey (1½m NW of Dolgellau, off A470) Remains of a 12th-c Cistercian abbey, beautifully set in a partly wooded valley; free; Cadw. The George III at Penmaenpool is quite handy for something to eat.

LLANFAIRPWLLGWYNGYLL SH5372

The record books add another 39 letters (gocherychwyrndrobwllllantysiliogogo goch) to this village's name, but locals cut it even shorter, to Llanfair PG, or Llanfairpwll. Excellent views of Snowdonia and the Menai Strait from the top of the Marquess of Anglesey's Column, built in 1816 to commemorate the military achievements of Wellington's second-in-command at the Battle of Waterloo. The nearby village of Penmynydd was the ancient home of the Tudor family. The Liverpool Arms at Menai Bridge is the nearest good place for lunch.

Plas Newydd 🏛 (A4080, 2m S) Lovely mountain views from the elegant 18th-c former home of the Marquess of Anglesey, known best for association with Rex Whistler where largest painting is here; there is also an exhibition about his work. A military museum contains the campaign relics of the first Marquess of Anglesey who commanded the cavalry at the Battle of Waterloo. A fine spring garden (the rhododendron garden is open Apr-

early Jun), summer terrace, and australasian arboretum; a woodland walk gives access to a marine walk on the Menai Strait, and the adventure play trail has been extended; boat trips from the jetty (weather permitting). Meals, snacks, shop, disabled access; cl Thurs, Fri, all Nov-Mar; (01248) 714795; £4.60; NT.

LLANGEFNI SH4576

Right in the centre of Anglesey, and its 'capital', with a big open-air market every Thurs and Sat.

Oriel Ynys Mon (Rhosmeirch, B5111 N) Excellent gallery with imaginative changing displays on the history of Anglesey, as well as a collection of wildlife paintings by C F Tunnicliffe. You can spend a surprising amount of time here. Meals, snacks, shop, disabled access; cl Mon (exc bank hols), 25 Dec-1 Jan; (01248) 724444; £2.50.

LLANGOLLEN SJ2142

Not special in itself despite a good few solid and gracious Georgian and Victorian villas; what makes it attractive is its charming valley setting above the River Dee. It has discreet hotels that cater for the generally older people to whom the area most appeals - though it comes vividly alive during the Eisteddfod. The strikingly converted riverside Corn Mill has interesting enjoyable food, and Abbey Grange, Royal and Wild Pheasant hotels are all pleasant for lunch, too.

Castell Dinas Bran The place for walkers to head for from Llangollen. This hill fort commands views over the vale and is close to the Panorama Walk (actually a surfaced minor road). Walks can be linked to the canal towpath below, where the Sun Trevor (A539) is handy for enjoyable food, with good views.

Horse-drawn boat trips (Llangollen Wharf) Trips along the lovely Vale of Llangollen; meals and snacks at the Wharf Café, shop, disabled access; cl Nov-Easter and may cl Thurs and Fri in Apr and Oct; (01978) 860702;*£4.

Llangollen Railway (Abbey Rd) Runs eight miles, with steam and diesel trains from the pleasantly preserved station (renovations here may continue into 2004) to the village of Carrog up the Dee, where the Grouse in a lovely setting above the river does reasonably priced food all day; special events inc Santa specials. Snacks, shop, special coach for the disabled (you have to book); cl mid-Oct to mid-Apr; (01978) 860951 for talking timetable; £8 full return fare, less for shorter trips.

Motor Museum and Canal Exhibition 🏛 (A542 N) Classic cars and motorcycles, and an exhibition on the canal network. Shop, disabled access; cl Mon and Nov to mid-Feb; (01978) 860324; *£2.50.

Plas Newydd 🏛 Lady Eleanor Butler and Sarah Ponsonby, the Ladies of Llangollen, lived here 1780-1831. The beautiful house has stained glass, leather wall coverings and domestic paraphernalia of the period, and pleasant gardens. Shop; cl Nov-Apr; (01978) 861314; £3.

Pontcysyllte aqueduct (off A5/A539 E) The longest in Britain, very spectacular to cross - by boat or on foot.

Valle Crucis Abbey (A542 2m N) Substantial remains of the early 13th-c Cistercian abbey church, one of the most complete in Wales, a vaulted roof chapter house and some beautifully carved grave slabs. Shop, limited disabled access; cl late Sept to mid-Mar - you can still get into the abbey then, but not into the dormitory or exhibitions; (01978) 860326; £2; Cadw. The ruins stand at the bottom of the Horseshoe Pass, a nerve-wrackingly steep but extremely scenic mountain drive; the Britannia Inn just above the abbey has exceptional views.

LLANGWM SH9845

Ewe-phoria 🏛 As well as seeing the sheepdogs put through their paces at these enjoyable shows, you can watch shearing demonstrations, and learn about a dozen or more different breeds of sheep in their ram parade. The best time to visit is spring when there are lots of baby lambs (you may be able to feed them); picnic and indoor play areas. Meals, snacks, shop, disabled access; (01490) 460369; cl Mon (exc bank hols), Sat, and all Nov-Easter; £4.20.

LLANGYBI SH4241

St Cybi's Well Known to the Welsh as Fynnon Gybi, this has been reckoned to have healing properties for over a thousand years. Look out for the corbelled beehive vaulting inside the roofless stone structure, which is ancient Irish in style.

LLANRWST SH7961 Pretty little town with old stone bridge over the Conwy river, said to be the work of Inigo Jones. The friendly Pen y Bont has enjoyable food. Gwydir Chapel, added by the influential Wynn family to the parish church in the 17th c, has a stone coffin reputedly that of Llewelyn the Great, as well as a magnificent rood screen from the ruins of Maenan Abbey. The Wynns also constructed the nearby Gwydir Uchaf Chapel, with intriguing ceiling paintings.

Gwydir Castle Splendid Tudor courtyard house with later additions, partly built of Maenan Abbey stone after the Dissolution. The former ancestral home of the Wynn family, it is set in Grade I listed gardens in the Conwy Valley. Cl Nov-Feb, and some Sats for weddings - best to phone; (01492) 641687; £3.

LLANUWCHLLYN SH8829

Bala Lake Railway 🏛 Some of the carriages on trains using this delightful 4½-mile route are open to the elements, which seems to make the views of the lake and mountains more vivid. The locomotives were once used to haul slate in the local quarries. Snacks, shop, disabled access (but no facilities); cl Oct-Easter, and Mon and Fri during Apr, May, Jun and Sept; (01678) 540666 for timetable; £6.70. The Eagles has good home-made food and nice views.

LLANYSTUMDWY SH4738

Lloyd George Memorial Museum (A497) Audio-visual displays and memorabilia relating to the life and times of Lloyd George. Between 1864 and 1880 he lived in nearby Highgate Cottage, with its shoemaking workshop, which has been restored to the way it was then, and Victorian garden; a library is devoted to books about him. Shop, disabled access; cl Nov-May (exc Easter), May-Oct wknds, Sun in Jun; (01766) 522071; £3. The old-fashioned bar opposite is good value, and it's a short stroll from here to where he's buried.

Rabbit Farm (just off A497) Children enjoy this, with hundreds of rabbits (you can buy bags of food; 50p), as well as other small animals such as chipmunks, chinchillas, pygmy goats and guinea-pigs; also pony rides, and picnic and play areas. Snacks, shop, disabled access; cl end Oct-Mar; (01766) 523136; £2.50.

LLEYN PENINSULA SH3235
Well worth carrying on to the very end of this long peninsula for the best of the cliff-top walks, starting W from Aberdaron, with fine windswept views from Mynydd Mawr (where there is a useful hilltop car park), and E of here is the spectacular bay of Hell's Mouth; the beaches along here have clean bathing water. For a stiffer walk, try Yr Eifl (the Rivals), a 563-metre (1,849-ft) mountain close to the N coast.

LLYN IDWAL SH6460
This superbly sited Snowdonia lake beneath Glyder Fach gives pleasant walks along a signed nature trail.

MENAI BRIDGE SH5571
The village takes its name from Thomas Telford's magnificent iron suspension bridge linking Anglesey to the mainland, the first such bridge in the world. The waterside Liverpool Arms has good value fresh food.

Butterfly Palace £ (A5025) Exotic butterflies from all corners of the globe, as well as bird house, insectarium, reptile house, and adventure playground. Meals, snacks, shop, disabled access; cl Jan-Feb; (01248) 712474; £4.75.

MOEL FAMAU SJ1662
The highest point of the Clwydian Range, a bulging massif with clearly marked paths; walk up from the car park on the minor road E of Llanbedr DC through colour-coded forest trails or over open land, for views of much of Snowdonia, the edge of the Peak District and the Wirral. The Offa's Dyke Path returns over the moor S to the road, just after which it continues up the Iron Age hill fort of Foel Fennli, another fine viewpoint.

MOLD SJ2364
A good theatre, and a richly decorated parish church built to commemorate the victory of Henry Tudor at Bosworth Field in 1485. The Druid out at Llanferres on the Ruthin road and the Bryn Awel on the Denbigh road are reliable dining pubs.

PENMACHNO SH7752
Ty Mawr Wybrnant (forest rd NW) Picturesque, lonely thick-walled medieval cottage, birthplace of Bishop William Morgan who first translated the Bible into Welsh (see also St Asaph). Shop, disabled access; cl Mon-Weds, and Nov-Mar; (01690) 760213; £2.20. NT.

Ty'n-y-Coed Uchaf Reached by a pleasant walk along the river from the Woollen Mill's car park, a fully furnished 19th-c farmhouse, good for showing the traditional way of life in this area. Shop, disabled parking in yard. Cl am, also Mon-Weds, Sat and Nov-Mar; (01690) 760229; *£2.40; NT.

PENMAENPOOL SH6717
Its small waterside nature reserve has a very useful nature information centre pointing out promising places throughout this whole area, a good region for walks. One is the walk along the old railway track beside the Mawddach estuary to Fairbourne, giving magnificent views. The George III is a pleasant place for lunch.

Abergwynant Farm Trekking Centre (A493, about a mile SW) Will take beginners out on ponies (experienced riders, too), over scenic routes. Snacks, disabled riding and access; (01341) 422377; from £10 an hour, £15 for two hours. You can stay at the farm in self-catering cottages and flats; fishing.

PENMON SH6279
A tiny place near the NE corner of Anglesey, notable for its ruined priory. This was a Norman rebuild, but there are earlier Celtic crosses, a 17th-c dovecote and a hermitage well. From here it is well worth driving the final mile along the road to the car park at the cliff edge, for a fine view of Puffin Island, ½m offshore. Uninhabited apart from visiting cormorants, shags and seals, the island is known in Welsh as Ynys Seiriol, after St Seiriol whose monastic settlement is now a few scant ruins.

PORTHMADOG SH5638
Quite a busy shopping town of low slate-roofed houses, with a spacious harbour and long causeway road (5p toll) across the estuary. The Royal Sportsman does good value bar and restaurant lunches, and nearby Black

Rock Golden Sands is one of the area's finest beaches.

Ffestiniog Railway (Harbour Station) The famous narrow-gauge railway opened in 1836 to carry slate from Blaenau Ffestiniog to Porthmadog by gravity. Closed in 1946, it reopened in 1955 and has gradually been extended to climb the 13½ miles to Blaenau Ffestiniog. There are plans to extend it further. Stop off at stations along the way for good walks and views. The railway links with the main line Cambrian Coast Line, hugging the coast from Pwllheli to Machynlleth, with many stops along the way. Good meals and snacks (appealing station bar with seats out on terrace), shop, some disabled access; cl 22-25 Dec and limited winter service, best to phone; (01766) 516073; full return fare £14 (or travel first class for an extra £5 return).

Welsh Highland Railway 🔲 (opposite main line station) Overshadowed by its more famous neighbour in size but certainly not in spirit, this enthusiastically restored line runs trains daily; a two-mile extension should be completed by May 2004. Meals, snacks, shop, disabled access; cl Jan-Mar, Nov (they run all-day courses then, which include driving a steam engine); (01766) 513402 for timetable or (0151) 608 1950; *£3.75.

PORTMEIRION SH5837 🔲 On the steep wooded shores of an inlet from Tremadog Bay, this fairytale 20th-c holiday village designed by Williams-Ellis is set in 70 hectares (175 acres) of lush coastal cliff and woodland gardens. Quite charming, it's an italianate folly - pastel-washed cottages interlaced with grottoes and cobbled squares, a bell tower, castle and lighthouse, and long picturesque flights of steps zigzagging down to the water, which at low tide dries to miles of sand. Enveloping the village are the steeply spreading Gwyllt gardens, with fine displays of rhododendrons, azaleas, hydrangeas and subtropical plants; good wild woodlands, too. You have to pay a toll to enter the village, but once in can see the house where Noel Coward wrote *Blithe Spirit* and the locations for the cult TV series *The Prisoner*; children can play in the playground, on a make-believe schooner

apparently moored by the hotel, or, tide permitting, on the beach. A lovely relaxing place, quite unlike anywhere else. Meals, snacks, shops (one specialising in Portmeirion pottery); cl 25 Dec; (01766) 770000; *£5.70. No dogs - though there's a touching dog cemetery in the woods nearby.

Plas Brondanw (Llanfrothen, A4085 N of Penrhyndeudraeth) The ancestral home of Portmeirion's architect Sir Clough Williams-Ellis, you can visit the architectural garden he designed there - great views. Open daily; (01766) 770228; £5.50. The nearby Brondanw Arms has popular food.

PRECIPICE WALK SH7321 Signposted N of Dolgellau, this is an attractive Snowdonia walk.

PRESTATYN SJ0683 Bustling seaside resort standing at one end of the 168-mile walkable route of Offa's Dyke, marked by a stone pillar above the main beach. At Gwaenysgor in the hills just behind, the Eagle & Child has good value food and fine views. There are plans for a huge wind farm out at sea down the coast towards Rhyl.

PWLLHELI SH3231 **Plas Glyn-Y-Weddw** (Llanbedrog) Fine gallery in a stunning Victorian Gothic Grade II mansion. Tearoom, shop; cl Tues (exc July and Aug) and following bank hols, cl Christmas-end Jan; (01758) 740763; *£2.50. The nearby Glynyweddw Arms does enjoyable food.

RHIW SH2328 **Plas yn Rhiw** Charming if unassuming little manor house at the tip of the Lleyn Peninsula, with all the furniture and kitchen utensils exactly as they were originally; lovely gardens and woodland, inc a waterfall, spring snowdrop wood and subtropical specimens. Shop, very limited disabled access; cl Tues, plus Weds 23 Mar-13 May, cl wkdys Oct (open all week half-term), cl all Nov-Mar; (01758) 780219; £3.20; NT. The setting is great, overlooking one of the area's wildest coasts. The beautifully placed Sun over at Llanengan does decent food.

RHUDDLAN SJ0478 **Bodrhyddan Hall** 🔲 (A5151 Rhuddlan—Dyserth) Lovely doll's-house front, and some wonderfully elaborate fireplaces in the drawing room. Also formal french garden, a woodland garden with four ponds and a Palladian-styled summer house, and an interesting well-house built by Inigo Jones. Teas (meals by appointment), disabled access to ground floor only; open pm Tues and Thurs Jun-Sept (or to parties by appointment at any time); (01745) 590414; *£4.

Dyserth church (off A5151 E) Partly 13th-c, with a Jesse window; not far from a plunging 18-metre (60-ft) waterfall.

Rhuddlan Castle Fine old castle, adapted by Edward I from an earlier Norman structure, to guard what was once a busy port (now a sleepy little town). Overlooking the river, it's a pretty spot. Shop, mostly disabled access; cl end Sept-Easter; (01745) 590777; £2.50; Cadw.

RHYL SJ0081
Rather brash seaside resort; if you're passing with children, they'll enjoy the Terror Tomb, a walk-through ghost train.

Seaquarium (East Parade) One of the very good sea life centres that we've described in several english resorts, with a dramatic Shark Encounter as well as the usual walk-through underwater tunnel. They have an interesting new project for 2004, still under wraps as we go to press (they say this may put the price up). Meals, snacks, shop, disabled access; cl 25 Dec; (01745) 344660; £5.50.

SNOWDON SH6455
The highest mountain in England or Wales, Snowdon is the most famous of the diverse mountain shapes in Snowdonia National Park. This whole area has enough fine walking, both gentle and taxing, to fill a walking holiday. Snowdon itself has a number of ways up ranging from the easy path alongside the mountain railway (see Llanberis) to the enthralling Horseshoe Route, which makes its way along knife-edge ridges; the Pyg Track and Watkin Path are among the favourites. For a taste of the mountain without actually going up it, follow the start of the Miners' Track (from the Pen-y-Pass car park on the A4086), which really is a track as far as Glaslyn, the last of four lakes passed. The National Trust now

owns large areas of the mountain, and is carrying out path improvements alongside careful conservation of the landscape, with long-term plans for regeneration of some former oak forest. A planning application has also been made for a replacement for the summit's inelegant café, one of the less successful works of Portmeirion architect Sir Clough Williams-Ellis.

SOUTH STACK SH2182
Seabird Centre The spectacular cliffs near the lighthouse are full of seabird breeding colonies, and this RSPB reserve covering over a square mile has guillemots, razorbills and puffins (esp around May, June and July). Lots of colourful wild flowers too, and perhaps the odd seal. The visitor centre has CCTV of nesting birds; guided walks leave here at 2pm most Suns May-Aug. Visitor centre cl mid-Sept to Easter; (01407) 764973; free. A second newer RSPB seabird centre is at the lighthouse itself, which also has CCTV; cl Oct-Easter; (01248) 724444; £3. Nearby is a large group of the foundations of **hut circles**, probably around 2,000 years old, still with some visible traces of stone sleeping slabs.

ST ASAPH SJ0374
St Asaph Cathedral To match its tiny little city, this is the smallest in Britain, founded in 537. A column in the grounds commemorates its most famous cleric Bishop Morgan (see also Penmachno) and his work translating the Bible into Welsh. A little museum has finds from the site, open by appointment; shop, disabled access; (01745) 583429; free. The Farmers Arms (The Waen) does proper food.

TAL-Y-CAFN SH7972
Bodnant Garden (off A470) Started in 1875 but improved in 1900, this garden is among Britain's greatest. Part of the 32-hectare (80-acre) grounds have a beautiful woodland garden in a sheltered valley, notable for its rhododendrons and azaleas, while below the private house are five terraces in the italian style, with a canal pool, reconstructed pin mill and an open-air stage on the lowest. Many fine rare plants inc unusual trees and shrubs. Meals, snacks, disabled access (but it is steep in places); cl Nov to mid-Mar;

(01492) 650460; £5.20; NT. The nearby Tal-y-Cafn Hotel is good for lunch.

TAN-Y-BWLCH SH6945

Plas Tan-y-Bwlch 🏛 (off A487) The grounds of the Snowdonia National Park's environmental study centre have rewarding strolls through gardens and extensive woodland; in places the paths cross the Ffestiniog Railway. Woods open all year, gardens summer only. Shop, some disabled access; (01766) 590324; *£2.50.

TRE'R CEIRI HILL FORT SH3744

Off B4417, just up the hill from Llanaelhaearn, a signed path leads to this evocative place, occupied from the Bronze Age through to the Dark Ages; a massive stone wall, lots of hut foundations, and fine views. At Morfa Nefyn nearby, the Bryncynan and (overlooking a lovely sandy bay) Cliff Hotel do good lunches.

TREFRIW SH7863

Used to be a spa, and you can still see the wells on the N outskirts of the village (the water is said to treat rheumatism, indigestion, and homesickness). The village also has a 14th-c church; the Princes Arms has decent food.

Trefriw Woollen Mill (B5106) The same family have run this woollen mill for over 140 years; two hydro-electric turbines are driven by the fast-flowing Afon Crafnant, and there's a weaver's garden (best Jun-Sept). Weaving demonstrations and turbine house wkdys all year (even Nov-Easter when the mill itself is closed). Snacks, shop (selling traditional welsh bedspreads and tweeds made here); cl Sun (exc Easter and spring bank hol); no weaving over Christmas hols; (01492) 640462; free.

WREXHAM SJ3350

Mostly an industrial town, but its 15th-c church is worth a look, with its magnificent steeple. The A525 to Ruthin is a pleasant drive.

Erddig See *separate family panel on p.861.*

A few miles S of Erddig the Cross Foxes at Overton Bridge has good food.

Bersham Heritage Centre & Ironworks (B5099/B5098 W) Well re-created 18th-c ironworks, with a good overview of other local industries, and occasional demonstrations of various

traditional skills. Snacks, shop, limited disabled access; Heritage Centre open all year (exc 25-26 Dec, 1 Jan); Ironworks cl Sept-Easter, best to phone for opening hours; (01978) 261529; free.

Farm World (adjacent to Erddig) Well liked by readers, a 120-hectare (300-acre) working dairy farm with all the necessary ingredients. Cl Nov-Feb, but best to phone; (01978) 840697; £4.95.

Y FELINHELI SH5367

Greenwood Forest Park (off B4366 NE of Caernarfon) This developing centre is an unexpected delight, taking a lively look at trees and wood from trunks and rainforests to ethiopian wooden pillows. You can handle most of the exhibits, and there's 7 hectares (17 acres) of woodland to explore. They've a giant 70-metre (230-ft) slide, longbow shooting, toddlers' village and play barn, a forest theatre (shows in school hols), boat rides and mini tractors (£1). Lots is doors, so enjoyable even if the weather isn't great. Meals, teas and picnic areas, shop, some disabled access; usually cl Nov to mid-Mar; (01248) 670076; £4.50-£6.30. The Vaynol Arms at Pentir has good food.

Attractive villages, almost all with decent pubs and in general tending to appeal for their surroundings more than for the beauty of their buildings, include Betws-yn-Rhos SH9174, Cilcain SJ1865, Erbistock SJ3542, Halkyn SJ2172, Hanmer SJ4639, Llanarmon DC SJ1633, Llanarmon-yn-Ial SJ1856, Llanasa SJ1082, Llandwrog SH4456, Llanelidan SJ1150, Llangedwyn SJ1924 in the Tanat Valley, Llanrhaeadr-ym-Mochnant SJ1326, Llansannan SH9466, Pontblyddyn SJ2761, Porth Dinllaen SH2741 (an idyllic seaside spot, but you have to walk to it) and St George SH9576. **Other pubs** and inns in attractive areas or with notable views include the Porth Tocyn Hotel above the sea at Abersoch SH3226 (excellent clean beach for families), Castell Cidwm at Betws Garmon SH5458, Sportsmans Arms up on the A543 S of Bylchau SH9863, Grouse at Carrog SJ1144, T'yn-y-Groes at Ganllwyd SH7224, Three Pigeons at Graig Fechan SJ1454, Eagle & Child in the hilltop village of Gwaenysgor SJ0881, Druid at

Llanferres SJ1961, Ship by acres of sand on the shore of Red Wharf Bay SH5281, Cwellyn Arms at Rhyd Ddu SH5753 (big playground), White Eagle on Holy Island at Rhoscolyn SH2676 and Caerffynon Hall at Talsarnau SH6236.

Where to eat

BEAUMARIS SH6076 **Sailors Return** *Church St (01248) 811314* Bright and cheerful, more or less open-plan pub, with a collection of car-shaped teapots, naval memorabilia and maps and old prints, comfortable furnishings in rich colours, a good mix of customers, well kept real ales, and enjoyable food inc daily specials; disabled access. £20|**£6.95**

COLWYN BAY SH8478 **Pen-y-Bryn** *Wentworth Ave (01492) 533360* (B5113 S) Big modern bar with plenty of space, well spaced tables in varying sizes, oriental rugs on pale stripped boards, big pot plants and a profusion of pictures, shelves of books, two coal fires, and thoughtful friendly service; interesting modern food, well kept real ales, thoughtfully chosen wines, proper coffee, and freshly squeezed orange machine; big windows look down over the town to the sea (with a telescope), and there are tables out on terraces. £21.75|**£7.45**

GRESFORD SJ3453 **Pant-yr-Ochain** *Old Wrexham Rd (01978) 853525* Stylishly decorated spacious pub in attractive grounds, with a gently upmarket atmosphere in the light and airy main room, a wide range of interesting prints and bric-a-brac, and a good mix of individually chosen country furnishings; open fires, a big dining area set out as a library, excellent food from a daily changing menu, a good range of decent wines, well kept real ales, lots of malt whiskies, and polite efficient service; one room is no smoking; children until 6pm. £24.65|**£7.95**

LLANBERIS SH5760 **Y Bistro** *43-45 High St (01286) 871278* Friendly no smoking restaurant (both rooms are no smoking) using the best local produce for its welsh and english cooking - fine fish and enjoyable puddings; cl Sun, Mon; partial disabled access. £30

LLANDUDNO JUNCTION SH8180 **Queens Head** *Glanwydden (01492) 546570* Busy but comfortable dining pub with a spacious and comfortable modern lounge bar, carefully prepared and generously served enjoyable food from a weekly changing menu (lots of fine seafood and tempting puddings), real ales, and decent wines; cl 25 Dec; children over 7. £25|**£7.95**

LLANGEDWYN SJ1924 **Green** *(01691) 828234* Country dining pub in lovely spot in the Tanat Valley and open all day at weekends; lots of nooks, alcoves and crannies, a blazing log fire, a good mix of furnishings, pleasant upstairs no smoking evening restaurant, impressive range of tasty bar food, half-a-dozen real ales, and a good choice of malt whiskies and wines; attractive garden over road with picnic-sets by the river, and fishing permits. £20|**£5.95**

LLANGOLLEN SJ2142 **Corn Mill** *Dee Lane (01978) 869555* Remarkable conversion of big watermill, handsomely refitted inside with several uncluttered levels of new pale pine flooring, a striking open stairway with gleaming timber and tensioned steel rails, mainly stripped stone walls, and quite a bit of the old mill machinery; a great waterwheel turns between the building and external decking cantilevered over the River Dee, and a terrace has lots of good teak tables and chairs, and a superb view over the river; a lively bustling chatty feel, quick service from plenty of neat young staff, nicely chosen pictures (many to do with water), good changing food, well kept real ales, and careful choice of wines. £24.75|**£7.95**

LLANRWST SH7961 **Ty-Hwnt-i'r-Bont** *(01492) 640138* Charming little 500-year-old cottage by bridge with nice old country furniture under the beams and joists, interesting knick-knacks, light lunches, home-made cakes, shortbread and scones for enjoyable afternoon teas, and quite a choice of teas, coffees and milk shakes; home-made mustards to take away, and old books and bric-a-brac upstairs; cl Mon (exc bank hols), cl end Oct to mid-Mar.|**£6.10**

OVERTON BRIDGE SJ3542 **Cross Foxes** *(01978) 780380* (A539) Substantial, carefully reworked 18th-c coaching inn with several linked but distinct areas, each with its own character, and framed pictures in abundance; a good mix of individual tables in varying sizes (big candles at night), grey carpet here, bare boards there, oriental rugs on quarry tiles elsewhere, mixed dining chairs in some places, built-in padded banquettes in others; good log fires; a wide choice of consistently good food, well kept real ales, a changing choice of wines by the glass, and kind and efficient service; fine view of the River Dee from the end room on the left, and from picnic-sets out on a crazy-paved terrace. £23.95|**£8.95**

PWLLHELI SH3535 **Plas Bodegroes** *(01758) 612363* Lovely Georgian manor house, aptly described as a restaurant-with-rooms, in tree-filled grounds and fronted by a 200-year-old beech avenue; comfortably restful rooms, enjoyable food using superb fresh local produce (esp fish) and very good wine list; bdrms; cl Sun pm, Mon (but open bank hol wknds), Dec-Feb, children allowed but not encouraged. £45

RED WHARF BAY SH5281 **Ship Inn** *(01248) 852568* Solidly built old pub looking over miles of cockle-sands, with enterprising bar food, big old-fashioned bars, coal fires, friendly cheerful service, no smoking dining room and cellar room, well kept real ales, quite a few whiskies, and plenty of seats outside. £20|**£5.50**

TY'N-Y-GROES SH7774 **Groes** *(01492) 650545* Particularly well run family inn with wonderful views from airy no smoking conservatory, rambling low-beamed and thick-walled rooms with welcoming atmosphere and interesting old furnishings, winter log fires, a fine range of good traditional country cooking, well kept real ales, and efficient friendly service; stylish bdrms; children over 5; disabled access (and one specially equipped bdrm). £35|**£10**

West Wales

**Open-air Wales at its cheerful best - beautiful unspoilt coastline,
some splendid gardens and ruins, and ample opportunities
for family fun**

This part of Wales scores high for undemanding (and cheap) family holidays, and relaxing short breaks. With its sheltered sandy beaches, civilised Tenby is a welcoming little resort, ideal for a laid-back weekend. Further W, St David's (with a fun aquarium as well as the fine cathedral) preserves some of its ancient calm, and is ideally placed for exploring the rugged coast. There are enjoyable boat trips from both these places, and also from Dale to spectacularly wild Skomer (watch out for seals), Grassholm and Skokholm. In tiny inlets along the coast, ports like Solva and Porthgain, once busy with transatlantic trade, are fascinating to explore.

Families enjoy Manor House Wild Animal Park in St Florence (the nearby country park has a range of activities), and there are friendly farm animals at Begelly and Castle Morris (a good place to buy cheese); in Gwbert you might catch sight of seals and even dolphins. Wales's premiere theme park in Narberth has more than enough for an action-packed day out. You can visit goldmines in Pumsaint, and (new to this edition) the Gun Tower Museum in Pembroke is interesting.

The spectacular Stackpole Estate at Bosherston and the numerous attractions at Burry Port's Pembrey Country Park are excellent in fine weather. The no-expense-spared National Botanic Garden of Wales at Llanarthne with its knock-out giant glasshouse is well worth a visit, and it's not just gardeners who are entranced by the haunting ancient garden among ruins at Llangathen. The woollen industry museum at Drefach Felindre will be worth a look when it reopens.

The coast is relatively gentle in the S, with level cliffs, sinuous estuaries and some lovely sandy beaches. In the W and N it's much more rugged. The Pembrokeshire Coast Path and the Celtic Cycle Trail (part of the national Sustrans network) make the most of it, snaking around the intricate seaboard.

Where to stay

BROAD HAVEN SM8616 **Druidstone Hotel** *Broad Haven, Haverfordwest, Dyfed SA62 3NE* (01437) 781221 **£90**; 11 rms, some with sea view, shared bthrms. Alone on the coast above an effectively private beach with exhilarating cliff walks, this roomy and very informally friendly hotel, run by a very nice family, has something of a folk-club and Outward Bound feel at times; it's extremely winning and relaxing if you take to its unique combination of good wholesome and often memorably inventive food, slightly fend-for-yourself approach amid elderly furniture, and glorious seaside surroundings; self-catering cottages, two with wheelchair access; disabled access; dogs welcome ☺

CAREW SN0403 **Old Stable Cottage** *Carew, Tenby, Dyfed SA70 8SL* (01646) 651889 **£28***; 3 charming rms. Originally a stable and carthouse for the castle, this attractive place has an inglenook fireplace and original bread oven, a lovely sitting room with teak beams (probably from former shipyards), games room, conservatory overlooking the garden, and good Aga-cooked food; cl Dec-Jan inc; children over 3

CRUGYBAR SN6437 **Glanrannell Park** *Crugybar, Llanwrda, Dyfed SA19 8SA* (01558) 685230 **£80***; 7 rms. Surrounded by lawns and overlooking a small private lake, this peaceful place has two comfortable lounges and a small library, a well stocked bar, good varied food using fresh local produce where possible, and friendly helpful owners; excellent area for walks and esp bird-watching, also lots of wildlife, pony-trekking, and fishing nearby; cl 24 Dec-1 Mar; children over 8; dogs welcome in bedrooms

FISHGUARD SM9736 **Gilfach Goch** *Fishguard, Dyfed SA65 9SR* (01348) 873871 **£60***; 5 rms. Traditional carefully modernised 18th-c welsh stone farmhouse on 18-acre smallholding near Pembrokeshire coastal path, with sheep, donkeys, cats and fowl; lovely views, log fires, homely lounge, good country cooking, and a safe garden for children; no smoking; cl Oct-Easter; partial disabled access

FISHGUARD SM9537 **Manor House Hotel** *Main St, Fishguard, Dyfed SA65 9HG* (01348) 873260 **£54***; 6 comfortable rms, most with sea views. Georgian house with fine views of harbour from sheltered garden, a guests' lounge with books, an attractive, well planned basement restaurant with delicious home-made food using fresh local produce, and enjoyable breakfasts (and pre-dinner drinks), out on the terrace overlooking the sea in good weather; cl Christmas and restricted opening Nov-Feb; dogs welcome in bedrooms

GLYNARTHEN SN3049 **Penbontbren Farm** *Glynarthen, Llandysul, Dyfed SA44 6PE* (01239) 810248 **£96**, plus special breaks; 10 rms in converted stone farm outbuildings. Victorian farmhouse in lovely countryside with a little farm museum, and nearby beaches; period pine furnishings in bar, lounge and well liked restaurant, good honest country cooking and hearty breakfasts; cl 24-28 Dec; disabled access; dogs welcome in bedrooms

LLANDELOY SM8527 **Lochmeyler Farm** *Llandeloy, Haverfordwest, Dyfed SA62 6LL* (01348) 837724 **£55***; plus special winter breaks; 15 pretty rms with videos (they have a video library). Attractive creeper-covered 16th-c farmhouse on 220-acre working dairy farm; two lounges (one no smoking), traditional farmhouse cooking in pleasant dining room, mature garden, and welsh cakes on arrival; can walk around the farm trails; cl Christmas; disabled access; dogs welcome in bedrooms

LLANELLI SS5499 **Llwyn Hall** *Llwynhendy, Llanelli, Dyfed SA14 9LJ* (01554)

777754 **£60**; 9 rms, 5 in main house. Attractively furnished and spacious country house hotel, with a welcoming, relaxed atmosphere, plenty of antiques, good enjoyable food from a varied menu, and very handy for the Wildfowl & Wetlands Trust, also in Llwynhendy; children over 10; cl first 2 wks Jan; disabled access

SPITTAL SM9822 **Lower Haythog** *Spittal, Haverfordwest, Dyfed SA62 5QL (01437) 731279* **£50**; 6 rms. Centuries-old farmhouse on working dairy farm in 250 acres of unspoilt countryside, with comfortable lounge, log fire, books and games, traditional breakfasts, good cooking in the dining room, and friendly owners; swing and slide in the garden, trout ponds in the woods; self-catering also; dogs welcome in bedrooms

ST DAVID'S SM7524 **Warpool Court** *St David's, Haverfordwest, Dyfed SA62 6BN (01437) 720300* **£150***, plus special breaks; 25 rms. Originally built as St David's cathedral school in the 1860s and bordering NT land, this popular hotel has lovely views over St Bride's Bay; Ada Williams's collection of lovely hand-painted tiles can be seen in the public rooms, food in the spacious elegant restaurant is imaginative (good for vegetarians too), and staff are helpful and friendly; quiet gardens, heated summer swimming pool, tennis, exercise room, table-tennis, pool and croquet; cl Jan; dogs welcome in bedrooms

To see and do

ABERAERON SN4562
The line of colour-washed houses facing the harbour is very pretty; there's a good craft centre here too, and the Harbourmaster is a useful food stop.
Llanerchaeron (2 miles E) Little-changed 1790s house by John Nash in a lovely, small-scale gentleman's estate, with a dairy, brewery and laundry among the service buildings - all subject to painstaking restoration by the National Trust. It now operates as a working organic farm, with estate walks, stables and walled gardens, and captivating views of the wooded valleys of the Aeron and Mydr. Cl Mon (exc bank hols), Tues, and all Nov-Mar; (01545) 570200; *£5; NT.
AMROTH SN1508
Colby Woodland Gardens 🖾 (off A477) Beautiful woodland gardens in sheltered valley - very pleasant and colourful, esp in spring; a walled garden has a 'gothick' gazebo and colourful herbaceous plants. Snacks, gallery, shop, disabled access; cl early Nov-Mar; (01834) 811885; £3; NT. In the village the 16th-c New Inn near the lovely beach has decent food inc local seafood.
BEGELLY SN1109
Folly Farm (A478) Busy working dairy farm - you can watch the cows being milked. There's a daily horse parade, pony and donkey barn, pets to handle, and a circus workshop; also large indoor traditional fairground, good play

areas, a pirate ship, and go-karts. Meals, snacks, shop, disabled access; cl 22 Dec-2 Jan, wkdays Nov-Mar; (01834) 812731; £4.95. A working pottery is nearby; (01834) 811204; cl Oct-Easter.
BOSHERSTON SR9394
Elegug Stacks (3m W) A pair of great rock pinnacles harbouring vast numbers of guillemots, herring gulls and kittiwakes. Unless the artillery ranges are in use (red warning flags, etc) you can get here by the coast path from St Govan's Chapel, or by a lonely road through the ranges. Just W is the Green Bridge of Wales, a fine natural arch.
St Govan's chapel (SE of Bosherston, towards St Govan's Head) A simple reroofed 14th-c ruin, dramatically set halfway down the sea cliffs, and reached via rough rock steps; the holy well has now dried up.
Stackpole Estate & Bosherston Lakes E of Bosherston, this spectacular estate covering several square miles is a real delight to wander through, with lily ponds, woodlands, cliffs, dunes and beaches offering a range of landscapes to suit every taste and mood.
Bosherston Lakes make a particularly easy strolling-ground, with level paths around them; a fine sight when the lilies are in bloom in summer; several car parks - but they do fill up at peak holiday times; free. At the S end you can cross dunes to emerge on to a

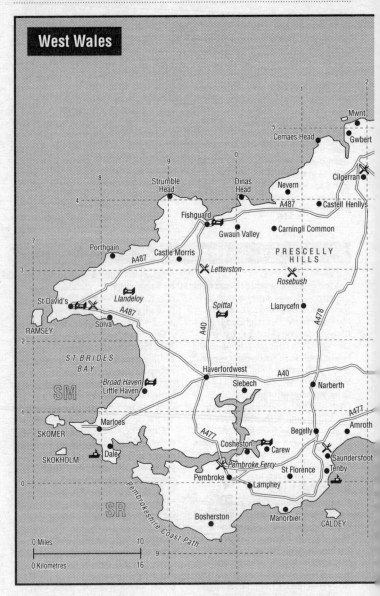

West Wales

(map of West Wales showing locations including Mwnt, Cemaes Head, Gwbert, Cilgerran, Strumble Head, Dinas Head, Nevern, Castell Henllys, Fishguard, Gwaun Valley, Carningli Common, Porthgain, Castle Morris, Letterston, PRESCELLY HILLS, Rosebush, St David's, Llandeloy, Spittal, Llanycefn, Solva, RAMSEY, ST BRIDES BAY, SM, Broad Haven, Little Haven, Haverfordwest, Slebech, Narberth, Marloes, SKOMER, Dale, SKOKHOLM, Cosheston, Carew, Begelly, Amroth, Pembroke Ferry, St Florence, Saundersfoot, Tenby, Pembroke, Lamphey, Bosherston, Manorbier, CALDEY, SR, Pembrokeshire Coast Path)

0 Miles 10
0 Kilometres 16

large sandy beach, Broad Haven. Barafundle Bay is a lovely relatively undiscovered beach. Snacks (at Stackpole Quay); (01646) 661359; car park (which can be very busy bank hols and summer) open Easter-Sept, £2 (free to NT members); NT. The Armstrong Arms does good food.

BURRY PORT SN4100
Pembrey Country Park Good for families to unwind in, with nearly a square mile of woodland, pitch-and-putt, orienteering, adventure playground, visitor centre, dry ski slope, toboggan run, miniature railway - and 8 miles of clean sandy beach (no dogs on one

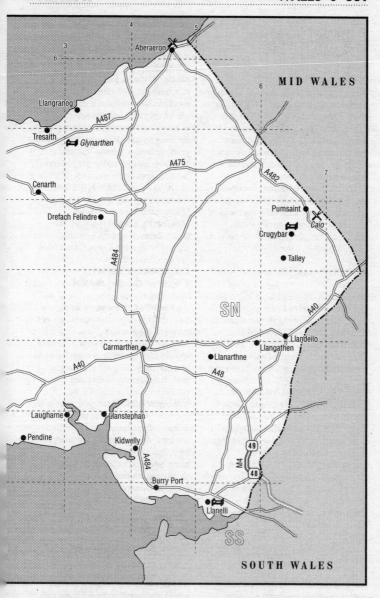

MID WALES

Aberaeron

Llangranog

A487

Tresaith

Glynarthen

A475

Cenarth

A482

Pumsaint

Drefach Felindre

Caio

Crugybar

A484

Talley

7

SN

A40

Llandeilo

Carmarthen

Llangathen

A40

Llanarthne

A48

Laugharne

Llanstephan

Pendine

Kidwelly

A484

M4

49

48

Burry Port

Llanelli

SS

SOUTH WALES

stretch in summer). Adjacent, Pembrey Burrows is a huge sweep of sands flanked by dunes and forest. Meals, snacks, shop, disabled access; park open all year exc 25 Dec, though most attractions cl winter; (01554) 833913; parking £3.30 (£5.50 July-Aug, £1.60 Oct-Mar, charges for some attractions).

CAREW SN0403
Carew Castle & Tidal Mill
Magnificent Norman castle (the setting for the Great Tournament of 1507), with esp handsome ivy-clad SE tower. The mill is one of just four restored tidal mills in Britain, with records dating back to 1558. Shop, some disabled access; cl

Nov-Mar; (01646) 651782; £2.80 both, £1.90 each. By the good Carew Inn nearby is the Carew Cross, an impressive 4-metre (13-ft) Celtic cross dating from the 11th c.

CARMARTHEN SN4120
Busy regional market town, according to legend the birthplace of Merlin, with the remains of a 13th-c castle, and on Priory St an unusual 2nd-c Roman amphitheatre. The Salutation along the A40 E in the pretty village of Pont-ar-Gothi (pleasant riverside walks) has been a good food stop.

Carmarthen Museum (Abergwili, just E) Good museum in a former palace of the Bishop of St David's, in extensive attractive grounds. Snacks, shop, disabled access to ground floor only; cl Sun, 25-26 Dec, 1 Jan; (01267) 231691; free.

Gwili Railway 🎫 (Bronwydd, A484 N) Steam-train trips along 2½m of scenic standard-gauge branch line of the old Great Western Railway. Snacks, shop, mostly disabled access; cl Jan-Mar and Nov; (01267) 230666; £4.50.

CARNINGLI COMMON SN0637
(S of Newport) Pleasant walks on moorland capped by ancient cairns and other antiquities.

CASTELL HENLLYS SN1138
(signed off A487 E of Newport) Iron Age hill fort in beautiful countryside overlooking River Gwaun, with interesting reconstruction of three big conical roundhouses; you may remember the BBC fly-on-the-wall documentary *Surviving the Iron Age*, which was made here. Also a forge, smithy, primitive looms and herb garden. Snacks, shop, some disabled access; cl Nov-Mar; (01239) 891319; £2.80.

CASTLE MORRIS SM9032
Llangloffan Farmhouse Cheese (Llangloffan Farm, just N) Delicious traditional farmhouse hard cheeses are hand-made here, and cheese-making demonstrations run from 10am to 12.45pm (Mon-Fri Apr-Oct); also friendly animals, a museum-cum-restaurant, children's play area and a picnic spot. The farm shop sells samples of the cheeses and other locally pro-duced foods; cl Sun, Nov-Mar; (01348) 891241; *£2.30. The excellent value fish restaurant at Letterston is handy.

CEMAES HEAD SN1249
Gives walkers good views over the mouth of the Teifi estuary and out over the Irish Sea.

CENARTH SN2641
National Coracle Centre 🎫 (Cenarth Falls) Unique collection of small hand-made boats from all over the world; they may have demonstrations of how they're made, and there are also various tools used for poaching. A 200-year-old bridge, salmon leap and a pretty waterfall provide the backdrop. Snacks, shop, disabled access; cl Sat, and all Nov-1 Apr; (01239) 710980; *£3. In the appealing village, the beamed Three Horseshoes has decent food.

Newcastle Emlyn (nearby) The attractive main street leads down to an ancient bridge; the Three Compasses has good value food.

CILGERRAN SN1943
Cilgerran Castle (off A484) Picturesquely placed on a crag above the River Teifi, these remains include a pair of highly defensible round towers dating to the first half of the 13th c, with Norman origins; good views from the towers and high walls, though, as usual, you have to go up a spiral staircase. Shop (not Sat), some disabled access; (01239) 615007; £2.50; Cadw.

Welsh Wildlife Centre Covering 110 hectares (270 acres), this nature reserve is one of the richest areas of wetland in the area - the reed bed is the second biggest in Wales. There are various trails, hides and information boards; you'll probably see more towards dusk, but even then some bashful creatures might not emerge. Meals, snacks, shop, disabled access; cl Nov- Easter; (01239) 621600; free, £3 car park.

COSHESTON SN0104
Upton Castle Gardens (off A477 E of Pembroke Dock; signed from Cosheston) Lovely woodland gardens surrounding a medieval castle (not open), with wide variety of trees and shrubs, formal terraces with herbaceous borders, and rose gardens. Picnic area; cl Sat and Nov-Mar; £2.

CRUGYBAR SN6638
Felin Newydd Watermill & Gardens 200-year-old watermill, still capable of grinding flour; interesting graffiti link it to the 19th-c welsh

colonists of South America; attractive gardens with chickens and ducks. Snacks, craft shop, disabled access; cl Tues (exc school summer hols), Weds, and Nov-Good Fri; (01558) 650375; *£2.

DALE SM8104

Dale Sea Safari Lots of varied boat trips to the islands of Skomer, Grassholm and Skokholm to see wonderful seabirds, flowers, seals, dolphins, and porpoises; sailing times (usually Apr-Oct only); (0800) 028 4090; £20.

Grassholm The island has 30,000 pairs of gannets: on a clear sunny morning even from the coast you can see it's white with them.

Skokholm This island has Britain's first bird observatory, still tracking migrations.

Skomer More than a mile across, spectacular wild scenery with countless birds (inc breeding pairs of short-eared owls, puffins and more than half the world's population of manx shearwaters) and flowers, as well as seals playing on the shore - perhaps common seals briefly in June or July, more likely grey seals and their pups in Sept and Oct; it's also remarkable for the easily traced remains of the Iron Age settlement here. The Wildlife Trust West Wales has accommodation on Skomer and Skokholm (contact Mrs Glenisteron, (01834) 870011), letting visitors see the amazing spectacle of the thousands of shearwaters leaving their nests in the evening.

Dale peninsula At the entrance to the huge natural harbour of Milford Haven, with gentle level-topped terrain giving walkers a bird's-eye view of the shipping activities, reducing the giant oil tankers to a pleasantly toy-like scale. The waterside Griffin in Dale itself is useful for something to eat.

DINAS HEAD SN0039

A classic north Pembrokeshire headland: the path around it takes about an hour's walking from the car park. The Old Sailors has food from sandwiches to local seafood inc summer cream teas.

DREFACH FELINDRE SN3539

Museum of the Welsh Woollen Industry Reopening in spring 2004 (the £1¾ million facelift took longer than expected), this working Teifi Valley textile mill focuses on the industry's 19th-c heyday, when this area, with 50 mills open, was known as the Huddersfield of Wales. Shop, snacks, disabled access; phone for opening times; (01559) 370929; free.

FISHGUARD SM9537

Joined on to Goodwick, from where ferries leave to Rosslare in Ireland, Fishguard has narrow, winding streets of cottages leading down from the attractive upper town to the old harbour (the Ship here has lots of atmosphere). The Royal Oak was the scene of the final surrender of the French in a bungled attempt to invade the mainland in 1797; the cannon fired then still stand on the now-ruined fort.

GWAUN VALLEY SN0034

Pretty walks along the lushly wooded river either upstream or downstream of Pontfaen.

GWBERT SN1648

Cardigan Island Coastal Farm Park Most notable for its fine clifftop setting overlooking Cardigan Island; there are a good few friendly animals for children, as well as plenty of wild flowers, and a coastal walk to caves where seals breed (best Mar-Nov). You may even see dolphins leaping. Cl Nov to mid-Mar; (01239) 612196; £3.

HAVERFORDWEST SM9515

Conveniently sited for exploring the Pembrokeshire National Park (although outside it), this hilly town is dominated by its castle ruins. Rising from the river towards Castle Sq, the High St has some attractive buildings, and there is a decent covered market (cl Sun), and books, crafts and antique shops along Market St, where Georges has a good choice of home-made food, with a Celtic arts shop in front.

Castle Museum 🔲 An english stronghold throughout its history, repulsing an attack in 1405 during Owain Glyndwr's rebellion; most of the surviving stonework dates from the late 13th c. A little museum in the old Governor's House (it was a prison in the 18th and 19th c) has local history displays. Shop, disabled access to ground floor only (though you can see the upstairs rooms on computer); open

Mon-Sat Easter-end Oct; (01437) 763087; *£1.

KIDWELLY SN4007

Kidwelly Castle Remarkably well preserved, this fine castle was built as an earth-and-timber stronghold in 1106, and rebuilt in stone in 1270. Four massive towers, the tremendous gatehouse and much of the impressive outer walls still remain, with steps up to the battlements and turrets. From the walls, the narrow medieval street layout of Kidwelly itself is very obvious. Shop, some disabled access; cl 24-26 Dec, 1 Jan; (01554) 890104; £2.50 inc audio tour; Cadw.

Kidwelly Industrial Museum (Mynyddygarreg, NE; clearly signposted from A484 Kidwelly by-pass) Looks at two great welsh industries, coal and tinplate. The original tinplate working buildings are still here, and there's an exhibition of coal-mining with pithead gear and a winding engine. Snacks, shop, disabled access; cl all Oct-May, and am wknds; (01554) 891078; free. The nearby Gwenllian Court Hotel has decent food.

LAMPHEY SN0101

Lamphey Palace (A4139) Ruined 13th-c palace once belonging to the Bishops of St David's. Shop; cl 25 Dec; (01646) 672224; £2.50; Cadw.

LAUGHARNE SN3011

The setting on the Taf estuary makes this a rewarding spot for wandering - past Laugharne Castle, Dylan Thomas's Boat House and along the cliff walk (known as Dylan's Walk); in the other direction there's a pleasant walk via Roche Castle. Thomas and his wife are buried in the village churchyard, their grave marked by a simple white cross. Browns Hotel (King St) seems not much changed since Thomas drank there; splendid second-hand bookshop opposite.

Dylan Thomas's Boat House 🆓 (Dylan's Walk) Wales's best-known recent poet lived here while he was writing *Under Milk Wood*, and there are still some of his family photographs and furniture. The writing shed he used for so many poems is nearby. Snacks, shop; cl a few days over Christmas and New Year, limited hours in winter; (01994) 427420; £2.95.

Laugharne Castle The ruin Dylan Thomas described as 'brown as owls' is a massive battlemented compilation of styles from 12th- to 16th-c; it has Victorian and Georgian gardens, and good views over the estuary. Cl Oct-Apr; (01994) 427906; £2.50; Cadw.

LITTLE HAVEN SM8512

Attractive village, with boats pulled up on to the sand, and a good base for seaside walks on the Pembrokeshire Coast Path. The Swan and Castle overlooking the bay do good lunches. There are some attractive sandy-floored rock coves to explore at low tide around here and the Druidstone Hotel to the N, with a good cliff walk N from there to the long sweep of sand and surf at Newgale Sands (food all day from the Duke of Edinburgh).

LLANARTHNE SN5320

National Botanic Garden of Wales (well signed from A48 - signing from the A40 needs improvement!) The first national botanic garden to be made in Britain for two centuries, this £43m showpiece is developing around 18th-c Middleton Hall, in the heart of the attractive Tywi Valley. The centrepiece is the awesome Norman Foster-designed Great Glasshouse - made from 1,000 panes (controlled by computer to vary the climate in different parts) and Europe's biggest. Plants in here come from as far afield as southern California, western Australia and the Canary Islands, and include Britain's rarest tree, the ley's whitebeam, of which there are only 11 known examples left in the wild. Outside, visitors are treated to a mediterranean-style landscape with a 5-metre (16-ft) deep ravine, rock terraces, waterfalls and a lake (one of seven on the site). Highlights include a genetic garden and a physic garden displaying herbs and their medicinal uses around the world. The centre has a hands-on science centre and an audio-visual theatre. Meals, snacks, shop, good disabled access; cl 25 Dec; (01558) 668768; £6.95. The Golden Grove Arms (B4300) has good food.

LLANDEILO SN6222

An attractive sloping town; the Castle Hotel has popular food, and past it the Plough at Rhosmaen (B4300) is a favourite local dining pub.

Dinefwr Park 🏛 (20 mins' walk from riverside lodge at S edge of Llandeilo; follow Dyfed Wildlife Trust path) Pleasant walks through wooded Capability Brown parkland around isolated, largely 13th-c castle and Newton House. Plenty of deer (a feature of the estate for over 1,000 years), but no trace of the medieval town which is known to have stood outside the walls. Meals, snacks, disabled access; cl Tues, Weds, Nov-Mar; (01558) 823902; *£3.30.

Gelli Aur Country Park (3m W, off B4300) Very relaxing: 24 hectares (60 acres) of wooded parkland around a splendid mansion, with an arboretum, nature trails, and specimen trees and shrubs. Meals, snacks, shop, disabled access; cl 25-26 Dec; (01558) 668885; *£1.50 parking charge.

LLANELLI SS5099

Millennium Coastal Park 14 miles of coastline, once heavily scarred by industry, transformed into an appealing park. Attractions between Loughor Bridge and Pembrey (where the Burry Port harbour is being restored) include several wetland nature reserves, a golf course designed by Jack Nicklaus, a national angling centre, a restored historic dockyard, and the seafront promenade at Llanelli. Lots of public sculpture has been commissioned, gardens and community woodlands have been landscaped, and there are plenty of rewarding viewpoints over the estuary. The sites are linked by a continuous traffic-free cycleway/ footpath which hooks up with the **Celtic Trail**, a 220-mile cycle route that winds its way across South and West Wales, from the Severn Bridge to the Pembrokeshire Coast National Park.

National Wetlands Centre for Wales (Llwynhendy, 3m E) By Wales's main estuary for wildfowl and waders, with plenty of observation hides and special walkways, and home to thousands of spectacular ducks, geese and swans. Many of the birds will feed from your hand, and at their summer Duckery you can hear ducklings calling from inside their eggs. The Millennium Wetlands is a 100-hectare (250-acre) reserve, with a discovery centre. Meals, snacks, shop, disabled access;

cl 24-25 Dec; (01554) 741087; £5.50.

Parc Howard Art Gallery & Museum In pleasant parkland, the largest collection of the distinctive local pottery in existence, as well as local history, and pictures by local artist J Dickson Innes. Snacks during school hols; shop; cl 1-2 pm, cl am all year at wknds, and 25-26 Dec, 1 Jan; (01554) 772029; free. The Stepney (Park St) is handy for lunch.

LLANGATHEN SN5822

Garden Lost in Time 🏛 (Aberglasney) Exciting garden restoration project with six different gardens (inc three walled ones) in 3½ hectares (9 acres); at its heart, a unique and fully restored Elizabethan/Jacobean cloister and parapet walk. Shop with plant sales, meals, snacks, disabled access; cl 25 Dec; (01558) 668998; *£5.50. The Cottage at Pentrefelin does good lunches.

LLANGRANOG SN3154

Attractive fishing village with a nice family beach backed by cliffs; there's a pleasant stroll to a headland to the N (otherwise, Cardiganshire lacks a coast path for much of the way). Further N Cwmtydu Cove is pretty - spectacular at sunset.

LLANSTEPHAN SN3410

Llanstephan Castle Sprawling 11th/13th-c ruin, majestically overlooking the Tywi estuary and Carmarthen Bay from an isolated ridge high over the water. Impressive gatehouse with fine vaulted ceiling, and you can still see the slots for drenching intruders with boiling fat or lead. Disabled access; free.

LLANYCEFN SN1024

Penrhos Cottage (off B4313) There can't have been many housing problems around here if local tradition is to be believed; anyone who built a house overnight on common land was entitled to claim it, and this old cottage was such a one, frantically constructed by friends and family. Disabled access; open by appointment only; (01437) 731328; donations.

MANORBIER SS0697

Manorbier Castle 🏛 Still in the hands of the family who have owned it for over 300 years, this impressive partly 12th-c fortress looking down to the beach has massive medieval outer walls and an early round tower, with a 13th-c chapel (where music is played) and other buildings, and more modern constructions within the walls. Self-catering house. Snacks, shop; cl Oct-Easter; (01834) 871394; £3. The quiet village is attractive, with a particularly good clean beach, and there's a striking view of the castle from the church. The Castle Inn (open all day in summer) is useful for lunch, and children are made very welcome at the friendly Chives tearoom. Springfields Farm (off A4139) has pick-your-own strawberries and a decent farm shop; (01834) 871746.

MARLOES SM7508

Marloes Deer Park Not actually a deer park, but a wild cliffy headland a couple of miles W, joined to the mainland by quite a narrow isthmus showing steep Iron Age defences; a place to watch birds (choughs breed here) and maybe seals on the offshore rocks. The Lobster Pot is a useful informal family pub, and the beaches are safe for bathing as well as gloriously remote.

Marloes peninsula Gentle terrain above the cliffs, giving views of Skomer Island, and memorable walkers' routes that need only minimal inland walking to complete the circuit.

MWNT SN1951

Tiny, idyllic chisel-shaped cove with a sandy beach, enclosed by sheer cliffs, beneath a whitewashed church and a NT car park at the end of a narrow lane NE of Cardigan.

NARBERTH SN1014

Pleasant small town standing on the imaginary Landsker line separating the Little England of South Pembrokeshire from the more properly welsh areas to the N. The Angel has good food inc local fish and lamb.

Black Pool Mill (Canaston Bridge, 3m W) Striking three-storeyed former corn mill with working machinery, and pleasant walks along the fish-filled river that powered it. Snacks, shop; cl Oct-Easter; (01437) 541233; £2. The nearby Bridge and Bush both have decent food.

CC2000 (Canaston Bridge, 3m W) 10-pin bowling, amusements and a reconstruction of TV's *Crystal Maze*; cl 24-26 Dec, New Year, Mon and Tues Sept-Apr exc school hols; (01834)

891622; separate charges for individual attractions.

Cwm Deri Vineyard (Martletwy, off A4075 SW) Self-guided vineyard walk; 350 teddy bears lurking in a shed, and tastings of speciality wines, liqueurs and mead; winery and shop; picnic area. May be cl Sun am, wkdys Oct-Mar, and all Jan and Feb; (01834) 891274; free.

Llawhaden Castle 12th-c ruins, surrounded by a deep moat, with the remains of the 13th/14th-c bishop's hall, kitchen and bakehouse; free; Cadw.

Oakwood Park (A4075 W) Wales's premier theme park, with rides from the world's No 1 wooden roller-coaster Megafobia to the sky-coaster, Vertigo: you're strapped in a harness and winched to a height of up to 50 metres (165 ft), then free-fall at 70mph back towards the ground - just in time you'll start swinging like a frantic pendulum. A nightmare cross between bungee-jumping and a parachute drop, this obviously wouldn't suit everyone, so rather than bump up the entry price, there's an extra charge of £11 per person (3 flyers). There's a real mix of other things, with younger children having their own little roller-coaster (there's another medium-sized one aimed at families), carousels and the like. During the school holidays, the park stays open until 10pm and the evening ends with a spectacular firework and waterscreen light show. Meals, snacks, shop, disabled access; cl Oct-Apr (exc school hols); (0845) 3455667; £12.95.

NEVERN SN0839

Interesting old riverside village with a medieval bridge over the Nyfer. The church has a tall 10th-c carved Celtic cross and other carved stones, some with Viking patterns, in the graveyard, where the massive yew trees are reputed to weep tears of blood if the priest is not Welsh-speaking. The Trewern Arms is handy for lunch.

Pentre Ifan Burial Chamber (SE towards Brynberian) One of the most impressive ancient monuments in Wales: a striking former long barrow with the enormous capstone still held up by three of the four surviving great upright megaliths. Great views over the Nyfer Valley.

PEMBROKE SM9603

Gun Tower Museum 🏛 Martello tower with interesting museum which tells the story of the garrison and shows the workings of a gun tower. Replica howitzer, models of flying boats and an introductory video. Shop, disabled access (some spiral stairs); cl Oct-Mar; *£2.

Museum of the Home (Westgate Hill) Intriguing private collection of all sorts of everyday objects from the past 300 years, in a pleasant domestic setting. Closing at the end of Sept 2004. No under-5s; open Mon-Thurs May-Sept; (01646) 681200; £1.20.

Pembroke Castle 🏛 The birthplace of Henry VII and thus the Tudor dynasty, this impressive 13th-c castle is largely intact, and its endless passages, tunnels and stairways are great fun to explore. The 23-metre (75-ft) tower is one of the finest in Britain; there's also a brass rubbing centre (from £1.95, not Sat), six exhibition rooms and an introductory video. Summer snacks, shop, disabled access to ground floor; cl 24-26 Dec, 1 Jan; (01646) 681510; *£3 (guided tours Jun-Aug exc Sat, 50p extra). The Pembroke Ferry pub by the water at the foot of the bridge over the estuary does good fresh fish.

PENDINE SN2307

Museum of Speed The hard flat sand on the beaches here made it a favourite spot for attempting new speed records; in 1926 J G Parry Thomas and his 27-litre car Babs set a short-lived land-speed record of 168 mph, but the careers of both ended the following year in a grisly accident. The car spent the next 40 years buried in the sand but has now been restored, and in July and Aug (perhaps longer) forms the centrepiece of this small museum overlooking the beach; a good introductory video will tell you more. Also local and natural history. Shop, disabled access; cl 1-1.30pm, all Nov-Easter, Tues-Thurs Oct-beginning Jun; (01994) 453488; free.

PORTHGAIN SM8132

Quaint small working harbour in tiny village carefully preserved by the National Park authorities, former granite and slate centre - bastions of former stone works still tower over water. The Sloop is a good pub, and

there are fine coastal walks.

PRESCELLY HILLS SN0529 (Mynydd Preseli) Celebrated as the place where Stonehenge's bluestones came from - brought by either man or glacial action. Appropriately it has a primeval, windswept ruggedness, the gorse and heather clad upland dotted with Bronze Age cairns (most memorably, Carn Arthur) and an Iron Age hill fort. A fine path follows the length of the ridge E to W, though circular walks are a bit hard to devise. A layby a mile SW of Crymych (off A478 on the road to Mynachlog-ddu) makes a useful starting point.

PUMSAINT SN6640

Dolaucothi Gold Mines 🏛 (off A482) 2,000 years of gold-mining are the focus of this unusual mine, in use since Roman times; tours of the Roman adits and the Victorian (no under-5s) and 1930s workings, complete with miners' lamps and helmets. New exhibition about gold, visitor centre, woodland walks, and the chance to have a go at panning for gold. Stout footwear recommended. Meals, snacks, shop; site open Apr to mid-Sept; £2.90; NT. Underground tours (01558) 650177; estate events inc Victorian, Roman and archaeology family activity days, fishing, self-catering, B&B and cycle hire; (01558) 650707. The nearby Brunant Arms in fine scenery at Caio has good food (inc prime welsh black steak), and opposite the pub is a Roman fort and red kite information centre.

SAUNDERSFOOT SN1304

Relaxed extended seaside village, with a lighthouse on the spit sheltering the harbour and sandy beach; good fresh fish at the Royal Oak - which has heaters for its outside tables.

SLEBECH SN0013

Picton Castle In 16 hectares (40 acres) of gardens, inc a maze, woodland and walled gardens, gallery and garden shop. It started as a massive medieval castle, then during the 1750s the influential and philanthropic Philipps family attuned it to gracious living by adding lavish Georgian interiors with ornate plasterwork and fireplaces. Castle cl Mon (exc bank hol), Oct-Mar, garden and gallery cl Mon exc bank hol and all Nov-Mar; (01437) 751326;

*£3.95 castle (guided tour only), £4.95 castle, garden and gallery.

Slebech church (off A40 5m E of Haverfordwest) Gloriously isolated ruined 12th-c church, formerly a temple of the Knights Hospitaller, by the tidal waters of the East Cleddau. Though there is a track from the main road, it's more enjoyable to turn down the A4075, take the next right turn and park by the mill, walk over the bridge and down the track through the woods above the river.

SOLVA SM8024

One of the prettiest villages on the coast, with a great deal of character. From the harbour a good interesting shortish path running E to Dinas Fawr, the opposite headland. This high crag (enclosed by the ramparts of an Iron Age fort) gives pretty views of the attractive little fishing village and the coast. The Cambrian Arms is a reliable dining pub.

ST DAVID'S SM7525

The cathedral here has had a community in residence around it for longer than any other in Britain, but thanks to the relative isolation of the place it's stayed undeveloped, so that St David's today is little more than a village - with lots of colourful flowers in spring. Parking can be a problem, and the wardens are assiduous. It's a good area for coastal walks, perhaps to ancient sites such as the neolithic burial chambers up by St David's Head to the S or over towards Solva, to St Non's Chapel, or W to St Justinian (another chapel here, looking over Ramsey Island). The cheerful Farmers Arms by the cathedral gate has good value food. The beach at Whitesands Bay is good. In summer there are boat trips from the lifeboat station around or to rocky Ramsey Island, where seabirds nest in great numbers.

Bishop's Palace Impressive ruins, clearly once very grand: plenty of quadrangles, stairways and splendid arcaded walls, with all sorts of intricate and often entertaining details (like the carvings below the arcaded parapets). Atmospheric and tranquil, particularly out of season when you may have it largely to yourself. Shop, limited disabled access; cl winter Sun am, 24-26 Dec, 1 Jan; (01437) 720517; £2.50; Cadw.

Oceanarium (New St) Excellent insight into sea and shore life; highlights include the shark tank and rock pool. Talks and demonstrations for children during school hols. Snacks, shop, limited disabled access; cl 24-26 Dec; (01437) 720453; *£3.

St David's Cathedral The Norman church had largely collapsed by the 15th c, and elaborate repairs had to be made; the resulting roof is an impressive lace-like oak affair, and oak features in most of the rest of the church too. There's a fine collection of Celtic sculptured crosses. Shop, disabled access; cl Sun am; free, though £2 donation welcome.

St David's Open Farm (NE edge, off A487) Commercial farm with rare breed animals as well, and a network of grassy paths giving a view into most fields; playgrounds and picnic areas. Cl Nov-Mar; (01437) 721601; £2 suggested donation.

St Non's chapel (about ½m N) Reputed birthplace of St Non, the mother of St David; there are lovely sea views from the very scant ruins of the simple coastal chapel here, signed down a track from the useful St Non's Hotel, with a holy well nearby. The walk from St David's is pleasant.

TYF Adventure Organise well supervised abseiling, canoeing, rock-climbing and other activities - ideal for off-loading active children for the day (over-8s only); (01437) 721611.

ST FLORENCE SN0802

Manor House Wild Animal Park ▣ (B4318) Around 15 hectares (40 acres) of wooded grounds and gardens with exotic birds, mammals, reptiles and fish, a pets corner, handling unit, playground, model railway exhibition and falconry displays (2pm); also natural history museum. Meals, snacks, shop, disabled access; cl Oct-Mar; (01646) 651201; £4.80. The Old Parsonage Farm does quick family food. At **Heatherton Country Sports Park** (B4318 towards Tenby), you'll find a range of different activities from pitch-and-putt golf to karting and coarse fishing or archery; you can also book horseriding and paintballing, and they have a summer maize maze. Meals, snacks, shop, some disabled access; phone for details; (01646) 651055.

STRUMBLE HEAD SM8941
Remote, but well worth the drive from
Fishguard through a maze of very minor
roads. Beyond the car park the seas boil
through the narrow neck cutting off the
rock on which Strumble Head
lighthouse stands. Down on the rocks
there you quite often see seals even in
the spring, though they're more
common in late summer. The scenery
typifies the rocky, big-dipper coastline
of north Pembrokeshire: outstanding
walking in both directions. Garn Fawr,
2m S, is a splendidly sited hill fort right
by a car park, with a path leading W to
join the coast path.

TALLEY SN6332

Talley Abbey (off B4302) Ruins of
once-magnificent 12th-c abbey, still
very fine, esp the two pointed
archways; open daily; free; Cadw.

TENBY SN1300

Pleasantly restrained family seaside
resort, with nice sheltered beaches and
rock coves. It's a walled town, the
splendidly preserved 13th-c wall still
with many of its towers left, as well as a
magnificent 14th-c arched barbican
gateway; a moat used to run the whole
length of what is now a tree-lined
street. The medieval Plantagenet House
has good interesting food.

Caldey Island boat trips 🖼 Reached
by summer boat trips from Tenby
harbour (look out for seals), still a
monastic island, where the Cistercian
monks have good shortbread and
chocolates for sale (though catering on
the island could be better), as well as
herbs, more durable crafts and old-
fashioned perfume. Besides the modern
abbey, there's a 13th-c church with a
simple cobbled floor, still in use, on one
side of the small cloister of the original
priory; these ancient priory buildings,
which you can see from outside but not
enter, give a better sense of the past
than almost anywhere else in West
Wales. Sailing times Apr-Sept, weather
permitting, cl Sun and some Sats;
(01834) 844453; £8.

Dinosaur Park (Great Wedlock
Farm, Gumfreston - B4318 W) Family-
run, in a rural setting: over 20 life-size
dinosaurs in glades and swamps along a
woodland trail; outdoor and indoor

adventure playgrounds, an organised
daily activity programme, pets, rides,
and computer games. Restaurant,
indoor and outdoor snack kiosks, and
picnic facilities, shop, disabled access; cl
Nov-end Mar; (01834) 842668; *£4.50.

Hoyle's Mouth Cave (off A4139 just
SW, Trefloyne Lane towards St
Florence; short path through wood on
left after 500 yds) Running more than
30 metres (100 ft) back into the hillside,
this spooky place has yielded Ice Age
mammoth bones, as well as human
tools dating back over 10,000 years.
Take a torch, but don't go in winter -
you'd disturb the hibernating bats.

St Mary's church Interesting 13th-c
building with a huge steeple and a
plaque commemorating a local
invention that many of us use every day
- the equals sign.

Tenby Museum and Art Gallery
Some remains of a 13th-c castle stand
on the headland above the yachting
harbour; this site houses a local history
and geology museum, with prehistoric
finds, and two art galleries with
Augustus and Gwen John collections.
Shop; cl winter wknds and Christmas
week; (01834) 842809; £2.

Tudor Merchant's House (Quay Hill)
Fine example of gabled 15th-c
architecture, with a good flemish
chimney and the remains of frescoes on
three walls; small herb garden. Shop; cl
every Weds and Sun am, all day Sat in Oct
(this may change so best to phone), and
all Nov-Mar; (01834) 842279; £2; NT.

TRESAITH SN2751

Attractive coastal village down steep
roads, with a decent pub (and a
waterfall to its beach).

Pubs and inns doing food that are
noteworthy for their fine positions
include the Black Lion at Abergorlech
SN5833 (lots of good walks nearby),
Forest Arms at Brechfa SN5230,
Cresselly Arms by the water at
Cresswell Quay SN0406, Ship at
Freshwater East SS0298, Stanley Arms
on the Cleddau estuary opposite Picton
Castle at Landshipping SN0111 and
Cennen Arms at Trapp SN6518. The
Teifi Netpool at St Dogmaels SN1645 is
handy for a walk along to Poppitt Sands.

Where to eat

ABERAERON SN4562 **Hive on the Quay** *Cadwgan Pl* (01545) 570445 Cheerful harbourside place on the wharf, based around family honey business (their home-made honey ice-cream is delicious), with lunchtime buffet and popular café relying heavily on organic produce, and with quite an emphasis on fish from their own boat; also bee exhibition and shop; evening opening too during July seafood festival and in Aug; cl mid-Sept to Whitsun. £28|£7.50

CAIO SN6739 **Brunant Arms** (01558) 650483 Unpretentious place with charming youngish licensees, convivial smallish lounge bar, booths formed by high-backed winged settles, a good log fire and plenty of house plants; small Perspex-roofed verandah, pub games in stone public bar, and picnic-sets on the terrace; good interesting freshly cooked food using the best local produce (the meat is delicious), a fine choice of real ales and other drinks, and friendly service. £23|£6.50

CILGERRAN SN1942 **Pendre** *High St* (01239) 614223 Ancient pub with massive stripped 14th-c medieval stone walls above a panelled dado in the original bar area, some beautifully polished slate flooring, and a comfortable lounge bar and restaurant area; astonishingly cheap and really good interesting food, well kept real ales, prompt welcoming service; a small terrace and enclosed play area; babies and well behaved young children lunchtime and early evening only; cl Sun. £13|£3.50

LETTERSTON SM9429 **Something Cooking** *Haverfordwest Rd* (01348) 840621 Enthusiastically run and very friendly fish restaurant with truly outstanding fresh fish, served by neat uniformed waitresses - very reasonable prices too; cl winter Sun, 2 wks Christmas; disabled access. £17|£4.99

PEMBROKE FERRY SM9704 **Ferry Inn** (01646) 682947 Former sailors' haunt by the water below Cleddau Bridge (not by the new ferry), with wide choice of very fresh fish dishes - non-fishy things too - nautical décor, good views, a relaxed pubby atmosphere, well kept real ales, decent malt whiskies, and efficient service; restaurant cl 25-26 Dec; disabled access. £23|£3.95

ROSEBUSH SN0729 **Old Post Office** (01437) 532205 Quaint bistro with lots of local photos, farming tools and teapots on the ceiling, good value lunches, well prepared traditional cooking in the candlelit dining room, and coffee and afternoon tea; bdrms; cl Sun and Mon pm; some disabled access. £16|£4.50

SAUNDERSFOOT SN1304 **Royal Oak** *Wogan Terrace* (01834) 812546 In a good spot in the village centre above the harbour, this very well run pub has friendly attentive staff, a buoyant atmosphere in the dining area and carpeted no smoking lounge bar, and enjoyable food inc eight or so fresh fish dishes (increasing to well over a dozen in summer), well kept real ales, 25 malts, an interesting choice of wines with a dozen by the glass, and seats outside, with overhead heaters for cold days; cl 25 Dec pm; children must be well behaved; disabled access. £24|£7.95

ST DAVID'S SM7525 **Morgan's Brasserie** *20 Nun St* (01437) 720508 Smart little brasserie specialising in good fresh fish from a shortish menu, supplemented by daily specials and using good fresh local produce; friendly service, and good value wines; cl Sun, Jan, Feb; well behaved children welcome. £30

We welcome reports from readers

This *Guide* depends on readers' reports. Do help us if you can – in return, we offer a discount on the next edition to people who've helped us with reports for it. Tell us what you think about places already in it, and anything extra you think we should say about them. And send us your ideas for inclusion in the next edition: places to visit, eat at or stay in, attractive drives or walks, maybe even unusual shops you know of. Use the card in the middle, the report forms at the end, or just write – no stamp needed: *The Good Britain Guide*, FREEPOST TN1569, Wadhurst, E Sussex TN5 7BR. Or log on to www.goodguides.co.uk

Mid Wales

**Location, location, location - here it's the great scenery
which counts most, with untouched landscapes and dramatic natural
features; some spectacular steam trips too**

This is one of the best parts of Britain for feeling you've escaped it all, in the scenic hills or in the splendid river valleys, such as the friendly Usk, the rather more imposing Upper Wye, and, above Aberystwyth, the beautiful Vale of Rheidol. Sparsely populated, the whole area is great for walkers. The rewarding target for most is the Brecon Beacons National Park: the western Black Mountain, the Brecon Beacons themselves (with some memorable waterfalls in their southern reaches), and the eastern Black Mountains. You can also cherry-pick the best bits of two national trails - the Offa's Dyke Path (coast to coast up the welsh border) and Glyndwr's Way (121 miles from Knighton to Welshpool). There are plenty of other areas where you can really strike out on your own, though you'll need careful map-reading to make the most of these little-frequented wildernesses.

You can stay in your car throughout and still get a tremendous amount out of this heart of Wales. The roads here are often completely empty (great for cyclists, too), including some glorious Cambrian Mountain drives threading through moorland and forest, scarcely encountering a single building along the way.

The friendly towns include a string of dignified slightly old-fashioned inland spa towns, with excellently restored historic buildings in Brecon (good annual jazz festival) and Presteigne. Llandrindod Wells is charming, and Hay-on-Wye is a joy for book-lovers.

Dotted about are some good family attractions. These include several picturesque steam railway lines, the intriguing caves at Craig-y-Nos, underground tours of the Llywernog Silver Lead Mine in Ponterwyd, the friendly Borth Animalarium, and two unusual new entries this year - the rather aptly named Museum of Mechanical Magic at Llanbrynmair, and Knighton's defence HQ in the war against attack by asteroids. Magnificent Powis Castle at Welshpool is well worth a visit, and there are haunting ruins in Carreg Cennen. A good investment for families is the Dyfi Valley Pass (£13.40) covering lively Celtica and the Centre for Alternative Technology (both in Machynlleth, with a good art gallery here too), as well as the Arthurian legends in the caves of Corris (thrilling for children); and you get a 20% discount on the Talyllyn Railway in Tywyn.

We have tracked down some very comfortable places to stay in, with glorious countryside more or less on their doorsteps.

Where to stay

ABERDOVEY SN6196 **Penhelig Arms** *Terrace Rd, Aberdovey, Gwynedd LL35 0LT (01654) 767215* **£90**, plus special breaks; 14 comfortable rms, 4 impressively furnished ones in annexe with fine harbour views. Newly refurbished building in fine spot overlooking sea, with cosy bar, open fires, delicious food with emphasis on daily-delivered fresh local fish in no smoking restaurant, extensive (and fairly priced) wine list with 30 by the glass (champagne, too), splendid breakfasts, and charming friendly service; lovely views of Dovey estuary; cl 25-26 Dec; dogs welcome in bedrooms

ABERDOVEY SN6196 **Preswylfa** *Aberdovey, Gwynedd LL35 0LE (01654) 767239* **£65***; 3 super rms with lovely views. Friendly and relaxed Edwardian house in pretty, mature garden, courteous genuinely helpful owners, period drawing room with grand piano (all welcome to play), enjoyable evening meals (by arrangement) using home-grown produce in dining room with fine views, and footpath leading to village and beach (4 mins); no children

CHURCH STOKE SO2689 **Drewin Farm** *Church Stoke, Montgomery, Powys SY15 6TW (01588) 620325* **£44**; 2 rms. Attractive 17th-c farmhouse with panoramic views, warm welcome, comfortable beamed lounge, traditional cooking in newly decorated dining room; Offa's Dyke footpath runs through the mixed farm of sheep, cattle and crops; cl Nov-Feb

CRICKHOWELL SO2118 **Bear** *High St, Crickhowell, Powys NP8 1BW (01873) 810408* **£92**; 35 rms, the back ones are the best, and some have jacuzzis. Particularly friendly coaching inn with calmly civilised atmosphere, excellent food using local produce and home-grown herbs (some welsh specialities), fine wines and ports, well kept real ales, and prompt attentive service; lots of antiques, deeply comfortable seats, and a roaring log fire in the heavily beamed lounge, and a partly no smoking family room; children over 8 in restaurant; disabled access

CRICKHOWELL SO1719 **Gliffaes Hotel** *Gliffaes Rd, Crickhowell, Powys NP8 1RH (01874) 730371* **£126.30**, plus special breaks; 22 rms. Run by the same family since 1948, this imposing house stands in 33 wonderfully peaceful acres, with fine rare trees; enjoyably informal and relaxed atmosphere, comfortable big sitting room, elegant drawing room, pleasant conservatory, glorious Usk Valley views from terrace, good cooking, and cheerful staff; fishing, hard tennis court, golf practice net, and a putting and croquet lawn; cl 2 wks Jan; limited disabled access

EGLWYSFACH SN6796 **Ynyshir Hall** *Eglwysfach, Machynlleth, Dyfed SY20 8TA (01654) 781209* **£160***, plus special breaks; 9 individually decorated, no smoking rms, two with four-posters. Carefully run Georgian manor house in 14 acres of landscaped gardens adjoining the Ynyshir coastal bird reserve, with particularly good service, antiques, log fires and paintings in the light and airy public rooms, extremely good food using home-grown vegetables, and delicious breakfasts; lots to do nearby; cl 3 wks Jan; children over 9; disabled access to ground floor rms; dogs welcome in bedrooms

GUILSFIELD SJ2110 **Lower Trelydan** *Guilsfield, Welshpool, Powys SY21 9PH (01938) 553105* **£54**; 3 rms. Charming black and white farmhouse on beef cattle and sheep farm, with lovely heavily beamed ceilings, fine antiques and comfortable seating, a cosy licensed bar, warm and friendly atmosphere, and delicious farmhouse cooking; pretty garden; also self-catering cottages; cl Christmas and New Year; disabled access

HAY-ON-WYE SO2342 **Old Black Lion** *26 Lion St, Hay-on-Wye, Hereford, Herefordshire HR3 5AD (01497) 820841* **£80**, plus special breaks; 10 individually designed rms, some in modern coach house. Smartly civilised hotel with low beams and panelling, convivial bar, wide choice of carefully prepared food in bar and no smoking beamed restaurant, and an extensive wine list; close to fishing (private salmon and trout fishing) and riding; cl 25-26 Dec; children over 5

KNIGHTON SO3371 **Milebrook House** *Stanage, Knighton, Herefordshire LD7 1LT (01547) 528632* **£86**, plus special breaks; 10 spacious, refurbished rms.

Charming 18th-c house in three acres surrounded by really unspoilt countryside with River Teme trout fishing; log fires, residents' sitting room, bar (where light lunches are served), and good sound cooking using home-grown vegetables; children over 8; disabled access

LLANGAMMARCH WELLS SN9447 **Lake** *Llangammarch Wells, Powys LD4 4BS* *(01591) 620202* **£170***; plus special breaks; 19 charming, pretty rms with fruit and decanter of sherry. Particularly well run 1860 half-timbered hotel in 50 acres with plenty of wildlife, well stocked trout lake, clay pigeon shoots, tennis and riding, or walk their two friendly labradors; deeply comfortable tranquil drawing room with antiques, paintings and log fire, wonderful afternoon teas (in summer under the chestnut tree overlooking the river), courteous discreet service, fine wines and very good modern british cooking in elegant candlelit dining room, and liberal breakfasts; children over 7 in evening dining room; disabled access; dogs welcome in bedrooms ☺

LLANWRTYD WELLS SN8746 **Carlton House** *Dolycoed Rd, Llanwrtyd Wells, Powys LD5 4RA (01591) 610248* **£65***, plus special breaks; 6 well equipped rms. Warmly friendly owners run this comfortable Edwardian restaurant-with-rooms, and there's a relaxing little sitting room with plants and antiques, an attractive dining room with original panelling and log fire, exceptionally good modern british cooking using top-quality local produce (delicious puddings and home-made canapés and petits fours), super breakfasts with home-made bread and marmalade, and a thoughtful wine list; cl 10-29 Dec; dogs welcome in bedrooms

LLYSWEN SO1240 **Llangoed Hall** *Llyswen, Brecon, Powys LD3 0YP (01874) 754525* **£160**, plus special breaks; 23 very pretty rms with luxurious touches. Fine Edwardian mansion beautifully converted into a first-class hotel with lovely house-party atmosphere, handsome hall, elegant and spacious public rooms with antiques, pictures, fresh flowers and views over the grounds, imaginative modern cooking in charming restaurant (non-residents most welcome), an excellent wine list, and very good welsh breakfasts; marvellous surrounding countryside; children over 8

MONTGOMERY SO2296 **Dragon** *Market Sq, Montgomery, Powys SY15 6PA (01686) 668359* **£79.50**, plus special breaks; 20 rms. Attractive black and white timbered small hotel with a pleasant grey-stone tiled hall, comfortable residents' lounge, beamed bar, restaurant using local produce; indoor swimming pool, sauna; dogs welcome in bedrooms

OLD RADNOR SO2559 **Harp** *Old Radnor, Presteigne, Powys LD8 2RH (01544) 350655* **£60**; 5 pretty rms, most with own bthrm. 15th-c inn in superb tranquil hilltop position, with lovely views and good walks nearby; friendly attentive owners, traditional bars with good log fires, some slate flooring and antique settles, character dining room, good value home cooking inc good breakfasts, well kept ales; self-catering bungalow; seats outside with play area; cl wkdy lunchtimes

PENNAL SN6799 **Gogarth Hall Farm** *Pennal, Machynlleth, Powys SY20 9LB (01654) 791235* **£54**; 4 rms. 17th-c house on working farm of suckler cows and sheep with marvellous views of Dovey estuary - guests welcome to walk around the farm; dining room and lounge, and enjoyable breakfasts and evening meals; babysitting available; self-catering also; disabled access

PRESTEIGNE SO3164 **Radnorshire Arms** *High St, Presteigne, Powys LD8 2BE (01544) 267406* **£72.90**, plus special breaks; 19 rms. Rambling handsomely timbered 17th-c hotel with old-fashioned charm and an unchanging atmosphere, elegantly moulded beams and fine dark panelling in the lounge bar, latticed windows, enjoyable food (inc morning coffee and afternoon tea), separate no smoking restaurant, well kept real ales, and politely attentive service; partial disabled access; dogs welcome in bedrooms

RHAYADER SN9969 **Beili Neuadd** *Rhayader, Powys LD6 5NS (01597) 810211* **£48**; 3 rms with log fires, and newly converted stone barn with 3 bunkhouse rms. Charming partly 16th-c stone-built farmhouse in quiet countryside (they have their own trout pools and woodland), with beams, polished oak floorboards, and nice breakfasts in new garden room; self-catering also; cl Christmas; children over 8; dogs by arrangement

To see and do

ABERDOVEY SN6196

Attractive, restrained resort with very pleasant sheltered beaches but none of the crowds or tat they usually bring. Legend has it there's a lost city beneath the sea, inundated by the crashing waves in a great storm 1,500 years ago. Sometimes at night imaginative people can hear the mournful tolling of its bells. The Penhelig Arms Hotel, with tables out by the harbour walls, is an excellent food stop.

ABERYSTWYTH SN5981

Low-key resort, scarcely changed in 20 years, with long shingle beaches and sedate cliff railway to large camera obscura high above. Quite a scholarly university town, too, with a good museum, and one of the very few of Edward I's castles in this part of Wales. Yr Hen Orsaf (Alexandra Rd) has sensibly priced food all day. The university has a large agricultural college attached and, as well as the usual sheep, you may see llamas in some of the surrounding fields. There's a pleasant walk along the straight stretch of coast to Borth; you can use the train for the other half of a round trip.

National Library of Wales (Penglais Hill) Imposing neo-classical building looking over the town, with exhibitions of fine early welsh and celtic manuscripts and more modern art. Meals, snacks, shop, disabled access; cl Sun, first full wk Oct, 25-26 Dec, 1 Jan; (01970) 632800; free.

Vale of Rheidol Railway (Alexander Rd) The town's main attraction for families, with steam trains for several miles along the picturesque twists of the Rheidol Valley to the dramatic beauty-spot gorge of Devil's Bridge. You can use the railway for attractive round-trip walks. Snacks, shop; trains run most days Easter-Oct (not Sun in Sept, not Fri or Sun in Oct); (01970) 625819 for timetable; £11 full return fare.

BERRIEW SJ1800

Andrew Logan Museum of Sculpture 🔁 The only museum in Europe dedicated to a living artist, with witty glittery sculptures and Alternative Miss World memorabilia from throughout his career. Meals, snacks,

shop, disabled access; cl am, and Mon, Tues and all Jan-Mar, but will open any time for group bookings and education visits; (01686) 640689; *£2.50. The village is attractive, with the river tumbling over rocks below a high bridge, and enjoyable food in the Lion.

Glansevern Hall Gardens In parkland by the River Severn around a Greek Revival house, this 7-hectare (18-acre) formal garden has a newly restored walled garden and some notable and unusual trees. Snacks, shop and plant sales, disabled access; cl Sun-Thurs, Oct-Apr; (01686) 640200; £3.

BLACK MOUNTAIN SN8123

The westernmost range in the Brecon Beacons National Park - not to be confused with the Black Mountains to the E. Much of the high terrain is a long way from the road, so this part is more the preserve of the committed long-distance walker. The craggy ridge known as Carmarthen Fan protrudes dramatically above the moors and provides the high point of a long but rewarding walk from the N.

BLACK MOUNTAINS SO2632

Making up the E part of the Brecon Beacons National Park, these finger-shaped ridges have steep-sided valleys between. Most of the best views are from the Offa's Dyke Path along the E flanks: the land eastwards slopes abruptly down to low-lying agricultural Herefordshire, and views far into England give you a feeling of true border country. Circular walks here tend to be long and hefty, often with two major ascents to get you up on to the different ridges, but the scenic Gospel Pass road from Hay-on-Wye lets you drive to within reasonable striking distance of Hay Bluff (670 metres, 2,200 ft). Twmpa (690 metres, 2,263 ft) is better known by its intriguing english name of Lord Hereford's Knob; though it's not itself on the Offa's Dyke Path, it is nearby, and you can combine it with Hay Bluff in a longer walk. Llanthony Abbey, with an unusual cellar bar, makes a beautiful objective in the valley below, where diligent map-reading is needed for a cross-fields route from Cwmyoy, with extensions on to the Offa's Dyke Path on the ridge to complete a satisfying circuit. There have been recent sightings of a puma-like beast near Llangadog.

BORTH SN6086

Borth Animalarium 🖼 Just a short walk from this low-key resort's big beach (pebbly when the tide is in), this friendly little place packs in so much that it keeps children happy for a good half-day. Committed to conserving endangered animals, it has lemurs and small primates, wallabies, bats, parrots, owls, rheas, and a family of geoffroy's cats; also iguana and crocodiles, daily snake-handling and pony rides. Daily demonstrations, good play and picnic areas, snacks, shop, disabled access; open daily; (01970) 871224; *£4.20.

BRECON SO0428

Enjoyable and interesting small town despite too much traffic, with some fine old buildings around its main square and narrow streets. The striking Norman priory was grandly restored in the 19th c and became a cathedral in 1923. Also the rather sad remnants of a castle, and a couple of decent little museums. The George (George St) has reasonably priced food all day and an attractive dining conservatory, and some of the highest peaks in the area are a short drive away.

Brecknock Museum and Art Gallery 🖼 (Captain's Walk) The town's excellently preserved assize court with an interpretative exhibition, as well as plenty of love spoons and some interesting Celtic crosses. Extensive programme of art, craft, and historical exhibitions. Shop, disabled access; cl 1-2pm Sat, Sun Oct-Mar, Good Fri, 25-26 Dec, 1 Jan; (01874) 624121; *£1.

BRECON BEACONS SO0121

The highest land in Wales outside Snowdonia, this fine area for walking is crowned by a pair of graceful pointed summits connected by a short ridge that seems to be visible from most of South and Mid Wales. There's a magnificent high-level walk along the crest, which has massive drops on the N side. Pen y Fan (886 metres, 2,906 ft) is the highest welsh summit outside Snowdonia, and the main E-W upland spine effectively stretches about 5

miles. The most popular walk up from Pont ar Daf, from the A470 to the W, is straightforward enough although there has been some serious footpath erosion, but the N approaches are more exciting and surprisingly little walked.

Brecon Beacons Mountain Centre (Libanus) Useful National Parks visitor centre; (01874) 623366; free. They can advise on local walks, inc how to get to the spectacular waterfalls near Glyn Neath (see next entry), and from the centre there's free access to the surrounding area known as Illtud Common, with fine views of the Beacons and an Iron Age hill fort to make for; this can also be used as a starting-point for walking up to Craig Cerrig-gleisiad a Fan Frynach national nature reserve SN9522, home to arctic/alpine flora and some 80 bird species.

Brecon Beacons Waterfall Country A series of mighty waterfalls with few rivals in Britain grace the deep wooded gorges of the Nedd, Hepste and Mellte, just inside the southern Brecon Beacons park boundary (within easy reach of South Wales, too). An easy path leads along the River Nedd from Pontneddfechan, where the Angel and Old White Horse do enjoyable food. The Porth yr Ogof car park nr Ystradfellte is convenient for the Mellte. Dire warning notices ward you off getting too close to the edge (it is certainly hazardously slippery), but you can accompany the river most of the way to its junction with the Hepste. Here, a path crosses the river by going behind the curtain of Sgwd yr Eira waterfall - a rock ledge holds you in safely, but it's an excitingly damp experience. Note the forest tracks may be closed during felling operations.

BUILTH WELLS SO0451

Pleasant small spa town, with good walks in attractive scenery. Just N, the knobbly upland of Carneddau has some bracing moorland tracks linking up Iron Age hill forts.

CADAIR IDRIS SH7112

This great peak in the S of the National Park offers walkers various ways up its friendly slopes; for a really dramatic ascent, take the Minffordd Path from the car park E of Tal-y-llyn lake (A487);

it rises past Llyn Cau, a striking lake in a huge glaciated scoop below the mountain. Good strolling and picnicking opportunities to the W near the car park by the little Cregennen Lakes above Arthog.

CARREG CENNEN CASTLE
SN6619

🏛 Few castles can boast as excellent a setting as these old ruins (nr Trapp, SE of Llandeilo), dramatically dominating their limestone crag high above the river, and overlooking the unspoilt countryside towards the Black Mountains. Rebuilt in the 13th c (and again in the 19th - you can easily distinguish the new stonework), the castle has a mysterious passage in the side of the cliff. Part of the reason readers like this so much is the friendliness of the staff. Meals, snacks, shop; cl 25 Dec; (01558) 822291; *£3; Cadw. The Cennen Arms nearby has good simple food.

CORRIS SH7408
Attractive and nicely set beneath the towering crags of Cadair Idris, with lakes and pine forests in the surrounding valley. The whole village seems to be made of slate.

Corris Craft Centre (off A487 towards Corris Uchaf) Craft workshops inc working potter, toymaker, jeweller, leatherworker, and candlemaker, with a restaurant, shop, disabled access, picnic and play areas; best to check winter opening; (01654) 761584; free.

King Arthur's Labyrinth 🏛 (Upper Corris, off A487 towards Corris Uchaf) Fun for families; a boat trip takes you to the heart of the underground tunnels and caverns, then it's a half-mile walk through passageways punctuated with scenes from the local version of the Arthurian legends. Wrap up well: it can get cold down here. Meals, snacks, shop; cl Nov-Mar (may open half-term Feb); (01654) 761584; £4.85.

CRAIG-Y-NOS SN8316
Craig-y-Nos Country Park Ideal for a picnic or a stroll: 16 hectares (40 acres) of woodland, lake and meadow, landscaped and developed in the last century by the opera singer Adelina Patti. Interactive displays and exhibitions in the visitor centre. Shop, limited disabled access; cl 25 Dec; (01639)

730395; park free, though £2.40 parking all day. The Gwyn Arms nearby, open all day, has good generous food.

National Showcave Centre for Wales (A4067 just N) Fascinating series of caves, well lit to emphasise the extraordinary rock formations. The Cathedral Cave is the largest single chamber open to the public in any british showcave, while 3,000 years ago Bone Cave was lived in by humans. There's also a dinosaur park, Iron Age farm, shire horse centre, and artificial ski-slope, so lots to see. Meals, snacks, shops; cl end Oct-Apr (open Feb half-term); (01639) 730284; £8.50. The Tafarn y Garreg just N does decent food.

CRICKHOWELL SO2118
Pleasant village-sized 'town', with an excellent inn in the Bear, and a fine ancient bridge over the Usk (which the popular Bridge End Inn overlooks).

DEVIL'S BRIDGE SN7477
Three bridges stacked one on top of another, with a dramatic waterfall far below, tucked away in a beauty-spot wooded gorge near the meeting of two rivers. Well marked paths supply the ingredients for a decent circular walk, taking in the former lead-mining village of Ystumtuen. The oldest bridge gave this place its name, when it was built by the Devil in order to trap an old woman into giving him her soul; she outwitted him. For the Vale of Rheidol Railway, see Aberystwyth entry. The Halfway Inn at Pisgah on the A4120 to Aberystwyth is a useful stop.

ELAN VALLEY SN9365
These four lakes W of Rhayader are the most majestic of the many man-made reservoirs in Wales. Built at the turn of the last century, they have weathered in well now - even the dams look good, and there are splendid valley and Cambrian Mountain views, especially from high-level trackbeds of the long-vanished railway. It's a good spot for bird-watching, particularly in summer, with red kites usually prominent - huge birds with forked tails, often flying above the lakes. The exciting drive beyond the reservoirs to Devil's Bridge follows an old drovers' route through the startlingly empty scenery of the Cambrian Mountains. The Elan Valley Hotel (B4518) has decent food.

Elan Valley Visitor Centre (Elan village) Good opening to this attractive area, with an audio-visual show and displays, and children's play area. Meals, snacks, shop, disabled access. Cl Nov to mid-Mar; (01597) 810880; free (£1 car parking charge). Outside is a statue of Shelley, who lived in a house now lost beneath the reservoirs. Walks from here include woodland walks and strolls along the old railway track by the water's edge - very attractive, and fine for wheelchairs, cyclists, and horse-riders.

FAIRBOURNE SH6112

Fairbourne & Barmouth Steam Railway (Beach Rd) Running the spectacular 2½m to the end of the peninsula and the ferry for Barmouth, this started life in 1890 as a horse-drawn railway used to carry building materials for the seaside resort of Fairbourne. Meals, snacks, shop; cl Jan to mid-Apr, mid-Sept to mid-Oct, Nov-Dec; (01341) 250362 for timetable; *£6.40. The Fairbourne Hotel is quite useful for lunch, as is the 15th-c Last Inn on Barmouth Harbour. The attractively set George III along the estuary at Penmaenpool is quite handy too. Fairbourne and Barmouth both have good clean beaches.

FURNACE SN6895

On the edge of the woods are the eerie ruins of Dyfi Furnace that gave the village its name. Now partly restored by Cadw as a monument, it's a rare example of an 18th-c charcoal-fired blast furnace, where iron ore was smelted; later on, the use of coke made such furnaces redundant. Free. Up the road at Derwenlas the Black Lion is a pleasant food stop.

HAY-ON-WYE SO2342

This pleasant small town has become a world centre for second-hand and antiquarian books. There are plenty of print, junk and antiques shops too, as well as a rather jolly puzzle and teddy bear shop on Broad St. Celtic Canoes (01497) 847422 offers canoe hire and instruction (Jun-Aug). Hay Bluff nearby has lovely walks, and it's within easy reach of the Black Mountains, the Golden Valley over the english border, and the attractive unspoilt countryside just over the Gwent border that we've mentioned in the South Wales section.

Kilverts and the Blue Boar have enjoyable food. Black Mountain Activities just up the road (technically in Herefordshire) can arrange all sorts of exertions; (01497) 847897.

KNIGHTON SO2872

Pleasantly hilly town with the ubiquitous welsh-style clock tower. At the junction of two national trails, the Offa's Dyke Path and Glyndwyr's Way, so there are usually rucksack-clad hikers about. The George & Dragon (Broad St) is a useful stop.

Spaceguard Centre (Llanshay Lane) A 90-min guided tour of this working astronomical observatory puts the emphasis on Spaceguard, the threat to earth posed by asteroids; also planetarium, camera obscura, and live weather satellite link. Shop, disabled access; open Weds-Sun and bank hols (tours 10.30am, 2 and 4pm); (01547) 520247; £5.

LLANBISTER SO0974

Llananno church Remarkable, with an astonishingly elaborate rood screen that wouldn't be out of place in a cathedral.

Llanbister church Interesting, with a chimney instead of the usual tower, and presumably a warmer congregation.

LLANBRYNMAIR SH8902

Museum of Mechanical Magic 🔲 Unusual and growing automata collection (powered by electricity, clockwork, wind-driven or hand-turned), with subjects ranging from abstract appeal to entertainment and social commentary, often in the form of 3D cartoons; from a drummer and dragon to a man having his tooth pulled and a maid sweeping the floor. Shop selling timberkits, good café, and chance to view the workshop; cl 25-26 Dec; (01650) 511514; £2.75.

LLANDRINDOD WELLS SO0661

A delightful Victorian period piece, with red and yellow brick hotels and turreted villas nestling in the green landscape. The former spa town is immaculately preserved with period shop fronts, imposing buildings on broad avenues and terraces, wrought-iron frills everywhere, elegant flower displays and Victorian parks, antique shop-fronts and little canopies along the shopping streets. Middleton, the main shopping street, is now one way, with

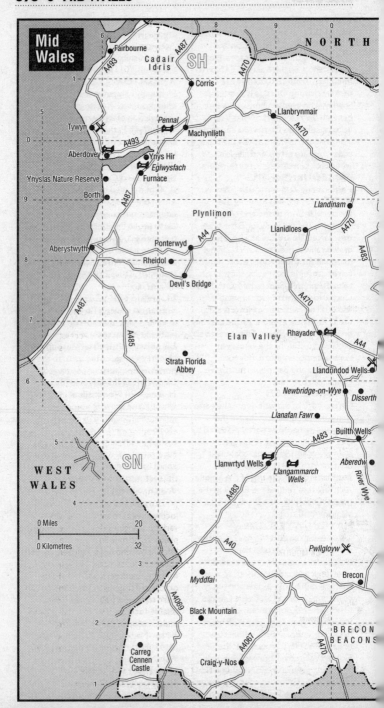

Mid Wales

NORTH

Fairbourne
Cadair Idris
SH
Corris
A487
A470
A493
Llanbrynmair
Pennal
A470
Tywyn
Machynlleth
A493
Aberdovey
Ynys Hir
Eglwysfach
Ynyslas Nature Reserve
Furnace
A487
Borth
Plynlimon
Llandinam
A470
Llanidloes
A483
Ponterwyd
A44
Aberystwyth
Rheidol
Devil's Bridge
A485
A470
Elan Valley
Rhayader
A44
A487
Strata Florida Abbey
Llandrindod Wells
Newbridge-on-Wye
Disserth
Llanafan Fawr
WEST WALES
SN
Builth Wells
A483
Llanwrtyd Wells
Llangammarch Wells
Aberedw
River Wye
A483
0 Miles   20
0 Kilometres   32
A40
Pwllgloyw
A4069
Myddfai
Brecon
Black Mountain
BRECON BEACONS
A4067
A470
Carreg Cennen Castle
Craig-y-Nos

wider pavements and better parking. It was clearly a resort for temperance - though there are places to drink, they're tucked discreetly away. The former spa pump room in Rock Park has reopened as a restaurant, with a small museum about the spa alongside; there are sedate walks around a very old-fashioned boating lake, and a very helpful Tourist Information Centre is housed in the Old Town Hall. The Metropole Hotel generally does some food all day, and the 16th-c Llanerch has plenty of atmosphere.

Cefnllys Castle A good walk from the town to this impressively sited hill fort with a lonely church below, close to Shaky Bridge (no longer shaky); a nature trail here takes you along the banks of the River Ithon.

National Cycle Collection 🏛 (Temple St) Over 250 cycles, reconstructions of Victorian and Edwardian cycle shops, early lamp collections, displays on past racing stars, and artist exhibitions. Meals, snacks, shop, disabled access; best to ring for winter opening hours; (01597) 825531; *£2.50.

Radnorshire Museum (Temple St) Charming district museum, well worth a look, with a gallery showing varying exhibits from early Christian carvings to Victorian paintings; medieval log boat, too. Shop; cl 1-2pm, Mon, Sun am Apr-Sept (all day Sun in winter), and Christmas bank hols; (01597) 824513; *£1.

LLANFAIR CAEREINION SJ1006
Welshpool & Llanfair Railway (A458) Colonial and austrian steam locomotives are among the wide variety of engines that dawdle along this pretty eight-mile line, and the Welshpool end has a handsomely done station reconstruction. It's run by friendly volunteers, and they hold occasional training days when you can learn to drive a train. Snacks, shop, disabled access; cl wkdys mid-Sept to mid-Oct (open daily half-term), cl Nov-Mar exc Dec Santa Specials; (01938) 810441 for timetable; £8.90. The Goat has good home cooking.

LLANIDLOES SN9584
Engagingly old-fashioned and surprisingly untouristy small town, with

unique Elizabethan timbered market hall; the Great Oak Bookshop (Great Oak St) is a wonderfully rambling place, with a wealth of new and second-hand books (cl Sun).

LLANWRTYD WELLS SN8746
Pleasant small spa town, said to be Britain's smallest town, with good walks in attractive scenery, also mountain bike hire. The nicely laid-back Neuadd Arms is the focus for all sorts of activities inc man v horse v mountain bike marathons, and bog-snorkelling championships.

MACHYNLLETH SH7400
Wide main street with tall, dark and handsome 19th-c clock tower and a very relaxed feel. The good value Dyfi Valley Days pass (see Celtica, below) covers several of the places to visit nearby, and Greenstiles (Maegwyn St) does bike hire; the White Lion and Wynnstay Arms do enjoyable lunches.
Celtica Very enjoyable look at the history and legends of the Celts, in an 18th-c mansion. There's a traditionalish museum upstairs, but more fun is the lively walk-through exhibition on the ground floor, special effects bringing ancient villages and druids' prophecies vividly to life. Also a good themed indoor play area for under-8s. It's popular with school trips the last couple of weeks of term. Meals, snacks, good shop, disabled access; cl 24-26 Dec, 1 Jan; (01654) 702702; £4.95, joint ticket with other attractions inc Talyllyn Railway, the Centre for Alternative Technology and King Arthur's Labyrinth £13.40.
Centre for Alternative Technology (A487 3m N) Reached by a water-balanced cliff railway with lovely views, the 3-hectare (7-acre) display gardens are crammed with exhibitions, displays and information. The centre is concerned with presenting solutions to environmental problems in an interesting and informative way, and shows sustainable ways of living through environmental technologies - and how to save energy and money in your home. Wholesome vegetarian restaurant, good bookshop, partial disabled access; cl 25-26 Dec and 2 wks mid-Jan; (01654) 705950/702400; £7 summer, £5 winter. They do good

value family tickets, and you can save 10% if you arrive by bus, bike or foot; you can also halve the cost of hiring a bike from Greenstiles (Heol Maengwyn); (01654) 703543.
Museum of Modern Art, Wales (Penrallt St) Lively place with six galleries inc works by Wales's top contemporary artists, a permanent collection of post-1900 art, and shows devoted to individual artists. Year-round recitals and performances in the adjacent auditorium (a converted Wesleyan chapel) include the Aug Machynlleth Festival, with special events for children. Occasional snacks, shop, disabled access; cl Sun, 24-26 Dec, 1 Jan; (01654) 703355; free.
Parliament House Local history museum in 15th-c building, with a particular emphasis on Owain Glyndwr's 1404 rebellion (it's on the spot where he held parliament); great events planned for this 600th anniversary, such as battle re-enactments, archery, and concerts. Brass rubbing centre, shop, disabled access; cl 12.30-1.30pm, Sun (exc bank hols), and all Oct-Easter; (01654) 702827; free.

MONTGOMERY SO2793
Tiny town, not much more than a handsome Georgian square, with great views from its castle perched above; Brickys (B4386 - see *Where to eat*) has good food mainly from local smallholdings, and the comfortable Dragon Hotel (Market Sq) is open all day. Montgomeryshire consists of the quintessential sheep-grazed lands of rural Wales - generally not prime walking country, with few major objectives for walkers, and fair distances between villages.

OFFA'S DYKE PATH SO2455
The major walkers' attraction in this part; on its coast-to-coast route pretty much along the welsh border it takes in some very attractive hill-farm country between Hay-on-Wye and Knighton, inc the breezily open Hergest Ridge (access from Kington or Gladestry; in the latter, the Royal Oak is a useful walker's pub) and some well preserved stretches of Offa's 9th-c boundary marker between Knighton and Kington.

OLD RADNOR SO2559
Old Radnor church Handsome

screen and roof, Britain's oldest organ-case and font; delightful hilltop surroundings, with beautiful views. The attractive Harp up in this peaceful spot has good home cooking.

PLYNLIMON SN7687

One of the big peaks of Mid Wales, this is the source of both the Wye and the Severn; its bog-strewn top doesn't make it the most appealing summit, but there are fine views of the range from two scenic roads - from Nant-y-moch Reservoir (at the end of a tortuous road off the A487 at Talybont, NE of Aberystwyth) and from the back road off the B4518 N of Staylittle, via Dylife towards Machynlleth.

PONTERWYD SN7281

Bwlch Nant-yr-Arian Forest Centre (A44 just W) Designated Kite Country centre, with feeding daily all year (3pm summer, 2pm winter); Explore the forest on the way-marked walks and enjoy breathtaking valley views. There's a mountain bike trail and a lakeside walk even wheelchairs can manage. Visitor centre (01970) 890694 with snacks, shop, disabled access; picnic areas and children's play area; cl Christmas period. Free (parking £1).

Llywernog Silver Lead Mine (A434 just W) A lively place, set against a beautiful sweeping mountainside backdrop. Regular displays of silver panning, an underground tour past sound and light tableaux in the caves and tunnels, and working water-wheels; you can try panning for fool's gold or dowsing for mineral veins; good trails. Wear sensible shoes in wet weather. Snacks, shop, some disabled access; cl Nov-Mar; (01970) 890620; £5.95.

Mountain drive An eye-opening mountain drive runs from Ponterwyd N past the partly wooded Nant-y-moch reservoir below the slopes of Plynlimon, and on to Talybont.

PRESTEIGNE SO3164

Attractive former county town of Radnorshire, with some fine timbered houses, a handsome church, and a good town trail. The handsome Radnorshire Arms is good value, as is the Hat Shop restaurant, with its exhibitions by local artists.

Judge's Lodging 🏛 (Broad St) Enjoyable restoration of the judge's living quarters. Unlike in most historic reconstructions you can sit on the chairs and try out the beds for comfort. A lively audio tour leads you to trial in the Victorian court; children's guides and family fun boxes. Shop, disabled access to ground floor only; cl Mon and Tues Nov-Dec, all Jan-Feb; (01544) 260650; *£4.50.

RADNOR FOREST SO2160

Open walking country for the most part, with conifers on the northern slopes. Walks include New Radnor to the modest summit of the quaintly named Whimble, and from the A44 between Llanfihangel-nant-Melan (where the Red Lion has decent food) and New Radnor to Water-break-its-neck waterfall (car park just above A44).

RADNORSHIRE HILLS SO1551

Away from Offa's Dyke, Radnorshire is less well known than it deserves to be, with old drovers' tracks providing some enjoyable escapist walking, and a reasonable network of field paths. There are few major objectives, but this part between Aberedw (good honest food at the Seven Stars), Glascwm and Gladestry is all very pleasant walking.

RHAYADER SN9867

Gigrin Farm (A470, just outside) Farm trail with excellent views and red kite feeding station with hides (the birds are fed daily at 3pm in summer, 2pm in winter); children's play area and picnic site. A new wetland site also has a hide, and you can watch badgers on CCTV. Also B&B, self-catering and camping. Snacks, shop, disabled access; cl am in winter, 25 Dec; (01597) 810243; *£2.50. In the pleasant unhurried town the mainly 16th-c Triangle (B4518) has enjoyable food.

Gilfach Nature Reserve (St Harmon, just N) Includes farmland virtually unchanged in 200 years in fine craggy mountain backdrops (look out for red kites); several well signed paths include the Monks' Trod and the nature trail from Gilfach Farm - leading across a defunct railway and close to the otter-populated River Marteg, eventually emerging on the A470 by Pont Marteg, a delightful shady place with a footbridge over the River Wye. Longhouse and visitor centre, snacks, shop, disabled access; cl Tues-Thurs

May, Jun and Sept, and end Oct-Mar; (01597) 823298; free.

Welsh Royal Crystal (Brynberth Industrial Estate) Workshop tours; no glass-cutting demonstrations wknds or some wkdys, best to check first on (01597) 811005. Snacks, shop, disabled access; cl 25-26 Dec, 1 Jan; free.

RHEIDOL SN7079

Rheidol Hydro-electric Scheme (off A44 at Capel Bangor) Guided tours of power station with unexpected fish farm. Good nature trails, scenic lakes and reservoirs, trout fishing. Snacks, disabled access; cl end Sept-1 May but open Easter; (01970) 880667; free, fishing permits from £7 (get them at the gate of the fish farm).

STRATA FLORIDA ABBEY SN7465

Little is left of this once-important centre of learning, exc the ruined church and cloister, but the surroundings are lovely. 14th-c poet Dafyd ap Gwilym is thought to be buried here. Teas, shop, disabled access; cl end Sept-Apr; (01974) 831261; £2; Cadw. From Tregaron down the B4343 a steep road climbs through the pine forests into the mountains, eventually reaching the Llyn Brianne reservoir.

TALYBONT-ON-USK SO1122

Attractive village, with friendly boat hire on the Monmouthshire & Brecon Canal, opposite the Travellers Rest (generous food). It's on the Taff Trail waymarked path.

TRETOWER SO1821

Tretower Court & Castle (off A40) The medieval manor house dates from the 14th c, though it has been developed over the centuries; beside it is the substantial ruin of an 11th-c motte and bailey, with massively thick walls and a three-storey tower. Limited disabled access; cl end Oct-beg Mar; (029) 2082 6185; £2.50; Cadw. The friendly Farmers Arms at Cwmdu has good value food, or for an excellent lunch go to the Nantyffin Cider Mill.

TYWYN SH5800

Talyllyn Railway This railway journey gives glorious views, climbing from the little seaside resort up the steep sides of the Fathew Valley and stopping for passengers to get off and admire Dolgoch Falls and the Nant Gwernol Forest (there's a waterfall two mins away from the platform at this end). The 27-in-gauge railway, the oldest of this gauge in the world, was built in 1865 to serve the slate mine at Abergynolwyn (where the Railway Inn does decent food in a lovely setting). Snacks, shop, disabled access with prior notice; cl 9 Nov-19 Dec, 4 Jan-27 Mar; (01654) 710472 for timetable; £9.50 full return. A big lottery grant is to provide a new museum at Tywyn Station for the locomotives, wagons and other equipment on show there.

WELSHPOOL SJ2106

Powis Castle (A483, 1m S) In magnificent gardens with splendid 18th-c terraces, this dramatic-looking castle was built in the 13th c, but far from falling into decay like so many others, has developed into a grand house. It's been constantly occupied since its construction, once by the son of Clive of India - there are displays about his father's life. You can now also see the opulent 19th-c state coach used by the 3rd Earl of Powis, and mannequins show off the sumptuous garb of his coachman and footmen. Meals, snacks, shop; cl Mon, Tues (exc July-Aug), and Nov-beginning Apr (castle and museum cl am); (01938) 551944 information line, (01938) 551920 property office; £8, garden only £5.50; NT.

Powysland Museum and Canal Centre (Canal Wharf) Decent local history museum, with temporary exhibitions and canal material too; disabled access; cl 1-2pm, Weds; (01938) 554656; *£1. The big Royal Oak Hotel has enjoyable bar food, and the main station is rather unusual.

YNYS HIR SN6895

(1m N) Intriguingly diverse RSPB reserve with reedbeds, saltmarsh, oak woods, freshwater pools and peat bogs, on low-lying land on the southern flank of the Dyfi estuary. Dragonflies, damselflies and butterflies as well as breeding woodland birds and wintering wildfowl. Daily until dusk; (01654) 781265.

YNYSLAS NATURE RESERVE SN6094

(just N of Borth) A major scenic highlight of the coast, with watery views across the vast sands of the Dovey estuary, lots of birds inc red kites, and an important dune system, habitat for orchids. You can walk round the tip of land jutting into the mouth of the Dovey and then along the shore. **Attractive villages and small towns** in the area, all with decent pubs, include Llanafan Fawr SN9655, Llanbedr SO2420, Llandinam SO0388, Llangenny SO2417, Llyswen SO1337, Myddfai SN7730 and Newbridge-on-Wye SO0158. Other pubs doing food that are particularly worth noting for their positions include the Neuadd Fawr at Cilycwm SN7540, Admiral Rodney at Criggion SJ2915, Farmers Arms at Cwmdu SO1823, Dolfor Inn at Dolfor SO1187, White Swan at Llanfrynach SO0725, Coach & Horses above the canal at Llangynidr SO1519 (lovely walks), Stables Hotel at Neuadd Fawr SO2322 (good hill walking), canalside Royal Oak at Pencelli SO0925, Royal Oak at Rhandirmwyn SN7843 and Goose & Cuckoo at Rhyd-y-Meirch SO2907. **Some unspoilt and humble rustic churches in beautiful settings** include Aberedw SO0847, Bleddfa SO2168 (the Hundred House is a good base for walkers), Disserth SO0358, Llanbadarn-y-garreg SO1148, Maesyronnen Chapel SO1740 NW of Hay, and Rhulen SO1349.

Where to eat

CRICKHOWELL SO1920 **Nantyffin Cider Mill** *Talgarth Rd (01873) 801775* Handsome pink-washed dining pub with striking raftered restaurant, smart relaxed atmosphere, fresh and dried flowers, woodburner, comfortable tables and chairs, beautifully presented imaginative food (much organic produce), excellent service, well kept real ales, good wines and charming views; cl Mon; disabled access. £28/ 2-course weekday lunch £10

FELINFACH SO0933 **Griffin** *(01874) 620111* Brightly painted opened-up roadside restaurant with good imaginative modern cooking using only local ingredients in two formally set out bare-boards or flagstoned no smoking front dining rooms with big modern prints; back bar area with stripped furniture and floors, mustard walls and bright blue dado, and leather sofas by the log fire; six good house wines in three glass sizes, polite service, and no smoking area; comfortable bdrms; cl Mon am, 25 Dec; disabled access. £29.50|£11.50

HAY-ON-WYE SO2342 **Kilverts** *Bullring (01497) 821042* Friendly town pub with an informal relaxed atmosphere in the airy high-beamed bar, candles on the good mix of tables, some stripped stone walls and standing timbers, interesting enjoyable food (esp the daily specials) from a thoughtful menu, a dozen wines by the glass, well kept real ales, local welsh wines, and efficient easy-going service; bdrms; cl 25 Dec. £24.95|£6.95

LLANDRINDOD WELLS SO0561 **Llanerch** *High St (01597) 822086* Welcoming low-ceilinged 16th-c inn with old-fashioned settles in cheerful beamed main bar, communicating lounges (one no smoking), popular bar food, well kept real ales, prompt service, peaceful mountain views from the back terrace, and boules in the orchard garden; bdrms; cl 25 Dec, 1 Jan. £20|£6.50

LLOWES SO1941 **Radnor Arms** *(01497) 847460* Small, modest and very old place with log fire in the bar, neat little cottagey dining room, enjoyable food (nice puddings), friendly staff, and tables in imaginatively planted garden; cl Sun pm, Mon (exc bank hols), 2 wks Nov, 2 wks Jun; well behaved children welcome; partial disabled access. £22.50|£7.50

MONTGOMERY SO2296 **Brickys** *Chirbury Rd (01686) 668177* Plain-looking pub hiding really special food, from a short and interesting choice using unusually carefully chosen ingredients cooked with real imagination, and served attractively on big plates; the bar (shiny red flooring tiles throughout) has an area on the left for eating, with seven or eight pub tables, a few modern prints, a big woodburner, real ales, organic cider, and a short but interesting choice of wines inc good ones by the glass; linen-set restaurant, and friendly and quietly helpful service; picnic-sets out in front. £27|£6.25

PWLLGLOYW SO0333 **Seland Newydd** *(01874) 690282* Popular with a good mix of people, this friendly former pub has a comfortable lounge, a huge fireplace in the bar, and attractive no smoking dining room with good modern cooking using the best local produce; good value little wine list; bdrms; peaceful setting with own woodland and plenty of fine walks; cl Sun pm, Mon, Tues am. £30

TYWYN SH5800 **Proper Gander** *High St (01654) 711270* Popular little pink tea shop on two floors with morning coffee, lunches, and good afternoon teas, more elaborate evening restaurant (may be closed Sun-Weds pm), and good Sun lunch; no smoking. £18|**£6.30**

South Wales

Rich and rewarding variety of outings, for all ages

From an impressive roster of good family attractions, we'd particularly pick out the unforgettable re-creations and underground tours at the former coal mines in Trehafod and free Blaenavon, magnificent Tredegar House in Newport, the lively museum at Nelson, and busy Margam Park. Historic buildings with family appeal include picture-book Castell Coch in Tongwynlais, mighty moated Caerphilly Castle, and the first recorded Norman stone castle, in Chepstow. There's no shortage of atmospheric ruins: favourites are the striking Roman remains at Caerleon, and beautiful 14th-c Tintern Abbey, but there are many more.

Cardiff has some great attractions, from the over-the-top castle and engaging museum in its centre to the hands-on science centre in the increasingly visitor-friendly Bay. The fascinating Museum of Welsh Life (enough here to keep children happy for most of the day) is just outside. Swansea has several places of interest, and the Gower peninsula offers visitors quite a lot - its broad sands are ideal for uncomplicated beach holidays. Monmouth is an attractive small town with good nearby walks, and there's a busy market in Abergavenny.

The former coal-mining valleys N of Cardiff are not conventionally pretty, but are interesting to drive through. And even quite close to the built-up and industrialised areas are some unspoilt pockets of attractive scenery.

Where to stay

CARDIFF ST1974 **St David's Hotel & Spa** *Havannah St, Cardiff, South Glamorgan CF10 5SD (029) 2045 4045* **£200**; 132 well equipped, comfortable rms with ship-style balcony decks overlooking the water. Luxurious hotel on Millennium Waterfront with lovely views over the bay, impressive and stylish public rooms with italian furniture and lovely flower arrangements, imaginative food in Marco Pierre White's Tides restaurant, and superb hydrotherapy spa with swimming pool and 14 treatment rms

GILWERN SO2413 **Wenallt Farm** *Twyn-wenallt, Gilwern, Abergavenny, Gwent NP7 0HP (01873) 830694* **£48**; 8 rms. Friendly and relaxing 16th-c welsh longhouse on 50 acres of farmland, with oak beams and inglenook fireplace in big drawing room, a TV room, good food in dining room, and lots to do nearby; cl Christmas; dogs welcome in bedrooms

MONMOUTH SO5012 **Riverside Hotel** *Cinderhill St, Monmouth, Gwent NP25*

5EY (01600) 715577 **£68***, plus special breaks; 17 rms. Comfortable, warmly welcoming bustling hotel overlooking River Monnow and the 13th-c fortified gatehouse, with good value bar meals, extensive restaurant menu, a bustling lounge bar, and conservatory; disabled access; dogs welcome in bedrooms

MUMBLES SS6087 **Hillcrest House** *1 Higher Lane, Langland, Swansea, West Glamorgan SA3 4NS* (01792) 363700 **£85***; 6 individually decorated rms, each themed to represent a different country. Friendly white house with stone terrace two mins from beach yet handy for Swansea; informal welcoming atmosphere, thoughtful individual service, comfortable lounge with newspapers, and enjoyable breakfasts; cl 23-26 Dec

OXWICH SS4986 **Oxwich Bay Hotel** *Oxwich, Swansea, West Glamorgan SA3 1LS* (01792) 390329 **£60***, plus special breaks; 13 rms. Comfortable hotel on edge of beach in a lovely area, with dedicated friendly staff, food served all day, restaurant/lounge bar with panoramic views, summer outdoor dining area, and a welcome for families; cl 24-25 Dec; dogs welcome in bedrooms

PARKMILL SS5389 **Parc-Le-Breos House** *Penmaen, Swansea, West Glamorgan SA3 2HA (01792) 371636* **£50**, plus special breaks; 10 rms. 19th-c former hunting lodge in 70 acres, down a long wooded drive; open log fire, relaxing lounge, games room, enjoyable meals using home-grown fruit and vegetables in period dining room, and helpful owners; pony trekking, and they can arrange all manner of water sports; wonderful walks and wildlife, and historic sites; cl 25-26 Dec

REYNOLDSTON SS4691 **Fairyhill** *Reynoldston, Swansea, West Glamorgan SA3 1BS* (01792) 390139 **£140**, plus special breaks; 8 rms. 18th-c hotel in 24 wooded acres with croquet, trout stream and wild duck on the lake; log fire in comfortable drawing room, cosy bar, lovely food in attractive dining room, hearty breakfasts, a leafy terrace, and personal friendly service; cl 1-16 Jan; children over 8

ST BRIDES WENTLOOG ST2982 **West Usk Lighthouse** *St Brides Wentloog, Newport, Gwent NP10 8SF* (01633) 810126 **£95**; 3 rms. Unusual ex-lighthouse - squat rather than tall - that was on an island in the Bristol Channel (the land has since been reclaimed); modern stylish furnishings, lots of framed record sleeves (Mr Sheahan used to work for a record company), informal atmosphere, good big breakfasts, and a Rolls-Royce drive to good local restaurant; flotation tank, aromatherapy and reflexology sessions, roof garden with palm trees, vines and a barbecue, and lots of nearby walks; dogs welcome in bedrooms

TINTERN PARVA SO5200 **Parva Farmhouse Hotel** *Tintern, Chepstow, Gwent NP16 6SQ (01291) 689411* **£76***, plus special breaks; 9 comfortable rms. Friendly stone farmhouse built in 17th c, with leather chesterfields, woodburner and honesty bar in large beamed lounge, books (no TV downstairs), and very good food and wine (inc wine using locally grown grapes) in cosy restaurant; 50 yds from River Wye and lovely surrounding countryside; partial disabled access; dogs welcome in bedrooms

WHITEBROOK SO5306 **Crown at Whitebrook** *Whitebrook, Monmouth, Gwent NP25 4TX (01600) 860254* **£90***, plus special breaks; 10 neat rms. Small modernised restaurant-with-rooms in beautiful Wye Valley, with friendly caring service, relaxed atmosphere, comfortable lounge and bar; small cosy restaurant with fine wines and excellent food combining welsh ingredients and french style, very good breakfasts; cl 2 wks Christmas and New Year; children over 12; dogs welcome in bedrooms

To see and do

ABERDULAIS SS7799
Aberdulais Falls (A465) Since the 16th c this splendid waterfall has been used to power a range of industries from copper-smelting to tinplate. A magnificent water-wheel now generates electricity. Snacks, shop,

disabled access (right to the top of the falls thanks to a lift powered by the electricity generated on site); cl Nov-Dec wknds, Jan-Feb, Mar wknds; (01639) 636674;* £3.20; NT.
ABERGAVENNY SO2914
There are some attractive ancient

buildings in Nevill St and particularly Market St, with its busy Tues market and smaller produce market on Fri. The **church** has a remarkable collection of memorials. Out on the A40 NW the Lamb & Flag is useful for a meal.

Abergavenny Castle 12th- and 14th-c remains inc the walls, towers and rebuilt gatehouse; the early 19th-c keep and adjoining house now contain a local history museum inc Victorian farm kitchen, saddler's workshop and 1950s grocer's, and the grounds are good for picnics. Shop, limited disabled access; cl 1-2pm, all day Sun (exc pm Nov-Feb), 24-26 Dec, 1 Jan; (01873) 854282; free.

BARRY ST1166

Lively seaside resort which, along with its jutting-out peninsula Barry Island, grew as a centre for the coal industry. Remains of 13th-c castle, and usual fairground attractions for children. The suburban Glenbrook (Dobbins Rd) has good value food.

Welsh Hawking Centre (A4226 N) Cheery centre with over 200 birds of prey. Regular flying demonstrations (11.30am, 1.30pm, 3.30pm), baby birds (May-July), adventure playground, and animals for children to fuss over. Snacks, shop, some disabled access; best to phone for winter opening; (01446) 734687; £5. The Green Dragon over at Llancadle has good value food.

BETTWS NEWYDD SO3605

Bettws Newydd church Largely unaltered from the 15th c, with a choir gallery and fine screen; the village is peaceful.

BLAENAVON SO2509

The former centre for mining and ironwork in the Gwent valleys, this industrial village is now a World Heritage Site.

Afon Lwyd Valley Interesting example of post-mining land reclamation between here and Cwmbran New Town, with plantings designed for re-establishment of nature (and for pleasant walking).

Big Pit Mining Museum (B4248) For 200 years until 1980 this was a working pit, and the tour guides are all former miners; their anecdotes and expertise, and the underground atmosphere, make a visit here quite special. There are plenty of colliery workings to

explore on the surface, but it's the hour-long pit tours that stand out; armed with a hard hat and lamp, you get into the pit cage and descend 90 metres (300 ft) into the inky blackness that was daily life for generations of local men. Wrap up warmly (even in summer) and wear sensible footwear. They don't allow under-5s, or anyone under a metre tall. Back on the surface there's a reconstructed miner's cottage, and an exhibition in the old pithead baths. The whole site takes around 2½ hrs to see properly. Meals, snacks, shop, disabled access (even underground, though you must book); usually cl Dec to mid-Feb; (01495) 790311; free.

Blaenavon Ironworks (North St) Appreciable ruins of five 1788-89 steam-powered blast furnaces, driven out of business by the advent of steel in the following century. A water-balance tower (which provided power to move materials around the site) and workers' cottages also survive. Shop, disabled access; site exhibition; open Apr-Oct; tours through on-site Tourist Information Centre; (01495) 792615; £2; Cadw.

BRIDGEND SS9084

Bryngarw Country Park (just N) Unexpectedly tranquil refuge from the M4, with woodland walks, formal gardens, ornamental lakes and a japanese garden. Playground, snacks, shop; usually only cl 25-26 Dec; (01656) 725155; free (£2 parking wknds and bank hols, and school hols Apr-Sept). The Masons Arms (A4061 at Bryncethin) does good lunches.

Ewenny Priory (just S) This riverside ruin is one of the finest fortified religious buildings in Britain.

Newcastle (Newcastle Hill) Ruined 12th-c castle with surviving rectangular tower, richly carved Norman gateway and massive curtain walls; open daily; free; Cadw. The prosperous industrial town below isn't much of a place for visitors.

CAERLEON ST3490

Roman Fortress Baths, Amphitheatre & Barracks The site of the 20-hectare (50-acre) Roman fortress of Isca, established in AD 75 as the permanent base of the 5,500-strong 2nd Augustan Legion. One of the best examples of an amphitheatre in the country, alongside impressive remains of the fortress baths, barrack blocks (the only examples currently visible in all Europe), and fortress wall. Shop, disabled access; cl 24-26 Dec, 1 Jan; (01554) 890104; £2.50; Cadw. Caerleon is reckoned in these parts to have been the site of the court of King Arthur. Near the Tourist Information Centre on the High St is a little art gallery, with various craft workshops in an 18th-c walled garden; the Hanbury Arms has generous food.

Roman Legionary Museum (High St) Gives some idea of the daily life of the garrison; quite a few hands-on activities at wknds and school hols. Shop, disabled access; cl am Sun, 24-26 Dec, 1 Jan; (01633) 423134; free.

CAERPHILLY ST1587

Caerphilly Castle One of the largest medieval fortresses in Britain, begun in 1268, with extensive land and water defences. Rising sheer from its broad outer moat, it's a proper picture-book castle, pleasing for this reason to the most casual visitor. It also enthrals serious students of castle architecture with its remarkably complex design of concentric defences. Look out for the incredible leaning tower, which appears ready to topple any second; audio-visual display and replica medieval siege engines; new visitor centre. Shop, disabled access to ground floor; cl 24-26 Dec, 1 Jan; (029) 2088 3143; £3; Cadw. In the oddly strung-out small town, the ancient Courthouse overlooking the castle has reasonably priced food.

CAERWENT ROMAN WALLS ST4790

These massive walls, still some 4½ metres (15 ft) high in places, enclosed the large site of Venta Silurum - big enough for a sizeable town, though none of that's left now; free. The Carpenters Arms up in the attractive village of Shirenewton does good value food.

CALDICOT ST4888

Caldicot Castle 🏰 (off B4245) Founded by the Normans, developed in Royal hands as a stronghold in the Middle Ages, restored as a Victorian family home, and now surrounded by

22 hectares (55 acres) of parkland. It's a pleasant place for a relaxed afternoon, with hands-on activities and games for children, a new play area, picnic facilities and barbecue hearths; special events. Snacks, shop, limited disabled access; cl Nov-Feb; (01291) 420241; £3 inc audio tour.

CARDIFF ST1876

Cardiff's bustling centre, much of it pedestrianised, has a good friendly feel; there are several interesting Victorian covered shopping arcades, as well as modern ones, and near the medieval church of St John the Baptist is a bustling two-storey Victorian market hall. In summer a lively place to head is Mill Lane, where lots of the cafés and bars have outside tables; for food, we also recommend the Celtic Cauldron (in pretty Castle Arcade), where you can try traditional welsh dishes such as lavabread, and La Fosse (The Hayes) does a good value lunch. The magnificent riverside Millennium Stadium is surprisingly central (and dominates the city skyline from most approaches), and on match days the roar of the crowds can be heard right across the city; there are enthusiastic hourly tours every day; (029) 2082 2228; £5. Slightly aloof from the bustle of the centre lie the impressive neo-classical buildings of **Cathays Park**. The City Hall, with its dome and ornate clock tower, is flanked by the porticoed National Museum of Wales and the imposing Law Courts. Beyond this trio are more grand buildings, grouped around formal Alexandra Gardens and the Welsh National War Memorial. The two broad, tree-lined avenues liven up at New Year and during the Aug festival, when there's a fairground and outdoor concerts.

Cardiff Bay (Britannia Park) The attempt to reconnect Cardiff with its waterfront has had considerable success, and although the bay is still semi-detached from city centre activity there are regular buses from the centre. A space-age, cylindrical **Visitor Centre** at Harbour Drive (shop, disabled access; cl 24-26, 31 Dec and 1 Jan; (029) 2046 3833; free) tells of the continuing transformation of Cardiff's waterfront and docklands. A huge freshwater lake, separated from the sea by a 1,000-metre barrage, is fringed by new residential, commercial and leisure developments. At the heart of the bay work has at last begun on the National Assembly building, while the imposing new slate-clad Millenium Centre (for cultural events and organisations inc opera) is due to open in Jan. These two landmark buildings, along with the fine Victorian Pierhead building, will provide a counterbalance to the Mermaid Quay development, with its restaurants, cafés and bars leading down to the waterfront; there's a nearby multi-screen cinema too (Atlantic Wharf). Roald Dahl Basin and Britannia Park are a focus for outdoor events. There are boat trips (and a land train) to the barrage, and to Penarth Marina (usually daily); (029) 2048 8842; £3.50 return.

Cardiff Castle (Castle St) With its romantic towers, formidable walls, and lavishly decorated interiors much of the castle realises the medieval fantasies of Victorian architect William Burges and the super-rich 3rd Marquess of Bute. Some parts though are much older: a section of wall remains from the original Roman fort (3 metres thick, it stretches for 270 metres), and the Norman keep survives (you can climb to the top), as does a 13th-c tower; other medieval buildings had been casually razed by Capability Brown, while landscaping the grounds for an earlier Marquess. There are also two military museums. Snacks, shop; usually cl 25-26 Dec, 1 Jan, though major development over the next few years may affect opening times, best to phone; (029) 2087 8100; £5.80 for full guided tour, £2.90 grounds only. Beyond the castle stretches the extensive **Bute Park**. Along with Sophia Gardens, Pontcanna Fields and Llandaff Fields, on the opposite bank of the Taff, the park forms a green corridor stretching to Llandaff, and beyond. The Taff trail for walkers and cyclists follows this corridor, S to Cardiff Bay and N to Brecon.

Craft in the Bay (Lloyd George Ave) Demonstrations by potters, jewellers and glass workers, and a large gallery and shop; cl 25-26 Dec, 1 Jan; free.

Llandaff Cathedral (W of centre)

Rebuilt several times, it's survived neglect, the depredations of Cromwell's armies, and a landmine; it nestles snugly in a hollow. Jacob Epstein's controversial Christ in Majesty, on its uncompromising concrete arch, dominates the modest but atmospheric interior, which includes some delightful medieval masonry, Pre-Raphaelite works, and a marvellous modern timber roof. Disabled access; (029) 2056 4554; suggested donation £2.50. The nearby green has an attractive collection of buildings around it, including the sparse remains of the medieval bishops' palace, and the good Black Lion.

Museum of Welsh Life (St Fagans, A4232 4m W) Excellent 100 acre open-air museum, with reconstructed buildings from all over Wales illustrating living conditions and life styles throughout the ages, from a Celtic village, medieval church and 17th-c farmhouse to a Victorian schoolroom and 1960s prefab. You can shop at a pre-war grocery, ride on horse and cart, make your own pot, and watch a blacksmith at work; native breeds of sheep and cattle too. It stands in the grounds of St Fagan's Castle (a fine Elizabethan manor, which they're currently restoring to reflect the life of its Edwardian occupant the Earl of Plymouth; it should reopen in the spring), and the lovely formal gardens, include a recently restored italian garden (cl Oct-Apr), and medieval fishponds. Also crafts, regular demonstrations, changing exhibitons, and lots of seasonal events. Meals and snacks (in 1920s tearoom), shops, limited disabled access; cl 24-25 Dec; (029) 2057 3500; free. The Plymouth Arms is very handy for good value food.

National Museum & Gallery (Cathays Park) Lively, with interactive displays and exhibitions on subjects as diverse as ceramics, coins and prehistoric sea monsters. The East Wing has an impressive collection of paintings, with notable french Impressionists, and there's an excellent section on the evolution of the welsh landscape. Meals, snacks, shop, disabled access; cl Mon (exc bank hols), 25-26 Dec; (029) 2039 7951; free.

Techniquest 🏛 (Stuart St) An excellent family excursion, with fun as well as interest at this hi-tech science centre; around 160 hands-on exhibits and activities, and a planetarium - all exceptionally well done, and the staff are friendly. Snacks, shop, very good disabled access; cl 24-26 Dec, 1 Jan; (029) 2047 5475; *£6.75.

CHEPSTOW ST5294

A steep but civilised small town, still with its battlemented 13th-c town gate. Stuart Crystal have a workshop opposite the castle, and there's a working pottery on Lower Church St (cl Sun). The Castle View is useful for lunch.

Chepstow Castle The first recorded Norman stone castle, proudly standing on an easily defended spot above the Wye, overlooking the gorge, which here is spanned by a handsome Regency iron bridge. Splendid gatehouse with portcullis grooves and ancient gates, and exhibitions on siege warfare and the Civil War, with models of both the medieval lords and a Civil War battle scene. Shop, limited disabled access; cl 24-26 Dec, 1 Jan; £3; Cadw.

Chepstow Museum (Bridge St) Good local history in an elegant 18th-c house. Shop, some disabled access; cl Sun am, and 25-26 Dec, 1 Jan; free.

CRYNANT SN7904

Cefn Coed Colliery Museum (A4109) On the site of former Cefn Coed Colliery, the story of mining in the Dulais Valley. It still has a steam winding-engine, though the winding gear is now run by electricity. Also a simulated underground mining gallery, boiler house and compressor house. Shop; cl Nov-Mar; (01639) 750556; free.

CWM DARRAN SO1203

(Rhymney Valley, nr Bargoed) Interesting example of post-mining land reclamation, which now provides a wide variety of habitats for wildlife and plants, with scenery ranging from the valley floor through forest areas to upland moors giving walkers superb views of the Brecon Beacons.

CWMBRAN ST2795

Greenmeadow Community Farm 🏛 (1m W) Founded to protect one of the encroaching new town's last green

areas, this friendly farm has a wide range of animals - traditional, rare and cuddly - as well as a deer enclosure, bluebell wood, and craft workshops. Meals, snacks, shop, disabled access; cl 25 Dec; (01633) 862202; *£3.50. Up towards Pontypool the canalside Open Hearth (Griffithstown) has good food.

CYNONVILLE SS8194

Afan Forest Park (A4107) 25 tranquil square miles of forest, with trails for walking or cycling (you can hire mountain bikes in summer) inc challenging mountain bike trails, picnic and barbecue areas, and visitor centre; disabled access with scooters available; (01639) 850564; free, parking from £1, miners' museum £1.20.

Welsh Miners Museum (Afan Forest Park) Illustrates life as a miner, with coal faces, pit gear and mining equipment among the displays. Meals, snacks, shop, disabled access; maybe cl Christmas wk - best to check in winter; (01639) 850564; £1.20.

EBBW VALE SO1508

Victoria Park (Victoria, A4046 2m S) Pleasant lakeside walks and trails through gardens, wetlands and woodland, with woodland craft centre, owl sanctuary and some quite extraordinary sculptures, one made from 30,000 individually modelled clay bricks. Also a large factory shopping centre. Land train rides at wknds during the summer and school hols, weather permitting. Meals, snacks, disabled access; centre cl 25 Dec; (01495) 350010; free.

GOVILON SO2414

Monmouthshire & Brecon Canal A walk along the Monmouthshire & Brecon Canal to Llanfoist (SO2813) can tie in with a return along the track of the former Abergavenny—Merthyr Tydfil railway line, making a level 4 miles in all. The lower section of the canal has a heritage and activity centre at Goytre Wharf, Llanover. Snacks, shop, disabled access; (01873) 881069; free, charges for activities. You can hire boats nearby.

GOWER SS4990

This peninsula stretching W of Swansea has quite a bit of off-putting ribbon development along the roads leading in, but it's well worth persevering into what was designated as the first of

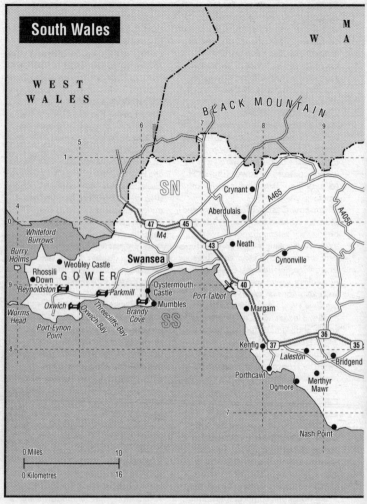

Britain's Areas of Outstanding Natural Beauty. It encapsulates on a small scale many different types of welsh landscape, with lots of walking opportunities, and parts of the coast are lovely (the N coast though is attractive only at its western end). Busy in summer with quite a young feel in parts, though even the main places tend to be virtually empty out of season.

Brandy Cove This tiny cove makes an attractive destination for a walk down the wooded Bishopston Valley, perhaps from the good Joiners Arms.

Burry Holms Islet with ruined chapel and Iron Age fort; you can walk out across the sands at low tide.

Gower Heritage Centre (Parkmill) Based round a 12th-c water-powered cornmill (you can still see it working), this developing centre includes a re-created mill cottage, farm museum, a display of coracles, blacksmith, wheelwright and pottery (you can have a go at making your own pot, £2.50) and hatchery; also picnic and play areas, and you can feed the fish. They have a puppet theatre, craft shops and hold special events. Tearoom, snacks, shops, disabled access; cl 25-26 Dec, 1 Jan;

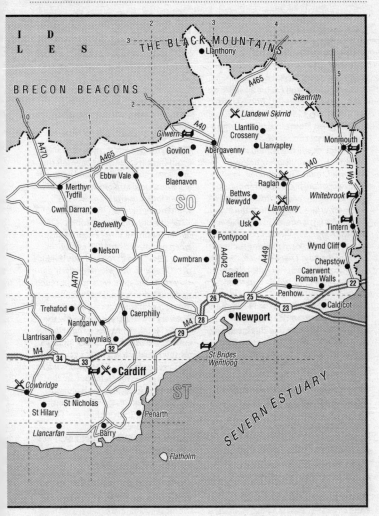

(01792) 371206; £3.60.
Mumbles Pleasantly unspoilt resort with a gallery collection of traditional welsh love spoons (cl Sun; (01792) 360132), and a surprisingly active night-life; around 14 pubs line the stretch of Mumbles Rd near Mumbles Head, and Swansea students like to 'go mumbling' between them. Claudes Restaurant (Newton Rd) does good value set meals; the Park Inn (Park St) is also good value, with lots of photographs of the old Mumbles Railway.
Oxwich Bay Dunes and broad sands, presided over by Oxwich Point on its

W side; good walking. It's also good for windsurfing - you can hire wet suits from a windsurfing school at Oxwich Bay - though the water will never be more than what might euphemistically be called invigorating. The seaview Oxwich Bay Hotel has above-average food all day.
Oxwich Castle 16th-c courtyard house, luxurious in its day and built as a mock-fortified manor; now an atmospheric ruin. Shop, disabled access to ground floor; open Easter-end Sept; (029) 2082 6185; £2; Cadw.
Oystermouth Castle (Mumbles)

Very complete ruins of the de Breose family castle, in a small park overlooking the bay. The gatehouse, chapel and great hall date from the 13th/14th-c. Cl Sept-Apr; (01792) 368732; £1; Cadw.

Pony trekking (Park-Le-Breos, Parkmill) Family-run centre, based in a 19th-c hunting lodge; (01792) 371636; half a day from £15.

Port-Eynon Point Interesting, with a huge medieval rock-dove dovecot in the cliff (birds still use it), and cliff walks on either side; windsurfing below.

Rhossili Down This rounded windswept rough-cropped moorland seems a million miles from Swansea (yet as the crow flies is only about ten from the outskirts); it offers Gower walkers breathtaking coast views. From Rhossili walks can also take in the long surfers' sands of the bay. There's an informative NT visitor centre at Rhossili; cl Mon-Tues Nov-Dec, and wkdys Jan to mid-Mar.

Threecliffs Bay From the NT car park near Penmaen church a good walk follows the lane down to this lovely bay, then heads W along the coast as far as Nicholaston Farm to end with the mild ascent of Cefn Bryn, a rounded moorland hill giving breathtaking views of both - or all three - Gower coasts.

Weobley Castle (Llanrhidian) 12th/14th-c fortified manor house with an exhibition on the area's history, and superb views. Cl 24-26 Dec, 1 Jan; (01792) 390012; £2; Cadw. This is a lovely spot above the estuary and its long glistening cockle sands - full of interest for walkers.

Whiteford Burrows An extensive nature reserve, with sand dunes, marshy slacks and pine trees - good walks.

Worms Head Nature reserve where you may see seals on the tidal rocks in late summer; walks here can also take in Mewslade Bay, where the south-facing sands are enclosed by limestone cliffs. The Worms Head Hotel with clifftop views over Rhossili Bay has enjoyable food.

KENFIG SS8081

Kenfig National Nature Reserve (off A48 W of Bridgend) A thriving medieval town till huge storms buried it in sand (the only remaining trace is the castle keep), this is one of the last

remnants of a huge dune system that stretched for miles along the South Wales coast (a haven for wild orchids); bird hides overlook a 28-hectare (70-acre) freshwater pool, and the little visitor centre has a hands-on exhibition. Shop, snacks, disabled access to shop only; cl am and 25 Dec; free. The ancient Prince of Wales has good home cooking.

LLANTHONY SO2923

Cwmyoy church (Llanthony Valley road) Repeated landslips have left the medieval church twisted, and its tower leans at an angle that makes the Tower of Pisa look positively sober.

Llanthony Priory Graceful ruins of 12th-c priory, the money for its construction put up by Hugh de Lacey when he decided he'd had enough of being a bold bad baron and was thinking of retiring into these lonely hills. It's a very romantic spot, with nothing much to disturb the peace. The remains cover a variety of architectural styles; free. The very ancient crypt bar below the Abbey Hotel, right among the priory buildings, is useful for a snack lunch - a most unusual place. This is a good start or objective for Black Mountains walks.

Partrishow church (about 3m S, in next valley) A remarkable building in the Black Mountains, with a musicians' gallery and a mural of a figure of Death wielding a shovel.

LLANTILIO CROSSENY SO3914

Attractive village with a lovely view of the 13th-c church from the former moat of Hen Cwrt nearby; the Halfway House and Hostry are good for lunch.

White Castle (NW) The remains of the most substantial of the trio of moated castles Hubert de Burgh built to defend the Welsh Marches; £2; Cadw. Among the narrow hilly lanes N of here, the Hunters Moon at Llangattock Lingoed has good food. The other ruins stand at Skenfrith (the Bell by an old mill here is good) and Grosmont, an attractive hillside village with another 13th-c church (the Angel here is good value).

LLANTRISANT ST0483

The **ancient church** in this attractive hill town has a window by Burne-Jones. Overlooking the Bullring in the centre of the old town, the decent **Model**

House Craft & Design Centre has around ten contemporary craft exhibitions every year; shop; cl Mon (exc bank hols); (01443) 237758; free. The Miskin Arms out at Miskin has good value food.

LLANVAPLEY SO3614
Interesting village, with a church dating from 860; the friendly Red Hart by the cricket green has good food.

MARGAM SS8086
Margam Park (A48) Pretty country park spreading over more than a square mile around a splendid Gothic mansion; all sorts of natural and historic features and various themed areas, inc a scaled-down nursery-rhyme village for young children. Also a ruined abbey and Iron Age hill fort, marked walks among the parkland and forests, deer and cattle, a light railway and good adventure playground. Meals, snacks, shop, disabled access; the centre is cl Sept-Mar but parkland is open; (01639) 881635; free, but car park £2.

MERTHYR MAWR SS8877
Delightful village of thatched cottages, bordered by meadows and woodlands. Nearby Merthyr Mawr Warren is Europe's largest sand dune system, a site of special scientific interest; the ruined 15th-c Candleston Castle stands at the edge of the dunes.

MERTHYR TYDFIL SO0511
Brecon Mountain Railway (off A465) This narrow-gauge railway starts at Pant Station, 3m N of Merthyr Tydfil, and runs for 3½ miles into the Brecon Beacons to the end of the Taf Fechan reservoir; there's a footpath to a picnic site with lovely panoramic valley views. Meals, snacks, shop, disabled access; cl Nov-Mar exc Dec; (01685) 722988 for timetable; *£7.50. On a stretch of disused line nearby, the Ponsarn Viaduct is a striking sight, well worth a detour.

Cyfarthfa Castle (Cyfarthfa Park) Impressive early 19th-c castellated Gothic mansion, in beautiful gardens. Now restored to their full Regency glory, the state rooms contain a museum with displays on Egyptology and archaeology, also fine art and ceramics. Snacks, shop, disabled access; cl wknd ams and Mon Oct-Mar, 24-26 Dec, 1 Jan; (01685) 723112; free.

Garwnant Forest Centre (5m NW, off A470) Looking out over the Llwyn-On reservoir on the S edge of the National Park, carefully restored old farm buildings with displays on forestry, wildlife and conservation, and information on nature trails and cycle routes (you can hire bikes). They run some summer activities for children, and this year there will be a new ropes course for older children; also play equipment. Meals, snacks, shop, disabled access; (01685) 384060; £1.50 car parking charge. Thye Nant Ddu Lodge just S has imaginative reasonably priced food.

Joseph Parry's Cottage (Chapel Row, Georgetown) The composer of Myfanwy was born here, and the ground floor has been restored and decorated in the style of the 1840s. Shop; cl am, also Mon-Weds and all Oct-Mar; (01685) 723112; free. The Butchers Arms up at Pontsticill has good home cooking.

MONMOUTH SO5113
Attractive market town of considerable character; below the remains of the 12th-c castle where Henry V was born, and the 17th-c Great Castle House (built in its precincts with enormous blocks of masonry), the main Agincourt Sq is surrounded by handsome buildings, inc the imposing central Shire Hall with its arcaded market floor. The town nestles in the crook formed by the River Wye and the River Monnow, with a splendid 13th-c gatehouse bridge over the Monnow. The Punch House is the most enjoyable place here for lunch, and the May Hill (where Offa's Dyke Path crosses the Wye) is useful for walkers.

Fairview Rock Lofty crag near the Biblins suspension bridge, making a good riverside walk from Monmouth, with a level track giving an easy route along the picturesque Lower Wye gorge.

Naval Temple and Round House A pair of whimsical Georgian buildings in grounds on top of the Kymin, the hill just E of Monmouth, commanding views over the Forest of Dean and Black Mountains. The Naval Temple is a delightful rustic conceit, built in 1800 to commemorate the admirals of the Napoleonic Wars, while the

Roundhouse is a circular banqueting house. Roundhouse open Sun and Mon, Apr-Oct; (01600) 719241; *£2.10; NT.

Nelson Museum (Priory St) Tremendous collection relating to Nelson, inc letters, medals and best of all his fighting sword. Nelson has nothing to do with Monmouth, but the collection was originally put together by Lady Llangattock who lived nearby, and whose son was one of the founders of Rolls-Royce; also local history collections and temporary exhibitions. Shop, mostly disabled access; cl 1-2pm, Sun am, 24-26 Dec, 1 Jan; (01600) 710630; free.

NANTGARW ST1285

Nantgarw China Works Museum (Treforest Industrial Estate, off A470) For a brief period early in the 19th c, Nantgarw porcelain was among the finest in the world. Snacks, shop; opening times are being revised - best to phone; (01443) 841703; free.

NASH POINT SS9168

The curious striped cliffs of the Glamorgan coast look over the Bristol Channel to Exmoor. It is worth getting down to shore level to see the cliffs in their full glory. The coast path provides a number of possibilities, inc walking E past the lighthouse to St Donat's Castle (now a college) and back.

NEATH SS7597

Borough Museum (Gwyn Hall, Orchard St) Includes finds from a nearby Roman fort and hands-on activities for children, inc using a Celtic loom and the chance to dress up as a Roman soldier. Shop, disabled access; cl Sun, Mon (exc bank hols) Good Fri, 24 Dec-2 Jan; (01639) 645726; free.

Gnoll Estate (B4434 NE) Enchanting landscaped grounds beautifully restored by the local council, with some lovely features; there's also an adventure playground, and you can fish in one of the four lakes. Snacks, shop, disabled access; visitors centre cl 24 Dec-2 Jan; (01639) 635808; free.

Neath Abbey Remains of Cistercian abbey founded in 1130 by Richard de Grainville. Disabled access; free.

NELSON ST1196

Llancaiach Fawr 🏛 (B4254) Splendidly entertaining and carefully organised living history museum, the

Elizabethan manor's Civil War days brought vividly to life by costumed guides who rarely step out of character - they even speak in 17th-c style. Children actually enjoy visiting a stately home when it's like this - there are no ropes or barriers (it's all firmly hands-on) and they can try on historic clothes, handle armour, or even languish in the stocks for a while. Extra activities summer wknds. Meals, snacks, shop, some disabled access; cl Mon Nov-Feb, and 24 Dec-2 Jan; (01443) 412248; £4.50.

NEWPORT ST3187

Museum and Art Gallery (John Frost Sq) Worthwhile collections, inc a mass of teapots, and a display on the Chartist uprising. Shop, snacks, disabled access; (01633) 840064; cl Sun and bank hols; free. Newport was raised to city status as part of the Jubilee celebrations, and down by the docks (B4237) its 1906 transporter bridge is back in action - an extraordinary sight. Out at Bassaleg (A468 W) the Tredegar Arms has well cooked food.

Transporter Bridge Opened in 1906, this is one of only three working transporter bridges in Britain; designed to allow vehicles and pedestrians to cross the river without obstructing shipping, a suspended gondola is driven by two electric motors nearly 200 metres (645 ft) across the River Usk (cl am Sun; free, 50p for cars). An interactive model at the Visitor Centre shows you how it works; shop, disabled access; cl am Sun, plus wkdys Oct-Mar; free.

Tredegar House (Coedkernew; off A48 SW) Magnificent 17th-c house and gardens in 36-hectare (90-acre) landscaped park on the edge of this industrial town. The Morgans, later Lords Tredegar, lived here for five centuries, and the household's above and below stairs activities are well illustrated in the 30 or so rooms on show. In the grounds are self-guided trails, craft workshops, an Edwardian sunken garden, as well as boating and an adventure playground. Meals, snacks, shop, disabled access; cl Mon and Tues, and Oct-Easter; (01633) 815880; £5.25. Past here on the B4239 the Lighthouse Inn at St Brides Wentlooge has good food upstairs, and great Severn views.

OGMORE SS8876
Ogmore Castle Three-storeyed
12th-c keep with a preserved hooded
fireplace, a dry moat surrounding the
inner ward, and a surviving 12-metre
(40-ft) W wall. The setting of this ruin is
attractive: odd to think that what this
impressive fortress was built to defend
was the row of stepping stones which
still cross the river; free. The cheery
Three Golden Cups along the road at
Southerndown gives sea views to
Devon on a clear day. Just past it is a car
park by the interestingly preserved
remains of the seaside gardens of
entirely demolished Dunraven Castle,
with walks by the cliffs over the sands
and rock pools, and around to the
fragmentary remains of an Iron Age
promontory hill fort above the sea.
PENARTH ST1971
An unspoilt seaside resort of some
charm, with the usual attractions.
Cosmeston Medieval Village ⬚
(Lavernock Rd towards Sully) Living
museum of medieval life, reconstructed
on the site of an actual village which was
deserted during the 14th c. Hens and
sheep wander between the cottages.
Meals, snacks, shop, disabled access; cl
25 Dec; (029) 2070 1678; *£3. It's in the
Cosmeston Lakes country park, with
lakes, woodland and wildlife.
Turner House (Plymouth Rd)
Changing exhibits from the National
Museum of Wales. Shop, disabled
access to ground floor; cl all day Mon
(exc bank hols), between exhibitions,
and occasional lunchtimes; (029) 2070
8870; free.
PENHOW ST4290
Penhow Castle (A48) The oldest
lived-in castle in Wales, with tours of
the restored rooms taking you from the
12th-c ramparts and Norman
bedchamber through the 15th-c Great
Hall with its minstrels' gallery to the
Victorian housekeeper's room. There's
a choice of several good audio tours,
one specially for children, and others
concentrating on a particular topic,
such as the musical or domestic history
of the building. You can stay here.
Snacks, shop; cl Mon (exc bank hols),
Tues, and all end Sept-Good Fri exc
Weds and pm Sun, best to check;
(01633) 400800; *£3.80. The 16th-c

Rock & Fountain has popular food.
PONTYPOOL SO2801
Pontypool Museum (Pontypool
Park, off A4042) The story of a typical
South Wales valley, well shown in the
Georgian stable block of Pontypool
Park House. Galleries inc exhibitions of
fine art, Victorian life and Pontypool
and Usk japanware. Snacks, shop,
disabled access; cl Sat and Sun am,
Christmas and New Year; (01495)
752036; *£1.20, free Weds and Sun
(and they have hopes of abolishing the
entrance fee altogether). The
surrounding country park (formerly the
mansions's grounds) is a microcosm of
the welsh valleys scenery: patches of
conifer plantation and rather scrappy
moorland rising high above the
industrial valleys - not exactly pretty,
but its gruff sense of place appeals to
some, and it has two unique follies
(open summer wknds), a shell grotto
and Folly Tower with far-reaching
views. The Open Hearth just below the
canal at Griffithstown is good for lunch.
PORTHCAWL SS8176
Developing summer resort, with broad
sandy beaches, well placed golf club,
fairground, fishing from the pier, and
what's said to be the largest caravan
park in Wales; it's quieter on the W
side of the harbour.
RAGLAN SO4108
Raglan Castle Quite magnificent ruins
of 15th-c castle, particularly notable for
its Yellow Tower of Gwent. Its intricate
history is displayed in the closet tower
and two rooms of the gatehouse. Shop,
some disabled access; cl 24-26 Dec, 1
Jan; (01291) 690228; £2.50; Cadw. The
Clytha Arms (Abergavenny road) has
good food.
ST HILARY ST0171
Beaupre Castle Well preserved
ruined Elizabethan courtyard mansion
with an extraordinarily elaborate three-
storey italianate porch; free. The Bush
is good for lunch, and the village with its
thatched houses is pretty.
ST NICHOLAS ST0971
Dyffryn Gardens (off A48) These
lovely Grade I Edwardian gardens are
being restored with help from a lottery
grant. Small themed gardens and seasonal
bedding displays help break up the 22
hectares (55 acres) of rare plants and

shrubs, and there's an arboretum and a visitor centre. Summer snacks, shop, limited disabled access; gardens cl 25-26 Dec, visitor centre cl Nov-Mar (when entry is free); (029) 2059 3328; £3.

SWANSEA SS6593

Largely post-industrial and commercial, so there are few buildings of any age or great appeal to visitors, but long sandy beaches have made it something of a family summer resort (and there's a good fresh-food covered market with cockles and lavabread). Work is proceeding on what may turn out to be a fabulous new waterfront museum, but we have to wait until 2005 for its opening. Among some current high spots is the 1934 Guildhall, containing the Brangwyn Hall with its 16 huge British Empire murals painted by Sir Frank Brangwyn for the House of Lords - Wales's gain, as they were judged too controversial. There are some castle ruins (you can't go inside, but can see them from outside), inc a striking 14th-c first-floor arcade. The handsome **Dylan Thomas Centre** (Somerset Pl, Marina) is devoted to welsh literature, with changing exhibitions as well as a permanent exhibition on Dylan Thomas. Restaurant and good bookshop, café (you can peruse the books over your coffee), disabled access; cl Mon, and some bank hols; (01792) 463980; free, charges for events. From the marina, a cycle- and footpath takes you around the bay to Mumbles and Gowerton beyond. The Hanbury in Kingsway is popular for lunch, and the Bankers Draft (Wind St) and Potters Wheel (Kingsway) have good value food all day.

Egypt Centre (University Campus, off Oystermouth Rd) An important collection of egyptian artefacts. Snacks, shop, disabled access; cl Sun and Mon, bank hols, Christmas-New Year; (01792) 295960; free.

Glynn Vivian Art Gallery & Museum (Alexandra Rd) Displays of porcelain from Swansea's all-too-brief but brilliant period of production between 1814 and 1824, and paintings, drawings and sculptures by british, french and, above all, welsh artists, especially the locally born Ceri Richards. Good changing exhibitions.

Shop, disabled access to ground and first floors; cl Mon (exc bank hols), 25-26 Dec, 1 Jan; (01792) 516900; free.

Plantasia 🏛 (Parc Tawe) Tropical and desert plants in big futuristic landscaped glasshouse, also monkey house, reptiles and various creepy-crawlies. Snacks, shop, disabled access; (01792) 474555; cl Mon Sept-May (exc bank hols), 25-26 Dec, 1 Jan and perhaps 2 wks mid-Jan; £2.95.

Swansea Museum (Victoria Rd, Maritime Quarter) The oldest in Wales (Dylan Thomas called it 'the museum which should have been in a museum') with local history and replicas of the oldest human bones found in Wales. Shop, limited disabled access; cl Mon (exc bank hols), and a few days over Christmas and New Year; (01792) 653763; free.

TINTERN SO5300

Tintern Abbey (off A466) Remarkably well preserved, these 14th-c ruins were considered an essential spot for 18th-c artists and poets to visit, lying as they do in a lovely part of the steeply wooded Wye Valley. Wordsworth was just one of many to find inspiration here. Shop, disabled access; cl 24-25 Dec, 1 Jan; (01291) 689251; £2.50; Cadw. The Moon & Sixpence overlooking it and the river has good value food, and the ancient tucked-away Cherry Tree (signed off the main road) does bargain lunches. The Abbey Mill has been converted into a craft and visitor centre. Demonstrations, restaurant and coffee shop; cl 25-26 Dec and 10 days in Jan; free. A visitor centre at Tintern Old Station can help you make the most of the surrounding hills and woodland; open Apr-Oct; free.

TONGWYNLAIS ST1382

Castell Coch (off A470) This spectacular triangular hillside landmark, designed in 1875 by William Burges for the Marquess of Bute, is actually based on a 13th-c castle in spite of its improbable appearance, like something by Disney out of Wagner - red sandstone, conical towers, drawbridge and portcullis. Though never finished, it's a very successful pastiche, and inside is just as impressive: an astonishingly elaborate mock-medieval idyll of gilt, gorgeous colours, statues, murals and carvings. The bedroom of Lady Bute is decorated on the theme of Sleeping Beauty. Shop, disabled access to ground floor only; cl 24-26 Dec, 1 Jan, mid-Jan to end Feb (best to check); (029) 2081 0101; £3; Cadw. The Travellers Rest (A469, Thornhill) has decent food all day.

TREHAFOD ST0290

Rhondda Heritage Park 🏛 (off the A470) Based around the last colliery buildings in the area, this well organised centre uses lively multi-media exhibitions to re-create the golden days of the coal-mining industry, evoking sights, sounds and smells from the life and work of the miners. The excellent underground tour showing what it was like to work a shift is uncannily realistic, and the twisting simulated trip back to the surface is a definite highlight. Other displays look at the wider social heritage of the valley, with art by locals, a re-created village street, and (Easter-Sept) an excellent themed adventure play area. A good excursion whatever the weather. Meals, snacks, shop, good disabled access (even underground); cl Mon Oct-Apr, and 25 Dec-1 Jan; (01443) 682036; £5.60.

USK SO3700

Rural Life Museum 🏛 (New Market St) Interesting collection, in three old barns; one shows life in the area from Victorian times to World War II, inc a typical farmhouse kitchen, laundry and dairy, and the others have machinery and waggons. Cl am wknds and all Nov-Mar; £2. The little town is attractive, with an interesting church and good river walks; the Nags Head is currently the best pub.

WYND CLIFF ST5297

This viewpoint gives walkers an extensive panorama, a short detour up steps. Elsewhere, the Wye Valley Walk between Chepstow and Tintern gives only occasional views down to the river, which in this picturesque Lower Wye gorge makes the boundary between England and Wales.

Attractive villages or small towns, all with decent pubs, include Bedwellty SO1600, Cowbridge SS9974 and Laleston SS8879. The church and churchyard of Llancarfan ST0570 are worth a look.

Pubs or inns elsewhere which are particularly useful for their attractive surroundings or views include the Goose & Cuckoo at Rhyd-y-Meirch SO2907 (follow Upper Llanover sign up narrow track off A4042 S of Abergavenny), Bridgend by the canal at Gilwern SO2414, Old Glais at Glais SN7000, Old House at Llangynwyd SS8588, Greyhound at Llantrisant ST3997, Brynfynnon at Llanwonno ST0295, Plough & Harrow at Monknash SS9270, Rowan Tree at Nelson ST1195, Halfway House at Talycoed SO4115, Trekkers at The Narth SO5206 and Fountain at Trelleck Grange SO4902.

Where to eat

CARDIFF ST1676 **Gallois** *6-8 Romilly Crescent* (029) 2034 1264 Small and stylish split-level restaurant with a loyal following, bustling cheerful atmosphere, delicious imaginative food from a modern menu, a good wine list with ten by the glass, and helpful staff; good value lunch; must book; cl Sun, Mon, 2 wks Aug, 1 wk Christmas-New Year; disabled access. £40/2-course meal £14.95

CARDIFF ST1974 **Izakaya Japanese Tavern** *Mermaid Quay* (029) 2049 2939 Japanese tavern with views over Cardiff Bay, eating and drinking bars, more formal rooms with sunken tables, and colourful décor; a choice of up to 60 items with english descriptions, a relaxed atmosphere, and some fine sakes served warm or cold; disabled access. £20|**£5.90**

COWBRIDGE SS9974 **Farthings** *54 High St* (01446) 772990 Attractively decorated restaurant with stripped stone and black beams, candles and soft lighting, partly flagstoned front part, spreading far back up one or two steps into a cosily divided area with french prints on white walls and mix of carpet and quarry tiles, good freshly made modern food including tender welsh black steaks, elaborate cakes, well chosen wines at rather low mark-ups, and friendly informal service; cl Sun and Mon pm, 25-26 Dec, 1 Jan, bank hol Mon; disabled access. £22|**£6.95**

LLANDENNY SO4103 **Raglan Arms** *(01291)* 690800 Dining pub with extensive series of sturdily furnished linked rooms inc a conservatory, as well as a terracotta-walled flagstoned bar with leather sofas, daily papers and *Country Living* to read, and a big log fire in the handsome stone fireplace; good fresh food (plenty of fish and seafood cooked to order), well kept real ales, a well chosen wine list, and pleasant efficient service; best to book at wknds; garden tables. £25|£8

LLANDEWI SKIRRID SO3416 **Walnut Tree** *(01873)* 852797 Simply furnished dining pub with a small white-walled bar, some polished settles and country chairs around biggish tables on its flagstones, and a log-effect gas fire; it opens into an airy and relaxed dining lounge with dark wooden chairs and tables; excellent modern food, and a tempting choice of wines (particularly good italian ones); cl Mon (exc bank hol), 24 Dec-1 Jan; disabled access. £35/2-course set lunch £16.50

PORT TALBOT SS7489 **Aberavon Beach Hotel** *Princess Margaret Way (01639)* 884949 Popular modern hotel opposite wide sandy beach, with enjoyable modern cooking in no smoking restaurant, thoughtful wine list, helpful staff, and attractive public rooms; all-weather leisure centre; comfortable bdrms; good disabled access. £25|£7.95

RAGLAN SO3608 **Clytha Arms** *(01873)* 840206 Fine old country inn with a tastefully and solidly comfortable bar, cheerful helpful staff, good carefully prepared food inc delicious puddings and good value Sun lunch in no smoking restaurant, log fires, well kept real ales, and neat garden; bdrms; cl Mon am (open bank hols), 25 Dec. £30|£5.95

SKENFRITH SO4520 **Bell** *(01600)* 750235 Attractively reworked inn in beautiful setting by bridge over the River Monnow; flagstones and canary walls in linked areas with settees, pews and carved settles among more conventional pub furniture, church candles on tables, a log fire in big fireplace, and welcoming enthusiastic owners; good wines by the glass, real ales, and interesting food using the best local produce in both bar and extensive bare-boards restaurant (must book); picnic-sets out on the terrace; bdrms. £30|£10

USK SO3700 **Nags Head** *4-6 Twyn Sq (01291)* 672820 Run by the same warmly welcoming family for 36 years, this relaxed old coaching inn has enjoyable interesting food inc plenty of seasonal game and well kept beers, with plenty of character in its traditional beamed bar, and (cl winter) a separate coffee bar; disabled access. £22|£5.50

Special thanks to Corinne Goughtly, Peter and Audrey Dowsett, Mr and Mrs P Smith, Paul Kennedy, B and K Hypher, Michael and Jenny Back, James Morrell

INDEX

This index includes the main places in the **To see and Do** sections.

936 • INDEX

LONDON INDEX

REPORT FORMS

Please report to us: you can use the card in the middle of the book, tear-out forms on the following pages, or just plain paper - whichever's easiest for you. Or you can send reports on our web site www.goodguides.co.uk. Please tell us what you think about places already in the *Guide*. And about other places worthy of inclusion. We try to answer all letters, and readers who send us reports will be offered a discount on forthcoming editions.

If you are recommending a new place to stay or eat in, the more detail you can give, the better. Imagine you're writing about it for the *Guide* itself, and put in the sorts of things you'd want to know yourself before deciding on a visit. A full address and telephone number is also an enormous help.

We'd also very much like to know about places you've enjoyed visiting - anything from a little village to a stately home, from a peaceful wood or a nature reserve or a stretch of unspoilt coastal cliff to a theme park or a zoo or a pleasure beach. Whatever it is, if you've enjoyed it, please tell us about it. We'll assume we can print your name or initials as a recommender unless you tell us otherwise.

When you write to *The Good Britain Guide*, FREEPOST TN1569, WADHURST, E. Sussex, TN5 7BR, you don't need a stamp in the UK. The information you send us will be stored in our computer files.

We will reply to your letters but we would ask for your patience if there's a delay, particularly from June well into autumn, when we are fully extended getting the next edition to the printers. The end of May is pretty much the cut-off date for reasoned consideration of reports for the next edition - the earlier the better, if they're suggestions for new entries.

The Good Britain Guide: Endorsement Form

I have been to the following hotels/restaurants/attractions/places in *The 2004 Good Britain Guide* in the last few months, found them as described, and confirm that they deserve continued inclusion:

✂ PLEASE GIVE YOUR NAME AND ADDRESS ON THE BACK OF THIS FORM

Your own name and address (*block capitals please*)

Please return to:
The Good Britain Guide
FREEPOST TN1569
WADHURST
E. Sussex
TN5 7BR

The Good Britain Guide: Report Form

Please use this form to tell us about anything that you think should or should not be included in the next edition of *The Good Britain Guide*. Just fill it in and send it to us - no stamp needed.

ALISDAIR AIRD

☐ Please tick this box if you would like extra report forms

Report on *(its name)*

Its address:

Postcode: Telephone:

What is this? (e.g. *hotel, restaurant, garden, village, drive, walk*)

Description/why it appeals

PLEASE GIVE YOUR NAME AND ADDRESS ON THE BACK OF THIS FORM

...ur own name and address (*block capitals please*)

Please return to:

> *The Good Britain Guide*
> FREEPOST TN1569
> WADHURST
> E. Sussex
> TN5 7BR